Less managing. More teaching. Greater learning.

INSTRUCTORS...

Would you like your **students** to show up for class **more prepared**?
(Let's face it, class is much more fun if everyone is engaged and prepared...)

Want an **easy way to assign** homework online and track student **progress**?
(Less time grading means more time teaching...)

Want an **instant view** of student or class performance relative to learning objectives? *(No more wondering if students understand...)*

Need to **collect data and generate reports** required for administration or accreditation? *(Say goodbye to manually tracking student learning outcomes...)*

Want to **record and post your lectures** for students to view online?

With **McGraw-Hill's *Connect Plus Accounting*,**

INSTRUCTORS GET:

- Simple **assignment management**, allowing you to spend more time teaching.
- **Auto-graded** assignments, quizzes, and tests.
- **Detailed Visual Reporting** where student and section results can be viewed and analyzed.
- Sophisticated **online testing** capability.
- A **filtering and reporting** function that allows you to easily assign and report on materials that are correlated to accreditation standards, learning outcomes, and Bloom's taxonomy.
- An easy-to-use **lecture capture** tool.
- The option to **upload course documents** for student access.

Want an online, **searchable version** of your textbook?

Wish your textbook could be **available online** while you're doing your assignments?

Connect Plus Accounting eBook

If you choose to use *Connect Plus Accounting*, you have an affordable and searchable online version of your book integrated with your other online tools.

Connect Plus Accounting eBook offers features like:

- Topic search
- Direct links from assignments
- Adjustable text size
- Jump to page number
- Print by section

Want to get more **value** from your textbook purchase?

Think learning accounting should be a bit more **interesting**?

Check out the STUDENT RESOURCES section under the *Connect* Library tab.

Here you'll find a wealth of resources designed to help you achieve your goals in the course. You'll find things like **quizzes, PowerPoints, and Internet activities** to help you study. Every student has different needs, so explore the STUDENT RESOURCES to find the materials best suited to you.

Eighth Edition

Fundamental Financial Accounting Concepts

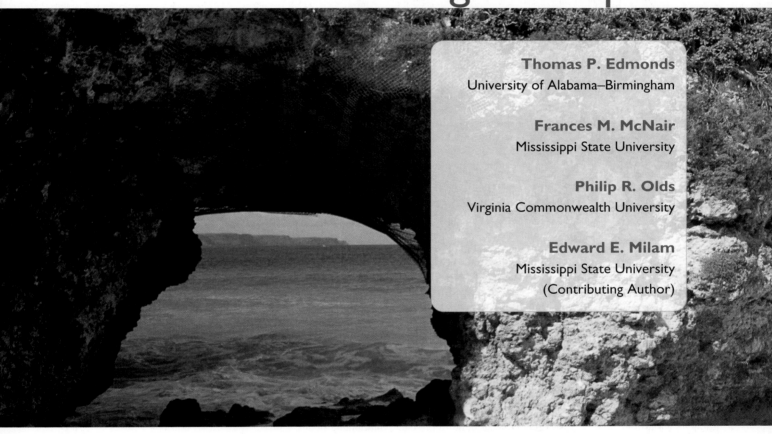

Thomas P. Edmonds
University of Alabama–Birmingham

Frances M. McNair
Mississippi State University

Philip R. Olds
Virginia Commonwealth University

Edward E. Milam
Mississippi State University
(Contributing Author)

McGraw-Hill
Irwin

FUNDAMENTAL FINANCIAL ACCOUNTING CONCEPTS

2 3 4 5 6 7 8 9 0 DOW/DOW 1 0 9 8 7 6 5 4 3 2

ISBN   978-0-07-802536-5
MHID   0-07-802536-2

Vice president and editor-in-chief: *Brent Gordon*
Publisher: *Tim Vertovec*
Senior sponsoring editor: *Dana L. Woo*
Executive director of development: *Ann Torbert*
Development editor II: *Katie Jones*
Vice president and director of marketing: *Robin J. Zwettler*
Marketing director: *Brad Parkins*
Senior marketing manager: *Kathleen Klehr*
Vice president of editing, design, and production: *Sesha Bolisetty*
Senior project manager: *Diane L. Nowaczyk*
Senior buyer: *Carol A. Bielski*
Interior designer: *Pam Verros*
Senior photo research coordinator: *Jeremy Cheshareck*
Photo researcher: *Ira C. Roberts*
Lead media project manager: *Allison Souter*
Media project manager: *Ron Nelms*
Cover and interior design: *Pam Verros*
Typeface: *10.5/12 Times New Roman MT Regular*
Compositor: *Aptara®, Inc.*
Printer: *R. R. Donnelley*

Library of Congress Cataloging-in-Publication Data

Edmonds, Thomas P.
   Fundamental financial accounting concepts / Thomas P. Edmonds, Frances M. McNair, Philip R. Olds; Edward E. Milam, contributing author.—8th ed.
      p. cm.
   Includes index.
   ISBN-13: 978-0-07-802536-5 (alk. paper)
   ISBN-10: 0-07-802536-2 (alk. paper)
   1. Accounting. I. McNair, Frances M., 1945– II. Olds, Philip R. III. Title.
HF5636.F86 2013
657—dc23

                                                                    2011037655

This book is dedicated to our students, whose questions have so frequently caused us to reevaluate our method of presentation that they have, in fact, become major contributors to the development of this text.

Why should you adopt this textbook? Because it does a better job of teaching traditional introductory accounting concepts. Indeed, we view ourselves as innovative traditionalists. We don't aim to radically transform accounting education, but instead to make it more effective. Consider the following features that distinguish this book from its competitors.

THE LINK BETWEEN EVENTS AND STATEMENTS

We not only teach students how to journalize transactions but we also explain how the journal entries affect the financial statements. The text provides coverage of debits and credits, journal entries, T-accounts, and trial balances. Beyond these traditional topics, we employ a *financial statements model* to ensure that students learn how accounting events affect financial statements. The model arranges the balance sheet income statement and statement of cash flows horizontally across a single line of text as shown below:

Assets	=	Liab.	+	Equity	Rev.	−	Exp.	=	Net Inc.	Cash Flow

Typically, we show the statements model immediately after each journal entry. For example, the settlement of a liability for interest would be shown as follows:

Account Title	Debit	Credit
Interest Payable	8,400	
Cash		8,400

Assets	=	Liab.	+	Equity	Rev.	−	Exp.	=	Net Inc.	Cash Flow	
(8,400)		(8,400)		NA	NA	NA			NA	(8,400)	OA

This approach provides a direct visual connection between journal entries and financial statements. It enables students to see how each individual accounting event affects decision making. Executives make few decisions without considering how those decisions affect "bottom line" financial performance measures. The statements model approach encourages students to develop real-world thinking patterns.

A UNIQUE APPROACH TO THE STATEMENT OF CASH FLOWS

We not only cover the income statement, statement of stockholders' equity, and the balance sheet, but we also provide comprehensive coverage of the statement of cash flows. Coverage of the statement of cash flows starts in Chapter I and is discussed throughout the text. While the statement of cash flows is critically important in the real world, coverage of the statement is often slighted and usually relegated to the last chapter in the text. The primary reason for this treatment is that teaching students to convert accrual accounting data into cash flow is complicated. We remove this complexity by introducing the statement through a highly simplified teaching approach.

We begin by teaching students to classify an individual cash transaction as a financing, investing, or operating activity. Students then compile the classified transactions into a formal statement of cash flows. Preparing the statement under this direct, transaction-by-transaction approach reduces the learning task to a simple classification scheme. Later, in Chapter 12, we introduce the more complex task of converting accrual accounting data to a statement of cash flows.

UNDERSTANDING FINANCIAL STATEMENT ANALYSIS

We not only show how to calculate financial ratios but also explain how those ratios are used to evaluate businesses. We provide unparalleled coverage of financial statement analysis. A separate section titled the "Financial Analyst" is included in each chapter of the text. Further, a summary of financial ratios is included in an appendix at the end of the text. Finally, a complete chapter covering financial statement analysis is available online. Providing coverage in multiple formats allows the instructor to establish the level of emphasis placed on this subject.

Is a gross margin percentage of 25% good or bad? Clearly, the answer depends on the type of company under consideration. While most textbooks show students how to calculate financial ratios, this text goes a step beyond by providing real-world industry data that facilitates an understanding of the ratios. Exercises, problems, and real-world cases that reference real-world data are included in each chapter. Further, the text includes two financial statement analysis projects. One pertains to Target's 10-K report that is included in the text. The other is a open-ended project that allows the instructor to choose the company to be evaluated.

IFRS AND OTHER INTERNATIONAL ACCOUNTING ISSUES

We not only provide comprehensive coverage of generally accepted accounting principles (GAAP) but also expose students to International Financial Reporting Standards (IFRS). Clearly, GAAP is the predominant practice in the United States. However, ever-increasing globalization requires awareness of international standards as well. The book contains textboxes titled "Focus on International Issues." These boxes include content regarding IFRS and other interesting international topics. Specially marked exercises allow the instructor to reinforce the international content through homework assignments. The textbox approach allows flexibility in the level of emphasis instructors choose to place on this subject.

DEMONSTRATING EVENT EFFECTS OVER MULTIPLE ACCOUNTING CYCLES

We not only show how an accounting event effects a single accounting period but also how that event affects multiple accounting cycles. The text uses a vertical statements model that shows financial statements from top to bottom on a single page. This model displays financial results for consecutive accounting cycles in adjacent columns, thereby enabling the instructor to show how related events are reported *over multiple accounting cycles.*

CONCLUDING REMARKS

We appreciate your taking time to read this note. We encourage your questions or comments. Contact information for members of the author team are as follows:

Tom Edmonds
205-934-8875
tedmonds@uab.edu

Frances McNair
662-325-1636
fmcnair@cobilan.msstate.edu

Phil Olds
804-828-7120
prolds@vcu.edu

"I especially like the fact that, for most transactions, the authors give the type of transaction (asset source, etc.), followed by the journal entry and horizontal mode. It gives instructors lots of flexibility and continually reinforces concepts throughout."

MARY MANKTELOW,
JAMES MADISON UNIVERSITY

"I like the coverage of certain critical Generally Accepted Accounting Principles, such as the Matching Concept) and the Conservatism Principle. . . . It helps the students to have perspective on how material of a given chapter fits into the larger picture of accrual basis accounting and GAAP."

STACEY ADAMS,
ANTELOPE VALLEY CC

EXHIBIT 8.3	Financial Statements under Straight-Line Depreciation				
DRYDEN ENTERPRISES Financial Statements					
	2013	2014	2015	2016	2017
Income Statements					
Rent revenue	$ 8,000	$ 8,000	$ 8,000	$ 8,000	$ 0
Depreciation expense	(5,000)	(5,000)	(5,000)	(5,000)	0
Operating income	3,000	3,000	3,000	3,000	0
Gain on sale of van	0	0	0	0	500
Net income	$ 3,000	$ 3,000	$ 3,000	$ 3,000	$ 500
Balance Sheets					
Assets					
Cash	$ 9,000	$17,000	$25,000	$33,000	$37,500
Van	24,000	24,000	24,000	24,000	0
Accumulated depreciation	(5,000)	(10,000)	(15,000)	(20,000)	0
Total assets	$28,000	$31,000	$34,000	$37,000	$37,500
Stockholders' equity					
Common stock	$25,000	$25,000	$25,000	$25,000	$25,000
Retained earnings	3,000	6,000	9,000	12,000	12,500
Total stockholders' equity	$28,000	$31,000	$34,000	$37,000	$37,500
Statements of Cash Flows					
Operating Activities					
Inflow from customers	$ 8,000	$ 8,000	$ 8,000	$ 8,000	$ 0
Investing Activities					
Outflow to purchase van	(24,000)				
Inflow from sale of van					4,500
Financing Activities					
Inflow from stock issue	25,000				
Net Change in Cash	9,000	8,000	8,000	8,000	4,500
Beginning cash balance	0	9,000	17,000	25,000	33,000
Ending cash balance	$ 9,000	$17,000	$25,000	$33,000	$37,500

Thomas P. Edmonds

Thomas P. Edmonds, is the Friends and Alumni Professor of Accounting at the University of Alabama at Birmingham (UAB). Dr. Edmonds has taught in the introductory area throughout his career. He has coordinated the accounting principles courses at the University of Houston and UAB. He currently teaches introductory accounting in mass sections and in UAB's distance learning program. He is actively involved in the accounting education change movement. He has conducted more than 50 workshops related to teaching introductory accounting during the last decade. Dr. Edmonds has received numerous prestigious teaching awards including the Alabama Society of CPAs Outstanding Educator Award and the UAB President's Excellence in Teaching Award. Dr. Edmonds's current research is education based. He has written articles that appeared in many publications including, among others, the *Accounting Review, Issues in Accounting Education, Journal of Accounting Education,* and *Advances in Accounting Education.* Dr. Edmonds has been a successful entrepreneur. He has worked as a management accountant for a transportation company and as a commercial lending officer for the Federal Home Loan Bank. Dr. Edmonds began his academic training at Young Harris Community College. His PhD degree was awarded by Georgia State University. Dr. Edmonds's work experience and academic training has enabled him to bring a unique perspective to the classroom.

Frances M. McNair

Frances M. McNair holds the KPMG Peat Marwick Professorship in Accounting at Mississippi State University (MSU). She has been involved in teaching principles of accounting for the past 12 years and currently serves as the coordinator for the principles of accounting courses at MSU. She joined the MSU faculty in 1987 after receiving her PhD from the University of Mississippi. The author of various articles that have appeared in the *Journal of Accountancy, Management Accounting, Business and Professional Ethics Journal, The Practical Accountant, Taxes,* and other publications, she also coauthored the book *The Tax Practitioner* with Dr. Denzil Causey. Dr. McNair is currently serving on committees of the American Taxation Association, the American Accounting Association, and the Institute of Management Accountants as well as numerous School of Accountancy and MSU committees.

Philip R. Olds

Philip R. Olds is associate professor of accounting at Virginia Commonwealth University (VCU). He serves as the coordinator of the introduction to accounting courses at VCU. Dr. Olds has also received the Distinguished Service Award and the Distinguished Teaching Award from VCU School of Business. Dr. Olds received his A.S. degree from Brunswick Junior College in Brunswick, Georgia (now Costal Georgia Community College). He received a BBA in Accounting from Georgia Southern College (now Georgia Southern University) and his MPA and PhD degrees from Georgia State University. After graduating from Georgia Southern, he worked as an auditor with the U.S. Department of Labor in Atlanta, Georgia. Dr. Olds has published articles in various professional journals and presented papers at national and regional conferences. He also served as the faculty adviser to the VCU chapter of Beta Alpha Psi for five years. In 1989, he was recognized with an Outstanding Faculty Vice-President Award by the national Beta Alpha Psi organization.

This edition offers new opportunities for instructors to determine the scope and pace of coverage. You can now choose to introduce depreciation and interest computations in Chapter 2. Alternatively, you can delay coverage of these subjects thereby providing more time to introduce basic concepts in a simpler environment. In addition, Chapters 1 and 2 have been subdivided into parts that allow you to effectively control the pace of coverage. Also, the revision delivers enhanced coverage of financial statement analysis.

In preparation for the development of this edition we surveyed instructors who use the text to assess their experiences with the revisions made in the previous edition. Overall, we received positive feedback and strong support for the changes we implemented previously. One area where reviewers' comments were more varied related to the delay of coverage of depreciation and interest computations. Roughly 65 percent of the respondents ranked delaying coverage of depreciation as very or moderately effective, leaving 35 percent who classified the delay as not very effective. Similarly, 74 percent found delaying coverage of interest computations to be very or moderately effective, while 26 percent classified the delay as not very effective. Clearly, many of our adopters are happy to have coverage of these subjects delayed while others would prefer to have those topics covered in Chapters 2 and 3.

In response, we have created an appendix for Chapter 2 that covers depreciation and the computation of interest. Also, numerous exercises and problems covering these topics have been added to the end-of-chapter materials. These exercises and problems have been clearly labeled as being related to the "Appendix." Identifying them is easy and coverage is left to the discretion of the instructor. Coverage of these topics continues in an appendix to Chapter 3. Accordingly, individual instructors have the opportunity to decide the appropriate time to introduce these pivotal topics.

Virtually everyone is happy that the text addresses issues of substance immediately; there is very little fluff in Chapter 1. While the majority of respondents felt the pace of coverage was on target, some suggested it was overly challenging for their students. The proper pace is, of course, dependent on student aptitude. Since student aptitude varies widely across schools, the pace of coverage must also vary. In recognition of the need for flexibility, we divided Chapter 1 into two sections.

Chapter 1, Section 1 covers basic terminology, introduces the accounting equation, and demonstrates how business events are recorded under the equation. Section 2 introduces students to financial statements. The end-of-chapter exercises and problems are also segregated in separate sections. With this arrangement it is easy for instructors to treat the chapter as two separate chapters, thereby slowing the pace and allowing more time to cover key conceptual issues. Chapter 2 has also been divided into two sections: Chapter 2, Section 1 covers accruals, while Section 2 covers deferrals.

Breaking the chapters into sections offers an added benefit of promoting a stepwise learning environment. The primary concepts are isolated and introduced in a simple environment. More complex relationships and details are then added to the basic foundation. Stepwise learning is a hallmark of our teaching strategy.

The Target annual report project contained in Appendix D has been redesigned and includes many new features that promote ease of use. Specifically, Target's 2008, 2009, and 2010 financial statements have been loaded into an Excel spreadsheet that is available on the textbook's website. The income statement shown in the spreadsheet has been revised to better reflect the income statement format and wording used in the textbook. The revision moves credit card revenues (interest income) to the nonoperating section and enables the project solution for gross margin percentages to agree to those identified in the Management Discussion & Analysis section of the annual report. This Excel spreadsheet provides an excellent starting point for the vertical and horizontal analysis required in the project. Also, to simplify grading,

"I think Edmonds is the best financial accounting book on the market."

MARK CAMMA,
ATLANTIC CAPE
COMMUNITY COLLEGE

"I really like all of the recaps of financial statements after presenting a number of transactions. I always tell students that the financial statements are our ultimate outcome so it's good that they see them often."

EILEEN SHIFFLETT,
JAMES MADISON
UNIVERSITY

"As a result of using the horizontal model, students have a much better understanding of the accrual effect and the cash effect of a transaction. It is well-written with interesting examples and illustrations."

NANCY SNOW,
UNIVERSITY OF TOLEDO

"Good, easy-to-read book for students."

CAROLINE FALCONETTI,
NASSAU COMMUNITY
COLLEGE

we provide a multiple choice project quiz. This quiz is available in the instructor's manual, as well as in *Connect*®.

Specific revisions for each chapter are described below.

● SPECIFIC CHAPTER CHANGES

Chapter 1 An Introduction to Accounting

- Divided chapter into two sections, thereby providing more flexibility to set the pace of instruction.
- Added new *Curious Accountant* featuring new high-profile companies and products.
- Updated *Focus on International Issues* textbox that includes IFRS coverage.
- Added new *Reality Bytes*.
- Updated *The Financial Analyst* content.
- Updated exercises, problems, and cases.

Chapter 2 Accounting for Accruals and Deferrals

- Divided chapter into two sections, thereby providing more flexibility to set the pace of instruction.
- Added an appendix and related end-of-chapter materials covering the introduction of depreciation and the computation of interest.
- Revised learning objectives.
- Added new *Curious Accountant* featuring new high-profile companies and products.
- Added new *Reality Bytes*.
- Updated *The Financial Analyst* content.
- Updated exercises, problems, and cases.

Chapter 3 The Double-Entry Accounting System

- Added an appendix and related end-of-chapter materials that provide continuing coverage of depreciation and the computation of interest.
- Added new *Curious Accountant* featuring new high-profile companies and products.
- Added new *Focus on International Issues* textbox that includes IFRS coverage.
- Updated *The Financial Analyst* content.
- Updated exercises, problems, and cases.

Chapter 4 Accounting for Merchandising Businesses

- Added new *Curious Accountant* featuring new high-profile companies and products.
- Updated *The Financial Analyst* content.
- Updated exercises, problems, and cases.

Chapter 5 Accounting for Inventories

- Added new *Curious Accountant* featuring new high-profile companies and products.
- Updated *Focus on International Issues* textbox that includes IFRS coverage.
- Updated *The Financial Analyst* content.
- Updated exercises, problems, and cases.

Chapter 6 Internal Control and Accounting for Cash

- Added coverage of the framework for internal controls and enterprise risk management developed by the Committee of Sponsoring Organizations of the Treadway Commission (COSO).
- Updated *Curious Accountant*.
- Updated exercises, problems, and cases.

Chapter 7 Accounting for Receivables

- Added new *Curious Accountant* featuring new high-profile companies and products.
- Updated *Reality Bytes.*
- Updated *The Financial Analyst* content.
- Updated exercises, problems, and cases.

Chapter 8 Accounting for Long-Term Operational Assets

- Added new *Curious Accountant* featuring new high-profile companies and products.
- Updated *Focus on International Issues* textbox that includes IFRS coverage.
- Added new *Reality Bytes.*
- Updated *The Financial Analyst* content.
- Updated exercises, problems, and cases.

Chapter 9 Accounting for Current Liabilities and Payroll

- Updated *Reality Bytes.*
- Updated *Focus on International Issues* textbox that includes IFRS coverage.
- Updated *The Financial Analyst* content.
- Updated exercises, problems, and cases.

Chapter 10 Accounting for Long-Term Debt

- Added new *Curious Accountant* featuring new high-profile companies and products.
- Added new *Reality Bytes.*
- Updated *The Financial Analyst* content.
- Updated exercises, problems, and cases.

Chapter 11 Proprietorships, Partnerships, and Corporations

- Added new *Curious Accountant* featuring new high-profile companies and products.
- Added new *Reality Bytes.*
- Updated *Focus on International Issues* textbox that includes IFRS coverage.
- Updated *The Financial Analyst* content.
- Updated exercises, problems, and cases.

Chapter 12 Statement of Cash Flows

- Added new *Curious Accountant* featuring new high-profile companies and products.
- Updated *Reality Bytes.*
- Updated *The Financial Analyst* content.
- Updated exercises, problems, and cases.

Chapter 13 Financial Statement Analysis (Available online only at www.mhhe.com/edmonds8e)

- Updated *Curious Accountant.*
- Updated exercises, problems, and cases.

Real-World Examples

The text provides a variety of real-world examples of financial accounting as an essential part of the management process. There are descriptions of accounting practices from real organizations such as Coca-Cola, Enron, General Motors, and Amazon.com. These companies are highlighted in blue in the text.

The Curious Accountant

Each chapter opens with a short vignette. These pose a question about a real-world accounting issue related to the topic of the chapter. The answer to the question appears in a separate sidebar a few pages further into the chapter.

Focus on International Issues

These boxed inserts expose students to IFRS and other international issues in accounting.

The Financial Analyst

Financial statement analysis is highlighted in each chapter under this heading.

Check Yourself

These short question/answer features occur at the end of each main topic and ask students to stop and think about the material just covered. The answer follows to provide immediate feedback before students go on to a new topic.

The Curious Accountant

Richard recently purchased a new Ford automobile from a dealer near his home. When he told his friend Jeff that he was able to purchase the car for $1,000 less than the sticker price, Jeff told Richard he had gotten a lousy deal. "Everybody knows there is a huge markup on cars," Jeff said. "You could have gotten a much lower price if you'd shopped around."

Richard responded, "If there is such a big profit margin on cars, why did so many of the car manufacturers get into financial trouble?" Jeff told him that he was confusing the maker of the car with the dealer. Jeff argued that although the manufacturers may not have high profit margins, the dealers do, and told him again that he had paid too much.

Exhibit 4.1 presents the income statements for AutoNation, Inc., and Ford Motor Company. Based on these statements, do you think either of these guys is correct? For example, if you pay $20,000 for

Answers to The Curious Accountant

As data from the income statement for AutoNation show, automobile dealers do not have big markups on the cars they sell. The new vehicles the company sold for $6,669.1 million in 2010 cost the company $6,217.9 to purchase, resulting in a gross margin of $451.2, or 6.8%. In other words, if you bought an "average" car from AutoNation for $20,000, the company's gross profit on it was only $1,360 ($20,000 × .068), meaning it paid Ford $18,640 ($20,000 − $1,360). Furthermore, the company still had other expenses to pay besides its cost of goods sold. In 2010, only 1.8% of each dollar of AutoNation's sales was net profit ($226.6 ÷ $12,461.0) Remember, the amount shown for sales on AutoNation's income statement is based on what customers

FOCUS ON INTERNATIONAL ISSUES

HOW DO IFRS DIFFER FROM U.S. GAAP?

Chapter 1 discussed the progression toward a single global GAAP in the form of International Financial Reporting Standards (IFRS). That discussion noted that the United States does not currently allow domestic companies to use IFRS; they must follow GAAP. Let's briefly consider just how U.S. GAAP differs from IFRS.

The differences can be summarized in a few broad categories. First, some differences are relatively minor. Consider the case of bank overdrafts. Under IFRS some bank overdrafts are included as a cash inflow and reported on the statement of cash flows. U.S. GAAP does not permit this. Conversely, some differences relate to very significant issues. Both IFRS and GAAP use historical cost as their primary method for reporting information on financial statements, but both allow exceptions in some circumstances. However, IFRS permit more exceptions to historical cost than do GAAP. Some of these differences will be discussed in later chapters.

Some of the differences affect how financial statements are presented in annual reports. IFRS require companies to report all financial statements for the current year and the prior year—two years of comparative data. Rules of the Securities and Exchange Commission

THE FINANCIAL ANALYST

CORPORATE GOVERNANCE

Corporate governance is the set of relationships between the board of directors, management, shareholders, auditors, and other stakeholders that determine how a company is operated. Clearly, financial analysts are keenly interested in these relationships. This section discusses the key components of corporate governance.

LO 9

Discuss the primary components of corporate governance.

Importance of Ethics

The accountant's role in society requires trust and credibility. Accounting information is worthless if the accountant is not trustworthy. Similarly, tax and consulting advice is useless if it comes from an incompetent person. The high ethical standards required by the profession state "

✓ CHECK YOURSELF 3.1

What are the three sources of assets? Which accounts are debited and credited when a business acquires an asset?

Answer The three sources of assets are creditors, investors, and earnings. When a company acquires an asset, the asset account is debited and the source account is credited. For example, if a company earns revenue on account, the receivables account is debited and the revenue account is credited.

Reality Bytes

This feature expands on the topics by showing how companies use the concepts discussed in the chapter to make real-world business decisions.

Annual Reports

The 2010 annual report for Target Corporation is shown in Appendix B.

Business Application Problems related to the annual report are included at the end of each chapter.

A financial statement analysis project for the annual report is located in Appendix D. Also, a general purpose annual report project is included for instructors to assign for any company.

Chapter Focus Company

Each chapter introduces important managerial accounting topics within the context of a realistic company. Students see the impact of managerial accounting decisions on the company as they work through the chapter. When the Focus Company is presented in the chapter, its logo is shown so the students see its application to the text topics.

A Look Back/A Look Forward

Students need a roadmap to make sense of where the chapter topics fit into the "whole" picture. A Look Back reviews the chapter materials and a look forward introduces students to what is to come.

REALITY BYTES

Do all accounting systems require using debits and credits? The answer is a definite no. Many small businesses use a single-entry system. A checkbook constitutes a sufficient accounting system for many business owners. Deposits represent revenues, and payments constitute expenses. Many excellent automated accounting systems do not require data entry through a debit/credit recording scheme. **QuickBooks** is a good example of this type of system. Data are entered into the QuickBooks software program through a user-friendly computer interface that does not require knowledge of debit/credit terminology. Even so, the QuickBooks program produces traditional financial reports such as an income statement, balance sheet, and statement of cash flows. How is this possible? Before you become too ingrained in the debit/credit system, recall that throughout the first two chapters of this text, we illustrated accounting records without using debits and credits. Financial reports can be produced in many ways without using a double-entry system. Having recognized this point, we also note that the vast majority of medium- to large-size companies use the double-entry system. Indeed, debit/credit terminology is a part of common culture. Most people have an understanding of what is happening when a business tells them that their account is being debited o...
well a...

Appendix B

Portion of the Form 10-K for Target Corporation

This appendix contains a portion of the Form 10-K for the Target Corporation that was filed with the Securities and Exchange Commission on March 11, 2011. The document included in this appendix is Target's annual report, which was included *as a part* of its complete Form 10-K for the company's fiscal year ended January 29, 2011. Throughout this text this is referred to as the company's 2010 fiscal year.

This document is included for illustrative purposes, and it is intended to be used for educational purposes only. It should not be used for making investment decisions. Target Corporation's complete Form 10-K may be obtained from the SEC's EDGAR website, using the procedures explained in Appendix A. The Form 10-K may also be found on the company's website at www.target.com.

UNITED STATES
SECURITIES AND EXCHANGE COMMISSION
Washington, D.C. 20549

FORM 10-K

(Mark One)
☒ ANNUAL REPORT PURSUANT
    For the
☐ TRANSITION REPORT PURSU
    For the transition period

TARG

Minnesota   (State or other jurisdiction of   incor
1000 Nicollet Mall, Minneapolis, Min
of principal executive off

Securities Registered Pursuant To Section (12)(B) Of The Act:

Title of Each Class
Common Stock, par value $0.0833 p
Securities re

Name and Type of Company Used as Main Chapter Example			
Chapter Title	Company Used as Main Chapter Example	Company Logo	Type of Company
1. An Introduction to Accounting	Rustic Camp Sites		Rents land
2. Accounting for Accruals and Deferrals	Cato Consultants		Provides training services
3. The Double-Entry Accounting System	Collins Brokerage Services, Inc.		Investment consulting firm
4. Accounting for Merchandising Businesses	June's Plant Shop		Sells gardening supplies
5. Accounting for Inventories	The Mountain Bike Company		Sells bicycles
6. Internal Control and Accounting for Cash	Green Shades Resorts, Inc.		Rents resort facilities
7. Accounting for Receivables	Allen's Tutoring Services		Provides tutoring services
8. Accounting for Long-Term Operational Assets	Dryden Enterprises		Van rental company
9. Accounting for Current Liabilities and Payroll	Herrera Supply Company		Supply company
10. Accounting for Long-Term Debt	Mason Company		Leases land
11. Proprietorships, Partnerships, and Corporations	Nelson Incorporated		Software development company
12. Statement of Cash Flows	New South Corporation		Retail gift shop

---

A Look Back <<

Merchandising companies earn profits by selling inventory at prices that are higher than the cost paid for the goods. Merchandising companies include *retail companies* (companies that sell goods to the final consumer) and *wholesale companies* (companies that sell to other merchandising companies). The products sold by merchandising companies

>> A Look Forward

To this point, the text has explained the basic accounting cycle for service and merchandising businesses. Future chapters more closely address specific accounting issues. For example, in Chapter 6 you will learn how to deal with inventory items that are purchased at differing prices. Other chapters will discuss a variety of specific practices that are widely used by real-world companies.

Regardless of the instructional approach, there is no shortcut to learning accounting. Students must practice to master basic accounting concepts. The text includes a prodigious supply of practice materials and exercises and problems.

Self-Study Review Problem

These example problems include a detailed, worked-out solution and provide support for students before they work problems on their own. These review problems are included in an animated audio presentation, on the text website.

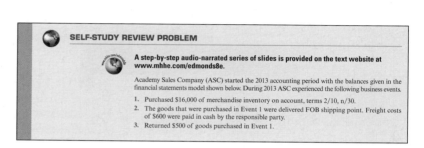

Exercise Series A & B and Problem Series A & B

There are two sets of problems and exercises, Series A and B. Instructors can assign one set for homework and another set for classwork.

● Check Figures

The figures provide key answers for selected problems.

● Excel

Many problems can be solved using the Excel™ templates contained on the text's Online Learning Center. A logo appears in the margins next to these problems.

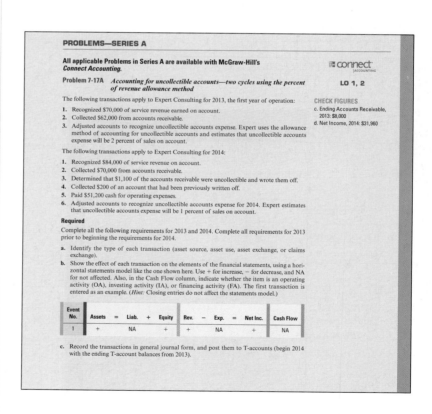

"The self study problems and supplements on the web are very useful for students."

BARRY BUCHOFF,
TOWSON UNIVERSITY

"Exercises and problems are great and provide a variety as well as multiple examples for students to practice."

PATRICIA BANCROFT, BRIDGEWATER
STATE UNIVERSITY

REINFORCED?

Analyze, Think, Communicate (ATC)

Each chapter includes an innovative section entitled Analyze, Think, Communicate (ATC). This section offers Business Applications Cases, Group Assignments, Real World Cases, Writing Assignments, Ethical Dilemma Problems, Research Assignments, and Spreadsheet Assignments.

We use logos to help students identify the type of question being asked.

- **Target Corp.**

- **Group Work** • **Ethics**

- **Real World Company**

- **Research** • **Writing**

- **Excel**

Comprehensive Problem

Beginning in Chapter 1, a comprehensive problem builds in each successive chapter, with the ending account balances in one chapter becoming the beginning account balances in the next chapter.

Mastering Excel and Using Excel

The Excel applications are used to make students comfortable with this analytical tool and to show its use in accounting.

"Lots of good exercises and problems at the end of each chapter with A and B choices."

CAROL SHAVER,
LOUISIANA TECH UNIVERSITY

"I love the spreadsheet assignments and the comprehensive problems at the end of each chapter. I love the check figures that are available on some of the problems."

JANE GARVIN,
IVY TECH COMMUNITY COLLEGE

● McGRAW-HILL *CONNECT® ACCOUNTING*

McGraw-Hill *Connect® Accounting* is an online assignment and assessment solution that connects you with the tools and resources necessary to achieve success through faster learning, more efficient studying, and higher retention of knowledge.

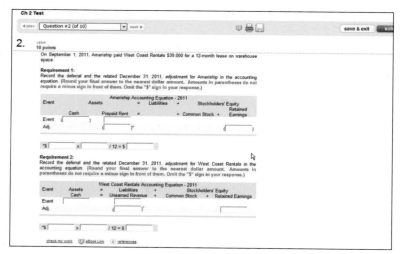

Online Assignments

McGraw-Hill *Connect Accounting* helps students learn more efficiently by providing feedback and practice material when and where they need it. *Connect Accounting* grades homework automatically and gives immediate feedback on any questions students may have missed.

Student Library

The *Connect Accounting* Student Library gives students access to additional resources such as recorded lectures, Self-Quiz and Study practice materials, an eBook, and more.

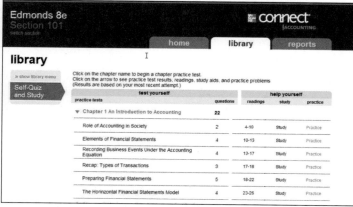

Self-Quiz and Study

Self-Quiz and Study connects students to the learning resources they need to succeed in the course. For each chapter, students can take a practice quiz and immediately see how well they performed. A study plan then recommends specific readings from the text, supplemental study material, and practice exercises that will improve students' understanding and mastery of each learning objective.

SUCCESS? ●━━━━━━━━━━━

● LESS MANAGING. MORE TEACHING. GREATER LEARNING.

McGraw-Hill *Connect Accounting* offers a number of powerful tools and features to make managing assignments easier, so faculty can spend more time teaching. With *Connect Accounting,* students can engage with their coursework anytime, anywhere, making the learning process more accessible and efficient. Please see the previous page for a description of the student tools available within *Connect Accounting.*

McGraw-Hill's *Connect Accounting* for Instructors

Simple Assignment Management and Smart Grading. With McGraw-Hill *Connect Accounting,* creating assignments is easier than ever, so you can spend more time teaching and less time managing. *Connect Accounting* enables you to:

- Create and deliver assignments easily with selectable end-of-chapter questions and test bank items.
- Go paperless with the eBook and online submission and grading of student assignments.
- Have assignments scored automatically, giving students immediate feedback on their work and comparisons with correct answers.
- Reinforce classroom concepts with practice tests and instant quizzes.

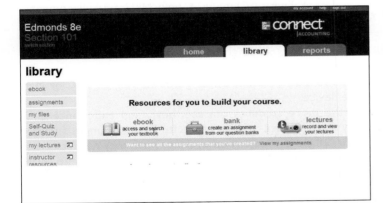

Instructor Library

The *Connect Accounting* Instructor Library is your repository for additional resources to improve student engagement in and out of class. You can select and use any asset that enhances your lecture. The *Connect Accounting* Instructor Library includes access to:

- Solutions Manual
- Instructor's Manual
- Test Bank
- Instructor PowerPoint® slides
- The eBook version of the text

Student Reports

McGraw-Hill's *Connect Accounting* keeps instructors informed about how each student, section, and class is performing, allowing for more productive use of lecture and office hours. The reports tab enables you to:

- View scored work immediately and track individual or group performance with assignment and grade reports.
- Access an instant view of student or class performance relative to learning objectives.
- Collect data and generate reports required by many accreditation organizations, such as AACSB and AICPA.

McGraw-Hill's *Connect® Plus Accounting*

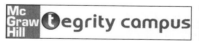

McGraw-Hill reinvents the textbook learning experience for the modern student with *Connect Plus Accounting*, which provides a seamless integration of the eBook and *Connect Accounting*. *Connect Plus Accounting* provides all of the *Connect Accounting* features, as well as:

- An integrated eBook, allowing for anytime, anywhere access to the textbook.
- Dynamic links between the problems or questions you assign to your students and the location in the eBook where the concept related to that problem or question is covered.
- A powerful search function to pinpoint and connect key concepts in a snap.

For more information about *Connect Accounting*, go to **www.mcgrawhillconnect.com,** or contact your local McGraw-Hill sales representative.

● TEGRITY CAMPUS: LECTURES 24/7

Tegrity Campus, a new McGraw-Hill company, provides a service that makes class time available 24/7 by automatically capturing every lecture. With a simple one-click start-and-stop process, you capture all computer screens and corresponding audio in a format that is easily searchable, frame by frame. Students can replay any part of any class with easy-to-use browser-based viewing on a PC or Mac, iPad, iPod, or other mobile device.

Educators know that the more students can see, hear, and experience class resources, the better they learn. In fact, studies prove it. Tegrity Campus's unique search feature helps students efficiently find what they need, when they need it, across an entire semester of class recordings. Help turn your students' study time into learning moments immediately supported by your lecture. With Tegrity Campus, you also increase intent listening and class participation by easing students' concerns about note-taking. Lecture Capture will make it more likely you will see students' faces, not the tops of their heads. To learn more about Tegrity, watch a 2-minute Flash demo at **http://tegritycampus.mhhe.com.**

● ONLINE COURSE MANAGEMENT

McGraw-Hill Higher Education and Blackboard have teamed up. What does this mean for you?

1. **Your life, simplified.** Now you and your students can access McGraw-Hill *Connect* and Create™ right from within your Blackboard course—all with one single sign-on. Say goodbye to the days of logging in to multiple applications.

2. **Deep integration of content and tools.** Not only do you get single sign-on with *Connect* and Create, you also get deep integration of McGraw-Hill content and content engines right in Blackboard. Whether you're choosing a book for your course or building *Connect* assignments, all the tools you need are right where you want them—inside of Blackboard.

3. **Seamless grade books.** Are you tired of keeping multiple grade books and manually synchronizing grades into Blackboard? We thought so. When a student completes an integrated *Connect* assignment, the grade for that assignment automatically (and instantly) feeds your Blackboard grade center.

4. **A solution for everyone.** Whether your institution is already using Blackboard or you just want to try Blackboard on your own, we have a solution for you. McGraw-Hill and Blackboard can now offer you easy access to industry-leading technology and content, whether your campus hosts it, or we do. Be sure to ask your local McGraw-Hill representative for details or visit **www.domorenow.com.**

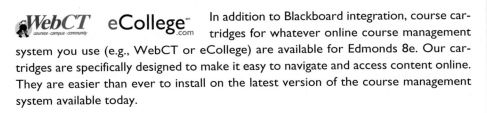

In addition to Blackboard integration, course cartridges for whatever online course management system you use (e.g., WebCT or eCollege) are available for Edmonds 8e. Our cartridges are specifically designed to make it easy to navigate and access content online. They are easier than ever to install on the latest version of the course management system available today.

● McGRAW-HILL/IRWIN CARES

At McGraw-Hill/Irwin, we understand that getting the most from new technology can be challenging. That's why our services don't stop after you purchase our book. You can e-mail our Product Specialists 24 hours a day, get product training online, or search our knowledge bank of Frequently Asked Questions on our support website. For Customer Support, call 800-331-5094 or visit **www.mhhe.com/support.** One of our Technical Support Analysts will assist you in a timely fashion.

Assurance of Learning Ready

Many educational institutions today are focused on the notion of *assurance of learning*, an important element of many accreditation standards. *Fundamental Financial Accounting Concepts 8e* is designed specifically to support your assurance of learning initiatives with a simple, yet powerful, solution.

Each chapter in the book begins with a list of numbered learning objectives, which appear throughout the chapter as well as in the end-of-chapter assignments. Every Test Bank question for *Fundamental Financial Accounting Concepts* maps to a specific chapter learning objective in the textbook. Each Test Bank question also identifies topic area, level of difficulty, Bloom's Taxonomy level, AICPA and AACSB skill area. You can use our Test Bank software, *EZ Test Online*, or *Connect Accounting* to easily search for learning objectives that directly relate to the learning objectives for your course. You can then use the reporting features of *EZ Test* to aggregate student results in similar fashion, making the collection and presentation of Assurance of Learning data simple and easy.

AACSB Statement

McGraw-Hill/Irwin is a proud corporate member of AACSB International. Understanding the importance and value of AACSB accreditation, *Fundamental Financial Accounting Concepts 8e* recognizes the curricula guidelines detailed in the AACSB standards for business accreditation by connecting selected questions in the text and the Test Bank to the general knowledge and skill guidelines in the AACSB standards.

The statements contained in *Fundamental Financial Accounting Concepts 8e* are provided only as a guide for the users of this textbook. The AACSB leaves content coverage and assessment within the purview of individual schools, the mission of the school, and the faculty. While *Fundamental Financial Accounting Concepts 8e* and the teaching package make no claim of any specific AACSB qualification or evaluation, we have, within the text and test bank labeled selected questions according to the six general knowledge and skills areas.

McGraw-Hill's *Connect®* Accounting

 McGraw-Hill *Connect Accounting* offers a number of powerful tools and features to make managing your classroom easier. *Connect Accounting* with Edmonds 8e offers enhanced features and technology to help both you and your students make the most of your time inside and outside the classroom. See page xiv for more details.

Online Learning Center
(www.mhhe.com/edmonds8e)

The password protected instructor side of the book's Online Learning Center (OLC) houses all the instructor resources you need to administer your course, including:

• Solutions Manual

• Instructor's Manual

• Test Bank

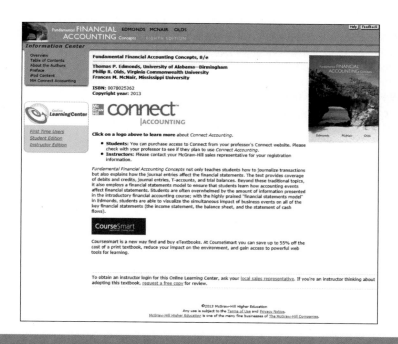

- Instructor PowerPoints
- Excel Templates and Solutions

If you choose to use *Connect Accounting* with Edmonds, you will have access to these same resources via the Instructor Library.

Instructor's Manual

This comprehensive manual includes step-by-step, explicit instructions on how the text can be used to implement alternative teaching methods. It also provides guidance for instructors who use the traditional lecture method. The guide includes lesson plans and demonstration problems with student work papers, as well as solutions.

Solutions Manual

Prepared by the authors, the manual contains complete solutions to all the text's end-of-chapter exercises, problems, and cases.

PowerPoint Presentation

These audio-narrated slides can serve as interactive class discussions.

Test Bank

This test bank in Word™ format contains multiple-choice questions, essay questions, and short problems. Each test item is coded for level of difficulty learning objective AACSB, AICPA and Bloom's.

EZ Test Online

Available through the Online Learning Center, *Connect* Instructor Library, and at www.eztestonline, McGraw-Hill's EZ Test Online allows you to quickly create customized exams. This user-friendly program allows instructors to sort questions by format; edit existing questions or add new ones. It also can scramble questions for multiple versions of the same test.

McGraw-Hill *Connect*® *Accounting* and *Connect*® *Plus Accounting*

McGraw-Hill *Connect Accounting* helps prepare you for your future by enabling faster learning, more efficient studying, and higher retention of knowledge. *Connect Plus Accounting* includes everything in *Connect* plus access to a searchable, integrated online version of the text. If your instructor chooses to use *Connect Accounting*, you can purchase access from the Online Learning Center at www.mhhe.com/edmonds8e.

CourseSmart

CourseSmart is a new way to find and buy eTextbooks. At Course-Smart you can save up to 55 percent off the cost of a print textbook, reduce your impact on the environment, and gain access to powerful web tools for learning. CourseSmart has the largest selection of eTextbooks available anywhere, offering thousands of the most commonly adopted textbooks from a wide variety of higher education publishers. CourseSmart eTextbooks are available in one standard online reader with full text search, notes and highlighting, and e-mail tools for sharing notes between classmates.

Online Learning Center
www.mhhe.com/edmonds8e

The Online Learning Center (OLC) follows Edmonds 8e chapter by chapter, offering all kinds of supplementary help for you as you read. The OLC includes the following resources to help you study more efficiently:

- Online Quizzes
- Student PowerPoint slides
- Narrated PowerPoint lectures
- Self-Study Review slides
- Excel Templates
- Video Library
- Appendices
- Links to Accounting Resources

If your instructor chooses to use *Connect Accounting* in this course, you will have access to these same resources via the Student Library.

Study Guide

ISBN-10: 0077433874   ISBN-13: 9780077433871
This proactive guide incorporates many of the accounting skills essential to student success. Each chapter contains a review and explanation of the chapter's learning objectives, as well as multiple-choice problems and short exercises. Unique to this Study Guide is a series of articulation problems that require students to indicate how accounting events affect the elements of financial statements.

Working Papers

ISBN-10: 0077433882   ISBN-13: 9780077433888
This study aid contains forms that help students organize their solutions to homework exercises and problems and is also available through McGraw-Hill *Create*.

Excel Templates

These templates allow students to develop spreadsheet skills to solve selected assignments identified by an icon in the end-of-chapter material.

● ACKNOWLEDGMENTS ●

Our grateful appreciation is extended to those who reviewed previous editions:

Special thanks to the talented people who prepared the supplements. These take a great deal of time and effort to write and we appreciate their efforts. Molly Brown of James Madison University prepared the Test Bank and accuracy checked the Instructor's Manual and PowerPoints. Anna Lusher of Slippery Rock University wrote the Instructors Manual. Jack Terry developed the Excel Templates. LuAnn Bean of Florida Institute of Technology prepared the online quizzes and PowerPoints. Loretta Manktelow of James Madison University accuracy checked the Test Bank and quizzes. We also thank our accuracy checkers Ilene Persoff of CW Post Campus/Long Island University and LuAnn Bean of Florida Institute of Technology. A special thanks to Linda Bell of William Jewell College for her contribution to the Financial Statement Analysis material that appears in Appendix D.

We extend our sincere appreciation to Tim Vertovec, Dana Woo, Diane Nowaczyk, Katie Jones, Kathleen Klehr, Jeremy Cheshareck, Pam Verros, Carol Bielski, Allison Souter, and Ron Nelms. We deeply appreciate the long hours that you committed to the formation of a high-quality text.

• Thomas P. Edmonds • Frances M. McNair • Philip R. Olds

We would like to express our appreciation to the people who have provided assistance in the development of this textbook.

We express our sincere thanks to the following individuals who provided extensive reviews for the seventh and eighth editions:

Reviewers

Stacey Adams, *Antelope Valley College*
Susan Anderson, *Appalachian State University*
Patricia Bancroft, *Bridgewater State University*
Debbie Benson, *Kennesaw State University*
J. Lawrence Bergin, *Winona State University*
Eddy Birrer, *Gonzaga University*
Lindsey Boyer, *Central Piedmont Community College*
Amy Bourne, *Oregon State University*
Barry Buchoff, *Towson University*
Georgia Buckles, *Manchester Community College*
Jackie Burke, *Hofstra University*
Roscoe Eugene Bryson, *University of Alabama in Huntsville*
Sandra Byrd, *Missouri State University*
Mark Camma, *Atlantic Cape Community College*
Elizabeth Cannata, *Johnson & Wales University*
Guenther Dermanelian, *Johnson & Wales University*
Caroline Falconetti, *Nassau Community College*
Jane Garvin, *Ivy Tech Community College*
Abo-El-Yazeed Habib, *Minnesota State University, Mankato*
Deborah Hanks, *Cardinal Stritch University*

David Juriga, *Saint Louis Community College*
Cindi Khanlarian, *University of North Carolina Greensboro*
Leah Kratz, *Eastern Mennonite University*
Joan Lacher, *Nassau Community College*
Steven LaFave, *Augsburg College*
Joseph Larkin, *Saint Joseph's University*
Laurie Larson, *Valencia Community College*
Nancy Lynch, *West Virginia University*
Mary Manktelow, *James Madison University*
Lynn Mazzola, *Nassau Community College*
Sara Melendy, *Gonzaga University*
Patrick Montgomery, *University of Wisconsin, Platteville*
Gerald Motl, *Xavier University*
Steve Muller, *Valencia Community College*
Christine Noel, *Colorado State University—Pueblo*
Ron O'Brien, *Fayetteville Technical Community College*
Viola Persia, *SUNY Stony Brook*
Jack Peterson, *Utah State University*
Atul Rai, *Wichita State University*
Ann Rowell, *Central Piedmont Community College*
Joanne Segovia, *Minnesota State University, Moorhead*

Carol Shaver, *Louisiana Tech University*
Mary Sheil, *Kennesaw State University*
Eileen Shifflett, *James Madison University*
Nathan Slavin, *Hofstra University*
Sondra Smith, *University of West Georgia*
Nancy Snow, *University of Toledo*
Vic Stanton, *University of California Berkeley*

Gloria Stuart, *Georgia Southern University*
Jan Sweeney, *Baruch College CUNY*
Kerri Tassin, *Missouri State University*
Steve Teeter, *Utah Valley State College*
Peter Theuri, *Northern Kentucky University*
Ada Till, *Prairie View A&M University*
Marjorie Yuschak, *Rutgers University*

Focus Group Participants

Mark Anderson, *University of Texas at Dallas*
Brenda Benson, *Blinn College*
Anna Marie Boulware, *St. Charles Community College*
Norris Dorsey, *California State University, Northridge*
Caroline Falconetti, *Nassau Community College*
Judith Harris, *Nova Southeastern University*
Carol Hutchinson, *AB Tech*
Douglas Larson, *Salem State College*
Joseph Lupino, *St. Mary's College of California*
Al Nagy, *John Carroll University*
Ron Pierno, *Florida State University*
Linda Poulson, *Elon University*
Atul Rai, *Wichita State University*

Gayle Richardson, *Bakersfield College*
Dwight Riley, *Richland College*
Megan Schaupp, *West Virginia University—Morgantown*
Rex Schildhouse, *Miramar College*
Virginia Smith, *Saint Mary's College of California*
Warren Smock, *Ivy Tech Community College*
Kathy Sobieralski, *University of Maryland, University College*
Rasoul Taghizadeh, *Bluegrass Community and Technical College*
LaVerne Thomas-Vertrees, *St. Louis Community College*
Al Wallace, *Owensboro Community & Technical College*

Past Edition Reviewers

Our grateful appreciation is extended to those who reviewed previous editions:

Charles Richard Aldridge, *Western Kentucky University*
Mary Allen, *Boise State University*
Sheila Ammons, *Austin Community College*
Marie Archambault, *Marshall University*
Kashi Balachandran, *Stern School, New York University*
Debra Barbeau, *Southern Illinois University-Carbondale*
Charles Baril, *James Madison University*
Beryl Barkman, *University of Massachusetts-Dartmouth*
Cheryl Bartlett, *Albuquerque TVI Community College*
Ira Bates, *Florida A&M University*
Jim Bates, *Mountain Empire Community College*
Deborah Beard, *Southeast Missouri State University*
Judy Beebe, *Western Oregon University*
Linda Bell, *William Jewell College*
Judy Benish, *Fox Valley Tech*
Wilbur Berry, *Jacksonville State University*
Nancy Bledsoe, *Millsaps College*
Cendy Boyd, *Northeast Louisiana State*
Arthur Boyett, *Francis Marion University*
Cassie Bradley, *Troy State University*
Rodger Brannan, *University of Minnesota, Duluth*

Connie Buchanan, *Southwest Texas Junior College*
Radie Bunn, *Southwest Missouri State University*
Gregory Bushong, *Wright State University*
Judith Cadle, *Tarleton State University*
James Cahsell, *Miami University*
Scott Cairns, *Shippensburg College*
Eric Carlsen, *Kean University*
Frederic J. Carlson, *LeTourneau University*
Joan Carroll, *SUNY-College at Oswego*
Valrie Chambers, *Texas A&M University, Corpus Christi*
Bruce Chase, *Radford University*
Bea Chiang, *College of New Jersey*
Alan Cherry, *Loyola Marymount University*
Ginger Clark, *University of Cincinnati*
Paul Clikeman, *University of Richmond*
Ronald Colley, *State University of West Georgia*
Cheryl Corke, *Genesse Community College*
Samantha Cox, *Wake Technical Community College*
William Cress, *University of Wisconsin-La Cross*
Kathy Crusto-Way, *Tarrant County College Southeast*
Sue Cullers, *Tarleton State University*
Jill D'Aquila, *Iona College*
Wagih Dafashy, *College of William & Mary*
Laura DeLaune, *Louisiana State University*

Robert Derstine, *Villanova University*
Walter Doehring, *Genesee Community College*
George Dow, *Valencia Community College*
Lola Dudley, *Eastern Illinois University*
Melanie Earls, *Mississippi State University*
Catherine Eason, *Queens University of Charlotte*
Alan Eastman, *Indiana University of Pennsylvania*
M. J. Edwards, *Adirondack Community College*
Susan Eldridge, *University of Nebraska, Omaha*
Terry Elliott, *Morehead State University*
Tom English, *Boise State University*
Denise English, *Boise State University*
Ruth Epps, *Virginia Commonwealth University*
John Farlin, *Ohio Dominican University*
Philip Fink, *University of Toledo*
Ralph Fritzsch, *Midwestern State University*
David Fordham, *James Madison University*
Ken Fowler, *San Jose State University*
Lou Fowler, *Missouri Western State College*
Peter Frischmann, *Idaho State University*
Mark Fronke, *Cerritos College*
Ross Fuerman, *Suffolk University*
Mary Anne Gaffney, *Temple University*
David Ganz, *University of Missouri-Saint Louis*
Michael Garner, *Salisbury State University*
William T. Geary, *College of William and Mary*
Lucille Genduso, *Nova Southeastern University*
Frank Gersich, *Gustavus Adolphus College*
Daniel Gibbons, *Waubonsee Community College*
Frank Giove, *Niagara University*
Claudia Gilbertson, *North Hennepin Community College*
Lorraine Glasscock, *University of North Alabama*
Diane Glowacki, *Tarrant County College*
John Gould, *Western Carolina University*
Joseph Guardino, *Kingsborough Community College*
Jeffry Haber, *Iona College*
Larry Hagler, *East Carolina University*
Penny Hanes, *Virginia Tech University*
Leon Hanouille, *Syracuse University*
Coby Harmon, *University of California, Santa Barbara*
Judith Harris, *Nova Southeastern University*
Phillip Harsha, *Southwest Missouri State University*
Charles Hart, *Copiah-Lincoln Community College*
Paul Haugen, *Wisconsin Indianhead Technical College*
Thomas Hayes, *University of Louisiana, Monroe*
Inez Heal, *Youngstown State University*
Kenneth Hiltebeitel, *Villanova*
Nitham Hindi, *Shippensburg College*
Jan Holmes, *Louisiana State University*
Bambi Hora, *University of Central Oklahoma*
M. A. Houston, *Wright State University*
Susan Hughes, *Butler University*
Kurt Hull, *California State University, Los Angeles*

Karen Hull, *Kansas Wesleyan University*
Richard Hulme, *California State Polytechnic University-Pomona*
Sharon Jackson, *Samford University*
Gary Todd Jackson, *Northeastern State University*
Agatha Jeffers, *Montclair State University*
Scott Jerris, *San Francisco State University*
Pamela Jones, *Mississippi State University*
Shelley Stall Kane, *Wake Technical Community College*
Khondkar Karim, *Monmouth University*
Bonita Kramer, *Montana State University*
Nathan Kranowski, *Radford University*
Helen LaFrancois, *University of Massachusetts-Dartmouth*
Ellen Landgraf, *Loyola University, Chicago*
Robert Landry, *Massasoit Community College*
William Lathen, *Boise State University*
Doug Laufer, *Metropolitan State College of Denver*
Daniel Law, *Gonzaga University*
Marilynn Leathart, *John Carroll University*
Patsy Lee, *University of Texas, Arlington*
June Li, *University of Minnesota, Duluth*
David Law, *Youngstown State University*
William Link, *University of Missouri-Saint Louis*
Larry Logan, *University of Massachusetts-Dartmouth*
Patricia Lopez, *Valencia Community College*
James Lukawitz, *University of Memphis*
Catherine Lumbattis, *Southern Illinois University-Carbondale*
Mary MacAusland, *Reading Area Community College*
Mostafa Maksy, *Northeastern Illinois University*
Joseph Marcheggiani, *Butler University*
Herb Martin, *Hope College*
Elizabeth Matz, *University of Pittsburgh, Bradford*
Alan Mayer-Sommer, *Georgetown University*
Ruth Ann McEwen, *Suffolk University*
Dwight McIntyre, *Clemson University*
Shaen McMurtrie, *Northern Oklahoma College*
Dawn McKinley, *William Rainey Harper College*
Nancy Meade, *Radford University*
Trini Melcher, *California State University, San Marcos*
Pam Meyer, *University of Louisiana, Lafayette*
R. L. C. Miller, *California State University, Fullerton*
Elizabeth Minbiole, *Northwood University*
Susan Minke, *Indiana University-Purdue University, Ft. Wayne*
George Minmier, *University of Memphis*
Cheryl Mitchem, *Virginia State University*
Lu Montondon, *Southwest Texas State University*
Elizabeth Mulig, *Columbus State University*
Steven Muller, *Valencia Community College*
Carol Murphy, *Quinsigamond Community College*
Irvin Nelson, *Utah State University*
Bruce Neumann, *University of Colorado, Denver*
Tim Nygaard, *Madisonville Community College*

Brian O'Doherty, *East Carolina University*
Bruce Oliver, *Rochester Institute of Technology*
Joseph Onyeocha, *South Carolina State University*
Ashton Oravetz, *Tyler Junior College*
Stephen Owusu-Ansah, *University of Texas, Pan American*
Lawrence Ozzello, *University of Wisconsin-Eau Claire*
Eileen Peacock, *Oakland University*
Kathy Perdue, *DeVry Institute of Technology at Decatur*
Thomas Phillips, Jr., *Louisiana Tech University*
Cynthia Phipps, *Lake Land College*
Ronald Pierno, *Florida State University*
Cathy Pitts, *Highline Community College*
Mary Raven, *Mount Mary College*
Craig Reeder, *Florida A&M University*
Thomas Rearick, *Indiana University*
Jane Reimers, *Florida State University*
Ann Rich, *Quinnipiac University*
Laura Rickett, *Kent State University*
Michael Riordan, *James Madison University*
Patricia Robinson, *Johnson and Wales University*
Luther Ross, *Central Piedmont Community College*
Nadine Russell
Ken Ruby, *Idaho State University*
P. N. Saksena, *Indiana University, South Bend*
Nancy Schneider, *Lynchburg College*
Henry Schulman, *Grossmont College*
Jeffrey Schwartz, *Montgomery College*
Lewis Shaw, *Suffolk University*
Cindy Seipel, *New Mexico State University*
Suzanne Sevalstad, *University of Nevada-Las Vegas*
Kim Shaughnessy, *James Madison University*
John Shaver, *Louisiana Tech University*
Lewis Shaw, *Suffolk University*
Jill Smith, *Idaho State University*
Talitha Smith, *Auburn University*
Paul E. Solomon
John Sperry, *Virginia Commonwealth University*
Barbara Squires, *Corning Community College*
Mary Soroko, *St. Cloud State University*
Linda Specht, *Trinity University*

Paul Steinbart, *Saint Louis University-Saint Louis*
Scott Steinkamp, *College of Lake County*
Tim Stephens, *DeVry Institute of Technology at Addison*
Mary Stevens, *University of Texas-El Paso*
Sue Stickland, *University of Texas, Arlington*
Leonard Stokes, *Siena College*
Janice Swanson, *Southern Oregon University*
James Swayze, *University of Nevada, Las Vegas*
Ellen Sweatt, *Georgia Perimeter College*
Rasoul Taghizadeh, *Lexington Community College*
Bill Talbot, *Montgomery College*
James Thompson, *Oklahoma City University*
Karen Turner, *University of Northern Colorado*
Maurice Tassin, *Louisiana Tech University*
Kim Temme, *Maryville University*
Suneel Udpa, *St. Mary's College of California*
Donna Ulmer, *St. Louis Community College, Meramec*
Denise Dickins Veitch, *Florida Atlantic University*
George Violette, *University of Southern Maine*
Beth Vogel, *Mount Mary College*
Sharon Walters, *Morehead State University*
Andrea Weickgenannt, *Northern Kentucky University*
J. D. Weinhold, *Concordia College*
Judith Welch, *University of Central Florida*
T. Sterling Wetzel, *Oklahoma State University, Stillwater*
Thomas Whalen, *Suffolk University*
Thomas Whitacre, *University of South Carolina*
Jennifer Wilbanks, *State Fair Community College*
Macil C. Wilkie, Jr., *Grambling State University*
Marvin Williams, *University of Houston*
Stephen Willits, *Bucknell University*
Marie Winks, *Lynchburg College*
Kenneth Winter, *University of Wisconsin-La Cross.*
Alan Winters, *Clemson University*
Gail Wright, *Bryant University*
Judith Zander, *Grossmont College*
Haiwen Zhang, *University of Minnesota*
Ping Zhon, *Baruch College*

Brief Contents

Chapter 1   An Introduction to Accounting   2

Chapter 2   Accounting for Accruals and Deferrals   62

Chapter 3   The Double-Entry System   138

Chapter 4   Accounting for Merchandising Businesses   206

Chapter 5   Accounting for Inventories   268

Chapter 6   Internal Control and Accounting for Cash   312

Chapter 7   Accounting for Receivables   360

Chapter 8   Accounting for Long-Term Operational Assets   416

Chapter 9   Accounting for Current Liabilities and Payroll   476

Chapter 10   Accounting for Long-Term Debt   534

Chapter 11   Proprietorships, Partnerships, and Corporations   592

Chapter 12   Statement of Cash Flows   640

Chapter 13   Financial Statement Analysis (Available online only at www.mhhe.com/edmonds8e)   13-0

Appendix A   Accessing the EDGAR Database through the Internet   696

Appendix B   Portion of the Form 10-K for Target Corporation   697

Appendix C   Summary of Financial Radios   754

Appendix D   Annual Report and Financial Statement Analysis Projects   757

Appendix E   Accounting for Investment Securities   764

Appendix F   Time Value of Money   773

Glossary   781

Photo Credits   792

Index   793

Contents

Note from the Authors   iv

Chapter 1   An Introduction to Accounting   2

Chapter Opening   2
Section 1: Collecting and Organizing Information   3
Role of Accounting in Society   4
   Using Free Markets to Set Resource Priorities   4
   Accounting Provides Information   6
   Types of Accounting Information   6
   Nonbusiness Resource Usage   6
   Careers in Accounting   7
   Measurement Rules   8
   Reporting Entities   9
Elements of Financial Statements   10
   Using Accounts to Gather Information   11
   Accounting Equation   12
Recording Business Events under the Accounting Equation   14
   Asset Source Transactions   14
   Asset Exchange Transactions   15
   Another Asset Source Transaction   16
   Asset Use Transactions   16
   Summary of Transactions   18
Recap: Types of Transactions   19
Section 2: Reporting Information   19
Preparing Financial Statements   20

   Income Statement and the Matching Concept   20
   Statement of Changes in Stockholders' Equity   22
   Balance Sheet   22
   Statement of Cash Flows   23
   The Closing Process   24
The Horizontal Financial Statements Model   25
The Financial Analyst   26
   Real-World Financial Reports   26
   Annual Report for Target Corporation   26
   Special Terms in Real-World Reports   27
A Look Back   28
A Look Forward   29
Self-Study Review Problem   29
Key Terms   30
Questions   31
Multiple-Choice Questions   31
Exercises—Series A   31
Problems—Series A   40
Exercises—Series B   44
Problems—Series B   52
Analyze, Think, Communicate   55
Comprehensive Problem   61

Chapter 2   Accounting for Accruals and Deferrals   62

Chapter Opening   62
Section 1: Accounting for Accruals   63
Accrual Accounting   64
   Accounting for Accounts Receivable   65
   Other Events   65
   Accounting for Accrued Salary Expense (Adjusting Entry)   66
   Summary of Events and General Ledger   67
   Vertical Statements Model   67
   The Closing Process   70

   Steps in an Accounting Cycle   70
   The Matching Concept   70
   The Conservation Principle   72
Section 2: Accounting for Deferrals   72
Second Accounting Cycle   72
   Accounting for Supplies Purchase   72
   Prepaid Items (Cost versus Expense)   73
   Accounting for Receipt of Unearned Revenue   74

Other 2014 Events 74

Adjusting Entries 76

Accounting for Supplies (Adjusting Entry) 76

Accounting for Prepaid Rent (Adjusting Entry) 76

Accounting for Unearned Revenue (Adjusting Entry) 77

Accounting for Accrued Salary Expense (Adjusting Entry) 80

Summary of Events and General Ledger 80

Vertical Statements Model 80

Transaction Classification 84

The Financial Analyst 85

Corporate Governance 85

Importance of Ethics 85

Sarbanes-Oxley Act 85

Common Features of Criminal and Ethical Misconduct 86

A Look Back 88

A Look Forward 89

Appendix 89

Self-Study Review Problem 93

Key Terms 95

Questions 95

Multiple-Choice Questions 95

Section 1 Exercises—Series A 96

Section 2 Exercises—Series A 98

Problems—Series A 107

Section 1 Exercises—Series B 113

Section 2 Exercises—Series B 116

Problems—Series B 125

Analyze, Think, Communicate 131

Comprehensive Problem 136

Chapter 3   The Double-Entry Accounting System   138

Chapter Opening 138

Debit/Credit Terminology 140

Recording Transactions in T-Accounts 140

Asset Source Transactions 140

Asset Exchange Transactions 143

Asset Use Transactions 144

Claims Exchange Transactions 146

Adjusting the Accounts 147

Overview of Debit/Credit Relationships 149

The General Journal 149

Trial Balance and Financial Statements 153

Closing Entries 155

Post-Closing Trial Balance 156

The Financial Analyst 157

Assessing the Effective Use of Assets 157

Assessing Debt Risk 158

Real-World Data 159

Scope of Coverage 160

A Look Back 160

A Look Forward 161

Appendix 161

Self-Study Review Problem 163

Key Terms 166

Questions 166

Multiple-Choice Questions 167

Exercises—Series A 167

Problems—Series A 175

Exercises—Series B 182

Problems—Series B 191

Analyze, Think, Communicate 198

Comprehensive Problem 204

Chapter 4   Accounting for Merchandising Businesses   206

Chapter Opening   206

Accounting for Inventory Transactions   209

Allocating Inventory Cost between Asset and Expense Accounts   210

Perpetual Inventory System   210

Effects of 2013 Events on Financial Statements   210

Ledger Accounts and Financial Statements   212

Transportation Cost, Purchase Returns and Allowances, and Cash Discounts Related to Inventory Purchases   214

Effects of 2014 Events on Financial Statements   214

Accounting for Purchase Returns and Allowances   215

Purchase Discounts   216

The Cost of Financing Inventory   217

Accounting for Transportation Costs   217

Recognizing Gains and Losses   220

Multistep Income Statement   222

Lost, Damaged, or Stolen Inventory   224

Events Affecting Sales   225

Accounting for Sales Returns and Allowances   226

Accounting for Sales Discounts   227

The Financial Analyst   228

Common Size Financial Statements   228

Ratio Analysis   229

Real-World Data   230

A Look Back   231

A Look Forward   232

Appendix   232

Self-Study Review Problem   234

Key Terms   236

Questions   236

Multiple-Choice Questions   237

Exercises—Series A   237

Problems—Series A   245

Exercises—Series B   249

Problems—Series B   257

Analyze, Think, Communicate   261

Comprehensive Problem   266

Chapter 5   Accounting for Inventories   268

Chapter Opening   268

Inventory Cost Flow Methods   270

Specific Identification   270

First-In, First-Out (FIFO)   270

Last-In, First-Out (LIFO)   270

Weighted Average   270

Physical Flow   270

Effect of Cost Flow on Financial Statements   271

Multiple Layers with Multiple Quantities   272

Allocating Cost of Goods Available for Sale   272

Effect of Cost Flow on Financial Statements   274

Inventory Cost Flow When Sales and Purchases Occur Intermittently   276

Lower-of-Cost-or-Market Rule   278

Avoiding Fraud in Merchandising Businesses   280

Estimating the Ending Inventory Balance   282

The Financial Analyst   283
  Average Number of Days to Sell Inventory   284
  Is It a Marketing or an Accounting Decision?   284
  Real-World Data   284
  Effects of Cost Flow on Ratio Analysis   285
A Look Back   285
A Look Forward   286
Self-Study Review Problem   286

Key Terms   287
Questions   287
Multiple-Choice Questions   287
Exercises—Series A   288
Problems—Series A   293
Exercises—Series B   297
Problems—Series B   302
Analyze, Think, Communicate   306
Comprehensive Problem   310

Chapter 6   Internal Control and Accounting for Cash   312

Chapter Opening   312
Key Features of Internal Control Systems   314
  Separation of Duties   315
  Quality of Employees   315
  Bonded Employees   315
  Required Absences   315
  Procedures Manual   315
  Authority and Responsibility   316
  Prenumbered Documents   316
  Physical Control   316
  Performance Evaluations   317
  Limitations   317
Accounting for Cash   317
  Controlling Cash   318
  Checking Account Documents   320
Reconciling the Bank Account   321
  Determining True Cash Balance   321
  Adjustments to the Bank Balance   322
  Adjustments to the Book Balance   322
  Correction of Errors   323
  Certified Checks   323
  Illustrating a Bank Reconciliation   323
  Updating GSRI's Accounting Records   324
  Cash Short and Over   326

Using Petty Cash Funds   327
The Financial Analyst   329
Notes to the Financial Statements   329
Management's Discussion and Analysis   330
Role of the Independent Auditor   330
  The Financial Statements Audit   330
  Materiality and Financial Statements Audits   331
  Types of Audit Opinions   332
  Confidentiality   332
The Securities and Exchange Commission   332
A Look Back   333
A Look Forward   334
Self-Study Review Problem   335
Key Terms   336
Questions   336
Multiple-Choice Questions   336
Exercises—Series A   337
Problems—Series A   341
Exercises—Series B   345
Problems—Series B   349
Analyze, Think, Communicate   354
Comprehensive Problem   358

Chapter 7 Accounting for Receivables 360

Chapter Opening 360

Allowance Method of Accounting for Uncollectible Accounts 362

Accounting Events Affecting the 2013 Period 362

Recording and Reporting Uncollectible Accounts Events in the Double-Entry System 364

Financial Statements 364

Accounting Events Affecting the 2014 Period 365

Estimating Uncollectible Accounts Expense Using the Percent of Revenue (Sales) Method 368

Recording and Reporting Uncollectible Accounts Events in the Double-Entry System 369

Analysis of Financial Statements 370

Estimating Uncollectible Accounts Expense Using the Percent of Receivables Method 370

Matching Revenues and Expenses versus Asset Measurement 372

Recognizing Uncollectible Accounts Expense Using the Direct Write-Off Method 372

Accounting for Notes Receivable 373

Recording and Reporting Transactions Related to Notes Receivable 374

Financial Statements 377

Accounting for Credit Card Sales 378

The Financial Analyst 379

Costs of Credit Sales 379

Average Number of Days to Collect Accounts Receivable 380

Real-World Data 381

A Look Back 383

A Look Forward 384

Self-Study Review Problem 384

Key Terms 385

Questions 385

Multiple-Choice Questions 386

Exercises—Series A 386

Problems—Series A 393

Exercises—Series B 398

Problems—Series B 405

Analyze, Think, Communicate 410

Comprehensive Problem 414

Chapter 8 Accounting for Long-Term Operational Assets 416

Chapter Opening 416

Tangible versus Intangible Assets 418

Tangible Long-Term Assets 418

Intangible Assets 419

Determining the Cost of Long-Term Assets 419

Basket Purchase Allocation 419

Methods of Recognizing Depreciation Expense 420

Dryden Enterprises Illustration 421

Straight-Line Depreciation 421

Financial Statements 423

Double-Declining-Balance Depreciation 425

Units-of-Production Depreciation 427

Comparing the Depreciation Methods 429

Income Tax Considerations 429

Revision of Estimates 431

Revision of Life 431

Revision of Salvage 432

Continuing Expenditures for Plant Assets   432

Costs that Are Expensed   432

Costs that Are Capitalized   432

Natural Resources   434

Intangible Assets   435

Trademarks   436

Patents   436

Copyrights   436

Franchises   437

Goodwill   437

Expense Recognition for Intangible Assets   438

Balance Sheet Presentation   439

The Financial Analyst   440

Effect of Judgment and Estimation   440

Effect of Industry Characteristics   441

A Look Back   441

A Look Forward   442

Self-Study Review Problem   442

Key Terms   443

Questions   444

Multiple-Choice Questions   444

Exercises—Series A   445

Problems—Series A   451

Exercises—Series B   456

Problems—Series B   463

Analyze, Think, Communicate   468

Comprehensive Problem   474

Chapter 9   Accounting for Current Liabilities and Payroll   476

Chapter Opening   476

Accounting for Notes Payable   478

Accounting for Sales Tax   480

Contingent Liabilities   481

Warranty Obligations   482

General Ledger T-Accounts and Financial Statements   484

Accounting for Payroll   485

Identifying Employees   485

Employees' Gross Earnings   486

Deductions from Employees' Gross Earnings   486

Federal Income Taxes   486

Federal Income Tax Documents   487

Social Security and Medicare Taxes (FICA)   488

Voluntary Withholdings (Deductions)   489

Computing Employee Net Pay   490

Employer Payroll Taxes   491

Recording and Reporting Payroll Taxes   491

Employee Fringe Benefits   492

The Financial Analyst   492

Current versus Noncurrent   492

Liquidity versus Solvency   495

Real-World Data   496

A Look Back   496

A Look Forward   497

Appendix   497

Self-Study Review Problem   503

Key Terms   505

Questions   506

Multiple-Choice Questions   506

Exercises—Series A   506

Problems—Series A   513

Exercises—Series B   517

Problems—Series B   524

Analyze, Think, Communicate   528

Comprehensive Problem   532

xxxii

Chapter 10   Accounting for Long-Term Debt   534

Chapter Opening   534

Installment Notes Payable   536

Line of Credit   539

Bond Liabilities   539

    Advantages of Issuing Bonds   540

    Security of Bonds   541

    Timing of Maturity   541

    Special Features   542

    Bond Ratings   543

    Restrictive Covenants   543

    Bonds Issued at Face Value   543

    Journal Entries and Financial Statement Effects   543

    Effect of Events on Financial Statements   543

    Financial Statements   545

Amortization Using the Straight-Line Method   546

    Bonds Issued at a Discount   546

    Bonds Issued at a Premium   551

    Bond Redemptions   552

Amortization Using the Effective Interest Rate Method   553

    Amortizing Bond Discounts   554

    Amortizing Bond Premiums   555

The Financial Analyst   557

    Financial Leverage and Tax Advantage of Debt Financing   557

    EBIT and Ratio Analysis   558

    Times Interest Earned Ratio   559

A Look Back   560

A Look Forward   560

Self-Study Review Problem   560

Key Terms   561

Questions   561

Multiple-Choice Questions   562

Exercises—Series A   562

Problems—Series A   569

Exercises—Series B   573

Problems—Series B   580

Analyze, Think, Communicate   583

Comprehensive Problem   590

Chapter 11   Proprietorships, Partnerships, and Corporations   592

Chapter Opening   592

Forms of Business Organizations   594

    Regulation   594

    Double Taxation   595

    Limited Liability   596

    Continuity   596

    Transferability of Ownership   596

    Management Structure   596

    Ability to Raise Capital   597

    Appearance of Capital Structure in Financial Statements   597

Accounting for Capital Stock   599

    Par Value   599

    Stated Value   599

    Other Valuation Terminology   599

    Stock: Authorized, Issued, and Outstanding   599

    Classes of Stock   599

    Accounting for Stock Transactions   601

    Financial Statement Presentation   603

Treasury Stock   603

Dividends, Stock Splits, and Appropriations of Retained Earnings   605

    Cash Dividend   605

    Stock Dividend   606

    Stock Split   607

    Appropriation of Retained Earnings   608

    Financial Statement Presentation   609

The Financial Analyst   610

    Receiving Dividends   610

    Increasing the Price of Stock   610

    Price Earnings Ratio   611

    Exercising Control through Stock Ownership   612

A Look Back   612

A Look Forward   613

Self-Study Review Problem   613

Key Terms   614

Questions   614

Multiple-Choice Questions   615

Exercises—Series A   615

Problems—Series A   620

Exercises—Series B   624

Problems—Series B   628

Analyze, Think, Communicate   632

Comprehensive Problem   638

Chapter 12   Statement of Cash Flows   640

Chapter Opening   640

An Overview of the Statement of Cash Flows   642

    Operating Activities   642

    Investing Activities   643

    Financing Activities   643

    Noncash Investing and Financing Activities   644

    Reporting Format for the Statement of Cash Flows   644

Preparing a Statement of Cash Flows   645

Preparing the Operating Activities Section of a Statement of Cash Flows Using the Indirect Method   646

    Indirect Method—Reconciliation Approach   648

    Indirect Method—Rule-Based Approach   652

Preparing the Operating Activities Section of a Statement of Cash Flows Using the Direct Method   655

Preparing the Investing Activities Section of a Statement of Cash Flows   656

    Reconciliation of Investment Securities   656

    Reconciliation of Store Fixtures   657

    Reconciliation of Land   657

Preparing the Financing Activities Section of a Statement of Cash Flows   658

    Reconciliation of Mortgage Payable   659

    Reconciliation of Bonds Payable   659

    Reconciliation of Common Stock   660

    Reconciliation of Retained Earnings   660

    Reconciliation of Treasury Stock   660

Preparing the Schedule of Noncash Investing and Financing Activities   663

The Financial Analyst   663

    Real-World Data   663

A Look Back   665

A Look Forward   666

Self-Study Review Problem   666
Key Terms   668
Questions   669
Multiple-Choice Questions   669
Exercises—Series A   669

Problems—Series A   674
Exercises—Series B   680
Problems—Series B   684
Analyze, Think, Communicate   690

Chapter 13   Financial Statement Analysis (Available online only at www.mhhe.com/edmonds8e)   13-0

Chapter Opening   13-0
Factors in Communicating Useful Information   13-2
   The Users   13-2
   The Types of Decisions   13-2
   Information Analysis   13-2
Methods of Analysis   13-2
   Horizontal Analysis   13-3
   Vertical Analysis   13-6
Ratio Analysis   13-6
   Objectives of Ratio Analysis   13-7
Measures of Debt-Paying Ability   13-7
   Liquidity Ratios   13-7
   Solvency Ratios   13-11
Measures of Profitability   13-13
   Measures of Managerial Effectiveness   13-13
   Stock Market Ratios   13-15

Limitations of Financial Statement Analysis   13-18
   Different Industries   13-18
   Changing Economic Environment   13-19
   Accounting Principles   13-19
A Look Back   13-20
A Look Forward   13-20
Self-Study Review Problem   13-21
Key Terms   13-23
Questions   13-23
Multiple-Choice Questions   13-23
Exercises—Series A   13-23
Problems—Series A   13-29
Exercises—Series B   13-35
Problems—Series B   13-40
Analyze, Think, Communicate   13-46

Appendix A   Accessing the EDGAR Database through the Internet   696
Appendix B   Portion of the Form 10-K for Target Corporation   697
Appendix C   Summary of Financial Ratios   754
Appendix D   Annual Report and Financial Statement Analysis Projects   757

Appendix E   Accounting for Investment Securities   764
Appendix F   Time Value of Money   773
Glossary   781
Photo Credits   792
Index   793

CHAPTER I

An Introduction to Accounting

LEARNING OBJECTIVES

After you have mastered the material in this chapter, you will be able to:

SECTION 1: COLLECTING AND ORGANIZING INFORMATION

LO1 Explain the role of accounting in society.

LO2 Construct an accounting equation using elements of financial statements terminology.

LO3 Record business events in general ledger accounts organized under an accounting equation.

LO4 Classify business events as asset source, use, or exchange transactions.

SECTION 2: REPORTING INFORMATION

LO5 Use general ledger account information to prepare four financial statements.

LO6 Record business events using a horizontal financial statements model.

The Curious Accountant

Who owns **Google**? Who owns the **American Heart Association** (AHA)? Many people and organizations other than owners are interested in the operations of Google and the AHA. These parties are called *stakeholders*. Among others, they include lenders, employees, suppliers, customers, benefactors, research institutions, local governments, heart patients, lawyers, bankers, financial analysts, and government agencies such as the Internal Revenue Service and the Securities and Exchange Commission. Organizations communicate information to stakeholders through *financial reports*.

How do you think the financial reports of Google differ from those of the AHA? (Answer on page 11.)

SECTION I:

COLLECTING AND ORGANIZING INFORMATION

Why should you study accounting? You should study accounting because it can help you succeed in business. Businesses use accounting to keep score. Imagine trying to play football without knowing how many points a touchdown is worth. Like sports, business is competitive. If you do not know how to keep score, you are not likely to succeed.

Accounting is an information system that reports on the economic activities and financial condition of a business or other organization. Do not underestimate the importance of accounting information. If you had information that enabled you to predict business success, you could become a very wealthy Wall Street investor. Communicating economic information is so important that accounting is frequently called the *language of business.*

ROLE OF ACCOUNTING IN SOCIETY

How should society allocate its resources? Should we spend more to harvest food or cure disease? Should we build computers or cars? Should we invest money in IBM or General Motors? Accounting provides information that helps answer such questions.

Using Free Markets to Set Resource Priorities

Suppose you want to start a business. You may have heard "you have to have money to make money." In fact, you will need more than just money to start and operate a business. You will likely need such resources as equipment, land, materials, and employees. If you do not have these resources, how can you get them? In the United States, you compete for resources in open markets.

A **market** is a group of people or entities organized to exchange items of value. The market for business resources involves three distinct participants: consumers, conversion agents, and resource owners. *Consumers* use resources. Resources are frequently not in a form consumers want. For example, nature provides trees but consumers want furniture. *Conversion agents* (businesses) transform resources such as trees into desirable products such as furniture. *Resource owners* control the distribution of resources to conversion agents. Thus resource owners provide resources (inputs) to conversion agents who provide goods and services (outputs) to consumers.

For example, a home builder (conversion agent) transforms labor and materials (inputs) into houses (output) that consumers use. The transformation adds value to the inputs, creating outputs worth more than the sum of the inputs. A house that required

$220,000 of materials and labor to build could have a market value of $250,000.

Common terms for the added value created in the transformation process include **profit, income,** or **earnings.** Accountants measure the added value as the difference between the cost of a product or service and the selling price of that product or service. The profit on the house described above is $30,000, the difference between its $220,000 cost and $250,000 market value.

Conversion agents who successfully and efficiently (at low cost) satisfy consumer preferences are rewarded with high earnings. These earnings are shared with resource owners, so conversion agents who exhibit high earnings potential are more likely to compete successfully for resources.

Return to the original question. How can you get the resources you need to start a business? You must go to open markets and convince resource owners that you can produce profits. Exhibit 1.1 illustrates the market trilogy involved in resource allocation.

The specific resources businesses commonly use to satisfy consumer demand are financial resources, physical resources, and labor resources.

Financial Resources

Businesses (conversion agents) need **financial resources** (money) to get started and to operate. *Investors* and *creditors* provide financial resources.

■ **Investors** provide financial resources in exchange for ownership interests in businesses. Owners expect businesses to return to them a share of the business including a portion of earned income.

■ **Creditors** lend financial resources to businesses. Instead of a share of the business, creditors expect the businesses to repay borrowed resources plus a specified fee called **interest.**

The resources controlled by a business are called **assets.** If a business ceases to operate, its remaining assets are sold and the sale proceeds are returned to the creditors

EXHIBIT 1.1

Market Trilogy in Resource Allocation

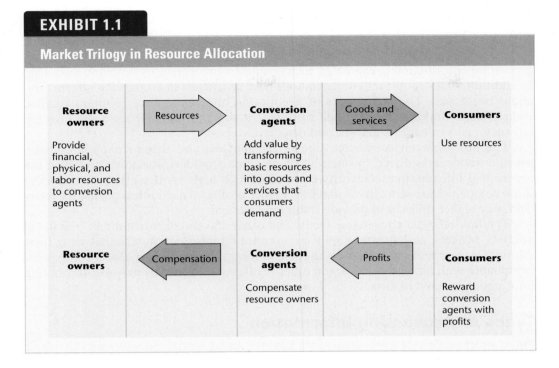

and investors through a process called business **liquidation.** Creditors have priority in business liquidations. This means the business uses its assets first to settle the obligations to the creditors. Any assets remaining after the creditors have been paid are then distributed to the investors.

To illustrate, suppose a business acquired $100 cash from investors and $200 cash from creditors. Assume the business lost $75 and returned the remaining $225 ($300 − $75) to the resource providers. The creditors would receive $200; the owners would receive only $25. If the business lost $120, the creditors would receive only $180 ($300 − $120); the investors would receive nothing.

As this illustration suggests, both creditors and investors can lose resources when businesses fail. Creditors, however, are in a more secure position because of their priority claim on resources. In exchange for their more secure position, creditors normally do not share business profits. Instead, they receive a fixed amount of money called interest.

Investors and creditors prefer to provide financial resources to businesses with high earnings potential because such companies are better able to share profits and make interest payments. Profitable businesses are also less likely to experience bankruptcy and liquidation.

Physical Resources

In their most primitive form, **physical resources** are natural resources. Physical resources often move through numerous stages of transformation. For example, standing timber may be successively transformed into harvested logs, raw lumber, and finished furniture. Owners of physical resources seek to sell those resources to businesses with high earnings potential because profitable businesses are able to pay higher prices and make repeat purchases.

Labor Resources

Labor resources include both intellectual and physical labor. Like other resource providers, workers prefer businesses that have high income potential because these businesses are able to pay higher wages and offer continued employment.

Accounting Provides Information

How do providers of financial, physical, and labor resources identify conversion agents (businesses) with high profit potential? Investors, creditors, and workers rely heavily on accounting information to evaluate which businesses are worthy of receiving resources. In addition, other people and organizations have an interest in accounting information about businesses. The many **users** of accounting information are commonly called **stakeholders.** Stakeholders include resource providers, financial analysts, brokers, attorneys, government regulators, and news reporters.

The link between conversion agents (businesses) and those stakeholders who provide resources is direct: businesses pay resource providers. Resource providers use accounting information to identify companies with high earnings potential because those companies are more likely to return higher profits, make interest payments, repay debt, pay higher prices, and provide stable employment.

The link between conversion agents and other stakeholders is indirect. Financial analysts, brokers, and attorneys may use accounting information when advising their clients. Government agencies may use accounting information to assess companies' compliance with income tax laws and other regulations. Reporters may use accounting information in news reports.

Types of Accounting Information

Stakeholders such as investors, creditors, lawyers, and financial analysts exist outside of and separate from the businesses in which they are interested. The accounting information these *external users* need is provided by **financial accounting.** In contrast, the accounting information needed by *internal users,* stakeholders such as managers and employees who work within a business, is provided by **managerial accounting.**

The information needs of external and internal users frequently overlap. For example, external and internal users are both interested in the amount of income a business earns. Managerial accounting information, however, is usually more detailed than financial accounting reports. Investors are concerned about the overall profitability of Wendy's versus Burger King; a Wendy's regional manager is interested in the profits of individual Wendy's restaurants. In fact, a regional manager is also interested in nonfinancial measures, such as the number of employees needed to operate a restaurant, the times at which customer demand is high versus low, and measures of cleanliness and customer satisfaction.

Nonbusiness Resource Usage

The U.S. economy is not *purely* market based. Factors other than profitability often influence resource allocation priorities. For example, governments allocate resources to national defense, to redistribute wealth, or to protect the environment. Foundations, religious groups, the Peace Corps, and other benevolent organizations prioritize resource usage based on humanitarian concerns.

Like profit-oriented businesses, civic or humanitarian organizations add value through resource transformation. For example, a soup kitchen adds value to uncooked meats and vegetables by converting them into prepared meals. The individuals who consume the meals, however, are unable to pay for the kitchen's operating costs, much less for the added value. The soup kitchen's motivation is to meet humanitarian needs, not to earn profits. Organizations that are not motivated by profit are called **not-for-profit entities** (also called *nonprofit* or *nonbusiness organizations*).

Stakeholders interested in nonprofit organizations also need accounting information. Accounting systems measure the cost of the goods and services not-for-profit organizations provide, the efficiency and effectiveness of the organizations' operations, and the ability of the organizations to continue to provide goods and services. This information serves a host of stakeholders, including taxpayers, contributors, lenders, suppliers, employees, managers, financial analysts, attorneys, and beneficiaries.

The focus of accounting, therefore, is to provide information that is useful to a variety of business and nonbusiness user groups for decision-making. The different

EXHIBIT 1.2

Accounting as Information Provider

Accounting Information

Financial accounting
- Investors
- Creditors
- Brokers

Managerial accounting
- Managers
- Employees
- Unions

Nonprofit accounting
- Benefactors and beneficiaries
- Legislators
- Citizens

types of accounting information and the stakeholders that commonly use the information are summarized in Exhibit 1.2.

Careers in Accounting

An accounting career can take you to the top of the business world. *Bloomberg Businessweek* studied the backgrounds of the chief executive officers (CEOs) of the 1,000 largest public corporations. More CEOs had backgrounds in finance and accounting than any other field. Exhibit 1.3 provides additional detail regarding the career paths followed by these executives.

What do accountants do? Accountants identify, record, analyze, and communicate information about the economic events that affect organizations. They may work in either public accounting or private accounting.

Public Accounting

You are probably familiar with the acronym CPA. CPA stands for certified *public* accountant. Public accountants provide services to various clients. They are usually paid a fee that varies depending on the service provided. Services typically offered by public accountants include (1) audit services, (2) tax services, and (3) consulting services.

- *Audit services* involve examining a company's accounting records in order to issue an opinion about whether the company's financial statements conform to generally accepted accounting principles. The auditor's opinion adds credibility to the statements, which are prepared by the company's management.

EXHIBIT 1.3

Career Paths of Chief Executive Officers

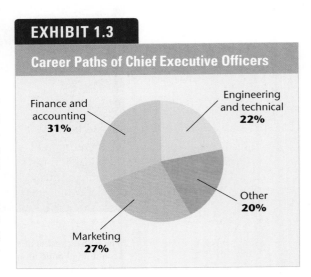

Finance and accounting **31%**

Engineering and technical **22%**

Other **20%**

Marketing **27%**

- *Tax services* include both determining the amount of tax due and tax planning to help companies minimize tax expense.
- *Consulting services* cover a wide range of activities that includes everything from installing sophisticated computerized accounting systems to providing personal financial advice.

All public accountants are not certified. Each state government establishes certification requirements applicable in that state. Although the requirements vary from state to state, CPA candidates normally must have a college education, pass a demanding technical examination, and obtain work experience relevant to practicing public accounting.

Private Accounting

Accountants employed in the private sector usually work for a specific company or nonprofit organization. Private sector accountants perform a wide variety of functions for their employers. Their duties include classifying and recording transactions, billing customers and collecting amounts due, ordering merchandise, paying suppliers, preparing and analyzing financial statements, developing budgets, measuring costs, assessing performance, and making decisions.

Private accountants may earn any of several professional certifications. For example, the Institute of Management Accountants issues the *Certified Management Accounting (CMA)* designation. The Institute of Internal Auditors issues the *Certified Internal Auditor (CIA)* designation. These designations are widely recognized indicators of technical competence and integrity on the part of individuals who hold them. All professional accounting certifications call for meeting education requirements, passing a technical examination, and obtaining relevant work experience.

Measurement Rules

Suppose a store sells a MP3 player in December to a customer who agrees to pay for it in January. Should the business *recognize* (report) the sale as a December transaction or as a January transaction? It really does not matter as long as the storeowner discloses the rule the decision is based on and applies it consistently to other transactions. Because businesses may use different reporting rules, however, clear communication also requires full and fair disclosure of the accounting rules chosen.

Communicating business results would be simpler if each type of business activity were reported using only one measurement method. World economies and financial reporting practices, however, have not evolved uniformly. Even in highly sophisticated countries such as the United States, companies exhibit significant diversity in reporting methods. Providers of financial reports assume that users are educated about accounting practices.

The **Financial Accounting Standards Board (FASB)**[1] is a privately funded organization with the primary authority for establishing accounting standards in the United States. The measurement rules established by the FASB are called **generally accepted accounting principles (GAAP).** Financial reports issued to the public must follow GAAP. This textbook introduces these principles so you will be able to understand business activity reported by companies in the USA.

[1]The FASB consists of seven full-time members appointed by the supporting organization, the Financial Accounting Foundation (FAF). The FAF membership is intended to represent the broad spectrum of individuals and institutions that have an interest in accounting and financial reporting. FAF members include representatives of the accounting profession, industry, financial institutions, the government, and the investing public.

FOCUS ON INTERNATIONAL ISSUES

IS THERE GLOBAL GAAP?

As explained in this chapter, accounting is a measurement and communication discipline based on rules referred to as *generally accepted accounting principles (GAAP)*. The rules described in this text are based on GAAP used in the United States, but what rules do the rest of the world use? Is there a global GAAP, or does each country establish its own unique GAAP?

Until recently, each country developed its own unique GAAP. Global companies were required to prepare multiple sets of financial statements to satisfy each country's GAAP. The use of multiple accounting standards across the globe made comparing company performance difficult and expensive. To address the need for a common set of financial standards, the International Accounting Standards Committee was formed in 1973. The committee was reorganized as the **International Accounting Standards Board (IASB)** in 2001. The IASB issues **International Financial Reporting Standards (IFRS)**, which are rapidly gaining support worldwide. In 2005, companies in the countries who were members of the European Union were required to use the IFRS as established by the IASB, which is headquartered in London. Today, over 100 countries require or permit companies to prepare their financial statements using IFRS.

As of 2012 most of the major economic countries had switched from their local GAAP to IFRS. One notable exception is the United States, but even here, the Securities and Exchange Commission announced in 2008 that it was seriously considering adopting rules that would allow our companies to use either GAAP or IFRS. Although not finalized when this book was being prepared, many accountants in the United States believe this will occur. Additionally, there is an active process in place to reduce the differences between IFRS and U.S. GAAP.

There are many similarities between the IASB and the FASB. Both the FASB and the IASB are required to include members with a variety of backgrounds, including auditors, users of financial information, academics, and so forth. Also, both groups primarily require that their members work full-time for their respective boards; they cannot serve on the board while being compensated by another organization. (The IASB does allow up to three of its members to be part-time.) Members of each board serve five-year terms, and can be reappointed once. The funds to support both boards, and the large organizations that support them are obtained from a variety of sources, including selling publications and private contributions. To help maintain independence of the board's members, fundraising is performed by separate sets of trustees.

There are significant differences between the IASB and the FASB, and one of these relates to size and geographic diversity. The FASB has only seven members, all from the United States. The IASB has sixteen members, and these must include at least four from Asia, four from Europe, four from North America, one from Africa, and one from South America.

Not only is the structure of the standards-setting boards different but the standards and principles they establish may also differ significantly. In this chapter, you will learn that GAAP employs the *historical cost concept*. This means that the assets of most U.S. companies are shown on the balance sheet at the amount for which they were purchased. For example, land that has a market value of millions of dollars may be shown on US Steel's financial statements with a value of only a few hundred thousand dollars. This occurs because GAAP requires US Steel to show the land at its cost rather than its market value. In contrast, IFRS permits companies to show market values on their financial statements. This means that the exact same assets may show radically different values if the statements are prepared under IFRS rather than GAAP.

Throughout this text, where appropriate, we will note the differences between U.S. GAAP and IFRS. However, by the time you graduate, it is likely that among the major industrialized nations, there will be a global GAAP.

Companies are not required to follow GAAP when preparing *management accounting* reports. Although there is considerable overlap between financial and managerial accounting, managers are free to construct internal reports in whatever fashion best suits the effective operation of their companies.

Reporting Entities

Think of accountants as you would of news reporters. A news reporter gathers and discloses information about some person, place, or thing. Likewise, an accountant gathers and discloses financial information about specific people or businesses. The people or businesses accountants report on are called **reporting entities.** When studying accounting you should think of yourself as the accountant. Your first step is to identify the person or business on which you are reporting. This is not always as easy as it may seem. To illustrate, consider the following scenario.

Jason Winston recently started a business. During the first few days of operation, Mr. Winston transferred cash from his personal account into a business account for a company he named Winston Enterprises. Mr. Winston's brother, George, invested cash in Winston Enterprises for which he received an ownership interest in the company. Winston Enterprises borrowed cash from First Federal Bank. Winston Enterprises paid cash to purchase a building from Commercial Properties, Inc. Winston Enterprises earned cash revenues from its customers and paid its employees cash for salaries expense.

How many reporting entities are described in this scenario? Assuming all of the customers are counted as a single entity and all of the employees are counted as a single entity, there are a total of seven entities named in the scenario. These entities include: (1) Jason Winston, (2) Winston Enterprises (3) George Winston, (4) First Federal Bank, (5) Commercial Properties, Inc., (6) the customers, and (7) the employees. A separate set of accounting records would be maintained for each entity.

Your ability to learn accounting will be greatly influenced by how you approach the entity concept. Based on your everyday experiences you likely think from the perspective of a customer. In contrast, this text is written from the perspective of a business entity. These opposing perspectives dramatically affect how you view business events. For example, as a customer you consider a sales discount a great bargain. The view is different from the perspective of the business granting the discount. A sales discount means an item did not sell at the expected price. To move the item, the business had to accept less money than it originally planned to receive. From this perspective, a sales discount is not a good thing. To understand accounting, train yourself to interpret transactions from the perspective of a business rather than a consumer. Each time you encounter an accounting event ask yourself, how does this affect the business?

✓ **CHECK YOURSELF 1.1**

In a recent business transaction, land was exchanged for cash. Did the amount of cash increase or decrease?

Answer   The answer depends on the reporting entity to which the question pertains. One entity sold land. The other entity bought land. For the entity that sold land, cash increased. For the entity that bought land, cash decreased.

ELEMENTS OF FINANCIAL STATEMENTS

LO 2

Construct an accounting equation using elements of financial statements terminology.

The individuals and organizations that need information about a business are called *stakeholders.* Stakeholders include owners, lenders, government agencies, employees, news reporters, and others. Businesses communicate information to stakeholders through four financial statements:[2] (1) an income statement, (2) a statement of changes in equity, (3) a balance sheet, and (4) a statement of cash flows.

---

[2]In practice these statements have alternate names. For example, the income statement may be called *results of operations* or *statement of earnings.* The balance sheet is sometimes called the *statement of financial position.* The statement of changes in equity might be called *statement of capital* or *statement of stockholders' equity.* Since the Financial Accounting Standards Board (FASB) called for the title *statement of cash flows,* companies do not use alternate names for that statement.

Answers to The Curious Accountant

Anyone who owns stock in Google owns a part of the company. Google has many owners. In contrast, nobody actually owns the American Heart Association (AHA). The AHA has a board of directors that is responsible for overseeing its operations, but the board is not its owner.

Ultimately, the purpose of a business entity is to increase the wealth of its owners. To this end, it "spends money to make money." The expense that Google incurs for developing software is a cost incurred in the hope that it will generate revenues when it sells advertising. The financial statements of a business show, among other things, whether and how the company made a profit during the current year. For example, Google's income statements show how much expense was incurred from "research and development" operations versus from "sales and marketing."

The AHA is a not-for-profit entity. It operates to provide services to society at large, not to make a profit. It cannot increase the wealth of its owners, because it has no owners. When the AHA spends money to conduct CPR classes, it does not spend this money in the expectation that it will generate revenues. The revenues of the AHA come from contributors who wish to support efforts related to fighting heart disease. Because the AHA does not spend money to make money, it has no reason to prepare an *income statement* like that of Google. The AHA's statement of activities shows how much revenue was received from "contributions" versus from "special events."

Not-for-profit entities do prepare financial statements that are similar in appearance to those of commercial enterprises. The financial statements of not-for-profit entities are called the *statement of financial position,* the *statement of activities,* and the *cash flow statement.*

The information reported in **financial statements** is organized into ten categories known as **elements.** Eight financial statement elements are discussed in this chapter: assets, liabilities, equity, contributed capital, revenue, expenses, distributions, and net income. The other two elements, gains and losses, are discussed in a later chapter. In practice, the business world uses various titles to identify several of the financial statement elements. For example, business people use net income, net *earnings,* and net *profit* interchangeably to describe the same element. Contributed capital may be called *common stock* and equity may be called *stockholders' equity, owner's capital,* and *partners' equity.* Furthermore, the transfer of assets from a business to its owners may be called *distributions, withdrawals,* or *dividends.* Think of accounting as a language. Different terms can describe the same business event. Detailed definitions of the elements and their placement on financial statements will be discussed in the following sections of the chapter.

Using Accounts to Gather Information

Detailed information about the elements is maintained in records commonly called **accounts.** For example, information regarding the element *assets* may be organized in separate accounts for cash, equipment, buildings, land, and so forth. The types and number of accounts used by a business depends on the information needs of its stakeholders. Some businesses provide very detailed information; others report highly summarized information. The more detail desired, the greater number of accounts needed. Think of accounts like the notebooks students keep for their classes. Some students keep detailed notes about every class they take in a separate notebook. Other students keep only the key points for all of their classes in a single notebook. Similarly, some businesses use more accounts than other businesses.

Diversity also exists regarding the names used for various accounts. For example, employee pay may be called salaries, wages, commissions, and so forth. Do not become frustrated with the diversity of terms used in accounting. Remember, accounting is a language. The same word can have different meanings. Similarly, different words can be used to describe the same phenomenon. The more you study and use accounting, the more familiar it will become to you.

Accounting Equation

You have probably heard the adage "you have to have money to make money." Indeed, you usually need a lot more than just money. For example, Carmike Cinemas, Inc., uses buildings, seating, screens, projection equipment, vending machines, cash registers, and so on in order to make money from ticket sales. The resources a business uses to make money are called *assets*. So, where do businesses get assets? There are three distinct sources.

First, a business can borrow assets from creditors. Usually a business acquires cash from creditors and then uses the cash to purchase the assets it needs to conduct its operations. When a business receives cash from creditors it accepts an obligation to return the cash to the creditors at some future date. In accounting terms, the obligations a business has to its creditors are called **liabilities.**

The second source of assets is investors. When a business acquires assets from investors it commits to keep the assets safe and to use the assets in a manner that benefits the investors. The business also grants the investor an ownership interest in the business thereby allowing the investor (owner) to share in the profits generated by the business. The specific commitments made to the investors are described in certificates called **common stock.** In accounting terms investors are called **stockholders.** Further, the business' commitment to the stockholders is called **stockholders' equity.**

The third source of assets is operations. Businesses use assets in order to produce higher amounts of other assets. For example, Best Buy may sell a TV that cost the company $500 for $600. The $100 difference between the sales price and the cost of the TV results in an increase in Best Buy's total assets. This explains how operations can be a source of assets. Of course operations may also result in a decrease in assets. If Best Buy has to discount the sales price of the TV to $450 in order to sell it, the company's total assets decrease by $50.

Increases in assets generated from operations are commonly called *earnings* or *income*. Decreases in assets caused by operations are called *losses*. As a result of their ownership status, the stockholders reap the benefits and suffer the sacrifices that a business experiences from its operations. A business may distribute all or part of the assets generated through operations to the shareholders. The distribution of assets generated through earnings is called a *dividend*.

Notice that paying dividends is an option not a legal requirement. Instead of paying dividends, a business may retain the assets it generates through operations. If a business retains the assets, it commits to use those assets for the benefit of the stockholders. This increase in the business's commitments to its stockholders is normally called **retained earnings.** Also, note that earnings that have been retained in the past can be used to pay dividends in the future. However, a company that does not have current or retained earnings cannot pay dividends. Remember, dividends are distributions of assets that have been generated through earnings. Without earnings there can be no dividends or retained earnings.

As a result of providing assets to a business the creditors and investors are entitled to make potential **claims**[3] on the assets owned by the business. The relationship between a business's assets and the claims on its assets is frequently expressed in an equality

[3]A claim is a legal action to obtain money, property, or the enforcement of a right against another party.

called the **accounting equation.** Based on the relationships described above the accounting equation can be developed as follows:

Assets =   Claims

Assets = Liabilities   +   Stockholders' equity

Assets = Liabilities + Common stock + Retained earnings

To illustrate the relationships associated with the accounting equation assume Educate Inc. acquires $600 cash from creditors, $300 cash from investors, and $100 cash from operations. This information can be organized under an accounting equation as follows:

Assets   = Liabilities + Common stock + Retained earnings
$1,000 Cash = $600   + $300   + $100

Now assume that Educate Inc. uses its cash to purchase land. Immediately after Educate pays $1,000 cash to purchase land, the company's accounting equation is a follows:

Assets   = Liabilities + Common stock + Retained earnings
$1,000 Land = $600   + $300   + $100

At this point the company has zero cash. This highlights the fact that the amounts in Liabilities, Common stock, and Retained earnings do not represent cash. Instead they represent the organization's obligations and commitments to its creditors and investors. Indeed, the right side of the accounting equation could be expressed as percentages instead of dollars. Specifically, the equation could be written as

Assets   = Liabilities + Common stock + Retained earnings
$1,000 Land =   60%   +   30%   +   10%

As this equation suggests it would require 60% of Educate's assets to satisfy the company's obligations to its creditors, thereby leaving 40% available to support its commitments to the stockholders. Recall that in business liquidations assets are first used to satisfy creditors' claims. If there are insufficient assets to settle the company's liabilities, the investors receive nothing. Bankruptcy proceedings can lead to legal fees and losses on the sale of assets that end up hurting creditors as well as investors. As a result, maintaining stockholders' equity is essential to creditors as well as investors. All other things being equal, the higher the percentage of stockholders' equity to total assets, the less likely the company is to experience bankruptcy. A company becomes bankrupt when its liabilities exceed its assets.

The treatment of retained earnings is a critical component of maintaining a healthy level of stockholders' equity. To further examine the treatment of earnings we will assume that Educate Inc. earns an additional $150 of cash earnings. This event would cause assets and retained earnings to increase, thereby resulting in the following accounting equation:

Assets   = Liabilities + Common stock + Retained earnings
$150 Cash + $1,000 Land   = $600   + $300   + $250

Given that the company has $250 in retained earnings, can the company pay a $200 cash dividend? The answer is no. Remember there is no cash in retained earnings. The only cash the company has is listed on the left side of the equation. In this case, the maximum cash dividend that can be paid is $150 because that is all the cash the company has.

Suppose Educate decides it no longer needs the land and sells it for $1,000 cash. Immediately after this event the accounting equation appears as follows:

Assets   = Liabilities + Common stock + Retained earnings
$1,150 Cash = $600   + $300   + $250

Given that Educate now has $1,150 in cash, can the company pay a $400 dividend? The answer is no. Based on the information in the accounting equation, Educate has only increased its assets by $250 as a result of its operations. Since dividends are a distribution of assets that were generated through earnings, the maximum dividend Educate can distribute at this time is $250. By definition, a company cannot pay dividends in excess of its current and prior earnings. This does not mean that retained earnings cannot become negative. Operating activities that result in losses can cause deficit balances in retained earnings even when a company does not pay dividends.

Finally, assume Educate decides once again to purchase land. This time the company pays $1,150 cash to buy land. The equation now appears as follows:

$$\text{Assets} = \text{Liabilities} + \text{Common stock} + \text{Retained earnings}$$
$$\$1,150 \text{ Land} = \$600 + \$300 + \$250$$

Suppose it is now time to repay creditors. At this point Educate has no cash. It only has land. As a result, Educate cannot satisfy its obligations and may be forced to liquidate. This scenario demonstrates that even profitable companies can be forced to liquidate. A company must properly manage its assets as well as its liabilities and stockholders' equity in order to remain a **going concern.** The going concern doctrine assumes that a business is able to continue its operations into the foreseeable future. Many procedures and practices used by accountants are based on a going concern assumption. If a company's going concern status becomes uncertain, accountants are required to notify creditors and investors.

In practice, the relationships between a business and its creditors and investors are determined by complex legal documents that may conflict with the general conditions described above. We will discuss some of these details in later chapters. However, it is important to clearly establish the basic guidelines before we begin discussing the refinements.

✓ CHECK YOURSELF 1.2

Gupta Company has $250,000 of assets, $60,000 of liabilities, and $90,000 of common stock. What percentage of the assets was provided by retained earnings?

Answer   First, using algebra, determine the dollar amount of retained earnings:

Assets = Liabilities + Common stock + Retained earnings
Retained earnings = Assets − Liabilities − Common stock
Retained earnings = $250,000 − $60,000 − $90,000
Retained earnings = $100,000

Second, determine the percentage:

Percentage of assets provided by retained earnings = Retained earnings/Total assets
Percentage of assets provided by retained earnings = $100,000/$250,000 = 40%

RECORDING BUSINESS EVENTS UNDER THE ACCOUNTING EQUATION

LO 3

Record business events in general ledger accounts organized under an accounting equation.

An **accounting event** is an economic occurrence that changes an enterprise's assets, liabilities, or stockholders' equity. A **transaction** is a particular kind of event that involves transferring something of value between two entities. Examples of transactions include acquiring assets from owners, borrowing money from creditors, and purchasing or selling goods and services. The following section of the text explains how several different types of accounting events affect a company's accounting equation.

Asset Source Transactions

As previously mentioned, businesses obtain assets (resources) from three sources. They acquire assets from owners (stockholders); they borrow assets from creditors; and they earn assets through profitable operations. Asset source transactions increase total assets and total claims. A more detailed discussion of the effects of asset source transactions is provided below:

EVENT 1 Rustic Camp Sites (RCS) was formed on January 1, 2013, when it acquired $120,000 cash from issuing common stock.

When RCS issued stock, it received cash and gave each investor (owner) a stock certificate as a receipt. Since this transaction provided $120,000 of assets (cash) to the business, it is an **asset source transaction.** It increases the business's assets (cash) and its stockholders' equity (common stock).

	Assets			=	Liab.	+	Stockholders' Equity		
	Cash	+	Land	=	N. Pay.	+	Com. Stk.	+	Ret. Earn.
Acquired cash through stock issue	120,000	+	NA	=	NA	+	120,000	+	NA

Notice the elements have been divided into accounts. For example, the element *assets* is divided into a Cash account and a Land account. Do not be concerned if some of these account titles are unfamiliar. They will be explained as new transactions are presented. Recall that the number of accounts a company uses depends on the nature of its business and the level of detail management needs to operate the business. For example, Sears would have an account called Cost of Goods Sold although GEICO Insurance would not. Why? Because Sears sells goods (merchandise) but GEICO does not.

Also, notice that a stock issue transaction affects the accounting equation in two places, both under an asset (cash) and also under the source of that asset (common stock). All transactions affect the accounting equation in at least two places. It is from this practice that the **double-entry bookkeeping** system derives its name.

EVENT 2 RCS acquired an additional $400,000 of cash by borrowing from a creditor.

This transaction is also an asset source transaction. It increases assets (cash) and liabilities (notes payable). The account title Notes Payable is used because the borrower (RCS) is required to issue a promissory note to the creditor (a bank). A promissory note describes, among other things, the amount of interest RCS will pay and for how long it will borrow the money.[4] The effect of the borrowing transaction on the accounting equation is indicated below.

	Assets			=	Liab.	+	Stockholders' Equity		
	Cash	+	Land	=	N. Pay.	+	Com. Stk.	+	Ret. Earn.
Beginning balances	120,000	+	NA	=	NA	+	120,000	+	NA
Acquired cash by issuing note	400,000	+	NA	=	400,000	+	NA	+	NA
Ending balances	520,000	+	NA	=	400,000	+	120,000	+	NA

The beginning balances above came from the ending balances produced by the prior transaction. This practice is followed throughout the illustration.

Asset Exchange Transactions

Businesses frequently trade one asset for another asset. In such cases, the amount of one asset decreases and the amount of the other asset increases. Total assets are unaffected by asset exchange transactions. Event 3 is an asset exchange transaction.

[4]For simplicity, the computation of interest is ignored in this chapter. Interest computation is discussed in the appendix to Chapter 2 and in subsequent chapters.

EVENT 3   RCS paid $500,000 cash to purchase land.

This asset exchange transaction reduces the asset account Cash and increases the asset account Land. The amount of total assets is not affected. An **asset exchange transaction** simply reflects changes in the composition of assets. In this case, the company traded cash for land. The amount of cash decreased by $500,000 and the amount of land increased by the same amount.

	Assets			=	Liab.	+	Stockholders' Equity		
	Cash	+	Land	=	N. Pay.	+	Com. Stk.	+	Ret. Earn.
Beginning balances	520,000	+	NA	=	400,000	+	120,000	+	NA
Paid cash to buy land	(500,000)	+	500,000	=	NA	+	NA	+	NA
Ending balances	20,000	+	500,000	=	400,000	+	120,000	+	NA

Another Asset Source Transaction

EVENT 4   RCS obtained $85,000 cash by leasing camp sites to customers.

Revenue represents an economic benefit a company obtains by providing customers with goods and services. In this example the economic benefit is an increase in the asset cash. Revenue transactions can therefore be viewed as *asset source transactions*. The asset increase is balanced by an increase in the retained earnings section of stockholders' equity because producing revenue increases the amount of earnings that can be retained in the business.

	Assets			=	Liab.	+	Stockholders' Equity			
	Cash	+	Land	=	N. Pay.	+	Com. Stk.	+	Ret. Earn.	Acct. Title
Beginning balances	20,000	+	500,000	=	400,000	+	120,000	+	NA	
Acquired cash by earning revenue	85,000	+	NA	=	NA	+	NA	+	85,000	Revenue
Ending balances	105,000	+	500,000	=	400,000	+	120,000	+	85,000	

Note carefully that the $85,000 ending balance in the retained earnings column is *not* in the Retained Earnings account. It is in the Revenue account. It will be transferred to the Retained Earnings account at the end of the accounting period. Transferring the Revenue account balance to the Retained Earnings account is part of a process called *closing the accounts.*

Asset Use Transactions

Businesses use assets for a variety of purposes. For example, assets may be used to pay off liabilities or they may be transferred to owners. Assets may also be used in the process of generating earnings. All **asset use transactions** decrease the total amount of assets and the total amount of claims on assets (liabilities or stockholders' equity).

EVENT 5   RCS paid $50,000 cash for operating expenses such as salaries, rent, and interest. (RCS could establish a separate account for each type of expense. However, the management team does not currently desire this level of detail. Remember, the number of accounts a business uses depends on the level of information managers need to make decisions.)

In the normal course of generating revenue, a business consumes various assets and services. The assets and services consumed to generate revenue are called **expenses.** Revenue results from providing goods and services to customers. In exchange, the business acquires assets from its customers. Since the owners bear the ultimate risk and reap the rewards of operating the business, revenues increase stockholders' equity (retained earnings), and expenses decrease retained earnings. In this case, the asset account, Cash, decreased. This decrease is balanced by a decrease in the retained earnings section of stockholders' equity because expenses decrease the amount of earnings retained in the business.

	Assets			=	Liab.	+	Stockholders' Equity			
	Cash	+	Land	=	N. Pay.	+	Com. Stk.	+	Ret. Earn.	Acct. Title
Beginning balances	105,000	+	500,000	=	400,000	+	120,000	+	85,000	
Used cash to pay expenses	(50,000)	+	NA	=	NA	+	NA	+	(50,000)	Expense
Ending balances	55,000	+	500,000	=	400,000	+	120,000	+	35,000	

Like revenues, expenses are not recorded directly into the Retained Earnings account. The $50,000 of expense is recorded in the Expense account. It will be transferred to the Retained Earnings account at the end of the accounting period as part of the closing process. The $35,000 ending balance in the retained earnings column shows what would be in the Retained Earnings account after the balances in the Revenue and Expense accounts have been closed. The current balance in the Retained Earnings account is zero.

EVENT 6   RCS paid $4,000 in cash dividends to its owners.

To this point the enterprise's total assets and equity have increased by $35,000 ($85,000 of revenue − $50,000 of expense) as a result of its earnings activities. RCS can keep the additional assets in the business or transfer them to the owners. If a business transfers some or all of its earned assets to owners, the transfer is frequently called a **dividend.** Since assets distributed to stockholders are not used for the purpose of generating revenue, *dividends are not expenses.* Furthermore, dividends are a transfer of *earnings,* not a return of the assets acquired from the issue of common stock.

	Assets			=	Liab.	+	Stockholders' Equity			
	Cash	+	Land	=	N. Pay.	+	Com. Stk.	+	Ret. Earn.	Acct. Title
Beginning balances	55,000	+	500,000	=	400,000	+	120,000	+	35,000	
Used cash to pay dividends	(4,000)	+	NA	=	NA	+	NA	+	(4,000)	Dividends
Ending balances	51,000	+	500,000	=	400,000	+	120,000	+	31,000	

Like revenues and expenses, dividends are not recorded directly into the Retained Earnings account. The $4,000 dividend is recorded in the Dividends account. It will be transferred to retained earnings at the end of the accounting period as part of the closing process. The $31,000 ending balance in the retained earnings column shows what would be in the Retained Earnings account after the balances in the Revenue, Expense, and Dividend accounts have been closed. The current balance in the Retained Earnings account is zero.

EVENT 7   The land that RCS paid $500,000 to purchase had an appraised market value of $525,000 on December 31, 2013.

Although the appraised value of the land is higher than the original cost, RCS will not increase the amount recorded in its accounting records above the land's $500,000 historical cost. In general, accountants do not recognize changes in market value. The **historical cost concept** requires that most assets be reported at the amount paid for them (their historical cost) regardless of increases in market value.

Surely investors would rather know what an asset is worth instead of how much it originally cost. So why do accountants maintain records and report financial information based on historical cost? Accountants rely heavily on verification. Information is considered to be more useful if it can be independently verified. For example, two people looking at the legal documents associated with RCS's land purchase will both conclude that RCS paid $500,000 for the land. That historical cost is a verifiable fact. The appraised value, in contrast, is an opinion. Even two persons who are experienced appraisers are not likely to come up with the same amount for the land's market value. Accountants do not report market values in financial statements because such values are not reliable.

There are exceptions to the application of the historical cost rule. When market value can be clearly established, GAAP not only permits but requires its use. For example, securities that are traded on the New York Stock Exchange must be shown at market value rather than historical cost. We will discuss other notable exceptions to the historical cost principle later in the text. However, as a general rule you should assume that assets shown in a company's financial statements are valued at historical cost.

Summary of Transactions

The complete collection of a company's accounts is called the **general ledger.** A summary of the accounting events and the general ledger account information for RCS's 2013 accounting period is shown in Exhibit 1.4. The Revenue, Expense, and Dividend account data appear in the retained earnings column. These account titles are shown immediately to the right of the dollar amounts listed in the retained earnings column.

EXHIBIT 1.4

Accounting Events

1.	RCS issued common stock, acquiring $120,000 cash from its owners.
2.	RCS borrowed $400,000 cash.
3.	RCS paid $500,000 cash to purchase land.
4.	RCS received $85,000 cash from earning revenue.
5.	RCS paid $50,000 cash for expenses.
6.	RCS paid dividends of $4,000 cash to the owners.
7.	The land that RCS paid $500,000 to purchase had an appraised market value of $525,000 on December 31, 2013.

General Ledger Accounts Organized Under the Accounting Equation

Event No.	Assets			=	Liabilities	+	Stockholders' Equity			Other Account Titles
	Cash	+	Land	=	Notes Payable	+	Common Stock	+	Retained Earnings	
Beg. bal.	0		0		0		0		0	
1.	120,000						120,000			
2.	400,000				400,000					
3.	(500,000)		500,000							
4.	85,000								85,000	Revenue
5.	(50,000)								(50,000)	Expense
6.	(4,000)								(4,000)	Dividend
7.	NA		NA		NA		NA		NA	
	51,000	+	500,000	=	400,000	+	120,000	+	31,000	

RECAP: TYPES OF TRANSACTIONS

The transactions described above have each been classified into one of three categories: (1) asset source transactions; (2) asset exchange transactions; and (3) asset use transactions. A fourth category, claims exchange transactions, is introduced in a later chapter. In summary:

LO 4

Classify business events as asset source, use, or exchange transactions.

- **Asset source transactions** increase the total amount of assets and increase the total amount of claims. In its first year of operation, RCS acquired assets from three sources: first, from owners (Event 1); next, by borrowing (Event 2); and finally, through earnings activities (Event 4).

- **Asset exchange transactions** decrease one asset and increase another asset. The total amount of assets is unchanged by asset exchange transactions. RCS experienced one asset exchange transaction; it used cash to purchase land (Event 3).

- **Asset use transactions** decrease the total amount of assets and the total amount of claims. RCS used assets to pay expenses (Event 5) and to pay dividends (Event 6).

As you proceed through this text, practice classifying transactions into one of the four categories. Businesses engage in thousands of transactions every day. It is far more effective to learn how to classify the transactions into meaningful categories than to attempt to memorize the effects of thousands of transactions.

SECTION 2: Reporting Information

The RCS case includes only seven business events, one of which is not recognized in the ledger accounts. These events are assumed to have taken place over the course of a year. In contrast, real-world companies engage in thousands, even millions, of transactions in a single day. For example, think of the number of sales events Walmart processes in a day or how many tickets Delta Airlines sells. Presenting this many events in accounting equation format would produce such a volume of data that users would be overwhelmed with details. To facilitate communication accountants summarize and organize the transaction data into reports called financial statements. This section discusses the information contained in financial statements and explains how they are prepared. While the RCS illustration contains only a few transactions, the financial statements prepared for this company contain the same basic content as those of much larger companies.

PREPARING FINANCIAL STATEMENTS

LO 5

Use general ledger account information to prepare four financial statements.

As indicated earlier, accounting information is normally presented to external users in four general-purpose financial statements. The information in the ledger accounts is used to prepare these financial statements. The data in the ledger accounts in Exhibit 1.4 are color coded to help you understand the source of information in the financial statements. The numbers in *green* are used in the *statement of cash flows.* The numbers in *red* are used to prepare the *balance sheet.* Finally, the numbers in *blue* are used to prepare the *income statement.* The numbers reported in the statement of changes in stockholders' equity have not been color coded because they appear in more than one statement. The next section explains how the information in the accounts is presented in financial statements.

The financial statements for RCS are shown in Exhibit 1.5. The information used to prepare these statements was drawn from the ledger accounts. Information in one statement may relate to information in another statement. For example, the amount of net income reported on the income statement also appears on the statement of changes in stockholders' equity. Accountants use the term **articulation** to describe the interrelationships among the various elements of the financial statements. The key articulated relationships in RCS's financial statements are highlighted with arrows (Exhibit 1.5). A description of each statement follows.

Income Statement and the Matching Concept

A business must make sacrifices in order to obtain benefits. For example, RCS must sacrifice cash to pay for employee salaries, rent, and interest. In turn, RCS receives a benefit when it collects cash from its customers. As this example implies, sacrifices are defined as decreases in assets; and benefits are increases in assets. In accounting terms sacrifices are called expenses; and benefits are called revenues. *Therefore, expenses are decreases in assets; and revenues are increases in assets.*[5]

The **income statement** matches the expenses with the revenues that occur during a period when operating a business. If revenues exceed expenses, the difference is called **net income.** If expenses are greater than revenues, the difference is called **net loss.** The practice of pairing revenues with expenses on the income statement is called the **matching concept.**

The income statement in Exhibit 1.5 indicates that RCS has earned more assets than it has used. The statement shows that RCS has increased its assets by $35,000 (net income) as a result of operating its business. Observe the phrase *For the Year Ended December 31, 2013,* in the heading of the income statement. Income is measured for a span of time called the **accounting period.** While accounting periods of one year are normal for external financial reporting, income can be measured weekly, monthly, quarterly, semiannually, or over any other desired time period. Notice that the cash RCS paid to its stockholders (dividends) is not reported as expense. The decrease in assets for dividend payments is not incurred for the purpose of generating revenue. Instead, dividends are transfers of wealth to the owners of the business. Dividend payments are not reported on the income statement.

---

[5]The definitions for revenue and expense are expanded in subsequent chapters as additional relationships among the elements of financial statements are introduced.

EXHIBIT 1.5   Financial Statements

RUSTIC CAMP SITES
Income Statement
For the Year Ended December 31, 2013

Rental revenue (*asset increases*)	$ 85,000
Operating expenses (*asset decreases*)	(50,000)
Net income	$ 35,000

RUSTIC CAMP SITES
Statement of Changes in Stockholders' Equity
For the Year Ended December 31, 2013

Beginning common stock	$ 0	
Plus: common stock issued	120,000	
Ending common stock		$120,000
Beginning retained earnings	0	
Plus: Net income	35,000	
Less: Dividends	(4,000)	
Ending retained earnings		31,000
Total stockholders' equity		$151,000

RUSTIC CAMP SITES
Balance Sheet
As of December 31, 2013

Assets		
Cash	$ 51,000	
Land	500,000	
Total assets		$551,000
Liabilities		
Notes payable		$400,000
Stockholders' equity		
Common stock	$120,000	
Retained earnings	31,000	
Total stockholders' equity		151,000
Total liabilities and stockholders' equity		$551,000

RUSTIC CAMP SITES
Statement of Cash Flows
For the Year Ended December 31, 2013

Cash flows from operating activities:		
Cash receipts from revenue	$ 85,000	
Cash payments for expenses	(50,000)	
Net cash flow from operating activities		$ 35,000
Cash flows from investing activities:		
Cash payments to purchase land		(500,000)
Cash flows from financing activities:		
Cash receipts from borrowing funds	400,000	
Cash receipts from issuing common stock	120,000	
Cash payments for dividends	(4,000)	
Net cash flow from financing activities		516,000
Net increase in cash		51,000
Plus: beginning cash balance		0
Ending cash balance		$ 51,000

Statement of Changes in Stockholders' Equity

The **statement of changes in stockholders' equity** explains the effects of transactions on stockholders' equity during the accounting period. It starts with the beginning balance in the common stock account. In the case of RCS, the beginning balance in the common stock account is zero because the company did not exist before the 2013 accounting period. The $120,000 of stock issued during the accounting period is added to the beginning balance to determine the ending balance in the common stock account.

In addition to reporting the changes in common stock, the statement describes the changes in retained earnings for the accounting period. RCS had no beginning balance in retained earnings. During the period, the company earned $35,000 and paid $4,000 in dividends to the stockholders, producing an ending retained earnings balance of $31,000 ($0 + $35,000 − $4,000). Since equity consists of common stock and retained earnings, the ending total equity balance is $151,000 ($120,000 + $31,000). This statement is also dated with the phrase *For the Year Ended December 31, 2013*, because it describes what happened to stockholders' equity during 2013.

Balance Sheet

The **balance sheet** draws its name from the accounting equation. Total assets balance with (equal) liabilities and stockholders' equity. The balance sheet for RCS is shown in Exhibit 1.5. In this case, total assets equals total liabilities plus stockholders' equity ($551,000 = $551,000).

Note the order of the assets in the balance sheet. Cash appears first, followed by land. Assets are displayed in the balance sheet based on their level of **liquidity.** This means that assets are listed in the order of how rapidly they can be converted into cash. Finally, note that the balance sheet is dated with the phrase *As of December 31, 2013*, indicating that it describes the company's financial condition on the last day of the accounting period.

Statement of Cash Flows

The **statement of cash flows** explains how a company obtained and used *cash* during the accounting period. Receipts of cash are called *cash inflows,* and payments are *cash outflows.* The statement classifies cash receipts (inflows) and payments (outflows) into three categories: financing activities, investing activities, and operating activities.

Businesses normally start with an idea. Implementing the idea usually requires cash. For example, suppose you decide to start an apartment rental business. First, you would need cash to finance acquiring the apartments. Acquiring cash to start a business is a financing activity. **Financing activities** include obtaining cash (inflow) from owners or paying cash (outflow) to owners (dividends). Financing activities also include borrowing cash (inflow) from creditors and repaying the principal (outflow) to creditors. Because interest on borrowed money is an expense, however, cash paid to creditors for interest is reported in the operating activities section of the statement of cash flows.

After obtaining cash from financing activities, you would invest the money by building or buying apartments. **Investing activities** involve paying cash (outflow) to purchase long-term assets or receiving cash (inflow) from selling long-term assets. Long-term assets are normally used for more than one year. Cash outflows to purchase land or cash inflows from selling a building are examples of investing activities.

After investing in the productive assets (apartments), you would engage in operating activities. **Operating activities** involve receiving cash (inflow) from revenue and paying cash (outflow) for expenses. Note that cash spent to purchase short-term assets such as office supplies is reported in the operating activities section because the office supplies would likely be used (expensed) within a single accounting period.

The primary cash inflows and outflows related to the types of business activity introduced in this chapter are summarized in Exhibit 1.6. The exhibit will be expanded as additional types of events are introduced in subsequent chapters.

The statement of cash flows for Rustic Camp Sites in Exhibit 1.5 shows that the amount of cash increased by $51,000 during the year. The beginning balance in the Cash account was zero; adding the $51,000 increase to the beginning balance results in a $51,000 ending balance. Notice that the $51,000 ending cash balance on the statement of cash flows is the same as the amount of cash reported in the asset section on the December 31 year-end balance sheet. Also, note that the statement of cash flows is dated with the phrase *For the Year Ended December 31, 2013,* because it describes what happened to cash over the span of the year.

EXHIBIT 1.6

Classification Scheme for Statement of Cash Flows

Cash flows from operating activities:
Cash receipts (inflows) from customers
Cash payments (outflows) to suppliers

Cash flows from investing activities:
Cash receipts (inflows) from the sale of long-term assets
Cash payments (outflows) for the purchase of long-term assets

Cash flows from financing activities:
Cash receipts (inflows) from borrowing funds
Cash receipts (inflows) from issuing common stock
Cash payments (outflows) to repay borrowed funds
Cash payments (outflows) for dividends

✓ CHECK YOURSELF 1.5

Classify each of the following cash flows as an operating activity, investing activity, or financing activity.

1. Acquired cash from owners.
2. Borrowed cash from creditors.
3. Paid cash to purchase land.
4. Earned cash revenue.
5. Paid cash for salary expenses.
6. Paid cash dividend.
7. Paid cash for interest.

Answer   (1) financing activity; (2) financing activity; (3) investing activity; (4) operating activity; (5) operating activity; (6) financing activity; (7) operating activity.

The Closing Process

As previously indicated, transaction data are recorded in the Revenue, Expense, and Dividend accounts during the accounting period. At the end of the accounting period the data in these accounts are transferred to the Retained Earnings account. The process of transferring the balances is called **closing.** Since the Revenue, Expense, and Dividend accounts are closed each period, they are called **temporary accounts.** At the beginning of each new accounting period, the temporary accounts have zero balances. The Retained Earnings account carries forward from one accounting period to the next. Since this account is not closed, it is called a **permanent account.**

Since RCS started operations on January 1, 2013, the beginning Retained Earnings account balance was zero. In other words, there were no previous earnings available to be retained by the business. During 2013, amounts were recorded in the Revenue, Expense, and Dividend accounts. Since the Retained Earnings account is separate from the Revenue, Expense, and Dividend accounts, the entries in these temporary accounts did not affect the Retained Earnings balance. Specifically, the *before closing* balance in the Retained Earnings account on December 31, 2013, is still zero. In contrast, the Revenue account has a balance of $85,000; the Expense account has a balance of $50,000; and the Dividends account has a balance of $4,000. The closing process transfers the balances in the Revenue, Expense, and Dividend accounts to the Retained Earnings account. Therefore, *after closing* the balance in the Retained Earnings account is $31,000 ($85,000 − $50,000 − $4,000) and the Revenue, Expense, and Dividend accounts have zero balances.

Since the asset, liability, common stock, and retained earnings accounts are permanent accounts, they are not closed at the end of the accounting period. After the closing account process, RCS's general ledger will contain the following account balances as of December 31, 2013.

Cash	+	Land	=	Notes Payable	+	Common Stock	+	Retained Earnings
51,000	+	500,000	=	400,000	+	120,000	+	31,000

Take note that the December 31, 2013, ending account balances become the January 1, 2014, beginning account balances. So, RCS will start the 2014 accounting period with these same accounts balances. In other words, the current period's after closing ending balances become the next period's beginning balances.

 CHECK YOURSELF 1.6

After closing on December 31, 2013, Walston Company had $4,600 of assets, $2,000 of liabilities, and $700 of common stock. During January of 2014, Walston earned $750 of revenue and incurred $300 of expense. Walston closes it books each year on December 31.

1. Determine the balance in the Retained Earnings account as of December 31, 2013.
2. Determine the balance in the Retained Earnings account as of January 1, 2014.
3. Determine the balance in the Retained Earnings account as of January 31, 2014.

Answer

1. Assets = Liabilities + Common Stock + Retained Earnings

   $4,600 = $2,000 + $700 + Retained Earnings

   Retained Earnings = $1,900

2. The balance in the Retained Earnings account on January 1, 2014, is the same as it was on December 31, 2013. This year's ending balance becomes next year's beginning balance. Therefore, the balance in the Retained Earnings account on January 1, 2014, is $1,900.

3. The balance in the Retained Earnings account on January 31, 2014, is still $1,900. The revenue earned and expenses incurred during January are not recorded in the Retained Earnings account. Revenue is recorded in a Revenue account and expenses are recorded in an Expense account during the accounting period. The balances in the Revenue and Expense accounts are transferred to the Retained Earnings account during the closing process at the end of the accounting period (December 31, 2014).

THE HORIZONTAL FINANCIAL STATEMENTS MODEL

Financial statements are the scorecard for business activity. If you want to succeed in business, you must know how your business decisions affect your company's financial statements. This text uses a **horizontal statements model** to help you understand how business events affect financial statements. This model shows a set of financial statements horizontally across a single page of paper. The balance sheet is displayed first, adjacent to the income statement, and then the statement of cash flows. Because the effects of equity transactions can be analyzed by referring to certain balance sheet columns, and because of limited space, the statement of changes in stockholders' equity is not shown in the horizontal statements model.

The model frequently uses abbreviations. For example, activity classifications in the statement of cash flows are identified using OA for operating activities, IA for investing activities, and FA for financing activities. NC designates the net change in cash. The statements model uses "NA" when an account is not affected by an event. The background of the *balance sheet* is red, the *income statement* is blue, and the *statement of cash flows* is green. To demonstrate the usefulness of the horizontal statements model, we use it to display the seven accounting events that RCS experienced during its first year of operation (2013).

Record business events using a horizontal financial statements model.

1. RCS acquired $120,000 cash from the issuance of common stock.
2. RCS borrowed $400,000 cash.
3. RCS paid $500,000 cash to purchase land.
4. RCS received $85,000 cash from earning revenue.
5. RCS paid $50,000 cash for expenses.
6. RCS paid $4,000 of cash dividends to the owners.
7. The market value of the land owned by RCS was appraised at $525,000 on December 31, 2013.

Event No.	Balance Sheet																Income Statement						Statement of Cash Flows	
	Assets			=	Liab.	+	Stockholders' Equity									Rev.	−	Exp.	=	Net Inc.			
	Cash	+	Land	=	N. Pay.	+	Com. Stk.	+	Ret. Earn.														
Beg. bal.	0	+	0	=	0	+	0	+	0							0	−	0	=	0		NA	
1.	120,000	+	NA	=	NA	+	120,000	+	NA							NA	−	NA	=	NA		120,000	FA
2.	400,000	+	NA	=	400,000	+	NA	+	NA							NA	−	NA	=	NA		400,000	FA
3.	(500,000)	+	500,000	=	NA	+	NA	+	NA							NA	−	NA	=	NA		(500,000)	IA
4.	85,000	+	NA	=	NA	+	NA	+	85,000							85,000	−	NA	=	85,000		85,000	OA
5.	(50,000)	+	NA	=	NA	+	NA	+	(50,000)							NA	−	50,000	=	(50,000)		(50,000)	OA
6.	(4,000)	+	NA	=	NA	+	NA	+	(4,000)							NA	−	NA	=	NA		(4,000)	FA
7.	NA	+	NA	=	NA	+	NA	+	NA							NA	−	NA	=	NA		NA	
Totals	51,000	+	500,000	=	400,000	+	120,000	+	31,000							85,000	−	50,000	=	35,000		51,000	NC

Recognize that statements models are learning tools. Because they are helpful in understanding how accounting events affect financial statements, they are used extensively in this book. However, the models omit many of the details used in published financial statements. For example, the horizontal model shows only a partial set of statements. Also, since the statements are presented in aggregate, the description of dates (i.e., "as of" versus "for the period ended") does not distinguish periodic from cumulative data.

THE FINANCIAL ANALYST

This section of each chapter introduces topics related to analyzing real-world financial reports. We focus first on the types of businesses that operate in the real world. We also discuss the annual report that is used to communicate information to stakeholders.

Real-World Financial Reports

As previously indicated, organizations exist in many different forms, including *business* entities and *not-for-profit* entities. Business entities are typically service, merchandising, or manufacturing companies. **Service businesses,** which include doctors, attorneys, accountants, dry cleaners, and housekeepers, provide services to their customers. **Merchandising businesses,** sometimes called *retail* or *wholesale companies,* sell goods to customers that other entities make. **Manufacturing businesses** make the goods that they sell to their customers.

Some business operations include combinations of these three categories. For example, an automotive repair shop might change oil (service function), sell parts such as oil filters (retail function), and rebuild engines (manufacturing function). The nature of the reporting entity affects the form and content of the information reported in an entity's financial statements. For example, governmental entities provide statements of activities while business entities provide income statements. Similarly, income statements of retail companies show an expense item called *cost of goods sold,* but service companies that do not sell goods have no such item in their income statements. You should expect some diversity when reviewing real-world financial statements.

Throughout this book we usually present income statements that end with "Net income." Due to an accounting rule that became effective at the end of 2009, income statements of large, real-world companies often appear to have three lines for net income. The partial income statements for Merck & Company, a large pharmaceutical company, shown in Exhibit 1.7, illustrate this issue. Notice that the third line from the bottom of the statement is called "Net income." However, "Net income attributable to noncontrolling interest" is subtracted from this first net income to arrive at "Net income attributable to Merck & Co., Inc." The illustrations in this text always assume that there is no net income attributable to noncontrolling interests, therefore our examples simply end with the term "Net income."

Some real-world companies with complex operations report information related to *comprehensive income.* Comprehensive income is determined by adding or subtracting certain items to or from net income. A description of the items used to determine comprehensive income is complex and beyond the scope of this course. Even so, the reader should be aware that, as of 2011, companies that must report comprehensive income may do so in one of two ways. First, comprehensive income items can be added to the bottom of the primary statement of earnings. Alternatively, a separate statement showing the determination of comprehensive income can be presented immediately following the primary statement of earnings. If a company chooses to report comprehensive income in a separate statement, the company's annual report will contain five financial statements. This text limits coverage to the four financial statements that traditionally appear in real-world annual reports. The optional statement of comprehensive income is not covered.

Annual Report for Target Corporation

Organizations normally provide information, including financial statements, to *stakeholders* yearly in a document known as an **annual report.** The annual report for Target Corporation is reproduced in Appendix B of this text. This report includes the company's financial statements (see pages 721–726). Immediately following the statements are a set of notes that provide additional details about the items described in the statements (see pages 727–753). The annual report contains the *auditors' report,* which is discussed in Chapter 6. Annual reports also include written commentary describing management's assessment of significant events that affected the company during the reporting period. This commentary is called *management's discussion and analysis* (MD&A).

The U.S. Securities and Exchange Commission (SEC) requires public companies to file an annual report in a document known as a 10-K. The SEC is discussed in more detail later. Even though the annual report is usually flashier (contains more color and pictures) than the 10-K, the 10-K is normally more comprehensive with respect to content. As a result, the 10-K report frequently substitutes for the annual report, but the annual report cannot substitute for the 10-K. In an effort to reduce costs, many companies now use the 10-K report as their annual report.

Special Terms in Real-World Reports

The financial statements of real-world companies include numerous items relating to advanced topics that are not covered in introductory accounting textbooks, especially the first chapter of an introductory accounting textbook. Do not, however, be discouraged from browsing through real-world annual reports. You will significantly enhance your learning if you look at many annual reports and attempt to identify as many items

EXHIBIT 1.7   Real-World Financial Reporting

MERCK & CO., INC. AND SUBSIDIARIES
Consolidated Statement of Income (partial)
Years Ended December 31
($ in millions except per share amounts)

	2010	2009	2008
Sales	$45,987	$27,428	$23,850
Costs, expenses, and other			
Materials and production	18,396	9,019	5,583
Marketing and administrative	13,245	8,543	7,377
Research and development	10,991	5,845	4,805
Restructuring costs	985	1,634	1,033
Equity income from affiliates	(587)	(2,235)	(2,561)
Other (income) expense, net	1,304	(10,668)	(2,318)
	44,334	12,138	13,919
Income before taxes	1,653	15,290	9,931
Taxes on income	671	2,268	1,999
	982	13,022	7,932
Net income			
Less: Net Income attributable to noncontrolling interests	121	123	124
Net income attributable to Merck & Co., Inc.	$ 861	$12,899	$ 7,808

REALITY BYTES

On April 19, 2010, the stock of BP, Plc. (formally known as British Petroleum) was trading at $59.48 per share. On that same day the stock of Chevron Corp. was trading at $81.32 and the stock of Exxon Mobil Corp. was trading at $68.23. About six weeks later, on June 4, 2010, these companies' stocks had fallen to $37.16, $71.28, and $59.53 per share, respectively. Why did this happen? Did the companies report a large drop in their net earnings during these six weeks? No. What happened was that on April 20, 2010, the Deepwater Horizon oil well, owned by BP, failed and began discharging 60,000 barrels of oil daily into the Gulf of Mexico.

While it is easy to see why this event could cause BP's stock to lose 38 percent of its value, why would this cause Chevron's stock to fall 12 percent and Exxon's stock to fall 13 percent? These two companies did not have any oil spills during this time. One reason that the stock price of most oil companies declined significantly after BP's problems was that investors were concerned the failure would result in tighter regulation of all oil companies. Additionally, there was the concern that the government would ban, or seriously reduce, all future deepwater drilling. More regulations, and certainly a ban on future drilling, could drastically reduce the future earnings potential of all oil companies, not just BP.

As this situation illustrates, investors frequently use information not yet reported in a company's annual report. The annual report focuses on historical data, but investors are more concerned about the future. The historical information contained in the annual report is important because the past is frequently a strong predictor of what will occur in the future. However, current negative news, such as an oil spill, may give investors more information about a company's future than last year's annual report. For example, while the oil spill was bad news for the oil companies, it was, in financial terms, good news for companies that manufacture the oil-booms used to prevent oil from reaching the beaches. Similarly, a new company that has never earned a profit may have such an innovative idea that investors rush to buy its stock, even though they expect it to be a few years before the company has positive earnings. Also, investors and creditors may be motivated by nonfinancial considerations such as social consciousness, humanitarian concerns, or personal preferences. While accounting information is critically important, it is only one dimension of the information pool that investors and creditors use to make decisions.

as you can. As your accounting knowledge grows, you will likely experience increased interest in real-world financial reports and the businesses they describe.

We encourage you to look for annual reports in the library or ask your employer for a copy of your company's report. The Internet is another excellent source for obtaining annual reports. Most companies provide links to their annual reports on their home pages. Look for links labeled "about the company" or "investor relations" or other phrases that logically lead to the company's financial reports. The best way to learn accounting is to use it. Accounting is the language of business. Learning the language will serve you well in almost any area of business that you pursue.

◀◀ A Look Back

This chapter introduced the role of accounting in society and business: to provide information helpful to operating and evaluating the performance of organizations. Accounting is a measurement discipline. To communicate effectively, users of accounting must agree on the rules of measurement. *Generally accepted accounting principles (GAAP)* constitute the rules used by the accounting profession in the United States to govern financial reporting. GAAP is a work in progress that continues to evolve.

This chapter has discussed eight elements of financial statements: *assets, liabilities, equity, common stock (contributed capital), revenue, expenses, dividends (distributions),* and *net income.* The elements represent broad classifications reported on financial statements. Four basic financial statements appear in the reports of public companies: the *balance sheet,* the *income statement,* the *statement of changes in stockholders' equity,* and the *statement of cash flows.* The chapter discussed the form and content of each statement as well as the interrelationships among the statements.

This chapter introduced a *horizontal financial statements model* as a tool to help you understand how business events affect a set of financial statements. This model is used throughout the text. You should carefully study this model before proceeding to Chapter 2.

A Look Forward >>

To keep matters as simple as possible and to focus on the interrelationships among financial statements, this chapter considered only cash events. Obviously, many real-world events do not involve an immediate exchange of cash. For example, customers use telephone service throughout the month without paying for it until the next month. Such phone usage represents an expense in one month with a cash exchange in the following month. Events such as this are called *accruals.* Understanding the effects that accrual events have on the financial statements is included in Chapter 2.

 ## SELF-STUDY REVIEW PROBLEM

A step-by-step audio-narrated series of slides is provided on the text website at www.mhhe.com/edmonds8e.

During 2014 Rustic Camp Sites experienced the following transactions.

1. RCS acquired $32,000 cash by issuing common stock.
2. RCS received $116,000 cash for providing services to customers (leasing camp sites).
3. RCS paid $13,000 cash for salaries expense.
4. RCS paid a $9,000 cash dividend to the owners.
5. RCS sold land that had cost $100,000 for $100,000 cash.
6. RCS paid $47,000 cash for other operating expenses.

Required

a. Record the transaction data in a horizontal financial statements model like the following one. In the Cash Flow column, classify the cash flows as operating activities (OA), investing activities (IA), or financing activities (FA). The beginning balances have been recorded as an example. They are the ending balances shown on RCS's December 31, 2013, financial statements illustrated in the chapter. Note that the revenue and expense accounts have a zero beginning balance. Amounts in these accounts apply only to a single accounting period. Revenue and expense account balances are not carried forward from one accounting period to the next.

	Balance Sheet									Income Statement					
	Assets			**=**	**Liab.**	**+**	**Stockholders' Equity**								**Statement of Cash Flows**
Event No.	Cash	+	Land	=	N. Pay.	+	Com. Stk.	+	Ret. Earn.	Rev.	−	Exp.	=	Net Inc.	
Beg. bal.	51,000	+	500,000	=	400,000	+	120,000	+	31,000	NA	−	NA	=	NA	NA

b. Explain why there are no beginning balances in the Income Statement columns.
c. What amount of net income will RCS report on the 2014 income statement?
d. What amount of total assets will RCS report on the December 31, 2014, balance sheet?
e. What amount of retained earnings will RCS report on the December 31, 2014, balance sheet?
f. What amount of net cash flow from operating activities will RCS report on the 2014 statement of cash flows?

Solution

a.

Event No.	Balance Sheet											Income Statement				Statement of Cash Flows	
	Assets			=	Liab.	+	Stockholders' Equity										
	Cash	+	Land	=	N. Pay.	+	Com. Stk.	+	Ret. Earn.			Rev.	−	Exp.	=	Net Inc.	
Beg. bal.	51,000	+	500,000	=	400,000	+	120,000	+	31,000			NA	−	NA	=	NA	NA
1.	32,000	+	NA	=	NA	+	32,000	+	NA			NA	−	NA	=	NA	32,000 FA
2.	116,000	+	NA	=	NA	+	NA	+	116,000			116,000	−	NA	=	116,000	116,000 OA
3.	(13,000)	+	NA	=	NA	+	NA	+	(13,000)			NA	−	13,000	=	(13,000)	(13,000) OA
4.	(9,000)	+	NA	=	NA	+	NA	+	(9,000)			NA	−	NA	=	NA	(9,000) FA
5.	100,000	+	(100,000)	=	NA	+	NA	+	NA			NA	−	NA	=	NA	100,000 IA
6.	(47,000)	+	NA	=	NA	+	NA	+	(47,000)			NA	−	47,000	=	(47,000)	(47,000) OA
Totals	230,000	+	400,000	=	400,000	+	152,000	+	78,000			116,000	−	60,000	=	56,000	179,000 NC*

*The letters NC on the last line of the column designate the net change in cash.

b. The revenue and expense accounts are temporary accounts used to capture data for a single accounting period. They are closed (amounts removed from the accounts) to retained earnings at the end of the accounting period and therefore always have zero balances at the beginning of the accounting cycle.

c. RCS will report net income of $56,000 on the 2014 income statement. Compute this amount by subtracting the expenses from the revenue ($116,000 Revenue − $13,000 Salaries expense − $47,000 Other operating expense).

d. RCS will report total assets of $630,000 on the December 31, 2014, balance sheet. Compute total assets by adding the cash amount to the land amount ($230,000 Cash + $400,000 Land).

e. RCS will report retained earnings of $78,000 on the December 31, 2014, balance sheet. Compute this amount using the following formula: Beginning retained earnings + Net income − Dividends = Ending retained earnings. In this case, $31,000 + $56,000 − $9,000 = $78,000.

f. Net cash flow from operating activities is the difference between the amount of cash collected from revenue and the amount of cash spent for expenses. In this case, $116,000 cash inflow from revenue − $13,000 cash outflow for salaries expense − $47,000 cash outflow for other operating expenses = $56,000 net cash inflow from operating activities.

KEY TERMS

accounting 3
accounting equation 13
accounting event 14
accounting period 20
accounts 11
annual report 26
articulation 20
asset exchange transaction 16
asset source transaction 15
asset use transaction 16
assets 4
balance sheet 22
claims 12
closing 24
common stock 12
creditors 4
dividend 17
double-entry bookkeeping 15
earnings 4

elements 11
expenses 16
financial accounting 6
Financial Accounting Standards Board (FASB) 8
financial resources 4
financial statements 11
financing activities 23
general ledger 18
generally accepted accounting principles (GAAP) 8
going concern 14
historical cost concept 17
horizontal statements model 25
income 4
income statement 20
interest 4

International Accounting Standards Board (IASB) 9
International Financial Reporting Standards (IFRS) 9
investing activities 23
investors 4
labor resources 5
liabilities 12
liquidation 5
liquidity 22
managerial accounting 6
manufacturing businesses 26
market 4
matching concept 20
merchandising businesses 26
net income 20
net loss 20
not-for-profit entities 6

operating activities 23
permanent accounts 24
physical resources 5
profit 4
reporting entities 10
retained earnings 12
revenue 16
service businesses 26
stakeholders 6
statement of cash flows 23
statement of changes in stockholders' equity 22
stockholders 12
stockholders' equity 12
temporary accounts 24
transaction 14
users 6

QUESTIONS

1. Explain the term *stakeholder*. Distinguish between stakeholders with a direct versus an indirect interest in the companies that issue financial reports.
2. Why is accounting called the *language of business?*
3. What is the primary mechanism used to allocate resources in the United States?
4. In a business context, what does the term *market* mean?
5. What market trilogy components are involved in the process of transforming resources into finished products?
6. Give an example of a financial resource, a physical resource, and a labor resource.
7. What type of income or profit does an investor expect to receive in exchange for providing financial resources to a business? What type of income does a creditor expect from providing financial resources to an organization or business?
8. How do financial and managerial accounting differ?
9. Describe a not-for-profit or nonprofit enterprise. What is the motivation for this type of entity?
10. What are the U.S. rules of accounting information measurement called?
11. Explain how a career in public accounting differs from a career in private accounting.
12. Distinguish between elements of financial statements and accounts.
13. What role do assets play in business profitability?
14. To whom do the assets of a business belong?
15. Describe the differences between creditors and investors.
16. Name the accounting term used to describe a business's obligations to creditors.
17. What is the accounting equation? Describe each of its three components.
18. Who ultimately bears the risk and collects the rewards associated with operating a business?
19. What does a *double-entry bookkeeping system* mean?
20. How does acquiring capital from owners affect the accounting equation?
21. What is the difference between assets that are acquired by issuing common stock and those that are acquired using retained earnings?
22. How does earning revenue affect the accounting equation?
23. What are the three primary sources of assets?
24. What is the source of retained earnings?
25. How does distributing assets (paying dividends) to owners affect the accounting equation?
26. What are the similarities and differences between dividends and expenses?
27. What four general-purpose financial statements do business enterprises use?
28. Which of the general-purpose financial statements provides information about the enterprise at a specific designated date?
29. What causes a net loss?
30. What three categories of cash receipts and cash payments do businesses report on the statement of cash flows? Explain the types of cash flows reported in each category.
31. How are asset accounts usually arranged in the balance sheet?
32. Discuss the term *articulation* as it relates to financial statements.
33. How do temporary accounts differ from permanent accounts? Name three temporary accounts. Is retained earnings a temporary or a permanent account?
34. What is the historical cost concept and how does it relate to verifiability?
35. Identify the three types of accounting transactions discussed in this chapter. Provide an example of each type of transaction, and explain how it affects the accounting equation.
36. What type of information does a business typically include in its annual report?
37. What is U.S. GAAP? What is IFRS?

MULTIPLE-CHOICE QUESTIONS

Multiple-choice questions are provided on the text website at www.mhhe.com/edmonds8e.

EXERCISES—SERIES A

All applicable Exercises in Series A are available with McGraw-Hill's *Connect® Accounting.*

Exercise 1-1A   *The role of accounting in society*

LO 1

Resource owners provide three types of resources to conversion agents that transform the resources into products or services that satisfy consumer demands.

Required

Identify the three types of resources. Write a brief memo explaining how resource owners select the particular conversion agents to which they will provide resources. Your memo should include answers to the following questions: If you work as a private accountant, what role would you play in the allocation of resources? Which professional certification would be most appropriate to your career?

LO 1

Exercise 1-2A   *Careers in accounting*

Accounting is commonly divided into two sectors. One sector is called public accounting. The other sector is called private accounting.

Required

a. Identify three areas of service provided by public accountants.
b. Describe the common duties performed by private accountants.

LO 1

Exercise 1-3A   *Identifying the reporting entities*

Ray Steen recently started a business. During the first few days of operation, Mr. Steen transferred $100,000 from his personal account into a business account for a company he named Steen Enterprises. Steen Enterprises borrowed $60,000 from First Bank. Mr. Steen's father-in-law, Stan Rhoades, invested $75,000 into the business for which he received a 25 percent ownership interest. Steen Enterprises purchased a building from Zoro Realty Company. The building cost $150,000 cash. Steen Enterprises earned $56,000 in revenue from the company's customers and paid its employees $31,000 for salaries expense.

Required

Identify the entities that were mentioned in the scenario and explain what happened to the cash accounts of each entity that you identify.

LO 1

Exercise 1-4A   *Distribution in a business liquidation*

Assume that Clinton Company acquires $1,200 cash from creditors and $1,700 cash from investors.

Required

a. Explain the primary differences between investors and creditors.
b. If Clinton has net income of $800 and then liquidates, what amount of cash will the creditors receive? What amount of cash will the investors receive?
c. If Clinton has a net loss of $800 cash and then liquidates, what amount of cash will the creditors receive? What amount of cash will the investors receive?
d. If Clinton has a net loss of $1,900 cash and then liquidates, what amount of cash will the creditors receive? What amount of cash will the investors receive?

LO 1

Exercise 1-5A   *Differences between interest and dividends*

The following account balances were drawn from the financial records of Crystal Company (CC) as of January 1, 2013. Assets, $14,000; Liabilities, $4,000; Common Stock, $7,000; and Retained Earnings, $3,000. CC has agreed to pay the creditors $400 of interest per year. Further, CC agrees that for the 2013 fiscal year any annual earnings remaining after the interest charges will be paid out as dividends to the owners.

Required

a. Assuming CC earns a before interest expense recognition profit of $900 during 2013, determine the amount of interest and dividends paid.
b. Assuming CC earns a before interest expense recognition profit of $500 during 2013, determine the amount of interest and dividends paid.
c. Assuming CC earns a before interest expense recognition profit of $100 during 2013, determine the amount of interest and dividends paid.

Exercise 1-6A   *Components of the accounting equation*   LO 2

Lang Enterprises was started when it acquired $4,000 cash from creditors and $6,000 from owners. The company immediately purchased land that cost $9,000.

Required

a. Record the events under an accounting equation.

b. After all events have been recorded, Lang's obligations to creditors represents what percent of total assets?

c. After all events have been recorded, Lang's stockholder's equity represents what percent of total assets?

d. Assume the debt is due. Given that Lang has $6,000 in stockholders' equity, can the company repay the creditors at this point? Why or why not?

Exercise 1-7A   *Components of the accounting equation*   LO 2

The financial condition of GreyCo Inc. is expressed in the following accounting equation:

$$\text{Assets} = \text{Liabilities} + \text{Common stock} + \text{Retained earnings}$$
$$\$800 \text{ Cash} + \$9,200 \text{ Land} = \$7,000 + \$2,000 + \$1,000$$

Required

a. Are dividends paid to creditors or investors? Explain why.

b. How much cash is in the Retained Earnings account?

c. Determine the maximum dividend GreyCo can pay.

d. If the obligation to creditors is due, can GreyCo repay the loan? Why or why not?

e. Suppose the land sinks into the sea as a result of an earthquake and a resulting tsunami. The business is then liquidated. How much cash will creditors receive? How much cash will investors receive? (Assume there are no legal fees or other costs of liquidation.)

Exercise 1-8A   *Missing information in the accounting equation*   LO 2

Required

Calculate the missing amounts in the following table.

					Stockholders' Equity		
Company	Assets	=	Liabilities	+	Common Stock	+	Retained Earnings
A	$?		$30,000		$ 50,000		$62,000
B	50,000		?		10,000		25,000
C	85,000		20,000		?		40,000
D	215,000		60,000		100,000		?

Exercise 1-9A   *Missing information and recording events*   LO 2, 3

As of December 31, 2013, Post Company had total cash of $156,000, notes payable of $85,600, and common stock of $52,400. During 2014, Post earned $36,000 of cash revenue, paid $20,000 for cash expenses, and paid a $3,000 cash dividend to the stockholders.

Required

a. Determine the amount of retained earnings as of December 31, 2013.

b. Create an accounting equation and record the beginning account balances under the appropriate elements.

c. Record the revenue, expense, and dividend events under the appropriate elements of the accounting equation created in Requirement *b*.

d. Prove the equality of the accounting equation as of December 31, 2014.

e. Identify the beginning and ending balances in the Cash and Common Stock accounts. Explain why the beginning and ending balances in the Cash account are different, but the beginning and ending balances in the Common Stock account remain the same.

34   Chapter 1

LO 2, 3

Exercise 1-10A *Effect of events on the accounting equation*

Hansen Enterprises experienced the following events during 2013:

1. Acquired cash from the issue of common stock.
2. Provided services to clients for cash.
3. Paid utilities expenses with cash.
4. Paid cash to reduce the principal on a bank note.
5. Sold land for cash at an amount equal to its cost.
6. Paid a cash dividend to the stockholders.

Required

Explain how each of the events would affect the accounting equation by writing the letter I for increase, the letter D for decrease, and NA for does not affect under each of the components of the accounting equation. The first event is shown as an example.

Event Number	Assets	= Liabilities +	Common Stock	+ Retained Earnings
1	I	NA	I	NA

LO 2, 3

Exercise 1-11A *Effect of transactions on general ledger accounts*

At the beginning of 2013, Foster Corp.'s accounting records had the following general ledger accounts and balances.

	FOSTER CORP. Accounting Equation						
Event	Assets		=	Liabilities	+	Stockholders' Equity		Acct. Titles for RE
	Cash	Land		Notes Payable		Common Stock	Retained Earnings	
Balance 1/1/2013	30,000	16,000		10,000		20,000	16,000	

Foster Corp. completed the following transactions during 2013:

1. Purchased land for $20,000 cash.
2. Acquired $10,000 cash from the issue of common stock.
3. Received $90,000 cash for providing services to customers.
4. Paid cash operating expenses of $65,000.
5. Borrowed $20,000 cash from the bank.
6. Paid a $5,000 cash dividend to the stockholders.
7. Determined that the market value of the land purchased in event 1 is $30,000.

Required

a. Record the transactions in the appropriate general ledger accounts. Record the amounts of revenue, expense, and dividends in the Retained Earnings column. Provide the appropriate titles for these accounts in the last column of the table.
b. As of December 31, 2013, determine the total amount of assets, liabilities, and stockholder's equity and present this information in the form of an accounting equation.
c. What is the amount of total assets, liabilities, and stockholders' equity as of January 1, 2014?

Exercise 1-12A   *Accounts titles and the accounting equation*   **LO 3**

The following account titles were drawn from the general ledger of Gutter Control, Incorporated (GCI): Cash, Notes Payable, Land, Accounts Payable, Office Furniture, Salaries Expense, Common Stock, Service Revenue, Interest Expense, Utilities Payable, Utilities Expense, Trucks, Supplies, Operating Expenses, Rent Revenue, Dividends, Computers, Building, Supplies Expense, Gasoline Expense, Retained Earnings, Dividends.

Required

a. Create an accounting equation using the elements assets, liabilities, and stockholders' equity. List each account title under the element of the accounting equation to which it belongs.

b. Will all businesses have the same number of accounts? Explain your answer.

Exercise 1-13A   *Classifying events as asset source, use, or exchange*   **LO 4**

Dale's Business Services experienced the following events during its first year of operations:

1. Acquired $20,000 cash from the issue of common stock.
2. Borrowed $12,000 cash from First Bank.
3. Paid $5,000 cash to purchase land.
4. Received $25,000 cash for providing boarding services.
5. Acquired an additional $5,000 cash from the issue of common stock.
6. Purchased additional land for $4,000 cash.
7. Paid $10,000 cash for salary expense.
8. Signed a contract to provide additional services in the future.
9. Paid $1,200 cash for rent expense.
10. Paid a $1,000 cash dividend to the stockholders.
11. Determined the market value of the land to be $18,000 at the end of the accounting period.

Required

Classify each event as an asset source, use, or exchange transaction or as not applicable (NA).

Exercise 1-14A   *Historical cost versus market value*   **LO 5**

Mountain View, Inc., purchased land in January 2009 at a cost of $250,000. The estimated market value of the land is $425,000 as of December 31, 2013.

Required

a. Name the December 31, 2013, financial statement(s) on which the land will be shown.

b. At what dollar amount will the land be shown in the financial statement(s)?

c. Name the key concept that will be used in determining the dollar amount that will be reported for land that is shown in the financial statement(s).

Exercise 1-15A   *Preparing an income statement and a balance sheet*   **LO 2, 3, 5**

Topez Company was started on January 1, 2013. During 2013, the company experienced the following three accounting events: (1) earned cash revenues of $14,500, (2) paid cash expenses of $9,200, and (3) paid a $500 cash dividend to its stockholders. These were the only events that affected the company during 2013.

Required

a. Create an accounting equation and record the effects of each accounting event under the appropriate general ledger account headings.

b. Prepare an income statement and a balance sheet dated December 31, 2013, for Topez Company.

c. Explain why the income statement uses different terminology to date the income statement than is used to date the balance sheet.

LO 5

Exercise 1-16A   *Statement of cash flows*

On January 1, 2013, Palmetto, a fast-food company, had a balance in its Cash account of $32,000. During the 2013 accounting period, the company had (1) net cash inflow from operating activities of $15,600, (2) net cash outflow for investing activities of $23,000, and (3) net cash outflow from financing activities of $4,500.

Required

a. Prepare a statement of cash flows.

b. Provide a reasonable explanation as to what may have caused the net cash inflow from operating activities.

c. Provide a reasonable explanation as to what may have caused the net cash outflow from investing activities.

d. Provide a reasonable explanation as to what may have caused the net cash outflow from financing activities.

LO 5

Exercise 1-17A   *Prepare a statement of cash flows*

American General Company experienced the following accounting events during 2013:

1. Paid $4,000 cash for salary expense.
2. Borrowed $8,000 cash from State Bank.
3. Received $30,000 cash from the issue of common stock.
4. Purchased land for $8,000 cash.
5. Performed services for $14,000 cash.
6. Paid $4,200 cash for utilities expense.
7. Sold land for $7,000 cash.
8. Paid a cash dividend of $1,000 to the stockholders.
9. Hired an accountant to keep the books.
10. Paid $3,000 cash on the loan from State Bank.

Required

a. Indicate how each of the events would be classified on the statement of cash flows as operating activities (OA), investing activities (IA), financing activities (FA), or not applicable (NA).

b. Prepare a statement of cash flows for 2013. Assume American General had a beginning cash balance of $9,000 on January 1, 2013.

LO 1, 4, 5

Exercise 1-18A   *Relating accounting events to entities*

Arnett Company was started in 2013 when it acquired $30,000 cash by issuing common stock to Dan Arnett.

Required

a. Was this event an asset source, use, or exchange transaction for Arnett Company?

b. Was this event an asset source, use, or exchange transaction for Dan Arnett?

c. Was the cash flow an operating, investing, or financing activity on Arnett Company's 2013 statement of cash flows?

d. Was the cash flow an operating, investing, or financing activity on Dan Arnett's 2013 statement of cash flows?

LO 2, 3, 5

Exercise 1-19A   *Preparing financial statements*

Carolina Company experienced the following events during 2013.

1. Acquired $50,000 cash from the issue of common stock.
2. Paid $15,000 cash to purchase land.
3. Borrowed $25,000 cash.
4. Provided services for $60,000 cash.

5. Paid $12,000 cash for rent expense.
6. Paid $22,000 cash for other operating expenses.
7. Paid a $5,000 cash dividend to the stockholders.
8. Determined that the market value of the land purchased in Event 2 is now $16,500.

Required

a. The January 1, 2013, general ledger account balances are shown in the following accounting equation. Record the eight events in the appropriate general ledger accounts. Record the amounts of revenue, expense, and dividends in the Retained Earnings column. Provide the appropriate titles for these accounts in the last column of the table. The first event is shown as an example.

		CAROLINA COMPANY Accounting Equation						
Event	Assets		=	Liabilities	+	Stockholders' Equity		Acct. Titles for RE
	Cash	Land		Notes Payable		Common Stock	Retained Earnings	
Balance 1/1/2013 1.	15,000 50,000	10,000		0		20,000 50,000	5,000	

b. Prepare an income statement, statement of changes in equity, year-end balance sheet, and statement of cash flows for the 2013 accounting period.

c. Determine the percentage of assets that were provided by retained earnings. How much cash is in the retained earnings account?

Exercise 1-20A *Preparing financial statements—cash flow emphasis*

LO 2, 3, 5

As of January 1, 2013, Concepts Inc. had a balance of $4,500 in Cash, $2,500 in Common Stock, and $2,000 in Retained Earnings. These were the only accounts with balances in the ledger on January 1, 2013. Further analysis of the company's cash account indicated that during the 2013 accounting period, the company had (1) net cash inflow from operating activities of $5,100, (2) net cash outflow for investing activities of $13,000, and (3) net cash inflow from financing activities of $7,600. All revenue and expense events were cash events. The following accounts and balances represent the general ledger of Concepts Inc. as of December 31, 2013, before closing.

CONCEPTS INC.
General Ledger

Assets	=	Liabilities	+	Stockholders' Equity	
Cash		**Notes Payable**		**Common Stock**	**Revenue**
Bal. 4,200		Bal. 3,000		Bal. 8,000	Bal. 9,900
Land				**Retained Earnings**	**Expenses**
Bal. 13,000				Bal. 2,000	Bal. 4,800
					Dividends
					Bal. 900

Required

a. Assume that the net cash inflow from financing activities of $7,600 was caused by three events. Based on the information above, identify these events and determine the cash flow associated with each event.

b. What did the company purchase that resulted in the cash outflow from investing activities?

c. Prepare an income statement, statement of changes in stockholders' equity, balance sheet, and statement of cash flows.

LO 2, 3, 5

Exercise 1-21A   *Preparing financial statements—retained earnings emphasis*

On January 1, 2013, the following information was drawn from the accounting records of Wilson Company: cash of $200; land of $1,800; notes payable of $600; and common stock of $1,000.

Required

a. Determine the amount of retained earnings as of January 1, 2013.

b. After looking at the amount of retained earnings, the chief executive officer (CEO) wants to pay a $300 cash dividend to the stockholders. Can the company pay this dividend? Why or why not?

c. As of January 1, 2013, what percent of the assets were acquired from creditors?

d. As of January 1, 2013, what percent of the assets were acquired from investors?

e. As of January 1, 2013, what percent of the assets were acquired from retained earnings?

f. Create an accounting equation using percentages instead of dollar amounts on the right side of the equation.

g. During 2013, Wilson Company earned cash revenue of $500, paid cash expenses of $300, and paid a cash dividend of $50. Prepare an income statement, statement of changes in stockholders' equity, a balance sheet, and a statement of cash flows dated December 31, 2013? (*Hint:* It is helpful to record these events under an accounting equation before preparing the statements.)

h. Comment on the terminology used to date each statement.

i. An appraiser determines that as of December 31, 2013, the market value of the land is $2,000. How will this fact change the financial statements?

j. What is the balance in the Revenue account on January 1, 2014?

LO 2

Exercise 1-22A   *Missing information for determining net income*

The December 31, 2012, balance sheet for Thomas Company showed total stockholders' equity of $156,000. Total stockholders' equity increased by $65,000 between December 31, 2012, and December 31, 2013. During 2013 Thomas Company acquired $20,000 cash from the issue of common stock. Thomas Company paid an $5,000 cash dividend to the stockholders during 2013.

Required

Determine the amount of net income or loss Thomas reported on its 2013 income statement. (*Hint:* Remember that stock issues, net income, and dividends all change total stockholders' equity.)

EXERCISES—SERIES A

LO 5

Exercise 1-23A   *The closing process*

Sammy's Pizza opened on January 1, 2013. Sammy's reported the following for cash revenues and cash expenses for the years 2013 to 2015:

	Cash Revenues	Cash Expenses
2013	$20,000	$11,000
2014	$30,000	$14,000
2015	$40,000	$22,000

Required

a. What would Sammy's Pizza report for net income and retained earnings for the years 2013, 2014, and 2015?

b. Explain the difference between net income and retained earnings.

c. Assume that Sammy's Pizza paid a $5,000 dividend to stockholders in 2014. What would Sammy's Pizza report for net income and retained earnings for 2014 and 2015?

Exercise 1-24A   *Retained earnings and the closing process*

LO 5

Davis Company was started on January 1, 2013. During the month of January, Davis earned $4,600 of revenue and incurred $3,000 of expense. During the remainder of 2013, Davis earned $52,000 and incurred $42,000 of expenses. Davis closes its books on December 31 of each year.

Required

a. Determine the balance in the Retained Earnings account as of January 31, 2013.

b. Determine the balance in the Revenue and Expense accounts as of January 31, 2013.

c. Determine the balance in the Retained Earnings account as of December 31, 2013, before closing.

d. Determine the balances in the Revenue and Expense accounts as of December 31, 2013, before closing.

e. Determine the balance in the Retained Earnings and Revenue accounts as of January 1, 2014.

Exercise 1-25A   *Comparing common stock with retained earnings*

LO 5

As of December 31, 2013, Blue Hen Company had total assets of $100,000, total liabilities of $30,000, and common stock of $50,000.

Required

a. Determine the amount of retained earnings as of December 31, 2013, after closing.

b. Explain the difference between common stock and retained earnings.

c. On January 1, 2014, Blue Hen raised $40,000 by issuing additional common stock. Immediately after the additional capital was raised, Blue Hen reported total equity of $110,000. Are the stockholders of Blue Hen in a better financial position than they were on December 31, 2013?

Exercise 1-26A   *Types of transactions and the horizontal statements model*

LO 4, 6

Happy Pet Store experienced the following events during its first year of operations, 2013:

1. Acquired cash by issuing common stock.
2. Borrowed cash from a bank.
3. Signed a contract to provide services in the future.
4. Purchased land with cash.
5. Paid cash for operating expenses.
6. Paid a cash dividend to the stockholders.
7. Determined that the market value of the land is higher than the historical cost.

Required

a. Indicate whether each event is an asset source, use, or exchange transaction.

b. Use a horizontal statements model to show how each event affects the balance sheet, income statement, and statement of cash flows. Indicate whether the event increases (I), decreases (D), or does not affect (NA) each element of the financial statements. Also, in the Cash

Flows column, classify the cash flows as operating activities (OA), investing activities (IA), or financing activities (FA). The first transaction is shown as an example.

Event No.	Balance Sheet									Income Statement					Statement of Cash Flows
	Cash	+	Land	=	N. Pay	+	C. Stock.	+	Ret. Ear.	Rev.	−	Exp.	=	Net Inc.	
1.	I	+	NA	=	NA	+	I	+	NA	NA	−	NA	=	NA	I FA

LO IFRS

Exercise 1-27A   *International Financial Reporting Standards*

Corrugated Boxes Inc. is a U.S.–based company that develops its financial statements under GAAP. The total amount of the company's assets shown on its December 31, 2013, balance sheet was approximately $305 million. The president of Corrugated is considering the possibility of relocating the company to a country that practices accounting under IFRS. The president has hired an international accounting firm to determine what the company's statements would look like if they were prepared under IFRS. One striking difference is that under IFRS the assets shown on the balance sheet would be valued at approximately $345 million.

Required

a. Would Corrugated Boxes' assets really be worth $40 million more if it moves its headquarters?

b. Discuss the underlying conceptual differences between U.S. GAAP and IFRS that cause the difference in the reported asset values.

PROBLEMS—SERIES A

All applicable Problems in Series A are available with McGraw-Hill's *Connect® Accounting.*

LO 1

Problem 1-28A   *Accounting's role in not-for-profits*

Karen White is struggling to pass her introductory accounting course. Karen is intelligent but she likes to party. Studying is a low priority for Karen. When one of her friends tells her that she is going to have trouble in business if she doesn't learn accounting, Karen responds that she doesn't plan to go into business. She says that she is arts oriented and plans someday to be a director of a museum. She is in the school of business to develop her social skills, not her quantitative skills. Karen says she won't have to worry about accounting, since museums are not intended to make a profit.

Required

a. Write a brief memo explaining whether you agree or disagree with Karen's position regarding accounting and not-for-profit organizations.

b. Distinguish between financial accounting and managerial accounting.

c. Identify some of the stakeholders of not-for-profit institutions that would expect to receive financial accounting reports.

d. Identify some of the stakeholders of not-for-profit institutions that would expect to receive managerial accounting reports.

LO 1

CHECK FIGURE
a1. Entities mentioned: Chris Hann and Classic Auto Sales

Problem 1-29A   *Accounting entities*

The following business scenarios are independent from one another:

1. Chris Hann purchased an automobile from Classic Auto Sales for $10,000.
2. Sal Pearl loaned $15,000 to the business in which he is a stockholder.

3. First State Bank paid interest to Strong Co. on a certificate of deposit that Strong Co. has invested at First State Bank.

4. Cindy's Restaurant paid the current utility bill of $135 to Midwest Utilities.

5. Sun Corp., borrowed $50,000 from City National Bank and used the funds to purchase land from Carriage Realty.

6. Sue Wang purchased $10,000 of common stock of International Sales Corporation from the corporation.

7. Chris Gordon loaned $6,000 cash to his daughter.

8. Motor Service Co. earned $20,000 in cash revenue.

9. Poy Imports paid $4,000 for salaries to each of its four employees.

10. Borg Inc. paid a cash dividend of $4,000 to its sole shareholder, Mark Borg.

Required

a. For each scenario, create a list of all of the entities that are mentioned in the description.

b. Describe what happens to the cash account of each entity that you identified in Requirement *a*.

Problem 1-30A   *Classifying events as asset source, use, or exchange*   LO 4

The following unrelated events are typical of those experienced by business entities:

1. Pay cash for operating expenses.
2. Pay an office manager's salary with cash.
3. Receive cash for services that have been performed.
4. Pay cash for utilities expense.
5. Acquire land by accepting a liability (financing the purchase).
6. Pay cash to purchase a new office building.
7. Discuss plans for a new office building with an architect.
8. Repay part of a bank loan.
9. Acquire cash by issuing common stock.
10. Purchase land with cash.
11. Purchase equipment with cash.
12. Pay monthly rent on an office building.
13. Hire a new office manager.
14. Borrow cash from a bank.
15. Pay a cash dividend to stockholders.

Required

Identify each of the events as an asset source, use, or exchange transaction. If an event would not be recorded under generally accepted accounting principles, identify it as not applicable (NA). Also indicate for each event whether total assets would increase, decrease, or remain unchanged. Organize your answer according to the following table. The first event is shown in the table as an example.

Event No.	Type of Event	Effect on Total Assets
1	Asset use	Decrease

Problem 1-31A   *Relating titles and accounts to financial statements*   LO 2, 5

Required

Identify the financial statements on which each of the following items (titles, date descriptions, and accounts) appears by placing a check mark in the appropriate column. If an item appears on more than one statement, place a check mark in every applicable column.

Item	Income Statement	Statement of Changes in Stockholders' Equity	Balance Sheet	Statement of Cash Flows
For the period ended (date)				
Net income				
Investing activities				
Net loss				
Ending cash balance				
Salary expense				
Consulting revenue				
Dividends				
Financing activities				
Ending common stock				
Interest expense				
As of (date)				
Land				
Beginning cash balance				
Notes payable				
Beginning common stock				
Service revenue				
Utility expense				
Stock issue				
Operating activities				

LO 2, 3, 5, 6

CHECK FIGURES

a. Net Income 2013: $40,000

b. Retained Earnings 2014: $80,000

Problem 1-32A *Preparing financial statements for two complete accounting cycles*

Susan's Consulting experienced the following transactions for 2013, its first year of operations, and 2014. *Assume that all transactions involve the receipt or payment of cash.*

Transactions for 2013

1. Acquired $50,000 by issuing common stock.
2. Received $100,000 cash for providing services to customers.
3. Borrowed $15,000 cash from creditors.
4. Paid expenses amounting to $60,000.
5. Purchased land for $40,000 cash.

Transactions for 2014

Beginning account balances for 2014 are:

Cash	$65,000
Land	40,000
Notes payable	15,000
Common stock	50,000
Retained earnings	40,000

1. Acquired an additional $20,000 from the issue of common stock.
2. Received $130,000 for providing services.

3. Paid $10,000 to creditors to reduce loan.
4. Paid expenses amounting to $75,000.
5. Paid a $15,000 dividend to the stockholders.
6. Determined that the market value of the land is $50,000.

Required

a. Write an accounting equation, and record the effects of each accounting event under the appropriate headings for each year. Record the amounts of revenue, expense, and dividends in the Retained Earnings column. Provide appropriate titles for these accounts in the last column of the table.

b. Prepare an income statement, statement of changes in stockholders' equity, year-end balance sheet, and statement of cash flows for each year.

c. Determine the amount of cash that is in the retained earnings account at the end of 2013 and 2014.

d. Examine the balance sheets for the two years. How did assets change from 2013 to 2014?

e. Determine the balance in the Retained Earnings account immediately after Event 2 in 2013 and in 2014 are recorded.

Problem 1-33A *Interrelationships among financial statements*

Crawford Enterprises started the 2013 accounting period with $75,000 of assets (all cash), $15,000 of liabilities, and $25,000 of common stock. During the year, Crawford earned cash revenues of $46,000, paid cash expenses of $26,000, and paid a cash dividend to stockholders of $5,000. Crawford also acquired $15,000 of additional cash from the sale of common stock and paid $10,000 cash to reduce the liability owed to a bank.

Required

a. Prepare an income statement, statement of changes in stockholders' equity, period-end balance sheet, and statement of cash flows for the 2013 accounting period. (*Hint:* Determine the amount of beginning retained earnings before considering the effects of the current period events. It also might help to record all events under an accounting equation before preparing the statements.)

b. Determine the percentage of total assets that were provided by creditors, investors, and earnings.

Problem 1-34A *Recording events in a horizontal statements model*

Davidson Company was started on January 1, 2013, and experienced the following events during its first year of operation:

1. Acquired $52,000 cash from the issue of common stock.
2. Borrowed $20,000 cash from National Bank.
3. Earned cash revenues of $42,000 for performing services.
4. Paid cash expenses of $23,000.
5. Paid a $6,000 cash dividend to the stockholders.
6. Acquired an additional $10,000 cash from the issue of common stock.
7. Paid $10,000 cash to reduce the principal balance of the bank note.
8. Paid $45,000 cash to purchase land.
9. Determined that the market value of the land is $55,000.

Required

a. Record the preceding transactions in the horizontal statements model. Also, in the Cash Flows column, classify the cash flows as operating activities (OA), investing activities (IA), or financing activities (FA). The first event is shown as an example.

Event No.	Balance Sheet								Income Statement					Statement of Cash Flows
	Cash	+	Land	=	N. Pay	+	C. Stock.	+	Ret. Ear.	Rev.	−	Exp.	=	Net Inc.	
1.	52,000	+	NA	=	NA	+	52,000	+	NA	NA	−	NA	=	NA	52,000 FA

b. Determine the amount of total assets that Davidson would report on the December 31, 2013, balance sheet.

c. Identify the asset source transactions and related amounts for 2013.

d. Determine the net income that Davidson would report on the 2013 income statement. Explain why dividends do not appear on the income statement.

e. Determine the net cash flows from operating activities, financing activities, and investing activities that Davidson would report on the 2013 statement of cash flows.

f. Determine the percentage of assets that were provided by investors, creditors, and earnings.

g. What is the balance in the Retained Earnings account immediately after Event 3 is recorded?

EXERCISES—SERIES B

LO 1

Exercise 1-1B   *The role of accounting in society*

Free economies use open markets to allocate resources.

Required

Identify the three participants in a free business market. Write a brief memo explaining how these participants interact to ensure that goods and services are distributed in a manner that satisfies consumers. Your memo should include answers to the following questions: If you work as a public accountant, what role would you play in the allocation of resources? Which professional certification would be most appropriate to your career?

LO 1

Exercise 1-2B   *Careers in accounting*

While public and private accounting overlap, various professional certifications are designed to attest to competency for specific areas of interest.

Required

a. Name the most common professional certification held by public accountants. Describe the general requirements for attaining this certification.

b. Name two types of professional certification, other than CPA, held by private accountants. Describe the general requirements for attaining these certifications.

LO 1

Exercise 1-3B   *Identifying the reporting entities*

Karen White helped organize a charity fund to help cover the medical expenses of a friend of hers who was seriously injured in a bicycle accident. The fund was named Vicky Hill Recovery Fund (VHRF). Karen contributed $1,000 of her own money to the fund. The $1,000 was paid to WKUX, a local radio station that designed and played an advertising campaign to educate the public as to the need for help. The campaign resulted in the collection of $20,000 cash. VHRF paid $12,000 to Mercy Hospital to cover Vicky's outstanding hospital cost. The remaining $8,000 was contributed to the National Cyclist Fund.

Required

Identify the entities that were mentioned in the scenario and explain what happened to the cash accounts of each entity that you identify.

LO 1

Exercise 1-4B   *Distribution in a business liquidation*

Assume that Martin Company acquires $2,400 cash from creditors and $3,400 cash from investors.

Required

a. Explain the primary differences between investors and creditors.

b. If Martin has net income of $1,500 and then liquidates, what amount of cash will the creditors receive? What amount of cash will the investors receive?

c. If Martin has a net loss of $1,500 cash and then liquidates, what amount of cash will the creditors receive? What amount of cash will the investors receive?

d. If Martin has a net loss of $3,900 cash and then liquidates, what amount of cash will the creditors receive? What amount of cash will the investors receive?

Exercise 1-5B   Differences between interest and dividends

The following account balances were drawn from the financial records of Kerr Company (KC) as of January 1, 2013. Assets, $25,000; Liabilities, $8,000; Common Stock, $10,000; and Retained Earnings, $7,000. Kerr has agreed to pay the creditors $600 of interest per year. Further, Kerr agrees that for the 2013 fiscal year, any annual earnings remaining after the interest charges will be paid out as dividends to the owners.

Required

a. Assuming Kerr earns a before interest expense recognition profit of $1,500 during 2013, determine the amount of interest and dividends paid.

b. Assuming Kerr earns a before interest expense recognition profit of $800 during 2013, determine the amount of interest and dividends paid.

c. Assuming Kerr earns a before interest expense recognition profit of $400 during 2013, determine the amount of interest and dividends paid.

Exercise 1-6B   Components of the accounting equation

Josey Enterprises was started when it acquired $4,000 cash from creditors and $8,000 from owners. The company immediately purchased land that cost $10,000.

Required

a. Record the events under an accounting equation.

b. After all events have been recorded, Josey's obligations to creditors represents what percent of total assets?

c. After all events have been recorded, Josey's stockholders' equity represents what percent of total assets?

d. Assume the debt is due. Given that Josey has $8,000 in stockholders' equity, can the company repay the creditors at this point? Why or why not?

Exercise 1-7B   Components of the accounting equation

	Assets	=	Liabilities	+	Common Stock	+	Retained Earnings
Abbot	$10,000	=	$7,500	+	$2,000	+	$ 500
Wayne	$12,000	=	$3,000	+	$7,200	+	$1,800

Required

a. Based on this information alone, can you determine whether Wayne can pay a $2,000 cash dividend? Why or why not?

b. Reconstruct the accounting equation for each company using percentages on the right side of the equation instead of dollar values. Which company is more financially stable? Why?

c. Assume Abbot incurs a $3,500 operating loss. The remaining assets are sold for the value shown on the books, and the cash proceeds are distributed to the creditors and investors. How much money will be paid to creditors and how much will be paid to investors?

d. Assume Wayne incurs a $3,500 operating loss. The remaining assets are sold for the value shown on the books, and the cash proceeds are distributed to the creditors and investors. How much money will be paid to creditors and how much will be paid to investors?

Exercise 1-8B   Missing information in the accounting equation

Required

Calculate the missing amounts in the following table:

Company	Assets	=	Liabilities	+	Common Stock	+	Retained Earnings
A	$?		$25,000		48,000		$50,000
B	40,000		?		7,000		30,000
C	75,000		15,000		?		42,000
D	125,000		45,000		60,000		?

LO 2, 3

Exercise 1-9B   *Missing information and recording events*

As of December 31, 2013, Gibbs Company had total cash of $89,000, notes payable of $25,600, and common stock of $41,000. During 2014, Gibbs earned $52,000 of cash revenue, paid $34,000 for cash expenses, and paid a $6,000 cash dividend to the stockholders.

Required

a. Determine the amount of retained earnings as of December 31, 2013.
b. Create an accounting equation and record the beginning account balances under the appropriate elements.
c. Record the revenue, expense, and dividend events under the appropriate elements of the accounting equation created in Requirement *b*.
d. Prove the equality of the accounting equation as of December 31, 2014.
e. Identify the beginning and ending balances in the Cash and Common Stock accounts. Explain why the beginning and ending balances in the Cash account are different, but the beginning and ending balances in the Common Stock account remain the same.

LO 2, 3

Exercise 1-10B   *Effect of events on the accounting equation*

Grayson Co. experienced the following events during 2013:

1. Acquired cash from the issue of common stock.
2. Borrowed cash.
3. Collected cash from providing services.
4. Purchased land with cash.
5. Paid operating expenses with cash.
6. Paid a cash dividend to the stockholders.

Required

Explain how each of these events affect the accounting equation by writing the letter I for increase, the letter D for decrease, and NA for does not affect under each of the components of the accounting equation. The first event is shown as an example.

Event Number	Assets	=	Liabilities	+	Common Stock	+	Retained Earnings
					Stockholders' Equity		
1	I		NA		I		NA

LO 2, 3

Exercise 1-11B   *Effect of transactions on general ledger accounts*

At the beginning of 2013, Sauder Company's accounting records had the following general ledger accounts and balances.

SAUDER COMPANY								
Accounting Equation								
Event	Assets		=	Liabilities	+	Stockholders' Equity		Acct. Titles for RE
	Cash	Land		Notes Payable		Common Stock	Retained Earnings	
Balance 1/1/2013	10,000	20,000		12,000		7,000	11,000	

Paramount completed the following transactions during 2013:

1. Purchased land for $5,000 cash.
2. Acquired $25,000 cash from the issue of common stock.
3. Received $75,000 cash for providing services to customers.
4. Paid cash operating expenses of $42,000.
5. Paid $10,000 cash on notes payable.
6. Paid a $5,000 cash dividend to the stockholders.
7. Determined that the market value of the land is $35,000.

Required

a. Record the transactions in the appropriate general ledger accounts. Record the amounts of revenue, expense, and dividends in the Retained Earnings column. Provide the appropriate titles for these accounts in the last column of the table.

b. As of December 31, 2013, determine the total amount of assets, liabilities, and stockholders' equity and present this information in the form of an accounting equation.

c. What is the amount of total assets, liabilities, and stockholders' equity as of January 1, 2014?

Exercise 1-12B *Accounts titles and the accounting equation*

LO 3

The following account titles were drawn from the general ledger of Holt Food Supplies, Incorporated (HFSI): Computers, Operating Expenses, Rent Revenue, Building, Cash, Notes Payable, Land, Utilities Payable, Utilities Expense, Trucks, Gasoline Expense, Retained Earnings, Supplies, Accounts Payable, Office Furniture, Salaries Expense, Common Stock, Service Revenue, Interest Expense, Dividends, Supplies Expense.

Required

a. Create an accounting equation using the elements assets, liabilities, and stockholders' equity. List each account title under the element of the accounting equation to which it belongs.

b. Will all businesses have the same type of accounts? Explain your answer.

Exercise 1-13B *Classifying events as asset source, use, or exchange*

LO 4

Texas Company experienced the following events during its first year of operations:

1. Acquired an additional $1,000 cash from the issue of common stock.
2. Paid $2,400 cash for utilities expense.
3. Paid a $1,500 cash dividend to the stockholders.
4. Provided additional services for $6,000 cash.
5. Purchased additional land for $2,500 cash.
6. The market value of the land was determined to be $24,000 at the end of the accounting period.
7. Acquired $16,000 cash from the issue of common stock.
8. Paid $3,500 cash for salary expense.
9. Borrowed $10,000 cash from New South Bank.
10. Paid $6,000 cash to purchase land.
11. Provided boarding services for $10,500 cash.

Required

Classify each event as an asset source, use, or exchange transaction.

Exercise 1-14B *Historical cost versus market value*

LO 5

Sung Company purchased land in April 2008 at a cost of $500,000. The estimated market value of the land is $800,000 as of December 31, 2013. Sung purchased marketable equity securities (bought the common stock of a company that is independent of Sung) in May 2008 at a cost of $340,000. These securities have a market value of $360,000 as of December 31, 2013. Generally accepted accounting principles require that the land be shown on the December 31, 2013, balance sheet at $500,000, while the marketable equity securities are required to be reported at $360,000.

Required

Write a brief memo that explains the contradiction regarding why GAAP requires Sung to report historical cost with respect to the land versus market value with respect to the marketable securities. This answer may require speculation on your part. Use your knowledge about the historical cost and verifiability to formulate a logical response.

LO 2, 3, 5

Exercise 1-15B   *Preparing an income statement and a balance sheet*

Majka Company was started on January 1, 2013. During 2013, the company experienced the following three accounting events: (1) earned cash revenues of $28,600, (2) paid cash expenses of $13,200, and (3) paid a $1,500 cash dividend to its stockholders. These were the only events that affected the company during 2013.

Required

a. Create an accounting equation, and record the effects of each accounting event under the appropriate general ledger account headings.

b. Prepare an income statement and a balance sheet dated December 31, 2013, for Majka Company.

c. Explain why the income statement uses different terminology to date the income statement than is used to date the balance sheet.

LO 5

Exercise 1-16B   *Statement of cash flows*

On January 1, 2013, Moore, a fast-food company, had a balance in its Cash account of $45,800. During the 2013 accounting period, the company had (1) net cash inflow from operating activities of $24,800, (2) net cash outflow for investing activities of $16,000, and (3) net cash outflow from financing activities of $6,800.

Required

a. Prepare a statement of cash flows.

b. Provide a reasonable explanation as to what may have caused the net cash inflow from operating activities.

c. Provide a reasonable explanation as to what may have caused the net cash outflow from investing activities.

d. Provide a reasonable explanation as to what may have caused the net cash outflow from financing activities.

LO 5

Exercise 1-17B   *Prepare a statement of cash flows*

All-Star Automotive Company experienced the following accounting events during 2013:

1. Performed services for $25,000 cash.
2. Purchased land for $6,000 cash.
3. Hired an accountant to keep the books.
4. Received $50,000 cash from the issue of common stock.
5. Borrowed $5,000 cash from State Bank.
6. Paid $14,000 cash for salary expense.
7. Sold land for $9,000 cash.
8. Paid $10,000 cash on the loan from State Bank.
9. Paid $2,800 cash for utilities expense.
10. Paid a cash dividend of $5,000 to the stockholders.

Required

a. Indicate how each of the events would be classified on the statement of cash flows as operating activities (OA), investing activities (IA), financing activities (FA), or not applicable (NA).

b. Prepare a statement of cash flows. Assume All-Star Automotive had a beginning cash balance of $9,000.

Exercise 1-18B   *Relating accounting events to entities*

Metal Works borrowed $100,000 cash from First State Bank in 2013:

Required

a. Was this event an asset source, use, or exchange transaction for Metal Works?

b. Was this event an asset source, use, or exchange transaction for First State Bank?

c. Was the cash flow an operating, investing, or financing activity on Metal Works's 2013 statement of cash flows?

d. Was the cash flow an operating, investing, or financing activity on First State Bank's 2013 statement of cash flows?

Exercise 1-19B   *Preparing financial statements*

Dakota, Inc., experienced the following events during 2013:

1. Acquired $30,000 cash from the issue of common stock.
2. Paid $12,000 cash to purchase land.
3. Borrowed $10,000 cash from First Bank.
4. Provided services for $20,000 cash.
5. Paid $1,000 cash for utilities expense.
6. Paid $15,000 cash for other operating expenses.
7. Paid a $2,000 cash dividend to the stockholders.
8. Determined that the market value of the land purchased in Event 2 is $12,700.

Required

a. The January 1, 2013, general ledger account balances are shown in the following accounting equation. Record the eight events in the appropriate general ledger accounts. Record the amounts of revenue, expense, and dividends in the Retained Earnings column. Provide the appropriate titles for these accounts in the last column of the table. The first event is shown as an example.

DAKOTA, INC.									
Accounting Equation									
Event	Assets		=	Liabilities	+	Stockholders' Equity		Acct. Titles for RE	
	Cash	Land		Notes Payable		Common Stock	Retained Earnings		
Balance 1/1/2013 1.	2,000 30,000	12,000		0		6,000 30,000	8,000		

b. Prepare an income statement, statement of changes in stockholders' equity, year-end balance sheet, and statement of cash flows for the 2013 accounting period.

c. Determine the percentage of assets that were provided by retained earnings. How much cash is in the retained earnings account?

Exercise 1-20B   *Preparing financial statements—cash flow emphasis*

As of January 1, 2013, Floor Design Inc. had a balance of $9,900 in Cash, $3,500 in Common Stock and $6,400 in Retained Earnings. These were the only accounts with balances in the ledger on January 1, 2013. Further analysis of the company's cash account indicated that during the 2013 accounting period, the company had (1) net cash inflow from operating activities of $9,800, (2) net cash outflow for investing activities of $16,500, and (3) net cash inflow from financing activities of $11,000. All revenue and expense events were cash events. The following accounts and balances represent the general ledger of Floor Design Inc. as of December 31, 2013, before closing.

FLOOR DESIGN INC.
General Ledger

Assets	=	Liabilities	+		Stockholders' Equity	

Cash		Notes Payable		Common Stock		Revenue
Bal. 14,200		Bal. 9,000		Bal. 7,500		Bal. 18,100

Land				Retained Earnings		Expenses
Bal. 16,500				Bal. 6,400		Bal. 8,300

						Dividends
						Bal. 2,000

Required

a. Assume that the net cash inflow from financing activities of $11,000 was caused by three events. Based on the information above, identify these events and determine the cash flow associated with each event.

b. What did the company purchase that resulted in the cash outflow from investing activities?

c. Prepare an income statement, statement of changes in stockholders' equity, balance sheet, and statement of cash flows.

LO 2, 3, 5

Exercise 1-21B *Preparing financial statements—retained earnings emphasis*

On January 1, 2013, the following information was drawn from the accounting records of Craven Company: cash of $800; land of $3,500; notes payable of $1,600; and common stock of $1,000.

Required

a. Determine the amount of retained earnings as of January 1, 2013.

b. After looking at the amount of retained earnings, the chief executive officer (CEO) wants to pay a $1,000 cash dividend to the stockholders. Can the company pay this dividend? Why or why not?

c. As of January 1, 2013, what percent of assets were acquired from creditors?

d. As of January 1, 2013, what percent of the assets were acquired from investors?

e. As of January 1, 2013, what percent of the assets were acquired from retained earnings?

f. Create an accounting equation using percentages instead of dollar amounts on the right side of the equation.

g. During 2013, Craven Company earned cash revenue of $1,800, paid cash expenses of $1,200, and paid a cash dividend of $500. Prepare an income statement, statement of changes in stockholders' equity, a balance sheet, and a statement of cash flows dated December 31, 2013? (*Hint:* It is helpful to record these events under an accounting equation before preparing the statements.)

h. Comment on the terminology used to date each statement?

i. An appraiser determines that as of December 31, 2013, the market value of the land is $5,000. How will this fact change the financial statements?

j. What is the balance in the Revenue account on January 1, 2014?

LO 2

Exercise 1-22B *Missing information for determining revenue*

Total stockholders' equity of Davis Company increased by $42,250 between December 31, 2013, and December 31, 2014. During 2014 Davis acquired $15,000 cash from the issue of common stock. The company paid a $2,500 cash dividend to the stockholders during 2014. Total expenses during 2014 amounted to $18,000.

Required

Determine the amount of revenue that Davis reported on its 2014 income statement. (*Hint:* Remember that stock issues, net income, and dividends all change total stockholders' equity.)

Exercise 1-23B   *The closing process*   LO 5

Laura's Flowers opened on January 1, 2013. Laura's reported the following for cash revenues and cash expenses for the years 2013 to 2015:

	Cash Revenues	Cash Expenses
2013	$30,000	$18,000
2014	$50,000	$26,000
2015	$70,000	$38,000

Required

a. What would Laura's Flowers report for net income and retained earnings for the years 2013, 2014, and 2015?

b. Explain the difference between net income and retained earnings.

c. Assume that Laura's Flowers paid a $6,000 dividend to stockholders in 2014. What would Laura's Flowers report for net income and retained earnings for 2014 and 2015?

EXERCISES—SERIES B

Exercise 1-24B   *Retained earnings and the closing process*   LO 5

Critz Company was started on January 1, 2013. During the month of January, Critz earned $7,500 of revenue and incurred $4,800 of expense. During the remainder of 2013, Critz earned $86,000 and incurred $51,000 of expenses. Critz closes its books on December 31 of each year.

Required

a. Determine the balance in the Retained Earnings account as of January 31, 2013.

b. Determine the balance in the Revenue and Expense accounts as of January 31, 2013.

c. Determine the balance in the Retained Earnings account as of December 31, 2013, before closing.

d. Determine the balances in the Revenue and Expense accounts as of December 31, 2013, before closing.

e. Determine the balance in the Retained Earnings and Revenue accounts as of January 1, 2014.

Exercise 1-25B   *Comparing common stock with retained earnings*   LO 5

As of December 31, 2013, Zip Express Company had total assets of $80,000, total liabilities of $20,000, and common stock of $25,000.

Required

a. Determine the amount of retained earnings as of December 31, 2013, after closing.

b. Explain the difference between common stock and retained earnings.

c. On January 1, 2014, Zip Express raised $50,000 by issuing additional common stock. Immediately after the additional capital was raised, Zip Express reported total equity of $110,000. Are the stockholders of Zip Express in a better financial position than they were on December 31, 2013?

Exercise 1-26B   *Types of transactions and the horizontal statements model*   LO 4, 6

The Candle Shop experienced the following events during its first year of operations, 2013:

1. Acquired cash by issuing common stock.
2. Paid a cash dividend to the stockholders.
3. Paid cash for operating expenses.
4. Borrowed cash from a bank.

5. Provided services and collected cash.
6. Purchased land with cash.
7. Determined that the market value of the land is higher than the historical cost.

Required

a. Indicate whether each event is an asset source, use, or exchange transaction.

b. Use a horizontal statements model to show how each event affects the balance sheet, income statement, and statement of cash flows. Indicate whether the event increases (I), decreases (D), or does not affect (NA) each element of the financial statements. Also, in the Cash Flows column, classify the cash flows as operating activities (OA), investing activities (IA), or financing activities (FA). The first transaction is shown as an example.

Event No.	Balance Sheet										Income Statement						Statement of Cash Flows
	Cash	+	Land	=	N. Pay	+	C. Stock.	+	Ret. Ear.		Rev.	−	Exp.	=	Net Inc.		
1.	I	+	NA	=	NA	+	I	+	NA		NA	−	NA	=	NA		I FA

LO IFRS

Exercise 1-27B   *International financial reporting standards*

Accounting is a social science. It reflects the cultural differences of the countries in which it is developed. The reporting standards in one country may be very different than those used in another country. These differences thwart communication and limit trade among international business people. As globalization progresses, the need for standardization intensifies.

Required

a. Comment on the history and development of a global GAAP.

b. Identify the similarities and differences in the organizational structure of the Financial Accounting Standards Board (FASB) and the International Accounting Standards Board (IASB). Speculate as to why there may be structural differences between the two boards.

c. Are the differences between the FASB and the IASB limited to the variation in structure? Explain your answer with a specific example.

PROBLEMS—SERIES B

LO 1

Problem 1-28B   *Applying GAAP to financial reporting*

Jan Perkins is a business consultant. She analyzed the business processes of one of her clients, Diamond Companies, in November 2013. She prepared a report containing her recommendation for changes in some of the company's business practices. She presented Diamond with the report in December 2013. Jan guarantees that her clients will save money by following her advice. She does not collect for the services she provides until the client is satisfied with the results of her work. In this case she received cash payment from Diamond in February 2014.

Required

a. Define the acronym GAAP.

b. Assume that Jan's accountant tells her that GAAP permits Jan to recognize the revenue from Diamond in either 2013 or 2014. What GAAP rule would justify reporting the same event in two different ways? Write a brief memo explaining the logic behind this rule.

c. If Jan were keeping records for managerial reporting purposes, would she be bound by GAAP rules? Write a brief memo to explain how GAAP applies to financial versus managerial reporting.

LO 1

Problem 1-29B   *Accounting entities*

The following business scenarios are independent from one another:

1. Bob Wilder starts a business by transferring $10,000 from his personal checking account into a checking account for his business, Wilder Co.
2. A business that Sam Pace owns earns $4,600 of cash revenue.

3. Jim Sneed borrows $30,000 from the National Bank and uses the money to purchase a car from Iuka Ford.

4. OZ Company pays its five employees $2,500 each to cover their salaries.

5. Gil Roberts loans his son Jim $5,000 cash.

6. Gane, Inc., paid $100,000 cash to purchase land from Atlanta Land Co.

7. Rob Moore and Gil Thomas form a partnership by contributing $20,000 each from their personal bank accounts to a partnership bank account.

8. Stephen Woo pays cash to purchase $5,000 of common stock that is issued by Izzard, Inc.

9. Natural Stone pays a $5,000 cash dividend to each of its seven shareholders.

10. Billows, Inc., borrowed $5,000,000 from the National Bank.

Required

a. For each scenario create a list of all of the entities that are mentioned in the description.

b. Describe what happens to the cash account of each entity that you identified in Requirement *a*.

Problem 1-30B   *Classifying events as asset source, use, or exchange*

The following unrelated events are typical of those experienced by business entities:

1. Acquire cash by issuing common stock.

2. Pay other operating supplies expense.

3. Agree to represent a client in an IRS audit and to receive payment when the audit is complete.

4. Receive cash from customers for services rendered.

5. Pay employee salaries with cash.

6. Pay back a bank loan with cash.

7. Pay interest to a bank with cash.

8. Transfer cash from a checking account to a money market account.

9. Sell land for cash at its original cost.

10. Pay a cash dividend to stockholders.

11. Learn that a financial analyst determined the company's price-earnings ratio to be 26.

12. Borrow cash from the local bank.

13. Pay office supplies expense.

14. Make plans to purchase office equipment.

15. Trade a used car for a computer with the same value.

Required

Identify each of the events as an asset source, asset use, or asset exchange transaction. If an event would not be recorded under generally accepted accounting principles, identify it as not applicable (NA). Also indicate for each event whether total assets would increase, decrease, or remain unchanged. Organize your answer according to the following table. The first event is shown in the table as an example.

Event No.	Type of Event	Effect on Total Assets
1	Asset source	Increase

LO 4

CHECK FIGURE
Event 2: Asset Use

Problem 1-31B   *Relating titles and accounts to financial statements*

A random list of various financial statements components follows: (1) Common Stock account ending balance, (2) common stock issued during the period, (3) liabilities, (4) financing activities, (5) investing activities, (6) Retained Earnings account beginning balance, (7) assets, (8) expenses, (9) Retained Earnings account ending balance, (10) revenues, (11) Common Stock account beginning balance, (12) operating activities, and (13) dividends.

Required

Set up a table with the following headings. Identify the financial statements on which each of the preceding components appears by placing a check mark in the appropriate column. If an item

LO 2, 5

appears on more than one statement, place the reference number in every applicable column. The first component is shown as an example.

Income Statement	Statement of Changes in Stockholders' Equity	Balance Sheet	Statement of Cash Flows
	✓	✓	

LO 2, 3, 5, 6

Problem 1-32B   *Preparing financial statements for two complete accounting cycles*

Mabry's Consulting Services experienced the following transactions for 2013, the first year of operations, and 2014. *Assume that all transactions involve the receipt or payment of cash.*

Transactions for 2013

1. Acquired $20,000 by issuing common stock.
2. Received $35,000 for providing services to customers.
3. Borrowed $25,000 cash from creditors.
4. Paid expenses amounting to $22,000.
5. Purchased land for $30,000 cash.

Transactions for 2014

Beginning account balances for 2014 are:

Cash	$28,000
Land	30,000
Notes payable	25,000
Common stock	20,000
Retained earnings	13,000

1. Acquired an additional $24,000 from the issue of common stock.
2. Received $95,000 for providing services in 2014.
3. Paid $15,000 to reduce notes payable.
4. Paid expenses amounting to $71,500.
5. Paid a $3,000 dividend to the stockholders.
6. Determined that the market value of the land is $47,000.

Required

a. Write an accounting equation, and record the effects of each accounting event under the appropriate headings for each year. Record the amounts of revenue, expense, and dividends in the Retained Earnings column. Provide appropriate titles for these accounts in the last column of the table.
b. Prepare an income statement, statement of changes in stockholders' equity, year-end balance sheet, and statement of cash flows for each year.
c. Determine the amount of cash that is in the retained earnings account at the end of 2013 and 2014.
d. Compare the information provided by the income statement with the information provided by the statement of cash flows. Point out similarities and differences.
e. Determine the balance in the Retained Earnings account immediately after Event 2 in 2013 and in 2014 are recorded.

LO 2, 3, 5, 6

Problem 1-33B   *Interrelationships among financial statements*

Pratt Corp. started the accounting period with $30,000 of assets, $12,000 of liabilities, and $5,000 of retained earnings. During the period, the Retained Earnings account increased by $7,550. The bookkeeper reported that Pratt paid cash expenses of $26,000 and paid a $2,000 cash dividend to stockholders, but she could not find a record of the amount of cash that Pratt received for performing services. Pratt also paid $3,000 cash to reduce the liability owed to a bank, and the business acquired $4,000 of additional cash from the issue of common stock.

Required

a. Prepare an income statement, statement of changes in stockholders' equity, year-end balance sheet, and statement of cash flows for the accounting period. (*Hint:* Determine the beginning balance in the common stock account before considering the effects of the current period events. It also might help to record all events under an accounting equation before preparing the statements.)

b. Determine the percentage of total assets that were provided by creditors, investors, and earnings.

Problem 1-34B   *Recording events in a horizontal statements model*

LO 5, 6

Molpus Company was started January 1, 2013, and experienced the following events during its first year of operation:

1. Acquired $30,000 cash from the issue of common stock.
2. Borrowed $40,000 cash from National Bank.
3. Earned cash revenues of $48,000 for performing services.
4. Paid cash expenses of $25,000.
5. Paid a $1,000 cash dividend to the stockholders.
6. Acquired $20,000 cash from the issue of additional common stock.
7. Paid $10,000 cash to reduce the principal balance of the bank note.
8. Paid $53,000 cash to purchase land.
9. Determined that the market value of the land is $75,000.

Required

a. Record the preceding transactions in the horizontal statements model. Also, in the Cash Flows column, classify the cash flows as operating activities (OA), investing activities (IA), or financing activities (FA). The first event is shown as an example.

Event No.	Balance Sheet										Income Statement						Statement of Cash Flows
	Cash	+	Land	=	N. Pay	+	C. Stock.	+	Ret. Ear.		Rev.	−	Exp.	=	Net Inc.		
1.	30,000	+	NA	=	NA	+	30,000	+	NA		NA	−	NA	=	NA		30,000 FA

b. Determine the amount of total assets that Molpus would report on the December 31, 2013, balance sheet.

c. Identify the asset source transactions and related amounts for 2013.

d. Determine the net income that Molpus would report on the 2013 income statement. Explain why dividends do not appear on the income statement.

e. Determine the net cash flows from operating activities, investing activities, and financing activities that Molpus would report on the 2013 statement of cash flows.

f. Determine the percentage of assets that were provided by investors, creditors, and earnings.

g. What is the balance in the Retained Earnings account immediately after Event 3 is recorded?

ANALYZE, THINK, COMMUNICATE

ATC 1-1   Business Applications Case   *Understanding real-world annual reports*

Required

Use the Target Corporation's annual report in Appendix B to answer the following questions.

Target Corporation

a. What was Target's net income for 2010 (the year ended January 29, 2011)?

b. Did Target's net income increase or decrease from 2009 to 2010, and by how much?

c. What was Target's accounting equation for 2010?

d. Which of the following had the largest percentage change from 2009 to 2010: sales, cost of sales, or selling, general, and administrative expenses? Show all computations.

ATC 1-2   Group Assignment   *Missing information*

The following selected financial information is available for Best, Inc. Amounts are in millions of dollars.

Income Statements	2016	2015	2014	2013
Revenue	$ 860	$1,520	$ (a)	$1,200
Cost and expenses	(a)	(a)	(2,400)	(860)
Income from continuing operations	(b)	450	320	(a)
Unusual items	-0-	175	(b)	(b)
Net income	$ 20	$ (b)	$ 175	$ 300
Balance Sheets				
Assets				
Cash and marketable securities	$ 350	$1,720	$ (c)	$ 940
Other assets	1,900	(c)	2,500	(c)
Total assets	2,250	$2,900	$ (d)	$3,500
Liabilities	$ (c)	$ (d)	$1,001	$ (d)
Stockholders' equity				
Common stock	880	720	(e)	800
Retained earnings	(d)	(e)	800	(e)
Total stockholders' equity	1,520	1,345	(f)	2,200
Total liabilities and stockholders' equity	$2,250	$ (f)	$3,250	$3,500

Required

a. Divide the class into groups of four or five students each. Organize the groups into four sections. Assign Task 1 to the first section of groups, Task 2 to the second section, Task 3 to the third section, and Task 4 to the fourth section.

Group Tasks

(1) Fill in the missing information for 2013.

(2) Fill in the missing information for 2014.

(3) Fill in the missing information for 2015.

(4) Fill in the missing information for 2016.

b. Each section should select two representatives. One representative is to put the financial statements assigned to that section on the board, underlining the missing amounts. The second representative is to explain to the class how the missing amounts were determined.

c. Each section should list events that could have caused the unusual items category on the income statement.

ATC 1-3   Real-World Case   *Classifying cash flow activities at five companies*

The following cash transactions occurred in five real-world companies:

1. In June 2010, Dow Chemical Company sold its Styron subsidiary to Bain Capital Partners for $1.6 billion.

2. General Motors Company issued $16 billion in common stock in November 2010.

3. Consolidated Edison, Inc., paid $8 million of dividends in December 2010.

4. In January 2011, Qualcomm, Inc., announced plans to purchase Atheros Communications, Inc., for $3.2 billion in cash. Assume the deal was completed as announced.

5. Abercrombie & Fitch Co. reported $886 million in cash sales during August, September, and October of 2010.

Required

Determine if each of the above transactions should be classified as an *operating, investing,* or *financing* activity. Also, identify the amount of each cash flow and whether it was an *inflow* or an *outflow*.

ATC 1-4   Business Applications Case   *Forecasting from financial reports*

The following information was drawn from the annual report of Active Wilderness Adventures (AWA).

	For the Years	
	2013	**2014**
Income Statement		
Revenues	$ 720,000	$ 792,000
Operating expenses	576,000	633,600
Income from continuing operations	144,000	158,400
*Extraordinary item—lottery win		81,600
Net income	$ 144,000	$ 240,000
Balance Sheet		
Assets	$1,056,000	$1,056,000
Liabilities	$ 240,000	$ 0
Stockholders' equity:		
Common stock	456,000	456,000
Retained earnings	360,000	600,000
Total liabilities and stockholders' equity	$1,056,000	$1,056,000

*By definition, extraordinary items are not likely to recur in the future.

Required

a. Compute the percentage of growth in net income from 2013 to 2014. Can stockholders expect a similar increase between 2014 and 2015?

b. Assuming that AWA collected $240,000 cash from earnings (i.e., net income), explain how this money was spent in 2014.

c. Assuming that AWA experiences the same percentage of growth from 2014 to 2015 as it did from 2013 to 2014, determine the amount of income from continuing operations that the owners can expect to see on the 2015 income statement.

d. During 2015, AWA experienced a $50,000 loss due to storm damage (note that this would be shown as an extraordinary loss on the income statement). Liabilities and common stock were unchanged from 2014 to 2015. Use the information that you computed in Requirement *c* plus the additional information provided in the previous two sentences to prepare an income statement and balance sheet as of December 31, 2015.

ATC 1-5   Writing Assignment   *Elements of financial statements defined*

Sam and his sister Blair both attend the state university. As a reward for their successful completion of the past year (Sam had a 3.2 GPA in business, and Blair had a 3.7 GPA in art), their father gave each of them 100 shares of The Walt Disney Company stock. They have just received their first annual report. Blair does not understand what the information means and has asked Sam to explain it to her. Sam is currently taking an accounting course, and she knows he will understand the financial statements.

Required

Assume that you are Sam. Write Blair a memo explaining the following financial statement items to her. In your explanation, describe each of the two financial statements and explain the financial information each contains. Also define each of the elements listed for each financial statement and explain what it means.

Balance Sheet
Assets
Liabilities
Stockholders' equity
Income Statement
Revenue
Expense
Net income

ATC 1-6   Ethical Dilemma   *Loyalty versus the bottom line*

Assume that Kevin has been working for you for five years. He has had an excellent work history and has received generous pay raises in response. The raises have been so generous that Kevin is quite overpaid for the job he is required to perform. Unfortunately, he is not qualified to take on other, more responsible jobs available within the company. A recent job applicant is willing to accept a salary $5,000 per year less than the amount currently being paid to Kevin. The applicant is well qualified to take over Kevin's duties and has a very positive attitude. The following financial statements were reported by your company at the close of its most recent accounting period.

Required

a. Reconstruct the financial statements (shown below), assuming that Kevin was replaced at the beginning of the most recent accounting period. Both Kevin and his replacement are paid in cash. No other changes are to be considered.

b. Discuss the short- and long-term ramifications of replacing Kevin. There are no right answers. However, assume that you are required to make a decision. Use your judgment and common sense to support your choice.

Financial Statements		
Income Statement		
Revenue		$ 57,000
Expense		(45,000)
Net income		$ 12,000
Statement of Changes in Stockholders' Equity		
Beginning common stock	$ 20,000	
Plus: stock issued	5,000	
Ending common stock		$25,000
Beginning retained earnings	50,000	
Net income	12,000	
Dividends	(2,000)	
Ending retained earnings		60,000
Total stockholders' equity		$85,000

continued

Balance Sheet	
Assets	
Cash	$85,000
Equity	
Common stock	$25,000
Retained earnings	60,000
Total stockholders' equity	$85,000

Statement of Cash Flows		
Operating activities		
Inflow from customers	$ 57,000	
Outflow to suppliers expenses	(45,000)	
Net inflow from operations		$12,000
Investing activities		0
Financing activities		
Inflow from stock issue	5,000	
Outflow for dividends	(2,000)	
Net inflow from financing activities		3,000
Net change in cash		15,000
Plus: beginning cash balance		70,000
Ending cash balance		$85,000

ATC 1-7 Research Assignment *Finding real-world accounting information*

This chapter introduced the basic four financial statements companies use annually to keep their stakeholders informed of their accomplishments and financial situation. Complete the requirements below using the most recent (20xx) financial statements available on the Sonic Drive-In's website. Obtain the statements on the Internet by following the steps below. (The formatting of the company's website may have changed since these instructions were written.)

1. Go to www.sonicdrivein.com.
2. Click on the "Strictly Business" link at the top of the page. (Most companies have a link titled "investors relations" that leads to their financial statements; Sonic uses "strictly business" instead.)
3. Click on the "INVESTORS INFO" link at the left side of the page.
4. Click on *"Annual Reports"* and then on *"20xx Financial Report."*
5. Go to the company's financial statements that begin around page 30 of the annual report.

Required

a. What was the company's net income in each of the last 3 years?
b. What amount of total assets did the company have at the end of the most recent year?
c. How much retained earnings did the company have at the end of the most recent year?
d. For the most recent year, what was the company's cash flow from operating activities, cash flow from investing activities, and cash flow from financing activities?

ATC 1-8 Spreadsheet Assignment *Using Excel*

The financial statements for Simple Company are reported here using an Excel spreadsheet.

Required

Recreate the financial statements using your own Excel spreadsheet.

a. For each number with an arrow by it, enter a formula in that particular cell address to solve for the number shown. (Do not enter the arrow.)
b. When complete, print the spreadsheet with formulas rather than absolute numbers.

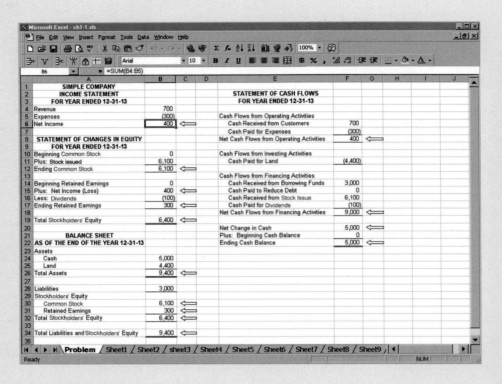

Spreadsheet Tips

(1) Widen a column by positioning the cursor on the vertical line between two column headings until cross-hairs appear. Either double click to automatically widen, or click and drag the crosshair to the desired width.

(2) Negative numbers can be parenthesized by choosing Format and then Cells. Under Number, choose Custom and under Type, choose the first option containing parentheses.

(3) The SUM function is one way to add a series of numbers. For example, the formula for net income in cell B6 is SUM(B4:B5).

(4) Single and double lines can be drawn using the Borders icon.

(5) Print a spreadsheet on one page by choosing File, Page Setup, and Fit to 1.

(6) Print without gridlines by choosing File, Page Setup, and Sheet and uncheck Gridlines. Another option is to choose Tools and Options and uncheck Gridlines.

(7) Print formulas by choosing Tools, Options, and Formulas.

ATC 1-9   Spreadsheet Assignment   *Mastering Excel*

Required

a. Enter the following headings for the horizontal statements model onto a blank spreadsheet.

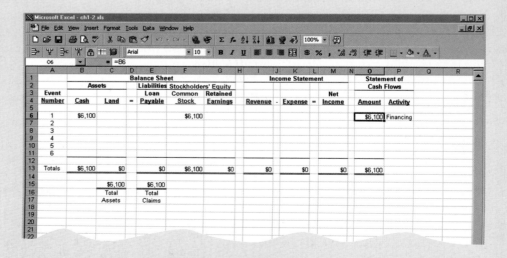

b. Under the appropriate headings, record the effects of each of the following accounting events for the first month of operations. The first event has been recorded as an example.

(1) Acquired $6,100 from the issue of common stock.

(2) Paid $4,400 to purchase land.

(3) Borrowed $3,000 cash.

(4) Provided services to customers and received $700 in cash.

(5) Paid $300 for expenses.

(6) Paid a $100 dividend to the stockholders.

(*Note:* The amounts on the statement of cash flows can be referenced to the Cash account on the balance sheet. In other words, recording the cash amounts twice is not necessary. Instead enter formulas in the Statement of Cash Flows column equating those cell addresses to the respective cell in the Cash column. Notice that the formula in cell O6 (statement of cash flows) is set equal to cell B6 (cash on the balance sheet). Once the formula is completed for cell O6, it can be easily copied to cells O7 through O11.)

c. Using formulas, sum each of the quantitative columns to arrive at the end-of-month amounts reported on the financial statements.

Spreadsheet Tips

(1) Center the heading *Balance Sheet* across columns by entering the entire heading in cell B1. Position the cursor on B1 until a fat cross appears. Click and drag the cursor across B1 through G1. Click on the Merge and Center icon (it is highlighted in the screen in the toolbar).

(2) Enter arithmetic signs as headings by placing an apostrophe in front of the sign. For example, to enter the equal sign in cell D4, enter '=.

(3) Copy cells by positioning the cursor in the bottom right corner of the cell to copy from (such as cell O6) until a thin cross appears. Click and drag the cursor down through the desired locations to copy to (through cell O11).

(4) To enter the dollar sign, choose Format, Cells, and Currency.

COMPREHENSIVE PROBLEM

The following information is available for Pacilio Security Services Inc. for 2011, its first year of operations. Pacilio provides security services for local sporting events.

The following summary transactions occurred during 2011:

1. Acquired $6,000 from the issue of common stock.
2. Borrowed $5,000 from the Small Business Government Agency. The loan is interest free.
3. Performed security services at local sporting events during the year for $9,000 cash.
4. Paid salaries expense of $3,000 for the year.
5. Purchased land for $4,000.
6. Paid other operating expenses of $2,000 for the year.
7. Paid a cash dividend to the shareholders of $2,500.
8. The market value of the land was determined to be $4,500 at December 31, 2011.

Required

a. Record the above transactions in an accounting equation. Provide the appropriate account titles for the amounts shown in the Retained Earnings column.

b. Prepare an income statement, statement of changes in stockholders' equity, balance sheet, and statement of cash flows for 2011.

CHAPTER 2

Accounting for Accruals and Deferrals

LEARNING OBJECTIVES

After you have mastered the material in this chapter, you will be able to:

SECTION 1: SHOW HOW ACCRUALS AFFECT FINANCIAL STATEMENTS

LO1 Show how receivables affect financial statements.

LO2 Show how payables affect financial statements.

SECTION 2: SHOW HOW DEFERRALS AFFECT FINANCIAL STATEMENTS

LO3 Show how supplies affect financial statements.

LO4 Show how prepaid items affect financial statements.

LO5 Show how unearned revenues affect financial statements.

LO6 Explain the accounting cycle including adjustments and the closing process.

LO7 Prepare financial statements based on accrual accounting.

LO8 Classify accounting events into one of four categories:

- Asset source transactions.
- Asset use transactions.
- Asset exchange transactions.
- Claims exchange transactions.

LO9 Discuss the primary components of corporate governance.

APPENDIX

LO10 Compute depreciation expense and show how it affects financial statements.

LO11 Compute interest expense and show how it affects financial statements.

SECTION 1:

ACCOUNTING FOR ACCRUALS

Users of financial statements must distinguish between the terms *recognition* and *realization*. **Recognition** means formally *reporting* an economic item or event in the financial statements. **Realization** refers to collecting money, generally from the sale of products or services. Companies may recognize (report) revenue in the income statement in a different accounting period from the period in which they collect the cash related to the revenue. Furthermore, companies frequently make cash payments for expenses in accounting periods other than the periods in which the expenses are recognized in the income statement.

To illustrate assume Johnson Company provides services to customers in 2013 but collects cash for those services in 2014. In this case, realization occurs in 2014. When should Johnson recognize the services revenue?

Users of *cash basis* accounting recognize (report) revenues and expenses in the period in which cash is collected or paid. Under cash basis accounting Johnson would recognize the revenue in 2014. When it collects the cash. In contrast, users of **accrual accounting** recognize revenues and expenses in the period in which they occur, regardless of when cash is collected or paid. Under accrual accounting Johnson would recognize the revenue in 2013 (the period in which it performed the services) even though it does not collect (realize) the cash until 2014.

Accrual accounting is required by generally accepted accounting principles. Virtually all major companies operating in the United States use it. Its two distinguishing features are called *accruals* and *deferrals*

■ The term **accrual** describes a revenue or an expense event that is recognized **before** cash is exchanged. Johnson's recognition of revenue in 2013 related to cash realized in 2014 is an example of an accrual.

■ The term **deferral** describes a revenue or an expense event that is recognized **after** cash has been exchanged. Suppose Johnson pays cash in 2013 to purchase office supplies it uses in 2014. In this case the cash payment occurs in 2013 although supplies expense is recognized in 2014. This example is a deferral.

The Curious Accountant

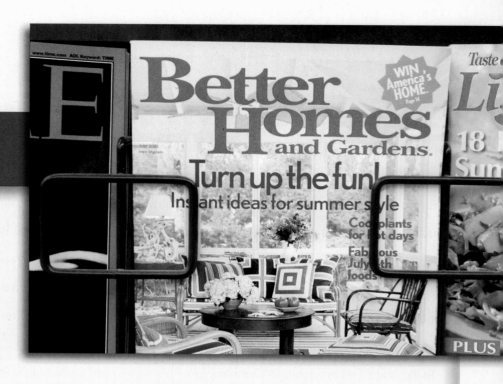

On September 15, 2013, Janet McGeorge purchased a subscription to *Better Homes and Gardens* magazine for her mother's birthday. She paid $12 for a one-year subscription to the **Meredith Corporation**, the company that publishes *Fitness, American Baby, Better Homes and Gardens, The Ladies Home Journal,* and several other magazines. The company also owns 12 television stations. Janet's mother will receive her first issue of the magazine in October.

How should Meredith Corporation account for the receipt of this cash? How would this event be reported on its December 31, 2013, financial statements? (Answer on page 78.)

ACCRUAL ACCOUNTING

LO 1

Show how receivables affect financial statements.

This section of the text describes seven events experienced by Cato Consultants, a training services company that uses accrual accounting.

EVENT 1   **Cato Consultants was started on January 1, 2013, when it acquired $5,000 cash by issuing common stock.**

The issue of stock for cash is an **asset source transaction.** It increases the company's assets (cash) and its equity (common stock). The transaction does not affect the income statement. The cash inflow is classified as a financing activity (acquisition from owners). These effects are shown in the following financial statements model:

Assets	=	Liab.	+	Stockholders' Equity							
Cash	=			Com. Stk.	+	Ret. Earn.	Rev.	−	Exp.	=	Net Inc.	Cash Flow
5,000	=	NA	+	5,000	+	NA	NA	−	NA	=	NA	5,000 FA

Accounting for Accounts Receivable

EVENT 2   During 2013 Cato Consultants provided $84,000 of consulting services to its clients. The business has completed the work and sent bills to the clients, but not yet collected any cash. This type of transaction is frequently described as providing services *on account.*

Accrual accounting requires companies to recognize revenue in the period in which the work is done regardless of when cash is collected. In this case, revenue is recognized in 2013 even though cash has not been realized (collected). Recall that revenue represents the economic benefit that results in an increase in assets from providing goods and services to customers. The specific asset that increases is called **Accounts Receivable.** The balance in Accounts Receivable represents the amount of cash the company expects to collect in the future. Since the revenue recognition causes assets (accounts receivable) to increase, it is classified as an asset source transaction. Its effect on the financial statements follows:

Assets			=	Liab.	+	Stockholders' Equity				Rev.	−	Exp.	=	Net Inc.	Cash Flow
Cash	+	Accts. Rec.	=			Com. Stk.	+	Ret. Earn.							
NA	+	84,000	=	NA	+	NA	+	84,000		84,000	−	NA	=	84,000	NA

Notice that the event affects the income statement but not the statement of cash flows. The statement of cash flows will be affected in the future when cash is collected.

EVENT 3   Cato collected $60,000 cash from customers in partial settlement of its accounts receivable.

The collection of an account receivable is an **asset exchange transaction.** One asset account (Cash) increases and another asset account (Accounts Receivable) decreases. The amount of total assets is unchanged. The effect of the $60,000 collection of receivables on the financial statements is as follows:

Assets			=	Liab.	+	Stockholders' Equity				Rev.	−	Exp.	=	Net Inc.	Cash Flow
Cash	+	Accts. Rec.	=			Com. Stk.	+	Ret. Earn.							
60,000	+	(60,000)	=	NA	+	NA	+	NA		NA	−	NA	=	NA	60,000 OA

Notice that collecting the cash did not affect the income statement. The revenue was recognized when the work was done (see Event 2). Revenue would be double counted if it were recognized again when the cash is collected. The statement of cash flows reflects a cash inflow from operating activities.

Other Events

EVENT 4   Cato paid the instructor $10,000 for teaching training courses (salary expense).

Cash payment for salary expense is an **asset use transaction.** Both the asset account Cash and the equity account Retained Earnings decrease by $10,000. Recognizing the expense decreases net income on the income statement. Since Cato paid cash for the expense, the statement of cash flows reflects a cash outflow from operating activities. These effects on the financial statements follow:

Assets			=	Liab.	+	Stockholders' Equity				Rev.	−	Exp.	=	Net Inc.	Cash Flow
Cash	+	Accts. Rec.	=			Com. Stk.	+	Ret. Earn.							
(10,000)	+	NA	=	NA	+	NA	+	(10,000)		NA	−	10,000	=	(10,000)	(10,000) OA

EVENT 5 Cato paid $2,000 cash for advertising costs. The advertisements appeared in 2013.

Cash payments for advertising expenses are asset use transactions. Both the asset account Cash and the equity account Retained Earnings decrease by $2,000. Recognizing the expense decreases net income on the income statement. Since the expense was paid with cash, the statement of cash flows reflects a cash outflow from operating activities. These effects on the financial statements follow:

Assets			=	Liab.	+	Stockholders' Equity								
Cash	+	Accts. Rec.	=			Com. Stk.	+	Ret. Earn.	Rev.	−	Exp.	=	Net Inc.	Cash Flow
(2,000)	+	NA	=	NA	+	NA	+	(2,000)	NA	−	2,000	=	(2,000)	(2,000) OA

EVENT 6 Cato signed contracts for $42,000 of consulting services to be performed in 2014.

The $42,000 for consulting services to be performed in 2014 is not recognized in the 2013 financial statements. Revenue is recognized for work actually completed, *not* work expected to be completed. This event does not affect any of the financial statements.

Assets			=	Liab.	+	Stockholders' Equity								
Cash	+	Accts. Rec.	=			Com. Stk.	+	Ret. Earn.	Rev.	−	Exp.	=	Net Inc.	Cash Flow
NA	+	NA	=	NA	+	NA	+	NA	NA	−	NA	=	NA	NA

Accounting for Accrued Salary Expense (Adjusting Entry)

It is impractical to record many business events as they occur. For example, Cato incurs salary expense continually as the instructor teaches courses. Imagine the impossibility of trying to record salary expense second by second! Companies normally record transactions when it is most convenient. The most convenient time to record many expenses is when they are paid. Often, however, a single business transaction pertains to more than one accounting period. To provide accurate financial reports in such cases, companies may need to recognize some expenses before paying cash for them. Expenses that are recognized before cash is paid are called **accrued expenses.** The accounting for Event 7 illustrates the effect of recognizing accrued salary expense.

EVENT 7 At the end of 2013. Cato recorded accrued salary expense of $6,000 (the salary expense is for courses the instructor taught in 2013 that Cato will pay cash for in 2014).

Accrual accounting requires that companies recognize expenses in the period in which they are incurred regardless of when cash is paid. Cato must recognize all salary expense in the period in which the instructor worked (2013) even though Cato will not pay the instructor again until 2014. Cato must also recognize the obligation (liability) it has to pay the instructor. To accurately report all 2013 salary expense and year-end obligations, Cato must record the unpaid salary expense and salary liability before preparing its financial statements. The entry to recognize the accrued salary expense is called an **adjusting entry.** Like all adjusting entries, it is only to update the accounting records; it does not affect cash.

This adjusting entry decreases stockholders' equity (Retained Earnings) and increases a liability account called **Salaries Payable.** The balance in the Salaries Payable account represents the amount of cash the company is obligated to pay the instructor in the future. The effect of the expense recognition on the financial statements follows:

Assets			=	Liab.	+	Stockholders' Equity				Rev.	–	Exp.	=	Net Inc.	Cash Flow
Cash	+	Accts. Rec.	=	Sal. Pay.	+	Com. Stk.	+	Ret. Earn.		Rev.	–	Exp.	=	Net Inc.	Cash Flow
NA	+	NA	=	6,000	+	NA	+	(6,000)		NA	–	6,000	=	(6,000)	NA

This event is a **claims exchange transaction.** The claims of creditors (liabilities) increase and the claims of stockholders (retained earnings) decrease. Total claims remain unchanged. The salary expense is reported on the income statement. The statement of cash flows is not affected.

Be careful not to confuse liabilities with expenses. Although liabilities may increase when a company recognizes expenses, liabilities are not expenses. Liabilities are obligations. They can arise from acquiring assets as well as recognizing expenses. For example, when a business borrows money from a bank, it recognizes an increase in assets (cash) and liabilities (notes payable). The borrowing transaction does not affect expenses.

✓ CHECK YOURSELF 2.1

During 2013, Anwar Company earned $345,000 of revenue on account and collected $320,000 cash from accounts receivable. Anwar paid cash expenses of $300,000 and cash dividends of $12,000. Determine the amount of net income Anwar should report on the 2013 income statement and the amount of cash flow from operating activities Anwar should report on the 2013 statement of cash flows.

Answer   Net income is $45,000 ($345,000 revenue – $300,000 expenses). The cash flow from operating activities is $20,000, the amount of revenue collected in cash from customers (accounts receivable) minus the cash paid for expenses ($320,000 – $300,000). Dividend payments are classified as financing activities and do not affect the determination of either net income or cash flow from operating activities.

Summary of Events and General Ledger

The previous section of this chapter described seven events Cato Consultants experienced during the 2013 accounting period. These events are summarized in Exhibit 2.1. The associated general ledger accounts are also shown in the exhibit. The information in these accounts is used to prepare the financial statements. The revenue and expense items appear in the Retained Earnings column with their account titles immediately to the right of the dollar amounts. The amounts are color coded to help you trace the data to the financial statements. Data in red appear on the balance sheet, data in blue on the income statement, and data in green on the statement of cash flows.

Vertical Statements Model

The financial statements for Cato Consultants' 2013 accounting period are represented in a vertical statements model in Exhibit 2.2. A vertical statements model arranges a set of financial statement information vertically on a single page. Like horizontal statements models, vertical statements models are learning tools. They illustrate interrelationships among financial statements. The models do not, however, portray the full, formal presentation formats companies use in published financial statements. For example, statements models may use summarized formats with abbreviated titles and dates. As you read the following explanations of each financial statement, trace the color coded financial data from Exhibit 2.1 to Exhibit 2.2.

EXHIBIT 2.1

Transaction Data for 2013 Recorded in General Ledger Accounts

1	Cato Consultants acquired $5,000 cash by issuing common stock.
2	Cato provided $84,000 of consulting services on account.
3	Cato collected $60,000 cash from customers in partial settlement of its accounts receivable.
4	Cato paid $10,000 cash for salary expense.
5	Cato paid $2,000 cash for 2013 advertising costs.
6	Cato signed contracts for $42,000 of consulting services to be performed in 2014.
7	Cato recognized $6,000 of accrued salary expense.

	Assets			=	Liabilities	+		Stockholders' Equity		
Event No.	Cash	+	Accounts Receivable	=	Salaries Payable	+	Common Stock	+	Retained Earnings	Other Account Titles
Beg. bal.	0		0		0		0		0	
1	5,000						5,000			
2			84,000						84,000	Consulting revenue
3	60,000		(60,000)							
4	(10,000)								(10,000)	Salary expense
5	(2,000)								(2,000)	Advertising expense
6										
7					6,000				(6,000)	Salary Expense
End bal.	53,000	+	24,000	=	6,000	+	5,000	+	66,000	

Income Statement

The income statement reflects accrual accounting. Consulting revenue represents the price Cato charged for all the services it performed in 2013, even though Cato had not by the end of the year received cash for some of the services performed. Expenses include all costs incurred to produce revenue, whether paid for by year-end or not. We can now expand the definition of expenses introduced in Chapter 1. Expenses were previously defined as assets consumed in the process of generating revenue. Cato's adjusting entry to recognize accrued salaries expense did not reflect consuming assets. Instead of a decrease in assets, Cato recorded an increase in liabilities (salaries payable). An **expense** can therefore be more precisely defined as *a decrease in assets or an increase in liabilities resulting from operating activities undertaken to generate revenue.*

Statement of Changes in Stockholders' Equity

The statement of changes in stockholders' equity reports the effects on equity of issuing common stock, earning net income, and paying dividends to stockholders. It identifies how an entity's equity increased and decreased during the period as a result of transactions with stockholders and operating the business. In the Cato case, the statement shows that equity increased when the business acquired $5,000 cash by issuing common stock. The statement also reports that equity increased by $66,000 from earning income and that none of the $66,000 of net earnings was distributed to owners (no dividends were paid). Equity at the end of the year is $71,000 ($5,000 + $66,000).

Balance Sheet

The balance sheet discloses an entity's assets, liabilities, and stockholders' equity at particular point in time. As of December 31, 2013, Cato Consultants had total assets of $77,000 ($53,000 cash + $24,000 accounts receivable). These assets are equal to the

EXHIBIT 2.2   Vertical Statements Model

CATO CONSULTANTS
Financial Statements*
Income Statement
For the Year Ended December 31, 2013

Consulting revenue	$84,000
Salary expense	(16,000)
Advertising expense	(2,000)
Net income	$66,000

Statement of Changes in Stockholders' Equity
For the Year Ended December 31, 2013

Beginning common stock	$ 0	
Plus: Common stock issued	5,000	
Ending common stock		$ 5,000
Beginning retained earnings	0	
Plus: Net income	66,000	
Less: Dividends	0	
Ending retained earnings		66,000
Total stockholders' equity		$71,000

Balance Sheet
As of December 31, 2013

Assets		
Cash	$53,000	
Accounts receivable	24,000	
Total assets		$77,000
Liabilities		
Salaries payable		$ 6,000
Stockholders' equity		
Common stock	$ 5,000	
Retained earnings	66,000	
Total stockholders' equity		71,000
Total liabilities and stockholders' equity		$77,000

Statement of Cash Flows
For the Year Ended December 31, 2013

Cash flows from operating activities		
Cash receipts from customers	$60,000	
Cash payments for salary expense	(10,000)	
Cash payments for advertising expenses	(2,000)	
Net cash flow from operating activities		$48,000
Cash flow from investing activities		0
Cash flows from financing activities		
Cash receipt from issuing common stock	5,000	
Net cash flow from financing activities		5,000
Net change in cash		53,000
Plus: Beginning cash balance		0
Ending cash balance		$53,000

*In real-world annual reports, financial statements are normally presented separately with appropriate descriptions of the date to indicate whether the statement applies to the entire accounting period or a specific point in time.

obligations and commitments Cato has to its creditors and investors. Specifically, Cato has a $6,000 obligation (liability) to creditors, with the remaining $71,000 of assets available to support commitments (stockholders' equity) to stockholders.

Statement of Cash Flows

The statement of cash flows explains the change in cash from the beginning to the end of the accounting period. It can be prepared by analyzing the Cash account. Since Cato Consultants was established in 2013, its beginning cash balance was zero. By the end of the year, the cash balance was $53,000. The statement of cash flows explains this increase. The Cash account increased because Cato collected $60,000 from customers and decreased because Cato paid $12,000 for expenses. As a result, Cato's net cash inflow from operating activities was $48,000. Also, the business acquired $5,000 cash through the financing activity of issuing common stock, for a cumulative cash increase of $53,000 ($48,000 + $5,000) during 2013.

Comparing Cash Flow from Operating Activities with Net Income

The amount of net income measured using accrual accounting differs from the amount of cash flow from operating activities. For Cato Consulting in 2013, the differences are summarized below.

	Accrual Accounting	Cash Flow
Consulting revenue	$84,000	$60,000
Salary expense	(16,000)	(10,000)
Advertising expense	(2,000)	(2,000)
Net income	$66,000	$48,000

Many students begin their first accounting class with the misconception that revenue and expense items are cash equivalents. The Cato illustration demonstrates that a company may recognize a revenue or expense without a corresponding cash collection or payment in the same accounting period.

The Closing Process

Recall that the temporary accounts (revenue, expense, and dividend) are closed prior to the start of the next accounting cycle. The closing process transfers the amount in each of these accounts to the Retained Earnings account, leaving each temporary account with a zero balance.

Exhibit 2.3 shows the general ledger accounts for Cato Consultants after the revenue and expense accounts have been closed to retained earnings. The closing entry labeled C1.1 transfers the balance in the Consulting Revenue account to the Retained Earnings account. Closing entries C1.2 and C1.3 transfer the balances in the expense accounts to retained earnings.

Steps in an Accounting Cycle

An accounting cycle, which is represented graphically in Exhibit 2.4, involves several steps. The four steps identified to this point are (1) recording transactions; (2) adjusting the accounts; (3) preparing financial statements; and (4) closing the temporary accounts. The first step occurs continually throughout the accounting period. Steps 2, 3, and 4 normally occur at the end of the accounting period.

The Matching Concept

Cash basis accounting can distort reported net income because it sometimes fails to match expenses with the revenues they produce. To illustrate, consider the $6,000 of accrued salary expense that Cato Consultants recognized at the end of 2013. The instructor's teaching produced revenue in 2013. If Cato waited until 2014 (when it paid

EXHIBIT 2.3

General Ledger Accounts for Cato Consultants

Assets		=	Liabilities		+	Stockholders' Equity	

Cash

(1)	5,000
(3)	60,000
(4)	(10,000)
(5)	(2,000)
Bal.	53,000

Salaries Payable

| (7) | 6,000 |
| Bal. | 6,000 |

Common Stock

| (1) | 5,000 |

Accounts Receivable

(2)	84,000
(3)	(60,000)
Bal.	24,000

Retained Earnings

Cl.1	84,000
Cl.2	(16,000)
Cl.3	(2,000)
Bal.	66,000

Consulting Revenue

(2)	84,000
Cl.1	(84,000)
Bal.	0

Salary Expense

(4)	(10,000)
(7)	(6,000)
Cl.2	16,000
Bal.	0

Advertising Expense

(5)	(2,000)
Cl.3	2,000
Bal.	0

the instructor) to recognize $6,000 of the total $16,000 salary expense, then $6,000 of the expense would not be matched with the revenue it generated. By using accrual accounting, Cato recognized all the salary expense in the same accounting period in which the consulting revenue was recognized. A primary goal of accrual accounting is to appropriately match expenses with revenues, the **matching concept.**

Appropriately matching expenses with revenues can be difficult even when using accrual accounting. For example, consider Cato's advertising expense. Money spent on advertising may generate revenue in future accounting periods as well as in the current period. A prospective customer could save an advertising brochure for several years before calling Cato for training services. It is difficult to know when and to what extent advertising produces revenue. When the connection between an expense and the corresponding revenue is vague, accountants commonly match the expense with the period in which it is incurred. Cato matched (recognized) the entire $2,000 of advertising cost with the 2012 accounting period even though some of that cost might generate revenue in future accounting periods. Expenses that are matched with the period in which they are incurred are frequently called **period costs.**

Matching is not perfect. Although it would be more accurate to match expenses with revenues than with periods, there is sometimes no obvious direct connection between expenses and revenue.

EXHIBIT 2.4

The Accounting Cycle

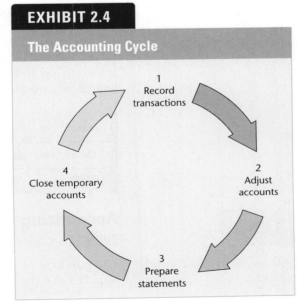

1 Record transactions
2 Adjust accounts
3 Prepare statements
4 Close temporary accounts

Accountants must exercise judgment to select the accounting period in which to recognize revenues and expenses. The concept of conservatism influences such judgment calls.

The Conservatism Principle

When faced with a recognition dilemma, **conservatism** guides accountants to select the alternative that produces the lowest amount of net income. In uncertain circumstances, accountants tend to delay revenue recognition and accelerate expense recognition. The conservatism principle holds that it is better to understate net income than to overstate it. If subsequent developments suggest that net income should have been higher, investors will respond more favorably than if they learn it was really lower. This practice explains why Cato recognized all of the advertising cost as expense in 2013 even though some of that cost may generate revenue in future accounting periods.

SECTION 2: Accounting for Deferrals

As previously discussed cash may be exchanged before revenue or expense is recognized. In this case the business defers recognition. This section introduces three common deferrals.

SECOND ACCOUNTING CYCLE

The effects of Cato Consultants' 2014 events are as follows:

EVENT 1   Cato paid $6,000 to the instructor to settle the salaries payable obligation.

Cash payments to creditors are *asset use transactions.* When Cato pays the instructor, both the asset account Cash and the liability account Salaries Payable decrease. The cash payment does not affect the income statement. The salary expense was recognized in 2013 when the instructor taught the classes. The statement of cash flows reflects a cash outflow from operating activities. The effects of this transaction on the financial statements are shown here.

Assets	=	Liab.	+	Stk. Equity						
Cash	=	Sal. Pay.				Rev.	−	Exp.	=	Net Inc.	Cash Flow
(6,000)	=	(6,000)	+	NA		NA	−	NA	=	NA	(6,000) OA

LO 3

Show how supplies affect financial statements.

Accounting for Supplies Purchase

EVENT 2   Cato purchased $800 of supplies on account.

The purchase of supplies on account is an *asset source transaction.* The asset account Supplies and the liability account Accounts Payable increase. The income statement is unaffected. Expense recognition is deferred until the supplies are used. The statement of cash flows is not affected. The effects of this transaction on the financial statements are shown here.

Assets	=	Liab.	+	Stk. Equity		Rev.	–	Exp.	=	Net Inc.	Cash Flow
Supplies	=	Accts. Pay.				Rev.	–	Exp.	=	Net Inc.	Cash Flow
800	=	800	+	NA		NA	–	NA	=	NA	NA

Prepaid Items (Cost versus Expense)

EVENT 3   On March 1, 2014, Cato signed a one-year lease agreement and paid $12,000 cash in advance to rent office space. The one-year lease term began on March 1.

LO 4

Show how prepaid items affect financial statements.

Accrual accounting draws a distinction between the terms *cost* and *expense*. *A* **cost** *might be either an asset or an expense.* If a company has already consumed a purchased resource in the process of earning revenue, the cost of the resource is an *expense*. For example, companies normally pay for electricity the month after using it. The cost of electric utilities is therefore usually recorded as an expense. In contrast, if a company purchases a resource it will use in the future to generate revenue, the cost of the resource represents an *asset*. Accountants record such a cost in an asset account and **defer** recognizing an expense until the resource is used to produce revenue. Deferring the expense recognition provides more accurate **matching** of revenues and expenses.

The cost of the office space Cato leased in Event 2 is an asset. It is recorded in the asset account *Prepaid Rent*. Cato expects to benefit from incurring this cost for the next twelve months. Expense recognition is deferred until Cato uses the office space to help generate revenue. Other common deferred expenses include *prepaid insurance* and *prepaid taxes*. As these titles imply, deferred expenses are frequently called **prepaid items.** Exhibit 2.5 illustrates the relationship between costs, assets, and expenses.

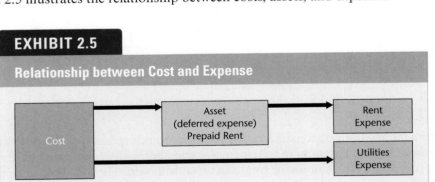

EXHIBIT 2.5

Relationship between Cost and Expense

Purchasing prepaid rent is an asset exchange transaction. The asset account Cash decreases and the asset account Prepaid Rent increases. The amount of total assets is unaffected. The income statement is unaffected. Expense recognition is deferred until the office space is used. The statement of cash flows reflects a cash outflow from operating activities. The effects of this transaction on the financial statements are shown here.

Assets			=	Liab.	+	Stk. Equity		Rev.	–	Exp.	=	Net Inc.	Cash Flow
Cash	+	Prep. Rent						Rev.	–	Exp.	=	Net Inc.	Cash Flow
(12,000)	+	12,000	=	NA	+	NA		NA	–	NA	=	NA	(12,000) OA

LO 5

Show how unearned revenues affect financial statements.

Accounting for Receipt of Unearned Revenue

EVENT 4   Cato received $18,000 cash in advance from Westberry Company for consulting services Cato agreed to perform over a one-year period beginning June 1, 2014.

Cato must defer (delay) recognizing any revenue until it performs (does the work) the consulting services for Westberry. From Cato's point of view, the deferred revenue is a liability because Cato is obligated to perform services in the future. The liability is called **unearned revenue.** The cash receipt is an *asset source transaction.* The asset account Cash and the liability account Unearned Revenue both increase. Collecting the cash has no effect on the income statement. The revenue will be reported on the income statement after Cato performs the services. The statement of cash flows reflects a cash inflow from operating activities. The effects of this transaction on the financial statements are shown here.

Assets	=	Liab.	+	Stk. Equity		Rev.	−	Exp.	=	Net Inc.	Cash Flow
Cash	=	Unearn. Rev.				Rev.	−	Exp.	=	Net Inc.	Cash Flow
18,000	=	18,000	+	NA		NA	−	NA	=	NA	18,000 OA

Other 2014 Events

EVENT 5   Cato provided $96,400 of consulting services on account.

Providing services on account is an *asset source transaction.* The asset account Accounts Receivable and the stockholders' equity account Retained Earnings increase. Revenue and net income increase. The statement of cash flows is not affected. The effects of this transaction on the financial statements are shown here.

Assets	=	Liab.	+	Stk. Equity		Rev.	−	Exp.	=	Net Inc.	Cash Flow
Accts. Rec.	=			Ret. Earn.		Rev.	−	Exp.	=	Net Inc.	Cash Flow
96,400	=	NA	+	96,400		96,400	−	NA	=	96,400	NA

EVENT 6   Cato collected $105,000 cash from customers as partial settlement of accounts receivable.

Collecting money from customers who are paying accounts receivable is an *asset exchange transaction.* One asset account (Cash) increases and another asset account (Accounts Receivable) decreases. The amount of total assets is unchanged. The income statement is not affected. The statement of cash flows reports a cash inflow from operating activities. The effects of this transaction on the financial statements are shown here.

Assets			=	Liab.	+	Stk. Equity		Rev.	−	Exp.	=	Net Inc.	Cash Flow
Cash	+	Accts. Rec.						Rev.	−	Exp.	=	Net Inc.	Cash Flow
105,000	+	(105,000)	=	NA	+	NA		NA	−	NA	=	NA	105,000 OA

EVENT 7   Cato paid $32,000 cash for salary expense.

Cash payments for salary expense are *asset use transactions.* Both the asset account Cash and the equity account Retained Earnings decrease by $32,000. Recognizing the expense decreases net income on the income statement. The statement of cash flows reflects a cash outflow from operating activities. The effects of this transaction on the financial statements are shown here.

Assets	=	Liab.	+	Stk. Equity						
Cash	=			Ret. Earn.	Rev.	−	Exp.	=	Net Inc.	Cash Flow
(32,000)	=	NA	+	(32,000)	NA	−	32,000	=	(32,000)	(32,000) OA

EVENT 8   Cato incurred $21,000 of other operating expenses on account.

Recognizing expenses incurred on account are *claims exchange transactions.* One claims account (Accounts Payable) increases and another claims account (Retained Earnings) decreases. The amount of total claims is not affected. Recognizing the expenses decreases net income. The statement of cash flows is not affected. The effects of this transaction on the financial statements are shown here.

Assets	=	Liab.	+	Stk. Equity						
		Accts. Pay.	+	Ret. Earn.	Rev.	−	Exp.	=	Net Inc.	Cash Flow
NA	=	21,000	+	(21,000)	NA	−	21,000	=	(21,000)	NA

EVENT 9   Cato paid $18,200 in partial settlement of accounts payable.

Paying accounts payable is an *asset use transaction.* The asset account Cash and the liability account Accounts Payable decrease. The statement of cash flows reports a cash outflow for operating activities. The income statement is not affected. The effects of this transaction on the financial statements are shown here.

Assets	=	Liab.	+	Stk. Equity						
Cash	=	Accts. Pay.			Rev.	−	Exp.	=	Net Inc.	Cash Flow
(18,200)	=	(18,200)	+	NA	NA	−	NA	=	NA	(18,200) OA

EVENT 10   Cato paid $79,500 to purchase land it planned to use in the future as a building site for its home office.

Purchasing land with cash is an *asset exchange transaction.* One asset account, Cash, decreases and another asset account, Land, increases. The amount of total assets is unchanged. The income statement is not affected. The statement of cash flows reports a cash outflow for investing activities. The effects of this transaction on the financial statements are shown here.

Assets			=	Liab.	+	Stk. Equity					
Cash	+	Land					Rev.	−	Exp.	=	Net Inc.	Cash Flow
(79,500)	+	79,500	=	NA	+	NA	NA	−	NA	=	NA	(79,500) IA

EVENT 11   Cato paid $21,000 in cash dividends to its stockholders.

Cash payments for dividends are *asset use transactions.* Both the asset account Cash and the equity account Retained Earnings decrease. Recall that dividends are wealth transfers from the business to the stockholders, not expenses. They are not incurred in the process of generating revenue. They do not affect the income statement. The statement of cash flows reflects a cash outflow from financing activities. The effects of this transaction on the financial statements are shown here.

Assets	=	Liab.	+	Stk. Equity						
Cash	=			Ret. Earn.	Rev.	−	Exp.	=	Net Inc.	Cash Flow
(21,000)	=	NA	+	(21,000)	NA	−	NA	=	NA	(21,000) FA

EVENT 12   Cato acquired $2,000 cash from issuing additional shares of common stock.

Issuing common stock is an *asset source transaction.* The asset account Cash and the stockholders' equity account Common Stock increase. The income statement is unaffected. The statement of cash flows reports a cash inflow from financing activities. The effects of this transaction on the financial statements are shown here.

Assets	=	Liab.	+	Stk. Equity		Rev.	−	Exp.	=	Net Inc.	Cash Flow
Cash	=			Com. Stk.		Rev.	−	Exp.	=	Net Inc.	Cash Flow
2,000	=	NA	+	2,000		NA	−	NA	=	NA	2,000 FA

Adjusting Entries

Recall that companies make adjusting entries at the end of an accounting period to update the account balances before preparing the financial statements. Adjusting entries ensure that companies report revenues and expenses in the appropriate accounting period; adjusting entries never affect the Cash account.

Accounting for Supplies (Adjusting Entry)

EVENT 13   After determining through a physical count that it had $150 of unused supplies on hand as of December 31, Cato recognized supplies expense.

Companies would find the cost of recording supplies expense each time a pencil, piece of paper, envelope, or other supply item is used to far outweigh the benefit derived from such tedious recordkeeping. Instead, accountants transfer to expense the total cost of all supplies used during the entire accounting period in a single year-end adjusting entry. The cost of supplies used is determined as follows:

> Beginning supplies balance + Supplies purchased = Supplies available for use
> Supplies available for use − Ending supplies balance = Supplies used

Companies determine the ending supplies balance by physically counting the supplies on hand at the end of the period. Cato used $650 of supplies during the year (zero beginning balance + $800 supplies purchase = $800 available for use; $800 available for use − $150 ending balance = $650). Recognizing Cato's supplies expense is an *asset use transaction.* The asset account Supplies and the stockholders' equity account Retained Earnings decrease. Recognizing supplies expense reduces net income. The statement of cash flows is not affected. The effects of this transaction on the financial statements are shown here.

Assets	=	Liab.	+	Stk. Equity		Rev.	−	Exp.	=	Net Inc.	Cash Flow
Supplies	=			Ret. Earn.		Rev.	−	Exp.	=	Net Inc.	Cash Flow
(650)	=	NA	+	(650)		NA	−	650	=	(650)	NA

Accounting for Prepaid Rent (Adjusting Entry)

EVENT 14   Cato recognized rent expense for the office space used during the accounting period.

Recall that Cato paid $12,000 on March 1, 2014, to rent office space for one year (see Event 3). The portion of the lease cost that represents using office space from March 1 through December 31 is computed as follows:

> $12,000 Cost of annual lease ÷ 12 Months = $1,000 Cost per month
> $1,000 Cost per month × 10 Months used = $10,000 Rent expense

Recognizing the rent expense decreases the asset account Prepaid Rent and the stockholders' equity account Retained Earnings. Recognizing rent expense reduces net income. The statement of cash flows is not affected. The cash flow effect was recorded in the March 1 event. These effects on the financial statements follow:

Assets	=	Liab.	+	Stk. Equity					
Prep. Rent	=			Ret. Earn.	Rev.	−	Exp.	=	Net Inc.	Cash Flow
(10,000)	=	NA	+	(10,000)	NA	−	10,000	=	(10,000)	NA

✓ CHECK YOURSELF 2.2

Rujoub Inc. paid $18,000 cash for one year of insurance coverage that began on November 1, 2013. Based on this information alone, determine the cash flow from operating activities that Rujoub would report on the 2013 and 2014 statements of cash flows. Also, determine the amount of insurance expense Rujoub would report on the 2013 income statement and the amount of prepaid insurance (an asset) that Rujoub would report on the December 31, 2013, balance sheet.

Answer Since Rujoub paid all of the cash in 2013, the 2013 statement of cash flows would report an $18,000 cash outflow from operating activities. The 2014 statement of cash flows would report zero cash flow from operating activities. The expense would be recognized in the periods in which the insurance is used. In this case, insurance expense is recognized at the rate of $1,500 per month ($18,000 ÷ 12 months). Rujoub used two months of insurance coverage in 2013 and therefore would report $3,000 (2 months × $1,500) of insurance expense on the 2013 income statement. Rujoub would report a $15,000 (10 months × $1,500) asset, prepaid insurance, on the December 31, 2013, balance sheet. The $15,000 of prepaid insurance would be recognized as insurance expense in 2014 when the insurance coverage is used.

Accounting for Unearned Revenue (Adjusting Entry)

EVENT 15 Cato recognized the portion of the unearned revenue it earned during the accounting period.

Recall that Cato received an $18,000 cash advance from Westberry Company to provide consulting services from June 1, 2014, to May 31, 2015 (see Event 4). By December 31, Cato had earned 7 months (June 1 through December 31) of the revenue related to this contract. Rather than recording the revenue continuously as it performed the consulting services, Cato can simply recognize the amount earned in a single adjustment to the accounting records at the end of the accounting period. The amount of the adjustment is computed as follows:

$$\$18,000 \div 12 \text{ months} = \$1,500 \text{ revenue earned per month}$$

$$\$1,500 \times 7 \text{ months} = \$10,500 \text{ revenue to be recognized in 2014}$$

The adjusting entry moves $10,500 from the Unearned Revenue account to the Consulting Revenue account. This entry is a *claims exchange transaction.* The liability account Unearned Revenue decreases and the equity account Retained Earnings increases. The effects of this transaction on the financial statements are shown here.

Assets	=	Liab.	+	Stk. Equity					
		Unearn. Rev.	+	Ret. Earn.	Rev.	−	Exp.	=	Net Inc.	Cash Flow
NA	=	(10,500)	+	10,500	10,500	−	NA	=	10,500	NA

Recall that revenue was previously defined as an economic benefit a company obtains by providing customers with goods and services. In this case the economic benefit is a decrease in the liability account Unearned Revenue. **Revenue** can therefore be more precisely defined as *an increase in assets or a decrease in liabilities that a company obtains by providing customers with goods or services.*

 CHECK YOURSELF 2.3

Sanderson & Associates received a $24,000 cash advance as a retainer to provide legal services to a client. The contract called for Sanderson to render services during a one-year period beginning October 1, 2013. Based on this information alone, determine the cash flow from operating activities Sanderson would report on the 2013 and 2014 statements of cash flows. Also determine the amount of revenue Sanderson would report on the 2013 and 2014 income statements.

Answer Since Sanderson collected all of the cash in 2013, the 2013 statement of cash flows would report a $24,000 cash inflow from operating activities. The 2014 statement of cash flows would report zero cash flow from operating activities. Revenue is recognized in the period in which it is earned. In this case revenue is earned at the rate of $2,000 per month ($24,000 ÷ 12 months = $2,000 per month). Sanderson rendered services for three months in 2013 and nine months in 2014. Sanderson would report $6,000 (3 months × $2,000) of revenue on the 2013 income statement and $18,000 (9 months × $2,000) of revenue on the 2014 income statement.

Answers to The Curious Accountant

Because the Meredith Corporation receives cash from customers before actually sending any magazines to them, the company has not earned any revenue when it receives the cash. Meredith has a liability called *unearned revenue*. If Meredith closed its books on December 31, then $3 of Janet's subscription would be recognized as revenue in 2013. The remaining $9 would appear on the balance sheet as a liability.

Meredith actually ends its accounting year on June 30 each year. The actual June 30, 2010, balance sheet for the company is presented in Exhibit 2.6. The liability for unearned revenue was $290 million ($159.3 + $130.7)—which represented about 27.9 percent of total liabilities!

Will Meredith need cash to pay these subscription liabilities? Not exactly. The liabilities will not be paid directly with cash. Instead, they will be satisfied by providing magazines to the subscribers. However, Meredith will need cash to pay for producing and distributing the magazines supplied to the customers. Even so, the amount of cash required to provide magazines will probably differ significantly from the amount of unearned revenues. In most cases, subscription fees do not cover the cost of producing and distributing magazines. By collecting significant amounts of advertising revenue, publishers can provide magazines to customers at prices well below the cost of publication. The amount of unearned revenue is not likely to coincide with the amount of cash needed to cover the cost of satisfying the company's obligation to produce and distribute magazines. Even though the association between unearned revenues and the cost of providing magazines to customers is not direct, a knowledgeable financial analyst can use the information to make estimates of future cash flows and revenue recognition.

EXHIBIT 2.6	Balance Sheet for Meredith Corporation

MEREDITH CORPORATION AND SUBSIDIARIES
Consolidated Balance Sheets
As of June 30, (amounts in thousands)

	2010	2009
Assets		
Current assets		
Cash and cash equivalents	$ 48,574	$ 27,910
Accounts receivable		
(net of allowances of $23,944 in 2008 and $21,002 in 2007)	223,630	192,367
Inventories	26,807	28,151
Current portion of subscription acquisition costs	57,917	60,017
Current portion of broadcast rights	5,423	8,297
Other current assets	19,076	23,398
Total current assets	381,427	340,140
Property, plant, and equipment		
Land	19,594	19,500
Buildings and improvements	127,043	125,779
Machinery and equipment	286,860	276,376
Leasehold improvements	14,409	14,208
Construction in progress	3,060	9,041
Total property, plant, and equipment	450,966	444,904
Less accumulated depreciation	(263,964)	(253,597)
Net property, plant, and equipment	187,002	191,307
Subscription acquisition costs	55,228	63,444
Broadcast rights	2,977	4,545
Other assets	59,138	45,907
Intangible assets, net	552,210	561,581
Goodwill	489,334	462,379
Total assets	$1,727,316	$1,669,303
Liabilities and Shareholders' Equity		
Current liabilities		
Current portion of long-term debt	$ 50,000	$ —
Current portion of long-term broadcast rights payable	9,892	10,560
Accounts payable	109,897	86,381
Accrued expenses		
Compensation and benefits	54,203	42,667
Distribution expenses	14,193	12,224
Other taxes and expenses	40,829	26,653
Total accrued expenses	109,225	81,544
Current portion of unearned subscription revenues	159,292	170,731
Total current liabilities	438,306	349,216
Long-term debt	250,000	380,000
Long-term broadcast rights payable	8,961	11,851
Unearned subscription revenues	130,699	148,393
Deferred income taxes	114,240	64,322
Other noncurrent liabilities	96,765	106,138
Total liabilities	1,038,971	1,059,920
Shareholders' equity		
Series preferred stock, par value $1 per share	—	—
Common stock, par value $1 per share	36,329	35,934
Class B stock, par value $1 per share, convertible to common stock	9,086	9,133
Additional paid-in capital	66,311	53,938
Retained earnings	604,624	542,006
Accumulated other comprehensive income (loss)	(28,005)	(31,628)
Total shareholders' equity	688,345	609,383
Total liabilities and shareholders' equity	$1,727,316	$1,669,303

Accounting for Accrued Salary Expense (Adjusting Entry)

EVENT 16 Cato recognized $4,000 of accrued salary expense.

The adjusting entry to recognize the accrued salary expense is a ***claims exchange transaction.*** One claims account, Retained Earnings, decreases and another claims account, Salaries Payable, increases. The expense recognition reduces net income. The statement of cash flows is not affected. The effects of this transaction on the financial statements are shown here.

Assets	=	Liab.	+	Stk. Equity						
		Sal. Pay.	+	Ret. Earn.	Rev.	−	Exp.	=	Net Inc.	Cash Flow
NA	=	4,000	+	(4,000)	NA	−	4,000	=	(4,000)	NA

Summary of Events and General Ledger

The previous section of this chapter described sixteen events Cato Consultants experienced the during the 2014 accounting period. These events are summarized in Exhibit 2.7 on page 81. The associated general ledger accounts are also shown in the exhibit. The account balances at the end of 2013, shown in Exhibit 2.3, become the beginning balances for the 2014 accounting period. The 2014 transaction data are referenced to the accounting events with numbers in parentheses. The information in the ledger accounts is the basis for the financial statements in Exhibit 2.8 on pages 82 and 83. Before reading further, trace each event in the summary of events into Exhibit 2.7.

Vertical Statements Model

Financial statement users obtain helpful insights by analyzing company trends over multiple accounting cycles. Exhibit 2.8 presents for Cato Consultants a multicycle **vertical statements model** of 2013 and 2014 accounting data. To conserve space, we have combined all the expenses for each year into single amounts labeled "Operating Expenses," determined as follows:

	2013	2014
Other operating expenses	$ 0	$21,000
Salary expense	16,000	36,000
Rent expense	0	10,000
Advertising expense	2,000	0
Supplies expense	0	650
Total operating expenses	$18,000	$67,650

Similarly, we combined the cash payments for operating expenses on the statement of cash flows as follows:

	2013	2014
Supplies and other operating expenses	$ 0	$18,200*
Salary expense	10,000	38,000
Rent expense	0	12,000
Advertising expense	2,000	0
Total cash payments for operating expenses	$12,000	$68,200

*Amount paid in partial settlement of accounts payable

Recall that the level of detail reported in financial statements depends on user information needs. Most real-world companies combine many account balances together to report highly summarized totals under each financial statement caption. Before

EXHIBIT 2.7

Ledger Accounts with 2014 Transaction Data

1. Cato paid $6,000 to the instructor to settle the salaries payable obligation.
2. Cato purchased $800 of supplies on account.
3. On March 1, Cato paid $12,000 cash to lease office space for one year.
4. Cato received $18,000 cash in advance from Westberry Company for consulting services to be performed for one year beginning June 1.
5. Cato provided $96,400 of consulting services on account.
6. Cato collected $105,000 cash from customers as partial settlement of accounts receivable.
7. Cato paid $32,000 cash for salary expense.
8. Cato incurred $21,000 of other operating expenses on account.
9. Cato paid $18,200 in partial settlement of accounts payable.
10. Cato paid $79,500 to purchase land it planned to use in the future as a building site for its home office.
11. Cato paid $21,000 in cash dividends to its stockholders.
12. Cato acquired $2,000 cash from issuing additional shares of common stock.

The year-end adjustments are:

13. After determining through a physical count that it had $150 of unused supplies on hand as of December 31, Cato recognized supplies expense.
14. Cato recognized rent expense for the office space used during the accounting period.
15. Cato recognized the portion of the unearned revenue it earned during the accounting period.
16. Cato recognized $4,000 of accrued salary expense.

Assets		=	Liabilities	+	Stockholders' Equity	

Cash

Bal.	53,000
(1)	(6,000)
(3)	(12,000)
(4)	18,000
(6)	105,000
(7)	(32,000)
(9)	(18,200)
(10)	(79,500)
(11)	(21,000)
(12)	2,000
Bal.	9,300

Accounts Receivable

Bal.	24,000
(5)	96,400
(6)	(105,000)
Bal.	15,400

Supplies

Bal.	0
(2)	800
(13)	(650)
Bal.	150

Prepaid Rent

Bal.	0
(3)	12,000
(14)	(10,000)
Bal.	2,000

Land

Bal.	0
(10)	79,500
Bal.	79,500

Accounts Payable

Bal.	0
(2)	800
(8)	21,000
(9)	(18,200)
Bal.	3,600

Unearned Revenue

Bal.	0
(4)	18,000
(15)	(10,500)
Bal.	7,500

Salaries Payable

Bal.	6,000
(1)	(6,000)
(16)	4,000
Bal.	4,000

Common Stock

Bal.	5,000
(12)	2,000
Bal.	7,000

Retained Earnings

Bal.	66,000

Dividends

Bal.	0
(11)	(21,000)
Bal.	(21,000)

Consulting Revenue

Bal.	0
(5)	96,400
(15)	10,500
Bal.	106,900

Other Operating Expenses

Bal.	0
(8)	(21,000)
Bal.	(21,000)

Salary Expense

Bal.	0
(7)	(32,000)
(16)	(4,000)
Bal.	(36,000)

Rent Expense

Bal.	0
(14)	(10,000)
Bal.	(10,000)

Supplies Expense

Bal.	0
(13)	(650)
Bal.	(650)

EXHIBIT 2.8   Vertical Statements Model

CATO CONSULTANTS
Financial Statements
Income Statements
For the Years Ended December 31

	2013	2014
Consulting revenue	$84,000	$106,900
Operating expenses	(18,000)	(67,650)
Net income	$66,000	$ 39,250

Statements of Changes in Stockholders' Equity
For the Years Ended December 31

	2013	2014
Beginning common stock	$ 0	$ 5,000
Plus: Common stock issued	5,000	2,000
Ending common stock	5,000	7,000
Beginning retained earnings	0	66,000
Plus: Net income	66,000	39,250
Less: Dividends	0	(21,000)
Ending retained earnings	66,000	84,250
Total stockholders' equity	$71,000	$ 91,250

Balance Sheets
As of December 31

	2013	2014
Assets		
Cash	$53,000	$ 9,300
Accounts receivable	24,000	15,400
Supplies	0	150
Prepaid rent	0	2,000
Land	0	79,500
Total assets	$77,000	$106,350
Liabilities		
Accounts payable	$ 0	$ 3,600
Unearned revenue	0	7,500
Salaries payable	6,000	4,000
Total liabilities	6,000	15,100
Stockholders' equity		
Common stock	5,000	7,000
Retained earnings	66,000	84,250
Total stockholders' equity	71,000	91,250
Total liabilities and stockholders' equity	$77,000	$106,350

continued

EXHIBIT 2.8   *Concluded*

Statements of Cash Flows For the Years Ended December 31	2013	2014
Cash Flows from Operating Activities		
Cash receipts from customers	$60,000	$123,000
Cash payments for operating expenses	(12,000)	(68,200)
Net cash flow from operating activities	48,000	54,800
Cash Flows from Investing Activities		
Cash payment to purchase land	0	(79,500)
Cash Flows from Financing Activities		
Cash receipts from issuing common stock	5,000	2,000
Cash payments for dividends	0	(21,000)
Net cash flow from financing activities	5,000	(19,000)
Net change in cash	53,000	(43,700)
Plus: Beginning cash balance	0	53,000
Ending cash balance	$53,000	$ 9,300

reading further, trace the remaining financial statement items from the ledger accounts in Exhibit 2.7 to where they are reported in Exhibit 2.8.

The vertical statements model in Exhibit 2.8 shows significant interrelationships among the financial statements. For each year, trace the amount of net income from the income statement to the statement of changes in stockholders' equity. Next, trace the ending balances of common stock and retained earnings reported on the statement of changes in stockholders' equity to the stockholders' equity section of the balance sheet. Also, confirm that the amount of cash reported on the balance sheet equals the ending cash balance on the statement of cash flows.

Other relationships connect the two accounting periods. For example, trace the ending retained earnings balance from the 2013 statement of stockholders' equity to the beginning retained earnings balance on the 2014 statement of stockholders' equity. Also, trace the ending cash balance on the 2013 statement of cash flows to the beginning cash balance on the 2014 statement of cash flows. Finally, confirm that the change in cash between the 2013 and 2014 balance sheets ($53,000 − $9,300 = $43,700 decrease) agrees with the net change in cash reported on the 2014 statement of cash flows.

CHECK YOURSELF 2.4

Treadmore Company started the 2013 accounting period with $580 of supplies on hand. During 2013 the company paid cash to purchase $2,200 of supplies. A physical count of supplies indicated that there was $420 of supplies on hand at the end of 2013. Treadmore pays cash for supplies at the time they are purchased. Based on this information alone, determine the amount of supplies expense to be recognized on the income statement and the amount of cash flow to be shown in the operating activities section of the statement of cash flows.

Answer The amount of supplies expense recognized on the income statement is the amount of supplies that were used during the accounting period. This amount is computed below:

$580 Beginning balance + $2,200 Supplies purchases = $2,780 Supplies available for use

$2,780 Supplies available for use − $420 Ending supplies balance = $2,360 supplies used

The cash flow from operating activities is the amount of cash paid for supplies during the accounting period. In this case, Treadmore paid $2,200 cash to purchase supplies. This amount would be shown as a cash outflow.

REALITY BYTES

REVENUE VERSUS CASH FLOW: THE GAMES PEOPLE PLAY

Most banks have a sign on their door that says "FDIC Insured." The FDIC on the sign refers to the Federal Deposit Insurance Corporation. Insurance provided by the FDIC protects the bank's depositors up to $250,000 per account in the event the bank should fail. To pay for this insurance, the FDIC charges participating banks a fee.

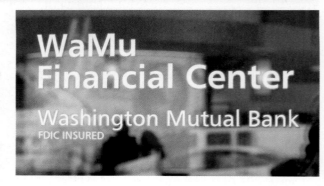

After 164 banks failed during the economic and banking crisis of 2007 and 2008 the FDIC was concerned that its reserves available to pay potential claims were running low. To address this, it required banks to prepay three years of premiums in 2009, rather than pay them in 2009, 2010, and 2011. Although such measures improved the FDIC's cash reserves, it does not mean they earned three year's worth of revenue in 2009, and it did not change the fact that cash payments would still have to be made over the next three years with moneys collected in 2009. And, even though the banks paid three years of premiums in 2009, they spread the expense recognition over 2009, 2010, and 2011.

The FDIC was not the first entity to use such tactics. State and local governments have sometimes delayed payments due near the end of their fiscal year into the next year so as not to show a deficit in the current year.

Near the end of their fiscal year, business entities sometimes try to convince customers to buy more goods and services than they need immediately. The company tells the customer that they can always return the goods next year if they do not need them. The goal is to increase this year's revenues, and profits, and executive bonuses. This tactic, called "trade loading" is at best a violation of GAAP, and in some situations may be illegal.

The problems these tactics create are rather obvious. Cash collected in advance in 2009 by the FDIC means less cash will be collected in 2010 and 2011. Expenses deferred into the next fiscal year by a state government means that next year will have higher expenses to pay than it otherwise would have. These schemes are sometimes referred to as, "kicking the can down the road." Such plans are seldom successful in the long run.

Source of FDIC information: *Birmingham Business Journal,* October 2, 2009.

TRANSACTION CLASSIFICATION

LO 8

Classify accounting events into one of four categories:

■ Asset source transactions.
■ Asset use transactions.
■ Asset exchange transactions.
■ Claims exchange transactions.

Chapters 1 and 2 introduced four types of transactions. Although businesses engage in an infinite number of different transactions, all transactions fall into one of four types. By learning to identify transactions by type, you can understand how unfamiliar events affect financial statements. The four types of transactions are

1. *Asset source transactions:* An asset account increases, and a corresponding claims account increases.

2. *Asset use transactions:* An asset account decreases, and a corresponding claims account decreases.

3. *Asset exchange transactions:* One asset account increases, and another asset account decreases.

4. *Claims exchange transactions:* One claims account increases, and another claims account decreases.

THE FINANCIAL ANALYST

CORPORATE GOVERNANCE

Corporate governance is the set of relationships between the board of directors, management, shareholders, auditors, and other stakeholders that determine how a company is operated. Clearly, financial analysts are keenly interested in these relationships. This section discusses the key components of corporate governance.

Importance of Ethics

The accountant's role in society requires trust and credibility. Accounting information is worthless if the accountant is not trustworthy. Similarly, tax and consulting advice is useless if it comes from an incompetent person. The high ethical standards required by the profession state "a certified public accountant assumes an obligation of self-discipline above and beyond requirements of laws and regulations." The **American Institute of Certified Public Accountants** (AICPA) requires its members to comply with the **Code of Professional Conduct.** Section I of the Code includes six articles that are summarized in Exhibit 2.9. The importance of ethical conduct is universally recognized across a broad spectrum of accounting organizations. The Institute of Management Accountants requires its members to follow a set of Standards of Ethical Conduct. The Institute of Internal Auditors also requires its members to subscribe to the organization's Code of Ethics.

Sarbanes-Oxley Act

Credible financial reporting relies on a system of checks and balances. Corporate management is responsible for preparing financial reports while outside, independent accountants (CPAs) audit the reports. The massive surprise bankruptcies of Enron in late 2001 and WorldCom several months later suggested major audit failures on the part of the independent auditors. An audit failure means a company's auditor does not detect,

LO 9

Discuss the primary components of corporate governance.

EXHIBIT 2.9

Articles of AICPA Code of Professional Conduct

Article I Responsibilities
In carrying out their responsibilities as professionals, members should exercise sensitive professional and moral judgments in all their activities.

Article II The Public Interest
Members should accept the obligation to act in a way that will serve the public interest, honor the public trust, and demonstrate commitment to professionalism.

Article III Integrity
To maintain and broaden public confidence, members should perform all professional responsibilities with the highest sense of integrity.

Article IV Objectivity and Independence
A member should maintain objectivity and be free of conflicts of interest in discharging professional responsibilities. A member in public practice should be independent in fact and appearance when providing auditing and other attestation services.

Article V Due Care
A member should observe the profession's technical and ethical standards, strive continually to improve competence and the quality of services, and discharge professional responsibility to the best of the member's ability.

Article VI Scope and Nature of Services
A member in public practice should observe the principles of the Code of Professional Conduct in determining the scope and nature of services to be provided.

or fails to report, that the company's financial reports are not in compliance with GAAP. The audit failures at Enron, WorldCom, and others prompted Congress to pass the Sarbanes-Oxley Act (SOX).

Prior to SOX, independent auditors often provided nonaudit services, such as installing computer systems, for their audit clients. The fees they earned for these services sometimes greatly exceeded the fees charged for the audit itself. This practice had been questioned prior to the audit failures at Enron and WorldCom. Critics felt the independent audit firm was subject to pressure from the company to conduct a less rigorous audit, or risk losing lucrative nonaudit work. To strengthen the audit function, SOX included the following provisions:

■ Prior to the enactment of SOX, independent auditors were self-regulated by the membership of the American Institute of Certified Public Accountants and by state boards of accountancy. Beyond self-regulation, SOX established the Public Company Accounting Oversight Board (PCAOB) to regulate accounting professionals that audit the financial statements of public companies.

■ Independent auditors must register with the PCAOB or cease all participation in public company audits and abide by the board's pronouncements.

■ The PCAOB has the responsibility to conduct inspections of registered firms. To ensure enforcement, the board has a full range of sanctions at its disposal, including suspension or revocation of registration, censure, and significant fines.

■ To reduce the likelihood of conflicts of interest, SOX prohibits all registered public accounting firms from providing audit clients, contemporaneously with the audit, certain nonaudit services, including internal audit outsourcing, financial-information-system design and implementation services, and expert services.

■ SOX provides significant corporate governance reforms regarding audit committees and their relationship to the auditor, making the audit committee responsible for the appointment, compensation, and oversight of the issuer's auditor.

Other provisions of SOX clarify the legal responsibility that company management has for a company's financial reports. The company's chief executive officer (CEO) and chief financial officer (CFO) must certify in writing that they have reviewed the financial reports being issued, and that the reports present fairly the company's financial status. An executive who falsely certifies the company's financial reports is subject to a fine up to $5 million and imprisonment up to 20 years.

Common Features of Criminal and Ethical Misconduct

Unfortunately, it takes more than a code of conduct to stop fraud. People frequently engage in activities that they know are unethical or even criminal. The auditing profession has identified three elements that are typically present when fraud occurs including:

1. The availability of an opportunity.
2. The existence of some form of pressure leading to an incentive.
3. The capacity to rationalize.

The three elements are frequently arranged in the shape of a triangle as shown in Exhibit 2.10.

Opportunity is shown at the top of the triangle because without opportunity fraud could not exist. The most effective way to reduce opportunities for ethical or criminal misconduct is to implement an effective set of internal controls. **Internal controls** are policies and procedures that a business implements to reduce opportunities for fraud and to assure that its objectives will be accomplished. Specific controls are tailored to meet the individual needs of particular businesses. For example, banks use elaborate vaults to protect cash and safety deposit boxes, but universities have little use for this type of equipment. Even so, many of the same procedures are used by a wide variety of businesses. The internal control policies and procedures that have gained widespread acceptance are discussed in a subsequent chapter.

EXHIBIT 2.10

The Fraud Triangle

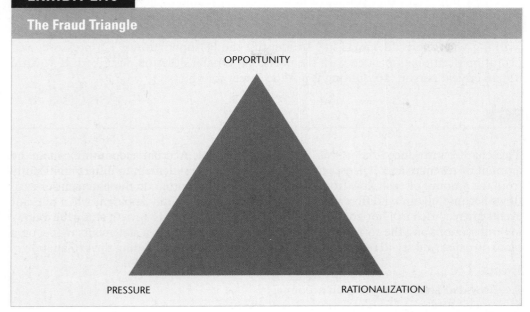

Only a few employees turn to the dark side even when internal control is weak and opportunities abound. So, what causes one person to commit fraud and another to remain honest? The second element of the fraud triangle recognizes **pressure** as a key ingredient of misconduct. A manager who is told "either make the numbers or you are fired" is more likely to cheat than one who is told to "tell it like it is." Pressure can come from a variety of sources, including:

- Personal vices such as drug addiction, gambling, and promiscuity.
- Intimidation from superiors.
- Personal debt from credit cards, consumer and mortgage loans, or poor investments.
- Family expectations to provide a standard of living that is beyond one's capabilities.
- Business failure caused by poor decision making or temporary factors such as a poor economy.
- Loyalty or trying to be agreeable.

The third and final element of the fraud triangle is **rationalization.** Few individuals think of themselves as evil. They develop rationalizations to justify their misconduct. Common rationalizations include the following:

- Everybody does it.
- They are not paying me enough. I'm only taking what I deserve.
- I'm only borrowing the money. I'll pay it back.
- The company can afford it. Look what they are paying the officers.
- I'm taking what my family needs to live like everyone else.

Most people are able to resist pressure and the tendency to rationalize ethical or legal misconduct. However, some people will yield to temptation. What can accountants do to protect themselves and their companies from unscrupulous characters? The answer lies in personal integrity. The best indicator of personal integrity is past performance. Accordingly, companies must exercise due care in performing appropriate background investigations before hiring people to fill positions of trust.

Ethical misconduct is a serious offense in the accounting profession. A single mistake can destroy an accounting career. If you commit a white-collar crime, you normally lose the opportunity to hold a white-collar job. Second chances are rarely granted; it is extremely important that you learn how to recognize and avoid the common features of ethical misconduct. To help you prepare for the real-world situations you are likely to encounter, we include ethical dilemmas in the end-of-chapter materials. When working with these dilemmas, try to identify the (1) opportunity, (2) pressure, and (3) rationalization associated with the particular ethical situation described. If you are not an ethical person, accounting is not the career for you.

<< A Look Back

This chapter introduced the *accrual accounting* concept. Accrual accounting causes the amount of revenues and expenses reported on the income statement to differ significantly from the amount of cash flow from operating activities reported on the statement of cash flows because of timing differences. These differences are readily apparent when relevant events are recorded in a horizontal financial statements model. To review, study the following transactions and the corresponding statements model. Set up a statements model on a piece of paper and try to record the effects of each event before reading the explanation.

Events

1. Provided $600 of services on account.
2. Collected $400 cash from accounts receivable.
3. Accrued $350 of salary expense.
4. Paid $225 cash in partial settlement of salaries payable.

Event No.	Balance Sheet									Income Statement					Statement of Cash Flows	
	Cash	+	Accts. Rec.	=	Sal. Pay.	+	Ret. Earn.		Rev.	−	Exp.	=	Net Inc.			
1	NA	+	600	=	NA	+	600		600	−	NA	=	600		NA	
2	400	+	(400)	=	NA	+	NA		NA	−	NA	=	NA		400	OA
3	NA	+	NA	=	350	+	(350)		NA	−	350	=	(350)		NA	
4	(225)	+	NA	=	(225)	+	NA		NA	−	NA	=	NA		(225)	OA
Totals	175	+	200	=	125	+	250		600	−	350	=	250		175	NC

Notice the $250 of net income differs from the $175 cash flow from operating activities. The entries in the statements model demonstrate the reasons for the difference. Although $600 of revenue is recognized, only $400 of cash was collected. The remaining $200 will be collected in the future and is currently shown on the balance sheet as Accounts Receivable. Also, although $350 of salary expense is recognized, only $225 was paid in cash. The remaining $125 will be paid in the future. This obligation is shown as Salaries Payable on the balance sheet. Study these relationships carefully to develop a clear understanding of how accrual accounting affects financial reporting.

Also, the definitions of revenue and expense have been expanded. The complete definitions of these two elements are as follows:

1. **Revenue:** Revenue is the *economic benefit* derived from operating the business. Its recognition is accompanied by an increase in assets or a decrease in liabilities resulting from providing products or services to customers.

2. **Expense:** An expense is an *economic sacrifice* incurred in the process of generating revenue. Its recognition is accompanied by a decrease in assets or an increase in liabilities resulting from consuming assets and services in an effort to produce revenue.

Finally, this chapter introduced the issues surrounding corporate governance. Codes of ethics, the relevant provisions of Sarbanes-Oxley, and the fraud triangle are discussed.

To this point, we have used plus and minus signs to illustrate the effects of business events on financial statements. In real businesses, so many transactions occur that recording them with simple mathematical notations is impractical. In practice, accountants usually maintain records using a system of rules known as *double-entry bookkeeping*. Chapter 3 introduces the basic components of this bookkeeping system. You will learn how to record business events using a debit/credit format. You will be introduced to ledgers, journals, and trial balances. When you finish Chapter 3, you will have a clear understanding of how accountants maintain records of business activity.

APPENDIX

Companies frequently purchase assets that are used for several years. These assets are frequently called long-term assets. Also, companies incur liabilities that require the computation of interest. Accounting for these issues is introduced in this appendix. A more detailed discussion of these subjects will be included in subsequent chapters.

Accounting Events for 2013

Assume that on January 1, 2013, Libby Company had beginning balances of $43,000 in its Cash and Retained Earnings accounts. During 2013 Libby experienced the following transactions:

EVENT 1   On January 1, 2013, Libby paid $43,000 cash to purchase a forklift.

Libby expected to rent the forklift to its customers during the coming four years and then to sell the used forklift for $3,000. The expected period of use is commonly called the **useful life.** The amount Libby expects to receive from the sale of the asset at the end of its useful life is called the **salvage value.**

The purchase of the forklift is an asset exchange transaction. The balance in the Cash account decreases and the balance in a new asset account called Forklift increases. The purchase does not affect the income statement. Since the asset has a long-term useful life, the cash outflow necessary to buy the asset is an investing activity. The effects of the purchase on the financial statements are shown here:

Assets			=	Liab.	+	Equity						
Cash	+	Forklift	=				Rev.	−	Exp.	=	Net Inc.	Cash Flow
(43,000)	+	43,000	=	NA	+	NA	NA	−	NA	=	NA	(43,000) IA

EVENT 2   On February 1, 2013, Libby borrowed $5,000 cash from the State Bank.

As evidence of the debt, Libby issues a promissory note that describes the company's obligations to the bank. The note stipulates a one-year term and an annual interest rate of 6 percent. Issuing the note is an asset source transaction. The asset account Cash increases and a new liability account called Notes Payable increases. The income statement is not affected. The statement of cash flows shows a $5,000 cash inflow from financing activities. The effects on the financial statements are shown here:

Assets			=	Liab.	+	Equity						
Cash	+	Forklift	=	Note Payable			Rev.	−	Exp.	=	Net Inc.	Cash Flow
5,000	+	NA	=	5,000	+	NA	NA	−	NA	=	NA	5,000 FA

EVENT 3   During 2013 Libby earned $16,000 cash by renting the forklift to its customers.

The effects of this event on the financial statements are shown here:

Assets		=	Liab.	+	Equity					
Cash	+ Forklift	=		+	Retained Earnings	Rev.	− Exp.	= Net Inc.	Cash Flow	
16,000	+ NA	=	NA	+	16,000	16,000	− NA	= 16,000	16,000	OA

EVENT 4   On December 31, 2013 Libby adjusts its accounts to recognize the expense of using the forklift during 2013.

LO 10

Compute depreciation expense and show how it affects financial statements.

To measure the net economic benefit of running the business, Libby must estimate how much of the cost of the forklift it used in the process of earning revenue. Recall that the forklift has a four-year useful life and a $3,000 salvage value. Since the salvage value is expected to be recovered at the end of the forklift's useful life, only $40,000 ($43,000 cost − $3,000 salvage) worth of the forklift is ultimately expected to be used. Assuming the forklift is used evenly over its four-year life, it is logical to allocate an equal amount of the $40,000 to expense each year the forklift is used. The allocation is computed as follows:

$$(\text{Asset cost} - \text{Salvage value})/\text{Useful life} = \text{Depreciation expense}$$
$$(\ \$43,000\ -\ \$3,000\ )/\ 4\ \text{years}\ =\ \$10,000\ \text{per year}$$

As indicated above, the portion of the cost that represents the use of the asset is commonly called **depreciation expense.** The method of computing the depreciation expense that is described above is called **straight-line depreciation.** Recognizing depreciation expense is an asset use transaction. Assets and equity decrease. On the income statement, expenses increase and net income decreases. There are no cash flow consequences. Recall that the cash outflow occurred at the time the asset was purchased. There is no cash flow when the expense is recognized. The effects on the financial statements are shown here:

Assets		=	Liab.	+	Equity				
Cash	+ Book Value of Forklift	=		+	Retained Earnings	Rev.	− Exp.	= Net Inc.	Cash Flow
NA	+ (10,000)	=	NA	+	(10,000)	NA	− 10,000	= (10,000)	NA

The asset account, Forklift, is not decreased directly. Instead, the asset reduction is recorded in a contra asset account called Accumulated Depreciation. This approach is used because it increases the usefulness of the information. The book value of the asset is the difference between the balances in the Forklift account and the related Accumulated Depreciation account as follows:

Forklift	$43,000
Accumulated Depreciation	(10,000)
Book Value	$33,000

The book value may also be called the **carrying value.** On the balance sheet the book value of the asset is added to the other asset account balances to determine the total amount of assets.

Depreciation expense is recognized each year the forklift is used. Like other expense accounts, the Depreciation Expense account is a temporary account that is closed to retained earnings at the end of each accounting cycle. In other words, each year $10,000 is recognized in the Depreciation Expense account and then closed to the Retained Earnings account. In this case, the Depreciation Expense account will be $10,000 each year.

In contrast, the Accumulated Depreciation account is a permanent account. As its name implies, the total amount in the Accumulated Depreciation account increases (accumulates) each time depreciation expense is recognized. For example, at the end of 2014, Libby will recognize $10,000 of depreciation expense and the balance in the Accumulated Depreciation account will increase to $20,000. At the end of 2015, Libby will recognize $10,000 of depreciation expense and the balance in the Accumulated Depreciation account will increase to $30,000, and so on.

EVENT 5 **On December 31, 2013, Libby adjusts its books to recognize the amount of interest expense incurred during 2013.**

Recall that Libby borrowed $5,000 on February 1, 2013. As a result, Libby owes the bank interest for the eleven months the loan was outstanding during the year. The accrued interest is $275 ($5,000 × .06 × 11/12). The adjusting entry is a claims exchange event. The liability account Interest Payable increases, and the equity account Retained Earnings decreases. The income statement would report interest expense. However, there is no effect on cash flow because the actual cash payment for interest will be made on the maturity date in 2014. The effects on the financial statements are shown here:

LO 11

Compute interest expense and show how it affects financial statements.

Assets			=	Liab.	+	Equity						
Cash	+	Forklift	=	Interest Payable	+	Retained Earnings	Rev.	−	Exp.	=	Net Inc.	Cash Flow
NA	+	NA	=	275	+	(275)	NA	−	275	=	(275)	NA

The events experienced by Libby during 2013 are summarized in Exhibit 2.11.

EXHIBIT 2.11

Transaction Data Recorded in Accounts

Event No.		Assets			=	Liabilities			+	Equity	
		Cash	+	Forklift	=	Notes Payable	+	Interest Payable	+	Retained Earnings	
Beg. bal.		43,000		0		0		0		43,000	
1	Purchase forklift	(43,000)		43,000							
2	Borrowed cash	5,000				5,000					
3	Recognize revenue	16,000								16,000	Revenue
4	Recognize depreciation			(10,000)						(10,000)	Depreciation Expense
5	Accrued interest							275		(275)	Interest Expense
End bal.		21,000	+	33,000	=	5,000	+	275	+	48,725	

Accounting Events for 2014

Libby would record three journal entries on January 31, 2014 (the maturity date). The first entry recognizes $25 ($5,000 × .06 × 1/12) of interest expense that accrued in 2014 for the month of January. The effects on the financial statements are shown here:

Assets			=	Liab.	+	Equity						
Cash	+	Forklift	=	Interest Payable	+	Retained Earnings	Rev.	−	Exp.	=	Net Inc.	Cash Flow
NA	+	NA	=	25	+	(25)	NA	−	25	=	(25)	NA

The second entry records Libby's cash payment for interest payable. This entry is an asset use transaction that reduces both the Cash and Interest Payable accounts for the total amount of interest due, $300. The interest payment includes the eleven months interest accrued in 2013 and one month accrued in 2014 ($275 + $25 = $300). There is no effect on the income statement because Libby recognized the interest expense previously. The statement of cash flows would report a $300 cash outflow from operating activities. The effects on the financial statements are shown here:

Assets			=	Liab.	+	Equity							
				Interest									
Cash	+	Forklift	=	Payable			Rev.	−	Exp.	=	Net Inc.	Cash Flow	
(300)	+	NA	=	(300)	+	NA	NA	−	NA	=	NA	(300)	OA

The third entry on January 31, 2014, reflects repaying the principal. This entry is an asset use transaction. The Cash account and the Notes Payable account each decrease by $5,000. There is no effect on the income statement. The statement of cash flows would show a $5,000 cash outflow from financing activities. The effects on the financial statements are shown here:

Assets			=	Liab.	+	Equity							
				Note									
Cash	+	Forklift	=	Payable			Rev.	−	Exp.	=	Net Inc.	Cash Flow	
(5,000)	+	NA	=	(5,000)	+	NA	NA	−	NA	=	NA	(5,000)	FA

Libby's balance sheets, income statements, and statements of cash flows for 2013 and 2014 are shown in Exhibit 2.12. The statements assume revenue for 2014 is also $16,000 cash and the company made the appropriate adjusting entry to recognize depreciation expense.

EXHIBIT 2.12	Financial Statements

LIBBY COMPANY
Financial Statements
December 31, 2013 and 2014

	2013	2014
Income Statements		
Revenue	$16,000	$16,000
Depreciation expense	(10,000)	(10,000)
Interest expense	(275)	(25)
Net income	$ 5,725	$ 5,975
Balance Sheets		
Assets		
Cash	$21,000	$31,700
Forklift less accumulated depreciation	33,000	23,000
Total Assets	$54,000	$54,700
Liabilities		
Notes Payable	$ 5,000	$ 0
Interest Payable	275	0
Total Liabilities	5,275	0
Stockholders' Equity		
Retained Earnings	48,725	54,700
Total Liab. and Stockholders' Equity	$54,000	$54,700

continued

EXHIBIT 2.12   *Concluded*

Statements of Cash Flows		
	2013	**2014**
Cash flows from operations activities		
Inflow from customers	$16,000	$16,000
Cash flow from investing activities		
Outflow to purchase forklift	(43,000)	0
Cash flows from financing activities		
Inflow (outflow) from issue of note	5,000	(5,000)
Outflow for interest	0	(300)
Net change in cash	(22,000)	10,700
Plus beginning cash balance	43,000	21,000
Ending cash balance	$21,000	$31,700

SELF-STUDY REVIEW PROBLEM

A step-by-step audio-narrated series of slides is provided on the text website at edmonds8e.

www.mhhe.com/edmonds8e

Gifford Company experienced the following accounting events during 2013:

1. Started operations on January 1 when it acquired $20,000 cash by issuing common stock.
2. Earned $18,000 of revenue on account.
3. On March 1 collected $36,000 cash as an advance for services to be performed in the future.
4. Paid cash operating expenses of $17,000.
5. Paid a $2,700 cash dividend to stockholders.
6. On December 31, 2013, adjusted the books to recognize the revenue earned by providing services related to the advance described in Event 3. The contract required Gifford to provide services for a one-year period starting March 1.
7. Collected $15,000 cash from accounts receivable.

Gifford Company experienced the following accounting events during 2014:

1. Recognized $38,000 of cash revenue.
2. On April 1 paid $12,000 cash for an insurance policy that provides coverage for one year beginning immediately.
3. Collected $2,000 cash from accounts receivable.
4. Paid cash operating expenses of $21,000.
5. Paid a $5,000 cash dividend to stockholders.
6. On December 31, 2014, adjusted the books to recognize the remaining revenue earned by providing services related to the advance described in Event 3 of 2013.
7. On December 31, 2014, Gifford adjusted the books to recognize the amount of the insurance policy used during 2014.

Required

a. Record the events in a financial statements model like the following one. The first event is recorded as an example.

Event No.	Assets			=	Liab.	+	Stockholders' Equity							Cash Flow
	Cash	+ Accts. Rec.	+ Prep. Ins.	=	Unearn. Rev.	+	Com. Stk.	+ Ret. Earn.	Rev.	− Exp.	= Net Inc.				
1	20,000 +	NA	+ NA	=	NA	+	20,000	+ NA	NA	− NA	= NA			20,000 FA

b. What amount of revenue would Gifford report on the 2013 income statement?

c. What amount of cash flow from customers would Gifford report on the 2013 statement of cash flows?

d. What amount of unearned revenue would Gifford report on the 2013 and 2014 year-end balance sheets?

e. What are the 2014 opening balances for the revenue and expense accounts?

f. What amount of total assets would Gifford report on the December 31, 2013 balance sheet?

g. What obligations and commitments would Gifford report on the December 31, 2014 balance sheet?

Solution to Requirement a

The financial statements model follows:

	Assets			=	Liab.	+	Stockholders' Equity						
Event No.	Cash +	Accts. Rec. +	Prep. Ins. =		Unearn. Rev. +		Com. Stk. +	Ret. Earn.	Rev. −	Exp. =	Net Inc.	Cash Flow		
2013													
1	20,000 +	NA +	NA =		NA +		20,000 +	NA	NA −	NA =	NA	20,000 FA		
2	NA +	18,000 +	NA =		NA +		NA +	18,000	18,000 −	NA =	18,000	NA		
3	36,000 +	NA +	NA =		36,000 +		NA +	NA	NA −	NA =	NA	36,000 OA		
4	(17,000) +	NA +	NA =		NA +		NA +	(17,000)	NA −	17,000 =	(17,000)	(17,000) OA		
5	(2,700) +	NA +	NA =		NA +		NA +	(2,700)	NA −	NA =	NA	(2,700) FA		
6*	NA +	NA +	NA =		(30,000) +		NA +	30,000	30,000 −	NA =	30,000	NA		
7	15,000 +	(15,000) +	NA =		NA +		NA +	NA	NA −	NA =	NA	15,000 OA		
Bal.	51,300 +	3,000 +	NA =		6,000 +		20,000 +	28,300	48,000 −	17,000 =	31,000	51,300 NC		
	Asset, liability, and equity account balances carry forward								Rev. & exp. accts. are closed				
2014													
Bal.	51,300 +	3,000 +	NA =		6,000 +		20,000 +	28,300	NA −	NA =	NA	NA		
1	38,000 +	NA +	NA =		NA +		NA +	38,000	38,000 −	NA =	38,000	38,000 OA		
2	(12,000) +	NA +	12,000 =		NA +		NA +	NA	NA −	NA =	NA	(12,000) OA		
3	2,000 +	(2,000) +	NA =		NA +		NA +	NA	NA −	NA =	NA	2,000 OA		
4	(21,000) +	NA +	NA =		NA +		NA +	(21,000)	NA −	21,000 =	(21,000)	(21,000) OA		
5	(5,000) +	NA +	NA =		NA +		NA +	(5,000)	NA −	NA =	NA	(5,000) FA		
6*	NA +	NA +	NA =		(6,000) +		NA +	6,000	6,000 −	NA =	6,000	NA		
7†	NA +	NA +	(9,000) =		NA +		NA +	(9,000)	NA −	9,000 =	(9,000)	NA		
Bal.	53,300 +	1,000 +	3,000 =		0 +		20,000 +	37,300	44,000 −	30,000 =	14,000	2,000 NC		

*Revenue is earned at the rate of $3,000 ($36,000 ÷ 12 months) per month. Revenue recognized in 2013 is $30,000 ($3,000 × 10 months). Revenue recognized in 2014 is $6,000 ($3,000 × 2 months).

†Rent expense is incurred at the rate of $1,000 ($12,000 ÷ 12 months) per month. Rent expense recognized in 2014 is $9,000 ($1,000 × 9 months).

Solutions to Requirements b–g

b. Gifford would report $48,000 of revenue in 2013 ($18,000 revenue on account plus $30,000 of the $36,000 of unearned revenue).

c. The cash inflow from customers in 2013 is $51,000 ($36,000 when the unearned revenue was received plus $15,000 collection of accounts receivable).

d. The December 31, 2013, balance sheet will report $6,000 of unearned revenue, which is the amount of the cash advance less the amount of revenue recognized in 2013 ($36,000 − $30,000). The December 31, 2014, unearned revenue balance is zero.

e. Since revenue and expense accounts are closed at the end of each accounting period, the beginning balances in these accounts are always zero.

f. Assets on the December 31, 2013, balance sheet are $54,300 [Gifford's cash at year end plus the balance in accounts receivable ($51,300 + $3,000)].

g. Since all unearned revenue would be recognized before the financial statements were prepared at the end of 2014, there would be no liabilities on the 2014 balance sheet. In this case, all of the assets are committed to the investors.

KEY TERMS

accounts receivable 65	asset source transaction 64	depreciation expense 90	realization 63
accrual 63	asset use transaction 65	expense 68	recognition 63
accrual accounting 63	claims exchange transaction 67	internal controls 86	revenue 78
accrued expenses 66	carrying value 90	matching concept 71	salaries payable 66
adjusting entry 66	Code of Professional	opportunity 86	salvage value 89
American Institute of	Conduct 85	period costs 71	straight-line depreciation 90
Certified Public	conservatism 72	prepaid items 73	unearned revenue 74
Accountants 85	cost 73	pressure 87	useful life 89
asset exchange transaction 65	deferral 64	rationalization 87	vertical statements model 80

QUESTIONS

1. What does accrual accounting attempt to accomplish?

2. Define *recognition*. How is it independent of collecting or paying cash?

3. What does the term *deferral* mean?

4. If cash is collected in advance of performing services, when is the associated revenue recognized?

5. What does the term *asset source transaction* mean?

6. What effect does the issue of common stock have on the accounting equation?

7. How does the recognition of revenue on account (accounts receivable) affect the income statement compared to its effect on the statement of cash flows?

8. Give an example of an asset source transaction. What is the effect of this transaction on the accounting equation?

9. When is revenue recognized under accrual accounting?

10. Give an example of an asset exchange transaction.

What is the effect of this transaction on the accounting equation?

11. What is the effect on the right side of the accounting equation when cash is collected in advance of performing services?

12. What does the term *unearned revenue* mean?

13. What effect does expense recognition have on the accounting equation?

14. What does the term *claims exchange transaction* mean?

15. What type of transaction is a cash payment to creditors? How does this type of transaction affect the accounting equation?

16. When are expenses recognized under accrual accounting?

17. Why may net cash flow from operating activities on the cash flow statement be different from the amount of net income reported on the income statement?

18. What is the relationship between the income statement and changes in assets and liabilities?

19. How does net income affect the stockholders' claims on the business's assets?

20. What is the difference between a cost and an expense?

21. When does a cost become an expense? Do all costs become expenses?

22. How and when is the cost of the *supplies used* recognized in an accounting period?

23. What does the term *expense* mean?

24. What does the term *revenue* mean?

25. What is the purpose of the statement of changes in stockholders' equity?

26. What is the main purpose of the balance sheet?

27. Why is the balance sheet dated *as of* a specific date when the income statement, statement of changes in stockholders' equity, and statement of cash flows are dated with the phrase *for the period ended?*

28. In what order are assets listed on the balance sheet?

29. What does the statement of cash flows explain?

30. What does the term *adjusting entry* mean? Give an example.

31. What types of accounts are closed at the end of the accounting period? Why is it necessary to close these accounts?

32. Give several examples of period costs.

33. Give an example of a cost that can be directly matched with the revenue produced by an accounting firm from preparing a tax return.

34. List and describe the four stages of the accounting cycle discussed in Chapter 2.

35. Name and comment on the three elements of the fraud triangle.

36. What is the maximum penalty and prison term that can be charged to a CEO and/or CFO under the Sarbanes-Oxley Act?

MULTIPLE-CHOICE QUESTIONS

Multiple-choice questions are provided on the text website at www.mhhe.com/edmonds8e.

EXERCISES—SERIES A

All applicable Exercises in Series A are available with McGraw-Hill's
Connect® Accounting.

Where applicable in all exercises, round computations to the nearest dollar.

LO 1, 2, 6, 7

Exercise 2-1A *Effect of accruals on the financial statements*

Coates Inc. experienced the following events in 2013, in its first year of operation:

1. Received $20,000 cash from the issue of common stock.
2. Performed services on account for $38,000.
3. Paid the utility expense of $2,500.
4. Collected $21,000 of the accounts receivable.
5. Recorded $15,000 of accrued salaries at the end of the year.
6. Paid a $2,000 cash dividend to the shareholders.

Required

a. Record the events in general ledger accounts under an accounting equation. In the last column of the table, provide appropriate account titles for the Retained Earnings amounts. The first transaction has been recorded as an example.

COATES INC.							
General Ledger Accounts							
Event	Assets		=	Liabilities	+	Stockholders' Equity	Acct. Titles for Ret. Earn.
	Cash	Accounts Receivable		Salaries Payable		Common Stock	Retained Earnings	
1.	20,000					20,000		

b. Prepare the income statement, statement of changes in stockholders' equity, balance sheet, and statement of cash flows for the 2013 accounting period.

c. Why is the amount of net income different from the amount of net cash flow from operating activities?

LO 1

Exercise 2-2A *Effect of collecting accounts receivable on the accounting equation and financial statements*

Burke Company earned $12,000 of service revenue on account during 2013. The company collected $9,800 cash from accounts receivable during 2013.

Required

Based on this information alone, determine the following for Burke Company. (*Hint:* Record the events in general ledger accounts under an accounting equation before satisfying the requirements.)

a. The balance of the accounts receivable that Burke would report on the December 31, 2013, balance sheet.

b. The amount of net income that Burke would report on the 2013 income statement.

c. The amount of net cash flow from operating activities that would be reported on the 2013 statement of cash flows.

d. The amount of retained earnings that would be reported on the 2013 balance sheet.

e. Why are the answers to Requirements *b* and *c* different?

Exercise 2-3A   *Effect of accrued expenses on the accounting equation and financial statements*

LO 2, 7

During 2013, Crest Corporation earned $5,000 of cash revenue and accrued $3,000 of salaries expense.

Required

(*Hint:* Record the events in general ledger accounts under an accounting equation before satisfying the requirements.) Based on this information alone:

a. Prepare the December 31, 2013, balance sheet.

b. Determine the amount of net income that Crest would report on the 2013 income statement.

c. Determine the amount of net cash flow from operating activities that Crest would report on the 2013 statement of cash flows.

d. Why are the answers to Requirements *b* and *c* different?

Exercise 2-4A   *Effect of accruals on the financial statements*

LO 1, 2, 6

Valmont Inc. experienced the following events in 2013, its first year of operation:

1. Received $50,000 cash from the issue of common stock.
2. Performed services on account for $67,000.
3. Paid a $5,000 cash dividend to the stockholders.
4. Collected $45,000 of the accounts receivable.
5. Paid $49,000 cash for other operating expenses.
6. Performed services for $10,000 cash.
7. Recognized $2,000 of accrued utilities expense at the end of the year.

Required

a. Identify the events that result in revenue or expense recognition:

b. Based on your response to Requirement *a*, determine the amount of net income reported on the 2013 income statement.

c. Identify the events that affect the statement of cash flows.

d. Based on your response to Requirement *c*, determine the amount of cash flow from operating activities reported on the 2013 statement of cash flows.

e. What is the before- and after-closing balance in the service revenue account? What other accounts would be closed at the end of the accounting cycle?

f. What is the balance of the retained earnings account that appears on the 2013 balance sheet?

Exercise 2-5A   *Effect of accounts receivable and accounts payable transactions on financial statements*

LO 1, 2

The following events apply to Brown and Birgin, a public accounting firm, for the 2013 accounting period:

1. Performed $96,000 of services for clients on account.
2. Performed $65,000 of services for cash.
3. Incurred $45,000 of other operating expenses on account.
4. Paid $26,000 cash to an employee for salary.
5. Collected $70,000 cash from accounts receivable.
6. Paid $38,000 cash on accounts payable.
7. Paid a $10,000 cash dividend to the stockholders.
8. Accrued salaries were $3,000 at the end of 2013.

Required

a. Show the effects of the events on the financial statements using a horizontal statements model like the following one. In the Cash Flow column, use OA to designate operating activity, IA for investment activity, FA for financing activity, and NC for net change in cash. Use

NA to indicate the element is not affected by the event. The first event is recorded as an example.

Event No.	Assets		=	Liabilities			+	Equity						
	Cash	+ Accts. Rec.	=	Accts. Pay.	+	Sal. Pay	+	Ret. Earn.	Rev.	−	Exp.	=	Net Inc.	Cash Flow
1	NA	+ 96,000	=	NA	+	NA	+	96,000	96,000	−	NA	=	96,000	NA

   b. What is the amount of total assets at the end of 2013?
   c. What is the balance of accounts receivable at the end of 2013?
   d. What is the balance of accounts payable at the end of 2013?
   e. What is the difference between accounts receivable and accounts payable?
   f. What is net income for 2013?
   g. What is the amount of net cash flow from operating activities for 2013?

LO 1, 2

Exercise 2-6A *Missing information related to accruals*

Panoramic Inc. had a beginning balance of $2,000 in its Accounts Receivable account. The ending balance of Accounts Receivable was $2,400. During the period, Panoramic recognized $40,000 of revenue on account. Panoramic's Salaries Payable account has a beginning balance of $1,300 and an ending balance of $900. During the period, the company recognized $35,000 of accrued salaries expense.

Required

   a. Based on the information provided, determine the amount of net income.
   b. Based on the information provided, determine the amount of net cash flow from operating activities.

EXERCISES—SERIES A

LO 3, 6, 7

Exercise 2-7A *Supplies on financial statements*

Accounting Professionals Inc. experienced the following events in 2013, its first year of operation:

   1. Performed services for $20,000 cash.
   2. Purchased $4,000 of supplies on account.
   3. A physical count on December 31, 2013, found that there was $1,000 of supplies on hand.

Required

Based on this information alone

   a. Record the events under an accounting equation.
   b. Prepare an income statement, balance sheet, and statement of cash flows for the 2013 accounting period.
   c. What is the balance in the Supplies account as of January 1, 2014?
   d. What is the balance in the Supplies Expense account as of January 1, 2014?

LO 2, 3, 6

Exercise 2-8A *Supplies and the financial statements model*

Copy Express Inc. began the 2013 accounting period with $9,000 cash, $5,000 of common stock, and $4,000 of retained earnings. Copy Express was affected by the following accounting events during 2013:

   1. Purchased $9,500 of paper and other supplies on account.
   2. Earned and collected $32,500 of cash revenue.
   3. Paid $7,200 cash on accounts payable.
   4. Adjusted the records to reflect the use of supplies. A physical count indicated that $1,700 of supplies was still on hand on December 31, 2013.

Required

a. Show the effects of the events on the financial statements using a horizontal statements model like the following one. In the Cash Flows column, use OA to designate operating activity, IA for investing activity, FA for financing activity, and NC for net change in cash. Use NA to indicate accounts not affected by the event. The beginning balances are entered in the following example:

Event No.	Assets		=	Liab.	+	Stockholders' Equity				Rev.	−	Exp.	=	Net Inc.	Cash Flows
	Cash	+ Supplies	=	Accts. Pay.	+	Com. Stk.	+	Ret. Earn.		Rev.	−	Exp.	=	Net Inc.	Cash Flows
Beg. bal.	9,000	+ 0	=	0	+	5,000	+	4,000		0	−	0	=	0	0

b. Explain the difference between the amount of net income and amount of net cash flow from operating activities.

Exercise 2-9A *Prepaid items on financial statements*

LO 4, 6, 7

Therapy Inc. experienced the following events in 2013, its first year of operation:

1. Performed counseling services for $18,000 cash.
2. On February 1, 2013, paid $12,000 cash to rent office space for the coming year.
3. Adjusted the accounts to reflect the amount of rent used during the year.

Required

Based on this information alone

a. Record the events under an accounting equation.
b. Prepare an income statement, balance sheet, and statement of cash flows for the 2013 accounting period.
c. Ignoring all other future events, what is the amount of rent expense that would be recognized in 2014?

Exercise 2-10A *Effect of an error on financial statements*

LO 4, 6

On June 1, 2013, Cole Corporation paid $8,400 to purchase a 24-month insurance policy. Assume that Cole records the purchase as an asset and that the books are closed on December 31.

Required

a. Show the purchase of the insurance policy and the related adjusting entry to recognize insurance expense in the accounting equation.
b. Assume that Cole Corporation failed to record the adjusting entry to reflect the expiration of insurance. How would the error affect the company's 2013 income statement and balance sheet?

Exercise 2-11A *Unearned items on financial statements*

LO 5, 6, 7

Interior Design Consultants (IDC) experienced the following events in 2013, its first year of operation:

1. On October 1, 2013, IDC collected $24,000 for consulting services it agreed to provide during the coming year.
2. Adjusted the accounts to reflect the amount of consulting service revenue recognized in 2013.

Required

Based on this information alone

a. Record the events under an accounting equation.
b. Prepare an income statement, balance sheet, and statement of cash flows for the 2013 accounting period.
c. Ignoring all other future events, what is the amount of service revenue that would be recognized in 2014?

LO 5, 6

Exercise 2-12A   *Unearned revenue and the financial statements model*

Ed Arnold started a personal financial planning business when he accepted $120,000 cash as advance payment for managing the financial assets of a large estate. Arnold agreed to manage the estate for a one-year period beginning May 1, 2013.

Required

a. Show the effects of the advance payment and revenue recognition on the 2013 financial statements using a horizontal statements model like the following one. In the Cash Flows column, use OA to designate operating activity, IA for investing activity, FA for financing activity, and NC for net change in cash. Use NA if the account is not affected.

Event	Assets	=	Liab.	+	Stockholders' Equity		Rev.	−	Exp.	=	Net Inc.	Cash Flows
	Cash	=	Unearn. Rev.	+	Ret. Earn.							

b. How much revenue would Ed recognize on the 2014 income statement?

c. What is the amount of cash flow from operating activities in 2014?

LO 5

Exercise 2-13A   *Unearned revenue defined as a liability*

Kim Wong received $800 in advance for tutoring fees when she agreed to help Joe Pratt with his introductory accounting course. Upon receiving the cash, Kim mentioned that she would have to record the transaction as a liability on her books. Joe asked, "Why a liability? You don't owe me any money, do you?"

Required

Respond to Joe's question regarding Wong's liability.

LO 2, 3, 5, 6

Exercise 2-14 A   *Supplies, unearned revenue, and the financial statements model*

Ross, Attorney at Law, experienced the following transactions in 2013, the first year of operations:

1. Purchased $1,500 of office supplies on account.
2. Accepted $36,000 on February 1, 2013, as a retainer for services to be performed evenly over the next 12 months.
3. Performed legal services for cash of $84,000.
4. Paid cash for salaries expense of $32,000.
5. Paid a cash dividend to the stockholders of $8,000.
6. Paid $1,200 of the amount due on accounts payable.
7. Determined that at the end of the accounting period, $150 of office supplies remained on hand.
8. On December 31, 2013, recognized the revenue that had been earned for services performed in accordance with Transaction 2.

Required

Show the effects of the events on the financial statements using a horizontal statements model like the following one. In the Cash Flow column, use the initials OA to designate operating activity, IA for investing activity, FA for financing activity, and NC for net change in cash. Use NA to indicate accounts not affected by the event. The first event has been recorded as an example.

Event No.	Assets			=	Liabilities			+	Stk. Equity		Rev.	−	Exp.	=	Net Inc.	Cash Flow
	Cash	+	Supplies	=	Accts. Pay.	+	Unearn. Rev.	+	Ret. Earn.		Rev.	−	Exp.	=	Net Inc.	Cash Flow
1	NA	+	1,500	=	1,500	+	NA	+	NA		NA	−	NA	=	NA	NA

Exercise 2-15A   *Prepaid vs. unearned, the entity concept*

On October 1, 2013, Caldonia Company paid East Alabama Rentals $4,800 for a 12-month lease on warehouse space.

Required

a. Record the deferral and the related December 31, 2013, adjustment for Caldonia Company in the accounting equation.

b. Record the deferral and the related December 31, 2013, adjustment for East Alabama Rentals in the accounting equation.

Exercise 2-16A   *Identifying transaction type and effect on the financial statements*

Required

Identify whether each of the following transactions is an asset source (AS), asset use (AU), asset exchange (AE), or claims exchange (CE). Also show the effects of the events on the financial statements using the horizontal statements model. Indicate whether the event increases (I), decreases (D), or does not affect (NA) each element of the financial statements. In the Cash Flows column, designate the cash flows as operating activities (OA), investing activities (IA), or financing activities (FA). The first two transactions have been recorded as examples.

					Stockholders' Equity						
Event No.	Type of Event	Assets	= Liabilities	+	Common Stock	+	Retained Earnings	Rev.	− Exp.	= Net Inc.	Cash Flows
a	AE	I/D	NA		NA		NA	NA	NA	NA	D IA
b	AS	I	NA		I		NA	NA	NA	NA	I FA

a. Purchased land for cash.

b. Acquired cash from the issue of common stock.

c. Collected cash from accounts receivable.

d. Paid cash for operating expenses.

e. Recorded accrued salaries.

f. Purchased supplies on account.

g. Performed services on account.

h. Paid cash in advance for rent on office space.

i. Adjusted the books to record supplies used during the period.

j. Performed services for cash.

k. Paid cash for salaries accrued at the end of a prior period.

l. Paid a cash dividend to the stockholders.

m. Adjusted books to reflect the amount of prepaid rent expired during the period.

n. Incurred operating expenses on account.

o. Paid cash on accounts payable.

p. Received cash advance for services to be provided in the future.

q. Recorded accrued interest revenue earned at the end of the accounting period.

Exercise 2-17A   *Asset versus expense*

A cost can be either an asset or an expense.

Required

a. Distinguish between a cost that is an asset and a cost that is an expense.

b. List three costs that are assets.

c. List three costs that are expenses.

LO 1–6

Exercise 2-18A   *Identifying deferral and accrual events*

Required

Identify each of the following events as an accrual, deferral, or neither:

a. Incurred other operating expenses on account.
b. Recorded expense for salaries owed to employees at the end of the accounting period.
c. Paid a cash dividend to the stockholders.
d. Paid cash to purchase supplies to be used over the next several months.
e. Paid cash to purchase land.
f. Provided services on account.
g. Collected accounts receivable.
h. Paid one year's rent in advance.
i. Paid cash for utilities expense.
j. Collected $2,400 in advance for services to be performed over the next 12 months.
k. Recorded interest revenue earned for the period.

LO 6

Exercise 2-19A   *Adjusting the accounts*

Mikita Inc. experienced the following accounting events during its 2013 accounting period:

1. Paid cash to settle an account payable.
2. Collected a cash advance for services that will be provided during the coming year.
3. Paid a cash dividend to the stockholders.
4. Paid cash for a one-year lease to rent office space.
5. Collected cash from accounts receivable.
6. Recognized cash revenue.
7. Issued common stock.
8. Paid cash to purchase land.
9. Paid cash to purchase supplies.
10. Recognized operating expenses on account.

Required

a. Identify the events that would require a year-end adjusting entry.
b. Are adjusting or closing entries recorded first? Why?

LO 6

Exercise 2-20A   *Revenue and expense recognition*

Required

a. Describe a revenue recognition event that results in an increase in assets.
b. Describe a revenue recognition event that results in a decrease in liabilities.
c. Describe an expense recognition event that results in an increase in liabilities.
d. Describe an expense recognition event that results in a decrease in assets.

LO 6, 7

Exercise 2-21A   *Classifying events on the statement of cash flows*

The following transactions pertain to the operations of Blair Company for 2013:

1. Acquired $30,000 cash from the issue of common stock.
2. Performed services for $12,000 cash.
3. Paid a $7,200 cash advance for a one year contract to rent equipment.
4. Recognized $15,000 of accrued salary expense.
5. Accepted a $21,000 cash advance for services to be performed in the future.
6. Provided $60,000 of services on account.
7. Incurred $28,000 of other operating expenses on account.
8. Collected $51,000 cash from accounts receivable.
9. Paid a $5,000 cash dividend to the stockholders.
10. Paid $22,000 cash on accounts payable.

Required

a. Classify the cash flows from these transactions as operating activities (OA), investing activities (IA), or financing activities (FA). Use NA for transactions that do not affect the statement of cash flows.

b. Prepare a statement of cash flows. (There is no beginning cash balance.)

Exercise 2-22A   *Net income versus changes in cash*

In 2013, Zoe Inc. billed its customers $62,000 for services performed. The company collected $51,000 of the amount billed. Zoe incurred $39,000 of other operating expenses on account. Zoe paid $31,000 of the accounts payable. Zoe acquired $40,000 cash from the issue of common stock. The company invested $21,000 cash in the purchase of land.

Required

(*Hint:* Identify the six events described in the paragraph and record them in general ledger accounts under an accounting equation before attempting to answer the questions.) Use the preceding information to answer the following questions:

a. What amount of revenue will Zoe report on the 2013 income statement?

b. What amount of cash flow from revenue will Zoe report on the statement of cash flows?

c. What is the net income for the period?

d. What is the net cash flow from operating activities for the period?

e. Why is the amount of net income different from the net cash flow from operating activities for the period?

f. What is the amount of net cash flow from investing activities?

g. What is the amount of net cash flow from financing activities?

h. What amounts of total assets, liabilities, and equity will Zoe report on the year-end balance sheet?

Exercise 2-23A   *Relationship of accounts to financial statements*

Required

Identify whether each of the following items would appear on the income statement (IS), statement of changes in stockholders' equity (SE), balance sheet (BS), or statement of cash flows (CF). Some items may appear on more than one statement; if so, identify all applicable statements. If an item would not appear on any financial statement, label it NA.

a. Consulting Revenue

b. Market Value of Land

c. Supplies Expense

d. Salaries Payable

e. Notes Payable

f. Ending Common Stock

g. Beginning Cash Balance

h. Prepaid Rent

i. Net Change in Cash

j. Land

k. Operating Expenses

l. Total Liabilities

m. "As of" Date Notation

n. Salaries Expense

o. Net Income

p. Service Revenue

q. Cash Flow from Operating Activities

r. Operating Income

s. Interest Receivable

t. Interest Revenue

u. Rent Expense

v. Salary Expense

w. Total Stockholders' Equity

x. Unearned Revenue

y. Cash Flow from Investing Activities

z. Insurance Expense

aa. Ending Retained Earnings

bb. Interest Revenue

cc. Supplies

dd. Beginning Retained Earnings

ee. Utilities Payable

ff. Cash Flow from Financing Activities

gg. Accounts Receivable

hh. Prepaid Insurance

ii. Ending Cash Balance

jj. Utilities Expense

kk. Accounts Payable

ll. Beginning Common Stock

mm. Dividends

nn. Total Assets

LO 1, 2, 3, 4, 5, 6

Exercise 2-24A   *Effect of accounting events on the income statement and statement of cash flows*

Required

Explain how each of the following events or series of events and the related adjusting entry will affect the amount of *net income* and the amount of *cash flow from operating activities* reported on the year-end financial statements. Identify the direction of change (increase, decrease, or NA) and the amount of the change. Organize your answers according to the following table. The first event is recorded as an example. If an event does not have a related adjusting entry, record only the effects of the event.

	Net Income		Cash Flows from Operating Activities	
Event	Direction of Change	Amount of Change	Direction of Change	Amount of Change
a	NA	NA	NA	NA

a. Acquired $60,000 cash from the issue of common stock.

b. Earned $20,000 of revenue on account. Collected $15,000 cash from accounts receivable.

c. Paid $4,800 cash on October 1 to purchase a one-year insurance policy.

d. Collected $12,000 in advance for services to be performed in the future. The contract called for services to start on August 1 and to continue for one year.

e. Accrued salaries amounting to $5,000.

f. Sold land that cost $15,000 for $15,000 cash.

g. Provided services for $9,200 cash.

h. Purchased $2,000 of supplies on account. Paid $1,500 cash on accounts payable. The ending balance in the Supplies account, after adjustment, was $800.

i. Paid cash for other operating expenses of $2,200.

LO 6

Exercise 2-25A   *Closing the accounts*

The following information was drawn from the accounting records of Swanson Company as of December 31, 2013, before the temporary accounts had been closed. The Cash balance was $6,000, and Notes Payable amounted to $3,000. The company had revenues of $7,000 and expenses of $4,200. The company's Land account had a $4,000 balance. Dividends amounted to $1,000. There was $2,000 of common stock issued.

Required

a. Identify which accounts would be classified as permanent and which accounts would be classified as temporary.

b. Assuming that Swanson's beginning balance (as of January 1, 2013) in the Retained Earnings account was $5,200, determine its balance after the temporary accounts were closed at the end of 2013.

c. What amount of net income would Swanson Company report on its 2013 income statement?

d. Explain why the amount of net income differs from the amount of the ending Retained Earnings balance.

e. What are the balances in the revenue, expense, and dividend accounts on January 1, 2014?

LO 6

Exercise 2-26A   *Closing accounts and the accounting cycle*

Required

a. Identify which of the following accounts are temporary (will be closed to Retained Earnings at the end of the year) and which are permanent:

   (1) Service Revenue

   (2) Dividends

   (3) Common Stock

(4) Notes Payable

(5) Cash

(6) Rent Expense

(7) Accounts Receivable

(8) Utilities Expense

(9) Prepaid Insurance

(10) Retained Earnings

b. List and explain the four stages of the accounting cycle. Which stage must be first? Which stage is last?

Exercise 2-27A   *Closing entries*

LO 6

Rollins Company's accounting records show an after-closing balance of $19,400 in its Retained Earnings account on December 31, 2013. During the 2013 accounting cycle, Rollins earned $15,100 of revenue, incurred $9,200 of expense, and paid $1,500 of dividends. Revenues and expenses were recognized evenly throughout the accounting period.

Required

a. Determine the balance in the Retained Earnings account as of January 1, 2014.

b. Determine the balance in the temporary accounts as of January 1, 2013.

c. Determine the after-closing balance in the Retained Earnings account as of December 31, 2012.

d. Determine the balance in the Retained Earnings account as of June 30, 2013.

Exercise 2-28A   *Matching concept*

LO 6

Companies make sacrifices known as *expenses* to obtain benefits called *revenues*. The accurate measurement of net income requires that expenses be matched with revenues. In some circumstances, matching a particular expense directly with revenue is difficult or impossible. In these circumstances, the expense is matched with the period in which it is incurred.

Required

Distinguish the following items that could be matched directly with revenues from the items that would be classified as period expenses:

a. Sales commissions paid to employees.

b. Advertising expense.

c. Supplies.

d. The cost of land that has been sold.

Exercise 2-29A   *Transactions that affect the elements of financial statements*

LO 8

Required

Give an example of a transaction that will

a. Increase an asset and decrease another asset (asset exchange event).

b. Increase an asset and increase a liability (asset source event).

c. Decrease an asset and decrease a liability (asset use event).

d. Decrease an asset and decrease equity (asset use event).

e. Increase a liability and decrease equity (claims exchange event).

f. Increase an asset and increase equity (asset source event).

g. Decrease a liability and increase equity (claims exchange event).

Exercise 2-30A   *Identifying source, use, and exchange transactions*

LO 8

Required

Indicate whether each of the following transactions is an asset source (AS), asset use (AU), asset exchange (AE), or claims exchange (CE) transaction:

a. Performed services for clients on account.

b. Paid cash for salary expense.

c. Acquired cash from the issue of common stock.

d. Incurred other operating expenses on account.

e. Performed services for cash.

f. Paid cash on accounts payable.

g. Collected cash from accounts receivable.

h. Paid a cash dividend to the stockholders.

i. Received cash for services to be performed in the future.

j. Purchased land with cash.

LO 8

Exercise 2-31A   *Identifying asset source, use, and exchange transactions*

Required

a. Name an asset use transaction that will affect the income statement.

b. Name an asset use transaction that will *not* affect the income statement.

c. Name an asset exchange transaction that will *not* affect the statement of cash flows.

d. Name an asset exchange transaction that will affect the statement of cash flows.

e. Name an asset source transaction that will *not* affect the income statement.

LO 9

Exercise 2-32A   *Ethical conduct*

Required

Name and provide a brief explanation of the six articles of the AICPA Code of Professional Conduct.

LO 11

Exercise 2-33A   *Effects of recognizing accrued interest on financial statements (Appendix)*

Joe Hughes started Hughes Company on January 1, 2013. The company experienced the following events during its first year of operation:

1. Earned $1,500 of cash revenue for performing services.

2. Borrowed $3,000 cash from the bank.

3. Adjusted the accounting records to recognize accrued interest expense on the bank note. The note, issued on August 1, 2013, had a one-year term and a 6 percent annual interest rate.

Required

a. What is the amount of interest expense in 2013?

b. What amount of cash was paid for interest in 2013?

c. Use a horizontal statements model to show how each event affects the balance sheet, income statement, and statement of cash flows. Indicate whether the event increases (I), decreases (D), or does not affect (NA) each element of the financial statements. Also, in the Cash Flows column, designate the cash flows as operating activities (OA), investing activities (IA), or financing activities (FA). The first transaction has been recorded as an example.

Event No.	Balance Sheet										Income Statement						Statement of Cash Flows
	Cash	=	Note Pay.	+	Int. Pay.	+	C. Stk.	+	Ret. Earn.		Rev.	−	Exp.	=	Net Inc.		
1	I	=	NA	+	NA	+	NA	+	I		I	−	NA	=	I		I OA

LO 11

Exercise 2-34A   *Recognizing accrued interest revenue (Appendix)*

Leach Company invested $80,000 in a certificate of deposit on June 1, 2013. The certificate had a 6 percent annual rate of interest and a one-year term to maturity.

Required

a. What amount of interest revenue will Leach recognize for the year ending December 31, 2013?

b. Show how the December 31, 2013, adjusting entry to recognize the accrued interest revenue affects the accounting equation.

c. What amount of cash will Leach collect for interest revenue in 2013?

d. What is the amount of interest receivable as of December 31, 2013?

e. What amount of cash will Leach collect for interest revenue in 2014, assuming it does not renew the CD?

f. What amount of interest revenue will Leach recognize in 2014, assuming it does not renew the CD?

g. What is the amount of interest receivable as of December 31, 2014, assuming it does not renew the CD?

Exercise 2-35A Effect of depreciation on the accounting equation and financial statements (Appendix)

LO 10

The following events apply to The Taco Factory for the 2013 fiscal year:

1. Started the company when it acquired $21,000 cash from the issue of common stock.
2. Purchased a new cooktop that cost $18,000 cash.
3. Earned $32,000 in cash revenue.
4. Paid $16,000 cash for salaries expense.
5. Paid $7,000 cash for operating expenses.
6. Adjusted the records to reflect the use of the cooktop. The cooktop, purchased on January 1, 2013, has an expected useful life of five years and an estimated salvage value of $3,000. Use straight-line depreciation. The adjusting entry was made as of December 31, 2013.

Required

a. Write an accounting equation and record the effects of each accounting event under the appropriate general ledger account headings.

b. What amount of depreciation expense would The Taco Factory report on the 2014 income statement?

c. What amount of accumulated depreciation would The Taco Factory report on the December 31, 2014, balance sheet?

d. Would the cash flow from operating activities be affected by depreciation in 2014?

Exercise 2-36A Depreciation affecting multiple cycles (Appendix)

LO 10

On January 1, 2013, Metro Maxx Inc. paid $23,000 cash to purchase a taxi cab. The taxi had a four-year useful life and a $3,000 salvage value.

Required

a. Determine the amount of depreciation expense that would appear on the 2013 and 2014 income statements.

b. Determine the amount of accumulated depreciation that would appear on the 2013 and 2014 balance sheets.

c. Explain how the purchase of equipment would affect the 2013 and 2014 statements of cash flows.

PROBLEMS—SERIES A

All applicable Problems in Series A are available with McGraw-Hill's Connect® Accounting.

Problem 2-37A Recording events in a horizontal statements model

LO 1, 2, 3, 4, 5, 6

The following events pertain to James Cleaning Company:

1. Acquired $15,000 cash from the issue of common stock.
2. Provided services for $6,000 cash.
3. Provided $18,000 of services on account.

CHECK FIGURES
Net Income: $15,200
Ending Cash Balance: $24,600

4. Collected $11,000 cash from the account receivable created in Event 3.

5. Paid $1,400 cash to purchase supplies.

6. Had $100 of supplies on hand at the end of the accounting period.

7. Received $3,600 cash in advance for services to be performed in the future.

8. Performed one-half of the services agreed to in Event 7.

9. Paid $6,500 for salaries expense.

10. Incurred $2,800 of other operating expenses on account.

11. Paid $2,100 cash on the account payable created in Event 10.

12. Paid a $1,000 cash dividend to the stockholders.

Required

Show the effects of the events on the financial statements using a horizontal statements model like the following one. In the Cash Flows column, use the letters OA to designate operating activity, IA for investing activity, FA for financing activity, and NC for net change in cash. Use NA to indicate accounts not affected by the event. The first event is recorded as an example.

Event No.			Assets			=	Liabilities			+	Stockholders' Equity								
	Cash	+	Accts. Rec.	+	Supp.	=	Accts. Pay.	+	Unearn. Rev.	+	Com. Stk.	+	Ret. Earn.		Rev.	−	Exp.	= Net Inc.	Cash Flows
1	15,000	+	NA	+	NA	=	NA	+	NA	+	15,000	+	NA		NA	−	NA	= NA	15,000 FA

LO 2, 3, 4, 5, 6

Problem 2-38A   *Effect of adjusting entries on the accounting equation*

CHECK FIGURE

b. adjustment amount: $2,200

Required

Each of the following independent events requires a year-end adjusting entry. Show how each event and its related adjusting entry affect the accounting equation. Assume a December 31 closing date. The first event is recorded as an example.

	Total Assets						**Stockholders Equity**		
Event/ Adjustment	Cash	+	Other Assets	=	Liabilities	+	Common Stock	+	Retained Earnings
a	−6,000		+6,000		NA		NA		NA
Adj.	NA		−4,500		NA		NA		−4,500

a. Paid $6,000 cash in advance on April 1 for a one-year insurance policy.

b. Purchased $2,400 of supplies on account. At year's end, $200 of supplies remained on hand.

c. Paid $7,200 cash in advance on March 1 for a one-year lease on office space.

d. Received an $18,000 cash advance for a contract to provide services in the future. The contract required a one-year commitment starting September 1.

LO 6

Problem 2-39A   *Closing the accounts*

The following selected accounts and account balances were taken from the records of Bates Company. Except as otherwise indicated, all balances are as of December 31, 2013, before the closing entries were recorded.

Cash received from common stock issued during 2013	$ 4,500
Cash	10,500
Revenue	18,000
Salary expense	13,000
Cash flow from operating activities	4,500
Notes payable	6,000
Utility expense	1,800
Dividends	1,000
Cash flow from financing activities	5,000
Rent expense	1,600
Land	25,000
Retained earnings, January 1, 2013	19,700
Common stock, December 31, 2013	20,000

Required

a. Prepare the income statement Black would include in its 2013 annual report.

b. Identify the accounts that should be closed to the Retained Earnings account.

c. Determine the Retained Earnings account balance at December 31, 2013. Identify the reasons for the difference between net income and the ending balance in Retained Earnings.

d. What are the balances in the Revenue, Expense, and Dividend accounts on January 1, 2014? Explain.

Problem 2-40A *Effect of events on financial statements*

Davis Company had the following balances in its accounting records as of December 31, 2013:

Assets		Liabilities and Equity	
Cash	$ 60,000	Accounts Payable	$ 32,000
Accounts Receivable	45,000	Common Stock	60,000
Land	35,000	Retained Earnings	48,000
Totals	$140,000		$140,000

The following accounting events apply to Davis for 2014:

Jan.   1   Acquired an additional $30,000 cash from the issue of common stock.
April 1   Paid $7,200 cash in advance for a one-year lease for office space.
June   1   Paid a $5,000 cash dividend to the stockholders.
July   1   Purchased additional land that cost $40,000 cash.
Aug.   1   Made a cash payment on accounts payable of $21,000.
Sept.   1   Received $9,600 cash in advance as a retainer for services to be performed monthly during the next eight months.
Sept. 30 Sold land for $20,000 cash that had originally cost $20,000.
Oct.   1   Purchased $1,200 of supplies on account.
Dec. 31   Earned $75,000 of service revenue on account during the year.
        31   Received $62,000 cash collections from accounts receivable.
        31   Incurred $27,000 other operating expenses on account during the year.
        31   Recognized accrued salaries expense of $18,000.
        31   Had $100 of supplies on hand at the end of the period.
        31   The land purchased on July 1 had a market value of $56,000.
        31   Recognized $120 of accrued interest revenue.

Required

Based on the preceding information for Davis Company answer the following questions. All questions pertain to the 2014 financial statements. (*Hint:* Record the events in general ledger accounts under an accounting equation before answering the questions.)

a. What two additional adjusting entries need to be made at the end of the year?

b. What amount would be reported for land on the balance sheet?

c. What amount of net cash flow from operating activities would be reported on the statement of cash flows?

d. What amount of rent expense would be reported in the income statement?

e. What amount of total liabilities would be reported on the balance sheet?

f. What amount of supplies expense would be reported on the income statement?

g. What amount of unearned revenue would be reported on the balance sheet?

h. What amount of net cash flow from investing activities would be reported on the statement of cash flows?

i. What amount of total expenses would be reported on the income statement?

j. What total amount of service revenue would be reported on the income statement?

k. What amount of cash flows from financing activities would be reported on the statement of cash flows?

l. What amount of net income would be reported on the income statement?

m. What amount of retained earnings would be reported on the balance sheet?

LO 7

CHECK FIGURES
a. Total Assets $91,700
b. Net Income $20,000

Problem 2-41A   *Identifying and arranging elements on financial statements*

The following accounts and balances were drawn from the records of Dawkins Company at December 31, 2013:

Cash	$22,100	Accounts receivable	$21,000
Land	43,000	Cash flow from operating act.	8,600
Insurance expense	2,500	Beginning retained earnings	47,200
Dividends	5,000	Beginning common stock	5,500
Prepaid insurance	3,500	Service revenue	86,000
Accounts payable	15,000	Cash flow from financing act.	9,000
Supplies	2,100	Ending common stock	14,500
Supplies expense	1,000	Cash flow from investing act.	(6,000)
Rent expense	3,500	Other operating expenses	59,000

Required

Use the accounts and balances from Dawkins Company to construct an income statement, statement of changes in stockholders' equity, balance sheet, and statement of cash flows (show only totals for each activity on the statement of cash flows).

LO 7

Problem 2-42A   *Missing information in financial statements*

Required

Fill in the blanks (indicated by the alphabetic letters in parentheses) in the following financial statements. Assume the company started operations January 1, 2013, and all transactions involve cash.

	For the Years		
	2013	2014	2015
Income Statements			
Revenue	$ 400	$ 500	$ 800
Expense	(250)	(l)	(425)
Net income	$ (a)	$ 100	$ 375
Statement of Changes in Stockholders' Equity			
Beginning common stock	$ 0	$ (m)	$ 9,100
Plus: Common stock issued	(b)	1,100	310
Ending common stock	$8,000	9,100	(s)
Beginning retained earnings	0	25	75
Plus: Net income	(c)	100	375
Less: Dividends	(d)	(50)	(150)
Ending retained earnings	25	(n)	300
Total stockholders' equity	$ (e)	$ 9,175	$ (t)

continued

Balance Sheets

Assets			
Cash	$ (f)	$ (o)	$ (u)
Land	0	(p)	2,500
Total assets	$11,000	$11,650	$10,550
Liabilities	$ (g)	$ (q)	$ 840
Stockholders' equity			
Common stock	(h)	(r)	9,410
Retained earnings	(i)	75	300
Total stockholders' equity	8,025	9,175	9,710
Total liabilities and stockholders' equity	$11,000	$11,650	$10,550

Statements of Cash Flows

Cash flows from operating activities			
Cash receipts from customers	$ (j)	$ 500	$ (v)
Cash payments for expenses	(k)	(400)	(w)
Net cash flows from operating activities	150	100	375
Cash flows from investing activities			
Cash payments for land	0	(5,000)	0
Cash receipt from sale of land	0	0	2,500
Net cash flows from investing activities	0	(5,000)	2,500
Cash flows from financing activities			
Cash receipts from borrowed funds	2,975	0	0
Cash payments to reduce debt	0	(500)	(x)
Cash receipts from stock issue	8,000	1,100	(y)
Cash payments for dividends	(125)	(50)	(z)
Net cash flows from financing activities	10,850	550	(1,475)
Net change in cash	11,000	(4,350)	1,400
Plus: Beginning cash balance	0	11,000	6,650
Ending cash balance	$11,000	$ 6,650	$ 8,050

Problem 2-43A   *Events for two complete accounting cycles*

LO 1-8

Alabama Service Company was formed on January 1, 2013.

Events Affecting the 2013 Accounting Period

1. Acquired cash of $60,000 from the issue of common stock.
2. Purchased $1,200 of supplies on account.
3. Purchased land that cost $18,000 cash.
4. Paid $800 cash to settle accounts payable created in Event 2.
5. Recognized revenue on account of $42,000.
6. Paid $21,000 cash for other operating expenses.
7. Collected $38,000 cash from accounts receivable.

Information for 2013 Adjusting Entries

8. Recognized accrued salaries of $3,200 on December 31, 2013.
9. Had $200 of supplies on hand at the end of the accounting period.

Events Affecting the 2014 Accounting Period

1. Acquired an additional $20,000 cash from the issue of common stock.
2. Paid $3,200 cash to settle the salaries payable obligation.
3. Paid $3,600 cash in advance for a lease on office facilities.
4. Sold land that had cost $15,000 for $15,000 cash.
5. Received $4,800 cash in advance for services to be performed in the future.

6. Purchased $1,000 of supplies on account during the year.

7. Provided services on account of $32,000.

8. Collected $33,000 cash from accounts receivable.

9. Paid a cash dividend of $5,000 to the stockholders.

10. Paid other operating expenses of $19,500.

Information for 2014 Adjusting Entries

11. The advance payment for rental of the office facilities (see Event 3) was made on March 1 for a one-year lease term.

12. The cash advance for services to be provided in the future was collected on October 1 (see Event 5). The one-year contract started October 1.

13. Had $300 of supplies on hand at the end of the period.

14. Recognized accrued salaries of $3,900 at the end of the accounting period.

15. Recognized $400 of accrued interest revenue.

Required

a. Identify each event affecting the 2013 and 2014 accounting periods as asset source (AS), asset use (AU), asset exchange (AE), or claims exchange (CE). Record the effects of each event under the appropriate general ledger account headings of the accounting equation.

b. Prepare an income statement, statement of changes in stockholders' equity, balance sheet, and statement of cash flows for 2013 and 2014, using the vertical statements model.

LO 9

Problem 2-44A   *Ethics*

Raula Kato discovered a material reporting error in accounting records of Sampoon, Inc. (SI), during the annual audit. The error was so significant that it will certainly have an adverse effect on the price of the client's stock which is actively traded on the western stock exchange. After talking to his close friend, and president of SI, Kato agreed to withhold the information until the president had time to sell his SI stock. Kato leaked the information to his parents so that they could sell their shares of stock as well. The reporting matter was a relatively complex issue that involved recently issued reporting standards. Kato told himself that if he were caught he would simply plead ignorance. He would simply say that he did not have time to keep up with the rapidly changing standards and he would be off the hook.

Required

a. Write a memo that identifies specific articles of the AICPA Code of Professional Conduct that were violated by Kato.

b. Would pleading ignorance relieve Kato from his audit responsibilities?

LO 1, 2, 3, 4, 5, 6

CHECK FIGURES
b. $1,400
h. $(81,000)

Problem 2-45A   *Effect of events on financial statements (Appendix)*

Oaks Company had the following balances in its accounting records as of December 31, 2013:

Assets		Claims	
Cash	$ 61,000	Accounts payable	$ 25,000
Accounts receivable	45,000	Common stock	90,000
Land	27,000	Retained earnings	18,000
Totals	$133,000		$133,000

The following accounting events apply to Oak's 2013 fiscal year:

Jan.   1   Acquired an additional $70,000 cash from the issue of common stock.

        1   Purchased a delivery van that cost $26,000 and that had an $7,000 salvage value and a five-year useful life.

Mar.   1   Borrowed $21,000 by issuing a note that had an 8 percent annual interest rate and a one-year term.

April   1   Paid $6,600 cash in advance for a one-year lease for office space.

June   1   Paid a $3,000 cash dividend to the stockholders.
July   1   Purchased land that cost $25,000 cash.
Aug.   1   Made a cash payment on accounts payable of $13,000.
Sept. 1   Received $8,400 cash in advance as a retainer for services to be performed monthly
           during the next eight months.
Oct.   1   Purchased $900 of supplies on account.
Nov.   1   Purchased a one-year $30,000 certificate of deposit that paid a 4 percent annual rate
           of interest.
Dec. 31   Earned $80,000 of service revenue on account during the year.
      31   Received $56,000 cash collections from accounts receivable.
      31   Incurred $16,000 other operating expenses on account during the year.
      31   Incurred accrued salaries expense of $5,000.
      31   Had $250 of supplies on hand at the end of the period.

Required

Based on the preceding information, answer the following questions. All questions pertain to the
2014 financial statements. (*Hint:* Record the events in general ledger accounts under an accounting equation before answering the questions.)

a. What additional five adjusting entries are required at the end of the year?
b. What amount of interest expense would Oaks report on the income statement?
c. What amount of net cash flow from operating activities would Oaks report on the statement
    of cash flows?
d. What amount of rent expense would Oaks report in the income statement?
e. What amount of total liabilities would Oaks report on the balance sheet?
f. What amount of supplies expense would Oaks report on the income statement?
g. What amount of unearned revenue would Oaks report on the balance sheet?
h. What amount of net cash flow from investing activities would Oaks report on the statement
    of cash flows?
i. What amount of interest payable would Oaks report on the balance sheet?
j. What amount of total expenses would Oaks report on the income statement?
k. What amount of retained earnings would Oaks report on the balance sheet?
l. What total amount of service revenues would Oaks report on the income statement?
m. What amount of cash flows from financing activities would Oaks report on the statement of
    cash flows?
n. What amount of net income would Oaks report on the income statement?

EXERCISES—SERIES B

Where applicable in all exercises, round computations to the nearest dollar.

Exercise 2-1B   *Effect of accruals on the financial statements*   LO 1, 2, 6, 7

Able Inc. experienced the following events in 2013, its first year of operations:

1. Received $20,000 cash from the issue of common stock.
2. Performed services on account for $56,000.
3. Paid the utility expense of $2,500.
4. Collected $48,000 of the accounts receivable.
5. Recorded $10,000 of accrued salaries at the end of the year.
6. Paid a $2,000 cash dividend to the stockholders.

Required

a. Record these events in general ledger accounts under an accounting equation. In the last
    column of the table, provide appropriate account titles for the Retained Earnings amounts.
    The first transaction has been recorded as an example.

	ABLE INC.						
	General Ledger Accounts						
Event	Assets		=	Liabilities	+	Stockholders' Equity		Acct. Titles for Ret. Earn.
	Cash	Accounts Receivable		Salaries Payable		Common Stock	Retained Earnings	
1.	20,000					20,000		

b. Prepare the income statement, statement of changes in stockholders' equity, balance sheet, and statement of cash flows for the 2013 accounting period.

c. Why is the ending cash balance the same as the net change in cash on the statement of cash flows?

LO 1

Exercise 2-2B *Effect of collecting accounts receivable on the accounting equation and financial statements*

Capaning Company earned $18,000 of revenue on account during 2013. The company collected $14,000 cash from accounts receivable during 2013.

Required

Based on this information alone, determine the following. (*Hint:* Record the events in general ledger accounts under an accounting equation before satisfying the requirements.)

a. The balance of accounts receivable that Capaning would report on the December 31, 2013, balance sheet.

b. The amount of net income that Capaning would report on the 2013 income statement.

c. The amount of net cash flow from operating activities that Capaning would report on the 2013 statement of cash flows.

d. The amount of retained earnings that Capaning would report on the December 31, 2013, balance sheet.

e. Why are the answers to Requirements *b* and *c* different?

LO 2

Exercise 2-3B *Effect of accrued expenses on the accounting equation and financial statements*

During 2013, Chung Corporation earned $8,000 of cash revenue and accrued $5,000 of salaries expense.

Required

Based on this information alone: (*Hint:* Record the events in general ledger accounts under an accounting equation before satisfying the requirements.)

a. Prepare the December 31, 2013, balance sheet.

b. Determine the amount of net income that Chung would report on the 2013 income statement.

c. Determine the amount of net cash flow from operating activities that Chung would report on the 2013 statement of cash flows.

d. Why are the answers to Requirements *b* and *c* different?

LO 1, 2, 6

Exercise 2-4B *Effect of accruals on the financial statements*

Bricca Inc. experienced the following events in 2013, its first year of operation:

1. Received $40,000 cash from the issue of common stock.
2. Performed services on account for $82,000.
3. Paid a $6,000 cash dividend to the stockholders.
4. Collected $76,000 of the accounts receivable.

5. Paid $53,000 cash for other operating expenses.
6. Performed services for $19,000 cash.
7. Recognized $3,500 of accrued utilities expense at the end of the year.

Required

a. Identify the events that result in revenue or expense recognition.
b. Based on your response to Requirement *a*, determine the amount of net income reported on the 2013 income statement.
c. Identify the events that affect the statement of cash flows.
d. Based on your response to Requirement *c*, determine the amount of cash flow from operating activities reported on the 2013 statement of cash flows.
e. What is the before- and after-closing balance in the service revenue account? What other accounts would be closed at the end of the accounting cycle?
f. What is the balance of the retained earnings account that appears on the 2013 balance sheet?

Exercise 2-5B *Effect of accounts receivable and accounts payable transactions on financial statements*   **LO 1, 2**

The following events apply to Culvin and Piper, a public accounting firm, for the 2013 accounting period:

1. Performed $70,000 of services for clients on account.
2. Performed $40,000 of services for cash.
3. Incurred $36,000 of other operating expenses on account.
4. Paid $10,000 cash to an employee for salary.
5. Collected $47,000 cash from accounts receivable.
6. Paid $16,000 cash on accounts payable.
7. Paid an $8,000 cash dividend to the stockholders.
8. Accrued salaries were $2,000 at the end of 2013.

Required

a. Show the effects of the events on the financial statements using a horizontal statements model like the following one. In the Case Flow column, use OA to designate operating activity, IA for investment activity, FA for financing activity, and NC for net change in cash. Use NA to indicate the element is not affected by the event. The first event is recorded as an example.

Event No.	Assets		=	Liabilities			+	Stk. Equity							Cash Flow
	Cash	+ Accts. Rec.	=	Accts. Pay.	+	Sal. Pay.	+	Ret. Earn.	Rev.	−	Exp.	=	Net Inc.		
1	NA	+ 70,000	=	NA	+	NA	+	70,000	70,000	−	NA	=	70,000		NA

b. What is the amount of total assets at the end of 2013?
c. What is the balance of accounts receivable at the end of 2013?
d. What is the balance of accounts payable at the end of 2013?
e. What is the difference between accounts receivable and accounts payable?
f. What is net income for 2013?
g. What is the amount of net cash flow from operating activities for 2013?

Exercise 2-6B *Missing information related to accruals*   **LO 1, 2**

Carver Inc. had a beginning balance of $4,000 in its Accounts Receivable account. The ending balance of Accounts Receivable was $4,500. During the period, Carver recognized $68,000 of revenue on account. Carver's Salaries Payable account has a beginning balance of $2,600 and an ending balance of $1,500. During the period, the company recognized $46,000 of accrued salaries expense.

Required

a. Based on the information provided, determine the amount of net income.

b. Based on the information provided, determine the amount of net cash flow from operating activities.

EXERCISES—SERIES B

LO 3, 6, 7

Exercise 2-7B   *Supplies on financial statements*

Expert Janitorial Services Inc. experienced the following events in 2013, its first year of operation:

1. Performed services for $35,000 cash.
2. Purchased $6,000 of supplies on account.
3. A physical count on December 31, 2013, found that there was $1,800 of supplies on hand.

Required

Based on this information alone

a. Record the events under an accounting equation.

b. Prepare an income statement, balance sheet, and statement of cash flows for the 2013 accounting period.

c. What is the balance in the Supplies account as of January 1, 2014?

d. What is the balance in the Supplies Expense account as of January 1, 2014?

LO 2, 3, 6

Exercise 2-8B   *Supplies and the financial statements model*

Copy Magic began the 2013 accounting period with $2,500 cash, $1,400 of common stock, and $1,100 of retained earnings. Copy Magic was affected by the following accounting events during 2013:

1. Purchased $3,600 of copier toner and other supplies on account.
2. Earned and collected $12,300 of cash revenue.
3. Paid $2,700 cash on accounts payable.
4. Adjusted the records to reflect the use of supplies. A physical count indicated that $250 of supplies was still on hand on December 31, 2013.

Required

a. Show the effects of the events on the financial statements using a horizontal statements model like the following one. In the Cash Flows column, use OA to designate operating activity, IA for investing activity, FA for financing activity, and NC for net change in cash. Use NA to indicate accounts not affected by the event. The beginning balances are entered in the following example:

Event No.	Assets			=	Liab.	+	Stockholders' Equity							
	Cash	+	Supplies	=	Accts. Pay.	+	Com. Stk.	+	Ret. Earn.	Rev.	−	Exp.	=	Net Inc.	Cash Flows
Beg. bal.	2,500	+	0	=	0	+	1,400	+	1,100	0	−	0	=	0	0

b. Explain the difference between the amount of net income and amount of net cash flow from operating activities.

LO 4, 6, 7

Exercise 2-9B   *Prepaid items on financial statements*

Secret Services Inc. experienced the following events in 2013, its first year of operation:

1. Performed counseling services for $36,000 cash.
2. On February 1, 2013, paid $18,000 cash to rent office space for the coming year.
3. Adjusted the accounts to reflect the amount of rent used during the year.

Required

Based on this information alone

a. Record the events under an accounting equation.

b. Prepare an income statement, balance sheet, and statement of cash flows for the 2013 accounting period.

c. Ignoring all other future events, what is the amount of rent expense that would be recognized in 2014?

Exercise 2-10B *Effect of an error on financial statements*   LO 4, 6

On April 1, 2013, Idaho Corporation paid $18,000 cash in advance for a one-year lease on an office building. Assume that Idaho records the prepaid rent as an asset and that the books are closed on December 31.

Required

a. Show the payment for the one-year lease and the related adjusting entry to recognize rent expense in the accounting equation.

b. Assume that Idaho Corporation failed to record the adjusting entry to reflect using the office building. How would the error affect the company's 2013 income statement and balance sheet?

Exercise 2-11B *Unearned items on financial statements*   LO 5, 6, 7

Young and Associates experienced the following events in 2013, its first year of operation:

1. On October 1, 2013, Young collected $54,000 for consulting services it agreed to provide during the coming year.

2. Adjusted the accounts to reflect the amount of consulting service revenue recognized in 2013.

Required

Based on this information alone

a. Record the events under an accounting equation.

b. Prepare an income statement, balance sheet, and statement of cash flows for the 2013 accounting period.

c. Ignoring all other future events, what is the amount of service revenue that would be recognized in 2014?

Exercise 2-12B *Unearned revenue and the financial statements model*   LO 5, 6

Chris Holmes started a personal financial planning business when he accepted $36,000 cash as advance payment for managing the financial assets of a large estate. Chris agreed to manage the estate for a 12-month period, beginning June 1, 2013.

Required

a. Show the effects of the advance payment and revenue recognition on the 2013 financial statements using a horizontal statements model like the following one. In the Cash Flows column, use OA to designate operating activity, IA for investing activity, FA for financing activity, and NC for net change in cash. Use NA if the account is not affected.

Event	Assets	=	Liab.	+	Stockholders' Equity	Rev.	−	Exp.	=	Net Inc.	Cash Flows
	Cash	=	Unearn. Rev.	+	Ret. Earn.						

b. How much revenue would Holmes recognize on the 2014 income statement?

c. What is the amount of cash flow from operating activities in 2014?

LO 5

Exercise 2-13B   *Unearned revenue defined as a liability*

Lan, an accounting major, and Pat, a marketing major, are watching a *Matlock* rerun on late-night TV. Of course, there is a murder and the suspect wants to hire Matlock as the defense attorney. Matlock will take the case but requires an advance payment of $150,000. Pat remarks that Matlock has earned a cool $150,000 without lifting a finger. Lan tells Pat that Matlock has not earned anything but has a $150,000 liability. Pat asks "How can that be?"

Required

Assume you are Lan. Explain to Pat why Matlock has a liability and when Matlock would actually earn the $150,000.

LO 2, 3, 5, 6

Exercise 2-14B   *Supplies, unearned revenue, and the financial statements model*

Roe, Attorney at Law, experienced the following transactions in 2013, the first year of operations:

1. Accepted $36,000 on April 1, 2013, as a retainer for services to be performed evenly over the next 12 months.
2. Performed legal services for cash of $54,000.
3. Purchased $2,800 of office supplies on account.
4. Paid $2,400 of the amount due on accounts payable.
5. Paid a cash dividend to the stockholders of $5,000.
6. Paid cash for operating expenses of $31,000.
7. Determined that at the end of the accounting period $200 of office supplies remained on hand.
8. On December 31, 2013, recognized the revenue that had been earned for services performed in accordance with Transaction 1.

Required

Show the effects of the events on the financial statements using a horizontal statements model like the following one. In the Cash Flows column, use the initials OA to designate operating activity, IA for investing activity, FA for financing activity, and NC for net change in cash. Use NA to indicate accounts not affected by the event. The first event has been recorded as an example.

Event No.	Assets			=	Liabilities			+	Stk. Equity							
	Cash	+	Supplies	=	Accts. Pay.	+	Unearn. Rev.	+	Ret. Earn.		Rev.	−	Exp.	=	Net Inc.	Cash Flow
1	36,000	+	NA	=	NA	+	36,000	+	NA		NA	−	NA	=	NA	36,000 OA

LO 4, 5, 6

Exercise 2-15B   *Prepaid vs. Unearned, the entity concept*

On October 1, 2013, Josh Smith, attorney, accepted an $10,800 cash advance from his client, James Company, for services to be performed over the next six months.

Required

a. Record the deferral and the related December 31, 2013, adjustment for Josh Smith in an accounting equation.
b. Record the deferral and the related December 31, 2013, adjustment for James Company in an accounting equation.

LO 6, 8

Exercise 2-16B   *Identifying transaction type and effect on the financial statements*

Required

Identify whether each of the following transactions is an asset source (AS), asset use (AU), asset exchange (AE), or claims exchange (CE). Also show the effects of the events on the financial statements using the horizontal statements model. Indicate whether the event increases (I), decreases (D), or does not affect (NA) each element of the financial statements. In the Cash Flows column, designate the cash flows as operating activities (OA), investing activities (IA), or financing activities (FA). The first two transactions have been recorded as examples.

Event No.	Type of Event	Assets	=	Liabilities	+	Stockholders' Equity Common Stock	+	Retained Earnings	Rev.	−	Exp.	=	Net Inc.	Cash Flows
a	AS	I		NA		NA		I	I		NA		I	I OA
b	AS	I		I		NA		NA	NA		NA		NA	NA

a. Provided services and collected cash.

b. Purchased supplies on account to be used in the future.

c. Paid cash in advance for one year's rent.

d. Paid cash to purchase land.

e. Paid a cash dividend to the stockholders.

f. Received cash from the issue of common stock.

g. Paid cash on accounts payable.

h. Collected cash from accounts receivable.

i. Received cash advance for services to be provided in the future.

j. Incurred other operating expenses on account.

k. Performed services on account.

l. Adjusted books to reflect the amount of prepaid rent expired during the period.

m. Paid cash for operating expenses.

n. Adjusted the books to record the supplies used during the period.

o. Recorded accrued salaries.

p. Paid cash for salaries accrued at the end of a prior period.

q. Recorded accrued interest revenue earned at the end of the accounting period.

Exercise 2-17B *Distinguishing between an expense and a cost*   LO 6

Amber Gray tells you that the accountants where she works are real hair splitters. For example, they make a big issue over the difference between a cost and an expense. She says the two terms mean the same thing to her.

Required

a. Explain to Amber the difference between a cost and an expense from an accountant's perspective.

b. Explain whether each of the following events produces an asset or an expense:

   (1) Purchased a building for cash.

   (2) Paid cash to purchase supplies.

   (3) Used supplies on hand to produce revenue.

   (4) Paid cash in advance for insurance.

   (5) Recognized accrued salaries.

Exercise 2-18B *Identifying deferral and accrual events*   LO 1, 2, 3, 4, 5, 6

Required

Identify each of the following events as an accrual, a deferral, or neither:

a. Paid cash in advance for a one-year insurance policy.

b. Paid cash to settle an account payable.

c. Collected accounts receivable.

d. Paid cash for current salaries expense.

e. Paid cash to purchase supplies.

f. Provided services on account.

g. Provided services and collected cash.

h. Paid cash to purchase land.

    i. Recognized accrued salaries at the end of the accounting period.

    j. Paid a cash dividend to the stockholders.

    k. Recognized accrued interest revenue at the end of the period.

LO 6

Exercise 2-19B *Adjusting the accounts*

Victory Associates experienced the following accounting events during its 2013 accounting period.

  1. Recognized revenue on account.

  2. Issued common stock.

  3. Paid cash to purchase supplies.

  4. Collected a cash advance for services that will be provided during the coming year.

  5. Paid a cash dividend to the stockholders.

  6. Paid cash for an insurance policy that provides coverage during the next year.

  7. Collected cash from accounts receivable.

  8. Paid cash for operating expenses.

  9. Paid cash to settle an account payable.

10. Paid cash to purchase land.

Required

a. Identify the events that would require a year-end adjusting entry.

b. Explain why adjusting entries are made at the end of the accounting period.

LO 6

Exercise 2-20B *Revenue and expense recognition*

Required

a. Describe an expense recognition event that results in an increase in liabilities.

b. Describe an expense recognition event that results in a decrease in assets.

c. Describe a revenue recognition event that results in a decrease in liabilities.

d. Describe a revenue recognition event that results in an increase in assets.

LO 6, 7

Exercise 2-21B *Classifying events on the statement of cash flows*

The following transactions pertain to the operations of Luckett Company for 2013:

  1. Acquired $30,000 cash from the issue of common stock.

  2. Provided $65,000 of services on account.

  3. Paid $22,000 cash on accounts payable.

  4. Performed services for $8,000 cash.

  5. Collected $51,000 cash from accounts receivable.

  6. Incurred $37,000 of operating expenses on account.

  7. Paid $6,500 cash for one year's rent in advance.

  8. Paid a $4,000 cash dividend to the stockholders.

  9. Paid $1,200 cash for supplies to be used in the future.

10. Recognized $3,100 of accrued salaries expense.

Required

a. Classify the cash flows from each of these transactions as operating activities (OA), investing activities (IA), or financing activities (FA). Use NA for transactions that do not affect the statement of cash flows.

b. Prepare a statement of cash flows. (This is the first year of operations.)

LO 1, 2, 6

Exercise 2-22B *Net income versus changes in cash*

In 2013, Ring Company billed its customers $90,000 for services performed. The company subsequently collected $73,000 of the amount billed. Ring incurred $72,000 of operating expenses on account. Ring paid $65,000 of that amount. Ring acquired $30,000 cash from the issue of common stock. The company invested $25,000 cash in the purchase of land.

Required

Use the preceding information to answer the following questions. (*Hint:* Identify the six events described in the paragraph and record them in general ledger accounts under an accounting equation before answering the questions.)

a. What amount of revenue will Ring report on the 2013 income statement?

b. What is the net income for the period?

c. What amount of cash flow from revenue will Ring report on the statement of cash flows?

d. What is the net cash flow from operating activities for the period?

e. Why is the amount of net income different from the net cash flow from operating activities for the period?

f. What is the amount of net cash flow from investing activities?

g. What is the amount of net cash flow from financing activities?

h. What amount of total equity will Ring report on the year-end balance sheet?

Exercise 2-23B   *Relationship of accounts to financial statements*   LO 7

Required

Identify whether each of the following items would appear on the income statement (IS), statement of changes in stockholders' equity (SE), balance sheet (BS), or statement of cash flows (CF). If some items appear on more than one statement, identify all applicable statements. If an item will not appear on any financial statement, label it NA.

a. Supplies

b. Cash Flow from Financing Activities

c. "As of" Date Notation

d. Ending Retained Earnings

e. Net Income

f. Dividends

g. Net Change in Cash

h. "For the Period Ended"

i. Land

j. Ending Common Stock

k. Salaries Expense

l. Prepaid Rent

m. Accounts Payable

n. Total Assets

o. Salaries Payable

p. Insurance Expense

q. Notes Payable

r. Accounts Receivable

s. Accrued Interest Receivable

t. Interest Revenue

u. Rent Expense

v. Price/earnings Ratio

w. Taxes Payable

x. Unearned Revenue

y. Service Revenue

z. Cash Flow from Investing Activities

aa. Consulting Revenue

bb. Utilities Expense

cc. Ending Common Stock

dd. Total Liabilities

ee. Operating Cycle

ff. Cash Flow from Operating Activities

gg. Operating Expenses

hh. Supplies Expense

ii. Beginning Retained Earnings

jj. Beginning Common Stock

kk. Prepaid Insurance

ll. Salary Expense

mm. Beginning Cash Balance

nn. Ending Cash Balance

Exercise 2-24B   *Effect of accounting events on the income statement and statement*   LO 1, 2, 3, 4, 5, 6
of cash flows

Required

Explain how each of the following events or series of events and any related adjusting entry will affect the amount of *net income* and the amount of *cash flow from operating activities* reported on the year-end financial statements. Identify the direction of change (increase, decrease, or NA) and the amount of the change. Organize your answers according to the following table. The first event is recorded as an example. If an event does not have a related adjusting entry, record only the effects of the event.

	Net Income		Cash Flows from Operating Activities	
Event No.	Direction of Change	Amount of Change	Direction of Change	Amount of Change
a	NA	NA	Decrease	$9,000
Adj	Decrease	$2,250	NA	NA

a. Paid $9,000 cash on October 1 to purchase a one-year insurance policy.

b. Purchased $2,000 of supplies on account. Paid $500 cash on accounts payable. The ending balance in the Supplies account, after adjustment, was $300.

c. Provided services for $10,000 cash.

d. Collected $2,400 in advance for services to be performed in the future. The contract called for services to start on May 1 and to continue for one year.

e. Accrued salaries amounting to $5,600.

f. Sold land that cost $3,000 for $3,000 cash.

g. Acquired $15,000 cash from the issue of common stock.

h. Earned $12,000 of revenue on account. Collected $8,000 cash from accounts receivable.

i. Paid cash operating expenses of $4,500.

LO 6

Exercise 2-25B   *Closing the accounts*

The following information was drawn from the accounting records of Dorman Company as of December 31, 2013, before the temporary accounts had been closed. The company's cash balance was $3,600, and its land account had a $8,000 balance. Notes payable amounted to $4,000. The balance in the Common Stock account was $2,000. The company had revenues of $7,500 and expenses of $3,400, and dividends amounted to $1,000.

Required

a. Identify the accounts that would be closed to Retained Earnings at the end of the accounting period.

b. Assuming that Dorman's beginning balance (as of January 1, 2013) in the Retained Earnings account was $2,500, determine its balance after the temporary accounts were closed at the end of 2013.

c. What amount of net income would Dorman Company report on its 2013 income statement?

d. Explain why the amount of net income differs from the amount of the ending Retained Earnings balance.

e. What are the balances in the revenue, expense, and dividend accounts on January 1, 2014?

LO 6

Exercise 2-26B   *Closing accounts and the accounting cycle*

Required

a. Identify which of the following accounts are temporary (will be closed to Retained Earnings at the end of the year) and which are permanent:

(1) Other Operating Expenses

(2) Utilities Expense

(3) Retained Earnings

(4) Salaries Expense

(5) Land

(6) Dividends

(7) Service Revenue

(8) Cash

(9) Salaries Payable

(10) Common Stock

b. Sam bragged that he had five years of accounting experience. Susan disagreed, responding, "No. You have had one year of accounting experience five times." Explain what Susan meant. (*Hint:* Refer to the accounting cycle.)

Exercise 2-27B *Closing entries*

LO 6

Baker Company's accounting records show a $42,100 balance in its Retained Earnings account on January 1, 2013. During the 2013 accounting cycle Baker earned $19,400 of revenue, incurred $9,800 of expense, and paid $500 of dividends. Revenues and expenses were recognized evenly throughout the accounting period.

Required

a. Determine the after-closing balance in the Retained Earnings account as of December 31, 2012.
b. Determine the before-closing balance in the temporary accounts as of December 31, 2013.
c. Determine the after-closing balance in the Retained Earnings account as of December 31, 2013.
d. Determine the balance in the Retained Earnings account as of June 30, 2013.

Exercise 2-28B *Matching concept*

LO 6

Companies make sacrifices known as *expenses* to obtain benefits called *revenues*. The accurate measurement of net income requires that expenses be matched with revenues. In some circumstances matching a particular expense directly with revenue is difficult or impossible. In these circumstances, the expense is matched with the period in which it is incurred.

Required

a. Identify an expense that could be matched directly with revenue.
b. Identify a period expense that would be difficult to match with revenue. Explain why.

Exercise 2-29B *Transactions that affect the elements of financial statements*

LO 8

Required

Give an example of a transaction that will do the following:

a. Increase an asset and increase equity (asset source event).
b. Decrease an asset and decrease equity (asset use event).
c. Increase an asset and decrease another asset (asset exchange event).
d. Decrease a liability and increase equity (claims exchange event).
e. Increase a liability and decrease equity (claims exchange event).
f. Increase an asset and increase a liability (asset source event).
g. Decrease an asset and decrease a liability (asset use event).

Exercise 2-30B *Identifying source, use, and exchange transactions*

LO 8

Required

Indicate whether each of the following transactions is an asset source (AS), asset use (AU), asset exchange (AE), or claims exchange (CE) transaction.

a. Acquired cash from the issue of stock.
b. Paid a cash dividend to the stockholders.
c. Paid cash on accounts payable.
d. Incurred other operating expenses on account.
e. Paid cash for rent expense.
f. Performed services for cash.
g. Performed services for clients on account.
h. Collected cash from accounts receivable.
i. Received cash for services to be performed in the future.
j. Purchased land with cash.

LO 8

Exercise 2-31B   *Identifying asset source, use, and exchange transactions*

Required

a. Name an asset use transaction that will *not* affect the income statement.

b. Name an asset exchange transaction that will affect the statement of cash flows.

c. Name an asset source transaction that will *not* affect the income statement.

d. Name an asset source transaction that will *not* affect the statement of cash flows.

e. Name an asset source transaction that will affect the income statement.

LO 9

Exercise 2-32B   *Ethical conduct*

In February 2006, former senator Warren Rudman of New Hampshire completed a 17-month investigation of an $11 billion accounting scandal at Fannie Mae (a major enterprise involved in home-mortgage financing). The Rudman investigation concluded that Fannie Mae's CFO and controller used an accounting gimmick to manipulate financial statements in order to meet earning-per-share (EPS) targets. Meeting the EPS targets triggered bonus payments for the executives.

Required

Comment on the provisions of SOX that pertain to intentional misrepresentation and describe the maximum penalty that the CFO could face.

LO 11

Exercise 2-33B   *Effects of recognizing accrued interest on financial statements (Appendix)*

Arthur Troy started Troy Company on January 1, 2013. The company experienced the following events during its first year of operation:

1. Earned $6,200 of cash revenue.

2. Borrowed $5,000 cash from the bank.

3. Adjusted the accounting records to recognize accrued interest expense on the bank note. The note, issued on September 1, 2013, had a one-year term and a 9 percent annual interest rate.

Required

a. What is the amount of interest payable at December 31, 2013?

b. What is the amount of interest expense in 2013?

c. What is the amount of interest paid in 2013?

d. Use a horizontal statements model to show how each event affects the balance sheet, income statement, and statement of cash flows. Indicate whether the event increases (I) decreases (D), or does not affect (NA) each element of the financial statements. Also, in the Cash Flows column, designate the cash flows as operating activities (OA), investing activities (IA), or financing activities (FA). The first transaction has been recorded as an example.

Event No.	Balance Sheet										Income Statement							Statement of Cash Flows
	Cash	=	Note Pay.	+	Int. Pay.	+	C. Stk.	+	Ret. Earn.		Rev.	−	Exp.	=	Net Inc.			
1	I	=	NA	+	NA	+	NA	+	I		I	−	NA	=	I			I OA

LO 11

Exercise 2-34B   *Recognizing accrued interest revenue (Appendix)*

Texas Company invested $90,000 in a certificate of deposit on August 1, 2013. The certificate had a 6 percent annual rate of interest and a one-year term to maturity.

Required

a. What amount of interest revenue will Texas recognize for the year ending December 31, 2013?

b. Show how the December 31, 2013, adjusting entry to recognize the accrued interest revenue affect the accounting equation.

c. What amount of cash will Texas collect for interest revenue in 2013?

d. What is the amount of interest receivable as of December 31, 2013?

e. What amount of cash will Texas collect for interest revenue in 2014, assuming it does not renew the CD?

f. What amount of interest revenue will Texas recognize in 2014, assuming it does not renew the CD?

g. What is the amount of interest receivable as of December 31, 2014, assuming it does not renew the CD?

Exercise 2-35B   *Effect of depreciation on the accounting equation and financial statements (Appendix)*

LO 10

The following events apply to Dill's Diner for the 2013 fiscal year:

1. Started the company when it acquired $40,000 cash by issuing common stock.
2. Purchased a new stove that cost $26,000 cash.
3. Earned $21,000 in cash revenue.
4. Paid $3,500 of cash for salaries expense.
5. Adjusted the records to reflect the use of the stove. Purchased on January 1, 2013, the stove has an expected useful life of four years and an estimated salvage value of $4,000. Use straight-line depreciation. The adjusting entry was made as of December 31, 2013.

Required

a. Write an accounting equation and record the effects of each accounting event under the appropriate general ledger account headings.

b. Prepare a balance sheet and a statement of cash flows for the 2013 accounting period.

c. What is the net income for 2013?

d. What is the amount of depreciation expense Dill's would report on the 2014 income statement?

e. What amount of accumulated depreciation would Dill's report on the December 31, 2014, balance sheet?

f. Would the cash flow from operating activities be affected by depreciation in 2014?

Exercise 2-36B   *Depreciation affecting multiple cycles*

LO 10

On January 1, 2013, Hartland Inc. paid $34,000 cash to purchase a taxi cab. The taxi had a four-year useful life and a $4,000 salvage value.

Required

a. Determine the amount of depreciation expense that would appear on the 2013 and 2014 income statements.

b. Determine the amount of accumulated depreciation that would appear on the 2013 and 2014 balance sheets.

c. Explain how the purchase of equipment would affect the 2013 and 2014 statements of cash flows.

PROBLEMS—SERIES B

Problem 2-37B   *Recording events in a horizontal statements model*

LO 1, 2, 3, 4, 5, 6

The following events pertain to Jack's Inc.:

1. Acquired $10,000 cash from the issue of common stock.
2. Provided $15,000 of services on account.
3. Provided services for $5,000 cash.
4. Received $2,800 cash in advance for services to be performed in the future.
5. Collected $12,200 cash from the account receivable created in Event 2.
6. Paid $1,900 for cash expenses.
7. Performed $1,400 of the services agreed to in Event 4.

8. Incurred $3,600 of expenses on account.

9. Paid $4,800 cash in advance for one-year contract to rent office space.

10. Paid $2,800 cash on the account payable created in Event 8.

11. Paid a $1,500 cash dividend to the stockholders.

12. Recognized rent expense for nine months' use of office space acquired in Event 9.

Required

Show the effects of the events on the financial statements using a horizontal statements model like the following one. In the Cash Flows column, use the letters OA to designate operating activity, IA for investing activity, FA for financing activity, and NC for net change in cash. Use NA to indicate accounts not affected by the event. The first event is recorded as an example.

Event No.	Assets			=	Liabilities			+	Stockholders' Equity						
	Cash +	Accts. Rec. +	Prep. Rent =		Accts. Pay. +	Unearn. Rev. +			Common Stock +	Ret. Earn.	Rev. −	Exp. =	Net Inc.		Cash Flows
1	10,000 +	NA +	NA =		NA +	NA +			10,000 +	NA	NA −	NA =	NA		10,000 FA

LO 2, 3, 4, 5, 6

Problem 2-38B *Effect of adjusting entries on the accounting equation*

Required

Each of the following independent events requires a year-end adjusting entry. Show how each event and its related adjusting entry affects the accounting equation. Assume a December 31 closing date. The first event is recorded as an example.

	Total Assets						Stockholders' Equity		
Event/ Adjustment	Cash	+	Other Assets	=	Liabilities	+	Common Stock	+	Retained Earnings
a	−4,800		+4,800		NA		NA		NA
Adj.	NA		−1,200		NA		NA		−1,200

a. Paid $4,800 cash in advance on October 1 for a one-year insurance policy.

b. Received an $3,600 cash advance for a contract to provide services in the future. The contract required a one-year commitment, starting April 1.

c. Purchased $1,200 of supplies on account. At year's end, $175 of supplies remained on hand.

d. Paid $9,600 cash in advance on August 1 for a one-year lease on office space.

LO 6

Problem 2-39B *Closing the accounts*

The following data were taken from the records of Wathen Company. Except as otherwise indicated, all balances are as of December 31, 2013, before the closing entries had been recorded.

Consulting revenue	$18,200
Cash	35,600
Cash received from common stock issued during 2013	6,000
Travel expense	2,100
Dividends	4,000
Cash flow from investing activities	5,200
Rent expense	3,500
Payment to reduce debt principal	10,000
Retained earnings, January 1, 2013	16,200
Salary expense	7,200
Cash flow from operating activities	2,600
Common stock, December 31, 2013	16,000
Other operating expenses	2,300

Required

a. Identify the accounts that should be closed to the Retained Earnings account.

b. Prepare the income statement that Wathen would include in its 2013 annual report.

c. Determine the Retained Earnings account balance at December 31, 2013. Explain how the company could pay cash dividends in excess of the amount of net income earned in 2013.

d. Name the stages of the accounting cycle in the order in which they normally occur.

Problem 2-40B   *Effect of events on financial statements*   LO 1, 2, 3, 4, 5, 6

Barker Company had the following balances in its accounting records as of December 31, 2012:

Assets		Liabilities and Equity	
Cash	$35,000	Accounts Payable	$ 7,500
Accounts Receivable	9,000	Common Stock	40,000
Land	51,000	Retained Earnings	47,500
Total	$95,000	Total	$95,000

The following accounting events apply to Barker Company's 2013 fiscal year:

Jan.   1   Acquired $20,000 cash from the issue of common stock.
Feb.   1   Paid $6,000 cash in advance for a one-year lease for office space.
Mar.   1   Paid a $2,000 cash dividend to the stockholders.
April 1   Purchased additional land that cost $15,000 cash.
May   1   Made a cash payment on accounts payable of $5,500.
July   1   Received $9,600 cash in advance as a retainer for services to be performed monthly over the coming year.
Sept. 1   Sold land for $30,000 cash that had originally cost $30,000.
Oct.   1   Purchased $2,500 of supplies on account.
Dec. 31   Earned $58,000 of service revenue on account during the year.
       31   Received cash collections from accounts receivable amounting to $46,000.
       31   Incurred other operating expenses on account during the year that amounted to $28,000.
       31   Recognized accrued salaries expense of $6,500.
       31   Had $50 of supplies on hand at the end of the period.
       31   The land purchased on April 1 had a market value of $20,000.
       31   Recognized $500 of accrued interest revenue.

Required

Based on the preceding information, answer the following questions for Barker Company. All questions pertain to the 2013 financial statements. (*Hint:* Enter items in general ledger accounts under the accounting equation before answering the questions.)

a. Based on the preceding transactions, identify two additional adjustments and describe them.

b. What amount would Barker report for land on the balance sheet?

c. What amount of net cash flow from operating activities would be reported on the statement of cash flows?

d. What amount of rent expense would be reported in the income statement?

e. What amount of total liabilities would be reported on the balance sheet?

f. What amount of supplies expense would be reported on the income statement?

g. What amount of unearned revenue would be reported on the balance sheet?

h. What amount of net cash flow from investing activities would be reported on the statement of cash flows?

i. What amount of total expenses would be reported on the income statement?

j. What amount of service revenue would be reported on the income statement?

k. What amount of cash flows from financing activities would be reported on the statement of cash flows?

l. What amount of net income would be reported on the income statement?

m. What amount of retained earnings would be reported on the balance sheet?

LO 7

Problem 2-41B   *Preparing financial statements*

The following accounts and balances were drawn from the records of Griffin Company:

Required

The following accounts and balances were drawn from the 2013 accounting records of Griffin Company. Use the information to construct an income statement, statement of changes in stockholders' equity, balance sheet, and statement of cash flows. (Show only totals for each activity on the statement of cash flows.)

Supplies	$ 1,000	Beginning retained earnings	$ 9,300
Cash flow from investing act.	(5,200)	Cash flow from financing act.	(5,000)
Prepaid insurance	1,200	Rent expense	2,500
Service revenue	65,200	Dividends	3,000
Other operating expenses	41,000	Cash	48,000
Supplies expense	1,100	Accounts receivable	14,200
Insurance expense	2,100	Prepaid rent	4,800
Beginning common stock	40,000	Unearned revenue	6,400
Cash flow from operating act.	15,600	Land	24,000
Common stock issued	5,000	Accounts payable	17,000

LO 7

CHECK FIGURES
a. ($500)
o. $600

Problem 2-42B   *Missing information in financial statements*

Required

Fill in the blanks (as indicated by the alphabetic letters in parentheses) in the following financial statements. Assume the company started operations January 1, 2013, and that all transactions involve cash.

	For the Years		
	2013	2014	2015
Income Statements			
Revenue	$ 700	$ 1,300	$ 2,000
Expense	(a)	(700)	(1,300)
Net income	$ 200	$ (m)	$ 700
Statements of Changes in Stockholders' Equity			
Beginning common stock	$ 0	$ (n)	$ 6,000
Plus: Common stock issued	5,000	1,000	2,000
Ending common stock	5,000	6,000	(t)
Beginning retained earnings	0	100	200
Plus: Net income	(b)	(o)	700
Less: Dividends	(c)	(500)	(300)
Ending retained earnings	100	(p)	600
Total stockholders' equity	$ (d)	$ 6,200	$ 8,600
Balance Sheets			
Assets			
Cash	$ (e)	$ (q)	$ (u)
Land	0	(r)	8,000
Total assets	$ (f)	$11,200	$10,600
Liabilities	$ (g)	$ 5,000	$ 2,000
Stockholders' equity			
Common stock	(h)	(s)	8,000
Retained earnings	(i)	200	600
Total stockholders' equity	(j)	6,200	8,600
Total liabilities and stockholders' equity	$8,100	$11,200	$10,600

continued

Statements of Cash Flows			
Cash flows from operating activities			
Cash receipts from customers	$ (k)	$ 1,300	$ (v)
Cash payments for expenses	(l)	(700)	(w)
Net cash flows from operating activities	200	600	700
Cash flows from investing activities			
Cash payments for land	0	(8,000)	0
Cash flows from financing activities			
Cash receipts from loan	3,000	3,000	0
Cash payments to reduce debt	0	(1,000)	(x)
Cash receipts from stock issue	5,000	1,000	(y)
Cash payments for dividends	(100)	(500)	(z)
Net cash flows from financing activities	7,900	2,500	(1,300)
Net change in cash	8,100	(4,900)	(600)
Plus: Beginning cash balance	0	8,100	3,200
Ending cash balance	$8,100	$ 3,200	$ 2,600

Problem 2-43B   *Events for two complete accounting cycles*   LO 1–8

Andrews Company was formed on January 1, 2013.

Events Affecting the 2013 Accounting Period

1. Acquired $20,000 cash from the issue of common stock.
2. Purchased $800 of supplies on account.
3. Purchased land that cost $14,000 cash.
4. Paid $800 cash to settle accounts payable created in Event 2.
5. Recognized revenue on account of $10,500.
6. Paid $3,800 cash for other operating expenses.
7. Collected $7,000 cash from accounts receivable.

Information for 2013 Adjusting Entries

8. Recognized accrued salaries of $3,600 on December 31, 2013.
9. Had $100 of supplies on hand at the end of the accounting period.

Events Affecting the 2014 Accounting Period

1. Acquired $15,000 cash from the issue of common stock.
2. Paid $3,600 cash to settle the salaries payable obligation.
3. Paid $9,000 cash in advance to lease office space.
4. Sold the land that cost $14,000 for $14,000 cash.
5. Received $6,000 cash in advance for services to be performed in the future.
6. Purchased $2,400 of supplies on account during the year.
7. Provided services on account of $14,500.
8. Collected $12,600 cash from accounts receivable.
9. Paid a cash dividend of $2,000 to the stockholders.

Information for 2014 Adjusting Entries

10. The advance payment for rental of the office space (see Event 3) was made on March 1 for a one-year term.
11. The cash advance for services to be provided in the future was collected on October 1 (see Event 5). The one-year contract started on October 1.
12. Had $300 of supplies remaining on hand at the end of the period.
13. Recognized accrued salaries of $4,800 at the end of the accounting period.

Required

a. Identify each event affecting the 2013 and 2014 accounting periods as an asset source (AS), asset use (AU), asset exchange (AE), or claims exchange (CE). Record the effects of each event under the appropriate general ledger account headings of the accounting equation.

b. Prepare an income statement, statement of changes in stockholders' equity, balance sheet, and statement of cash flows for 2013 and 2014, using the vertical statements model.

LO 9

Problem 2-44B *Ethics*

Pete Chalance is an accountant with a shady past. Suffice it to say that he owes some very unsavory characters a lot of money. Despite his past, Pete works hard at keeping up a strong professional image. He is a manager at Smith and Associates, a fast-growing CPA firm. Pete is highly regarded around the office because he is a strong producer of client revenue. Indeed, on several occasions he exceeded his authority in establishing prices with clients. This is typically a partner's job but who could criticize Pete, who is most certainly bringing in the business. Indeed, Pete is so good that he is able to pull off the following scheme. He bills clients at inflated rates and then reports the ordinary rate to his accounting firm. Say for example, the normal charge for a job is $2,500. Pete will smooth talk the client, then charge him $3,000. He reports the normal charge of $2,500 to his firm and keeps the extra $500 for himself. He knows it isn't exactly right because his firm gets its regular charges and the client willingly pays for the services rendered. He thinks to himself, as he pockets his ill-gotten gains, who is getting hurt anyway?

Required

The text discusses three common features (conditions) that motivate ethical misconduct. Identify and explain each of the three features as they appear in the above scenario.

LO 1–6, 10, 11

Problem 2-45B *Effect of events on financial statements (Appendix)*

Porser Company had the following balances in its accounting records as of December 31, 2013:

Assets		Claims	
Cash	$26,000	Accounts payable	$ 5,000
Accounts receivable	9,000	Common stock	28,000
Land	42,000	Retained earnings	44,000
Total	$77,000	Total	$77,000

The following accounting events apply to Porser Company's 2014 fiscal year:

Jan. 1 Acquired $15,000 cash from the issue of common stock.
      1 Purchased a truck that cost $22,000 and had a $2,000 salvage value and a four-year useful life.
Feb. 1 Borrowed $12,000 by issuing a note that had a 9 percent annual interest rate and a one-year term.
      1 Paid $3,000 cash in advance for a one-year lease for office space.
Mar. 1 Paid a $2,000 cash dividend to the stockholders.
April 1 Purchased land that cost $28,000 cash.
May   1 Made a cash payment on accounts payable of $4,000.
July 1 Received $5,400 cash in advance as a retainer for services to be performed monthly over the next 12 months.
Sept. 1 Sold land for $42,000 that originally cost $42,000.
Oct. 1 Purchased $5,000 of supplies on account.

Nov. 1   Purchased a one-year $50,000 certificate of deposit that paid a 6 percent annual rate of interest.

Dec. 31   Earned $42,000 of service revenue on account during the year.

     31   Received cash collections from accounts receivable amounting to $40,000.

     31   Incurred other operating expenses on account during the year that amounted to $6,000.

     31   Incurred accrued salaries expense of $5,200.

     31   Had $200 of supplies on hand at the end of the period.

Required

Based on the preceding information, answer the following questions. All questions pertain to the 2014 financial statements. (*Hint:* Enter items in general ledger accounts under the accounting equation before answering the questions.)

a. Based on the preceding transaction, identify five additional adjustments and describe them.

b. What amount of interest expense would Porser report on the income statement?

c. What amount of net cash flow from operating activities would Porser report on the statement of cash flows?

d. What amount of rent expense would Porser report in the income statement?

e. What amount of total liabilities would Porser report on the balance sheet?

f. What amount of supplies expense would Porser report on the income statement?

g. What amount of unearned revenue would Porser report on the balance sheet?

h. What amount of net cash flow from investing activities would Porser report on the statement of cash flows?

i. What amount of interest payable would Porser report on the balance sheet?

j. What amount of total expenses would Porser report on the income statement?

k. What amount of retained earnings would Porser report on the balance sheet?

l. What amount of service revenues would Porser report on the income statement?

m. What amount of cash flows from financing activities would Porser report on the statement of cash flows?

n. What amount of net income would Porser report on the income statement?

ANALYZE, THINK, COMMUNICATE

ATC 2-1 Business Applications Case   *Understanding real-world annual reports*

Required

Use the Target Corporation annual report in Appendix B to answer the following questions:

Target Corporation

a. Which accounts on Target's balance sheet are accrual type accounts?

b. Which accounts on Target's balance sheet are deferral type accounts?

c. Compare Target's *net income* to its *cash provided by operating activities* for the fiscal-year ended January 29, 2011 (2010). Which is larger?

d. First, compare Target's 2009 net income to its 2010 net income. Next, compare Target's 2009 cash provided by operating activities to its 2010 cash provided by operating activities. Which changed the most from 2009 to 2010, net income or cash provided by operating activities?

ATC 2-2 Group Assignment   *Missing information*

Verizon Communications, Inc., is one of the world's largest providers of communication services. The following information, taken from the company's annual reports, is available for the years 2010, 2009, and 2008:

	2010	2009	2008
Revenues	$106,565	$107,808	$97,354
Operating expenses	91,920	91,830	94,742

In 2007, Verizon's operating income was $15,578. Operating income is a subcategory of net income.

Required

a. Divide the class into groups of four or five students. Organize the groups into three sections. Assign each section of groups the financial data for one of the preceding accounting periods.

Group Tasks

(1) Determine the amount of net income for the year assigned.

(2) How does the result in item 1 above affect the retained earnings of the company?

(3) Compute the percentage growth rate for each year.

(4) Have representatives from each section put the income statement for their respective year on the board.

Class Discussion

b. Have the class discuss the trend in revenue and net income.

ATC 2-3   Business Application Case   *Analyzing earnings information using real-world data*

The following data are based on information in the 2010 annual report of Cracker Barrel Old Country Store. As of September 30, 2010, Cracker Barrel operated 595 restaurants and gift shops in 41 states. Dollar amounts are in thousands.

	2010	2009
Assets	$1,292,067	$1,245,181
Liabilities	1,100,450	1,109,559
Stockholders' equity	191,617	135,622
Revenues	2,404,515	2,367,285
Expenses	2,319,257	2,301,359
Dividends	18,465	18,131
Retained earnings at end of 2008		$ 119,450

Required

a. Calculate the company's net income and retained earnings for 2009 and 2010.

b. Which increased (or decreased) by the greatest percentage amount: revenues or net income? Show your computations.

c. For each year, calculate the company's net income as a percentage of its revenues. Show your computations.

d. Did the company perform better in 2009 or 2010? Explain your answer.

ATC 2-4   Business Application Case   *Analyzing cash flow information using real-world data*

The following data are based on information in the 2010 annual report of Buffalo Wild Wings, Inc. As of December 26, 2010, there were 732 Buffalo Wild Wings restaurants in 44 states. The parent company owned 259 and 473 were franchised. Dollar amounts are in thousands.

	2010	2009
Assets	$380,357	$309,073
Liabilities	123,536	99,240
Stockholders' equity	256,821	209,833
Revenues	613,256	538,924
Expenses	574,856	508,253
Cash flows from operating activities	89,699	79,286
Cash flows from investing activities	(85,226)	(79,172)
Cash flows from financing activities	1,265	1,119
Cash balance at the beginning of 2009 was $8,347		

Required

a. Calculate the company's net change in cash for 2009 and 2010.

b. Calculate the company's ending cash balance for 2009 and 2010.

c. Notice that cash flows from investing activities were negative for each year. Do you think this represents something positive or negative about the company? Explain your answer.

ATC 2-5   Business Application Case   *Analyzing earnings information at two real-world companies*

The following data are based on information in the 2010 annual reports of Aéropostale, Inc., and American Eagle Outfitters, Inc. Dollar amounts are in thousands.

Aéropostale, Inc. is a retailer of casual apparel and accessories, targeting 14- to 17-year-old young women and young men. As of January 31, 2010, it operated 894 stores in 49 states and Puerto Rico, and 44 in Canada.

American Eagle Outfitters, Inc., is a retailer of clothing, accessories targeting 15- to 25-year-old customers. As of January 31, 2010, it operated 938 American Eagle Outfitters stores in the United States and Canada.

	Aeropostale	American Eagle Outfitters
Assets	$ 792,309	$2,138,148
Liabilities	357,820	559,631
Stockholders' equity	434,489	1,578,517
Revenues	2,230,105	2,990,520
Expenses	2,000,648	2,821,498
Dividends	—	83,906
Retained earnings at end of 2009	693,333	1,694,161

Required

a. Calculate each company's net income and retained earnings for 2010.

b. For each company, calculate its net earnings as a percentage of its revenues. Show your computations.

c. Which company performed better in 2010? Explain your answer.

ATC 2-6   Business Application Case   *Analyzing cash flow information at two real-world companies*

The following data are based on information in the 2010 annual reports of H&R Block, Inc., and Jackson Hewitt Tax Services, Inc. Dollar amounts are in thousands.

H&R Block, Inc., has subsidiaries that provide tax, investment, retail banking, accounting, and business consulting services and products in the United States, Canada, and Australia. For the fiscal year ended June 30, 2010, the company served approximately 23.2 million customers.

In the fiscal year ended April 30, 2010, Jackson Hewitt Tax Services, Inc., had a network of 6,407 franchised and company-owned offices that provided computerized preparation of individual income tax returns in the United States. These offices prepared 2.53 million tax returns.

	H&R Block	Jackson Hewitt
Assets	$5,234,318	$346,424
Liabilities	3,793,688	371,559
Stockholders' equity	1,440,630	(25,135)
Revenues	3,874,332	213,762
Expenses	3,395,090	486,021
Cash flows from operating activities	587,469	(5,013)
Cash flows from investing activities	31,353	(20,942)
Cash flows from financing activities	(481,118)	36,495
Cash balance at the beginning of 2010	1,654,663	306

Required

a. Calculate each company's net income and net change in cash for 2010.

b. Calculate each company's ending cash balance for 2010.

c. Notice that cash flows from investing activities were negative for Jackson Hewitt. Do you think this represents something positive or negative about the company? Write a brief explanation of your answer.

d. Notice that cash flows from financing activities were negative for H&R Block. Write a brief explanation as to what might have caused this.

ATC 2-7   Ethical Dilemma   *What is a little deceit among friends?*

Glenn's Cleaning Services Company is experiencing cash flow problems and needs a loan. Glenn has a friend who is willing to lend him the money he needs provided she can be convinced that he will be able to repay the debt. Glenn has assured his friend that his business is viable, but his friend has asked to see the company's financial statements. Glenn's accountant produced the following financial statements:

Income Statement		Balance Sheet	
Service Revenue	$ 38,000	Assets	$85,000
Operating Expenses	(70,000)	Liabilities	$35,000
Net Loss	$(32,000)	Stockholders' Equity	
		Common Stock	82,000
		Retained Earnings	(32,000)
		Total Liabilities and Stockholders' Equity	$85,000

Glenn made the following adjustments to these statements before showing them to his friend. He recorded $82,000 of revenue on account from Barrymore Manufacturing Company for a contract to clean its headquarters office building that was still being negotiated for the next month.

Barrymore had scheduled a meeting to sign a contract the following week, so Glenn was sure that he would get the job. Barrymore was a reputable company, and Glenn was confident that he could ultimately collect the $82,000. Also, he subtracted $30,000 of accrued salaries expense and the corresponding liability. He reasoned that since he had not paid the employees, he had not incurred any expense.

Required

a. Reconstruct the income statement and balance sheet as they would appear after Glenn's adjustments. Comment on the accuracy of the adjusted financial statements.

b. Suppose you are Glenn and the $30,000 you owe your employees is due next week. If you are unable to pay them, they will quit and the business will go bankrupt. You are sure you will be able to repay your friend when your employees perform the $82,000 of services for Barrymore and you collect the cash. However, your friend is risk averse and is not likely to make the loan based on the financial statements your accountant prepared. Would you make the changes that Glenn made to get the loan and thereby save your company? Defend your position with a rational explanation.

c. Discuss the elements of the fraud triangle as they apply to Glenn's decision to change the financial statements to reflect more favorable results.

ATC 2-8   Research Assignment   *Identifying accruals and deferrals at Netflix, Inc.*

This chapter defined and discussed accrual and deferral transactions. Complete the requirements below using the most recent financial statements available on the Internet for Netflix, Inc. Obtain the statements by following the steps below. (Be aware that the formatting of the company's website may have changed since these instructions were written.)

1. Go to www.netflix.com.
2. Click on "Investor Relations," which is at the bottom of the page in very small print.
3. Click on the "Annual Reports and Proxies" link at the left side of the page.
4. Click on the "20xxAnnual Report." Use the .pdf version of the annual report.
5. Find the company's balance sheet and complete the requirements below. In recent years this has been shown toward the end of the Form 10-K section of the company's annual report, on page F-3. The "Index" near the beginning of the report can help you locate the financial statements.

Required

a. Make a list of all the accounts on the balance sheet that you believe are accrual type accounts.

b. Make a list of all the accounts on the balance sheet that you believe are deferral type accounts.

ATC 2-9   Spreadsheet Assignment   *Using Excel*

Required

a. Refer to Problem 2-41A. Use an Excel spreadsheet to construct the required financial statements. To complete Requirement *b*, use formulas where normal arithmetic calculations are made within the financial statements (in particular the statement of changes in stockholders' equity).

b. It is interesting to speculate about what would happen if certain operating results change for better or worse. After completing Requirement *a*, change certain account balances for each of the following independent operating adjustments. After each adjustment, notice how the financial statements would differ if the change in operations were to occur. After noting the effect of each adjustment, return the data to the original amounts in Problem 2-37A and then go to the next operating adjustment.

In the following table, note the new amounts on the financial statements for the various operating changes listed:

Original	1	2	3	4	5
Net income					
Total assets					
Total liabilities					
Total stockholders' equity					
Total liabilities & stockholders' equity					

Independent Operating Adjustments

1. Revenue and the related Accounts Receivable increased $10,000.
2. Revenue and the related Accounts Receivable decreased $10,000.
3. Operating Expenses and the related Accounts Payable decreased $400.
4. Operating Expenses and the related Accounts Payable increased $400.
5. Dividends paid decreased $500 and cash changed accordingly.

ATC 2-10   Spreadsheet Assignment   *Mastering Excel*

Refer to Problem 2-37A. Complete the requirements using an Excel spreadsheet. Refer to Chapter 1 problem ATC 1-8 for ideas on how to structure the spreadsheet.

COMPREHENSIVE PROBLEM

The trial balance of Pacilio Security Services Inc. as of January 1, 2012, was as follows:

Cash	$8,500
Land	4,000
Notes Payable	5,000
Common Stock	6,000
Retained Earnings	1,500

During 2012, Pacilio Security Services experienced the following transactions:

1. Acquired an additional $2,000 from the issue of common stock.
2. Paid $3,000 on the debt owed to the Small Business Government Agency. The loan is interest free.
3. Performed $21,000 of security services for numerous local events during the year; $15,000 was on account and $6,000 was cash.
4. On May 1, rented a small office building. Paid $2,400 for 12 months' rent in advance.
5. Purchased supplies on account for $650.
6. Paid salaries expense for the year of $8,000.
7. Incurred other operating expenses on account, $6,200.
8. On September 1, 2012, a customer paid $600 for services to be provided over the next six months.
9. Collected $13,500 of accounts receivable during the year.
10. Paid $5,800 on accounts payable.
11. Paid $1,500 of advertising expenses for the year.
12. Paid a cash dividend to the shareholders of $1,000.
13. The market value of the land was determined to be $5,000 at December 31, 2012.

Information for Adjustments

14. There was $65 of supplies on hand at the end of the year.

15. Recognized the expired rent.

16. Recognized the revenue earned from Transaction 8.

17. Accrued salaries were $1,200 at December 31, 2012.

Required

a. Record the above transactions in an accounting equation. Provide the appropriate account titles for the amounts shown in the Retained Earnings column.

b. Prepare an income statement, statement of changes in stockholders' equity, balance sheet, and statement of cash flows for 2012.

CHAPTER 3

The Double-Entry Accounting System

LEARNING OBJECTIVES

After you have mastered the material in this chapter, you will be able to:

LO1 Describe business events using debit/credit terminology.

LO2 Record transactions in T-accounts and show their effect on financial statements.

LO3 Record transactions using the general journal format and show their effect on financial statements.

LO4 Prepare a trial balance and explain how it is used to prepare financial statements.

LO5 Use a return on assets ratio, debt to assets ratio, and a return on equity ratio to analyze financial statements.

APPENDIX

LO6 Record depreciation and interest using journal entries and T-accounts, and show how these entries affect financial statements.

CHAPTER OPENING

To prepare financial statements, a company must have a system for accurately capturing the vast numbers of business transactions in which it engages each year. The most widely used such system, double-entry accounting, is so effective it has been in use for hundreds of years! This chapter explains the rules for recording transactions using double-entry accounting.

Double-entry accounting rules are analogous to other rules people adopt to achieve various goals, such as rules governing traffic signals. A red signal means "stop," but it could just as easily mean "go." What matters is that all drivers agree on what red means. Similarly, double-entry accounting rules could have developed differently. In fact, the rules sometimes seem backwards at first. You likely use accounting terms like "debit" or "credit" from a consumer's point of view. To learn the accounting rules, however, you must view them from a business perspective. With practice, they will become second nature and you will know them as well as you know traffic signals.

The Curious Accountant

Most companies prepare financial statements at least once each year. The year about which financial statements report is called a **fiscal year**. Illustrations in this textbook usually assume the fiscal year coincides with the calendar year; that is, it ends on December 31. In practice, the fiscal years of many companies do not end on December 31. For example, Polo Ralph Lauren, a company that produces clothing, ends its fiscal year on the first Sunday in April. Abercrombie & Fitch, a company that sells clothing, ends its fiscal year on the last Sunday in January.

Why would these companies choose these dates to end their fiscal years? (Answers on pages 155 and 156.)

DEBIT/CREDIT TERMINOLOGY

Describe business events using debit/credit terminology.

An account form known as a **T-account** is a good starting point for learning double-entry recording procedures. A T-account looks like the letter "T" drawn on a piece of paper. The account title is written across the top of the horizontal bar of the T. The left side of the vertical bar is the **debit** side, and the right side is the **credit** side. An account has been *debited* when an amount is written on the left side and *credited* when an amount is written on the right side. Accountants often abbreviate the term *debit* as "dr." and *credit* as "cr." For any given account, the difference between the total debit and credit amounts is the **account balance.**

The rules for using debits and credits to record transactions in T-accounts are as follows:

Assets		=	Liabilities		+	Equity	
Debit	Credit		Debit	Credit		Debit	Credit
+	−		−	+		−	+

Notice that a debit can represent an increase or a decrease. Likewise, a credit can represent an increase or a decrease. Whether a debit or credit is an increase or a decrease depends on the type of account (asset, liability, or stockholders' equity) in question. The rules of debits and credits are summarized as follows:

1. Debits increase asset accounts; credits decrease asset accounts.
2. Debits decrease liability and stockholders' equity accounts; credits increase liability and stockholders' equity accounts.

RECORDING TRANSACTIONS IN T-ACCOUNTS

Record transactions in T-accounts and show their effect on financial statements.

To illustrate the rules for debits and credits we record the 2013 accounting events for a small business, Collins Brokerage Services, Inc. Collins begins the accounting period with the following balances in its permanent accounts: Cash, $5,000; Common Stock, $4,000; and Retained Earnings, $1,000. The beginning balances for the temporary accounts (Revenues, Expenses, and Dividends) are zero because these accounts were closed at the end of the previous period. The events are organized into four categories including: asset source, asset exchange, asset use, and claims exchange.

Asset Source Transactions

A business may obtain assets from three primary sources: (1) from stockholders, (2) from creditors, or (3) through operating activities (earning revenue). An asset source transaction increases an asset account and a corresponding liability or stockholders' equity account. The increase in the asset account is recorded with a debit entry. The increase in a liability or stockholders' equity account is recorded with a credit entry. The following section demonstrates recording procedures for common asset source transactions.

EVENT 1   Acquired $25,000 cash from the issue of common stock.

This accounting event increases both assets and stockholders' equity. The increase in assets (Cash) is recorded with a debit, and the increase in stockholders' equity (Common Stock) with a credit, shown in T-account form as follows:

Assets		=	Liabilities	+	Equity	
Cash					Common Stock	
Debit	Credit				Debit	Credit
+						+
(1) 25,000						25,000 (1)

Notice the entry included both debiting an account and crediting an account. This system is called **double-entry accounting.** Recording any transaction requires at least one debit and at least one credit. The total of the debit amounts must equal the total of the credit amounts. These requirements provide accountants with a built-in error detection tool. For your convenience, the event number is shown parenthetically in the T-accounts beside the transactions amounts.

This entry has the following effects on the financial statements:

Assets	=	Liab.	+	Equity	Rev.	−	Exp.	=	Net Inc.	Cash Flow
Cash	=			Com. Stk.						
25,000	=	NA	+	25,000	NA	−	NA	=	NA	25,000 FA

EVENT 2   Purchased $850 of supplies on account.

Purchasing supplies on account increases both assets and liabilities. The increase in assets (Supplies) is recorded with a debit, and the increase in liabilities (Accounts Payable) is recorded with a credit, as shown in the following T-accounts:

Assets		=	Liabilities		+	Equity	
Supplies			Accounts Payable				
Debit	Credit		Debit	Credit			
+				+			
(2) 850				850 (2)			

This entry has the following effects on the financial statements:

Assets	=	Liab.	+	Equity	Rev.	−	Exp.	=	Net Inc.	Cash Flow
Supplies	=	Accts. Pay.								
850	=	850	+	NA	NA	−	NA	=	NA	NA

EVENT 3   Collected $1,800 cash as an advance to provide future services over a one year period starting March 1.

Accepting the $1,800 in advance creates an obligation for Collins. The obligation is to provide future services to a customer. Collins will recognize a liability called *unearned revenue.* Recording the event increases both assets and liabilities. The increase in assets

(Cash) is recorded with a debit, and the increase in liabilities (Unearned Revenue) is recorded with a credit, as shown in the following T-accounts:

Assets		=	Liabilities		+	Equity	
Cash			Unearned Revenue				
Debit +	Credit		Debit	Credit +			
(3) 1,800				1,800 (3)			

This entry has the following effects on the financial statements:

Assets	=	Liab.	+	Equity	Rev.	−	Exp.	=	Net Inc.	Cash Flow
Cash	=	Unearned Revenue								
1,800	=	1,800	+	NA	NA	−	NA	=	NA	1,800 OA

EVENT 4   **Provided $15,760 of services on account.**

Recognizing revenue earned on account increases both assets and stockholders' equity. The increase in assets (Accounts Receivable) is recorded with a debit, and the increase in stockholders' equity (Service Revenue) is recorded with a credit, as shown in the following T-accounts:

Assets		=	Liabilities	+	Equity	
Accounts Receivable					Service Revenue	
Debit +	Credit				Debit	Credit +
(4) 15,760						15,760 (4)

This entry has the following effects on the financial statements:

Assets	=	Liab.	+	Equity	Rev.	−	Exp.	=	Net Inc.	Cash Flow
Accts. Rec.	=			Ret. Earn.						
15,760	=	NA	+	15,760	15,760	−	NA	=	15,760	NA

Summary of the Previous Asset Source Transactions

Events 1 through 4 are asset source transactions. In each case, an asset account and a corresponding liability or equity account increased. The increase in the asset account was recorded with a debit and the increase in the liability or stockholders' equity account was recorded with a credit. Any transaction that provides assets to a business is recorded similarly.

Asset Exchange Transactions

Asset exchange transactions involve trading one asset for another asset. One asset account increases; the other decreases. The total amount of assets remains unchanged. Asset exchange transactions are recorded by debiting the asset account that is increasing and crediting the asset account that is decreasing. In T-account form, asset exchange transactions have the following effects on the accounting equation:

Assets				=	Claims
Asset 1		**Asset 2**			
Debit	Credit	Debit	Credit		
+			−		

EVENT 5   **Purchased land for $26,000 cash.**

The increase in assets (Land) is recorded with a debit, and the decrease in assets (Cash) is recorded with a credit, as shown in the following T-accounts:

Assets				=	Claims
Cash		**Land**			
Debit	Credit	Debit	Credit		
	−	+			
	26,000 (5)	(5) 26,000			

This entry has the following effects on the financial statements:

Assets			=	Liab.	+	Equity	Rev.	−	Exp.	=	Net Inc.	Cash Flow
Cash	+	Land										
(26,000)	+	26,000	=	NA	+	NA	NA	−	NA	=	NA	(26,000) IA

EVENT 6   Paid $1,200 cash for a one-year insurance policy with coverage starting August 1.

The increase in assets (Prepaid Insurance) is recorded with a debit, and the decrease in assets (Cash) is recorded with a credit, as shown in the following T-accounts:

Assets				=	Claims
Cash		**Prepaid Insurance**			
Debit	Credit	Debit	Credit		
	−	+			
	1,200 (6)	(6) 1,200			

This entry has the following effects on the financial statements:

Assets			= Liab.	+ Equity	Rev.	− Exp.	= Net Inc.	Cash Flow
Cash	+	Prepaid Insurance						
(1,200)	+	1,200	= NA	+ NA	NA	− NA =	NA	(1,200) OA

EVENT 7   Collected $13,400 cash from accounts receivable.

The increase in assets (Cash) is recorded with a debit, and the decrease in assets (Accounts Receivable) is recorded with a credit, as shown in the following T-accounts:

Assets				=	Claims
Cash		**Accounts Receivable**			
Debit	Credit	Debit	Credit		
+			−		
(7) 13,400			13,400 (7)		

This entry has the following effects on the financial statements:

Assets			= Liab.	+ Equity	Rev.	− Exp.	= Net Inc.	Cash Flow
Cash	+	Accts. Rec.						
13,400	+	(13,400)	= NA	+ NA	NA	− NA =	NA	13,400 OA

Summary of the Previous Asset Exchange Transactions

Events 6 and 7 are both asset exchange transactions. In each case, one asset account increased and another decreased. The asset account that increased was debited, and the asset account that decreased was credited. These asset exchange transactions did not affect the total amounts of assets, liabilities, or equity.

Asset Use Transactions

There are three primary asset use transactions: (1) expenses may use assets, (2) settling liabilities may use assets, or (3) paying dividends may use assets. An asset use transaction decreases an asset account and also decreases a liability or equity account. The decrease in the asset account is recorded with a credit and the decrease in the liability or equity account is recorded with a debit.

EVENT 8   **Paid $9,500 cash for salaries expense.**

The decrease in assets (Cash) is recorded with a credit, and the decrease in stockholders' equity (Salaries Expense) is recorded with a debit, as shown in the following T-accounts:

Assets	=	Liabilities	+	Equity

Cash				Salaries Expense

Debit	Credit		Debit + Expense − Equity	Credit
	− 9,500 (8)		(8) 9,500	

The debit to Salaries Expense represents an *increase* in the salaries expense account which is actually a *decrease* in stockholders' equity (Retained Earnings). Debit entries increase expense accounts. Expenses, however, decrease stockholders' equity (Retained Earnings). Debiting an expense account, therefore, reduces stockholders' equity.

This entry has the following effects on the financial statements:

Assets	=	Liab.	+	Equity	Rev.	−	Exp.	=	Net Inc.	Cash Flow
Cash	=			Ret. Earn.						
(9,500)	=	NA	+	(9,500)	NA	−	9,500	=	(9,500)	(9,500) OA

EVENT 9   **Paid an $800 cash dividend.**

The decrease in assets (Cash) is recorded with a credit, and the decrease in stockholders' equity (Dividends) is recorded with a debit, as shown in the following T-accounts:

Assets	=	Liabilities	+	Equity

Cash				Dividends

Debit	Credit		Debit + Div − Equity	Credit
	− 800 (9)		(9) 800	

The debit to Dividends represents both an increase in the dividends account and a decrease in stockholders' equity (Retained Earnings). Since dividends decrease stockholders' equity, an increase in the dividends account reduces stockholders' equity. Recall that dividends are wealth transfers, not expenses.

This entry has the following effects on the financial statements:

Assets	=	Liab.	+	Equity	Rev.	−	Exp.	=	Net Inc.	Cash Flow
Cash	=			Ret. Earn.						
(800)	=	NA	+	(800)	NA	−	NA	=	NA	(800) FA

EVENT 10   Paid $850 cash to settle accounts payable.

The decrease in assets (Cash) is recorded with a credit, and the decrease in liabilities (Accounts Payable) is recorded with a debit, as shown in the following T-accounts:

Assets		=	Liabilities		+	Equity
Cash			**Accounts Payable**			
Debit	Credit		Debit	Credit		
	—		—			
	850 (10)		(10) 850			

This entry has the following effects on the financial statements:

Assets	=	Liab.	+	Equity	Rev.	−	Exp.	=	Net Inc.	Cash Flow
Cash	=	Accts. Pay.								
(850)	=	(850)	+	NA	NA	−	NA	=	NA	(850) OA

Summary of Asset Use Transactions

Events 8 through 10 each reduced an asset account and also either a liability or stockholders' equity account. Even though debit entries to expense and dividends accounts represent increases in those accounts, the balances in expense and dividends accounts reduce stockholders' equity. Any asset use transaction is recorded with a debit to a liability or a stockholders' equity account and a credit to an asset account.

Claims Exchange Transactions

Certain transactions involve exchanging one claims account for another claims account. The total amount of claims remains unchanged. Such transactions are recorded by debiting the claims account which is decreasing and crediting the claims account which is increasing.

EVENT 11   Recognized $1,900 other operating expenses on account.

The event increases liabilities and decreases stockholders' equity. The increase in liabilities (Accounts Payable) is recorded with a credit, and the decrease in stockholders' equity (Other Operating Expense) is recorded with a debit, as shown in the following T-accounts:

Assets	=	Liabilities		+	Equity	
		Accounts Payable			**Other Operating Expense**	
		Debit	Credit		Debit	Credit
			+		+ Expense	
			1,900 (11)		− Equity	
					(11) 1,900	

This entry has the following effects on the financial statements:

Assets	=	Liab.	+	Equity	Rev.	−	Exp.	=	Net Inc.	Cash Flow
		Accts. Pay.	+	Ret. Earn.						
NA	=	1,900	+	(1,900)	NA	−	1,900	=	(1,900)	NA

Summary of Claims Exchange Transactions

Event 11 reflects an exchange on the claims side of the accounting equation. In each case, one claims account was debited, and another claims account was credited. Claims exchange transactions do not affect the total amounts of either assets or claim.

Adjusting the Accounts

Assume Collins' fiscal year ends on December 31, 2013. Collins has several unrecorded accruals and deferrals that must be recognized before the financial statements can be prepared. The appropriate adjustments are discussed below.

ADJUSTMENT 1 **As of December 31, 2013, Collins had earned $750 of accrued interest revenue.**

Recognizing the revenue increases both assets and stockholders' equity. The increase in assets (Accrued Interest Receivable) is recorded with a debit, and the increase in stockholders' equity (Accrued Interest Revenue) is recorded with a credit, as shown in the following T-accounts:

Assets	=	Liabilities	+	Equity

Accrued Interest Receivable					Accrued Interest Revenue	
Debit	Credit				Debit	Credit
+						+
(Adj. 1) 750						750 (Adj. 1)

This entry has the following effects on the financial statements:

Assets	=	Liab.	+	Equity	Rev.	−	Exp.	=	Net Inc.	Cash Flow
Int. Rec.	=			Ret. Earn.						
750	=	NA	+	750	750	−	NA	=	750	NA

ADJUSTMENT 2 **As of December 31, 2013, Collins had earned $1,500 of the $1,800 of the revenue it deferred in Event 3.**

Recall that Collins collected $1,800 in advance for a one-year contract starting March 1. By December 31, 2013, Collins would have provided professional services for 10 months, earning $1,500 ($1,800 ÷ 12 = $150; $150 × 10 = $1,500) of the revenue during 2013. This amount must be transferred from the liability account (Unearned Revenue) to an equity account (Service Revenue). Recognizing the revenue decreases liabilities and increases stockholders' equity. The decrease in liabilities (Unearned Revenue) is recorded with a debit, and the increase in stockholders' equity (Service Revenue) is recorded with a credit, as shown in the following T-accounts:

Assets	=	Liabilities	+	Equity

		Unearned Revenue			Service Revenue	
		Debit	Credit		Debit	Credit
		−				+
		(Adj. 2) 1,500				1,500 (Adj. 2)

This adjustment has the following effects on the financial statements:

Assets	=	Liab.	+	Equity	Rev.	−	Exp.	=	Net Inc.	Cash Flow
		Unearned Revenue	+	Ret. Earn.						
NA	=	(1,500)	+	1,500	1,500	−	NA	=	1,500	NA

ADJUSTMENT 3   As of December 31, 2013, Collins had $800 of accrued salary expenses that will be paid in 2014.

Assume that Collins owes $800 to employees for work done in 2013. Collins will pay these salaries in 2014. The required adjusting entry increases liabilities and decreases stockholders' equity. The increase in liabilities (Salaries Payable) is recorded with a credit, and the decrease in stockholders' equity (Salaries Expense) is recorded with a debit, as shown in the following T-accounts:

Assets	=	Liabilities	+	Equity
		Salaries Payable		**Salaries Expense**
		Debit	Credit + 800 (Adj. 3)	Debit + Expense − Equity (Adj. 3) 800	Credit

This adjustment has the following effects on the financial statements:

Assets	=	Liab.	+	Equity	Rev.	−	Exp.	=	Net Inc.	Cash Flow
		Sal. Pay.	+	Ret. Earn.						
NA	=	800	+	(800)	NA	−	800	=	(800)	NA

ADJUSTMENT 4   As of December 31, 2013, Collins had used $500 of the $1,200 of insurance coverage that was prepaid in Event 6.

Recall that Collins paid $1,200 in advance for insurance coverage for one year. The monthly insurance cost is therefore $100 ($1,200 ÷ 12 months). By December 31, Collins had *used* the insurance coverage for five months in 2013. Insurance expense for those five months is therefore $500 ($100 × 5). Recognizing the insurance expense decreases both assets and stockholders' equity. The decrease in assets (Prepaid Insurance) is recorded with a credit, and the decrease in stockholders' equity (Insurance Expense) is recorded with a debit, as shown in the following T-accounts:

Assets	=	Liabilities	+	Equity
Prepaid Insurance				**Insurance Expense**
Debit	Credit − 500 (Adj. 4)			Debit + Expense − Equity (Adj. 4) 500	Credit

This adjustment has the following effects on the financial statements:

Assets	=	Liab.	+	Equity	Rev.	−	Exp.	=	Net Inc.	Cash Flow
Prep. Ins.	=			Ret. Earn.						
(500)	=	NA	+	(500)	NA	−	500	=	(500)	NA

ADJUSTMENT 5 As of December 31, 2013, a physical count of the supplies on hand revealed that $125 of unused supplies were available for future use.

Collins used $725 ($850 − $125) of supplies during the period. Recognizing the supplies expense decreases both assets and stockholders' equity. The decrease in assets (Supplies) is recorded with a credit and the decrease in stockholders' equity (Supplies Expense) is recorded with a debit, as shown in the following T-accounts:

Assets	=	Liabilities	+	Equity

Supplies

Debit	Credit
	−
	725 (Adj. 5)

Supplies Expense

Debit	Credit
+ Expense	
− Equity	
(Adj. 5) 725	

This adjustment has the following effects on the financial statements:

Assets	=	Liab.	+	Equity	Rev.	−	Exp.	=	Net Inc.	Cash Flow
Supplies	=			Ret. Earn.						
(725)	=	NA	+	(725)	NA	−	725	=	(725)	NA

✓ CHECK YOURSELF 3.2

Can an asset exchange transaction be an adjusting entry?

Answer No. Adjusting entries always involve revenue or expense accounts. Since an asset exchange transaction involves only asset accounts, it cannot be an adjusting entry.

Overview of Debit/Credit Relationships

Panel A of Exhibit 3.1 summarizes the rules for debits and credits. Panel B illustrates these rules in T-account form.

The balance in each account, which is the difference between all the debit entries and all the credit entries, is written on the plus (increase) side of that account. Asset, expense, and dividend accounts normally have *debit balances;* liability, stockholders' equity, and revenue accounts normally have *credit balances.*

THE GENERAL JOURNAL

LO 3

Businesses find it impractical to record every individual transaction directly into general ledger accounts. Imagine the number of cash transactions a grocery store has each day. To simplify recordkeeping, businesses rely on **source documents** such as cash register

Record transactions using the general journal format and show their effect on financial statements.

EXHIBIT 3.1

Debit/Credit Relationships

Panel A

Account	Debits	Credits
Assets	Increase	Decrease
Liabilities	Decrease	Increase
Equity	Decrease	Increase
Common Stock	Decrease	Increase
Revenue	Decrease	Increase
Expenses	Increase	Decrease
Dividends	Increase	Decrease

Panel B

Assets = Liabilities + Equity

Assets		Liabilities		Equity	
Debit +	Credit −	Debit −	Credit +	Debit −	Credit +

Common Stock

Debit −	Credit +

Dividends

Debit − Equity + Div.	Credit + Equity − Div.

Revenue

Debit −	Credit +

Expense

Debit − Equity + Exp.	Credit + Equity − Exp.

tapes as the basis for entering transaction data into the accounting system. Other source documents include invoices, time cards, check registers, and deposit tickets.

Accountants further simplify recordkeeping by initially recording data from source documents into **journals.** Journals provide a chronological record of business transactions. *Transactions are recorded in journals before they are entered into ledger accounts.* Journals are therefore **books of original entry.** Companies may use different **special journals** to record specific types of recurring transactions. For example, a company may use one special journal to record sales on account, another to record purchases on account, a third to record cash receipts, and a fourth to record cash payments. Transactions that do not fall into any of these categories are recorded in the **general journal.** Although special journals are useful, companies can keep records without them by recording all transactions in the general journal. For simplicity, this text illustrates a general journal only.

At a minimum, the general journal shows the dates, the account titles, and the amounts of each transaction. The date is recorded in the first column, followed by the title of the account to be debited. The title of the account to be credited is indented and written on the line directly below the account to be debited. The dollar amount of the transaction is recorded in the Debit and Credit columns. Dollar signs are not used when

REALITY BYTES

Do all accounting systems require using debits and credits? The answer is a definite no. Many small businesses use a single-entry system. A checkbook constitutes a sufficient accounting system for many business owners. Deposits represent revenues, and payments constitute expenses. Many excellent automated accounting systems do not require data entry through a debit/credit recording scheme. **QuickBooks** is a good example of this type of system. Data are entered into the QuickBooks software program through a user-friendly computer interface that does not require knowledge of debit/credit terminology. Even so, the QuickBooks program produces traditional financial reports such as an income statement, balance sheet, and statement of cash flows. How is this possible? Before you become too ingrained in the debit/credit system, recall that throughout the first two chapters of this text, we illustrated accounting records without using debits and credits. Financial reports can be produced in many ways without using a double-entry system. Having recognized this point, we also note that the vast majority of medium- to large-size companies use the double-entry system. Indeed, debit/credit terminology is a part of common culture. Most people have an understanding of what is happening when a business tells them that their account is being debited or credited. It is important for you to embrace the double-entry system as well as other financial reporting systems.

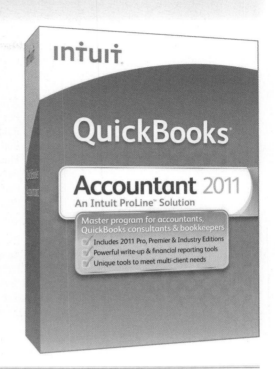

recording journal entries. For example, providing services for $1,000 cash on August 1 would be recorded in general journal format as follows:

Date	Account Title	Debit	Credit
Aug. 1	Cash	1,000	
	Service Revenue		1,000

Exhibit 3.2 shows a summary of Collins's 2013 transactions and demonstrates how the transactions are recorded in general journal format. For easy reference the journal column normally used for the transaction date contains the event numbers and the references for the adjusting entries. After transactions are initially recorded in a journal, the dollar amounts of each debit and credit are copied into the ledger accounts through a process called **posting.**

Most companies today use computer technology to record transactions and prepare financial statements. Computers can record and post data pertaining to vast numbers of transactions with incredible speed and unparalleled accuracy. Both manual and computerized accounting systems, however, use the same underlying design. Analyzing a manual accounting system is a useful way to gain insight into how computer-based systems work.

The collection of all the accounts used by a particular business is called the **general ledger.** The general ledger for Collins is displayed in Exhibit 3.3. In a manual system, the ledger could be a book with pages for each account where entries are recorded by hand. In more sophisticated systems, the general ledger is maintained in electronic form. Data are entered into electronic ledgers using computer keyboards or scanners. Companies typically assign each ledger account a name and a number. A list of all ledger accounts and their account numbers is called the **chart of accounts.**

EXHIBIT 3.2

Transaction Summary

Event 1 Acquired $25,000 cash from the issue of common stock.
Event 2 Purchased $850 of supplies on account.
Event 3 Collected $1,800 cash as an advance to provide future services over a one year period starting March 1.
Event 4 Provided $15,760 of services on account.
Event 5 Purchased land for $26,000 cash.
Event 6 Paid $1,200 cash for a one-year insurance policy with coverage starting August 1.
Event 7 Collected $13,400 cash from accounts receivable.
Event 8 Paid $9,500 cash for salaries expense.
Event 9 Paid an $800 cash dividend.
Event 10 Paid $850 cash to settle accounts payable.
Event 11 Recognized $1,900 other operating expenses on account.

Adjustments

Adj. 1 Recognized $750 of accrued interest revenue.
Adj. 2 Recognized $1,500 of deferred service revenue.
Adj. 3 Recognized $800 of accrued salaries expense.
Adj. 4 Recognized $500 of deferred insurance expense.
Adj. 5 Recognized $725 of deferred supplies expense.

General Journal Entries

Event No.	Account Titles	Debit	Credit
1	Cash	25,000	
	Common Stock		25,000
2	Supplies	850	
	Accounts Payable		850
3	Cash	1,800	
	Unearned Service Revenue		1,800
4	Accounts Receivable	15,760	
	Service Revenue		15,760
5	Land	26,000	
	Cash		26,000
6	Prepaid Insurance	1,200	
	Cash		1,200
7	Cash	13,400	
	Accounts Receivable		13,400
8	Salaries Expense	9,500	
	Cash		9,500
9	Dividends	800	
	Cash		800
10	Accounts Payable	850	
	Cash		850
11	Other Operating Expenses	1,900	
	Accounts Payable		1,900
Adj. 1	Accrued Interest Receivable	750	
	Accrued Interest Revenue		750
Adj. 2	Unearned Service Revenue	1,500	
	Service Revenue		1,500
Adj. 3	Salaries Expense	800	
	Salaries Payable		800
Adj. 4	Insurance Expense	500	
	Prepaid Insurance		500
Adj. 5	Supplies Expense	725	
	Supplies		725

EXHIBIT 3.3

General Ledger

Assets   =   Liabilities   +   Stockholders' Equity

Cash

Bal.	5,000	26,000	(5)
(1)	25,000	1,200	(6)
(3)	1,800	9,500	(8)
(7)	13,400	800	(9)
		850	(10)
Bal.	6,850		

Accounts Payable

(10)	850	850	(2)	
		1,900	(11)	
		1,900	Bal.	

Common Stock

	4,000	Bal.
	25,000	(1)
	29,000	Bal.

Service Revenue

	15,760	(4)
	1,500	(Adj. 2)
	17,260	Bal.

Accounts Receivable

(4)	15,760	13,400	(7)
Bal.	2,360		

Salaries Payable

	800	(Adj. 3)

Retained Earnings

	1,000	Bal.

Accrued Interest Revenue

	750	(Adj. 1)

Accrued Interest Receivable

(Adj. 1)	750

Unearned Service Revenue

(Adj. 2)	1,500	1,800	(3)	
		300	Bal.	

Dividends

(9)	800

Salaries Expense

(8)	9,500
(Adj. 3)	800
Bal.	10,300

Prepaid Insurance

(6)	1,200	500	(Adj. 4)
Bal.	700		

Other Operating Expenses

(11)	1,900

Insurance Expense

(Adj. 4)	500

Supplies

(2)	850	725	(Adj. 5)
Bal.	125		

Supplies Expense

(Adj. 5)	725

Land

(5)	26,000

TRIAL BALANCE AND FINANCIAL STATEMENTS

To test whether debits equal credits in the general ledger, accountants regularly prepare an internal accounting schedule called a **trial balance.** A trial balance lists every ledger account and its balance. Debit balances are listed in one column and credit balances are listed in an adjacent column. The columns are totaled and the totals are compared. Exhibit 3.4 displays the trial balance for Collins Brokerage Services, Inc., after the adjusting entries have been posted to the ledger.

If the debit total does not equal the credit total, the accountant knows to search for an error. Even if the totals are equal, however, there may be errors in the accounting records. For example, equal trial balance totals would not disclose errors like the following: failure to record transactions; misclassifications, such as debiting the wrong account; or incorrectly recording the amount of a transaction, such as recording a $200 transaction as $2,000. Equal debits and credits in a trial balance provide evidence rather than proof of accuracy.

Supplemented with details from the Cash and Common Stock ledger accounts, the adjusted trial balance (Exhibit 3.4) provides the information to prepare the financial statements for Collins Brokerage Services, Inc. The income statement, statement of changes in stockholders' equity, balance sheet, and statement of cash flows are shown in Exhibits 3.5, 3.6, 3.7, and 3.8.

LO 4

Prepare a trial balance and explain how it is used to prepare financial statements.

EXHIBIT 3.4

COLLINS BROKERAGE SERVICES, INC.
Adjusted Trial Balance
December 31, 2013

Account Title	Debit	Credit
Cash	$ 6,850	
Accounts receivable	2,360	
Accrued interest receivable	750	
Prepaid insurance	700	
Supplies	125	
Land	26,000	
Accounts payable		$ 1,900
Salaries payable		800
Unearned service revenue		300
Common stock		29,000
Retained earnings		1,000
Dividends	800	
Service revenue		17,260
Accrued interest revenue		750
Salaries expense	10,300	
Insurance expense	500	
Supplies expense	725	
Other operating expense	1,900	
Totals	$51,010	$51,010

EXHIBIT 3.5

COLLINS BROKERAGE SERVICES, INC.
Income Statement
For the Year Ended December 31, 2013

Revenues		
Service revenue	$17,260	
Interest revenue	750	
Total revenue		$18,010
Expenses		
Salaries expense	(10,300)	
Other operating expenses	(1,900)	
Insurance expense	(500)	
Supplies expense	(725)	
Total expenses		(13,425)
Net income		$ 4,585

EXHIBIT 3.6

COLLINS BROKERAGE SERVICES, INC.
Statement of Changes in Stockholders' Equity
For the Year Ended December 31, 2013

Beginning common stock	$ 4,000	
Plus: Common stock issued	25,000	
Ending common stock		$29,000
Beginning retained earnings	1,000	
Plus: Net income	4,585	
Less: Dividends	(800)	
Ending retained earnings		4,785
Total stockholders' equity		$33,785

EXHIBIT 3.7

COLLINS BROKERAGE SERVICES, INC.
Balance Sheet
As of December 31, 2013

Assets		
Cash	$ 6,850	
Accounts receivable	2,360	
Accrued interest receivable	750	
Prepaid insurance	700	
Supplies	125	
Land	26,000	
Total assets		$36,785
Liabilities:		
Accounts payable	$ 1,900	
Salaries payable	800	
Unearned service revenue	300	
Total liabilities		$ 3,000
Stockholders equity		
Common stock	29,000	
Retained earnings	4,785	
Total stockholders' equity		33,785
Total liabilities and stockholders' equity		$36,785

EXHIBIT 3.8

COLLINS BROKERAGE SERVICES, INC.
Statement of Cash Flows
For the Year Ended December 31, 2013

Cash flows from operating activities		
Cash receipts from customers	$15,200*	
Cash payments for salaries expense	(9,500)	
Cash payments for insurance expense	(1,200)	
Cash payments for supplies	(850)	
Net cash flow from operating activities		$ 3,650
Cash flows from investing activities		
Cash payment to purchase land		(26,000)
Cash flows from financing activities		
Cash receipts from issue of common stock	25,000	
Cash payment for dividends	(800)	
Net cash flow from financing activities		24,200
Net increase in cash		1,850
Plus: Beginning cash balance		5,000
Ending cash balance		$ 6,850

*$13,400 accounts receivable collections + $1,800 unearned service revenue collection.

Answers to The Curious Accountant

Part 1

The process of closing the books and going through a year-end audit is time consuming for a business. Also, it is time spent that does not produce revenue. Thus, companies whose business is highly seasonal often choose "slow" periods to end their fiscal year. Abercrombie & Fitch does heavy business during the Christmas season, so it might find December 31 an inconvenient time to close its books. Toward the end of January, business activity is slow, and inventory levels are at their low points. This is a good time to count the inventory and to assess the financial condition of the company. For these reasons, Abercrombie & Fitch has chosen to close its books to end its fiscal year around the end of January.

Now that you know why a business like Abercrombie & Fitch might choose to end its fiscal year at the end of January, can you think of a reason why Polo Ralph Lauren closes its books at the end of April? (See page 156.)

Closing Entries

Exhibit 3.9 shows **closing entries** for Collins Brokerage Services, Inc. These entries move all 2013 data from the temporary accounts (revenues, expenses, and dividends) into the Retained Earnings account. For example, the first closing entry in Exhibit 3.9 moves the balance in the Service Revenue account to the Retained Earnings account. As shown in the adjusted trial balance (Exhibit 3.4), the Service Revenue account has a $17,260 credit balance before it is closed. Debiting the account for $17,260 brings its after-closing balance to zero. The corresponding $17,260 credit to Retained Earnings increases the balance in that account.

The third closing entry moves the balance in the Salaries Expense account to the Retained Earnings account. Before closing, the Salaries Expense account has a $10,300 debit balance; crediting the account for $10,300 leaves it with an after-closing balance

EXHIBIT 3.9

Closing Entries

Date	Account Titles	Debit	Credit
Dec. 31	Service Revenue	17,260	
	Retained Earnings		17,260
31	Accrued Interest Revenue	750	
	Retained Earnings		750
31	Retained Earnings	10,300	
	Salaries Expense		10,300
31	Retained Earnings	1,900	
	Other Operating Expenses		1,900
31	Retained Earnings	500	
	Insurance Expense		500
31	Retained Earnings	725	
	Supplies Expense		725
31	Retained Earnings	800	
	Dividends		800

Answers to The Curious Accountant

Part 2

Early April probably is a relatively slow time of year for Polo Ralph Lauren. Polo sells most of its goods through retailers. It must deliver clothing to stores such as Abercrombie & Fitch weeks before they will be sold to holiday shoppers. By April, the Christmas season has passed and much of the spring clothing will have already been shipped to retailers, so this is a good time for Polo to close its books. Tommy Hilfiger, another clothing manufacturer, closes its books on March 31 of each year.

of zero. The corresponding $10,300 debit to the Retained Earnings account reduces the balance in that account. The remaining entries close the other revenue, expense and the dividends accounts to the Retained Earnings account.

Closing entries can be recorded more efficiently than in Exhibit 3.9. For example, the two revenue accounts could be closed with one compound journal entry, like the one below.

Date	Account Title	Debit	Credit
Dec. 31	Service Revenue	17,260	
	Accrued Interest Revenue	750	
	Retained Earnings		18,010

Furthermore, revenue, expense, and dividend accounts could all be closed in a single compound journal entry. The form of the closing entries is not important. What matters is that all revenue, expense, and dividend amounts be moved to the Retained Earnings account. After the closing entries are posted to the ledger accounts, all revenue, expense, and dividends accounts have zero balances. The temporary accounts are then ready to capture revenue, expense, and dividend data for the next fiscal year.

If all companies closed their books on December 31 each year, accountants, printers, lawyers, government agencies, and others would be overburdened by the effort to produce the accounting reports of all companies at the same time. In an effort to balance the workload, many companies close their books at the end of the natural business year. A natural business year ends when operating activities are at their lowest point. For many companies the lowest point in the operating cycle occurs on a date other than December 31. A recent survey found that almost one-half of the companies sampled closed their books in months other than December (see Exhibit 3.10).

EXHIBIT 3.10

Distribution of Fiscal Closing Dates

Data Source: AICPA Accounting Trends and Techniques.

Post-Closing Trial Balance

How often should companies prepare a trial balance? Some companies prepare a trial balance daily; others may prepare one monthly, quarterly, or annually, depending on the needs of management. The heading of a trial balance describes the status of the account balances in it. For example, the trial balance in Exhibit 3.11 is described as a *Post-Closing Trial Balance* because it reflects the account balances immediately after the closing entries were posted. In contrast, the trial balance in Exhibit 3.4 is described as an *Adjusted Trial Balance* because it shows the account balances immediately after the adjusting entries were posted. A trial balance prepared at the end of each day may be described as a *Daily Trial Balance*.

✓ CHECK YOURSELF 3.3

Describe an error that would not cause a trial balance to be out of balance.

Answer   Many potential errors would not cause a trial balance to be out of balance, such as debiting or crediting the wrong account. For example, if revenue earned on account were recorded with a debit to Cash instead of Accounts Receivable, total assets would be correct and the totals in the trial balance would equal each other even though the balances in the Cash and Accounts Receivable accounts would be incorrect. Recording the same incorrect amount in both the debit and credit part of an entry also would not cause a trial balance to be out of balance. For example, if $20 of revenue earned on account were recorded as a $200 debit to Accounts Receivable and a $200 credit to Consulting Revenue, the totals in the trial balance would equal each other although Accounts Receivable and Consulting Revenue amounts would be incorrect.

THE FINANCIAL ANALYST

Suppose a company earned net income of $1,000,000. Is the company's performance good or poor? If the company is Comcast, the performance is poor. If it is a small shoe store, the performance is outstanding. So, how do financial analysts compare the performance of differing size companies? Financial ratios are helpful in this regard.

Assessing the Effective Use of Assets

LO 5

Use a return on assets ratio, debt to assets ratio, and a return on equity ratio to analyze financial statements.

Evaluating performance requires considering the size of the investment base used to produce the income. In other words, you expect someone who has a $10 million investment base to earn more than someone who has a $10 thousand base. The relationship between the level of income and the size of the investment can be expressed as the **return on assets ratio,** as follows:

$$\frac{\text{Net income}^{1}}{\text{Total assets}}$$

This ratio permits meaningful comparisons between different-size companies. Compare Dollar Tree, Inc., a retailer that prices all of its merchandise at $1.00, to Wal-Mart Stores, Inc. In their 2011 fiscal years, Dollar Tree reported net income of $397.3 million, while Walmart reported net income of $15.4 billion. Walmart earnings were almost 39 times the earnings of Dollar Tree. However, the return on asset ratios for the two companies reveal that Dollar Tree produced higher earnings relative to the assets invested. Walmart ratio was 8.4 percent while Dollar Tree's was 16.7 percent. Even though Dollar Tree's earned fewer dollars of net income, the company did a better job than Walmart of managing its assets.

The preceding example demonstrates the usefulness of the relationship between income and assets. Two more ratios that enhance financial statement analysis are discussed in the following paragraphs.

EXHIBIT 3.11

COLLINS BROKERAGE SERVICES, INC.
Post-Closing Trial Balance
December 31, 2013

Account Title	Debit	Credit
Cash	$ 6,850	
Accounts receivable	2,360	
Accrued interest receivable	750	
Prepaid insurance	700	
Supplies	125	
Land	26,000	
Accounts payable		$ 1,900
Salaries payable		800
Unearned service revenue		300
Common stock		29,000
Retained earnings		4,785
Totals	$36,785	$36,785

---

[1]The use of net income in this ratio ignores the effects of debt financing and income taxation. The effect of these variables on the return on assets ratio is explained in a later chapter.

Assessing Debt Risk

Borrowing money can be a risky business. To illustrate, assume two companies have the following financial structures:

	Assets	=	Liabilities	+	Stockholders' Equity
Eastern Company	100	=	20	+	80
Western Company	100	=	80	+	20

Which company has the greater financial risk? If each company incurred a $30 loss, the financial structures would change as follows:

	Assets	=	Liabilities	+	Stockholders' Equity
Eastern Company	70	=	20	+	50
Western Company	70	=	80	+	(10)

Clearly, Western Company is at greater risk. Eastern Company could survive a $30 loss that reduced assets and stockholders' equity. It would still have a $50 balance in stockholders' equity and more than enough assets ($70) to satisfy the $20 obligation to creditors. In contrast, a $30 loss would throw Western Company into bankruptcy. The company would have a $10 deficit (negative) balance in stockholders' equity and the remaining assets ($70) would be less than the $80 obligation to creditors.

The level of debt risk can be measured in part by using a **debt to assets ratio,** as follows:

$$\frac{\text{Total debt}}{\text{Total assets}}$$

For example, Eastern Company's debt to assets ratio is 20 percent ($20 ÷ $100) while Western Company's is 80 percent ($80 ÷ $100). Why would the owners of Western Company be willing to accept greater debt risk? Assume that both companies produce $12 of revenue and each must pay 10 percent interest on money owed to creditors. Income statements for the two companies appear as follows:[2]

	Eastern Company	Western Company
Revenue	$12	$12
Interest Expense	2	8
Net Income	$10	$ 4

At first glance, the owners of Eastern Company appear better off because Eastern produced higher net income. In fact, however, the owners of *Western* Company are better off. The owners of Eastern Company get $10 of income for investing $80 of their own money into the business, a return on their invested funds of 12.5 percent ($10 ÷ $80). In contrast, the owners of Western Company obtain $4 of net income for their $20 investment, a return on invested funds of 20 percent ($4 ÷ $20).

The relationship between net income and stockholders' equity used above is the **return on equity ratio,** computed as

$$\frac{\text{Net income}}{\text{Stockholders' equity}}$$

Using borrowed money to increase the return on stockholders' investment is called **financial leverage.** Financial leverage explains why companies are willing to accept the risk of debt. Companies borrow money to make money. If a company can borrow money at 10 percent and invest it at 12 percent, the owners will be better off by 2 percent

---

[2]This illustration ignores the effect of income taxes on debt financing. This subject is discussed in a later chapter.

FOCUS ON INTERNATIONAL ISSUES

HOW DO IFRS DIFFER FROM U.S. GAAP?

Chapter 1 discussed the progression toward a single global GAAP in the form of International Financial Reporting Standards (IFRS). That discussion noted that the United States does not currently allow domestic companies to use IFRS; they must follow GAAP. Let's briefly consider just how U.S. GAAP differs from IFRS.

The differences can be summarized in a few broad categories. First, some differences are relatively minor. Consider the case of bank overdrafts. Under IFRS some bank overdrafts are included as a cash inflow and reported on the statement of cash flows. U.S. GAAP does not permit this. Conversely, some differences relate to very significant issues. Both IFRS and GAAP use historical cost as their primary method for reporting information on financial statements, but both allow exceptions in some circumstances. However, IFRS permit more exceptions to historical cost than do GAAP. Some of these differences will be discussed in later chapters.

Some of the differences affect how financial statements are presented in annual reports. IFRS require companies to report all financial statements for the current year and the prior year—two years of comparative data. Rules of the Securities and Exchange Commission require U.S. companies to report two years of balance sheets, the current and prior year, and three years of all other statements. See the financial statements of Target Corporation in Appendix B as an example. Of course, companies can show additional years if they wish.

As you would expect in the first course of accounting, some of the differences between IFRS and GAAP are simply too complex to be covered. Examples of such items relate to business combinations (when one company buys another) and to foreign currency translations (when a company has subsidiaries that operate outside the United States).

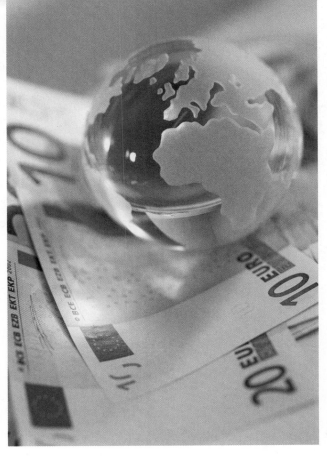

Do not be overwhelmed by the differences between IFRS and GAAP. There are many more rules that are alike than are different. A person who has a reasonable understanding of U.S. GAAP should be able to read financial statements prepared under IFRS without too much difficulty. If you wish more detailed, up-to-date information about IFRS versus GAAP, the large international accounting firms have websites that can help. Two examples are: www.iasplus.com, which is presented by the firm of Deloitte Touche Tohmatsu, and www.kpmgifrg.com, which is presented by the firm of KPMG.

---

of the amount borrowed. A business that does not borrow may be missing an opportunity to increase its return on equity.

Real-World Data

Exhibit 3.12 shows the debt to assets, return on assets, and return on equity ratios for six real-world companies in two different industries. The data are drawn from the companies' 2010 annual reports. Notice that Aflac's return on assets ratio was 2.3 percent and Aetna's was 4.7 percent. Neither ratio seems good; banks sometimes pay more than 2.3 percent interest on deposits in savings accounts. The *return on equity* ratios, however, show a different picture; Aflac's was 21.2 percent and Aetna's was 17.9 percent—much better than banks pay depositors.

Exhibit 3.12 shows that while ExxonMobil's return on assets ratio was more than four times higher than Aflac's (10.1 percent versus 2.3 percent), its return on equity ratio was about the same (20.0 percent versus 21.2 percent). How did this happen? Compare their debt to assets ratios. Aflac financed 89 percent of its assets with debt compared to Exxon's 50 percent. Financial leverage is the biggest factor causing these results, but it is not the only factor that affects this ratio.

EXHIBIT 3.12

Three Ratios (in Percentages) for Six Real-World Companies

Industry	Company	Debt to Assets	Return on Assets	Return on Equity
Insurance	Aetna	74	4.7	17.9
	Aflac	89	2.3	21.2
	Progressive	71	5.1	17.7
Oil	Chevron	43	10.3	18.0
	ExxonMobil	50	10.1	20.0
	Marathon Oil	52	5.1	10.8

Since financial leverage offers the opportunity to increase return on equity, why doesn't every company leverage itself to the maximum? There is a down side. When the economy turns down, companies may not be able to produce investment returns that exceed interest rates. A company that has borrowed money at a fixed rate of 8 percent that can only earn 6 percent on its investments will suffer from financial leverage. In

other words, financial leverage is a double-edged sword. It can have a negative as well as a positive impact on a company's return on equity ratio.

Finally, compare the ratios in Exhibit 3.12 for companies in the oil industry to the same ratios for companies in the insurance industry. There are significant differences *between* industries, but there are considerable similarities *within* each industry. The debt to assets ratio is much higher for the insurance industry than for the oil industry. However, within each industry, the ratios are clustered fairly close together. Distinct differences between industries and similarities within industries are common business features. When you compare accounting information for different companies, you must consider the industries in which those companies operate.

SCOPE OF COVERAGE

Throughout this text, we introduce ratios directly related to chapter topics. Only a few of the many ratios available to users of financial statements are introduced. Introductory finance courses typically include a more extensive study of ratios and other topics related to financial statement analysis. Many business programs offer an entire course on financial statement analysis. These courses help students learn to judge whether the ratio results signal good or poor performance. Developing such judgment requires understanding how accounting policies and procedures can affect financial ratios. The ratios introduced in this text will enhance your understanding of accounting as a basis for studying more advanced topics in subsequent courses.

<< A Look Back

This chapter introduced the *double-entry accounting system*. This system was first documented in the 1400s, and is used by most companies today. Key components of the double-entry system are summarized below.

1.   Business events can be classified concisely using debit/credit terminology. *Debits* are used to record increases in asset accounts and decreases in liability and stockholders' equity accounts. *Credits* are used to record decreases in asset accounts and increases in liability and stockholders' equity accounts.

2. *T-accounts* are frequently used to analyze and communicate account activity. The account title is placed at the top of the horizontal bar of the T, and increases and decreases are placed on either side of the vertical bar. In a T-account, debits are recorded on the left side and credits are recorded on the right side.

3. Accountants initially record transaction data in journals. The *general journal* is used not only for data entry but also as a shorthand communication tool. Each journal entry includes at least one debit and one credit. An entry is recorded using at least two lines, with the debit recorded on the top line and the credit on the bottom line. The credit is indented to distinguish it from the debit. The general journal format is illustrated here:

| Debit | | xxx | |
| Credit | | | xxx |

4. Information is posted (copied) from the journals to *ledger* accounts. The ledger accounts provide the information used to prepare the financial statements.

5. *Trial balances* are used to check the mathematical accuracy of the recording process. Ledger accounts with their associated debit and credit balances are listed in the trial balance. The debit and credit amounts are totaled and compared. An equal amount of debits and credits provides evidence but not proof that transactions have been recorded correctly. If the debits and credits are *not* equal, it is proof that errors exist.

The double-entry system is just a way to organize accounting data. No matter how we organize the data, the objective is to summarize and report it in a way that is useful for making decisions.

A Look Forward >>

Chapters 1 through 3 focused on businesses that generate revenue by providing services to their customers. Examples of these types of businesses include consulting, real estate sales, medical services, and legal services. The next chapter introduces accounting practices for businesses that generate revenue by selling goods. Examples of these companies include Walmart, Best Buy, Office Depot, and Lowe's.

APPENDIX

Journal Entries for Long-Term Assets and Depreciation

To illustrate the journal entries associated with the acquisition and depreciation of long-term assets, assume Evans Company paid $34,000 cash to purchase a computer. The computer has a $4,000 salvage value and a 3-year useful life. The journal entry necessary to record the purchase of the computer is shown here.

Record depreciation and interest using journal entries and T-accounts, and show how these entries affect financial statements.

Account Title	Debit	Credit
Computer	34,000	
Cash		34,000

Depreciation expense is determined as follows:

($34,000 cost − $4,000 salvage) / 3-year useful life = $10,000 per year

The journal entry to record the depreciation expense at the end of each year is shown here.

Account Title	Debit	Credit
Depreciation Expense	10,000	
Accumulated Depreciation		10,000

Journal Entries for Notes Payable and Interest Expense

To illustrate the journal entries associated with issuing a promissory note and associated interest, assume Evans Company acquired $20,000 cash by issuing a note to the State Bank. The note was dated October 1, 2013. It stipulated a 1-year term and a 9 percent annual interest rate. The entry necessary to record the issue of the note on October 1 is shown here.

Account Title	Debit	Credit
Cash	20,000	
Note Payable		20,000

Accrued interest as of December 31, 2013, is computed as follows:

$20,000 principal × .09 annual interest × 3/12 = $450

The journal entry required to record the accrued interest as of December 31, 2013, is shown here.

Account Title	Debit	Credit
Accrued Interest Expense	450	
Interest Payable		450

The note matures on September 30, 2014. The accrued interest expense for the nine months the note was outstanding in 2014 is computed as follows:

$20,000 principal × .09 annual interest × 9/12 = $1,350

The journal entry required to record the accrued interest is shown here.

Account Title	Debit	Credit
Accrued Interest Expense	1,350	
Interest Payable		1,350

The journal entry required to pay the interest due and the principal balance of the note on September 30, 2014, is shown here:

Account Title	Debit	Credit
Interest Payable	1,800	
Notes Payable	20,000	
Cash		21,800

SELF-STUDY REVIEW PROBLEM

A step-by-step audio-narrated series of slides is provided on the text website at www.mhhe.com/edmonds8e.

The following events apply to the first year of operations for Mestro Financial Services Company:

1. Acquired $28,000 cash by issuing common stock on January 1, 2013.
2. Purchased $1,100 of supplies on account.
3. Paid $12,000 cash in advance for a one-year lease on office space.
4. Earned $23,000 of consulting revenue on account.
5. Incurred $16,000 of general operating expenses on account.
6. Collected $20,000 cash from receivables.
7. Paid $13,000 cash on accounts payable.
8. Paid a $1,000 cash dividend to stockholders.

Information for Adjusting Entries

9. There was $200 of supplies on hand at the end of the accounting period.
10. The one-year lease on the office space was effective beginning on October 1, 2013.
11. There was $1,200 of accrued salaries at the end of 2013.

Required

a. Record the preceding events in general journal format.
b. Post the transaction data from the general journal into general ledger T-accounts.
c. Prepare an adjusted trial balance.
d. Prepare an income statement, statement of changes in stockholders' equity, balance sheet, and statement of cash flows.
e. Prepare the appropriate closing entries in general journal format.

Solution to Requirement a

Event No.	Account Title	Debit	Credit
1	Cash	28,000	
	Common Stock		28,000
2	Supplies	1,100	
	Accounts Payable		1,100
3	Prepaid Rent	12,000	
	Cash		12,000
4	Accounts Receivable	23,000	
	Consulting Revenue		23,000
5	General Operating Expenses	16,000	
	Accounts Payable		16,000
6	Cash	20,000	
	Accounts Receivable		20,000
7	Accounts Payable	13,000	
	Cash		13,000
8	Dividends	1,000	
	Cash		1,000
9	Supplies Expense	900	
	Supplies		900
10	Rent Expense	3,000	
	Prepaid Rent		3,000
11	Salaries Expense	1,200	
	Salaries Payable		1,200

Solution to Requirement b

MESTRO FINANCIAL SERVICES COMPANY
T-Accounts, 2013

| Assets | | = | Liabilities | | + | Equity | |

Cash

1.	28,000	3.	12,000
6.	20,000	7.	13,000
		8.	1,000
Bal.	22,000		

Accounts Receivable

| 4. | 23,000 | 6. | 20,000 |
| Bal. | 3,000 | | |

Supplies

| 2. | 1,100 | 9. | 900 |
| Bal. | 200 | | |

Prepaid Rent

| 3. | 12,000 | 10. | 3,000 |
| Bal. | 9,000 | | |

Accounts Payable

7.	13,000	2.	1,100
		5.	16,000
		Bal.	4,100

Salaries Payable

| | | 11. | 1,200 |
| | | Bal. | 1,200 |

Common Stock

| | | 1. | 28,000 |
| | | Bal. | 28,000 |

Dividends

| 8. | 1,000 | |

Consulting Revenue

| | | 4. | 23,000 |

General Operating Expenses

| 5. | 16,000 | |

Salaries Expense

| 11. | 1,200 | |

Supplies Expense

| 9. | 900 | |

Rent Expense

| 10. | 3,000 | |

Solution to Requirement c

MESTRO FINANCIAL SERVICES COMPANY
Trial Balance
December 31, 2013

Account Titles	Debit	Credit
Cash	$22,000	
Accounts receivable	3,000	
Supplies	200	
Prepaid rent	9,000	
Accounts payable		$ 4,100
Salaries payable		1,200
Common stock		28,000
Dividends	1,000	
Consulting revenue		23,000
General operating expenses	16,000	
Salaries expense	1,200	
Supplies expense	900	
Rent expense	3,000	
Totals	$56,300	$56,300

Solution to Requirement d

MESTRO FINANCIAL SERVICES COMPANY
Financial Statements
For 2013

Income Statement
For the Year Ended December 31, 2013

Consulting revenue		$23,000
Expenses		
General operating expenses	$16,000	
Salaries expense	1,200	
Supplies expense	900	
Rent expense	3,000	
Total expenses		(21,100)
Net income		$ 1,900

Statement of Changes in Stockholders' Equity
For the Year Ended December 31, 2013

Beginning common stock	$ 0	
Plus: Common stock issued	28,000	
Ending common stock		$28,000
Beginning retained earnings	0	
Plus: Net income	1,900	
Less: Dividends	(1,000)	
Ending retained earnings		900
Total stockholders' equity		$28,900

Balance Sheet
As of December 31, 2013

Assets		
Cash	$22,000	
Accounts receivable	3,000	
Supplies	200	
Prepaid rent	9,000	
Total assets		$34,200
Liabilities		
Accounts payable	$ 4,100	
Salaries payable	1,200	
Total liabilities		$ 5,300
Stockholders' equity		
Common stock	28,000	
Retained earnings	900	
Total stockholders' equity		28,900
Total liabilities and stockholders' equity		$34,200

continued

Statement of Cash Flows For the Year Ended December 31, 2013		
Cash flows from operating activities		
Inflow from customers	$20,000	
Outflow for expenses	(25,000)	
Net cash flow from operating activities		$(5,000)
Cash flows from investing activities		0
Cash flows from financing activities		
Inflow from issue of common stock	28,000	
Outflow for dividends	(1,000)	
Net cash flow from financing activities		27,000
Net change in cash		22,000
Plus: Beginning cash balance		0
Ending cash balance		$22,000

Solution to Requirement e

Date	Account Title	Debit	Credit
Dec. 31	Consulting Revenue	23,000	
	Retained Earnings		23,000
Dec. 31	Retained Earnings	21,100	
	General Operating Expenses		16,000
	Salaries Expense		1,200
	Supplies Expense		900
	Rent Expense		3,000
Dec. 31	Retained Earnings	1,000	
	Dividends		1,000

KEY TERMS

account balance 140
books of original entry 150
chart of accounts 151
closing entries 155
credit 140

debit 140
debt to assets ratio 158
double-entry accounting 141
financial leverage 158
fiscal year 139

general journal 150
general ledger 151
journals 150
posting 151
return on assets ratio 157

return on equity ratio 158
source documents 149
special journals 150
T-account 140
trial balance 153

QUESTIONS

1. What are the two fundamental equality requirements of the double-entry accounting system?

2. Define *debit* and *credit*. How are assets, liabilities, common stock, retained earnings, revenues, expenses, and dividends affected (increased or decreased) by debits and by credits?

3. How is the balance of an account determined?

4. What are the three primary sources of business assets?

5. What are the three primary ways a business may use assets?

6. Give an example of an asset exchange transaction.

7. How does a debit to an expense account ultimately affect retained earnings? Stockholders' equity?

8. What accounts normally have debit balances?

What accounts normally have credit balances?

9. What is the primary source of information for preparing the financial statements?

10. What is the purpose of a journal?

11. What is the difference between the *general journal* and special journals?

12. What is a ledger? What is its function in the accounting system?

13. What is the purpose of closing entries?

14. Do all companies close their books on December 31? Why or why not?

15. At a minimum, what information is recorded in the general journal?

16. What is the purpose of a trial balance?

17. When should a trial balance be prepared?

18. What does the term *posting* mean?

19. What information does the return on assets ratio provide about a company?

20. What information does the debt to assets ratio provide about a company?

21. What is financial leverage?

22. Explain how financial leverage impacts the return on equity ratio.

MULTIPLE-CHOICE QUESTIONS

Multiple-choice questions are provided on the text website at www.mhhe.com/edmonds8e.

EXERCISES—SERIES A

All applicable Exercises in Series A are available with McGraw-Hill's
Connect® Accounting.

Exercise 3-1A   *Matching debit and credit terminology with accounts*

LO 1

Required

Complete the following table by indicating whether a debit or credit is used to increase or decrease the balance of the following accounts. The appropriate debit/credit terminology has been identified for the first account as an example.

Account Titles	Used to Increase This Account	Used to Decrease This Account
Accounts Receivable	Debit	Credit
Accounts Payable		
Common Stock		
Land		
Unearned Revenue		
Service Revenue		
Retained Earnings		
Insurance Expense		
Rent Expense		
Prepaid Rent		
Interest Revenue		

Exercise 3-2A   *Debit/credit rules*

LO 1

Chris, Patty, and Devon, three accounting students, were discussing the rules of debits and credits. Chris says that debits increase account balances and credits decrease account balances. Patty says that Chris is wrong, that credits increase account balances and debits decrease account balances. Devon interrupts and declares that they are both correct.

Required

Explain what Devon meant and give examples of transactions where debits increase account balances, credits decrease account balances, credits increase account balances, and debits decrease account balances.

Exercise 3-3A   *Matching debit and credit terminology with account titles*

LO 1

Required

Indicate whether each of the following accounts normally has a debit balance or a credit balance.

a. Common Stock
b. Prepaid Rent
c. Supplies
d. Accounts Payable
e. Interest Revenue
f. Rent Expense

g. Unearned Revenue
h. Service Revenue
i. Dividends
j. Land
k. Accounts Receivable
l. Cash

LO 1

Exercise 3-4A *Applying debit/credit terminology to accounting events*

Required

a. In parallel columns, list the accounts that would be debited and credited for each of the following unrelated transactions:

(1) Purchased land for cash.

(2) Paid a cash dividend to the stockholders.

(3) Provided services for cash.

(4) Recognized accrued salaries at the end of the period.

(5) Recognized accrued interest revenue.

(6) Provided services on account.

(7) Paid cash for operating expenses.

(8) Acquired cash from the issue of common stock.

(9) Purchased supplies on account.

b. Show how each transaction affects the financial statements by placing a + for increase, − for decrease, and NA for not affected under each component in a horizontal statements model like the one shown below. Also, in the Cash Flow column, use the letters OA to designate operating activity, IA for investing activity, and FA for financing activity. The first event is recorded as an example.

Assets	=	Liab.	+	Equity	Rev.	−	Exp.	=	Net Inc.	Cash Flow
+ −		NA		NA	NA		NA		NA	− IA

LO 1

Exercise 3-5A *Debit/credit terminology*

Required

For each of the following independent events, identify the account that would be debited and the account that would be credited. The accounts for the first event are identified as an example.

Event	Account Debited	Account Credited
a	Cash	Common Stock

a. Received cash by issuing common stock.

b. Provided services on account.

c. Paid accounts payable.

d. Received cash for services to be performed in the future.

e. Purchased supplies on account.

f. Paid cash in advance for one year's rent.

g. Recognized revenue for services completed; previously collected the cash in Event *d*.

h. Paid cash for operating expenses.

i. Paid salaries payable.

j. Paid cash dividends to the stockholders.

k. Recognized accrued interest revenue.

l. Recognized expense for prepaid rent that had been used up by the end of the accounting period.

m. Paid salaries expense.

n. Received cash in payment of accounts receivable.

LO 1

Exercise 3-6A *Identifying transaction type, its effect on the accounting equation, and whether the effect is recorded with a debit or credit*

Required

Identify whether each of the following transactions is an asset source (AS), asset use (AU), asset exchange (AE), or claims exchange (CE). Also explain how each event affects the accounting equation by placing a + for *increase,* − for *decrease,* and NA for *not affected* under each of the components of the accounting equation. Finally, indicate whether the effect requires a debit or credit entry. The first event is recorded as an example.

| | | | | | | Stockholders Equity | | |
Event	Type of Event	Assets	=	Liabilities	+	Common Stock	+	Retained Earnings
a	AS	+ Debit		+ Credit		NA		NA

a. Received cash for services to be performed in the future.
b. Paid a cash dividend to the stockholders.
c. Paid cash in advance for one year's rent.
d. Provided services on account.
e. Provided services for cash.
f. Received cash in payment of accounts receivable.
g. Recognized revenue for services completed; cash collected previously.
h. Purchased land by paying cash.
i. Recognized accrued interest revenue.
j. Purchased supplies on account.
k. Paid salaries payable.
l. Recognized expense for prepaid rent that had been used up by the end of the accounting period.
m. Incurred other operating expenses on account.
n. Recognized expense for supplies used during the period.

Exercise 3-7A   *Identifying increases and decreases in T-accounts*   LO 1, 2

Required

For each of the following T-accounts, indicate the side of the account that should be used to record an increase or decrease in the financial statement element:

Assets		=	Liabilities		+	Stockholders' Equity	
Debit	Credit		Debit	Credit		Debit	Credit
						Revenue	
						Debit	Credit
						Expense	
						Debit	Credit

Exercise 3-8A   *T-accounts and the accounting equation*   LO 2

Required

Record each of the following Jackson Co. events in T-accounts and then explain how the event affects the accounting equation:

a. Received $40,000 cash by issuing common stock.
b. Purchased supplies for $1,800 cash.
c. Performed services on account for $14,000.
d. Paid cash for $8,000 of salaries expense.

Exercise 3-9A   *Recording receivables and identifying their effect on financial statements*   LO 2

Rice Company performed services on account for $30,000 in 2013, its first year of operations. Rice collected $24,000 cash from accounts receivable during 2013 and the remaining $6,000 in cash during 2014.

Required

a. Record the 2013 transactions in T-accounts.

b. Record the 2013 transactions in a horizontal statements model like the following one:

Assets		= Liab. +	Equity	Rev.	−	Exp.	=	Net Inc.	Cash Flow
Cash	+ Accts. Rec. =		Ret. Earn.						

c. Determine the amount of revenue Rice would report on the 2013 income statement.

d. Determine the amount of cash flow from operating activities Rice would report on the 2013 statement of cash flows.

e. Open a T-account for Retained Earnings, and close the 2013 Service Revenue account to the Retained Earnings account.

f. Record the 2014 cash collection in the appropriate T-accounts.

g. Record the 2014 transaction in a horizontal statements model like the one shown in Requirement *b*.

h. Assuming no other transactions occur in 2014, determine the amount of net income and the net cash flow from operating activities for 2014.

LO 2, 4

Exercise 3-10A *Recording supplies and identifying their effect on financial statement*

Nickie Hern started and operated a small family consulting firm in 2013. The firm was affected by two events: (1) Hern provided $36,000 of services on account, and (2) she purchased $10,000 of supplies on account. There were $1,800 of supplies on hand as of December 31, 2013.

Required

a. Open T-accounts and record the two transactions in the accounts.

b. Record the required year-end adjusting entry to reflect the use of supplies.

c. Record the above transactions in a horizontal statements model like the following one:

Assets			= Liab.	+	Equity	Rev.	−	Exp.	=	Net Inc.	Cash Flow
Accts. Rec.	+	Supplies =	Accts. Pay.	+	Ret. Earn.						

d. Explain why the amounts of net income and net cash flow from operating activities differ.

e. Record and post the required closing entries, and prepare a post-closing trial balance.

LO 2

Exercise 3-11A *Recording unearned revenue and identifying its effect on financial statements*

Ditto received a $90,000 cash advance on March 1, 2013, for legal services to be performed in the future. Services were to be provided for a one-year term beginning March 1, 2013.

Required

a. Record the March 1 cash receipt in T-accounts.

b. Record in T-accounts the adjustment required as of December 31, 2013.

c. Record the preceding transaction and related adjustment in a horizontal statements model like the following one:

Assets	=	Liab.	+	Equity	Rev.	−	Exp.	=	Net Inc.	Cash Flow

d. Determine the amount of net income on the 2013 income statement. What is the amount of net cash flow from operating activities for 2013?

e. What amount of unearned revenue would Ditto report on the December 31, 2013, balance sheet?

Exercise 3-12A   *Using a T-account to determine cash flow from operating activities*   **LO 2**

Farris Inc. began the accounting period with a $105,000 debit balance in its Accounts Receivable account. During the accounting period, Farris earned revenue on account of $448,000. The ending Accounts Receivable balance was $86,000.

Required

Based on this information alone, determine the amount of cash inflow from operating activities during the accounting period. (*Hint:* Use a T-account for Accounts Receivable. Enter the debits and credits for the given events, and solve for the missing amount.)

Exercise 3-13A   *Using a T-account to determine cash flow from operating activities*   **LO 2**

Ray Company began the accounting period with a $36,000 credit balance in its Accounts Payable account. During the accounting period, Ray incurred expenses on account of $108,000. The ending Accounts Payable balance was $48,000.

Required

Based on this information, determine the amount of cash outflow for expenses during the accounting period. (*Hint:* Use a T-account for Accounts Payable. Enter the debits and credits for the given events, and solve for the missing amount.)

Exercise 3-14A   *Recording events in the general journal and the effect on financial statements*   **LO 3**

Required

Record each of the following transactions in general journal form and then show the effect of the transaction in the horizontal statements model. The first transaction is shown as an example.

Account Title	Debit	Credit
Cash	4,000	
Unearned Revenue		4,000

Assets	=	Liab.	+	Equity	Rev.	−	Exp.	=	Net Inc.	Cash Flow
4,000		4,000		NA	NA		NA		NA	4,000 OA

a. Received $4,000 cash for services to be performed at a later date.
b. Purchased supplies for $2,400 cash.
c. Performed $50,000 worth of services on account.
d. Charged $2,000 on account for operating expense.
e. Collected $27,000 cash on accounts receivable.
f. Paid $700 on accounts payable.
g. Paid $6,800 cash in advance for an insurance policy.
h. Recorded the adjusting entry to recognize $4,500 of insurance expense.
i. Recorded the adjusting entry to recognize $800 of accrued interest revenue.

Exercise 3-15A   *Recording accrued salaries and identifying their effect on financial statements*   **LO 3**

On December 31, 2013, Blue Bayou Company had accrued salaries of $12,000.

Required

a. Record in general journal format the adjustment required as of December 31, 2013.

b. Record the above adjustment in a horizontal statements model like the following one:

Assets	=	Liab.	+	Equity	Rev.	−	Exp.	=	Net Inc.	Cash Flow
		Sal. Pay.	+	Ret. Earn.						

c. Determine the amount of net income Blue Bayou would report on the 2013 income statement, assuming that Blue Bayou received $29,000 of cash revenue. What is the amount of net cash flow from operating activities for 2013?

d. What amount of salaries payable would Blue Bayou report on the December 31, 2013, balance sheet?

LO 3

Exercise 3-16A   *Recording prepaid items and identifying their effect on financial statements*

Washington Mining began operations by issuing common stock for $150,000. The company paid $135,000 cash in advance for a one-year contract to lease machinery for the business. The lease agreement was signed on March 1, 2013, and was effective immediately. Washington Mining received $172,500 of cash revenue in 2013.

Required

a. Record the March 1 cash payment in general journal format.

b. Record in general journal format the adjustment required as of December 31, 2013.

c. Record all 2013 events in a horizontal statements model like the following one:

Assets			=	Liab.	+	Equity			Rev.	−	Exp.	=	Net Inc.	Cash Flow
Cash	+	Prep. Rent	=			Common Stock	+	Ret. Earn.						

d. What amount of net income would Washington Mining report on the 2013 income statement? What is the amount of net cash flow from operating activities for 2013?

e. Determine the amount of prepaid rent Washington Mining would report on the December 31, 2013, balance sheet.

LO 3

Exercise 3-17A   *Preparing closing entries*

The following financial information was taken from the books of Walker Spa:

Account Balances as of December 31, 2013	
Accounts Receivable	$54,000
Accounts Payable	15,000
Advertising Expense	7,000
Cash	80,600
Common Stock	40,000
Dividends	10,000
Land	27,000
Prepaid Rent	6,400
Rent Expense	15,600
Retained Earnings 1/1/2013	38,800
Salaries Expense	64,000
Salaries Payable	23,600
Service Revenue	153,000
Supplies	800
Supplies Expense	5,000

Required

a. Prepare the journal entries necessary to close the temporary accounts December 31, 2013, for Walker Spa.

b. What is the balance in the Retained Earnings account after the closing entries are posted?

Exercise 3-18A   Recording transactions in general journal and T-accounts   LO 2, 3

The following events apply to Sanford Service Co. for 2013, its first year of operation:

1. Received cash of $60,000 from the issue of common stock.
2. Performed $100,000 worth of services on account.
3. Paid $74,000 cash for salaries expense.
4. Purchased supplies for $13,000 on account.
5. Collected $79,000 of accounts receivable.
6. Paid $9,500 of the accounts payable.
7. Paid a $6,000 dividend to the stockholders.
8. Had $2,500 of supplies on hand at the end of the period.

Required

a. Record these events in general journal form.

b. Post the entries to T-accounts and determine the ending balance in each account.

c. Determine the amount of total assets at the end of 2013.

d. Determine the amount of net income for 2013.

Exercise 3-19A   Preparing a trial balance   LO 4

Required

On December 31, 2013, Magee Company had the following normal account balances in its general ledger. Use this information to prepare a trial balance.

Common Stock	$ 50,000
Salaries Expense	32,000
Office Supplies	3,600
Advertising Expense	5,000
Retained Earnings, 1/1/2013	28,400
Unearned Revenue	36,000
Accounts Receivable	13,000
Cash	120,000
Service Revenue	152,000
Dividends	10,000
Prepaid Insurance	12,800
Land	44,000
Rent Expense	30,000
Accounts Payable	4,000

Exercise 3-20A   Determining the effect of errors on the trial balance   LO 4

Required

Explain how each of the following posting errors affects a trial balance. State whether the trial balance will be out of balance because of the posting error, and indicate which side of the trial balance will have a higher amount after each independent entry is posted. If the posting error does not affect the equality of debits and credits in the trial balance, state that the error will not cause an inequality and explain why.

a. A $2,500 credit to Accounts Payable was posted as a credit to Cash.

b. The collection of $400 of accounts receivable was posted to Accounts Receivable twice.

c. A $2,000 credit to Salaries Payable was not posted.

d. A $5,400 debit to Cash was posted as a $4,500 debit.

e. A $3,000 debit to Prepaid Rent was debited to Rent Expense.

Exercise 3-21A   *Recording events in the general journal, posting to T-accounts, and preparing a trial balance*

The following events apply to Davis Dry Cleaners in 2013, its first year of operations:

1. Received $45,000 cash from the issue of common stock.
2. Earned $37,500 of service revenue on account.
3. Incurred $15,000 of operating expenses on account.
4. Received $30,000 cash for performing services.
5. Paid $12,000 cash to purchase land.
6. Collected $33,000 of cash from accounts receivable.
7. Received a $9,000 cash advance for services to be provided in the future.
8. Purchased $1,350 of supplies on account.
9. Made an $11,250 payment on accounts payable.
10. Paid a $7,500 cash dividend to the stockholders.
11. Recognized $750 of supplies expense.
12. Recognized $7,500 of revenue for services provided to the customer in Event 7.
13. Recognized $1,350 of accrued interest revenue.

Required

a. Record the events in the general journal.
b. Post the events to T-accounts and determine the ending account balances.
c. Test the equality of the debit and credit balances of the T-accounts by preparing a trial balance.

Exercise 3-22A   *Recording events in the general journal, posting to T-accounts, and preparing closing entries*

At the beginning of 2013, Eva Event Service had the following normal balances in its accounts:

Account	Balance
Cash	$60,000
Accounts Receivable	38,000
Accounts Payable	24,800
Common Stock	48,000
Retained Earnings	25,200

The following events apply to Eva Event Service for 2013:

1. Provided $130,000 of services on account.
2. Incurred $6,200 of operating expenses on account.
3. Collected $112,000 of accounts receivable.
4. Paid $72,000 cash for salaries expense.
5. Paid $30,000 cash as a partial payment on accounts payable.
6. Paid an $16,000 cash dividend to the stockholders.

Required

a. Record these events in a general journal.
b. Open T-accounts and post the beginning balances and the preceding transactions to the appropriate accounts. Determine the balance of each account.
c. Record the beginning balances and the events in a horizontal statements model such as the following one:

Assets		=	Liab.	+	Equity		Rev.	−	Exp.	=	Net Inc.	Cash Flow
Cash	Accts. Rec.	=	Accts. Pay.	+	Common Stock	Ret. Earn.						

d. Record the closing entries in the general journal and post them to the T-accounts. What is the amount of net income for the year?

e. What is the amount of *change* in retained earnings for the year? Is the change in retained earnings different from the amount of net income? If so, why?

f. Prepare a post-closing trial balance.

Exercise 3-23A *Using ratio analysis to assess financial risk*

LO 5

The following information was drawn from the balance sheets of two companies:

Company	Assets	=	Liabilities	+	Equity
North	$416,000		$178,500		$237,500
South	164,000		57,500		106,500

Required

a. Compute the debt to assets ratio to measure the level of financial risk of both companies.

b. Compare the two ratios computed in Requirement *a* to identify which company has the higher level of financial risk.

Exercise 3-24A *IFRS and U.S. GAAP*

IFRS

Using one of the websites referenced in the Focus on International Issues feature on page 159, define the IASB and describe its function.

PROBLEMS—SERIES A

All applicable Problems in Series A are available with McGraw-Hill's *Connect® Accounting*.

McGraw Hill connect
|ACCOUNTING

Problem 3-25A *Identifying debit and credit balances*

LO 1

Required

Indicate whether each of the following accounts normally has a debit or credit balance:

CHECK FIGURES
a. Interest Receivable: Debit
o. Salaries Payable: Credit

a. Interest Receivable
b. Interest Revenue
c. Dividends
d. Operating Expense
e. Unearned Revenue
f. Accounts Payable
g. Supplies
h. Service Revenue
i. Prepaid Rent
j. Supplies Expense

k. Retained Earnings
l. Prepaid Insurance
m. Insurance Expense
n. Accounts Receivable
o. Salaries Payable
p. Cash
q. Common Stock
r. Rent Expense
s. Salaries Expense
t. Land

Problem 3-26A *Transaction type and debit/credit terminology*

LO 1

The following events apply to Box Enterprises:

1. Acquired $30,000 cash from the issue of common stock.
2. Recognized $28,000 of service revenue on account.
3. Paid cash to rent office space for the next 12 months, $7,800.
4. Paid cash of $9,200 for operating expenses.
5. Collected $9,000 cash for services to be performed in the future.
6. Paid salaries to employees, $8,000 cash.
7. Paid cash for utilities expense, $1,200.

8. Paid on accounts payable, $1,200.

9. Paid a $5,000 cash dividend to the stockholders.

10. Purchased $2,000 of supplies on account.

11. Received $18,000 cash for services rendered.

12. Recognized $400 of accrued interest revenue.

13. Recognized $3,250 of rent expense related to cash paid in a prior transaction (see Event 3).

14. Recognized $6,000 of revenue for services performed for which cash had been previously collected (see Event 5).

15. Recognized $4,800 of accrued salaries expense.

Required

Identify each event as asset source (AS), asset use (AU), asset exchange (AE), or claims exchange (CE). Also identify the account to be debited and the account to be credited when the transaction is recorded. The first event is recorded as an example.

Event No.	Type of Event	Account Debited	Account Credited
1	AS	Cash	Common Stock

LO 2, 4

CHECK FIGURE
b. Total debits: $78,250

Problem 3-27A *Recording events in a statements model and T-accounts and preparing a trial balance*

The following accounting events apply to Barnes Co. for the year 2013:

Asset Source Transactions

1. Began operations when the business acquired $40,000 cash from the issue of common stock.

2. Performed services and collected cash of $2,000.

3. Collected $9,000 of cash in advance for services to be provided over the next 12 months.

4. Provided $24,000 of services on account.

5. Purchased supplies of $840 on account.

Asset Exchange Transactions

6. Purchased $8,000 of land for cash.

7. Collected $17,000 of cash from accounts receivable.

8. Purchased $1,000 of supplies with cash.

9. Paid $7,200 in advance for one year's rent.

Asset Use Transactions

10. Paid $4,000 cash for salaries of employees.

11. Paid a cash dividend of $4,000 to the stockholders.

12. Paid $840 for supplies that had been purchased on account.

Claims Exchange Transactions

13. Placed an advertisement in the local newspaper for $300 and agreed to pay for the ad later.

14. Incurred utilities expense of $250 on account.

Adjusting Entries

15. Recognized $6,000 of revenue for performing services. The collection of cash for these services occurred in a prior transaction. (See Event 3.)

16. Recorded $1,800 of accrued salary expense at the end of 2013.

17. Recorded supplies expense. Had $240 of supplies on hand at the end of the accounting period.

18. Recognized that three months of prepaid rent had been used up during the accounting period.

19. Recognized $900 of accrued interest revenue.

Required

a. Record each of the preceding transactions in T-accounts and determine the balance of each account.

b. Prepare a before-closing trial balance.

c. Use a horizontal statements model to show how each event affects the balance sheet, income statement, and statement of cash flows. Indicate whether the event increases (+), decreases (−), or does not affect (NA) each element of the financial statements. Also, in the Cash Flow column, use the letters OA to designate operating activity, IA for investing activity, and FA for financing activity. The first event is recorded as an example.

Assets	=	Liab.	+	Equity	Rev.	−	Exp.	=	Net Inc.	Cash Flow
+		NA		+	NA		NA		NA	+ FA

Problem 3-28A *Effect of journal entries on financial statements*   LO 3

Event No.	Account Title	Debit	Credit
1	Cash	xxx	
	Common Stock		xxx
2	Accounts Receivable	xxx	
	Service Revenue		xxx
3	Cash	xxx	
	Accounts Receivable		xxx
4	Supplies	xxx	
	Accounts Payable		xxx
5	Cash	xxx	
	Unearned Revenue		xxx
6	Cash	xxx	
	Service Revenue		xxx
7	Property Tax Expense	xxx	
	Cash		xxx
8	Prepaid Rent	xxx	
	Cash		xxx
9	Salaries Expense	xxx	
	Cash		xxx
10	Unearned Revenue	xxx	
	Service Revenue		xxx
11	Rent Expense	xxx	
	Prepaid Rent		xxx
12	Supplies Expense	xxx	
	Supplies		xxx
13	Dividends	xxx	
	Cash		xxx

Required

The preceding 13 different accounting events are presented in general journal format. Use a horizontal statements model to show how each event affects the balance sheet, income statement, and statement of cash flows. Indicate whether the event increases (+), decreases (−), or does not affect (NA) each element of the financial statements. Also, in the Cash Flow column, use the letters OA to designate operating activity, IA for investing activity, and FA for financing activity. The first event is recorded as an example.

Assets	=	Liab.	+	Equity	Rev.	−	Exp.	=	Net Inc.	Cash Flow
+		NA		+	NA		NA		NA	+ FA

LO 3

Problem 3-29A *Identifying accounting events from journal entries*

Required

The following information is from the records of Floral Design. Write a brief explanation of the accounting event represented in each of the general journal entries.

Date	Account Titles	Debit	Credit
Jan. 1	Cash	18,750	
	Common Stock		18,750
Feb. 1	Prepaid Rent	15,300	
	Cash		15,300
Mar. 1	Supplies	2,325	
	Accounts Payable		2,325
Apr. 1	Cash	19,500	
	Unearned Revenue		19,500
May 20	Accounts Receivable	27,600	
	Service Revenue		27,600
June 30	Salaries Expense	9,150	
	Cash		9,150
30	Property Tax Expense	4,500	
	Cash		4,500
Aug. 1	Cash	13,000	
	Service Revenue		13,000
Oct. 2	Cash	16,000	
	Accounts Receivable		16,000
Dec. 1	Dividends	4,000	
	Cash		4,000
Dec. 31	Supplies Expense	2,100	
	Supplies		2,100
31	Rent Expense	9,600	
	Prepaid Rent		9,600
31	Unearned Revenue	12,500	
	Service Revenue		12,500

LO 3

CHECK FIGURE
d. Adjustment amount: $3,200

Problem 3-30A *Recording adjusting entries in general journal format*

Required

Each of the following independent events requires a year-end adjusting entry. Record each event and the related adjusting entry in general journal format. The first event is recorded as an example. Assume a December 31 closing date.

Date	Account Titles	Debit	Credit
Oct. 1	Prepaid Rent	8,400	
	Cash		8,400
Dec. 31	Rent Expense (8,400 × 3/12)	2,100	
	Prepaid Rent		2,100

a. Paid $8,400 cash in advance on October 1 for a one-year lease on office space.

b. Purchased $1,600 of supplies on account on June 15. At year end, $200 of supplies remained on hand.

c. Received a $4,800 cash advance on September 1 for a contract to provide services for one year beginning immediately..

d. Paid $4,800 cash in advance on May 1 for a one-year insurance policy.

Problem 3-31A   *Effect of errors on the trial balance*

The following trial balance was prepared from the ledger accounts of Smith Inc.:

LO 4

CHECK FIGURE
Corrected cash balance: $9,200

SMITH INC.
Trial Balance
May 31, 2013

Account Titles	Debit	Credit
Cash	$ 7,200	
Accounts Receivable	1,770	
Supplies	420	
Prepaid Insurance	2,400	
Land	5,000	
Accounts Payable		$ 1,500
Common Stock		1,800
Retained Earnings		7,390
Dividends	400	
Service Revenue		19,600
Rent Expense	3,600	
Salaries Expense	9,000	
Operating Expenses	2,500	
Totals	$32,290	$30,290

The accountant for Smith, Inc., made the following errors during May 2013:

1. The cash purchase of land for $3,000 was recorded as a $5,000 debit to Land and a $3,000 credit to Cash.

2. A $1,600 purchase of supplies on account was properly recorded as a debit to the Supplies account but was incorrectly recorded as a credit to the Cash account.

3. The company provided services valued at $7,800 to a customer on account. The accountant recorded the transaction in the proper accounts but in the incorrect amount of $8,700.

4. A $1,200 cash receipt from a customer on an account receivable was not recorded.

5. An $800 cash payment of an account payable was not recorded.

6. The May utility bill, which amounted to $1,050 on account, was not recorded.

Required

a. Identify the errors that would cause a difference in the total amounts of debits and credits that would appear in a trial balance. Indicate whether the Debit or Credit column would be larger as a result of the error.

b. Indicate whether each of the preceding errors would overstate, understate, or have no effect on the amount of total assets, liabilities, and equity. Your answer should take the following form:

Event No.	Assets	=	Liabilities	+	Stockholders' Equity
1	Overstate		No effect		No effect

c. Prepare a corrected trial balance.

LO 2, 3, 4

CHECK FIGURES
d. Net Income: $6,450
   Total Assets: $38,150

Problem 3-32A   *Comprehensive problem: single cycle*

The following transactions pertain to Boykin Corporation for 2013:

Jan.   1   Began operations when the business acquired $25,000 cash from the issue of common stock.
Mar.   1   Paid rent for office space for two years, $8,400 cash.
Apr. 14   Purchased $400 of supplies on account.
June 30   Received $12,000 cash in advance for services to be provided over the next year.
July   5   Paid $300 of the accounts payable from April 14.
Aug.   1   Billed a customer $4,800 for services provided during July.
       8   Completed a job and received $1,600 cash for services rendered.
Sept. 1   Paid employee salaries of $18,000 cash.
       9   Received $4,250 cash from accounts receivable.
Oct.   5   Billed customers $17,000 for services rendered on account.
Nov.   2   Paid a $500 cash dividend to the stockholders.
Dec. 31   Adjusted records to recognize the services provided on the contract of June 30.
      31   Recorded $1,100 of accrued salaries as of December 31.
      31   Recorded the rent expense for the year. (See March 1.)
      31   Physically counted supplies; $50 was on hand at the end of the period.

Required

a.   Record the preceding transactions in the general journal.
b.   Post the transactions to T-accounts and calculate the account balances.
c.   Prepare a trial balance.
d.   Prepare the income statement, statement of changes in stockholders' equity, balance sheet, and statement of cash flows.
e.   Prepare the closing entries at December 31.
f.   Prepare a trial balance after the closing entries are posted.

LO 2, 3, 4

CHECK FIGURES
b. Ending Cash Balance, 2013: $111,400
g. Net Income, 2014: $53,300

Problem 3-33A   *Two complete accounting cycles*

Allantis Machining experienced the following events during 2013:

1. Started operations by acquiring $100,000 of cash from the issue of common stock.
2. Paid $12,000 cash in advance for rent during the period from February 1, 2013, to February 1, 2014.
3. Received $9,600 cash in advance for services to be performed evenly over the period from September 1, 2013, to September 1, 2014.
4. Performed services for customers on account for $130,400.
5. Incurred operating expenses on account of $63,000.
6. Collected $113,800 cash from accounts receivable.
7. Paid $44,000 cash for salaries expense.
8. Paid $56,000 cash as a partial payment on accounts payable.

Adjusting Entries

9. Made the adjusting entry for the expired rent. (See Event 2.)
10. Recognized revenue for services performed in accordance with Event 3.
11. Recorded $4,200 of accrued salaries at the end of 2013.

Events for 2014

1. Paid $4,200 cash for the salaries accrued at the end of the previous year.
2. Performed services for cash, $81,000.
3. Paid $50,000 cash to purchase land.
4. Paid $10,800 cash in advance for rent during the period from February 1, 2014, to February 1, 2015.
5. Performed services for customers on account for $164,000.
6. Incurred operating expenses on account of $98,200.
7. Collected $152,600 cash from accounts receivable.
8. Paid $96,000 cash as a partial payment on accounts payable.

9. Paid $82,000 cash for salaries expense.

10. Paid a $10,000 cash dividend to the stockholders.

Adjusting Entries

11. Recognized revenue for services performed in accordance with Event 3 in 2013.

12. Made the adjusting entry for the expired rent. (*Hint:* Part of the rent was paid in 2013.)

13. Recorded $7,000 of accrued salaries at the end of 2014.

Required

a. Record the events and adjusting entries for 2013 in general journal form.

b. Post the events for 2013 to T-accounts.

c. Prepare a trial balance for 2013.

d. Prepare an income statement, statement of changes in stockholders' equity, balance sheet, and statement of cash flows for 2013.

e. Record the entries to close the 2013 temporary accounts to Retained Earnings in the general journal and post to the T-accounts.

f. Prepare a post-closing trial balance for December 31, 2013.

g. Repeat requirements *a* through *f* for 2014.

Problem 3-34A   *Using ratio analysis to make comparisons between companies*   LO 5

At the end of 2013 the following information is available for the Boise Company and the Tucson Company:

	Boise Co.	Tucson Co.
Total assets	$127,000	$753,000
Total liabilities	93,000	452,000
Stockholders' equity	34,000	301,000
Net income	8,000	45,000

Required

a. For each company, compute the debt to assets ratio and the return on equity ratio.

b. Determine what percentage of each company's assets were financed by the owners.

c. Which company has the greatest level of financial risk?

d. Based on profitability alone, which company performed better?

e. Do the above ratios support the concept of financial leverage? Explain.

Problem 3-35A   *Notes payable*   LO 6

Bombay Inc. acquired $10,000 cash by issuing a promissory note to the National Bank on November 1, 2013. The note stipulated a one-year term and a 9% annual interest rate.

Required

Prepare the general journal entries to record

a. The issue of the note on November 1, 2013.

b. Accrued interest on December 31, 2013.

c. Accrued interest on October 31, 2014.

d. Cash paid to settle the amount of interest payable on October 31, 2014.

e. Cash paid to settle the principal balance of the obligation to the bank on October 31, 2014.

Problem 3-36A   *Comprehensive problem including depreciation*   LO 6

Lee Company started the period with cash of $22,000, common stock of $12,000, and retained earnings of $10,000. Lee engaged in the following transactions in 2013:

Transactions During 2013

1. On January 1, 2013, purchased a computer for $7,500 cash.

2. On February 1, paid $6,600 cash for rent for a 12-month period beginning immediately.

3. Purchased $1,100 of supplies for cash.

4. Provided $56,000 of services for cash.

5. Paid $18,000 cash for salaries expense.

6. On May 1, received $9,000 for services that will be performed over the next 12 months.

Information for Adjusting Entries

7. The computer had an estimated life of three years and a $2,400 salvage value.

8. Recognized the expired rent.

9. An inventory of supplies showed $120 of supplies on hand as of December 31.

10. Recognized the revenue associated with Event 6 as of December 31.

Required

a. Record the 10 events in general journal format.

b. Prepare an income statement, balance sheet, and statement of cash flows.

EXERCISES—SERIES B

LO 1

Exercise 3-1B *Matching debit and credit terminology with accounting elements*

Required

Complete the following table by indicating whether a debit or credit is used to increase or decrease the balance of accounts belonging to each category of financial statement elements. The appropriate debit/credit terminology has been identified for the first category (assets) as an example.

Category of Elements	Used to Increase This Element	Used to Decrease This Element
Assets	Debit	Credit
Liabilities		
Common Stock		
Retained Earnings		
Revenue		
Expense		
Dividends		

LO 1

Exercise 3-2B *Debit/credit terminology*

Two introductory accounting students were arguing about how to record a transaction involving an exchange of cash for land. Trisha stated that the transaction should have a debit to Land and a credit to Cash; Tony argued that the reverse (debit to Cash and credit to Land) represented the appropriate treatment.

Required

Which student was correct? Defend your position.

LO 1

Exercise 3-3B *Matching debit and credit terminology with account titles*

Required

Indicate whether each of the following accounts normally has a debit balance or a credit balance:

a. Salaries Payable

b. Cash

c. Prepaid Insurance

d. Common Stock

e. Interest Revenue

f. Rent Expense

g. Salaries Expense

h. Consulting Revenue

i. Unearned Revenue

j. Accounts Payable

k. Dividends

l. Land

Exercise 3-4B   *Applying debit/credit terminology to accounting events*   **LO 1**

Required

a. In parallel columns, list the accounts that would be debited and credited for each of the following unrelated transactions:

   (1) Acquired cash from the issue of common stock.

   (2) Provided services on account.

   (3) Purchased supplies for cash.

   (4) Provided services for cash.

   (5) Paid cash for salaries expense.

   (6) Paid in advance for two-year lease on office space.

   (7) Recorded accrued salaries at the end of the accounting period.

   (8) Recognized expense for prepaid rent that had been used up by the end of the accounting period.

   (9) Recognized accrued interest revenue.

b. Show how each transaction affects the financial statements by placing a + for increase, − for decrease, and NA for not affected under each component in a horizontal statements model like the one shown below. Also, in the Cash Flow column, use the letters OA to designate operating activity, IA for investing activity, and FA for financing activity. The first event is recorded as an example.

Assets	=	Liab.	+	Equity	Rev.	−	Exp.	=	Net Inc.	Cash Flow
+		NA		+	NA		NA		NA	+ FA

Exercise 3-5B   *Debit/credit terminology*   **LO 1**

Required

For each of the following independent events, identify the account that would be debited and the account that would be credited. The accounts for the first event are identified as an example.

Event	Account Debited	Account Credited
a	Accounts Payable	Cash

a. Paid accounts payable.

b. Received cash in payment of accounts receivable.

c. Received cash by issuing common stock.

d. Received cash for services to be performed in the future.

e. Paid salaries payable.

f. Provided services on account.

g. Paid cash for operating expenses.

h. Purchased supplies on account.

i. Recognized revenue for services completed. Cash had been collected in Event *d*.

j. Recognized accrued salaries expense.

k. Recognized expense for supplies used during the period.

l. Performed services for cash.

m. Recognized accrued interest revenue.

n. Paid a cash dividend to the stockholders.

Exercise 3-6B   *Identifying transaction type, its effect on the accounting equation, and whether the effect is recorded with a debit or credit*   **LO 1**

Required

Identify whether each of the following transactions is an asset source (AS), asset use (AU), asset exchange (AE), or claims exchange (CE). Also explain how each event affects the accounting equation by placing a + for *increase,* − for *decrease,* and NA for *not affected* under each of the components of the accounting equation. Finally, indicate whether the effect requires a debit or credit entry. The first event is recorded as an example.

						Stockholders' Equity		
Event	Type of Event	Assets	=	Liabilities	+	Common Stock	+	Retained Earnings
a	AE	+ Debit − Credit		NA		NA		NA

a. Purchased land with cash.
b. Purchased supplies on account.
c. Acquired cash from the issue of common stock.
d. Paid cash in advance for one year of rent.
e. Paid salaries payable.
f. Received cash for services to be performed in the future.
g. Paid a cash dividend to the stockholders.
h. Received cash in payment of accounts receivable.
i. Paid accounts payable.
j. Provided services for cash.
k. Recognized expense for supplies used during the period.
l. Recognized revenue for services completed for which cash had been collected previously.
m. Recognized accrued interest revenue.
n. Incurred other operating expenses on account.

LO 1, 2

Exercise 3-7B   *Identifying increases and decreases in T-accounts*

Required

For each of the following T-accounts, indicate the side of the account that should be used to record an increase or decrease in the account balance:

Cash		Accounts Payable		Common Stock	
Debit	Credit	Debit	Credit	Debit	Credit

Accounts Receivable		Salaries Payable		Dividends	
Debit	Credit	Debit	Credit	Debit	Credit

Supplies				Service Revenue	
Debit	Credit			Debit	Credit

				Other Operating Expense	
				Debit	Credit

LO 2

Exercise 3-8B   *T-accounts and the accounting equation*

Required

Record each of the following Zeke Co. events in T-accounts, and then explain how the event affects the accounting equation:

a. Received $10,000 cash by issuing common stock.
b. Purchased supplies for $500 cash.
c. Purchased land for $20,000 cash.
d. Performed services for $1,600 cash.

Exercise 3-9B   *Recording receivables and identifying their effect on financial statements*

Grant Company performed services on account for $80,000 in 2013. Grant collected $50,000 cash from accounts receivable during 2013, and the remaining $30,000 was collected in cash during 2014.

Required

a. Record the 2013 transactions in T-accounts.

b. Record the 2013 transactions in a horizontal statements model like the following one:

Assets		=	Liab.	+	Equity	Rev.	−	Exp.	=	Net Inc.	Cash Flow
Cash	+ Accts. Rec.	=			Ret. Earn.						

c. Determine the amount of revenue Grant would report on the 2013 income statement.

d. Determine the amount of cash flow from operating activities Grant would report on the 2013 statement of cash flows.

e. Open a T-account for Retained Earnings, and close the 2013 Service Revenue account to the Retained Earnings account.

f. Record the 2014 cash collection in the appropriate T-accounts.

g. Record the 2014 transaction in a horizontal statements model like the one shown in Requirement *b*.

h. Assuming no other transactions occur in 2014, determine the amount of net income and the net cash flow from operating activities for 2014.

Exercise 3-10B   *Recording supplies and identifying their effect on financial statements*

Ben Parker started and operated a small family architectural firm in 2013. The firm was affected by two events: (1) Parker provided $12,500 of services on account, and (2) he purchased $3,000 of supplies on account. There were $250 of supplies on hand as of December 31, 2013.

Required

a. Open T-accounts and record the two transactions in the accounts.

b. Record the required year-end adjusting entry to reflect the use of supplies.

c. Record the preceding transactions in a horizontal statements model like the following one:

Assets			=	Liab.	+	Equity	Rev.	−	Exp.	=	Net Inc.	Cash Flow
Accts. Rec.	+	Supplies	=	Accts. Pay.	+	Ret. Earn.						

d. Explain why the amounts of net income and net cash flow from operating activities differ.

e. Record and post the required closing entries, and prepare a post-closing trial balance.

Exercise 3-11B   *Recording unearned revenue and identifying its effect on financial statements*

Jackie received a $30,000 cash advance payment on June 1, 2013, for consulting services to be performed in the future. Services were to be provided for a one-year term beginning June 1, 2013.

Required

a. Record the June 1 cash receipt in T-accounts.

b. Record in T-accounts the adjustment required as of December 31, 2013.

c. Record the preceding transaction and related adjustment in a horizontal statements model like the following one:

Assets	=	Liab.	+	Equity	Rev.	−	Exp.	=	Net Inc.	Cash Flow

d. Determine the amount of net income on the 2013 income statement. What is the amount of net cash flow from operating activities for 2013?

e. What amount of liabilities would Jackie report on the 2013 balance sheet?

LO 2

Exercise 3-12B   *Using a T-account to determine cash flow from operating activities*

Delta Co. began the accounting period with a $116,000 debit balance in its Accounts Receivable account. During the accounting period, Delta Co. earned revenue on account of $152,000. The ending Accounts Receivable balance was $108,000.

Required

Based on this information alone, determine the amount of cash inflow from operating activities during the accounting period. (*Hint:* Use a T-account for Accounts Receivable. Enter the debits and credits for the given events, and solve for the missing amount.)

LO 2

Exercise 3-13B   *Using a T-account to determine cash flow from operating activities*

The Flower Company began the accounting period with an $80,000 credit balance in its Accounts Payable account. During the accounting period, Flower Co. incurred expenses on account of $190,000. The ending Accounts Payable balance was $56,000.

Required

Based on this information, determine the amount of cash outflow for expenses during the accounting period. (*Hint:* Use a T-account for Accounts Payable. Enter the debits and credits for the given events, and solve for the missing amount.)

LO 3

Exercise 3-14B   *Recording events in the general journal and effect on financial statements*

Required

Record each of the following transactions in general journal form and then show the effect of the transaction in a horizontal statements model. The first transaction is shown as an example.

Account Title	Debit	Credit
Accounts Receivable	9,500	
Service Revenue		9,500

Assets	=	Liab.	+	Equity	Rev.	−	Exp.	=	Net Inc.	Cash Flow
9,500				9,500	9,500		NA		9,500	NA

a. Performed $9,500 of services on account.

b. Purchased land for $12,000 cash.

c. Purchased supplies for $265 cash.

d. Received $1,500 cash for services to be performed at a later date.

e. Collected $4,200 cash on accounts receivable.

f. Paid $1,150 cash in advance for an insurance policy.

g. Paid $600 on accounts payable.

h. Recorded the adjusting entry to recognize $400 of insurance expense.

i. Recorded the adjusting entry to recognize $300 accrued interest revenue.

Exercise 3-15B   *Recording prepaid items and identifying their effect on financial statements*   LO 3

Southern Company began operations when it issued common stock for $100,000 cash. It paid $96,000 cash in advance for a one-year contract to lease delivery equipment for the business. It signed the lease agreement on March 1, 2013, which was effective immediately. Southern received $120,000 of cash revenue in 2013.

Required

a. Record the March 1 cash payment in general journal format.

b. Record in general journal format the adjustment required as of December 31, 2013.

c. Record all events in a horizontal statements model like the following one:

Assets		=	Liab.	+	Equity		Rev.	−	Exp.	=	Net Inc.	Cash Flow
	Prep.				Common	Ret.						
Cash	+ Rent	=			Stock	+ Earn.						

d. What amount of net income will Southern Company report on the 2013 income statement? What is the amount of net cash flow from operating activities for 2013?

e. Determine the amount of prepaid rent Southern Company would report on the December 31, 2013, balance sheet.

Exercise 3-16B   *Recording accrued salaries and identifying their effect on financial statements*   LO 3

On December 31, 2011, CST Company had accrued salaries of $4,800.

Required

a. Record in general journal format the adjustment required as of December 31, 2013.

b. Record the above adjustment in a horizontal statements model like the following one:

Assets	=	Liab.	+	Equity	Rev.	−	Exp.	=	Net Inc.	Cash Flow
		Sal. Pay.	+	Ret. Earn.						

c. Determine the amount of net income CST would report on the 2013 income statement, assuming that CST received $24,000 of cash revenue. What is the amount of net cash flow from operating activities for 2013?

d. What amount of salaries payable would CST report on the December 31, 2013, balance sheet?

LO 3

Exercise 3-17B *Preparing closing entries*

The following financial information was taken from the books of Get Fit Health Club, a small spa and health club:

Account Balances as of December 31, 2013	
Accounts Receivable	$16,150
Accounts Payable	5,500
Salaries Payable	2,150
Cash	20,725
Dividends	1,750
Operating Expense	31,550
Prepaid Rent	600
Rent Expense	9,200
Retained Earnings 1/1/2013	32,650
Salaries Expense	16,200
Service Revenue	58,400
Supplies	450
Supplies Expense	4,240
Common Stock	6,515
Unearned Revenue	8,050
Land	12,400

Required

a. Prepare the journal entries necessary to close the temporary accounts at December 31, 2013, the Get Fit Health Club.

b. What is the balance in the Retained Earnings account after the closing entries are posted?

LO 2, 3

Exercise 3-18B *Recording transactions in the general journal and T-accounts*

The following events apply to Goodman Company for 2013, its first year of operation:

1. Received cash of $24,000 from the issue of common stock.
2. Performed $42,500 of services on account.
3. Incurred $4,000 of other operating expenses on account.
4. Paid $17,000 cash for salaries expense.
5. Collected $32,500 of accounts receivable.
6. Paid a $2,500 dividend to the stockholders.
7. Performed $4,600 of services for cash.
8. Paid $2,200 of the accounts payable.

Required

a. Record the preceding transactions in general journal form.
b. Post the entries to T-accounts and determine the ending balance in each account.
c. Determine the amount of total assets at the end of 2013.
d. Determine the amount of net income for 2013.

LO 4

Exercise 3-19B *Preparing a trial balance*

Required

On December 31, 2013, Green Company had the following normal account balances in its general ledger. Use this information to prepare a trial balance.

Land	$40,000
Unearned Revenue	26,000
Dividends	10,000
Prepaid Rent	9,600
Cash	29,000
Salaries Expense	15,000
Accounts Payable	6,000
Common Stock	40,000
Operating Expense	35,000
Office Supplies	5,000
Advertising Expense	2,000
Retained Earnings, 1/1/2013	9,000
Service Revenue	92,000
Accounts Receivable	27,400

Exercise 3-20B   *Determining the effect of errors on the trial balance*   LO 4

Required

Explain how each of the following posting errors affects a trial balance. State whether the trial balance will be out of balance because of the posting error, and indicate which side of the trial balance will have a higher amount after each independent entry is posted. If the posting error does not affect the equality of debits and credits in the trial balance, state that the error will not cause an inequality and explain why.

a. A $1,040 debit to Office Supplies was debited to Office Supplies Expense.

b. A $400 debit to Cash was posted as a $4,000 debit.

c. An $800 credit to Unearned Revenue was credited to Service Revenue.

d. A $2,400 credit to Accounts Payable was not posted.

e. An $800 debit to Rent Expense was posted twice.

Exercise 3-21B   *Recording events in the general journal, posting to T-accounts,*   LO 2, 3, 4
                      and preparing a trial balance

The following events apply to Computer Services Inc. in its first year of operation:

1. Acquired $40,000 cash from the issue of common stock.
2. Earned $28,000 of service revenue on account.
3. Incurred $15,200 of operating expenses on account.
4. Collected $26,400 cash from accounts receivable.
5. Made a $13,600 payment on accounts payable.
6. Paid a $2,000 cash dividend to the stockholders.
7. Received a $7,100 cash advance for services to be provided in the future.
8. Purchased $1,600 of supplies on account.
9. Recognized $2,400 of revenue for services provided to the customer in Event 7.
10. Recognized $1,200 of supplies expense.
11. Recorded $1,600 of accrued salaries expense.
12. Recognized $450 of accrued interest revenue.

Required

a. Record the events in T-accounts and determine the ending account balances.

b. Test the equality of the debit and credit balances of the T-accounts by preparing a trial balance.

Exercise 3-22B   *Recording events in the general journal, posting to T-accounts, and*   LO 2, 3, 4
                      preparing closing entries

At the beginning of 2013, Ron's Consulting had the following normal balances in its accounts:

Account	Balance
Cash	$26,000
Accounts Receivable	19,000
Accounts Payable	7,200
Common Stock	19,800
Retained Earnings	18,000

The following events apply to Ron's Consulting for 2013:

1. Provided $236,000 of services on account.
2. Incurred $23,960 of operating expenses on account.
3. Collected $248,000 of accounts receivable.
4. Paid $142,000 cash for salaries expense.
5. Paid $27,200 cash as a partial payment on accounts payable.
6. Paid an $22,000 cash dividend to the stockholders.

Required

a. Record these transactions in a general journal.
b. Open T-accounts, and post the beginning balances and the preceding transactions to the appropriate accounts.
c. Record the beginning balances and the transactions in a horizontal statements model such as the following one:

Assets		=	Liab.	+	Equity		Rev.	−	Exp.	=	Net Inc.	Cash Flow
Cash	+ Accts. Rec.	=	Accts. Pay.	+	Common Stock	+ Ret. Earn.						

d. Record the closing entries in the general journal and post them to the T-accounts. What is the amount of net income for the year?
e. What is the amount of *change* in retained earnings for the year? Is the change in retained earnings different from the amount of net income? If so, why?
f. Prepare a post-closing trial balance.

LO 5

Exercise 3-23B *Using ratio analysis to assess financial risk*

The following information was drawn from the balance sheets of two companies:

Company	Assets	=	Liabilities	+	Equity
Ever-Well	215,000		58,000		157,000
Eat-Right	675,000		256,500		418,500

Required

a. Compute the debt to assets ratio to measure the level of financial risk of both companies.
b. Compare the two ratios computed in Requirement *a* to identify which company has the higher level of financial risk.

IFRS

Exercise 3-24B *IFRS and U.S. GAAP*

a. Describe some way that U.S. GAAP and IFRS are different.
b. How are U.S. GAAP and IFRS alike for reporting purposes?

PROBLEMS—SERIES B

Problem 3-25B   *Identifying debit and credit balances*   **LO 2**

Required

Indicate whether each of the following accounts normally has a debit or credit balance:

a. Service Revenue
b. Accounts Payable
c. Operating Expense
d. Unearned Revenue
e. Dividends
f. Cash
g. Insurance Expense
h. Accounts Receivable
i. Land
j. Retained Earnings
k. Common Stock

l. Interest Receivable
m. Interest Revenue
n. Prepaid Insurance
o. Land
p. Salaries Payable
q. Salaries Expense
r. Supplies Expense
s. Consulting Revenue
t. Utilities Payable
u. Supplies

Problem 3-26B   *Transaction type and debit/credit terminology*   **LO 1, 2**

The following events apply to Kate Enterprises:

1. Acquired $50,000 cash from the issue of common stock.
2. Paid salaries to employees, $3,500 cash.
3. Collected $16,200 cash for services to be performed in the future.
4. Paid cash for utilities expense, $804.
5. Recognized $45,000 of service revenue on account.
6. Paid a $2,500 cash dividend to the stockholders.
7. Purchased $3,200 of supplies on account.
8. Received $12,500 cash for services rendered.
9. Paid cash to rent office space for the next 12 months, $12,000.
10. Paid cash of $17,500 for other operating expenses.
11. Paid on account payable, $1,752.
12. Recognized $3,000 of rent expense. Cash had been paid in a prior transaction (see Event 9).
13. Recognized $5,000 of revenue for services performed. Cash had been previously collected (see Event 3).
14. Recognized $5,200 of accrued salaries expense.
15. Recognized $1,300 of accrued interest revenue.

Required

Identify each event as asset source (AS), asset use (AU), asset exchange (AE), or claims exchange (CE). Also identify the account that is to be debited and the account that is to be credited when the transaction is recorded. The first event is recorded as an example.

Event No.	Type of Event	Account Debited	Account Credited
1	AS	Cash	Common Stock

Problem 3-27B   *Recording events in a statements model and T-accounts and preparing a trial balance*

The following accounting events apply to Lee's Designs for the year 2013:

Asset Source Transactions

1. Began operations by acquiring $80,000 of cash from the issue of common stock.
2. Performed services and collected cash of $4,000.
3. Collected $24,000 of cash in advance for services to be provided over the next 12 months.
4. Provided $48,000 of services on account.
5. Purchased supplies of $6,000 on account.

Asset Exchange Transactions

6. Purchased $16,000 of land for cash.
7. Collected $28,000 of cash from accounts receivable.
8. Purchased $2,520 of supplies with cash.
9. Paid $9,600 for one year's rent in advance.

Asset Use Transactions

10. Paid $16,000 cash for salaries of employees.
11. Paid a cash dividend of $8,000 to the stockholders.
12. Paid off $2,520 of the accounts payable with cash.

Claims Exchange Transactions

13. Placed an advertisement in the local newspaper for $3,200 on account.
14. Incurred utility expense of $2,400 on account.

Adjusting Entries

15. Recognized $17,600 of revenue for performing services. The collection of cash for these services occurred in a prior transaction. (See Event 3.)
16. Recorded $6,000 of accrued salary expense at the end of 2013.
17. Recorded supplies expense. Had $2,400 of supplies on hand at the end of the accounting period.
18. Recognized four months' of expense for prepaid rent that had been used up during the accounting period.
19. Recognized $600 of accrued interest revenue.

Required

a. Record each of the preceding events in T-accounts.
b. Prepare a before-closing trial balance.
c. Use a horizontal statements model to show how each event affects the balance sheet, income statement, and statement of cash flows. Indicate whether the event increases (+), decreases (−), or does not affect (NA) each element of the financial statements. Also, in the Cash Flow column, use the letters OA to designate operating activity, IA for investing activity, and FA for financing activity. The first event is recorded as an example.

Assets	=	Liab.	+	Equity	Rev.	−	Exp.	=	Net Inc.	Cash Flow
+		NA		+	NA		NA		NA	+ FA

Problem 3-28B *Effect of journal entries on financial statements*   LO 3

Event No.	Account Title	Debit	Credit
1	Cash	xxx	
	Common Stock		xxx
2	Cash	xxx	
	Service Revenue		xxx
3	Prepaid Rent	xxx	
	Cash		xxx
4	Accounts Receivable	xxx	
	Service Revenue		xxx
5	Cash	xxx	
	Unearned Revenue		xxx
6	Cash	xxx	
	Accounts Receivable		xxx
7	Supplies	xxx	
	Accounts Payable		xxx
8	Salaries Expense	xxx	
	Cash		xxx
9	Utilities Expense	xxx	
	Cash		xxx
10	Supplies Expense	xxx	
	Supplies		xxx
11	Unearned Revenue	xxx	
	Service Revenue		xxx
12	Rent Expense	xxx	
	Prepaid Rent		xxx
13	Dividends	xxx	
	Cash		xxx

Required

The preceding 13 different accounting events are presented in general journal format. Use a horizontal statements model to show how each event affects the balance sheet, income statement, and statement of cash flows. Indicate whether the event increases (+), decreases (−), or does not affect (NA) each element of the financial statements. Also, in the Cash Flow column, use the letters OA to designate operating activity, IA for investing activity, and FA for financing activity. The first event is recorded as an example.

Assets	=	Liab.	+	Equity	Rev.	−	Exp.	=	Net Inc.	Cash Flow
+		NA		+	NA		NA		NA	+ FA

Problem 3-29B *Identifying accounting events from journal entries*   LO 3

Required

The following information is from the records of attorney Matt Black. Write a brief explanation of the accounting event represented in each of the general journal entries.

Date	Account Titles	Debit	Credit
Jan. 1	Cash	40,000	
	Common Stock		40,000
Feb. 1	Accounts Receivable	48,000	
	Service Revenue		48,000
Mar. 1	Cash	24,000	
	Service Revenue		24,000
Apr. 1	Prepaid Rent	1,600	
	Cash		1,600
May 10	Cash	8,000	
	Unearned Revenue		8,000
June 30	Supplies	2,000	
	Cash		2,000
July 1	Salaries Expense	4,000	
	Cash		4,000
Aug. 10	Cash	8,800	
	Accounts Receivable		8,800
Oct. 1	Property Tax Expense	3,000	
	Cash		3,000
Dec. 1	Dividends	2,000	
	Cash		2,000
Dec. 31	Supplies Expense	800	
	Supplies		800
31	Rent Expense	4,400	
	Prepaid Rent		4,400
31	Unearned Revenue	2,240	
	Service Revenue		2,240

LO 3

Problem 3-30B *Recording adjusting entries in general journal format*

Required

Each of the following independent events requires a year-end adjusting entry. Record each event and the related adjusting entry in general journal format. The first event is recorded as an example. Assume a December 31 closing date.

Event No.	Date	Account Titles	Debit	Credit
a	Sept. 1	Prepaid Rent	30,000	
		Cash		30,000
a	Dec. 31	Rent Expense (30,000 × 4/12)	10,000	
		Prepaid Rent		10,000

a. Paid $30,000 cash in advance on September 1 for a one-year lease on office space.

b. Purchased $4,000 of supplies on account on April 15. At year-end, $300 of supplies remained on hand.

c. Received a $7,200 cash advance on July 1 for a contract to provide services for one year beginning immediately.

d. Paid $10,200 cash in advance on February 1 for a one-year insurance policy.

LO 4

Problem 3-31B *Effect of errors on the trial balance*

The following trial balance was prepared from the ledger accounts of Zumba Company:

ZUMBA COMPANY
Trial Balance
April 30, 2013

Account Title	Debit	Credit
Cash	$ 41,500	
Accounts Receivable	40,000	
Supplies	2,400	
Prepaid Insurance	3,200	
Land		$ 10,000
Accounts Payable		8,500
Common Stock		96,000
Retained Earnings		56,720
Dividends	6,000	
Service Revenue		40,000
Rent Expense	7,200	
Salaries Expense	26,400	
Operating Expense	65,240	
Totals	$191,940	$211,220

When the trial balance failed to balance, the accountant reviewed the records and discovered the following errors:

1. The company received $470 as payment for services rendered. The credit to Service Revenue was recorded correctly, but the debit to Cash was recorded as $740.

2. An $860 receipt of cash that was received from a customer on accounts receivable was not recorded.

3. A $450 purchase of supplies on account was properly recorded as a debit to the Supplies account. However, the credit to Accounts Payable was not recorded.

4. Land valued at $10,000 was contributed to the business in exchange for common stock. The entry to record the transaction was recorded as a $10,000 credit to both the Land account and the Common Stock account.

5. A $400 rent payment was properly recorded as a credit to Cash. However, the Salaries Expense account was incorrectly debited for $400.

Required

Based on this information, prepare a corrected trial balance for Zumba Company.

Problem 3-32B   *Comprehensive problem: single cycle*   LO 2, 3, 4

The following transactions pertain to Chef Training Company for 2013:

Jan.	30	Established the business when it acquired $37,500 cash from the issue of common stock.
Feb.	1	Paid rent for office space for two years, $12,000 cash.
Apr.	10	Purchased $2,650 of supplies on account.
July	1	Received $25,000 cash in advance for services to be provided over the next year.
	20	Paid $900 of the accounts payable from April 10.
Aug.	15	Billed a customer $16,000 for services provided during August.
Sept.	15	Completed a job and received $9,500 cash for services rendered.
Oct.	1	Paid employee salaries of $10,000 cash.
	15	Received $12,500 cash from accounts receivable.
Nov.	16	Billed customers $37,000 for services rendered on account.
Dec.	1	Paid a dividend of $18,500 cash to the stockholders.
	31	Adjusted records to recognize the services provided on the contract of July 1.
	31	Recorded $2,250 of accrued salaries as of December 31.
	31	Recorded the rent expense for the year. (See February 1.)
	31	Physically counted supplies; $240 was on hand at the end of the period.

Required

a. Record the preceding transactions in the general journal.

b. Post the transactions to T-accounts and calculate the account balances.

c. Prepare a trial balance.

d. Prepare the income statement, statement of changes in stockholders' equity, balance sheet, and statement of cash flows.

e. Prepare the closing entries at December 31.

f. Prepare a trial balance after the closing entries are posted.

LO 2, 3, 4   **Problem 3-33B**   *Two complete accounting cycles*

Heckel Enterprises experienced the following events for 2013, the first year of operation:

1. Acquired $26,000 cash from the issue of common stock.
2. Paid $8,000 cash in advance for rent. The payment was for the period April 1, 2013, to March 31, 2014.
3. Performed services for customers on account for $54,000.
4. Incurred operating expenses on account of $27,000.
5. Collected $50,300 cash from accounts receivable.
6. Paid $17,000 cash for salary expense.
7. Paid $23,000 cash as a partial payment on accounts payable.

Adjusting Entries

8. Made the adjusting entry for the expired rent. (See Event 2.)
9. Recorded $1,800 of accrued salaries at the end of 2013.

Events for 2014

1. Paid $1,800 cash for the salaries accrued at the end of the prior accounting period.
2. Performed services for cash of $17,000.
3. Purchased $2,400 of supplies on account.
4. Paid $9,000 cash in advance for rent. The payment was for one year beginning April 1, 2014.
5. Performed services for customers on account for $84,000.
6. Incurred operating expenses on account of $38,500.
7. Collected $81,000 cash from accounts receivable.
8. Paid $40,000 cash as a partial payment on accounts payable.
9. Paid $28,000 cash for salary expense.
10. Paid a $12,000 cash dividend to stockholders.

Adjusting Entries

11. Made the adjusting entry for the expired rent. (*Hint:* Part of the rent was paid in 2013.)
12. Recorded supplies expense. A physical count showed that $300 of supplies were still on hand.

Required

a. Record the events and adjusting entries for 2013 in general journal form.

b. Post the 2013 events to T-accounts.

c. Prepare a trial balance for 2013.

d. Prepare an income statement, statement of changes in stockholders' equity, balance sheet, and statement of cash flows for 2013.

e. Record the entries to close the 2013 temporary accounts to Retained Earnings in the general journal and post to the T-accounts.

f. Prepare a post-closing trial balance for December 31, 2013.

g. Repeat requirements *a* through *f* for 2014.

Problem 3-34B   *Using ratio analysis to make comparisons between companies*

LO 5

At the end of 2014, the following information is available for Teton Co. and Glacier, Inc:

	Teton Co.	Glacier Co.
Total assets	$945,000	$273,000
Total liabilities	585,000	191,000
Stockholders' equity	360,000	82,000
Net income	61,000	17,000

Required

a. For each company, compute the debt to assets ratio and the return on equity ratio.

b. Determine what percentage of each company's assets were financed by the owners.

c. Which company has the greatest level of financial risk?

d. Based on profitability alone, which company performed better?

e. Do the above ratios support the concept of financial leverage? Explain.

Problem 3-35B   *Notes payable*

LO 6

Duval Inc. acquired $50,000 cash by issuing a promissory note to the National Bank on May 1, 2013. Duval issued a promissory note with a one-year term and a 6% annual interest rate.

Required

Prepare the general journal entries to record

a. The issue of the note on May 1, 2013.

b. Accrued interest on December 31, 2013.

c. Accrued interest on April 30, 2014.

d. Cash paid to settle the amount of interest payable on April 30, 2014.

e. Cash paid to settle the principal balance of the obligation to the bank on April 30, 2014.

Problem 3-36B   *Comprehensive problem including depreciation*

LO 6

Bower Consulting Company started the period with cash of $25,000, common stock of $13,000, and retained earnings of $12,000. Bower engaged in the following transactions in 2013:

Transactions during 2013

1. On January 1, 2013, purchased office furniture for $12,000.
2. On March 1, paid $5,400 for an insurance policy that provides coverage for 12 months beginning immediately.
3. Purchased $1,800 of supplies for cash.
4. Provided $39,000 of services for cash.
5. Paid $9,000 for salaries expense.
6. On April 1, received $12,000 for services that will be performed over the next 12 months beginning immediately.

Information for Adjusting Entries

7. The furniture had an estimated life of four years and a $2,000 salvage value.
8. Recognized the expired insurance.
9. An inventory of supplies showed $250 of supplies on hand as of December 31.
10. Recognized the revenue associated with Event 6 as of December 31.

Required

a. Record the 10 events in general journal format.

b. Prepare an income statement, balance sheet, and statement of cash flows.

ANALYZE, THINK, COMMUNICATE

ATC 3-1 Business Applications Case *Understanding real-world annual reports*

Required

Use the Target Corporation's annual report in Appendix B to answer the following questions:

a. What was Target's debt to assets ratio for its fiscal-year ended January 29, 2011 (2010) and 2009?

b. What was Target's return on assets ratio for 2010 and 2009?

c. What was Target's return on equity ratio for 2010 and 2009?

d. Why was Target's return on equity ratio higher than its return on assets ratio for 2010 and 2009?

ATC 3-2 Group Assignment *Financial statement analysis*

The beginning account balances for Miller Company were as follows for 2013, 2014, and 2015:

	January 1		
	2013	2014	2015
Cash	$12,000	$19,000	$42,600
Accounts Receivable	6,000	10,000	6,000
Land	9,000	9,000	9,000
Prepaid Rent	0	1,000	1,400
Accounts Payable	12,300	11,300	15,300
Salaries Payable	0	0	2,100
Common Stock	10,000	10,000	10,000
Retained Earnings	4,700	17,700	31,600

Miller Company experienced the following events for the accounting periods 2013, 2014, and 2015:

2013

1. Performed services for $36,000 on account.
2. Paid rent of $6,000 for the period March 1, 2013, to March 1, 2014.
3. Incurred operating expenses of $18,000 on account.
4. Collected $32,000 of accounts receivable.
5. Paid $19,000 of accounts payable.
6. Recorded expired rent.

2014

1. Performed services on account of $48,000.
2. Paid rent of $8,400 for the period March 1, 2014, to March 1, 2015, and recorded the expired rent for the period January 1, 2014, to March 1, 2014.
3. Incurred operating expenses of $24,000 on account.
4. Collected $52,000 of accounts receivable.
5. Paid $20,000 of accounts payable.
6. Recorded expired rent.
7. Recorded accrued salaries of $2,100.

2015

1. Paid accrued salaries.
2. Performed services on account of $56,000.
3. Paid rent of $9,000 for the period March 1, 2015, to March 1, 2016, and recorded the expired rent for the period January 1, 2015, to March 1, 2015.

4. Incurred operating expenses of $32,000 on account.

5. Collected $55,000 of accounts receivable.

6. Paid $33,000 of accounts payable.

7. Sold land for $5,000; the land had a cost of $5,000.

8. Recorded expired rent.

Required

Divide the class into groups of four or five students. Organize the groups into three sections. Assign each section of groups the financial data for one of the preceding accounting periods.

Group Task

a. Prepare an income statement, balance sheet, and statement of cash flows. It may be helpful to open T-accounts and post transactions to these accounts before attempting to prepare the statements.

Class Discussion

b. Review the cash flows associated with the collection of receivables and the payment of payables. Comment on the company's collection and payment strategy.

c. Did net income increase or decrease between 2013 and 2014? What were the primary causes?

d. Did net income increase or decrease between 2014 and 2015? What were the primary causes?

ATC 3-3   Real-World Case   *Choice of fiscal year*

Consider the following brief descriptions of four companies, listed alphabetically, from different industries. Six Flags, Inc. operates regional theme-parks. It operates 17 parks in the United States, one in Mexico, and one in Canada. Toll Brothers, Inc., is a homebuilder. In 2010 it had almost 35,000 home sites in 407 communities. Toys R Us, Inc. is the well-known, international retailer of toys. Vail Resorts, Inc., operates several ski resorts in Colorado, including Vail Mountain, the largest in the United States, and Breckenridge Mountain Resort.

The chapter explained that companies often choose to close their books when business is slow. Each of these companies ends its fiscal year on a different date. The closing dates, listed chronologically, are as follows:

January 31

July 31

October 31

December 31

Required

a. Try to determine which fiscal year-end matches which company. Write a grief explanation of the reason for your decisions.

b. Because many companies deliberately choose to prepare their financial statements at a slow time of year, try to identify problems this may present for someone trying to analyze the balance sheet for Michaels Stores. Write a brief explanation of the issues you identify.

ATC 3-4   Business Applications Case   *Performing ratio analysis using real-world data*

The following data were taken from Netflix, Inc.'s 2010 annual report. *All dollar amounts are in millions.*

	Fiscal Years Ending	
	December 31, 2010	**December 31, 2009**
Total assets	$982,067	$679,734
Total liabilities		
Stockholders' equity	290,164	199,143
Net income	160,853	115,860

Required

a. For each year, compute Netflix's debt to assets ratio, return on assets ratio, and return on equity ratio. You will need to compute total liabilities.

b. Did the company's level of financial risk increase or decrease from 2009 to 2010?

c. In which year did the company appear to manage its assets most efficiently?

d. Do the above ratios support the concept of financial leverage? Explain.

ATC 3-5   Business Applications Case   *Performing ratio analysis using real-world data*

The following data were taken from the 2010 annual reports of Biogen Idec, Inc., and Amgen Inc. Both companies are leaders in biotechnology. *All dollar amounts are in millions.*

	Biogen Idec	Amgen
	December 31, 2010	December 31, 2010
Total assets	$8,093	$43,486
Total liabilities	2,643	19,542
Stockholders' equity	5,449	23,944
Net income	1,005	4,627

Required

a. For each company, compute the debt to assets ratio, return on assets ratio, and return on equity ratio.

b. Which company has the greatest level of financial risk? Explain.

c. Which company appears to have managed its assets most efficiently? Explain.

d. Which company performed better from the perspective of the owners? Explain.

ATC 3-6   Writing Assignment   *Effect of land sale on return on assets*

Toyo Company is holding land that cost $900,000 for future use. However, plans have changed and the company may not need the land in the foreseeable future. The president is concerned about the return on assets. Current net income is $425,000 and total assets are $3,500,000.

Required

a. Write a memo to the company president explaining the effect of disposing of the land, assuming that it has a current value of $1,500,000.

b. Write a memo to the company president explaining the effect of disposing of the land, assuming that it has a current value of $600,000.

ATC 3-7   Ethical Dilemma   *Choice of brothers: ethics, risk, and accounting numbers in a medieval setting*

In the late 1400s, a wealthy land owner named Caster was trying to decide which of his twin sons, Rogan or Argon, to designate as the first heir to the family fortune. He decided to set up each son with a small farm consisting of 300 sheep and 20 acres of land. Each twin would be allowed to manage his property as he deemed appropriate. After a designated period, Caster would call his sons before him to account for their actions. The heir to the family fortune would be chosen on the basis of which son had produced a larger increase in wealth during the test period.

On the appointed day of reckoning, Argon boasted that he had 714 sheep under his control while Rogan had only 330. Furthermore, Argon stated that he had increased his land holdings to 27 acres. The seven-acre increase resulted from two transactions: first, on the day the contest started, Argon used 20 sheep to buy 10 additional acres; and second, he sold three of these acres for a total of 9 sheep on the day of reckoning. Also, Argon's flock had produced 75 newborn sheep during the period of accounting. He had been able to give his friends 50 sheep in return for the help that they had given him in building a fence, thereby increasing not only his own wealth but the wealth of his neighbors as well. Argon boasted that the fence was strong and would keep his herd safe from predatory creatures for five years (assume the fence had been used for one year during the contest period). Rogan countered that Argon was holding 400 sheep that belonged to another herder. Argon had borrowed these sheep on the day that the contest had started. Furthermore, Argon had agreed to return 424 sheep to the herder. The 24 additional sheep represented consideration for the use of the herder's flock. Argon had agreed to return the sheep immediately after the day of reckoning.

During the test period, Rogan's flock had produced 37 newborn sheep, but 2 sheep had gotten sick and died during the accounting period. Rogan had also lost 5 sheep to predatory creatures. He had no fence, and some of his sheep strayed from the herd, thereby exposing themselves to danger. Knowing that he was falling behind, Rogan had taken a wife in order to boost his productivity. His wife owned 170 sheep on the day they were married; her sheep had produced 16 newborn sheep since the date of her marriage to Rogan. Argon had not included the wife's sheep in his count of Rogan's herd. If his wife's sheep had been counted, Rogan's herd would contain 516 instead of 330 sheep suggested by Argon's count.

Argon charged that seven of Rogan's sheep were sick with symptoms similar to those exhibited by the two sheep that were now dead. Rogan interjected that he should not be held accountable for acts of nature such as illness. Furthermore, he contended that by isolating the sick sheep from the remainder of the herd, he had demonstrated prudent management practices that supported his case to be designated first heir.

Required

a. Prepare an income statement, balance sheet, statement of sheep flow (cash flow) for each twin, using contemporary (2011) accounting standards. Note that you have to decide whether to include the sheep owned by Rogan's wife when making his financial statements (what is the accounting entity?). (*Hint:* Use the number of sheep rather than the number of dollars as the common unit of measure.)

b. Refer to the statements you prepared in Requirement *a* to answer the following questions:
   (1) Which twin has more owner's equity at the end of the accounting period?
   (2) Which twin produced the higher net income during the accounting period?
   (3) Which son should be designated heir based on conventional accounting and reporting standards?

c. What is the difference in the value of the land of the twins if the land is valued at market value (that is, three sheep per acre) rather than historical cost (that is, two sheep per acre)?

d. Did Argon's decision to borrow sheep increase his profitability? Support your answer with appropriate financial data.

e. Was Argon's decision to build a fence financially prudent? Support your answer with appropriate financial data.

f. Assuming that the loan resulted in a financial benefit to Argon, identify some reasons that the shepherd who owned the sheep may have been willing to loan them to Argon.

g. Which twin is likely to take risks to improve profitability? What would be the financial condition of each twin if one-half of the sheep in both flocks died as a result of illness? How should such risk factors be reported in financial statements?

h. Should Rogan's decision to "marry for sheep" be considered from an ethical perspective, or should the decision be made solely on the basis of the bottom-line net income figure?

i. Prepare a report that recommends which twin should be designated heir to the family business. Include a set of financial statements that supports your recommendation. Since this is a managerial report that will not be distributed to the public, you are not bound by generally accepted accounting principles.

ATC 3-8   Research Assignment   *Investigating Nike's 10-K report*

Many companies must file financial reports with the SEC. Many of these reports are available electronically through the EDGAR database. EDGAR is an acronym for Electronic Data Gathering, Analysis, and Retrieval system, and it is accessible through the World Wide Web on the Internet. Instructions for using EDGAR are in Appendix A.

Using the most current 10-K available on EDGAR or on the company's website at www.nikebiz.com, answer the following questions about **Nike Company**:

a. In what year did Nike begin operations?

b. Other than the Nike brand, what business does Nike operate?

c. How many employees does Nike have?

d. Describe, in dollar amounts, Nike's accounting equation at the end of the most recent year.

e. Has Nike's performance been improving or deteriorating over the past three years? Explain your answer.

ATC 3-9   Spreadsheet Assignment   *Use of Excel*

Adams Company started operations on January 1, 2013. Six months later on June 30, 2013, the company decided to prepare financial statements. The company's accountant decided to problem solve for the adjusting journal entries and the final adjusted account balances by using an electronic spreadsheet. Once the spreadsheet is complete, she will record the adjusting entries in the general journal and post to the ledger. The accountant has started the following spreadsheet but wants you to finish it for her.

Required

a. On a blank spreadsheet, enter the following trial balance in Columns A through C. Also enter the headings for Columns E through I.

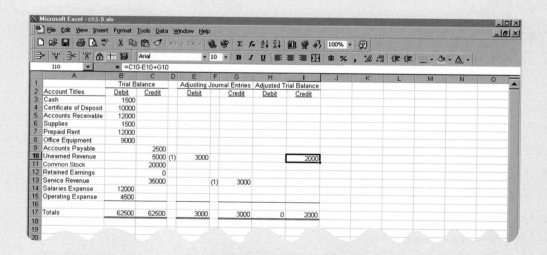

b. Each of the following events requires an adjusting journal entry. Instead of recording entries in general journal format, record the adjusting entries in the Debit and Credit columns under the heading Adjusting Journal Entries. Entry (1) has already been recorded as an example. Be sure to number your adjusting entries on the spreadsheet. It will be necessary to insert new accounts for the adjustments. Recall that the accounting period is for six months.

   (1) Received a $5,000 cash advance on April 1 for a contract to provide five months of service.

   (2) Had accrued salaries on June 30 amounting to $1,500.

(3) On January 1 invested in a one-year, $10,000 certificate of deposit that had a 5 percent interest rate.

(4) On January 1 paid $12,000 in advance for a one-year lease on office space.

(5) Received in the mail a utility bill dated June 30 for $150.

(6) Purchased $1,500 of supplies on January 1. As of June 30, $700 of supplies remained on hand.

(7) Paid $9,000 for office equipment on January 1. The equipment was expected to have a four-year useful life and a $1,000 salvage value. Depreciation is computed on a straight-line basis.

c. Develop formulas to sum both the Debit and Credit columns under the Adjusting Journal Entries heading.

d. Develop formulas to derive the adjusted balances for the adjusted trial balance. For example, the formula for the ending balance of Unearned Revenue is =C10−E10+G10. In other words, a credit balance minus debit entries plus credit entries equals the ending balance. Once an ending balance is formulated for one credit account, that formula can be copied to all other credit accounts; the same is true for debit accounts. Once an ending balance is formulated for a debit account, that formula can be copied to all other debit accounts.

e. Develop formulas to sum both the Debit and Credit columns under the Adjusted Trial Balance heading.

Spreadsheet Tips

1. Rows and columns can be inserted by positioning the mouse on the immediate row or column after the desired position. Click on the *right* mouse button. With the *left* mouse button, choose Insert and then either Entire Column or Entire Row. Use the same method to delete columns or rows.

2. Enter the sequential numbering of the adjusting entries as labels rather than values by positioning an apostrophe in front of each entry. The first adjusting entry should be labeled '(1).

ATC 3-10 Spreadsheet Assignment *Mastery of Excel*

At the end of the accounting period, Adams Company's general ledger contained the following adjusted balances:

Required

1. Set up the preceding spreadsheet format. (The spreadsheet tips for ATC 3-9 also apply for this problem.)
2. Record the closing entries in the Closing Entries column of the spreadsheet.
3. Compute the Ending Trial Balance amounts.

COMPREHENSIVE PROBLEM

The trial balance of Pacilio Security Services Inc. as of January 1, 2013 had the following normal balances:

Cash	$8,900
Accounts Receivable	1,500
Supplies	65
Prepaid Rent	800
Land	4,000
Accounts Payable	1,050
Unearned Revenue	200
Salaries Payable	1,200
Notes Payable	2,000
Common Stock	8,000
Retained Earnings	2,815

During 2013, Pacilio Security Services experienced the following transactions:

1. Paid the salaries payable from 2012.
2. Paid the balance of $2,000 on the debt owed to the Small Business Government Agency. The loan is interest free.
3. Performed $32,000 of security services for numerous local events during the year; $21,000 was on account and $11,000 was for cash.
4. On May 1, paid $3,000 for 12 months' rent in advance.
5. Purchased supplies on account for $700.
6. Paid salaries expense for the year of $9,000.
7. Incurred other operating expenses on account, $4,200.
8. On October 1, 2013, a customer paid $1,200 for services to be provided over the next 12 months.
9. Collected $19,000 of accounts receivable during the year.
10. Paid $5,950 on accounts payable.
11. Paid $1,800 of advertising expenses for the year.
12. Paid a cash dividend to the shareholders of $4,650.
13. The market value of the land was determined to be $5,500 at December 31, 2013.

Adjustments

14. There was $120 of supplies on hand at the end of the year.
15. Recognized the expired rent.
16. Recognized the earned revenue from 2012 and transaction no. 8.
17. Accrued salaries were $1,000 at December 31, 2013.

Required

a. Record the above transactions in general journal form.

b. Post the transactions to T-accounts and determine the account balances.

c. Prepare a trial balance.

d. Prepare an income statement, statement of changes in stockholders' equity, balance sheet, and statement of cash flows for 2013.

e. Prepare the closing entries and post to the T-accounts.

f. Prepare a post-closing trial balance.

CHAPTER 4

Accounting for Merchandising Businesses

LEARNING OBJECTIVES

After you have mastered the material in this chapter, you will be able to:

LO1 Record and report on inventory transactions using a perpetual system.

LO2 Explain the meaning of terms used to describe transportation costs, cash discounts, returns or allowances, and financing costs.

LO3 Explain how gains and losses differ from revenues and expenses.

LO4 Compare and contrast single and multistep income statements.

LO5 Show the effect of lost, damaged, or stolen inventory on financial statements.

LO6 Determine the amount of net sales.

LO7 Use common size financial statements and ratio analysis to evaluate managerial performance.

LO8 Identify the primary features of the periodic inventory system. (Appendix)

CHAPTER OPENING

Previous chapters have discussed accounting for service businesses. These businesses obtain revenue by providing some kind of service such as medical or legal advice to their customers. Other examples of service companies include dry cleaning companies, housekeeping service companies, and car washes. This chapter introduces accounting for merchandising businesses. **Merchandising businesses** generate revenue by selling goods. They buy the merchandise they sell from companies called suppliers. The goods purchased for resale are called **merchandise inventory.** Merchandising businesses include **retail companies** (companies that sell goods to the final consumer) and **wholesale companies** (companies that sell to other businesses). Sears, JCPenney, Target, and Sam's Club are real-world merchandising businesses.

The Curious Accountant

Richard recently purchased a new Ford automobile from a dealer near his home. When he told his friend Jeff that he was able to purchase the car for $1,000 less than the sticker price, Jeff told Richard he had gotten a lousy deal. "Everybody knows there is a huge markup on cars," Jeff said. "You could have gotten a much lower price if you'd shopped around."

Richard responded, "If there is such a big profit margin on cars, why did so many of the car manufacturers get into financial trouble?" Jeff told him that he was confusing the maker of the car with the dealer. Jeff argued that although the manufacturers may not have high profit margins, the dealers do, and told him again that he had paid too much.

Exhibit 4.1 presents the income statements for AutoNation, Inc., and Ford Motor Company. Based on these statements, do you think either of these guys is correct? For example, if you pay $20,000 for a vehicle from a dealership operated by AutoNation, the largest auto retailer in the United States, how much did the car cost the company? Also, how much did the car cost the Ford Motor Company to manufacture? (Answers on page 230.)

EXHIBIT 4.1   Comparative Income Statements

AUTONATION, INC.
Consolidated Statements of Operations (partial)
For the Years Ended December 31,
(In millions, except per share data)

	2010	2009	2008
Revenue:			
New vehicle	$6,669.1	$5,674.6	$7,339.4
Used vehicle	3,116.1	2,485.9	3,111.7
Parts and service	2,209.1	2,109.8	2,271.1
Finance and insurance, net	418.9	348.6	455.7
Other	47.8	47.1	60.8
Total revenue	12,461.0	10,666.0	13,238.7
Cost of sales:			
New vehicle	6,217.9	5,290.6	6,854.3
Used vehicle	2,849.4	2,257.2	2,850.7
Parts and service	1,245.9	1,187.6	1,281.8
Other	20.3	20.8	26.9
Total cost of sales	10,333.5	8,756.2	11,013.7
Gross Profit:			
New vehicle	451.2	384.0	485.1
Used vehicle	266.7	228.7	261.0
Parts and service	963.2	922.2	989.3
Finance and insurance	418.9	348.6	455.7
Other	27.5	26.3	33.9
Total gross profit	2,127.5	1,909.8	2,225.0
Selling, general & administrative expenses	1,552.1	1,446.9	1,675.1
Depreciation and amortization	76.8	76.7	84.0
Goodwill impairment	—	—	1,610.0
Franchise rights impairment	—	1.5	127.4
Other expenses (income), net	2.0	(23.3)	9.6
Operating income (loss)	496.6	408.0	(1,281.1)
Floorplan interest expense	(42.5)	(35.7)	(79.8)
Other interest expense	(56.1)	(42.6)	(89.4)
Loss on debt extinguishment	(19.6)	—	—
Gain on senior note repurchases	—	13.0	51.3
Interest income	1.4	1.1	2.2
Other gains (losses), net	1.5	5.4	(4.7)
Income (loss) from continuing operations before income taxes	381.3	349.2	(1,401.5)
Income tax provision (benefit)	146.0	116.1	(189.2)
Net income (loss) from continuing operations	235.3	233.1	(1,212.3)
Loss from discontinued operations, net of income taxes	(8.7)	(35.1)	(30.8)
Net income (loss)	$ 226.6	$ 198.0	$(1,243.1)

continued

EXHIBIT 4.1   *Concluded*

FORD MOTOR COMPANY AND SUBSIDIARIES
Consolidated Statement of Operations (Partial)
For the Years Ended December 31, 2010, 2009, and 2008
(in millions, except per share amounts)

	2010	2009	2008
Sales and revenues			
Automotive sales	$119,280	$103,868	$127,635
Financial Services revenues	9,674	12,415	15,949
Total sales and revenues	128,954	116,283	143,584
Costs and expenses			
Automotive cost of sales	104,451	98,866	126,620
Selling, administrative and other expenses	11,909	13,029	21,065
Interest expense	6,152	6,790	9,737
Financial Services provision for credit and insurance losses	(216)	1,030	1,874
Total costs and expenses	122,296	119,715	159,296
Automotive interest income and other non-operating income/(expense), net	(362)	5,284	(713)
Financial Services other income/(loss), net	315	552	1,149
Equity in net income/(loss) of affiliated companies	538	195	381
Income/(Loss) before income taxes	7,149	2,599	(14,895)
Provision for/(Benefit from) income taxes	592	(113)	(62)
Income/(Loss) from continuing operations	6,557	2,712	(14,833)
Income/(Loss) from discontinued operations	—	5	9
Net income/(loss)	6,557	2,717	(14,824)
Less: Income/(Loss) attributable to noncontrolling interests	(4)	—	(58)
Net income/(loss) attributable to Ford Motor Company	$ 6,561	$ 2,717	$ (14,766)

ACCOUNTING FOR INVENTORY TRANSACTIONS

Companies report inventory costs on the balance sheet in the asset account Merchandise Inventory. All costs incurred to acquire merchandise and ready it for sale are included in the inventory account. Examples of inventory costs include the price of goods purchased, shipping and handling costs, transit insurance, and storage costs. Since inventory items are referred to as products, inventory costs are frequently called **product costs.**

Costs that are not included in inventory are usually called **selling and administrative costs.** Examples of selling and administrative costs include advertising, administrative salaries, sales commissions, and insurance. Since selling and administrative costs are usually recognized as expenses *in the period* in which they are incurred, they are sometimes called **period costs.** In contrast, product costs are expensed when inventory is sold regardless of when it was purchased. In other words, product costs are matched directly with sales revenue, while selling and administrative costs are matched with the period in which they are incurred.

LO 1

Record and report on inventory transactions using a perpetual system.

Allocating Inventory Cost Between Asset and Expense Accounts

The cost of inventory that is available for sale during a specific accounting period is determined as follows:

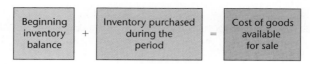

Beginning inventory balance + Inventory purchased during the period = Cost of goods available for sale

The **cost of goods available for sale** is allocated between the asset account Merchandise Inventory and an expense account called **Cost of Goods Sold.** The cost of inventory items that have not been sold (Merchandise Inventory) is reported as an asset on the balance sheet, and the cost of the items sold (Cost of Goods Sold) is expensed on the income statement. This allocation is depicted graphically as follows.

Cost of goods available for sale → Merchandise inventory (balance sheet) / Cost of goods sold (income statement)

The difference between the sales revenue and the cost of goods sold is called **gross margin** or **gross profit.** The selling and administrative expenses (period costs) are subtracted from gross margin to obtain the net income.

Exhibit 4.1 displays income statements from the annual reports of AutoNation and Ford. For each company, review the most current income statement and determine the amount of gross margin. You should find a gross profit of $2,127.5 for AutoNation and a gross margin of $14,829 ($119,280 − $104,451) for Ford.

Perpetual Inventory System

Most modern companies maintain their inventory records using the **perpetual inventory system,** so-called because the inventory account is adjusted perpetually (continually) throughout the accounting period. Each time merchandise is purchased, the inventory account is increased; each time it is sold, the inventory account is decreased. The following illustration demonstrates the basic features of the perpetual inventory system.

June Gardener loved plants and grew them with such remarkable success that she decided to open a small retail plant store. She started June's Plant Shop (JPS) on January 1, 2013. The following discussion explains and illustrates the effects of the five events the company experienced during its first year of operation.

Effects of 2013 Events on Financial Statements

EVENT 1   JPS acquired $15,000 cash by issuing common stock.

This event is an asset source transaction. It increases both assets (cash) and stockholders' equity (common stock). The income statement is not affected. The statement of cash flows reflects an inflow from financing activities. The journal entry and its effects on the financial statements are shown here:

Account Title	Debit	Credit
Cash	15,000	
Common Stock		15,000

Assets			=	Liab.	+	Stockholders' Equity							
Cash	+ Inventory	+ Land	=	Accts. Pay.	+	Com. Stk.	+ Ret. Earn.	Rev.	−	Exp.	=	Net Inc.	Cash Flow
15,000	+ NA	+ NA	=	NA	+	15,000	+ NA	NA	−	NA	=	NA	15,000 FA

EVENT 2 JPS purchased merchandise inventory (plants) for $14,000 cash.

This event is an asset exchange transaction. One asset, cash, decreases and another asset, merchandise inventory, increases; total assets remain unchanged. Because product costs are expensed when inventory is sold, not when the goods are purchased, the event does not affect the income statement. The cash outflow, however, is reported in the operating activities section of the statement of cash flows. The journal entry and its effects on the financial statements are shown here:

Account Title	Debit	Credit
Merchandise Inventory	14,000	
Cash		14,000

Assets			=	Liab.	+	Stockholders' Equity							
Cash	+ Inventory	+ Land	=	Accts. Pay.	+	Com. Stk.	+ Ret. Earn.	Rev.	−	Exp.	=	Net Inc.	Cash Flow
(14,000)	+ 14,000	+ NA	=	NA	+	NA	+ NA	NA	−	NA	=	NA	(14,000) OA

EVENT 3a JPS recognized sales revenue from selling inventory for $12,000 cash.

The revenue recognition is the first part of a two-part transaction. The *sales part* represents a source of assets (cash increases from earning sales revenue). Both assets (cash) and stockholders' equity (retained earnings) increase. Sales revenue on the income statement increases. The $12,000 cash inflow is reported in the operating activities section of the statement of cash flows. The journal entry and its effects on the financial statements are shown here:

Account Title	Debit	Credit
Cash	12,000	
Sales Revenue		12,000

Assets			=	Liab.	+	Stockholders' Equity							
Cash	+ Inventory	+ Land	=	Accts. Pay.	+	Com. Stk.	+ Ret. Earn.	Rev.	−	Exp.	=	Net Inc.	Cash Flow
12,000	+ NA	+ NA	=	NA	+	NA	+ 12,000	12,000	−	NA	=	12,000	12,000 OA

EVENT 3b JPS recognized $8,000 of cost of goods sold.

The expense recognition is the second part of the two-part transaction. The *expense part* represents a use of assets. Both assets (merchandise inventory) and stockholders' equity (retained earnings) decrease. An expense account, Cost of Goods Sold, is reported on the income statement. This part of the transaction does not affect the statement of cash flows. A cash outflow occurred when these goods were bought, not when they were sold. The journal entry and its effects on the financial statements are shown here:

Account Title	Debit	Credit
Cost of Goods Sold	8,000	
Merchandise Inventory		8,000

	Assets			=	Liab.	+	Stockholders' Equity								
Cash	+	Inventory	+	Land	=	Accts. Pay.	+	Com. Stk.	+	Ret. Earn.	Rev.	−	Exp.	=	Net Inc.	Cash Flow
NA	+	(8,000)	+	NA	=	NA	+	NA	+	(8,000)	NA	−	8,000	=	(8,000)	NA

EVENT 4   JPS paid $1,000 cash for selling and administrative expenses.

This event is an asset use transaction. The payment decreases both assets (cash) and stockholders' equity (retained earnings). The increase in selling and administrative expenses decreases net income. The $1,000 cash payment is reported in the operating activities section of the statement of cash flows. The journal entry and its effects on the financial statements are shown here:

Account Title	Debit	Credit
Selling and Administrative Expenses	1,000	
Cash		1,000

	Assets			=	Liab.	+	Stockholders' Equity								
Cash	+	Inventory	+	Land	=	Accts. Pay.	+	Com. Stk.	+	Ret. Earn.	Rev.	−	Exp.	=	Net Inc.	Cash Flow
(1,000)	+	NA	+	NA	=	NA	+	NA	+	(1,000)	NA	−	1,000	=	(1,000)	(1,000) OA

EVENT 5   JPS paid $5,500 cash to purchase land for a place to locate a future store.

Buying the land increases the Land account and decreases the Cash account on the balance sheet. This is an asset exchange transaction. The income statement is not affected. The statement of cash flow shows a cash outflow to purchase land in the investing activities section of the statement of cash flows. The journal entry and its effects on the financial statements are shown here:

Account Title	Debit	Credit
Land	5,500	
Cash		5,500

	Assets			=	Liab.	+	Stockholders' Equity								
Cash	+	Inventory	+	Land	=	Accts. Pay.	+	Com. Stk.	+	Ret. Earn.	Rev.	−	Exp.	=	Net Inc.	Cash Flow
(5,500)	+	NA	+	5,500	=	NA	+	NA	+	NA	NA	−	NA	=	NA	(5,500) IA

Ledger Accounts and Financial Statements

Panel A of Exhibit 4.2 provides a summary of the 2013 accounting events. Panel B of Exhibit 4.2 shows the general ledger T-accounts after the journal entries have been posted to them. The ledger accounts provide the data for the financial statements in Exhibit 4.3.

Although Exhibit 4.2 does not include the 2013 year-end closing entries, recall that the closing entries will transfer the amounts from the revenue and expense accounts to the Retained Earnings account. The balance in the Retained Earnings account after closing will be $3,000. Before reading further, trace the transaction data from each journal entry in Panel A to the ledger accounts in Panel B and then from the ledger accounts to the financial statements in Exhibit 4.3.

EXHIBIT 4.2

Journal Entries and General Ledger Accounts for 2013

Panel A Accounting Events

The 2013 transactions JPS experienced are summarized below.

Event 1   JPS acquired $15,000 cash by issuing common stock.
Event 2   JPS purchased merchandise inventory (plants) for $14,000 cash.
Event 3a JPS recognized sales revenue from selling inventory for $12,000 cash.
Event 3b JPS recognized $8,000 of cost of goods sold.
Event 4   JPS paid $1,000 cash for selling and administrative expenses.
Event 5   JPS paid $5,500 cash to purchase land.

Panel B General Ledger Accounts

Assets				=	Liabilities		+	Equity		

Cash

(1)	15,000	14,000	(2)
(3a)	12,000	1,000	(4)
		5,500	(5)
Bal.	6,500		

Accounts Payable

	0	Bal.

Common Stock

	15,000	(1)
	15,000	Bal.

Merchandise Inventory

(2)	14,000	8,000	(3b)
Bal.	6,000		

Retained Earnings

Land

(5)	5,500

Sales Revenue

	12,000	(3a)

Cost of Goods Sold

(3b)	8,000

Selling and Admin. Expenses

(4)	1,000

EXHIBIT 4.3

Financial Statements

2013 Income Statement			12/31/13 Balance Sheet			2013 Statement of Cash Flows		
Sales revenue	$12,000		Assets			Operating activities		
Cost of goods sold	(8,000)		Cash	$ 6,500		Inflow from customers	$12,000	
Gross margin	4,000		Merchandise inventory	6,000		Outflow for inventory	(14,000)	
Less: Operating exp.			Land	5,500		Outflow for selling		
Selling and			Total assets		$18,000	& admin. exp.	(1,000)	
admin. exp.	(1,000)		Liabilities		$ 0	Net cash outflow from		
Net income	$ 3,000		Stockholders' equity			operating activities		$ (3,000)
			Common stock	$15,000		Investing activities		
			Retained earnings	3,000		Outflow to purchase land		(5,500)
			Total stockholders' equity		18,000	Financing activities		
			Total liab. and stk. equity		$18,000	Inflow from stock issue		15,000
						Net change in cash		6,500
						Plus: Beginning cash balance		0
						Ending cash balance		$ 6,500

JPS had no beginning inventory in its first year, so the cost of merchandise inventory available for sale was $14,000 (the amount of inventory purchased during the period). Recall that JPS must allocate the *Cost of Goods (Inventory) Available for Sale* between the *Cost of Goods Sold* ($8,000) and the ending balance ($6,000) in the *Merchandise Inventory* account. The cost of goods sold is reported as an expense on the income statement and the ending balance of merchandise inventory is reported as an asset on the balance sheet. The difference between the sales revenue ($12,000) and the cost of goods sold ($8,000) is labeled *gross margin* ($4,000) on the income statement.

✓ CHECK YOURSELF 4.1

Phambroom Company began 2013 with $35,600 in its Inventory account. During the year, it purchased inventory costing $356,800 and sold inventory that had cost $360,000 for $520,000. Based on this information alone, determine (1) the inventory balance as of December 31, 2013, and (2) the amount of gross margin Phambroom would report on its 2013 income statement.

Answer

1. Beginning inventory + Purchases = Goods available − Ending inventory = Cost of goods sold

   $35,600 + $356,800 = $392,400 − Ending inventory = $360,000

   Ending inventory = $32,400

2. Sales revenue − Cost of goods sold = Gross margin

   $520,000 − $360,000 = $160,000

TRANSPORTATION COST, PURCHASE RETURNS AND ALLOWANCES, AND CASH DISCOUNTS RELATED TO INVENTORY PURCHASES

LO 2

Explain the meaning of terms used to describe transportation costs, cash discounts, returns or allowances, and financing costs.

Purchasing inventory often involves: (1) incurring transportation costs, (2) returning inventory or receiving purchase allowances (cost reductions), and (3) taking cash discounts (also cost reductions). During its second accounting cycle, JPS encountered these kinds of events. The final account balances at the end of the 2013 fiscal year become the beginning balances for 2014: Cash, $6,500; Merchandise Inventory, $6,000; Land, 5,500; Common Stock, $15,000; and Retained Earnings, $3,000.

Effects of 2014 Events on Financial Statements

JPS experienced the following events during its 2014 accounting period. The effects of each of these events are explained and illustrated in the following discussion.

EVENT 1   JPS borrowed $4,000 cash by issuing a note payable.

JPS borrowed the money to enable it to purchase an additional plot of land for a future site for a store it planned to build in the near future. Borrowing the money increases the Cash account and the Notes Payable account on the balance sheet. The income statement is not affected. The statement of cash flow shows a cash flow from financing activities. The journal entry and its effects on the financial statements are shown here:

Account Title	Debit	Credit
Cash	4,000	
Notes Payable		4,000

	Assets				=	Liabilities			+	Stockholders' Equity							
Cash	+	Accts. Rec.	+ Inventory	+ Land	=	Accts. Pay.	+	Notes Pay.	+	Com. Stk.	+ Ret. Earn.	Rev.	− Exp.	= Net Inc.		Cash Flow	
4,000	+	NA	+ NA	+ NA	=	NA	+	4,000	+	NA	+ NA	NA	− NA	= NA		4,000	FA

EVENT 2 JPS purchased on account merchandise inventory with a list price of $11,000.

The inventory purchase increases both assets (merchandise inventory) and liabilities (accounts payable) on the balance sheet. The income statement is not affected until later, when inventory is sold. Since the inventory was purchased on account, there was no cash outflow. The journal entry and its effects on the financial statements are shown here:

Account Title	Debit	Credit
Merchandise Inventory	11,000	
Accounts Payable		11,000

	Assets				=	Liab.			+	Stockholders' Equity						
Cash	+	Accts. Rec.	+ Inventory	+ Land	=	Accts. Pay.	+	Notes Pay.	+	Com. Stk.	+ Ret. Earn.	Rev.	− Exp.	= Net Inc.		Cash Flow
NA	+	NA	+ 11,000	+ NA	=	11,000	+	NA	+	NA	+ NA	NA	− NA	= NA		NA

Accounting for Purchase Returns and Allowances

EVENT 3 JPS returned some of the inventory purchased in Event 2. The list price of the returned merchandise was $1,000.

To promote customer satisfaction, many businesses allow customers to return goods for reasons such as wrong size, wrong color, wrong design, or even simply because the purchaser changed his mind. The effect of a purchase return is the *opposite* of the original purchase. For JPS the **purchase return** decreases both assets (merchandise inventory) and liabilities (accounts payable). There is no effect on either the income statement or the statement of cash flows. The journal entry and its effects on the financial statements are shown here:

Account Title	Debit	Credit
Accounts Payable	1,000	
Merchandise Inventory		1,000

	Assets				=	Liab.			+	Stockholders' Equity						
Cash	+	Accts. Rec.	+ Inventory	+ Land	=	Accts. Pay.	+	Notes Pay.	+	Com. Stk.	+ Ret. Earn.	Rev.	− Exp.	= Net Inc.		Cash Flow
NA	+	NA	+ (1,000)	+ NA	=	(1,000)	+	NA	+	NA	+ NA	NA	− NA	= NA		NA

Sometimes dissatisfied buyers will agree to keep goods instead of returning them if the seller offers to reduce the price. Such reductions are called allowances. **Purchase allowances** affect the financial statements the same way purchase returns do.

Purchase Discounts

EVENT 4   JPS received a cash discount on goods purchased in Event 2. The credit terms were 2/10, n/30.

To encourage buyers to pay promptly, sellers sometimes offer **cash discounts.** To illustrate, assume JPS purchased the inventory in Event 2 under terms **2/10, n/30** (two-ten, net thirty). These terms mean the seller will allow a 2 percent cash discount if the purchaser pays cash within 10 days from the date of purchase. The amount not paid within the first 10 days is due at the end of 30 days from date of purchase. Recall that in Event 3 JPS returned $1,000 of the inventory purchased in Event 2 leaving a $10,000 balance ($11,000 list price − $1,000 purchase return). If JPS pays for the inventory within 10 days, the amount of the discount is $200 ($10,000 × .02).

When a cash discount is applied to a purchase it is called a **purchase discount.** When it is applied to a sale, it is called a sales discount. Sales discounts will be discussed later in the chapter. A *purchase discount* reduces the cost of the inventory and the associated account payable on the balance sheet. A purchase discount does not directly affect the income statement or the statement of cash flow. The journal entry and its effects on the financial statements are shown here:

Account Title	Debit	Credit
Accounts Payable	200	
Merchandise Inventory		200

	Assets				=	Liab.			+	Stockholders' Equity							
Cash	+	Accts. Rec.	+	Inventory	+	Land	=	Accts. Pay.	+	Notes Pay.	+	Com. Stk.	+	Ret. Earn.	Rev. − Exp. = Net Inc.	Cash Flow
NA	+	NA	+	(200)	+	NA	=	(200)	+	NA	+	NA	+	NA	NA − NA = NA	NA

If JPS paid the account payable after 10 days, there would be no purchase discount. In this case the balances in the Inventory and Account Payable accounts would remain at $10,000.

EVENT 5   JPS paid the $9,800 balance due on the account payable.

The remaining balance in the accounts payable is $9,800 ($10,000 list price − $200 purchase discount). Paying cash to settle the liability reduces cash and accounts payable on the balance sheet. The income statement is not affected. The cash outflow is shown in the operating section of the statement of cash flows. The journal entry and its effects on the financial statements are shown here:

Account Title	Debit	Credit
Accounts Payable	9,800	
Cash		9,800

Cash	+	Accts. Rec.	+	Inventory	+	Land	=	Accts. Pay.	+	Notes Pay.	+	Com. Stk.	+	Ret. Earn.	Rev. − Exp. = Net Inc.	Cash Flow
(9,800)	+	NA	+	NA	+	NA	=	(9,800)	+	NA	+	NA	+	NA	NA − NA = NA	(9,800) OA

REALITY BYTES

Many real-world companies have found it more effective to impose a penalty for late payment than to use a cash discount to encourage early payment. The invoice from Arley Water Works is an example of the penalty strategy. Notice that the amount due, if paid by the due date, is $18.14. A $1.88 late charge is imposed if the bill is paid after the due date. The $1.88 late charge is in fact interest. If Arley Water Works collects the payment after the due date, the utility will receive cash of $20.02. The collection will increase cash ($20.02), reduce accounts receivable ($18.14), and increase interest revenue ($1.88).

ARLEY WATER WORKS				
P.O. BOX 146				
ARLEY, ALABAMA 35541				
(205) 387-0156				

TYPE OF SERVICE	METER READING		USED	CHARGES
	PRESENT	PREVIOUS		
WAT	33030	30950	2080	17.44
Sales Tax				0.70

PLEASE   CLEAN   OUT   AROUND   YOUR   METER

ACCOUNT   #   2054   09-26-13

METER READ			TOTAL DUE UPON RECEIPT	LATE CHARGE AFTER DUE DATE	PAST DUE AMOUNT
MONTH	DAY	CLASS			
9	17	1	18.14	1.88	20.02

The Cost of Financing Inventory

Suppose you buy inventory this month and sell it next month. Where do you get the money to pay for the inventory at the time you buy it? One way to finance the purchase is to buy it on account and withhold payment until the last day of the term for the account payable. For example, suppose you buy inventory under terms 2/10, net/30. Under these circumstances you could delay payment for 30 days after the day of purchase. This way you may be able to collect enough money from the inventory you sell to pay for the inventory you purchased. Refusing the discount allows you the time needed to generate the cash necessary to pay off the liability (account payable). Unfortunately, this is usually a very expensive way to finance the purchase of inventory.

While the amount of a cash discount may appear small, the discount period is short. Consider the terms 2/10, net/30. Since you can pay on the tenth day and still receive the discount, you obtain financing for only 20 days (30-day full credit term − 10-day discount term). In other words, you must forgo a 2 percent discount to obtain a loan with a 20-day term. What is the size of the discount in annual terms? The answer is determined by the following formula.

$$\text{Annual rate} = \text{Discount rate} \times (365 \text{ days} \div \text{Term of the loan})$$

$$\text{Annual rate} = 2\% \times (365 \div 20)$$

$$\text{Annual rate} = 36.5\%$$

This means that a 2 percent discount rate for 20 days is equivalent to a 36.5 percent annual rate of interest. So, if you do not have the money to pay the account payable, but can borrow money from a bank at less than 36.5 percent annual interest, you should borrow the money and pay off the account payable within the discount period.

Accounting for Transportation Costs

EVENT 6   The shipping terms for the inventory purchased in Event 2 were FOB shipping point. JPS paid the freight company $300 cash for delivering the merchandise.

The terms **FOB shipping point** and **FOB destination** identify whether the buyer or the seller is responsible for transportation costs. If goods are delivered FOB shipping point, the buyer is responsible for the freight cost. If goods are delivered FOB destination, the seller is responsible. When the buyer is responsible, the freight cost is called **transportation-in.**

When the seller is responsible, the cost is called **transportation-out.** The following table summarizes freight cost terms:

Responsible Party	Buyer	Seller
Freight terms	FOB shipping point	FOB destination
Account title	Merchandise inventory	Transportation-out

Event 6 indicates the inventory was delivered FOB shipping point, so JPS (the buyer) is responsible for the $300 freight cost. Since incurring transportation-in costs is necessary to obtain inventory, these costs are added to the inventory account. The freight cost increases one asset account (Merchandise Inventory) and decreases another asset account (Cash). The income statement is not affected by this transaction because transportation-in costs are not expensed when they are incurred. Instead they are expensed as part of *cost of goods sold* when the inventory is sold. However, the cash paid for transportation-in costs is reported as an outflow in the operating activities section of the statement of cash flows. The journal entry and its effects on the financial statements are shown here:

Account Title	Debit	Credit
Merchandise Inventory	300	
Cash		300

		Assets			=	Liab.		+	Stockholders' Equity							
Cash	+	Accts. Rec.	+ Inventory +	Land	=	Accts. Pay.	+ Notes Pay.	+	Com. Stk.	+ Ret. Earn.		Rev.	− Exp.	= Net Inc.		Cash Flow
(300)	+	NA	+ 300 +	NA	=	NA	+ NA	+	NA	+ NA		NA	− NA	= NA		(300) OA

EVENT 7a   **JPS recognized $24,750 of revenue on the cash sale of merchandise that cost $11,500.**

The sale increases assets (cash) and stockholders' equity (retained earnings). The revenue recognition increases net income. The $24,750 cash inflow from the sale is reported in the operating activities section of the statement of cash flows. The journal entry and its effects on the financial statements are shown here:

Account Title	Debit	Credit
Cash	24,750	
Sales		24,750

		Assets			=	Liab.		+	Stockholders' Equity							
Cash	+	Accts. Rec.	+ Inventory +	Land	=	Accts. Pay.	+ Notes Pay.	+	Com. Stk.	+ Ret. Earn.		Rev.	− Exp.	= Net Inc.		Cash Flow
24,750	+	NA	+ NA +	NA	=	NA	+ NA	+	NA	+ 24,750		24,750	− NA	= 24,750		24,750 OA

EVENT 7b   **JPS recognized $11,500 of cost of goods sold.**

When goods are sold, the product cost—*including a proportionate share of transportation-in and adjustments for purchase returns and allowances*—is transferred from the Merchandise Inventory account to the expense account, Cost of Goods Sold. Recognizing cost of goods sold decreases both assets (merchandise inventory) and stockholders' equity (retained earnings). The expense recognition for cost of goods sold decreases net income. Cash flow is not affected. The journal entry and its effects on the financial statements are shown here:

Account Title	Debit	Credit
Cost of Goods Sold	11,500	
Merchandise Inventory		11,500

		Assets			**=**	**Liab.**		**+**	**Stockholders' Equity**						
Cash	**+**	**Accts. Rec.**	**+ Inventory**	**+ Land**	**=**	**Accts. Pay.**	**+ Notes Pay.**	**+ Com. Stk.**	**+ Ret. Earn.**		**Rev.**	**− Exp.**	**= Net Inc.**		**Cash Flow**
NA	+	NA	+ (11,500)	+ NA	=	NA	+ NA	+ NA	+ (11,500)		NA	− 11,500	= (11,500)		NA

EVENT 8   JPS paid $450 cash for freight costs on inventory delivered to customers.

Assume the merchandise sold in Event 7a was shipped FOB destination. Also assume JPS paid the freight cost in cash. FOB destination means the seller is responsible for the freight cost, which is called transportation-out. Transportation-out is reported on the income statement as an operating expense in the section below gross margin. The cost of freight on goods shipped to customers is incurred *after* the goods are sold. It is not part of the costs to obtain goods or ready them for sale. Recognizing the expense of transportation-out reduces assets (cash) and stockholders' equity (retained earnings). Operating expenses increase and net income decreases. The cash outflow is reported in the operating activities section of the statement of cash flows. The journal entry and its effects on the financial statements are shown here:

Account Title	Debit	Credit
Transportation-Out	450	
Cash		450

		Assets			**=**	**Liab.**		**+**	**Stockholders' Equity**						
Cash	**+**	**Accts. Rec.**	**+ Inventory**	**+ Land**	**=**	**Accts. Pay.**	**+ Notes Pay.**	**+ Com. Stk.**	**+ Ret. Earn.**		**Rev.**	**− Exp.**	**= Net Inc.**		**Cash Flow**
(450)	+	NA	+ NA	+ NA	=	NA	+ NA	+ NA	+ (450)		NA	− 450	= (450)		(450) OA

If the terms had been FOB shipping point, the customer would have been responsible for the transportation cost and JPS would not have recorded an expense.

EVENT 9   JPS paid $5,000 cash for selling and administrative expenses.

The effect on the balance sheet is to decrease both assets (cash) and stockholders' equity (retained earnings). Recognizing the selling and administrative expenses decreases net income. The $5,000 cash outflow is reported in the operating activities section of the statement of cash flows. The journal entry and its effects on the financial statements are shown here:

Account Title	Debit	Credit
Selling and Administrative Expenses	5,000	
Cash		5,000

Assets				=	Liab.		+	Stockholders' Equity							
Cash	+ Accts. Rec.	+ Inventory	+ Land	=	Accts. Pay.	+ Notes Pay.	+	Com. Stk.	+ Ret. Earn.		Rev.	− Exp.	= Net Inc.		Cash Flow
(5,000)	+ NA	+ NA	+ NA	=	NA	+ NA	+	NA	+ (5,000)		NA	− 5,000	= (5,000)		(5,000) OA

EVENT 10 JPS paid $360 cash for interest expense on the note payable described in Event 1.

The effect on the balance sheet is to decrease both assets (cash) and stockholders' equity (retained earnings). Recognizing the interest expense decreases net income. The $360 cash outflow is reported in the operating activities section of the statement of cash flows. The journal entry and its effects on the financial statements are shown here:

Account Title	Debit	Credit
Interest Expense	360	
Cash		360

Assets				=	Liab.		+	Stockholders' Equity							
Cash	+ Accts. Rec.	+ Inventory	+ Land	=	Accts. Pay.	+ Notes Pay.	+	Com. Stk.	+ Ret. Earn.		Rev.	− Exp.	= Net Inc.		Cash Flow
(360)	+ NA	+ NA	+ NA	=	NA	+ NA	+	NA	+ (360)		NA	− 360	= (360)		(360) OA

RECOGNIZING GAINS AND LOSSES

LO 3

Explain how gains and losses differ from revenues and expenses.

EVENT 11 JPS sold the land that had cost $5,500 for $6,200 cash.

When JPS sells merchandise inventory for more than it cost, the difference between the sales revenue and the cost of the goods sold is called the *gross margin*. In contrast, when JPS sells land for more than it cost, the difference between the sales price and the cost of the land is called a **gain**. Why is one called *gross margin* and the other a *gain*? The terms are used to alert financial statement users to the fact that the nature of the underlying transactions is different.

JPS' primary business is selling inventory, not land. The term *gain* indicates profit resulting from transactions that are not likely to regularly recur. Similarly, had the land sold for less than cost the difference would have been labeled **loss** rather than expense. This term also indicates the underlying transaction is not from normal, recurring operating activities. Gains and losses are shown separately on the income statement to communicate the expectation that they are nonrecurring.

The presentation of gains and losses in the income statement is discussed in more detail in a later section of the chapter. At this point note that the sale increases cash, decreases land, and increases retained earnings on the balance sheet. The income statement shows a gain on the sale of land and net income increases. The $6,200 cash inflow is shown as an investing activity on the statement of cash flows. The journal entry and its effects on the financial statements are shown here:

Account Title	Debit	Credit
Cash	6,200	
Land		5,500
Gain on Sale of Land		700

	Assets			=	Liab.		+	Stockholders' Equity						
Cash +	Accts. Rec. +	Inventory +	Land =		Accts. Pay. +	Notes Pay. +		Com. Stk. +	Ret. Earn.	Gain −	Exp. =	Net Inc.	Cash Flow	
6,200 +	NA +	NA +	(5,500) =		NA +	NA +		NA +	700	700 −	NA =	700	6,200 IA	

✓ CHECK YOURSELF 4.2

Tsang Company purchased $32,000 of inventory on account with payment terms of 2/10, n/30 and freight terms FOB shipping point. Freight costs were $1,100. Tsang obtained a $2,000 purchase allowance because the inventory was damaged upon arrival. Tsang paid for the inventory within the discount period. Based on this information alone, determine the balance in the inventory account.

Answer

List price of inventory	$32,000
Plus: Transportation-in costs	1,100
Less: Purchase returns and allowances	(2,000)
Less: Purchase discount [($32,000 − $2,000) × .02]	(600)
Balance in inventory account	$30,500

Exhibit 4.4 summarizes the accounting events and ledger T-accounts for the 2014 accounting period. Before reading further, trace the effects of each event to the ledger accounts. Then trace the information in the ledger accounts to the 2014 financial statements displayed in Exhibits 4.5, 4.7, and 4.8.

EXHIBIT 4.4

Accounting Events and Ledger Accounts for 2014

Panel A Accounting Events

Event 1	JPS borrowed $4,000 cash by issuing a note payable.
Event 2	JPS purchased on account merchandise inventory with a list price of $11,000.
Event 3	JPS returned some of the inventory purchased in Event 2. The list price of the returned merchandise was $1,000.
Event 4	JPS received a cash discount on goods purchased in Event 2. The credit terms were 2/10, n/30.
Event 5	JPS paid the $9,800 balance due on the account payable.
Event 6	The inventory purchased in Event 2 was delivered FOB shipping point. JPS paid the freight company $300 cash for delivering the merchandise.
Event 7a	JPS recognized $24,750 of revenue on the cash sale of merchandise that cost $11,500.
Event 7b	JPS recognized $11,500 of cost of goods sold.
Event 8	JPS paid $450 cash for freight costs on inventory delivered to customers.
Event 9	JPS paid $5,000 cash for selling and administrative expenses.
Event 10	JPS paid $360 cash for interest expense on the note payable described in Event 1.
Event 11	JPS sold the land that had cost $5,500 for $6,200 cash.

continued

Panel B Ledger Accounts

| | Assets | | | = | | Liabilities | | + | | Equity | |

Assets

Cash

Bal.	6,500	9,800	(5)
(1)	4,000	300	(6)
(7a)	24,750	450	(8)
(11)	6,200	5,000	(9)
		360	(10)
Bal.	25,540		

Merchandise Inventory

Bal.	6,000	1,000	(3)
(2)	11,000	200	(4)
(6)	300	11,500	(7b)
Bal.	4,600		

Land

Bal.	5,500	5,500	(11)
Bal.	0		

Liabilities

Accounts Payable

(3)	1,000	11,000	(2)
(4)	200		
(5)	9,800		
		0	Bal.

Notes Payable

		4,000	(1)
		4,000	Bal.

Equity

Common Stock

		15,000	Bal.

Retained Earnings

		3,000	Bal.
		8,140	(CI)
		11,140	Bal.

Sales Revenue

(CI)	24,750	24,750	(7a)
		–0–	Bal.

Gain on Sale of Land

(CI)	700	700	(11)
		–0–	Bal.

Cost of Goods Sold

(7b)	11,500	11,500	(CI)
Bal.	–0–		

Transportation-out

(8)	450	450	(CI)
Bal.	–0–		

Selling and Admin. Expenses

(9)	5,000	5,000	(CI)
Bal.	–0–		

Interest Expense

(10)	360	360	(CI)
Bal.	–0–		

Total Assets		Total Liabilities		Total Equity
$30,140	=	$4,000	+	$26,140

MULTISTEP INCOME STATEMENT

LO 4

Compare and contrast single and multistep income statements.

JPS' 2014 income statement is shown in Exhibit 4.5. Observe the form of this statement carefully. It is more informative than one that simply subtracts expenses from revenues. First, it compares sales revenue with the cost of the goods that were sold to produce that revenue. The difference between the sales revenue and the cost of goods sold is called *gross margin*. Next, the operating expenses are subtracted from the gross margin to determine the *operating income*. **Operating income** is the amount of income that is generated from the normal recurring operations of a business. Items that are not expected to recur on a regular basis are subtracted from the operating income to determine the amount of *net income*.[1]

Income statements that show these additional relationships are called **multistep income statements.** Income statements that display a single comparison of all revenues

[1]Revenue and expense items with special characteristics may be classified as discontinued or extraordinary items. These items are shown separately just above net income regardless of whether a company uses a single-step or multistep format. Further discussion of these items is beyond the scope of this text.

EXHIBIT 4.5

JUNE'S PLANT SHOP
Income Statement
For the Period Ended December 31, 2014

Sales revenue	$ 24,750
Cost of goods sold	(11,500)
Gross margin	13,250
Less: Operating expenses	
Selling and administrative expense	(5,000)
Transportation-out	(450)
Operating income	7,800
Nonoperating items	
Interest expense	(360)
Gain on the sale of land	700
Net income	$ 8,140

EXHIBIT 4.6

Income Statement Format Used by U.S. Companies

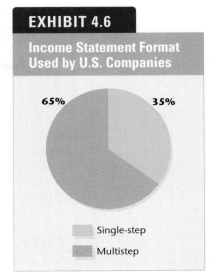

65%   35%

- Single-step
- Multistep

Data Source: AICPA, *Accounting Trends and Techniques.*

EXHIBIT 4.7

JUNE'S PLANT SHOP
Balance Sheet
As of December 31, 2014

Assets		
Cash	$25,540	
Merchandise inventory	4,600	
Total assets		$30,140
Liabilities		
Notes payable		$ 4,000
Stockholders' equity		
Common stock	$15,000	
Retained earnings	11,140	
Total stockholders' equity		26,140
Total liabilities and stockholders' equity		$30,140

EXHIBIT 4.8

JUNE'S PLANT SHOP
Statement of Cash Flows
For the Period Ended December 31, 2014

Operating activities		
Inflow from customers	$ 24,750	
Outflow for inventory*	(10,100)	
Outflow for transportation-out	(450)	
Outflow for selling and		
administrative expense	(5,000)	
Outflow for interest expense	(360)	
Net cash outflow for operating		
activities		$ 8,840
Investing activities		
Inflow from sale of land		6,200
Financing activities		
Inflow from issue of note payable		4,000
Net change in cash		19,040
Plus beginning cash balance		6,500
Ending cash balance		$25,540

*Net cost on inventory 9,800 + transportation-in $300 = $10,100

minus all expenses are called **single-step income statements.** To this point in the text we have shown only single-step income statements to promote simplicity. However, the multistep form is used more frequently in practice. Exhibit 4.6 shows the percentage of companies that use the multistep versus the single-step format. Go to Exhibit 4.1 and identify the company that presents its income statement in the multistep format. You should have identified AutoNation as the company using the multistep format. Ford's statement is shown in the single-step format.

Note that interest is reported as a nonoperating item on the income statement in Exhibit 4.5. In contrast, it is shown in the *operating* activities section of the statement of cash flows in Exhibit 4.8. When the FASB issued *Statement of Financial Accounting*

Standard (SFAS) 95, it required interest to be reported in the operating activities section of the statement of cash flows. There was no corresponding requirement for the treatment of interest on the income statement. Prior to *SFAS 95,* interest was considered to be a nonoperating item. Most companies continued to report interest as a nonoperating item on their income statements even though they were required to change how it was reported on the statement of cash flows. As a result, there is frequent inconsistency in the way interest is reported on the two financial statements.

Also note that while the gain on the sale of land is shown on the income statement, it is not included in the operating activities section of the statement of cash flows. Since the gain is a nonoperating item, it is included in the cash inflow from the sale of land shown in the investing activities section. In this case the full cash inflow from the sale of land ($6,200) is shown in the investing activities section of the statement of cash flows in Exhibit 4.8.

LOST, DAMAGED, OR STOLEN INVENTORY

LO 5

Show the effect of lost, damaged, or stolen inventory on financial statements.

Most merchandising companies experience some level of inventory **shrinkage,** a term that reflects decreases in inventory for reasons other than sales to customers. Inventory may be stolen by shoplifters, damaged by customers or employees, or even simply lost or misplaced. Since the *perpetual* inventory system is designed to record purchases and sales of inventory as they occur, the balance in the merchandise inventory account represents the amount of inventory that *should* be on hand at any given time. By taking a physical count of the merchandise inventory at the end of the accounting period and comparing that amount with the book balance in the Merchandise Inventory account, managers can determine the amount of any inventory shrinkage. If goods have been lost, damaged, or stolen, the book balance will be higher than the actual amount of inventory on hand and an adjusting entry is required to reduce assets and equity. The Merchandise Inventory account is reduced, and an expense for the amount of the lost, damaged, or stolen inventory is recognized.

To illustrate, assume that Midwest Merchandising Company maintains perpetual inventory records. Midwest determined, through a physical count, that it had $23,500 of merchandise inventory on hand at the end of the accounting period. The balance in the Inventory account was $24,000. Midwest must make an adjusting entry to write down the Inventory account so the amount reported on the financial statements agrees with the amount actually on hand at the end of the period. The write-down decreases both assets (inventory) and stockholders' equity (retained earnings). The write-down

REALITY BYTES

"Closed for Inventory Count" is a sign you frequently see on retail stores sometime during the month of January. Even if companies use a perpetual inventory system, the amount of inventory on hand may be unknown because of lost, damaged, or stolen goods. The only way to determine the amount of inventory on hand is to count it. Why count it in January? Christmas shoppers and many after-Christmas sales shoppers are satiated by mid-January, leaving the stores low on both merchandise and customers. Accordingly, stores have less merchandise to count and "lost sales" are minimized during January. Companies that do not depend on seasonal sales (e.g., a plumbing supplies wholesale business) may choose to count inventory at some other time during the year. Counting inventory is not a revenue-generating activity; it is a necessary activity that should be conducted when it least disrupts operations.

increases expenses and decreases net income. Cash flow is not affected. The effects on the statements are as follows:

Assets	=	Liab.	+	Equity	Rev.	–	Exp.	=	Net Inc.	Cash Flow
(500)	=	NA	+	(500)	NA	–	500	=	(500)	NA

In general journal form, the entry is as follows:

Account Title	Debit	Credit
Inventory Loss (Cost of Goods Sold)	500	
Inventory		500

Theoretically, inventory losses are operating expenses. However, because such losses are normally immaterial in amount, they are usually added to cost of goods sold for external reporting purposes.

EVENTS AFFECTING SALES

To this point we assumed JPS did not offer cash discounts to its customers. However, sales, as well as purchases of inventory, can be affected by returns, allowances, and discounts. **Sales discounts** are price reductions offered by sellers to encourage buyers to pay promptly. To illustrate, assume JPS engaged in the following selected events during 2015.

Determine the amount of net sales.

EVENT 1a   JPS sold on account merchandise with a list price of $8,500. Payment terms were 1/10, n/30. The merchandise had cost JPS $4,000.

The sale increases both assets (accounts receivable) and shareholders' equity (retained earnings). Recognizing revenue increases net income. The statement of cash flows is not affected. The journal entry for this event and its effects on the financial statements follow:

Account Title	Debit	Credit
Accounts Receivable	8,500	
Sales Revenue		8,500

Assets					=	Liab.	+	Stockholders' Equity			Rev.	–	Exp.	=	Net Inc.	Cash Flow
Cash	+	Accts. Rec.	+	Inventory	=	Note Pay.	+	Com. Stk.	+	Retained Earnings						
NA	+	8,500	+	NA	=	NA	+	NA	+	8,500	8,500	–	NA	=	8,500	NA

EVENT 1b   JPS recognized $4,000 of cost of goods sold.

Recognizing the expense decreases assets (merchandise inventory) and stockholders' equity (retained earnings). Cost of goods sold increases and net income decreases. Cash flow is not affected. The journal entry for this event and its effects on the financial statements follow:

Account Title	Debit	Credit
Cost of Goods Sold	4,000	
Merchandise Inventory		4,000

Assets				=	Liab.	+	Stockholders' Equity			Rev.	−	Exp.	=	Net Inc.	Cash Flow
Cash	+	Accts. Rec.	+ Inventory	=	Note Pay.	+	Com. Stk.	+	Retained Earnings						
NA	+	NA	+ (4,000)	=	NA	+	NA	+	(4,000)	NA	−	4,000	=	(4,000)	NA

Accounting for Sales Returns and Allowances

EVENT 2a   A customer from Event 1a returned inventory with a $1,000 list price. The merchandise had cost JPS $450.

The sales return decreases both assets (accounts receivable) and stockholders' equity (retained earnings) on the balance sheet. Sales and net income decrease. Cash flow is not affected. The journal entry for this event and its effects on the financial statements follow:

Account Title	Debit	Credit
Sales Revenue	1,000	
Accounts Receivable		1,000

Assets				=	Liab.	+	Stockholders' Equity			Rev.	−	Exp.	=	Net Inc.	Cash Flow
Cash	+	Accts. Rec.	+ Inventory	=	Note Pay.	+	Com. Stk.	+	Retained Earnings						
NA	+	(1,000)	+ NA	=	NA	+	NA	+	(1,000)	(1,000)	−	NA	=	(1,000)	NA

EVENT 2b   The cost of the goods ($450) is returned to the inventory account.

Since JPS got the inventory back, the sales return increases both assets (merchandise inventory) and stockholders' equity (retained earnings). The expense (cost of goods sold) decreases and net income increases. Cash flow is not affected. The journal entry for this event and its effects on the financial statements follow:

Account Title	Debit	Credit
Merchandise Inventory	450	
Cost of Goods Sold		450

Assets				=	Liab.	+	Stockholders' Equity			Rev.	−	Exp.	=	Net Inc.	Cash Flow
Cash	+	Accts. Rec.	+ Inventory	=	Note Pay.	+	Com. Stk.	+	Retained Earnings						
NA	+	NA	+ 450	=	NA	+	NA	+	450	NA	−	(450)	=	450	NA

Accounting for Sales Discounts

EVENT 3 JPS collected the balance of the accounts receivable generated in Event 1a. Recall the goods were sold under terms 1/10, net/30.

ALTERNATIVE 1 The collection occurs before the discount period has expired (within 10 days from the date of the sale).

JPS would give the buyer a 1 percent discount. Given the original sales amount of $8,500 and a sales return of $1,000, the amount of the discount is $75 [($8,500 − $1,000) × .01]. The sales discount reduces the amount of accounts receivable and retained earnings on the balance sheet. It also reduces the amount of revenue and the net income shown on the balance sheet. It does not affect the statement of cash flows. These effects are shown below.

Account Title	Debit	Credit
Sales Revenue	75	
Accounts Receivable		75

	Assets				=	Liab.	+	Stockholders' Equity			Rev.	−	Exp.	=	Net Inc.	Cash Flow
Cash	+	Accts. Rec.	+	Inventory	=	Note Pay.	+	Com. Stk.	+	Retained Earnings					
NA	+	(75)	+	NA	=	NA	+	NA	+	(75)	(75)	−	NA	=	(75)	NA

The balance due on the account receivable is $7,425 ($8,500 original sales − $1,000 sales return − $75 discount). The collection increases the Cash account and decreases the Accounts Receivable account. The income statement is not affected. The cash inflow is shown in the operating activities section of the statement of cash flows. The journal entry for this event and its effects on the financial statements follow:

Account Title	Debit	Credit
Cash	7,425	
Accounts Receivable		7,425

	Assets				=	Liab.	+	Stockholders' Equity			Rev.	−	Exp.	=	Net Inc.	Cash Flow
Cash	+	Accts. Rec.	+	Inventory	=	Accts. Pay.	+	Com. Stk.	+	Retained Earnings					
7,425	+	(7,425)	+	NA	=	NA	+	NA	+	NA	NA	−	NA	=	NA	7,425 OA

Net Sales

The gross amount of sales minus **sales returns and allowances** and sales discounts is commonly called **net sales**. Companies are not required by GAAP to show sales returns and allowances and sales discounts on their income statement. Indeed, most companies show only the amount of *net sales* on the income statement. In this case the net sales amount to $7,425 ($8,500 original sales − $1,000 sales return − $75 discount).

ALTERNATIVE 2   The collection occurs after the discount period has expired (after 10 days from the date of the sale).

Under these circumstances there is no sales discount. The amount collected is $7,500 ($8,500 original sale − $1,000 sales return). Net sales shown on the income statement would also be $7,500.

THE FINANCIAL ANALYST

Merchandising is a highly competitive business. In order to succeed, merchandisers develop different strategies to distinguish themselves in the marketplace. For example, some companies like Walmart, Kmart, and Costco focus on price competition while others such as Neiman Marcus and Saks Fifth Avenue sell high-priced goods that offer high quality, style, and strong guaranties. Financial analysts have developed specific tools that are useful in scrutinizing the success or failure of a company's sales strategy. The first step in the analytical process is to develop common size statements so that comparisons can be made between companies.

Common Size Financial Statements

LO 7

Use common size financial statements and ratio analysis to evaluate managerial performance.

How good is a $1,000,000 increase in net income? The answer is not clear because there is no indication as to the size of the company. A million dollar increase may be excellent for a small company but would be virtually meaningless for a company the size of Exxon. To enable meaningful comparisons analysts prepare **common size financial statements.** Common size statements display information in percentages as well as absolute dollar amounts.

To illustrate, we expand the income statements for JPS to include percentages. The results are shown in Exhibit 4.9. The percentage data are computed by defining net

EXHIBIT 4.9	Common Size Financial Statements			
JUNE'S PLANT SHOP Income Statement For the Period Ended				
	2013		**2014**	
Net sales*	$12,000	100.0%	$ 24,750	100.0%
Cost of goods sold	(8,000)	66.7	(11,500)	46.5
Gross margin	4,000	33.3	13,250	53.5
Less: Operating expenses				
Selling and administrative expense	(1,000)	8.3	(5,000)	20.2
Transportation-out			(450)	1.8
Operating income	3,000	25.0	7,800	31.5
Nonoperating items				
Interest expense			(360)	(1.5)
Gain on the sale of land			700	2.8
Net income	$ 3,000	25.0	$ 8,140	32.9

*Since JPS did not offer sales discounts or have sales returns and allowances during 2013 or 2014, the amount of sales revenue is equal to the amount of net sales. We use the term *net sales* here because it is more commonly used in business practice. Percentages do not add exactly because they have been rounded.

sales as the base figure, or 100 percent. The other amounts on the statements are then shown as a percentage of net sales. For example, the *cost of goods sold percentage* is the dollar amount of *cost of goods sold* divided by the dollar amount of *net sales,* which produces a percentage of 66.7 percent ($8,000 ÷ $12,000) for 2013 and 46.5 percent ($11,500 ÷ $24,750) for 2014. Other income statement items are computed using the same approach.

Ratio Analysis

Two of the percentages shown in Exhibit 4.9 are used frequently in business to make comparisons within a specific company or between two or more different companies. These two commonly used percentages are the **gross margin percentage** and the **net income percentage.** These percentages are calculated as follows:

$$\text{Gross margin percentage} = \frac{\text{Gross margin}}{\text{Net sales}}$$

The gross margin percentage provides insight about a company's pricing strategy. All other things being equal, a high gross margin percentage means that a company is charging high prices in relation to its cost of goods sold.

$$\text{Net income percentage} = \frac{\text{Net income}}{\text{Net sales}}$$

In practice, the *net income percentage* is frequently called the **return on sales** ratio. The return on sales ratio provides insight as to how much of each sales dollar remains as net income after all expenses are paid. All other things being equal, companies with high ratios are doing a better job of controlling expenses.

Comparisons within a Particular Company

To illustrate comparisons within a particular company, assume that JPS relocated its store in an upscale mall in early 2014. Management realized that the company would have to pay more for operating expenses but believed those expenses could be offset by charging significantly higher prices. We use the gross margin percentage and the net income percentage to assess the success of JPS's strategy. Exhibit 4.9 shows an increase in the *gross margin percentage* from 33.3 to 53.5. This confirms that JPS was able to increase prices relative to its cost of goods sold. The increase in the *return on sales* ratio (25 percent to 32.9 percent) confirms that the increase in gross margin was larger than the increase in total expenses. We therefore conclude that JPS's strategy to relocate was successful. As a side note this may also explain why JPS sold its land in late 2014. Considering the success the company experienced at the new location, there was no motive to build a store on the land.

Since net income is affected by nonoperating items, some financial analysts would prefer to use *operating income* instead of *net income* when computing the *return on sales* ratio. In this case the nonoperating items were immaterial. Indeed, to simplify the discussion in this chapter we always assume immateriality when computing this ratio. However, when nonoperating items are significant, it is more insightful to use *operating income* as the numerator of the *return on sales* ratio.

Comparisons between Companies

Does Walmart sell merchandise at a higher or lower price than Target? The *gross margin percentage* is useful in answering questions such as this. Since Walmart's 2011 fiscal year annual report shows a gross margin percentage of 25.3 while Target's report shows a gross margin percentage of 32.2, we conclude that there is validity to Walmart's claim of having low prices. The next section of the chapter provides insight as to how the *gross margin percentage* and the *return on sales* ratio can be used to gain insight about the operations of several real-world companies.

✓ CHECK YOURSELF 4.3

The following sales data are from the records of two retail sales companies. All amounts are in thousands.

	Company A	Company B
Sales	$ 21,234	$ 43,465
Cost of goods sold	(14,864)	(34,772)
Gross margin	$ 6,370	$ 8,693

One company is an upscale department store, and the other is a discount store. Which company is the upscale department store?

Answer   The gross margin percentage for Company A is approximately 30 percent ($6,370 ÷ $21,234). The gross margin percentage for Company B is 20 percent ($8,693 ÷ $43,465). These percentages suggest that Company A is selling goods with a higher markup than Company B, which implies that Company A is the upscale department store.

Answers to The Curious Accountant

As data from the income statement for AutoNation show, automobile dealers do not have big markups on the cars they sell. The new vehicles the company sold for $6,669.1 million in 2010 cost the company $6,217.9 to purchase, resulting in a gross margin of $451.2, or 6.8%. In other words, if you bought an "average" car from AutoNation for $20,000, the company's gross profit on it was only $1,360 ($20,000 × .068), meaning it paid Ford $18,640 ($20,000 − $1,360). Furthermore, the company still had other expenses to pay besides its cost of goods sold. In 2010, only 1.8% of each dollar of AutoNation's sales was net profit ($226.6 ÷ $12,461.0) Remember, the amount shown for sales on AutoNation's income statement is based on what customers actually paid for the cars the company sold, not the "sticker price."

Meanwhile, if Ford sold the car to AutoNation for $18,640, it earned a gross margin on the sale of 12.4%, or $2,311 [$14,829 ÷ $119,280 = 12.4%; ($119,280 − $104,451 = $14,829)] [$18,640 × .124 = $2.311]. Like AutoNation, Ford still had other expenses to pay for besides the cost of goods sold. In 2010, Ford earned 5.1% of net profit on each dollar of sales ($6,561 ÷ $128,954).

Most consumers significantly overestimate the profit margins of the companies from which they buy goods. Retailers, especially, operate with small profit margins, so inventory management, discussed in Chapter 5, is very important to their success.

REAL-WORLD DATA

Exhibit 4.10 shows the gross margin percentages and return on sales ratios for 10 companies. Three of the companies are manufacturers that produce pharmaceutical products, and the remaining seven companies sell various products at the retail level. These data are for the companies' 2010 or 2011 fiscal years.

EXHIBIT 4.10

Industry/Company	Gross Margin %	Return on Sales %
Pharmaceutical manufacturers		
GlaxoSmithKline	73.3	9.7
Johnson & Johnson	69.5	21.7
Merck & Co.	60.0	1.9
Retail pharmacies		
CVS	21.0	3.6
Rite Aid	26.6	−2.0
Walgreens	28.1	3.1
Department stores		
Macy's	41.3	8.1
Walmart	25.3	3.6
Office supplies		
Office Depot	28.9	0.3
Staples	26.9	3.6

A review of the data confirms our earlier finding that ratios for companies in the same industry are often more similar than are ratios for companies from different industries. For example, note that the manufacturers have much higher margins, both for gross profit and for net earnings, than do the retailers. Manufacturers are often able to charge higher prices than are retailers because they obtain patents which give them a legal monopoly on the products they create. When a company such as Merck develops a new drug, no one else can produce that drug until the patent expires, giving it lots of control over its price at the wholesale level. Conversely, when Walgreen sells Merck's drug at the retail level, it faces price competition from CVS Caremark (CVS), a company that is trying to sell the same drug to the same consumers. One way CVS can try to get customers to shop at its store is to charge lower prices than its competitors, but this reduces its profit margins, since it must pay the same price to get Merck's drug as did Walgreen. As the data in Exhibit 4.10 show, in 2010 CVS had a lower gross margin percentage than did Walgreen, indicating it is charging lower prices for similar goods.

In the examples presented in Exhibit 4.10, some companies with higher gross margin percentages have higher return on sales ratios than their competitors, but this is not always the case. Office Depot, had a gross margin percentage that was 7 percent greater than Staples [(28.9 − 26.9) ÷ 28.9], but its return on sales ratio was lower.

A Look Back

Merchandising companies earn profits by selling inventory at prices that are higher than the cost paid for the goods. Merchandising companies include *retail companies* (companies that sell goods to the final consumer) and *wholesale companies* (companies that sell to other merchandising companies). The products sold by merchandising companies are called *inventory.* The costs to purchase inventory, to receive it, and to ready it for sale are *product costs,* which are first accumulated in an inventory account (balance sheet asset account) and then recognized as cost of goods sold (income statement expense account) in the period in which goods are sold. Purchases and sales of inventory can be recorded continually as goods are bought and sold (perpetual system) or at the end of the accounting period (periodic system, discussed in the chapter appendix).

Accounting for inventory includes the treatment of cash discounts, transportation costs, and returns and allowances. The cost of inventory is the list price less any purchase returns and allowances and purchase discounts, plus transportation-in costs. The cost of freight paid to acquire inventory (*transportation-in*) is considered a product cost. The cost of freight paid to deliver inventory to customers (*transportation-out*) is a selling expense. *Sales returns and allowances* and *sales discounts* are subtracted from sales revenue to determine the amount of *net sales* reported on the income statement. Purchase returns and allowances reduce product cost. Theoretically, the cost of lost, damaged, or stolen inventory is an operating expense. However, because these costs are usually immaterial in amount they are typically included as part of cost of goods sold on the income statement.

Some companies use a *multistep income statement* which reports product costs separately from selling and administrative costs. Cost of goods sold is subtracted from sales revenue to determine *gross margin.* Selling and administrative expenses are subtracted from gross margin to determine income from operations. Other companies report income using a *single-step format* in which the cost of goods sold is listed along with selling and administrative items in a single expense category that is subtracted in total from revenue to determine income from operations.

Managers of merchandising businesses operate in a highly competitive environment. They must manage company operations carefully to remain profitable. *Common size financial statements* (statements presented on a percentage basis) and ratio analysis are useful monitoring tools. Common size financial statements permit ready comparisons among different-size companies. Although a $1 million increase in sales may be good for a small company and bad for a large company, a 10 percent increase can apply to any size company. The two most common ratios used by merchandising companies are the *gross margin percentage* (gross margin ÷ net sales) and the *net income percentage* (net income ÷ net sales). Interpreting these ratios requires an understanding of industry characteristics. For example, a discount store such as Walmart would be expected to have a much lower gross margin percentage than an upscale store such as Neiman Marcus.

Managers should be aware of the financing cost of carrying inventory. By investing funds in inventory, a firm loses the opportunity to invest them in interest-bearing assets. The cost of financing inventory is an *opportunity cost.* To minimize financing costs, a company should minimize the amount of inventory it carries, the length of time it holds the inventory, and the time it requires to collect accounts receivable after the inventory is sold.

>> A Look Forward

To this point, the text has explained the basic accounting cycle for service and merchandising businesses. Future chapters more closely address specific accounting issues. For example, in Chapter 6 you will learn how to deal with inventory items that are purchased at differing prices. Other chapters will discuss a variety of specific practices that are widely used by real-world companies.

APPENDIX

Periodic Inventory System

LO 8

Identify the primary features of the periodic inventory system.

Under certain conditions, it is impractical to record inventory sales transactions as they occur. Consider the operations of a fast-food restaurant. To maintain perpetual inventory records, the restaurant would have to transfer from the Inventory account to the Cost of Goods Sold account the *cost* of each hamburger, order of fries, soft drink, or other food items as they were sold. Obviously, recording the cost of each item at the point of sale would be impractical without using highly sophisticated computer equipment.

EXHIBIT 4.11

General Journal Entries for 2014 (Periodic Method)

Event No.	Account Title	Debit	Credit
1	Cash	4,000	
	Notes Payable		4,000
2	Purchases	11,000	
	Accounts Payable		11,000
3	Accounts Payable	1,000	
	Purchase Returns and Allowances		1,000
4	Accounts Payable	200	
	Purchase Discounts		200
5	Accounts Payable	9,800	
	Cash		9,800
6	Transportation-In	300	
	Cash		300
7a	Cash	24,750	
	Sales		24,750
8	Transportation-Out	450	
	Cash		450
9	Selling and Administrative Expenses	5,000	
	Cash		5,000
10	Interest Expense	360	
	Cash		360
11	Cash	6,200	
	Land		5,500
	Gain on Sale of Land		700
Adj	Cost of Goods Sold	11,500	
	Merchandise Inventory (Ending Balance)	4,600	
	Purchase Returns and Allowances	1,000	
	Purchase Discounts	200	
	Purchases		11,000
	Transportation-In		300
	Merchandise Inventory (Beginning Balance)		6,000
CL	Revenue	24,750	
	Gain on Sale of Land	700	
	Cost of Goods Sold		11,500
	Transportation-Out		450
	Selling and Administrative Expenses		5,000
	Interest Expense		360
	Retained Earnings		8,140

Recording the selling price the customer pays is captured by cash registers; the difficulty lies in capturing inventory cost.

The **periodic inventory system** offers a practical solution for recording inventory transactions in a low-technology, high-volume environment. As shown in Exhibit 4.11, inventory costs are recorded in a Purchases account at the time of purchase. Purchase returns and allowances and transportation-in are recorded in separate accounts. No entries for the cost of merchandise purchases or sales are recorded in the Inventory account during the period. The cost of goods sold is determined at the end of the period as shown in Exhibit 4.12.

The perpetual and periodic inventory systems represent alternative procedures for recording the same information. The amounts of cost of goods sold and ending

EXHIBIT 4.12

Schedule of Cost of Goods Sold for 2014

Beginning inventory	$ 6,000
Purchases	11,000
Purchase returns and allowances	(1,000)
Purchase discounts	(200)
Transportation-in	300
Cost of goods available for sale	16,100
Ending inventory	(4,600)
Cost of goods sold	$11,500

inventory reported in the financial statements will be the same regardless of the method used. Exhibit 4.11 presents the general journal entries JPS would make if it used the periodic inventory method for the 2014 transactions. Cost of goods sold is recorded in an adjusting entry at the end of the accounting period.

The **schedule of cost of goods sold** presented in Exhibit 4.12 is used for internal reporting purposes. It is normally not shown in published financial statements. The amount of cost of goods sold is reported as a single line item on the income statement. The income statement in Exhibit 4.5 will be the same whether JPS maintains perpetual or periodic inventory records.

Advantages and Disadvantages of the Periodic System versus the Perpetual System

The chief advantage of the periodic method is recording efficiency. Recording inventory transactions occasionally (periodically) requires less effort than recording them continually (perpetually). Historically, practical limitations offered businesses like fast-food restaurants or grocery stores no alternative to using the periodic system. The sheer volume of transactions made recording individual decreases to the Inventory account balance as each item was sold impossible. Imagine the number of transactions a grocery store would have to record every business day to maintain perpetual records.

Although the periodic system provides a recordkeeping advantage over the perpetual system, perpetual inventory records provide significant control advantages over periodic records. With perpetual records, the book balance in the Inventory account should agree with the amount of inventory in stock at any given time. By comparing that book balance with the results of a physical inventory count, management can determine the amount of lost, damaged, destroyed, or stolen inventory. Perpetual records also permit more timely and accurate reorder decisions and profitability assessments.

When a company uses the *periodic* inventory system, lost, damaged, or stolen merchandise is automatically included in cost of goods sold. Because such goods are not included in the year-end physical count, they are treated as sold regardless of the reason for their absence. Since the periodic system does not separate the cost of lost, damaged, or stolen merchandise from the cost of goods sold, the amount of any inventory shrinkage is unknown. This feature is a major disadvantage of the periodic system. Without knowing the amount of inventory losses, management cannot weigh the costs of various security systems against the potential benefits.

Advances in such technology as electronic bar code scanning and increased computing power have eliminated most of the practical constraints that once prevented merchandisers with high-volume, low dollar-value inventories from recording inventory transactions on a continual basis. As a result, use of the perpetual inventory system has expanded rapidly in recent years and continued growth can be expected. This text, therefore, concentrates on the perpetual inventory system.

SELF-STUDY REVIEW PROBLEM

A step-by-step audio-narrated series of slides is provided on the text website at www.mhhe.com/edmonds8e.

Academy Sales Company (ASC) started the 2013 accounting period with the balances given in the financial statements model shown below. During 2013 ASC experienced the following business events.

1. Purchased $16,000 of merchandise inventory on account, terms 2/10, n/30.
2. The goods that were purchased in Event 1 were delivered FOB shipping point. Freight costs of $600 were paid in cash by the responsible party.
3. Returned $500 of goods purchased in Event 1.

4a. Recorded the cash discount on the goods purchased in Event 1.

4b. Paid the balance due on the account payable within the discount period.

5a. Recognized $21,000 of cash revenue from the sale of merchandise.

5b. Recognized $15,000 of cost of goods sold.

6. The merchandise in Event 5a was sold to customers FOB destination. Freight costs of $950 were paid in cash by the responsible party.

7. Paid cash of $4,000 for selling and administrative expenses.

8. Sold the land for $5,600 cash.

Required

a. Record the above transactions in a financial statements model like the one shown below.

Event No.	Cash	+	Inventory	+	Land	=	Accts. Pay.	+	Com. Stk.	+	Ret. Earn.	Rev./ Gain	–	Exp.	=	Net Inc.	Cash Flow
Bal.	25,000	+	3,000	+	5,000	=	–0–	+	18,000	+	15,000	NA	–	NA	=	NA	NA

b. Prepare a schedule of cost of goods sold. (Appendix)

c. Prepare a multistep income statement. Include common size percentages on the income statement.

d. ASC's gross margin percentage in 2012 was 22%. Based on the common size data in the income statement, did ASC raise or lower its prices in 2013? (Appendix)

e. Assuming a 10 percent rate of growth, what is the amount of net income expected for 2014?

Answer

a.

Event No.	Cash	+	Inventory	+	Land	=	Accts. Pay.	+	Com. Stk.	+	Ret. Earn.	Rev./ Gain	–	Exp.	=	Net Inc.	Cash Flow
Bal.	25,000	+	3,000	+	5,000	=	–0–	+	18,000	+	15,000	NA	–	NA	=	NA	NA
1		+	16,000			=	16,000	+		+			–		=		
2	(600)	+	600			=		+		+			–		=		(600) OA
3		+	(500)			=	(500)	+		+			–		=		
4a		+	(310)			=	(310)	+		+			–		=		
4b	(15,190)	+				=	(15,190)	+		+			–		=		(15,190) OA
5a	21,000	+				=		+		+	21,000	21,000	–		=	21,000	21,000 OA
5b		+	(15,000)			=		+		+	(15,000)		–	15,000	=	(15,000)	
6	(950)	+				=		+		+	(950)		–	950	=	(950)	(950) OA
7	(4,000)	+				=		+		+	(4,000)		–	4,000	=	(4,000)	(4,000) OA
8	5,600	+			(5,000)	=		+		+	600	600	–		=	600	5,600 IA
Bal.	30,860	+	3,790		–0–	=	–0–	+	18,000	+	16,650	21,600	–	19,950	=	1,650	5,860 NC

b.

ACADEMY SALES COMPANY
Schedule of Cost of Goods Sold
For the Period Ended December 31, 2013

Beginning inventory	$ 3,000
Plus purchases	16,000
Less: Purchase returns and allowances	(500)
Less: Purchases discounts	(310)
Plus: Transportation-in	600
Goods available for sale	18,790
Less: Ending inventory	(3,790)
Cost of goods sold	$15,000

c.

ACADEMY SALES COMPANY
Income Statement*
For the Period Ended December 31, 2013

Net sales	$ 21,000	100.0%
Cost of goods sold	(15,000)	71.4
Gross margin	6,000	28.6
Less: Operating expenses		
Selling and administrative expense	(4,000)	19.0
Transportation-out	(950)	4.5
Operating income	1,050	5.0
Nonoperating items		
Gain on the sale of land	600	2.9
Net income	$ 1,650	7.9

*Percentages do not add exactly because they have been rounded.

d. All other things being equal, the higher the gross margin percentage, the higher the sales prices. Since the gross margin percentage increased from 22% to 28.6%, the data suggest that Academy raised its sales prices.

e. $1,155 [$1,050 + (.10 × $1,050)]. Note that the gain is not expected to recur.

KEY TERMS

cash discount 216
common size financial statements 228
cost of goods available for sale 210
cost of goods sold 210
FOB (free on board) destination 217
FOB (free on board) shipping point 217
gain 220
gross margin 210

gross margin percentage 229
gross profit 210
loss 220
merchandise inventory 207
merchandising businesses 206
multistep income statement 222
net income percentage 229
net sales 227
operating income (or loss) 222
period costs 209
periodic inventory system 233

perpetual inventory system 210
product costs 209
purchase discount 216
purchase returns and allowances 215
retail companies 207
return on sales 229
sales discounts 225
sales returns and allowances 227
schedule of cost of goods sold 234

selling and administrative costs 209
shrinkage 224
single-step income statement 223
transportation-in (freight-in) 217
transportation-out (freight-out) 218
2/10, n/30 216
wholesale companies 207

QUESTIONS

1. Define *merchandise inventory*. What types of costs are included in the Merchandise Inventory account?

2. What is the difference between a product cost and a selling and administrative cost?

3. How is the cost of goods available for sale determined?

4. What portion of cost of goods available for sale is shown on the balance sheet? What portion is shown on the income statement?

5. When are period costs expensed? When are product costs expensed?

6. If PetCo had net sales of $600,000, goods available for sale of $450,000, and cost of goods sold of $375,000, what is its gross margin? What amount of inventory will be shown on its balance sheet?

7. Describe how the perpetual inventory system works. What are some advantages of using the perpetual inventory system? Is it necessary to

take a physical inventory when using the perpetual inventory system?

8. What are the effects of the following types of transactions on the accounting equation? Also identify the financial statements that are affected. (Assume that the perpetual inventory system is used.)
   a. Acquisition of cash from the issue of common stock.
   b. Contribution of inventory by an owner of a company.

c. Purchase of inventory with cash by a company.

d. Sale of inventory for cash.

9. Northern Merchandising Company sold inventory that cost $12,000 for $20,000 cash. How does this event affect the accounting equation? What financial statements and accounts are affected? (Assume that the perpetual inventory system is used.)

10. If goods are shipped FOB shipping point, which party (buyer or

seller) is responsible for the shipping costs?

11. Define *transportation-in*. Is it a product or a period cost?

12. Quality Cellular Co. paid $80 for freight on merchandise that it had purchased for resale to customers (transportation-in) and paid $135 for freight on merchandise delivered to customers (transportation-out). What account is debited for the $80 payment? What account is debited for the $135 payment?

13. Why would a seller grant an allowance to a buyer of the seller's merchandise?

14. Dyer Department Store purchased goods with the terms 2/10, n/30. What do these terms mean?

15. Eastern Discount Stores incurred a $5,000 cash

cost. How does the accounting for this cost differ if the cash were paid for inventory versus commissions to sales personnel?

16. What is the purpose of giving a cash discount to charge customers?

17. Define *transportation-out*. Is it a product cost or a period cost for the seller?

18. Ball Co. purchased inventory with a list price of $4,000 with the terms 2/10, n/30. What amount will be debited to the Merchandise Inventory account?

19. Explain the difference between gains and revenues.

20. Explain the difference between losses and expenses.

21. Suda Company sold land that cost $40,000 for

$37,000 cash. Explain how this transaction would be shown on the statement of cash flows.

22. Explain the difference between purchase returns and sales returns. How do purchase returns affect the financial statements of both buyer and seller? How do sales returns affect the financial statements of both buyer and seller?

23. How is net sales determined?

24. What is the difference between a multistep income statement and a single-step income statement?

25. What is the advantage of using common size income statements to present financial information for several accounting periods?

26. What information is provided by the net income percentage (return on sales ratio)?

27. What is the purpose of preparing a schedule of cost of goods sold? (Appendix)

28. Explain how the periodic inventory system works. What are some advantages of using the periodic inventory system? What are some disadvantages of using the periodic inventory system? Is it necessary to take a physical inventory when using the periodic inventory system? (Appendix)

29. Why does the periodic inventory system impose a major disadvantage for management in accounting for lost, stolen, or damaged goods? (Appendix)

MULTIPLE-CHOICE QUESTIONS

Multiple-choice questions are provided on the text website at www.mhhe.com/edmonds8e.

EXERCISES—SERIES A

All applicable Exercises in Series A are available with McGraw-Hill's *Connect® Accounting*.

When the instructions for *any* exercise or problem call for the preparation of an income statement, use the *multistep format* unless otherwise indicated.

Exercise 4-1A   *Comparing a merchandising company with a service company*

LO 1

The following information is available for two different types of businesses for the 2013 accounting period. Blake Consulting is a service business that provides consulting services to small businesses. University BookMart is a merchandising business that sells books to college students.

Data for Blake Consulting

1. Borrowed $80,000 from the bank to start the business.
2. Performed services for clients and collected $60,000 cash.
3. Paid salary expense of $38,400.

Data for University BookMart

1. Borrowed $80,000 from the bank to start the business.
2. Purchased $38,000 of inventory for cash.

3. Inventory costing $33,600 was sold for $60,000 cash.
4. Paid $4,800 cash for operating expenses.

Required

a. Prepare an income statement, balance sheet, and statement of cash flows for each of the companies.
b. What is different about the income statements of the two businesses?
c. What is different about the balance sheets of the two businesses?
d. How are the statements of cash flow different for the two businesses?

LO 1, 4

Exercise 4-2A   *Effect of inventory transactions on journals, ledgers, and financial statements: Perpetual system*

Justin Swords started a small merchandising business in 2013. The business experienced the following events during its first year of operation. Assume that Swords uses the perpetual inventory system.

1. Acquired $30,000 cash from the issue of common stock.
2. Purchased inventory for $60,000 cash.
3. Sold inventory costing $48,000 for $82,000 cash.

Required

a. Record the events in general journal format.
b. Post the entries to T-accounts.
c. Prepare an income statement for 2013 (use the multistep format).
d. What is the amount of total assets at the end of the period?

LO 1

Exercise 4-3A   *Effect of inventory transactions on the income statement and statement of cash flows: Perpetual system*

During 2013, Sistronk Merchandising Company purchased $40,000 of inventory on account. The company sold inventory on account that cost $30,000 for $50,000. Cash payments on accounts payable were $24,500. There was $38,000 cash collected from accounts receivable. Sistronk also paid $9,000 cash for operating expenses. Assume that Sistronk started the accounting period with $20,000 in both cash and common stock.

Required

a. Identify the events described in the preceding paragraph and record them in a horizontal statements model like the following one:

Assets				=	Liab.	+	Equity			Rev.	−	Exp.	=	Net Inc.	Cash Flow
Cash	+	Accts. Rec.	+	Inv. =	Accts. Pay.	+	Com. Stk.	+	Ret. Earn.						
20,000	+	NA	+	NA =	NA	+	20,000	+	NA	NA	−	NA	=	NA	NA

b. What is the balance of accounts receivable at the end of 2013?
c. What is the balance of accounts payable at the end of 2013?
d. What are the amounts of gross margin and net income for 2013?
e. Determine the amount of net cash flow from operating activities.
f. Explain any differences between net income and net cash flow from operating activities.

LO 1

Exercise 4-4A   *Recording inventory transactions in the general journal and posting entries to T-accounts: Perpetual system*

Tripp's Toner Supply experienced the following events during 2013, its first year of operation:

1. Acquired $25,000 cash from the issue of common stock.
2. Purchased inventory for $32,000 cash.

3. Sold inventory costing $19,000 for $36,000 cash.

4. Paid $3,100 for advertising expense.

Required

a. Record the general journal entries for the preceding transactions.

b. Post each of the entries to T-accounts.

c. Prepare a trial balance to prove the equality of debits and credits.

Exercise 4-5A   *Determining which party is responsible for freight cost*   LO 2

Required

Determine which party, buyer or seller, is responsible for freight charges in each of the following situations:

a. Sold merchandise, freight terms, FOB destination.

b. Sold merchandise, freight terms, FOB shipping point.

c. Purchased merchandise, freight terms, FOB destination.

d. Purchased merchandise, freight terms, FOB shipping point.

Exercise 4-6A   *Purchase discounts and transportation costs*   LO 2

Callegari Basket Company had an $8,500 beginning balance in its Merchandise Inventory account. The following information regarding Callegari's purchases and sales of inventory during its 2013 accounting period was drawn from the company's accounting records:

1. Purchased $45,000 of inventory under terms 1/10, net/60. Transportation costs amounted to $700. The goods were delivered FOB shipping point. Callegari paid for the inventory within the discount period.

2. Purchased $40,000 of inventory under terms 2/10, net/30. Transportation costs amounted to $900. The goods were delivered to Callegari FOB destination. Callegari paid for the inventory after the discount period had expired.

3. Sold inventory that cost $56,000 for $94,000. Transportation costs for goods delivered to customers amounted to $3,200. The goods were delivered FOB destination.

Required

a. Determine the balance in the Inventory account at the end of the accounting period.

b. Is Callegari or its customers responsible for the transportation costs described in Event 3?

c. Determine the gross margin.

Exercise 4-7A   *Effect of purchase returns and allowances and freight costs on the*   LO 1, 2
journal, ledger, and financial statements: Perpetual system

The trial balance for The Box Shop as of January 1, 2013, was as follows:

Account Titles	Debit	Credit
Cash	$12,000	
Inventory	6,000	
Common Stock		$15,000
Retained Earnings		3,000
Total	$18,000	$18,000

The following events affected the company during the 2013 accounting period:

1. Purchased merchandise on account that cost $8,200.

2. The goods in event 1 were purchased FOB shipping point with freight cost of $600 cash.

3. Returned $800 of damaged merchandise for credit on account.

4. Agreed to keep other damaged merchandise for which the company received a $400 allowance.

5. Sold merchandise that cost $5,500 for $9,500 cash.

6. Delivered merchandise to customers under terms FOB destination with freight costs amounting to $300 cash.

7. Paid $5,000 on the merchandise purchased in Event 1.

Required

a. Record the transactions in general journal format.

b. Open general ledger T-accounts with the appropriate beginning balances, and post the journal entries to the T-accounts.

c. Prepare an income statement and statement of cash flows for 2013.

d. Explain why a difference does or does not exist between net income and net cash flow from operating activities.

LO 1, 2

Exercise 4-8A   Accounting for product costs: Perpetual inventory system

Which of the following would be *debited* to the Inventory account for a merchandising business using the perpetual inventory system?

Required

a. Purchase of office supplies.

b. Transportation-out.

c. Cash discount given on goods sold.

d. Transportation-in.

e. Allowance received for damaged inventory.

f. Purchase of inventory.

LO 1, 2

Exercise 4-9A   Effect of product cost and period cost: Horizontal statements model

Wilson Co. experienced the following events for the 2013 accounting period:

1. Acquired $20,000 cash from the issue of common stock.

2. Purchased $36,000 of inventory on account.

3. Received goods purchased in Event 2 FOB shipping point. Freight cost of $900 paid in cash.

4. Returned $4,000 of goods purchased in Event 2 because of poor quality.

5. Sold inventory on account that cost $28,000 for $82,000.

6. Freight cost on the goods sold in Event 5 was $200. The goods were shipped FOB destination. Cash was paid for the freight cost.

7. Collected $33,000 cash from accounts receivable.

8. Paid $27,000 cash on accounts payable.

9. Paid $4,500 for advertising expense.

10. Paid $7,200 cash for insurance expense.

Required

a. Which of these transactions affect period (selling and administrative) costs? Which result in product costs? If neither, label the transaction NA.

b. Record each event in a horizontal statements model like the following one. The first event is recorded as an example.

Assets			=	Liab.	+	Equity			Rev.	−	Exp.	=	Net Inc.	Cash Flow
Cash	+	Accts. Rec.	+	Inv.	=	Accts. Pay.	+	C. Stk.	+	Ret. Earn.						
20,000	+	NA	+	NA	=	NA	+	20,000	+	NA	NA	−	NA	=	NA	20,000 FA

Exercise 4-10A   *Cash discounts and purchase returns*   LO 1, 2

On March 6, 2013, Cobb's Imports purchased merchandise from Games Inc. with a list price of $19,000, terms 2/10, n/45. On March 10, Cobb's returned merchandise to Games Inc. for credit. The list price of the returned merchandise was $8,500. Cobb's paid cash to settle the accounts payable on March 15, 2013.

Required

a. What is the amount of the check that Cobb's must write to Games Inc. on March 15?
b. Record the events in a horizontal statements model like the following one.

Assets			=	Liab.	+	Equity				Rev.	−	Exp.	=	Net Inc.	Cash Flow
Cash	+	Inv.	=	Accts. Pay.	+	C. Stk.	+	Ret. Earn.							

c. How much would Cobb's pay for the merchandise purchased if the payment is not made until March 20, 2013?
d. Record the payment of the merchandise in Requirement *c* in a horizontal statements model like the one shown above.
e. Why would Games Inc. sell merchandise with the terms 2/10, n/45?

Exercise 4-11A   *Determining the effect of inventory transactions on the financial statements model: Perpetual system*   LO 2

Mario Company experienced the following events:

1. Purchased merchandise inventory for cash.
2. Sold merchandise inventory on account. Label the revenue recognition 2a and the expense recognition 2b.
3. Returned merchandise purchased on account.
4. Purchased merchandise inventory on account.
5. Paid cash on accounts payable within the discount period.
6. Paid cash for selling and administrative expenses.
7. Sold merchandise inventory for cash. Label the revenue recognition 7a and the expense recognition 7b.
8. Paid cash for transportation-out.
9. Paid cash for transportation-in.
10. Collected cash from accounts receivable not within the discount period.

Required

Identify each event as asset source (AS), asset use (AU), asset exchange (AE), or claims exchange (CE). Also explain how each event affects the financial statements by placing a + for increase, − for decrease, or NA for not affected under each of the components in the following statements model. Assume the company uses the perpetual inventory system. The first event is recorded as an example.

Event No.	Event Type	Assets	=	Liab.	+	Equity	Rev.	−	Exp.	=	Net Inc.	Cash Flow
1	AE	+ −	=	NA	+	NA	NA	−	NA	=	NA	− OA

Exercise 4-12A   *Multistep income statement*   LO 3, 4, 7

In 2013, Byrd Incorporated sold land for $82,000 cash. The land had originally cost $50,000. Also, Byrd sold inventory that had cost $176,000 for $265,000 cash. Operating expenses amounted to $41,000.

Required

a. Prepare a 2013 multistep income statement for Byrd Incorporated.

b. Assume that normal operating activities grow evenly by 10% during 2014. Prepare a 2014 multistep income statement of Byrd Incorporated.

c. Determine the percentage change in net income between 2013 and 2014.

d. Should the stockholders have expected the results determined in Requirement *c*? Explain your answer.

LO 2, 3, 4

Exercise 4-13A   *Purchase returns, discounts, loss, and a multistep income statement*

The following information was drawn from the 2013 accounting records of Sawyer Merchandisers.

1. Inventory with a list price of $40,000 was purchased under terms 2/10, net/30.
2. Sawyer returned $4,200 of the inventory to the supplier.
3. The accounts payable was settled within the discount period.
4. The inventory was sold for $69,000.
5. Selling and administrative expenses amounted to $12,000.
6. Interest expense amounted to $800.
7. Land that cost $15,000 was sold for $20,000 cash.

Required

a. Determine the cost of the inventory sold.

b. Prepare a multistep income statement.

c. Where would the interest expense be shown on the statement of cash flows?

d. How would the sale of the land be shown on the statement of cash flows?

e. Explain the difference between a loss and an expense.

LO 2, 3, 4, 7

Exercise 4-14A   *Comprehensive exercise with purchases discounts*

The Wedding Shop (TWS) started the 2013 accounting period with the balances given in the financial statements model shown below. During 2013 TWS experienced the following business events:

1. Purchased $60,000 of merchandise inventory on account, terms 2/10, n/30.
2. The goods that were purchased in Event 1 were delivered FOB shipping point. Freight costs of $1,500 were paid in cash by the responsible party.
3. Returned $3,000 of goods purchased in Event 1.
4a. Recorded the cash discount on the goods purchased in Event 1.
4b. Paid the balance due on the account payable within the discount period.
5a. Recognized $59,000 of cash revenue from the sale of merchandise.
5b. Recognized $45,000 of cost of goods sold.
6. The merchandise in Event 5a was sold to customers FOB destination. Freight costs of $1,400 were paid in cash by the responsible party.
7. Paid cash of $9,000 for selling and administrative expenses.
8. Sold the land for $14,500 cash.

Required

a. Record the above transactions in a financial statements model like the one shown below.

Event No.	Cash	+	Inventory	+	Land	=	Accts. Pay.	+	Com. Stk.	+	Ret. Earn.	Rev./ Gain	–	Exp.	=	Net Inc.	Cash Flow
Bal.	60,000	+	8,000	+	12,000	=	–0–	+	50,000	+	30,000	NA	–	NA	=	NA	NA

b. Prepare a multistep income statement. Include common size percentages on the income statement.

c. TWS's gross margin percentage in 2012 was 34%. Based on the common size data in the income statement, did TWS raise or lower its prices in 2013?

d. Assuming a 5% rate of growth, what is the amount of net income expected for 2014?

Exercise 4-15A   Single-step and multistep income statements   LO 4

The following information was taken from the accounts of Healthy Eats, a delicatessen, at December 31, 2013. The accounts are listed in alphabetical order, and each has a normal balance.

Accounts payable	$1,200
Accounts receivable	800
Advertising expense	400
Cash	820
Common stock	400
Cost of goods sold	1,200
Interest expense	140
Merchandise inventory	900
Prepaid rent	80
Retained earnings	1,000
Sales revenue	2,000
Salaries expense	260
Rent expense	220
Loss on sale of land	50

Required

First, prepare an income statement for the year using the single-step approach. Then prepare another income statement using the multistep approach.

Exercise 4-16A   Effect of inventory losses: Perpetual system   LO 5

Royal Sales experienced the following events during 2013, its first year of operation:

1. Started the business when it acquired $80,000 cash from the issue of common stock.
2. Paid $35,000 cash to purchase inventory.
3. Sold inventory costing $21,000 for $40,500 cash.
4. Physically counted inventory showing $13,500 inventory was on hand at the end of the accounting period.

Required

a. Open appropriate ledger T-accounts, and record the events in the accounts.

b. Prepare an income statement and balance sheet for 2013.

c. Explain how differences between the book balance and the physical count of inventory could arise. Why is being able to determine whether differences exist useful to management?

Exercise 4-17A   Effect of sales returns and allowances and freight costs on the   LO 6
               journal, ledger, and financial statements: Perpetual system

Poole Company began the 2013 accounting period with $36,000 cash, $80,000 inventory, $70,000 common stock, and $46,000 retained earnings. During the 2013 accounting period, Poole experienced the following events:

1. Sold merchandise costing $51,500 for $92,900 on account to Mable's General Store.
2. Delivered the goods to Mable's under terms FOB destination. Freight costs were $500 cash.
3. Received returned goods from Mable's. The goods cost Poole Company $3,200 and were sold to Mable's for $4,700.
4. Granted Mable's a $1,500 allowance for damaged goods that Mable's agreed to keep.
5. Collected partial payment of $71,000 cash from accounts receivable.

Required

a. Record the transactions in general journal format.

b. Open general ledger T-accounts with the appropriate beginning balances and post the journal entries to the T-accounts.

c. Prepare an income statement, balance sheet, and statement of cash flows.

d. Why would Poole grant the $1,500 allowance to Mable's? Who benefits more?

LO 7

Exercise 4-18A   *Using ratios to make comparisons*

The following income statements were drawn from the annual reports of the Pines Company and the Yew Company:

	Pines*	Yew*
Net sales	$32,600	$86,200
Cost of goods sold	17,930	64,650
Gross margin	14,670	21,550
Less: Operating exp.		
Selling and admin. exp.	13,040	18,960
Net income	$ 1,630	$ 2,590

*All figures are reported in thousands of dollars.

Required

a. One of the companies is a high-end retailer that operates in exclusive shopping malls. The other operates discount stores that are located in low-cost, stand-alone buildings. Identify the high-end retailer and the discounter. Support your answer with appropriate ratios.

b. If Pines and Yew have equity of $16,200 and $20,400, respectively, which company is in the more profitable business?

LO 7

Exercise 4-19A   *Using common size statements and ratios to make comparisons*

At the end of 2013 the following information is available for Badger and Marmot companies:

	Badger	Marmot
Sales	$1,000,000	$1,000,000
Cost of goods sold	650,000	550,000
Operating expenses	250,000	375,000
Total assets	1,200,000	1,200,000
Stockholders' equity	450,000	300,000

Required

a. Prepare a common size income statement for each company.

b. Compute the return on assets and return on equity for each company.

c. Which company is more profitable from the stockholders' perspective?

d. One company is a high-end retailer, and the other operates a discount store. Which is the discounter? Support your selection by referring to the appropriate ratios.

LO 8

Exercise 4-20A   *Effect of inventory transactions on the income statement and balance sheet: Periodic system (Appendix)*

Sara Hitt is the owner of SH Cleaning. At the beginning of the year, Hitt had $4,800 in inventory. During the year, Hitt purchased inventory that cost $26,000. At the end of the year, inventory on hand amounted to $3,600.

Required

Calculate the following:

a. Cost of goods available for sale during the year.
b. Cost of goods sold for the year.
c. Inventory amount SH Cleaning would report on its year-end balance sheet.

Exercise 4-21A Determining cost of goods sold: Periodic system (Appendix)   LO 8

India Retailers uses the periodic inventory system to account for its inventory transactions. The following account titles and balances were drawn from India's records for the year 2013: beginning balance in inventory, $46,200; purchases, $352,400; purchase returns and allowances, $14,600; sales, $840,000; sales returns and allowances, $7,520; transportation-in, $2,150; and operating expenses, $65,100. A physical count indicated that $35,100 of merchandise was on hand at the end of the accounting period.

Required

a. Prepare a schedule of cost of goods sold.
b. Prepare a multistep income statement.

Exercise 4-22A Basic transactions: Periodic system, single cycle (Appendix)   LO 8

The following events apply to Mia's Gift Shop for 2013, its first year of operation:

1. Acquired $60,000 cash from the issue of common stock.
2. Issued common stock to Mia Smart, one of the owners, in exchange for merchandise inventory worth $3,200 Mia had acquired prior to opening the shop.
3. Purchased $56,200 of inventory on account.
4. Paid $4,500 for advertising expense.
5. Sold inventory for $98,300 cash.
6. Paid $12,000 in salary to a part-time salesperson.
7. Paid $47,000 on accounts payable (see Event 3).
8. Physically counted inventory, which indicated that $16,000 of inventory was on hand at the end of the accounting period.

Required

a. Record each of these events in general journal form. Mia's Gift Shop uses the periodic system.
b. Post each of the events to ledger T-accounts.
c. Prepare an income statement, statement of changes in stockholders' equity, balance sheet, and statement of cash flows for 2013.
d. Prepare the necessary closing entries at the end of 2013, and post them to the appropriate T-accounts.
e. Prepare a post-closing trial balance.
f. Discuss an advantage of using the periodic system instead of the perpetual system.
g. Why is the common stock issued on the statement of changes in stockholders' equity different from the common stock issued in the cash flow from financing activities section of the cash flow statement?

PROBLEMS—SERIES A

All applicable Problems in Series A are available with McGraw-Hill's *Connect® Accounting.*

Problem 4-23A Basic transactions for three accounting cycles: Perpetual system   LO 1, 4

Cushing Company was started in 2013 when it acquired $40,000 from the issue of common stock. The following data summarize the company's first three years' operating activities. Assume that all transactions were cash transactions.

CHECK FIGURES
2013 Net Income: $1,500
2014 Total Assets: $61,400

	2013	2014	2015
Purchases of inventory	$30,000	$36,000	$57,000
Sales	42,000	56,000	72,000
Cost of goods sold	22,000	39,000	51,000
Selling and administrative expenses	6,500	9,100	11,200

Required

Prepare an income statement (use the multistep format) and balance sheet for each fiscal year. (*Hint:* Record the transaction data for each accounting period in T-accounts before preparing the statements for that year.)

LO 2

Problem 4-24A   *Identifying freight cost*

Required

For each of the following events, determine the amount of freight paid by Tom's Parts House. Also indicate whether the freight is classified as a product or period cost.

a. Purchased inventory with freight costs of $1,400, FOB destination.
b. Shipped merchandise to customers with freight costs of $300, FOB destination.
c. Purchased additional merchandise with costs of $500, FOB shipping point.
d. Sold merchandise to a customer. Freight costs were $800, FOB shipping point.

LO 2

Problem 4-25A   *Identifying product and period costs*

Required

Indicate whether each of the following costs is a product cost or a period cost:

a. Advertising expense.
b. Insurance on vans used to deliver goods to customers.
c. Salaries of sales supervisors.
d. Monthly maintenance expense for a copier.
e. Goods purchased for resale.
f. Cleaning supplies for the office.
g. Freight on goods purchased for resale.
h. Salary of the marketing director.
i. Freight on goods sold to customer with terms FOB destination.
j. Utilities expense incurred for office building.

LO 4, 7

Problem 4-26A   *Multistep and common size income statements*

The following information was drawn from the records of Moore Sales Company:

	2013	2014
Net sales	$60,000	$70,000
Cost of goods sold	(25,000)	(26,500)
Operating expenses	(13,200)	(16,100)
Gain on the sale of land	0	5,000

Required

a. Prepare a multistep income statement for each year.
b. Prepare a common size income statement for each year.
c. Assume that the operating trends between 2013 and 2014 continue through 2015. Write a brief memo indicating whether you expect net income to increase or decrease in 2015.

Problem 4-27A *Comprehensive cycle problem: Perpetual system*

LO 1, 2, 3, 4, 5, 6

At the beginning of 2013, P & D Enterprises had the following balances in its accounts:

CHECK FIGURES
d. Net Income: $3,642
Total Assets: $26,442

Cash	$16,800
Inventory	4,000
Land	2,000
Common stock	12,000
Retained earnings	10,800

During 2013, P & D Enterprises experienced the following events:

1. Purchased inventory costing $11,200 on account from Stone Company under terms 2/10, n/30. The merchandise was delivered FOB shipping point. Freight costs of $800 were paid in cash.

2. Returned $600 of the inventory that it had purchased because the inventory was damaged in transit. The seller agreed to pay the return freight cost.

3. Paid the amount due on its account payable to Stone Company within the cash discount period.

4. Sold inventory that had cost $8,000 for $13,500. The sale was on account under terms 2/10, n/45.

5. Received merchandise returned from a customer. The merchandise had originally cost $1,200 and had been sold to the customer for $2,100 cash. The customer was paid $2,100 cash for the returned merchandise.

6. Delivered goods in Event 4 FOB destination. Freight costs of $800 were paid in cash.

7. Collected the amount due on accounts receivable within the discount period.

8. Sold the land for $3,500.

9. Recognized $500 of accrued interest revenue.

10. Took a physical count indicating that $6,500 of inventory was on hand at the end of the accounting period.

Required

a. Identify each of these events as asset source (AS), asset use (AU), asset exchange (AE), or claims exchange (CE). Also explain how each event affects the financial statements by placing a + for increase, − for decrease, or NA for not affected under each of the components in the following statements model. Assume that the perpetual inventory method is used. When an event has more than one part, use letters to distinguish the effects of each part. The first event is recorded as an example.

Event No.	Event Type	Assets	=	Liab.	+	Stk. Equity	Rev.	−	Exp.	=	Net Inc.	Cash Flow
1a	AS	+	=	+	+	NA	NA	−	NA	=	NA	NA
1b	AE	+ −	=	NA	+	NA	NA	−	NA	=	NA	− OA

b. Record the events in general journal format.

c. Open ledger T-accounts and post the beginning balances and the events to the accounts.

d. Prepare a multistep income statement, statement of changes in stockholders' equity, balance sheet, and statement of cash flows.

e. Record and post the closing entries, and prepare a post-closing trial balance.

Problem 4-28A *Preparing a schedule of cost of goods sold and multistep and single-step income statements: Periodic system (Appendix)*

LO 4, 8

The following account titles and balances were taken from the adjusted trial balance of Gaskin Sales Co. at December 31, 2013. The company uses the periodic inventory method.

Account Title	Balance
Advertising expense	$ 20,800
Interest expense	10,000
Merchandise inventory, January 1	36,000
Merchandise inventory, December 31	40,200
Miscellaneous expense	1,600
Purchases	300,000
Purchase returns and allowances	5,400
Rent expense	36,000
Salaries expense	106,000
Sales	640,000
Sales returns and allowances	16,000
Transportation-in	12,400
Transportation-out	21,600
Gain on sale of land	8,000
Utilities expense	22,400

Required

a. Prepare a schedule to determine the amount of cost of goods sold.

b. Prepare a multistep income statement.

c. Prepare a single-step income statement.

LO 8

Problem 4-29A   *Comprehensive cycle problem: Periodic system (Appendix)*

The following trial balance pertains to Feazell Hardware as of January 1, 2013:

Account Title	Debit	Credit
Cash	$ 28,000	
Accounts receivable	18,000	
Merchandise inventory	120,000	
Accounts payable		$ 10,000
Common stock		140,000
Retained earnings		16,000
Total	$166,000	$166,000

The following events occurred in 2013. Assume that Feazell Hardware uses the periodic inventory system.

1. Purchased land for $16,000 cash.

2. Purchased merchandise on account for $46,000, terms 2/10 n/30.

3. The merchandise purchased by Feazell was shipped FOB shipping point for $460 cash.

4. Returned $4,000 of defective merchandise purchased in Event 2.

5. Sold merchandise for $54,000 cash.

6. Sold merchandise on account for $100,000, terms 1/20 n/30.

7. Paid cash within the discount period on accounts payable due on merchandise purchased in Event 2.

8. Paid $2,400 cash for selling expenses.

9. Collected $70,000 of accounts receivable within the discount period.

10. Collected $24,000 of accounts receivable but not within the discount period.

11. Paid $6,400 of other operating expenses.

12. Performed a physical count indicating that $60,000 of inventory was on hand at the end of the accounting period.

Required

a. Record these transactions in a general journal.

b. Post the transactions to ledger T-accounts.

c. Prepare a schedule of cost of goods sold, an income statement, a statement of changes in stockholders' equity, a balance sheet, and a statement of cash flows for 2013.

EXERCISES—SERIES B

When the instructions for *any* exercise or problem call for the preparation of an income statement, use the *multistep format* unless otherwise indicated.

Exercise 4-1B   *Comparing a merchandising company with a service company*   **LO 1**

The following information is available for two different types of businesses for the 2013 accounting period. Lewis CPAs is a service business that provides accounting services to small businesses. Casual Clothing is a merchandising business that sells sports clothing to college students.

Data for Lewis CPAs

1. Borrowed $80,000 from the bank to start the business.
2. Provided $60,000 of services to clients and collected $60,000 cash.
3. Paid salary expense of $40,000.

Data for Casual Clothing

1. Borrowed $80,000 from the bank to start the business.
2. Purchased $50,000 inventory for cash.
3. Inventory costing $32,000 was sold for $60,000 cash.
4. Paid $7,200 cash for operating expenses.

Required

a. Prepare an income statement, balance sheet, and statement of cash flows for each of the companies.

b. Which of the two businesses would have product costs? Why?

c. Why does Lewis CPAs not compute gross margin on its income statement?

d. Compare the assets of both companies. What assets do they have in common? What assets are different? Why?

Exercise 4-2B   *Effect of inventory transactions on journals, ledgers, and financial statements: Perpetual system*   **LO 1, 4**

John Tyler started a small merchandising business in 2014. The business experienced the following events during its first year of operation. Assume that Tyler uses the perpetual inventory system.

1. Acquired $20,000 cash from the issue of common stock.
2. Purchased inventory for $15,000 cash.
3. Sold inventory costing $12,000 for $28,000 cash.

Required

a. Record the events in general journal format.

b. Post the entries to T-accounts.

c. Prepare an income statement for 2014 (use the multistep format).

d. What is the amount of net cash flow from operating activities for 2014?

Exercise 4-3B   *Effect of inventory transactions on the income statement and statement of cash flows: Perpetual system*   **LO 1**

During 2013, King Merchandising Company purchased $30,000 of inventory on account. King sold inventory on account that cost $22,500 for $31,000. Cash payments on accounts payable were $18,000. There was $22,000 cash collected from accounts receivable. King also paid $4,200 cash for operating expenses. Assume that King started the accounting period with $18,000 in both cash and common stock.

Required

a. Identify the events described in the preceding paragraph and record them in a horizontal statements model like the following one:

Assets			=	Liab.	+	Equity			Rev.	−	Exp.	=	Net Inc.	Cash Flow
Cash	+	Accts. Rec.	+ Inv. =	Accts. Pay.	+	Com. Stk.	+	Ret. Earn.						
18,000	+	NA	+ NA =	NA	+	18,000	+	NA	NA	−	NA	=	NA	NA

b. What is the balance of accounts receivable at the end of 2013?

c. What is the balance of accounts payable at the end of 2013?

d. What are the amounts of gross margin and net income for 2013?

e. Determine the amount of net cash flow from operating activities.

f. Explain why net income and retained earnings are the same for King. Normally would these amounts be the same? Why or why not?

LO 1

Exercise 4-4B   Recording inventory transactions in the general journal and posting entries to T-accounts: Perpetual system

Hilo Clothing experienced the following events during 2013, its first year of operation:

1. Acquired $25,000 cash from the issue of common stock.
2. Purchased inventory for $12,000 cash.
3. Sold inventory costing $8,000 for $15,000 cash.
4. Paid $1,200 for advertising expense.

Required

a. Record the general journal entries for the preceding transactions.

b. Post each of the entries to T-accounts.

c. Prepare a trial balance to prove the equality of debits and credits.

LO 2

Exercise 4-5B   Understanding the freight terms FOB shipping point and FOB destination

Required

For each of the following events, indicate whether the freight terms are FOB destination or FOB shipping point.

a. Sold merchandise and paid the freight costs.

b. Purchased merchandise and paid the freight costs.

c. Sold merchandise and the buyer paid the freight costs.

d. Purchased merchandise and the seller paid the freight costs.

LO 2

Exercise 4-6B   Determining the cost of inventory

Required

For each of the following cases determine the ending balance in the inventory account. (*Hint:* First, determine the total cost of inventory available for sale. Next, subtract the cost of the inventory sold to arrive at the ending balance.)

a. Mona's Dress Shop had a beginning balance in its inventory account of $20,000. During the accounting period Mona's purchased $68,000 of inventory, returned $4,000 of inventory, and obtained $640 of purchases discounts. Mona's incurred $1,200 of transportation-in cost and $1,600 of transportation-out cost. Salaries of sales personnel amounted to $26,500. Administrative expenses amounted to $42,000. Cost of goods sold amounted to $65,800.

b. Ben's Boat Shop had a beginning balance in its inventory account of $8,000. During the accounting period Ben's purchased $36,900 of inventory, obtained $1,200 of purchases allowances, and received $360 of purchases discounts. Sales discounts amounted to $640. Ben's incurred $900 of transportation-in cost and $260 of transportation-out cost. Selling and administrative cost amounted to $12,300. Cost of goods sold amounted to $33,900.

Exercise 4-7B Effect of purchase returns and allowances and freight costs on the journal, ledger, and financial statements: Perpetual system

LO 1, 2

The trial balance for Austin's Auto Shop as of January 1, 2013, follows:

Account Titles	Debit	Credit
Cash	$14,000	
Inventory	7,000	
Common stock		$18,000
Retained earnings		3,000
Total	$21,000	$21,000

The following events affected the company during the 2013 accounting period:

1. Purchased merchandise on account that cost $12,000.
2. The goods in Event 1 were purchased FOB shipping point with freight cost of $800 cash.
3. Returned $2,600 of damaged merchandise for credit on account.
4. Agreed to keep other damaged merchandise for which the company received an $1,100 allowance.
5. Sold merchandise that cost $12,000 for $21,500 cash.
6. Delivered merchandise to customers in Event 5 under terms FOB destination with freight costs amounting to $500 cash.
7. Paid $8,000 on the merchandise purchased in Event 1.

Required

a. Record the events in general journal format.
b. Open general ledger T-accounts with the appropriate beginning balances, and post the journal entries to the T-accounts.
c. Prepare an income statement, balance sheet, and statement of cash flows. (Assume that closing entries have been made.)
d. Explain why a difference does or does not exist between net income and net cash flow from operating activities.

Exercise 4-8B Accounting for product costs: Perpetual inventory system

LO 1, 2

Which of the following would be *debited* to the Inventory account for a merchandising business using the perpetual inventory system?

Required

a. Purchase of a new computer to be used by the business.
b. Purchase of inventory.
c. Allowance received for damaged inventory.
d. Transportation-out.
e. Purchase discount.
f. Transportation-in.

Exercise 4-9B Effect of product cost and period cost: Horizontal statements model

LO 1, 2

The Sports Store experienced the following events for the 2013 accounting period:

1. Acquired $40,000 cash from the issue of common stock.
2. Purchased $78,000 of inventory on account.
3. Received goods purchased in Event 2 FOB shipping point; freight cost of $900 paid in cash.

4. Sold inventory on account that cost $46,000 for $72,000.

5. Freight cost on the goods sold in Event 4 was $560. The goods were shipped FOB destination. Cash was paid for the freight cost.

6. Customer in Event 4 returned $5,100 worth of goods that had a cost of $2,950.

7. Collected $61,500 cash from accounts receivable.

8. Paid $66,100 cash on accounts payable.

9. Paid $2,600 for advertising expense.

10. Paid $3,100 cash for insurance expense.

Required

a. Which of these events affect period (selling and administrative) costs? Which result in product costs? If neither, label the transaction NA.

b. Record each event in a horizontal statements model like the following one. The first event is recorded as an example.

Assets				=	Liab.	+	Equity				Rev.	−	Exp.	=	Net Inc.	Cash Flow	
Cash	+	Accts. Rec.	+	Inv.	=	Accts. Pay.	+	C. Stk.	+	Ret. Earn.							
40,000	+	NA	+	NA	=	NA	+	40,000	+	NA	NA	−	NA	=	NA	40,000	FA

LO 1, 2

Exercise 4-10B *Cash discounts and purchase returns*

On April 6, 2013, Fashion Furnishings purchased $24,800 of merchandise from James' Imports, terms 2/10 n/45. On April 8, Fashion returned $2,400 of the merchandise to James' Imports for credit. Fashion paid cash for the merchandise on April 15, 2013.

Required

a. What is the amount that Fashion must pay James' Imports on April 15?

b. Record the events in a horizontal statements model like the following one.

Assets			=	Liab.	+	Equity				Rev.	−	Exp.	=	Net Inc.	Cash Flow
Cash	+	Inv.	=	Accts. Pay.	+	C. Stock.	+	Ret. Earn.							

c. How much must Fashion pay for the merchandise purchased if the payment is not made until April 20, 2013?

d. Record the payment in Requirement *c* in a horizontal statements model like the one above.

e. Why would Fashion want to pay for the merchandise by April 15?

LO 2

Exercise 4-11B *Determining the effect of inventory transactions on the horizontal statements model: Perpetual system*

Dahl Sales Company experienced the following events:

1. Purchased merchandise inventory on account.

2. Sold merchandise inventory for cash. Label the revenue recognition 2a and the expense recognition 2b.

3. Purchased merchandise inventory for cash.

4. Returned merchandise purchased on account.

5. Sold merchandise inventory on account. Label the revenue recognition 5a and the expense recognition 5b.

6. Paid cash on accounts payable not within the discount period.

7. Paid cash for transportation-in.

8. Paid cash for selling and administrative expenses.

9. Paid cash for transportation-out.

10. Collected cash from accounts receivable.

Required

Identify each event as asset source (AS), asset use (AU), asset exchange (AE), or claims exchange (CE). Also explain how each event affects the financial statements by placing a + for increase, − for decrease, or NA for not affected under each of the components in the following statements model. Assume the use of the perpetual inventory system. The first event is recorded as an example.

Event No.	Event Type	Assets	=	Liab.	+	Equity	Rev.	−	Exp.	=	Net Inc.	Cash Flow
1	AE	+	=	+	+	NA	NA	−	NA	=	NA	NA

Exercise 4-12B   *Multistep income statement*

LO 3, 4, 7

In 2013, York Company sold land for $95,000 cash. The land had originally cost $60,000. Also, York sold inventory that had cost $120,000 for $210,000 cash. Operating expenses amounted to $36,000.

Required

a. Prepare a 2013 multistep income statement for York Company.

b. Assume that normal operating activities grow evenly by 10% during 2014. Prepare a 2014 multistep income statement of York Company.

c. Determine the percentage change in net income between 2013 and 2014.

d. Should the stockholders have expected the results determined in Requirement *c*? Explain your answer.

Exercise 4-13B   *Sales returns, discounts, gain, and a multistep income statement*

LO 2, 3, 4, 6

The following information was drawn from the 2013 accounting records of Foster Merchandisers:

1. Inventory that had cost $19,400 was sold for $31,500 under terms 2/20, net/30.

2. Customers returned merchandise to Foster. The merchandise had been sold for a price of $1,350. The merchandise had cost Foster $920.

3. All customers paid their accounts within the discount period.

4. Selling and administrative expenses amounted to $4,700.

5. Interest expense amounted to $420.

6. Land that had cost $7,000 was sold for $9,250 cash.

Required

a. Determine the amount of net sales.

b. Prepare a multistep income statement.

c. Where would the interest expense be shown on the statement of cash flows?

d. How would the sale of the land be shown on the statement of cash flows?

e. Explain the difference between a gain and revenue.

Exercise 4-14B   *Comprehensive exercise with sales discounts*

LO 2, 3, 4, 6, 7

Power Buys started the 2013 accounting period with the balances given in the financial statements model shown below. During 2013 Power Buys experienced the following business events:

1. Paid cash to purchase $60,000 of merchandise inventory.

2. The goods that were purchased in Event 1 were delivered FOB destination. Freight costs of $1,100 were paid in cash by the responsible party.

3a. Sold merchandise for $65,000 under terms 1/10, n/30.

3b. Recognized $42,500 of cost of goods sold.

4a. Power Buys customers returned merchandise that was sold for $1,900.

4b. The merchandise returned in Event 4a had cost Power Buys $1,300.

5. The merchandise in Event 3a was sold to customers FOB destination. Freight costs of $1,800 were paid in cash by the responsible party.

6a. The customers paid for the merchandise sold in Event 3a within the discount period. Recognized the sales discount.

6b. Collected the balance in the accounts receivable account.

7. Paid cash of $6,500 for selling and administrative expenses.

8. Sold the land for $9,100 cash.

Required

a. Record the above transactions in a financial statements model like the one shown below:

Event No.	Cash	+	Accts. Rec.	+	Inventory	+	Land	=	Com. Stk.	+	Ret. Earn.	Rev./ Gain	−	Exp.	=	Net Inc.	Cash Flow
Bal.	70,000	+	0	+	12,000	+	10,000	=	50,000	+	42,000	NA	−	NA	=	NA	NA

b. Determine the amount of net sales.

c. Prepare a multistep income statement. Include common size percentages on the income statement.

d. Power Buys return on sales ratio in 2012 was 12 percent. Based on the common size data in the income statement, did Power Buys' expenses increase or decrease in 2013?

e. Explain why the term *loss* is used to describe the results due to the sale of land.

LO 4

Exercise 4-15B *Single-step and multistep income statements*

The following information was taken from the accounts of Super Foods Market, a small grocery store at December 31, 2013. The accounts are listed in alphabetical order, and all have normal balances. Dollar amounts are given in thousands.

Accounts payable	$ 600
Accounts receivable	2,080
Advertising expense	400
Cash	1,640
Common stock	1,200
Cost of goods sold	1,800
Interest expense	280
Merchandise inventory	1,000
Prepaid rent	560
Retained earnings, 1/1/2013	1,950
Sales revenue	4,800
Salaries expense	520
Rent expense	420
Gain on sale of land	150

Required

First, prepare an income statement for the year using the single-step approach. Then prepare another income statement using the multistep approach.

Exercise 4-16B   *Effect of inventory losses: Perpetual system*

LO 5

Bullard Designs experienced the following events during 2013, its first year of operation:

1. Started the business when it acquired $50,000 cash from the issue of common stock.
2. Paid $32,000 cash to purchase inventory.
3. Sold inventory costing $26,500 for $48,100 cash.
4. Physically counted inventory; had inventory of $4,800 on hand at the end of the accounting period.

Required

a. Open appropriate ledger T-accounts, and record the events in the accounts.
b. Prepare an income statement and balance sheet.
c. If all purchases and sales of merchandise are reflected as increases or decreases to the Merchandise Inventory account, why is it necessary for management to even bother to take a physical count of goods on hand (ending inventory) at the end of the year?

Exercise 4-17B   *Effect of sales returns and allowances and freight costs on the journal, ledger, and financial statements: Perpetual system*

LO 6

Skruggs Company began the 2013 accounting period with $20,000 cash, $76,000 inventory, $50,000 common stock, and $46,000 retained earnings. During 2013, Skruggs experienced the following events:

1. Sold merchandise costing $56,000 for $92,000 on account to Mark's Furniture Store.
2. Delivered the goods to Mark's under terms FOB destination. Freight costs were $800 cash.
3. Received returned goods from Mark's. The goods cost Skruggs $4,000 and were sold to Mark's for $5,900.
4. Granted Mark's a $3,000 allowance for damaged goods that Mark's agreed to keep.
5. Collected partial payment of $81,000 cash from accounts receivable.

Required

a. Record the events in general journal format.
b. Open general ledger T-accounts with the appropriate beginning balances and post the journal entries to the T-accounts.
c. Prepare an income statement, balance sheet, and statement of cash flows.
d. Why would Mark's agree to keep the damaged goods? Who benefits more?

Exercise 4-18B   *Using ratios to make comparisons*

LO 7

The following income statements were drawn from the annual reports of the Rocky Company and the Sandy Company:

	Rocky*	Sandy*
Net sales	$95,700	$52,300
Cost of goods sold	68,900	31,400
Gross margin	26,800	20,900
Less: Operating exp.		
Selling and admin. exp.	22,000	18,800
Net income	$ 4,800	$ 2,100

*All figures are reported in thousands of dollars.

Required

a. One of the companies is a high-end retailer that operates in exclusive shopping malls. The other operates discount stores that are located in low-cost, stand-alone buildings. Identify the high-end retailer and the discounter. Support your answer with appropriate ratios.

b. If Rocky and Sandy have equity of $40,000 and $21,000, respectively, which company is in the more profitable business?

LO 7

Exercise 4-19B *Using common size statements and ratios to make comparisons*

At the end of 2014 the following information is available for Fargo and Huston companies:

	Fargo	Huston
Sales	$2,000,000	$2,000,000
Cost of goods sold	1,600,000	1,200,000
Operating expenses	300,000	640,000
Total assets	2,500,000	2,500,000
Stockholders' equity	700,000	1,500,000

Required

a. Prepare a common size income statement for each company.

b. Compute the return on assets and return on equity for each company.

c. Which company is more profitable from the stockholders' perspective?

d. One company is a high-end retailer, and the other operates a discount store. Which is the discounter? Support your selection by referring to the appropriate ratios.

LO 8

Exercise 4-20B *Effect of inventory transactions on the income statement and balance sheet: Periodic system (Appendix)*

Edd Gant owns Edd's Sporting Goods. At the beginning of the year, Edd's had $16,000 in inventory. During the year, Edd's purchased inventory that cost $65,000. At the end of the year, inventory on hand amounted to $26,300.

Required

Calculate the following:

a. Cost of goods available for sale during the year.

b. Cost of goods sold for the year.

c. Amount of inventory Edd's would report on the year-end balance sheet.

LO 8

Exercise 4-21B *Determining cost of goods sold: Periodic system (Appendix)*

Belk Antiques uses the periodic inventory system to account for its inventory transactions. The following account titles and balances were drawn from Belk's records for the year 2013: beginning balance in inventory, $42,000; purchases, $128,000; purchase returns and allowances, $12,000; sales, $520,000; sales returns and allowances, $3,900; freight-in, $1,000; and operating expenses, $130,000. A physical count indicated that $26,000 of merchandise was on hand at the end of the accounting period.

Required

a. Prepare a schedule of cost of goods sold.

b. Prepare a multistep income statement.

Exercise 4-22B *Basic transactions: Periodic system, single cycle (Appendix)*   **LO 8**

The following transactions apply to Sue's Specialties Shop for 2014, its first year of operations:

1. Acquired $35,000 cash from the issue of common stock.
2. Acquired $9,600 of merchandise from Sue Hall, the owner, who had acquired the merchandise prior to opening the shop. Issued common stock to Sue in exchange for the merchandise inventory.
3. Purchased $85,000 of inventory on account.
4. Paid $2,800 for radio ads.
5. Sold inventory for $165,000 cash.
6. Paid $28,000 in salary to a part-time salesperson.
7. Paid $65,000 on accounts payable (see Event 3).
8. Physically counted inventory, which indicated that $28,500 of inventory was on hand at the end of the accounting period.

Required

a. Record each of these transactions in general journal form using the periodic method.
b. Post each of the transactions to ledger T-accounts.
c. Prepare an income statement, statement of changes in stockholders' equity, balance sheet, and statement of cash flows for 2014.
d. Prepare the necessary closing entries at the end of 2014, and post them to the appropriate T-accounts.
e. Prepare a post-closing trial balance.
f. Give an example of a business that may want to use the periodic system. Give an example of a business that may use the perpetual system.
g. Give some examples of assets other than cash that are commonly contributed to a business in exchange for stock.

PROBLEMS—SERIES B

Problem 4-23B *Basic transactions for three accounting cycles:*   **LO 1, 4**
Perpetual system

Amber's Flower Company was started in 2013 when it acquired $80,000 cash from the issue of common stock. The following data summarize the company's first three years' operating activities. Assume that all transactions were cash transactions.

	2013	2014	2015
Purchases of inventory	$40,000	$55,000	$ 95,000
Sales	75,000	88,000	146,000
Cost of goods sold	38,000	49,000	82,000
Selling and administrative expenses	29,000	35,000	42,000

Required

Prepare an income statement (use multistep format) and balance sheet for each fiscal year. (*Hint:* Record the transaction data for each accounting period in T-accounts before preparing the statements for that year.)

LO 2

Problem 4-24B   *Identifying freight costs*

Required

For each of the following events, determine the amount of freight paid by The Cake Shop. Also indicate whether the freight cost would be classified as a product or period (selling and administrative) cost.

a. Purchased merchandise with freight costs of $520. The merchandise was shipped FOB shipping point.

b. Shipped merchandise to customers, freight terms FOB shipping point. The freight costs were $250.

c. Purchased inventory with freight costs of $1,300. The goods were shipped FOB destination.

d. Sold merchandise to a customer. Freight costs were $750. The goods were shipped FOB destination.

LO 2

Problem 4-25B   *Identifying product and period costs*

Required

Indicate whether each of the following costs is a product cost or a period (selling and administrative) cost:

a. Transportation-in.
b. Insurance on the office building.
c. Office supplies.
d. Costs incurred to improve the quality of goods available for sale.
e. Goods purchased for resale.
f. Salaries of salespersons.
g. Advertising costs.
h. Transportation-out.
i. Interest on a note payable.
j. Salary of the company president.

LO 4, 7

Problem 4-26B   *Multistep and common size income statements*

The following information was drawn from the records of Harper Sales Company:

	2013	2014
Net sales	$200,000	$200,000
Cost of goods sold	(90,000)	(80,000)
Operating expenses	(60,000)	(50,000)
Loss on the sale of land	–0–	(24,000)

Required

a. Prepare a multistep income statement for each year.

b. Prepare a common size income statement for each year.

c. At a recent meeting of the stockholders, Harper's president stated 2015 would be a very good year with net income rising significantly. Write a brief memo explaining whether you agree or disagree with the president. Assume that the operating trends between 2013 and 2014 continue through 2015.

Problem 4-27B   *Comprehensive cycle problem: Perpetual system*

At the beginning of 2013, the Bradley Company had the following balances in its accounts:

Cash	$ 8,600
Inventory	18,000
Land	5,000
Common stock	20,000
Retained earnings	11,600

During 2013, the company experienced the following events:

1. Purchased inventory that cost $4,400 on account from Bivins Company under terms 1/10, n/30. The merchandise was delivered FOB shipping point. Freight costs of $190 were paid in cash.
2. Returned $400 of the inventory that it had purchased because the inventory was damaged in transit. The seller agreed to pay the return freight cost.
3. Paid the amount due on its account payable to Bivins Company within the cash discount period.
4. Sold inventory that had cost $6,000 for $11,000 on account, under terms 2/10, n/45.
5. Received merchandise returned from a customer. The merchandise originally cost $800 and was sold to the customer for $1,450 cash. The customer was paid $1,450 cash for the returned merchandise.
6. Delivered goods FOB destination in Event 4. Freight costs of $120 were paid in cash.
7. Collected the amount due on the account receivable within the discount period.
8. Sold the land for $8,500.
9. Recognized accrued interest income of $900.
10. Took a physical count indicating that $15,500 of inventory was on hand at the end of the accounting period.

Required

a. Identify each of these events as asset source (AS), asset use (AU), asset exchange (AE), or claims exchange (CE). Also explain how each event would affect the financial statements by placing a + for increase, − for decrease, or NA for not affected under each of the components in the following statements model. Assume that the perpetual inventory method is used. When an event has more than one part, use letters to distinguish the effects of each part. The first event is recorded as an example.

Event No.	Event Type	Assets	=	Liab.	+	Stk. Equity	Rev.	−	Exp.	=	Net Inc.	Cash Flow
1a	AS	+	=	+	+	NA	NA	−	NA	=	NA	NA
1b	AE	+ −	=	NA	+	NA	NA	−	NA	=	NA	− OA

b. Record the events in general journal format.
c. Open ledger T-accounts, and post the beginning balances and the events to the accounts.
d. Prepare a multistep income statement, a statement of changes in stockholders' equity, a balance sheet, and a statement of cash flows.
e. Record and post the closing entries, and prepare an post-closing trial balance.

LO 4, 8

Problem 4-28B *Preparing schedule of cost of goods sold and multistep and single-step income statements: Periodic system (Appendix)*

The following account titles and balances were taken from the adjusted trial balance of Omar Farm Co. for 2013. The company uses the periodic inventory system.

Account Title	Balance
Sales returns and allowances	$ 6,500
Miscellaneous expense	800
Transportation-out	1,400
Sales	139,500
Advertising expense	5,500
Salaries expense	17,000
Transportation-in	3,450
Purchases	84,000
Interest expense	720
Merchandise inventory, January 1	12,400
Rent expense	10,000
Merchandise inventory, December 31	8,100
Purchase returns and allowances	2,500
Loss on sale of land	6,800
Utilities expense	1,420

Required

a. Prepare a schedule to determine the amount of cost of goods sold.
b. Prepare a multistep income statement.
c. Prepare a single-step income statement.

LO 8

Problem 4-29B *Comprehensive cycle problem: Periodic system (Appendix)*

The following trial balance pertains to Cal's Grocery as of January 1, 2013:

Account Title	Debit	Credit
Cash	$ 52,000	
Accounts receivable	8,000	
Merchandise inventory	100,000	
Accounts payable		$ 8,000
Common stock		86,000
Retained earnings		66,000
Totals	$160,000	$160,000

The following events occurred in 2013. Assume that Cal's uses the periodic inventory method.

1. Purchased land for $40,000 cash.
2. Purchased merchandise on account for $252,000, terms 1/10 n/45.
3. Paid freight of $2,000 cash on merchandise purchased FOB shipping point.
4. Returned $7,200 of defective merchandise purchased in Event 2.
5. Sold merchandise for $172,000 cash.
6. Sold merchandise on account for $240,000, terms 2/10 n/30.
7. Paid cash within the discount period on accounts payable due on merchandise purchased in Event 2.

8. Paid $23,200 cash for selling expenses.
9. Collected $95,000 of the accounts receivable from Event 6 within the discount period.
10. Collected $62,000 of the accounts receivable but not within the discount period.
11. Paid $13,200 of other operating expenses.
12. A physical count indicated that $53,100 of inventory was on hand at the end of the accounting period.

Required

a. Record these transactions in a general journal.
b. Post the transactions to ledger T-accounts.
c. Prepare a schedule of costs of goods sold, an income statement, statement of changes in stockholders' equity, balance sheet, and statement of cash flows for 2013.

ANALYZE, THINK, COMMUNICATE

ATC 4-1   Business Applications Case   *Understanding real-world annual reports*

Required

a. Use the Target Corporation's annual report in Appendix B to answer the following questions:
   (1) What was Target's gross margin percentage for the fiscal year ended January 29, 2011 (2010) and 2009?
   (2) What was Target's return on sales percentage for 2010 and 2009?
   (3) Target's return on sales percentage for 2009 was lower than it was in 2010. Ignoring taxes, how much higher would Target's 2009 net income have been if its return on sales percentage in 2009 had been the same as for 2010?

ATC 4-2   Group Exercise   *Multistep income statement*

The following quarterly information is given for Rossie for the year ended 2013 (amounts shown are in millions):

	First Quarter	Second Quarter	Third Quarter	Fourth Quarter
Net Sales	$736.0	$717.4	$815.2	$620.1
Gross Margin	461.9	440.3	525.3	252.3
Net Income	37.1	24.6	38.6	31.4

Required

a. Divide the class into groups and organize the groups into four sections. Assign each section financial information for one of the quarters.
   (1) Each group should compute the cost of goods sold and operating expenses for the specific quarter assigned to its section and prepare a multistep income statement for the quarter.
   (2) Each group should compute the gross margin percentage and cost of goods sold percentage for its specific quarter.
   (3) Have a representative of each group put that quarter's sales, cost of goods sold percentage, and gross margin percentage on the board.

Class Discussion

b. Have the class discuss the change in each of these items from quarter to quarter and explain why the change might have occurred. Which was the best quarter and why?

ATC 4-3 Real-World Case *Identifying companies based on financial statement information*

Presented here is selected information from the 2010 fiscal-year 10-K reports of four companies. The four companies, in alphabetical order, are: Advanced Micro Devices, a company that manufactures semiconductors; AT&T, Inc, a large telecommunications company; Deere & Company, a company that manufactures heavy equipment for construction and farming; and Pfizer, Inc, a pharmaceutical company. The data for the companies, presented in the order of the amount of their sales in millions of dollars, are:

	A	B	C	D
Sales	$124,280	$ 67,809	$23,573	$6,494
Cost of goods sold	52,263	16,279	17,399	3,533
Net income	19,864	8,257	1,865	471
Inventory	0	14,612	3,063	632
Accounts receivable	13,610	8,405	26,848	968
Total assets	268,488	195,014	43,267	4,964

Required

Based on these financial data and your knowledge and assumptions about the nature of the businesses that the companies operate, determine which data relate to which companies. Write a memorandum explaining your decisions. Include a discussion of which ratios you used in your analysis, and show the computations of these ratios in your memorandum.

ATC 4-4 Business Applications Case *Performing ratio analysis using real-world data*

The following data were taken from California Pizza Kitchen's (CPK) 2010 annual report. All dollar amounts are in millions.

	Fiscal Years Ending	
	January 2, 2011	January 3, 2010
Total sales	$630,606	$652,185
Cost of goods sold	528,285	543,504
Net income	(406)	4,581

Required

a. Compute CPK's gross margin percentage for 2010 and 2009.
b. Compute CPK's return on sales percentage for 2010 and 2009.
c. Based on the percentages computed in Requirements *a* and *b*, did CPK's performance get better or worse from 2009 to 2010?
d. Compare CPK's gross margin percentages and return on sales percentages to those of the other real-world companies discussed in this chapter and discuss whether or not it appears to have better than average financial performance or not.

ATC 4-5 Business Applications Case *Performing ratio analysis using real-world data*

Supervalu, Inc., claims to be the largest publicly held food wholesaler in the United States. In addition to being a food wholesaler, it operates "extreme value" retail grocery stores under the name Save-A-Lot. Most of these discount stores are located in inner-city areas not served by others.

Whole Food Markets claims to be the world's largest retailer of natural and organic foods. Unlike Save-A-Lot stores that focus on low-income customers, Whole Foods offers specialty products to customers with sufficient disposable income to spend on such goods.

The following data were taken from these companies' 2010 annual reports. All dollar amounts are in millions.

	Supervalu, Inc. February 27, 2010	Whole Foods September 26, 2010
Sales	$40,597	$9,905.8
Cost of goods sold	31,444	5,870.4
Net income	393	245.8

Required

a. Before performing any calculations, speculate as to which company will have the highest gross margin and return on sales percentage. Explain the rationale for your decision.

b. Calculate the gross margin percentages for Supervalu and Whole Foods Market.

c. Calculate the return on sales percentages for Supervalu and Whole Foods Market.

d. Do the calculations from Requirements *b* and *c* confirm your speculations in Requirement *a*?

ATC 4-6 Written Assignment, Critical Thinking *Effect of sales returns on financial statements*

Bell Farm and Garden Equipment reported the following information for 2013:

Net sales of equipment	$2,450,567
Other income	6,786
Cost of goods sold	(1,425,990)
Selling, general, and administrative expense	(325,965)
Depreciation and amortization	(3,987)
Net operating income	$ 701,411

Selected information from the balance sheet as of December 31, 2013, follows:

Cash and marketable securities	$113,545
Inventory	248,600
Accounts receivable	82,462
Property, plant, and equipment—net	335,890
Other assets	5,410
Total assets	$785,907

Assume that a major customer returned a large order to Bell on December 31, 2013. The amount of the sale had been $146,800 with a cost of sales of $94,623. The return was recorded in the books on January 1, 2014. The company president does not want to correct the books. He argues that it makes no difference as to whether the return is recorded in 2013 or 2014. Either way, the return has been duly recognized.

Required

a. Assume that you are the CFO for Bell Farm and Garden Equipment Co. Write a memo to the president explaining how omitting the entry on December 31, 2013, could cause the financial statements to be misleading to investors and creditors. Explain how omitting the return from the customer would affect net income and the balance sheet.

b. Why might the president want to record the return on January 1, 2014, instead of December 31, 2013?

c. Would the failure to record the customer return violate the AICPA Code of Professional Conduct? (See Exhibit 2.9 in Chapter 2.)

d. If the president of the company refuses to correct the financial statements, what action should you take?

ATC 4-7   Ethical Dilemma   *Wait until I get mine*

Ada Fontanez is the president of a large company that owns a chain of athletic shoe stores. The company was in dire financial condition when she was hired three years ago. In an effort to motivate Fontanez, the board of directors included a bonus plan as part of her compensation package. According to her employment contract, on January 15 of each year, Fontanez is paid a cash bonus equal to 5 percent of the amount of net income reported on the preceding December 31 income statement. Fontanez was sufficiently motivated. Through her leadership, the company prospered. Her efforts were recognized throughout the industry, and she received numerous lucrative offers to leave the company. One offer was so enticing that she decided to change jobs. Her decision was made in late December 2013. However, she decided to resign effective February 1, 2014, to ensure the receipt of her January bonus. On December 31, 2013, the chief accountant, Walter Smith, advised Fontanez that the company had a sizable quantity of damaged inventory. A warehouse fire had resulted in smoke and water damage to approximately $600,000 of inventory. The warehouse was not insured, and the accountant recommended that the loss be recognized immediately. After examining the inventory, Fontanez argued that it could be sold as *damaged goods* to customers at reduced prices. Accordingly, she refused to allow the write-off the accountant recommended. She stated that so long as she is president, the inventory stays on the books at cost. She told the accountant that he could take up the matter with the new president in February.

Required

a. How would an immediate write-off of the damaged inventory affect the December 31, 2013, income statement, balance sheet, and statement of cash flows?

b. How would the write-off affect Fontanez's bonus?

c. If the new president is given the same bonus plan, how will Fontanez's refusal to recognize the loss affect his or her bonus?

d. Assuming that the damaged inventory is truly worthless, comment on the ethical implications of Fontanez's refusal to recognize the loss in the 2013 accounting period.

e. Assume that the damaged inventory is truly worthless and that you are Smith. How would you react to Fontanez's refusal to recognize the loss?

ATC 4-8   Research Assignment   *Analyzing Alcoa's profit margins*

Using either Alcoa's most current Form 10-K or the company's annual report, answer the questions below. To obtain the Form 10-K you can use either use the EDGAR system following the instructions in Appendix A, or it can be found on the company's website. The company's annual report is available on its website.

Required

a. What was Alcoa's gross margin percentage for the most current year?

b. What was Alcoa's gross margin percentage for the previous year? Has it changed significantly?

c. What was Alcoa's return on sales percentage for the most current year?

d. What percentage of Alcoa's total sales for the most current year was from operations in the United States?

e. Comment on the appropriateness of comparing Alcoa's gross margin with that of Microsoft. If Microsoft has a higher/lower margin, does that mean that Microsoft is a better managed company?

ATC 4-9   Spreadsheet Analysis   *Using Excel*

The following accounts, balances, and other financial information are drawn from the records of Vong Company for the year 2013:

Net sales revenue	$18,800	Beginning common stock	$ 9,000
Unearned revenue	2,600	Land	8,000
Accounts receivable	6,000	Certificate of deposit	10,000
Cost of goods sold	6,000	Interest revenue	100
Inventory	5,000	Interest receivable	100
Accounts payable	5,800	Dividends	1,500
Notes payable	6,000	Beginning retained earnings	8,500
Interest expense	550	Cash from stock issued	3,000
Interest payable	550	Cash	7,200
Supplies	50	Gain on sale of land	1,050
Supplies expense	750	Loss on sale of property	50
Office equipment	3,500	Salaries expense	1,400
Depreciation expense	500	Salaries payable	400
Accumulated depreciation	1,000	Rent expense	1,100
Transportation-out expense	500	Prepaid rent	100
Miscellaneous operating expense	4,500		

The Cash account revealed the following cash flows:

Received cash from advances from customers	$ 2,600
Purchased office equipment	(3,500)
Received cash from issuing stock	3,000
Collected cash from accounts receivable	3,800
Purchased land	(8,000)
Received cash from borrowing funds	6,000
Paid cash for rent	(1,200)
Sold land	10,000
Paid cash for dividends	(1,500)
Paid cash for operating expenses	(1,000)
Purchased certificate of deposit	(10,000)

Required

Build an Excel spreadsheet to construct a multistep income statement, statement of changes in stockholders' equity, balance sheet, and statement of cash flows for the year 2013.

ATC 4-10   Spreadsheet Analysis   *Mastering Excel*

At the end of 2013, the following information is available for Short and Wise Companies:

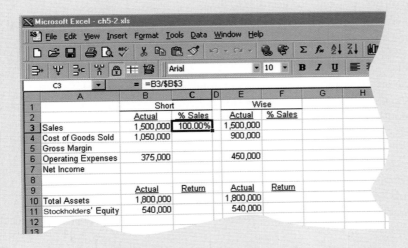

Required

a. Set up the spreadsheet shown here. Complete the income statements by using Excel formulas.

b. Prepare a common size income statement for each company by completing the % Sales columns.

c. One company is a high-end retailer, and the other operates a discount store. Which is the discounter? Support your selection by referring to the common size statements.

d. Compute the return on assets and return on equity for each company.

e. Which company is more profitable from the stockholders' perspective?

f. Assume that a shortage of goods from suppliers is causing cost of goods sold to increase 10 percent for each company. Change the respective cost of goods sold balances in the Actual income statement column for each company. Note the new calculated amounts on the income statement and in the ratios. Which company's profits and returns are more sensitive to inventory price hikes?

COMPREHENSIVE PROBLEM

The trial balance of Pacilio Security Services Inc. as of January 1, 2014, had the following normal balances:

Cash	$12,500
Accounts Receivable	3,500
Supplies	120
Prepaid Rent	1,000
Land	4,000
Unearned Revenue	900
Salaries Payable	1,000
Common Stock	8,000
Retained Earnings	11,220

In 2014, Pacilio Security Services decided to expand its business to sell security systems and offer 24-hour alarm monitoring services. It plans to phase out its current service of providing security personnel at various events. The following summary transactions occurred during 2014.

1. Paid the salaries payable from 2013.
2. Acquired an additional $42,000 cash from the issue of common stock.
3. Rented a larger building on May 1; paid $6,000 for 12 months' rent in advance.
4. Paid $800 cash for supplies to be used over the next several months by the business.
5. Purchased 50 alarm systems for resale at a cost of $12,000. The alarm systems were purchased on account with the terms 2/10, n/30.
6. Returned one of the alarm systems that had a cost of $240.
7. Installed 40 alarm systems during the year for a total sales amount of $20,000. The cost of these systems amounted to $9,440. $15,000 of the sales were on account and $5,000 were cash sales.
8. Paid the installers and other employees a total of $9,500 in salaries.
9. Sold $36,000 of monitoring services for the year. The services are billed to the customers each month.
10. Paid cash on accounts payable. The payment was made before the discount period expired. At the time of purchase, the inventory had a cost of $8,000.
11. Paid cash to settle additional accounts payable. The payment was made after the discount period expired. At the time of purchase, the inventory had a cost of $2,780.
12. Collected $43,000 of accounts receivable during the year.
13. Performed $12,000 of security services for area events; $9,000 was on account and $3,000 was for cash.

14. Paid advertising cost of $1,620 for the year.
15. Paid $1,100 for utilities expense for the year.
16. Paid a dividend of $12,000 to the shareholders.

Adjustment Information

17. Supplies of $150 were on hand at the end of the year.
18. Recognized the expired rent for the year.
19. Recognized the balance of the unearned revenue; cash was received in 2013.
20. Accrued salaries at December 31, 2014, were $1,500.

Required

a. Record the above transactions in general journal form. (Round amounts to the nearest dollar.)
b. Post the transactions to T-accounts.
c. Prepare a trial balance.
d. Prepare an income statement, statement of changes in stockholders' equity, balance sheet, and statement of cash flows.
e. Close the temporary accounts to retained earnings.
f. Post the closing entries to the T-accounts and prepare a post-closing trial balance.

CHAPTER 5

Accounting for Inventories

LEARNING OBJECTIVES

After you have mastered the material in this chapter, you will be able to:

LO1 Determine the amount of cost of goods sold and ending inventory using the FIFO, LIFO, weighted average, and specific identification cost flow methods.

LO2 Apply the lower-of-cost-or-market rule to inventory valuation.

LO3 Explain how fraud can be avoided through inventory control.

LO4 Use the gross margin method to estimate ending inventory.

LO5 Explain the importance of inventory turnover to a company's profitability.

CHAPTER OPENING

In the previous chapter we used the simplifying assumption that identical inventory items cost the same amount. In practice, businesses often pay different amounts for identical items. Suppose The Mountain Bike Company (TMBC) sells high-end Model 201 helmets. Since all Model 201 helmets are identical, does the helmet supplier charge TMBC the same amount for each helmet? Probably not. You have likely observed that prices change frequently.

Assume TMBC purchases one Model 201 helmet at a cost of $100. Two weeks later TMBC purchases a second Model 201 helmet. Because the supplier has raised prices, the second helmet costs $110. If TMBC sells one of its two helmets, should it record $100 or $110 as cost of goods sold? The following section of this chapter discusses several acceptable alternative methods for determining the amount of cost of goods sold from which companies may choose under generally accepted accounting principles.

The Curious Accountant

Safeway, Inc. is one of the largest food store chains in the United States, operating about 1,700 stores. As of January 1, 2011, the company reported approximately $2.6 billion of inventory on its balance sheet. In the notes to its financial statements, Safeway reported that it uses an inventory method that assumes its newest goods are sold first and its oldest goods are kept in inventory.

Can you think of any reason why a company selling perishable goods such as milk and vegetables uses an inventory method that assumes older goods are kept while newer goods are sold? (Answer on page 283.)

INVENTORY COST FLOW METHODS

LO 1

Determine the amount of cost of goods sold and ending inventory using the FIFO, LIFO, weighted average, and specific identification cost flow methods.

Recall that when goods are sold, product costs flow (are transferred) from the Inventory account to the Cost of Goods Sold account. Four acceptable methods for determining the amount of cost to transfer are (1) specific identification; (2) first-in, first-out (FIFO); (3) last-in, first-out (LIFO); and (4) weighted average.

Specific Identification

Suppose The Mountain Bike Company (TMBC) tags inventory items so that it can identify which one is sold at the time of sale. TMBC could then charge the actual cost of the specific item sold to cost of goods sold. Recall that the first inventory item TMBC purchased cost $100 and the second item cost $110. Using **specific identification,** cost of goods sold would be $100 if the first item purchased was sold or $110 if the second item purchased was sold.

When a company's inventory consists of many low-priced, high-turnover goods the record keeping necessary to use specific identification isn't practical. Imagine the difficulty of recording the cost of each specific food item in a grocery store. Another disadvantage of the specific identification method is the opportunity for managers to

manipulate the income statement. For example, TMBC can report a lower cost of goods sold by selling the first instead of the second item. Specific identification is, however, frequently used for high-priced, low-turnover inventory items such as automobiles. For big ticket items like cars, customer demands for specific products limit management's ability to select which merchandise is sold and volume is low enough to manage the recordkeeping.

First-In, First-Out (FIFO)

The **first-in, first-out (FIFO) cost flow method** requires that the cost of the items purchased *first* be assigned to cost of goods sold. Using FIFO, TMBC's cost of goods sold is $100.

Last-In, First-Out (LIFO)

The **last-in, first-out (LIFO) cost flow method** requires that the cost of the items purchased *last* be charged to cost of goods sold. Using LIFO, TMBC's cost of goods sold is $110.

Weighted Average

To use the **weighted-average cost flow method,** first calculate the average cost per unit by dividing the *total cost* of the inventory available by the *total number* of units available. In the case of TMBC, the average cost per unit of the inventory is $105 [($100 + $110) ÷ 2]. Cost of goods sold is then calculated by multiplying the average cost per unit by the number of units sold. Using weighted average, TMBC's cost of goods sold is $105 ($105 × 1).

Physical Flow

The preceding discussion pertains to the flow of *costs* through the accounting records, *not* the actual **physical flow of goods.** Goods usually move physically on a FIFO basis, which means that the first items of merchandise acquired by a company (first-in) are the first items sold to its customers (first-out). The inventory items on hand at the end of the accounting period are typically the last items in (the most recently acquired goods). If companies did not sell their oldest inventory items first, inventories would include dated, less marketable merchandise. *Cost flow,* however, can differ from *physical flow.* For example, a company may use LIFO or weighted average for financial reporting even if its goods flow physically on a FIFO basis.

Effect of Cost Flow on Financial Statements

Effect on Income Statement

The cost flow method a company uses can significantly affect the gross margin reported in the income statement. To demonstrate, assume that TMBC sold the inventory item discussed previously for $120. The amounts of gross margin using the FIFO, LIFO, and weighted-average cost flow assumptions are shown in the following table:

	FIFO	LIFO	Weighted Average
Sales	$120	$120	$120
Cost of goods sold	100	110	105
Gross margin	$ 20	$ 10	$ 15

Even though the physical flow is assumed to be identical for each method, the gross margin reported under FIFO is double the amount reported under LIFO. Companies experiencing identical economic events (same units of inventory purchased and sold) can report significantly different results in their financial statements. Meaningful financial analysis requires an understanding of financial reporting practices.

Effect on Balance Sheet

Since total product costs are allocated between costs of goods sold and ending inventory, the cost flow method a company uses affects its balance sheet as well as its income statement. Since FIFO transfers the first cost to the income statement, it leaves the last cost on the balance sheet. Similarly, by transferring the last cost to the income statement, LIFO leaves the first cost in ending inventory. The weighted-average method bases both cost of goods sold and ending inventory on the average cost per unit. To illustrate, the ending inventory TMBC would report on the balance sheet using each of the three cost flow methods is shown in the following table:

	FIFO	LIFO	Weighted Average
Ending inventory	$110	$100	$105

The FIFO, LIFO, and weighted-average methods are all used extensively in business practice. The same company may even use one cost flow method for some of its products and different cost flow methods for other products. Exhibit 5.1 illustrates the relative use of the different cost flow methods among U.S. companies.

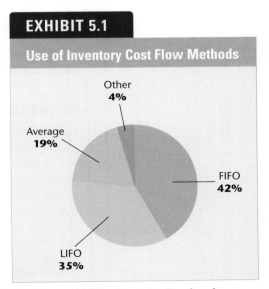

EXHIBIT 5.1

Use of Inventory Cost Flow Methods

Other 4%
Average 19%
FIFO 42%
LIFO 35%

Data Source: AICPA, *Accounting Trends and Techniques.*

CHECK YOURSELF 5.1

Nash Office Supply (NOS) purchased two Model 303 copiers at different times. The first copier purchased cost $400 and the second copier purchased cost $450. NOS sold one of the copiers for $600. Determine the gross margin on the sale and the ending inventory balance assuming NOS accounts for inventory using (1) FIFO, (2) LIFO, and (3) weighted average.

Answer

	FIFO	LIFO	Weighted Average
Sales	$600	$600	$600
Cost of goods sold	(400)	(450)	(425)
Gross margin	$200	$150	$175
Ending inventory	$450	$400	$425

Multiple Layers with Multiple Quantities

The previous example illustrates different **inventory cost flow methods** using only two cost layers ($100 and $110) with only one unit of inventory in each layer. Actual business inventories are considerably more complex. Most real-world inventories are composed of multiple cost layers with different quantities of inventory in each layer. The underlying allocation concepts, however, remain unchanged.

For example, a different inventory item The Mountain Bike Company (TMBC) carries in its stores is a bike called the Eraser. TMBC's beginning inventory and two purchases of Eraser bikes are described below.

Jan. 1	Beginning inventory	10 units @ $200	=	$ 2,000
Mar. 18	First purchase	20 units @ $220	=	4,400
Aug. 21	Second purchase	25 units @ $250	=	6,250
Total cost of the 55 bikes available for sale				$12,650

The accounting records for the period show that TMBC paid cash for all Eraser bike purchases and that it sold 43 bikes at a cash price of $350 each.

Allocating Cost of Goods Available for Sale

The following discussion shows how to determine the cost of goods sold and ending inventory amounts under FIFO, LIFO, and weighted average. We show all three methods to demonstrate how they affect the financial statements differently; TMBC would actually use only one of the methods.

Regardless of the cost flow method chosen, TMBC must allocate the cost of goods available for sale ($12,650) between cost of goods sold and ending inventory. The amounts assigned to each category will differ depending on TMBC's cost flow method. Computations for each method are shown below.

FIFO Inventory Cost Flow

Recall that TMBC sold 43 Eraser bikes during the accounting period. The FIFO method transfers to the Cost of Goods Sold account the *cost of the first 43 bikes* TMBC had available to sell. The first 43 bikes acquired by TMBC were the 10 bikes in the beginning inventory (these were purchased in the prior period) plus the 20 bikes purchased in March and 13 of the bikes purchased in August. The expense recognized for the cost of these bikes ($9,650) is computed as follows:

Jan. 1	Beginning inventory	10 units @ $200	=	$2,000
Mar. 18	First purchase	20 units @ $220	=	4,400
Aug. 21	Second purchase	13 units @ $250	=	3,250
Total cost of the 43 bikes sold				$9,650

Since TMBC had 55 bikes available for sale it would have 12 bikes (55 available − 43 sold) in ending inventory. The cost assigned to these 12 bikes (the ending balance in the Inventory account) equals the cost of goods available for sale minus the cost of goods sold as shown below:

Cost of goods available for sale	$12,650
Cost of goods sold	9,650
Ending inventory balance	$ 3,000

We show the allocation of the cost of goods available for sale between cost of goods sold and ending inventory graphically below.

LIFO Inventory Cost Flow

Under LIFO, the cost of goods sold is the cost of the last 43 bikes acquired by TMBC, computed as follows:

Aug. 21	Second purchase	25 units @ $250	=	$ 6,250
Mar. 18	First purchase	18 units @ $220	=	3,960
Total cost of the 43 bikes sold				$10,210

The LIFO cost of the 12 bikes in ending inventory is computed as shown below:

Cost of goods available for sale	$12,650
Cost of goods sold	10,210
Ending inventory balance	$ 2,440

We show the allocation of the cost of goods available for sale between cost of goods sold and ending inventory graphically below.

Weighted-Average Cost Flow

The weighted-average cost per unit is determined by dividing the *total cost of goods available for sale* by the *total number of units* available for sale. For TMBC, the weighted-average cost per unit is $230 ($12,650 ÷ 55). The weighted-average cost of goods sold is determined by multiplying the average cost per unit by the number of units sold ($230 × 43 = $9,890). The cost assigned to the 12 bikes in ending inventory is $2,760 (12 × $230).

We show the allocation of the cost of goods available for sale between cost of goods sold and ending inventory graphically below.

Cost of goods available for sale $12,650 → Cost of goods sold $9,890 / Ending inventory balance $2,760

Effect of Cost Flow on Financial Statements

Exhibit 5.2 displays partial financial statements for The Mountain Bike Company (TMBC). This exhibit includes only information pertaining to the Eraser bikes inventory item described above. Other financial statement data are omitted.

Recall that assets are reported on the balance sheet in order of liquidity (how quickly they are expected to be converted to cash). Since companies frequently sell inventory on account, inventory is less liquid than accounts receivable. As a result, companies commonly report inventory below accounts receivable on the balance sheet.

Exhibit 5.2 demonstrates that the amounts reported for gross margin on the income statement and inventory on the balance sheet differ significantly. The cash flow from operating activities on the statement of cash flows, however, is identical under all three methods. Regardless of cost flow reporting method, TMBC paid $10,650 cash ($4,400 first purchase + $6,250 second purchase) to purchase inventory and received $15,050 cash for inventory sold.

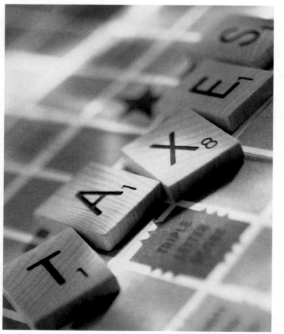

The Impact of Income Tax

Based on the financial statement information in Exhibit 5.2, which cost flow method should TMBC use? Most people initially suggest FIFO because FIFO reports the highest gross margin and the largest balance in ending inventory. However, other factors are relevant. FIFO produces the highest gross margin; it also produces the highest net income and the highest income tax expense. In contrast, LIFO results in recognizing the lowest gross margin, lowest net income, and the lowest income tax expense.[1]

Will investors favor a company with more assets and higher net income or one with lower tax expense? Recognize that specific identification, FIFO, LIFO, and weighted average are *different methods of reporting the same information.* TMBC experienced only one set of events pertaining to Eraser bikes. Exhibit 5.2 reports those same events three different ways. However, if the FIFO reporting method causes TMBC to pay more taxes than the LIFO method, using FIFO will cause a real reduction in the value of the company. Paying more money in taxes leaves less money in the company. Knowledgeable investors would be more attracted to TMBC if it uses LIFO because the lower tax payments allow the company to keep more value in the business.

[1]At the time of this revision, there is serious consideration in Congress for legislation that denies the use of LIFO for tax purposes. Since it is costly to maintain two separate cost flow systems for the same inventory, passage of this legislation would likely eliminate the use of LIFO for financial reporting purposes as well as for the determination of taxable income.

EXHIBIT 5.2

TMBC COMPANY
Comparative Financial Statements

Partial Income Statements

	FIFO	LIFO	Weighted Average
Sales	$15,050	$15,050	$15,050
Cost of goods sold	(9,650)	(10,210)	(9,890)
Gross margin	5,400	4,840	5,160

Partial Balance Sheets

	FIFO	LIFO	Weighted Average
Assets			
Cash	$ xx	$ xx	$ xx
Accounts receivable	xx	xx	xx
Inventory	3,000	2,440	2,760

Partial Statements of Cash Flows

	FIFO	LIFO	Weighted Average
Operating Activities			
Cash inflow from customers	$15,050	$15,050	$15,050
Cash outflow for inventory	(10,650)	(10,650)	(10,650)

Research suggests that, as a group, investors are knowledgeable. They make investment decisions based on economic substance regardless of how information is reported in financial statements.

The Income Statement versus the Tax Return

In some instances companies may use one accounting method for financial reporting and a different method to compute income taxes (the tax return must explain any differences). With respect to LIFO, however, the Internal Revenue Service requires that companies using LIFO for income tax purposes must also use LIFO for financial reporting. A company could not, therefore, get both the lower tax benefit provided by LIFO and the financial reporting advantage offered under FIFO.

Inflation versus Deflation

Our illustration assumes an inflationary environment (rising inventory prices). In a deflationary environment, the impact of using LIFO versus FIFO is reversed. LIFO produces tax advantages in an inflationary environment, while FIFO produces tax advantages in a deflationary environment. Companies operating in the computer industry where prices are falling would obtain a tax advantage by using FIFO. In contrast, companies that sell medical supplies in an inflationary environment would obtain a tax advantage by using LIFO.

Full Disclosure and Consistency

Generally accepted accounting principles allow each company to choose the inventory cost flow method best suited to its reporting needs. Because results can vary considerably among methods, however, the GAAP principle of **full disclosure** requires that financial statements disclose the method chosen. In addition, so that a company's financial statements are comparable from year to year, the GAAP principle of **consistency** generally requires that companies use the same cost flow method each period. The limited exceptions to the consistency principle are described in more advanced accounting courses.

✓ CHECK YOURSELF 5.2

The following information was drawn from the inventory records of Fields, Inc.

Beginning inventory	200 units @ $20
First purchase	400 units @ $22
Second purchase	600 units @ $24

Assume that Fields sold 900 units of inventory.

1. Determine the amount of cost of goods sold using FIFO.

2. Would using LIFO produce a higher or lower amount of cost of goods sold? Why?

Answer

1. Cost of goods sold using FIFO

Beginning inventory	200 units @ $20	=	$ 4,000
First purchase	400 units @ $22	=	8,800
Second purchase	300 units @ $24	=	7,200
Total cost of goods sold			$20,000

2. The inventory records reflect an inflationary environment of steadily rising prices. Since LIFO charges the latest costs (in this case the highest costs) to the income statement, using LIFO would produce a higher amount of cost of goods sold than would using FIFO.

Inventory Cost Flow When Sales and Purchases Occur Intermittently

In the previous illustrations, all purchases were made before any goods were sold. This section addresses more realistic conditions, when sales transactions occur intermittently with purchases. Consider a third product The Mountain Bike Company (TMBC) carries in its inventory, an energy bar called NeverStop. NeverStop is sold at concession booths sponsored by TMBC at bike races. TMBC purchases and sells NeverStop in bulk boxes. It refers to each box as a unit of product. TMBC's beginning inventory, purchases, and sales of NeverStop for the period are described below.

Date	Transaction	Description
Jan. 1	Beginning inventory	100 units @ $20.00
Feb. 14	Purchased	200 units @ $21.50
Apr. 5	Sold	220 units @ $30.00
June 21	Purchased	160 units @ $22.50
Aug. 18	Sold	100 units @ $30.00
Sept. 2	Purchased	280 units @ $23.50
Nov. 10	Sold	330 units @ $30.00

FIFO Cost Flow

Exhibit 5.3 displays the computations for cost of goods sold and inventory if TMBC uses the FIFO cost flow method. The inventory records are maintained in layers. Each time a sales transaction occurs, the unit cost in the first layer of inventory is assigned to the items sold. If the number of items sold exceeds the number of items in the first

EXHIBIT 5.3

Inventory Balance and Cost of Goods Sold using FIFO Cost Flow

Date	Description	Units		Cost		Total	Cost of Goods Sold
Jan. 1	Beginning balance	100	@	$20.00	=	$2,000	
Feb. 14	Purchase	200	@	21.50	=	4,300	
Apr. 5	Sale of 220 units	(100)	@	20.00	=	(2,000)	
		(120)	@	21.50	=	(2,580)	$ 4,580
	Inventory balance after sale	80	@	21.50	=	1,720	
June 21	Purchase	160	@	22.50	=	3,600	
Aug. 18	Sale of 100 units	(80)	@	21.50	=	(1,720)	
		(20)	@	22.50	=	(450)	2,170
	Inventory balance after sale	140	@	22.50	=	3,150	
Sept. 2	Purchase	280	@	23.50	=	6,580	
Nov. 10	Sale of 330 units	(140)	@	22.50	=	(3,150)	
		(190)	@	23.50	=	(4,465)	7,615
	Ending inventory balance	90	@	23.50	=	$2,115	
	Total cost of goods sold						$14,365

layer, the unit cost of the next layer is assigned to the remaining number of units sold, and so on. For example, the cost assigned to the 220 units of inventory sold on April 5 is determined as follows:

100 units of inventory in the first layer × $20.00 per unit	=	$2,000
+ 120 units of inventory in the second layer × $21.50 per unit	=	2,580
220 units for total cost of goods sold for the April 5 sale	=	$4,580

The cost of goods sold for subsequent sales transactions is similarly computed.

Using FIFO, and assuming a selling price of $30 per unit, gross margin for the period is computed as follows:

Sales (650 units @ $30 each)	$19,500
Cost of goods sold	14,365
Gross margin	$ 5,135

Weighted-Average and LIFO Cost Flows

When maintaining perpetual inventory records, using the weighted-average or LIFO cost flow methods leads to timing difficulties. For example, under LIFO, the cost of the *last* items purchased *during an accounting period* is the first amount transferred to cost of goods sold. When sales and purchases occur intermittently, the cost of the last items purchased isn't known at the time earlier sales occur. For example, when TMBC sold merchandise in April, it did not know what the replacement inventory purchased in September would cost.

Accountants can solve cost flow timing problems by keeping perpetual records of the quantities (number of units) of items purchased and sold separately from the

FOCUS ON INTERNATIONAL ISSUES

LIFO IN OTHER COUNTRIES

This chapter introduced a rather strange inventory cost flow assumption called LIFO. As explained, the primary advantage of LIFO is to reduce a company's income taxes. Given the choice, companies that use LIFO to reduce their taxes would probably prefer to use another method when preparing their GAAP—based financial statements, but the IRS does not permit this. Thus, they are left with no choice but to use the seemingly counterintuitive LIFO assumption for GAAP as well tax reporting.

What happens in countries other than the United States? International Financial Reporting Standards (IFRS) do not allow the use of LIFO. Most industrialized nations are now using IFRS. You can see the impact of this disparity if you review the annual report of a U.S. company that uses LIFO *and* has significant operations in other countries. Very often it will explain that LIFO is used to calculate inventory (and cost of goods sold) for domestic operations, but another method is used for activities outside the United States.

For example, here is an excerpt from General Electric's 2010 Form 10-K, Note 1.

All inventories are stated at the lower of cost or realizable values. Cost for a significant portion of GE U.S. inventories is determined on a last-in, first-out (LIFO) basis. Cost of other GE inventories is determined on a first-in, first-out (FIFO) basis. LIFO was used for 39% of GE inventories at December 31, 2010 and 2009.

If the company has its headquarters in the United States, why not simply use LIFO in its foreign operations? In addition to having to prepare financial statements for the United States, the company probably has to prepare statements for its local operations using the reporting standards of the local country.

Prior to the establishment of IFRS each country was responsible for issuing its own, local GAAP. Even then, most countries did not allow for the use of LIFO.

---

related costs. Keeping records of quantities moving in and out of inventory, even though cost information is unavailable, provides many of the benefits of a perpetual inventory system. For example, management can determine the quantity of lost, damaged, or stolen goods and the point at which to reorder merchandise. At the end of the accounting period, when the cost of all inventory purchases is available, costs are assigned to the quantity data that have been maintained perpetually. Although further discussion of the weighted-average and LIFO cost flow methods is beyond the scope of this text, recognize that timing problems associated with intermittent sales are manageable.

LOWER-OF-COST-OR-MARKET RULE

LO 2

Apply the lower-of-cost-or-market rule to inventory valuation.

Regardless of whether a company uses FIFO, LIFO, weighted average, or specific identification, once the cost of ending inventory has been determined, generally accepted accounting principles require that the cost be compared with the end of period market value and that the inventory be reported at *lower of cost or market. Market* is defined as the amount the company would have to pay to *replace* the merchandise. If the replacement cost is less than the actual cost, regardless of whether the decline in market value is due to physical damage, deterioration, obsolescence, or a general price-level decline, the loss must be recognized in the current period.

The **lower-of-cost-or-market rule** can be applied to (1) each individual inventory item, (2) major classes or categories of inventory, or (3) the entire stock of inventory in the aggregate. The most common practice is the individualized application. To illustrate applying

REALITY BYTES

To avoid spoilage or obsolescence, most companies use a first-in, first-out (FIFO) approach for the flow of physical goods. The older goods (first units purchased) are sold before the newer goods are sold. For example, Kroger's and other food stores stack older merchandise at the front of the shelf where customers are more likely to pick it up first. As a result, merchandise is sold before it becomes dated. However, when timing is not an issue, convenience may dictate the use of the last-in, first-out (LIFO) method. Examples of products that frequently move on a LIFO basis include rock, gravel, dirt, or other nonwasting assets. Indeed, rock, gravel, and dirt are normally stored in piles that are unprotected from weather. New inventory is simply piled on top of the old. Inventory that is sold is taken from the top of the pile because it is convenient to do so. Accordingly, the last inventory purchased is the first inventory sold. For example, Vulcan Materials Co., which claims to be the nation's largest producer of construction aggregates (stone and gravel), uses LIFO. Regardless of whether the flow of physical goods occurs on a LIFO or FIFO basis, costs can flow differently. The flow of inventory through the physical facility is a separate issue from the flow of costs through the accounting system.

the rule to individual inventory items, assume that The Mountain Bike Company (TMBC) has in ending inventory 100 T-shirts it purchased at a cost of $14 each. If the year-end replacement cost of the shirts is above $14, TMBC will report the ending inventory at cost (100 × $14 = $1,400). However, if outsourcing permits the manufacturer to reduce the unit price of the shirts to $11, then TMBC's replacement cost falls below the historical cost, and the inventory must be written down to $1,100 (100 × $11).

Exhibit 5.4 illustrates computing the ending inventory value on an item-by-item basis for a company that has four different inventory items. The company must write down the $30,020 historical cost of its ending inventory to $28,410. This $1,610 write-down reduces the company's gross margin for the period. If the company keeps perpetual inventory records, the effect of the write-down and the journal entry to record it are as follows:

Assets	=	Liab.	+	Equity	Rev.	−	Exp.	=	Net Inc.	Cash Flow
(1,610)	=	NA	+	(1,610)	NA	−	1,610	=	(1,610)	NA

EXHIBIT 5.4

Determination of Ending Inventory at Lower of Cost or Market

Item	Quantity (a)	Unit Cost (b)	Unit Market (c)	Total Cost (a × b)	Total Market (a × c)	Lower of Cost or Market
A	320	$21.50	$22.00	$ 6,880	$ 7,040	$ 6,880
B	460	18.00	16.00	8,280	7,360	7,360
C	690	15.00	14.00	10,350	9,660	9,660
D	220	20.50	23.00	4,510	5,060	4,510
				$30,020	$29,120	$28,410

FOCUS ON INTERNATIONAL ISSUES

THE LOWER-OF-COST-OR-MARKET RULE AND IFRS

Suppose a company has inventory with a historical cost of $1,000,000, the market value of which falls to $700,000. The company would have to write down the inventory and take a loss of $300,000. Now suppose that before the inventory was sold the market value recovered to $900,000. What would the company do? Nothing under U.S. GAAP; the inventory would remain on the books at $700,000 until it is sold or its market value declines further. However, under IFRS the inventory would be written up from $700,000 to $900,000 and a gain of $200,000 would be recognized.

Account Title	Debit	Credit
Cost of Goods Sold (Inventory Loss)	1,610	
Inventory		1,610

Conceptually, the loss should be reported as an operating expense on the income statement. However, if the amount is immaterial, it can be included in cost of goods sold.

AVOIDING FRAUD IN MERCHANDISING BUSINESSES

Explain how fraud can be avoided through inventory control.

For merchandising businesses, inventory is often the largest single asset reported on the balance sheet and cost of goods sold is normally the largest single expense reported on the income statement. For example, a recent income statement for Publix (a large grocery store chain) reported $16.0 billion of sales and approximately $11.6 billion of cost of goods sold, which means cost of goods sold for Publix was about 72% of revenue. In contrast, the next largest expense (operating and administrative expense) was approximately $3.4 billion, or 21% of revenue. While cost of goods sold represents only one expense account, the operating and administrative expense category actually combines many, perhaps hundreds, of individual expense accounts, such as depreciation, salaries, utilities, and so on. Because the inventory and cost of goods sold accounts are so significant, they are attractive targets for concealing fraud. For example, suppose a manager attempts to perpetrate a fraud by deliberately understating expenses. The understatement is less likely to be detected if it is hidden in the $11.6 billion Cost of Goods Sold account than if it is recorded in one of the smaller operating expense accounts.

Because the inventory and cost of goods sold accounts are susceptible to abuse, auditors and financial analysts carefully examine them for signs of fraud. Using tools to detect possible inventory misstatements requires understanding how overstatement or understatement of inventory affects the financial statements. To illustrate, assume that a company overstates its year-end inventory balance by $1,000. This inventory overstatement results in a $1,000 understatement of cost of goods sold, as shown in the following schedule:

	Ending Inventory Is Accurate	Ending Inventory Is Overstated	Effect
Beginning inventory	$ 4,000	$ 4,000	
Purchases	6,000	6,000	
Cost of goods available for sale	10,000	10,000	
Ending inventory	(3,000)	(4,000)	$1,000 Overstated
Cost of goods sold	$ 7,000	$ 6,000	$1,000 Understated

The understatement of cost of goods sold results in the overstatement of gross margin, which leads to an overstatement of net earnings, as indicated in the following income statement:

	Ending Inventory Is Accurate	Ending Inventory Is Overstated	Effect
Sales	$11,000	$11,000	
Cost of goods sold	(7,000)	(6,000)	$1,000 Understated
Gross margin	$ 4,000	$ 5,000	$1,000 Overstated

On the balance sheet, assets (inventory) and stockholders' equity (retained earnings) are overstated as follows:

	Ending Inventory Is Accurate	Ending Inventory Is Overstated	Effect
Assets			
Cash	$1,000	$ 1,000	
Inventory	3,000	4,000	$1,000 Overstated
Other assets	5,000	5,000	
Total assets	$9,000	$10,000	
Stockholders' equity			
Common stock	$5,000	$ 5,000	
Retained earnings	4,000	5,000	$1,000 Overstated
Total stockholders' equity	$9,000	$10,000	

Managers may be tempted to overstate the physical count of the ending inventory in order to report higher amounts of gross margin on the income statement and larger amounts of assets on the balance sheet. How can companies discourage managers from deliberately overstating the physical count of the ending inventory? The first line of defense is to assign the task of recording inventory transactions to different employees from those responsible for counting inventory.

Recall that under the perpetual system, increases and decreases in inventory are recorded at the time inventory is purchased and sold. If the records are maintained accurately, the balance in the inventory account should agree with the amount of physical inventory on hand. If a manager were to attempt to manipulate the financial statements by overstating the physical count of inventory, there would be a discrepancy between the accounting records and the physical count. In other words, a successful fraud requires controlling both the physical count and the recording process. If the counting and recording duties are performed by different individuals, fraud requires collusion, which reduces the likelihood of its occurrence. The separation of duties is an internal control procedure discussed further in the next chapter.

Because motives for fraud persist, even the most carefully managed companies cannot guarantee that no fraud will ever occur. As a result, auditors and financial analysts have developed tools to test for financial statement manipulation. The gross margin method of estimating the ending inventory balance is such a tool.

ESTIMATING THE ENDING INVENTORY BALANCE

The **gross margin method** assumes that the percentage of gross margin to sales remains relatively stable over time. To the extent that this assumption is accurate, the gross margin ratio from prior periods can be used to accurately estimate the current period's ending inventory. To illustrate, first review the information in Exhibit 5.5 which pertains to the T-Shirt Company.

The estimated cost of ending inventory can be computed as follows:

1. Calculate the expected gross margin ratio using financial statement data from prior periods. Accuracy may be improved by averaging gross margin and sales data over several accounting periods. For the T-Shirt Company, assume the average gross margin for the prior five years ÷ the average sales for the same five-year period = 25% expected gross margin ratio.

2. Multiply the expected gross margin ratio by the current period's sales ($22,000 × 0.25 = $5,500) to estimate the amount of gross margin.

3. Subtract the estimated gross margin from sales ($22,000 − $5,500 = $16,500) to estimate the amount of cost of goods sold.

4. Subtract the estimated cost of goods sold from the amount of goods available for sale ($23,600 − $16,500 = $7,100) to estimate the amount of ending inventory.

The estimated amount of ending inventory ($7,100) can be compared to the book balance and the physical count of inventory. If the book balance or the physical count is significantly higher than the estimated inventory balance, the analysis suggests the possibility of financial statement manipulation.

Other analytical comparisons are also useful. For example, the current year's gross margin ratio can be compared to last year's ratio. If cost of goods sold has been understated (ending inventory overstated), the gross margin ratio will be inflated. If this year's ratio is significantly higher than last year's, further analysis is required.

Although it may seem common because of the intense publicity generated when it occurs, fraud is the exception rather than the norm. In fact, growth in the inventory account balance usually results from natural business conditions. For example, a company that is adding new stores is expected to report growth in its inventory balance. Nevertheless, significant growth in inventory that is not explained by accompanying sales growth signals the need to analyze further for evidence of manipulation.

Since one year's ending inventory balance becomes the next year's beginning inventory balance, inaccuracies carry forward from one accounting period to the next. Persistent inventory overstatements result in an inventory account balance that spirals higher and higher. A fraudulently increasing inventory balance is likely to be discovered eventually.

EXHIBIT 5.5

THE T-SHIRT COMPANY		
Schedule for Estimating the Ending Inventory Balance		
For the Six Months Ending June 30, 2013		
Beginning inventory	$ 5,100	
Purchases	18,500	
Cost of goods available for sale		$23,600
Sales through June 30, 2013	22,000	
Less: Estimated gross margin*	?	
Estimated cost of goods sold		?
Estimated ending inventory		$?

*Historically, gross margin has amounted to approximately 25 percent of sales.

Answers to The Curious Accountant

Even though Safeway uses the last-in, first-out *cost flow assumption* for financial reporting purposes, it, like most other companies, actually sells its oldest inventory first. As explained in the text material, GAAP allows a company to report its costs of goods sold in an order that is different from the actual physical flow of its goods. The primary reason some companies use the LIFO assumption is to reduce income taxes. Over the years, Safeway has saved approximately $12 million in taxes by using the LIFO versus the FIFO cost flow assumption when computing its taxable income.

To avoid detection, a manager who has previously overstated inventory will need to write the inventory back down in a subsequent accounting period. Therefore significant decreases, as well as increases, in the inventory balance or the gross margin ratio should be investigated. A manager may try to justify inventory write-downs by claiming that the inventory was lost, damaged, stolen, or had declined in value below historical cost. While there are valid reasons for writing down inventory, the possibility of fraud should be investigated.

✓ CHECK YOURSELF 5.3

A physical count of Cantrell Inc.'s inventory revealed an ending balance of $6,020. The company's auditor decided to use the gross margin method to test the accuracy of the physical count. The accounting records indicate that the beginning inventory balance had been $20,000. During the period Cantrell had purchased $70,000 of inventory and had recognized $140,000 of sales revenue. Cantrell's gross margin percentage is normally 40 percent of sales. Develop an estimate of the amount of ending inventory and comment on the accuracy of the physical count.

Answer   Goods available for sale is $90,000 ($20,000 beginning inventory + $70,000 purchases). Estimated cost of goods sold is $84,000 [$140,000 sales − ($140,000 × 0.40) gross margin]. Estimated ending inventory is $6,000 ($90,000 goods available for sale − $84,000 cost of goods sold). The difference between the physical count and the estimated balance ($6,020 − $6,000 = $20) is immaterial. Therefore the gross margin estimate is consistent with the physical count.

THE FINANCIAL ANALYST

Assume a grocery store sells two brands of kitchen cleansers, Zjax and Cosmos. Zjax costs $1 and sells for $1.25, resulting in a gross margin of $0.25 ($1.25 − $1.00). Cosmos costs $1.20 and sells for $1.60, resulting in a gross margin of $0.40 ($1.60 − $1.20). Is it more profitable to stock Cosmos than Zjax? Not if the store can sell significantly more cans of Zjax.

Suppose the lower price results in higher customer demand for Zjax. If the store can sell 7,000 units of Zjax but only 3,000 units of Cosmos, Zjax will provide a total gross margin of $1,750 (7,000 units × $0.25 per unit), while Cosmos will provide only $1,200 (3,000 units × $0.40 per unit). How fast inventory sells is as important as the spread between cost and selling price. To determine how fast inventory is selling, financial analysts calculate a ratio that measures the *average number of days it takes to sell inventory.*

LO 5

Explain the importance of inventory turnover to a company's profitability.

Average Number of Days to Sell Inventory

The first step in calculating the average number of days it takes to sell inventory is to compute the **inventory turnover,** as follows:

$$\frac{\text{Cost of goods sold}}{\text{Inventory}}$$

The result of this computation is the number of times the balance in the Inventory account is turned over (sold) each year. To more easily interpret the inventory turnover ratio, analysts often take a further step and determine the **average number of days to sell inventory** (also called the **average days in inventory**), computed as

$$\frac{365}{\text{Inventory turnover}}$$

Is It a Marketing or an Accounting Decision?

As suggested, overall profitability depends upon two elements: gross margin and inventory turnover. The most profitable combination would be to carry high margin inventory that turns over rapidly. To be competitive, however, companies must often concentrate on one or the other of the elements. For example, *discount merchandisers* such as Costco offer lower prices to stimulate greater sales. In contrast, fashionable stores such as Neiman Marcus charge higher prices to compensate for their slower inventory turnover. These upscale stores justify their higher prices by offering superior style, quality, convenience, service, etc. While decisions about pricing, advertising, service, and so on are often viewed as marketing decisions, effective choices require understanding the interaction between the gross margin percentage and inventory turnover.

Real-World Data

Exhibit 5.6 shows the *average number of days to sell inventory* for seven real-world companies in three different industries. The numbers pertain to the 2010 fiscal year. The data raise several questions.

First, why do Concha y Toro and Willamette Valley Vineyards take so long to sell their inventories compared with the other companies? Both of these companies produce and sell wine. Quality wine is aged before it is sold; time spent in inventory is actually a part of the production process. In the wine world, wines produced by Willamette Valley Vineyards are, on average, considered to be of higher quality than those produced by Concha y Toro. This higher quality results, in part, from the longer time Willamette Valley Vineyards wines spend aging prior to sale.

Why does Starbucks hold its inventory so much longer than the other two fast-food businesses? Starbucks' inventory is mostly coffee. It is more difficult for Starbucks to obtain coffee than it is for McDonald's to obtain beef or Yum! Brands to obtain flour, cheese, and fresh vegetables for its Pizza Hut pizza. Very little coffee is grown in the United States (Hawaii is the only state that produces coffee). Since purchasing coffee requires

EXHIBIT 5.6

Industry	Company	Average Number of Days to Sell Inventory
Fast Food	McDonald's	8
	Starbucks	44
	Yum! Brands	22
Department Stores	Target	61
	Walmart	42
Wineries	Concha y Toro	162
	Willamette Valley Vineyards	404

substantial delivery time, Starbucks cannot order its inventory at the last minute. This problem is further complicated by the fact that coffee harvests are seasonal. Cattle, on the other hand, can be processed into hamburgers year-round. As a result, Starbucks must hold inventory longer than McDonald's or Yum! Brands.

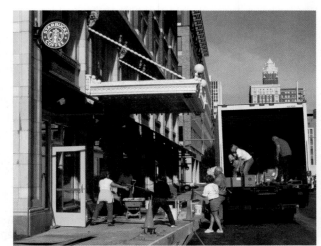

Why do department stores such as **Target** and **Walmart** take longer to sell inventory than McDonald's? Part of the answer is that food is perishable and clothing is not. But there is also the fact that department stores carry many more inventory items than do fast-food restaurants. It is much easier to anticipate customer demand if a company sells only 20 different items than if the company sells 20,000 different items. The problem of anticipating customer demand is solved by holding larger quantities of inventory.

Finally, notice that Walmart sells it merchandise in 42 days while Target takes 61. This would seem to be an advantage for Walmart, but recall from Chapter 4 that in its 2011 fiscal year Walmart's gross margin percentage was 25.3 while Target's was 32.2. Target's higher gross margin percentage helps to make up for the additional time it takes to sell merchandise. Different companies use different business strategies to achieve their objectives. In the end, Target's return on sales percentage, at 4.3%, was higher than Walmart's which was 3.6%.

Effects of Cost Flow on Ratio Analysis

Since the amounts of ending inventory and cost of goods sold are affected by the cost flow method (FIFO, LIFO, etc.) a company uses, the gross margin and inventory turnover ratios are also affected by the cost flow method used. Further, since cost of goods sold affects the amount of net income and retained earnings, many other ratios are also affected by the inventory cost flow method that a company uses. Financial analysts must consider that the ratios they use can be significantly influenced by which accounting methods a company chooses.

A Look Back

This chapter discussed the inventory cost flow methods of first-in, first-out (FIFO), last-in, first-out (LIFO), weighted average, and specific identification. Under *FIFO,* the cost of the items purchased first is reported on the income statement, and the cost of the items purchased last is reported on the balance sheet. Under *LIFO,* the cost of the items purchased last is reported on the income statement, and the cost of the items purchased first is reported on the balance sheet. Under the *weighted-average method,* the average cost of inventory is reported on both the income statement and the balance sheet. Finally, under specific identification the actual cost of the goods is reported on the income statement and the balance sheet.

Generally accepted accounting principles often allow companies to account for the same types of events in different ways. The different cost flow methods presented in this chapter—FIFO, LIFO, weighted average, and specific identification—are examples of alternative accounting procedures allowed by GAAP. Financial analysts must be aware that financial statement amounts are affected by the accounting methods that a company uses as well as the economic activity it experiences.

This chapter also explained how to calculate the time it takes a company to sell its inventory. The measure of how fast inventory sells is called *inventory turnover;* it is computed by dividing cost of goods sold by inventory. The result of this computation is the number of times the balance in the inventory account is turned over each year. The *average number of days to sell inventory* can be determined by dividing the number of days in a year (365) by the inventory turnover ratio.

A Look Forward

Chapter 6 examines accounting for cash and the system of internal controls. Internal controls are the accounting practices and procedures that companies use to protect assets and to ensure that transactions are recorded accurately. You will learn that companies account for small disbursements of cash, called *petty cash disbursements*, differently than they do for large disbursements. You will also learn how to prepare a formal bank reconciliation.

SELF-STUDY REVIEW PROBLEM

A step-by-step audio-narrated series of slides is provided on the text website at www.mhhe.com/edmonds8e.

Erie Jewelers sells gold earrings. Its beginning inventory of Model 407 gold earrings consisted of 100 pairs of earrings at $50 per pair. Erie purchased two batches of Model 407 earrings during the year. The first batch purchased consisted of 150 pairs at $53 per pair; the second batch consisted of 200 pairs at $56 per pair. During the year, Erie sold 375 pairs of Model 407 earrings.

Required

Determine the amount of product cost Erie would allocate to cost of goods sold and ending inventory assuming that Erie uses (a) FIFO, (b) LIFO, and (c) weighted average.

Solution to Requirements a–c

Goods Available for Sale					
Beginning inventory	100	@	$50	=	$ 5,000
First purchase	150	@	53	=	7,950
Second purchase	200	@	56	=	11,200
Goods available for sale	450				$24,150

a. FIFO

Cost of Goods Sold	Pairs		Cost per Pair		Cost of Goods Sold
From beginning inventory	100	@	$50	=	$ 5,000
From first purchase	150	@	53	=	7,950
From second purchase	125	@	56	=	7,000
Total pairs sold	375				$19,950

Ending inventory = Goods available for sale − Cost of goods sold
Ending inventory = $24,150 − $19,950 = $4,200

b. LIFO

Cost of Goods Sold	Pairs		Cost per Pair		Cost of Goods Sold
From second purchase	200	@	$56	=	$11,200
From first purchase	150	@	53	=	7,950
From beginning inventory	25	@	50	=	1,250
Total pairs sold	375				$20,400

Ending inventory = Goods available for sale − Cost of goods sold
Ending inventory = $24,150 − $20,400 = $3,750

c. Weighted average

Goods available for sale ÷ Total pairs = Cost per pair

$24,150   ÷   450   = $53.6667

Cost of goods sold   375 units @ $53.6667 = $20,125

Ending inventory   75 units @ $53.6667 = $4,025

KEY TERMS

**average number of days
  to sell inventory** (also
  called **the average days
  in inventory) 284**
consistency 275

**first-in, first-out (FIFO) cost
  flow method 270**
full disclosure 275
gross margin method 282
inventory cost flow methods 272

inventory turnover 284
**last-in, first-out (LIFO) cost
  flow method 270**
**lower-of-cost-or-market
  rule 278**

physical flow of goods 270
specific identification 270
**weighted-average cost flow
  method 270**

QUESTIONS

1. Name and describe the four cost flow methods discussed in this chapter.

2. What are some advantages and disadvantages of the specific identification method of accounting for inventory?

3. What are some advantages and disadvantages of using the FIFO method of inventory valuation?

4. What are some advantages and disadvantages of using the LIFO method of inventory valuation?

5. In an inflationary period, which inventory cost flow method will produce the highest net income? Explain.

6. In an inflationary period, which inventory cost flow method will produce the largest amount of total assets on the balance sheet? Explain.

7. What is the difference between the flow of costs and the physical flow of goods?

8. Does the choice of cost flow method (FIFO, LIFO, or weighted average) affect the statement of cash flows? Explain.

9. Assume that Key Co. purchased 1,000 units of merchandise in its first year of operations for $25 per unit. The company sold 850 units for $40. What is the amount of cost of goods sold using FIFO? LIFO? Weighted average?

10. Assume that Key Co. purchased 1,500 units of merchandise in its second year of operation for $27 per unit. Its beginning inventory was determined in Question 9. Assuming that 1,500 units are sold, what is the amount of cost of goods sold using FIFO? LIFO? Weighted average?

11. Refer to Questions 9 and 10. Which method might be preferable for financial statements? For income tax reporting? Explain.

12. In an inflationary period, which cost flow method, FIFO or LIFO, produces the larger cash flow? Explain.

13. Which inventory cost flow method produces the highest net income in a deflationary period?

14. How does the phrase *lower-of-cost-or-market* apply to inventory valuation?

15. If some merchandise declined in value because of damage or obsolescence, what effect will the lower-of-cost-or-market rule have on the income statement? Explain.

16. What is a situation in which estimates of the amount of inventory may be useful or even necessary?

17. How can management manipulate net income using inventory fraud?

18. If the amount of goods available for sale is $123,000, the amount of sales is $130,000, and the gross margin is 25 percent of sales, what is the amount of ending inventory?

19. Assume that inventory is overstated by $1,500 at the end of 2013 but is corrected in 2014. What effect will this have on the 2013 income statement? The 2013 balance sheet? The 2014 income statement? The 2014 balance sheet?

20. What information does inventory turnover provide?

21. What is an example of a business that would have a high inventory turnover? A low inventory turnover?

MULTIPLE-CHOICE QUESTIONS

**Multiple-choice questions are provided on the text website at
www.mhhe.com/edmonds8e.**

EXERCISES—SERIES A

All applicable Exercises in Series A are available with McGraw-Hill's Connect® Accounting.

LO 1

Exercise 5-1A   *Effect of inventory cost flow assumption on financial statements*

Required

For each of the following situations, fill in the blank with *FIFO, LIFO,* or *weighted average:*

a. _____ would produce the highest amount of net income in an inflationary environment.

b. _____ would produce the highest amount of assets in an inflationary environment.

c. _____ would produce the lowest amount of net income in a deflationary environment.

d. _____ would produce the same unit cost for assets and cost of goods sold in an inflationary environment.

e. _____ would produce the lowest amount of net income in an inflationary environment.

f. _____ would produce an asset value that was the same regardless of whether the environment was inflationary or deflationary.

g. _____ would produce the lowest amount of assets in an inflationary environment.

h. _____ would produce the highest amount of assets in a deflationary environment.

LO 1

Exercise 5-2A   *Allocating product cost between cost of goods sold and ending inventory*

Spice Co. started the year with no inventory. During the year, it purchased two identical inventory items. The inventory was purchased at different times. The first purchase cost $3,600 and the other, $4,200. One of the items was sold during the year.

Required

Based on this information, how much product cost would be allocated to cost of goods sold and ending inventory on the year-end financial statements, assuming use of

a. FIFO?

b. LIFO?

c. Weighted average?

LO 1

Exercise 5-3A   *Allocating product cost between cost of goods sold and ending inventory: multiple purchases*

Suggs Company sells coffee makers used in business offices. Its beginning inventory of coffee makers was 400 units at $50 per unit. During the year, Suggs made two batch purchases of coffee makers. The first was a 500-unit purchase at $55 per unit; the second was a 600-unit purchase at $58 per unit. During the period, Suggs sold 1,200 coffee makers.

Required

Determine the amount of product costs that would be allocated to cost of goods sold and ending inventory, assuming that Suggs uses

a. FIFO.

b. LIFO.

c. Weighted average.

LO 1

Exercise 5-4A   *Effect of inventory cost flow (FIFO, LIFO, and weighted average) on gross margin*

The following information pertains to Baxter Company for 2013:

Beginning inventory	90 units @ $15
Units purchased	320 units @ $19

Ending inventory consisted of 40 units. Baxter sold 370 units at $30 each. All purchases and sales were made with cash.

Required

a. Compute the gross margin for Baxter Company using the following cost flow assumptions: (1) FIFO, (2) LIFO, and (3) weighted average.

b. What is the dollar amount of difference in net income between using FIFO versus LIFO? (Ignore income tax considerations.)

c. Determine the cash flow from operating activities, using each of the three cost flow assumptions listed in Requirement a. Ignore the effect of income taxes. Explain why these cash flows have no differences.

Exercise 5-5A   Effect of inventory cost flow on ending inventory balance and gross margin   LO 1

Dugan Sales had the following transactions for jackets in 2013, its first year of operations:

Jan. 20	Purchased 80 units @ $15	=	$1,200
Apr. 21	Purchased 420 units @ $16	=	6,720
July 25	Purchased 250 units @ $20	=	5,000
Sept. 19	Purchased 150 units @ $22	=	3,300

During the year, Dugan Sales sold 830 jackets for $40 each.

Required

a. Compute the amount of ending inventory Dugan would report on the balance sheet, assuming the following cost flow assumptions: (1) FIFO, (2) LIFO, and (3) weighted average.

b. Record the above transactions in general journal form and post to T-accounts using (1) FIFO, (2) LIFO, and (3) weighted average. Use a separate set of journal entries and T-accounts for each method. Assume all transactions are cash transactions.

c. Compute the difference in gross margin between the FIFO and LIFO cost flow assumptions.

Exercise 5-6A   Income tax effect of shifting from FIFO to LIFO   LO 1

The following information pertains to the inventory of the Windjammer Company:

Jan. 1	Beginning Inventory	300 units @ $25
Apr. 1	Purchased	2,800 units @ $30
Oct. 1	Purchased	1,000 units @ $32

During the year, Windjammer sold 3,500 units of inventory at $50 per unit and incurred $21,000 of operating expenses. Windjammer currently uses the FIFO method but is considering a change to LIFO. All transactions are cash transactions. Assume a 30 percent income tax rate. Windjammer started the period with cash of $36,000, inventory of $7,500, common stock of $20,000 and retained earnings of $23,500.

Required

a. Record the above transactions in general journal form and post to T-accounts using (1) FIFO and (2) LIFO. Use a separate set of journal entries and T-accounts for each method.

b. Prepare income statements using FIFO and LIFO.

c. Determine the amount of income tax Windjammer would save if it changed cost flow methods.

d. Determine the cash flow from operating activities under FIFO and LIFO.

e. Explain why cash flow from operating activities is lower under FIFO when that cost flow method produced the higher gross margin.

LO 1

Exercise 5-7A *Effect of FIFO versus LIFO on income tax expense*

Garden Gifts Inc. had cash sales of $112,500 for 2013, its first year of operation. On April 2, the company purchased 150 units of inventory at $180 per unit. On September 1, an additional 200 units were purchased for $200 per unit. The company had 50 units on hand at the end of the year. The company's income tax rate is 40 percent. All transactions are cash transactions.

Required

a. The preceding paragraph describes five accounting events: (1) a sales transaction, (2) the first purchase of inventory, (3) a second purchase of inventory, (4) the recognition of cost of goods sold expense, and (5) the payment of income tax expense. Record the amounts of each event in horizontal statements models like the following ones, assuming first a FIFO and then a LIFO cost flow.

Effect of Events on Financial Statements
Panel 1: FIFO Cost Flow

Event No.	Balance Sheet						Income Statement					Statement of Cash Flows
	Cash	+	Inventory	=	Com. Stk.	+	Ret. Earn.	Rev.	−	Exp.	=	Net Inc.	

Panel 2: LIFO Cost Flow

Event No.	Balance Sheet						Income Statement					Statement of Cash Flows
	Cash	+	Inventory	=	Com. Stk.	+	Ret. Earn.	Rev.	−	Exp.	=	Net Inc.	

b. Compute net income using FIFO.

c. Compute net income using LIFO.

d. Explain the difference, if any, in the amount of income tax expense incurred using the two cost flow assumptions.

e. How does the use of the FIFO versus the LIFO cost flow assumptions affect the statement of cash flows?

LO 1

Exercise 5-8A *Recording inventory transactions using the perpetual system: intermittent sales and purchases*

The following inventory transactions apply to Star Glass Company for 2013:

Jan. 1	Purchased	200 units @ $12
Apr. 1	Sold	150 units @ $20
Aug. 1	Purchased	300 units @ $15
Dec. 1	Sold	450 units @ $25

The beginning inventory consisted of 180 units at $10 per unit. All transactions are cash transactions.

Required

a. Record these transactions in general journal format assuming Star Glass Company uses the FIFO cost flow assumption and keeps perpetual records.

b. Compute the ending balance in the Inventory account.

Exercise 5-9A   *Effect of cost flow on ending inventory: intermittent sales and purchases*

LO 1

Tull Auto Parts, Inc., had the following transactions for 2013:

Date	Transaction	Description
Jan. 1	Beginning inventory	40 units @ $22
Mar. 15	Purchased	150 units @ $24
May 30	Sold	175 units @ $48
Aug. 10	Purchased	320 units @ $26
Nov. 20	Sold	300 units @ $50

Required

a. Determine the quantity and dollar amount of inventory at the end of the year, assuming Tull Auto Parts Inc. uses the FIFO cost flow assumption and keeps perpetual records.

b. Write a memo explaining why Tull Auto Parts, Inc., would have difficulty applying the LIFO method on a perpetual basis. Include a discussion of how to overcome these difficulties.

Exercise 5-10A   *Lower-of-cost-or-market rule: perpetual system*

LO 2

The following information pertains to Wroten Hardware's ending inventory for the current year:

Item	Quantity	Unit Cost	Unit Market Value
M	200	$10	$ 8
N	100	12	10
0	40	8	9
P	30	5	10

Required

a. Determine the value of the ending inventory using the lower-of-cost-or-market rule applied to (1) each individual inventory item and (2) the inventory in aggregate.

b. Prepare any necessary journal entries, assuming the decline in value is immaterial, using the (1) individual method and (2) aggregate method. Wroten Hardware uses the perpetual inventory system.

Exercise 5-11A   *Lower-of-cost-or-market rule*

LO 2

Scheiner Company carries three inventory items. The following information pertains to the ending inventory:

Item	Quantity	Unit Cost	Unit Market Value
A	400	$20	$18
B	500	25	24
C	300	10	12

Required

a. Determine the ending inventory that will be reported on the balance sheet, assuming that Scheiner applies the lower-of-cost-or-market rule to individual inventory items.

b. Prepare the necessary journal entry, assuming the decline in value is immaterial.

LO 3, 4

Exercise 5-12A   *Estimating ending inventory using the gross margin method*

Donnie Mills, the owner of Donnie's Fishing Supplies, is surprised at the amount of actual inventory at the end of the year. He thought there should be more inventory on hand based on the amount of sales for the year. The following information is taken from the books of Donnie's Fishing Supplies:

Beginning inventory	$250,000
Purchases for the year	500,000
Sales for the year	850,000
Inventory at the end of the year (based on actual count)	40,000

Historically, Donnie has made a 20 percent gross margin on his sales. Donnie thinks there may be some problem with the inventory. Evaluate the situation based on the historical gross profit percentage.

Required

Estimate the following:

a. Gross margin in dollars.

b. Cost of goods sold in dollars.

c. Estimated ending inventory.

d. Inventory shortage.

e. Give an explanation for the shortage.

LO 4

Exercise 5-13A   *Estimating ending inventory: perpetual system*

Kate Mullin owned a small company that sold boating equipment. The equipment was expensive, and a perpetual system was maintained for control purposes. Even so, lost, damaged, and stolen merchandise normally amounted to 5 percent of the inventory balance. On June 14, Kate's warehouse was destroyed by fire. Just prior to the fire, the accounting records contained a $130,000 balance in the Inventory account. However, inventory costing $20,000 had been sold and delivered to customers the day of the fire but had not been recorded in the books at the time of the fire. The fire did not affect the showroom, which contained inventory that cost $50,000.

Required

Estimate the amount of inventory destroyed by fire.

LO 4

Exercise 5-14A   *Effect of inventory error on financial statements: perpetual system*

Grayson Company failed to count $22,000 of inventory in its 2013 year-end physical count.

Required

Explain how this error will affect Grayson's 2013 financial statements, assuming that Grayson uses the perpetual inventory system.

LO 4

Exercise 5-15A   *Effect of inventory misstatement on elements of financial statements*

The ending inventory for Pine Co. was erroneously written down causing an understatement of $6,500 at the end of 2013.

Required

Was each of the following amounts overstated, understated, or not affected by the error?

Item No.	Year	Amount
1	2013	Beginning inventory
2	2013	Purchases
3	2013	Goods available for sale
4	2013	Cost of goods sold
5	2013	Gross margin
6	2013	Net income
7	2014	Beginning inventory
8	2014	Purchases
9	2014	Goods available for sale
10	2014	Cost of goods sold
11	2014	Gross margin
12	2014	Net income

Exercise 5-16A *Explaining multiple inventory methods at one real-world company*

LO 1, IFRS

The following footnote related to accounting for inventory was taken from the 2010 annual report of Walmart Stores, Inc.:

Inventories The Company values inventories at the lower of cost or market as determined primarily by the retail method of accounting, using the last-in, first-out ("LIFO") method for substantially all of the Walmart U.S. segment's merchandise inventories. Sam's Club merchandise and merchandise in our distribution warehouses are valued based on the weighted average cost using the LIFO method. Inventories of foreign operations are primarily valued by the retail method of accounting, using the first-in, first-out ("FIFO") method. At January 31, 2010 and 2009, our inventories valued at LIFO approximate those inventories as if they were valued at FIFO.

Required

Write a brief report explaining the reason or reasons that best explain why Walmart uses the LIFO cost flow method for its operations in the United States, but the FIFO method for its non-U.S. operations.

Exercise 5-17A *GAAP vs IFRS*

IFRS

Hillside Winery Inc. has inventory that cost $600,000. The aging process for the inventory requires several years. At the company's closing date (December 31, 2013) the inventory had a market value of $500,000. During 2014 the market value recovered to an estimated $580,000.

Required

a. Assuming Hillside uses GAAP, determine the book value and the amount of any gain or loss recognized on the 2013 and 2014 financial statements.

b. Assuming Hillside uses IFRS, determine the book value and the amount of any gain or loss recognized on the 2013 and 2014 financial statements.

PROBLEMS—SERIES A

All applicable Problems in Series A are available with McGraw-Hill's *Connect® Accounting*.

Problem 5-18A *Effect of different inventory cost flow methods on financial statements*

LO 1

The accounting records of Roberts Insulation, Inc., reflected the following balances as of January 1, 2013:

Cash	$36,000
Beginning inventory	24,000 (200 units @ $120)
Common stock	25,000
Retained earnings	35,000

CHECK FIGURES
a. Cost of Goods Sold—
FIFO: $42,680
c. Net Income—LIFO: $26,232

The following five transactions occurred in 2013:

1. First purchase (cash)   130 units @ $124
2. Second purchase (cash)   220 units @ $128
3. Sales (all cash)   350 units @ $320
4. Paid $24,000 cash for operating expenses.
5. Paid cash for income tax at the rate of 40 percent of income before taxes.

Required

a. Compute the cost of goods sold and ending inventory, assuming (1) FIFO cost flow, (2) LIFO cost flow, and (3) weighted-average cost flow. Compute income tax expense for each method.

b. Record the above transactions in general journal form and post to T-accounts assuming (1) FIFO cost flow, (2) LIFO cost flow, and (3) weighted-average cost flow.

c. Use a vertical model to show the 2013 income statement, balance sheet, and statement of cash flows under FIFO, LIFO, and weighted average.

LO 1

CHECK FIGURES
b. Cost of Goods Sold: $17,700
c. Ending Inventory: $5,650

Problem 5-19A   *Allocating product costs between cost of goods sold and ending inventory: intermittent purchases and sales of merchandise*

Action, Inc., had the following sales and purchase transactions during 2013. Beginning inventory consisted of 120 items at $80 each. Action uses the FIFO cost flow assumption and keeps perpetual inventory records.

Date	Transaction	Description
Mar. 5	Purchased	100 items @ $90
Apr. 10	Sold	70 items @ $175
June 19	Sold	80 items @ $175
Sept. 16	Purchased	50 items @ $95
Nov. 28	Sold	60 items @ $180

Required

a. Record the inventory transactions in general journal format.

b. Calculate the gross margin Action would report on the 2013 income statement.

c. Determine the ending inventory balance Action would report on the December 31, 2013, balance sheet.

LO 2

eXcel

CHECK FIGURES
a. $5,680
c. $6,030

Problem 5-20A   *Inventory valuation based on the lower-of-cost-or-market rule*

At the end of the year, Clausel Jewelers had the following items in inventory:

Item	Quantity	Unit Cost	Unit Market Value
D1	30	$80	$90
D2	10	60	55
D3	41	30	32
D4	20	90	75

Required

a. Determine the amount of ending inventory using the lower-of-cost-or-market rule applied to each individual inventory item.

b. Provide the general journal entry necessary to write down the inventory based on Requirement *a*. Assume that Clausel Jewelers uses the perpetual inventory system.

c. Determine the amount of ending inventory, assuming that the lower-of-cost-or-market rule is applied to the inventory in aggregate.

d. Provide the general journal entry necessary to write down the inventory based on Requirement *c*. Assume that Clausel Jewelers uses the perpetual inventory system.

Problem 5-21A   *Estimating ending inventory: gross margin method*

LO 4

A hurricane destroyed the inventory of Franklin Feed Store on September 21 of the current year. Although some of the accounting information was destroyed, the following information was discovered for the period of January 1 through September 21:

CHECK FIGURES
a. Gross Margin: $280,000
b. Total Inventory Loss: $42,000

Beginning inventory, January 1	$120,000
Purchases through September 21	450,000
Sales through September 21	800,000

The gross margin for Franklin Feed Store has traditionally been 35 percent of sales.

Required

a. For the period ending September 21, compute the following:
   (1) Estimated gross margin.
   (2) Estimated cost of goods sold.
   (3) Estimated inventory at September 21.
b. Assume that $8,000 of the inventory was not damaged. What is the amount of the loss from the hurricane?
c. Franklin Feed Store uses the perpetual inventory system. If some of the accounting records had not been destroyed, how would Franklin determine the amount of the inventory loss?

Problem 5-22A   *Estimating ending inventory: gross margin method*

LO 4

Bill Money, owner of Money Company, is reviewing the quarterly financial statements and thinks the cost of goods sold is out of line with past years. The following historical data is available for 2013 and 2014:

CHECK FIGURE
b. Estimated ending inventory:
$151,200

	2013	2014
Net sales	$220,000	$250,000
Cost of goods sold	99,000	117,200

At the end of the first quarter of 2014, Money Company's ledger had the following account balances:

Sales	$280,000
Purchases	210,000
Beginning inventory, January 1, 2013	70,000

Required

Using the information provided, estimate the following for the first quarter of 2015:

a. Cost of goods sold. (Use average cost of goods sold percentage.)
b. Ending inventory at March 31 based on the historical cost of goods sold percentage.
c. Inventory shortage if the inventory balance as of March 31 is $125,000.

Problem 5-23A   *Effect of inventory errors on financial statements*

LO 3

The following income statement was prepared for Hughes Company for the year 2013:

HUGHES COMPANY
Income Statement
For the Year Ended December 31, 2013

Sales	$75,000
Cost of goods sold	(41,250)
Gross margin	33,750
Operating expenses	(10,120)
Net income	$23,630

During the year-end audit, the following errors were discovered:

1. An $1,800 payment for repairs was erroneously charged to the Cost of Goods Sold account. (Assume that the perpetual inventory system is used.)
2. Sales to customers for $3,400 at December 31, 2013, were not recorded in the books for 2013. Also, the $1,870 cost of goods sold was not recorded. The error was not discovered in the physical count because the goods had not been delivered to the customer.
3. A mathematical error was made in determining ending inventory. Ending inventory was understated by $1,700. (The Inventory account was written down in error to the Cost of Goods Sold account.)

Required

Determine the effect, if any, of each of the errors on the following items. Give the dollar amount of the effect and whether it would overstate (O), understate (U), or not affect (NA) the account. The effect on sales is recorded as an example.

Error No. 1	Amount of Error	Effect
Sales, 2013	NA	NA
Ending inventory, December 31, 2013		
Gross margin, 2013		
Beginning inventory, January 1, 2014		
Cost of goods sold, 2013		
Net income, 2013		
Retained earnings, December 31, 2013		
Total assets, December 31, 2013		

Error No. 2	Amount of Error	Effect
Sales, 2013	$2,400	U
Ending inventory, December 31, 2013		
Gross margin, 2013		
Beginning inventory, January 1, 2014		
Cost of goods sold, 2013		
Net income, 2013		
Retained earnings, December 31, 2013		
Total assets, December 31, 2013		

Error No. 3	Amount of Error	Effect
Sales, 2013	NA	NA
Ending inventory, December 31, 2013		
Gross margin, 2013		
Beginning inventory, January 1, 2014		
Cost of goods sold, 2013		
Net income, 2013		
Retained earnings, December 31, 2013		
Total assets, December 31, 2013		

LO 6

Problem 5-24A   *Using ratios to make comparisons*

The following accounting information pertains to Calgary Co. and Toronto Co. companies at the end of 2014. The only difference between the two companies is that Calgary Co. uses FIFO while Toronto Co. uses LIFO.

	Calgary Co.	Toronto Co.
Cash	$ 80,000	$ 80,000
Accounts receivable	320,000	320,000
Merchandise inventory	240,000	180,000
Accounts payable	220,000	220,000
Cost of goods sold	1,200,000	1,260,000
Building	400,000	400,00
Sales	2,000,000	2,000,000

Required

a. Compute the gross margin percentage for each company and identify the company that *appears* to be charging the higher prices in relation to its cost.

b. For each company, compute the inventory turnover ratio and the average days to sell inventory. Identify the company that *appears* to be incurring the higher inventory financing cost.

c. Explain why a company with the lower gross margin percentage has the higher inventory turnover ratio.

EXERCISES—SERIES B

Exercise 5-1B   *Effect of inventory cost flow assumption on financial statements*   LO 1

Required

For each of the following situations, indicate whether FIFO, LIFO, or weighted average applies:

a. In a period of rising prices, net income would be highest.

b. In a period of rising prices, cost of goods sold would be highest.

c. In a period of rising prices, ending inventory would be highest.

d. In a period of falling prices, net income would be highest.

e. In a period of falling prices, the unit cost of goods would be the same for ending inventory and cost of goods sold.

Exercise 5-2B   *Allocating product cost between cost of goods sold and ending inventory*   LO 1

Adams Co. started the year with no inventory. During the year, it purchased two identical inventory items at different times. The first purchase cost $950 and the other, $1,250. Adams sold one of the items during the year.

Required

Based on this information, how much product cost would be allocated to cost of goods sold and ending inventory on the year-end financial statements, assuming use of

a. FIFO?

b. LIFO?

c. Weighted average?

Exercise 5-3B   *Allocating product cost between cost of goods sold and ending inventory: multiple purchases*   LO 1

Perez Company sells chairs that are used at computer stations. Its beginning inventory of chairs was 100 units at $50 per unit. During the year, Perez made two batch purchases of this chair. The first was a 150-unit purchase at $55 per unit; the second was a 200-unit purchase at $58 per unit. During the period, it sold 260 chairs.

Required

Determine the amount of product costs that would be allocated to cost of goods sold and ending inventory, assuming that Perez uses

a. FIFO.

b. LIFO.

c. Weighted average.

LO 1

Exercise 5-4B *Effect of inventory cost flow (FIFO, LIFO, and weighted average) on gross margin*

The following information pertains to King Company for 2013:

Beginning inventory	80 units @ $30
Units purchased	300 units @ $35

Ending inventory consisted of 30 units. King sold 350 units at $60 each. All purchases and sales were made with cash. Operating expenses amounted to $3,000.

Required

a. Compute the gross margin for King Company using the following cost flow assumptions: (1) FIFO, (2) LIFO, and (3) weighted average.

b. What is the amount of net income using FIFO, LIFO, and weighted average? (Ignore income tax considerations.)

c. Compute the amount of ending inventory using (1) FIFO, (2) LIFO, and (3) weighted average.

LO 1

Exercise 5-5B *Effect of inventory cost flow on ending inventory balance and gross margin*

Silver Sales had the following transactions for T-shirts for 2013, its first year of operations:

Jan. 20	Purchased 350 units @ $ 6	=	$2,100
Apr. 21	Purchased 150 units @ $ 8	=	1,200
July 25	Purchased 200 units @ $10	=	2,000
Sept. 19	Purchased 80 units @ $11	=	880

During the year, Silver Sales sold 650 T-shirts for $20 each.

Required

a. Compute the amount of ending inventory Silver would report on the balance sheet, assuming the following cost flow assumptions: (1) FIFO, (2) LIFO, and (3) weighted average.

b. Record the above transactions in general journal form and post to T-accounts assuming (1) FIFO, (2) LIFO, and (3) weighted average methods. Use a separate set of journal entries and T-accounts for each method. Assume all transactions are cash transactions.

c. Compute the difference in gross margin between the FIFO and LIFO cost flow assumptions.

LO 1

Exercise 5-6B *Income tax effect of shifting from FIFO to LIFO*

The following information pertains to the inventory of Anniola Company:

Jan. 1	Beginning inventory	600 units @ $20
Apr. 1	Purchased	3,000 units @ $22
Oct. 1	Purchased	900 units @ $28

During 2013, Anniola sold 4,000 units of inventory at $40 per unit and incurred $38,000 of operating expenses. Anniola currently uses the FIFO method but is considering a change to LIFO. All transactions are cash transactions. Assume a 30 percent income tax rate. Anniola started the period with cash of $80,000, inventory of $12,000, common stock of $50,000, and retained earnings of $42,000.

Required

a. Record the above transactions in general journal form and post to T-accounts using (1) FIFO and (2) LIFO. Use a separate set of journal entries and T-accounts for each method.

b. Prepare income statements using FIFO and LIFO.

c. Determine the amount of income tax that Anniola would pay using each cost flow method.

d. Determine the cash flow from operating activities under FIFO and LIFO.

e. Why is the cash flow from operating activities different under FIFO and LIFO?

Exercise 5-7B   *Effect of FIFO versus LIFO on income tax expense*

LO 1

The Gold Company had cash sales of $350,000 for 2013, its first year of operation. On April 2, the company purchased 200 units of inventory at $375 per unit. On September 1, an additional 150 units were purchased for $400 per unit. The company had 100 units on hand at the end of the year. The company's income tax rate is 40 percent. All transactions are cash transactions.

Required

a. The preceding paragraph describes five accounting events: (1) a sales transaction, (2) the first purchase of inventory, (3) a second purchase of inventory, (4) the recognition of cost of goods sold expense, and (5) the payment of income tax expense. Record the amounts of each event in horizontal statements models like the following ones, assuming first a FIFO and then a LIFO cost flow.

colspan over	**Effect of Events on Financial Statements**													
	Panel 1: FIFO Cost Flow													
Event No.	**Balance Sheet**						**Income Statement**						**Statement of Cash Flows**	
	Cash	+	Inventory	=	Ret. Earn.		Rev.	−	Exp.	=	Net Inc.			
	Panel 2: LIFO Cost Flow													
Event No.	**Balance Sheet**						**Income Statement**						**Statement of Cash Flows**	
	Cash	+	Inventory	=	Ret. Earn.		Rev.	−	Exp.	=	Net Inc.			

b. Compute net income using FIFO.

c. Compute net income using LIFO.

d. Explain the difference, if any, in the amount of income tax expense incurred using the two cost flow assumptions.

e. Which method, FIFO or LIFO, produced the larger amount of assets on the balance sheet?

Exercise 5-8B   *Recording inventory transactions using the perpetual method: intermittent sales and purchases*

LO 1

The following inventory transactions apply to Apac Company for 2013:

Jan. 1	Purchased	250 units @ $60
Apr. 1	Sold	125 units @ $90
Aug. 1	Purchased	400 units @ $65
Dec. 1	Sold	500 units @ $95

The beginning inventory consisted of 175 units at $55 per unit. All transactions are cash transactions.

Required

a. Record these transactions in general journal format assuming Apac uses the FIFO cost flow assumption and keeps perpetual records.

b. Compute cost of goods sold for 2013.

LO 1

Exercise 5-9B *Effect of cost flow on ending inventory: intermittent sales and purchases*

The Party Store, had the following series of transactions for 2013:

Date	Transaction	Description
Jan. 1	Beginning inventory	50 units @ $35
Mar. 15	Purchased	200 units @ $40
May 30	Sold	170 units @ $90
Aug. 10	Purchased	275 units @ $45
Nov. 20	Sold	340 units @ $92

Required

a. Determine the quantity and dollar amount of inventory at the end of the year, assuming The Party Store uses the FIFO cost flow assumption and keeps perpetual records.

b. Write a memo explaining why The Party Store, would have difficulty applying the weighted-average method on a perpetual basis.

LO 2

Exercise 5-10B *Lower-of-cost-or-market rule: perpetual system*

The following information pertains to Smith Woodwork Co.'s ending inventory for the current year:

Item	Quantity	Unit Cost	Unit Market Value
C	80	$20	$16
D	70	22	20
K	30	25	28
M	20	15	17

Required

a. Determine the value of the ending inventory using the lower-of-cost-or-market rule applied to (1) each individual inventory item and (2) the inventory in aggregate.

b. Prepare any necessary journal entries, assuming the decline in value is immaterial. Smith Woodwork Co. uses the perpetual inventory system. (Make entries for both methods.)

LO 2

Exercise 5-11B *Lower-of-cost-or-market rule*

Waldron Company carries three inventory items. The following information pertains to the ending inventory:

Item	Quantity	Unit Cost	Unit Market Value
A	100	$60	$55
F	150	80	75
K	90	30	40

Required

a. Determine the ending inventory that Waldron will report on the balance sheet, assuming that it applies the lower-of-cost-or-market rule to individual inventory items.

b. Prepare the necessary journal entry, assuming the decline in value was immaterial.

LO 3, 4

Exercise 5-12B *Estimating ending inventory*

A substantial portion of inventory owned by Alcorn Sporting Goods was recently destroyed when the roof collapsed during a rainstorm. Alcorn also lost some of its accounting records. Alcorn must estimate the loss from the storm for insurance reporting and financial statement purposes. Alcorn uses the periodic inventory system. The following accounting information was recovered from the damaged records:

Beginning inventory	$ 50,000
Purchases to date of storm	175,000
Sales to date of storm	240,000

The value of undamaged inventory counted was $4,000. Historically Alcorn's gross margin percentage has been approximately 25 percent of sales.

Required

Estimate the following:

a. Gross margin in dollars.
b. Cost of goods sold.
c. Ending inventory.
d. Amount of lost inventory.

Exercise 5-13B   *Estimating ending inventory: perpetual system*

LO 3, 4

Bill Phillips owned a small company that sold garden equipment. The equipment was expensive, and a perpetual system was maintained for control purposes. Even so, lost, damaged, and stolen merchandise normally amounted to 5 percent of the inventory balance. On June 14, Phillips' warehouse was destroyed by fire. Just prior to the fire, the accounting records contained a $320,000 balance in the Inventory account. However, inventory costing $36,000 had been sold and delivered to customers but had not been recorded in the books at the time of the fire. The fire did not affect the showroom, which contained inventory that cost $62,000.

Required

Estimate the amount of inventory destroyed by fire.

Exercise 5-14B   *Effect of inventory error on financial statements: perpetual system*

LO 3

Shook Company failed to count $60,000 of inventory in its 2013 year-end physical count.

Required

Write a memo explaining how Shook Company's balance sheet will be affected in 2013. Assume Shook uses the perpetual inventory system.

Exercise 5-15B   *Effect of inventory error on elements of financial statements*

LO 3

The ending inventory for Oak Co. was incorrectly adjusted, which caused it to be understated by $18,500 for 2013.

Required

Was each of the following amounts overstated, understated, or not affected by the error?

Item No.	Year	Amount
1	2013	Beginning inventory
2	2013	Purchases
3	2013	Goods available for sale
4	2013	Cost of goods sold
5	2013	Gross margin
6	2013	Net income
7	2014	Beginning inventory
8	2014	Purchases
9	2014	Goods available for sale
10	2014	Cost of goods sold
11	2014	Gross margin
12	2014	Net income

LO 1, IFRS

Exercise 5-16B *Explaining multiple inventory methods at one real-world company*

The following footnote related to accounting for inventory was taken from the 2010 annual report of Alcoa, Inc.:

> **Inventory Valuation** Inventories are carried at the lower of cost or market, with cost for a substantial portion of U.S. and Canadian inventories determined under the last-in, first-out (LIFO) method. The cost of other inventories is principally determined under the average-cost method. See Note G for additional information.

Required

Write a brief report explaining the reason or reasons that best explain why Alcoa uses the LIFO cost flow method for its inventories kept in the United States and Canada, but the average cost method for its other inventories.

IFRS

Exercise 5-17B *GAAP vs IFRS*

Generally accepted accounting principles (GAAP) and International Financial Reporting Standards (IFRS) treat the LIFO inventory cost flow method differently.

Required

a. Briefly describe the position GAAP takes with respect to LIFO.
b. Briefly describe the position IFRS takes with respect to LIFO.
c. Explain the primary force that motivates the different positions.

PROBLEMS—SERIES B

LO 1

Problem 5-18B *Effect of different inventory cost flow methods on financial statements*

The accounting records of Carrol's Lamp Shop reflected the following balances as of January 1, 2013:

Cash	$90,500
Beginning inventory	28,000 (200 units @ $140)
Common stock	40,000
Retained earnings	78,500

The following five transactions occurred in 2013:

1. First purchase (cash)   120 units @ $150
2. Second purchase (cash)   140 units @ $160
3. Sales (all cash)   400 units @ $320
4. Paid $40,000 cash for salaries expense.
5. Paid cash for income tax at the rate of 25 percent of income before taxes.

Required

a. Compute the cost of goods sold and ending inventory, assuming (1) FIFO cost flow, (2) LIFO cost flow, and (3) weighted-average cost flow. Compute the income tax expense for each method.
b. Record the five transactions in general journal form and post to T-accounts assuming (1) FIFO cost flow, (2) LIFO cost flow, and (3) weighted-average cost flow.
c. Use a vertical model to show the 2013 income statement, balance sheet, and statement of cash flows under FIFO, LIFO, and weighted average. (*Hint:* Record the events under an accounting equation before preparing the statements.)

Problem 5-19B   *Allocating product costs between cost of goods sold and ending inventory: intermittent purchases and sales of merchandise*

Creative Awnings had the following sales and purchase transactions during 2013. Beginning inventory consisted of 50 items at $350 each. The company uses the FIFO cost flow assumption and keeps perpetual inventory records.

Date	Transaction	Description
Mar. 5	Purchased	40 items @ $370
Apr. 10	Sold	30 items @ $450
June 19	Sold	55 items @ $450
Sept. 16	Purchased	60 items @ $390
Nov. 28	Sold	45 items @ $470

Required

a. Record the inventory transactions in general journal format.

b. Calculate the gross margin Creative Awnings would report on the 2013 income statement.

c. Determine the ending inventory balance Creative Awnings would report on the December 31, 2013, balance sheet.

Problem 5-20B   *Inventory valuation based on the lower-of-cost-or-market rule*

At the end of the year, Ray's Repair Service had the following items in inventory:

Item	Quantity	Unit Cost	Unit Market Value
P1	70	$ 80	$ 90
P2	50	60	66
P3	90	140	130
P4	60	130	140

Required

a. Determine the amount of ending inventory using the lower-of-cost-or-market rule applied to each individual inventory item.

b. Provide the general journal entry necessary to write down the inventory based on Requirement *a*. Assume that Ray's Repair Service uses the perpetual inventory system.

c. Determine the amount of ending inventory, assuming that the lower-of-cost-or-market rule is applied to the total inventory in aggregate.

d. Provide the general journal entry necessary to write down the inventory based on Requirement *c*. Assume that Ray's Repair Service uses the perpetual inventory system.

e. Explain how the inventory loss would be reported when the periodic inventory system is used.

Problem 5-21B   *Estimating ending inventory: gross margin method*

The inventory of Bent & Dent Grocery was destroyed by a tornado on October 6 of the current year. Fortunately, some of the accounting records were at the home of one of the owners and were not damaged. The following information was available for the period of January 1 through October 6:

Beginning inventory, January 1	$ 138,000
Purchases through October 6	650,000
Sales through October 6	1,050,000

Gross margin for Bent & Dent has traditionally been 30 percent of sales.

Required

a. For the period ending October 6, compute the following:

(1) Estimated gross margin.

(2) Estimated cost of goods sold.

(3) Estimated inventory at October 6.

b. Assume that $15,000 of the inventory was not damaged. What is the amount of the loss from the tornado?

c. If Bent & Dent had used the perpetual inventory system, how would it have determined the amount of the inventory loss?

LO 4

Problem 5-22B *Estimating ending inventory: gross margin method*

Babyland wishes to produce quarterly financial statements, but it takes a physical count of inventory only at year end. The following historical data were taken from the 2013 and 2014 accounting records:

	2013	2014
Net sales	$120,000	$140,000
Cost of goods sold	62,000	65,300

At the end of the first quarter of 2015, Babyland's ledger had the following account balances:

Sales	$160,000
Purchases	90,000
Beginning inventory 1/1/2015	24,500
Ending inventory 3/31/2015	19,000

Based on purchases and sales, the Babyland accountant thinks inventory is low.

Required

Using the information provided, estimate the following for the first quarter of 2015:

a. Cost of goods sold. (Use the average cost of goods sold percentage.)

b. Ending inventory at March 31.

c. What could explain the difference between actual and estimated inventory?

LO 3

Problem 5-23B *Effect of inventory errors on financial statements*

The following income statement was prepared for Cool Pool Supplies for the year 2013:

COOL POOL SUPPLIES
Income Statement
For the Year Ended December 31, 2013

Sales	$280,000
Cost of goods sold	(155,000)
Gross margin	125,000
Operating expenses	(81,200)
Net income	$ 43,800

During the year-end audit, the following errors were discovered:

1. A $3,000 payment for repairs was erroneously charged to the Cost of Goods Sold account. (Assume that the perpetual inventory system is used.)

2. Sales to customers for $1,500 at December 31, 2013, were not recorded in the books for 2013. Also, the $900 cost of goods sold was not recorded. The error was not discovered in the physical count because the goods had not been delivered to the customers.

3. A mathematical error was made in determining ending inventory. Ending inventory was understated by $2,350. (The Inventory account was mistakenly written down to the Cost of Goods Sold account.)

Required

Determine the effect, if any, of each of the errors on the following items. Give the dollar amount of the effect and whether it would overstate (O), understate (U), or not affect (NA) the account. The first item for each error is recorded as an example.

Error No. 1	Amount of Error	Effect
Sales, 2013	NA	NA
Ending inventory, December 31, 2013		
Gross margin, 2013		
Beginning inventory, January 1, 2014		
Cost of goods sold, 2013		
Net income, 2013		
Retained earnings, December 31, 2013		
Total assets, December 31, 2013		

Error No. 2	Amount of Error	Effect
Sales, 2013	$500	U
Ending inventory, December 31, 2013		
Gross margin, 2013		
Beginning inventory, January 1, 2014		
Cost of goods sold, 2013		
Net income, 2013		
Retained earnings, December 31, 2013		
Total assets, December 31, 2013		

Error No. 3	Amount of Error	Effect
Sales, 2013	NA	NA
Ending inventory, December 31, 2013		
Gross margin, 2013		
Beginning inventory, January 1, 2014		
Cost of goods sold, 2013		
Net income, 2013		
Retained earnings, December 31, 2013		
Total assets, December 31, 2013		

Problem 5-24B   *Using ratios to make comparisons*

LO 5

The following accounting information pertains to Jasper and Banff companies at the end of 2013. The only difference between the two companies is that Jasper uses FIFO while Banff uses LIFO.

	Jasper	Banff
Cash	$ 60,000	$ 60,000
Accounts receivable	190,000	190,000
Merchandise Inventory	185,000	155,000
Accounts payable	175,000	175,000
Cost of goods sold	1,125,000	1,155,000
Building	250,000	250,000
Sales	1,500,000	1,500,000

Required

a. Compute the gross margin percentage for each company and identify the company that *appears* to be charging the higher prices in relation to its cost.

b. For each company, compute the inventory turnover ratio and the average days to sell inventory. Identify the company that *appears* to be incurring the higher inventory financing cost.

c. Explain why a company with the lower gross margin percentage has the higher inventory turnover ratio.

ANALYZE, THINK, COMMUNICATE

ATC 5-1   Business Applications Case   *Understanding real world annual reports*

Required

Use the Target Corporation's annual report in Appendix B to answer the following questions.

a.   What was Target's inventory turnover ratio and average days to sell inventory for the fiscal-year ended January 29, 2011 (2010) and 2009?

b.   Is the company's management of inventory getting better or worse?

c.   What cost flow method(s) did Target use to account for inventory?

ATC 5-2   Group Assignment   *Inventory cost flow*

The accounting records of Blue Bird Co. showed the following balances at January 1, 2013:

Cash	$30,000
Beginning inventory (100 units @ $50, 70 units @ $55)	8,850
Common stock	20,000
Retained earnings	18,850

Transactions for 2013 were as follows:

> Purchased 100 units @ $54 per unit.
> Sold 220 units @ $80 per unit.
> Purchased 250 units @ $58 per unit.
> Sold 200 units @ $90 per unit.
> Paid operating expenses of $3,200.
> Paid income tax expense. The income tax rate is 30%.

Required

a.   Organize the class into three sections, and divide each section into groups of three to five students. Assign each section one of the cost flow methods, FIFO, LIFO, or weighted average. The company uses the perpetual inventory system.

Group Tasks

Determine the amount of ending inventory, cost of goods sold, gross margin, and net income after income tax for the cost flow method assigned to your section. Also prepare an income statement using that cost flow assumption.

Class Discussion

b.   Have a representative of each section put its income statement on the board. Discuss the effect that each cost flow method has on assets (ending inventory), net income, and cash flows. Which method is preferred for tax reporting? For financial reporting? What restrictions are placed on the use of LIFO for tax reporting?

ATC 5-3   Real-World Case   *Inventory management issues at the Penske Automotive Group*

The following data were extracted from the 2010 financial statements of Penske Automotive Group, Inc. This company operates automobile dealerships, mostly in the United States and the United Kingdom. The company had 323 dealerships as of the end of 2010.

	December 31, 2010	December 31, 2009
Revenue from car sales	$8,396,098	$7,251,724
Cost of sales—cars	7,721,961	6,652,349
Gross profit—car sales	674,137	599,375
Operating income before taxes	170,168	128,958
Net income (loss)	108,281	76,461
Ending inventory—cars	1,524,226	1,302,495

Required

a. Compute Penske's gross margin percentage for 2010 and 2009.

b. Compute Penske's average days to sell inventory for 2010 and 2009.

c. How much higher or lower would Penske's *earnings before taxes* have been in 2010 if its gross margin percentage had been the same as it was in 2009? Show all supporting computations.

ATC 5-4   Business Applications Case   *Performing ratio analysis using real-world data*

Safeway, Inc., operated 1,700 stores as of January 1, 2011. The following data were taken from the company's annual report. All dollar amounts are in millions.

	Fiscal Years Ending	
	January 1, 2011	**January 2, 2010**
Revenue	$41,050.0	$40,850.7
Cost of goods sold	29,442.5	29,157.2
Net income	589.8	(1,097.5)
Merchandise inventory	2,623.4	2,508.9

Required

a. Compute Safeway's inventory turnover ratio for 2010 and 2009.

b. Compute Safeway's average days to sell inventory for 2010 and 2009.

c. Based on your computations in Requirements *a* and *b*, did Safeway's inventory management get better or worse from 2009 to 2010?

ATC 5-5   Business Applications Case   *Performing ratio analysis using real-world data*

Ruby Tuesday's, Inc., operated 656 casual dining restaurants across the United States as of June 1, 2010. Zale Corporation claims to be a leading supplier retailer of fine jewelry. The following data were taken from these companies' 2010 annual reports. All dollar amounts are in thousands.

	Ruby Tuesday's June 1, 2010	Zale Corporation July 31, 2010
Revenue	$1,188,043	$1,616,305
Cost of goods sold	344,462	802,172
Net income	45,344	(93,672)
Merchandise inventory	21,145	703,115

Required

a. Before performing any calculations, speculate as to which company will take the longest to sell its inventory. Explain the rationale for your decision.

b. Calculate the inventory turnover ratios for Ruby Tuesday's and Zale Corporation.

c. Calculate the average days to sell inventory for Ruby Tuesday's and Zale Corporation.

d. Do the calculations from Requirements *b* and *c* confirm your speculations in Requirement *a*?

ATC 5-6 Writing Assignment   *Use of LIFO*

The following information is available for Leno Company:

Sales	$695,000
Goods available for sale	$535,000
Ending inventory (using FIFO)	$246,000

Leno Company currently uses the FIFO cost flow method for financial statement reporting and for tax reporting. It is considering changing to the LIFO cost flow method for tax reporting purposes. If Leno uses LIFO, its ending inventory would be $175,000.

Required

a. Why would Leno want to change to LIFO for tax reporting?

b. Discuss any changes that Leno would have to make for GAAP reporting if it does change to LIFO for tax reporting.

ATC 5-7   Ethical Dilemma   *Show them only what you want them to see*

Clair Coolage is the chief accountant for a sales company called Far Eastern Imports. The company has been highly successful and is trying to increase its capital base by attracting new investors. The company operates in an inflationary environment and has been using the LIFO inventory cost flow method to minimize its net earnings and thereby reduce its income taxes. Katie Bailey, the vice president of finance, asked Coolage to estimate the change in net earnings that would occur if the company switched to FIFO. After reviewing the company's books, Coolage estimated that pretax income would increase by $1,200,000 if the company adopted the FIFO cost flow method. However, the switch would result in approximately $400,000 of additional taxes. The overall effect would result in an increase of $800,000 in net earnings. Bailey told Coolage to avoid the additional taxes by preparing the tax return on a LIFO basis but to prepare a set of statements on a FIFO basis to be distributed to potential investors.

Required

a. Comment on the legal and ethical implications of Bailey's decision.

b. How will the switch to FIFO affect Far Eastern's balance sheet?

c. If Bailey reconsiders and makes a decision to switch to FIFO for tax purposes as well as financial reporting purposes, net income will increase by $800,000. Comment on the wisdom of paying $400,000 in income taxes to obtain an additional $800,000 of net income.

ATC 5-8   Research Assignment   *Analyzing inventory at Gap Company*

Using either Gap's most current Form 10-K or the company's annual report, answer the questions below. To obtain the Form 10-K use either the EDGAR system following the instructions in Appendix A, or the company's website. The company's annual report is available on its website.

Required

a. What was the average amount of inventory per store? Use *all* stores operated by The Gap, Inc., not just those called *The Gap*. (*Hint:* The answer to this question must be computed. The number of stores in operation at the end of the most recent year can be found in the MD&A of the 10-K.)

b. How many stores did Gap operate at year-end?

c. Using the quarterly financial information in the 10-K, complete the following chart.

Quarter	Sales During Each Quarter
1	$
2	
3	
4	

d. Referring to the chart in Requirement *c*, explain why Gap's sales vary so widely throughout its fiscal year. Do you believe that Gap's inventory level varies throughout the year in relation to sales?

ATC 5-9   Spreadsheet Analysis   *Using Excel*

At January 1, 2013, the accounting records of Ginger's Boutique had the following balances:

Cash	$1,000
Inventory	2,250 (150 units @ $15)
Common stock	2,000
Retained earnings	1,250

During January, Ginger's Boutique entered into five cash transactions:

1. Purchased 120 units of inventory @ $16 each.
2. Purchased 160 units of inventory @ $17 each.
3. Sold 330 units of inventory @ $30 each.
4. Incurred $1,700 of operating expenses.
5. Paid income tax at the rate of 30 percent of income before taxes.

Required

a. Set up rows 1 through 10 of the following spreadsheet to compute cost of goods sold and ending inventory, assuming (1) FIFO, (2) LIFO, and (3) weighted-average cost flows. Notice that the FIFO cost flow has already been completed for you. Use columns O through W to complete the LIFO and weighted-average cost flow computations. Be sure to use formulas for all calculations.

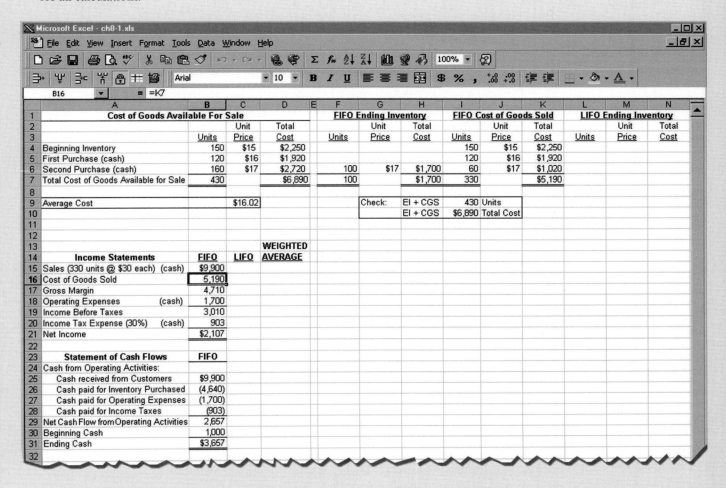

b. In rows 13 through 31, compute the amount of net income and net cash flow from operations under FIFO, LIFO, and weighted average. The FIFO column has been provided as an example.

ATC 5-10   Spreadsheet Assignment   *Mastering Excel*

Required

Complete ATC 5-5 using an Excel spreadsheet. Use Excel problem ATC 5-9 as a resource for structuring the spreadsheet.

COMPREHENSIVE PROBLEM

The trial balance of Pacilio Security Services Inc. as of January 1, 2015, had the following normal balances:

Cash	$62,860
Accounts receivable	20,500
Supplies	150
Prepaid rent	2,000
Merchandise inventory (9 @ $240)	2,160
Land	4,000
Accounts payable	980
Salaries payable	1,500
Common stock	50,000
Retained earnings	39,190

During 2015, Pacilio Security Services experienced the following transactions:

1. Paid the salaries payable from 2014.
2. On January 15, purchased 20 standard alarm systems for cash at a cost of $250 each.
3. On February 1, paid the accounts payable of $980, but not within the discount period. (The company uses the gross method.)
4. On March 1, leased a business van. Paid $4,800 for one year's lease in advance.
5. Paid $7,200 on May 1 for one year's rent on the office in advance.
6. Purchased with cash $500 of supplies to be used over the next several months by the business.
7. Purchased with cash another 25 alarm systems on August 1 for resale at a cost of $260 each.
8. On September 5, purchased on account 30 standard alarm systems at a cost of $265.
9. Installed 60 standard alarm systems for $33,000. $22,000 of the sales were on account and $11,000 were cash sales. (*Note:* Be sure to record cost of goods sold using the perpetual FIFO method.)
10. Made a full refund to a dissatisfied customer who returned her alarm system. The sale had been a cash sale for $550 with a cost of $260.
11. Paid installers and other employees a total of $21,000 cash for salaries.
12. Sold $45,000 of monitoring services during the year. The services are billed to the customers each month.
13. Sold an additional monitoring service for $1,200 for one year's service. The customer paid the full amount of $1,200 on October 1.
14. Collected $74,000 of accounts receivable during the year.
15. Paid an additional $6,000 to settle some of the accounts payable.
16. Paid $3,500 of advertising expense during the year.
17. Paid $2,320 of utilities expense for the year.
18. Paid a dividend of $15,000 to the shareholders.

Adjustments

19. There was $200 of supplies on hand at the end of the year.
20. Recognized the expired rent for both the van and the office building for the year.
21. Recognized the revenue earned from transaction 13.
22. Accrued salaries at December 31, 2015, were $1,000.

Required

a. Record the above transactions in general journal form.
b. Post the transactions to T-accounts.
c. Prepare a trial balance.
d. Prepare an income statement, statement of changes in stockholders' equity, balance sheet, and statement of cash flows.
e. Close the temporary accounts to retained earnings.
f. Post the closing entries to the T-accounts and prepare an after-closing trial balance.

CHAPTER 6

Internal Control and Accounting for Cash

LEARNING OBJECTIVES

After you have mastered the material in this chapter, you will be able to:

LO1 Identify the key elements of a strong system of internal control.

LO2 Identify special internal controls for cash.

LO3 Prepare a bank reconciliation.

LO4 Explain the use of a petty cash fund.

LO5 Describe the auditor's role in financial reporting.

CHAPTER OPENING

To operate successfully, businesses must establish systems of control. How can **Walmart's** upper-level managers ensure that every store will open on time? How can the president of **General Motors** be confident that the company's financial reports fairly reflect the company's operations? How can the owner of a restaurant prevent a waiter from serving food to his friends and relatives without charging them for it? The answer: by exercising effective control over company activities. The policies and procedures used to provide reasonable assurance that the objectives of an enterprise will be accomplished are called **internal controls.**

Internal controls can be divided into two categories: (1) **accounting controls** are designed to safeguard company assets and ensure reliable accounting records; and (2) **administrative controls** are concerned with evaluating performance and assessing the degree of compliance with company policies and public laws.

The Curious Accountant

On December 11, 2008, Bernard Madoff was arrested on suspicion of having defrauded the clients of his investment company, Bernard L. Madoff Investments (BMI), of $50 billion. Later estimates would put the losses at over $60 billion. Although his clients believed the money they sent to BMI was being invested in the stock market, it was actually just being deposited into bank accounts.

Mr. Madoff was accused of operating the largest Ponzi scheme in history. Clients were sent monthly statements falsely showing that their investments were earning income and growing at a steady rate, even when the overall stock market was falling. When individual investors asked to withdraw their funds, they were simply given money that had been deposited by other investors.

This fraudulent system works as long as more new money is being deposited than is being withdrawn. Unfortunately for BMI, with the severe stock-market decline of 2008 too many clients got nervous and asked to withdraw their money, including the gains they believed they had earned over the years. At this point the Ponzi scheme failed.

How could such a pervasive fraud go undetected for so long? (Answer on page 318.)

KEY FEATURES OF INTERNAL CONTROL SYSTEMS

LO 1

Identify the key elements of a strong system of internal control.

During the early 2000s a number of accounting related scandals cost investors billions. In 2001, Enron's share price went from $85 to $0.30 after it was revealed that the company had billions of dollars in losses that were not reported on the financial statements. Several months later, WorldCom reported an $11 billion accounting fraud, which included hundreds of millions in personal loans to then CEO, Bernie Ebbers.

The Enron and WorldCom accounting scandals had such devastating effects that they led Congress to pass the Sarbanes-Oxley Act of 2002 (SOX). SOX requires public companies to evaluate their *internal control* and to publish those findings with their SEC filings. **Internal control** is the process designed to ensure reliable financial reporting, effective and efficient operations, and compliance with applicable laws and regulations. Safeguarding assets against theft and unauthorized use, acquisition, or disposal is also part of internal control.

Section 404 of Sarbanes-Oxley requires a statement of management's responsibility for establishing and maintaining adequate internal control over financial reporting by public companies. This section includes an assessment of the controls and the identification of the framework used for the assessment. The framework established by The Committee of Sponsoring Organizations of the Treadway Commission (COSO) in 1992 is the de facto standard by which SOX compliance is judged. COSO's framework titled *Internal Control—An Integrated Framework* recognizes five interrelated components including:

1. *Control Environment.* The integrity and ethical values of the company, including its code of conduct, involvement of the board of directors, and other actions that set the tone of the organization.

2. *Risk Assessment.* Management's process of identifying potential risks that could result in misstated financial statements and developing actions to address those risks.

3. *Control Activities.* These are the activities usually thought of as "the internal controls." They include such things as segregation of duties, account reconciliations, and information processing controls that are designed to safeguard assets and enable an organization to prepare reliable financial statements in a timely manner.

4. *Information and Communication.* The internal and external reporting process, and includes an assessment of the technology environment.

5. *Monitoring.* Assessing the quality of a company's internal control over time and taking actions as necessary to ensure it continues to address the risks of the organization.

In 2004, COSO updated the framework to help entities design and implement effective enterprise-wide approaches to risk management. The updated document is titled *Enterprise Risk Management (ERM)—An Integrated Framework.* The ERM framework introduces an enterprisewide approach to risk management as well as concepts such as risk appetite, risk tolerance, and portfolio view. While SOX applies only to U.S. public companies, the ERM framework has been adopted by both public and private organizations around the world.

The ERM framework does not replace the internal control framework. Instead, it incorporates the internal control framework within it. Accordingly, companies may decide to look to the ERM framework both to satisfy their internal control needs and to move toward a fuller risk management process.

While a detailed discussion of the COSO documents is beyond the scope of this text, the following overview of the more common *control activities* of the internal control framework is insightful.

Separation of Duties

The likelihood of fraud or theft is reduced if employees must work together to accomplish it. Clear **separation of duties** is frequently used as a deterrent to corruption. When duties are separated, the work of one employee can act as a check on the work of another employee. For example, a person selling seats to a movie may be tempted to steal money received from customers who enter the theater. This temptation is reduced if the person staffing the box office is required to issue tickets that a second employee collects as people enter the theater. If ticket stubs collected by the second employee are compared with the cash receipts from ticket sales, any cash shortages would become apparent. Furthermore, friends and relatives of the ticket agent could not easily enter the theater without paying. Theft or unauthorized entry would require collusion between the ticket agent and the usher who collects the tickets. Both individuals would have to be dishonest enough to steal, yet trustworthy enough to convince each other they would keep the embezzlement secret. Whenever possible, the functions of *authorization, recording,* and *custody of assets* should be performed by separate individuals.

Quality of Employees

A business is only as good as the people it employs. Cheap labor is not a bargain if the employees are incompetent. Employees should be properly trained. In fact, they should be trained to perform a variety of tasks. The ability of employees to substitute for one another prevents disruptions when co-workers are absent because of illnesses, vacations, or other commitments. The capacity to rotate jobs also relieves boredom and increases respect for the contributions of other employees. Every business should strive to maximize the productivity of every employee. Ongoing training programs are essential to a strong system of internal control.

Bonded Employees

The best way to ensure employee honesty is to hire individuals with *high levels of personal integrity.* Employers should screen job applicants using interviews, background checks, and recommendations from prior employers or educators. Even so, screening programs may fail to identify character weaknesses. Further, unusual circumstances may cause honest employees to go astray. Therefore, employees in positions of trust should be bonded. A **fidelity bond** provides insurance that protects a company from losses caused by employee dishonesty.

Required Absences

Employees should be required to take regular vacations and their duties should be rotated periodically. Employees may be able to cover up fraudulent activities if they are always present at work. Consider the case of a parking meter collection agent who covered the same route for several years with no vacation. When the agent became sick, a substitute collected more money each day than the regular reader usually reported. Management checked past records and found that the ill meter reader had been understating the cash receipts and pocketing the difference. If management had required vacations or rotated the routes, the embezzlement would have been discovered much earlier.

Procedures Manual

Appropriate accounting procedures should be documented in a **procedures manual.** The manual should be routinely updated. Periodic reviews should be conducted to ensure that employees are following the procedures outlined in the manual.

Nordstrom, known for its service, empowers its employees to make on-the-spot decisions to satisfy customers.

Authority and Responsibility

Employees are motivated by clear lines of authority and responsibility. They work harder when they have the authority to use their own judgment and they exercise reasonable caution when they are held responsible for their actions. Businesses should prepare an **authority manual** that establishes a definitive *chain of command.* The authority manual should guide both specific and general authorizations. **Specific authorizations** apply to specific positions within the organization. For example, investment decisions are authorized at the division level while hiring decisions are authorized at the departmental level. In contrast, **general authority** applies across different levels of management. For example, employees at all levels may be required to fly economy class or to make purchases from specific vendors.

Prenumbered Documents

How would you know if a check were stolen from your check book? If you keep a record of your check numbers, the missing number would tip you off immediately. Businesses also use prenumbered checks to avoid the unauthorized use of their bank accounts. In fact, prenumbered forms are used for all important documents such as purchase orders, receiving reports, invoices, and checks. To reduce errors, prenumbered forms should be as simple and easy to use as possible. Also, the documents should allow for authorized signatures. For example, credit sales slips should be signed by the customer to clearly establish who made the purchase, reducing the likelihood of unauthorized transactions.

Physical Control

Employees walk away with billions of dollars of business assets each year. To limit losses, companies should establish adequate physical control over valuable assets. For example, inventory should be kept in a storeroom and not released without proper authorization. Serial numbers on equipment should be recorded along with the name of the individual who is responsible for the equipment. Unannounced physical counts should be conducted randomly to verify the presence of company-owned equipment. Certificates of deposit and marketable securities should be kept in fireproof vaults. Access to these vaults should be limited to authorized personnel. These procedures protect the documents from fire and limit access to only those individuals who have the appropriate security clearance to handle the documents.

In addition to safeguarding assets, there should be physical control over the accounting records. The accounting journals, ledgers, and supporting documents should be kept in a fireproof safe. Only personnel responsible for recording transactions in the journals should have access to them. With limited access, there is less chance that someone will change the records to conceal fraud or embezzlement.

Performance Evaluations

Because few people can evaluate their own performance objectively, internal controls should include independent verification of employee performance. For example, someone other than the person who has control over inventory should take a physical count of inventory. Internal and external audits serve as independent verification of performance. Auditors should evaluate the effectiveness of the internal control system as well as verify the accuracy of the accounting records. In addition, the external auditors attest to the company's use of generally accepted accounting principles in the financial statements.

Limitations

A system of internal controls is designed to prevent or detect errors and fraud. However, no control system is foolproof. Internal controls can be circumvented by collusion among employees. Two or more employees working together can hide embezzlement by covering for each other. For example, if an embezzler goes on vacation, fraud will not be reported by a replacement who is in collusion with the embezzler. No system can prevent all fraud. However, a good system of internal controls minimizes illegal or unethical activities by reducing temptation and increasing the likelihood of early detection.

 CHECK YOURSELF 6.1

What are nine features of an internal control system?

Answer   The nine features follow:

1. Separating duties so that fraud or theft requires collusion.
2. Hiring and training competent employees.
3. Bonding employees to recover losses through insurance.
4. Requiring employees to be absent from their jobs so that their replacements can discover errors or fraudulent activity that might have occurred.
5. Establishing proper procedures for processing transactions.
6. Establishing clear lines of authority and responsibility.
7. Using prenumbered documents.
8. Implementing physical controls such as locking cash in a safe.
9. Conducting performance evaluations through independent internal and external audits.

ACCOUNTING FOR CASH

For financial reporting purposes, **cash** generally includes currency and other items that are payable *on demand,* such as checks, money orders, bank drafts, and certain savings accounts. Savings accounts that impose substantial penalties for early withdrawal should be classified as *investments* rather than cash. Postdated checks or IOUs represent *receivables* and should not be included in cash. As illustrated in Exhibit 6.1, most companies combine currency and other payable on demand items in a single balance sheet account with varying titles.

LO 2

Identify special internal controls for cash.

Answers to The Curious Accountant

As this chapter explains, separation of duties is one of the primary features of a good system of internal controls. However, separation of duties is not designed to detect fraud at the very top level of management. Mr. Madoff ran BMI with almost complete control; he had no boss.

Even with a good system of internal controls, there is always some level of trust required in business. Mr. Madoff had an excellent reputation in the investment community. He had even been the president of the NASDAQ. His investors trusted him and assumed they could depend on his independent auditor to detect any major problems with the way BMI was investing, or not investing, their money.

Federal prosecutors believe that BMI's auditor, David Friehling, did very little in the way of properly auditing BMI's books. In fact, on March 18, 2009, he also was arrested and charged with falsely certifying BMI's financial statements.

On March 12, 2009, the 70-year-old Mr. Madoff pled guilty to 11 felony charges. He entered his guilty pleas without the benefit of a plea bargain and was sentenced to 150 years in prison. On Saturday, December 11, 2010, exactly two years after Bernard Madoff's arrest, his oldest son committed suicide. His death was attributed to personal problems related to his father's scandal.

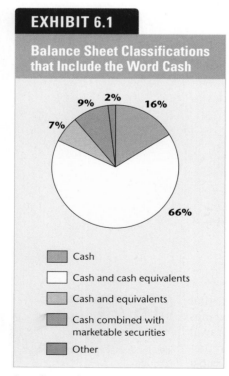

EXHIBIT 6.1

Balance Sheet Classifications that Include the Word Cash

- Cash
- Cash and cash equivalents
- Cash and equivalents
- Cash combined with marketable securities
- Other

Data Source: AICPA, *Accounting Trends and Techniques.*

Companies must maintain a sufficient amount of cash to pay employees, suppliers, and other creditors. When a company fails to pay its legal obligations, its creditors can force the company into bankruptcy. Even so, management should avoid accumulating more cash than is needed. The failure to invest excess cash in earning assets reduces profitability. Cash inflows and outflows must be managed to prevent a shortage or surplus of cash.

Controlling Cash

Controlling cash, more than any other asset, requires strict adherence to internal control procedures. Cash has universal appeal. A relatively small suitcase filled with high-denomination currency can represent significant value. Furthermore, the rightful owner of currency is difficult to prove. In most cases, possession constitutes ownership. As a result, cash is highly susceptible to theft and must be carefully protected. Cash is most susceptible to embezzlement when it is received or disbursed. The following controls should be employed to reduce the likelihood of theft.

Cash Receipts

A record of all cash collections should be prepared immediately upon receipt. The amount of cash on hand should be counted regularly. Missing amounts of money can be detected by comparing the actual cash on hand with the book balance. Employees who receive cash should give customers a copy of a written receipt. Customers usually review their receipts to ensure they have gotten credit for the amount paid and call any errors to the receipts clerk's attention. This not only reduces errors but also provides a control on the clerk's honesty. Cash receipts should be deposited in a bank on a timely

REALITY BYTES

THE COST OF PROTECTING CASH

Could you afford to buy a safe like the one shown here? The vault is only one of many expensive security devices used by banks to safeguard cash. By using checking accounts, companies are able to avoid many of the costs associated with keeping cash safe. In addition to providing physical control, checking accounts enable companies to maintain a written audit trail of cash receipts and payments. Checking accounts represent the most widely used internal control device in modern society. It is difficult to imagine a business operating without the use of checking accounts.

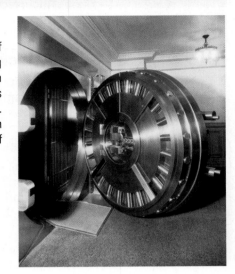

basis. Cash collected late in the day should be deposited in a night depository. Every effort should be made to minimize the amount of cash on hand. Keeping large amounts of cash on hand not only increases the risk of loss from theft but also places employees in danger of being harmed by criminals who may be tempted to rob the company.

Cash Payments

To effectively control cash, a company should make all disbursements using checks, thereby providing a record of cash payments. All checks should be prenumbered, and unused checks should be locked up. Using prenumbered checks allows companies to easily identify lost or stolen checks by comparing the numbers on unused and canceled checks with the numbers used for legitimate disbursements.

The duties of approving disbursements, signing checks, and recording transactions should be separated. If one person is authorized to approve, sign, and record checks, he or she could falsify supporting documents, write an unauthorized check, and record a cover-up transaction in the accounting records. By separating these duties, the check signer reviews the documentation provided by the approving individual before signing the check. Likewise, the recording clerk reviews the work of both the approving person and the check signer when the disbursement is recorded in the accounting records. Thus writing unauthorized checks requires trilevel collusion.

Supporting documents with authorized approval signatures should be required when checks are presented to the check signer. For example, a warehouse receiving order should be matched with a purchase order before a check is approved to pay a bill from a supplier. Before payments are approved, invoice amounts should be checked and payees verified as valid vendors. Matching supporting documents with proper authorization discourages employees from creating phony documents for a disbursement to a friend or fictitious business. Also, the approval process serves as a check on the accuracy of the work of all employees involved.

Supporting documents should be marked *Paid* when the check is signed. If the documents are not indelibly marked, they could be retrieved from the files and resubmitted for a duplicate, unauthorized payment. A payables clerk could collude with the payee to split extra cash paid out by submitting the same supporting documents for a second payment.

All spoiled and voided checks should be defaced and retained. If defaced checks are not retained, an employee could steal a check and then claim that it was written incorrectly and thrown away. The clerk could then use the stolen check to make an unauthorized payment.

Checking Account Documents

The previous section explained the need for businesses to use checking accounts. A description of four main types of forms associated with a bank checking account follows:

Signature Card

A bank **signature card** shows the bank account number and the signatures of the people authorized to sign checks. The card is retained in the bank's files. If a bank employee is unfamiliar with the signature on a check, he or she can refer to the signature card to verify the signature before cashing the check.

Deposit Ticket

Each deposit of cash or checks is accompanied by a **deposit ticket,** which normally identifies the account number and the name of the account. The depositor lists the individual amounts of currency, coins, and checks, as well as the total deposited, on the deposit ticket.

Bank Check

A written check affects three parties: (1) the person or business writing the check (the *payer*); (2) the bank on which the check is drawn; and (3) the person or business to whom the check is payable (the *payee*). Companies often write **checks** using multicopy, prenumbered forms, with the name of the issuing business preprinted on the face of each check. A remittance notice is usually attached to the check forms. This portion of the form provides the issuer space to record what the check is for (e.g., what invoices are being paid), the amount being disbursed, and the date of payment. When signed by the person whose signature is on the signature card, the check authorizes the bank to transfer the face amount of the check from the payer's account to the payee.

Bank Statement

Periodically, the bank sends the depositor a **bank statement.** The bank statement is presented from the bank's point of view. Checking accounts are liabilities to a bank because the bank is obligated to pay back the money that customers have deposited in their accounts. Therefore, in the bank's accounting records a customer's checking account has a *credit* balance. As a result, **bank statement debit memos** describe transactions that reduce the customer's account balance (the bank's liability). **Bank statement credit memos** describe activities that increase the customer's account balance (the bank's liability). Since a checking account is an asset (cash) to the depositor, a *bank statement debit memo* requires a *credit entry* to the Cash account on the depositor's books. Likewise, when a bank tells you that it has credited your account, you will debit your Cash account in response.

Bank statements normally report (a) the balance of the account at the beginning of the period; (b) additions for customer deposits made during the period; (c) other additions described in credit memos (e.g., for interest earned); (d) subtractions for the payment of checks drawn on the account during the period; (e) other subtractions described in debit memos (e.g., for service charges); (f) a running balance of the account; and (g) the balance of the account at the end of the period. The sample bank statement in Exhibit 6.2 illustrates these items with references to the preceding letters in parentheses. Normally, the canceled checks or copies of them are enclosed with the bank statement.

EXHIBIT 6.2

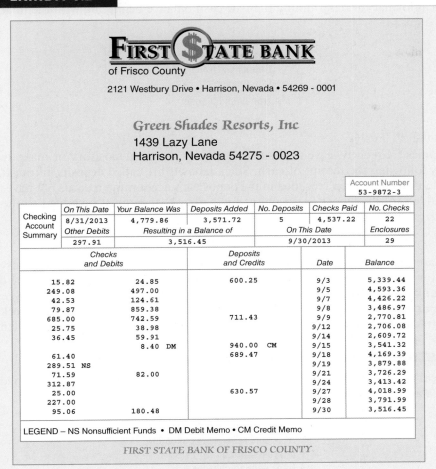

FIRST STATE BANK
of Frisco County

2121 Westbury Drive • Harrison, Nevada • 54269 - 0001

Green Shades Resorts, Inc
1439 Lazy Lane
Harrison, Nevada 54275 - 0023

Account Number
53-9872-3

Checking Account Summary	On This Date	Your Balance Was	Deposits Added	No. Deposits	Checks Paid	No. Checks
	8/31/2013	4,779.86	3,571.72	5	4,537.22	22
	Other Debits	Resulting in a Balance of			On This Date	Enclosures
	297.91	3,516.45			9/30/2013	29

Checks and Debits		Deposits and Credits	Date	Balance
15.82	24.85	600.25	9/3	5,339.44
249.08	497.00		9/5	4,593.36
42.53	124.61		9/7	4,426.22
79.87	859.38		9/8	3,486.97
685.00	742.59	711.43	9/9	2,770.81
25.75	38.98		9/12	2,706.08
36.45	59.91		9/14	2,609.72
	8.40 DM	940.00 CM	9/15	3,541.32
61.40		689.47	9/18	4,169.39
289.51 NS			9/19	3,879.88
71.59	82.00		9/21	3,726.29
312.87			9/24	3,413.42
25.00		630.57	9/27	4,018.99
227.00			9/28	3,791.99
95.06	180.48		9/30	3,516.45

LEGEND – NS Nonsufficient Funds • DM Debit Memo • CM Credit Memo

FIRST STATE BANK OF FRISCO COUNTY

RECONCILING THE BANK ACCOUNT

Usually the ending balance reported on the bank statement differs from the balance in the depositor's Cash account as of the same date. The discrepancy is normally attributable to timing differences. For example, a depositor deducts the amount of a check from its Cash account when it writes the check. However, the bank does not deduct the amount of the check from the depositor's account until the payee presents it for payment, which may be days, weeks, or even months after the check is written. As a result, the balance on the depositor's books is lower than the balance on the bank's books. Companies prepare a **bank reconciliation** to explain the differences between the cash balance reported on the bank statement and the cash balance recorded in the depositor's accounting records.

LO 3

Prepare a bank reconciliation.

Determining True Cash Balance

A bank reconciliation normally begins with the cash balance reported by the bank, which is called the **unadjusted bank balance.** The adjustments necessary to determine the amount of cash that the depositor actually owns as of the date of the bank statement are then added to and subtracted from the unadjusted bank balance. The final total is the **true cash balance.** The true cash balance is independently reached a second time by making adjustments to the **unadjusted book balance.** The bank account is reconciled when the true cash balance determined from the perspective of the unadjusted *bank* balance agrees with the true cash balance determined from the perspective of the unadjusted *book* balance. The procedures a company uses to determine the *true cash balance* from the two different perspectives are outlined here.

Adjustments to the Bank Balance

A typical format for determining the true cash balance beginning with the unadjusted bank balance is

```
  Unadjusted bank balance
+ Deposits in transit
- Outstanding checks
= True cash balance
```

Deposits in Transit

Companies frequently leave deposits in the bank's night depository or make them on the day following the receipt of cash. Such deposits are called **deposits in transit.** Since these deposits have been recorded in the depositor's accounting records but have not yet been added to the depositor's account by the bank, they must be added to the unadjusted bank balance.

Outstanding Checks

These are disbursements that have been properly recorded as cash deductions on the depositor's books. However, the bank has not deducted the amounts from the depositor's bank account because the checks have not yet been presented by the payee to the bank for payment; that is, the checks have not cleared the bank. **Outstanding checks** must be subtracted from the unadjusted bank balance to determine the true cash balance.

Adjustments to the Book Balance

A typical format for determining the true cash balance beginning with the unadjusted book balance is as follows:

```
  Unadjusted book balance
+ Accounts receivable collections
+ Interest earned
- Bank service charges
- Non-sufficient-funds (NSF) checks
= True cash balance
```

Accounts Receivable Collections

To collect cash as quickly as possible, many companies have their customers send payments directly to the bank. The bank adds the collection directly to the depositor's account and notifies the depositor about the collection through a credit memo that is included on the bank statement. The depositor adds the amount of the cash collections to the unadjusted book balance in the process of determining the true cash balance.

Interest Earned

Banks pay interest on certain checking accounts. The amount of the interest is added directly to the depositor's bank account. The bank notifies the depositor about the interest through a credit memo that is included on the bank statement. The depositor adds the amount of the interest revenue to the unadjusted book balance in the process of determining the true cash balance.

Service Charges

Banks frequently charge depositors fees for services performed. They may also charge a penalty if the depositor fails to maintain a specified minimum cash balance throughout the period. Banks deduct such fees and penalties directly from the depositor's account and advise the depositor of the deduction through a debit memo that is included on the bank statement. The depositor deducts such **service charges** from the unadjusted book balance to determine the true cash balance.

Non-Sufficient-Funds (NSF) Checks

Non-sufficient-funds (NSF) checks are checks that a company obtains from its customers and deposits in its checking account. However, when the checks are submitted to the customers' banks for payment, the banks refuse payment because there is insufficient money in the customers' accounts. When such checks are returned, the amounts of the checks are deducted from the company's bank account balance. The company is advised of NSF checks through debit memos that appear on the bank statement. The depositor deducts the amounts of the NSF checks from the unadjusted book balance in the process of determining the true cash balance.

Correction of Errors

In the course of reconciling the bank statement with the Cash account, the depositor may discover errors in the bank's records, the depositor's records, or both. If an error is found on the bank statement, an adjustment for it is made to the unadjusted bank balance to determine the true cash balance, and the bank should be notified immediately to correct its records. Errors made by the depositor require adjustments to the book balance to arrive at the true cash balance.

Certified Checks

A **certified check** is guaranteed for payment by a bank. Whereas a regular check is deducted from the customer's account when it is presented for payment, a certified check is deducted from the customer's account when the bank certifies that the check is good. Certified checks, therefore, *have* been deducted by the bank in determining the unadjusted bank balance, whether they have cleared the bank or remain outstanding as of the date of the bank statement. Since certified checks are deducted both from bank and depositor records immediately, they do not cause differences between the depositor and bank balances. As a result, certified checks are not included in a bank reconciliation.

Illustrating a Bank Reconciliation

The following example illustrates preparing the bank reconciliation for Green Shades Resorts, Inc. (GSRI). The bank statement for GSRI is displayed in Exhibit 6.2. Exhibit 6.3 illustrates the completed bank reconciliation. The items on the reconciliation are described on the next page.

Adjustments to the Bank Balance

As of September 30, 2013, the bank statement showed an unadjusted balance of $3,516.45. A review of the bank statement disclosed three adjustments that had to be made to the unadjusted bank balance to determine GSRI's true cash balance.

1. Comparing the deposits on the bank statement with deposits recorded in GSRI's accounting records indicated there was $724.11 of deposits in transit.

2. An examination of the returned checks disclosed that the bank had erroneously deducted a $25 check written by Green Valley Resorts from GSRI's bank account. This amount must be added back to the unadjusted bank balance to determine the true cash balance.

3. The checks returned with the bank statement were sorted and compared to the cash records. Three checks with amounts totaling $235.25 were outstanding.

After these adjustment are made GSRI's true cash balance is determined to be $4,030.31.

EXHIBIT 6.3

GREEN SHADES RESORTS, INC.
Bank Reconciliation
September 30, 2013

Unadjusted bank balance, September 30, 2013			$3,516.45
Add: Deposits in transit			724.11
Bank error: Check drawn on Green Valley Resorts charged to GSRI			25.00
Less: Outstanding checks			

Check No.	Date	Amount
639	Sept. 18	$ 13.75
646	Sept. 20	29.00
672	Sept. 27	192.50

Total	(235.25)
True cash balance, September 30, 2013	$4,030.31
Unadjusted book balance, September 30, 2013	$3,361.22
Add: Receivable collected by bank	940.00
Error made by accountant (Check no. 633 recorded as $63.45 instead of $36.45)	27.00
Less: Bank service charges	(8.40)
NSF check	(289.51)
True cash balance, September 30, 2013	$4,030.31

Adjustments to the Book Balance

As indicated in Exhibit 6.3, GSRI's unadjusted book balance as of September 30, 2013, was $3,361.22. This balance differs from GSRI's true cash balance because of four unrecorded accounting events:

1. The bank collected a $940 account receivable for GSRI.
2. GSRI's accountant made a $27 recording error.
3. The bank charged GSRI an $8.40 service fee.
4. GSRI had deposited a $289.51 check from a customer who did not have sufficient funds to cover the check.

Two of these four adjustments increase the unadjusted cash balance. The other two decrease the unadjusted cash balance. After the adjustments have been recorded, the Cash account reflects the true cash balance of $4,030.31 ($3,361.22 unadjusted cash balance + $940.00 receivable collection + $27.00 recording error − $8.40 service charge − $289.51 NSF check). Since the true balance determined from the perspective of the bank statement agrees with the true balance determined from the perspective of GSRI's books, the bank statement has been successfully reconciled with the accounting records.

Updating GSRI's Accounting Records

Each of the adjustments to the book balance must be recorded in GSRI's financial records. The effects of each adjustment on the financial statements are as follows.

ADJUSTMENT 1   Recording the $940 receivable collection increases Cash and reduces Accounts Receivable.

The event is an asset exchange transaction. The journal entry and its effects on the financial statements are shown here:

Account Title	Debit	Credit
Cash	940.00	
Accounts Receivable		940.00

Assets		= Liab. + Equity			Rev.	–	Exp.	=	Net Inc.	Cash Flow
Cash	+ Accts. Rec.									
940.00	+ (940.00)	= NA	+	NA	NA	–	NA	=	NA	940.00 OA

ADJUSTMENT 2 Assume the $27 recording error occurred because GSRI's accountant accidentally transposed two numbers when recording check no. 633 for utilities expense.

The check was written to pay utilities expense of $36.45 but was recorded as a $63.45 disbursement. Since cash payments are overstated by $27.00 ($63.45 − $36.45), this amount must be added back to GSRI's Cash balance and deducted from the Utilities Expense account, which increases net income. The journal entry and its effects on the financial statements are shown here:

Account Title	Debit	Credit
Cash	27.00	
Utilities Expense		27.00

Assets	=	Liab.	+	Equity	Rev.	–	Exp.	=	Net Inc.	Cash Flow
Cash	=			Ret. Earn.						
27.00	=	NA	+	27.00	NA	–	(27.00)	=	27.00	27.00 OA

ADJUSTMENT 3 The $8.40 service charge is an expense that reduces assets, stockholders' equity, net income, and cash.

The journal entry and its effects on the financial statements are shown here:

Account Title	Debit	Credit
Bank Service Charge Expense	8.40	
Cash		8.40

Assets	=	Liab.	+	Equity	Rev.	–	Exp.	=	Net Inc.	Cash Flow
Cash	=			Ret. Earn.						
(8.40)	=	NA	+	(8.40)	NA	–	8.40	=	(8.40)	(8.40) OA

ADJUSTMENT 4 The $289.51 NSF check reduces GSRI's cash balance.

When it originally accepted the customer's check, GSRI increased its Cash account. Since there is not enough money in the customer's bank account to pay the check, GSRI didn't actually receive cash so GSRI must reduce its Cash account. GSRI will still try to collect the money from the customer. In the meantime, it will show the amount of the NSF check as an account receivable. The adjusting entry to record the NSF check is an asset exchange transaction. Cash decreases and Accounts

Receivable increases. The journal entry and its effects on the financial statements are shown here:

Account Title	Debit	Credit
Accounts Receivable	289.51	
Cash		289.51

Assets			= Liab.	+ Equity	Rev.	− Exp.	= Net Inc.	Cash Flow	
Cash	+	Accts. Rec.							
(289.51)	+	289.51	= NA	+ NA	NA	− NA	= NA	(289.51)	OA

Cash Short and Over

Sometimes employees make mistakes when collecting cash from or making change for customers. When such errors occur, the amount of money in the cash register will not agree with the amount of cash receipts recorded on the cash register tape. For example, suppose that when a customer paid for $17.95 of merchandise with a $20 bill, the sales clerk returned $3.05 in change instead of $2.05. If, at the end of the day, the cash register tape shows total receipts of $487.50, the cash drawer would contain only $486.50. The actual cash balance is less than the expected cash balance by $1. Any shortage of cash or excess of cash is recorded in a special account called **Cash Short and Over.** In this example, the shortage is recorded with the following journal entry:

Account Title	Debit	Credit
Cash	486.50	
Cash Short and Over	1.00	
Sales		487.50

A cash shortage is an expense. It is recorded by debiting the Cash Short and Over account. An overage of cash represents revenue and is recorded by crediting the Cash Short and Over account. As with other expense and revenue items, the balance of the Cash Short and Over account is closed to the Retained Earnings account at the end of the accounting period.

✓ CHECK YOURSELF 6.2

The following information was drawn from Reliance Company's October bank statement. The unadjusted bank balance on October 31 was $2,300. The statement showed that the bank had collected a $200 account receivable for Reliance. The statement also included $20 of bank service charges for October and a $100 check payable to Reliance that was returned NSF. A comparison of the bank statement with company accounting records indicates that there was a $500 deposit in transit and $1,800 of checks outstanding at the end of the month. Based on this information, determine the true cash balance on October 31.

Answer Since the unadjusted book balance is not given, start with the unadjusted bank balance to determine the true cash balance. The collection of the receivable, the bank service charges, and the NSF check are already recognized in the unadjusted bank balance, so these items are not used to determine the true cash balance. Determine the true cash balance by adding the deposit in transit to and subtracting the outstanding checks from the unadjusted bank balance. The true cash balance is $1,000 ($2,300 unadjusted bank balance + $500 deposit in transit − $1,800 outstanding checks).

USING PETTY CASH FUNDS

Although businesses use checks for most disbursements, they often pay for small items such as postage, delivery charges, taxi fares, employees' supper money, and so on with currency. They frequently establish a **petty cash fund** to maintain effective control over these small cash disbursements. The fund is established for a specified dollar amount, such as $300, and is controlled by one employee, called the *petty cash custodian.*

Petty cash funds are usually maintained on an **imprest basis,** which means that the money disbursed is periodically replenished. The fund is created by drawing a check on the regular checking account, cashing it, and giving the currency to the petty cash custodian. The custodian normally keeps the currency under lock and key. The amount of the petty cash fund depends on what it is used for, how often it is used, and how often it is replenished. It should be large enough to handle disbursements for a reasonable time period, such as several weeks or a month.

Establishing a petty cash fund merely transfers money from a bank to a safety box inside the company offices. The establishment is an asset exchange event. The Cash account decreases, and an account called Petty Cash increases. The journal entry and its effects on the financial statements are shown here:

LO 4

Explain the use of a petty cash fund.

Account Title	Debit	Credit
Petty Cash	300.00	
Cash		300.00

Assets			=	Liab.	+	Equity	Rev.	−	Exp.	=	Net Inc.	Cash Flow
Cash	+	Petty Cash										
(300.00)	+	300.00	=	NA	+	NA	NA	−	NA	=	NA	NA

When money is disbursed from the petty cash fund, the custodian should complete a **petty cash voucher,** such as the one in Exhibit 6.4. Any supporting documents, such as an invoice, restaurant bill, or parking fee receipt, should be attached to the petty cash voucher. The person who receives the currency should sign the voucher as evidence of receiving the money. The total of the amounts recorded on the petty cash vouchers plus the remaining coins and currency should equal the balance of the petty cash ledger account. *No journal entry is made in the accounting records when petty cash funds are disbursed.* The effects on the financial statements are recorded when the petty cash fund is replenished (when additional currency is put into the petty cash safety box).

When the amount of currency in the petty cash fund is relatively low, the fund is replenished. The petty cash vouchers are totaled, the amount of any cash short or over is determined, and a check is issued to the bank to obtain the currency needed to return

EXHIBIT 6.4

Petty cash voucher no. _____

To: _____   Date _____, 20_____

Explanation: Account No. _____   Amount _____

Approved by _____   Received by _____

the fund to its imprest balance. For example, suppose the $300 petty cash fund is replenished when the total of the petty cash vouchers is $216. The vouchers can be classified according to different types of expenses or listed in total as miscellaneous expense. Assuming the company classifies petty cash expenditures as miscellaneous expense, the journal entries to record replenishing the fund are as follows:

Account Title	Debit	Credit
Miscellaneous Expense	216.00	
Petty Cash		216.00
To record expenses paid from the petty cash fund		
Petty Cash	216.00	
Cash		216.00
To replenish the petty cash fund		

If desired, the effect of the entries could be recorded more efficiently. Since the credit to the Petty Cash account is offset by a debit to the same account, a single entry debiting miscellaneous expense and crediting cash would have the same effect on the accounts. The entry more frequently used in practice to record replenishing petty cash is:

Account Title	Debit	Credit
Miscellaneous Expense	216.00	
Cash		216.00

The replenishment affects the financial statements in the same manner as any other cash expense. It reduces assets, stockholders' equity, net income, and cash flow, as follows:

Assets	=	Liab.	+	Equity	Rev.	−	Exp.	=	Net Inc.	Cash Flow	
Cash	=			Ret. Earn.							
(216.00)	=	NA	+	(216.00)	NA	−	216.00	=	(216.00)	(216.00)	OA

If management desires more detailed information about petty cash expenditures, the vouchers can be sorted into postage, $66; delivery charges, $78.40; taxi fares, $28; and supper money, $43.60, in which case the journal entry to replenish the fund could be recorded as follows:

Account Title	Debit	Credit
Postage Expense	66.00	
Delivery Expense	78.40	
Taxi Fares Expense	28.00	
Employee Meal Expense	43.60	
Cash		216.00

Once the vouchers are checked, the fund replenished, and the journal entry recorded, the vouchers should be indelibly marked *Paid* so they cannot be reused.

Sometimes, cash shortages and overages are discovered when the money in the petty cash fund is physically counted. Suppose that a physical count discloses $212.30 in petty cash vouchers and only $87 in currency and coins. Assuming an imprest petty cash balance of $300, the journal entry necessary to replenish the fund is as follows:

Account Title	Debit	Credit
Miscellaneous Expense	212.30	
Cash Short and Over	.70	
Cash		213.00
To replenish the petty cash fund		

If cash shortages or overages do not occur frequently and are of insignificant amounts, companies are likely to include them in miscellaneous expense or miscellaneous revenue.

CHECK YOURSELF 6.3

Cornerstone Corporation established a $400 petty cash fund that was replenished when it contained $30 of currency and coins and $378 of receipts for miscellaneous expenses. Based on this information, determine the amount of cash short or over to be recognized. Explain how the shortage or overage would be reported in the financial statements. Also determine the amount of petty cash expenses that were recognized when the fund was replenished.

Answer   The fund contained $408 of currency and receipts ($30 currency + $378 of receipts), resulting in a cash overage of $8 ($408 − $400). The overage would be reported as miscellaneous revenue on the income statement. The amount of petty cash expenses recognized would equal the amount of the expense receipts, which is $378.

- -

THE FINANCIAL ANALYST

Companies communicate information to analysts and other users through a document called the *annual report*. These reports are usually printed in color on high quality paper and contain lots of photographs. However, in an effort to reduce cost, some companies issue their annual reports in black and white on low grade paper or in electronic form. A company's annual report contains much more than the financial statements. Annual reports often have 40 or more pages. The financial statements require only four to six pages. What is printed on all those other pages? In general, the annual report of a large company has four major sections: (1) financial statements, (2) notes to the financial statements, (3) management's discussion and analysis, and (4) auditors' report. The notes and management's discussion and analysis make up the bulk of the report.

- -

NOTES TO THE FINANCIAL STATEMENTS

Accountants frequently have to make estimates when preparing financial statements. Also, GAAP may offer alternative ways of reporting certain transactions. **Notes to the financial statements** explain some of the estimates that were made as well as which reporting options were used. Reading the notes is critical to understanding the financial statements. The financial statements often include a caveat such as "the accompanying notes are an integral part of these financial statements."

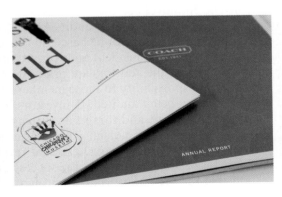

MANAGEMENT'S DISCUSSION AND ANALYSIS

Management's discussion and analysis (MD&A) is usually located at the beginning of the annual report. MD&A is the section of the annual report in which management explains the company's past performance and future plans. For example, MD&A typically compares current year earnings with those of past periods and explains the reasons for significant changes. If the company is planning significant acquisitions of assets or other businesses, this information is usually included in MD&A. Likewise, any plans to discontinue part of the existing business are outlined in MD&A.

ROLE OF THE INDEPENDENT AUDITOR

LO 5

Describe the auditor's role in financial reporting.

As previously explained, financial statements are prepared in accordance with certain rules called *generally accepted accounting principles (GAAP)*. Thus, when General Electric publishes its financial statements, it is saying, "here are our financial statements prepared according to GAAP." How can a financial analyst know that a company really did follow GAAP? Analysts and other statement users rely on **audits** conducted by **certified public accountants (CPAs).**

The primary roles of an independent auditor (CPA) are summarized below:

1. Conducts a financial audit (a detailed examination of a company's financial statements and underlying accounting records).

2. Assumes both legal and professional responsibilities to the public as well as to the company paying the auditor.

3. Determines if financial statements are *materially* correct rather than *absolutely* correct.

4. Presents conclusions in an audit report that includes an opinion as to whether the statements are prepared in conformity with GAAP. In rare cases, the auditor issues a disclaimer.

5. Maintains professional confidentiality of client records. The auditor is not, however, exempt from legal obligations such as testifying in court.

The Financial Statements Audit

What is an audit? There are several different types of audits. The type most relevant to this course is a **financial statements audit.** The financial audit is a detailed examination of a company's financial statements and the documents that support those statements. It also tests the reliability of the accounting system used to produce the financial reports. A financial audit is conducted by an **independent auditor** who must be a CPA.

The term *independent auditor* typically refers to a *firm* of certified public accountants. CPAs are licensed by state governments to provide services to the public. They are to be independent of the companies they audit. To help assure independence, CPAs may not be employees of the companies they audit. Further, they cannot have investments in the companies they audit. Although CPAs are paid by the companies they audit, the audit fee may not be based on the outcome of the audit.

Although the independent auditors are chosen by, paid by, and can be fired by their client companies, the auditors are primarily responsible to *the public.* In fact, auditors have a legal responsibility to those members of the public who have a financial interest in the company being audited. If investors in a company lose money, they sometimes sue the independent auditors in an attempt to recover their losses, especially if the losses were related to financial failure. A lawsuit against auditors will succeed only if the auditors failed in their professional responsibilities when conducting the audit. Auditors are not responsible for the success or failure of a company. Instead, they are responsible for the appropriate auditing of the reporting of that success or failure.

While recent debacles such as Bernard Madoff Investments produce spectacular headlines, auditors are actually not sued very often, considering the number of audits they perform.

Materiality and Financial Statements Audits

Auditors do not guarantee that financial statements are absolutely correct—only that they are *materially* correct. This is where things get a little fuzzy. What is a *material error?* The concept of materiality is very subjective. If Walmart inadvertently overstated its sales by $1 million, would this be material? In its 2011 fiscal-year, Walmart had approximately $419 billion of sales! A $1 million error in computing sales at Walmart is like a $1 error in computing the pay of a person who makes $419,000 per year—not material at all! An error, or other reporting problem, is **material** if knowing about it would influence the decisions of an *average prudent investor.*

Financial audits are not directed toward the discovery of fraud. Auditors are, however, responsible for providing *reasonable assurance* that statements are free from material misstatements, whether caused by errors or fraud. Also, auditors are responsible for evaluating whether internal control procedures are in place to help prevent fraud. If fraud is widespread in a company, normal audit procedures should detect it.

Accounting majors take at least one and often two or more courses in auditing to understand how to conduct an audit. An explanation of auditing techniques is beyond the scope of this course, but at least be aware that auditors do not review how the company accounted for every transaction. Along with other methods, auditors use statistics to choose representative samples of transactions to examine.

Types of Audit Opinions

Once an audit is complete, the auditors present their conclusions in a report that includes an *audit opinion.* There are three basic types of audit opinions.

An **unqualified opinion,** despite its negative-sounding name, is the most favorable opinion auditors can express. It means the auditor believes the financial statements are in compliance with GAAP without qualification, reservation, or exception. Most audits result in unqualified opinions because companies correct any material reporting deficiencies the auditors find before the financial statements are released.

The most negative report an auditor can issue is an **adverse opinion.** An adverse opinion means that one or more departures from GAAP are so material the financial statements do not present a fair picture of the company's status. The auditor's report explains the unacceptable accounting practice(s) that resulted in the adverse opinion being issued. Adverse opinions are very rare because public companies are required by law to follow GAAP.

A **qualified opinion** falls between an unqualified and an adverse opinion. A qualified opinion means that for the most part, the company's financial statements are in compliance with GAAP, but the auditors have reservations about something in the statements. The auditors' report explains why the opinion is qualified. A qualified opinion usually does not imply a serious accounting problem, but users should read the auditors' report and draw their own conclusions.

If an auditor is unable to perform the audit procedures necessary to determine whether the statements are prepared in accordance with GAAP, the auditor cannot issue an opinion on the financial statements. Instead, the auditor issues a **disclaimer of opinion.** A disclaimer is neither negative nor positive. It simply means that the auditor is unable to obtain enough information to confirm compliance with GAAP.

Regardless of the type of report they issue, auditors are only expressing their judgment about whether the financial statements present a fair picture of a company. They do not provide opinions regarding the investment quality of a company.

The ultimate responsibility for financial statements rests with the executives of the reporting company. Just like auditors, management can be sued by investors who believe they lost money due to improper financial reporting. This is one reason all business persons should understand accounting fundamentals.

Confidentiality

The **confidentiality** rules in the code of ethics for CPAs prohibits auditors from *voluntarily disclosing* information they have acquired as a result of their accountant-client relationships. However, accountants may be required to testify in a court of law. In general, federal law does not recognize an accountant-client privilege as it does with attorneys and clergy. Some federal courts have taken exception to this position, especially as it applies to tax cases. State law varies with respect to accountant-client privilege. Furthermore, if auditors terminate a client relationship because of ethical or legal disagreements and they are subsequently contacted by a successor auditor, they may be required to inform the successor of the reasons for the termination. In addition, auditors must consider the particular circumstances of a case when assessing the appropriateness of disclosing confidential information. Given the diverse legal positions governing accountant-client confidentiality, auditors should seek legal counsel prior to disclosing any information obtained in an accountant-client relationship.

To illustrate, assume that Joe Smith, CPA, discovers that his client Jane Doe is misrepresenting information reported in her financial statements. Smith tries to convince Doe to correct the misrepresentations, but she refuses to do so. Smith is required by the code of ethics to terminate his relationship with Doe. However, Smith is not permitted to disclose Doe's dishonest reporting practices unless he is called on to testify in a legal hearing or to respond to an inquiry by Doe's successor accountant.

With respect to the discovery of significant fraud, the auditor is required to inform management at least one level above the position of the employee who is engaged in the fraud and to notify the board of directors of the company. Suppose that Joe Smith, CPA, discovers that Jane Doe, employee of Western Company, is embezzling money from Western. Smith is required to inform Doe's supervisor and to notify Western's board of directors. However, Smith is prohibited from publicly disclosing the fraud.

THE SECURITIES AND EXCHANGE COMMISSION

The annual reports of public companies often differ from those of private companies because public companies are registered with the **Securities and Exchange Commission (SEC).** Public companies, sometimes called SEC companies, have to follow the reporting rules of the SEC as well as GAAP. SEC rules require some additional disclosures not required by GAAP. For example, an MD&A section is required by the SEC, but not by GAAP. As a result, annual reports of non-SEC companies usually do not include MD&A.

The SEC is a government agency authorized to establish and enforce the accounting rules for public companies. Although the SEC can overrule GAAP, it has very seldom done so. Recall that GAAP is established by the Financial Accounting Standards Board, a private professional accounting organization. While SEC rules seldom conflict with GAAP, they frequently require additional disclosures. All companies whose stock trades on public stock exchanges, and some whose do not, are required to register with the SEC. The SEC has no jurisdiction over non-SEC companies.

SEC companies must file specific information directly with the SEC annually, quarterly, and in-between if required. The most common reports are filed on Form 10-K (annually) and Form 10-Q (quarterly). The *10-Q*s are less detailed than the 10-Ks. While there is significant overlap between the 10-Ks (SEC report) and the annual reports that companies issue directly to the public, the 10-Ks usually contain more information but fewer photographs. Most of the reports filed with the SEC are available electronically through the SEC's EDGAR database. EDGAR is an acronym for Electronic Data Gathering, Analysis, and Retrieval system, and it is accessible through the World Wide Web on the Internet. Appendix A provides instructions for using EDGAR.

REALITY BYTES

The Curious Accountant for this chapter gives the story of the Ponzi scheme run by Bernard Madoff. It also noted that his auditor was arrested for falsely certifying the financial statements of Mr. Madoff's company. It is worth noting that the auditor was not charged with participating in the fraud, but of providing faulty audits. The specific complaints against the auditor were that (1) he did not verify that the investments Mr. Madoff claimed to have made actually existed; (2) he did not review the activity in the firm's primary checking account; and (3) the auditor and his family had investments with Mr. Madoff. Having investments with an audit client is a clear violation of the conflict of interest rules. Based on the information publicly available about the Madoff case, it seems any reasonably competent audit would have detected problems before so much money was lost.

In this case what appears to be an incompetent audit, coupled with a dishonest investment manager, cost thousands of clients billions of dollars. Many of Mr. Madoff's clients lost their entire life's saving and virtually all of their retirement income. Although auditors usually practice their profession unseen by the public, the results of their efforts can be almost unimaginably important to investors. In November 2009, the auditor, David Friehling, pled guilty to nine criminal charges and agreed to cooperate with investigators.

The SEC regulates audit standards as well as financial reporting. Prior to passage of the Sarbanes-Oxley Act in July 2002, the SEC left much of the regulation and oversight of independent auditors to the American Institute of Certified Public Accountants, a private professional organization. However, a key provision of Sarbanes-Oxley establishes the Public Company Accounting Oversight Board (PCAOB). This board assumes the primary responsibility for establishing and enforcing auditing standards for CPA firms that audit SEC companies. The board has five financially astute members, three of whom cannot be CPAs.

A Look Back

The policies and procedures used to provide reasonable assurance that the objectives of an enterprise will be accomplished are called *internal controls,* which can be subdivided into two categories: accounting controls and administrative controls. *Accounting controls* are composed of procedures designed to safeguard the assets and ensure that the accounting records contain reliable information. *Administrative controls* are designed to evaluate performance and the degree of compliance with company policies and public laws. While the mechanics of internal control systems vary from company to company, the more prevalent features include the following:

1. *Separation of duties.* Whenever possible, the functions of authorization, recording, and custody should be exercised by different individuals.

2. *Quality of employees.* Employees should be qualified to competently perform the duties that are assigned to them. Companies must establish hiring practices to screen out unqualified candidates. Furthermore, procedures should be established to ensure that employees receive appropriate training to maintain their competence.

3. *Bonded employees.* Employees in sensitive positions should be covered by a fidelity bond that provides insurance to reimburse losses due to illegal actions committed by employees.

4. *Required absences.* Employees should be required to take extended absences from their jobs so that they are not always present to hide unscrupulous or illegal activities.

5. *Procedures manual.* To promote compliance, the procedures for processing transactions should be clearly described in a manual.

6. *Authority and responsibility.* To motivate employees and promote effective control, clear lines of authority and responsibility should be established.

7. *Prenumbered documents.* Prenumbered documents minimize the likelihood of missing or duplicate documents. Prenumbered forms should be used for all important documents such as purchase orders, receiving reports, invoices, and checks.

8. *Physical control.* Locks, fences, security personnel, and other physical devices should be employed to safeguard assets.

9. *Performance evaluations.* Because few people can evaluate their own performance objectively, independent performance evaluations should be performed. Substandard performance will likely persist unless employees are encouraged to take corrective action.

Because cash is such an important business asset and because it is tempting to steal, much of the discussion of internal controls in this chapter focused on cash controls. Special procedures should be employed to control the receipts and payments of cash. One of the most common control policies is to use *checking accounts* for all except petty cash disbursements.

A *bank reconciliation* should be prepared each month to explain differences between the bank statement and a company's internal accounting records. A common reconciliation format determines the true cash balance based on both bank and book records. Items that typically appear on a bank reconciliation include the following:

Unadjusted bank balance	xxx	Unadjusted book balance	xxx
Add		Add	
Deposits in transit	xxx	Interest revenue	xxx
		Collection of receivables	xxx
Subtract		Subtract	
Outstanding checks	xxx	Bank service charges	xxx
		NSF checks	xxx
True cash balance	xxx	True cash balance	xxx

Agreement of the two true cash balances provides evidence that accounting for cash transactions has been accurate.

Another common internal control policy for protecting cash is using a *petty cash fund.* Normally, an employee who is designated as the petty cash custodian is entrusted with a small amount of cash. The custodian reimburses employees for small expenditures made on behalf of the company in exchange for authorized receipts from the employees at the time they are reimbursed. The total of these receipts plus the remaining currency in the fund should always equal the amount of funds entrusted to the custodian. Journal entries to recognize the expenses incurred are made at the time the fund is replenished.

Finally, the chapter discussed the auditor's role in financial reporting, including the materiality concept and the types of audit opinions that may be issued.

A Look Forward

Accounting for receivables and payables was introduced in Chapter 2 using relatively simple illustrations. For example, we assumed that customers who purchased services on account always paid their bills. In real business practice, some customers do not pay their bills. Among other topics, Chapter 7 examines how companies account for uncollectible accounts receivable.

SELF-STUDY REVIEW PROBLEM

A step-by-step audio-narrated series of slides is provided on the text website at www.mhhe.com/edmonds8e.

The following information pertains to Terry's Pest Control Company (TPCC) for July:

1. The unadjusted bank balance at July 31 was $870.
2. The bank statement included the following items:
   (a) A $60 credit memo for interest earned by TPCC.
   (b) A $200 NSF check made payable to TPCC.
   (c) A $110 debit memo for bank service charges.
3. The unadjusted book balance at July 31 was $1,400.
4. A comparison of the bank statement with company accounting records disclosed the following:
   (a) A $400 deposit in transit at July 31.
   (b) Outstanding checks totaling $120 at the end of the month.

Required

a. Prepare a bank reconciliation.
b. Prepare in general journal format the entries necessary to adjust TPCC's cash account to its true balance.

Solution to Requirement *a*

TERRY'S PEST CONTROL COMPANY
Bank Reconciliation
July 31

Unadjusted bank balance	$ 870
Add: Deposits in transit	400
Less: Outstanding checks	(120)
True cash balance	$1,150
Unadjusted book balance	$1,400
Add: Interest revenue	60
Less: NSF check	(200)
Less: Bank service charges	(110)
True cash balance	$1,150

Solution to Requirement *b*

Ref.	Account Title	Debit	Credit
1.	Cash	60	
	Interest Revenue		60
2.	Accounts Receivable	200	
	Cash		200
3.	Service Charge Expense	110	
	Cash		110

KEY TERMS

accounting controls 313
administrative controls 313
adverse opinion 331
audits 330
authority manual 316
bank reconciliation 321
bank statement 320
bank statement credit
   memo 320
bank statement debit memo 320
cash 317
cash short and over 326

certified check 323
certified public accountants
   (CPAs) 330
checks 320
confidentiality 332
deposit ticket 320
deposits in transit 322
disclaimer of opinion 331
fidelity bond 315
financial statements audit 330
general authority 316
imprest basis 327

independent auditor 336
internal controls 312
management's discussion and
   analysis (MD&A) 330
material 331
non-sufficient-funds (NSF)
   checks 323
notes to the financial
   statements 329
outstanding checks 322
petty cash fund 327
petty cash voucher 327

procedures manual 315
qualified opinion 331
Securities and Exchange
   Commission (SEC) 332
separation of duties 315
service charges 322
signature card 320
specific authorizations 316
true cash balance 321
unadjusted bank balance 321
unadjusted book balance 321
unqualified opinion 331

QUESTIONS

1. What motivated Congress to pass the Sarbanes-Oxley Act (SOX) of 2002?

2. Define the term *internal control*.

3. Explain the relationship between SOX and COSO.

4. Name and briefly define the five components of COSO's internal control framework.

5. Explain how COSO's *Enterprise Risk Management—An Integrated Framework* project relates to COSO's *Internal Control—An Integrated Framework* project.

6. What is the difference between accounting controls and administrative controls?

7. What are several features of an effective internal control system?

8. What is meant by *separation of duties*? Give an illustration.

9. What are the attributes of a high-quality employee?

10. What is a fidelity bond? Explain its purpose.

11. Why is it important that every employee periodically take a leave of absence or vacation?

12. What are the purpose and importance of a procedures manual?

13. What is the difference between specific and general authorizations?

14. Why should documents (checks, invoices, receipts) be prenumbered?

15. What procedures are important in the physical control of assets and accounting records?

16. What is the purpose of independent verification of performance?

17. What items are considered cash?

18. Why is cash more susceptible to theft or embezzlement than other assets?

19. Giving written copies of receipts to customers can help prevent what type of illegal acts?

20. What procedures can help to protect cash receipts?

21. What procedures can help protect cash disbursements?

22. What effect does a debit memo in a bank statement have on the Cash account? What effect does a credit memo in a bank statement have on the Cash account?

23. What information is normally included in a bank statement?

24. Why might a bank statement reflect a balance that is larger than the balance recorded in the depositor's books? What could cause the bank balance to be smaller than the book balance?

25. What is the purpose of a bank reconciliation?

26. What is an outstanding check?

27. What is a deposit in transit?

28. What is a certified check?

29. How is an NSF check accounted for in the accounting records?

30. What is the purpose of the Cash Short and Over account?

31. What is the purpose of a petty cash fund?

32. What types of expenditures are usually made from a petty cash fund?

33. What is a financial statement audit? Who is qualified to perform it?

34. What is an independent auditor? Why must auditors be independent?

35. What makes an error in the financial statements material?

36. What three basic types of auditors' opinions can be issued on audited financial statements? Describe each.

37. What are the implications of an unqualified audit opinion?

38. When might an auditor issue a disclaimer on financial statements?

39. In what circumstances can an auditor disclose confidential information about a client without the client's permission?

40. What is the purpose of internal controls in an organization?

MULTIPLE-CHOICE QUESTIONS

 Multiple-choice questions are provided on the text website at www.mhhe.com/edmonds8e.

EXERCISES—SERIES A

All applicable Exercises in Series A are available with McGraw-Hill's *Connect® Accounting*.

Exercise 6-1A   *SOX and COSO's internal control frameworks*

LO 1

Required

a. Explain what the acronym SOX refers to.
b. Define the acronym COSO and explain how it relates to SOX.
c. Name and briefly define the five components of COSO's internal control framework.
d. Define the acronym ERM and explain how it relates to COSO's internal control framework.

Exercise 6-2A   *Internal control procedures*

LO 1

Required

a. Name and describe the two categories of internal controls.
b. What is the purpose of internal controls?

Exercise 6-3A   *Internal control procedures*

LO 1

Dick Haney is opening a new business that will sell sporting goods. It will initially be a small operation, and he is concerned about the security of his assets. He will not be able to be at the business all of the time and will have to rely on his employees and internal control procedures to ensure that transactions are properly accounted for and assets are safeguarded. He will have a store manager and two other employees who will be sales personnel and stock personnel and who will also perform any other duties necessary. Dick will be in the business on a regular basis. He has come to you for advice.

Required

Write a memo to Dick outlining the procedures that he should implement to ensure that his store assets are protected and that the financial transactions are properly recorded.

Exercise 6-4A   *Internal controls to prevent theft*

LO 1

Rhonda Cox worked as the parts manager for State Line Automobiles, a local automobile dealership. Rhonda was very dedicated and never missed a day of work. Since State Line was a small operation, she was the only employee in the parts department. Her duties consisted of ordering parts for stock and as needed for repairs, receiving the parts and checking them in, distributing them as needed to the shop or to customers for purchase, and keeping track of and taking the year-end inventory of parts. State Line decided to expand and needed to secure additional financing. The local bank agreed to a loan contingent on an audit of the dealership. One requirement of the audit was to oversee the inventory count of both automobiles and parts on hand. Rhonda was clearly nervous, explaining that she had just inventoried all parts in the parts department. She supplied the auditors with a detailed list. The inventory showed parts on hand worth $225,000. The auditors decided they needed to verify a substantial part of the inventory. When the auditors began their counts, a pattern began to develop. Each type of part seemed to be one or two items short when the actual count was taken. This raised more concern. Although Rhonda assured the auditors the parts were just misplaced, the auditors continued the count. After completing the count of parts on hand, the auditors could document only $155,000 of actual parts. Suddenly, Rhonda quit her job and moved to another state.

Required

a. What do you suppose caused the discrepancy between the actual count and the count that Rhonda had supplied?
b. What procedures could be put into place to prevent this type of problem?

LO 2

Exercise 6-5A   *Features of internal control procedures for cash*

Required

List and discuss effective internal control procedures that apply to cash.

LO 1

Exercise 6-6A   *Internal controls for equipment*

Required

List the internal control procedures that pertain to the protection of business equipment.

LO 3

Exercise 6-7A   *Treatment of NSF check*

The bank statement of Stone Supplies included a $300 NSF check that one of Stone's customers had written to pay for services that were provided by Stone.

Required

a. Show the effects of recognizing the NSF check on the financial statements by recording the appropriate amounts in a horizontal statements model like the following one:

Assets		=	Liab.	+	Equity	Rev.	−	Exp.	=	Net Inc.	Cash Flow
Cash	+	Accts. Rec.									

b. Is the recognition of the NSF check on Stone's books an asset source, use, or exchange transaction?

c. Suppose the customer redeems the check by giving Stone $325 cash in exchange for the bad check. The additional $25 paid a service fee charged by Stone. Show the effects on the financial statements in the horizontal statements model in Requirement *a*.

d. Is the receipt of cash referred to in Requirement *c* an asset source, use, or exchange transaction?

e. Record in general journal form the adjusting entry for the NSF check and the subsequent entry for redemption of the check by the customer.

LO 3

Exercise 6-8A   *Adjustments to the balance per books*

Required

Identify which of the following items are added to or subtracted from the unadjusted *book balance* to arrive at the true cash balance. Distinguish the additions from the subtractions by placing a + beside the items that are added to the unadjusted book balance and a − beside those that are subtracted from it. The first item is recorded as an example.

Reconciling Items	Book Balance Adjusted?	Added or Subtracted?
Automatic debit for utility bill	Yes	−
Charge for printing new checks		
NSF check from customer		
ATM fee		
Outstanding checks		
Interest revenue earned on the account		
Deposits in transit		
Service charge		

LO 3

Exercise 6-9A   *Adjustments to the balance per bank*

Required

Identify which of the following items are added to or subtracted from the unadjusted *bank balance* to arrive at the true cash balance. Distinguish the additions from the subtractions by placing a + beside the items that are added to the unadjusted bank balance and a − beside those that are subtracted from it. The first item is recorded as an example.

Reconciling Items	Bank Balance Adjusted?	Added or Subtracted?
Credit memo	No	N/A
ATM fee		
Petty cash voucher		
NSF check from customer		
Interest revenue		
Bank service charge		
Outstanding checks		
Deposits in transit		
Debit memo		

Exercise 6-10A   *Adjusting the cash account*

LO 3

As of May 31, 2013, the bank statement showed an ending balance of $26,100. The unadjusted Cash account balance was $27,350. The following information is available:

1. Deposit in transit, $6,981.
2. Credit memo in bank statement for interest earned in May, $36.
3. Outstanding check, $5,720.
4. Debit memo for service charge, $25.

Required

a. Determine the true cash balance by preparing a bank reconciliation as of May 31, 2013, using the preceding information.

b. Record in general journal format the adjusting entries necessary to correct the unadjusted book balance.

Exercise 6-11A   *Determining the true cash balance, starting with the unadjusted bank balance*

LO 3

The following information is available for Young Company for the month of August:

1. The unadjusted balance per the bank statement on August 31 was $35,200.
2. Deposits in transit on August 31 were $3,750.
3. A debit memo was included with the bank statement for a service charge of $35.
4. A $2,120 check written in August had not been paid by the bank.
5. The bank statement included a $1,550 credit memo for the collection of a note. The principal of the note was $1,500, and the interest collected was $50.

Required

Determine the true cash balance as of August 31. (*Hint:* It is not necessary to use all of the preceding items to determine the true balance.)

Exercise 6-12A   *Determining the true cash balance, starting with the unadjusted book balance*

LO 3

Sanders Company had an unadjusted cash balance of $8,120 as of April 30. The company's bank statement, also dated April 30, included a $200 NSF check written by one of Sanders's customers. There were $1,525 in outstanding checks and $900 in deposits in transit as of April 30. According to the bank statement, service charges were $50, and the bank collected a $500 note receivable for Sanders. The bank statement also showed $31 of interest revenue earned by Sanders.

Required

Determine the true cash balance as of April 30. (*Hint:* It is not necessary to use all of the preceding items to determine the true balance.)

LO 4

Exercise 6-13A   *Effect of establishing a petty cash fund*

Smithville Timber Company established a $180 petty cash fund on January 1, 2013.

Required

a. Is the establishment of the petty cash fund an asset source, use, or exchange transaction?
b. Record the establishment of the petty cash fund in a horizontal statements model like the following one:

Assets		= Liab.	+ Equity	Rev.	− Exp.	= Net Inc.	Cash Flow
Cash	+ Petty Cash						

c. Record the establishment of the fund in general journal format.

LO 4

Exercise 6-14A   *Effect of petty cash events on the financial statements*

Lairo Inc. established a petty cash fund of $150 on January 2. On January 31, the fund contained cash of $8.20 and vouchers for the following cash payments:

Postage and office supplies	$76.30
Entertainment expense	36.50
Maintenance expense	25.00

The three distinct accounting events affecting the petty cash fund for the period were (1) establishment of the fund, (2) reimbursements made to employees, and (3) recognition of expenses and replenishment of the fund.

Required

a. Record each of the three events in a horizontal statements model like the following one. In the Cash Flow column, indicate whether the item is an operating activity (OA), investing activity (IA), or a financing activity (FA). Use NA to indicate that an account was not affected by the event.

Assets		= Liab.	+ Equity	Rev.	− Exp.	= Net Inc.	Cash Flow
Cash	+ Petty Cash						

b. Record the events in general journal format.

LO 4

Exercise 6-15A   *Determining the amount of petty cash expense*

Consider the following events:

1. A petty cash fund of $200 was established on April 1, 2013.
2. Employees were reimbursed when they presented petty cash vouchers to the petty cash custodian.
3. On April 30, 2013, the petty cash fund contained vouchers totaling $171.40 plus $26.10 of currency.

Required

Answer the following questions:

a. How did the establishment of the petty cash fund affect (increase, decrease, or have no effect on) total assets?

b. What is the amount of total petty cash expenses to be recognized during April?

c. When are petty cash expenses recognized (at the time of establishment, reimbursement, or replenishment)?

Exercise 6-16A   *Materiality and the auditor*

LO 5

Melissa Moore is an auditor. Her work at two companies disclosed inappropriate recognition of revenue. Both cases involved dollar amounts in the $200,000 range. In one case, Moore considered the item material and required her client to restate earnings. In the other case, Moore dismissed the misstatement as being immaterial.

Required

Write a memo that explains how a $200,000 misstatement of revenue is acceptable for one company but unacceptable for a different company.

PROBLEMS—SERIES A

All applicable Problems in Series A are available with McGraw-Hill's *Connect® Accounting*.

Problem 6-17A   *Using internal control to restrict illegal or unethical behavior*

LO 1, 2

Required

For each of the following fraudulent acts, describe one or more internal control procedures that could have prevented (or helped prevent) the problems.

a. Nina Wells, the administrative assistant in charge of payroll, created a fictitious employee, wrote weekly checks to the fictitious employee, and then personally cashed the checks for her own benefit.

b. Noel Rand, the receiving manager of Southern Lumber, created a fictitious supplier named F&M Building Supply. F&M regularly billed Southern Lumber for supplies purchased. Rand had printed shipping slips and billing invoices with the name of the fictitious company and opened a post office box as the mailing address. Rand simply prepared a receiving report and submitted it for payment to the accounts payable department. The accounts payable clerk then paid the invoice when it was received because Rand acknowledged receipt of the supplies.

c. Patty Smith works at a local hobby shop and usually operates the cash register. She has developed a way to give discounts to her friends. When they come by, she rings a lower price or does not charge the friend for some of the material purchased. At first, Smith thought she would get caught, but no one seemed to notice. Indeed, she has become so sure that there is no way for the owner to find out that she has started taking home some supplies for her own personal use.

Problem 6-18A   *Preparing a bank reconciliation*

LO 3

Joe Cushing owns a construction business, Cushing Supply Co. The following cash information is available for the month of October 2013.

As of October 31, the bank statement shows a balance of $21,400. The October 31 unadjusted balance in the Cash account of Cushing Supply Co. is $18,400. A review of the bank statement revealed the following information:

1. A deposit of $2,600 on October 31, 2011, does not appear on the October 31 bank statement.

2. A debit memo for $75 was included in the bank statement for the purchase of a new supply of checks.

CHECK FIGURE
a. True Cash Balance, October 31, 2013: $21,925

3. When checks written during the month were compared with those paid by the bank, three checks amounting to $2,075 were found to be outstanding.

4. It was discovered that a check to pay for repairs was correctly written and paid by the bank for $1,500 but was recorded on the books as $5,100.

Required

a. Prepare a bank reconciliation at the end of October showing the true cash balance.

b. Prepare any necessary journal entries to adjust the books to the true cash balance.

LO 3

Problem 6-19A   *Missing information in a bank reconciliation*

The following data apply to Vaughn Sports Inc. for April 2013:

1. Balance per the bank on April 30, $13,750.

2. Deposits in transit not recorded by the bank, $3,600.

3. Bank error; check written by Don Vaughn on his personal checking account was drawn on Vaughn Sports Inc.'s account, $800.

4. The following checks written and recorded by Vaughn Sports Inc. were not included in the bank statement:

CHECK FIGURE
True Cash Balance, April 30, 2013: $16,035

1901	$ 265
1920	650
1921	1,200

5. Credit memo for note collected by the bank, $1,100.

6. Service charge for collection of note, $50.

7. The bookkeeper recorded a check written for $760 to pay for April's office supplies as $670 in the cash disbursements journal.

8. Bank service charge in addition to the note collection fee, $45.

9. NSF checks returned by the bank, $175.

Required

Determine the amount of the unadjusted cash balance per Vaughan Sports Inc.'s books.

LO 3

CHECK FIGURE
h. Theft Loss: $800

Problem 6-20A   *Adjustments to the cash account based on the bank reconciliation*

Determine whether the following items in India Imports' bank reconciliation require adjusting or correcting entries on India Imports' books. When an entry is required, record it in general journal format.

a. The bank statement indicated that India Imports earned $60 of interest revenue.

b. India Imports' accountant mistakenly recorded a $430 check that was written to purchase supplies as $350.

c. Bank service charges for the month were $45.

d. The bank reconciliation disclosed that $800 had been stolen from India Imports' business.

e. Outstanding checks amounted to $2,600.

f. The bank collected $4,000 of India Imports' accounts receivable. India Imports had instructed its customers to send their payments directly to the bank.

g. The bank mistakenly gave Imports Inc. credit for a $800 deposit made by India Imports.

h. Deposits in transit were $6,200.

i. India Imports' bank statement contained a $525 NSF check. India Imports had received the check from a customer and had included it in one of its bank deposits.

Problem 6-21A *Bank reconciliation and adjustments to the cash account*   **LO 3**

The following information is available for Cooters Garage for March 2013:

BANK STATEMENT
HAZARD STATE BANK
215 MAIN STREET
HAZARD, GA 30321

Cooters Garage
629 Main Street
Hazard, GA 30321

Account number
62-00062
March 31, 2013

Beginning balance 3/1/2013	$15,000.00
Total deposits and other credits	7,000.00
Total checks and other debits	6,000.00
Ending balance 3/31/2013	16,000.00

Checks and Debits		Deposits and Credits	
Check No.	Amount	Date	Amount
1462	$1,163.00	March 1	$1,000.00
1463	62.00	March 2	1,340.00
1464	1,235.00	March 6	210.00
1465	750.00	March 12	1,940.00
1466	1,111.00	March 17	855.00
1467	964.00	March 22	1,480.00
DM	15.00	CM	175.00
1468	700.00		

The following is a list of checks and deposits recorded on the books of Cooters Garage for March 2013:

Date	Check No.	Amount of Check	Date	Amount of Deposit
March 1	1463	$ 62.00	March 1	$1,340.00
March 5	1464	1,235.00	March 5	210.00
March 6	1465	750.00		
March 9	1466	1,111.00	March 10	1,940.00
March 10	1467	964.00		
March 14	1468	70.00	March 16	855.00
March 19	1469	1,500.00	March 19	1,480.00
March 28	1470	102.00	March 29	2,000.00

Other Information

1. Check no. 1462 was outstanding from February.
2. A credit memo for collection of accounts receivable was included in the bank statement.
3. All checks were paid at the correct amount.
4. The bank statement included a debit memo for service charges.
5. The February 28 bank reconciliation showed a deposit in transit of $1,000.
6. Check no. 1468 was for the purchase of equipment.
7. The unadjusted Cash account balance at March 31 was $16,868.

Required

a. Prepare the bank reconciliation for Cooters Garage at the end of March.
b. Record in general journal form any necessary entries to the Cash account to adjust it to the true cash balance.

Problem 6-22A   *Effect of adjustments to cash on the accounting equation*

After reconciling its bank account, Ross Equipment Company made the following adjusting entries:

Entry No.	Account Titles	Debit	Credit

1	Accounts Receivable
	   Cash
	     To record NSF check from Wilson
		250	250

2	Rent Expense
	   Cash
	     To correct understatement of expense
		35	35

3	Service Charge Expense
	   Cash
	     To record bank service charge
		15	15

4	Cash
	   Accounts Receivable
	     To record bank collection
		175	175

5	Cash
	   Interest Revenue
	     To record interest revenue
		40	40

Required

Identify the event depicted in each journal entry as asset source (AS), asset use (AU), asset exchange (AE), or claims exchange (CE). Also explain how each entry affects the accounting equation by placing a + for increase, − for decrease, or NA for not affected under the following components of the accounting equation. The first event is recorded as an example.

Event No.	Type of Event	Assets	=	Liabilities	+	Common Stock	+	Retained Earnings
1	AE	+/−		NA		NA		NA

Stockholders' Equity spans Common Stock and Retained Earnings.

CHECK FIGURE
a. True Cash Balance, May 31, 2013: $21,650

Problem 6-23A   *Bank reconciliation and internal control*

Following is a bank reconciliation for Pizza Express for May 31, 2013:

	Cash Account	Bank Statement
Balance as of 5/31/2013	$25,000	$22,000
Deposit in transit		4,250
Outstanding checks		(465)
Note collected by bank	1,815	
Bank service charge	(30)	
Automatic payment on loan	(1,000)	
Adjusted cash balance as of 5/31/2013	$25,785	$25,785

Because of limited funds, Pizza Express employed only one accountant who was responsible for receiving cash, recording receipts and disbursements, preparing deposits, and preparing the bank reconciliation. The accountant left the company on June 8, 2013, after preparing the May 31 bank reconciliation. His replacement compared the checks returned with the bank statement to the cash disbursements journal and found the total of outstanding checks to be $4,600.

Required

a. Prepare a corrected bank reconciliation.

b. What is the total amount of cash missing, and how was the difference between the "true cash" per the bank and the "true cash" per the books hidden on the reconciliation prepared by the former employee?

c. What could Pizza Express do to avoid cash theft in the future?

Problem 6-24A *Petty cash fund*

LO 4

The following data pertain to the petty cash fund of Stanton Company:

1. The petty cash fund was established on an imprest basis at $250 on March 1.

2. On March 31, a physical count of the fund disclosed $13 in currency and coins, vouchers authorizing meal allowances totaling $120, vouchers authorizing purchase of postage stamps of $21, and vouchers for payment of delivery charges of $93.

Required

a. Prepare all general journal entries necessary to (1) establish the fund, (2) reimburse employees, and (3) recognize the expenses and replenish the fund as of March 31. (*Hint:* Journal entries may not be required for all three events.)

b. Explain how the Cash Short and Over account required in this case affects the income statement.

c. Identify the event depicted in each journal entry recorded in Requirement *a* as asset source (AS), asset use (AU), asset exchange (AE), or claims exchange (CE).

d. Record the effects on the financial statements of the events in Requirement *a* using a horizontal statements model like the following one. In the Cash Flow column, indicate whether the item is an operating activity (OA), investing activity (IA), or financing activity (FA). Use NA to indicate that an account was not affected by the event.

Assets		= Liab. + Equity	Rev. − Exp. = Net Inc.	Cash Flow
Cash +	Petty Cash			

Problem 6-25A *Types of audit reports*

LO 5

Ellen Norman is a partner of a regional accounting firm. Ms. Norman was hired by a client to audit the company's books. After extensive work, Ms. Norman determined that she was unable to perform the appropriate audit procedures.

Required

a. Name the type of audit report that Ms. Norman should issue with respect to the work that she did accomplish.

b. If Ms. Norman had been able to perform the necessary audit procedures, there are three types of audit reports that she could have issued depending on the outcome of the audit. Name and describe these three types of audit reports.

EXERCISES—SERIES B

Exercise 6-1B *SOX and COSO's internal control frameworks*

LO 1

Required

a. Discuss the requirements of Section 404 of the Sarbanes-Oxley Act and how it relates to COSO.

b. What type of companies do these rules apply to?

LO 1

Exercise 6-2B   *Features of a strong internal control system*

Required

List and describe nine features of a strong internal control system discussed in this chapter.

LO 1

Exercise 6-3B   *Internal control procedures to prevent embezzlement*

Jane Jones was in charge of the returns department at The Software Company. She was responsible for evaluating returned merchandise. She sent merchandise that was reusable back to the warehouse, where it was restocked in inventory. Jones was also responsible for taking the merchandise that she determined to be defective to the city dump for disposal. She had agreed to buy a friend a tax planning program at a discount through her contacts at work. That is when the idea came to her. She could simply classify one of the reusable returns as defective and bring it home instead of taking it to the dump. She did so and made a quick $150. She was happy, and her friend was ecstatic; he was able to buy a $400 software package for only $150. He told his friends about the deal, and soon Jones had a regular set of customers. She was caught when a retail store owner complained to the marketing manager that his pricing strategy was being undercut by The Software Company's direct sales to the public. The marketing manager was suspicious because The Software Company had no direct marketing program. When the outside sales were ultimately traced back to Jones, the company discovered that it had lost over $10,000 in sales revenue because of her criminal activity.

Required

Identify an internal control procedure that could have prevented the company's losses. Explain how the procedure would have stopped the embezzlement.

LO 1

Exercise 6-4B   *Internal control procedures to prevent deception*

Best Care Medical Centers (BCMC) hired a new physician, Sam Cole, who was an immediate success. Everyone loved his bedside manner; he could charm the most cantankerous patient. Indeed, he was a master salesman as well as an expert physician. Unfortunately, Cole misdiagnosed a case that resulted in serious consequences to the patient. The patient filed suit against BCMC. In preparation for the defense, BCMC's attorneys discovered that Cole was indeed an exceptional salesman. He had worked for several years as district marketing manager for a pharmaceutical company. In fact, he was not a physician at all! He had changed professions without going to medical school. He had lied on his application form. His knowledge of medical terminology had enabled him to fool everyone. BCMC was found negligent and lost a $3 million lawsuit.

Required

Identify the relevant internal control procedures that could have prevented the company's losses. Explain how these procedures would have prevented Cole's deception.

LO 2

Exercise 6-5B   *Internal control for cash*

Required

a. Why are special controls needed for cash?

b. What is included in the definition of *cash*?

LO 1, 2

Exercise 6-6B   *Internal controls for small businesses*

Required

Assume you are the owner of a small business that has only two employees.

a. Which of the internal control procedures are most important to you?

b. How can you overcome the limited opportunity to use the separation-of-duties control procedure?

LO 4

Exercise 6-7B   *Treatment of NSF check*

Montgomery Stationery's bank statement contained a $260 NSF check that one of its customers had written to pay for supplies purchased.

Required

a. Show the effects of recognizing the NSF check on the financial statements by recording the appropriate amounts in a horizontal statements model like the following one:

Assets		= Liab. + Equity	Rev. – Exp. = Net Inc.	Cash Flow
Cash +	Accts. Rec.			

b. Is the recognition of the NSF check on Montgomery's books an asset source, use, or exchange transaction?

c. Suppose the customer redeems the check by giving Montgomery $290 cash in exchange for the bad check. The additional $30 paid a service fee charged by Montgomery. Show the effects on the financial statements in the horizontal statements model in Requirement *a.*

d. Is the receipt of cash referenced in Requirement *c* an asset source, use, or exchange transaction?

e. Record in general journal form the adjusting entry for the NSF check and the entry for redemption of the check by the customer.

Exercise 6-8B *Adjustments to the balance per books*

LO 3

Required

Identify which of the following items are added to or subtracted from the unadjusted *book balance* to arrive at the true cash balance. Distinguish the additions from the subtractions by placing a + beside the items that are added to the unadjusted book balance and a – beside those that are subtracted from it. The first item is recorded as an example.

Reconciling Items	Book Balance Adjusted?	Added or Subtracted?
Charge for checks	Yes	–
NSF check from customer		
Note receivable collected by the bank		
Outstanding checks		
Credit memo		
Interest revenue		
Deposits in transit		
Debit memo		
Service charge		

Exercise 6-9B *Adjustments to the balance per bank*

LO 3

Required

Identify which of the following items are added to or subtracted from the unadjusted *bank balance* to arrive at the true cash balance. Distinguish the additions from the subtractions by placing a + beside the items that are added to the unadjusted bank balance and a – beside those that are subtracted from it. The first item is recorded as an example.

Reconciling Items	Bank Balance Adjusted?	Added or Subtracted?
Certified checks	NA	NA
Petty cash voucher		
NSF check from customer		
Interest revenue		
Bank service charge		
Outstanding checks		
Deposits in transit		
Debit memo		
Credit memo		

LO 3

Exercise 6-10B   *Adjusting the cash account*

As of June 30, 2013, the bank statement showed an ending balance of $15,246. The unadjusted Cash account balance was $14,720. The following information is available:

1. Deposit in transit, $1,390.
2. Credit memo in bank statement for interest earned in June, $22.
3. Outstanding check, $1,901.
4. Debit memo for service charge, $7.

Required

a. Determine the true cash balance by preparing a bank reconciliation as of June 30, 2013, using the preceding information.

b. Record in general journal format the adjusting entries necessary to correct the unadjusted book balance.

LO 3

Exercise 6-11B   *Determining the true cash balance, starting with the unadjusted bank balance*

The following information is available for Sharder Company for the month of June:

1. The unadjusted balance per the bank statement on June 30 was $71,230.
2. Deposits in transit on June 30 were $2,350.
3. A debit memo was included with the bank statement for a service charge of $25.
4. A $5,611 check written in June had not been paid by the bank.
5. The bank statement included a $930 credit memo for the collection of a note. The principal of the note was $900, and the interest collected amounted to $30.

Required

Determine the true cash balance as of June 30. (*Hint:* It is not necessary to use all of the preceding items to determine the true balance.)

LO 3

Exercise 6-12B   *Determining the true cash balance, starting with the unadjusted book balance*

Henderson Company had an unadjusted cash balance of $7,215 as of May 31. The company's bank statement, also dated May 31, included a $68 NSF check written by one of Henderson's customers. There were $750 in outstanding checks and $930 in deposits in transit as of May 31. According to the bank statement, service charges were $50, and the bank collected a $500 note receivable for Henderson. The bank statement also showed $13 of interest revenue earned by Henderson.

Required

Determine the true cash balance as of May 31. (*Hint:* It is not necessary to use all of the preceding items to determine the true balance.)

LO 4

Exercise 6-13B   *Effect of establishing a petty cash fund*

Manu Company established a $300 petty cash fund on January 1, 2013.

Required

a. Is the establishment of the petty cash fund an asset source, use, or exchange transaction?

b. Record the establishment of the petty cash fund in a horizontal statements model like the following one:

Assets		= Liab. + Equity	Rev. − Exp. = Net Inc.	Cash Flow
Cash +	Petty Cash			

c. Record the establishment of the fund in general journal format.

Exercise 6-14B   *Effect of petty cash events on the financial statements*

LO 4

Minor Medical Center established a petty cash fund of $200 on January 2. On January 31, the fund contained cash of $18.50 and vouchers for the following cash payments:

Maintenance expense	$56.30
Office supplies	75.10
Transportation expense	48.01

The three distinct accounting events affecting the petty cash fund for the period were (1) establishment of the fund, (2) reimbursements made to employees, and (3) recognition of expenses and replenishment of the fund.

Required

a. Record each of the three events in a horizontal statements model like the following one. In the Cash Flow column, indicate whether the item is an operating activity (OA), investing activity (IA), or a financing activity (FA). Use NA to indicate that an account was not affected by the event.

Assets	=	Liab.	+	Equity	Rev.	−	Exp.	=	Net Inc.	Cash Flow
Cash + Petty Cash										

b. Record the events in general journal format.

Exercise 6-15B   *Determining the amount of petty cash expense*

LO 4

Consider the following events:

1. A petty cash fund of $250 was established on April 1, 2013.
2. Employees were reimbursed when they presented petty cash vouchers to the petty cash custodian.
3. On April 30, 2013, the petty cash fund contained vouchers totaling $214.85 plus $32.15 of currency.

Required

Answer the following questions:

a. How did the establishment of the petty cash fund affect (increase, decrease, or have no effect on) total assets?
b. What is the amount of total petty cash expenses to be recognized during April?
c. When are petty cash expenses recognized (at the time of establishment, reimbursement, or replenishment)?

Exercise 6-16B   *Confidentiality and the auditor*

LO 5

West Aston discovered a significant fraud in the accounting records of a high profile client. The story has been broadcast on national airways. Aston was unable to resolve his remaining concerns with the company's management team and ultimately resigned from the audit engagement. Aston knows that he will be asked by several interested parties, including his friends and relatives, the successor auditor, and prosecuting attorneys in a court of law, to tell what he knows. He has asked you for advice.

Required

Write a memo that explains Aston's disclosure responsibilities to each of the interested parties.

PROBLEMS—SERIES B

Problem 6-17B   *Using internal control to restrict illegal or unethical behavior*

LO 1,2

Required

For each of the following fraudulent acts, describe one or more internal control procedures that could have prevented (or helped prevent) the problems.

a. Everyone in the office has noticed what a dedicated employee Sandy Mize is. She never misses work, not even for a vacation. Mize is in charge of the petty cash fund. She transfers funds from the company's bank account to the petty cash account on an as-needed basis. During a surprise audit, the petty cash fund was found to contain fictitious receipts. Over a three-year period, Mize had used more than $4,000 of petty cash to pay for personal expenses.

b. Joe Martin was hired as the vice president of the manufacturing division of a corporation. His impressive resume listed a master's degree in business administration from a large state university and numerous collegiate awards and activities, when in fact Martin had only a high school diploma. In a short time, the company was in poor financial condition because of his inadequate knowledge and bad decisions.

c. Redwood Manufacturing has good internal control over its manufacturing materials inventory. However, office supplies are kept on open shelves in the employee break room. The office supervisor has noticed that he is having to order paper, tape, staplers, and pens with increasing frequency.

LO 3 — Problem 6-18B *Preparing a bank reconciliation*

Hank Brock owns a card shop, Four Aces. The following cash information is available for the month of August 2013.

As of August 31, the bank statement shows a balance of $15,320. The August 31 unadjusted balance in the Cash account of Four Aces is $13,910. A review of the bank statement revealed the following information:

1. A deposit of $4,295 on August 31, 2013, does not appear on the August bank statement.
2. It was discovered that a check to pay for baseball cards was correctly written and paid by the bank for $3,650 but was recorded on the books as $4,400.
3. When checks written during the month were compared with those paid by the bank, three checks amounting to $5,030 were found to be outstanding.
4. A debit memo for $75 was included in the bank statement for the purchase of a new supply of checks.

Required

a. Prepare a bank reconciliation at the end of August showing the true cash balance.
b. Prepare any necessary journal entries to adjust the books to the true cash balance.

LO 3 — Problem 6-19B *Missing information in a bank reconciliation*

The following data apply to Larry's Auto Supply Inc. for May 2013:

1. Balance per the bank on May 31, $8,250.
2. Deposits in transit not recorded by the bank, $1,230.
3. Bank error; check written by L7 Auto Supply was charged to Larry's Auto Supply's account, $720.
4. The following checks written and recorded by Larry's Auto Supply were not included in the bank statement:

3013	$ 420
3054	650
3056	1,830

5. Note collected by the bank, $400.
6. Service charge for collection of note, $15.
7. The bookkeeper recorded a check written for $230 to pay for the May utilities expense as $430 in the cash disbursements journal.
8. Bank service charge in addition to the note collection fee, $35.
9. Customer checks returned by the bank as NSF, $275.

Required

Determine the amount of the unadjusted cash balance per Larry's Auto Supply's books.

Problem 6-20B *Adjustments to the cash account based on the bank reconciliation*

LO 3

Required

Determine whether the following items included in Sung Company's bank reconciliation will require adjusting or correcting entries on Sung's books. When an entry is required, record it in general journal format.

a. Service charges of $30 for the month of January were listed on the bank statement.

b. The bank charged a $350 check drawn on Yung Restaurant to Sung's account. The check was included in Sung's bank statement.

c. A check of $62 was returned to the bank because of insufficient funds and was noted on the bank statement. Sung received the check from a customer and thought that it was good when it was deposited into the account.

d. An $982 deposit was recorded by the bank as $928.

e. Four checks totaling $725 written during the month of January were not included with the January bank statement.

f. A $65 check written to Office Max for office supplies was recorded in the general journal as $56.

g. The bank statement indicated that the bank had collected a $450 note for Sung.

h. Sung recorded $700 of receipts on January 31, 2013, which was deposited in the night depository of the bank. These deposits were not included in the bank statement.

Problem 6-21B *Bank reconciliation and adjustments to the cash account*

LO 3

CHECK FIGURE
a. True Cash Balance, July 31, 2013: $16,234

The following information is available for Sunset Valley Hotel for July 2013:

Bank Statement

STATE BANK

Bolta Vista, NV 10001

Sunset Valley Hotel
10 Main Street
Bolta Vista, NV 10001

Account number
12-4567
July 31, 2013

Beginning balance 6/30/2013	$ 9,031
Total deposits and other credits	29,800
Total checks and other debits	23,902
Ending balance 7/31/2013	14,929

Checks and Debits		Deposits and Credits		
Check No.	Amount	Date		Amount
2350	$3,761	July	1	$1,102
2351	1,643	July	10	6,498
2352	8,000	July	15	4,929
2354	2,894	July	21	6,174
2355	1,401	July	26	5,963
2357	6,187	July	30	2,084
DM	16	CM		3,050

The following is a list of checks and deposits recorded on the books of the Sunset Valley Hotel for July 2013:

Date		Check No.	Amount of Check	Date		Amount of Deposit
July	2	2351	$1,643	July	8	$6,498
July	4	2352	8,000	July	14	4,929
July	10	2353	1,500	July	21	6,174
July	10	2354	2,894	July	26	5,963
July	15	2355	1,401	July	29	2,084
July	20	2356	745	July	30	3,550
July	22	2357	6,187			

Other Information

1. Check no. 2350 was outstanding from June.
2. The credit memo was for collection of notes receivable.
3. All checks were paid at the correct amount.
4. The debit memo was for printed checks.
5. The June 30 bank reconciliation showed a deposit in transit of $1,102.
6. The unadjusted Cash account balance at July 31 was $13,200.

Required

a. Prepare the bank reconciliation for Sunset Valley Hotel at the end of July.
b. Record in general journal form any necessary entries to the Cash account to adjust it to the true cash balance.

LO 3

Problem 6-22B *Effect of adjustments to cash on the accounting equation*

After reconciling its bank account, Scheiner Company made the following adjusting entries:

Entry No.	Account Titles	Debit	Credit
1	Service Charge Expense	35	
	Cash		35
	To record bank service charge		
2	Accounts Receivable	174	
	Cash		174
	To record NSF check from Beat		
3	Cash	20	
	Supplies Expense		20
	To correct overstatement of expense		
4	Cash	845	
	Accounts Receivable		845
	To record bank collection		
5	Cash	44	
	Interest Revenue		44
	To record interest revenue		

Required

Identify the event depicted in each journal entry as asset source (AS), asset use (AU), asset exchange (AE), or claims exchange (CE). Also explain how each entry affects the accounting equation by placing a + for increase, − for decrease, or NA for not affected under the following components of the accounting equation. The first event is recorded as an example.

Event No.	Type of Event	Assets	=	Liabilities	+	Common Stock	+	Retained Earnings
						Stockholders' Equity		
1	AU	−		NA		NA		−

LO 1, 2, 3

Problem 6-23B *Bank reconciliation and internal control*

Following is a bank reconciliation for The Gift Shop for June 30, 2013:

	Cash Account	Bank Statement
Balance as of 6/30/2013	$ 1,918	$ 3,000
Deposit in transit		600
Outstanding checks		(1,507)
Note collected by bank	2,000	
Bank service charge	(25)	
NSF check	(1,800)	
Adjusted cash balance as of 6/30/2013	$ 2,093	$ 2,093

When reviewing the bank reconciliation, The Gift Shop's auditor was unable to locate any reference to the NSF check on the bank statement. Furthermore, the clerk who reconciles the bank account and records the adjusting entries could not find the actual NSF check that should have been included in the bank statement. Finally, there was no specific reference in the accounts receivable supporting records identifying a party who had written a bad check.

Required

a. Prepare the adjusting entry that the clerk would have made to record the NSF check.

b. Assume that the clerk who prepares the bank reconciliation and records the adjusting entries also makes bank deposits. Explain how the clerk could use a fictitious NSF check to hide the theft of cash.

c. How could The Gift shop avoid the theft of cash that is concealed by the use of fictitious NSF checks?

Problem 6-24B *Petty cash fund*

LO 4

Quinn Co. established a petty cash fund by issuing a check for $200 and appointing Randy Moss as petty cash custodian. Moss had vouchers for the following petty cash payments during the month:

Stamps	$31
Miscellaneous items	10
Employee supper money	65
Taxi fare	40
Window-washing service	35

There was $21 of currency in the petty cash box at the time it was replenished.

Required

a. Prepare all general journal entries necessary to (1) establish the fund, (2) reimburse employees, (3) recognize expenses, and (4) replenish the fund. (*Hint:* Journal entries may not be required for all the events.)

b. Explain how the Cash Short and Over account required in this case will affect the income statement.

c. Identify the event depicted in each journal entry recorded in Requirement *a* as asset source (AS), asset use (AU), asset exchange (AE), or claims exchange (CE).

d. Record the effects of the events in Requirement *a* on the financial statements using a horizontal statements model like the following one. In the Cash Flow column, indicate whether the item is an operating activity (OA), investing activity (IA), or financing activity (FA). Use NA to indicate that an account was not affected by the event.

Assets		=	Liab.	+	Equity	Rev.	−	Exp.	=	Net Inc.	Cash Flow
Cash	+	Petty Cash									

LO 5

Problem 6-25B   *Auditor responsibilities*

You have probably heard it is unwise to bite the hand that feeds you. Independent auditors are chosen by, paid by, and can be fired by the companies they audit. What keeps the auditor independent? In other words, what stops an auditor from blindly following the orders of a client?

Required

Write a memo that explains the reporting responsibilities of an independent auditor.

ANALYZE, THINK, COMMUNICATE

ATC 6-1   Business Applications Case   *Understanding real-world annual reports*

Required

Use the Target Corporation's annual report in Appendix B to answer the following questions.

a. Who are the independent auditors for Target?

b. What type of opinion did the independent auditors issue on Target's financial statements?

c. On what date does it appear the independent auditors completed their work related to Target's financial statements for the fiscal-year ended January 29, 2011 (2010)?

d. Does the auditors' report give any information about how the audit was conducted? If so, what does it suggest was done?

e. Does the auditors' report tell the reader that the audit was concerned with materiality rather than absolute accuracy in the financial statements?

ATC 6-2   Group Assignment   *Bank reconciliations*

The following cash and bank information is available for three companies at June 30, 2014:

Cash and Adjustment Information	Peach Co.	Apple Co.	Pear Co.
Unadjusted cash balance per books, 6/30	$45,620	$32,450	$23,467
Outstanding checks	1,345	2,478	2,540
Service charge	50	75	35
Balance per bank statement, 6/30	48,632	37,176	24,894
Credit memo for collection of notes receivable	4,500	5,600	3,800
NSF check	325	145	90
Deposits in transit	2,500	3,200	4,800
Credit memo for interest earned	42	68	12

Required

a. Organize the class into three sections and divide each section into groups of three to five students. Assign Peach Co. to section 1, Apple Co. to section 2, and Pear Co. to section 3.

   Group Tasks

   (1) Prepare a bank reconciliation for the company assigned to your group.

   (2) Prepare any necessary journal entries for the company assigned to your group.

   (3) Select a representative from a group in each section to put the bank reconciliation and required journal entries on the board.

Class Discussion:

b. Discuss the cause of the difference between the unadjusted cash balance and the ending balance for the bank statement. Also, discuss types of adjustment that are commonly made to the bank balance and types of adjustment that are commonly made to the unadjusted book balance.

ATC 6-3   Real-World Case   *Evaluating management's responsibilities*

The following excerpt was taken from JCPenney's 10-K report for its 2010 fiscal year:

Management's Report on Internal Control over Financial Reporting

The management of our Company is responsible for establishing and maintaining adequate internal control over financial reporting.

The management of our Company has assessed the effectiveness of our Company's internal control over financial reporting as of January 30, 2010. In making this assessment, management used criteria set forth by the Committee of Sponsoring Organization of the Treadway Commission (COSO) in *Internal Control—Integrated Framework.* Based on its assessment, the management of our Company believes that, as of January 30, 2010, our Company's internal control over financial reporting is effective based on those criteria.

KPMG LLP, the registered public accounting firm that audited the financial statements included in this Annual Report on Form 10-K, has issued an attestation report on the effectiveness of our Company's internal control over financial reporting. Their report follows.

There were no changes in our Company's internal control over financial reporting during the fourth quarter ended January 30, 2010, that have materially affected, or are reasonably likely to materially affect, our Company's internal control over financial reporting.

Required

Based on information in the text, list some of the elements of internal control you would expect the company's management to have established. You do not need to read the report of the Treadway Commission.

ATC 6-4   Business Applications Case   *Decisions about materiality*

The accounting firm of Tucker & Connley, CPAs, recently completed the audits of three separate companies. During these audits, the following events were discovered, and Tucker & Connley is trying to decide if each event is material. If an item is material, the CPA firm will insist that the company modify the financial statements.

1. In 2013, Carter Company reported service revenues of $4,000,000 and earnings before tax of $240,000. Because of an accounting error, the company recorded $24,000 as revenue in 2013 for services that will not be performed until early 2014.
2. Avery Company plans to report a cash balance of $210,000. Because of an accounting error, this amount is $15,000 too high. Avery also plans to report total assets of $12,000 and net earnings of $1,245,000.
3. Lewis Company's 2013 balance sheet shows a cash balance of $250,000 and total assets of $9,500,000. For 2013, the company had a net income of $850,000. These balances are all correct, but they would have been $7,000 higher if the president of the company had not claimed business travel expenses that were, in fact, the cost of personal vacations for him and his family. He charged the costs of these trips on the company's credit card. The president of Lewis Company owns 25 percent of the business.

Required

Write a memorandum to the partners of Tucker & Connley, explaining whether each of these events is material.

ATC 6-5   Business Applications Case   *Limitations of audit opinion*

The statement of financial position (balance sheet) of Trident Company reports assets of $5,500,000. Lisa Kimpton advises you that a major accounting firm has audited the statements and attested that they were prepared in accordance with generally accepted accounting principles. She tells you that she can buy the total owner's interest in the business for only $3,800,000 and is seriously considering the opportunity. She says that the auditor's unqualified opinion validates the $5,500,000 value of the assets. Lisa believes she would be foolish to pass up the opportunity to purchase the assets at a price of only $3,800,000.

Required

a. What part of the accounting equation is Lisa failing to consider?

b. Comment on Lisa's misconceptions regarding the auditor's role in providing information that is useful in making investment decisions.

ATC 6-6   Writing Assignment   *Internal control procedures*

Sarah Johnson was a trusted employee of Evergreen Trust Bank. She was involved in everything. She worked as a teller, she accounted for the cash at the other teller windows, and she recorded many of the transactions in the accounting records. She was so loyal that she never would take a day off, even when she was really too sick to work. She routinely worked late to see that all the day's work was posted into the accounting records. She would never take even a day's vacation because they might need her at the bank. Adam and Jammie, CPAs, were hired to perform an audit, the first complete audit that had been done in several years. Johnson seemed somewhat upset by the upcoming audit. She said that everything had been properly accounted for and that the audit was a needless expense. When Adam and Jammie examined some of the bank's internal control procedures, the firm discovered problems. In fact, as the audit progressed, it became apparent that a large amount of cash was missing. Numerous adjustments had been made to customer accounts with credit memorandums, and many of the transactions had been posted several days late. In addition, there were numerous cash payments for "office expenses." When the audit was complete, it was determined that more than $100,000 of funds was missing or improperly accounted for. All fingers pointed to Johnson. The bank's president, who was a close friend of Johnson, was bewildered. How could this type of thing happen at this bank?

Required

Prepare a written memo to the bank president, outlining the procedures that should be followed to prevent this type of problem in the future.

ATC 6-7   Ethical Dilemma   *I need just a little extra money*

John Riley, a certified public accountant, has worked for the past eight years as a payroll clerk for Southeast Industries, a small furniture manufacturing firm in the northeast. John recently experienced unfortunate circumstances. His teenage son required minor surgery and the medical bills not covered by John's insurance have financially strained John's family.

John works hard and is a model employee. Although he received regular performance raises during his first few years with Southwest, John's wages have not increased in three years. John asked his supervisor, Bill Jameson, for a raise. Bill agreed that John deserved a raise, but told him he could not currently approve one because of sluggish sales.

A disappointed John returned to his duties while the financial pressures in his life continued. Two weeks later, Larry Tyler, an assembly worker at Southwest, quit over a dispute with management. John conceived an idea. John's duties included not only processing employee terminations but also approving time cards before paychecks were issued and then distributing the paychecks to firm personnel. John decided to delay processing Mr. Tyler's termination, to forge timecards for Larry Tyler for the next few weeks, and to cash the checks himself. Since he distributed paychecks, no one would find out, and John reasoned that he was really entitled to the extra money anyway. In fact, no one did discover his maneuver and John stopped the practice after three weeks.

Required

a. Does John's scheme affect Southwest's balance sheet? Explain your answer.

b. Review the AICPA's Articles of Professional Conduct (see Chapter 2) and comment on any of the standards that have been violated.

c. Identify the three elements of unethical and criminal conduct recognized in the fraud triangle.

ATC 6-8   Research Assignment   *Investigating cash and management issues at Smucker's*

Using the most current 10-K available on EDGAR, or the company's website, answer the following questions about the J. M. Smucker Company. Instructions for using EDGAR are in

Appendix A. *Note: In some years the financial statements, footnotes, etc. portion of Smucker's annual report have been located at the end of the Form 10-K in or just after "Item 15."*

Required

a. Instead of "Cash," the company's balance sheet uses the account name "Cash and cash equivalents." How does the company define cash equivalents?

b. The annual report has two reports in which management clearly acknowledges its responsibility for the company's financial reporting and internal controls. What are the names of these reports and on what pages are they located?

ATC 6-9   Spreadsheet Assignment   *Using Excel*

At the end of 2013, the following accounting information is available for Bainbridge and Crist Companies:

Required

a. Set up the preceding spreadsheet. Complete the balance sheet and income statement. Use Excel formulas for rows that "total" on the balance sheet and for gross margin and net income on the income statement.

b. Calculate the designated ratios using Excel formulas.

c. Which company is more likely to be able to pay its current liabilities?

d. Which company carries a greater financial risk?

e. Which company is more profitable from the stockholders' perspective?

f. Based on profitability alone, which company performed better?

g. Assume that sales increased 10 percent and that the additional sales were made on account. Adjust the balance sheet and income statement for the effects. Notice that Retained Earnings will also need to be adjusted to keep the balance sheet in balance. What is the resultant effect on the ratios?

COMPREHENSIVE PROBLEM

The trial balance of Pacilio Security Services Inc. as of January 1, 2016, had the following normal balances:

Cash	$74,210
Accounts Receivable	13,500
Supplies	200
Prepaid Rent	3,200
Merchandise Inventory (24 @ $265; 1 @ $260)	6,620
Land	4,000
Accounts Payable	1,950
Unearned Revenue	900
Salaries Payable	1,000
Common Stock	50,000
Retained Earnings	47,880

During 2016 Pacilio Security Services experienced the following transactions:

1. Paid the salaries payable from 2015.
2. On March 1, 2016, Pacilio established a $100 petty cash fund to handle small expenditures.
3. Paid $4,800 on March 1, 2016, for one year's lease on the company van in advance.
4. Paid $7,200 on May 2, 2016, for one year's office rent in advance.
5. Purchased $400 of supplies on account.
6. Purchased 100 alarm systems for $28,000 cash during the year.
7. Sold 102 alarm systems for $57,120. All sales were on account. (Compute cost of goods sold using the FIFO cost flow method.)
8. Paid $2,100 on accounts payable during the year.
9. Replenished the petty cash fund on August 1. At this time, the petty cash fund had only $7 of currency left. It contained the following receipts: office supplies expense $23, cutting grass $55, and miscellaneous expense $14.
10. Billed $52,000 of monitoring services for the year.
11. Paid installers and other employees a total of $25,000 cash for salaries.
12. Collected $89,300 of accounts receivable during the year.
13. Paid $3,600 of advertising expense during the year.
14. Paid $2,500 of utilities expense for the year.
15. Paid a dividend of $10,000 to the shareholders.

Adjustments

16. There was $160 of supplies on hand at the end of the year.
17. Recognized the expired rent for both the van and the office building for the year. (The rent for both the van and the office remained the same for 2015 and 2016.)
18. Recognized the balance of the revenue earned in 2016 where cash had been collected in 2015.
19. Accrued salaries at December 31, 2016, were $1,400.

Required

a. Record the above transactions in general journal form.
b. Post the transactions to the T-accounts.
c. Prepare a bank reconciliation at the end of the year. The following information is available for the bank reconciliation:
   (1) Checks written but not paid by the bank, $8,350.
   (2) A deposit of $6,500 made on December 31, 2016, had been recorded but was not shown on the bank statement.

(3) A debit memo for $55 for a new supply of checks. (*Hint:* Use Office Supplies Expense account.)

(4) A credit memo for $30 for interest earned on the checking account.

(5) An NSF check for $120.

(6) The balance shown on the bank statement was $80,822.

d. Record and post any adjustments necessary from the bank reconciliation.

e. Prepare a trial balance.

f. Prepare an income statement, statement of changes in stockholders' equity, balance sheet, and statement of cash flows.

g. Close the temporary accounts to retained earnings.

h. Post the closing entries to the T-accounts and prepare a post-closing trial balance.

CHAPTER 7

Accounting for Receivables

LEARNING OBJECTIVES

After you have mastered the material in this chapter, you will be able to:

LO1 Explain how the allowance method of accounting for uncollectible accounts affects financial statements.

LO2 Use the percent of revenue method to estimate uncollectible accounts expense.

LO3 Use the percent of receivables method to estimate uncollectible accounts expense.

LO4 Show how the direct write-off method of accounting for uncollectible accounts affects financial statements.

LO5 Explain how accounting for notes receivable and accrued interest affects financial statements.

LO6 Explain how accounting for credit card sales affects financial statements.

LO7 Explain the effects of the cost of financing credit sales.

CHAPTER OPENING

Many people buy on impulse. If they must wait, the desire to buy wanes. To take advantage of impulse buyers, most merchandising companies offer customers credit because it increases their sales. A disadvantage of this strategy occurs when some customers are unable or unwilling to pay their bills. Nevertheless, the widespread availability of credit suggests that the advantages of increased sales outweigh the disadvantages of some uncollectible accounts.

When a company allows a customer to "buy now and pay later," the company's right to collect cash in the future is called an **account receivable.** Typically, amounts due from individual accounts receivable are relatively small and the collection period is short.

Most accounts receivable are collected within 30 days. When a longer credit term is needed or when a receivable is large, the seller usually requires the buyer to issue a note reflecting a credit agreement between the parties. The note specifies the maturity date, interest rate, and other credit terms. Receivables evidenced by such notes are called **notes receivable.** Accounts and notes receivable are reported as assets on the balance sheet.

The Curious Accountant

Lockheed Martin develops and maintains various types of technology related to security. Its biggest customer, by far, is the U.S. government for whom it provides aeronautics and space-system products and services. In 2010, 83.8 percent of its revenue came from sales to the U.S. government, and another 14.5 percent came from sales to governments of other countries. Suppose the U.S. government contracted with Lockheed Martin Corporation to provide management services related to a governmental hardware and software system, and that the cost of these services will be $10 million per month. Assume the government offers to pay for the services on the day they are provided (a cash purchase) or 30 days later (a purchase on account).

Assume that Lockheed Martin is absolutely sure the government will pay its account when due. Do you think the company should care whether the government pays for the services upon delivery or 30 days later? Why? (Answer on page 363.)

ALLOWANCE METHOD OF ACCOUNTING FOR UNCOLLECTIBLE ACCOUNTS

LO 1

Explain how the allowance method of accounting for uncollectible accounts affects financial statements.

Most companies do not expect to collect the full amount (face value) of their accounts receivable. Even carefully screened credit customers sometimes don't pay their bills. The **net realizable value** of accounts receivable represents the amount of receivables a company estimates it will actually collect. The net realizable value is the *face value* less an *allowance for doubtful accounts*.

The **allowance for doubtful accounts** represents a company's estimate of the amount of uncollectible receivables. To illustrate, assume a company with total accounts receivable of $50,000 estimates that $2,000 of its receivables will not be collected. The net realizable value of receivables is computed as follows:

Accounts receivable	$50,000
Less: Allowance for doubtful accounts	(2,000)
Net realizable value of receivables	$48,000

A company cannot know today, of course, the exact amount of the receivables it will not be able to collect in the future. The *allowance for doubtful accounts* and the *net realizable value* are necessarily *estimated amounts.* The net realizable value, however, more closely measures the cash that will ultimately be collected than does the face value. To avoid overstating assets, companies report receivables on their balance sheets at the net realizable value.

Reporting accounts receivable in the financial statements at net realizable value is commonly called the **allowance method of accounting for uncollectible accounts.** The following section illustrates using the allowance method for Allen's Tutoring Services (ATS).

Accounting Events Affecting the 2013 Period

Allen's Tutoring Services is a small company that provides tutoring services to college students. Allen's started operations on January 1, 2013. During 2013, Allen's experienced three types of accounting events. These events are discussed below.

EVENT 1   Revenue Recognition

Allen's Tutoring Services recognized $14,000 of service revenue earned on account during 2013.

This is an asset source transaction. Allen's Tutoring Services obtained assets (accounts receivable) by providing services to customers. Both assets and stockholders' equity (retained earnings) increase. The event increases revenue and net income. Cash flow is not affected. The journal entry and its effects on the financial statements are shown here:

Account Title	Debit	Credit
Accounts Receivable	14,000	
Service Revenue		14,000

Assets	=	Liab.	+	Equity	Rev.	−	Exp.	=	Net Inc.	Cash Flow
Accts. Rec.	=			Ret. Earn.						
14,000	=	NA	+	14,000	14,000	−	NA	=	14,000	NA

Answers to The Curious Accountant

Lockheed Martin would definitely prefer to make the sale to the government in cash rather than on account. Even though it may be certain to collect its accounts receivable, the sooner the company gets its cash the sooner the cash can be reinvested.

The interest cost related to a small account receivable of $50 that takes 30 days to collect may seem immaterial; at 6 percent the lost interest amounts to $.25. However, when one considers that Lockheed Martin had approximately $5.8 billion of accounts receivable on December 31, 2010, and took an average of 46 days to collect them, the cost of financing receivables for a real-world company becomes apparent. At 6 percent the cost of waiting 46 days to collect $5.8 billion of cash is $43.9 million ($5.8 billion × .06 × 46/365). For a full year, the cost to Lockheed Martin would be $348 million ($5.8 billion × .06). In 2010 the weighted-average interest rate on Lockheed Martin's debt was approximately 6 percent.

EVENT 2   Collection of Receivables

Allen's Tutoring Services collected $12,500 cash from accounts receivable in 2013.

This event is an asset exchange transaction. The asset cash increases; the asset accounts receivable decreases. Total assets remains unchanged. Net income is not affected because the revenue was recognized in the previous transaction. The cash inflow is reported in the operating activities section of the statement of cash flows. The journal entry and its effects on the financial statements are shown here:

Account Title	Debit	Credit
Cash	12,500	
Accounts Receivable		12,500

Assets			=	Liab.	+	Equity	Rev.	−	Exp.	=	Net Inc.	Cash Flow	
Cash	+	Accts. Rec.											
12,500	+	(12,500)	=	NA	+	NA	NA	−	NA	=	NA	12,500	OA

EVENT 3   Recognizing Uncollectible Accounts Expense

Allen's Tutoring Services recognized uncollectible accounts expense for accounts expected to be uncollectible in the future.

The year-end balance in the accounts receivable account is $1,500 ($14,000 of revenue on account − $12,500 of collections). Although Allen's Tutoring Services has the legal right to receive this $1,500 in 2014, the company is not likely to collect the entire amount because some of its customers might not pay the amounts due. Allen's will not know the actual amount of uncollectible accounts until some future time when the customers default (fail to pay). However, the company can *estimate* the amount of receivables that will be uncollectible.

Suppose Allen's Tutoring Services estimates that $75 of the receivables is uncollectible. To improve financial reporting, the company would recognize the estimated expense in 2013. In this way, uncollectible accounts expense and the related revenue will be recognized in the same accounting period (2013). Recognizing an estimated expense is more useful than recognizing no expense. The *matching* of revenues and expenses is improved and the statements are, therefore, more accurate.

The estimated amount of **uncollectible accounts expense** is recognized in a year-end adjusting entry. The adjusting entry reduces the net realizable value of receivables, stockholders' equity, and the amount of reported net income. The statement of cash flows is not affected. The journal entry and its effects on the financial statements are shown here:

Account Title	Debit	Credit
Uncollectible Accounts Expense	75	
Allowance for Doubtful Accounts		75

Assets	=	Liab.	+	Equity	Rev.	−	Exp.	=	Net Inc.	Cash Flow
Net Realizable Value of Receivables	=			Ret. Earn.						
(75)	=	NA	+	(75)	NA	−	75	=	(75)	NA

The Accounts Receivable account is not reduced directly because none of the receivables have *actually* been determined to be uncollectible. The decrease in the net realizable value of receivables represents an *estimate* of what will be uncollectible some time in the future. To distinguish the actual balance in accounts receivable from the net realizable value, accountants use a **contra asset account** called Allowance or Doubtful Accounts. The allowance account is called a *contra account* because it has a credit balance instead of the debit balance normally seen in asset accounts. Indeed, the credit balance in the Allowance for Doubtful Accounts is subtracted from the debit balance in the Accounts Receivable account to determine the net realizable value of receivables that is shown on the balance sheet. The net realizable value of receivables for ATS is determined as follows:

Accounts receivable	$1,500
Less: Allowance for doubtful accounts	(75)
Net realizable value of receivables	$1,425

Generally accepted accounting principles require disclosure of both the net realizable value and the amount of the allowance account. Many companies disclose these amounts directly in the balance sheet in a manner similar to that shown in the text box above. Other companies disclose allowance information in the notes to the financial statements.

Recording and Reporting Uncollectible Accounts Events in the Double-Entry System

Exhibit 7.1, Panel A, shows a summary of the 2013 transactions. Panel B shows the general ledger T-accounts after the journal entries have been posted to them. Panel C contains the financial statements. Although Exhibit 7.1 does not illustrate the 2013 year-end closing entries, recall that the closing entries will transfer the amounts from the revenue and expense accounts to the Retained Earnings account. The balance in the Retained Earnings account after closing will be $13,925, as reported on the year-end balance sheet.

Financial Statements

As previously indicated, estimating uncollectible accounts improves the usefulness of the 2013 financial statements in two ways. First, the balance sheet reports the amount of cash ($1,500 − $75 = $1,425) the company actually expects to collect (net realizable value of accounts receivable). Second, the income statement provides a clearer picture of managerial performance because it better *matches* the uncollectible accounts expense with the revenue it helped produce. The statements in Exhibit 7.1 show that the cash flow from operating activities ($12,500) differs from net income ($13,925). The statement of cash flows reports only cash collections, whereas the income statement reports revenues earned on account less the estimated amount of uncollectible accounts expense.

EXHIBIT 7.1

The Big Picture

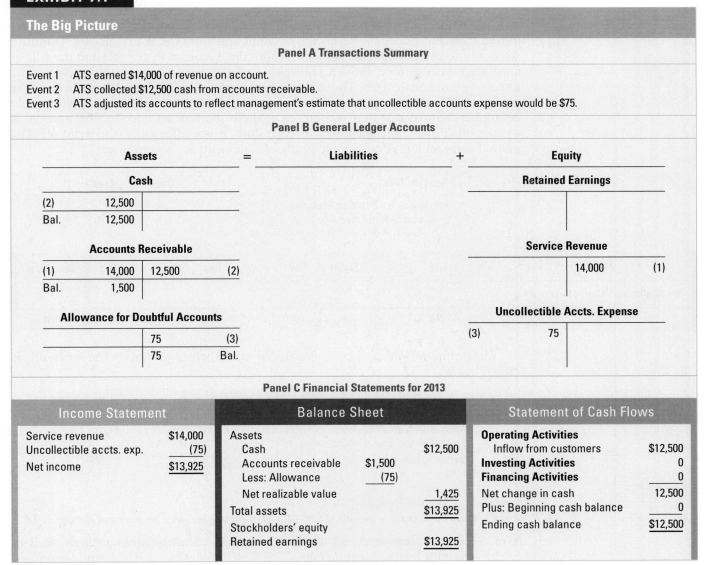

Panel A Transactions Summary

Event 1   ATS earned $14,000 of revenue on account.
Event 2   ATS collected $12,500 cash from accounts receivable.
Event 3   ATS adjusted its accounts to reflect management's estimate that uncollectible accounts expense would be $75.

Panel B General Ledger Accounts

Assets			=	Liabilities	+	Equity	

Cash

(2)	12,500	
Bal.	12,500	

Accounts Receivable

(1)	14,000	12,500	(2)
Bal.	1,500		

Allowance for Doubtful Accounts

	75	(3)
	75	Bal.

Retained Earnings

Service Revenue

	14,000	(1)

Uncollectible Accts. Expense

(3)	75	

Panel C Financial Statements for 2013

Income Statement		Balance Sheet			Statement of Cash Flows	
Service revenue	$14,000	Assets			**Operating Activities**	
Uncollectible accts. exp.	(75)	Cash		$12,500	Inflow from customers	$12,500
Net income	$13,925	Accounts receivable	$1,500		**Investing Activities**	0
		Less: Allowance	(75)		**Financing Activities**	0
		Net realizable value		1,425	Net change in cash	12,500
		Total assets		$13,925	Plus: Beginning cash balance	0
		Stockholders' equity			Ending cash balance	$12,500
		Retained earnings		$13,925		

✓ CHECK YOURSELF 7.1

Pamlico Inc. began operations on January 1, 2013. During 2013, it earned $400,000 of revenue on account. The company collected $370,000 of accounts receivable. At the end of the year, Pamlico estimates uncollectible accounts expense will be 1 percent of sales. Based on this information alone, what is the net realizable value of accounts receivable as of December 31, 2013?

Answer   Accounts receivable at year-end are $30,000 ($400,000 sales on account − $370,000 collection of receivables). The amount in the allowance for doubtful accounts would be $4,000 ($400,000 credit sales × 0.01). The net realizable value of accounts receivable is therefore $26,000 ($30,000 − $4,000).

Accounting Events Affecting the 2014 Period

To further illustrate accounting for uncollectible accounts, we discuss six accounting events affecting Allen's Tutoring Services during 2014.

EVENT 1   Write-Off of Uncollectible Accounts Receivable
Allen's Tutoring Services wrote off $70 of uncollectible accounts receivable.

This is an asset exchange transaction. The amount of the uncollectible accounts is removed from the Accounts Receivable account and from the Allowance for Doubtful Accounts account. Since the balances in both the Accounts Receivable and the Allowance accounts decrease, the net realizable value of receivables—and therefore total assets—remains unchanged. The write-off does not affect the income statement. Since the uncollectible accounts expense was recognized in the previous year, the expense would be double counted if it were recognized again at the time an uncollectible account is written off. Finally, the statement of cash flows is not affected by the write-off. The journal entry and its effects on the financial statements are shown here:

Account Title	Debit	Credit
Allowance for Doubtful Accounts	70	
Accounts Receivable		70

Assets	=	Liab.	+	Equity	Rev.	−	Exp.	=	Net Inc.	Cash Flow
Net Realizable Value of Receivables										
NA	=	NA	+	NA	NA	−	NA	=	NA	NA

The computation of the *net realizable value,* before and after the write-off, is shown below:

	Before Write-Off	After Write-Off
Accounts receivable	$1,500	$1,430
Less: Allowance for doubtful accounts	(75)	(5)
Net realizable value	$1,425	$1,425

EVENT 2   Revenue Recognition
Allen's Tutoring Services provided $10,000 of tutoring services on account during 2014.

Assets (accounts receivable) and stockholders' equity (retained earnings) increase. Recognizing revenue increases net income. Cash flow is not affected. The journal entry and its effects on the financial statements are shown here:

Account Title	Debit	Credit
Accounts Receivable	10,000	
Service Revenue		10,000

Assets	=	Liab.	+	Equity	Rev.	−	Exp.	=	Net Inc.	Cash Flow
Accts. Rec.	=			Ret. Earn.						
10,000	=	NA	+	10,000	10,000	−	NA	=	10,000	NA

EVENT 3   Collection of Accounts Receivable
Allen's Tutoring Services collected $8,430 cash from accounts receivable.

The balance in the Cash account increases, and the balance in the Accounts Receivable account decreases. Total assets are unaffected. Net income is not affected because revenue was recognized previously. The cash inflow is reported in the operating activities section of the statement of cash flows. The journal entry and its effects on the financial statements are shown here:

Account Title	Debit	Credit
Cash	8,430	
Accounts Receivable		8,430

Assets			=	Liab.	+	Equity	Rev.	−	Exp.	=	Net Inc.	Cash Flow	
Cash	+	Accts. Rec.											
8,430	+	(8,430)	=	NA	+	NA	NA	−	NA	=	NA	8,430	OA

EVENT 4   Recovery of an Uncollectible Account: Reinstate Receivable
Allen's Tutoring Services recovered a receivable that it had previously written off.

Occasionally, a company receives payment from a customer whose account was previously written off. In such cases, the customer's account should be reinstated and the cash received should be recorded the same way as any other collection on account. The account receivable is reinstated because a complete record of the customer's payment history may be useful if the customer requests credit again at some future date. To illustrate, assume that Allen's Tutoring Services received a $10 cash payment from a customer whose account had previously been written off. The first step is to **reinstate** the account receivable by reversing the previous write-off. The balances in the Accounts Receivable and the Allowance accounts increase. Since the Allowance is a contra asset account, the increase in it offsets the increase in the Accounts Receivable account, and total assets are unchanged. Net income and cash flow are unaffected. The journal entry and its effects on the financial statements are shown here:

Account Title	Debit	Credit
Accounts Receivable	10	
Allowance for Doubtful Accounts		10

Assets	=	Liab.	+	Equity	Rev.	−	Exp.	=	Net Inc.	Cash Flow
Net Realizable Value of Receivables										
NA	=	NA	+	NA	NA	−	NA	=	NA	NA

EVENT 5   Recovery of an Uncollectible Account: Collection of Receivable
Allen's Tutoring Services recorded collection of the reinstated receivable.

The collection of $10 is recorded like any other collection of a receivable account. Cash increases, and Accounts Receivable decreases. The journal entry and its effects on the financial statements are shown here:

Account Title	Debit	Credit
Cash	10	
Accounts Receivable		10

Assets			=	Liab.	+	Equity	Rev.	−	Exp.	=	Net Inc.	Cash Flow	
Cash	+	Accts. Rec.											
10	+	(10)	=	NA	+	NA	NA	−	NA	=	NA	10	OA

ESTIMATING UNCOLLECTIBLE ACCOUNTS EXPENSE USING THE PERCENT OF REVENUE (SALES) METHOD

LO 2

Use the percent of revenue method to estimate uncollectible accounts expense.

Companies recognize the estimated amount of uncollectible accounts expense in a period-end adjusting entry. Since Allen's Tutoring Service began operations in 2013, it had no previous credit history upon which to base its estimate. After consulting trade publications and experienced people in the same industry, ATS made an educated guess as to the amount of expense it should recognize for its first year. In its second year of operation, however, ATS can use its first-year experience as a starting point for estimating the second year (2014) uncollectible accounts expense.

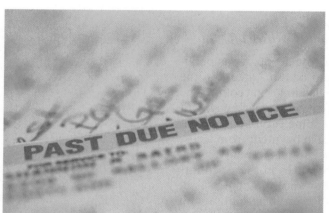

At the end of 2013 ATS estimated uncollectible accounts expense to be $75 on service revenue of $14,000. In 2014 ATS actually wrote off $70 of which $10 was later recovered. ATS therefore experienced actual uncollectible accounts of $60 on service revenue of $14,000 for an uncollectible accounts rate of approximately .43 percent of service revenue. ATS could apply this percentage to the 2014 service revenue to estimate the 2014 uncollectible accounts expense. In practice, many companies determine the percentage estimate of uncollectible accounts on a three- or five-year moving average.

Companies adjust the historical percentage for anticipated future circumstances. For example, they reduce it if they adopt more rigorous approval standards for new credit applicants. Alternatively, they may increase the percentage if economic forecasts signal an economic downturn that would make future defaults more likely. A company will also increase the percentage if it has specific knowledge one or more of its customers is financially distressed. Multiplying the service revenue by the percentage estimate of uncollectible accounts is commonly called the **percent of revenue method** of estimating uncollectible accounts expense.

EVENT 6   Adjustment for Recognition of Uncollectible Accounts Expense
Using the percent of revenue method, Allen's Tutoring Services recognized uncollectible accounts expense for 2014.

ATS must record this adjustment as of December 31, 2014, to update its accounting records before preparing the 2014 financial statements. After reviewing its credit history, economic forecasts, and correspondence with customers, management estimates uncollectible accounts expense to be 1.35 percent of service revenue, or $135 ($10,000 service revenue × .0135). Recognizing the $135 uncollectible accounts expense decreases both assets (net realizable value of receivables) and stockholders' equity (retained earnings). The expense recognition decreases net income. The statement of cash flows is not affected. The journal entry and its effects on the financial statements are shown here:

Account Title	Debit	Credit
Uncollectible Accounts Expense	135	
Allowance for Doubtful Accounts		135

Assets		Liab.	+	Equity	Rev.	–	Exp.	=	Net Inc.	Cash Flow
Net Realizable Value of Receivables	=			Ret. Earn.						
(135)	=	NA	+	(135)	NA	–	135	=	(135)	NA

Recording and Reporting Uncollectible Accounts Events in the Double-Entry System

Panel A of Exhibit 7.2 shows a summary of the 2014 accounting events. Panel B of the exhibit shows the general ledger T-accounts after the journal entries have been posted to them. Panel C contains the financial statements. Exhibit 7.2 does not include the closing entries. Closing the accounts will transfer the amounts from the revenue and expense accounts to the Retained Earnings account, resulting in a $23,790 ending balance in this account as shown on the 2014 balance sheet.

EXHIBIT 7.2

The Big Picture

Panel A Transactions Summary

Event 1   ATS wrote off $70 of uncollectible accounts receivable.
Event 2   ATS earned $10,000 of revenue on account.
Event 3   ATS collected $8,430 cash from accounts receivable.
Event 4   ATS reinstated a $10 account receivable it had previously written off.
Event 5   ATS recorded the collection of $10 from the reinstated receivable referenced in Event 4.
Event 6   ATS adjusted its accounts to recognize $135 of uncollectible accounts expense.

Panel B General Ledger Accounts

Assets   =   Liabilities   +   Equity

Cash

Bal.	12,500	
(3)	8,430	
(5)	10	
Bal.	20,940	

Retained Earnings

| | 13,925 | Bal. |

Accounts Receivable

Bal.	1,500	70	(1)
(2)	10,000	8,430	(3)
(4)	10	10	(5)
Bal.	3,000		

Service Revenue

| | 10,000 | (2) |

Allowance for Doubtful Accounts

(1)	70	75	Bal.
		10	(4)
		135	(6)
		150	Bal.

Uncollectible Accts. Expense

| (6) | 135 | |

Panel C Financial Statements for 2014

Income Statement

Service revenue	$10,000
Uncollectible accts. exp.	(135)
Net income	$ 9,865

Balance Sheet

Assets		
Cash		$20,940
Accounts receivable	$3,000	
Less: Allowance	(150)	
Net realizable value		2,850
Total assets		$23,790
Stockholders' equity		
Retained earnings		$23,790

Statement of Cash Flows

Operating Activities	
Inflow from customers	$ 8,440
Investing Activities	0
Financing Activities	0
Net change in cash	8,440
Plus: Beginning cash balance	12,500
Ending cash balance	$20,940

Analysis of Financial Statements

Exhibit 7.2 Panel C displays the 2014 financial statements. The amount of uncollectible accounts expense ($135) differs from the ending balance of the Allowance account ($150). The balance in the Allowance account was $15 before the 2014 adjusting entry for uncollectible accounts expense was recorded. At the end of 2013, Allen's Tutoring Services estimated there would be $75 of uncollectible accounts as a result of 2013 credit sales. Actual write-offs, however, amounted to $70 and $10 of that amount was recovered, indicating the actual uncollectible accounts expense for 2013 was only $60. Hindsight shows the expense for 2013 was overstated by $15. However, if no estimate had been made, the amount of uncollectible accounts expense would have been understated by $60. In some accounting periods estimated uncollectible accounts expense will likely be overstated; in others it may be understated. The allowance method cannot produce perfect results, but it does improve the accuracy of the financial statements.

Since no dividends were paid, retained earnings at the end of 2014 equals the December 31, 2013, retained earnings plus 2014 net income (that is, $13,925 + $9,865 = $23,790). Again, the cash flow from operating activities ($8,440) differs from net income ($9,865) because the statement of cash flows does not include the effects of revenues earned on account or the recognition of uncollectible accounts expense.

✓ CHECK YOURSELF 7.2

Maher Company had beginning balances in Accounts Receivable and Allowance for Doubtful Accounts of $24,200 and $2,000, respectively. During the accounting period Maher earned $230,000 of revenue on account and collected $232,500 of cash from receivables. The company also wrote off $1,950 of uncollectible accounts during the period. Maher estimates uncollectible accounts expense will be 1 percent of credit sales. Based on this information, what is the net realizable value of receivables at the end of the period?

Answer   The balance in the Accounts Receivable account is $19,750 ($24,200 + $230,000 − $232,500 − $1,950). The amount of uncollectible accounts expense for the period is $2,300 ($230,000 × 0.01). The balance in the Allowance for Doubtful Accounts is $2,350 ($2,000 − $1,950 + $2,300). The net realizable value of receivables is therefore $17,400 ($19,750 − $2,350).

ESTIMATING UNCOLLECTIBLE ACCOUNTS EXPENSE USING THE PERCENT OF RECEIVABLES METHOD

As an alternative to the percent of revenue method, which focuses on estimating the *expense* of uncollectible accounts, companies may estimate the amount of the adjusting entry to record uncollectible accounts expense using the **percent of receivables method.** The percent of receivables method focuses on estimating the most accurate amount for the balance sheet *Allowance for Doubtful Accounts* account.

The longer an account receivable remains outstanding, the less likely it is to be collected. Companies using the percent of receivables method typically determine the age of their individual accounts receivable accounts as part of estimating the allowance for doubtful accounts. An **aging of accounts receivable** schedule classifies all receivables by their due date. Exhibit 7.3 shows an aging schedule for Pyramid Corporation as of December 31, 2014.

A company estimates the required Allowance for Doubtful Accounts balance by applying different percentages to each category in the aging schedule. The percentage for each category is based on a company's previous collection experience for each of the categories. The percentages become progressively higher as the accounts become older. Exhibit 7.4 illustrates computing the allowance balance Pyramid Corporation requires.

EXHIBIT 7.3

PYRAMID CORPORATION
Accounts Receivable Aging Schedule
December 31, 2014

| Customer Name | Total Balance | Current | Number of Days Past Due | | | |
			0–30	31–60	61–90	Over 90
J. Davis	$ 6,700	$ 6,700				
B. Diamond	4,800	2,100	$ 2,700			
K. Eppy	9,400	9,400				
B. Gilman	2,200				$1,000	$1,200
A. Kelly	7,300	7,300				
L. Niel	8,600	1,000	6,000	$ 1,600		
L. Platt	4,600			4,600		
J. Turner	5,500			3,000	2,000	500
H. Zachry	6,900		3,000	3,900		
Total	$56,000	$26,500	$11,700	$13,100	$3,000	$1,700

EXHIBIT 7.4

Balance Required in the Allowance for Doubtful Accounts at December 31, 2014

Number of Days Past Due	Receivables Amount	Percentage Likely to Be Uncollectible	Required Allowance Account Balance
Current	$26,500	.01	$ 265
0–30	11,700	.05	585
31–60	13,100	.10	1,310
61–90	3,000	.25	750
Over 90	1,700	.50	850
Total	$56,000		$3,760

The computations in Exhibit 7.4 mean the *ending balance* in the Allowance for Doubtful Accounts account should be $3,760. This balance represents the amount Pyramid will subtract from total accounts receivable to determine the net realizable value of receivables. To determine the amount of the adjusting entry to recognize uncollectible accounts expense, Pyramid must take into account any existing balance in the allowance account *before* recording the adjustment. For example, if Pyramid Corporation had a $500 credit balance in the Allowance account before the year-end adjustment, the adjusting entry would need to add $3,260 ($3,760 − $500) to the account. The journal entry to record the uncollectible accounts expense and its effects on the financial statements are shown below:

Account Title	Debit	Credit
Uncollectible Accounts Expense	3,260	
Allowance for Doubtful Accounts		3,260

Assets	=	Liab.	+	Equity	Rev.	−	Exp.	=	Net Inc.	Cash Flow
Net Realizable Value of Receivables	=			Ret. Earn.						
(3,260)	=	NA	+	(3,260)	NA	−	3,260	=	(3,260)	NA

Matching Revenues and Expenses versus Asset Measurement

The *percent of revenue* method, with its focus on determining the uncollectible accounts expense, is often called the income statement approach. The *percent of receivables* method, focused on determining the best estimate of the allowance balance, is frequently called the balance sheet approach. Which estimating method is better? In any given year, the results will vary slightly between approaches. In the long run, however, the percentages used in either approach are based on a company's actual history of uncollectible accounts. Accountants routinely revise their estimates as more data become available, using hindsight to determine if the percentages should be increased or decreased. Either approach provides acceptable results.

RECOGNIZING UNCOLLECTIBLE ACCOUNTS EXPENSE USING THE DIRECT WRITE-OFF METHOD

LO 4

Show how the direct write-off method of accounting for uncollectible accounts affects financial statements.

If uncollectible accounts are not material, generally accepted accounting principles allow companies to account for them using the **direct write-off method.** Under the direct write-off method, a company simply recognizes uncollectible accounts expense *in the period in which it identifies and writes off uncollectible accounts.* No estimates, allowance account, or adjusting entries are needed.

The direct write-off method fails to match revenues with expenses. Revenues are recognized in one period and any related uncollectible accounts expense is recognized in a later period. Also, the direct write-off method overstates assets because receivables are reported at *face value* rather than *net realizable value.* If the amount of uncollectible accounts is immaterial, however, companies accept the minor reporting inaccuracies as a reasonable trade-off for recording convenience.

To illustrate the direct write-off method, return to the first year (2013) that Allen's Tutoring Service (ATS) operated. Assume ATS decided the direct write-off method was appropriate to account for its receivables. Recall that during 2013 ATS recognized $14,000 of revenue on account. The journal entry and its effects on the financial statements are shown below:

Account Title	Debit	Credit
Accounts Receivable	14,000	
Service Revenue		14,000

Assets	=	Liab.	+	Equity	Rev.	−	Exp.	=	Net Inc.	Cash Flow
Accts. Rec.	=			Ret. Earn.						
14,000	=	NA	+	14,000	14,000	−	NA	=	14,000	NA

ATS believed only an immaterial amount of the $14,000 of accounts receivable would prove uncollectible. It therefore made no year-end adjusting entry for estimated uncollectible accounts. Instead, ATS recognizes uncollectible accounts expense when it determines an account is uncollectible.

In its second accounting period (2014), ATS determined that $70 of accounts receivable were uncollectible. ATS recognized the uncollectible accounts expense in the entry to write off the uncollectible receivables. With the direct write-off method, the write-off reduces the asset account Accounts Receivable and decreases the stockholders' equity account Retained Earnings. On the income statement, expenses increase and net income decreases. The statement of cash flows is not affected by the write-off. The journal entry and its effects on the financial statements are shown below:

Account Title	Debit	Credit
Uncollectible Accounts Expense	70	
Accounts Receivable		70

Assets	=	Liab.	+	Equity	Rev.	−	Exp.	=	Net Inc.	Cash Flow
Accts. Rec.	=			Ret. Earn.						
(70)	=	NA	+	(70)	NA	−	70	=	(70)	NA

Also in 2014 ATS recovered a $10 account receivable it had previously written off. Recording the recovery of a previously written-off account requires two entries. First, ATS must *reinstate* the receivable (merely reverse the write-off entry above) because it has proven to be collectible after all. Second, ATS must record collecting the reinstated account. With the direct write-off method, reinstating the receivable increases the asset account Accounts Receivable and increases the stockholders' equity account Retained Earnings. On the income statement, expenses decrease and net income increases. The statement of cash flows is not affected. The journal entry and its effects on the financial statements are shown below:

Account Title	Debit	Credit
Accounts Receivable	10	
Uncollectible Accounts Expense		10

Assets	=	Liab.	+	Equity	Rev.	−	Exp.	=	Net Inc.	Cash Flow
Accts. Rec.	=			Ret. Earn.						
10	=	NA	+	10	NA	−	(10)	=	10	NA

Like the collection of any other receivable, collection of the reinstated account receivable increases the asset account Cash and decreases the asset account Accounts Receivable. The income statement is not affected. The cash inflow is reported in the operating activities section of the statement of cash flows. The journal entry and its effects on the financial statements are shown below:

Account Title	Debit	Credit
Cash	10	
Accounts Receivable		10

Assets		=	Liab.	+	Equity	Rev.	−	Exp.	=	Net Inc.	Cash Flow
Cash	− Accts. Rec.										
10	(10)	=	NA	+	NA	NA	−	NA	=	NA	10 OA

ACCOUNTING FOR NOTES RECEIVABLE

LO 5

Companies typically do not charge their customers interest on accounts receivable that are not past due. When a company extends credit for a long time or when the amount of credit it extends is large, however, the cost of granting free credit and the potential for disputes about payment terms both increase. To address these concerns, the parties

Explain how accounting for notes receivable and accrued interest affects financial statements.

EXHIBIT 7.5

Promissory Note

Promissory Note

$15,000 (3)   *November 1, 2013*

Amount   **Date**

For consideration received, Stanford Cummings (1) **hereby promises to pay to the order of:**

Allen's Tutoring Services (2)

Fifteen thousand and no/100 (3)   **Dollars**

payable on   October 31, 2014 (5)

plus interest thereon at the rate of 6 percent per year. (4)

Collateral Description   Automobile title (6)

Signature   *Stanford Cummings* (1)

frequently enter into a credit agreement, the terms of which are legally documented in a **promissory note.**

To illustrate, assume Allen's Tutoring Services (ATS) loans some of its idle cash to an individual, Stanford Cummings, so Cummings can buy a car. ATS and Cummings agree that Cummings will repay the money borrowed plus interest at the end of one year. They also agree that ATS will hold the title to the car to secure the debt. Exhibit 7.5 illustrates a promissory note that outlines this credit agreement. For ATS, the credit arrangement represents a *note receivable.*

Features of this note are discussed below. Each feature is cross referenced with a number that corresponds to an item on the promissory note in Exhibit 7.5. Locate each feature in Exhibit 7.5 and read the corresponding description of the feature below:

1. Maker—The person responsible for making payment on the due date is the **maker** of the note. The maker may also be called the *borrower* or *debtor.*

2. Payee—The person to whom the note is made payable is the **payee.** The payee may also be called the *creditor* or *lender.* The payee loans money to the maker and expects the return of the principal and the interest due.

3. Principal—The amount of money loaned by the payee to the maker of the note is the **principal.**

4. Interest—The economic benefit earned by the payee for loaning the principal to the maker is **interest,** which is normally expressed as an annual percentage of the principal amount. For example, a note with a 6 percent interest rate requires interest payments equal to 6 percent of the principal amount every year the loan is outstanding.

5. Maturity Date—The date on which the maker must repay the principal and make the final interest payment to the payee is the **maturity date.**

6. Collateral—Assets belonging to the maker that are assigned as security to ensure that the principal and interest will be paid when due are called **collateral.** In this example, if Cummings fails to pay ATS the amount due, ownership of the car Cummings purchased will be transferred to ATS.

Recording and Reporting Transactions Related to Notes Receivable

We illustrate accounting for notes receivable using the credit agreement evidenced by the promissory note in Exhibit 7.5. Allen's Tutoring Services engaged in many transactions during 2013; we discuss here only transactions directly related to the note receivable.

EVENT 1   Loan of Money

The note shows that ATS loaned $15,000 to Stanford Cummings on November 1, 2013. This event is an asset exchange. The asset account Cash decreases and the asset account Notes Receivable increases. The income statement is not affected. The statement of cash flows shows a cash outflow for investing activities. The journal entry and its effects on the financial statements are shown below:

Account Title	Debit	Credit
Notes Receivable	15,000	
Cash		15,000

	Assets					=	Liab.	+	Equity	Rev.	–	Exp.	=	Net Inc.	Cash Flow
Date	Cash	+	Notes Rec.	+	Int. Rec.	=			Ret. Earn.						
11/01/13	(15,000)	+	15,000	+	NA	=	NA	+	NA	NA	–	NA	=	NA	(15,000) IA

EVENT 2   Accrual of Interest

For ATS, loaning money represents an investment in the note receivable. ATS will collect the principal ($15,000) plus interest of 6 percent of the principal amount ($0.06 \times \$15,000 = \$900$), or a total of $15,900, on October 31, 2014, one year from the date the loan was made.

Conceptually, lenders *earn* interest continually even though they do not *collect* cash continually. Each day, the amount of interest due, called **accrued interest**, is greater than the day before. Companies would find it highly impractical to attempt to record (recognize) accrued interest continually as the amount due increased.

Businesses typically solve the recordkeeping problem by only recording accrued interest when it is time to prepare financial statements or when it is due. At such times, the accounts are *adjusted* to reflect the amount of interest currently due. For example, ATS recorded the asset exchange immediately upon investing in the Note Receivable on November 1, 2013. ATS did not, however, recognize any interest earned on the note until the balance sheet date, December 31, 2013. At year-end ATS made an entry to recognize the interest it had earned during the previous two months (November 1 through December 31). This entry is an **adjusting entry** because it adjusts (updates) the account balances prior to preparing financial statements.

ATS computed the amount of accrued interest by multiplying the principal amount of the note by the annual interest rate and by the length of time for which the note has been outstanding.

Principal × Annual interest rate × Time outstanding = Interest revenue
$15,000 ×   0.06   ×   (2/12)   = $150

ATS recognized the $150 of interest revenue in 2013 although ATS will not collect the cash until 2014. This practice illustrates the **matching concept.** Interest revenue is recognized in (matched with) the period in which it is earned regardless of when the related cash is collected. The adjusting entry is an asset source transaction. The asset account Interest Receivable increases, and the stockholders' equity account Retained Earnings increases. The income statement reflects an increase in revenue and net income. The statement of cash flows is not affected because ATS will not collect cash until the maturity date (October 31, 2014). The adjusting entry and its effects on the financial statements are shown below:

Account Title	Debit	Credit
Interest Receivable	150	
Interest Revenue		150

	Assets				=	Liab.	+	Equity	Rev.	–	Exp.	=	Net Inc.	Cash Flow
Date	Cash	+	Notes Rec.	+	Int. Rec.	=			Ret. Earn.					
12/31/13	NA	+	NA	+	150	=	NA	+	150	150	–	NA	=	150	NA

EVENT 3 Collection of Principal and Interest on the Maturity Date

ATS collected $15,900 cash on the maturity date. The collection included $15,000 for the principal plus $900 for the interest. Recall that ATS previously accrued interest in the December 31, 2013, adjusting entry for the two months in 2013 that the note was outstanding. Since year-end, ATS has earned an additional 10 months of interest revenue. ATS must recognize this interest revenue before recording the cash collection. The amount of interest earned in 2014 is computed as follows:

$$\text{Principal} \times \text{Annual interest rate} \times \text{Time outstanding} = \text{Interest revenue}$$
$$\$15,000 \times 0.06 \times (10/12) = \$750$$

The journal entry and effects on the financial statements are shown below:

Account Title	Debit	Credit
Interest Receivable	750	
Interest Revenue		750

	Assets				=	Liab.	+	Equity	Rev.	–	Exp.	=	Net Inc.	Cash Flow
Date	Cash	+	Notes Rec.	+	Int. Rec.	=			Ret. Earn.					
10/31/14	NA	+	NA	+	750	=	NA	+	750	750	–	NA	=	750	NA

The total amount of accrued interest is now $900 ($150 accrued in 2013 plus $750 accrued in 2014). The $15,900 cash collection is an asset exchange transaction. The asset account Cash increases and two asset accounts, Notes Receivable and Interest Receivable, decrease. The income statement is not affected. The statement of cash flows shows a $15,000 inflow from investing activities (recovery of principal) and a $900 inflow from operating activities (interest collection). The journal entry and effects on the financial statements are shown below:

Account Title	Debit	Credit
Cash	15,900	
Notes Receivable		15,000
Interest Receivable		900

	Assets				=	Liab.	+	Equity	Rev.	–	Exp.	=	Net Inc.	Cash Flow
Date	Cash	+	Notes Rec.	+	Int. Rec.	=			Ret. Earn.					
10/31/14	15,900	+	(15,900)	+	(900)	=	NA	+	NA	NA	–	NA	=	NA	15,000 IA 900 OA

To clarify the illustration, we showed the interest accrual and the cash collection as two separate entries. Experienced accountants often record the two events in a single journal entry as follows:

Account Title	Debit	Credit
Cash	15,900	
Notes Receivable		15,000
Interest Receivable		150
Interest Revenue		750

Financial Statements

The financial statements reveal key differences between the timing of revenue recognition and the exchange of cash. These differences are highlighted below:

	2013	2014	Total
Interest revenue recognized	$150	$750	$900
Cash inflow from operating activities	0	900	900

Accrual accounting calls for recognizing revenue in the period in which it is earned regardless of when cash is collected.

Income Statement

Although generally accepted accounting principles require reporting receipts of or payments for interest on the statement of cash flows as operating activities, they do not specify how to classify interest on the income statement. In fact, companies traditionally report interest on the income statement as a nonoperating item. Interest is therefore frequently reported in two different categories within the same set of financial statements.

Balance Sheet

As with other assets, companies report interest receivable and notes receivable on the balance sheet in order of their liquidity. **Liquidity** refers to how quickly assets are expected to be converted to cash during normal operations. In the preceding example, ATS expects to convert its accounts receivable to cash before it collects the interest receivable and note receivable. Companies commonly report interest and notes receivable after accounts receivable. Exhibit 7.6 shows a partial balance sheet for Southern Company to illustrate the presentation of receivables.

EXHIBIT 7.6

Typical Balance Sheet Presentation of Receivables

SOUTHERN COMPANY
Partial Balance Sheet
As of December 31, 2013

Cash		xxxx
Accounts receivable	xxxx	
Less: Allowance for doubtful accounts	(xxxx)	
Net realizable value of accounts receivable		xxxx
Interest receivable		xxxx
Notes receivable		xxxx

✓ CHECK YOURSELF 7.3

On October 1, 2013, Mei Company accepted a promissory note for a loan it made to the Asia Pacific Company. The note had a $24,000 principal amount, a four-month term, and an annual interest rate of 4 percent. Determine the amount of interest revenue and the cash inflow from operating activities Mei will report in its 2013 and 2014 financial statements. Also provide in general journal form the year-end adjusting entry needed to recognize 2013 interest revenue.

Answer   The computation of accrued interest revenue is shown below. The interest rate is stated in annual terms even though the term of the note is only four months. Interest rates are commonly expressed as an annual percentage regardless of the term of the note. The *time outstanding* in the following formulas is therefore expressed as a fraction of a year. Mei charged annual interest of 4 percent, but the note was outstanding for only 3/12 of a year in 2013 and 1/12 of a year in 2014.

2013

Principal	×	Annual interest rate	×	Time outstanding	=	Interest revenue
$24,000	×	0.04	×	(3/12)	=	$240

2014

Principal	×	Annual interest rate	×	Time outstanding	=	Interest revenue
$24,000	×	0.04	×	(1/12)	=	$80

In 2013, Mei's cash inflow from interest will be zero.

In 2014, Mei will report a $320 ($240 + $80) cash inflow from operating activities for interest. The adjusting entry to recognize 2013 accrued interest is as follows:

Interest Receivable	240	
Interest Revenue		240

ACCOUNTING FOR CREDIT CARD SALES

LO 6

Explain how accounting for credit card sales affects financial statements.

Maintaining accounts and notes receivable is expensive. In addition to uncollectible accounts expense, companies extending credit to their customers incur considerable costs for such clerical tasks as running background checks and maintaining customer records. Many businesses find it more efficient to accept third-party credit cards instead of offering

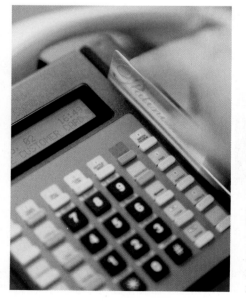

credit directly to their customers. Credit card companies service the merchant's credit sales for a fee that typically ranges between 2 and 8 percent of gross sales.

The credit card company usually provides customers with plastic cards that permit cardholders to charge purchases at various retail outlets. When a sale takes place, the seller records the transaction on a receipt the customer signs. The receipt is forwarded to the credit card company, which immediately pays the merchant.

The credit card company deducts its service fee from the gross amount of the sale and pays the merchant the net balance (gross amount of sale less credit card fee) in cash. The credit card company collects the gross sale amount directly from the customer. The merchant avoids the risk of uncollectible accounts as well as the cost of maintaining customer credit records. To illustrate, assume that Allen's Tutoring Service experiences the following events.

EVENT 1   Recognition of Revenue and Expense on Credit Card Sales
ATS accepts a credit card payment for $1,000 of services rendered.

Assume the credit card company charges a 5 percent fee for handling the transaction ($1,000 × 0.05 = $50). ATS's income increases by the amount of revenue ($1,000) and decreases by the amount of the credit card expense

($50). Net income increases by $950. The event increases an asset, accounts receivable, due from the credit card company, and stockholders' equity (retained earnings) by $950 ($1,000 revenue − $50 credit card expense). Cash flow is not affected. The journal entry and its effects on the financial statements are shown here:

Account Title	Debit	Credit
Accounts Receivable—Credit Card Company	950	
Credit Card Expense	50	
Service Revenue		1,000

Assets	=	Liab.	+	Equity	Rev.	−	Exp.	=	Net Inc.	Cash Flow
Accts. Rec.	=			Ret. Earn.						
950	=	NA	+	950	1,000	−	50	=	950	NA

EVENT 2   Collection of Credit Card Receivable

The collection of the receivable due from the credit card company is recorded like any other receivable collection.

When ATS collects the net amount of $950 ($1,000 − $50) from the credit card company, one asset account (Cash) increases and another asset account (Accounts Receivable) decreases. Total assets are not affected. The income statement is not affected. A $950 cash inflow is reported in the operating activities section of the statement of cash flows. The journal entry and its effects on the financial statements are shown here:

Account Title	Debit	Credit
Cash	950	
Accounts Receivable—Credit Card Company		950

Assets			=	Liab.	+	Equity	Rev.	−	Exp.	=	Net Inc.	Cash Flow
Cash	+	Accts. Rec.										
950	+	(950)	=	NA	+	NA	NA	−	NA	=	NA	950 OA

- -

THE FINANCIAL ANALYST

COSTS OF CREDIT SALES

As mentioned earlier, two costs of extending credit to customers are uncollectible accounts expense and recordkeeping costs. These costs can be significant. Large companies spend literally millions of dollars to buy the equipment and pay the staff necessary to operate entire departments devoted to managing accounts receivable. Further, there is an implicit interest cost associated with extending credit. When a customer is permitted to delay payment, the creditor forgoes the opportunity to invest the amount the customer owes.

Exhibit 7.7 presents part of a note from the 2010 annual report of Rent-A-Center. This excerpt provides insight into the credit costs real companies incur. First, observe that Rent-A-Center was owed $62.6 million of accounts receivable. These receivables represent money that could be in the bank earning interest if all sales had been made in cash. If Rent-A-Center could have earned interest at 5 percent on that money, the opportunity cost of this lost interest is approximately $3.1 million ($62.6 million × .05) a year. Next, observe that Rent-A-Center expects to have uncollectible accounts

LO 7

Explain the effects of the cost of financing credit sales.

EXHIBIT 7.7

RENT-A-CENTER, INC. December 31, 2010
PARTIAL NOTE B Regarding Accountants Receivable and Allowance for Doubtful Accounts (amounts shown in thousands)

Receivables consist of the following:

	2010	2009
Installment sales receivable	$ 42,839	$ 35,636
Financial service loans receivable	12,232	26,021
Trade and notes receivables	7,492	11,535
Total	62,563	73,192
Less allowance for doubtful accounts	(8,673)	(9,753)
Net receivables	$ 53,890	$ 63,439

Changes in the Company's allowance for doubtful accounts are as follows:

	2010	2009
Beginning balance	$ 9,753	$ 7,256
Bad debt expense	16,168	17,395
Accounts written off	(23,107)	(20,721)
Recoveries	5,859	5,823
Ending balance	$ 8,673	$ 9,753

amounting to $8.7 million (balance in the allowance account). These are significant costs to a company whose net income was $171.6 million in 2010.

Average Number of Days to Collect Accounts Receivable

The longer it takes to collect accounts receivable, the greater the opportunity cost of lost income. Also, business experience indicates that the older an account receivable becomes, the less likely it is to be collected. Finally, taking longer to collect an account typically costs more for salaries, equipment, and supplies used in the process of trying to collect it. Businesses are therefore concerned about how long it takes to collect their receivables.

Two ratios help management, or other users, measure a company's collection period. One is the **accounts receivable turnover ratio,** computed as:[1]

$$\frac{\text{Sales}}{\text{Accounts receivable}}$$

Dividing a company's sales by its accounts receivable tells how many times the accounts receivable balance is "turned over" (converted into cash) each year. The higher the turnover, the shorter the collection period. To simplify its interpretation, the accounts receivable turnover ratio is often taken one step further to determine the **average number of days to collect accounts receivable,** sometimes called the *average collection period.* This is computed as:

$$\frac{365}{\text{Accounts receivable turnover ratio}}$$

This ratio measures how many days, on average, it takes a company to collect its accounts receivable. Since longer collection periods increase costs, shorter periods are obviously more desirable. To illustrate computing the *average number of days to collect accounts receivable* for Allen's Tutoring Services, refer to the 2014 financial statements

---

[1]To be more precise, the ratio could be computed using only credit sales and average accounts receivable. Usually, however, companies do not report credit sales separately from cash sales in published financial statements. Average accounts receivable, if desired, is computed as [(beginning receivables + ending receivables) ÷ 2]. For this course, use the simpler computation shown here (sales ÷ accounts receivable).

in Exhibit 7.2. On average, the company takes 104 days to collect its receivables, computed in two steps:

1. The accounts receivable turnover is 3.509 ($10,000 ÷ $2,850) times.
2. The average number of days to collect receivables is 104 (365 ÷ 3.509) days.

In the preceding computations, the net realizable value of accounts receivable was used because that is the amount typically reported in published financial statements. The results would not have been materially different had total accounts receivable been used.

Real-World Data

What is the collection period for real companies? The time required to collect receivables varies among industries and among companies within industries. Column 4 in Exhibit 7.8 displays the average number of days to collect receivables for seven companies in three different industries. These numbers are for 2010.

Since fast-food restaurants require customers to pay cash when they purchase hamburgers or coffee, why do these companies have accounts receivable? The accounts receivable for McDonald's, Starbucks, and Yum! arise because these companies sell goods to restaurants that are independent franchisees. So, for example, McDonald's accounts receivable represents future collections from restaurant owners, not customers who purchase hamburgers.

Is the collection period for Concha y Toro, too long? The answer depends on its credit policies. If it is selling goods to customers on net 30-day terms, there may be reason for concern, but if it allows customers 120 days to pay and the cost of this policy has been built into its pricing structure, the collection period is not unreasonable.

Some companies allow their customers extended time to pay their bills because the customers would otherwise have difficulty coming up with the money. For example, Concha y Toro may sell to a wine retailer that does not have the cash available to pay immediately. If Concha y Toro allows the retailer sufficient time, the retailer can sell the wine to customers and obtain the cash it needs to pay Concha y Toro. Many small companies do not have cash available to pay up front. Buying on credit is the only way they can obtain the inventory they need. If a manufacturer or wholesaler wants to sell to such companies, credit sales represent the only option available.

The length of the **operating cycle** is the average time it takes a business to convert inventory to accounts receivable plus the time it takes to convert accounts receivable into cash. The average number of days to collect receivables is one component of the operating cycle for a particular company. The other component is the average number of days to sell inventory that was explained in Chapter 5. The length of the operating cycles for the real-world companies discussed herein is shown in the last column of Exhibit 7.8.

What is the significance of the different operating cycle lengths in Exhibit 7.8? As previously explained, the longer the operating cycle takes, the more it costs the company.

EXHIBIT 7.8

Industry	Company	Average Days to Sell Inventory	Average Days to Collect Receivables	Length of Operating Cycle
Fast Food	McDonald's	8	18	26
	Starbucks	44	10	54
	Yum! Brands	22	8	30
Department Stores	Target	61	33	94
	Walmart	42	4	46
Wine	Concha y Toro	162	106	268
	Willamette Valley Vineyards	404	27	431

REALITY BYTES

This chapter explains that, in general, companies want to collect their receivables as quickly as possible. There is a notable exception to this generalization. If a company charges its customers interest on unpaid receivables, the company makes money on the unpaid balance. Many sellers of "big-ticket" goods like furniture, large appliances, and automobiles offer to finance their customers' purchases, allowing customers extended time to pay off their receivables in exchange for the customers' paying additional charges for interest.

For example, most people probably think of Harley-Davidson as a company that makes its profits selling motorcycles, and that is largely true. However, Harley-Davidson also made a substantial amount of profit from financing the motorcycles that it sells. During 2006, 2007, and 2008, the company earned 88 percent of its operating income from motorcycle sales, and 12 percent from financing those sales. This amounted to $506 million of income before taxes. Therefore, the fact that it took Harley-Davidson 322 days to collect its receivables in 2008 was probably not a reason for concern. However, in recessionary times making payments on one's motorcycle loan is not a priority for some individuals. In 2009 Harley-Davidson had a $118 million operating loss from its financial operations, while motorcycle sales generated $314 million in pretax operating income.

Exhibit 7.8 shows it takes Target an average of 48 days longer than Walmart to complete an operating cycle. All other things being equal, approximately how much did this longer time reduce Target's earnings? Assume Target could invest excess cash at 8 percent (or alternatively, assume it pays 8 percent to finance its inventory and accounts receivable). Using the accounting information reported in Target's January 29, 2011, financial statements, we can answer the question as follows:

$$\text{Target's investment in inventory} \times \text{Interest rate} \times \text{Time} = \text{Cost}$$

$$\$7,576,000,000 \times 8\% \times 48/365 = \$79,703,671$$

With 3.9 operating cycles per year (365 ÷ 94), the extended operating cycle costs Target $311 million annually. Based on the assumptions used here, Target would have increased its after-tax earnings by approximately 8 percent, if it could have reduced its operating cycle by 48 days. Although this illustration is a rough estimate, it demonstrates that it is important for businesses to minimize the length of their operating cycles.

It should also be noted that one reason Target takes longer to collect its receivables than Walmart is because it has its own credit card. If a customer pays Walmart, or Target, with a third-party credit card such as Visa, the company gets its cash from the credit card company in a few days. However, Target will only receive cash from customers who use their Target credit card as the customers make monthly payments. Of course, if they do not pay off their card balance each month, Target will earn interest on their accounts. In its 2011 fiscal year, Target earned $1.6 billion in credit card revenue and cleared $541 million in pretax income from this revenue.

✓ CHECK YOURSELF 7.4

Randolph Corporation had sales for the year of $535,333 and an accounts receivable balance at year end of $22,000. Determine Randolph's average number of days to collect accounts receivable.

Answer   The accounts receivable turnover is 24.33 ($535,333 ÷ $22,000) times per year. The average number of days to collect accounts receivable is 15 (365 ÷ 24.33).

FOCUS ON INTERNATIONAL ISSUES

A ROSE BY ANY OTHER NAME ...

If a person who studied U.S. GAAP wanted to look at the financial statements of a non-U.S. company, choosing statements of a company from another English-speaking country might seem logical. Presumably, this would eliminate language differences, and only the differences in GAAP would remain. However, this is not true.

When an accountant in the United States uses the term *turnover,* she or he is usually thinking of a financial ratio, such as the accounts receivable turnover ratio. However, in the United Kingdom, the

term *turnover* refers to what U.S. accountants call *sales.* U.K. balance sheets do not usually show an account named *Inventory;* rather, they use the term *Stocks.* In the United States, accountants typically use the term *stocks* to refer to certificates representing ownership in a corporation. Finally, if an accountant or banker from the United Kingdom should ever ask you about your *gearing ratio,* he or she probably is not interested in your bicycle but in your debt to assets ratio.

Although IFRS have significantly increased the uniformity of financial reporting throughout the world, they do not seek to impose absolute uniformity. IFRS often allow alternate ways of accounting for the same business event, as will be discussed in Chapter 8. Even when different companies choose the same IFRS option for accounting for a given event, they are allowed some flexibility in the application of the IFRS rule, as are companies in the United States who follow GAAP. And, obviously, companies in different countries are allowed to prepare financial reports in their own language. As we will see in Chapter 9, companies in different countries may even use significantly different formats for their balance sheets.

A Look Back

We first introduced accounting for receivables in Chapter 2. This chapter presented additional complexities related to accounts receivable, such as the *allowance method of accounting for uncollectible accounts.* The allowance method improves matching of expenses with revenues. It also provides a more accurate measure of the value of accounts receivable on the balance sheet.

Under the allowance method, estimated uncollectible accounts expense is recorded in an adjusting entry at the end of the period in which a company has made credit sales. There are two methods commonly used to estimate the amount of uncollectible accounts expense: the percent of revenue method and the percent of receivables method. With the percent of revenue method, uncollectible accounts expense is measured as a percent of the period's sales. With the percent of receivables method, a company analyzes its accounts receivable at the end of the period, usually classifying them by age, to estimate the amount of the accounts receivable balance that is likely to be uncollectible. The balance in the Allowance for Doubtful Accounts account is then adjusted to equal the estimated amount of uncollectible accounts. Uncollectible accounts expense decreases the net realizable value of receivables (accounts receivable − allowance for doubtful accounts), stockholders' equity, and net income.

The allowance method of accounting for uncollectible accounts is conceptually superior to the *direct write-off method,* in which uncollectible accounts expense is recognized when an account is determined to be uncollectible. The direct write-off method fails to match revenues with expenses and overstates accounts receivable on the balance sheet. It is easier to use, however, and is permitted by generally accepted accounting principles if the amount of uncollectible accounts expense is immaterial.

The chapter also introduced notes receivable and accounting for *accrued interest.* When the term of a promissory note extends over more than one accounting period,

---

companies must record adjusting entries to recognize interest in the appropriate accounting period, even if the cash exchange of interest occurs in a different accounting period.

We also discussed accounting for credit card sales, a vehicle that shifts uncollectible accounts expense to the credit card issuer. Many companies find the benefits of accepting major credit cards to be worth the credit card expense consequently incurred.

Finally, we addressed the costs of making credit sales. In addition to uncollectible accounts expense, interest is a major cost of financing receivables. The length of the collection period provides a measure of the quality of receivables. Short collection periods usually indicate lower amounts of uncollectible accounts and interest cost. Long collection periods imply higher costs. The collection period can be measured in two steps. First, divide sales by the accounts receivable balance to determine the accounts receivable turnover ratio. Then divide the number of days in the year (365) by the accounts receivable turnover ratio.

>> A Look Forward

Chapter 8 discusses accounting for long-term assets such as buildings and equipment. As with inventory cost flow, discussed in Chapter 5, GAAP allows companies to use different accounting methods to report on similar types of business events. Life would be easier for accounting students if all companies used the same accounting methods. However, the business world is complex. For the foreseeable future, people are likely to continue to have diverse views as to the best way to account for a variety of business transactions. To function effectively in today's business environment, it is important for you to be able to recognize differences in reporting practices.

SELF-STUDY REVIEW PROBLEM

A step-by-step audio-narrated series of slides is provided on the text website at www.mhhe.com/edmonds8e.

During 2013 Calico Company experienced the following accounting events:

1. Provided $120,000 of services on account.
2. Collected $85,000 cash from accounts receivable.
3. Wrote off $1,800 of accounts receivable that were uncollectible.
4. Loaned $3,000 to an individual, Emma Gardner, in exchange for a note receivable.
5. Paid $90,500 cash for operating expenses.
6. Estimated that uncollectible accounts expense would be 2 percent of credit sales. Recorded the year-end adjusting entry.
7. Recorded the year-end adjusting entry for accrued interest on the note receivable (see Event 4). Calico made the loan on August 1. It had a six-month term and a 6 percent rate of interest.

Calico's ledger balances on January 1, 2013 were as follows:

Event No.	Assets				= Liab. +	Equity	
	Cash +	Net Realizable Value of Receivables +	Notes Rec. +	Int. Rec. =		Com. Stk. +	Ret. Earn.
Bal.	12,000	15,800	+ NA	+ NA	= NA +	20,000	+ 7,800

Required

a. Record the 2013 events in ledger accounts using the horizontal format shown above.
b. Determine net income for 2013.

c. Determine net cash flow from operating activities for 2013.

d. Determine the net realizable value of accounts receivable at December 31, 2013.

e. What amount of interest revenue will Calico recognize on its note receivable in 2014?

Solution to Requirement a.

Event No.	Cash	+	Net Realizable Value of Receivables	+	Notes Rec.	+	Int. Rec.	=	Liab.	+	Com. Stk.	+	Ret. Earn.
Bal.	12,000	+	15,800	+	NA	+	NA	=	NA	+	20,000	+	7,800
1	NA	+	120,000	+	NA	+	NA	=	NA	+	NA	+	120,000
2	85,000	+	(85,000)	+	NA	+	NA	=	NA	+	NA	+	NA
3	NA	+	NA	+	NA	+	NA	=	NA	+	NA	+	NA
4	(3,000)	+	NA	+	3,000	+	NA	=	NA	+	NA	+	NA
5	(90,500)	+	NA	+	NA	+	NA	=	NA	+	NA	+	(90,500)
6	NA	+	(2,400)	+	NA	+	NA	=	NA	+	NA	+	(2,400)
7	NA	+	NA	+	NA	+	75*	=	NA	+	NA	+	75
Totals	3,500	+	48,400	+	3,000	+	75	=	NA	+	20,000	+	34,975

*$3,000 × .06 × 5/12 = $75.

Solution to Requirements b–e.

b. Net income is $27,175 ($120,000 − $90,500 − $2,400 + $75).

c. Net cash flow from operating activities is an outflow of $5,500 ($85,000 − $90,500).

d. The net realizable value of accounts receivable is $48,400 ($51,200 − $2,800).

e. In 2014, Calico will recognize interest revenue for one month: $3,000 × .06 × 1/12 = $15.

KEY TERMS

account receivable 360
accounts receivable turnover ratio 380
accrued interest 375
adjusting entry 375
aging of accounts receivable 370
allowance for doubtful accounts 362

allowance method of accounting for uncollectible accounts 362
average number of days to collect accounts receivable 380
collateral 374
contra asset account 364
direct write-off method 372

interest 374
liquidity 377
maker 374
matching concept 375
maturity date 374
net realizable value 362
notes receivable 361
operating cycle 381
payee 374

percent of receivables method 370
percent of revenue method 368
principal 374
promissory note 374
reinstate 365
uncollectible accounts expense 364

QUESTIONS

1. What is the difference between accounts receivable and notes receivable?

2. What is the net realizable value of receivables?

3. What type of account is the Allowance for Doubtful Accounts?

4. What are two ways in which estimating uncollectible accounts improves the accuracy of the financial statements?

5. When using the allowance method, why is uncollectible accounts

expense an estimated amount?

6. What is the most common format for reporting accounts receivable on the balance sheet? What information does this method provide beyond

showing only the net amount?

7. Why is it necessary to make an entry to reinstate a previously written off account receivable before the collection is recorded?

8. What are some factors considered in estimating the amount of uncollectible accounts receivable?

9. What is the effect on the accounting equation of recognizing uncollectible accounts expense?

10. What is the effect on the accounting equation of writing off an uncollectible account receivable when the allowance method is used? When the direct write-off method is used?

11. How does the recovery of a previously written-off account affect the income statement when the allowance method is used? How does the recovery of a previously written-off account affect the statement of cash flows when the allowance method is used?

12. What is the advantage of using the allowance method of accounting for uncollectible accounts? What is the advantage of using the direct write-off method?

13. How do companies determine the percentage estimate of uncollectible accounts when using the percent of revenue method?

14. What is an advantage of using the percent of receivables method of estimating uncollectible accounts expense?

15. What is "aging of accounts receivable"?

16. What is the difference between the allowance method and the direct write-off method of accounting for uncollectible accounts?

17. When is it acceptable to use the direct write-off method of accounting for uncollectible accounts?

18. What is a promissory note?

19. Define the following terms:
   a. Maker
   b. Payee
   c. Principal
   d. Interest
   e. Maturity date
   f. Collateral

20. What is the formula for computing interest revenue?

21. What is accrued interest?

22. When is an adjusting entry for accrued interest generally recorded?

23. Assume that on July 1, 2013, Big Corp. loaned Little Corp. $12,000 for a period of one year at 6 percent interest. What amount of interest revenue will Big report for 2013? What amount of cash will Big receive upon maturity of the note?

24. In which section of the statement of cash flows will Big report the cash collected in question 23?

25. Why is it generally beneficial for a business to accept major credit cards as payment for goods and services even when the fee charged by the credit card company is substantial?

26. What types of costs do businesses avoid when they accept major credit cards as compared with handling credit sales themselves?

27. How is the accounts receivable turnover ratio computed? What information does the ratio provide?

28. How is the average number of days to collect accounts receivable computed? What information does the ratio provide?

29. Is accounting terminology standard in all countries? What term is used in the United Kingdom to refer to *sales?* What term is used to refer to *inventory?* What is a *gearing ratio?* Is it important to know about these differences?

30. What is the operating cycle of a business?

MULTIPLE-CHOICE QUESTIONS

Multiple-choice questions are provided on the text website at www.mhhe.com/edmonds8e.

EXERCISES—SERIES A

All applicable Exercises in Series A are available with McGraw-Hill's *Connect® Accounting.*

LO 4

Exercise 7-1A *Analysis of financial statement effects of accounting for uncollectible accounts under the direct write-off method*

Triplett Services Co. experienced the following events in 2013:

1. Provided services on account.
2. Collected cash for accounts receivable.
3. Attempted to collect an account and, when unsuccessful, wrote the amount off to uncollectible accounts expense.

Required

Show the effect of each event on the elements of the financial statements, using a horizontal statements model like the one shown here. Use the following coding scheme to record your answers: increase is +, decrease is −, not affected is NA. In the cash flow column, indicate whether the item is an operating activity (OA), investing activity (IA), or financing activity (FA).

Event No.	Assets	=	Liab.	+	Equity	Rev.	−	Exp.	=	Net Inc.	Cash Flow

Exercise 7-2A   *Accounting for bad debts: allowance method*   **LO 1**

Michelle's Accounting Service began operation on January 1, 2013. The company experienced the following events for its first year of operations:

Events Affecting 2013:

1. Provided $96,000 of accounting services on account.
2. Collected $80,000 cash from accounts receivable.
3. Paid salaries of $32,000 for the year.
4. Adjusted the accounts to reflect management's expectations that uncollectible accounts expense would be $1,600.

Required

a. Prepare general journal entries for the above events.
b. Post the general journal entries to T-accounts.
c. Prepare an income statement, balance sheet, and statement of cash flows for 2013.

Exercise 7-3A   *Analyzing account balances for a company using the allowance method of accounting for uncollectible accounts*   **LO 1**

The following account balances come from the records of King Company:

	Beginning Balance	Ending Balance
Accounts Receivable	$4,000	$4,500
Allowance for Doubtful Accounts	150	250

During the accounting period, King recorded $21,000 of service revenue on account. The company also wrote off a $180 account receivable.

Required

a. Determine the amount of cash collected from receivables.
b. Determine the amount of uncollectible accounts expense recognized during the period.

Exercise 7-4A   *Effect of recognizing uncollectible accounts expense on financial statements: percent of revenue allowance method*   **LO 1, 2**

Bulldog Auto Service was started on January 1, 2013. The company experienced the following events during its first two years of operation:

Events Affecting 2013

1. Provided $45,000 of repair services on account.
2. Collected $32,000 cash from accounts receivable.
3. Adjusted the accounting records to reflect the estimate that uncollectible accounts expense would be 1 percent of the service revenue on account.

Events Affecting 2014

1. Wrote off a $320 account receivable that was determined to be uncollectible.
2. Provided $65,000 of repair services on account.

3. Collected $66,000 cash from accounts receivable.
4. Adjusted the accounting records to reflect the estimate that uncollectible accounts expense would be 1 percent of the service revenue on account.

Required

a. Record the events for 2013 in general journal form and post them to T-accounts.
b. Determine the following amounts:
   (1) Net income for 2013.
   (2) Net cash flow from operating activities for 2013.
   (3) Balance of accounts receivable at the end of 2013.
   (4) Net realizable value of accounts receivable at the end of 2013.
c. Repeat Requirements *a* and *b* for the 2014 accounting period.

LO 1, 2   **Exercise 7-5A**   *Analyzing financial statement effects of accounting for uncollectible accounts using the percent of revenue allowance method*

Pate Bros. uses the allowance method to account for uncollectible accounts expense. Pate experienced the following four events in 2013:

1. Recognized $68,000 of revenue on account.
2. Collected $62,000 cash from accounts receivable.
3. Determined that $500 of accounts receivable were not collectible and wrote them off.
4. Recognized uncollectible accounts expense for the year. Pate estimates that uncollectible accounts expense will be 2 percent of its sales.

Required

a. Show the effect of each of these events on the elements of the financial statements, using a horizontal statements model like the following one. Use + for increase, − for decrease, and NA for not affected. In the cash flow column, indicate whether the item is an operating activity (OA), investing activity (IA), or financing activity (FA).

Event No.	Assets			=	Liab.	+	Equity	Rev.	−	Exp.	=	Net Inc.	Cash Flow
	Cash	+	Net Realizable Value of Rec.	=			Ret. Earn.						

b. Record the above transactions in general journal form.

LO 1, 2   **Exercise 7-6A**   *Effect of recovering a receivable previously written off*

The accounts receivable balance for Don's Shoe Repair at December 31, 2013, was $76,000. Also on that date, the balance in the Allowance for Doubtful Accounts was $3,200. During 2014, $2,900 of accounts receivable were written off as uncollectible. In addition, Don's Shoe Repair unexpectedly collected $200 of receivables that had been written off in a previous accounting period. Sales on account during 2014 were $210,000, and cash collections from receivables were $215,000. Uncollectible accounts expense was estimated to be 1 percent of the sales on account for the period.

Required

a. Record the transactions in general journal form and post them to T-accounts.
b. Based on the preceding information, compute (after year-end adjustment):
   (1) Balance of Allowance for Doubtful Accounts at December 31, 2014.
   (2) Balance of Accounts Receivable at December 31, 2014.
   (3) Net realizable value of Accounts Receivable at December 31, 2014.
c. What amount of uncollectible accounts expense will Don's Shoe Repair report for 2014?
d. Explain how the $200 recovery of receivables affected the accounting equation.

Exercise 7-7A   *Accounting for uncollectible accounts: percent of receivables*
allowance method   **LO 1, 3**

Tyler Service Co. experienced the following transactions for 2013, its first year of operations:

1. Provided $86,000 of services on account.
2. Collected $72,000 cash from accounts receivable.
3. Paid $39,000 of salaries expense for the year.
4. Tyler adjusted the accounts using the following information from an accounts receivable
    aging schedule:

Number of Days Past Due	Amount	Percent Likely to Be Uncollectible	Allowance Balance
Current	$7,500	.01	
0–30	2,000	.05	
31–60	1,500	.10	
61–90	1,000	.30	
Over 90 days	2,000	.50	

Required

a. Record the above transactions in general journal form and post them to T-accounts.
b. Prepare the income statement for Tyler Service Co. for 2013.
c. What is the net realizable value of the accounts receivable at December 31, 2013?

Exercise 7-8A   *Effect of recognizing uncollectible accounts on the financial*
statements: percent of receivables allowance method   **LO 1, 3**

Faello Inc. experienced the following events for the first two years of its operations:

2013:

1. Provided $80,000 of services on account.
2. Provided $22,000 of services and received cash.
3. Collected $65,000 cash from accounts receivable.
4. Paid $24,000 of salaries expense for the year.
5. Adjusted the accounting records to reflect uncollectible accounts expense for the year. Faello
    estimates that 5 percent of the ending accounts receivable balance will be uncollectible.

2014:

1. Wrote off an uncollectible account of $620.
2. Provided $95,000 of services on account.
3. Provided $15,000 of services and collected cash.
4. Collected $90,000 cash from accounts receivable.
5. Paid $35,000 of salaries expense for the year.
6. Adjusted the accounts to reflect uncollectible accounts expense for the year. Faello estimates
    that 5 percent of the ending accounts receivable balance will be uncollectible.

Required

a. Record the 2013 events in general journal form and post them to T-accounts.
b. Prepare the income statement, statement of changes in stockholders' equity, balance sheet,
    and statement of cash flows for 2013.
c. What is the net realizable value of the accounts receivable at December 31, 2013?
d. Repeat Requirements *a*, *b*, and *c* for 2014.

LO 4

Exercise 7-9A *Accounting for uncollectible accounts: direct write-off method*

Smart Business Systems has a small number of sales on account but is mostly a cash business. Consequently, it uses the direct write-off method to account for uncollectible accounts. During 2013 Smart Business Systems earned $46,000 of cash revenue and $9,000 of revenue on account. Cash operating expenses were $32,100. After numerous attempts to collect a $325 account receivable from T.M. Reed, the account was determined to be uncollectible in 2014.

Required

a. Record the effects of (1) cash revenue, (2) revenue on account, (3) cash expenses, and (4) write-off of the uncollectible account on the financial statements using a horizontal statements model like the one shown here. In the Cash Flow column, indicate whether the item is an operating activity (OA), investing activity (IA), or financing activity (FA). Use NA to indicate that an element is not affected by the event.

Assets		= Liab.	+ Equity	Rev.	− Exp.	= Net Inc.	Cash Flow
Cash	+ Accts. Rec.						

b. What amount of net income did Smart Business Systems report on the 2013 income statement?

c. Prepare the general journal entries for the four accounting events listed in Requirement *a*.

LO 2, 4

Exercise 7-10A *Accounting for uncollectible accounts: percent of revenue allowance versus direct write-off method*

Bing Auto Parts sells new and used auto parts. Although a majority of its sales are cash sales, it makes a significant amount of credit sales. During 2013, its first year of operations, Bing Auto Parts experienced the following:

Sales on account	$320,000
Cash sales	680,000
Collections of accounts receivable	295,000
Uncollectible accounts charged off during the year	1,400

Required

a. Assume that Bing Auto Parts uses the allowance method of accounting for uncollectible accounts and estimates that 1 percent of its sales on account will not be collected. Answer the following questions:

   (1) What is the Accounts Receivable balance at December 31, 2013?

   (2) What is the ending balance of the Allowance for Doubtful Accounts at December 31, 2013, after all entries and adjusting entries are posted?

   (3) What is the amount of uncollectible accounts expense for 2013?

   (4) What is the net realizable value of accounts receivable at December 31, 2013?

b. Assume that Bing Auto Parts uses the direct write-off method of accounting for uncollectible accounts. Answer the following questions:

   (1) What is the Accounts Receivable balance at December 31, 2013?

   (2) What is the amount of uncollectible accounts expense for 2013?

   (3) What is the net realizable value of accounts receivable at December 31, 2013?

LO 5

Exercise 7-11A *Accounting for notes receivable*

Poole Enterprises loaned $30,000 to Boyd Co. on September 1, 2013, for one year at 6 percent interest.

Required

a. Record these general journal entries for Poole Enterprises:

   (1) The loan to Boyd Co.

   (2) The adjusting entry at December 31, 2013.

   (3) The adjusting entry and collection of the note on September 1, 2014.

b. Show the effects of the three above transactions in a horizontal statements model like the one shown below.

Date	Assets						= Liab.	+	Equity	Rev.	−	Exp.	=	Net Inc.	Cash Flows
	Cash	+	Notes Rec.	+	Int. Rec.	=			Ret. Earn.						

Exercise 7-12A *Notes receivable—accrued interest*

LO 5

On March 1, 2013, Peppers Deli loaned $18,000 to Simms Supply for one year at 5 percent interest.

Required

Answer the following questions:

a. What is Peppers' interest income for 2013?

b. What is Peppers' total amount of receivables at December 31, 2013?

c. What amounts will be reported on Peppers' 2013 statement of cash flows?

d. What is Peppers' interest income for 2014?

e. What is the total amount of cash that Peppers will collect in 2014 from Simms Supply?

f. What amounts will be reported on Peppers' 2014 statement of cash flows?

g. What is the total amount of interest Peppers Deli earned from the loan to Simms Supply?

Exercise 7-13A *Effect of credit card sales on financial statements*

LO 6

Superior Carpet Cleaning provided $76,000 of services during 2013, its first year of operations. All customers paid for the services with major credit cards. Superior submitted the credit card receipts to the credit card company immediately. The credit card company paid Superior cash in the amount of face value less a 3 percent service charge.

Required

a. Record the credit card sales and the subsequent collection of accounts receivable in a horizontal statements model like the one shown here. In the Cash Flow column, indicate whether the item is an operating activity (OA), investing activity (IA), or financing activity (FA). Use NA to indicate that an element is not affected by the event.

Assets			= Liab.	+	Equity	Rev.	−	Exp.	=	Net Inc.	Cash Flow
Cash	+	Accts. Rec.									

b. Answer the following questions:

   (1) What is the amount of total assets at the end of the accounting period?

   (2) What is the amount of revenue reported on the income statement?

   (3) What is the amount of cash flow from operating activities reported on the statement of cash flows?

   (4) Why would Superior Carpet Cleaning accept credit cards instead of providing credit directly to its customers? In other words, why would Superior be willing to pay 3 percent of sales to have the credit card company handle its sales on account?

LO 6

Exercise 7-14A *Recording credit card sales*

Cassell Company accepted credit cards in payment for $8,650 of services performed during March 2013. The credit card company charged Cassell a 4 percent service fee. The credit card company paid Cassell as soon as it received the invoices.

Required

a. Prepare the general journal entry to record the service revenue.

b. Prepare the general journal entry for the collection of the receivable from the credit card company.

c. Based on this information alone, what is the amount of net income earned during the month of March?

LO 1, 2, 5, 6

Exercise 7-15A *Comprehensive single-cycle problem*

The following post-closing trial balance was drawn from the accounts of Hardwood Timber Co. as of December 31, 2012:

	Debit	Credit
Cash	$16,000	
Accounts receivable	18,000	
Allowance for doubtful accounts		$ 2,000
Inventory	25,000	
Accounts payable		9,200
Common stock		30,000
Retained earnings		17,800
Totals	$59,000	$59,000

Transactions for 2013

1. Acquired an additional $20,000 cash from the issue of common stock.
2. Purchased $80,000 of inventory on account.
3. Sold inventory that cost $61,000 for $98,000. Sales were made on account.
4. Wrote off $1,500 of uncollectible accounts.
5. On September 1, Hardwood loaned $10,000 to Pine Co. The note had a 6 percent interest rate and a one-year term.
6. Paid $24,500 cash for salaries expense.
7. Collected $99,000 cash from accounts receivable.
8. Paid $78,000 cash on accounts payable.
9. Paid a $5,000 cash dividend to the stockholders.
10. Accepted credit cards for sales amounting to $5,000. The cost of goods sold was $3,500. The credit card company charges a 4% service charge. The cash has not been received.
11. Estimated uncollectible accounts expense to be 1 percent of sales on account.
12. Recorded the accrued interest at December 31, 2013.

Required

a. Record the above transactions in general journal form.

b. Open T-accounts and record the beginning balances and the 2013 transactions.

c. Prepare an income statement, statement of changes in stockholders' equity, balance sheet, and statement of cash flows for 2013.

LO 7

Exercise 7-16A *Accounts receivable turnover and average days to collect accounts receivable*

The following information is available for L'Cole Inc. and Woodward Inc. at December 31, 2014:

Accounts	L'Cole	Woodward
Accounts Receivable	$115,500	$ 275,300
Allowance for Doubtful Accounts	4,050	10,120
Sales Revenue	895,600	2,472,700

Required

a. What is the accounts receivable turnover for each of the companies for 2014?

b. What is the average days to collect the receivables for 2014?

c. Assuming both companies use the percent of receivables allowance method, what is the estimated percentage of uncollectible accounts for each company?

PROBLEMS—SERIES A

All applicable Problems in Series A are available with McGraw-Hill's *Connect® Accounting.*

Problem 7-17A   *Accounting for uncollectible accounts—two cycles using the percent of revenue allowance method*

LO 1, 2

The following transactions apply to Expert Consulting for 2013, the first year of operation:

1. Recognized $70,000 of service revenue earned on account.
2. Collected $62,000 from accounts receivable.
3. Adjusted accounts to recognize uncollectible accounts expense. Expert uses the allowance method of accounting for uncollectible accounts and estimates that uncollectible accounts expense will be 2 percent of sales on account.

The following transactions apply to Expert Consulting for 2014:

1. Recognized $84,000 of service revenue on account.
2. Collected $70,000 from accounts receivable.
3. Determined that $1,100 of the accounts receivable were uncollectible and wrote them off.
4. Collected $200 of an account that had been previously written off.
5. Paid $51,200 cash for operating expenses.
6. Adjusted accounts to recognize uncollectible accounts expense for 2014. Expert estimates that uncollectible accounts expense will be 1 percent of sales on account.

CHECK FIGURES
c. Ending Accounts Receivable, 2013: $8,000
d. Net Income, 2014: $31,960

Required

Complete all the following requirements for 2013 and 2014. Complete all requirements for 2013 prior to beginning the requirements for 2014.

a. Identify the type of each transaction (asset source, asset use, asset exchange, or claims exchange).

b. Show the effect of each transaction on the elements of the financial statements, using a horizontal statements model like the one shown here. Use + for increase, − for decrease, and NA for not affected. Also, in the Cash Flow column, indicate whether the item is an operating activity (OA), investing activity (IA), or financing activity (FA). The first transaction is entered as an example. (*Hint:* Closing entries do not affect the statements model.)

Event No.	Assets	=	Liab.	+	Equity	Rev.	−	Exp.	=	Net Inc.	Cash Flow
1	+		NA		+	+		NA		+	NA

c. Record the transactions in general journal form, and post them to T-accounts (begin 2014 with the ending T-account balances from 2013).

d. Prepare the income statement, statement of changes in stockholders' equity, balance sheet, and statement of cash flows.

e. Prepare closing entries and post these closing entries to the T-accounts. Prepare a post-closing trial balance.

LO 1, 2

CHECK FIGURE
b. Net Realizable Value: $97,320

Problem 7-18A *Determining account balances and preparing journal entries: percent of revenue allowance method of accounting for uncollectible accounts*

The following information pertains to CJ's Cabinet Company's sales on account and accounts receivable:

Accounts Receivable Balance, January 1, 2013	$ 96,200
Allowance for Doubtful Accounts, January 1, 2013	6,250
Sales on Account, 2013	726,000
Cost of Goods Sold, 2013	473,000
Collections of Accounts Receivable, 2013	715,000

After several collection attempts, CJ's Cabinet Company wrote off $3,100 of accounts that could not be collected. CJ's estimates that uncollectible accounts expense will be 0.5 percent of sales on account.

Required

a. Prepare the general journal entries to:
   (1) Record sales on account for 2013.
   (2) Record cash collections from accounts receivable for 2013.
   (3) Write off the accounts that are not collectible.
   (4) Record the estimated uncollectible accounts expense for 2013.
b. Compute the following amounts:
   (1) Using the allowance method, the amount of uncollectible accounts expense for 2013.
   (2) Net realizable value of receivables at the end of 2013.
c. Explain why the uncollectible accounts expense amount is different from the amount that was written off as uncollectible.

LO 1, 3

CHECK FIGURE
d. Net Realizable Value $44,448

Problem 7-19A *Determination of account balances and preparation of journal entries—percent of receivables allowance method of accounting for uncollectible accounts*

During the first year of operation, 2013, Ferrell's Appliance recognized $261,000 of service revenue on account. At the end of 2013, the accounts receivable balance was $46,300. Even though this is his first year in business, the owner believes he will collect all but about 4 percent of the ending balance.

Required

a. What amount of cash was collected by Ferrell's during 2013?
b. Assuming the use of an allowance system to account for uncollectible accounts, what amount should Ferrell record as uncollectible accounts expense in 2013?
c. Prepare the journal entries to
   (1) Record service revenue on account.
   (2) Record collection of accounts receivable.
   (3) Record the entry to recognize uncollectible accounts expense.
d. What is the net realizable value of receivables at the end of 2013?
e. Show the effect of the transactions listed in Requirement *c* on the financial statements by recording the appropriate amounts in a horizontal statements model like the one shown here. When you record amounts in the Cash Flow column, indicate whether the item is an operating

activity (OA), investing activity (IA), or financing activity (FA). The letters NA indicate that an element is not affected by the event.

Assets		=	Liab.	+	Equity	Rev.	−	Exp.	=	Net Inc.	Cash Flow
Cash	+ Net Realizable Value of Receivables										

Problem 7-20A *Accounting for uncollectible accounts: percent of receivables allowance method*

LO 1, 3

Frankel Inc. experienced the following transactions for 2013, its first year of operations:

1. Issued common stock for $60,000 cash.
2. Purchased $210,000 of merchandise on account.
3. Sold merchandise that cost $165,000 for $310,000 on account.
4. Collected $288,000 cash from accounts receivable.
5. Paid $190,000 on accounts payable.
6. Paid $46,000 of salaries expense for the year.
7. Paid other operating expenses of $62,000.
8. Frankel adjusted the accounts using the following information from an accounts receivable aging schedule.

CHECK FIGURES
b. Net Income: $34,898
Total Assets: $114,898

Number of Days Past Due	Amount	Percent Likely to Be Uncollectible	Allowance Balance
Current	$15,700	.01	
0–30	8,500	.05	
31–60	4,000	.10	
61–90	2,600	.20	
Over 90 days	1,200	.50	

Required

a. Record the above transactions in general journal form and post them to T-accounts.
b. Prepare the income statement, statement of changes in stockholders' equity, balance sheet, and statement of cash flows for Frankel Inc. for 2013.
c. What is the net realizable value of the accounts receivable at December 31, 2013?

Problem 7-21A *Accounting for credit card sales and uncollectible accounts: percent of receivables allowance method*

LO 1, 3, 6

e**X**cel

Iupe Supply Company had the following transactions in 2013:

1. Acquired $50,000 cash from the issue of common stock.
2. Purchased $120,000 of merchandise for cash in 2013.
3. Sold merchandise that cost $95,000 for $180,000 during the year under the following terms:

CHECK FIGURES
c. Net Income: $29,865
Total Assets: $79,865

$ 50,000	Cash sales
115,000	Credit card sales (The credit card company charges a 3 percent service fee.)
15,000	Sales on account

4. Collected all the amount receivable from the credit card company.
5. Collected $11,300 of accounts receivable.
6. Paid selling and administrative expenses of $51,500.
7. Determined that 5 percent of the ending accounts receivable balance would be uncollectible.

Required

a. Show the effects of each of the transactions on the elements of the financial statements, using a horizontal statements model like the one shown here. Use + for increase, − for decrease, and NA for not affected. The first transaction is entered as an example. (*Hint:* Closing entries do not affect the statements model.)

Event No.	Assets	=	Liab.	+	Equity	Rev.	−	Exp.	=	Net Inc.	Cash Flow
1	+		NA		+	NA		NA		NA	+ FA

b. Prepare general journal entries for each of the transactions, and post them to T-accounts.

c. Prepare an income statement, statement of changes in stockholders' equity, balance sheet, and statement of cash flows for 2013.

LO 4, 5

Problem 7-22A *Accounting for notes receivable and uncollectible accounts using the direct write-off method*

The following transactions apply to Ard Co. for 2013, its first year of operations:

1. Issued $60,000 of common stock for cash.
2. Provided $94,000 of services on account.
3. Collected $84,500 cash from accounts receivable.
4. Loaned $10,000 to Swan Co. on October 1, 2013. The note had a one-year term to maturity and a 6 percent interest rate.
5. Paid $41,000 of salaries expense for the year.
6. Paid a $3,000 dividend to the stockholders.
7. Recorded the accrued interest on December 31, 2013 (see item 4).
8. Determined that $990 of accounts receivable were uncollectible. The company uses the direct write-off method.

Required

a. Record the above transactions in general journal form.
b. Post the entries to T-accounts.
c. Prepare the income statement, balance sheet, and statement of cash flows for 2013.
d. Show the effects of the above transactions in a horizontal statements model like the one shown below.

	Assets			= Liab. +	Equity		Rev. − Exp. = Net Inc.	Cash Flows
Event	Cash + Accts. Rec. + Notes Rec. + Int. Rec. =				Com. Stk. + Ret. Earn.			

LO 4, 5, 6

Problem 7-23A *Effect of transactions on the elements of financial statements*

Required

Identify each of the following independent transactions as asset source (AS), asset use (AU), asset exchange (AE), or claims exchange (CE). Also explain how each event affects assets, liabilities, stockholders' equity, net income, and cash flow by placing a + for increase, − for decrease, or NA for not affected under each of the categories. The first event is recorded as an example.

Event	Type of Event	Assets	Liabilities	Common Stock	Retained Earnings	Net Income	Cash Flow
a	AS/AU	+/−	NA	NA	+	+	NA

a. Sold merchandise at a price above cost. Accepted payment by credit card. The credit card company charges a service fee. The receipts have not yet been forwarded to the credit card company.

b. Sold land for cash at its cost.

c. Paid cash to satisfy salaries payable.

d. Submitted receipts to the credit card company (see *a* above) and collected cash.

e. Loaned Carl Maddox cash. The loan had a 5 percent interest rate and a one-year term to maturity.

f. Paid cash to creditors on accounts payable.

g. Accrued three months' interest on the note receivable (see *e* above).

h. Provided services for cash.

i. Paid cash for salaries expense.

j. Provided services on account.

k. Wrote off an uncollectible account (use direct write-off method).

l. Collected cash from customers paying their accounts.

m. Recovered an uncollectible account that was previously written off (assume direct write-off method was used).

n. Paid cash for land.

o. Paid cash for other operating expenses.

Problem 7-24A   *Multistep income statement and balance sheet*

LO 1, 5

eXcel

Required

Use the following information to prepare a multistep income statement and a balance sheet for Legg Company for 2013. (*Hint:* Some of the items will *not* appear on either statement, and ending retained earnings must be calculated.)

CHECK FIGURES
Total Assets: $289,800
Total Liabilities: $98,500

Operating Expenses	$ 45,000	Allowance for Doubtful Accounts	$ 6,500
Accounts Payable	48,000	Sales Revenue	350,000
Land	45,000	Uncollectible Accounts Expense	9,600
Dividends	10,000	Accounts Receivable	92,000
Beginning Retained Earnings	120,100	Salaries Payable	10,500
Interest Revenue	12,000	Supplies	4,500
Inventory	105,000	Prepaid Rent	16,000
Notes Receivable (short term)	15,000	Common Stock	60,000
Cash	16,700	Cost of Goods Sold	225,000
Interest Receivable (short term)	2,100	Salaries Expense	61,200
Cash Flow from Investing Activities	(91,600)	Unearned Revenue	40,000

Problem 7-25A   *Missing information*

LO 1, 5

The following information comes from the accounts of Sawyer Company:

CHECK FIGURES
a. Net Realizable Value: $29,800
b. Interest Revenue: $4,000

Account Title	Beginning Balance	Ending Balance
Accounts Receivable	$36,000	$32,000
Allowance for Doubtful Accounts	2,000	2,200
Notes Receivable	50,000	50,000
Interest Receivable	2,000	5,000

Required

a. There were $160,000 in sales on account during the accounting period. Write offs of uncollectible accounts were $1,200. What was the amount of cash collected from accounts receivable? What amount of uncollectible accounts expense was reported on the income statement? What was the net realizable value of receivables at the end of the accounting period?

b. The note has an 6 percent interest rate and 24 months to maturity. What amount of interest revenue was recognized for the year? How much cash was collected for interest?

Problem 7-26A   *Comprehensive accounting cycle problem (uses percent of revenue allowance method)*

The following trial balance was prepared for Village Cycle Sales and Service on December 31, 2013, after the closing entries were posted:

Account Title	Debit	Credit
Cash	$ 46,200	
Accounts Receivable	21,300	
Allowance for Doubtful Accounts		$ 1,350
Inventory	85,600	
Accounts Payable		28,000
Common Stock		80,000
Retained Earnings		43,750
Totals	$153,100	$153,100

Village Cycle had the following transactions in 2014:

1. Purchased merchandise on account for $260,000.
2. Sold merchandise that cost $243,000 on account for $340,000.
3. Performed $80,000 of services for cash.
4. Sold merchandise for $60,000 to credit card customers. The merchandise cost $41,250. The credit card company charges a 5 percent fee.
5. Collected $348,000 cash from accounts receivable.
6. Paid $265,000 cash on accounts payable.
7. Paid $115,000 cash for selling and administrative expenses.
8. Collected cash for the full amount due from the credit card company (see item 4).
9. Loaned $50,000 to Lee Supply. The note had an 9 percent interest rate and a one-year term to maturity.
10. Wrote off $830 of accounts as uncollectible.
11. Made the following adjusting entries:
    (a) Recorded three months' interest on the note at December 31, 2014 (see item 9).
    (b) Estimated uncollectible accounts expense to be .5 percent of sales on account.

Required

Prepare general journal entries for these transactions; post the entries to T-accounts; and prepare an income statement, a statement of changes in stockholders' equity, a balance sheet, and a statement of cash flows for 2014.

EXERCISES—SERIES B

LO 1

Exercise 7-1B   *Analysis of financial statement effects of accounting for uncollectible accounts under the allowance method*

Businesses using the allowance method for the recognition of uncollectible accounts expense commonly experience four accounting events:

1. Recognition of revenue on account.
2. Collection of cash from accounts receivable.
3. Recognition of uncollectible accounts expense through a year-end adjusting entry.
4. Write-off of uncollectible accounts.

Required

Show the effect of each event on the elements of the financial statements, using a horizontal statements model like the one shown here. Use the following coding scheme to record your answers: increase is +, decrease is −, not affected is NA. In the cash flow column, indicate whether the item is an operating activity (OA), investing activity (IA), or financing activity (FA). The first transaction is entered as an example.

Event No.	Assets	=	Liab.	+	Equity	Rev.	−	Exp.	=	Net Inc.	Cash Flow
1	+		NA		+	+		NA		+	NA

Exercise 7-2B *Accounting for uncollectible accounts: allowance method*

LO 1

Heffel's Cleaning Service began operation on January 1, 2013. The company experienced the following events for its first year of operations:

Events Affecting 2013:

1. Provided $96,000 of cleaning services on account.
2. Collected $81,000 cash from accounts receivable.
3. Paid salaries of $19,500 for the year.
4. Adjusted the accounts to reflect management's expectations that uncollectible accounts expense would be $1,100.

Required

a. Prepare general journal entries for the above events.
b. Post the general journal entries to T-accounts.
c. Prepare an income statement, balance sheet, and statement of cash flows for 2013.

Exercise 7-3B *Analyzing account balances for a company using the allowance method of accounting for uncollectible accounts*

LO 1

The following account balances come from the records of Cuevas Company:

	Beginning Balance	Ending Balance
Accounts Receivable	$2,500	$3,200
Allowance for Doubtful Accounts	225	300

During the accounting period, Cuevas recorded $11,000 of sales revenue on account. The company also wrote off an $120 account receivable.

Required

a. Determine the amount of cash collected from receivables.
b. Determine the amount of uncollectible accounts expense recognized during the period.

Exercise 7-4B *Effect of recognizing uncollectible accounts expense on financial statements: percent of revenue allowance method*

LO 1, 2

McCain Dry Cleaning was started on January 1, 2013. It experienced the following events during its first two years of operation:

Events Affecting 2013

1. Provided $40,000 of cleaning services on account.
2. Collected $38,000 cash from accounts receivable.
3. Adjusted the accounting records to reflect the estimate that uncollectible accounts expense would be 1 percent of the cleaning revenue on account.

Events Affecting 2014

1. Wrote off a $150 account receivable that was determined to be uncollectible.
2. Provided $65,000 of cleaning services on account.
3. Collected $62,000 cash from accounts receivable.
4. Adjusted the accounting records to reflect the estimate that uncollectible accounts expense would be 1 percent of the cleaning revenue on account.

Required

a. Record the events for 2013 in T-accounts.

b. Determine the following amounts:

(1) Net income for 2013.

(2) Net cash flow from operating activities for 2013.

(3) Balance of accounts receivable at the end of 2013.

(4) Net realizable value of accounts receivable at the end of 2013.

c. Repeat Requirements *a* and *b* for the 2014 accounting period.

LO 1, 2

Exercise 7-5B *Analyzing financial statement effects of accounting for uncollectible accounts using the percent of revenue allowance method*

Eccles Inc. uses the allowance method to account for uncollectible accounts expense. Eccles, Inc. experienced the following four accounting events in 2013:

1. Recognized $84,000 of revenue on account.
2. Collected $76,000 cash from accounts receivable.
3. Wrote off uncollectible accounts of $640.
4. Recognized uncollectible accounts expense. Eccles estimated that uncollectible accounts expense will be 1 percent of sales on account.

Required

a. Show the effect of each event on the elements of the financial statements, using a horizontal statements model like the one shown here. Use + for increase, − for decrease, and NA for not affected. In the cash flow column, indicate whether the item is an operating activity (OA), investing activity (IA), or financing activity (FA). The first transaction is entered as an example.

Event No.	Assets	=	Liab.	+	Equity	Rev.	−	Exp.	=	Net Inc.	Cash Flow
1	+		NA		+	+		NA		+	NA

b. Record the above transactions in general journal form.

LO 1, 2

Exercise 7-6B *Effect of recovering a receivable previously written off*

The accounts receivable balance for Diva Spa at December 31, 2012, was $56,000. Also on that date, the balance in the Allowance for Doubtful Accounts was $2,450. During 2013, $1,900 of accounts receivable were written off as uncollectible. In addition, Diva unexpectedly collected $600 of receivables that had been written off in a previous accounting period. Services provided on account during 2013 were $212,000, and cash collections from receivables were $214,000. Uncollectible accounts expense was estimated to be 2 percent of the sales on account for the period.

Required

a. Record the transactions in general journal form and post to T-accounts.

b. Based on the preceding information, compute (after year-end adjustment):

(1) Balance of Allowance for Doubtful Accounts at December 31, 2013.

(2) Balance of Accounts Receivable at December 31, 2013.

(3) Net realizable value of Accounts Receivable at December 31, 2013.

c. What amount of uncollectible accounts expense will Diva report for 2013?

d. Explain how the $600 recovery of receivables affects the income statement.

LO 1, 3

Exercise 7-7B *Accounting for uncollectible accounts: percent of receivables allowance method*

Butler Service Co. experienced the following transactions for 2013, its first year of operations:

1. Provided $84,000 of services on account.
2. Collected $71,000 cash from accounts receivable.

3. Paid $35,000 of salaries expense for the year.

4. Adjusted the accounts using the following information from an accounts receivable aging schedule:

Number of Days Past Due	Amount	Percent Likely to Be Uncollectible	Allowance Balance
Current	$6,300	.01	
0–30	3,000	.05	
31–60	1,500	.10	
61–90	1,200	.20	
Over 90 days	1,000	.50	

Required

a. Record the above transactions in general journal form and post to T-accounts.

b. Prepare the income statement for Butler Service Co. for 2013.

c. What is the net realizable value of the accounts receivable at December 31, 2013?

Exercise 7-8B *Effect of recognizing uncollectible accounts on the financial statements: percent of receivables allowance method*   **LO 1, 3**

Polledo Inc. experienced the following events for the first two years of its operations:

2013:

1. Provided $82,000 of services on account.
2. Provided $31,000 of services and received cash.
3. Collected $71,000 cash from accounts receivable.
4. Paid $40,000 of salaries expense for the year.
5. Adjusted the accounting records to reflect uncollectible accounts expense for the year. Polledo estimates that 5 percent of the ending accounts receivable balance will be uncollectible.

2014:

1. Wrote off an uncollectible account for $300.
2. Provided $91,000 of services on account.
3. Provided $24,000 of services and collected cash.
4. Collected $85,000 cash from accounts receivable.
5. Paid $44,000 of salaries expense for the year.
6. Adjusted the accounts to reflect uncollectible accounts expense for the year. Polledo estimates that 5 percent of the ending accounts receivable balance will be uncollectible.

Required

a. Record the 2013 events in general journal form and post them to T-accounts.

b. Prepare the income statement, statement of changes in stockholders' equity, balance sheet, and statement of cash flows for 2013.

c. What is the net realizable value of the accounts receivable at December 31, 2013?

d. Repeat Requirements a, b, and c for 2014.

Exercise 7-9B *Accounting for uncollectible accounts: direct write-off method*   **LO 4**

Nguyen Service Co. does make a few sales on account but is mostly a cash business. Consequently, it uses the direct write-off method to account for uncollectible accounts. During 2013 Nguyen Service Co. earned $25,000 of cash revenue and $3,000 of revenue on account. Cash operating expenses were $14,000. After numerous attempts to collect a $90 account receivable from Sam Stephens, the account was determined to be uncollectible in 2013.

Required

a. Record the effects of (1) cash revenue, (2) revenue on account, (3) cash expenses, and (4) write off of the uncollectible account on the financial statements using a horizontal statements model like the one shown here. In the Cash Flow column, indicate whether the item is an operating activity (OA), investing activity (IA), or financing activity (FA). Use NA to indicate that an element is not affected by the event.

Assets			=	Liab.	+	Equity	Rev.	−	Exp.	=	Net Inc.	Cash Flow
Cash	+	Accts. Rec.										

b. What amount of net income did Nguyen Service Co. report on the 2013 income statement?

c. Prepare the general journal entries for the four accounting events listed in Requirement *a*.

LO 2, 4

Exercise 7-10B *Accounting for uncollectible accounts: percent of revenue allowance versus direct write-off method*

Michael's Bike Shop sells new and used bicycle parts. Although a majority of its sales are cash sales, it makes a significant amount of credit sales. During 2013, its first year of operations, Michael's Bike Shop experienced the following:

Sales on account	$275,000
Cash sales	620,000
Collections of accounts receivable	240,000
Uncollectible accounts charged off during the year	400

Required

a. Assume that Michael's Bike Shop uses the allowance method of accounting for uncollectible accounts and estimates that 1 percent of its sales on account will not be collected. Answer the following questions:

   (1) What is the Accounts Receivable balance at December 31, 2013?

   (2) What is the ending balance of the Allowance for Doubtful Accounts at December 31, 2013, after all entries and adjusting entries are posted?

   (3) What is the amount of uncollectible accounts expense for 2013?

   (4) What is the net realizable value of accounts receivable at December 31, 2013?

b. Assume that Michael's Bike Shop uses the direct write-off method of accounting for uncollectible accounts. Answer the following questions:

   (1) What is the Accounts Receivable balance at December 31, 2013?

   (2) What is the amount of uncollectible accounts expense for 2013?

   (3) What is the net realizable value of accounts receivable at December 31, 2013?

LO 5

Exercise 7-11B *Accounting for notes receivable*

Fisher Enterprises loaned $15,000 to Hall Co. on June 1, 2013, for one year at 6 percent interest.

Required

a. Record these general journal entries for Fisher Enterprises:

   (1) The loan to Hall Co.

   (2) The adjusting entry at December 31, 2013.

   (3) The adjusting entry and collection of the note on June 1, 2014.

b. Show the effects of the three above transactions in a horizontal statements model like the one shown below:

	Assets					=	Liab.	+	Equity	Rev.	−	Exp.	=	Net Inc.	Cash Flows
Date	Cash	+	Notes Rec.	+	Int. Rec.	=			Ret. Earn.						

Exercise 7-12B   *Notes receivable—accrued interest*   **LO 5**

On May 1, 2013, Ozark's Sandwich Shop loaned $10,000 to Ben Spell for one year at 9 percent interest.

Required

Answer the following questions:

a. What is Ozark's interest income for 2013?
b. What is Ozark's total amount of receivables at December 31, 2013?
c. What amounts will be reported on Ozark's 2013 statement of cash flows?
d. What is Ozark's interest income for 2014?
e. What is the total amount of cash that Ozark's will collect in 2014 from Ben Spell?
f. What amounts will be reported on Ozark's 2014 statement of cash flows?
g. What is the total amount of interest that Ozark's earned on the loan to Ben Spell?

Exercise 7-13B   *Effect of credit card sales on financial statements*   **LO 6**

Bella Day Spa provided $110,000 of services during 2013. All customers paid for the services with credit cards. Bella submitted the credit card receipts to the credit card company immediately. The credit card company paid Bella cash in the amount of face value less a 5 percent service charge.

Required

a. Record the credit card sales and the subsequent collection of accounts receivable in a horizontal statements model like the one shown here. In the Cash Flow column, indicate whether the item is an operating activity (OA), investing activity (IA), or financing activity (FA). Use NA to indicate that an element is not affected by the event.

Assets		=	Liab.	+	Equity	Rev.	−	Exp.	=	Net Inc.	Cash Flow
Cash	+	Accts. Rec.									

b. Based on this information alone, answer the following questions:
   (1) What is the amount of total assets at the end of the accounting period?
   (2) What is the amount of revenue reported on the income statement?
   (3) What is the amount of cash flow from operating activities reported on the statement of cash flows?
   (4) What costs would a business incur if it maintained its own accounts receivable? What cost does a business incur by accepting credit cards?

Exercise 7-14B   *Recording credit card sales*   **LO 6**

Camp Company accepted credit cards in payment for $4,000 of services performed during July 2013. The credit card company charged Camp a 4 percent service fee; it paid Camp as soon as it received the invoices.

Required

a. Prepare the general journal entry to record the service revenue.
b. Prepare the general journal entry for the collection of the receivable from the credit card company.
c. Based on this information alone, what is the amount of net income earned during the month of July?

LO 1, 2, 5, 6

Exercise 7-15B   *Comprehensive single-cycle problem*

The following post-closing trial balance was drawn from the accounts of Gregg Grocery Supplier (GGS) as of December 31, 2012:

	Debit	Credit
Cash	$ 8,000	
Accounts Receivable	40,000	
Allowance for Doubtful Accounts		$ 2,000
Inventory	80,000	
Accounts Payable		20,000
Common Stock		40,000
Retained Earnings		66,000
Totals	$128,000	$128,000

Transactions for 2013

1. GGS acquired an additional $10,000 cash from the issue of common stock.
2. GGS purchased $90,000 of inventory on account.
3. GGS sold inventory that cost $91,000 for $150,000. Sales were made on account.
4. The company wrote off $800 of uncollectible accounts.
5. On September 1, GGS loaned $15,000 to Eden Co. The note had an 8 percent interest rate and a one-year term.
6. GGS paid $22,000 cash for operating expenses.
7. The company collected $152,000 cash from accounts receivable.
8. A cash payment of $96,000 was paid on accounts payable.
9. The company paid a $10,000 cash dividend to the stockholders.
10. Accepted credit cards for sales amounting to $6,000. The cost of goods sold was $4,000. The credit card company charges a 4% service charge. The cash has not been received.
11. Uncollectible accounts are estimated to be 1 percent of sales on account.
12. Recorded the accrued interest at December 31, 2013 (see item 5).

Required

a. Record the above transactions in general journal form.
b. Open T-accounts and record the beginning balances and the 2013 transactions.
c. Prepare an income statement, statement of changes in stockholders' equity, balance sheet, and statement of cash flows for 2013.

LO 7

Exercise 7-16B   *Accounts receivable turnover and average days to collect accounts receivable*

The following information is available for Adele Inc. and Chinstrap Inc. at December 31, 2013:

Accounts	Adele	Chinstrap
Accounts Receivable	$ 987,500	$ 675,100
Allowance for Doubtful Accounts	19,750	12,150
Sales Revenue	10,450,300	4,725,700

Required

a. What is the accounts receivable turnover for each of the companies for 2013?
b. What is the average days to collect the receivables for 2013?
c. Assuming both companies use the percent of receivables allowance method, what is the estimated percentage of uncollectible accounts for each company?

PROBLEMS—SERIES B

Problem 7-17B *Accounting for uncollectible accounts: two cycles using the percent of revenue allowance method*

The following transactions apply to Wade Company for 2013, the first year of operation:

1. Recognized $220,000 of service revenue earned on account.
2. Collected $162,000 from accounts receivable.
3. Paid $150,000 cash for operating expenses.
4. Adjusted the accounts to recognize uncollectible accounts expense. Wade uses the allowance method of accounting for uncollectible accounts and estimates that uncollectible accounts expense will be 1 percent of sales on account.

The following transactions apply to Wade for 2014:

1. Recognized $398,000 of service revenue on account.
2. Collected $402,000 from accounts receivable.
3. Determined that $2,400 of the accounts receivable were uncollectible and wrote them off.
4. Collected $1,000 of an account that had previously been written off.
5. Paid $210,000 cash for operating expenses.
6. Adjusted the accounts to recognize uncollectible accounts expense for 2014. Wade estimates uncollectible accounts expense will be 0.5 percent of sales on account.

Required

Complete the following requirements for 2013 and 2014. Complete all requirements for 2013 prior to beginning the requirements for 2014.

a. Identify the type of each transaction (asset source, asset use, asset exchange, or claims exchange).
b. Show the effect of each transaction on the elements of the financial statements, using a horizontal statements model like the one shown here. Use + for increase, − for decrease, and NA for not affected. Also, in the Cash Flow column, indicate whether the item is an operating activity (OA), investing activity (IA), or financing activity (FA). The first transaction is entered as an example. (*Hint:* Closing entries do not affect the statements model.)

Event No.	Assets	=	Liab.	+	Equity	Rev.	−	Exp.	=	Net Inc.	Cash Flow
1	+		NA		+	+		NA		+	NA

c. Record the transactions in general journal form, and post them to T-accounts (begin 2014 with the ending T-account balances from 2013).
d. Prepare the income statement, statement of changes in stockholders' equity, balance sheet, and statement of cash flows.
e. Prepare closing entries and post these closing entries to the T-accounts. Prepare the post-closing trial balance.

Problem 7-18B *Determining account balances and preparing journal entries: percent of revenue allowance method of accounting for uncollectible accounts*

During the first year of operation, 2013, Custom Appliance Co. recognized $320,000 of service revenue on account. At the end of 2013, the accounts receivable balance was $47,000. For this first year in business, the owner believes uncollectible accounts expense will be about 1 percent of sales on account.

Required

a. What amount of cash did Custom collect from accounts receivable during 2013?

b. Assuming Custom uses the allowance method to account for uncollectible accounts, what amount should Custom record as uncollectible accounts expense for 2013?

c. Prepare the general journal entries to:

   (1) Record service revenue on account.

   (2) Record collections from accounts receivable.

   (3) Record the entry to recognize uncollectible accounts expense.

d. What is the net realizable value of receivables at the end of 2013?

e. Show the effects of the transactions in Requirement *c* on the financial statements by recording the appropriate amounts in a horizontal statements model like the one shown here. In the Cash Flow column, indicate whether the item is an operating activity (OA), investing activity (IA), or financing activity (FA). Use NA for not affected.

Assets			=	Liab.	+	Equity	Rev.	−	Exp.	=	Net Inc.	Cash Flow
Cash	+	Net Realizable Value of Receivables										

LO 1, 3

Problem 7-19B *Determination of account balances and preparation of journal entries—percent of receivables allowance method of accounting for uncollectible accounts*

The following information is available for Campus Book Sales' sales on account and accounts receivable:

Accounts receivable balance, January 1, 2013	$ 92,500
Allowance for doubtful accounts, January 1, 2013	6,450
Sales on account, 2013	685,000
Collection on accounts receivable, 2013	691,000

After several collection attempts, Campus Book Sales wrote off $5,100 of accounts that could not be collected. Campus Book Sales estimates that 4 percent of the ending accounts receivable balance will be uncollectible.

Required

a. Compute the following amounts:

   (1) Using the allowance method, the amount of uncollectible accounts expense for 2013.

   (2) Net realizable value of receivables at the end of 2013.

b. Record the general journal entries to:

   (1) Record sales on account for 2013.

   (2) Record cash collections from accounts receivable for 2013.

   (3) Write off the accounts that are not collectible.

   (4) Record the estimated uncollectible accounts expense for 2013.

c. Explain why the uncollectible accounts expense amount is different from the amount that was written off as uncollectible.

LO 1, 3

Problem 7-20B *Accounting for uncollectible accounts: percent of receivables allowance method*

Shimi Inc. experienced the following transactions for 2013, its first year of operations:

1. Issued common stock for $60,000 cash.

2. Purchased $135,000 of merchandise on account.

3. Sold merchandise that cost $97,000 for $280,000 on account.

4. Collected $255,000 cash from accounts receivable.
5. Paid $122,000 on accounts payable.
6. Paid $47,000 of salaries expense for the year.
7. Paid other operating expenses of $21,000.
8. Shimi adjusted the accounts using the following information from an accounts receivable aging schedule:

Number of Days Past Due	Amount	Percent Likely to Be Uncollectible	Allowance Balance
Current	$13,000	.01	
0–30	5,000	.05	
31–60	3,000	.10	
61–90	2,500	.20	
Over 90 days	1,500	.50	

Required

a. Record the above transactions in general journal form and post to T-accounts.
b. Prepare the income statement, statement of changes in stockholders' equity, balance sheet, and statement of cash flows for Shimi Inc. for 2013.
c. What is the net realizable value of the accounts receivable at December 31, 2013?

Problem 7-21B *Accounting for credit card sales and uncollectible accounts: percent of receivables allowance method*   LO 1, 3, 6

New England Sales had the following transactions in 2013:

1. The business was started when it acquired $300,000 cash from the issue of common stock.
2. New England purchased $900,000 of merchandise for cash in 2013.
3. During the year, the company sold merchandise for $1,500,000. The merchandise cost $820,000. Sales were made under the following terms:

a. $530,000	Cash sales	
b. 450,000	Credit card sales (The credit card company charges a 4 percent service fee.)	
c. 520,000	Sales on account	

4. The company collected all the amount receivable from the credit card company.
5. The company collected $480,000 of accounts receivable.
6. The company paid $215,000 cash for selling and administrative expenses.
7. Determined that 5 percent of the ending accounts receivable balance would be uncollectible.

Required

a. Show the effects of each of the transactions on the elements of the financial statements, using a horizontal statements model like the one shown here. Use + for increase, − for decrease, and NA for not affected. The first transaction is entered as an example. (*Hint:* Closing entries do not affect the statements model.)

Event No.	Assets	=	Liab.	+	Equity	Rev.	−	Exp.	=	Net Inc.	Cash Flow
1	+		NA		+	NA		NA		NA	+ FA

b. Prepare general journal entries for each of the transactions, and post them to T-accounts.
c. Prepare an income statement, statement of changes in stockholders' equity, balance sheet, and statement of cash flows for 2013.

Problem 7-22B   *Accounting for notes receivable and uncollectible accounts using the direct write-off method*

The following transactions apply to Norris Co. for 2013, its first year of operations:

1. Issued $70,000 of common stock for cash.
2. Provided $95,000 of services on account.
3. Collected $81,000 cash from accounts receivable.
4. Loaned $20,000 to Scott Co. on November 30, 2013. The note had a one-year term to maturity and a 6 percent interest rate.
5. Paid $24,000 of salaries expense for the year.
6. Paid a $2,000 dividend to the stockholders.
7. Recorded the accrued interest on December 31, 2013 (see item 4).
8. Determined that $620 of accounts receivable were uncollectible.

Required

a. Record the above transactions in general journal form.
b. Post the entries to T-accounts.
c. Prepare the income statement, balance sheet, and statement of cash flows for 2013.
d. Show the effects of the above transactions in a horizontal statements model like the one shown below:

	Assets	= Liab. +	Equity	Rev. − Exp. = Net Inc.	Cash Flows
Event	Cash + Accts. Rec. + Notes Rec. + Int. Rec. =		Com. Stk. + Ret. Earn.		

Problem 7-23B   *Effect of transactions on the elements of financial statements*

Required

Identify each of the following independent transactions as asset source (AS), asset use (AU), asset exchange (AE), or claims exchange (CE). Also explain how each event affects assets, liabilities, stockholders' equity, net income, and cash flow by placing a + for increase, − for decrease, or NA for not affected under each of the categories. The first event is recorded as an example.

Event	Type of Event	Assets	Liabilities	Common Stock	Retained Earnings	Net Income	Cash Flow
a	AS	+	NA	NA	NA	+	+

a. Provided services for cash.
b. Paid cash for operating expenses.
c. Paid cash for salaries expense.
d. Recovered an uncollectible account that had been previously written off (assume the direct write-off method is used to account for uncollectible accounts).
e. Paid cash to creditors on accounts payable.
f. Loaned cash to H. Phillips for one year at 6 percent interest.
g. Provided services on account.
h. Wrote off an uncollectible account (use the direct write-off method).
i. Recorded three months of accrued interest on the note receivable (see *f* above).
j. Collected cash from customers paying their accounts.
k. Paid cash for land.
l. Sold merchandise at a price above cost. Accepted payment by credit card. The credit card company charges a service fee. The receipts have not yet been forwarded to the credit card company.

m. Submitted receipts to the credit card company (see *b* above) and collected cash.

n. Sold land at its cost.

Problem 7-24B   *Multistep income statement and balance sheet*

LO 1, 5

Required

Use the following information to prepare a multistep income statement and a balance sheet for Belmont Equipment Co. for 2013. (*Hint:* Some of the items will *not* appear on either statement, and ending retained earnings must be calculated.)

Salaries Expense	$ 78,000	Operating Expenses	$ 62,000
Common Stock	100,000	Cash Flow from Investing Activities	96,200
Notes Receivable (short term)	24,000	Prepaid Rent	11,200
Allowance for Doubtful Accounts	6,600	Land	40,000
Uncollectible Accounts Expense	9,400	Cash	48,100
Supplies	2,100	Inventory	98,300
Interest Revenue	5,400	Accounts Payable	52,000
Sales Revenue	345,000	Salaries Payable	7,500
Dividends	10,000	Cost of Goods Sold	128,000
Interest Receivable (short term)	1,200	Accounts Receivable	78,400
Beginning Retained Earnings	74,200		

Problem 7-25B   *Missing information*

LO 1, 5

The following information comes from the accounts of Posley Company:

Account Title	Beginning Balance	Ending Balance
Accounts Receivable	$34,000	$30,000
Allowance for Doubtful Accounts	1,600	1,800
Notes Receivable	40,000	40,000
Interest Receivable	1,400	4,200

Required

a. There were $180,000 of sales on account during the accounting period. Write-offs of uncollectible accounts were $1,450. What was the amount of cash collected from accounts receivable? What amount of uncollectible accounts expense was reported on the income statement? What was the net realizable value of receivables at the end of the accounting period?

b. The note receivable has a two-year term with a 7 percent interest rate. What amount of interest revenue was recognized during the period? How much cash was collected from interest?

Problem 7-26B   *Comprehensive accounting cycle problem (uses percent of sales allowance method)*

LO 1, 2, 3, 5, 6

The following trial balance was prepared for Gifts, Etc., Inc., on December 31, 2013, after the closing entries were posted:

Account Title	Debit	Credit
Cash	$128,000	
Accounts Receivable	162,000	
Allowance for Doubtful Accounts		$ 20,000
Inventory	650,000	
Accounts Payable		132,000
Common Stock		710,000
Retained Earnings		78,000
Totals	$940,000	$940,000

Gifts, Etc. had the following transactions in 2014:

1. Purchased merchandise on account for $405,000.
2. Sold merchandise that cost $310,000 for $490,000 on account.
3. Sold for $250,000 cash merchandise that had cost $156,000.
4. Sold merchandise for $190,000 to credit card customers. The merchandise had cost $112,000. The credit card company charges a 4 percent fee.
5. Collected $520,000 cash from accounts receivable.
6. Paid $495,000 cash on accounts payable.
7. Paid $145,000 cash for selling and administrative expenses.
8. Collected cash for the full amount due from the credit card company (see item 4).
9. Loaned $60,000 to L. Jones. The note had an 8 percent interest rate and a one-year term to maturity.
10. Wrote off $8,200 of accounts as uncollectible.
11. Made the following adjusting entries:
    (a) Recorded uncollectible accounts expense estimated at 1 percent of sales on account.
    (b) Recorded seven months of accrued interest on the note at December 31, 2014 (see item 9).

Required

a. Prepare general journal entries for these transactions; post the entries to T-accounts; and prepare an income statement, a statement of changes in stockholders' equity, a balance sheet, and a statement of cash flows for 2014.
b. Compute the net realizable value of accounts receivable at December 31, 2014.
c. If Candles, Etc. used the direct write-off method, what amount of uncollectible accounts expense would it report on the income statement?

ANALYZE, THINK, COMMUNICATE

ATC 7-1 Business Applications Case   *Understanding real-world annual reports*

Required

Use Target Corporation's annual report in Appendix B to answer the following questions:

a. How long did it take Target to collect credit card receivables during the fiscal-year ended January 29, 2011, (2010)?
b. Approximately what percentage of credit card receivables, did the company think would not be collected in 2010 and 2009?
c. What is Target's policy regarding when to write off credit card receivables?

ATC 7-2 Group Assignment   *Missing information*

The following selected financial information is available for three companies:

	Expo	White	Zina
Total sales	$125,000	$210,000	?
Cash sales	?	26,000	$120,000
Sales on account	40,000	?	75,000
Accounts receivable, January 1, 2013	6,200	42,000	?
Accounts receivable, December 31, 2013	5,600	48,000	7,500
Allowance for doubtful accounts, January 1, 2013	?	?	405
Allowance for doubtful accounts, December 31, 2013	224	1,680	?
Uncollectible accounts expense, 2013	242	1,200	395
Uncollectible accounts written off	204	1,360	365
Collections of accounts receivable, 2013	?	?	75,235

Required

a. Divide the class into three sections and divide each section into groups of three to five students. Assign one of the companies to each of the sections.

Group Tasks

(1) Determine the missing amounts for your company.

(2) Determine the percentage of accounts receivable estimated to be uncollectible at the end of 2012 and 2013 for your company.

(3) Determine the percentage of total sales that are sales on account for your company.

(4) Determine the accounts receivable turnover for your company.

Class Discussion

b. Have a representative of each section put the missing information on the board and explain how it was determined.

c. Which company has the highest percentage of sales that are on account?

d. Which company is doing the best job of collecting its accounts receivable? What procedures and policies can a company use to better collect its accounts receivable?

ATC 7-3 Real-World Case *Time needed to collect accounts receivable*

Presented here are the average days to collect accounts receivable for four companies in different industries. The data are for 2010.

Company	Average Days to Collect Accounts Receivable
Boeing (aircraft manufacturer)	31
Ford (automobile operations only)	23
Procter & Gamble (consumer products manufacturer)	25
Zale Corporation (jewelry retailer)	4

Required

Write a brief memorandum that provides possible answers to each of the following questions:

a. Why would a company that manufactures and sells airplanes (Boeing) and a company that manufacturers and sells automobiles (Ford) collect their accounts receivables in such relatively short times?

b. Why would a company that sells expensive jewelry (Zales) collect its receivables so much quicker than a company that sells toothpaste and soap (Procter & Gamble)?

ATC 7-4 Business Applications Case *Performing ratio analysis using real-world data*

The following data were taken from Hershey Foods Corporation's 2010 annual report. All dollar amounts are in thousands.

	Fiscal Years Ending	
	December 31, 2010	December 31, 2009
Sales	$5,671,009	$5,298,668
Accounts receivable	490,061	410,390

Required

a. Compute Hershey's accounts receivable turnover ratios for 2010 and 2009.

b. Compute Hershey's average days to collect accounts receivables for 2010 and 2009.

c. Based on the ratios computed in Requirements *a* and *b*, did Hershey's performance get better or worse from 2009 to 2010?

d. In 2010 Hershey issued long-term notes payable with an interest rate of 4.2 percent. Assume it took Hershey 30 days to collect its receivables. Using an interest rate of 4.2 percent, calculate how much it cost Hershey's to finance its receivables for 30 days in 2010.

ATC 7-5 Business Applications Case *Performing ratio analysis using real-world data*

AutoZone, Inc., claims to be "the nation's leading auto parts retailer." It sells replacement auto parts directly to the consumer. BorgWarner, Inc., has over 17,000 employees and produces automobile parts, such as transmissions and cooling systems, for the world's vehicle manufacturers. The following data were taken from these companies' 2010 annual reports. All dollar amounts are in thousands.

	AutoZone August 30, 2010	BorgWarner December 31, 2010
Sales	$7,362,618	$5,652,800
Accounts receivable	125,802	859,500

Required

a. Before performing any calculations, speculate as to which company will take the longest to collect its accounts receivables. Explain the rationale for your decision.

b. Calculate the accounts receivable turnover ratios for AutoZone and BorgWarner.

c. Calculate the average days to collect accounts receivables for AutoZone and BorgWarner.

d. Do the calculations from Requirements *b* and *c* confirm your speculations in Requirement *a*?

ATC 7-6 Writing Assignment *Cost of charge sales*

Paul Smith is opening a plumbing supply store in University City. He plans to sell plumbing parts and materials to both wholesale and retail customers. Since contractors (wholesale customers) prefer to charge parts and materials and pay at the end of the month, Paul expects he will have to offer charge accounts. He plans to offer charge sales to the wholesale customers only and to require retail customers to pay with either cash or credit cards. Paul wondered what expenses his business would incur relative to the charge sales and the credit cards.

Required

a. What issues will Paul need to consider if he allows wholesale customers to buy plumbing supplies on account?

b. Write a memo to Paul Smith outlining the potential cost of accepting charge customers. Discuss the difference between the allowance method for uncollectible accounts and the direct write-off method. Also discuss the cost of accepting credit cards.

ATC 7-7 Ethical Dilemma *How bad can it be?*

Alonzo Saunders owns a small training services company that is experiencing growing pains. The company has grown rapidly by offering liberal credit terms to its customers. Although his competitors require payment for services within 30 days, Saunders permits his customers to delay payment for up to 90 days. Saunders' customers thereby have time to fully evaluate the training that employees receive before they must pay for that training. Saunders guarantees satisfaction. If a customer is unhappy, the customer does not have to pay. Saunders works with reputable companies, provides top-quality training, and rarely encounters dissatisfied customers.

The long collection period, however, has created a cash flow problem. Saunders has a $100,000 accounts receivable balance, but needs cash to pay current bills. He has recently negotiated a loan agreement with National Bank of Brighton County that should solve his cash flow problems. The loan agreement requires that Saunders pledge the accounts receivable as collateral for the loan. The bank agreed to loan Saunders 70 percent of the receivables balance, thereby giving him access to $70,000 cash. Saunders is satisfied with this arrangement because he estimates he needs approximately $60,000.

On the day Saunders was to execute the loan agreement, he heard a rumor that his biggest customer was experiencing financial problems and might declare bankruptcy. The customer owed Saunders $45,000. Saunders promptly called the customer's chief accountant and learned "off the record" that the rumor was true. The accountant told Saunders that the company's net worth was negative and most of its assets were pledged as collateral for bank loans. In his opinion, Saunders was unlikely to collect the balance due. Saunders' immediate concern was the impact the circumstances would have on his loan agreement with the bank.

Saunders uses the direct write-off method to recognize uncollectible accounts expense. Removing the $45,000 receivable from the collateral pool would leave only $55,000 of receivables, reducing the available credit to $38,500 ($55,000 × 0.70). Even worse, recognizing the uncollectible accounts expense would so adversely affect his income statement that the bank might further reduce the available credit by reducing the percentage of receivables allowed under the loan agreement. Saunders will have to attest to the quality of the receivables at the date of the loan but reasons that since the information he obtained about the possible bankruptcy was "off the record" he is under no obligation to recognize the uncollectible accounts expense until the receivable is officially uncollectible.

Required

a. How are income and assets affected by the decision not to act on the bankruptcy information?

b. Review the AICPA's Articles of Professional Conduct (see Chapter 2) and comment on any of the standards that would be violated by the actions Saunders is contemplating.

c. Identify the elements of unethical and criminal conduct recognized in the fraud triangle (see Chapter 2), and explain how they apply to this case.

ATC 7-8 Research Assignment *Comparing Whirlpool Corporation's and Papa John's time to collect accounts receivable*

Using the most current annual reports or the Forms 10-K, for Whirlpool Corporation and for Papa John's International, Inc., complete the requirements below. To obtain the Forms 10-K, use either the EDGAR system following the instructions in Appendix A or the companies' websites. The annual reports can be found on the companies' websites.

Required

a. What was Whirlpool average days to collect accounts receivable? Show your computations.

b. What percentage of accounts receivable did Whirlpool estimate would not be collected?

c. What was Papa John's average days to collect accounts receivable? Show your computations.

d. What percentage of accounts receivable did Papa John's estimate would not be collected?

e. Briefly explain why Whirlpool would take longer than Papa John's to collect its accounts receivable.

ATC 7-9 Spreadsheet Analysis *Using Excel*

Set up the following spreadsheet comparing Vong and Crist Companies:

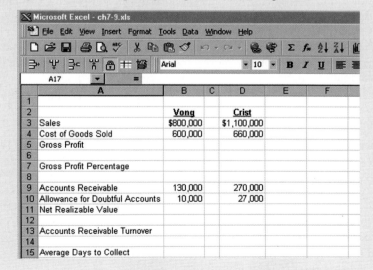

	A	B	C	D	E	F
1						
2		Vong		Crist		
3	Sales	$800,000		$1,100,000		
4	Cost of Goods Sold	600,000		660,000		
5	Gross Profit					
6						
7	Gross Profit Percentage					
8						
9	Accounts Receivable	130,000		270,000		
10	Allowance for Doubtful Accounts	10,000		27,000		
11	Net Realizable Value					
12						
13	Accounts Receivable Turnover					
14						
15	Average Days to Collect					

Required

a. For each company, compute gross profit, gross profit percentage, net realizable value, accounts receivable turnover, and average days to collect.

b. In relation to cost, which company is charging more for its merchandise?

c. Which company is likely to incur higher financial costs associated with granting credit to customers? Explain the reasons for your answer.

d. Which company appears to have more restrictive credit standards when authorizing credit to customers? How do you know?

COMPREHENSIVE PROBLEM

The trial balance of Pacilio Security Services Inc. as of January 1, 2017, had the following normal balances:

Cash	$78,972
Petty Cash	100
Accounts Receivable	33,440
Supplies	160
Prepaid Rent	3,200
Merchandise Inventory (23 @ $280)	6,440
Land	4,000
Accounts Payable	250
Salaries Payable	1,400
Common Stock	50,000
Retained Earnings	74,662

During 2017 Pacilio Security Services experienced the following transactions:

1. Paid the salaries payable from 2016.
2. Paid $4,800 on March 1, 2017, for one year's lease in advance on the company van.
3. Paid $8,400 on May 2, 2017, for one year's office rent in advance.
4. Purchased $550 of supplies on account.
5. Paid cash to purchase 105 alarm systems at a cost of $285 each.
6. Pacilio has noticed its accounts receivable balance is growing more than desired and some collection problems exist. It appears that uncollectible accounts expense is approximately 3 percent of total credit sales. Pacilio has decided it will, starting this year, adopt the allowance method of accounting for uncollectible accounts. It will record an adjusting entry to recognize the estimate at the end of the year.
7. In trying to collect several of its delinquent accounts, Pacilio has learned that these customers have either declared bankruptcy or moved and left no forwarding address. These uncollectible accounts amount to $1,900.
8. Sold 110 alarm systems for $63,800. All sales were on account. (Compute cost of goods sold using the FIFO cost flow method.)
9. Paid the balance of the accounts payable.
10. Pacilio began accepting credit cards for some of its monitoring service sales. The credit card company charges a fee of 4 percent. Total monitoring services for the year were $68,000. Pacilio accepted credit cards for $24,000 of this amount. The other $44,000 was sales on account.
11. On July 1, 2017, Pacilio replenished the petty cash fund. The fund contained $21 of currency and receipts of $50 for yard mowing, $22 for office supplies expense, and $9 for miscellaneous expenses.
12. Collected the amount due from the credit card company.

13. Paid installers and other employees a total of $45,000 cash for salaries.

14. Collected $116,800 of accounts receivable during the year.

15. Paid $9,500 of advertising expense during the year.

16. Paid $5,200 of utilities expense for the year.

17. Paid a dividend of $20,000 to the shareholders.

Adjustments

18. There was $250 of supplies on hand at the end of the year.

19. Recognized the expired rent for both the van and the office for the year.

20. Recognized the uncollectible accounts expense for the year using the allowance method.

21. Accrued salaries at December 31, 2017, were $2,100.

Required

a. Record the above transactions in general journal form.

b. Post the transactions to the T-accounts.

c. Prepare a trial balance.

d. Prepare an income statement, statement of changes in stockholders' equity, balance sheet, and statement of cash flows.

e. Close the temporary accounts to retained earnings.

f. Post the closing entries to the T-accounts and prepare a post-closing trial balance.

Accounting for Long-Term Operational Assets

CHAPTER OPENING

Companies use assets to produce revenue. Some assets, like inventory or office supplies, are called **current assets** because they are used relatively quickly (within a single accounting period). Other assets, like equipment or buildings, are used for extended periods of time (two or more accounting periods). These assets are called **long-term operational assets.**[1]

[1]Classifying assets as current versus long term is explained in more detail in Chapter 9.

Accounting for long-term assets raises several questions. For example, what is the cost of the asset? Is it the list price only or should the cost of transportation, transit insurance, setup, and so on be added to the list price? Should the cost of a long-term asset be recognized as expense in the period the asset is purchased or should the cost be expensed over the useful life of the asset? What happens in the accounting records when a long-term asset is retired from use? This chapter answers these questions. It explains accounting for long-term operational assets from the date of purchase through the date of disposal.

The Curious Accountant

Most companies have various types of long-term assets that they use to operate their business. Common types of long-term assets include buildings, machinery, and equipment. But there are other types as well. A major category of long-term assets for a mining company is the mineral reserves from which they extract ore.

Freeport-McMoRan Copper & Gold, Inc. (referred to as FCX) is one of the largest mining operations in the world. It produces copper, gold and molybdenum from 12 major mines located on four continents. As of December 31, 2010, it owned proven mineral reserves that cost $4.5 billion, and buildings, machinery, and equipment that cost $12.7 billion.

As you learned in Chapters 2 and 4, except for land, over time most assets are consumed in a company's efforts to produce revenues, and as they are consumed, the asset account is decreased and an expense account is increased. How do you think the way a mining company uses its buildings and equipment differs from the way it uses its mineral reserves, and how will these differences affect the way these assets are accounted for? (Answer on page 435.)

TANGIBLE VERSUS INTANGIBLE ASSETS

LO 1

Identify different types of long-term operational assets.

Long-term assets may be tangible or intangible. **Tangible assets** have a physical presence; they can be seen and touched. Tangible assets include equipment, machinery, natural resources, and land. In contrast, intangible assets have no physical form. Although they may be represented by physical documents, **intangible assets** are, in fact, rights or privileges. They cannot be seen or touched. For example, a patent represents an exclusive legal *privilege* to produce and sell a particular product. It protects inventors by making it illegal for others to profit by copying their inventions. Although a patent may be represented by legal documents, the privilege is the actual asset. Since the privilege cannot be seen or touched, the patent is an intangible asset.

Tangible Long-Term Assets

Tangible long-term assets are classified as (1) property, plant, and equipment; (2) natural resources, or (3) land.

Property, Plant, and Equipment

Property, plant, and equipment is sometimes called *plant assets* or *fixed assets.* Examples of property, plant, and equipment include furniture, cash registers, machinery, delivery trucks, computers, mechanical robots, and buildings. The level of detail used to account for these assets varies. One company may include all office equipment in one account, whereas another company might divide office equipment into computers, desks, chairs, and so on. The term used to recognize expense for property, plant, and equipment is **depreciation.**

Natural Resources

Mineral deposits, oil and gas reserves, timber stands, coal mines, and stone quarries are examples of **natural resources.** Conceptually, natural resources are inventories. When sold, the cost of these assets is frequently expensed as *cost of goods sold.* Although inventories are usually classified as short-term assets, natural resources are normally classified as long term because the resource deposits generally have long lives. For example, it may take decades to extract all of the diamonds from a diamond mine. The term used to recognize expense for natural resources is **depletion.**

Land

Land is classified separately from other property because land is not subject to depreciation or depletion. Land has an infinite life. It is not worn out or consumed as it is used. When buildings or natural resources are purchased simultaneously with land, the amount paid must be divided between the land and the other assets because of the non-depreciable nature of the land.

Intangible Assets

Intangible assets fall into two categories, those with *identifiable useful lives* and those with *indefinite useful lives.*

Intangible Assets with Identifiable Useful Lives

Intangible assets with identifiable useful lives include patents and copyrights. These assets may become obsolete (a patent may become worthless if new technology provides a superior product) or may reach the end of their legal lives. The term used when recognizing expense for intangible assets with identifiable useful lives is called **amortization.**

Intangible Assets with Indefinite Useful Lives

The benefits of some intangible assets may extend so far into the future that their useful lives cannot be estimated. For how many years will the Coca-Cola trademark attract customers? When will the value of a McDonald's franchise end? There are no answers to these questions. Intangible assets such as renewable franchises, trademarks, and goodwill have indefinite useful lives. The costs of such assets are not expensed unless the value of the assets becomes impaired.

DETERMINING THE COST OF LONG-TERM ASSETS

The **historical cost concept** requires that an asset be recorded at the amount paid for it. This amount includes the purchase price plus any costs necessary to get the asset in the location and condition for its intended use. Common cost components are:

LO 2

Determine the cost of long-term operational assets.

- **Buildings:** (1) purchase price, (2) sales taxes, (3) title search and transfer document costs, (4) realtor's and attorney's fees, and (5) remodeling costs.

- **Land:** (1) purchase price, (2) sales taxes, (3) title search and transfer document costs, (4) realtor's and attorney's fees, (5) costs for removal of old buildings, and (6) grading costs.

- **Equipment:** (1) purchase price (less discounts), (2) sales taxes, (3) delivery costs, (4) installation costs, and (5) costs to adapt for intended use.

The cost of an asset does not include payments for fines, damages, and so on that could have been avoided.

✓ CHECK YOURSELF 8.1

Sheridan Construction Company purchased a new bulldozer that had a $260,000 list price. The seller agreed to allow a 4 percent cash discount in exchange for immediate payment. The bull- dozer was delivered FOB shipping point at a cost of $1,200. Sheridan hired a new employee to operate the dozer for an annual salary of $36,000. The employee was trained to operate the dozer for a onetime training fee of $800. The cost of the company's theft insurance policy increased by $300 per year as a result of adding the dozer to the policy. The dozer had a five- year useful life and an expected salvage value of $26,000. Determine the asset's cost.

Answer

List price	$260,000
Less: Cash discount ($260,000 × 0.04)	(10,400)
Shipping cost	1,200
Training cost	800
Total asset cost (amount capitalized)	$251,600

Basket Purchase Allocation

Acquiring a group of assets in a single transaction is known as a **basket purchase.** The total price of a basket purchase must be allocated among the assets acquired. Accoun- tants commonly allocate the purchase price using the **relative fair market value method.** To illustrate, assume that Beatty Company purchased land and a building for $240,000 cash. A real estate appraiser determined the fair market value of each asset to be

Building	$270,000
Land	90,000
Total	$360,000

The appraisal indicates that the land is worth 25 percent ($90,000 ÷ $360,000) of the total value and the building is worth 75 percent ($270,000 ÷ $360,000). Using these percentages, the actual purchase price is allocated as follows:

Building	0.75 × $240,000 =	$180,000
Land	0.25 × $240,000 =	60,000
Total		$240,000

METHODS OF RECOGNIZING DEPRECIATION EXPENSE

LO 3

Explain how different depreciation methods affect financial statements.

The life cycle of an operational asset involves (1) acquiring the funds to buy the asset, (2) purchasing the asset, (3) using the asset, and (4) retiring (disposing of) the asset. These stages are illustrated in Exhibit 8.1. The stages involving (1) acquiring funds and (2) purchasing assets have been discussed previously. This section of the chapter describes how accountants recognize the *use* of assets (Stage 3). As they are used, assets suffer from wear and tear called *depreciation.* Ultimately, assets depreciate to the point that they are no longer useful in the process of earning revenue. This process usually takes several years. The amount of an asset's cost that is allocated to expense during an accounting period is called **depreciation expense.**

An asset that is fully depreciated by one company may still be useful to another company. For example, a rental car that is no longer useful to Hertz may still be useful to a local delivery company. As a result, companies are frequently able to sell their fully depreciated assets to other companies or individuals. The expected market value of a fully depreciated asset is called its **salvage value.** The total amount of depreciation a company recognizes for an asset, its **depreciable cost,** is the difference between its original cost and its salvage value.

For example, assume a company purchases an asset for $5,000. The company expects to use the asset for 5 years (the **estimated useful life**) and then to sell it for $1,000 (salvage value). The depreciable cost of the asset is $4,000 ($5,000 − $1,000). The portion of the depreciable cost ($4,000) that represents its annual usage is recognized as depreciation expense.

Accountants must exercise judgment to estimate the amount of depreciation expense to recognize each period. For example, suppose you own a personal computer. You know how much the computer cost, and you know you will eventually need to replace it. How would you determine the amount the computer depreciates each year you use it? Businesses may use any of several acceptable methods to estimate the amount of depreciation expense to recognize each year.

The method used to recognize depreciation expense should match the asset's usage pattern. More expense should be recognized in periods when the asset is used more and less in periods when the asset is used less. Since assets are used to produce revenue, matching expense recognition with asset usage also matches expense recognition with revenue recognition. Three alternative methods for recognizing depreciation expense are (1) straight-line, (2) double-declining-balance, and (3) units-of-production.

The *straight-line* method produces the same amount of depreciation expense each accounting period. *Double-declining-balance,* an accelerated method, produces more depreciation expense in the early years of an asset's life, with a declining amount of expense in later years. *Units-of-production* produces varying amounts of depreciation expense in different accounting periods (more in some accounting periods and less in others). Exhibit 8.2 contrasts the different depreciation methods that U.S. companies use.

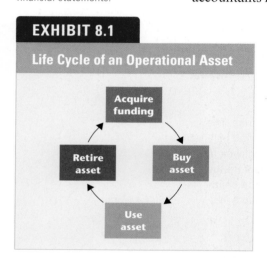

EXHIBIT 8.1

Life Cycle of an Operational Asset

Acquire funding → Buy asset → Use asset → Retire asset → (Acquire funding)

EXHIBIT 8.2

Depreciation Methods Used by U.S. Companies

Other 1%
Units-of-production 7%
Accelerated 14%
Straight-line 78%

Data Source: AICPA Accounting Trends and Techniques.

Dryden Enterprises Illustration

To illustrate the different depreciation methods, consider a van purchased by Dryden Enterprises. Dryden plans to use the van as rental property. The van had a list price of $23,500. Dryden obtained a 10 percent cash discount from the dealer. The van was delivered FOB shipping point, and Dryden paid an additional $250 for transportation costs. Dryden also paid $2,600 for a custom accessory package to increase the van's appeal as a rental vehicle. The cost of the van is computed as follows:

List price	$23,500	
Less: Cash discount	(2,350)	$23,500 × 0.10
Plus: Transportation costs	250	
Plus: Cost of customization	2,600	
Total	$24,000	

The van has an estimated *salvage value* of $4,000 and an *estimated useful life* of four years. The following section examines three different patterns of expense recognition for this van.

Straight-Line Depreciation

The first scenario assumes the van is used evenly over its four-year life. The revenue from renting the van is assumed to be $8,000 per year. The matching concept calls for the expense recognition pattern to match the revenue stream. Since the same amount of revenue is recognized in each accounting period, Dryden should use **straight-line depreciation** because it produces equal amounts of depreciation expense each year.

Life Cycle Phase 1

The first phase of the asset life cycle is to acquire funds to purchase the asset. Assume Dryden acquired $25,000 cash on January 1, 2013, by issuing common stock. The journal entry and its effects on the financial statements are shown here:

Account Title	Debit	Credit
Cash	25,000	
Common Stock		25,000

Assets			=	Equity			Rev.	−	Exp.	=	Net Inc.	Cash Flow	
Cash	+	Book Value of Van	=	Com. Stk.	+	Ret. Earn.							
25,000	+	NA	=	25,000	+	NA	NA	−	NA	=	NA	25,000	FA

Life Cycle Phase 2

The second phase of the life cycle is to purchase the van. Assume Dryden bought the van on January 1, 2013, using funds from the stock issue. The cost of the van, previously computed, was $24,000 cash. The journal entry and its effects on the financial statements are shown here:

Account Title	Debit	Credit
Van	24,000	
Cash		24,000

Assets			=	Equity			Rev.	−	Exp.	=	Net Inc.	Cash Flow	
Cash	+	Book Value of Van	=	Com. Stk.	+	Ret. Earn.							
(24,000)	+	24,000	=	NA	+	NA	NA	−	NA	=	NA	(24,000)	IA

Life Cycle Phase 3

Dryden used the van by renting it to customers. The rent revenue each year is $8,000 cash. The annual journal entry and its effects on the financial statements are shown here:

Account Title	Debit	Credit
Cash	8,000	
Rent Revenue		8,000

Assets			=	Equity			Rev.	−	Exp.	=	Net Inc.	Cash Flow
Cash	+	Book Value of Van	=	Com. Stk.	+	Ret. Earn.						
8,000	+	NA	=	NA	+	8,000	8,000	−	NA	=	8,000	8,000 OA

Although illustrated only once, these effects occur four times—once for each year Dryden earns revenue by renting the van.

At the end of each year, Dryden adjusts its accounts to recognize depreciation expense. The amount of depreciation recognized using the straight-line method is calculated as follows:

$$\text{(Asset cost − Salvage value)} \div \text{Useful life} = \text{Depreciation expense}$$
$$(\$24,000 − \$4,000) \div 4 \text{ years} = \$5,000 \text{ per year.}$$

Recognizing depreciation expense is an asset use transaction that reduces assets and equity. The asset reduction is reported using a **contra asset account** called **Accumulated Depreciation.** Like other contra asset accounts, the Accumulated Depreciation account has a credit balance. The **book value** of a long-term tangible asset is determined by subtracting the credit balance in the Accumulated Depreciation account from the debit balance in the associated asset account. The book value may also be called the **carrying value.**

While recognizing depreciation expense decreases net income, it *does not affect cash flow.* The $24,000 cash outflow occurred in January 2013 when Dryden purchased the van. In contrast, the $5,000 depreciation expense is recognized each year as the van is used. The December 31, 2013, journal entry recognizing depreciation expense and its effects on the financial statements are shown here:

Account Title	Debit	Credit
Depreciation Expense	5,000	
Accumulated Depreciation		5,000

Assets			=	Equity			Rev.	−	Exp.	=	Net Inc.	Cash Flow
Cash	+	Book Value of Van	=	Com. Stk.	+	Ret. Earn.						
NA	+	(5,000)	=	NA	+	(5,000)	NA	−	5,000	=	(5,000)	NA

The book value of the van as of December 31, 2013, is $19,000, computed as shown here:

Van	$24,000
Accumulated depreciation	(5,000)
Book value	$19,000

Depreciation expense is recognized each year the van is used. Like other expense accounts, the Depreciation Expense account is a temporary account that is closed to retained earnings at the end of each accounting cycle. In other words, each year $5,000 is recognized in the Depreciation Expense account and then closed to the Retained Earning account. As a result, the Depreciation Expense account will never have a balance that is larger than $5,000.

In contrast, the Accumulated Depreciation account is a permanent account. As its name implies, the total amount in the Accumulated Depreciation account increases (accumulates) each time depreciation expense is recognized. For example, at the end of 2014 Dryden will recognize $5,000 of depreciation expense and the balance in the Accumulated Depreciation account will increase to $10,000. At the end of 2015 Dryden will recognize $5,000 of depreciation expense and increase the balance in the Accumulated Depreciation account to $15,000, and so on.

Life Cycle Phase 4

The final stage in the life cycle of a tangible asset is its disposal and removal from the company's records. Dryden retired the van from service on January 1, 2017, selling it for $4,500 cash. The van's book value (cost − accumulated depreciation) when it was sold was $4,000 ($24,000 cost − $20,000 accumulated depreciation), so Dryden recognized a $500 gain ($4,500 − $4,000) on the sale.

Gains are *like* revenues in that they increase assets or decrease liabilities. Gains are *unlike* revenues in that gains result from peripheral (incidental) transactions rather than routine operating activities. Dryden is not in the business of selling vans. Dryden's normal business activity is renting vans. Since selling vans is incidental to Dryden's normal operations, gains are reported separately, after operating income, on the income statement.

If Dryden had sold the asset for less than book value, the company would have recognized a loss on the asset disposal. **Losses** are similar to expenses in that they decrease assets or increase liabilities. However, like gains, losses result from peripheral transactions. Losses are also reported as nonoperating items on the income statement.

The journal entry to record the asset disposal and its effects on the financial statements are shown here.

LO 4

Determine how gains and losses on disposals of long-term operational assets affect financial statements.

Account Title	Debit	Credit
Cash	4,500	
Accumulated Depreciation	20,000	
Van		24,000
Gain on Sale of Van		500

Assets			=	Equity			Rev. or Gain	−	Exp. or Loss	=	Net Inc.	Cash Flow
Cash	+	Book Value of Van	=	Com. Stk.	+	Ret. Earn.						
4,500	+	(4,000)	=	NA	+	500	500	−	NA	=	500	4,500 IA

Although the gain reported on the 2017 income statement is $500, the cash inflow from selling the van is $4,500. Gains and losses are not reported on the statement of cash flows. Instead they are included in the total amount of cash collected from the sale of the asset. In this case, the entire $4,500 is shown in the cash flow from investing activities section of the 2017 statement of cash flows.

Financial Statements

Exhibit 8.3 displays a vertical statements model that shows the financial results for the Dryden illustration from 2013 through 2017. Study the exhibit until you understand how all the figures were derived. The amount of depreciation expense ($5,000)

EXHIBIT 8.3	Financial Statements under Straight-Line Depreciation

DRYDEN ENTERPRISES
Financial Statements

	2013	2014	2015	2016	2017
Income Statements					
Rent revenue	$ 8,000	$ 8,000	$ 8,000	$ 8,000	$ 0
Depreciation expense	(5,000)	(5,000)	(5,000)	(5,000)	0
Operating income	3,000	3,000	3,000	3,000	0
Gain on sale of van	0	0	0	0	500
Net income	$ 3,000	$ 3,000	$ 3,000	$ 3,000	$ 500
Balance Sheets					
Assets					
Cash	$ 9,000	$17,000	$25,000	$33,000	$37,500
Van	24,000	24,000	24,000	24,000	0
Accumulated depreciation	(5,000)	(10,000)	(15,000)	(20,000)	0
Total assets	$28,000	$31,000	$34,000	$37,000	$37,500
Stockholders' equity					
Common stock	$25,000	$25,000	$25,000	$25,000	$25,000
Retained earnings	3,000	6,000	9,000	12,000	12,500
Total stockholders' equity	$28,000	$31,000	$34,000	$37,000	$37,500
Statements of Cash Flows					
Operating Activities					
Inflow from customers	$ 8,000	$ 8,000	$ 8,000	$ 8,000	$ 0
Investing Activities					
Outflow to purchase van	(24,000)				
Inflow from sale of van					4,500
Financing Activities					
Inflow from stock issue	25,000				
Net Change in Cash	9,000	8,000	8,000	8,000	4,500
Beginning cash balance	0	9,000	17,000	25,000	33,000
Ending cash balance	$ 9,000	$17,000	$25,000	$33,000	$37,500

reported on the income statement is constant each year from 2013 through 2016. The amount of accumulated depreciation reported on the balance sheet grows from $5,000 to $10,000, to $15,000, and finally to $20,000. The Accumulated Depreciation account is a *contra asset account* that is subtracted from the Van account in determining total assets.

Study the timing differences between cash flow and net income. Dryden spent $24,000 cash to acquire the van. Over the van's life cycle, Dryden collected $36,500 [($8,000 revenue × 4 years = $32,000) plus ($4,500 from the asset disposal) = $36,500]. The $12,500 difference between the cash collected and the cash paid ($36,500 − $24,000) equals the total net income earned during the van's life cycle.

Although the amounts are the same, the timing of the cash flows and the income recognition are different. For example, in 2013 there was a $24,000 cash outflow to purchase the van and an $8,000 cash inflow from customers. In contrast, the income statement reports net income of $3,000. In 2017, Dryden reported a $500 gain on the asset disposal, but the amount of operating income and the cash flow from operating activities is zero for that year. The gain is only indirectly related to cash flows. The $4,500 of cash received on disposal is reported as a cash inflow from investing activities. Since gains and losses result from peripheral transactions, they do not affect operatii income or cash flow from operating activities.

Double-Declining-Balance Depreciation

For the second scenario, assume demand for the van is strong when it is new, but fewer people rent the van as it ages. As a result, the van produces smaller amounts of revenue as time goes by. To match expenses with revenues, it is reasonable to recognize more depreciation expense in the van's early years and less as it ages.

Double-declining-balance depreciation produces a large amount of depreciation in the first year of an asset's life and progressively smaller levels of expense in each succeeding year. Since the double-declining-balance method recognizes depreciation expense more rapidly than the straight-line method does, it is called an **accelerated depreciation method.** Depreciation expense recognized using double-declining-balance is computed in three steps.

1. *Determine the straight-line rate.* Divide one by the asset's useful life. Since the estimated useful life of Dryden's van is four years, the straight-line rate is 25 percent (1 ÷ 4) per year.

2. *Determine the double-declining-balance rate.* Multiply the straight-line rate by 2 (*double* the rate). The double-declining-balance rate for the van is 50 percent (25 percent × 2).

3. *Determine the depreciation expense.* Multiply the double-declining-balance rate by the book value of the asset *at the beginning of the period* (recall that book value is historical cost minus *accumulated depreciation*). The following table shows the amount of depreciation expense Dryden will recognize over the van's useful life (2013–2016).

Year	Book Value at Beginning of Period	×	Double the Straight-Line Rate	=	Annual Depreciation Expense	
2013	($24,000 − $ 0) ×		0.50	=	$12,000	
2014	(24,000 − 12,000) ×		0.50	=	6,000	
2015	(24,000 − 18,000) ×		0.50	=	~~3,000~~	2,000
2016	(24,000 − 20,000) ×		0.50	=	~~2,000~~	0

Regardless of the depreciation method used, *an asset cannot be depreciated below its salvage value.* This restriction affects depreciation computations for the third and fourth years. Because the van had a cost of $24,000 and a salvage value of $4,000, the total amount of depreciable cost (historical cost − salvage value) is $20,000 ($24,000 − $4,000). Since $18,000 ($12,000 + $6,000) of the depreciable cost is recognized in the first two years, only $2,000 ($20,000 − $18,000) remains to be recognized after the second year. Depreciation expense recognized in the third year is therefore $2,000 even though double-declining-balance computations suggest that $3,000 should be recognized. Similarly, zero depreciation expense is recognized in the fourth year even though the computations indicate a $2,000 charge.

Effects on the Financial Statements

Exhibit 8.4 displays financial statements for the life of the asset assuming Dryden uses double-declining-balance depreciation. The illustration assumes a cash revenue stream of $15,000, $9,000, $5,000, and $3,000 for the years 2013, 2014, 2015, and 2016, respectively. Trace the depreciation expense from the table above to the income statements.

| EXHIBIT 8.4 | Financial Statements under Double-Declining-Balance Depreciation |

DRYDEN ENTERPRISES
Financial Statements

	2013	2014	2015	2016	2017
Income Statements					
Rent revenue	$15,000	$ 9,000	$ 5,000	$ 3,000	$ 0
Depreciation expense	(12,000)	(6,000)	(2,000)	0	0
Operating income	3,000	3,000	3,000	3,000	0
Gain on sale of van	0	0	0	0	500
Net income	$ 3,000	$ 3,000	$ 3,000	$ 3,000	$ 500
Balance Sheets					
Assets					
Cash	$16,000	$25,000	$30,000	$33,000	$37,500
Van	24,000	24,000	24,000	24,000	0
Accumulated depreciation	(12,000)	(18,000)	(20,000)	(20,000)	0
Total assets	$28,000	$31,000	$34,000	$37,000	$37,500
Stockholders' equity					
Common stock	$25,000	$25,000	$25,000	$25,000	$25,000
Retained earnings	3,000	6,000	9,000	12,000	12,500
Total stockholders' equity	$28,000	$31,000	$34,000	$37,000	$37,500
Statements of Cash Flows					
Operating Activities					
Inflow from customers	$15,000	$ 9,000	$ 5,000	$ 3,000	$ 0
Investing Activities					
Outflow to purchase van	(24,000)				
Inflow from sale of van					4,500
Financing Activities					
Inflow from stock issue	25,000				
Net Change in Cash	16,000	9,000	5,000	3,000	4,500
Beginning cash balance	0	16,000	25,000	30,000	33,000
Ending cash balance	$16,000	$25,000	$30,000	$33,000	$37,500

Reported depreciation expense is greater in the earlier years and smaller in the later years of the asset's life.

The double-declining-balance method smoothes the amount of net income reported over the asset's useful life. In the early years, when heavy asset use produces higher revenue, depreciation expense is also higher. Similarly, in the later years, lower levels of revenue are matched with lower levels of depreciation expense. Net income is constant at $3,000 per year.

The depreciation method a company uses *does not* affect how it acquires the financing, invests the funds, and retires the asset. For Dryden's van, the accounting effects of these life cycle phases are the same as under the straight-line approach. Similarly, the *recording procedures* are not affected by the depreciation method. Different depreciation methods affect only the amounts of depreciation expense recorded each year, not which accounts are used. The general journal entries are therefore not illustrated for the double-declining-balance or the units-of-production depreciation methods.

CHECK YOURSELF 8.2

Olds Company purchased an asset that cost $36,000 on January 1, 2013. The asset had an expected useful life of five years and an estimated salvage value of $5,000. Assuming Olds uses the double-declining-balance method, determine the amount of depreciation expense and the amount of accumulated depreciation Olds would report on the 2015 financial statements.

Answer

Year	Book Value at Beginning of Period	×	Double the Straight-Line Rate*	=	Annual Depreciation Expense
2013	($36,000 − $ 0)	×	0.40	=	$14,400
2014	(36,000 − 14,400)	×	0.40	=	8,640
2015	(36,000 − 23,040)	×	0.40	=	5,184
Total accumulated depreciation at December 31, 2015					$28,224

*Double-declining-balance rate = 2 × Straight-line rate = 2 × (1 ÷ 5 years) = 0.40

Units-of-Production Depreciation

Suppose rental demand for Dryden's van depends on general economic conditions. In a robust economy, travel increases, and demand for renting vans is high. In a stagnant economy, demand for van rentals declines. In such circumstances, revenues fluctuate from year to year. To accomplish the matching objective, depreciation should also fluctuate from year to year. A method of depreciation known as **units-of-production depreciation** accomplishes this goal by basing depreciation expense on actual asset usage.

Computing depreciation expense using units-of-production begins with identifying a measure of the asset's productive capacity. For example, the number of miles Dryden expects its van to be driven may be a reasonable measure of its productive capacity. If the depreciable asset were a saw, an appropriate measure of productive capacity could be the number of board feet the saw was expected to cut during its useful life. In other words, the basis for measuring production depends on the nature of the depreciable asset.

To illustrate computing depreciation using the units-of-production depreciation method, assume that Dryden measures productive capacity based on the total number of miles the van will be driven over its useful life. Assume Dryden estimates this productive capacity to be 100,000 miles. The first step in determining depreciation expense is to compute the cost per unit of production. For Dryden's van, this amount is total depreciable cost (historical cost − salvage value) divided by total units of expected productive capacity (100,000 miles). The depreciation cost per mile is therefore $0.20 [($24,000 cost − $4,000 salvage) ÷ 100,000 miles]. Annual depreciation expense is computed by multiplying the cost per mile by the number of miles driven. Odometer readings indicate the van was driven 40,000 miles, 20,000 miles, 30,000 miles, and 15,000 miles in 2013, 2014, 2015, and 2016, respectively. Dryden developed the following schedule of depreciation charges:

Year	Cost per Mile (a)	Miles Driven (b)	Depreciation Expense (a × b)
2013	$.20	40,000	$8,000
2014	.20	20,000	4,000
2015	.20	30,000	6,000
2016	.20	15,000	~~3,000~~ 2,000

As pointed out in the discussion of the double-declining-balance method, an asset cannot be depreciated below its salvage value. Since $18,000 of the $20,000 ($24,000 cost − $4,000 salvage) depreciable cost is recognized in the first three years of using the van, only $2,000 ($20,000 − $18,000) remains to be charged to depreciation in the fourth year, even though the depreciation computations suggest the charge should be $3,000. As the preceding table indicates, the general formula for computing units-of-production depreciation is

$$\frac{\text{Cost} - \text{Salvage value}}{\text{Total estimated units of production}} \times \begin{array}{c}\text{Units of production}\\ \text{in current}\\ \text{year}\end{array} = \begin{array}{c}\text{Annual}\\ \text{depreciation}\\ \text{expense}\end{array}$$

Exhibit 8.5 displays financial statements that assume Dryden uses units-of-production depreciation. The exhibit assumes a cash revenue stream of $11,000, $7,000, $9,000, and $5,000 for 2013, 2014, 2015, and 2016, respectively. Trace the depreciation expense from the schedule above to the income statements. Depreciation expense is greater in years the van is driven more and smaller in years the van is driven less, providing a reasonable matching of depreciation expense with revenue produced. Net income is again constant at $3,000 per year.

EXHIBIT 8.5   Financial Statements under Units-of-Production Depreciation

DRYDEN ENTERPRISES
Financial Statements

	2013	2014	2015	2016	2017
Income Statements					
Rent revenue	$11,000	$ 7,000	$ 9,000	$ 5,000	$ 0
Depreciation expense	(8,000)	(4,000)	(6,000)	(2,000)	0
Operating income	3,000	3,000	3,000	3,000	0
Gain on sale of van	0	0	0	0	500
Net income	$ 3,000	$ 3,000	$ 3,000	$ 3,000	$ 500
Balance Sheets					
Assets					
Cash	$12,000	$19,000	$28,000	$33,000	$37,500
Van	24,000	24,000	24,000	24,000	0
Accumulated depreciation	(8,000)	(12,000)	(18,000)	(20,000)	0
Total assets	$28,000	$31,000	$34,000	$37,000	$37,500
Stockholders' equity					
Common stock	$25,000	$25,000	$25,000	$25,000	$25,000
Retained earnings	3,000	6,000	9,000	12,000	12,500
Total stockholders' equity	$28,000	$31,000	$34,000	$37,000	$37,500
Statements of Cash Flows					
Operating Activities					
Inflow from customers	$11,000	$ 7,000	$ 9,000	$ 5,000	$ 0
Investing Activities					
Outflow to purchase van	(24,000)				
Inflow from sale of van					4,500
Financing Activities					
Inflow from stock issue	25,000				
Net Change in Cash	12,000	7,000	9,000	5,000	4,500
Beginning cash balance	0	12,000	19,000	28,000	33,000
Ending cash balance	$12,000	$19,000	$28,000	$33,000	$37,500

EXHIBIT 8.6

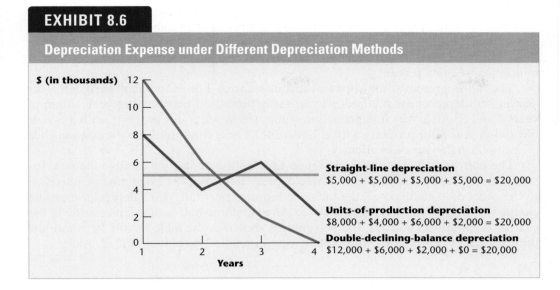

Depreciation Expense under Different Depreciation Methods

Straight-line depreciation
$5,000 + $5,000 + $5,000 + $5,000 = $20,000

Units-of-production depreciation
$8,000 + $4,000 + $6,000 + $2,000 = $20,000

Double-declining-balance depreciation
$12,000 + $6,000 + $2,000 + $0 = $20,000

Comparing the Depreciation Methods

The total amount of depreciation expense Dryden recognized using each of the three methods was $20,000 ($24,000 cost − $4,000 salvage value). The different methods affect the *timing*, but not the *total amount*, of expense recognized. The different methods simply assign the $20,000 to different accounting periods. Exhibit 8.6 presents graphically the differences among the three depreciation methods discussed above. A company should use the method that most closely matches expenses with revenues.

INCOME TAX CONSIDERATIONS

The matching principle is not relevant to income tax reporting. The objective of tax reporting is to minimize tax expense. For tax purposes the most desirable depreciation method is the one that produces the highest amount of depreciation expense. Higher expenses mean lower taxes.

Identify some of the tax issues that affect long-term operational assets.

   The maximum depreciation currently allowed by tax law is computed using an accelerated depreciation method known as the **modified accelerated cost recovery system (MACRS).** MACRS specifies the useful life for designated categories of assets. For example, under the law, companies must base depreciation computations for automobiles, light trucks, technological equipment, and other similar asset types on a 5-year useful life. In contrast, a 7-year life must be used for office furniture, fixtures, and many types of conventional machinery. The law classifies depreciable property, excluding real estate, into one of six categories: 3-year property, 5-year property, 7-year property, 10-year property, 15-year property, and 20-year property. Tables have been established for each category that specify the percentage of cost that can be expensed (deducted) in determining the amount of taxable income. A tax table for 5- and 7-year property is shown here as an example.

Year	5-Year Property, %	7-Year Property, %
1	20.00	14.29
2	32.00	24.49
3	19.20	17.49
4	11.52	12.49
5	11.52	8.93
6	5.76	8.92
7		8.93
8		4.46

The amount of depreciation a company can deduct each year for tax purposes is determined by multiplying the cost of a depreciable asset by the percentage shown in the table. For example, the depreciation expense for year 1 of a 7-year property asset is the cost of the asset multiplied by 14.29 percent. Depreciation for year 2 is the cost multiplied by 24.49 percent.

The tables present some apparent inconsistencies. For example, if MACRS is an accelerated depreciation method, why is less depreciation permitted in year 1 than in years 2 and 3? Also, why is depreciation computed in year 6 for property with a 5-year life and in year 8 for property with a 7-year life? These conditions are the consequence of using the **half-year convention.**

The half-year convention is designed to simplify computing taxable income. Instead of requiring taxpayers to calculate depreciation from the exact date of purchase to the exact date of disposal, the tax code requires one-half year's depreciation to be charged in the year in which an asset is acquired and one-half year's depreciation in the year of disposal. As a result, the percentages shown in the table for the first and last years represent depreciation for one-half year instead of the actual time of usage.

FOCUS ON INTERNATIONAL ISSUES

As you have learned, U.S. GAAP requires companies to use historical cost when accounting for property, plant, and equipment (PPE). Once a company begins depreciating its buildings and equipment, expenses increase (due to depreciation expense), which causes net income and retained earnings to decrease. This, of course, ignores the revenue the company hopes to generate by using the asset.

Under IFRS a company has two options regarding accounting of PPE. First, it can use a historical cost accounting method that is virtually identical to that required by U.S. GAAP. Second, it can use the "revaluation model," which reports PPE at its fair value. There can be different ways of determining fair value, but the preferred approach is to base fair value on a market-based appraisal, performed by professional appraisers. These revaluations must be conducted frequently enough that the fair value of an asset is not materially different from its recorded book value.

Basically, the revaluation model works as follows. The company periodically compares the current book value of its PPE to the fair value at that same date. This fair value relates to the value of the used asset, not the amount required to replace it with a new asset. If the fair value of an asset is higher than its currently recorded book value, the recorded amount for the asset is increased, which increases total assets. However, the increase in the asset's fair value is *not* reported on the company's income statement, as would a gain from selling the asset. Rather, the increase is reported in a special section of stockholders' equity, which balances the increase that was recorded for assets. However, if the new fair value is *lower* than the assets current book value, the decrease is charged to net income, as well as to assets. This is another example of the conservatism principle at work. Not surprisingly, there are exceptions to these rules. Once a new fair value is established, future depreciation expense is based on these values.

One concern might be that companies, hoping to manipulate earnings, would pick and choose some assets to account for under historical costs and others to account for under the revaluation model. This is not permitted. Although a company does not have to use a single method for all its assets, it must use a single method for all the assets in a given class of assets. For example, historical costs could be used for all factory equipment, and the revaluation model used for all its buildings.

As significant as the difference between the historical cost method and the fair value approach might be, the majority of companies continue to use historical costs. Professors H.B. Christensen and V. Nikolaev conducted a study of the use of revaluation accounting for nonfinancial assets by companies in Germany and the United Kingdom. Their research found that only 3.2 percent of the 1,539 companies surveyed used the revaluation model for property, plant, and equipment.*

*Source: Christensen, H.B. and Nikolaev, V., "Who Uses Fair Value Accounting for Nonfinancial Assets after IFRS Adoption?" The University of Chicago Booth School of Business Working Paper No. 09-12, February 2009.

To illustrate computing depreciation using MACRS, assume that Wilson Company purchased furniture (7-year property) for $10,000 cash on July 21. Tax depreciation charges over the useful life of the asset are computed as shown:

Year	Table Factor, %	×	Cost	=	Depreciation Amount
1	14.29		$10,000		$1,429
2	24.49		10,000		2,449
3	17.49		10,000		1,749
4	12.49		10,000		1,249
5	8.93		10,000		893
6	8.92		10,000		892
7	8.93		10,000		893
8	4.46		10,000		446
Total over useful life					$10,000

As an alternative to MACRS, the tax code permits using straight-line depreciation. For certain types of assets such as real property (buildings), the tax code requires using straight-line depreciation.

There is no requirement that depreciation methods used for financial reporting be consistent with those used in preparing the income tax return. For example, a company may use straight-line depreciation in its financial statements and MACRS for the tax return. A company making this choice would reduce taxes in the early years of an asset's life because it would report higher depreciation charges on the tax return than in the financial statements. In later years, however, taxes will be higher because under MACRS, the amount of depreciation declines as the asset becomes older. Taxes are delayed but not avoided. The amount of taxes delayed for future payment represent a **deferred tax liability.** Delaying tax payments is advantageous. During the delay period, the money that would have been used to pay taxes can be used instead to make revenue-generating investments.

REVISION OF ESTIMATES

In order to report useful financial information on a timely basis, accountants must make many estimates of future results, such as the salvage value and useful life of depreciable assets. Estimates are frequently revised when new information surfaces. Because revisions of estimates are common, generally accepted accounting principles call for incorporating the revised information into present and future calculations. Prior reports are not corrected.

LO 6

Show how revising estimates affects financial statements.

To illustrate, assume that McGraw Company purchased a machine on January 1, 2013, for $50,000. McGraw estimated the machine would have a useful life of eight years and a salvage value of $3,000. Using the straight-line method, McGraw determined the annual depreciation charge as follows:

($50,000 − $3,000) ÷ 8 years = $5,875 per year

At the beginning of the fifth year, accumulated depreciation on the machine is $23,500 ($5,875 × 4). The machine's book value is $26,500 ($50,000 − $23,500). At this point, what happens if McGraw changes its estimates of useful life or the salvage value? Consider the following revision examples independently of each other.

Revision of Life

Assume McGraw revises the expected life to 14, rather than 8, years. The machine's *remaining* life would then be 10 more years instead of 4 more years. Assume salvage value remains $3,000. Depreciation for each remaining year is:

($26,500 book value − $3,000 salvage) ÷ 10-year remaining life = $2,350

Revision of Salvage

Alternatively, assume the original expected life remained eight years, but McGraw revised its estimate of salvage value to $6,000. Depreciation for each of the remaining four years would be

$$(\$26,500 \text{ book value} - \$6,000 \text{ salvage}) \div 4\text{-year remaining life} = \$5,125$$

The revised amounts are determined for the full year, regardless of when McGraw revised its estimates. For example, if McGraw decides to change the estimated useful life on October 1, 2018, the change would be effective as of January 1, 2018. The year-end adjusting entry for depreciation would include a full year's depreciation calculated on the basis of the revised estimated useful life.

CONTINUING EXPENDITURES FOR PLANT ASSETS

LO 7

Explain how continuing expenditures for operational assets affect financial statements.

Most plant assets require additional expenditures for maintenance or improvement during their useful lives. Accountants must determine if these expenditures should be expensed or capitalized (recorded as assets).

Costs that Are Expensed

The costs of routine maintenance and minor repairs that are incurred to *keep* an asset in good working order are expensed in the period in which they are incurred. Because they reduce net income when incurred, accountants often call repair and maintenance costs **revenue expenditures** (companies subtract them from revenue).

With respect to the previous example, assume McGraw spent $500 for routine lubrication and to replace minor parts. The journal entry and its effects on the financial statements are shown here:

Account Title	Debit	Credit
Repairs Expense	500	
Cash		500

Assets	=		Equity			Rev.	−	Exp.	=	Net Inc.	Cash Flow
Cash	=	Com. Stk.	+	Ret. Earn.							
(500)	=	NA	+	(500)		NA	−	500	=	(500)	(500) OA

Costs that Are Capitalized

Substantial amounts spent to improve the quality or extend the life of an asset are described as **capital expenditures.** Capital expenditures are accounted for in one of two ways, depending on whether the cost incurred *improves the quality* or *extends the life* of the asset.

Improving Quality

Expenditures such as adding air conditioning to an existing building or installing a trailer hitch on a vehicle improve the quality of service these assets provide. If a capital expenditure improves an asset's quality, the amount is added to the historical cost of the asset. The additional cost is expensed through higher depreciation charges over the asset's remaining useful life.

To demonstrate, return to the McGraw Company example. Recall that the machine originally cost $50,000, had an estimated salvage of $3,000, and had a predicted life of eight years. Recall further that accumulated depreciation at the beginning of the fifth year is $23,500 ($5,875 × 4) so the book value is $26,500 ($50,000 − $23,500). Assume McGraw makes a major expenditure of $4,000 in the machine's fifth year to improve its productive capacity. The journal entry and its effects on the financial statements are shown here:

Account Title	Debit	Credit
Machine	4,000	
Cash		4,000

Assets			=	Equity			Rev.	−	Exp.	=	Net Inc.	Cash Flow
Cash	+	Book Value of Mach.	=	Com. Stk.	+	Ret. Earn.						
(4,000)	+	4,000	=	NA	+	NA	NA	−	NA	=	NA	(4,000) IA

After recording the expenditure, the machine account balance is $54,000 and the asset's book value is $30,500 ($54,000 − $23,500). The depreciation charges for each of the remaining four years are

($30,500 book value − $3,000 salvage) ÷ 4-year remaining life = $6,875

Extending Life

Expenditures such as replacing the roof of an existing building or putting a new engine in an older vehicle extend the useful life of these assets. If a capital expenditure extends the life of an asset rather than improving the asset's quality of service, accountants view the expenditure as canceling some of the depreciation previously charged to expense. The event is still an asset exchange; cash decreases, and the book value of the machine increases. However, the increase in the book value of the machine results from reducing the balance in the contra asset account, Accumulated Depreciation.

To illustrate, assume that instead of increasing productive capacity, McGraw's $4,000 expenditure had extended the useful life of the machine by two years. The journal entry and its effects on the financial statements are shown here:

Account Title	Debit	Credit
Accumulated Depreciation–Machine	4,000	
Cash		4,000

Assets			=	Equity			Rev.	−	Exp.	=	Net Inc.	Cash Flow
Cash	+	Book Value of Mach.	=	Com. Stk.	+	Ret. Earn.						
(4,000)	+	4,000	=	NA	+	NA	NA	−	NA	=	NA	(4,000) IA

After the expenditure is recorded, the book value is the same as if the $4,000 had been added to the Machine account ($50,000 cost − $19,500 adjusted balance in Accumulated Depreciation = $30,500). Depreciation expense for each of the remaining six years follows:

($30,500 book value − $3,000 salvage) ÷ 6-year remaining life = $4,583

CHECK YOURSELF 8.3

On January 1, 2013, Dager Inc. purchased an asset that cost $18,000. It had a five-year useful life and a $3,000 salvage value. Dager uses straight-line depreciation. On January 1, 2015, it incurred a $1,200 cost related to the asset. With respect to this asset, determine the amount of expense and accumulated depreciation Dager would report in the 2015 financial statements under each of the following assumptions.

1. The $1,200 cost was incurred to repair damage resulting from an accident.
2. The $1,200 cost improved the operating capacity of the asset. The total useful life and salvage value remained unchanged.
3. The $1,200 cost extended the useful life of the asset by one year. The salvage value remained unchanged.

Answer

1. Dager would report the $1,200 repair cost as an expense. Dager would also report depreciation expense of $3,000 [($18,000 − $3,000) ÷ 5]. Total expenses related to this asset in 2015 would be $4,200 ($1,200 repair expense + $3,000 depreciation expense). Accumulated depreciation at the end of 2015 would be $9,000 ($3,000 depreciation expense × 3 years).

2. The $1,200 cost would be capitalized in the asset account, increasing both the book value of the asset and the annual depreciation expense.

	After Effects of Capital Improvement
Amount in asset account ($18,000 + $1,200)	$19,200
Less: Salvage value	(3,000)
Accumulated depreciation on January 1, 2015	(6,000)
Remaining depreciable cost before recording 2015 depreciation	$10,200
Depreciation for 2015 ($10,200 ÷ 3 years)	$ 3,400
Accumulated depreciation at December 31, 2015 ($6,000 + $3,400)	$ 9,400

3. The $1,200 cost would be subtracted from the Accumulated Depreciation account, increasing the book value of the asset. The remaining useful life would increase to four years, which would decrease the depreciation expense.

	After Effects of Capital Improvement
Amount in asset account	$18,000
Less: Salvage value	(3,000)
Accumulated depreciation on January 1, 2015 ($6,000 − $1,200)	(4,800)
Remaining depreciable cost before recording 2015 depreciation	$10,200
Depreciation for 2015 ($10,200 ÷ 4 years)	$ 2,550
Accumulated depreciation at December 31, 2015 ($4,800 + $2,550)	$ 7,350

NATURAL RESOURCES

LO 8

Explain how expense recognition for natural resources (depletion) affects financial statements.

The cost of natural resources includes not only the purchase price but also related items such as the cost of exploration, geographic surveys, and estimates. The process of expensing natural resources is commonly called depletion.[2] The most common method used to calculate depletion is units-of-production.

[2]In practice, the depletion charge is considered a product cost and allocated between inventory and cost of goods sold. This text uses the simplifying assumption that all resources are sold in the same accounting period in which they are extracted. The full depletion charge is therefore expensed in the period in which the resources are extracted.

Answers to The Curious Accountant

As assets lose their productive capacity, either from being used or due to obsolescence, the asset account is reduced and an expense account is increased. Assets such as buildings and equipment may decline faster if they are used, but, due to obsolescence, they usually continue to decline even if they are not used. For this reason, a time-based depreciation method, such as straight-line or double-declining-balance, is almost always used for buildings and more often than not for equipment. In contrast, a mineral reserve does not lose its capacity unless ore is extracted. After all, the gold the FCX is mining today has been in the earth for millions of years. For this reason, companies typically use the units-of-production method to calculate depletion on mineral reserves. In both cases, the objective should be to achieve the best matching of expenses incurred with the revenues they generate.

To illustrate, assume Apex Coal Mining paid $4,000,000 cash to purchase a mine with an estimated 16,000,000 tons of coal. The unit depletion charge is

$$\$4,000,000 \div 16,000,000 \text{ tons} = \$0.25 \text{ per ton}$$

If Apex mines 360,000 tons of coal in the first year, the depletion charge is

$$360,000 \text{ tons} \times \$0.25 \text{ per ton} = \$90,000$$

The depletion of a natural resource has the same effect on the accounting equation as other expense recognition events. Assets (in this case, a *coal mine*) and stockholders' equity decrease. The depletion expense reduces net income. The journal entries necessary to record the acquisition and depletion of the coal mine and their effects on the financial statements are shown here:

Account Title	Debit	Credit
Coal Mine	4,000,000	
Cash		4,000,000
Depletion Expense	90,000	
Coal Mine		90,000

Assets			=	Equity			Rev.	−	Exp.	=	Net Inc.	Cash Flow
Cash	+	Coal Mine	=	Com. Stk.	+	Ret. Earn.						
(4,000,000)	+	4,000,000	=	NA	+	NA	NA	−	NA	=	NA	(4,000,000) IA
NA	+	(90,000)	=	NA	+	(90,000)	NA	−	90,000	=	(90,000)	NA

INTANGIBLE ASSETS

Intangible assets provide rights, privileges, and special opportunities to businesses. Common intangible assets include trademarks, patents, copyrights, franchises, and goodwill. Some of the unique characteristics of these intangible assets are described in the following sections.

Explain how expense recognition for intangible assets (amortization) affects financial statements.

FOCUS ON INTERNATIONAL ISSUES

RESEARCH *AND* DEVELOPMENT VS. RESEARCH *OR* DEVELOPMENT

For many years some thought the companies that followed U.S. GAAP were at a disadvantage when it came to research and development (R&D) costs, because these companies had to immediately expense such cost, while the accounting rules of some other countries allowed R&D cost to be capitalized. Remember, recording costs as an asset—capitalizing it—means that net income is not immediately reduced. The global movement toward using IFRS is reducing, but not eliminating, the different accounting treatments for R&D.

Like U.S. GAAP, IFRS require *research* costs to be expensed, but they allow *development* costs to be capitalized. This IFRS rule itself can present challenges, because sometimes it is not clear where research ends and development begins. Basically, once research has produced a product, patent, and so forth, that the company believes will result in a revenue generating outcome, any additional costs to get it ready for market are development costs.

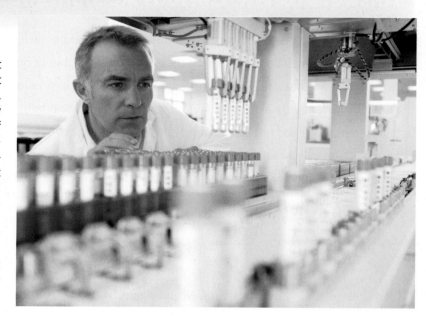

Trademarks

A **trademark** is a name or symbol that identifies a company or a product. Familiar trademarks include the Polo emblem, the name *Coca-Cola*, and the Nike slogan, "Just do it." Trademarks are registered with the federal government and have an indefinite legal lifetime.

The costs incurred to design, purchase, or defend a trademark are capitalized in an asset account called Trademarks. Companies want their trademarks to become familiar but also face the risk of a trademark being used as the generic name for a product. To protect a trademark, companies in this predicament spend large sums on legal fees and extensive advertising programs to educate consumers. Well-known trademarks that have been subject to this problem include Coke, Xerox, Kleenex, and Vaseline.

Patents

A **patent** grants its owner an exclusive legal right to produce and sell a product that has one or more unique features. Patents issued by the U.S. Patent Office have a legal life of 20 years. Companies may obtain patents through purchase, lease, or internal development. The costs capitalized in the Patent account are usually limited to the purchase price and legal fees to obtain and defend the patent. The research and development costs that are incurred to develop patentable products are usually expensed in the period in which they are incurred.

Copyrights

A **copyright** protects writings, musical compositions, works of art, and other intellectual property for the exclusive benefit of the creator or persons assigned the right by the

REALITY BYTES

For its fiscal year ended April 30, 2010, Jackson-Hewitt Tax Services, Inc. wrote off $274 million of its $419 million of goodwill due to "goodwill impairment." Without this write-off, the company would have reported positive earnings before taxes of $2.7 million. Because of the write-off, it reported a negative loss before taxes of $271.4 million. Below is an excerpt from the notes to its financial statements explaining the goodwill impairment.

GOODWILL AND OTHER INTANGIBLE ASSETS

Goodwill is the excess of the purchase price over the fair value assigned to the net assets acquired in a business combination. Goodwill is not amortized, but instead is subject to periodic testing for impairment. The Company assesses goodwill for impairment by comparing the carrying values of its reporting units to their estimated fair values. . . .

Due to the loss of approximately 50% of the Company's RAL [*refund anticipation loans*] program in the third quarter of fiscal 2010, the Company concluded that a goodwill impairment triggering event had occurred. . . .

Significant management judgment is required in assessing whether goodwill is impaired.

creator. The cost of a copyright includes the purchase price and any legal costs associated with obtaining and defending the copyright. Copyrights granted by the federal government extend for the life of the creator plus 70 years. A radio commercial could legally use a Bach composition as background music; it could not, however, use the theme song from the movie, *The Matrix,* without obtaining permission from the copyright owner. The cost of a copyright is often expensed early because future royalties may be uncertain.

Franchises

Franchises grant exclusive rights to sell products or perform services in certain geographic areas. Franchises may be granted by governments or private businesses. Franchises granted by governments include federal broadcasting licenses. Private business franchises include fast-food restaurant chains and brand labels such as Healthy Choice. The legal and useful lives of a franchise are frequently difficult to determine. Judgment is often crucial to establishing the estimated useful life for franchises.

Goodwill

Goodwill is the value attributable to favorable factors such as reputation, location, and superior products. Consider the most popular restaurant in your town. If the owner sold the restaurant, do you think the purchase price would be simply the total value of the chairs, tables, kitchen equipment, and building? Certainly not, because much of the restaurant's value lies in its popularity; in other words, its ability to generate a high return is based on the goodwill (reputation) of the business.

Calculating goodwill can be complex; here we present a simple example to illustrate how it is determined. Suppose the accounting records of a restaurant named Bendigo's show

Assets = Liabilities + Stockholders' equity
$200,000 = $50,000 + $150,000

Assume a buyer agrees to purchase the restaurant by paying the owner $300,000 cash and assuming the existing liabilities. In other words, the restaurant is purchased at a price of $350,000 ($300,000 cash + $50,000 assumed liabilities). Now assume that the assets of the business (tables, chairs, kitchen equipment, etc.) have a fair market value of only $280,000. Why would the buyer pay $350,000 to purchase assets with a market value of $280,000? Obviously, the buyer is purchasing more than just the assets. The buyer is purchasing the business's goodwill. The amount of the goodwill is the difference between the purchase price and the fair market value of the assets. In this case, the goodwill is $70,000 ($350,000 − $280,000). The journal entry to record the purchase and its effects on the financial statements are shown here:

Account Title	Debit	Credit
Restaurant Assets	280,000	
Goodwill	70,000	
Cash		300,000
Liabilities		50,000

Assets						=	Liab.	+	Equity	Rev.	−	Exp.	=	Net Inc.	Cash Flow	
Cash	+	Rest. Assets	+	Goodwill												
(300,000)	+	280,000	+	70,000	=		50,000	+	NA	NA	−	NA	=	NA	(300,000)	IA

The fair market value of the restaurant assets represents the historical cost to the new owner. It becomes the basis for future depreciation charges.

Expense Recognition for Intangible Assets

As mentioned earlier, intangible assets fall into two categories, those with *identifiable useful lives* and those with *indefinite useful lives.* Expense recognition for intangible assets depends on which classification applies.

Expensing Intangible Assets with Identifiable Useful Lives

The costs of intangible assets with identifiable useful lives are normally expensed on a straight-line basis using a process called *amortization.* An intangible asset should be amortized over the shorter of two possible time periods: (1) its legal life or (2) its useful life.

To illustrate, assume that Flowers Industries purchased a newly granted patent for $44,000 cash. Although the patent has a legal life of 20 years, Flowers estimates that it will be useful for only 11 years. The annual amortization charge is therefore $4,000 ($44,000 ÷ 11 years). The journal entries to record the patent purchase and first year amortization, and their effects on the financial statements are shown here:

Account Title	Debit	Credit
Patent	44,000	
Cash		44,000
Amortization Expense, Patent	4,000	
Patent		4,000

Assets			=	Equity			Rev.	−	Exp.	=	Net Inc.	Cash Flow	
Cash	+	Patent	=	Com. Stk.	+	Ret. Earn.							
(44,000)	+	44,000	=	NA	+	NA	NA	−	NA	=	NA	(44,000)	IA
NA	+	(4,000)	=	NA	+	(4,000)	NA	−	4,000	=	(4,000)	NA	

Impairment Losses for Intangible Assets with Indefinite Useful Lives

Intangible assets with indefinite useful lives must be tested for impairment annually. The impairment test consists of comparing the fair value of the intangible asset to its carrying value (book value). If the fair value is less than the book value, an impairment loss must be recognized.

To illustrate, return to the example of the Bendigo's restaurant purchase. Recall that the buyer of Bendigo's paid $70,000 for goodwill. Assume the restaurant experiences a significant decline in revenue because many of its former regular customers are dissatisfied with the food prepared by the new chef. Suppose the decline in revenue is so substantial that the new owner believes the Bendigo's name is permanently impaired. The owner decides to hire a different chef and change the name of the restaurant. In this case, the business has suffered a permanent decline in value of goodwill. The company must recognize an impairment loss.

The restaurant's name has lost its value, but the owner believes the location continues to provide the opportunity to produce above-average earnings. Some, but not all, of the goodwill has been lost. Assume the fair value of the remaining goodwill is determined to be $40,000. The impairment loss to recognize is $30,000 ($70,000 − $40,000). The loss reduces the intangible asset (goodwill), stockholder's equity (retained earnings), and net income. The statement of cash flows would not be affected. The journal entry and its effects on the financial statements follow:

Account Title	Debit	Credit
Impairment Loss	30,000	
Goodwill		30,000

Assets	=	Liab.	+	Equity	Rev.	−	Exp./Loss	=	Net Inc.	Cash Flow
Goodwill	=			Ret. Earn.						
(30,000)	=	NA	+	(30,000)	NA	−	30,000	=	(30,000)	NA

Balance Sheet Presentation

This chapter explained accounting for the acquisition, expense recognition, and disposal of a wide range of long-term assets. Exhibit 8.7 illustrates typical balance sheet presentation of many of the assets discussed.

EXHIBIT 8.7

Balance Sheet Presentation of Operational Assets

Partial Balance Sheet

Long-Term Assets			
Plant and equipment			
Buildings	$4,000,000		
Less: Accumulated depreciation	(2,500,000)	$1,500,000	
Equipment	1,750,000		
Less: Accumulated depreciation	(1,200,000)	550,000	
Total plant and equipment			$2,050,000
Land			850,000
Natural resources			
Mineral deposits (Less: Depletion)		2,100,000	
Oil reserves (Less: Depletion)		890,000	
Total natural resources			2,990,000
Intangibles			
Patents (Net of amortization)		38,000	
Goodwill		175,000	
Total intangible assets			213,000
Total long-term assets			$6,103,000

THE FINANCIAL ANALYST

Managers may have differing opinions about which allocation method (straight-line, accelerated, or units-of-production) best matches expenses with revenues. As a result, one company may use straight-line depreciation while another company in similar circumstances uses double-declining-balance. Since the allocation method a company uses affects the amount of expense it recognizes, analysts reviewing financial statements must consider the accounting procedures companies use in preparing the statements.

EFFECT OF JUDGMENT AND ESTIMATION

Assume that two companies, Alpha and Zeta, experience identical economic events in 2013 and 2014. Both generate revenue of $50,000 and incur cost of goods sold of $30,000 during each year. In 2013, each company pays $20,000 for an asset with an expected useful life of five years and no salvage value. How will the companies' financial statements differ if one uses straight-line depreciation and the other uses the double-declining-balance method? To answer this question, first compute the depreciation expense for both companies for 2013 and 2014.

If Alpha Company uses the straight-line method, depreciation for 2013 and 2014 is

$$(\text{Cost} - \text{Salvage}) \div \text{Useful life} = \text{Depreciation expense per year}$$
$$(\$20,000 - \$0) \div 5 \text{ years} = \$4,000$$

In contrast, if Zeta Company uses the double-declining-balance method, Zeta recognizes the following amounts of depreciation expense for 2013 and 2014

	(Cost − Accumulated Depreciation)	×	2 × (Straight-Line Rate)	=	Depreciation Expense
2013	($20,000 − $ 0)	×	[2 × (1 ÷ 5)]	=	$8,000
2014	($20,000 − $8,000)	×	[2 × (1 ÷ 5)]	=	$4,800

Based on these computations, the income statements for the two companies are:

Income Statements				
	2013		**2014**	
	Alpha Co.	Zeta Co.	Alpha Co.	Zeta Co.
Sales	$50,000	$50,000	$50,000	$ 50,000
Cost of goods sold	(30,000)	(30,000)	(30,000)	(30,000)
Gross margin	20,000	20,000	20,000	20,000
Depreciation expense	(4,000)	(8,000)	(4,000)	(4,800)
Net income	$16,000	$12,000	$16,000	$ 15,200

The relevant sections of the balance sheets are:

Plant Assets				
	2013		**2014**	
	Alpha Co.	Zeta Co.	Alpha Co.	Zeta Co.
Asset	$20,000	$20,000	$20,000	$ 20,000
Accumulated depreciation	(4,000)	(8,000)	(8,000)	(12,800)
Book value	$16,000	$12,000	$12,000	$ 7,200

EXHIBIT 8.8

Industry Data Reflecting the Use of Long-Term Tangible Assets		
Industry	**Company**	**Sales ÷ Property, Plant, and Equipment**
Broadband Communications	Comcast Corp.	1.61
	Verizon Communications	1.21
Airlines	Alaska Air Group	1.23
	Southwest Airlines	1.14
Employment Agencies	Kelly Services	47.60
	Manpower, Inc.	175.83

   The depreciation method is not the only aspect of expense recognition that can vary between companies. Companies may also make different assumptions about the useful lives and salvage values of long-term operational assets. Thus, even if the same depreciation method is used, depreciation expense may still differ.

   Since the depreciation method and the underlying assumptions regarding useful life and salvage value affect the determination of depreciation expense, they also affect the amounts of net income, retained earnings, and total assets. Financial statement analysis is affected if it is based on ratios that include these items. Previously defined ratios that are affected include the (1) debt to assets ratio, (2) return on assets ratio, (3) return on equity ratio, and (4) return on sales ratio.

   To promote meaningful analysis, public companies are required to disclose all significant accounting policies used to prepare their financial statements. This disclosure is provided in the notes that accompany the financial statements.

Effect of Industry Characteristics

As indicated in previous chapters, industry characteristics affect financial performance measures. For example, companies in manufacturing industries invest heavily in machinery while insurance companies rely more on human capital. Manufacturing companies therefore have relatively higher depreciation charges than insurance companies. To illustrate how the type of industry affects financial reporting, examine Exhibit 8.8. This exhibit compares the ratio of sales to property, plant, and equipment for two companies in each of three different industries. These data are for 2010.

   The table indicates that for every $1.00 invested in property, plant, and equipment, Manpower produced $175.83 of sales. In contrast, Verizon and Southwest Airlines produced only $1.21 and $1.14, respectively for each $1.00 they invested in operational assets. Does this mean the management of Manpower is doing a better job than the management of Verizon or Southwest Airlines? Not necessarily. It means that these companies operate in different economic environments. In other words, it takes significantly more equipment to operate a cable company or an airline than it takes to operate an employment agency.

   Effective financial analysis requires careful consideration of industry characteristics, accounting policies, and the reasonableness of assumptions such as useful life and salvage value.

A Look Back

This chapter explains that the primary objective of recognizing depreciation is to match the cost of a long-term tangible asset with the revenues the asset is expected to generate. The matching concept also applies to natural resources (depletion) and intangible assets (amortization). The chapter explains how alternative methods can be used to account for the same event (e.g., straight-line versus double-declining-balance depreciation). Companies experiencing exactly the same business events could produce different financial statements. The alternative accounting methods for depreciating, depleting, or amortizing assets include the (1) straight-line, (2) double-declining-balance, and (3) units-of-production methods.

The *straight-line method* produces equal amounts of expense in each accounting period. The amount of the expense recognized is determined using the formula [(cost − salvage) ÷ number of years of useful life]. The *double-declining-balance method* produces proportionately larger amounts of expense in the early years of an asset's useful life and increasingly smaller amounts of expense in the later years of the asset's useful life. The formula for calculating double-declining-balance depreciation is [book value at beginning of period × (2 × the straight-line rate)]. The *units-of-production method* produces expense in direct proportion to the number of units produced during an accounting period. The formula for the amount of expense recognized each period is [(cost − salvage) ÷ total estimated units of production = allocation rate × units of production in current accounting period].

The chapter also discussed *MACRS depreciation,* an accelerated tax reporting method. MACRS is not acceptable under GAAP for public reporting. A company may use MACRS depreciation for tax purposes and straight-line or one of the other methods for public reporting. As a result, differences may exist between the amount of tax expense and the amount of tax liability. Such differences are reported as *deferred income taxes.*

This chapter showed how to account for *changes in estimates* such as the useful life or the salvage value of a depreciable asset. Changes in estimates do not affect the amount of depreciation recognized previously. Instead, the remaining book value of the asset is expensed over its remaining useful life.

After an asset has been placed into service, companies typically incur further costs for maintenance, quality improvement, and extensions of useful life. *Maintenance costs* are expensed in the period in which they are incurred. *Costs that improve the quality* of an asset are added to the cost of the asset, increasing the book value and the amount of future depreciation charges. *Costs that extend the useful life* of an asset are subtracted from the asset's Accumulated Depreciation account, increasing the book value and the amount of future depreciation charges.

>> A Look Forward

In Chapter 9 we move from the assets section of the balance sheet to issues in accounting for short-term liabilities. You will also study the basic components of a payroll accounting system.

 ## SELF-STUDY REVIEW PROBLEM

 A step-by-step audio-narrated series of slides is provided on the text website at www.mhhe.com/edmonds8e.

The following information pertains to a machine purchased by Bakersfield Company on January 1, 2013:

Purchase price	$ 63,000
Delivery cost	$ 2,000
Installation charge	$ 3,000
Estimated useful life	8 years
Estimated units the machine will produce	130,000
Estimated salvage value	$ 3,000

The machine produced 14,400 units during 2013 and 17,000 units during 2014.

Required

Determine the depreciation expense Bakersfield would report for 2013 and 2014 using each of the following methods:

a. Straight-line.
b. Double-declining-balance.
c. Units-of-production.
d. MACRS assuming that the machine is classified as seven-year property.

Solution to Requirements a–d

a. Straight-line

Purchase price	$63,000
Delivery cost	2,000
Installation charge	3,000
Total cost of machine	68,000
Less: Salvage value	(3,000)
	$65,000 ÷ 8 = $8,125 Depreciation per year
2013	$ 8,125
2014	$ 8,125

b. Double-declining-balance

Year	Cost	−	Accumulated Depreciation at Beginning of Year	×	2 × S-L Rate	=	Annual Depreciation
2013	$68,000	−	$ 0	×	(2 × 0.125)	=	$17,000
2014	68,000	−	17,000	×	(2 × 0.125)	=	12,750

c. Units-of-production

(1) (Cost − Salvage value) ÷ Estimated units of production = Depreciation cost per unit produced

$$\frac{\$68,000 - \$3,000}{130,000} = \$0.50 \text{ per unit}$$

(2) Cost per unit × Annual units produced = Annual depreciation expense

$$2013 \quad \$0.50 \times 14,400 = \$7,200$$
$$2014 \quad 0.50 \times 17,000 = 8,500$$

d. MACRS

Cost × MACRS percentage = Annual depreciation

$$2013 \quad \$68,000 \times 0.1429 = \$ 9,717$$
$$2014 \quad 68,000 \times 0.2449 = 16,653$$

KEY TERMS

accelerated depreciation
  method 425
Accumulated
  Depreciation 422
amortization 418

basket purchase 419
book value 422
capital expenditures 432
carrying value 422
contra asset account 422

copyright 436
current assets 416
deferred tax
  liability 431
depletion 418

depreciable cost 420
depreciation 418
depreciation expense 420
double-declining-balance
  depreciation 425

estimated useful life 420
franchise 437
gain 423
goodwill 437
half-year convention 430
historical cost concept 419
intangible assets 418

long-term operational
   assets 416
loss 423
modified accelerated cost
   recovery system
   (MACRS) 429
natural resources 418

patent 436
property, plant, and
   equipment 418
relative fair market value
   method 419
revenue expenditures 432
salvage value 420

straight-line
   depreciation 421
tangible assets 418
trademark 436
units-of-production
   depreciation 427

QUESTIONS

1. What is the difference between the functions of long-term operational assets and investments?

2. What is the difference between tangible and intangible assets? Give an example of each.

3. What is the difference between goodwill and specifically identifiable intangible assets?

4. Define *depreciation*. What kind of asset depreciates?

5. Why are natural resources called *wasting assets?*

6. Is land a depreciable asset? Why or why not?

7. Define *amortization*. What kind of assets are amortized?

8. Explain the historical cost concept as it applies to long-term operational assets. Why is the book value of an asset likely to be different from the current market value of the asset?

9. What different kinds of expenditures might be included in the recorded cost of a building?

10. What is a basket purchase of assets? When a basket purchase is made, how is cost assigned to individual assets?

11. What are the stages in the life cycle of a long-term operational asset?

12. Explain straight-line, units-of-production, and double-declining-balance depreciation. When is it appropriate to use each of these depreciation methods?

13. What effect does the recognition of depreciation expense have on total assets? On total equity?

14. Does the recognition of depreciation expense affect cash flows? Why or why not?

15. MalMax purchased a depreciable asset. What would be the difference in total assets at the end of the first year if MalMax chooses straight-line depreciation versus double-declining-balance depreciation?

16. John Smith mistakenly expensed the cost of a long-term tangible fixed asset. Specifically, he charged the cost of a truck to a delivery expense account. How will this error affect the income statement and the balance sheet in the year in which the mistake is made?

17. What is *salvage value?*

18. What type of account (classification) is Accumulated Depreciation?

19. How is the book value of an asset determined?

20. Why is depreciation that has been recognized over the life of an asset shown in a contra account? Why not just reduce the asset account?

21. Assume that a piece of equipment cost $5,000 and had accumulated depreciation recorded of $3,000. What is the book value of the equipment? Is the book value equal to the fair market value of the equipment? Explain.

22. Why would a company choose to depreciate one piece of equipment using the double-declining-balance method and another piece of equipment using straight-line depreciation?

23. Explain MACRS depreciation. When is its use appropriate?

24. Does the method of depreciation required to be used for tax purposes reflect the use of a piece of equipment? Can you use double-declining-balance depreciation for tax purposes?

25. Define *deferred taxes*. Where does the account *Deferred Taxes* appear in the financial statements?

26. Why may it be necessary to revise the estimated life of a plant asset? When the estimated life is revised, does it affect the amount of depreciation per year? Why or why not?

27. How are capital expenditures made to improve the quality of a capital asset accounted for? Would the answer change if the expenditure extended the life of the asset but did not improve quality? Explain.

28. When a long-term operational asset is sold at a gain, how is the balance sheet affected? Is the statement of cash flows affected? If so, how?

29. Define *depletion*. What is the most commonly used method of computing depletion?

30. List several common intangible assets. How is the life determined that is to be used to compute amortization?

31. List some differences between U.S. GAAP and IFRS for long-term operational assets.

32. How do differences in expense recognition and industry characteristics affect financial performance measures?

MULTIPLE-CHOICE QUESTIONS

Multiple-choice questions are provided on the text website at www.mhhe.com/edmonds8e.

EXERCISES—SERIES A

All applicable Exercises in Series A are available with McGraw-Hill's
Connect® Accounting.

Unless specifically included, ignore income tax considerations in all exercises and problems.

Exercise 8-1A *Long-term operational assets used in a business*   LO 1

Required

Give some examples of long-term operational assets that each of the following companies is
likely to own: *(a)* Freds, *(b)* Princess Cruise Lines, *(c)* Southwest Airlines, and *(d)* Harley-
Davidson Co.

Exercise 8-2A *Identifying long-term operational assets*   LO 1

Required

Which of the following items should be classified as long-term operational assets?

a. Inventory
b. Patent
c. Tract of timber
d. Land
e. Computer
f. Goodwill

g. Cash
h. Buildings
i. Production machinery
j. Accounts receivable
k. Prepaid rent
l. Franchise

Exercise 8-3A *Classifying tangible and intangible assets*   LO 1

Required

Identify each of the following long-term operational assets as either tangible (T) or intangible (I).

a. 18-wheel truck
b. Timber
c. Log loader
d. Dental chair
e. Goodwill
f. Computer software

g. Retail store building
h. Shelving for inventory
i. Trademark
j. Gas well
k. Drilling rig
l. FCC license for TV station

Exercise 8-4A *Determining the cost of an asset*   LO 2

Louisiana Logging Co. purchased an electronic saw to cut various types and sizes of logs.
The saw had a list price of $160,000. The seller agreed to allow a 5 percent discount because
Louisiana paid cash. Delivery terms were FOB shipping point. Freight cost amounted to $3,200.
Louisiana had to hire an individual to operate the saw. Louisiana had to build a special platform
to mount the saw. The cost of the platform was $2,500. The saw operator was paid an annual
salary of $50,000. The cost of the company's theft insurance policy increased by $1,800 per year
as a result of acquiring of the saw. The saw had a five-year useful life and an expected salvage
value of $25,000.

Required

a. Determine the amount to be capitalized in an asset account for the purchase of the saw.
b. Record the purchase in general journal format.

Exercise 8-5A *Allocating costs on the basis of relative market values*   LO 2

Carolina Company purchased a building and the land on which the building is situated
for a total cost of $800,000 cash. The land was appraised at $300,000 and the building
at $700,000.

Required

  a. What is the accounting term for this type of acquisition?

  b. Determine the amount of the purchase cost to allocate to the land and the amount to allocate to the building.

  c. Would the company recognize a gain on the purchase? Why or why not?

  d. Record the purchase in a statements model like the following one.

Assets					=	Liab.	+	Equity	Rev.	−	Exp.	=	Net Inc.	Cash Flow
Cash	+	Land	+	Building										

  e. Record the purchases in general journal format.

LO 2

Exercise 8-6A *Allocating costs for a basket purchase*

Sneathen Company purchased a restaurant building, land, and equipment for $600,000 cash. The appraised value of the assets was as follows:

Land	$200,000
Building	480,000
Equipment	120,000
Total	$800,000

Required

  a. Compute the amount to be recorded on the books for each of the assets.

  b. Record the purchase in a horizontal statements model like the following one.

Assets							=	Liab.	+	Equity	Rev.	−	Exp.	=	Net Inc.	Cash Flow
Cash	+	Land	+	Building	+	Equip.										

  c. Prepare the general journal entry to record the purchase.

LO 3

Exercise 8-7A *Effect of depreciation on the accounting equation and financial statements*

The following events apply to The Ice Cream Parlor for the 2013 fiscal year:

  1. The company started when it acquired $20,000 cash from the issue of common stock.

  2. Purchased a new ice cream machine that cost $20,000 cash.

  3. Earned $36,000 in cash revenue.

  4. Paid $21,000 cash for salaries expense.

  5. Paid $6,000 cash for operating expenses.

  6. Adjusted the records to reflect the use of the ice cream machine. The machine, purchased on January 1, 2013, has an expected useful life of five years and an estimated salvage value of $5,000. Use straight-line depreciation. The adjusting entry was made as of December 31, 2013.

Required

  a. Record the events in general journal format and post to T-accounts.

  b. What amount of depreciation expense would The Ice Cream Parlor report on the 2014 income statement?

  c. What amount of accumulated depreciation would The Ice Cream Parlor report on the December 31, 2014, balance sheet?

  d. Would the cash flow from operating activities be affected by depreciation in 2014?

Exercise 8-8A   Effect of double-declining-balance depreciation on financial statements

LO 3

Posey Company started operations by acquiring $120,000 cash from the issue of common stock. On January 1, 2013, the company purchased equipment that cost $110,000 cash. The equipment had an expected useful life of five years and an estimated salvage value of $10,000. Posey Company earned $85,000 and $72,000 of cash revenue during 2013 and 2014, respectively. Posey Company uses double-declining-balance depreciation.

Required

Prepare income statements, balance sheets, and statements of cash flows for 2013 and 2014. Use a vertical statements format. (*Hint:* Record the events in T-accounts prior to preparing the statements.)

Exercise 8-9A   Events related to the acquisition, use, and disposal of a tangible plant asset: straight-line depreciation

LO 3, 4

Sam's Subs purchased a delivery van on January 1, 2013, for $35,000. In addition, Sam's paid sales tax and title fees of $1,500 for the van. The van is expected to have a four-year life and a salvage value of $6,500.

Required

a. Using the straight-line method, compute the depreciation expense for 2013 and 2014.

b. Prepare the general journal entry to record the 2013 depreciation.

c. Assume the van was sold on January 1, 2016, for $21,000. Prepare the journal entry for the sale of the van in 2016.

Exercise 8-10A   Computing and recording straight-line versus double-declining-balance depreciation

LO 3

At the beginning of 2013, Metal Manufacturing purchased a new computerized drill press for $75,000. It is expected to have a five-year life and a $15,000 salvage value.

Required

a. Compute the depreciation for each of the five years, assuming that the company uses

(1) Straight-line depreciation.

(2) Double-declining-balance depreciation.

b. Record the purchase of the drill press and the depreciation expense for the first year under the straight-line and double-declining-balance methods in a financial statements model like the following one:

Assets			=	Equity	Rev.	−	Exp.	=	Net Inc.	Cash Flow
Cash	+	Book Value of Drill Press	=	Ret. Earn.						

c. Prepare the journal entries to recognize depreciation for each of the five years, assuming that the company uses

(1) Straight-line depreciation.

(2) Double-declining-balance depreciation.

Exercise 8-11A   Effect of the disposal of plant assets on the financial statements

LO 4

A plant asset with a cost of $50,000 and accumulated depreciation of $41,000 is sold for $10,000.

Required

a. What is the book value of the asset at the time of sale?

b. What is the amount of gain or loss on the disposal?

c. How would the sale affect net income (increase, decrease, no effect) and by how much?

d. How would the sale affect the amount of total assets shown on the balance sheet (increase, decrease, no effect) and by how much?

e. How would the event affect the statement of cash flows (inflow, outflow, no effect) and in what section?

LO 4

Exercise 8-12A *Effect of gains and losses on the accounting equation and financial statements*

On January 1, 2013, Liken Enterprises purchased a parcel of land for $20,000 cash. At the time of purchase, the company planned to use the land for future expansion. In 2014, Liken Enterprises changed its plans and sold the land.

Required

a. Assume that the land was sold for $22,500 in 2014.
  (1) Show the effect of the sale on the accounting equation.
  (2) What amount would Liken report on the income statement related to the sale of the land?
  (3) What amount would Liken report on the statement of cash flows related to the sale of the land?

b. Assume that the land was sold for $18,500 in 2014.
  (1) Show the effect of the sale on the accounting equation.
  (2) What amount would Liken report on the income statement related to the sale of the land?
  (3) What amount would Liken report on the statement of cash flows related to the sale of the land?

LO 3, 4

Exercise 8-13A *Double-declining-balance and units-of-production depreciation: gain or loss on disposal*

Graphics Service Co. purchased a new color copier at the beginning of 2013 for $47,000. The copier is expected to have a five-year useful life and a $7,000 salvage value. The expected copy production was estimated at 2,000,000 copies. Actual copy production for the five years was as follows:

2013	560,000
2014	490,000
2015	430,000
2016	350,000
2017	210,000
Total	2,040,000

The copier was sold at the end of 2017 for $7,600.

Required

a. Compute the depreciation expense for each of the five years, using double-declining-balance depreciation.
b. Compute the depreciation expense for each of the five years, using units-of-production depreciation. (Round cost per unit to three decimal places.)
c. Calculate the amount of gain or loss from the sale of the asset under each of the depreciation methods.

LO 5

Exercise 8-14A *Computing depreciation for tax purposes*

Bruce Lumber Company purchased $240,000 of equipment on September 1, 2013.

Required

a. Compute the amount of depreciation expense that is deductible under MACRS for 2013 and 2014, assuming that the equipment is classified as seven-year property.
b. Compute the amount of depreciation expense that is deductible under MACRS for 2013 and 2014, assuming that the equipment is classified as five-year property.

LO 6

Exercise 8-15A *Revision of estimated useful life*

On January 1, 2013, Muoy Machining Co. purchased a compressor and related installation equipment for $72,500. The equipment had a three-year estimated life with a $12,500 salvage value. Straight-line depreciation was used. At the beginning of 2015, Muoy revised the expected life of the asset to four years rather than three years. The salvage value was revised to $2,500.

Required

Compute the depreciation expense for each of the four years.

Exercise 8-16A   Distinguishing between revenue expenditures and capital expenditures

Houston's Shredding Service has just completed a minor repair on a shredding machine. The repair cost was $1,900, and the book value prior to the repair was $6,000. In addition, the company spent $12,000 to replace the roof on a building. The new roof extended the life of the building by five years. Prior to the roof replacement, the general ledger reflected the Building account at $110,000 and related Accumulated Depreciation account at $30,000.

Required

After the work was completed, what book value should Houston's report on the balance sheet for the shredding machine and the building?

Exercise 8-17A   Effect of revenue expenditures versus capital expenditures on financial statements

Apac Construction Company purchased a forklift for $150,000 cash. It had an estimated useful life of four years and a $10,000 salvage value. At the beginning of the third year of use, the company spent an additional $9,000 that was related to the forklift. The company's financial condition just prior to this expenditure is shown in the following statements model:

Assets			=	Equity			Rev.	−	Exp.	=	Net Inc.	Cash Flow
Cash	+	Book Value of Forklift	=	Com. Stk.	+	Ret. Earn.						
15,000	+	80,000	=	45,000	+	50,000	NA	−	NA	=	NA	NA

Required

Record the $9,000 expenditure in the statements model under each of the following *independent* assumptions:

a. The expenditure was for routine maintenance.
b. The expenditure extended the forklift's life.
c. The expenditure improved the forklift's operating capacity.

Exercise 8-18A   Effect of revenue expenditures versus capital expenditures on financial statements

On January 1, 2013, Plains Power Company overhauled four turbine engines that generate power for customers. The overhaul resulted in a slight increase in the capacity of the engines to produce power. Such overhauls occur regularly at two-year intervals and have been treated as maintenance expense in the past. Management is considering whether to capitalize this year's $22,000 cash cost in the engine asset account or to expense it as a maintenance expense. Assume that the engines have a remaining useful life of two years and no expected salvage value. Assume straight-line depreciation.

Required

a. Determine the amount of additional depreciation expense Plains would recognize in 2013 and 2014 if the cost were capitalized in the Engine account.
b. Determine the amount of expense Plains would recognize in 2013 and 2014 if the cost were recognized as maintenance expense.
c. Determine the effect of the overhaul on cash flow from operating activities for 2013 and 2014 if the cost were capitalized and expensed through depreciation charges.
d. Determine the effect of the overhaul on cash flow from operating activities for 2013 and 2014 if the cost were recognized as maintenance expense.

LO 8

Exercise 8-19A *Computing and recording depletion expense*

Tishimingo Sand and Gravel paid $800,000 to acquire 1,200,000 cubic yards of sand reserves. The following statements model reflects Tishimingo's financial condition just prior to purchasing the sand reserves. The company extracted 650,000 cubic yards of sand in year 1 and 450,000 cubic yards in year 2.

Assets		=	Equity			Rev.	−	Exp.	=	Net Inc.	Cash Flow
Cash	+ Sand Res.	=	Com. Stk.	+	Ret. Earn.						
900,000	+ NA	=	900,000	+	NA	NA	−	NA	=	NA	NA

Required

a. Compute the depletion charge per cubic yard.

b. Record the acquisition of the sand reserves and the depletion expense for years 1 and 2 in a financial statements model like the preceding one.

c. Prepare the general journal entries to record the depletion expense for years 1 and 2.

LO 9

Exercise 8-20A *Computing and recording the amortization of intangibles*

Pacart Manufacturing paid cash to acquire the assets of an existing company. Among the assets acquired were the following items:

Patent with 5 remaining years of legal life	$48,000
Goodwill	35,000

Pacart's financial condition just prior to the purchase of these assets is shown in the following statements model:

Assets			=	Liab.	+	Equity	Rev.	−	Exp.	=	Net Inc.	Cash Flow
Cash	+ Patent	+ Goodwill										
94,000	+ NA	+ NA	=	NA	+	94,000	NA	−	NA	=	NA	NA

Required

a. Compute the annual amortization expense for these items if applicable.

b. Record the acquisition of the intangible assets and the related amortization expense for year 1 in a horizontal statements model like the preceding one.

c. Prepare the journal entries to record the acquisition of the intangible assets and the related amortization for year 1.

LO 9

Exercise 8-21A *Computing and recording goodwill*

Bill Yeates acquired the business Sun Supply Co. for $275,000 cash and assumed all liabilities at the date of acquisition. Sun's books showed tangible assets of $250,000, liabilities of $10,000, and equity of $240,000. An appraiser assessed the fair market value of the tangible assets at $265,000 at the date of acquisition. Yeates's financial condition just prior to the acquisition is shown in the following statements model:

Assets			=	Liab.	+	Equity	Rev.	−	Exp.	=	Net Inc.	Cash Flow
Cash	+ Tang. Assets	+ Goodwill										
450,000	+ NA	+ NA	=	NA	+	450,000	NA	−	NA	=	NA	NA

Required

a. Compute the amount of goodwill acquired.

b. Record the acquisition in a financial statements model like the preceding one.

c. Record the acquisition in general journal format.

Exercise 8-22A   *Depreciable assets under IFRS*

IFRS

The Global Transactions Inc. (GTI) purchased an asset that cost $90,000 on January 1, 2013. The asset had a four year useful life and a $15,000 salvage value.

Required

a. Determine the amount of expense recognized on the 2013 income statement assuming GTI uses U.S. GAAP.

b. Determine the amount of expense or gain recognized on the income statement assuming GTI uses the IFRS revaluation model and the asset is determined to have a fair value of $82,000 as of December 31, 2013.

c. Determine the amount of expense or gain recognized on the income statement assuming GTI uses the IFRS revaluation model and the asset is determined to have a fair value of $97,500 as of December 31, 2013.

Exercise 8-23A   *Accounting for land and buildings under IFRS*

IFRS

Assume the following. Deli Company purchased a parcel of land on January 1, 2008, for $600,000. It constructed a building on the land at a cost of $3,000,000. The building was occupied on January 1, 2011, and is expected to have a useful life of 40 years and an estimated salvage value of $900,000.

As of December 31, 2012 and 2013, the fair value of the land had not been formally revalued because the real estate market had not changed significantly. Due to a jump in real estate prices, during 2014 the value of the land had increased to $675,000, and the fair value of the building was $3,000,000. The salvage value of the building is still estimated at $900,000. The land and the building were reevaluated by the company in 2014.

Required

a. Under U.S. accounting rules, what amount would be reported on the company's 2013 and 2014 balance sheets for the land and for the building? Show any necessary computations.

b. Under U.S. accounting rules, what amount of depreciation expense would be reported in 2014 for the building? Show any necessary computations.

c. Under the IFRS revaluation model, what amount would be reported on the company's 2013 and 2014 balance sheets for the land and for the building? Show any necessary computations.

d. Under the IFRS revaluation model, what amount of depreciation expense would be reported in 2014 for the building? Show any necessary computations.

PROBLEMS—SERIES A

**All applicable Problems in Series A are available with McGraw-Hill's
*Connect® Accounting.***

Problem 8-24A   *Accounting for acquisition of assets including a basket purchase*

LO 2

Shay Company made several purchases of long-term assets in 2013. The details of each purchase are presented here.

CHECK FIGURES
Total cost of equipment: $51,700
Cost allocated to copier: $10,500

New Office Equipment

1. List price: $50,000; terms: 1/10 n/30; paid within the discount period.

2. Transportation-in: $1,200.

3. Installation: $1,000.

4. Cost to repair damage during unloading: $700.

5. Routine maintenance cost after eight months: $240.

Basket Purchase of Office Furniture, Copier, Computers, and Laser Printers for $70,000 with Fair Market Values

1. Office furniture, $48,000.
2. Copier, $12,000.
3. Computers and printers, $20,000.

Land for New Headquarters with Old Barn Torn Down

1. Purchase price, $100,000.
2. Demolition of barn, $7,000.
3. Lumber sold from old barn, $2,000.
4. Grading in preparation for new building, $11,000.
5. Construction of new building, $310,000.

Required

In each of these cases, determine the amount of cost to be capitalized in the asset accounts.

LO 3, 4

eXcel

CHECK FIGURES
Net Income, 2013: $500
Total Assets, 2016: $42,500

Problem 8-25A   *Accounting for depreciation over multiple accounting cycles: straight-line depreciation*

Zhao Company began operations when it acquired $40,000 cash from the issue of common stock on January 1, 2013. The cash acquired was immediately used to purchase equipment for $40,000 that had a $4,000 salvage value and an expected useful life of four years. The equipment was used to produce the following revenue stream (assume all revenue transactions are for cash). At the beginning of the fifth year, the equipment was sold for $4,500 cash. Zhao uses straight-line depreciation.

	2013	2014	2015	2016	2017
Revenue	$9,500	$10,000	$10,500	$8,500	$0

Required

Prepare income statements, statements of changes in stockholders' equity, balance sheets, and statements of cash flows for each of the five years.

LO 2, 3, 6, 7

CHECK FIGURES
c. Net Income, 2013: $48,520
Total Assets, 2015: $242,591

Problem 8-26A   *Purchase and use of tangible asset: three accounting cycles, double-declining-balance depreciation*

The following transactions pertain to Engineering Solutions Inc. Assume the transactions for the purchase of the computer and any capital improvements occur on January 1 each year.

2013

1. Acquired $80,000 cash from the issue of common stock.
2. Purchased a computer system for $35,000. It has an estimated useful life of five years and a $5,000 salvage value.
3. Paid $2,450 sales tax on the computer system.
4. Collected $65,000 in fees from clients.
5. Paid $1,500 in fees to service the computers.
6. Recorded double-declining-balance depreciation on the computer system for 2013.
7. Closed the revenue and expense accounts to Retained Earnings at the end of 2013.

2014

1. Paid $1,000 for repairs to the computer system.
2. Bought off-site backup services to maintain the computer system, $1,500.
3. Collected $68,000 in fees from clients.
4. Paid $1,500 in fees to service the computers.
5. Recorded double-declining-balance depreciation for 2014.
6. Closed the revenue and expense accounts to Retained Earnings at the end of 2014.

2015

1. Paid $6,000 to upgrade the computer system, which extended the total life of the system to six years. The salvage value did not change.
2. Paid $1,200 in fees to service the computers.
3. Collected $70,000 in fees from clients.
4. Recorded double-declining-balance depreciation for 2015.
5. Closed the revenue and expense accounts at the end of 2015.

Required

a. Use a horizontal statements model like the following one to show the effect of these transactions on the elements of financial statements. Use + for increase, − for decrease, and NA for not affected. The first event is recorded as an example.

2011 Event No.	Assets	=	Liabilities	+	Equity	Net Inc.	Cash Flow
1	+		NA		+	NA	+ FA

b. For each year, record the transactions in general journal form and post them to T-accounts.
c. Use a vertical model to present financial statements for 2013, 2014, and 2015.

Problem 8-27A *Calculating depreciation expense using four different methods*

Weir Service Company purchased a copier on January 1, 2013, for $25,000 and paid an additional $500 for delivery charges. The copier was estimated to have a life of four years or 1,000,000 copies. Salvage was estimated at $1,500. The copier produced 250,000 copies in 2013 and 270,000 copies in 2014.

Required

Compute the amount of depreciation expense for the copier for calendar years 2013 and 2014, using these methods:

a. Straight-line.
b. Units-of-production.
c. Double-declining-balance.
d. MACRS, assuming that the copier is classified as five-year property.

Problem 8-28A *Effect of straight-line versus double-declining-balance depreciation on the recognition of expense and gains or losses*

One Day Laundry Services purchased a new steam press on January 1, for $42,000. It is expected to have a five-year useful life and a $2,000 salvage value. One Day expects to use the steam press more extensively in the early years of its life.

Required

a. Calculate the depreciation expense for each of the five years, assuming the use of straight-line depreciation.
b. Calculate the depreciation expense for each of the five years, assuming the use of double-declining-balance depreciation.
c. Would the choice of one depreciation method over another produce a different amount of cash flow for any year? Why or why not?
d. Assume that One Day Laundry Services sold the steam press at the end of the third year for $22,000. Compute the amount of gain or loss using each depreciation method.

LO 3, 4

Problem 8-29A *Computing and recording units-of-production depreciation*

Renner Corporation purchased a delivery van for $28,500 in 2013. The firm's financial condition immediately prior to the purchase is shown in the following horizontal statements model:

Assets			=	Equity			Rev.	−	Exp.	=	Net Inc.	Cash Flow
Cash	+	Book Value of Van	=	Com. Stk.	+	Ret. Earn.						
50,000	+	NA	=	50,000	+	NA	NA	−	NA	=	NA	NA

CHECK FIGURES
a. Depreciation Expense, 2013: $7,800
c. Gain on Sale: $950

The van was expected to have a useful life of 200,000 miles and a salvage value of $2,500. Actual mileage was as follows:

2013	60,000
2014	50,000
2015	55,000

Required

a. Compute the depreciation for each of the three years, assuming the use of units-of-production depreciation.

b. Assume that Renner earns $26,000 of cash revenue during 2013. Record the purchase of the van and the recognition of the revenue and the depreciation expense for the first year in a financial statements model like the one shown above.

c. Assume that Renner sold the van at the end of the third year for $8,000. Record the general journal entry for the sale.

LO 3

Problem 8-30A *Determining the effect of depreciation expense on financial statements*

CHECK FIGURES
a. Company A, Net Income: $18,000
c. Company C, Book Value: $20,500

Three different companies each purchased a machine on January 1, 2013, for $64,000. Each machine was expected to last five years or 200,000 hours. Salvage value was estimated to be $4,000. All three machines were operated for 50,000 hours in 2013, 55,000 hours in 2014, 40,000 hours in 2015, 44,000 hours in 2016, and 31,000 hours in 2017. Each of the three companies earned $30,000 of cash revenue during each of the five years. Company A uses straight-line depreciation, company B uses double-declining-balance depreciation, and company C uses units-of-production depreciation.

Required

Answer each of the following questions. Ignore the effects of income taxes.

a. Which company will report the highest amount of net income for 2013?

b. Which company will report the lowest amount of net income for 2015?

c. Which company will report the highest book value on the December 31, 2015, balance sheet?

d. Which company will report the highest amount of retained earnings on the December 31, 2016, balance sheet?

e. Which company will report the lowest amount of cash flow from operating activities on the 2015 statement of cash flows?

LO 6, 8

Problem 8-31A *Accounting for depletion*

CHECK FIGURES
a. Coal Mine Depletion, 2013: $240,000
b. Total Natural Resources: $2,126,030

Cohen Exploration Corporation engages in the exploration and development of many types of natural resources. In the last two years, the company has engaged in the following activities:

Jan. 1, 2013   Purchased a coal mine estimated to contain 300,000 tons of coal for $900,000.
July 1, 2013   Purchased for $2,000,000 a tract of timber estimated to yield 3,000,000 board feet of lumber and to have a residual land value of $200,000.
Feb. 1, 2014   Purchased a silver mine estimated to contain 30,000 tons of silver for $850,000.
Aug. 1, 2014   Purchased for $875,000 oil reserves estimated to contain 270,000 barrels of oil, of which 20,000 would be unprofitable to pump.

Required

a. Prepare the journal entries to account for the following:

(1) The 2013 purchases.

(2) Depletion on the 2013 purchases, assuming that 80,000 tons of coal were mined and 1,000,000 board feet of lumber were cut.

(3) The 2014 purchases.

(4) Depletion on the four reserves, assuming that 68,000 tons of coal, 1,200,000 board feet of lumber, 9,000 tons of silver, and 80,000 barrels of oil were extracted.

b. Prepare the portion of the December 31, 2014, balance sheet that reports natural resources.

c. Assume that in 2015 the estimates changed to reflect only 50,000 tons of coal remaining. Prepare the depletion journal entry for 2015 to account for the extraction of 40,000 tons of coal.

Problem 8-32A   *Recording continuing expenditures for plant assets*

LO 3, 4, 6, 7

CHECK FIGURES
b. 2015 Depreciation
 Expense: $8,333
d. Loss on Sale: $2,916

Seaside Inc. recorded the following transactions over the life of a piece of equipment purchased in 2013:

Jan. 1, 2013	Purchased the equipment for $38,000 cash. The equipment is estimated to have a five-year life and $3,000 salvage value and was to be depreciated using the straight-line method.
Dec. 31, 2013	Recorded depreciation expense for 2013.
May 5, 2014	Undertook routine repairs costing $900.
Dec. 31, 2014	Recorded depreciation expense for 2014.
Jan. 1, 2015	Made an adjustment costing $4,000 to the equipment. It improved the quality of the output but did not affect the life and salvage value estimates.
Dec. 31, 2015	Recorded depreciation expense for 2015.
Mar. 1, 2016	Incurred $410 cost to oil and clean the equipment.
Dec. 31, 2016	Recorded depreciation expense for 2016.
Jan. 1, 2017	Had the equipment completely overhauled at a cost of $9,000. The overhaul was estimated to extend the total life to seven years and revised the salvage value to $2,500.
Dec. 31, 2017	Recorded depreciation expense for 2017.
July 1, 2018	Sold the equipment for $8,500 cash.

Required

a. Use a horizontal statements model like the following one to show the effects of these transactions on the elements of the financial statements. Use + for increase, − for decrease, and NA for not affected. The first event is recorded as an example.

Date	Assets	=	Liabilities	+	Equity	Net Inc.	Cash Flow
Jan. 1, 2013	+ −		NA		NA	NA	− IA

b. Determine amount of depreciation expense Seaside will report on the income statements for the years 2013 through 2017.

c. Determine the book value (cost − accumulated depreciation) Seaside will report on the balance sheets at the end of the years 2013 through 2017.

d. Determine the amount of the gain or loss Seaside will report on the disposal of the equipment on July 1, 2018.

e. Prepare the journal entry for the disposal of the equipment on July 1, 2018.

Problem 8-33 A   *Accounting for continuing expenditures*

LO 6, 7

Bird Manufacturing paid $62,000 to purchase a computerized assembly machine on January 1, 2013. The machine had an estimated life of eight years and a $2,000 salvage value. Bird's financial condition as of January 1, 2016, is shown in the following financial statements model. Bird uses the straight-line method for depreciation.

Assets			=	Equity			Rev.	–	Exp.	=	Net Inc.	Cash Flow
Cash	+	Book Value of Mach.	=	Com. Stk.	+	Ret. Earn.						
15,000	+	39,500	=	10,500	+	44,000	NA	–	NA	=	NA	NA

Bird Manufacturing made the following expenditures on the computerized assembly machine in 2016:

Jan. 2   Added an overdrive mechanism for $8,000 that would improve the overall quality of the performance of the machine but would not extend its life. The salvage value was revised to $2,500.

Aug. 1   Performed routine maintenance, $1,250.

Oct. 2   Replaced some computer chips (considered routine), $800.

Dec. 31   Recognized 2016 depreciation expense.

Required

a. Record the 2016 transactions in a statements model like the preceding one.

b. Prepare journal entries for the 2016 transactions.

LO 9

Problem 8-34A   *Accounting for intangible assets*

Cafe Olé Company acquired a fast-food restaurant for $1,500,000. The fair market values of the assets acquired were as follows. No liabilities were assumed.

Equipment	$380,000
Land	200,000
Building	680,000
Franchise (5-year life)	120,000

Required

a. Calculate the amount of goodwill acquired.

b. Prepare the journal entry to record the amortization of the franchise fee at the end of year 1.

LO 9

Problem 8-35A   *Accounting for goodwill*

Tri-State Co. acquired the assets of Riley Co. for $1,200,000 in 2013. The estimated fair market value of the assets at the acquisition date was $1,000,000. Goodwill of $200,000 was recorded at acquisition. In 2014, because of negative publicity, one-half of the goodwill acquired from Riley Co. was judged to be permanently impaired.

Required

a. How will Tri-State account for the impairment of the goodwill?

b. Prepare the journal entry to record the permanent impairment of goodwill.

EXERCISES—SERIES B

Unless specifically included, ignore income tax considerations in all exercises and problems.

LO 1

Exercise 8-1B   *Long-term operational assets used in a business*

Required

Give some examples of long-term operational assets that each of the following companies is likely to own: *(a)* UPS, *(b)* Greyhound, *(c)* Google, and *(d)* Prudential Insurance Co.

Exercise 8-2B   *Identifying long-term operational assets*   LO 1

Required

Which of the following items should be classified as long-term operational assets?

a. Delivery van
b. Land used in the business
c. Goodwill
d. Cash
e. Filing cabinet
f. Tax library of accounting firm

g. Prepaid insurance
h. Coal mine
i. Office equipment
j. Accounts receivable
k. Supplies
l. Copyright

Exercise 8-3B   *Classifying tangible and intangible assets*   LO 1

Required

Identify each of the following long-term operational assets as either tangible (T) or intangible (I):

a. Office building
b. Drill press
c. Patent
d. Oil well
e. Desk
f. Goodwill

g. Pizza oven
h. Land
i. Franchise
j. Filing cabinet
k. Copyright
l. Silver mine

Exercise 8-4B   *Determining the cost of an asset*   LO 2

Timber Milling Co. purchased a front-end loader to move stacks of lumber. The loader had a list price of $120,000. The seller agreed to allow a 4 percent discount because Timber Milling paid cash. Delivery terms were FOB shipping point. Freight cost amounted to $800. Timber Milling had to hire a consultant to train an employee to operate the loader. The training fee was $1,500. The loader operator is paid an annual salary of $45,000. The cost of the company's theft insurance policy increased by $900 per year as a result of acquiring the loader. The loader had a four-year useful life and an expected salvage value of $6,000.

Required

a. Determine the amount to be capitalized in an asset account for the purchase of the loader.
b. Record the purchase in general journal format.

Exercise 8-5B   *Allocating costs on the basis of relative market values*   LO 2

Estrada Inc. purchased a building and the land on which the building is situated for a total cost of $600,000 cash. The land was appraised at $210,000 and the building at $490,000.

Required

a. Determine the amount of the purchase cost to allocate to the land and the amount to allocate to the building.
b. Would the company recognize a gain on the purchase? Why or why not?
c. Record the purchase in a statements model like the following one.

Assets			=	Liab.	+	Equity	Rev.	−	Exp.	=	Net Inc.	Cash Flow
Cash	+ Land	+ Building										

d. Record the purchase in general journal format.

LO 2

Exercise 8-6B   *Allocating costs for a basket purchase*

Haskin Co. purchased an office building, land, and furniture for $400,000 cash. The appraised value of the assets was as follows:

Land	$100,000
Building	325,000
Furniture	75,000
Total	$500,000

Required

a. Compute the amount to be recorded on the books for each asset.

b. Record the purchase in a horizontal statements model like the following one.

Assets							=	Liab.	+	Equity	Rev.	−	Exp.	=	Net Inc.	Cash Flow
Cash	+	Land	+	Building	+	Furn.										

c. Prepare the general journal entry to record the purchase.

LO 3

Exercise 8-7B   *Effect of depreciation on the accounting equation and financial statements*

The following events apply to Sam's Seafood for the 2013 fiscal year:

1. The company started when it acquired $50,000 cash by issuing common stock.
2. Purchased a new cook top that cost $35,000 cash.
3. Earned $36,000 in cash revenue.
4. Paid $12,000 cash for salaries expense.
5. Adjusted the records to reflect the use of the cook top. Purchased on January 1, 2013, the cook top has an expected useful life of four years and an estimated salvage value of $3,000. Use straight-line depreciation. The adjusting entry was made as of December 31, 2013.

Required

a. Record the events in general journal format and post to T-accounts.

b. Prepare a balance sheet and a statement of cash flows for the 2013 accounting period.

c. What is the net income for 2013?

d. What amount of depreciation expense would Sam's report on the 2014 income statement?

e. What amount of accumulated depreciation would Sam's report on the December 31, 2014, balance sheet?

f. Would the cash flow from operating activities be affected by depreciation in 2014?

LO 3

Exercise 8-8B   *Effect of double-declining-balance depreciation on financial statements*

Katz Manufacturing Company started operations by acquiring $100,000 cash from the issue of common stock. On January 1, 2013, the company purchased equipment that cost $100,000 cash, had an expected useful life of six years, and had an estimated salvage value of $4,000. Katz Manufacturing earned $72,000 and $83,000 of cash revenue during 2013 and 2014, respectively. Katz Manufacturing uses double-declining-balance depreciation.

Required

Prepare income statements, balance sheets, and statements of cash flows for 2013 and 2014. Use a vertical statements format. (*Hint:* Record the events in T-accounts prior to preparing the statements.)

Exercise 8-9B   Events related to the acquisition, use, and disposal of a tangible plant asset: straight-line depreciation

Rod's Taxi Service purchased a new auto to use as a taxi on January 1, 2013, for $32,000. In addition, Rod's paid sales tax and title fees of $1,200 for the vehicle. The taxi is expected to have a five-year life and a salvage value of $3,200.

Required

a. Using the straight-line method, compute the depreciation expense for 2013 and 2014.

b. Prepare the general journal entry to record the 2013 depreciation.

c. Assume that the taxi was sold on January 1, 2015, for $22,000. Prepare the journal entry for the sale of the taxi in 2015.

Exercise 8-10B   Computing and recording straight-line versus double-declining-balance depreciation

At the beginning of 2013, Bayless Drugstore purchased a new computer system for $64,000. It is expected to have a five-year life and a $4,000 salvage value.

Required

a. Compute the depreciation for each of the five years, assuming that the company uses

(1) Straight-line depreciation.

(2) Double-declining-balance depreciation.

b. Record the purchase of the computer system and the depreciation expense for the first year under straight-line and double-declining-balance methods in a financial statements model like the following one:

Assets			=	Equity	Rev.	−	Exp.	=	Net Inc.	Cash Flow
Cash	+	Book Value of Comp. Sys.	=	Ret. Earn.						

c. Prepare the journal entries to recognize depreciation for each of the five years, assuming that the company uses

(1) Straight-line depreciation.

(2) Double-declining-balance depreciation.

Exercise 8-11B   Effect of the disposal of plant assets on the financial statements

Friel Company sold office equipment with a cost of $21,000 and accumulated depreciation of $9,000 for $14,000.

Required

a. What is the book value of the asset at the time of sale?

b. What is the amount of gain or loss on the disposal?

c. How would the sale affect net income (increase, decrease, no effect) and by how much?

d. How would the sale affect the amount of total assets shown on the balance sheet (increase, decrease, no effect) and by how much?

e. How would the event affect the statement of cash flows (inflow, outflow, no effect) and in what section?

Exercise 8-12B   Effect of gains and losses on the accounting equation and financial statements

On January 1, 2013, Alaska Enterprises purchased a parcel of land for $26,000 cash. At the time of purchase, the company planned to use the land for a warehouse site. In 2015, Alaska Enterprises changed its plans and sold the land.

Required

a. Assume that the land was sold for $28,500 in 2015.

  (1) Show the effect of the sale on the accounting equation.

  (2) What amount would Alaska report on the 2015 income statement related to the sale of the land?

  (3) What amount would Alaska report on the 2015 statement of cash flows related to the sale of the land?

b. Assume that the land was sold for $24,000 in 2015.

  (1) Show the effect of the sale on the accounting equation.

  (2) What amount would Alaska report on the 2015 income statement related to the sale of the land?

  (3) What amount would Alaska report on the 2015 statement of cash flows related to the sale of the land?

LO 3, 4   **Exercise 8-13B   Double-declining-balance and units-of-production depreciation: gain or loss on disposal**

Sure Shot Photo Service purchased a new color printer at the beginning of 2013 for $42,000. The printer is expected to have a four-year useful life and a $2,000 salvage value. The expected print production is estimated at 1,600,000 pages. Actual print production for the four years was as follows:

2013	370,000
2014	410,000
2015	420,000
2016	430,000
Total	1,630,000

The printer was sold at the end of 2016 for $1,600.

Required

a. Compute the depreciation expense for each of the four years, using double-declining-balance depreciation.

b. Compute the depreciation expense for each of the four years, using units-of-production depreciation.

c. Calculate the amount of gain or loss from the sale of the asset under each of the depreciation methods.

LO 5   **Exercise 8-14B   Computing depreciation for tax purposes**

Children's Eye Care Company purchased $50,000 of equipment on March 1, 2013.

Required

a. Compute the amount of depreciation expense that is deductible under MACRS for 2013 and 2014, assuming that the equipment is classified as seven-year property.

b. Compute the amount of depreciation expense that is deductible under MACRS for 2013 and 2014, assuming that the equipment is classified as five-year property.

LO 6   **Exercise 8-15B   Revision of estimated useful life**

On January 1, 2013, Food Storage Company purchased a freezer and related installation equipment for $38,000. The equipment had a three-year estimated life with a $5,000 salvage value. Straight-line depreciation was used. At the beginning of 2015, Food Storage revised the expected life of the asset to four years rather than three years. The salvage value was revised to $2,000.

Required

Compute the depreciation expense for each of the four years, 2013–2016.

Exercise 8-16B Distinguishing between revenue expenditures and capital expenditures

A-l Wrecker Service has just completed a minor repair on a tow truck. The repair cost was $830, and the book value prior to the repair was $7,200. In addition, the company spent $6,000 to replace the roof on a building. The new roof extended the life of the building by five years. Prior to the roof replacement, the general ledger reflected the Building account at $85,000 and related Accumulated Depreciation account at $32,000.

Required

After the work was completed, what book value should appear on the balance sheet for the tow truck and the building?

Exercise 8-17B Effect of revenue expenditures versus capital expenditures on financial statements

Thorp Construction Company purchased a compressor for $48,000 cash. It had an estimated useful life of four years and a $4,000 salvage value. At the beginning of the third year of use, the company spent an additional $5,000 related to the equipment. The company's financial condition just prior to this expenditure is shown in the following statements model:

Assets			=	Equity			Rev.	−	Exp.	=	Net Inc.	Cash Flow
Cash	+	Book Value of Compressor	=	Com. Stk.	+	Ret. Earn.						
34,000	+	26,000	=	40,000	+	20,000	NA	−	NA	=	NA	NA

Required

Record the $5,000 expenditure in the statements model under each of the following *independent* assumptions:

a. The expenditure was for routine maintenance.
b. The expenditure extended the compressor's life.
c. The expenditure improved the compressor's operating capacity.

Exercise 8-18B Effect of revenue expenditures versus capital expenditures on financial statements

On January 1, 2013, Kory Construction Company overhauled four cranes resulting in a slight increase in the life of the cranes. Such overhauls occur regularly at two-year intervals and have been treated as maintenance expense in the past. Management is considering whether to capitalize this year's $25,000 cash cost in the Cranes asset account or to expense it as a maintenance expense. Assume that the cranes have a remaining useful life of two years and no expected salvage value. Assume straight-line depreciation.

Required

a. Determine the amount of additional depreciation expense Kory would recognize in 2013 and 2014 if the cost were capitalized in the Cranes account.
b. Determine the amount of expense Kory would recognize in 2013 and 2014 if the cost were recognized as maintenance expense.
c. Determine the effect of the overhaul on cash flow from operating activities for 2013 and 2014 if the cost were capitalized and expensed through depreciation charges.
d. Determine the effect of the overhaul on cash flow from operating activities for 2013 and 2014 if the cost were recognized as maintenance expense.

Exercise 8-19B Computing and recording depletion expense

Green Mining paid $500,000 to acquire a mine with 25,000 tons of coal reserves. The following statements model reflects Green Mining financial condition just prior to purchasing the coal reserves. The company extracted 12,000 tons of coal in year 1 and 15,000 tons in year 2.

Assets			=	Equity			Rev.	–	Exp.	=	Net Inc.	Cash Flow
Cash	+	Coal Res.	=	Com. Stk.	+	Ret. Earn.						
600,000	+	NA	=	600,000	+	NA	NA	–	NA	=	NA	NA

Required

a. Compute the depletion charge per unit.

b. Record the acquisition of the coal reserves and the depletion expense for years 1 and 2 in a financial statements model like the preceding one.

c. Prepare the general journal entries to record the depletion expense for years 1 and 2.

LO 9   **Exercise 8-20B   *Computing and recording the amortization of intangibles***

Electronic Manufacturing paid cash to acquire the assets of an existing company. Among the assets acquired were the following items:

Patent with 4 remaining years of legal life	$35,000
Goodwill	25,000

Electronics financial condition just prior to the acquisition of these assets is shown in the following statements model:

Assets					=	Liab.	+	Equity	Rev.	–	Exp.	=	Net Inc.	Cash Flow
Cash	+	Patent	+	Goodwill										
85,000	+	NA	+	NA	=	NA	+	85,000	NA	–	NA	=	NA	NA

Required

a. Compute the annual amortization expense for these items.

b. Record the acquisition of the intangible assets and the related amortization expense for year 1 in a horizontal statements model like the one shown above.

c. Prepare the journal entries to record the acquisition of the intangible assets and the related amortization for year 1.

LO 9   **Exercise 8-21B   *Computing and recording goodwill***

Phoenix Corp acquired the business Data Resources for $300,000 cash and assumed all liabilities at the date of purchase. Data's books showed tangible assets of $260,000, liabilities of $40,000, and stockholders' equity of $220,000. An appraiser assessed the fair market value of the tangible assets at $235,000 at the date of acquisition. Phoenix Corp's financial condition just prior to the acquisition is shown in the following statements model:

Assets					=	Liab.	+	Equity	Rev.	–	Exp.	=	Net Inc.	Cash Flow
Cash	+	Tang. Assets	+	Goodwill										
400,000	+	NA	+	NA	=	NA	+	400,000	NA	–	NA	=	NA	NA

Required

a. Compute the amount of goodwill acquired.

b. Record the acquisition in a financial statements model like the preceding one.

c. When will the goodwill be written off under the impairment rules?

d. Record the acquisition in general journal format.

Exercise 8-22B   *R&D costs GAAP vs IFRS*

The Belgium Corp. incurred $3,000,000 of research cost and $2,200,000 of development cost during 2013.

Required

a. Determine the amount of expense recognized on the 2013 income statement assuming Belgium uses U.S. GAAP.

b. Determine the amount of expense recognized on the 2013 income statement assuming Belgium uses IFRS.

Exercise 8-23B   *Accounting for land and buildings under IFRS*

Assume the following. Paris Company purchased a parcel of land on January 1, 2008, for $900,000. It constructed a building on the land at a cost of $4,500,000. The building was occupied on January 1, 2011, and is expected to have a useful life of 40 years and an estimated salvage value of $1,500,000.

As of December 31, 2012, and 2013, the fair value of the land had not been formally revalued because the real estate market had not changed significantly. Due to a jump in real estate prices, during 2014 the value of the land had increased to $975,000, and the fair value of the building was $4,500,000. The salvage value of the building is still estimated at $1,500,000. The land and the building were reevaluated by the company in 2014.

Required

a. Under U.S. accounting rules, what amount would be reported on the company's 2013 and 2014 balance sheets for the land and for the building? Show any necessary computations.

b. Under U.S. accounting rules, what amount of depreciation expense would be reported in 2014 for the building? Show any necessary computations.

c. Under the IFRS revaluation model, what amount would be reported on the company's 2013 and 2014 balance sheets for the land and for the building? Show any necessary computations.

d. Under the IFRS revaluation model, what amount of depreciation expense would be reported in 2014 for the building? Show any necessary computations.

PROBLEMS—SERIES B

Problem 8-24B   *Accounting for acquisition of assets including a basket purchase*

Boone Co., Inc., made several purchases of long-term assets in 2013. The details of each purchase are presented here.

New Office Equipment

1. List price: $70,000; terms: 2/10 n/30; paid within discount period.

2. Transportation-in: $2,500.

3. Installation: $3,000.

4. Cost to repair damage during unloading: $800.

5. Routine maintenance cost after six months: $450.

Basket Purchase of Copier, Computer, and Scanner for $20,000 with Fair Market Values

1. Copier, $12,000.

2. Computer, $10,500.

3. Scanner, $7,500.

Land for New Warehouse with an Old Building Torn Down

1. Purchase price, $225,000.

2. Demolition of building, $15,000.

3. Lumber sold from old building, $5,000.
4. Grading in preparation for new building, $16,000.
5. Construction of new building, $450,000.

Required

In each of these cases, determine the amount of cost to be capitalized in the asset accounts.

LO 3, 4

Problem 8-25B *Accounting for depreciation over multiple accounting cycles: straight-line depreciation*

Regions Company started business by acquiring $50,000 cash from the issue of common stock on January 1, 2013. The cash acquired was immediately used to purchase equipment for $50,000 that had a $10,000 salvage value and an expected useful life of four years. The equipment was used to produce the following revenue stream (assume that all revenue transactions are for cash). At the beginning of the fifth year, the equipment was sold for $8,800 cash. Regions uses straight-line depreciation.

	2013	2014	2015	2016	2017
Revenue	$25,200	$27,300	$31,500	$26,000	$0

Required

Prepare income statements, statements of changes in stockholders' equity, balance sheets, and statements of cash flows for each of the five years. Present the statements in the form of a vertical statements model.

LO 3, 6, 7

Problem 8-26B *Purchase and use of tangible asset: three accounting cycles, straight-line depreciation*

The following transactions relate to Direct Towing Service. Assume the transactions for the purchase of the wrecker and any capital improvements occur on January 1 of each year.

2013

1. Acquired $60,000 cash from the issue of common stock.
2. Purchased a used wrecker for $28,000. It has an estimated useful life of three years and a $4,000 salvage value.
3. Paid sales tax on the wrecker of $3,000.
4. Collected $46,200 in towing fees.
5. Paid $8,000 for gasoline and oil.
6. Recorded straight-line depreciation on the wrecker for 2013.
7. Closed the revenue and expense accounts to Retained Earnings at the end of 2013.

2014

1. Paid for a tune-up for the wrecker's engine, $450.
2. Bought four new tires, $1,000.
3. Collected $56,000 in towing fees.
4. Paid $12,000 for gasoline and oil.
5. Recorded straight-line depreciation for 2014.
6. Closed the revenue and expense accounts to Retained Earnings at the end of 2014.

2015

1. Paid to overhaul the wrecker's engine, $3,500, which extended the life of the wrecker to a total of four years. The salvage value did not change.
2. Paid for gasoline and oil, $13,200.
3. Collected $62,000 in towing fees.
4. Recorded straight-line depreciation for 2015.
5. Closed the revenue and expense accounts at the end of 2015.

Required

a. Use a horizontal statements model like the following one to show the effect of these transactions on the elements of financial statements. Use + for increase, − for decrease, and NA for not affected. The first event is recorded as an example.

2013 Event No.	Assets	=	Liabilities	+	Equity	Net Inc.	Cash Flow
1	+		NA		+	NA	+ FA

b. For each year, record the transactions in general journal form and post them to T-accounts.
c. Use a vertical model to present financial statements for 2013, 2014, and 2015.

Problem 8-27B   *Calculating depreciation expense using four different methods*

LO 3

Ramer Inc. manufactures sporting goods. The following information applies to a machine purchased on January 1, 2013:

Purchase price	$ 80,000
Delivery cost	$ 2,500
Installation charge	$ 850
Estimated life	5 years
Estimated units	160,000
Salvage estimate	$ 3,350

During 2013, the machine produced 35,000 units and during 2014, it produced 36,000 units.

Required

Determine the amount of depreciation expense for 2013 and 2014 using each of the following methods:

a. Straight-line.
b. Double-declining-balance.
c. Units of production.
d. MACRS, assuming that the machine is classified as seven-year property.

Problem 8-28B   *Effect of straight-line versus double-declining-balance depreciation on the recognition of expense and gains or losses*

LO 3, 4

Sullivans Office Service purchased a new computer system in 2013 for $50,000. It is expected to have a five-year useful life and a $5,000 salvage value. The company expects to use the system more extensively in the early years of its life.

Required

a. Calculate the depreciation expense for each of the five years, assuming the use of straight-line depreciation.
b. Calculate the depreciation expense for each of the five years, assuming the use of double-declining-balance depreciation.
c. Would the choice of one depreciation method over another produce a different amount of cash flow for any year? Why or why not?
d. Assume that Sullivans Office Service sold the computer system at the end of the fourth year for $16,000. Compute the amount of gain or loss using each depreciation method.
e. Explain any differences in gain or loss due to using the different methods.

LO 3, 4

Problem 8-29B *Computing and recording units-of-production depreciation*

Angle Co. purchased assembly equipment for $600,000 on January 1, 2013. Angle's financial condition immediately prior to the purchase is shown in the following horizontal statements model:

Assets			=	Equity			Rev.	−	Exp.	=	Net Inc.	Cash Flow
Cash	+	Book Value of Equip.	=	Com. Stk.	+	Ret. Earn.						
800,000	+	NA	=	800,000	+	NA	NA	−	NA	=	NA	NA

The equipment is expected to have a useful life of 200,000 machine hours and a salvage value of $20,000. Actual machine-hour use was as follows:

2013	56,000
2014	61,000
2015	42,000
2016	36,000
2017	10,000

Required

a. Compute the depreciation for each of the five years, assuming the use of units-of-production depreciation.

b. Assume that Angle earns $210,000 of cash revenue during 2013. Record the purchase of the equipment and the recognition of the revenue and the depreciation expense for the first year in a financial statements model like the preceding one.

c. Assume that Angle sold the equipment at the end of the fifth year for $21,500. Record the general journal entry for the sale.

LO 3

Problem 8-30B *Determining the effect of depreciation expense on financial statements*

Three different companies each purchased trucks on January 1, 2013, for $45,000. Each truck was expected to last four years or 200,000 miles. Salvage value was estimated to be $5,000. All three trucks were driven 66,000 miles in 2013, 42,000 miles in 2014, 40,000 miles in 2015, and 60,000 miles in 2016. Each of the three companies earned $35,000 of cash revenue during each of the four years. Company A uses straight-line depreciation, company B uses double-declining-balance depreciation, and company C uses units-of-production depreciation.

Required

Answer each of the following questions. Ignore the effects of income taxes.

a. Which company will report the highest amount of net income for 2013?

b. Which company will report the lowest amount of net income for 2016?

c. Which company will report the highest book value on the December 31, 2015, balance sheet?

d. Which company will report the highest amount of retained earnings on the December 31, 2016, balance sheet?

e. Which company will report the lowest amount of cash flow from operating activities on the 2015 statement of cash flows?

LO 6, 8

Problem 8-31B *Accounting for depletion*

Patano Company engages in the exploration and development of many types of natural resources. In the last two years, the company has engaged in the following activities:

Jan. 1, 2013   Purchased for $1,800,000 a silver mine estimated to contain 100,000 tons of silver ore.

July 1, 2013   Purchased for $1,600,000 a tract of timber estimated to yield 1,000,000 board feet of lumber and the residual value of the land was estimated at $100,000.

Feb. 1, 2014   Purchased for $2,800,000 a gold mine estimated to yield 50,000 tons of gold-veined ore.

Sept. 1, 2014   Purchased oil reserves for $1,560,000. The reserves were estimated to contain 270,000 barrels of oil, of which 10,000 would be unprofitable to pump.

Required

a. Prepare the journal entries to account for the following:

(1) The 2013 purchases.

(2) Depletion on the 2013 purchases, assuming that 14,000 tons of silver were mined and 500,000 board feet of lumber were cut.

(3) The 2014 purchases.

(4) Depletion on the four natural resource assets, assuming that 20,000 tons of silver ore, 300,000 board feet of lumber, 4,000 tons of gold ore, and 50,000 barrels of oil were extracted.

b. Prepare the portion of the December 31, 2014, balance sheet that reports natural resources.

c. Assume that in 2015 the estimates changed to reflect only 20,000 tons of gold ore remaining. Prepare the depletion journal entry in 2015 to account for the extraction of 10,000 tons of gold ore.

Problem 8-32B *Recording continuing expenditures for plant assets*

LO 3, 4, 6, 7

Track Inc. recorded the following transactions over the life of a piece of equipment purchased in 2013:

Jan. 1, 2013	Purchased equipment for $80,000 cash. The equipment was estimated to have a five-year life and $5,000 salvage value and was to be depreciated using the straight-line method.
Dec. 31, 2013	Recorded depreciation expense for 2013.
Sept. 30, 2014	Undertook routine repairs costing $750.
Dec. 31, 2014	Recorded depreciation expense for 2014.
Jan. 1, 2015	Made an adjustment costing $3,000 to the equipment. It improved the quality of the output but did not affect the life and salvage value estimates.
Dec. 31, 2015	Recorded depreciation expense for 2015.
June 1, 2016	Incurred $620 cost to oil and clean the equipment.
Dec. 31, 2016	Recorded depreciation expense for 2016.
Jan. 1, 2017	Had the equipment completely overhauled at a cost of $8,000. The overhaul was estimated to extend the total life to seven years. The salvage value did not change.
Dec. 31, 2017	Recorded depreciation expense for 2017.
Oct. 1, 2018	Received and accepted an offer of $18,000 for the equipment.

Required

a. Use a horizontal statements model like the following one to show the effects of these transactions on the elements of the financial statements. Use + for increase, − for decrease, and NA for not affected. The first event is recorded as an example.

Date	Assets	=	Liabilities	+	Equity	Net Inc.	Cash Flow
Jan. 1, 2013	+ −		NA		NA	NA	− IA

b. Determine the amount of depreciation expense to be reported on the income statements for the years 2013 through 2017.

c. Determine the book value (cost − accumulated depreciation) Track will report on the balance sheets at the end of the years 2013 through 2018.

d. Determine the amount of the gain or loss Track will report on the disposal of the equipment on October 1, 2018.

e. Prepare the journal entry for the disposal of the equipment on October 1, 2018.

Problem 8-33B *Continuing expenditures with statements model*

LO 6, 7

Travel Company owned a service truck that was purchased at the beginning of 2013 for $28,000. It had an estimated life of three years and an estimated salvage value of $4,000. Travel Company uses straight-line depreciation. Its financial condition as of January 1, 2015, is shown in the following financial statements model:

Assets			=	Equity			Rev.	−	Exp.	=	Net Inc.	Cash Flow
Cash	+	Book Value of Truck	=	Com. Stk.	+	Ret. Earn.						
14,000	+	12,000	=	8,000	+	18,000	NA	−	NA	=	NA	NA

In 2015, Travel Company spent the following amounts on the truck:

Jan. 4   Overhauled the engine for $5,500. The estimated life was extended one additional year, and the salvage value was revised to $2,500.

July 6   Obtained oil change and transmission service, $180.

Aug. 7   Replaced the fan belt and battery, $290.

Dec. 31   Purchased gasoline for the year, $6,200.

31   Recognized 2015 depreciation expense.

Required

a. Record the 2015 transactions in a statements model like the preceding one.

b. Prepare journal entries for the 2015 transactions.

LO 9

Problem 8-34B   *Accounting for intangible assets*

Lopez Company acquired Atlantic Transportation Co. for $1,300,000. The fair market values of the assets acquired were as follows. No liabilities were assumed.

Equipment	$500,000
Land	150,000
Building	520,000
Franchise (10-year life)	30,000

Required

a. Calculate the amount of goodwill acquired.

b. Prepare the journal entry to record the amortization of the franchise fee at the end of year 1.

LO 9

Problem 8-35B   *Accounting for goodwill*

Casey Equipment Manufacturing Co. acquired the assets of Florence Inc., a competitor, in 2013. It recorded goodwill of $60,000 at acquisition. Because of defective machinery Florence had produced prior to the acquisition, it has been determined that all of the acquired goodwill has been permanently impaired.

Required

Prepare the journal entry to record the permanent impairment of the goodwill.

ANALYZE, THINK, COMMUNICATE

ATC 8-1   Business Applications Case   *Understanding real-world annual reports*

Required

Use the Target Corporation's annual report in Appendix B to answer the following questions.

a. What method of depreciation does Target use?

b. What types of intangible assets does Target have?

c. What are the estimated lives that Target uses for the various types of long-term assets?

d. As of January 29, 2011 (2010 fiscal-year), what is the original cost of Target's: Land; Buildings and improvements; and Fixtures and equipment?

e. What was Target's depreciation expense and amortization expense for 2010?

ATC 8-2   Group Assignment   *Different depreciation methods*

Sweet's Bakery makes cakes, pies, and other pastries that it sells to local grocery stores. The company experienced the following transactions during 2013.

1. Started business by acquiring $60,000 cash from the issue of common stock.
2. Purchased bakery equipment for $46,000.
3. Had sales in 2013 amounting to $42,000.
4. Paid $8,200 of cash for supplies which were all used during the year to make baked goods.
5. Incurred other operating expenses of $12,000 for 2013.
6. Recorded depreciation assuming the equipment had a four-year life and a $6,000 salvage value. The MACRS recovery period is five years.
7. Paid income tax. The rate is 30 percent.

Required

a. Organize the class into three sections and divide each section into groups of three to five students. Assign each section a depreciation method: straight-line, double-declining-balance, or MACRS.

Group Task

Prepare an income statement and balance sheet using the preceding information and the depreciation method assigned to your group.

Class Discussion

b. Have a representative of each section put its income statement on the board. Are there differences in net income? In the amount of income tax paid? How will these differences in the amount of depreciation expense change over the life of the equipment?

ATC 8-3   Real-World Case   *Identifying companies based on financial statement information*

The following ratios are for four companies in different industries. Some of these ratios have been discussed in the textbook, others have not, but their names explain how the ratio was computed. This data are for the companies' 2010 fiscal years. The four sets of ratios, presented randomly are:

	Company 1	Company 2	Company 3	Company 4
Current assets ÷ total assets	17%	50%	17%	20%
Operating cycle	33	269	96	15
Return on assets	18%	4%	6%	7%
Gross margin	54%	24%	44%	25%
Sales ÷ property, plant, and equipment	46.9	3.2	2.3	4.2
Sales ÷ number of full-time employees	25,929	381,539	221,992	47,693

The four companies to which these ratios relate, listed in alphabetical order, are:

Caterpillar, Inc. is a company that manufactures heavy construction equipment.

Denny's Corporation operated over 1,658 restaurants as of December 31, 2010.

Molson Coors Brewing, Inc. is a company that produces beer and related products.

Weight Watchers International, Inc. is a company that provides weight loss services and products.

Required

Determine which company should be matched with each set of ratios. Write a memorandum explaining the rationale for your decisions.

ATC 8-4   Business Applications Case   *Performing ratio analysis using real-world data*

American Greetings Corporation manufactures and sells greeting cards and related items such as gift wrapping paper. CSX Corporation is one of the largest railway networks in the nation. The following data were taken from one of the companies' December 25, 2010, annual report and from the other's February 28, 2010, annual report. Revealing which data relate to which company was intentionally omitted. For one company, the dollar amounts are in thousands, while for the other they are in millions.

	Company 1	Company 2
Sales	$10,636	$1,635,858
Depreciation costs	947	45,165
Net earnings	1,563	81,574
Current assets	2,855	677,424
Property, plant, and equipment	23,799	244,751
Total assets	28,141	1,529,651

Required

a. Calculate depreciation costs as a percentage of sales for each company.

b. Calculate property, plant, and equipment as a percentage of total assets for each company.

c. Based on the information now available to you, decide which data relate to which company. Explain the rationale for your decision.

d. Which company appears to be using its assets most efficiently? Explain your answer.

ATC 8-5   Business Applications Case   *Performing ratio analysis using real-world data*

Companies in the coal mining business use a lot of property, plant, and equipment. Not only is there the significant investment they must make in the equipment used to extract and process the coal, but they must also purchase the rights to the coal reserves themselves.

Cloud Peak Energy, Inc., claims to be the third largest coal company in the United States. Peabody Energy Corporation claims to be the largest private-sector coal company in the world. The following information was taken from these companies' December 31, 2010, annual reports. All dollar amounts are in thousands.

	Cloud Peak Energy, Inc.	Peabody Energy Corp.
Sales	$1,370,761	$6,331,300
Depreciation and depletion costs	100,023	440,900
Property, plant, and equipment (net of accumulated depreciation)	1,008,337	7,426,100
Total assets	1,915,107	11,363,100
Depreciation method	Straight-line or units of production	Straight-line
Depletion method	Units of production	Units of production
Estimated life of assets:		
Buildings	5 to 25 years	10 to 20 years
Machinery and equipment	3 to 20 years	3 to 33 years
Net income	$ 117,197*	$ 802,200*

*Includes income attributable to noncontrolling interest.

Required

a. Calculate depreciation costs as a percentage of sales for each company.

b. Calculate buildings, machinery, and equipment as a percentage of total assets for each company.

c. Based only on the percentages calculated in parts (a.) and (b.), which company appears to be using its assets most efficiently? Explain your answer.

d. Calculate the return on assets ratios for each company. Based on this ratio, which company appears to be using its assets most efficiently? Explain your answer.

e. Identify some of the problems a financial analyst encounters when trying to compare the use of long-term assets of Cloud Peak versus Peabody.

ATC 8-6   Writing Assignment *Impact of historical cost on asset presentation on the balance sheet*

Assume that you a... ...mining the balance sheets of two companies and note the following information:

	Company A	Company B
Equipment	$1,130,000	$900,000
Accumulated Depreciation	(730,000)	(500,000)
Book Value	$ 400,000	$400,000

Maxie Smith, a student who has had no accounting courses, remarks that Company A and Company B have the same amount of equipment.

Required

In a short paragraph, explain to Maxie that the two companies do not have equal amounts of equipment. You may want to include in your discussion comments regarding the possible age of each company's equipment, the impact of the historical cost concept on balance sheet information, and the impact of different depreciation methods on book value.

ATC 8-7   Ethical Dilemma *What's an expense?*

Several years ago, Wilson Blowhard founded a communications company. The company became successful and grew by expanding its customer base and acquiring some of its competitors. In fact, most of its growth resulted from acquiring other companies. Mr. Blowhard is adamant about continuing the company's growth and increasing its net worth. To achieve these goals, the business's net income must continue to increase at a rapid pace.

If the company's net worth continues to rise, Mr. Blowhard plans to sell the company and retire. He is, therefore, focused on improving the company's profit any way he can.

In the communications business, companies often use the lines of other communications companies. This line usage is a significant operating expense for Mr. Blowhard's company. Generally accepted accounting principles require operating costs like line use to be expensed as they are incurred each year. Each dollar of line cost reduces net income by a dollar.

After reviewing the company's operations, Mr. Blowhard concluded that the company did not currently need all of the line use it was paying for. It was really paying the owner of the lines now so that the line use would be available in the future for all of Mr. Blowhard's expected new customers. Mr. Blowhard instructed his accountant to capitalize all of the line cost charges and depreciate them over 10 years. The accountant reluctantly followed Mr. Blowhard's instructions and the company's net income for the current year showed a significant increase over the prior year's net income. Mr. Blowhard had found a way to report continued growth in the company's net income and increase the value of the company.

Required

a. How does Mr. Blowhard's scheme affect the amount of income that the company would otherwise report in its financial statements and how does the scheme affect the company's balance sheet? Explain your answer.

b. Review the AICPA's Articles of Professional Conduct (see Chapter 1) and comment on any of the standards that were violated.

c. Review Donald Cressey's identified features of unethical and criminal conduct (see Chapter 1) and comment on which of these features are evident in this case.

ATC 8-8 Research Assignment *Comparing Microsoft's and Intel's operational assets*

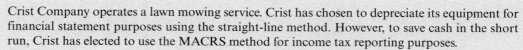

This chapter discussed how companies in different industries often use different proportions of current versus long-term assets to accomplish their business objective. The technology revolution resulting from the silicon microchip has often been led by two well-known companies: Microsoft and Intel. Although often thought of together, these companies are really very different. Using either the most current Forms 10-K or annual reports for Microsoft Corporation and Intel Corporation, complete the requirements below. To obtain the Forms 10-K, use either the EDGAR system following the instructions in Appendix A or the company's website. Microsoft's annual report is available on its website; Intel's annual report is its Form 10-K.

Required

a. Fill in the missing data in the following table. The percentages must be computed; they are not included in the companies' 10-Ks. (*Note:* The percentages for current assets and property, plant, and equipment will not sum to 100.)

	Current Assets	Property, Plant, and Equipment	Total Assets
Microsoft			
Dollar Amount	$ _____	$ _____	$ _____
% of Total Assets	_____ %	_____ %	100%
Intel			
Dollar Amount	$ _____	$ _____	$ _____
% of Total Assets	_____ %	_____ %	100%

b. Briefly explain why these two companies have different percentages of their assets in current assets versus property, plant, and equipment.

ATC 8-9 Spreadsheet Assignment *Reporting to the IRS versus financial statement reporting*

Crist Company operates a lawn mowing service. Crist has chosen to depreciate its equipment for financial statement purposes using the straight-line method. However, to save cash in the short run, Crist has elected to use the MACRS method for income tax reporting purposes.

Required

a. Set up the following spreadsheet to reflect the two different methods of reporting. Notice that the first two years of revenues and operating expenses are provided.

b. Enter the effects of the following items for 2013.

   (1) At the beginning of 2013, Crist purchased for $10,000 cash a lawn mower it expects to use for five years. Salvage value is estimated to be $2,000. As stated, Crist uses the straight-line method of depreciation for financial statement purposes and the MACRS method for income tax purposes. Use formulas to calculate depreciation expense for each method.

   (2) No equipment was sold during 2013; therefore, no gain or loss would be reported this year.

   (3) The income tax rate is 30 percent. For simplicity, assume that the income tax payable was paid in 2013.

   (4) Complete the schedules for income reporting, reporting of equipment, and reporting of cash flows for 2013. Use formulas for all calculations.

c. Enter the effects of the following items for 2014.

   (1) Crist used the mower for the entire 2014 year. Enter 2014 depreciation expense amounts for the income reporting section of your spreadsheet.

   (2) At December 31, Crist sold the lawn mower for $7,000. Calculate the gain or loss on the sale for the income reporting section. Use formulas to make the calculations.

   (3) The income tax rate is 30 percent. For simplicity, assume that the income tax payable was paid in 2014.

   (4) Complete the schedules for income reporting and reporting of cash flows for 2014.

d. Calculate the Total columns for the income reporting and reporting of cash flows sections.

e. Respond to the following.

(1) In 2013, by adopting the MACRS method of depreciation for tax purposes instead of the straight-line method, what is the difference in the amount of cash paid for income taxes?

(2) In the long term, after equipment has been disposed of, is there any difference in total income under the two methods?

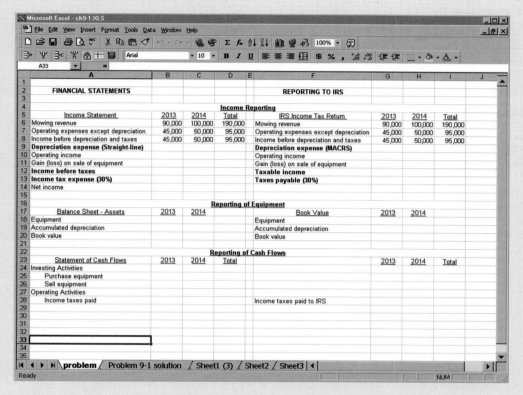

(3) In the long term, after equipment has been disposed of, is there any difference between total income tax expense and total income tax paid?

(4) Explain why Crist Company would use two different depreciation methods, particularly the straight-line method for the financial statements and an accelerated method (MACRS) for reporting to the IRS.

ATC 8-10   Spreadsheet Assignment   *Alternative methods of depreciation*

Short Company purchased a computer on January 1, 2013, for $5,000. An additional $100 was paid for delivery charges. The computer was estimated to have a life of five years or 10,000 hours. Salvage value was estimated at $300. During the five years, the computer was used as follows:

2013	2,500 hours
2014	2,400 hours
2015	2,000 hours
2016	1,700 hours
2017	1,400 hours

Required

a. Prepare a five-year depreciation schedule for the computer using the straight-line depreciation method. Be sure to use formulas for all computations including depreciation expense. Set up the following headings for your schedule:

		Beginning				Ending	
Year	Cost	Accumulated Depreciation	Book Value	Depreciation Expense	Cost	Accumulated Depreciation	Book Value

b. Prepare another five-year depreciation schedule for the computer using the units-of-production method. Use (copy) the headings used in Requirement *a*.

c. Prepare another five-year depreciation schedule for the computer using the double-declining-balance method. Use (copy) the headings used in Requirement *a*.

d. Prepare another five-year depreciation schedule for the computer using the MACRS method. Use (copy) the headings used in Requirement *a*.

Spreadsheet Tip

After the year 2013, enter subsequent dates automatically. Position the mouse in the lower right hand corner of the highlighted cell "2013" until a thin cross appears. Click and drag down four additional rows.

COMPREHENSIVE PROBLEM

The trial balance of Pacilio Security Services Inc. as of January 1, 2018, had the following normal balances:

Cash	$93,708
Petty cash	100
Accounts receivable	22,540
Allowance for doubtful accounts	1,334
Supplies	250
Prepaid rent	3,600
Merchandise inventory (18 @ $285)	5,130
Land	4,000
Salaries payable	2,100
Common stock	50,000
Retained earnings	75,894

During 2018 Pacillo Security Services experienced the following transactions:

1. Paid the salaries payable from 2017.
2. Purchased equipment and a van for a lump sum of $36,000 cash on January 2, 2018. The equipment was appraised for $10,000 and the van was appraised for $30,000.
3. Paid $9,000 on May 1, 2018, for one year's office rent in advance.
4. Purchased $300 of supplies on account.
5. Purchased 120 alarm systems at a cost of $280 each. Paid cash for the purchase.
6. After numerous attempts to collect from customers, wrote off $2,350 of uncollectible accounts receivable.
7. Sold 115 alarm systems for $580 each. All sales were on account. (Be sure to compute cost of goods sold using the FIFO cost flow method.)
8. Billed $86,000 of monitoring services for the year. Credit card sales amounted to $36,000, and the credit card company charged a 4 percent fee. The remaining $50,000 were sales on account.
9. Replenished the petty cash fund on June 30. The fund had $12 cash and receipts of $45 for yard mowing, $28 for office supplies expense, and $11 for miscellaneous expenses.
10. Collected the amount due from the credit card company.
11. Paid installers and other employees a total of $52,000 cash for salaries.
12. Collected $115,500 of accounts receivable during the year.
13. Paid $12,500 of advertising expense during the year.
14. Paid $6,800 of utilities expense for the year.
15. Sold the land, which was purchased in 2011, for $12,000.
16. Paid the accounts payable.
17. Paid a dividend of $10,000 to the shareholders.

Adjustments

18. Determined that $180 of supplies were on hand at the end of the year.

19. Recognized the expired rent for both the old van and the office building for the year. The lease on the van was not renewed. Rent paid on March 1, 2017, for the van was $4,800.

20. Recognized uncollectible accounts expense for the year using the allowance method. Pacilio estimates that 3 percent of sales on account will not be collected.

21. Recognized depreciation expense on the equipment and the van. The equipment has a five-year life and a $2,000 salvage value. The van has a four-year life and a $6,000 salvage value. The company uses double-declining-balance for the van and straight-line for the equipment.

22. Accrued salaries at December 31, 2018, were $1,500.

Required

a. Record the above transactions in general journal form.

b. Post the transactions to T-accounts.

c. Prepare a trial balance.

d. Prepare an income statement, statement of changes in stockholders' equity, balance sheet, and statement of cash flows.

e. Close the temporary accounts to retained earnings.

f. Post the closing entries to the T-accounts and prepare a post-closing trial balance.

CHAPTER 9

Accounting for Current Liabilities and Payroll

LEARNING OBJECTIVES

After you have mastered the material in this chapter, you will be able to:

LO1 Show how notes payable and related interest expense affect financial statements.

LO2 Show how sales tax liabilities affect financial statements.

LO3 Define contingent liabilities and explain how they are reported in financial statements.

LO4 Explain how warranty obligations affect financial statements.

LO5 Determine payroll taxes and explain how they affect financial statements.

LO6 Prepare a classified balance sheet.

LO7 Use the current ratio to assess the level of liquidity.

LO8 Show how discount notes and related interest charges affect financial statements. (Appendix)

CHAPTER OPENING

Chapter 7 explained the need to estimate the net realizable value of receivables (the amount of receivables a company expects to actually collect). Do companies also estimate the net realizable value of payables (the amount they expect to actually pay)? The answer is no. Unless there is evidence to the contrary, companies are assumed to be going concerns that will continue to operate. Under this **going concern assumption,** companies expect to pay their obligations in full. Accounts and notes payable are therefore reported at face value. In addition to reporting liabilities for which the amounts due are known, companies report liabilities for which the amounts due are uncertain. Liabilities that are uncertain as to amount are contingent liabilities.

Chapter 2 discussed several types of liabilities with known amounts due, including accounts payable, salaries payable, and unearned revenue. This chapter introduces other liabilities with known amounts due: notes payable, sales tax payable, and payroll liabilities; and contingent liabilities including warranties payable and vacation pay. We limit the discussion in this chapter to *current liabilities,* those that are payable within one year or the operating cycle, whichever is longer.

The Curious Accountant

Randy Moats had worked as a plumber or plumber's assistant since high school. When he turned 30, he started his own plumbing business. In addition to working himself, he hired two friends, each of whom he planned to pay $20 per hour plus reasonable benefits. One reason Randy wanted his own business was because he felt small companies often did not provide employees reasonable benefits. Randy planned to charge customers $40 per hour for plumbing services. He believed charging double the rate he paid his employees would cover his operating expenses and still provide a profit on the employees' work.

Randy hired a local accounting firm for his accounting needs, including handling his company's payroll records. After getting the business established, he and his employees kept busy, but the business was not as profitable as Randy had expected. His accountant explained that the total compensation cost of his employees was averaging around $26 per hour. Randy knew the employees would cost more than their $20 per hour wage rate because of their fringe benefits, but he had not expected the benefits cost to be 30 percent of their base pay.

What could cause Randy's compensation expenses to be so unexpectedly high? (Answers on page 493.)

ACCOUNTING FOR NOTES PAYABLE

LO 1

Show how notes payable and related interest expense affect financial statements.

Our discussion of promissory notes in Chapter 7 focused on the payee, the company with a note receivable on its books. In this chapter we focus on the maker of the note, the company with a note payable on its books. Since the maker of the note issues (gives) the note to the payee, the maker is sometimes called the **issuer.**

To illustrate, assume that on September 1, 2013, Herrera Supply Company (HSC) borrowed $90,000 from the National Bank. As evidence of the debt, Herrera issued a **note payable** that had a one-year term and an annual interest rate of 9 percent.

Issuing the note is an asset source transaction. The asset account Cash increases and the liability account Notes Payable increases. The income statement is not affected. The statement of cash flows shows a $90,000 cash inflow from financing activities. The journal entry and its effects on the financial statements are shown here:

Account Title	Debit	Credit
Cash	90,000	
Notes Payable		90,000

	Assets	=	Liabilities	+			Stockholders' Equity			Rev.	−	Exp.	=	Net Inc.	Cash Flow	
Date	Cash	=	Notes Pay.	+	Int. Pay.	+	Com. Stk.	+	Ret. Earn.							
09/01/13	90,000	=	90,000	+	NA	+	NA	+	NA	NA	−	NA	=	NA	90,000	FA

On December 31, 2013, HSC would record an adjusting entry to recognize four months (September 1 through December 31) of accrued interest expense. The accrued interest is $2,700 [$90,000 × 0.09 × (4 ÷ 12)]. The adjusting entry is a claims exchange. The liability account Interest Payable increases, and the equity account Retained Earnings decreases. The income statement would report interest expense although HSC had not paid any cash for interest in 2013. The journal entry and its effects on the financial statements are shown here:

Account Title	Debit	Credit
Interest Expense	2,700	
Interest Payable		2,700

	Assets	=	Liabilities	+			Stockholders' Equity			Rev.	−	Exp.	=	Net Inc.	Cash Flow
Date	Cash	=	Notes Pay.	+	Int. Pay.	+	Com. Stk.	+	Ret. Earn.						
12/31/13	NA	=	NA	+	2,700	+	NA	+	(2,700)	NA	−	2,700	=	(2,700)	NA

HSC would record three journal entries on August 31, 2014 (the maturity date). The first entry recognizes $5,400 of interest expense that accrued in 2014 from January 1 through August 31 [$90,000 × 0.09 × (8 ÷ 12)]. The entry and its effects on the financial statements are shown here:

Account Title	Debit	Credit
Interest Expense	5,400	
Interest Payable		5,400

	Assets	=	Liabilities			+	Stockholders' Equity			Rev.	−	Exp.	=	Net Inc.	Cash Flow
Date	Cash	=	Notes Pay.	+	Int. Pay.	+	Com. Stk.	+	Ret. Earn.						
08/31/14	NA	=	NA	+	5,400	+	NA	+	(5,400)	NA	−	5,400	=	(5,400)	NA

The second entry records HSC's cash payment for interest on August 31, 2014. This entry is an asset use transaction that reduces both the Cash and Interest Payable accounts for the total amount of interest due, $8,100 [$90,000 × 0.09 × (12 ÷ 12)]. The interest payment includes the four months' interest accrued in 2013 and the eight months accrued in 2014 ($2,700 + $5,400 = $8,100). There is no effect on the income statement because HSC recognized the interest expense in two previous journal entries. The statement of cash flows would report an $8,100 cash outflow from operating activities. The journal entry and its effects on the financial statements are shown here:

Account Title	Debit	Credit
Interest Payable	8,100	
Cash		8,100

	Assets	=	Liabilities			+	Stockholders' Equity			Rev.	−	Exp.	=	Net Inc.	Cash Flow
Date	Cash	=	Notes Pay.	+	Int. Pay.	+	Com. Stk.	+	Ret. Earn.						
08/31/14	(8,100)	=	NA	+	(8,100)	+	NA	+	NA	NA	−	NA	=	NA	(8,100) OA

The third entry on August 31, 2014, reflects repaying the principal. This entry is an asset use transaction. The Cash account and the Notes Payable account each decrease by $90,000. There is no effect on the income statement. The statement of cash flows would show a $90,000 cash outflow from financing activities. Recall that paying interest is classified as an operating activity even though repaying the principal is a financing activity. The journal entry and its effects on the financial statements are shown here:

Account Title	Debit	Credit
Notes Payable	90,000	
Cash		90,000

	Assets	=	Liabilities			+	Stockholders' Equity			Rev.	−	Exp.	=	Net Inc.	Cash Flow
Date	Cash	=	Notes Pay.	+	Int. Pay.	+	Com. Stk.	+	Ret. Earn.						
08/31/14	(90,000)	=	(90,000)	+	NA	+	NA	+	NA	NA	−	NA	=	NA	(90,000) FA

Alternatively, HSC could combine the three separate journal entries recorded on the maturity date (August 31, 2014) into a single compound journal entry as shown below:

Account Title	Debit	Credit
Interest Expense	5,400	
Interest Payable	2,700	
Notes Payable	90,000	
Cash		98,100

✓ CHECK YOURSELF 9.1

On October 1, 2013, Mellon Company issued an interest-bearing note payable to Better Banks Inc. The note had a $24,000 principal amount, a four-month term, and an annual interest rate of 4 percent. Determine the amount of interest expense and the cash outflow from operating activities Mellon will report in its 2013 and 2014 financial statements. Also provide in general journal form the adjusting entry necessary to recognize interest expense in 2013.

Answer   The computation of accrued interest expense is shown below. Unless otherwise specified, the interest rate is stated in annual terms even though the term of the note is only four months. Interest rates are commonly expressed as an annual percentage regardless of the term of the note. The *time outstanding* in the following formulas is therefore expressed as a fraction of a year. Mellon paid interest at an annual rate of 4 percent, but the note was outstanding for only 3/12 of a year in 2013 and 1/12 of a year in 2014.

2013

Principal	×	Annual interest rate	×	Time outstanding	=	Interest expense
$24,000	×	0.04	×	(3/12)	=	$240

2014

Principal	×	Annual interest rate	×	Time outstanding	=	Interest expense
$24,000	×	0.04	×	(1/12)	=	$80

Mellon will report a $320 ($240 + $80) cash outflow from operating activities for interest in 2014. The adjusting entry required to recognize accrued interest at the end of 2013 is as follows:

Interest Expense	240	
Interest Payable		240

ACCOUNTING FOR SALES TAX

Show how sales tax liabilities affect financial statements.

Most states require retail companies to collect a sales tax on items sold to their customers. The retailer collects the tax from its customers and remits the tax to the state at regular intervals. The retailer has a current liability for the amount of sales tax collected but not yet paid to the state.

To illustrate, assume Herrera Supply Company (HSC) sells merchandise to a customer for $2,000 cash in a state where the sales tax rate is 6 percent. The journal entry to record the sale and its effects on the financial statements are shown here:

Account Title	Debit	Credit
Cash	2,120	
Sales Tax Payable		120
Sales Revenue[1]		2,000

Assets	=	Liab.	+		Equity		Rev.	−	Exp.	=	Net Inc.	Cash Flow
Cash	=	Sales Tax Pay.	+	Com. Stk.	+	Ret. Earn.						
2,120	=	120	+	NA	+	2,000	2,000	−	NA	=	2,000	2,120 OA

[1]The entry to record cost of goods sold for this sale is intentionally omitted.

Remitting the tax (paying cash to the tax authority) is an asset use transaction. Both the Cash account and the Sales Tax Payable account decrease. The journal entry and its effects on the financial statements are shown here:

Account Title	Debit	Credit
Sales Tax Payable	120	
Cash		120

Assets	=	Liab.	+		Equity		Rev.	−	Exp.	=	Net Inc.	Cash Flow	
Cash	=	Sales Tax Pay.	+	Com. Stk.	+	Ret. Earn.							
(120)	=	(120)	+	NA	+	NA	NA	−	NA	=	NA	(120)	OA

CONTINGENT LIABILITIES

A **contingent liability** is a potential obligation arising from a past event. The amount or existence of the obligation depends on some future event. A pending lawsuit, for example, is a contingent liability. Depending on the outcome, a defendant company could be required to pay a large monetary settlement or could be relieved of any obligation. Generally accepted accounting principles require that companies classify contingent liabilities into three different categories depending on the likelihood of their becoming actual liabilities. The categories and the accounting for each are described below:

Define contingent liabilities and explain how they are reported in financial statements.

1. If the likelihood of a future obligation arising is *probable* (likely) and its amount can be *reasonably estimated,* a liability is recognized in the financial statements. Contingent liabilities in this category include warranties, vacation pay, and sick leave.

2. If the likelihood of a future obligation arising is *reasonably possible* but not likely or if it is probable but *cannot be reasonably estimated,* no liability is reported on the balance sheet. The potential liability is, however, disclosed in the notes to the financial statements. Contingent liabilities in this category include legal challenges, environmental damages, and government investigations.

3. If the likelihood of a future obligation arising is *remote,* no liability need be recognized in the financial statements or disclosed in the notes to the statements.[2]

Determining whether a contingent liability is probable, reasonably possible, or remote requires professional judgment. Even seasoned accountants seek the advice of attorneys, engineers, insurance agents, and government regulators before classifying significant contingent liabilities. Professional judgment is also required to distinguish between contingent liabilities and **general uncertainties.** All businesses face uncertainties such as competition and damage from floods or storms. Such uncertainties are not contingent liabilities, however, because they do not arise from past events.

Exhibit 9.1 summarizes the three categories of contingent liabilities and the accounting for each category.

[2]Companies may, if desired, voluntarily disclose contingent liabilities classified as remote.

EXHIBIT 9.1

Reporting Contingent Liabilities

```
                    Likelihood of a
                    contingent liability
                    becoming an
                    actual liability


    Probable and        Reasonably              Remote
    estimable           possible (or
                        probable but
                        not estimable)


    Recognize in the    Disclose                Need not
    financial           in the notes            recognize or
    statements          to the financial        disclose
                        statements
```

WARRANTY OBLIGATIONS

LO 4

Explain how warranty obligations affect financial statements.

To attract customers, many companies guarantee their products or services. Such guarantees are called **warranties.** Warranties take many forms. Usually, they extend for a specified period of time. Within this period, the seller promises to replace or repair defective products without charge. Although the amount and timing of warranty obligations are uncertain, warranties usually represent liabilities that must be reported in the financial statements.

To illustrate accounting for warranty obligations, assume Herrera Supply Company (HSC) had cash of $2,000, inventory of $6,000, common stock of $5,000, and retained earnings of $3,000 on January 1, 2013. The 2013 accounting period is affected by three accounting events: (1) sale of merchandise under warranty; (2) recognition of warranty obligations to customers who purchased the merchandise; and (3) settlement of a customer's warranty claim.

EVENT 1   Sale of Merchandise
HSC sold for $7,000 cash merchandise that had cost $4,000.

In the following statements model, revenue from the sale is referenced as 1a and the cost of the sale as 1b. The journal entries for the sales transaction and their effects on the financial statements are shown here:

Account Title	Debit	Credit
Cash	7,000	
Sales Revenue		7,000
Cost of Goods Sold	4,000	
Inventory		4,000

Event No.	Assets			=	Liab.	+	Equity	Rev.	−	Exp.	=	Net Inc.	Cash Flow
	Cash	+	Inventory	=			Ret. Earn.						
1a	7,000	+	NA	=	NA	+	7,000	7,000	−	NA	=	7,000	7,000 OA
1b	NA	+	(4,000)	=	NA	+	(4,000)	NA	−	4,000	=	(4,000)	NA

EVENT 2   Recognition of Warranty Expense
HSC guaranteed the merchandise sold in Event 1 to be free from defects for one year following the date of sale.

Although the exact amount of future warranty claims is unknown, HSC must inform financial statement users of the company's obligation. HSC must estimate the amount of the warranty liability and report the estimate in the 2013 financial statements. Assume the warranty obligation is estimated to be $100. Recognizing this obligation increases liabilities (warranties payable) and reduces stockholders' equity (retained earnings). Recognizing the warranty expense reduces net income. The statement of cash flows is not affected when the obligation and the corresponding expense are recognized. The journal entry and its effects on the financial statements are shown here:

Account Title	Debit	Credit
Warranty Expense	100	
Warranties Payable		100

Event No.	Assets	=	Liab.	+	Equity	Rev.	−	Exp.	=	Net Inc.	Cash Flow
			Warr. Pay.	+	Ret. Earn.						
2	NA	=	100	+	(100)	NA	−	100	=	(100)	NA

EVENT 3   Settlement of Warranty Obligation
HSC paid $40 cash to repair defective merchandise returned by a customer.

The cash payment for the repair is not an expense. Warranty expense was recognized in the period in which the sale was made (when the Warranties Payable account was credited). The payment reduces an asset (cash) and a liability (warranties payable). The income statement is not affected by the repairs payment. However, there is a $40 cash outflow reported in the operating activities section of the statement of cash flows. The journal entry and its effects on the financial statements are shown here:

Account Title	Debit	Credit
Warranties Payable	40	
Cash		40

Event No.	Assets	=	Liab.	+	Equity	Rev.	−	Exp.	=	Net Inc.	Cash Flow
	Cash	=	Warr. Pay.	+	Ret. Earn.						
3	(40)	=	(40)	+	NA	NA	−	NA	=	NA	(40) OA

General Ledger T-Accounts and Financial Statements

Panel A of Exhibit 9.2 summarizes the 2013 accounting events. Panel B presents the ledger accounts in T-account form. The event numbers are shown parenthetically in the T-accounts to facilitate your review. The closing entries are included and referenced with the abbreviation "cl." The financial statements are shown in Panel C of the exhibit. You should study Exhibit 9.2 to strengthen your understanding of how the warranty events affect the financial statements.

EXHIBIT 9.2

The Big Picture

Panel A: Transaction Summary

1. Sold merchandise that cost $4,000 for $7,000 cash.
2. Recognized a $100 warranty obligation and the corresponding expense.
3. Paid $40 to satisfy a warranty claim.
4. Closed the revenue and expense accounts (referenced cl.).

Panel B: General Ledger

Assets			=	Liabilities			+	Equity	

Cash

Bal.	2,000	40	(3)
(1a)	7,000		
Bal.	8,960		

Inventory

Bal.	6,000	4,000	(1b)
Bal.	2,000		

Warranties Payable

(3)	40	100	(2)
		60	Bal.

Common Stock

	5,000	Bal.

Retained Earnings

	3,000	Bal.
	2,900	(cl.)
	5,900	Bal.

Sales Revenue

(cl.)	7,000	7,000	(1a)
	0	Bal.	

Cost of Goods Sold

(1b)	4,000	4,000	(cl.)
		Bal.	0

Warranty Expense

(2)	100	100	(cl.)
Bal.	0		

Panel C: Financial Statements for 2013

Income Statement		Balance Sheet		Statement of Cash Flows	
Sales revenue	$7,000	Assets		**Operating Activities**	
Cost of goods sold	(4,000)	Cash	$ 8,960	Inflow from customers	$7,000
Gross margin	3,000	Inventory	2,000	Outflow for warranty	(40)
Warranty expense	(100)	Total assets	$10,960	Net Inflow from	
Net income	$2,900	Liabilities		Operating activities	6,960
		Warranties payable	$ 60	**Investing Activities**	0
		Stockholders' equity		**Financing Activities**	0
		Common stock	5,000	Net change in cash	6,960
		Retained earnings	5,900	Plus: Beginning cash balance	2,000
		Total liab. and stockholders' equity	$10,960	Ending cash balance	$8,960

The transaction data in the T-accounts for events 1 through 3 are referenced by event number shown in parentheses. Event 4 is referenced with the letters *cl* indicating that journal entry is for closing the accounts.

✓ CHECK YOURSELF 9.2

Flotation Systems Inc. (FSI) began operations in 2013. Its sales were $360,000 in 2013 and $410,000 in 2014. FSI estimates the cost of its one-year product warranty will be 2 percent of sales. Actual cash payments for warranty claims amounted to $5,400 during 2013 and $8,500 during 2014. Prepare the journal entries required to record warranty expense and cash paid to settle warranty claims for 2013 and 2014. Determine the amount of warranties payable FSI would report on its 2013 and 2014 year-end balance sheets.

Answer   Journal Entries for 2013

Account Title	Debit	Credit
Warranty Expense ($360,000 × .02)	7,200	
Warranties Payable		7,200
Warranties Payable	5,400	
Cash		5,400

Journal Entries for 2014

Account Title	Debit	Credit
Warranty Expense ($410,000 × .02)	8,200	
Warranties Payable		8,200
Warranties Payable	8,500	
Cash*		8,500

*The 2014 cash payment exceeds the 2014 accrued expense because some of the warranty expense accrued in 2013 was actually paid in 2014.

FSI would report Warranties Payable on the December 31, 2013, balance sheet of $1,800 ($7,200 − $5,400). Warranties Payable on the December 31, 2014, balance sheet is $1,500 ($1,800 + $8,200 − $8,500).

ACCOUNTING FOR PAYROLL

If you've had a job, you know the amount of your paycheck is less than the amount of your salary. Employers are required to withhold part of each employee's earnings. The money withheld is used to pay such items as income taxes, union dues, and medical insurance premiums for which the *employee* is responsible. The *employer* is also required to make matching payments for certain items such as social security and to pay additional amounts for unemployment taxes. This section of the chapter explains how employers account for *employee withholdings* as well as *employer payroll expenses*.

Determine payroll taxes and explain how they affect financial statements.

Identifying Employees

Businesses use the services of independent contractors as well as employees. They must distinguish between the two because payroll taxes apply only to employees. When a business supervises, directs, and controls an individual's work, the individual is an **employee** of the business. When a business pays an individual for specific services, but the individual supervises and controls the work, then that individual is an **independent contractor.**

REALITY BYTES

Many of the items we purchase come with a manufacturer's warranty, but companies that sell electronics and electrical appliances often offer to sell you an extended warranty that provides protection after the manufacturer's warranty has expired. Why do they offer this option to customers, and how do these warranties differ from the standard manufactures' warranties?

Companies such as Best Buy offer to sell customers extended warranties because they make a significant profit on them. If you buy an extended warranty from Best Buy, the retailer is not actually the one who is promising to repair your product; that will be done by a third party. Best Buy simply receives a commission for selling the warranty. In its 2010 fiscal-year such commissions accounted for 2.0 percent of the company's total revenues, and since it had to incur very little expense to earn these revenues, they are mostly profit.

The typical manufacturer's warranty, as you have learned in this chapter, is an expense recognized at the time of the sale. However, companies that provide extended warranties must recognize the warranty revenue over the life of the warranty, not immediately upon sale. Remember, this is referring to the third-party warranty provider, not Best Buy. Since Best Buy is simply earning a commission from selling the warranty, it gets to recognize all of the revenue at the time of the sale.

The distinction between independent contractor and employee depends upon control and supervision rather than the type of work performed. A company's chief financial officer (CFO) is a company *employee;* the company's outside auditor is an *independent contractor.* Although both individuals provide accounting services, the company controls the CFO's work while the auditor is independent. If a business hired Randy Moats's company (see The Curious Accountant at the start of the chapter) for plumbing services, Randy would be an independent contractor with respect to his customer. Randy's workers, however, are employees of Randy's plumbing company.

Employees' Gross Earnings

The compensation earned by employees who are paid based on the number of hours they work is normally called **wages.** The compensation earned by employees who are paid a set amount per week, month, or other earnings period regardless of the number of hours worked is normally called **salaries.** The total amount of wages or salaries earned, before any deductions for withholding, represents employees' **gross earnings.** Gross earnings is the sum of regular pay plus any bonuses, overtime, or other additions.

Deductions from Employees' Gross Earnings

Employers withhold money from employees' gross earnings. Employers are obligated (have liabilities) to pay the funds withheld on behalf of the employees. Employers determine each employee's net pay (cash paid to the employee) by *deducting* the withholdings from the gross earnings. This section of the chapter introduces common withholdings.

Federal Income Taxes

To help the federal government collect income taxes due on a timely basis, the tax laws adopted by Congress require employers to withhold income taxes from employee earnings. The employers then pay the withheld taxes directly to the government.

For example, assume an employee earns $2,000. Assume further the employee owes $300 of income tax on these earnings. On payday, the employer withholds $300 of the earnings and pays the employee $1,700 cash. The employer then has a $300 liability (obligation) to the federal government for the income tax withheld. The employer will use the money withheld to pay the employee's federal income tax liability. The journal entry to record paying the employee and its effects on the financial statements are shown here:

Account Title	Debit	Credit
Salary Expense	2,000	
Employee Income Tax Payable		300
Cash		1,700

Assets	=	Liab.	+		Equity			Rev.	−	Exp.	=	Net Inc.	Cash Flow
Cash	=	EIT Pay.	+	Com. Stk.	+	Ret. Earn.							
(1,700)	=	300	+	NA	+	(2,000)		NA	−	2,000	=	(2,000)	(1,700) OA

When the employer pays the liability, both cash and liabilities will decrease. The income statement will not be affected. The statement of cash flows will show a cash outflow from operating activities. The journal entry and its effects on the financial statements are shown here:

Account Title	Debit	Credit
Employee Income Tax Payable	300	
Cash		300

Assets	=	Liab.	+		Equity			Rev.	−	Exp.	=	Net Inc.	Cash Flow
Cash	=	EIT Pay.	+	Com. Stk.	+	Ret. Earn.							
(300)	=	(300)	+	NA	+	NA		NA	−	NA	=	NA	(300) OA

The federal tax laws require employers to withhold funds for employee Social Security (FICA) taxes and Medicare taxes as well as income taxes. Employers may also be required to withhold amounts to pay state, county, and municipal government taxes from employees' paychecks. These withholdings have the same effects on the financial statements as those described above for federal income taxes.

Federal Income Tax Documents

The amount withheld from an employee's salary depends on the employee's *gross pay* and the number of *withholding allowances* the employee claims. Each allowance reduces the amount the employer must withhold. Employees are generally allowed to claim one allowance for themselves and one for each legal dependent. For example, a married person with two dependent children could claim four allowances (the employee, the dependent spouse, and the two dependent children). Exhibit 9.3 shows an **Employee's Withholding Allowance Certificate, Form W-4,** the form used to document the number of allowances claimed by an employee.

The federal government provides tax withholding tables that indicate the amount to withhold for any amount of earnings and any number of allowances. At the end of the calendar year, the employer must notify each employee of the amount of his or her gross earnings for the year and of the amounts the employer withheld. Employers provide this information to employees on a **Wage and Tax Statement, Form W-2,** illustrated

EXHIBIT 9.3

Employee's Withholding Allowance Certificate Form W-4

Cut here and give Form W-4 to your employer. Keep the top part for your records.

Form **W-4**	**Employee's Withholding Allowance Certificate**	OMB No. 1545-0074
Department of the Treasury Internal Revenue Service	▶ Whether you are entitled to claim a certain number of allowances or exemption from withholding is subject to review by the IRS. Your employer may be required to send a copy of this form to the IRS.	2011

1 Type or print your first name and middle initial. Last name	2 Your social security number

Home address (number and street or rural route)	3 ☐ Single ☐ Married ☐ Married, but withhold at higher Single rate. **Note.** If married, but legally separated, or spouse is a nonresident alien, check the "Single" box.
City or town, state, and ZIP code	4 If your last name differs from that shown on your social security card, check here. You must call 1-800-772-1213 for a replacement card. ▶ ☐

5	Total number of allowances you are claiming (from line **H** above **or** from the applicable worksheet on page 2)	**5**	
6	Additional amount, if any, you want withheld from each paycheck	**6**	$
7	I claim exemption from withholding for 2011, and I certify that I meet **both** of the following conditions for exemption.		
	• Last year I had a right to a refund of **all** federal income tax withheld because I had **no** tax liability **and**		
	• This year I expect a refund of **all** federal income tax withheld because I expect to have **no** tax liability.		
	If you meet both conditions, write "Exempt" here . . . . ▶	**7**	

Under penalties of perjury, I declare that I have examined this certificate and to the best of my knowledge and belief, it is true, correct, and complete.

Employee's signature
(Form is not valid unless you sign it.) ▶ _____   Date ▶

8 Employer's name and address (Employer: Complete lines 8 and 10 only if sending to the IRS.)	9 Office code (optional)	10 Employer identification number (EIN)

For Privacy Act and Paperwork Reduction Act Notice, see page 2.	Cat. No. 10220Q	Form **W-4** (2011)

---

in Exhibit 9.4. The employer sends one copy of form W-2 to the Internal Revenue Service and other copies to the employee.

Employers are required to file the **Employer's Quarterly Federal Tax Return, Form 941** no later than one month after each quarter ends. This form reports the amounts due and paid to the government for federal withholdings. Failure to pay withheld taxes in a timely manner is serious. The government has the right to impose significant penalties and can even close a business, seize its assets, and take legal action against those who fail to pay taxes due.

Social Security and Medicare Taxes (FICA)

Congress adopted the Federal Insurance Contributions Act (FICA) to provide funding for the Social Security and Medicare programs. **Social Security** provides qualified individuals with old age, survivor's, and disability insurance (OASDI); **Medicare** provides

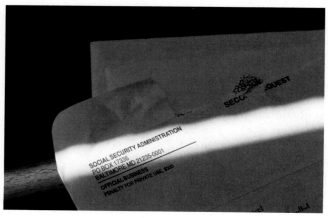

health insurance. During their working years, employees pay a percentage of their earnings (up to a specified limit) to the federal government for Social Security. At retirement, a qualified person is entitled to receive monthly Social Security payments. Workers who become disabled before retirement are eligible to receive disability benefits. If a worker or retired person dies, any legal dependents are eligible to receive survivor benefits.

In order to meet the required benefit payments, Congress has frequently increased the FICA tax rates and the amount of earnings to which the rates apply. Future changes in FICA tax rates and earnings maximums are likely. These changes will affect only the amount of FICA taxes, however, not how to account for them. *To simplify computations*

EXHIBIT 9.4

Wage and Tax Statement Form W-2

22222	Void ☐	a Employee's social security number	For Official Use Only ▶ OMB No. 1545-0008	

b Employer identification number (EIN)	1 Wages, tips, other compensation	2 Federal income tax withheld
c Employer's name, address, and ZIP code	3 Social security wages	4 Social security tax withheld
	5 Medicare wages and tips	6 Medicare tax withheld
	7 Social security tips	8 Allocated tips
d Control number	9 Advance EIC payment	10 Dependent care benefits
e Employee's first name and initial / Last name / Suff.	11 Nonqualified plans	12a See instructions for box 12
	13 Statutory employee ☐ Retirement plan ☐ Third-party sick pay ☐	12b
	14 Other	12c
		12d
f Employee's address and ZIP code		

15 State Employer's state ID number	16 State wages, tips, etc.	17 State income tax	18 Local wages, tips, etc.	19 Local income tax	20 Locality name

Form W-2 **Wage and Tax Statement** **2011**

Department of the Treasury—Internal Revenue Service

Copy A For Social Security Administration — Send this entire page with Form W-3 to the Social Security Administration; photocopies are **not** acceptable.

For Privacy Act and Paperwork Reduction Act Notice, see back of Copy D.

Cat. No. 10134D

Do Not Cut, Fold, or Staple Forms on This Page — Do Not Cut, Fold, or Staple Forms on This Page

this text assumes a Social Security rate of 6 percent on the first $110,000 of income and a Medicare rate of 1.5 percent on all earnings.[3] For example, an employee earning $100,000 per year will have the following FICA taxes withheld from his or her salary:

Social Security	$100,000	×	6.0%	=	$6,000
Medicare	100,000	×	1.5%	=	1,500
Total withheld					$7,500

Not only employees are required to pay FICA taxes; the FICA legislation requires employers to pay a matching amount. The total FICA tax paid to the federal government for an employee earning $100,000 per year is $15,000 ($7,500 × 2), half paid by the employee and half paid by the employer. We discuss accounting for employer taxes later in the chapter.

Voluntary Withholdings (Deductions)

One reason governments require employers to withhold taxes from employee earnings is that many people have difficulty managing their spending. If employees received their gross earnings amount, they might not be able to pay their taxes because they would spend the money on other things first. Many people have this tendency with regard to

[3]The actual rates are 6.2% and 1.45%.

other spending responsibilities as well. To ensure they make important payments, they voluntarily allow their employer to withhold money from their salaries. The employer then uses the money withheld to make payment in the employees' names for such items as medical insurance premiums, union dues, charitable contributions, and contributions to private retirement funds or savings accounts. Even employees who manage their personal finances without difficulty find it convenient to allow their employers to withhold funds and make payments on their behalf.

Withholding voluntary deductions from an employee's gross earnings represents a service on the employer's part. The employer must deduct the amounts authorized by each employee and remit the withheld money to the proper recipients. The employer must maintain additional records and undertake additional transactions to ensure the proper amounts are withheld and paid as specified on a timely basis. Employers normally itemize all deductions from gross pay on the pay stub to explain how an employee's net pay was determined.

Computing Employee Net Pay

Net pay is the employee's gross earnings less all deductions (withholdings). Net pay, often called take-home pay, is the amount of cash the employee receives from the employer.

To illustrate assume that Herrera Supply Company (HSC) has an employee named Sarah Jennings. Ms. Jennings earns a monthly salary of $6,000. Based on Ms. Jennings's Form W-4, the tax tables require withholding $450 per month for income taxes. Since Ms. Jennings earns less than $110,000 per year, her full monthly salary is subject to FICA withholdings. Ms. Jennings has authorized HSC to deduct $320 per month for medical insurance and $25 per month for a charitable contribution to the American Cancer Society. Ms. Jennings' net pay is computed as follows:

Gross monthly salary		$6,000
Deductions		
Federal income taxes	$450	
FICA Tax—Social Security ($6,000 × 6%)	360	
FICA Tax—Medicare ($6,000 × 1.5%)	90	
Medical insurance premiums	320	
American Cancer Society	25	
Total deductions		1,245
Net pay		$4,755

The journal entry to recognize salary expense for Ms. Jennings and its effects on HSC's financial statements are shown here:

Account Title	Debit	Credit
Salary Expense	6,000	
Employee Income Tax Payable		450
FICA Tax—Social Security Payable		360
FICA Tax—Medicare Payable		90
Medical Insurance Premiums Payable		320
American Cancer Society Payable		25
Cash		4,755

Assets =	Liab.	+	Equity		Rev.	−	Exp.	= Net Inc.	Cash Flow	
Cash	= Various Payables	+ Com. Stk.	+ Ret. Earn.							
(4,755) =	1,245	+ NA	+ (6,000)		NA	−	6,000	= (6,000)	(4,755)	OA

Employer Payroll Taxes

As mentioned above, employers are required to match employees' FICA taxes, and FICA tax rates are subject to change. This text uses the same assumed tax rates for employers as it uses for employees. *Assume a Social Security rate of 6% on the first $110,000 of each employee's earnings and a Medicare rate of 1.5% on all earnings.* The employers' portion of FICA taxes is a payroll tax expense to the employer.

Employers also incur a payroll tax expense for *unemployment* taxes. Congress adopted the **Federal Unemployment Tax Act (FUTA)** to finance temporary relief to qualified *unemployed* persons. The tax is determined by multiplying the wages of employees (up to a specified maximum limit) by a specified rate. The FUTA tax provides money to both state and federal government workforce agencies. States may enact supplemental unemployment tax laws based on higher maximum earnings or tax rates and could assess employees, rather than employers, for all or part of the supplemental coverage.

As of January 2011, the unemployment tax rate was 6.2 percent of the first $7,000 of wages earned by each employee during a calendar year. FUTA allows employers a credit of up to 5.4 percent for amounts paid to a state unemployment program, leaving a rate of .8 percent to be paid to the federal government. For example, on a tax of $434 (6.2% × $7,000), an employer would pay $56 (.8% × $7,000) to the federal government and $378 (5.4% × $7,000) to the state government. State governments receive a larger percentage because they are responsible for administering the unemployment programs. The rates may be reduced to reward employers with few or no unemployment claims.

Recording and Reporting Payroll Taxes

To illustrate computing employer payroll tax expense, return to HSC's employee, Ms. Jennings, who earns $6,000 per month. HSC's February payroll tax expense for Ms. Jennings is computed as follows:

FICA tax expense—Social Security ($6,000 × 6%)	$360
FICA tax expense—Medicare ($6,000 × 1.5%)	90
Federal unemployment tax expense ($1,000 × .8%)	8
State unemployment tax expense ($1,000 × 5.4%)	54
Total payroll tax expense	$512

The unemployment taxes apply only to the first $7,000 of income earned each year by each employee. Since Ms. Jennings earned $6,000 in January, unemployment tax only applies to $1,000 of her February salary. The journal entry to record the payroll tax expense and its effects on the financial statements are shown here:

Account Title	Debit	Credit
Payroll Tax Expense	512	
FICA Tax—Social Security Payable		360
FICA Tax—Medicare Payable		90
Federal Unemployment Tax Payable		8
State Unemployment Tax Payable		54

Assets	=	Liab.	+		Equity		Rev.	−	Exp.	=	Net Inc.	Cash Flow
Cash	=	Various Payables	+	Com. Stk.	+	Ret. Earn.						
NA	=	512	+	NA	+	(512)	NA	−	512	=	(512)	NA

Employee Fringe Benefits

In addition to salaries and wages, many employers provide their employees with a variety of fringe benefits such as paid vacations, sick leave, maternity leave, and medical, dental, life, and disability insurance. These benefits plus payroll taxes frequently amount to as much as 25% of the employees' gross salaries and wages. Fringe benefits are reported as expenses on the income statement.

To illustrate, assume HSC provides the following fringe benefits to an employee, Alice Worthington, who earns approximately $200 per day. Ms. Worthington earns one day of vacation for each month she works. HSC pays $250 per month for Ms. Worthington's medical insurance and contributes $150 per month to a pension (retirement) program for Ms. Worthington. The monthly entry to record the accrued fringe benefits expenses and its effects on the financial statements are shown here:

Account Title	Debit	Credit
Vacation Pay Expense	200	
Employee Medical Insurance Expense	250	
Employee Pension Expense	150	
Vacation Pay Payable		200
Employee Medical Insurance Payable		250
Employee Pension Liability		150

Assets	=	Liab.	+		Equity		Rev.	−	Exp.	=	Net Inc.	Cash Flow
Cash	=	Various Payables	+	Com. Stk.	+	Ret. Earn.						
NA	=	600	+	NA	+	(600)	NA	−	600	=	(600)	NA

- -

THE FINANCIAL ANALYST

CURRENT VERSUS NONCURRENT

LO 6

Prepare a classified balance sheet.

Because meeting obligations on time is critical to business survival, financial analysts and creditors are interested in whether companies will have enough money available to pay bills when they are due. Most businesses provide information about their bill-paying ability by classifying their assets and liabilities according to liquidity. The more quickly an asset is converted to cash or consumed, the more *liquid* it is. Assets are usually divided

Answers to The Curious Accountant

As the chapter has explained, not only do employees have 7.65% of their wages withheld for Social Security taxes, but the employer also must pay 7.65%, which is $1.53 per hour for someone being paid $20 per hour. Additionally, federal and state unemployment insurance taxes must be paid. While the amount paid varies from company to company even in a given state, a rate of 2.5% is not uncommon, which comes to $.50 per hour. Randy may also be contributing to his employees' 401(k) retirement funds. According to a study by the United States Chamber of Commerce released in March 2009, the average retirement costs incurred by small businesses were $2,694 per employee. Based on a 40 hour week, this would cost Randy $1.30 per hour, or 6.15% of his employees' wages. The same Chamber of Commerce study found that the average health care costs incurred by small businesses were $4,559 per employee. At this rate, Randy would be paying around $2.19, or 11% of wages, per hour for health care benefits. Employers' must also carry workers compensation insurance on their employees. This cost varies widely by state and type of job, but a study in the January/February 2008 issue of *Workers Compensation Policy Review* reported an average rate of 2.88%. This would amount to $.58 per hour for Randy's employees.

The costs included here would increase Randy's per hour cost by around $6.10, or 30% of the employees' base wages, and we have not even considered the costs of vacation time and sick leave. These figures also assume Randy's workers are working "billable hours" for 40 hours per week. Obviously this is not possible since plumbers must travel from job to job. The $20 markup Randy was charging his customers ($40 − $20) has to pay for these nonbillable hours as well as for the fringe benefits, other operating expenses, and, he hopes, a profit.

---

into two major classifications: *current* and *noncurrent*. Current items are also referred to as *short term* and noncurrent items as *long term*.

A **current (short-term) asset** is expected to be converted to cash or consumed within one year or an operating cycle, whichever is longer. An **operating cycle** is defined as the average time it takes a business to convert cash to inventory, inventory to accounts receivable, and accounts receivable back to cash. The financial tools used to measure the length of an operating cycle for particular businesses are discussed in Chapter 7. For most businesses, the operating cycle is less than one year. As a result, the one-year rule normally prevails with respect to classifying assets as current. The current assets section of a balance sheet typically includes the following items:

> Current Assets
>   Cash
>   Marketable securities
>   Accounts receivable
>   Short-term notes receivable
>   Interest receivable
>   Inventory
>   Supplies
>   Prepaid items

Given the definition of current assets, it seems reasonable to assume that **current (short-term) liabilities** would be those due within one year or an operating cycle, whichever is longer. This assumption is usually correct. However, an exception is made for long-term renewable debt. For example, consider a liability that was issued with a 20-year term to maturity. After 19 years, the liability becomes due within one year and is, therefore, a current liability. Even so, the liability will be classified as long term if the company plans to issue new long-term debt and to use the proceeds from that debt to repay the maturing liability. This situation is described as *refinancing short-term debt on a long-term basis.* In general, if a business does not plan to use any of its current assets to repay a debt, that debt is listed as long term even if it is due within one year. The current liabilities section of a balance sheet typically includes the following items:

> Current Liabilities
>   Accounts payable
>   Short-term notes payable
>   Wages payable
>   Taxes payable
>   Interest payable

Balance sheets that distinguish between current and noncurrent items are called **classified balance sheets.** To enhance the usefulness of accounting information, most real-world balance sheets are classified. Exhibit 9.5 displays an example of a classified balance sheet.

EXHIBIT 9.5

LIMBAUGH COMPANY
Classified Balance Sheet
As of December 31, 2013

Assets

Current Assets

Cash		$ 20,000	
Accounts receivable		35,000	
Inventory		230,000	
Prepaid rent		3,600	
Total current assets			$288,600
Property, Plant, and Equipment			
Office equipment	$ 80,000		
Less: Accumulated depreciation	(25,000)	55,000	
Building	340,000		
Less: Accumulated depreciation	(40,000)	300,000	
Land		120,000	
Total property, plant, and equipment			475,000
Total assets			$763,600

Liabilities and Stockholders' Equity

Current Liabilities

Accounts payable		$ 32,000	
Notes payable		120,000	
Salaries payable		32,000	
Unearned revenue		9,800	
Total current liabilities			$193,800
Long-Term Liabilities			
Note payable			100,000
Total liabilities			293,800
Stockholders' Equity			
Common stock		200,000	
Retained earnings		269,800	469,800
Total liabilities and stockholders' equity			$763,600

LIQUIDITY VERSUS SOLVENCY

LO 7

Use the current ratio to assess the level of liquidity.

Liquidity describes the ability to generate sufficient short-term cash flows to pay obligations as they come due. **Solvency** is the ability to repay liabilities in the long run. Liquidity and solvency are both important to the survival of a business. Financial analysts rely on several ratios to help them evaluate a company's liquidity and solvency. The *debt to assets* ratio introduced in Chapter 3 is one tool used to measure solvency. The primary ratio used to evaluate liquidity is the current ratio.

The **current ratio** is defined as

$$\frac{\text{Current assets}}{\text{Current liabities}}$$

Since current assets normally exceed current liabilities, this ratio is usually greater than 100 percent. For example, if a company has $250 in current assets and $100 in current liabilities, current assets are 250 percent of current liabilities. The current ratio is traditionally expressed as a decimal rather than as a percentage, however; most analysts would describe this example as a current ratio of 2.5 to 1 ($250 ÷ $100 = $2.50 in current assets for every $1 in current liabilities). This book uses the traditional format when referring to the current ratio.

The current ratio is among the most widely used ratios in analyzing financial statements. Current ratios can be too high as well as too low. A low ratio suggests that the company may have difficulty paying its short-term obligations. A high ratio suggests

FOCUS ON INTERNATIONAL ISSUES

WHY ARE THESE BALANCE SHEETS BACKWARD?

As discussed in earlier chapters, most industrialized countries require companies to use international financial accounting standards (IFRS), which are similar to the GAAP used in the United States. The globalization of accounting standards should, therefore, make it easier to read a company's annual report regardless of its country or origin. However, there are still language differences between companies; German companies prepare their financial reports using IFRS, but in German, while the UK companies use English.

Suppose language is not an issue. For example companies in the United States, the United Kingdom (U.K.), and even India, prepare their annual reports in English. Thus, one would expect to find few differences between financial reports prepared by companies in these countries. However, if a person who learned accounting in the United States looks at the balance sheet of a U.K. company he or she might think the statement is a bit "backwards," and if he or she reviews the balance sheet of an Indian company they may find it to be upside down.

Like U.S. companies, U.K. companies report assets at the top, or left, of the balance sheet, and liabilities and stockholders' equity on the bottom or right. However, unlike the United States, English companies typically show long-term assets before current assets. Even more different are balance sheets of Indian companies, which begin with stockholders' equity and then liabilities at the top or left, and then show assets on the bottom or right. Like the U.K. statements, those in India show long-term assets before current assets. Realize that most of the accounting rules established by IFRS or U.S. GAAP deal with measurement issues. Assets can be measured using the same rules, but be disclosed in different manners. IFRS require companies to classify assets and liabilities as current versus noncurrent, but the order in which these categories are listed on the balance sheet is not specified.

For an example of financial statement for a U.K. company, go to **www.itvplc.com**. Click on "Investors" and then "Reports and accounts." For an example of an Indian company's annual report, go to **www.tatamoters.co.in**. Click on "Investors," then "Financials and Filings," and then on "Annual Reports."

TATA MOTORS
65th Annual Report 2009-2010

that a company is not maximizing its earnings potential because investments in liquid assets usually do not earn as much money as investments in other assets. Companies must try to maintain an effective balance between liquid assets (so they can pay bills on time) and nonliquid assets (so they can earn a good return).

Real-World Data

Exhibit 9.6 presents the current ratios and debt to assets ratios for six companies in three different industries. These data are for the 2010 fiscal years.

EXHIBIT 9.6

Industry	Company	Current Ratio	Debt to Assets Ratio
Electric utilities	American Electric Power	0.77	0.73
	Dominion Resources	0.94	0.71
Clothing stores	American Eagle Outfitters	3.03	0.28
	The Gap	1.87	0.42
Building supplies	Home Depot	1.33	0.53
	Lowe's	1.40	0.46

Which of these companies has the highest level of financial risk? Perhaps American Electric Power because it has the highest debt to assets ratio. The electric utilities have higher debt to assets ratios and lower current ratios than those of the companies in the building supplies business. Does this mean that electric utilities are riskier investments? Not necessarily; since the companies are in different industries, the ratios may not be comparable. Utility companies have a more stable revenue base than building companies. If the economy turns downward, people are likely to continue to use electricity. However, they are less likely to buy a new home or to add on to their existing home. Because utility companies have a stable source of revenue, creditors are likely to feel comfortable with higher levels of debt for them than they would for building companies. As previously stated, the industry must be considered when interpreting ratios. American Eagle Outfitters appears to have the lowest financial risk based on its debt to assets ratio being lowest and its current ratio being the highest. Finally, note that the debt to assets ratios tend to be grouped by industry.

 # A Look Back

Chapter 9 discussed accounting for current liabilities and payroll. Current liabilities are obligations due within one year or the company's operating cycle, whichever is longer. The chapter expanded the discussion of promissory notes begun in Chapter 7. Chapter 7 introduced accounting for the note payee, the lender; Chapter 9 discussed accounting for the note maker (issuer), the borrower. Notes payable and related interest payable are reported as liabilities on the balance sheet. Chapter 9 also discussed accounting for sales tax liabilities, warranty obligations, and contingent liabilities.

Payroll costs and payroll taxes constitute a major expense for most businesses. An employer is responsible for withholding money from an employee's salary. The most common withholdings are for federal income taxes, FICA taxes, insurance premiums, savings or retirement contributions, union dues, and charitable donations. The employer uses the withholdings to pay the employees' obligations. The difference between the *gross pay* and the money withheld is called net pay. The *net pay* is the amount of cash the employer pays to the employee.

In addition to making payments for its employees, the employer is responsible for certain taxes on its employees' salaries and wages. These taxes are called payroll taxes. They include matching FICA Social Security and Medicare taxes, and federal and state unemployment taxes. Governments periodically change the rates of these taxes. The accounting for them, however, is not affected by rate changes. The rates used in this text are as follows: FICA Social Security—6 percent of the first $110,000 of each employee's wages with a matching payment for the employer; FICA Medicare—1.5 percent of the total wages of each employee with a matching payment for the employer; federal unemployment taxes—.8 percent (6.2 percent less a 5.4 percent credit for state unemployment taxes) of the first $7,000 of each employee's wages; and state unemployment—5.4 percent of the first $7,000 of each employee's wages.

Finally, Chapter 9 discussed assessing companies' liquidity. The current ratio is current assets divided by current liabilities. The higher the current ratio, the more liquid the business.

A Look Forward

Chapter 10 investigates issues related to accounting for long-term liabilities. As you will learn, income tax consequences enter into decisions to borrow money.

APPENDIX

Accounting for Discount Notes

All notes payable discussed previously have been "add-on" **interest-bearing notes.** The amount due at maturity for add-on notes is the *face value* of the note *plus accrued interest.* In contrast, the interest on a **discount note** is included in the face value of the note. A $5,000 face value discount note is repaid with $5,000 cash at maturity. This payment includes both principal and accrued interest.

Show how discount notes and related interest charges affect financial statements.

Accounting Events Affecting 2013

To illustrate, assume Beacon Management Services experienced the following events.

EVENT 1   Borrowed Money by Issuing a Discount Note
Beacon Management Services was started when it issued a $10,000 face value discount note to State Bank on March 1, 2013.

The note had a 9 percent *discount rate* and a one-year term to maturity. As with interest-bearing notes, the *issuer* of a discount note exchanges the promissory note for cash. Accounting for the discount note requires dividing the face amount between the **discount** and the **principal,** or **proceeds** (amount of cash borrowed). The discount is computed by multiplying the face value of the note by the interest rate by the time period. Subtracting the discount from the face value of the note determines the principal (proceeds). The computations follow:

Face value of note	$10,000
Less discount ($10,000 × 0.09 × 1) =	900
Proceeds (amount borrowed)	$ 9,100

On the issue date, both assets and liabilities increase by the amount borrowed (the $9,100 principal). The borrowing transaction on the issue date has no effect on the income statement. The $9,100 cash inflow is reported in the financing activities section of the statement of cash flows. The journal entry to record issuing the discount note and its effects on the financial statements are shown here:

Account Title	Debit	Credit
Cash	9,100	
Discount on Notes Payable	900	
Notes Payable		10,000

Event No.	Assets	=	Liabilities			+	Equity			Rev.	–	Exp.	=	Net Inc.	Cash Flow
	Cash	=	Notes Pay.	–	Disc. on N/P	+	Com. Stk.	+	Ret. Earn.						
1	9,100	=	10,000	–	900	+	NA	+	NA	NA	–	NA	=	NA	9,100 FA

The discount is recorded in a **contra liability account** called **Discount on Notes Payable.** The *carrying value* of the liability is the difference between the Notes Payable and Discount accounts. Carrying value, also called *book value,* is the amount at which the liability is carried on the books. In this case, the Notes Payable account in Beacon's ledger has a $10,000 credit balance and the Discount on Notes Payable account has a $900 debit balance. The carrying value on the issue date is as follows:

Notes payable	$10,000
Discount on notes payable	(900)
Carrying value of liability	$ 9,100

EVENT 2   Recognized Operating Expenses
Beacon incurred $8,000 of cash operating expenses.

Paying these expenses reduces both assets and stockholders' equity. The effect on the income statement is to increase expenses and decrease net income. The cash outflow is reported in the operating activities section of the statement of cash flows. The journal entry and its effects on the financial statements are shown here:

Account Title	Debit	Credit
Operating Expenses	8,000	
Cash		8,000

Event No.	Assets	=	Liabilities			+	Equity			Rev.	–	Exp.	=	Net Inc.	Cash Flow
	Cash	=	Notes Pay.	–	Disc. on N/P	+	Com. Stk.	+	Ret. Earn.						
2	(8,000)	=	NA	–	NA	+	NA	+	(8,000)	NA	–	(8,000)	=	(8,000)	(8,000) OA

EVENT 3   Recognized Revenue
Beacon recognized $12,000 of cash service revenue.

Recognizing revenue increases both assets and stockholders' equity. Net income increases. The cash inflow is reported in the operating activities section of the statement of cash flows. The journal entry and its effects on the financial statements are shown here:

Account Title	Debit	Credit
Cash	12,000	
Service Revenue		12,000

Event No.	Assets =		Liabilities	+		Equity		Rev. −	Exp. =	Net Inc.	Cash Flow
	Cash =	Notes Pay. −	Disc. on N/P +		Com. Stk. +	Ret. Earn.					
3	12,000 =	NA −	NA +		NA +	12,000	12,000 −	NA =	12,000	12,000 OA

EVENT 4   Recognized Accrued Interest
Beacon recorded an adjusting entry to recognize interest accrued since March 1.

On December 31, 2013, Beacon must adjust its accounting records to recognize the 10 months of interest expense it incurred in 2013. For this note, interest expense accrues at $75 per month ($900 discount ÷ 12). As of December 31, $750 ($75 × 10) of interest expense has accrued. Since no cash payment is due until the note matures in 2014, the reduction in equity from recognizing the interest expense is accompanied by an increase in liabilities.

The increase in liabilities is recorded by *reducing the contra liability account,* Discount on Notes Payable. Recall that the carrying value of the liability was $9,100 on the day the note was issued. The adjusting entry to record the accrued interest expense removes $750 from the Discount account, leaving a discount balance of $150 ($900 − $750) after the adjusting entry is posted.

The bookkeeping technique of converting the discount to interest expense over the term of the loan is described as **amortizing** the discount. After amortizing 10 months' interest expense, the carrying value of the liability reported on the December 31, 2013, balance sheet (see Exhibit 9.7) is $9,850 ($10,000 face value − $150 discount). The effect of the interest recognition on the income statement is to increase expenses and decrease net income by $750. The statement of cash flows is not affected by the accrual. Beacon recognizes the cash effects of the interest on the maturity date when it pays the maturity (face) value of the note to State Bank.

The journal entry to amortize the discount and its effects on the financial statements are shown here:

Account Title	Debit	Credit
Interest Expense	750	
Discount on Notes Payable		750

Event No.	Assets =		Liabilities	+		Equity		Rev. −	Exp. =	Net Inc.	Cash Flow
	Cash =	Notes Pay. −	Disc. on N/P +		Com. Stk. +	Ret. Earn.					
4	NA =	NA −	(750) +		NA +	(750)	NA −	750 =	(750)	NA

General Ledger T-Accounts and Financial Statements

Panel A of Exhibit 9.7 summarizes the 2013 accounting events. Panel B presents the ledger accounts in T-account form. The event numbers are shown in the T-accounts to facilitate your review. The closing entries are included and referenced with the abbreviation "cl." The financial statements are shown parenthetically in Panel C of the exhibit. You should study Exhibit 9.7 to strengthen your understanding of how the accounting for discount notes affects the financial statements.

EXHIBIT 9.7

The Big Picture

Panel A: Transaction Summary

1. Beacon issued a $10,000 face value, one-year, discount note with a 9 percent discount rate.
2. Beacon paid $8,000 cash for operating expenses.
3. Beacon earned cash service revenue of $12,000.
4. Beacon recognized $750 of accrued interest expense.
5. Beacon closed the revenue and expense accounts. The letters *cl* are the posting reference for the closing entry.

Panel B: General Ledger

Assets				=	Liabilities				+	Equity			

Cash

(1)	9,100	8,000	(2)
(3)	12,000		
Bal.	13,100		

Notes Payable

		10,000	(1)
		10,000	Bal.

Discount on Notes Payable

(1)	900	750	(4)
Bal.	150		

Retained Earnings

		3,250	(cl.)
		3,250	Bal.

Service Revenue

(cl.)	12,000	12,000	(3)
		0	Bal.

Operating Expenses

(2)	8,000	8,000	(cl.)
Bal.	0		

Interest Expense

(4)	750	750	(cl.)
Bal.	0		

Panel C: Financial Statements for 2013

Income Statement		Balance Sheet			Statement of Cash Flows	
Service revenue	$12,000	Assets			**Operating Activities**	
Operating expenses	(8,000)	Cash		$13,100	Inflow from customers	$12,000
Operating income	4,000	Liabilities			Outflow for expenses	(8,000)
Interest expense	(750)	Notes payable	$10,000		Net inflow from	
Net income	$ 3,250	Less: Disc. on notes pay.	(150)		operating activities	4,000
		Total liabilities		$ 9,850	**Investing Activities**	0
		Stockholders' equity			**Financing Activities**	
		Retained earnings		3,250	Inflow from creditors	9,100
		Total liab. and stockholders' equity		$13,100	Net change in cash	13,100
					Plus: Beginning cash balance	0
					Ending cash balance	$13,100

Accounting Events Affecting 2014

This section illustrates four accounting events that apply to Beacon's 2014 accounting cycle.

EVENT 1   Recognized Accrued Interest for 2014
Beacon recorded an adjusting entry to recognize interest accrued since December 31.

Since the note had a one-year term, interest for two months remains to be accrued at the maturity date on February 28, 2014. Interest on this note accrues at $75 per month

($900 discount ÷ 12), so there is $150 ($75 × 2) of interest expense to recognize in 2014. Recognizing the interest increases liabilities (the Discount account is reduced to zero) and decreases stockholders' equity. The effect on the income statement of recognizing interest is to increase expenses and decrease net income by $150. The statement of cash flows is not affected by the interest recognition. The journal entry and its effects on the financial statements are shown here:

Account Title	Debit	Credit
Interest Expense	150	
Discount on Notes Payable		150

Event No.	Assets	=	Liabilities			+	Equity			Rev.	−	Exp.	=	Net Inc.	Cash Flow
	Cash	=	Notes Pay.	−	Disc. on N/P	+	Com. Stk.	+	Ret. Earn.						
1	NA	=	NA	−	(150)	+	NA	+	(150)	NA	−	150	=	(150)	NA

EVENT 2   Payment of Face Value
Beacon paid the face value of the note.

The face value ($10,000) of the note is due on the maturity date. Paying the maturity value is an asset use transaction that decreases both assets and liabilities. The income statement is not affected by the payment. The $10,000 cash payment includes $900 for interest and $9,100 for principal. On the statement of cash flows a $900 outflow for interest is reported in the operating activities section and a $9,100 outflow for repaying the loan is reported in the financing activities section. The journal entry and its effects on the financial statements are shown here:

Account Title	Debit	Credit
Notes Payable	10,000	
Cash		10,000

Event No.	Assets	=	Liabilities			+	Equity			Rev.	−	Exp.	=	Net Inc.	Cash Flow
	Cash	=	Notes Pay.	−	Disc. on N/P	+	Com. Stk.	+	Ret. Earn.						
2	(10,000)	=	(10,000)	−	NA	+	NA	+	NA	NA	−	NA	=	NA	(900) OA (9,100) FA

EVENT 3   Recognized Revenue
Beacon recognized $13,000 of cash service revenue.

Recognizing the revenue increases both assets and stockholders' equity. Net income also increases. The cash inflow is reported in the operating activities section of the statement of cash flows. The journal entry and its effects on the financial statements are shown here:

Account Title	Debit	Credit
Cash	13,000	
Service Revenue		13,000

Event No.	Assets	=	Liabilities			+	Equity			Rev.	−	Exp.	=	Net Inc.	Cash Flow
	Cash	=	Notes Pay.	−	Disc. on N/P	+	Com. Stk.	+	Ret. Earn.						
3	13,000	=	NA	−	NA	+	NA	+	13,000	13,000	−	NA	=	13,000	13,000 OA

EVENT 4   Recognized Operating Expenses
Beacon incurred $8,500 of cash operating expenses.

This event decreases both assets and stockholders' equity. Net income also decreases. The cash outflow is reported in the operating activities section of the statement of cash flows. The journal entry and its effects on the financial statements are shown here:

Account Title	Debit	Credit
Operating Expenses	8,500	
Cash		8,500

Event No.	Assets =		Liabilities			+	Equity			Rev.	−	Exp.	=	Net Inc.	Cash Flow
	Cash	=	Notes Pay.	−	Disc. on N/P	+	Com. Stk.	+	Ret. Earn.						
4	(8,500)	=	NA	−	NA	+	NA	+	(8,500)	NA	−	8,500	=	(8,500)	(8,500) OA

General Ledger T-Accounts and Financial Statements

Panel A of Exhibit 9.8 summarizes the 2014 accounting events. Panel B presents the ledger accounts in T-account form. The event numbers are shown in the T-accounts

---

EXHIBIT 9.8

The Big Picture

Panel A: Transaction Summary

Event 1   Recognized accrued interest for 2014.
Event 2   Paid face value of note.
Event 3   Recognized revenue.
Event 4   Recognized operating expenses.

Panel B: General Ledger

	Assets			=		Liabilities			+		Equity	

Cash

Bal.	13,100	10,000	(2)
(3)	13,000	8,500	(4)
Bal.	7,600		

Notes Payable

(2)	10,000	10,000	Bal.
		0	Bal.

Discount on Notes Payable

Bal.	150	150	(1)
Bal.	0		

Retained Earnings

		3,250	Bal.
		4,350	(cl.)
		7,600	Bal.

Service Revenue

(cl.)	13,000	13,000	(3)
		0	Bal.

Operating Expenses

(4)	8,500	8,500	(cl.)
Bal.	0		

Interest Expense

(1)	150	150	(cl.)
Bal.	0		

continued

EXHIBIT 9.8	*Concluded*

Panel C: Financial Statements for 2014

Income Statement		Balance Sheet		Statement of Cash Flows	
Service revenue	$13,000	Assets		**Operating Activities**	
Operating expenses	(8,500)	Cash	$7,600	Inflow from customers	$13,000
Operating income	4,500	Liabilities	$ 0	Outflow for expenses	(8,500)
Interest expense	(150)	Stockholders' equity		Outflow for interest	(900)
Net income	$ 4,350	retained earnings	7,600	Net inflow from	
		Total liab. and stockholders' equity	$7,600	operating activities	3,600
				Investing Activities	0
				Financing Activities	
				Outflow to creditors	(9,100)
				Net change in cash	(5,500)
				Plus: Beginning cash balance	13,100
				Ending cash balance	$ 7,600

to facilitate your review. The closing entries are included and referenced with the abbreviation "cl." The financial statements are shown parenthetically in Panel C of the exhibit.

You should study Exhibit 9.8 to strengthen you understanding of how the accounting for discount notes affects the financial statements. Observe that no liabilities are reported in the balance sheet because Beacon has paid off the note and interest before the closing date. Since Beacon has not paid dividends since its inception, retained earning represents the sum of net income recognized for 2013 and 2014.

SELF-STUDY REVIEW PROBLEM

A step-by-step audio-narrated series of slides is provided on the text website at www.mhhe.com/edmonds8e.

Perfect Picture Inc. (PPI) experienced the following transactions during 2013. The transactions are summarized (transaction data pertain to the full year) and limited to those that affect the company's current liabilities.

1. PPI had cash sales of $820,000. The state requires that PPI charge customers an 8 percent sales tax (ignore cost of goods sold).
2. PPI paid the state sales tax authority $63,000.
3. On March 1, PPI issued a note payable to the County Bank. PPI received $50,000 cash (principal balance). The note had a one-year term and a 6 percent annual interest rate.
4. On December 31, PPI recognized accrued interest on the note issued in Event 3.
5. On December 31, PPI recognized warranty expense at the rate of 3 percent of sales.
6. PPI paid $22,000 cash to settle warranty claims.
7. PPI has five employees. Four of the employees each earn $40,000 per year. The fifth employee, the store manager, earns $120,000 per year. The annual amount withheld for income tax for all employees is $54,000. Each of the five employees has volunteered to have $50 per month withheld as a charitable contribution to the United Way. Record the net pay as a liability.
8. Based on the salary data described in Event 7, PPI recognized payroll tax expense for FICA and unemployment taxes.
9. During the year PPI remitted the following amounts of cash in partial settlement of the indicated liabilities.

Employee income tax payable	$ 52,000
FICA tax—Social Security payable	27,000
FICA tax—Medicare payable	7,000
United Way payable	2,500
Salaries payable	190,250
Federal unemployment tax payable	200
State unemployment tax payable	1,500

10. PPI pays $320 per month for medical insurance premiums for each employee. The company also contributes an amount equal to 4 percent of salaries to a pension fund for each employee. Each employee accrues vacation pay at a rate of $300 per month.

11. During the year PPI remitted the following amount of cash in partial settlement of the indicated liabilities.

Medical insurance payable	$18,000
Employee pension fund payable	8,200
Vacation pay payable	16,400

Required

a. Prepare in general journal form the entries to record the transactions described above.

b. Prepare the current liabilities section of the December 31, 2013, balance sheet.

Solution to Requirement a

Event No.	Account Title	Debit	Credit
1	Cash	885,600	
	Sales Revenue		820,000
	Sales Tax Payable		65,600
2	Sales Tax Payable	63,000	
	Cash		63,000
3	Cash	50,000	
	Notes Payable		50,000
4	Interest Expense ($50,000 × .06 × 10/12)	2,500	
	Interest Payable		2,500
5	Warranty Expense ($820,000 × 0.03)	24,600	
	Warranties Payable		24,600
6	Warranties Payable	22,000	
	Cash		22,000
7	Salary Expense [(4 × $40,000) + $120,000)]	280,000	
	Employee Income Tax Payable		54,000
	FICA Tax—Social Security Payable*		16,200
	FICA Tax—Medicare Payable ($280,000 × 0.015)		4,200
	United Way Payable ($50 × 5 × 12)		3,000
	Salaries Payable		202,600
8	Payroll Tax Expense	22,570	
	FICA Tax—Social Security Payable*		16,200
	FICA Tax—Medicare Payable ($280,000 × .015)		4,200
	Federal Unemployment Tax Payable ($7,000 × 5 × .008)		280
	State Unemployment Tax Payable ($7,000 × 5 × .054)		1,890
			continued

*Recall that the chapter assumes social security tax is applied to a maximum limit of $110,000.
[($40,000 × .06 = $2,400 × 4 = $9,600) + ($110,000 × .06 = $6,600)] = $16,200

Event No.	Account Title	Debit	Credit
9	Employee Income Tax Payable	52,000	
	FICA Tax—Social Security Payable	27,000	
	FICA Tax—Medicare Payable	7,000	
	United Way Payable	2,500	
	Salaries Payable	190,250	
	Federal Unemployment Tax Payable	200	
	State Unemployment Tax Payable	1,500	
	Cash		280,450
10	Fringe Benefits Expense	48,400	
	Medical Insurance Payable ($320 × 12 × 5)		19,200
	Employee Pension Fund Payable ($280,000 × .04)		11,200
	Vacation Pay Payable ($300 × 12 × 5)		18,000
11	Medical Insurance Payable	18,000	
	Employee Pension Fund Payable	8,200	
	Vacation Pay Payable	16,400	
	Cash		42,600

Solution to Requirement *b*

PERFECT PICTURE, INC.
Partial Balance Sheet
December 31, 2013

Current Liabilities

Sales tax payable ($65,600 − $63,000)	$ 2,600
Notes payable	50,000
Interest payable	2,500
Warranties payable ($24,600 − $22,000)	2,600
Employee income tax payable ($54,000 − $52,000)	2,000
FICA—Social Security payable ($16,200 + $16,200 − $27,000)	5,400
FICA—Medicare payable ($4,200 + $4,200 − $7,000)	1,400
United Way payable ($3,000 − $2,500)	500
Salaries payable ($202,600 − $190,250)	12,350
Federal unemployment tax payable ($280 − $200)	80
State unemployment tax payable ($1,890 − 1,500)	390
Medical insurance payable ($19,200 − $18,000)	1,200
Employee pension fund payable ($11,200 − $8,200)	3,000
Vacation pay payable ($18,000 − $16,400)	1,600
Total current liabilities	$85,620

KEY TERMS

amortizing 499
classified balance sheets 494
contingent liability 481
contra liability account 498
current (short-term) asset 493
current (short-term) liabilities 493
current ratio 495
discount 497
discount note 497

Discount on Notes Payable 498
employee 485
Employee's Withholding Allowance Certificate, Form W-4 487
Employer's Quarterly Federal Tax Return, Form 941 488
Federal Unemployment Tax Act (FUTA) 491

general uncertainties 481
going concern assumption 476
gross earnings 486
independent contractor 485
interest-bearing notes 497
issuer 478
liquidity 495
Medicare 488
net pay 490
note payable 478

operating cycle 493
principal 497
proceeds 497
salaries 486
Social Security 488
solvency 495
Wage and Tax Statement, Form W-2 487
wages 486
warranties 482

QUESTIONS

1. What type of transaction is a cash payment to creditors? How does this type of transaction affect the accounting equation?
2. What is a current liability? Distinguish between a current liability and a long-term debt.
3. What is included in the entry to record accrued interest expense? How does it affect the accounting equation?
4. Who is the maker of a note payable?
5. What is the going concern assumption? Does it affect the way liabilities are reported in the financial statements?
6. Why is it necessary to make an adjusting entry at the end of the accounting period for unpaid interest on a note payable?
7. Assume that on October 1, 2013, Big Company borrowed $10,000 from the local bank at 6 percent interest. The note is due on October 1, 2014. How much interest does Big pay in 2013? How much interest does Big pay in 2014? What amount of cash does Big pay back in 2014?

8. When a business collects sales tax from customers, is it revenue? Why or why not?
9. What is a contingent liability?
10. List the three categories of contingent liabilities.
11. Are contingent liabilities recorded on a company's books? Explain.
12. What is the difference in accounting procedures for a liability that is probable and estimable and one that is reasonably possible but not estimable?
13. What type of liabilities are not recorded on a company's books?
14. What does the term *warranty* mean?
15. What effect does recognizing future warranty obligations have on the balance sheet? On the income statement?
16. When is warranty cost reported on the statement of cash flows?
17. What is the difference between an employee and an independent contractor?
18. What is the difference between wages and salaries?

19. What is the purpose of the W-2 form? What is the purpose of the W-4 form?
20. What two taxes are components of the FICA tax? What programs do they fund?
21. Who pays the FICA tax? Is there a ceiling on the amount of tax that is paid?
22. What is the difference between gross pay and net pay for an employee?
23. Why are amounts withheld from employees' pay considered liabilities of the employer?
24. What is the purpose of the Federal Unemployment Tax? What are the maximum amount of wages subject to the tax?
25. What items are included in compensation cost for a company in addition to the gross salaries of the employees?
26. Give two examples of fringe benefits.
27. What is a classified balance sheet?
28. What is the difference between the liquidity and the solvency of a business?

29. The higher the company's current ratio, the better the company's financial condition. Do you agree with this statement? Explain.
30. What is the difference between an interest-bearing note and a discount note?
31. How is the carrying value of a discount note computed?
32. Will the effective rate of interest be the same on a $10,000 face value, 6 percent interest-bearing note and a $10,000 face value, 6 percent discount note? Is the amount of cash received upon making these two loans the same? Why or why not?
33. How does the *amortization* of a discount affect the income statement, balance sheet, and statement of cash flows?
34. How does issuing an $8,000 discount note with an 8 percent discount rate and a one-year term to maturity affect the accounting equation?
35. What type of account is Discount on Notes Payable?

MULTIPLE-CHOICE QUESTIONS

Multiple-choice questions are provided on the text website at www.mhhe.com/edmonds8e.

EXERCISES—SERIES A

All applicable Exercises in Series A are available with McGraw-Hill's *Connect® Accounting.*

LO 1

Exercise 9-1A   *Recognizing accrued interest expense*

Harveys Corporation borrowed $60,000 from the bank on November 1, 2013. The note had a 6 percent annual rate of interest and matured on April 30, 2014. Interest and principal were paid in cash on the maturity date.

Required

a. What amount of cash did Harveys pay for interest in 2013?

b. What amount of interest expense was reported on the 2013 income statement?

c. What amount of total liabilities was reported on the December 31, 2013, balance sheet?

d. What total amount of cash was paid to the bank on April 30, 2014, for principal and interest?

e. What amount of interest expense was reported on the 2014 income statement?

Exercise 9-2A   *Effects of recognizing accrued interest on financial statements*   LO 1

R.T. Jackson started Jackson Company on January 1, 2013. The company experienced the following events during its first year of operation:

1. Earned $3,000 of cash revenue for performing services.
2. Borrowed $4,800 cash from the bank.
3. Adjusted the accounting records to recognize accrued interest expense on the bank note. The note, issued on August 1, 2013, had a one-year term and a 6 percent annual interest rate.

Required

a. What is the amount of interest expense in 2013?

b. What amount of cash was paid for interest in 2013?

c. Use a horizontal statements model to show how each event affects the balance sheet, income statement, and statement of cash flows. Indicate whether the event increases (I), decreases (D), or does not affect (NA) each element of the financial statements. In the Cash Flows column, designate the cash flows as operating activities (OA), investing activities (IA), or financing activities (FA). The first transaction has been recorded as an example.

Event No.			Balance Sheet								Income Statement						Statement of Cash Flows
	Cash	=	Notes Pay.	+	Int. Pay.	+	Com. Stk.	+	Ret. Earn.		Rev.	−	Exp.	=	Net Inc.		
1	I	=	NA	+	NA	+	NA	+	I		I	−	NA	=	I		I OA

Exercise 9-3A   *Recording sales tax*   LO 2

The Rebel Book Store sells books and other supplies to students in a state where the sales tax rate is 7 percent. The Rebel Book Store engaged in the following transactions for 2013. Sales tax of 7 percent is collected on all sales.

1. Book sales, not including sales tax, for 2013 amounted to $215,000 cash.
2. Cash sales of miscellaneous items in 2013 were $160,000, not including tax.
3. Cost of goods sold amounted to $195,000 for the year.
4. Paid $95,000 in operating expenses for the year.
5. Paid the sales tax collected to the state agency.

Required

a. What is the total amount of sales tax the Rebel Book Store collected and paid for the year?

b. Prepare the journal entries for the above transactions.

c. What is the Rebel Book Store's net income for the year?

Exercise 9-4A   *Recognizing sales tax payable*   LO 2

The following selected transactions apply to Easy Stop for November and December 2013. November was the first month of operations. Sales tax is collected at the time of sale but is not paid to the state sales tax agency until the following month.

1. Cash sales for November 2013 were $85,000 plus sales tax of 8 percent.
2. Easy Stop paid the November sales tax to the state agency on December 10, 2013.
3. Cash sales for December 2013 were $98,000 plus sales tax of 8 percent.

Required

a. Record the above transactions in general journal form.

b. Show the effect of the above transactions on a statements model like the one shown below.

Assets	=	Liabilities	+	Equity		Income Statement			
Cash	=	Sales Tax Pay.	+	Com. Stk.	+ Ret. Earn.	Rev. − Exp.	= Net Inc.		Cash Flow

c. What was the total amount of sales tax paid in 2013?

d. What was the total amount of sales tax collected in 2013?

e. What is the amount of the sales tax liability as of December 31, 2013?

f. On what financial statement will the sales tax liability appear?

LO 3

Exercise 9-5A   *Contingent liabilities*

The following legal situations apply to Dabney Corp. for 2013:

1. A customer slipped and fell on a slick floor while shopping in the retail store. The customer has filed a $5 million lawsuit against the company. Dabney's attorney knows that the company will have to pay some damages but is reasonably certain that the suit can be settled for $750,000.

2. The EPA has assessed a fine against Dabney of $320,000 for hazardous emissions from one of its manufacturing plants. The EPA had previously issued a warning to Dabney and required Dabney to make repairs within six months. Dabney began to make the repairs, but was not able to complete them within the six-month period. Since Dabney has started the repairs, Dabney's attorney thinks the fine will be reduced to $120,000. He is approximately 80 percent certain that he can negotiate the fine reduction because of the repair work that has been completed.

3. One of Dabney's largest manufacturing facilities is located in "tornado alley." Property is routinely damaged by storms. Dabney estimates it may have property damage of as much as $450,000 this coming year.

Required

For each item above, determine the correct accounting treatment. Prepare any required journal entries.

LO 4

Exercise 9-6A   *Effect of warranties on income and cash flow*

To support himself while attending school, Devon James sold computers to other students. During the year Devon purchased computers for $150,000 and sold them for $280,000 cash. He provided his customers with a one-year warranty against defects in parts and labor. Based on industry standards, he estimated that warranty claims would amount to 5 percent of sales. During the year he paid $1,545 cash to replace a defective hard drive.

Required

a. Prepare the journal entries to record the
   (1) Purchase of inventory.
   (2) Sale of computers.
   (3) Warranty expense.
   (4) Payment for repairs.

b. Post the above transactions to T-accounts.

c. Prepare an income statement and statement of cash flows for Devon's first year of operation.

d. Explain the difference between net income and the amount of cash flow from operating activities.

Exercise 9-7A *Effect of warranty obligations and payments on financial statements*

The Wolf Appliance Co. provides a 120-day parts-and-labor warranty on all merchandise it sells. Wolf estimates the warranty expense for the current period to be $2,450. During the period a customer returned a product that cost $1,950 to repair.

Required

a. Show the effects of these transactions on the financial statements using a horizontal statements model like the example shown here. Use a + to indicate increase, a − for decrease, and NA for not affected. In the Cash Flow column, indicate whether the item is an operating activity (OA), investing activity (IA), or financing activity (FA).

Assets	=	Liab.	+	Equity	Rev.	−	Exp.	=	Net Inc.	Cash Flow

b. Prepare the journal entry to record the warranty expense for the period.
c. Prepare the journal entry to record payment for the actual repair costs.
d. Discuss the advantage of estimating the amount of warranty expense.

Exercise 9-8A *Current liabilities*

The following transactions apply to Midsouth Equipment Sales Corp. for 2013:

1. The business was started when Midsouth received $60,000 from the issue of common stock.
2. Purchased $160,000 of merchandise on account.
3. Sold merchandise for $220,000 cash (not including sales tax). Sales tax of 8 percent is collected when the merchandise is sold. The merchandise had a cost of $140,000.
4. Provided a six-month warranty on the merchandise sold. Based on industry estimates, the warranty claims would amount to 4 percent of merchandise sales.
5. Paid the sales tax to the state agency on $180,000 of the sales.
6. On September 1, 2013, borrowed $40,000 from the local bank. The note had a 6 percent interest rate and matures on March 1, 2014.
7. Paid $6,600 for warranty repairs during the year.
8. Paid operating expenses of $61,000 for the year.
9. Paid $145,000 of accounts payable.
10. Recorded accrued interest at the end of the year.

Required

a. Show the effect of these transactions on the financial statements using a horizontal statements model like the one shown here. Use a + to indicate increase, a − for decrease, and NA for not affected. In the Cash Flow column, indicate whether the item is an operating activity (OA), investing activity (IA), or financing activity (FA). The first transaction is recorded as an example.

Assets	=	Liabilities	+	Equity	Rev.	−	Exp.	=	Net Inc.	Cash Flow
+		NA		+	NA		NA		NA	+ FA

b. Prepare the journal entries for the above transactions and post them to the appropriate T-accounts.
c. Prepare the income statement, balance sheet, and statement of cash flows for 2013.
d. What is the total amount of current liabilities at December 31, 2013?

LO 5

Exercise 9-9A   *Calculating payroll*

Herring Enterprises has two hourly employees, Emily and Jash. Both employees earn overtime at the rate of 1½ times the hourly rate for hours worked in excess of 40 per week. Assume the Social Security tax rate is 6 percent on the first $110,000 of wages and the Medicare tax rate is 1.5 percent on all earnings. Federal income tax withheld for Emily and Jash was $280 and $250 respectively. The following information is for the first week in January 2013:

Employee	Hours Worked	Wage Rate per Hour
Emily	54	$25
Jash	48	$35

Required

a. Calculate the gross pay for each employee for the week.
b. Calculate the net pay for each employee for the week.
c. Prepare the general journal entry to record payment of the wages.

LO 5

Exercise 9-10A   *Calculating payroll*

Book Mart has two employees in 2013. Jessica earns $4,500 per month and Moses, the manager, earns $11,000 per month. Neither is paid extra if they work overtime. Assume the Social Security tax rate is 6 percent on the first $110,000 of earnings and the Medicare tax rate is 1.5 percent on all earnings. The federal income tax withholding is 15 percent of gross earnings for Jessica and 20 percent for Moses. Both Jessica and Moses have been employed all year.

Required

a. Calculate the net pay for both Jessica and Moses for March.
b. Calculate the net pay for both Jessica and Moses for December.
c. Is the net pay the same in March as December for both employees? Why or why not?
d. What amounts will Book Mart report on the 2013 W-2s for each employee?

LO 5

Exercise 9-11A   *Calculating employee and employer payroll taxes*

Panola Co. employed Jan Rao in 2013. Jan earned $5,200 per month and worked the entire year. Assume the Social Security tax rate is 6 percent on the first $110,000 of earnings and the Medicare tax rate is 1.5 percent. Jan's federal income tax withholding amount is $800 per month. Use 6.2 percent for the unemployment tax rate for the first $7,000 of earnings per employee.

Required

a. Answer the following questions:
   (1) What is Jan's net pay per month?
   (2) What amount does Jan pay monthly in FICA payroll taxes?
   (3) What is the total payroll tax expense for Panola Co. for January 2013? February 2013? March 2013? December 2013?
b. Assume that instead of $5,200 per month Jan earned $10,000 per month. Answer the questions in Requirement *a*.

LO 5

Exercise 9-12A   *Fringe benefits and payroll expense*

Watson Co. provides various fringe benefits for its three employees. It provides vacation and personal leave at the rate of one day for each month worked. Its employees earn a combined total of approximately $500 per day. In addition, Watson Co. pays $780 per month in medical insurance premiums for its employees. Watson also contributes $400 per month into a retirement plan for the employees. Assume the Social Security tax rate is 6% of the first $110,000 of salaries and the Medicare tax rate is 1.5%. The unemployment tax rate is 5.2% on the first $7,000 of earnings per employee.

Required

a. Prepare the monthly journal entry for the accrued fringe benefits.

b. Show the effect of the above transaction on a statements model like the one shown below:

Assets =	Liabilities	+	Equity		Income Statement		Cash Flow
Cash =	Various Payables +	Com. Stk. +	Ret. Earn.		Rev. − Exp. = Net Inc.		

c. If the three employees each worked 250 days for the year, what is Watson Co.'s total payroll cost (salary, payroll taxes, and fringe benefits) for the year? (Assume that each employee earns $250 per day.)

Exercise 9-13A   *Comprehensive single cycle problem*

LO 1, 2, 4, 5

The following transactions apply to Rocket Co. for 2013:

1. Received $40,000 cash from the issue of common stock.
2. Purchased inventory on account for $128,000.
3. Sold inventory for $200,000 cash that had cost $110,000. Sales tax was collected at the rate of 5 percent on the inventory sold.
4. Borrowed $40,000 from the First State Bank on October 1, 2013. The note had a 6 percent interest rate and a one-year term to maturity.
5. Paid the accounts payable (see transaction 2).
6. Paid the sales tax due on $160,000 of sales. Sales tax on the other $40,000 is not due until after the end of the year.
7. Salaries for the year for the one employee amounted $45,000. Assume the Social Security tax rate is 6 percent and the Medicare tax rate is 1.5 percent. Federal income tax withheld was $5,600.
8. Paid $3,200 for warranty repairs during the year.
9. Paid $24,000 of other operating expenses during the year.
10. Paid a dividend of $5,000 to the shareholders.

Adjustments:

11. The products sold in transaction 3 were warranted. Rocket estimated that the warranty cost would be 3 percent of sales.
12. Record the accrued interest at December 31, 2013.
13. Record the accrued payroll tax at December 31, 2013. Assume no payroll taxes have been paid for the year and that the unemployment tax rate is 6.2 percent (federal unemployment tax rate is .8 percent and the state unemployment tax rate is 5.4 percent on the first $7,000 of earnings per employee).

Required

a. Record the above transactions in general journal form.
b. Post the transactions to T-accounts.
c. Prepare an income statement, statement of changes in stockholders' equity, balance sheet, and statement of cash flows for 2013.

Exercise 9-14A   *Preparing a classified balance sheet*

LO 6

Required

Use the following information to prepare a classified balance sheet for Blackmon Co. at the end of 2013:

Accounts receivable	$36,200
Accounts payable	12,400
Cash	29,650
Common stock	50,000
Long-term notes payable	45,500
Merchandise inventory	38,300
Office equipment	36,400
Retained earnings	36,250
Prepaid insurance	3,600

LO 7

Exercise 9-15A *Using the current ratio to make comparisons*

The following information was drawn from the 2014 balance sheets of the Georgia and Nevada Companies:

	Georgia Company	Nevada Company
Current assets	$40,000	$70,000
Current liabilities	25,000	55,000

Required

a. Compute the current ratio for each company.

b. Which company has the greater likelihood of being able to pay its bills?

c. Assume that both companies have the same amount of total assets. Speculate as to which company would produce the higher return on assets ratio.

LO 8

Exercise 9-16A *Effect of a discount note on financial statements (Appendix)*

Ben Pratt started a moving company on January 1, 2013. On March 1, 2013, Pratt borrowed cash from a local bank by issuing a one-year $80,000 face value note with annual interest based on a 12 percent discount. During 2013, Pratt provided services for $65,400 cash.

Required

Answer the following questions. Record the events in T-accounts prior to answering the questions.

a. What is the amount of total liabilities on the December 31, 2013, balance sheet?

b. What is the amount of net income on the 2013 income statement?

c. What is the amount of cash flow from operating activities on the 2013 statement of cash flows?

d. Provide the general journal entries necessary to record issuing the note on March 1, 2013; recognizing accrued interest on December 31, 2013; and repaying the loan on February 28, 2014.

LO 1, 8

Exercise 9-17A *Comparing effective interest rates on discount versus interest-bearing notes (Appendix)*

Josey Wales borrowed money by issuing two notes on January 1, 2013. The financing transactions are described here.

1. Borrowed funds by issuing a $60,000 face value discount note to State Bank. The note had an 8 percent discount rate, a one-year term to maturity, and was paid off on December 31, 2013.

2. Borrowed funds by issuing a $60,000 face value, interest-bearing note to Community Bank. The note had an 8 percent stated rate of interest, a one-year term to maturity, and was paid off on December 31, 2013.

Required

a. Show the effects of issuing the two notes on the financial statements using separate horizontal financial statement models like the ones here. Record the transaction amounts under the appropriate categories. In the Cash Flow column, indicate whether the item is an operating activity (OA), investing activity (IA), or financing activity (FA). Record only the events occurring on the date of issue. Do not record accrued interest or the repayment at maturity.

Discount Note

Assets =	Liabilities	+ Equity	Rev. − Exp. = Net Inc.	Cash Flow
Cash = Notes Pay. − Disc. on Notes Pay. + Ret. Earn.				

Interest-Bearing Note

Assets	=	Liabilities	+	Equity		Rev.	−	Exp.	=	Net Inc.		Cash Flow
Cash	=	Notes Pay.	+	Ret. Earn.								

b. What is the total amount of interest to be paid on each note?

c. What amount of cash was received from each note when it was issued?

d. Which note has the higher effective interest rate? Support your answer with appropriate computations.

Exercise 9-18A *Recording accounting events for a discount note (Appendix)*

LO 8

Dawkins Co. issued a $60,000 face value discount note to First Bank on June 1, 2013. The note had a 6 percent discount rate and a one-year term to maturity.

Required

Prepare general journal entries for the following transactions:

a. The issuance of the note on June 1, 2013.

b. The adjustment for accrued interest at the end of the year, December 31, 2013.

c. Recording interest expense for 2014 and repaying the principal on May 31, 2014.

PROBLEMS—SERIES A

All applicable Problems in Series A are available with McGraw-Hill's *Connect® Accounting.*

Problem 9-19A *Effect of accrued interest on financial statements*

LO 1

Powell Co. borrowed $20,000 from the local bank on April 1, 2013, when the company was started. The note had an 8 percent annual interest rate and a one-year term to maturity. Powell Co. recognized $54,000 of revenue on account in 2013 and $65,000 of revenue on account in 2014. Cash collections from accounts receivable were $46,000 in 2013 and $63,000 in 2014. Powell Co. paid $27,000 of salaries expense in 2013 and $36,000 of salaries expense in 2014. Powell Co. paid the loan and interest at the maturity date.

CHECK FIGURES
a. $19,000
h. $54,400

Required

Based on the preceding information, answer the following questions. (*Hint:* Record the events in the accounting equation before answering the questions.)

a. What amount of net cash flow from operating activities would Powell report on the 2013 cash flow statement?

b. What amount of interest expense would Powell report on the 2013 income statement?

c. What amount of total liabilities would Powell report on the December 31, 2013, balance sheet?

d. What amount of retained earnings would Powell report on the December 31, 2013, balance sheet?

e. What amount of cash flow from financing activities would Powell report on the 2013 statement of cash flows?

f. What amount of interest expense would Powell report on the 2014 income statement?

g. What amount of cash flows from operating activities would Powell report on the 2014 cash flow statement?

h. What amount of total assets would Powell report on the December 31, 2014, balance sheet?

Problem 9-20A   *Accounting for short-term debt and sales tax—two accounting cycles*

The following transactions apply to Ocktoc Co. for 2013, its first year of operations:

1. Received $50,000 cash from the issue of a short-term note with a 5 percent interest rate and a one-year maturity. The note was made on April 1, 2013.
2. Received $140,000 cash plus applicable sales tax from performing services. The services are subject to a sales tax rate of 6 percent.
3. Paid $84,000 cash for other operating expenses during the year.
4. Paid the sales tax due on $110,000 of the service revenue for the year. Sales tax on the balance of the revenue is not due until 2014.
5. Recognized the accrued interest at December 31, 2013.

The following transactions apply to Ocktoc Co. for 2014:

1. Paid the balance of the sales tax due for 2013.
2. Received $155,000 cash plus applicable sales tax from performing services. The services are subject to a sales tax rate of 6 percent.
3. Repaid the principal of the note and applicable interest on April 1, 2014.
4. Paid $96,000 of other operating expenses during the year.
5. Paid the sales tax due on $135,000 of the service revenue. The sales tax on the balance of the revenue is not due until 2015.

Required

a. Record the 2013 transactions in general journal form.
b. Post the transactions to T-accounts.
c. Prepare a balance sheet, statement of changes in stockholders' equity, income statement, and statement of cash flows for 2013.
d. Prepare the closing entries and post them to the T-accounts.
e. Prepare a post-closing trial balance.
f. Repeat Requirements *a* through *e* for 2014.

Problem 9-21A   *Contingent liabilities*

Required

How should each of the following situations be reported in the financial statements?

a. It has been determined that one of the company's products has caused a safety hazard. It is considered probable that liabilities have been incurred and a reasonable estimate of the amount can be made.
b. A company warehouse is located in a section of the city that has routinely flooded in the past. Consequently the company can no longer find a source of insurance for the warehouse. No flood has yet occurred this year.
c. Because of newly passed legislation, a company will have to upgrade its facilities over the next two years. Significant expenditures will occur, but at this time the amount has not been determined.

Problem 9-22A   *Current liabilities*

The following selected transactions were taken from the books of Aliceville Company for 2013:

1. On March 1, 2013, borrowed $60,000 cash from the local bank. The note had a 6 percent interest rate and was due on September 1, 2013.
2. Cash sales for the year amounted to $240,000 plus sales tax at the rate of 7 percent.
3. Aliceville provides a 90-day warranty on the merchandise sold. The warranty expense is estimated to be 2 percent of sales.
4. Paid the sales tax to the state sales tax agency on $200,000 of the sales.
5. Paid the note due on September 1 and the related interest.
6. On October 1, 2013, borrowed $50,000 cash from the local bank. The note had a 7 percent interest rate and a one-year term to maturity.

7. Paid $3,800 in warranty repairs.

8. A customer has filed a lawsuit against Aliceville for $150,000 for breach of contract. The company attorney does not believe the suit has merit.

Required

a. Answer the following questions:

   (1) What amount of cash did Aliceville pay for interest during the year?

   (2) What amount of interest expense is reported on Aliceville's income statement for the year?

   (3) What is the amount of warranty expense for the year?

b. Prepare the current liabilities section of the balance sheet at December 31, 2013. (*Hint:* first post the liabilities transactions to T-accounts.)

c. Show the effect of these transactions on the financial statements using a horizontal statements model like the one shown here. Use a + to indicate increase, a − for decrease, and NA for not affected. In the Cash Flow column, indicate whether the item is an operating activity (OA), investing activity (IA), or financing activity (FA). The first transaction is recorded as an example.

Assets	=	Liabilities	+	Equity	Rev.	−	Exp.	=	Net Inc.	Cash Flow
+		+		NA	NA		NA		NA	+ FA

Problem 9-23A *Accounting for payroll and payroll taxes*

LO 5

CHECK FIGURE
a. Credit cash: $150,035

Milport Co. pays salaries monthly on the last day of the month. The following information is available from Milport Co. for the month ended December 31, 2013.

Administrative salaries	$85,000
Sales salaries	66,000
Office salaries	48,000

Assume the Social Security tax rate is 6 percent on the first $110,000 of salaries and the Medicare tax rate is 1.5 percent on all salaries. James reached the $110,000 amount in October. His salary in December amounted to $11,000 and is included in the $85,000. No one else will reach the $110,000 amount for the year. None of the employee salaries are subject to unemployment tax in December.

Other amounts withheld from salaries in December were as follows:

Federal income tax	$24,500
State income tax	7,200
Employee savings plan	3,000

Required

a. Prepare the journal entry to record the payment of payroll on December 31, 2013.

b. Prepare the journal entry to record the payroll tax expense for Milport Co. for December 2013.

Problem 9-24A *Computation of net pay and payroll expense*

LO 5

CHECK FIGURE
e. $3,877.00

The following information is available for the employees of Hoover Company for the first week of January 2013:

1. Tom earns $32 per hour and 1½ times his regular rate for hours over 40 per week. Tom worked 46 hours the first week in January. Tom's federal income tax withholding is equal to 10 percent of his gross pay. Hoover pays medical insurance of $75 per week for Tom and contributes $50 per week to a retirement plan for him.

2. Drake earns a weekly salary of $1,200. Drake's federal income tax withholding is 15 percent of his gross pay. Hoover pays medical insurance of $110 per week for Drake and contributes $100 per week to a retirement plan for him.

3. Vacation pay is accrued at the rate of 1/4 of the regular pay rate per hour for Tom and $60 per week for Drake.

Assume the Social Security tax rate is 6 percent on the first $110,000 of salaries and the Medicare tax rate is 1.5 percent of total salaries. The state unemployment tax rate is 4.2 percent and the federal unemployment tax rate is .8 percent of the first $7,000 of salary for each employee.

Required

a. Compute the gross pay for Tom for the first week in January.

b. Compute the net pay for both Tom and Drake for the first week in January.

c. Prepare the journal entry to record the payment of the payroll for the week.

d. Prepare the journal entry to record the payroll tax expense and fringe benefit expense for Hoover for the week.

e. What is the total cost of compensation expense for the first week of January 2013 for Hoover Company?

LO 6

e**X**cel

Problem 9-25A *Multistep income statement and classified balance sheet*

Required

Use the following information to prepare a multistep income statement and a classified balance sheet for Vernon Company for 2013. (*Hint:* Some of the items will *not* appear on either statement, and ending retained earnings must be calculated.)

CHECK FIGURES
Total Current Assets: $282,600
Total Current Liabilities: $120,500

Operating expenses	$ 45,000	Cash	$ 46,000
Land	75,000	Interest receivable (short term)	1,600
Accumulated depreciation	46,000	Cash flow from investing activities	(96,000)
Accounts payable	35,000	Allowance for doubtful accounts	14,000
Unearned revenue	27,000	Interest payable (short term)	6,000
Warranties payable (short term)	4,500	Sales revenue	900,000
Equipment	96,000	Uncollectible accounts expense	25,000
Notes payable (long term)	140,000	Interest expense	16,000
Salvage value of equipment	10,000	Accounts receivable	88,000
Dividends	15,000	Salaries payable	48,000
Warranty expense	7,200	Supplies	4,500
Beginning retained earnings	41,100	Prepaid rent	18,000
Interest revenue	4,200	Common stock	90,000
Gain on sale of equipment	7,000	Cost of goods sold	575,000
Inventory	126,000	Salaries expense	102,000
Notes receivable (short term)	12,500	Building	110,000

LO 7

CHECK FIGURE
a. Poe Current Ratio: 1.61 to 1

Problem 9-26A *Using ratios to make comparisons*

The following accounting information exists for Poe and Scott companies at the end of 2014:

	Poe	Scott
Cash	$ 110,000	$ 130,000
Wages payable	125,000	150,000
Merchandise inventory	135,000	170,000
Building	400,000	500,000
Accounts receivable	150,000	180,000
Long-term notes payable	450,000	500,000
Land	220,000	280,000
Accounts payable	120,000	130,000
Sales revenue	1,200,000	1,450,000
Expenses	1,090,000	1,350,000

Required

a. Identify the current assets and current liabilities and compute the current ratio for each company.

b. Assuming that all assets and liabilities are listed here, compute the debt to assets ratios for each company.

c. Determine which company has the greater financial risk in both the short term and the long term.

Problem 9-27A   *Accounting for a discount note—two accounting cycles (Appendix)*

Dona Corp. was started in 2013. The following summarizes transactions that occurred during 2013:

1. Issued a $40,000 face value discount note to Golden Savings Bank on April 1, 2013. The note had a 6 percent discount rate and a one-year term to maturity.
2. Recognized revenue from services performed for cash, $130,000.
3. Incurred and paid $98,000 cash for selling and administrative expenses.
4. Amortized the discount on the note at the end of the year, December 31, 2013.
5. Prepared the necessary closing entries at December 31, 2013.

The following summarizes transactions that occurred in 2014:

1. Recognized $215,000 of service revenue in cash.
2. Incurred and paid $151,000 for selling and administrative expenses.
3. Amortized the remainder of the discount for 2014 and paid the face value of the note.
4. Prepared the necessary closing entries at December 31, 2014.

Required

a. Show the effects of each of the transactions on the elements of the financial statements, using a horizontal statements model like the one shown here. Use + for increase, − for decrease, and NA for not affected. The first transaction is entered as an example. (*Hint:* Closing entries do not affect the statements model.)

Event No.	Assets	=	Liab.	+	Equity	Rev.	−	Exp.	=	Net Inc.	Cash Flow
1	+		+		NA	NA		NA		NA	+ FA

b. Prepare entries in general journal form for the transactions for 2013 and 2014, and post them to T-accounts.

c. Prepare an income statement, statement of changes in stockholders' equity, balance sheet, and statement of cash flows for 2013 and 2014.

LO 8

EXERCISES—SERIES B

Exercise 9-1B   *Recognizing accrued interest expense*

Bessemer Corporation borrowed $60,000 from the bank on October 1, 2013. The note had a 9 percent annual rate of interest and matured on March 31, 2014. Interest and principal were paid in cash on the maturity date.

LO 1

Required

a. What amount of cash did Bessemer pay for interest in 2013?

b. What amount of interest expense was recognized on the 2013 income statement?

c. What amount of total liabilities was reported on the December 31, 2013, balance sheet?

d. What total amount of cash was paid to the bank on March 31, 2014, for principal and interest?

e. What amount of interest expense was reported on the 2014 income statement?

LO 1

Exercise 9-2B   *Effects of recognizing accrued interest on financial statements*

Jim Macon started Macon Company on January 1, 2013. The company experienced the following events during its first year of operation:

1. Earned $8,800 of cash revenue.
2. Borrowed $10,000 cash from the bank.
3. Adjusted the accounting records to recognize accrued interest expense on the bank note. The note, issued on September 1, 2013, had a one-year term and a 8 percent annual interest rate.

Required

a. What is the amount of interest payable at December 31, 2013?
b. What is the amount of interest expense in 2013?
c. What is the amount of interest paid 2013?
d. Use a horizontal statements model to show how each event affects the balance sheet, income statement, and statement of cash flows. Indicate whether the event increases (I), decreases (D), or does not affect (NA) each element of the financial statements. In the Cash Flows column, designate the cash flows as operating activities (OA), investing activities (IA), or financing activities (FA). The first transaction has been recorded as an example.

Event No.	Balance Sheet											Income Statement					Statement of Cash Flows
	Cash	=	Notes Pay.	+	Int. Pay.	+	Com. Stk.	+	Ret. Earn.		Rev.	−	Exp.	=	Net Inc.		
1	I	=	NA	+	NA	+	NA	+	I		I	−	NA	=	I		I OA

LO 2

Exercise 9-3B   *Recording sales tax*

Reed Book Mart sells books and other supplies to students in a state where the sales tax rate is 8 percent. Reed Book Mart engaged in the following transactions for 2013. Sales tax of 8 percent is collected on all sales.

1. Book sales, not including sales tax, for 2013 amounted to $280,000 cash.
2. Cash sales of miscellaneous items in 2013 were $90,000, not including tax.
3. Cost of goods sold was $210,000 for the year.
4. Paid $110,000 in operating expenses for the year.
5. Paid the sales tax collected to the state agency.

Required

a. What is the total amount of sales tax Reed Book Mart collected and paid for the year?
b. Prepare the journal entries for the above transactions.
c. What is Reed Book Mart's net income for the year?

LO 2

Exercise 9-4B   *Recognizing sales tax payable*

The following selected transactions apply to Valley Supply for November and December 2013. November was the first month of operations. Sales tax is collected at the time of sale but is not paid to the state sales tax agency until the following month.

1. Cash sales for November 2013 were $146,000 plus sales tax of 7 percent.
2. Valley Supply paid the November sales tax to the state agency on December 10, 2013.
3. Cash sales for December 2013 were $175,000 plus sales tax of 7 percent.

Required

a. Record the above transactions in general journal form.
b. Show the effect of the above transactions on a statements model like the one shown on the next page.

Assets: =	Liabilities	+	Equity	Income Statement	Cash Flow
Cash =	Sales Tax Pay. +	Com. Stk. +	Ret. Earn.	Rev. − Exp. = Net Inc.	

c. What was the total amount of sales tax paid in 2013?

d. What was the total amount of sales tax collected in 2013?

e. What amount of sales tax expense will be reported on the 2013 income statement?

Exercise 9-5B *Contingent liabilities*

LO 3

The following three independent sets of facts relate to contingent liabilities:

1. In November of the current year an automobile manufacturing company recalled all Pickup Trucks manufactured during the past two years. A flaw in the battery cable was discovered and the recall provides for replacement of the defective cables. The estimated cost of this recall is $2 million.

2. The EPA has notified a company of violations of environmental laws relating to hazardous waste. These actions seek cleanup costs, penalties, and damages to property. The company is reasonably certain that the cleanup cost will be approximately $4 million. In addition, potential reimbursements for property damage could be as much as $1 million or as little as $100,000. There is no way to more accurately estimate the property damage at this time.

3. Jackson Company does not carry property damage insurance because of the cost. The company suffered substantial losses each year of the past three years. However, it has had no losses for the current year. Management thinks this is too good to be true and is sure there will be significant losses in the coming year. However, the exact amount cannot be determined.

Required

a. Discuss the various categories of contingent liabilities.

b. For each item above determine the correct accounting treatment. Prepare any required journal entries.

Exercise 9-6B *Effect of warranties on income and cash flow*

LO 4

To support herself while attending school, Young Shen sold stereo systems to other students. During the first year of operations, Shen purchased the stereo systems for $120,000 and sold them for $230,000 cash. She provided her customers with a one-year warranty against defects in parts and labor. Based on industry standards, she estimated that warranty claims would amount to 2 percent of sales. During the year she paid $2,450 cash to replace a defective tuner.

Required

Prepare an income statement and statement of cash flows for Shen's first year of operation. Based on the information given, what is Shen's total warranties liability at the end of the accounting period?

Exercise 9-7B *Effect of warranty obligations and payments on financial statements*

LO 4

The Boat Company provides a 120-day parts-and-labor warranty on all merchandise it sells. The Boat Company estimates the warranty expense for the current period to be $2,200. During the period a customer returned a product that cost $1,750 to repair.

Required

a. Show the effects of these transactions on the financial statements using a horizontal statements model like the example shown here. Use a + to indicate increase, a − for decrease, and NA for not affected. In the Cash Flow column, indicate whether the item is an operating activity (OA), investing activity (IA), or financing activity (FA).

Assets	=	Liab.	+	Equity	Rev.	−	Exp.	=	Net Inc.	Cash Flow

b. Prepare the journal entry to record the warranty expense for the period.

c. Prepare the journal entry to record payment for the actual repair costs.

d. Why do companies estimate warranty expense and record the expense before the repairs are actually made?

LO 1, 2, 4

Exercise 9-8B   *Current liabilities*

The following transactions apply to Tractor Sales for 2013:

1. The business was started when the company received $60,000 from the issue of common stock.
2. Purchased equipment inventory of $325,000 on account.
3. Sold equipment for $450,000 cash (not including sales tax). Sales tax of 8 percent is collected when the merchandise is sold. The merchandise had a cost of $305,000.
4. Provided a six-month warranty on the equipment sold. Based on industry estimates, the warranty claims would amount to 2 percent of sales.
5. Paid the sales tax to the state agency on $380,000 of the sales.
6. On September 1, 2013, borrowed $40,000 from the local bank. The note had a 4 percent interest rate and matured on March 1, 2014.
7. Paid $5,100 for warranty repairs during the year.
8. Paid operating expenses of $87,000 for the year.
9. Paid $300,000 of accounts payable.
10. Recorded accrued interest on the note issued in transaction no. 6.

Required

a. Show the effect of these transactions on the financial statements using a horizontal statements model like the one shown here. Use a + to indicate increase, a − for decrease, and NA for not affected. In the Cash Flow column, indicate whether the item is an operating activity (OA), investing activity (IA), or financing activity (FA). The first transaction is recorded as an example.

Assets	=	Liabilities	+	Equity	Rev.	−	Exp.	=	Net Inc.	Cash Flow
+		NA		+	NA		NA		NA	+ FA

b. Prepare the journal entries for the above transactions and post them to the appropriate T-accounts.

c. Prepare the income statement, balance sheet, and statement of cash flows for 2013.

d. What is the total amount of current liabilities at December 31, 2013?

LO 5

Exercise 9-9B   *Calculating payroll*

Vaughn Enterprises has two hourly employees, Lane and Adam. Both employees earn overtime at the rate of 1½ times the hourly rate for hours worked in excess of 40 per week. Assume the Social Security tax rate is 6 percent on the first $110,000 of wages and the Medicare tax rate is 1.5 percent on all earnings. Federal income tax withheld for Lane and Adam was $260 and $220 respectively for the first week of January. The following information is for the first week in January 2013:

Employee	Hours Worked	Wage Rate per Hour
Lane	54	$31
Adam	44	$28

Required

a. Calculate the gross pay for each employee for the week.

b. Calculate the net pay for each employee for the week.

c. Prepare the general journal entry to record payment of the wages.

Exercise 9-10B *Calculating payroll*

BJ Entertainment has two employees in 2013. Chad earns $3,800 per month and Jordan, the manager, earns $10,500 per month. Neither is paid extra for working overtime. Assume the Social Security tax rate is 6 percent on the first $110,000 of earnings and the Medicare tax rate is 1.5 percent on all earnings. The federal income tax withholding is 15 percent of gross earnings for Chad and 20 percent for Jordan. Both Chad and Jordan have been employed all year.

Required

a. Calculate the net pay for both Chad and Jordan for March.
b. Calculate the net pay for both Chad and Jordan for December.
c. Is the net pay the same in March as December for both employees? Why or why not?
d. What amounts will BJ's report on the 2013 W-2s for each employee?

Exercise 9-11B *Calculating employee and employer payroll taxes*

Woods Co. employed Brian Smith in 2013. Brian earned $5,400 per month and worked the entire year. Assume the Social Security tax rate is 6 percent for the first $110,000 of earnings and the Medicare tax rate is 1.5 percent. Brian's federal income tax withholding amount is $1,200 per month. Use 5.4 percent for the state unemployment tax rate and .8 percent for the federal unemployment tax rate on the first $7,000 of earnings per employee.

Required

a. Answer the following questions.
   (1) What is Brian's net pay per month?
   (2) What amount does Brian pay monthly in FICA payroll taxes?
   (3) What is the total payroll tax expense for Woods Co. for January 2013? February 2013? March 2013? December 2013?
b. Assume that instead of $5,400 per month Brian earned $9,800 per month. Answer the questions in Requirement *a*.

Exercise 9-12B *Fringe benefits and payroll expense*

Sneed Co. provides various fringe benefits for its three employees. It provides vacation and personal leave at the rate of one day for each month worked. Its employees earn a combined total of approximately $400 per day. In addition, Sneed Co. pays $650 per month in medical insurance premiums for its employees. Sneed also contributes $400 per month into a retirement plan for the employees. The federal unemployment tax rate is .8 percent and the state unemployment tax rate is 4.0 percent on the first $7,000 of earnings per employee.

Required

a. Prepare the monthly journal entry for the accrued fringe benefits.
b. Show the effect of the above transaction on a statements model like the one shown below.

Assets =	Liabilities	+	Equity	Income Statement	Cash Flow
Cash =	Various Payables	+ Com. Stk. +	Ret. Earn.	Rev. − Exp. = Net Inc.	

c. If the three employees each worked 250 days, what is Sneed Co.'s total payroll cost (salary, payroll taxes, and fringe benefits) for the year? (Assume that each employee earns $200 per day.)

Exercise 9-13B *Comprehensive single cycle problem*

The following transactions apply to York Co. for 2013:

1. Received $60,000 cash from the issue of common stock.
2. Purchased inventory on account for $240,000.
3. Sold inventory for $280,000 cash that had cost $150,000. Sales tax was collected at the rate of 5 percent on the inventory sold.

4. Borrowed $40,000 from the First State Bank on March 1, 2013. The note had a 7 percent interest rate and a one-year term to maturity.

5. Paid the accounts payable (see transaction 2).

6. Paid the sales tax due on $200,000 of sales. Sales tax on the other $80,000 is not due until after the end of the year.

7. Salaries for the year for the one employee amounted to $42,000. Assume the Social Security tax rate is 6 percent and the Medicare tax rate is 1.5 percent. Federal income tax withheld was $5,100.

8. Paid $6,200 for warranty repairs during the year.

9. Paid $41,000 of other operating expenses during the year.

10. Paid a dividend of $5,000 to the shareholders.

Adjustments:

11. The products sold in transaction 3 were warranted. York estimated that the warranty cost would be 3 percent of sales.

12. Record the accrued interest at December 31, 2013.

13. Record the accrued payroll tax at December 31, 2013. Assume no payroll taxes have been paid for the year and that the unemployment tax rate is 6.2 percent (federal unemployment tax rate is .8 percent and the state unemployment tax rate is 5.4 percent on the first $7,000 of earnings per employee).

Required

a. Record the above transactions in general journal form.

b. Post the transactions to T-accounts.

c. Prepare an income statement, statement of changes in stockholders' equity, balance sheet, and statement of cash flows for 2013.

LO 6

Exercise 9-14B   *Preparing a classified balance sheet*

Required

Use the following information to prepare a classified balance sheet for Watkins Co. at the end of 2013.

Accounts receivable	$24,300
Accounts payable	11,000
Cash	21,300
Common stock	24,000
Land	15,000
Long-term notes payable	18,500
Merchandise inventory	27,000
Retained earnings	34,100

LO 7

Exercise 9-15B   *Using the current ratio to make comparisons*

The following information was drawn from the 2013 balance sheets of the Copper and Iron companies:

	Copper	Iron
Current assets	$110,000	$140,000
Current liabilities	79,000	127,000

Required

a. Compute the current ratio for each company.

b. Which company has the greater likelihood of being able to pay its bills?

c. Assume that both companies have the same amount of total assets. Speculate as to which company would produce the higher return on assets ratio.

Exercise 9-16B   *Effect of a discount note on financial statements (Appendix)*

Chad Matson started a design company on January 1, 2013. On April 1, 2013, Matson borrowed cash from a local bank by issuing a one-year $100,000 face value note with annual interest based on an 8 percent discount. During 2013, Matson provided services for $64,000 cash.

Required

Answer the following questions. (*Hint:* Record the events in T-accounts prior to answering the questions.)

a. What is the amount of total liabilities on the December 31, 2013, balance sheet?

b. What is the amount of net income on the 2013 income statement?

c. What is the amount of cash flow from operating activities on the 2013 statement of cash flows?

d. Provide the general journal entries necessary to record issuing the note on April 1, 2013; recognizing accrued interest on December 31, 2013; and repaying the loan on March 31, 2014.

Exercise 9-17B   *Comparing effective interest rates on discount versus interest-bearing notes (Appendix)*

Patrick Owens borrowed money by issuing two notes on March 1, 2013. The financing transactions are described here.

1. Borrowed funds by issuing a $40,000 face value discount note to Farmers Bank. The note had an 8 percent discount rate, a one-year term to maturity, and was paid off on March 1, 2014.

2. Borrowed funds by issuing a $40,000 face value, interest-bearing note to Valley Bank. The note had an 8 percent stated rate of interest, a one-year term to maturity, and was paid off on March 1, 2014.

Required

a. Show the effects of issuing the two notes on the financial statements using separate horizontal financial statement models like the ones here. Record the transaction amounts under the appropriate categories. In the Cash Flow column, indicate whether the item is an operating activity (OA), investing activity (IA), or financing activity (FA). Record only the events occurring on the date of issue. Do not record accrued interest or the repayment at maturity.

Discount Note

Assets =	Liabilities	+ Equity	Rev. − Exp. = Net Inc.	Cash Flow
Cash = Notes Pay. − Disc. on Notes Pay. + Ret. Earn.				

Interest-Bearing Note

Assets	=	Liabilities	+	Equity	Rev.	−	Exp.	=	Net Inc.	Cash Flow
Cash	=	Notes Pay.	+	Ret. Earn.						

b. What is the total amount of interest to be paid on each note?

c. What amount of cash was received from each note when it was issued?

d. Which note has the higher effective interest rate? Support your answer with appropriate computations.

LO 8

Exercise 9-18B   *Recording accounting events for a discount note (Appendix)*

Ellison Co. issued a $50,000 face value discount note to National Bank on July 1, 2013. The note had a 10 percent discount rate and a one-year term to maturity.

Required

Prepare general journal entries for the following:

a. The issuance of the note on July 1, 2013.
b. The adjustment for accrued interest at the end of the year, December 31, 2013.
c. Recording interest expense for 2014 and repaying the principal on June 30, 2014.

PROBLEMS—SERIES B

LO 1

Problem 9-19B   *Effect of accrued interest on financial statements*

Talladega Enterprises borrowed $32,000 from a local bank on July 1, 2013, when the company was started. The note had a 10 percent annual interest rate and a one-year term to maturity. Talladega Enterprises recognized $61,500 of revenue on account in 2013 and $70,600 of revenue on account in 2014. Cash collections of accounts receivable were $54,300 in 2013 and $69,800 in 2014. Talladega paid $38,000 of other operating expenses in 2013 and $42,000 of other operating expenses in 2014. Repaid the loan and interest at the maturity date.

Required

Based on this information, answer the following questions. (*Hint:* Record the events in the accounting equation before answering the questions.)

a. What amount of interest expense would Talladega report on the 2013 income statement?
b. What amount of net cash flow from operating activities would Talladega report on the 2013 statement of cash flows?
c. What amount of total liabilities would Talladega report on the December 31, 2013, balance sheet?
d. What amount of retained earnings would Talladega report on the December 31, 2013, balance sheet?
e. What amount of net cash flow from financing activities would Talladega report on the 2013 statement of cash flows?
f. What amount of interest expense would Talladega report on the 2014 income statement?
g. What amount of net cash flow from operating activities would Talladega report on the 2014 statement of cash flows?
h. What amount of total assets would Talladega report on the December 31, 2014, balance sheet?
i. What amount of net cash flow from investing activities would Talladega report on the 2014 statement of cash flows?
j. If Talladega Enterprises paid a $2,000 dividend during 2014, what retained earnings balance would it report on the December 31, 2014, balance sheet?

LO 1, 2

Problem 9-20B   *Account for short-term debt and sales tax—two accounting cycles*

The following transactions apply to Cullman Enterprises for 2013, its first year of operations:

1. Received $60,000 cash from the issue of a short-term note with a 6 percent interest rate and a one-year maturity. The note was made on April 1, 2013.
2. Received $150,000 cash plus applicable sales tax from performing services. The services are subject to a sales tax rate of 6 percent.
3. Paid $75,000 cash for other operating expenses during the year.
4. Paid the sales tax due on $130,000 of the service revenue for the year. Sales tax on the balance of the revenue is not due until 2014.
5. Recognized the accrued interest at December 31, 2013.

The following transactions apply to Cullman Enterprises for 2014:

1. Paid the balance of the sales tax due for 2013.
2. Received $195,000 cash plus applicable sales tax from performing services. The services are subject to a sales tax rate of 6 percent.
3. Repaid the principal of the note and applicable interest on April 1, 2014.
4. Paid $106,500 of other operating expenses during the year.
5. Paid the sales tax due on $190,000 of the service revenue. The sales tax on the balance of the revenue is not due until 2015.

Required

a. Record the 2013 transactions in general journal form.
b. Post the transactions to T-accounts.
c. Prepare a balance sheet, statement of changes in stockholders' equity, income statement, and statement of cash flows for 2013.
d. Prepare the closing entries and post them to the T-accounts.
e. Prepare a post-closing trial balance.
f. Repeat Requirements *a* through *e* for 2014.

Problem 9-21B   *Contingent liabilities*   LO 3

Required

a. Give an example of a contingent liability that is probable and reasonably estimable. How would this type of liability be shown in the accounting records?
b. Give an example of a contingent liability that is reasonably possible or probable but not reasonably estimable. How would this type of liability be shown in the accounting records?
c. Give an example of a contingent liability that is remote. How is this type of liability shown in the accounting records?

Problem 9-22B   *Current liabilities*   LO 1, 2, 3, 4

The following selected transactions were taken from the books of Athens Company for 2013:

1. On February 1, 2013, borrowed $80,000 cash from the local bank. The note had a 6 percent interest rate and was due on June 1, 2013.
2. Cash sales for the year amounted to $290,000 plus sales tax at the rate of 7 percent.
3. Athens provides a 90-day warranty on the merchandise sold. The warranty expense is estimated to be 1 percent of sales.
4. Paid the sales tax to the state sales tax agency on $260,000 of the sales.
5. Paid the note due on June 1 and the related interest.
6. On November 1, 2013, borrowed $30,000 cash from the local bank. The note had a 6 percent interest rate and a one-year term to maturity.
7. Paid $2,400 in warranty repairs.
8. A customer has filed a lawsuit against Athens for $1 million for breach of contract. The company attorney does not believe the suit has merit.

Required

a. Answer the following questions:
   (1) What amount of cash did Athens pay for interest during 2013?
   (2) What amount of interest expense is reported on Athens's income statement for 2013?
   (3) What is the amount of warranty expense for 2013?
b. Prepare the current liabilities section of the balance sheet at December 31, 2013. (*Hint:* First post the liabilities transactions to T-accounts.)
c. Show the effect of these transactions on the financial statements using a horizontal statements model like the one on the next page. Use a + to indicate increase, a − for decrease, and NA for not affected. In the Cash Flow column, indicate whether the item is an operating

activity (OA), investing activity (IA), or financing activity (FA). The first transaction has been recorded as an example.

Assets	=	Liabilities	+	Equity	Rev.	−	Exp.	=	Net Inc.	Cash Flow
+		+		NA	NA		NA		NA	+ FA

LO 5

Problem 9-23B   *Accounting for payroll and payroll taxes*

Auto Service Co. pays salaries monthly on the last day of the month. The following information is available from Auto for the month ended December 31, 2013:

Administrative salaries	$86,000
Sales salaries	58,000
Office salaries	36,000

Assume the Social Security tax rate is 6 percent on the first $110,000 of salaries. Rane reached the $110,000 amount in September. His salary in December amounted to $11,500 and is included in the $86,000. No one else will reach the $110,000 amount for the year. None of the employee salaries are subject to unemployment tax in December.

Other amounts withheld from salaries in December were as follows:

Federal income tax	$21,500
State income tax	11,200
Employee savings plan	4,000

Required

a. Prepare the journal entry to record the payment of payroll on December 31, 2013.
b. Prepare the journal entry to record the payroll tax expense for Auto Service Co. for December 2013.

LO 5

Problem 9-24B   *Computation of net pay and payroll expense*

The following information is available for the employees of Bryan Packing Company for the first week of January 2013:

1. Cindy earns $26 per hour and 1½ times her regular rate for hours over 40 per week. Cindy worked 52 hours the first week in January. Cindy's federal income tax withholding is equal to 15 percent of her gross pay. Bryan pays medical insurance of $50 per week for Cindy and contributes $50 per week to a retirement plan for her.
2. Maggie earns a weekly salary of $1,800. Maggie's federal income tax withholding is 18 percent of her gross pay. Bryan pays medical insurance of $80 per week for Maggie and contributes $100 per week to a retirement plan for her.
3. Vacation pay is accrued at the rate of 2 hours per week (based on the regular pay rate) for Cindy and $60 per week for Maggie.

Assume the Social Security tax rate is 6 percent on the first $110,000 of salaries and the Medicare tax rate is 1.5 percent of total salaries. The state unemployment tax rate is 4.2 percent and the federal unemployment tax rate is .8 percent of the first $7,000 of salary for each employee.

Required

a. Compute the gross pay for Cindy for the first week in January.
b. Compute the net pay for both Cindy and Maggie for the first week in January.
c. Prepare the journal entry to record the payment of the payroll for the week.
d. Prepare the journal entry to record the payroll tax expense and fringe benefit expense for Bryan Packing Company for the week.
e. What is the total cost of compensation expense for the first week of January 2013 for Bryan Packing Company?

Problem 9-25B   *Multistep income statement and classified balance sheet*   LO 6

Required

Use the following information to prepare a multistep income statement and a classified balance sheet for Huggins Equipment Co. for 2013. (*Hint:* Some of the items will *not* appear on either statement, and ending retained earnings must be calculated.)

Salaries expense	$ 65,000	Beginning retained earnings	$ 70,150
Common stock	50,000	Warranties payable (short term)	1,500
Notes receivable (short term)	15,000	Gain on sale of equipment	8,500
Allowance for doubtful accounts	6,500	Operating expenses	75,000
Accumulated depreciation	42,300	Cash flow from investing activities	125,000
Notes payable (long term)	110,000	Prepaid rent	12,200
Salvage value of building	6,000	Land	50,000
Interest payable (short term)	1,500	Cash	26,300
Uncollectible accounts expense	8,650	Inventory	109,500
Supplies	1,800	Accounts payable	32,000
Equipment	93,500	Interest expense	8,600
Interest revenue	3,600	Salaries payable	5,200
Sales revenue	420,000	Unearned revenue	26,300
Dividends	10,000	Cost of goods sold	236,000
Warranty expense	8,400	Accounts receivable	56,000
Interest receivable (short term)	600	Depreciation expense	1,000

Problem 9-26B   *Using ratios to make comparisons*   LO 7

The following accounting information exists for Diamond and Emerald companies at the end of 2014:

	Diamond	Emerald
Cash	$ 230,000	$ 185,000
Wages payable	50,000	40,000
Merchandise inventory	430,000	315,000
Building	600,000	500,000
Accounts receivable	250,000	200,000
Long-term notes payable	550,000	600,000
Land	250,000	220,000
Accounts payable	350,000	300,000
Sales revenue	3,520,000	2,850,000
Expenses	3,230,000	2,615,000

Required

a. Identify the current assets and current liabilities and compute the current ratio for each company.

b. Assuming that all assets and liabilities are listed here, compute the debt to assets ratios for each company.

c. Determine which company has the greater financial risk in both the short term and the long term.

Problem 9-27B   *Accounting for a discount note across two accounting cycles (Appendix)*   LO 8

Precious Watson opened Precious & Company, an accounting practice, in 2013. The following summarizes transactions that occurred during 2013:

1. Issued a $100,000 face value discount note to First National Bank on July 1, 2013. The note had an 8 percent discount rate and a one-year term to maturity.

2. Recognized cash revenue of $275,000.

3. Incurred and paid $123,000 of operating expenses.

4. Adjusted the books to recognize interest expense at December 31, 2013.

5. Prepared the necessary closing entries at December 31, 2013.

The following summarizes transactions that occurred in 2014:

1. Recognized $326,000 of cash revenue.

2. Incurred and paid $143,000 of operating expenses.

3. Recognized the interest expense for 2014 and paid the face value of the note.

4. Prepared the necessary closing entries at December 31, 2014.

Required

a. Show the effects of each of the transactions on the elements of the financial statements, using a horizontal statements model like the one shown here. Use + for increase, − for decrease, and NA for not affected. The first transaction is entered as an example. (*Hint:* Closing entries do not affect the statements model.)

Event No.	Assets	=	Liab.	+	Equity	Rev.	−	Exp.	=	Net Inc.	Cash Flow
1	+		+		NA	NA		NA		NA	+ FA

b. Prepare entries in general journal form for the transactions for 2013 and 2014, and post them to T-accounts.

c. Prepare an income statement, statement of changes in stockholders' equity, balance sheet, and statement of cash flows for 2013 and 2014.

ANALYZE, THINK, COMMUNICATE

ATC 9-1   Business Applications Case   *Understanding real-world annual reports*

Required

Use the Target Corporation's annual report in Appendix B to answer the following questions.

a. What was Target's current ratio for its fiscal-year ended January 29, 2011 (2010) and 2009?

b. Did the current ratio get stronger or weaker from 2009 to 2010? Explain briefly why this happened.

c. Target's balance sheet reports "Accrued and other current liabilities." What is included in this category? (See the notes to the financial statements.)

ATC 9-2   Group Assignment   *Accounting for payroll*

The following payroll information is available for three companies for 2013. Each company has two employees. Assume that the Social Security tax rate is 6 percent on the first $110,000 of earnings and the Medicare tax rate is 1.5 percent on all earnings.

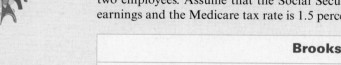

Brooks Company				
Brooks Company	Hourly Rate	Regular Hours	Overtime Rate	Overtime Hours
Employee No. 1	$40	2,000	$60	300
Employee No. 2	20	2,000	30	100

Other benefits provided for the employees:	
Medical insurance	$250 per month for each employee
Pension benefits	$100 per month for one employee

Federal income tax withheld is 15 percent of gross earnings for each employee. The state unemployment tax rate is 3.5 percent and the federal unemployment tax rate is .8 percent on the first $7,000 of earnings per employee.

Hill Company

Hill Company	Weekly Rate/Hourly Rate	Weeks/Hours Worked	Overtime Rate	Overtime Hours
Employee No. 1	$2,000	52	NA	NA
Employee No. 2	18	2,000	$27	60

> Other benefits provided for the employees:
> Medical and dental insurance $325 per month for each employee.
> Pension benefits $150 per month for one employee and
> $100 per month for the other employee.

Federal income tax withheld is 15 percent of gross earnings for each employee. The state unemployment tax rate is 3.5 percent and the federal unemployment tax rate is .8 percent on the first $7,000 of earnings per employee.

Valley Company

Valley Company	Monthly Rate/Hourly Rate	Monthly/Hours Worked	Overtime Rate	Overtime Hours
Employee No. 1	$10,500	12	NA	NA
Employee No. 2 (part time)	20	860	NA	NA

> Other benefits provided for the employees:
> Medical and dental insurance $375 per month for only one employee.
> Pension benefits   10% of Gross salary for the full time employee.

Federal income tax withheld is 15 percent of gross earnings for each employee. The state unemployment tax rate is 3.0 percent and the federal unemployment tax rate is .8 percent on the first $7,000 of earnings per employee.

Required

a. Divide the class into groups of four or five students. Organize the groups into three sections. Assign each section of groups the payroll data for one of the above companies.

Group Tasks

(1) Determine the gross and net payroll for your company for the year.

(2) Determine the total compensation cost for your company for the year.

(3) Have a representative from each section put the compensation on the board broken down by salaries cost, payroll tax, and fringe benefit cost.

Class Discussion

b. Have the class discuss how the categories of compensation cost are similar and why some are more or less than those of the other companies.

ATC 9-3   Real-World Case   *Unusual types of liabilities*

In the liabilities section of its 2010 balance sheet, Bank of America reported "noninterest-bearing deposits" of over $285 billion. Bank of America is a very large banking company. In the liabilities section of its 2010 balance sheet, Newmont Mining Corporation reported "reclamation and remediation liabilities" of more than $984 million. Newmont Mining is involved in gold mining and refining activities. In its 2010 balance sheet, Delta Air Lines' largest current liability reported was $3.3 billion for "air traffic liability."

Required

a. For each of the preceding liabilities, write a brief explanation of what you believe the nature of the liability to be and how the company will pay it off. To develop your answers, think about the nature of the industry in which each of the companies operates.

b. Of the three liabilities described, which do you think poses the most risk for the company? In other words, for which liability are actual costs most likely to exceed the liability reported on the balance sheet? Uncertainty creates risk.

ATC 9-4   Business Applications Case   *Performing ratio analysis using real-world data*

Not surprisingly, Newell Rubbermaid, Inc. is the marketer of the well known Rubbermaid plastic containers, but it also markets many other consumer brands, including Sharpie, Calphalon, Parker and Waterman writing instruments, and Lenox hand and power tools. The following data were taken from the company's 2010 annual report. Dollar amounts are in millions.

	Fiscal Years Ending	
	December 31, 2010	December 31, 2009
Current assets	$2,132.0	$2,182.1
Current liabilities	1,665.9	1,759.5
Total assets	6,405.3	6,423.9
Total liabilities	4,499.8	4,645.2

Required

a. Compute Rubbermaid's current ratios for 2010 and 2009.

b. Compute Rubbermaid's debt to assets ratios for 2010 and 2009.

c. Based on the ratios computed in Requirements *a* and *b*, did Rubbermaid's liquidity get better or worse from 2009 to 2010?

d. Based on the ratios computed in Requirements *a* and *b*, did Rubbermaid's solvency get better or worse from 2009 to 2010?

ATC 9-5   Business Applications Case   *Performing ratio analysis using real-world data*

National Semiconductor Corp claims to be ". . . one of the world's leading semiconductor companies focused on analog and mixed-signal integrated circuits and sub-systems, particularly in the area of power management." Texas Instruments, Inc., claims to be ". . . the world's fourth largest semiconductor company in 2009 as measured by revenue . . ." The following data were taken from the companies' 2010 annual reports. Dollar amounts are in millions.

	National Semiconductor	Texas Instruments
Current assets	$1,470.9	$ 7,060
Current liabilities	548.4	1,981
Total assets	2,274.8	13,401
Total liabilities	1,848.9	2,964

Required

a. Compute the current ratio for each company.

b. Compute the debt to assets ratio for each company.

c. Based on the ratios computed in Requirements *a* and *b*, which company had the better liquidity in 2010?

d. Based on the ratios computed in Requirements *a* and *b*, which company had the better solvency in 2010?

ATC 9-6   Writing Assignment   *Payroll tax costs*

Nancy, who graduated from State University in June 2013, has just landed her first real job. She is excited because her salary is $4,000 per month. Nancy is single and has been planning all month about how she will spend her $4,000. When she received her first paycheck on June 30, 2013, she was very disappointed. The amount of her check was only $3,100. Explain to Nancy why (generally) her check was not for $4,000.

ATC 9-7   Ethical Dilemma   *Who pays FICA taxes?*

Scott Putman owns and operates a lawn care company. Like most companies in the lawn care business, his company experiences a high level of employee turnover. However, he finds it relatively easy to replace employees because he pays above market wages. He attributes his ability to pay high wages to a little accounting trick he discovered several years ago. Instead of paying his half of each employee's FICA taxes to the government, he decided to pay that money to the employees in the form of higher wages. He then doubles their FICA tax payroll deduction and uses half of the deduction to pay his share of the Social Security tax. For example, suppose he plans to pay an employee $2,000 per month. Technically, the employee would have to pay 7.5 percent FICA and Medicare tax ($2,000 × .075 = $150) and Mr. Putman's company would have to make a $150 matching payment. Instead of doing it this way, he devised the following plan. He pays the employee $2,150 and then deducts $300 for FICA and Medicare tax from the employee's salary. The end result is the same. Either way the employee ends up with net pay of $1,850 ($2,000 − $150 = $1,850 or $2,150 − $300 = $1,850). Also, the government gets $300 FICA tax, regardless of how it gets divided between the employee and the employer. Mr. Putman is convinced that he is right in what he is doing. Certainly, it benefits his company by allowing him to offer higher starting salaries. Further, he believes it is a more honest way of showing the real cost of Social Security and Medicare.

Required

a. Is Mr. Putnam right in his assumption that the total tax paid is the same under his approach as it would be if proper accounting procedures were applied? Explain.

b. Assuming that Mr. Putman is a CPA, do his actions violate any of the articles of the AICPA Code of Professional Conduct shown in Chapter 2 (Exhibit 2.9)? If so, discuss some of the articles that are violated.

c. Discuss Mr. Putman's actions within the context of the fraud triangle's elements of ethical misconduct that were outlined in Chapter 2.

ATC 9-8   Research Assignment   *Analyzing Pep Boys' liquidity*

Using either the most current Form 10-K for The Pep Boys—Manny, Moe & Jack, or the company's annual report, answer the questions below. To obtain the Form 10-K either use the EDGAR system following the instructions in Appendix A, or the company's website. The company's annual report is available on its website.

Required

a. What is Pep Boys' current ratio?

b. Which of Pep Boys' current assets had the largest balance?

c. What percentage of Pep Boys' total assets consisted of current assets?

d. Did Pep Boys have any "currently maturing" long-term debt included in current liabilities on its balance sheet?

e. If Pep Boys were a company that manufactured auto parts rather than a retailer of auto parts, how do you think its balance sheet would be different?

ATC 9-9   Excel Assignment

The following information is available for Lumberton Co. for the week ending June 28, 2013. All employees are paid time and one-half for all hours over 40. Each employee has cumulative salary of over $7,000, but less than $110,000. Assume the Social Security tax rate is 6% on the first $110,000 of wages and the Medicare tax rate is 1.5% of total wages. The company contributes the retirement cost to a retirement plan for the employee.

Employee	Rate of Pay	Hours	Fed WH %	Contributions to Retirement Plans
Jillian	$15 per hour	32	12%	$20 per week
Carl	18	46	10	10% of gross pay
Yolanda	16	45	10	10% of gross pay

Required

a. Set up a spread sheet to compute the net pay for each of the above employees. You will need to insert the appropriate excel formulas.

b. What is the total amount of compensation cost (salary cost plus payroll tax cost) for Lumberton Co. for the week ending June 28, 2013?

c. Lumberton is considering adding group health insurance coverage for its employees to its benefits package. If the average cost of health insurance per employee is $3,900 per year, how much additional cost would be added to weekly compensation cost for Lumberton? Assume the addition of health insurance and recompute the total compensation cost for Lumberton for the week ending June 28, 2013.

ATC 9-10

Refer to Problem 9-17B. Complete requirement *a*, *b*, *c*, and *d*, using an Excel spreadsheet. Refer to Chapter 1, problem ATC 1-8 for ideas on how to structure the spreadsheet.

COMPREHENSIVE PROBLEM

The trial balance of Pacilio Security Services Inc. as of January 1, 2019, had the following normal balances:

Cash	$93,380
Petty cash	100
Accounts receivable	21,390
Allowance for doubtful accounts	2,485
Supplies	180
Prepaid rent	3,000
Merchandise inventory (23 @ $280)	6,440
Equipment	9,000
Van	27,000
Accumulated depreciation	14,900
Salaries payable	1,500
Common stock	50,000
Retained earnings	91,605

During 2019 Pacilio Security Services experienced the following transactions:

1. Paid the salaries payable from 2018.
2. Paid $9,000 on May 2, 2019, for one year's office rent in advance.
3. Purchased $425 of supplies on account.

4. Purchased 145 alarm systems at a cost of $290 each. Paid cash for the purchase.

5. After numerous attempts to collect from customers, wrote off $2,060 of uncollectible accounts receivable.

6. Sold 130 alarm systems for $580 each plus sales tax of 5 percent. All sales were on account. (Be sure to compute cost of goods sold using the FIFO cost flow method.)

7. Billed $107,000 of monitoring services for the year. Credit card sales amounted to $42,000, and the credit card company charged a 4 percent fee. The remaining $65,000 were sales on account. Sales tax is not charged on this service.

8. Replenished the petty cash fund on June 30. The fund had $5 cash and has receipts of $60 for yard mowing, $15 for office supplies expense, and $17 for miscellaneous expenses.

9. Collected the amount due from the credit card company.

10. Paid the sales tax collected on $69,600 of the alarm sales.

11. Paid installers and other employees a total of $65,000 for salaries for the year. Assume the Social Security tax rate is 6 percent and the Medicare tax rate is 1.5 percent. Federal income taxes withheld amounted to $7,500. Cash was paid for the net amount of salaries due.

12. Pacilio now offers a one-year warranty on its alarm systems. Paid $1,950 in warranty repairs during the year.

13. On September 1, borrowed $12,000 from State Bank. The note had an 8 percent interest rate and a one-year term to maturity.

14. Collected $136,100 of accounts receivable during the year.

15. Paid $15,000 of advertising expense during the year.

16. Paid $7,200 of utilities expense for the year.

17. Paid the payroll taxes, both the amounts withheld from the salaries plus the employer share of Social Security tax and Medicare tax, on $60,000 of the salaries plus $7,000 of the federal income tax that was withheld. (Unemployment taxes were not paid at this time.)

18. Paid the accounts payable.

19. Paid a dividend of $10,000 to the shareholders.

Adjustments

20. There was $165 of supplies on hand at the end of the year.

21. Recognized the expired rent for the office building for the year.

22. Recognized uncollectible accounts expense for the year using the allowance method. The company revised its estimate of uncollectible accounts based on prior years' experience. This year Pacilio estimates that 2.75 percent of sales on account will not be collected.

23. Recognized depreciation expense on the equipment and the van. The equipment has a 5-year life and a $2,000 salvage value. The van has a 4-year life and a $6,000 salvage value. The company uses double-declining-balance for the van and straight-line for the equipment. (A full year's depreciation was taken in 2018, the year of acquisition.)

24. The alarm systems sold in transaction 6 were covered with a one-year warranty. Pacilio estimated that the warranty cost would be 3 percent of alarm sales.

25. Recognized the accrued interest on the note payable at December 31, 2019.

26. The unemployment tax on salaries has not been paid. Record the accrued unemployment tax on the salaries for the year. The unemployment tax rate is 4.5 percent. ($14,000 of salaries is subject to this tax.)

27. Recognized the employer Social Security and Medicare payroll tax that has not been paid on $5,000 of salaries expense.

Required

a. Record the above transactions in general journal form. Round all amounts to nearest whole dollar.

b. Post the transactions to the T-accounts.

c. Prepare a trial balance.

d. Prepare an income statement, statement of changes in stockholders' equity, a classified balance sheet, and statement of cash flows.

e. Close the temporary accounts to retained earnings.

f. Post the closing entries to the T-accounts and prepare a post-closing trial balance.

Accounting for Long-Term Debt

CHAPTER OPENING

Most businesses finance their investing activities with long-term debt. Recall that current liabilities mature within one year or a company's operating cycle, whichever is longer. Other liabilities are **long-term liabilities.** Long-term debt agreements vary with respect to requirements for paying interest charges and repaying principal (the amount borrowed). Interest payments may be due monthly, annually, at some other interval, or at the maturity date. Interest charges may be based on a **fixed interest rate** that remains constant during the term of the loan or may be based on a **variable interest rate** that fluctuates up or down during the loan period.

Principal repayment is generally required either in one lump sum at the maturity date or in installments that are spread over the life of the loan. For example, each monthly payment on your car loan probably includes both paying interest and repaying some of the principal. Repaying a portion of the principal with regular payments that also include interest is often called loan **amortization.**[1] This chapter explains accounting for interest and principal with respect to the major forms of long-term debt financing.

[1]In Chapter 8 the term *amortization* described the expense recognized when the *cost of an intangible asset* is systematically allocated to expense over the useful life of the asset. This chapter shows that the term amortization refers more broadly to a variety of allocation processes. Here it means the systematic process of allocating the *principal repayment* over the life of a loan.

The Curious Accountant

In its 2010 fiscal year **BP p.l.c.** reported a net loss of $3.7 billion. During 2010, BP incurred $1.2 billion of interest expense. BP is the company formally named British Petroleum. Its net loss in 2010 was due to an oil spill at one of its wells in the Gulf of Mexico for which the company recorded a pretax expense of $40.9 billion.

With such a huge loss on its income statement, do you think BP was able to make the interest payments on its debt? If so, how? (Answer on page 537.)

INSTALLMENT NOTES PAYABLE

LO 1

Show how an installment note affects financial statements.

Loans that require payments of principal and interest at regular intervals (amortizing loans) are typically represented by **installment notes.** The terms of installment notes usually range from two to five years. To illustrate accounting for installment notes, assume Blair Company was started on January 1, 2013, when it borrowed $100,000 cash from the National Bank. In exchange for the money, Blair issued the bank a five-year installment note with a 9 percent fixed interest rate. The journal entry to record issuing the note and its effects on the financial statements are as follows:

Date	Account Title	Debit	Credit
2013 Jan. 1	Cash	100,000	
	Installment Note Payable		100,000

	Assets	=	Liab.	+		Equity			Rev.	−	Exp.	=	Net Inc.	Cash Flow	
Date	Cash	=	Note Pay.	+	Com. Stk.	+	Ret. Earn.								
2013 Jan. 1	100,000	=	100,000	+	NA	+	NA		NA	−	NA	=	NA	100,000	FA

The loan agreement required Blair to pay five equal installments of $25,709[2] on December 31 of each year from 2013 through 2017. Exhibit 10.1 shows the allocation of each payment between principal and interest. When Blair pays the final installment, both the principal and interest will be paid in full. The amounts shown in Exhibit 10.1 are computed as follows:

1. The Interest Expense (Column D) is computed by multiplying the Principal Balance on Jan. 1 (Column B) by the interest rate. For example, interest expense for 2013 is $100,000 \times .09 = $9,000; for 2014 it is $83,291 \times .09 = $7,496; and so on.
2. The Principal Repayment (Column E) is computed by subtracting the Interest Expense (Column D) from the Cash Payment on Dec. 31 (Column C). For example, the Principal Repayment for 2013 is $25,709 − $9,000 = $16,709; for 2014 it is $25,709 − $7,496 = $18,213; and so on.

EXHIBIT 10.1

Amortization Schedule for Installment Note Payable

Accounting Period Column A	Principal Balance on Jan. 1 Column B	Cash Payment on Dec. 31 Column C	Interest Expense Column D	Principal Repayment Column E	Principal Balance on Dec. 31 Column F
2013	$100,000	$25,709	$9,000	$16,709	$83,291
2014	83,291	25,709	7,496	18,213	65,078
2015	65,078	25,709	5,857	19,852	45,226
2016	45,226	25,709	4,070	21,639	23,587
2017	23,587	25,710*	2,123	23,587	0

*All computations are rounded to the nearest dollar. To fully liquidate the liability, the final payment is one dollar more than the others because of rounding differences.

[2]The amount of the annual payment is determined using the present value concepts presented in Appendix F (page 773) in the back of this text. Usually the lender (bank or other financial institution) calculates the amount of the payment for the customer.

Answers to The Curious Accountant

BP p.l.c. was able to make its interest payments in 2010 for two reasons.

(1) Interest is paid with cash, not accrued earnings. Many of the expenses on the company's income statement did not require the use of cash. The company's statement of cash flows shows that net cash flow from operating activities, *after making interest payments,* was a positive $13.6 billion in 2010, which is much greater than the $3.7 billion it reported as a net loss. Even though in 2010 BP recorded a pretax expense of $40.9 billion related to the oil spill, by the end of the year it had paid only $17.7 billion in cash related to this charge. The remaining amounts are for payments it expects to have to make in future years. Nevertheless, by the end of 2010, BP was trying to find buyers for some of its assets so as to have available the cash necessary to make the future payments related to the oil spill and also continue to explore for oil and run its operations. (2) The net loss the company incurred was *after* interest expense had been deducted. The capacity of operations to support interest payments is measured by the amount of earnings before interest deductions. For example, look at the 2013 income statement for Blair Company in Exhibit 10.2. This statement shows only $3,000 of net income, but $12,000 of cash revenue was available for the payment of interest. Similarly, BP's 2010 net loss is not an indication of the company's ability to pay interest in the short run.

3. The Principal Balance on Dec. 31 (Column F) is computed by subtracting the Principal Repayment (Column E) from the Principal Balance on Jan. 1 (Column B). For example, the Principal Balance on Dec. 31 for 2013 is $100,000 − $16,709 = $83,291; on December 31, 2014, the principal balance is $83,291 − $18,213 = $65,078; and so on. The Principal Balance on Dec. 31 (ending balance) for 2013 ($83,291) is also the Principal Balance on Jan. 1 (beginning balance) for 2014; the principal balance on December 31, 2014, is the principal balance on January 1, 2015, and so on.

Although the amounts for interest expense and principal repayment differ each year, the effects of the annual payment on the financial statements are the same. On the balance sheet, assets (cash) decrease by the total amount of the payment; liabilities (note payable) decrease by the amount of the principal repayment; and stockholders' equity (retained earnings) decreases by the amount of interest expense. Net income decreases from recognizing interest expense. On the statement of cash flows, the portion of the cash payment applied to interest is reported in the operating activities section and the portion applied to principal is reported in the financing activities section. The journal entry to record the December 31, 2013, cash payment and its effects on the financial statements is as follows:

Date	Account Title	Debit	Credit
2013 Dec. 31	Interest Expense	9,000	
	Installment Note Payable	16,709	
	Cash		25,709

	Assets	=	Liab.	+		Equity			Rev.	−	Exp.	=	Net Inc.	Cash Flow
Date	Cash	=	Note Pay.	+	Com. Stk.	+	Ret. Earn.							
2013 Dec. 31	(25,709)	=	(16,709)	+	NA	+	(9,000)		NA	−	9,000	=	(9,000)	(9,000) OA (16,709) FA

EXHIBIT 10.2

BLAIR COMPANY
Financial Statements

	2013	2014	2015	2016	2017
Income Statements					
Rent revenue	$12,000	$12,000	$12,000	$12,000	$12,000
Interest expense	(9,000)	(7,496)	(5,857)	(4,070)	(2,123)
Net income	$ 3,000	$ 4,504	$ 6,143	$ 7,930	$ 9,877
Balance Sheets					
Assets					
Cash	$86,291	$72,582	$58,873	$45,164	$31,454
Liabilities					
Note payable	$83,291	$65,078	$45,226	$23,587	$ 0
Stockholders' equity					
Retained earnings	3,000	7,504	13,647	21,577	31,454
Total liabilities and stk. equity	$86,291	$72,582	$58,873	$45,164	$31,454
Statements of Cash Flows					
Operating Activities					
Inflow from customers	$12,000	$12,000	$12,000	$12,000	$12,000
Outflow for interest	(9,000)	(7,496)	(5,857)	(4,070)	(2,123)
Investing Activities	0	0	0	0	0
Financing Activities					
Inflow from note issue	100,000	0	0	0	0
Outflow to repay note	(16,709)	(18,213)	(19,852)	(21,639)	(23,587)
Net change in cash	86,291	(13,709)	(13,709)	(13,709)	(13,710)
Plus: Beginning cash balance	0	86,291	72,582	58,873	45,164
Ending cash balance	$86,291	$72,582	$58,873	$45,164	$31,454

Exhibit 10.2 displays income statements, balance sheets, and statements of cash flows for Blair Company for the accounting periods 2013 through 2017. The illustration assumes that Blair earned $12,000 of rent revenue each year. Since some of the principal is repaid each year, the note payable amount reported on the balance sheet and the amount of the interest expense on the income statement both decline each year.

✓ CHECK YOURSELF 10.1

On January 1, 2013, Krueger Company issued a $50,000 installment note to State Bank. The note had a 10-year term and an 8 percent interest rate. Krueger agreed to repay the principal and interest in 10 annual payments of $7,451.47 at the end of each year. Determine the amount of principal and interest Krueger paid during the first and second year that the note was outstanding.

Answer

Accounting Period	Principal Balance January 1 A	Cash Payment December 31 B	Applied to Interest C = A × 0.08	Applied to Principal B − C
2013	$50,000.00	$7,451.47	$4,000.00	$3,451.47
2014	46,548.53	7,451.47	3,723.88	3,727.59

LINE OF CREDIT

A **line of credit** enables a company to borrow or repay funds as needed. For example, a business may borrow $50,000 one month and make a partial repayment of $10,000 the next month. Credit agreements usually specify a limit on the amount that can be borrowed. Exhibit 10.3 shows that credit agreements are widely used.

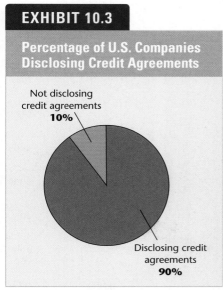

LO 2

Show how a line of credit affects financial statements.

Interest rates on lines of credit normally vary with fluctuations in some designated interest rate benchmark such as the rate paid on U.S. Treasury bills. For example, a company may pay 4 percent interest one month and 4.5 percent the next month, even if the principal balance remains constant.

Lines of credit typically have one-year terms. Although they are classified on the balance sheet as short-term liabilities, lines of credit are frequently extended indefinitely by simply renewing the credit agreement.

To illustrate accounting for a line of credit, assume Lagoon Company owns a wholesale jet-ski distributorship. In the spring, Lagoon borrows money using a line of credit to finance building up its inventory. Lagoon repays the loan over the summer months using cash generated from jet-ski sales. Borrowing or repaying events occur on the first of the month. Interest payments occur at the end of each month. Exhibit 10.4 presents all 2013 line of credit events.

Each borrowing event (March 1, April 1, and May 1) is an asset source transaction. Both cash and the line of credit liability increase. Each repayment (June 1, July 1, and August 1) is an asset use transaction. Both cash and the line of credit liability decrease. Each month's interest expense recognition and payment is an asset use transaction. Assets (cash) and stockholders' equity (retained earnings) decrease, as does net income. The journal entries to record the events are shown in Panel A of Exhibit 10.5. The effects of the events on the financial statements are shown in Panel B.

EXHIBIT 10.3

Percentage of U.S. Companies Disclosing Credit Agreements

Not disclosing credit agreements **10%**

Disclosing credit agreements **90%**

Data Source: AICPA, *Accounting Trends and Techniques.*

EXHIBIT 10.4

Summary of Line of Credit Events

Date	Amount Borrowed (Repaid)	Loan Balance at End of Month	Effective Interest Rate per Month (%)	Interest Expense (rounded to nearest $1)
Mar. 1	$20,000	$20,000	0.09 ÷ 12	$150
Apr. 1	30,000	50,000	0.09 ÷ 12	375
May 1	50,000	100,000	0.105 ÷ 12	875
June 1	(10,000)	90,000	0.10 ÷ 12	750
July 1	(40,000)	50,000	0.09 ÷ 12	375
Aug. 1	(50,000)	0	0.09 ÷ 12	0

BOND LIABILITIES

Many companies borrow money directly from the public by selling **bond certificates,** otherwise called *issuing* bonds. Bond certificates describe a company's obligation to pay interest and to repay the principal. The seller, or **issuer,** of a bond is the borrower; the buyer of a bond, or **bondholder,** is the lender.

LO 3

Describe bond features and show how bonds issued at face value affect financial statements.

From the issuer's point of view, a bond represents an obligation to pay a sum of money to the bondholder on the bond's maturity date. The amount due at maturity is the **face value** of the bond. Most bonds also require the issuer to make cash interest

EXHIBIT 10.5

Panel A: Journal Entries

Date	Account Titles	Debit	Credit
Mar. 1	Cash	20,000	
	Note Payable		20,000
Mar. 31	Interest Expense	150	
	Cash		150
Apr. 1	Cash	30,000	
	Note Payable		30,000
Apr. 30	Interest Expense	375	
	Cash		375
May 1	Cash	50,000	
	Note Payable		50,000
May 31	Interest Expense	875	
	Cash		875
June 1	Note Payable	10,000	
	Cash		10,000
June 30	Interest Expense	750	
	Cash		750
July 1	Note Payable	40,000	
	Cash		40,000
July 31	Interest Expense	375	
	Cash		375
Aug. 1	Note Payable	50,000	
	Cash		50,000

Panel B: Effects on Financial Statements

Date	Assets	=	Liabilities	+	Equity	Rev.	−	Exp.	=	Net Inc.	Cash Flow
Mar. 1	20,000	=	20,000	+	NA	NA	−	NA	=	NA	20,000 FA
31	(150)	=	NA	+	(150)	NA	−	150	=	(150)	(150) OA
Apr. 1	30,000	=	30,000	+	NA	NA	−	NA	=	NA	30,000 FA
30	(375)	=	NA	+	(375)	NA	−	375	=	(375)	(375) OA
May 1	50,000	=	50,000	+	NA	NA	−	NA	=	NA	50,000 FA
31	(875)	=	NA	+	(875)	NA	−	875	=	(875)	(875) OA
June 1	(10,000)	=	(10,000)	+	NA	NA	−	NA	=	NA	(10,000) FA
30	(750)	=	NA	+	(750)	NA	−	750	=	(750)	(750) OA
July 1	(40,000)	=	(40,000)	+	NA	NA	−	NA	=	NA	(40,000) FA
31	(375)	=	NA	+	(375)	NA	−	375	=	(375)	(375) OA
Aug. 1	(50,000)	=	(50,000)	+	NA	NA	−	NA	=	NA	(50,000) FA
31	NA	=	NA	+	NA	NA	−	NA	=	NA	NA

payments based on a **stated interest rate** at regular intervals over the life of the bond. Exhibit 10.6 shows a typical bond certificate.

Advantages of Issuing Bonds

Bond financing offers companies the following advantages:

EXHIBIT 10.6

Bond Certificate

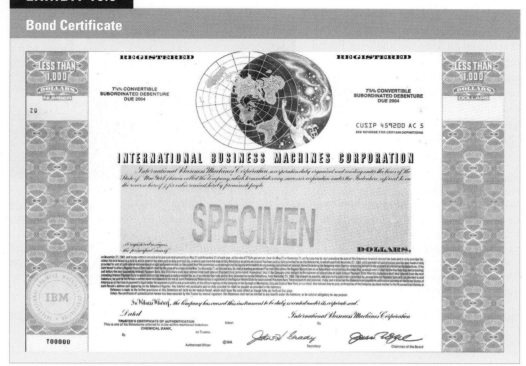

1. Bonds usually have longer terms than notes issued to banks. While typical bank loan terms range from 2 to 5 years, bonds normally have 20-year terms to maturity. Longer terms to maturity allow companies to implement long-term strategic plans without having to worry about frequent refinancing arrangements.

2. Bond interest rates may be lower than bank interest rates. Banks earn profits by borrowing money from the public (depositors) at low interest rates, then loaning that money to companies at higher rates. By issuing bonds directly to the public, companies can pay lower interest costs by eliminating the middleman (banks).

Security of Bonds

Bonds may be either secured or unsecured.

1. **Secured bonds** grant their holders a priority legal claim on specified identifiable assets should the issuer default. A common type of secured bond is a **mortgage bond,** which conditionally transfers the title of designated property to the bondholder until the bond is paid.

2. **Unsecured bonds,** also called **debentures,** are issued based on the general strength of the borrower's credit. Bond certificates often specify the priority of debenture holders' claims relative to other creditors. Holders of **subordinated debentures** have lower priority claims than other creditors, whereas holders of **unsubordinated debentures** have equal claims.

Timing of Maturity

The maturity dates of bonds can be specified in various ways. Even bonds sold as separate components of a single issue may have different maturity dates.

1. **Term bonds** mature on a specified date in the future.

2. **Serial bonds** mature at specified intervals throughout the life of the total issue. For example, bonds with a total face value of $1,000,000 may mature in increments of $100,000 every year for 10 years.

REALITY BYTES

Throughout this textbook various financial ratios have been discussed, including explanations of how they are used by financial analysts. Ratios are also often included as covenants in loan agreements when a company borrows money. If the company violates a ratio covenant in the loan agreement, the lender can force the company to renegotiate the loan, or pay back the borrowed funds much earlier than originally agreed. This can have dire consequences for the company. Consider the excerpts below taken from Note 2 of the 2010 Form 10-K of Las Vegas Sands Corporation.

... The U.S. credit facility, as amended in August 2010, requires the Company's Las Vegas operations to comply with certain financial covenants at the end of each quarter, including maintaining a maximum leverage ratio of net debt, as defined, to trailing twelve-month adjusted earnings before interest, income taxes, depreciation and amortization, as defined ("Adjusted EBITDA"). The maximum leverage ratio is 6.5x for the quarterly periods ended December 31, 2010 through June 30, 2011 ...

If the Company is unable to maintain compliance with the financial covenants under these credit facilities, it would be in default under the respective credit facilities. ... Any defaults ... would allow the lenders ... to exercise their rights and remedies as defined under their respective agreements. If the lenders were to exercise their rights to accelerate the due dates of the indebtedness outstanding, there can be no assurance that the Company would be able to repay or refinance any amounts that may become due ...

Simply put, the company is warning investors that if it violates the ratio covenants, which it seems likely to do, the company could go into bankruptcy. Ratios matter!

To ensure there is enough cash available at maturity to pay off the debt, a bond agreement may require the issuer to make regular payments into a **sinking fund.** Money deposited in the sinking fund is usually managed by an independent trustee who invests the funds until the bonds mature. At maturity, the funds and the proceeds from the investments are used to repay the bond debt.

Special Features

Some bonds feature one or both of the following characteristics.

1. **Convertible bonds** are liabilities that can be exchanged at the option of the bondholder for common stock or some other specified ownership interest. The issuing company benefits because bondholders (investors) are willing to accept a lower interest rate in exchange for the conversion feature. Bondholders benefit because they obtain the option to share in potential rewards of ownership. If the market value of the company's stock increases, bondholders can convert their bonds to stock. If the stock price does not increase, bondholders are still guaranteed interest payments and priority claims in bankruptcy settlements.

2. **Callable bonds** allow the issuing company to redeem (pay off) the bond debt before the maturity date. If interest rates decline, this feature benefits the issuing company because it could borrow additional money at a lower rate and use the proceeds to pay off its higher rate bonds. Since an early redemption would eliminate their higher interest bond investments, bondholders consider call features undesirable. To encourage investors to buy callable bonds, the **call price** normally exceeds the *face value* of the bonds. For example, the issuing company may agree to pay the holder of a $1,000 face value bond a call price of $1,050 if the bond is redeemed before its maturity date. The difference between the call price and the face value [$50 ($1,050 − $1,000) in this case] is commonly called a **call premium.**

Bond Ratings

Three financial services analyze the risk of default for corporate bond issues and publish ratings of the risk as guides to bond investors. These agencies are Fitch, Moody's, and Standard & Poor's. The highest rating (lowest risk) a company can achieve is AAA, the next highest AA, and so forth. Bond issuers try to maintain high credit ratings because lower ratings require them to pay higher interest rates.

Restrictive Covenants

In general, large loans with long terms to maturity pose more risk to lenders (creditors) than small loans with short terms. To reduce the risk that they won't get paid, lenders frequently require borrowers (debtors) to pledge designated assets as **collateral** for loans. For example, when a bank makes a car loan, it usually retains legal title to the car until the loan is fully repaid. If the borrower fails to make the monthly payments, the bank repossesses the car, sells it to someone else, and uses the proceeds to pay the original owner's debt. Similarly, assets like accounts receivable, inventory, equipment, buildings, and land may be pledged as collateral for business loans.

In addition to requiring collateral, creditors often obtain additional protection by including **restrictive covenants** in loan agreements. Such covenants may restrict additional borrowing, limit dividend payments, or restrict salary increases. If the loan restrictions are violated, the borrower is in default and the loan balance is due immediately.

Finally, creditors often ask key personnel to provide copies of their personal tax returns and financial statements. The financial condition of key executives is important because they may be asked to pledge personal property as collateral for business loans, particularly for small businesses.

Bonds Issued at Face Value

Assume Marsha Mason needs cash in order to seize a business opportunity. Mason knows of a company seeking a plot of land on which to store its inventory of crushed stone. Mason also knows of a suitable tract of land she could purchase for $100,000. The company has agreed to lease the land it needs from Mason for $12,000 per year. Mason lacks the funds to buy the land.

Some of Mason's friends recently complained about the low interest rates banks were paying on certificates of deposit. Mason suggested that her friends invest in bonds instead of CDs. She offered to sell them bonds with a 9 percent stated interest rate. The terms specified in the bond agreement Mason drafted included making interest payments in cash on December 31 of each year, a five-year term to maturity, and pledging the land as collateral for the bonds.[3] Her friends were favorably impressed, and Mason issued the bonds to them in exchange for cash on January 1, 2013.

Mason used the bond proceeds to purchase the land and immediately contracted to lease it for five years. On December 31, 2017, the maturity date of the bonds, Mason sold the land for its $100,000 book value and used the proceeds from the sale to repay the bond liability.

Journal Entries and Financial Statement Effects

Mason's business venture involved six distinct accounting events, described below.

Effect of Events on Financial Statements

EVENT 1   Issued Bonds for $100,000 Cash.

Assets (cash) and liabilities (bonds payable) increase. Net income is not affected. The $100,000 cash inflow is reported in the financing activities section of the statement

---

[3] In practice, bonds are usually issued for much larger sums of money, often hundreds of millions of dollars. Also, terms to maturity are normally long, with 20 years being common. Using such large amounts for such long terms is unnecessarily cumbersome for instructional purposes. The effects of bond issues can be illustrated efficiently by using smaller amounts of debt with shorter maturities, as assumed in the case of Marsha Mason.

of cash flows. The journal entry and its effects on the financial statements are shown here:

Account Title	Debit	Credit
Cash	100,000	
Bonds Payable		100,000

Assets	=	Liab.	+	Equity	Rev.	−	Exp.	=	Net Inc.	Cash Flow
Cash	=	Bonds Pay.								
100,000	=	100,000	+	NA	NA	−	NA	=	NA	100,000 FA

EVENT 2   Paid $100,000 cash to purchase land.

The asset cash decreases and the asset land increases. The income statement is not affected. The cash outflow is reported in the investing activities section of the statement of cash flows. The journal entry and its effects on the financial statements are shown here:

Account Title	Debit	Credit
Land	100,000	
Cash		100,000

Assets			=	Liab.	+	Equity	Rev.	−	Exp.	=	Net Inc.	Cash Flow
Cash	+	Land										
(100,000)	+	100,000	=	NA	+	NA	NA	−	NA	=	NA	(100,000) IA

EVENT 3   Recognized $12,000 cash revenue from renting the land.

This event is repeated each year from 2013 through 2017. The event increases assets and stockholders' equity. Recognizing revenue increases net income. The cash inflow is reported in the operating activities section of the statement of cash flows. The journal entry and its effects on the financial statements are shown here:

Account Title	Debit	Credit
Cash	12,000	
Rent Revenue		12,000

Assets	=	Liab.	+	Equity	Rev.	−	Exp.	=	Net Inc.	Cash Flow
Cash	=			Ret. Earn.						
12,000	=	NA	+	12,000	12,000	−	NA	=	12,000	12,000 OA

EVENT 4   Paid $9,000 cash for interest.

This event is also repeated each year from 2013 through 2017. The interest payment is an asset use transaction. Cash and stockholders' equity (retained earnings) decrease. The expense recognition decreases net income. The cash outflow is reported in the operating activities section of the statement of cash flows. The journal entry and its effects on the financial statements are shown here:

Account Title	Debit	Credit
Interest Expense	9,000	
Cash		9,000

Assets	=	Liab.	+	Equity	Rev.	−	Exp.	=	Net Inc.	Cash Flow
Cash	=			Ret. Earn.						
(9,000)	=	NA	+	(9,000)	NA	−	9,000	=	(9,000)	(9,000) OA

EVENT 5 Sold the land for cash equal to its $100,000 book value.

Cash increases and land decreases. Since there was no gain or loss on the sale, the income statement is not affected. The cash inflow is reported in the investing activities section of the statement of cash flows. The journal entry and its effects on the financial statements are shown here:

Account Title	Debit	Credit
Cash	100,000	
Land		100,000

Assets			=	Liab.	+	Equity	Rev.	−	Exp.	=	Net Inc.	Cash Flow
Cash	+	Land										
100,000	+	(100,000)	=	NA	+	NA	NA	−	NA	=	NA	100,000 IA

EVENT 6 Repaid the face value of the bond liability.

Cash and bonds payable decrease. The income statement is not affected. The cash outflow is reported in the financing activities section of the statement of cash flows. The journal entry and its effects on the financial statements are shown here:

Account Title	Debit	Credit
Bonds Payable	100,000	
Cash		100,000

Assets	=	Liab.	+	Equity	Rev.	−	Exp.	=	Net Inc.	Cash Flow
Cash	=	Bonds Pay.								
(100,000)	=	(100,000)	+	NA	NA	−	NA	=	NA	(100,000) FA

Financial Statements

Exhibit 10.7 displays Mason Company's financial statements. For simplicity, the income statement does not distinguish between operating and other items. Rent revenue and interest expense are constant across all accounting periods, so Mason recognizes $3,000 of net income in each accounting period. On the balance sheet, cash increases by $3,000 each year because cash revenue exceeds cash paid for interest. Land remains constant each year at its $100,000 historical cost until it is sold in 2017. Similarly, the bonds payable liability is reported at $100,000 from the date the bonds were issued in 2013 until they are paid off on December 31, 2017.

EXHIBIT 10.7

Mason Company Financial Statements

Bonds Issued at Face Value

	2013	2014	2015	2016	2017
Income Statements					
Rent revenue	$ 12,000	$ 12,000	$ 12,000	$ 12,000	$ 12,000
Interest expense	(9,000)	(9,000)	(9,000)	(9,000)	(9,000)
Net income	$ 3,000	$ 3,000	$ 3,000	$ 3,000	$ 3,000
Balance Sheets					
Assets					
Cash	$ 3,000	$ 6,000	$ 9,000	$ 12,000	$ 15,000
Land	100,000	100,000	100,000	100,000	0
Total assets	$103,000	$106,000	$109,000	$112,000	$ 15,000
Liabilities					
Bonds payable	$100,000	$100,000	$100,000	$100,000	$ 0
Stockholders' equity					
Retained earnings	3,000	6,000	9,000	12,000	15,000
Total liabilities and stockholders' equity	$103,000	$106,000	$109,000	$112,000	$ 15,000
Statements of Cash Flows					
Operating Activities					
Inflow from customers	$ 12,000	$ 12,000	$ 12,000	$ 12,000	$ 12,000
Outflow for interest	(9,000)	(9,000)	(9,000)	(9,000)	(9,000)
Investing Activities					
Outflow to purchase land	(100,000)				
Inflow from sale of land					100,000
Financing Activities					
Inflow from bond issue	100,000				
Outflow to repay bond liab.					(100,000)
Net change in cash	3,000	3,000	3,000	3,000	3,000
Plus: Beginning cash balance	0	3,000	6,000	9,000	12,000
Ending cash balance	$ 3,000	$ 6,000	$ 9,000	$ 12,000	$ 15,000

Compare Blair Company's income statements in Exhibit 10.2 with Mason Company's income statements in Exhibit 10.7. Both Blair and Mason borrowed $100,000 cash at a 9 percent stated interest rate for five-year terms. Blair, however, repaid its liability under the terms of an installment note while Mason did not repay any principal until the end of the five-year bond term. Because Blair repaid part of the principal balance on the installment loan each year, Blair's interest expense declined each year. The interest expense on Mason's bond liability, however, remained constant because the full principal amount was outstanding for the entire five-year bond term.

AMORTIZATION USING THE STRAIGHT-LINE METHOD

LO 4

Use the straight-line method to amortize bond discounts and premiums.

Bonds Issued at a Discount

Return to the Mason Company illustration with one change. Assume Mason's bond certificates have a 9 percent stated rate of interest printed on them. Suppose Mason's friends find they can buy bonds from another entrepreneur willing to pay a higher rate of interest. They explain to Mason that business decisions cannot be made on the basis of friendship. Mason provides a counteroffer. There is no time to change the bond certificates, so Mason offers to accept $95,000 for the bonds today and still repay the full face value of $100,000 at the maturity date. The $5,000 difference is called a **bond discount.** Mason's friends agree to buy the bonds for $95,000.

Effective Interest Rate

The bond discount increases the interest Mason must pay. First, Mason must still make the annual cash payments described in the bond agreement. In other words, Mason must pay cash of $9,000 (.09 × $100,000) annually even though she actually borrowed only $95,000. Second, Mason will have to pay back $5,000 more than she received ($100,000 − $95,000). The extra $5,000 (bond discount) is additional interest. Although the $5,000 of additional interest is not paid until maturity, when spread over the life of the bond, it amounts to $1,000 of additional interest expense per year.

The actual rate of interest that Mason must pay is called the **effective interest rate.** A rough estimate of the effective interest rate for the discounted Mason bonds is 10.5 percent [($9,000 annual stated interest + $1,000 annual amortization of the discount) ÷ $95,000 amount borrowed]. Selling the bonds at a $5,000 discount permits Mason to raise the 9 percent stated rate of interest to an effective rate of roughly 10.5 percent. Deeper discounts would raise the effective rate even higher. More shallow discounts would reduce the effective rate of interest. Mason can set the effective rate of interest to any level desired by adjusting the amount of the discount.

Bond Prices

It is common business practice to use discounts to raise the effective rate of interest above the stated rate. Bonds frequently sell for less than face value. Bond prices are normally expressed *as a percentage of the face value.* For example, Mason's discounted bonds sold for 95, meaning the bonds sold at 95 percent of face value ($100,000 × .95 = $95,000). Amounts of less than 1 percentage point are usually expressed as a fraction. Therefore, a bond priced at 98 3/4 sells for 98.75 percent of face value.

Journal Entries and Financial Statement Effects

To illustrate accounting for bonds issued at a discount, return to the Mason Company example using the assumption the bonds are issued for 95 instead of face value. We examine the same six events using this revised assumption. This revision changes some amounts reported on the financial statements. For example, Event 1 in year 2013 reflects receiving only $95,000 cash from the bond issue. Since Mason had only $95,000 available to invest in land, the illustration assumes that Mason acquired a less desirable piece of property which generated only $11,400 of rent revenue per year.

EVENT 1   Bonds with a face value of $100,000 are issued at 95.

Because Mason must pay the face value at maturity, the $100,000 face value of the bonds is recorded in the Bonds Payable account. The $5,000 discount is recorded in a separate contra liability account called **Discount on Bonds Payable.** As shown below, the contra account is subtracted from the face value to determine the **carrying value** (book value) of the bond liability on January 1, 2013.

Bonds payable	$100,000
Less: Discount on bonds payable	(5,000)
Carrying value	$ 95,000

The bond issue is an asset source transaction. Both assets and total liabilities increase by $95,000. Net income is not affected. The cash inflow is reported in the financing activities section of the statement of cash flows. The journal entry and its effects on the financial statements are shown here:

Account Title	Debit	Credit
Cash	95,000	
Discount on Bonds Payable	5,000	
Bonds Payable		100,000

Assets	=	Liabilities	+	Equity	Rev.	−	Exp.	=	Net Inc.	Cash Flow
Cash	=	Carrying Value of Bond Liability	+	Equity						
95,000	=	95,000	+	NA	NA	−	NA	=	NA	95,000 FA

EVENT 2   **Paid $95,000 cash to purchase land.**

The asset cash decreases and the asset land increases. The income statement is not affected. The cash outflow is reported in the investing activities section of the statement of cash flows. The journal entry and its effects on the financial statements are shown here:

Account Title	Debit	Credit
Land	95,000	
Cash		95,000

Assets			=	Liab.	+	Equity	Rev.	−	Exp.	=	Net Inc.	Cash Flow
Cash	+	Land										
(95,000)	+	95,000	=	NA	+	NA	NA	−	NA	=	NA	(95,000) IA

EVENT 3   **Recognized $11,400 cash revenue from renting the land.**

This event is repeated each year from 2013 through 2017. The event is an asset source transaction that increases assets and stockholders' equity. Recognizing revenue increases net income. The cash inflow is reported in the operating activities section of the statement of cash flows. The journal entry and its effects on the financial statements are shown here:

Account Title	Debit	Credit
Cash	11,400	
Rent Revenue		11,400

Assets	=	Liab.	+	Equity	Rev.	−	Exp.	=	Net Inc.	Cash Flow
Cash	=		+	Ret. Earn.						
11,400	=	NA	+	11,400	11,400	−	NA	=	11,400	11,400 OA

EVENT 4   **Recognized interest expense. The interest cost of borrowing has two components: the $9,000 paid in cash each year and the $5,000 discount paid at maturity.**

Using **straight-line amortization,** the amount of the discount recognized as expense in each accounting period is $1,000 ($5,000 discount ÷ 5 years). Mason will therefore recognize $10,000 of interest expense each year ($9,000 at the stated interest rate plus

$1,000 amortization of the bond discount). On the balance sheet, the asset cash decreases by $9,000, the carrying value of the bond liability increases by $1,000 (through a decrease in the bond discount), and retained earnings (interest expense) decreases by $10,000. The journal entry and its effects on the financial statements are shown here:

Account Title	Debit	Credit
Interest Expense	10,000	
Cash		9,000
Discount on Bonds Payable		1,000

Assets	=	Liabilities	+	Equity	Rev.	−	Exp.	=	Net Inc.	Cash Flow
Cash	=	Carrying Value of Bond Liability	+	Ret. Earn.						
(9,000)	=	1,000	+	(10,000)	NA	−	10,000	=	(10,000)	(9,000) OA

EVENT 5 Sold the land for cash equal to its $95,000 book value.

Cash increases and land decreases. Since there was no gain or loss on the sale, the income statement is not affected. The cash inflow is reported in the investing activities section of the statement of cash flows. The journal entry and its effects on the financial statements are shown here:

Account Title	Debit	Credit
Cash	95,000	
Land		95,000

Assets			=	Liab.	+	Equity	Rev.	−	Exp.	=	Net Inc.	Cash Flow
Cash	+	Land										
95,000	+	(95,000)	=	NA	+	NA	NA	−	NA	=	NA	95,000 IA

EVENT 6 Paid the bond liability.

Cash and bonds payable decrease. The income statement is not affected. For reporting purposes, the cash outflow is separated into two parts on the statement of cash flows: $95,000 of the cash outflow is reported in the financing activities section because it represents repaying the principal amount borrowed; the remaining $5,000 cash outflow is reported in the operating activities section because it represents the interest arising from issuing the bonds at a discount. In practice, the amount of the discount is frequently immaterial and is combined in the financing activities section with the principal repayment. The journal entry and its effects on the financial statements are shown here:

Account Title	Debit	Credit
Bond Payable	100,000	
Cash		100,000

Assets	=	Liab.	+	Equity	Rev.	−	Exp.	=	Net Inc.	Cash Flow
Cash	=	Bonds Pay.								
(100,000)	=	(100,000)	+	NA	NA	−	NA	=	NA	(95,000) FA (5,000) OA

Financial Statements

Exhibit 10.8 displays Mason Company's financial statements assuming the bonds were issued at a discount. Contrast the net income reported in Exhibit 10.8 (bonds issued at a discount) with the net income reported in Exhibit 10.7 (bonds sold at face value). Two factors cause the net income in Exhibit 10.8 to be lower. First, since the bonds were sold at a discount, Mason Company had less money to spend on its land investment. It bought less desirable land which generated less revenue. Second, the effective interest rate was higher than the stated rate, resulting in higher interest expense. Lower revenues coupled with higher expenses result in less profitability.

On the balance sheet, the carrying value of the bond liability increases each year until the maturity date, December 31, 2017, when it is equal to the $100,000 face value of the bonds (the amount Mason is obligated to pay). Because Mason did not pay any dividends, retained earnings ($7,000) on December 31, 2017, is equal to the total amount of net income reported over the five-year period ($1,400 × 5). All earnings were retained in the business.

EXHIBIT 10.8

Mason Company Financial Statements

Bonds Issued at a Discount

	2013	2014	2015	2016	2017
Income Statements					
Rent revenue	$ 11,400	$ 11,400	$ 11,400	$ 11,400	$ 11,400
Interest expense	(10,000)	(10,000)	(10,000)	(10,000)	(10,000)
Net income	$ 1,400	$ 1,400	$ 1,400	$ 1,400	$ 1,400
Balance Sheets					
Assets					
Cash	$ 2,400	$ 4,800	$ 7,200	$ 9,600	$ 7,000
Land	95,000	95,000	95,000	95,000	0
Total assets	$ 97,400	$ 99,800	$102,200	$104,600	$ 7,000
Liabilities					
Bonds payable	$100,000	$100,000	$100,000	$100,000	$ 0
Discount on bonds payable	(4,000)	(3,000)	(2,000)	(1,000)	0
Carrying value of bond liab.	96,000	97,000	98,000	99,000	0
Stockholders' equity					
Retained earnings	1,400	2,800	4,200	5,600	7,000
Total liabilities and stockholders' equity	$ 97,400	$ 99,800	$102,200	$104,600	$ 7,000
Statements of Cash Flows					
Operating Activities					
Inflow from customers	$ 11,400	$ 11,400	$ 11,400	$ 11,400	$ 11,400
Outflow for interest	(9,000)	(9,000)	(9,000)	(9,000)	(14,000)
Investing Activities					
Outflow to purchase land	(95,000)				
Inflow from sale of land					95,000
Financing Activities					
Inflow from bond issue	95,000				
Outflow to repay bond liab.					(95,000)
Net change in cash	2,400	2,400	2,400	2,400	(2,600)
Plus: Beginning cash balance	0	2,400	4,800	7,200	9,600
Ending cash balance	$ 2,400	$ 4,800	$ 7,200	$ 9,600	$ 7,000

Several factors account for the differences between net income and cash flow. First, although $10,000 of interest expense is reported on each income statement, only $9,000 of cash was paid for interest each year until 2017, when $14,000 was paid for interest ($9,000 based on the stated rate + $5,000 for discount). The $1,000 difference between interest expense and cash paid for interest in 2013, 2014, 2015, and 2016 results from amortizing the bond discount. The cash outflow for the interest related to the discount is included in the $100,000 payment made at maturity on December 31, 2017. Even though $14,000 of cash is paid for interest in 2017, only $10,000 is recognized as interest expense on the income statement that year. Although the total increase in cash over the five-year life of the business ($7,000) is equal to the total net income reported for the same period, there are significant timing differences between when the interest expense is recognized and when the cash outflows occur to pay for it.

✓ CHECK YOURSELF 10.2

On January 1, 2013, Moffett Company issued bonds with a $600,000 face value at 98. The bonds had a 9 percent annual interest rate and a 10-year term. Interest is payable in cash on December 31 of each year. What amount of interest expense will Moffett report on the 2015 income statement? What carrying value for bonds payable will Moffett report on the December 31, 2015, balance sheet?

Answer   The bonds were issued at a $12,000 ($600,000 × 0.02) discount. The discount will be amortized over the 10-year life at the rate of $1,200 ($12,000 ÷ 10 years) per year. The amount of interest expense for 2015 is $55,200 ($600,000 × .09 = $54,000 annual cash interest + $1,200 discount amortization).

The carrying value of the bond liability is equal to the face value less the unamortized discount. By the end of 2015, $3,600 of the discount will have been amortized ($1,200 × 3 years = $3,600). The unamortized discount as of December 31, 2015, will be $8,400 ($12,000 − $3,600). The carrying value of the bond liability as of December 31, 2015, will be $591,600 ($600,000 − $8,400).

Effect of Semiannual Interest Payments

The previous examples assumed that interest payments were made annually. In practice, most bond agreements call for interest to be paid semiannually, which means that interest is paid in cash twice each year. If Marsha Mason's bond certificate had stipulated semiannual interest payments, her company would have paid $4,500 ($100,000 × 0.09 = $9,000 ÷ 2 = $4,500) cash to bondholders for interest on June 30 and December 31 of each year. The journal entries to record semiannual interest payments each year (for the bonds issued at a discount) are as follows:

Date	Account Title	Debit	Credit
June 30	Interest Expense	5,000	
	Discount on Bonds Payable		500
	Cash		4,500
Dec. 31	Interest Expense	5,000	
	Discount on Bonds Payable		500
	Cash		4,500

Bonds Issued at a Premium

When bonds are sold for more than their face value, the difference between the amount received and the face value is called a **bond premium.** Bond premiums reduce the effective interest rate. For example, assume Mason Company issued its 9 percent bonds at 105, receiving $105,000 cash on the issue date. The company is still only required to repay the $100,000 face value of the bonds at the maturity date. The $5,000 difference between the amount received and the amount repaid at maturity reduces the total amount of interest expense. The premium is recorded in a separate liability account called **Premium on Bonds Payable.** This account is reported on the balance sheet as an addition to Bonds Payable, increasing the carrying value of the bond liability. On the issue date, the bond liability would be reported on the balance sheet as follows:

Bonds payable	$100,000
Plus: Premium on bonds payable	5,000
Carrying value	$105,000

The entire $105,000 cash inflow is reported in the financing activities section of the statement of cash flows even though the $5,000 premium is conceptually an operating activities cash flow because it pertains to interest. In practice, premiums are usually so small they are immaterial and the entire cash inflow is normally classified as a financing activity.

The journal entries to record issuing the bonds at a premium and the first interest payment are as follows (assume annual interest payments):

Date	Account Title	Debit	Credit
Jan. 1	Cash	105,000	
	Bonds Payable		100,000
	Premium on Bonds Payable		5,000
Dec. 31	Interest Expense	8,000	
	Premium on Bonds Payable	1,000	
	Cash		9,000

The effects on the financial statements are shown here:

Date	Assets	=	Liabilities	+	Equity	Rev.	−	Exp.	=	Net Inc.	Cash Flow
	Cash	=	Carrying Value of Bond Liability								
Jan. 1	105,000	=	105,000	+	NA	NA	−	NA	=	NA	105,000 FA
Dec. 31	(9,000)		(1,000)		(8,000)			8,000		(8,000)	9,000 OA

The Market Rate of Interest

When a bond is issued, the effective interest rate is determined by current market conditions. Market conditions are influenced by many factors such as the state of the economy, government policy, and the law of supply and demand. These conditions are collectively reflected in the **market interest rate.** The *effective rate of interest* investors are willing to accept *for a particular bond* equals the *market rate of interest* for other investments with similar levels of risk at the time the bond is issued. When the market rate of interest is higher than the stated rate of interest, bonds will sell at a discount so as to increase the effective rate of interest to the market rate. When the market rate is lower than the stated rate, bonds will sell at a premium so as to reduce the effective rate to the market rate.

Bond Redemptions

In the previous illustration, Mason Company's five-year, 9 percent bonds were redeemed (paid off) on the maturity date. After Mason Company paid the bondholders the face value of the bonds, the balance in the bonds payable account was zero. The balance in the fully amortized discount account was also zero.

Companies may redeem bonds with a *call provision* prior to the maturity date. If a company calls bonds prior to maturity, it must pay the bondholders the call price. As explained previously, the call price is normally above face value. For example, suppose Mason Company's bond certificate allows it to call the bonds at 103. Assume Marsha Mason's client breaks the land rental contract two years early, at the end of 2015. Mason is forced to sell the land and pay off the bonds. Assuming the bonds were originally issued at a $5,000 discount, Exhibit 10.8 shows there is a $2,000 balance in the Discount on Bonds Payable account at the end of 2015.

To redeem the bonds on January 1, 2016, Mason must pay the bondholders $103,000 ($100,000 face value × 1.03 call price). Since the book value of the bond liability is $98,000 ($100,000 face value − $2,000 remaining discount), Mason recognizes a $5,000 loss ($103,000 redemption price − $98,000 book value) when the bonds are called. The early redemption decreases cash, the carrying value of the bond liability, and stockholders' equity.

The entire $103,000 cash outflow is reported in the financing activities section of the statement of cash flows. Conceptually, some of this outflow is attributable to activities other than financing. In practice, the amounts paid in an early redemption which are not attributable to financing activities are usually immaterial and the entire cash outflow is therefore classified as a financing activity.

The general journal entry to record the bond redemption and its effects on the financial statements are shown here:

Account Title	Debit	Credit
Loss on Bond Redemption	5,000	
Bonds Payable	100,000	
Discount on Bonds Payable		2,000
Cash		103,000

Assets	=	Liabilities	+	Equity	Rev.	−	Exp.	=	Net Inc.	Cash Flow
Cash	=	Carrying Value of Bond Liability	+	Ret. Earn.						
(103,000)	=	(98,000)	+	(5,000)	NA	−	5,000	=	(5,000)	(103,000) FA

AMORTIZATION USING THE EFFECTIVE INTEREST RATE METHOD

To this point we have demonstrated the straight-line method for amortizing bond discounts and premiums. While this method is easy to understand, it is inaccurate because it does not show the correct amount of interest expense incurred during each accounting period. To illustrate, return to the case of Mason Company demonstrated in Exhibit 10.8 (page 550). Recall that the exhibit shows the effects of accounting for a $100,000 face value bond with a 9 percent stated rate of interest that was issued at a price of 95. The carrying value of the bond liability on the January 1, 2013, issue date was $95,000. The bond discount was amortized using the straight-line method.

LO 5

Use the effective interest rate method to amortize bond discounts and premiums.

Recall that the straight-line method amortizes the discount equally over the life of the bond. Specifically, there is a $5,000 discount which is amortized over a 5-year life resulting in a $1,000 amortization per year. As the discount is amortized the bond liability (carrying value of the bond) increases. Specifically, the carrying value of the bond liability shown in Exhibit 10.8 increases as follows:

Accounting Period	2013	2014	2015	2016
Carrying value as of December 31	$96,000	$97,000	$98,000	$99,000

While the carrying value of the bond liability increases steadily, the straight-line method recognizes the same amount of interest expense ($9,000 stated rate of interest + $1,000 discount amortization = $10,000 interest expense) per year. This straight-line recognition pattern is irrational because the amount of interest expense recognized should increase as the carrying value of the bond liability increases. A more accurate recognition pattern can be accomplished by using an approach called the **effective interest rate method.**

Amortizing Bond Discounts

The effective interest rate is determined by the price that the buyer of a bond is willing to pay on the issue date. In the case of Mason Company the issue price of $95,000 for bonds with a $100,000 face value, a 9 percent stated rate of interest, and a 5-year term produces an effective interest rate of approximately 10.33 percent.[4] Since the effective interest rate is based on the market price of the bonds on the day of issue, it is sometimes called *the market rate of interest.*

Interest recognition under the effective interest method is accomplished as follows:

1. Determine the cash payment for interest by multiplying the stated rate of interest times the face value of the bonds.
2. Determine the amount of interest expense by multiplying the effective rate of interest times the carrying value of the bond liability.
3. Determine the amount of the amortization of the bond discount by subtracting the cash payment from the interest expense.
4. Update the carrying value of the liability by adding the amount of the discount amortization to the amount of the carrying value at the beginning of the accounting period.

Applying these procedures to the Mason Company illustration produces the amortization schedule shown in Exhibit 10.9.

The recognition of interest expense at the end of each accounting period has the following effects on the financial statements. On the balance sheet, assets decrease, liabilities increase, and retained earnings decrease. On the income statement, expenses increase and

EXHIBIT 10.9

Amortization Schedule for Bond Discount

	(A) Cash Payment	(B) Interest Expense	(C) Discount Amortization	(D) Carrying Value
January 1, 2013				$ 95,000
December 31, 2013	$ 9,000	$ 9,814	$ 814	95,814
December 31, 2014	9,000	9,898	898	96,712
December 31, 2015	9,000	9,990	990	97,702
December 31, 2016	9,000	10,093	1,093	98,795
December 31, 2017	9,000	10,205	1,205	100,000
Totals	$45,000	$50,000	$5,000	

(A) Stated rate of interest times the face value of the bonds ($100,000 × .09).
(B) Effective interest rate times the carrying value at the beginning of the period. For the 2013 accounting period the amount is $9,814 ($95,000 × .1033).
(C) Interest Expense − Cash Payment. For 2013 the discount amortization is $814 ($9,814 − $9,000 = $814).
(D) Carrying value at beginning of period plus portion of discount amortized. For the accounting period ending December 31, 2013, the amount is $95,814 ($95,000 + $814).

[4]In practice the effective rate of interest is calculated using software programs, interest formulas, or interest tables. For further discussion see Appendix F, which is located at the end of the text.

net income decreases. There is a cash outflow in the operating activities of the statement of cash flows. The journal entry and its effects on the financial statements are shown here:

Account Title	Debit	Credit
Interest Expense	9,814	
Cash		9,000
Discount on Bonds Payable		814

Assets	=	Liabilities	+	Equity	Rev.	−	Exp.	=	Net Inc.	Cash Flow
Cash	=	Carrying Value of Bond Liab.	+	Ret. Earn.						
(9,000)	=	814	+	(9,814)	NA	−	9,814	=	(9,814)	(9,000) OA

Exhibit 10.10 shows the financial statements for Mason Company for 2013 through 2017. The statements assume the same events as described as those used to construct Exhibit 10.8 (page 550). These events are summarized below:

1. Mason issues a $100,000 face value bond with a 9 percent stated rate of interest. The bond has a 5-year term and is issued at a price of 95. Annual interest is paid with cash on December 31 of each year.
2. Mason uses the proceeds from the bond issue to purchase land.
3. Leasing the land produces rent revenue of $11,400 cash per year.
4. On the maturity date of the bond, the land is sold and the proceeds from the sale are used to repay the bond liability.

The only difference between the two exhibits is that Exhibit 10.8 was constructed assuming that the bond discount was amortized using the straight-line method while Exhibit 10.10 assumes that the discount was amortized using the effective interest rate method.

Notice that interest expense under the effective interest rate method (Exhibit 10.10) increases each year while interest expense under the straight-line method (Exhibit 10.8) remains constant for all years. This result occurs because the effective interest rate method amortizes increasingly larger amounts of the discount (see Column C of Exhibit 10.9) as the carrying value of the bond liability increases. In contrast, the straight-line method amortized the bond discount at a constant rate of $1,000 per year over the life of the bond. Even so, total amount of interest expense recognized over the life of the bond is the same ($50,000) under both methods. Since the effective interest rate method matches the interest expense with the carrying value of the bond liability, it is the theoretically preferred approach. Indeed, accounting standards require the use of the effective interest rate method when the differences between it and the straight-line method are material.

The amortization of the discount affects the carrying value of the bond as well as the amount of interest expense. Under the effective interest method the rate of growth of the carrying value of the bond increases as the maturity date approaches. In contrast, under the straight-line method the rate of growth of the carrying value of the bond remains constant at $1,000 per year throughout the life of the bond.

Finally, notice that cash flow is not affected by the method of amortization. The exact same cash flow consequences occur under both the straight-line (Exhibit 10.8) and the effective interest rate method (Exhibit 10.10).

Amortizing Bond Premiums

Bond premiums can also be amortized using the effective interest rate method. To illustrate, assume United Company issued a $100,000 face value bond with a 10 percent stated rate of interest. The bond had a 5-year term. The bond was issued at a price of

EXHIBIT 10.10

Financial Statements

Under the Assumption that Bonds Are Issued at a Discount

	2013	2014	2015	2016	2017
Income Statements					
Rent revenue	$ 11,400	$ 11,400	$ 11,400	$ 11,400	$ 11,400
Interest expense	(9,814)	(9,898)	(9,990)	(10,093)	(10,205)
Net income	$ 1,586	$ 1,502	$ 1,410	$ 1,307	$ 1,195
Balance Sheets					
Assets:					
Cash	$ 2,400	$ 4,800	$ 7,200	$ 9,600	$ 7,000
Land	95,000	95,000	95,000	95,000	0
Total assets	$ 97,400	$ 99,800	$102,200	$104,600	$ 7,000
Liabilities					
Bond payable	$100,000	$100,000	$100,000	$100,000	$ 0
Discount on bonds payable	(4,186)	(3,288)	(2,298)	(1,205)	0
Carrying value of bond liab.	95,814	96,712	97,702	98,795	0
Equity					
Retained earnings	1,586	3,088	4,498	5,805	7,000
Total liabilities and equity	$ 97,400	$ 99,800	$102,200	$104,600	$ 7,000
Statements of Cash Flows					
Operating Activities					
Inflow from customers	$ 11,400	$ 11,400	$ 11,400	$ 11,400	$ 11,400
Outflow for interest	(9,000)	(9,000)	(9,000)	(9,000)	(14,000)
Investing Activities					
Outflow to purchase land	(95,000)				
Inflow from sale of land					95,000
Financing Activities					
Inflow from bond issue	95,000				
Outflow to repay bond liab.					(95,000)
Net change in cash	2,400	2,400	4,800	7,200	(2,600)
Beginning cash balance	0	2,400	2,400	2,400	9,600
Ending cash balance	$ 2,400	$ 4,800	$ 7,200	$ 9,600	$ 7,000

$107,985. The effective rate of interest is 8 percent. United's accountant prepared the amortization schedule shown in Exhibit 10.11.

The recognition of interest expense at the end of each accounting period has the following effects on the financial statements. On the balance sheet assets decrease, liabilities decrease, and retained earnings decrease. On the income statement expenses increase and net income decreases. There is a cash outflow in the operating activities of the statement of cash flows. The journal entry and its effects on the financial statements are shown here.

Account Title	Debit	Credit
Interest Expense	8,639	
Premium on Bonds Payable	1,361	
Cash		10,000

EXHIBIT 10.11

Amortization Schedule for Bond Premium

	(A) Cash Payment	(B) Interest Expense	(C) Premium Amortization	(D) Carrying Value
January 1, 2013				$107,985
December 31, 2013	$10,000	$ 8,639	$1,361	106,624
December 31, 2014	10,000	8,530	1,470	105,154
December 31, 2015	10,000	8,413	1,587	103,567
December 31, 2016	10,000	8,285	1,715	101,852
December 31, 2017	10,000	8,148	1,852	100,000
Totals	$50,000	$42,015	$7,985	

(A) Stated rate of interest times the face value of the bonds ($100,000 × .10).

(B) Effective interest times the carrying value at the beginning of the period. For the 2013 accounting period the amount is $8,639 ($107,985 × .08).

(C) Cash Payment − Interest Expense. For 2013 the premium amortization is $1,361 ($10,000 − $8,639 = $1,361).

(D) Carrying value at beginning of period minus the portion of premium amortized. For the accounting period ending December 31, 2013, the amount is $106,624 ($107,985 − 1,361).

Assets	=	Liabilities	+	Equity	Rev.	−	Exp.	=	Net Inc.	Cash Flow
Cash	=	Carrying Value of Bond Liab.	+	Ret. Earn.						
(10,000)	=	(1,361)	+	(8,639)	NA	−	8,639	=	(8,639)	(10,000) OA

THE FINANCIAL ANALYST

Bond financing has advantages and disadvantages for the stockholders of a business. Assessing a company's investment potential requires understanding both the potential rewards and the potential risks of debt financing.

LO 6

Explain the advantages and disadvantages of debt financing.

Financial Leverage and Tax Advantage of Debt Financing

As with other forms of credit, bonds may provide companies increased earnings through **financial leverage.** If a company can borrow money at 7 percent through a bond issue and invest the proceeds at 12 percent, the company's earnings benefit from the 5 percent (12 percent − 7 percent) **spread.**

Also, bond interest expense, like other forms of interest expense, is tax deductible, making the effective cost of borrowing less than the interest expense because the interest expense reduces the tax expense. Because dividend payments are not tax deductible, equity financing (e.g., issuing common stock) does not offer this advantage.

To illustrate, assume its organizers obtain $100,000 to start Maduro Company. During its first year of operation, Maduro earns $60,000 of revenue and incurs $40,000 of expenses other than interest expense. Consider two different forms of financing. First, assume the initial $100,000 is obtained by issuing common stock (equity financing) and Maduro pays an 8 percent dividend ($100,000 × .08 = $8,000 dividend). Second, assume Maduro issues $100,000 of bonds that pay 8 percent annual interest

($100,000 × .08 = $8,000). Assuming a 30 percent tax rate, which form of financing produces the larger increase in retained earnings? Refer to the following computations:

Computation of Addition to Retained Earnings		
	Equity Financing	**Debt Financing**
Revenue	$ 60,000	$ 60,000
Expense (excluding interest)	(40,000)	(40,000)
Earnings before interest and taxes	20,000	20,000
Interest ($100,000 × 8%)	0	(8,000)
Pretax income	20,000	12,000
Income tax (30%)	(6,000)	(3,600)
Net income	14,000	8,400
Dividend	(8,000)	0
Addition to retained earnings	$ 6,000	$ 8,400

Debt financing produces $2,400 more retained earnings than equity financing. If equity financing is obtained, the company pays $6,000 in income taxes; debt financing requires only $3,600 of income taxes. Maduro's cost of financing, whether paid in dividends to investors or interest to creditors, is $8,000. With debt financing, however, the Internal Revenue Service receives $2,400 less.

The after-tax interest cost of debt can be computed as

$$\text{Total interest expense} \times (1.0 - \text{Tax rate})$$
$$\$8,000 \times (1.0 - 0.30) = \$5,600$$

The after-tax interest rate that Maduro is paying can be computed using the same logic:

$$\text{Debt interest rate} \times (1.0 - \text{Tax rate})$$
$$8\% \times (1.0 - 0.30) = 5.6\%$$

Unlike interest expense, there is no difference in the before-tax and after-tax effects of a dividend. For Maduro, $1 of dividends costs the company a full $1 of retained earnings, while $1 of interest has an after-tax cost of only $0.70 (assuming a 30 percent tax rate). This tax benefit only applies to profitable businesses. There are no tax savings if a company has no income because businesses that produce losses pay no taxes.

EBIT and Ratio Analysis

The tax consequences of debt financing can influence ratio analysis. For example, consider the *return on assets* (ROA) ratio discussed in Chapter 3. In that chapter ROA was defined as:

$$\text{Net income} \div \text{Total assets}$$

Recall that the ROA ratio is used to measure the effectiveness of asset management. In general, higher ROAs suggest better performance. However, the Maduro example demonstrates that a higher ROA can be obtained by using equity financing rather than debt financing without regard to how assets are managed. Recall that Maduro obtained $100,000 of assets whether through equity or debt financing. The assets were used exactly the same way regardless of the financing method used. With equity financing, Maduro's ROA is 14 percent ($14,000 ÷ $100,000) and with debt financing it is 8.4 percent ($8,400 ÷ $100,000). The difference in the ROA results from the financing approach rather than asset management.

The effects of the financing strategy can be avoided in ROA calculations by using *earnings before interest and taxes* (EBIT) rather than net income when computing the ratio. For example, if Maduro uses EBIT to compute ROA, the result is 20 percent ($20,000 ÷ $100,000) regardless of whether debt or equity financing is used. Using EBIT to compute ROA provides a less biased measure of asset utilization. For simplicity, however, this text uses net income to determine ROA unless otherwise indicated.

Times Interest Earned Ratio

Financing with bonds also has disadvantages. The issuer is legally obligated to make interest payments on time and to repay the principal at maturity. If a company fails to make scheduled payments, the creditors (bondholders) can force the company into bankruptcy. The claims on a company's assets held by bondholders and other creditors have priority over the claims of the owners. If a company in bankruptcy is forced to liquidate its assets, creditor claims must be fully paid before any owner claims can be paid. Bond issues therefore increase the owners' risk.

Financial analysts use several ratios to help assess the risk of bankruptcy. One is the *debt to assets ratio,* explained in Chapter 3. Another is the **times interest earned** ratio, defined as

$$\text{EBIT} \div \text{Interest expense}$$

This ratio measures *how many times* a company would be able to pay its interest using its earnings. The *times interest earned ratio* is based on EBIT rather than net income because it is the amount of earnings before interest and taxes that is available to pay interest. The higher the ratio, the less likely a company will be unable to make its interest payments. Higher times interest earned ratios suggest lower levels of risk. Examples of times interest earned ratios and debt to assets ratios for six real-world companies follow. These numbers are based on financial data for the year 2010.

Industry	Company	Times Interest Earned	Debt to Assets
Breakfast cereal	Kellogg's	8.05	0.82
	General Mills	6.74	0.68
Cosmetics	Avon	11.98	0.79
	Esteé Lauder	10.26	0.63
Hotels	Starwood Hotels	3.12	0.75
	Marriott	4.06	0.82

Since bills are paid with cash, not income, a company may be able to make interest payments even if it has a negative times interest earned ratio. A company with no EBIT may yet have cash. Meaningful financial statement analysis cannot rely on any single ratio or any set of ratios. Making sound business decisions requires considering other information in addition to the insights provided from analyzing ratios. A company with inferior ratios and a patent on a newly discovered drug that cures cancer may be a far better investment than a company with great ratios and a patent on a chemotherapy product that will soon be out of date. Ratio computations are based on historical data. They are useful only to the extent that history is likely to repeat itself.

✓ CHECK YOURSELF 10.3

Selected financial data pertaining to Shaver and Goode Companies follow (amounts are in thousands):

	Shaver Company	Goode Company
Earnings before interest and taxes	$750,720	$2,970,680
Interest expense	234,600	645,800

Based on this information, which company is more likely to be able to make its interest payments?

Answer The times interest earned ratio for Shaver Company is 3.2 ($750,720 ÷ $234,600) times. The times interest earned ratio for Goode Company is 4.6 ($2,970,680 ÷ $645,800) times. Based on this data, Goode Company is more likely to be able to make its interest payments.

<< A Look Back

This chapter explained basic accounting for long-term debt. *Long-term notes payable* usually mature in two to five years and require payments that include a return of principal plus interest. *Lines of credit* enable companies to borrow limited amounts on an as-needed basis. Although lines of credit normally have one-year terms, companies frequently renew them, extending the effective maturity date to the intermediate range of five or more years. Interest on a line of credit is normally paid monthly.

Long-term debt financing for more than 10 years usually requires issuing *bonds.* Bond agreements normally commit a company to pay *semiannual interest* at a fixed percentage of the bond face value. The amount of interest required by the bond agreement is based on the *stated interest rate.* If bonds are issued when the *market interest rate* is different from the stated interest rate, companies will receive more or less than the face value in order for the effective rate of interest to be consistent with market conditions. Selling bonds at a *discount* (below face value) increases the effective interest rate above the stated rate. Selling bonds at a *premium* decreases the effective rate of interest.

This chapter explained the tax advantages of using debt versus equity financing. Interest is a *tax-deductible expense* subtracted prior to determining taxable income. In contrast, dividends paid to owners are not deductible in determining taxable income.

>> A Look Forward

A company seeking long-term financing might choose to use debt, such as the types of bonds or term loans that were discussed in this chapter. Owners' equity is another source of long-term financing. Several equity alternatives are available, depending on the type of business organization the owners choose to establish. For example, a company could be organized as a sole proprietorship, partnership, or corporation. Chapter 11 presents accounting issues related to equity transactions for each of these types of business structures.

SELF-STUDY REVIEW PROBLEM

A step-by-step audio-narrated series of slides is provided on the text website at www.mhhe.com/edmonds8e.

During 2013 and 2014, Herring Corp. completed the following selected transactions relating to its bond issue. The corporation's fiscal year ends on December 31.

2013

Jan. 1   Sold $400,000 of 10-year, 9 percent bonds at 97. Interest is payable in cash on December 31 each year.

Dec. 31   Paid the bond interest and recorded the amortization of the discount using the straight-line method.

2014

Dec. 31   Paid the bond interest and recorded the amortization of the discount using the straight-line method.

Required

a.   Show how these events would affect Herring's financial statements by recording them in a financial statements model like the following one.

	Assets	=	Liab.	+	Equity	Rev.	−	Exp.	=	Net Inc.	Cash Flow
Date	Cash	=	Carrying Value of Bond Liability	+	Ret. Earn.						
1/1/13											
12/31/13											
12/31/14											

b. Determine the carrying value of the bond liability as of December 31, 2014.

c. Assuming Herring had earnings before interest and taxes of $198,360 in 2014, calculate the times interest earned ratio.

Solution

a.

	Assets	=	Liab.	+	Equity	Rev.	−	Exp.	=	Net Inc.	Cash Flow	
Date	Cash	=	Carrying Value of Bond Liability	+	Ret. Earn.							
1/1/13	388,000	=	388,000	+	NA	NA	−	NA	=	NA	388,000	FA
12/31/13	(36,000)	=	1,200	+	(37,200)	NA	−	37,200	=	(37,200)	(36,000)	OA
12/31/14	(36,000)	=	1,200	+	(37,200)	NA	−	37,200	=	(37,200)	(36,000)	OA

b. The unamortized discount as of December 31, 2014, is $9,600 ($12,000 − $1,200 − $1,200). The carrying value of the bond liability is $390,400 ($400,000 − $9,600).

c. The times interest earned ratio is 5.3 times ($198,360 ÷ $37,200).

KEY TERMS

amortization 535
bond certificates 539
bond discount 547
bondholder 539
bond premium 551
call premium 542
call price 542
callable bonds 542
carrying value 547
collateral 543
convertible bonds 542

debentures 541
Discount on Bonds
   Payable 547
effective interest rate 547
effective interest rate
   method 554
face value 539
financial leverage 557
fixed interest rate 534
installment notes 536
issuer 539

line of credit 539
long-term liabilities 534
market interest rate 552
mortgage bond 541
Premium on Bonds
   Payable 552
restrictive covenants 543
secured bonds 541
serial bonds 541
sinking fund 542
spread 557

stated interest rate 540
straight-line
   amortization 548
subordinated debentures 541
term bonds 541
times interest earned 559
unsecured bonds 541
unsubordinated
   debentures 541
variable interest rate 534

QUESTIONS

1. What is the difference between classification of a note as short term or long term?

2. At the beginning of year 1, B Co. has a note payable of $72,000 that calls for an annual payment of $16,246, which includes both principal and interest. If the interest rate is 8 percent, what is the amount of interest expense in year 1 and in year 2? What is the balance of the note at the end of year 2?

3. What is the purpose of a line of credit for a business? Why would a company choose to obtain a line of credit instead of issuing bonds?

4. What are the primary sources of debt financing for most large companies?

5. What are some advantages of issuing bonds

versus borrowing from a bank?

6. What are some disadvantages of issuing bonds?

7. Why can a company usually issue bonds at a lower interest rate than the company would pay if the funds were borrowed from a bank?

8. What effect does income tax have on the cost of borrowing funds for a business?

9. What is the concept of financial leverage?

10. Which type of bond, secured or unsecured, is likely to have a lower interest rate? Explain.

11. What is the function of restrictive covenants attached to bond issues?

12. What is the difference between term bonds and serial bonds?

13. What is the purpose of establishing a sinking fund?

14. What is the call price of a bond? Is it usually higher or lower than the face amount of the bond? Explain.

15. If Roc Co. issued $100,000 of 5 percent, 10-year bonds at the face amount, what is the effect of the issuance of the bonds on the financial statements? What amount of interest expense will Roc Co. recognize each year?

16. What mechanism is used to adjust the stated interest rate to the market rate of interest?

17. When the effective interest rate is higher than the stated interest rate on a bond issue, will the bond sell at a discount or premium? Why?

18. What type of transaction is the issuance of bonds by a company?

19. What factors may cause the effective interest rate

and the stated interest rate to be different?

20. If a bond is selling at 97 ½, how much cash will the company receive from the sale of a $1,000 bond?

21. How is the carrying value of a bond computed?

22. Gay Co. has a balance in the Bonds Payable account of $25,000 and a balance in the Discount on Bonds Payable account of $5,200. What is the carrying value of the bonds? What is the total amount of the liability?

23. When the effective interest rate is higher than the stated interest rate, will interest expense be higher or lower than the amount of interest paid?

24. Assuming that the selling price of the bond and the face value are the same, would the issuer of a

bond rather make annual or semiannual interest payments? Why?

25. Rato Co. called some bonds and had a loss on the redemption of the bonds of $2,850. How is this amount reported on the income statement?

26. Which method of financing, debt or equity, is generally more advantageous from a tax standpoint? Why?

27. If a company has a tax rate of 30 percent and interest expense was $10,000, what is the after-tax cost of the debt?

28. Which type of financing, debt or equity, increases the risk factor of a business? Why?

29. What information does the times interest earned ratio provide?

MULTIPLE-CHOICE QUESTIONS

Multiple-choice questions are provided on the text website at www.mhhe.com/edmonds8e.

EXERCISES—SERIES A

All applicable Exercises in Series A are available with McGraw-Hill's *Connect® Accounting.*

LO 1

Exercise 10-1A   *Interest only versus an installment note*

Dodson Co. is planning to finance an expansion of its operations by borrowing $120,000. City Bank has agreed to loan Dodson the funds. Dodson has two repayment options: (1) to issue a note with the principal due in 10 years and with interest payable annually or (2) to issue a note to repay $12,000 of the principal each year along with the annual interest based on the unpaid principal balance. Assume the interest rate is 8 percent for each option.

Required

a. What amount of interest will Dodson pay in year 1
   (1) Under option 1?
   (2) Under option 2?

b. What amount of interest will Dodson pay in year 2
   (1) Under option 1?
   (2) Under option 2?

c. Explain the advantage of each option.

Exercise 10-2A   *Amortization schedule for an installment note*

LO 1

On January 1, 2013, Hatch Co. borrowed $100,000 cash from First Bank by issuing a four-year, 6 percent note. The principal and interest are to be paid by making annual payments in the amount of $28,859. Payments are to be made December 31 of each year, beginning December 31, 2013.

Required

Prepare an amortization schedule for the interest and principal payments for the four-year period.

Exercise 10-3A   *Financial statement effects of an installment note*

LO 1

Jay Mills started a business by issuing a $60,000 face value note to State National Bank on January 1, 2013. The note had a 6 percent annual rate of interest and a 10-year term. Payments of $8,152 are to be made each December 31 for 10 years.

Required

a. What portion of the December 31, 2013, payment is applied to
   (1) Interest expense?
   (2) Principal?
b. What is the principal balance on January 1, 2014?
c. What portion of the December 31, 2014, payment is applied to
   (1) Interest expense?
   (2) Principal?

Exercise 10-4A   *Financial statement effects of an installment note*

LO 1

A partial amortization schedule for a five-year note payable that Holly Co. issued on January 1, 2013, is shown here:

Accounting Period	Principal Balance January 1	Cash Payment	Applied to Interest	Applied to Principal
2013	$50,000	$11,549	$2,500	$8,959
2014	41,041	11,549	2,052	9,497

Required

a. What rate of interest is Holly Co. paying on the note?
b. Using a financial statements model like the one shown below, record the appropriate amounts for the following two events:
   (1) January 1, 2013, issue of the note payable.
   (2) December 31, 2014, payment on the note payable.

Event No.	Assets	=	Liab.	+	Equity	Rev.	−	Exp.	=	Net Inc.	Cash Flow
1											

c. If the company earned $60,000 cash revenue and paid $30,000 in cash expenses in addition to the interest in 2013, what is the amount of each of the following?
   (1) Net income for 2013.
   (2) Cash flow from operating activities for 2013.
   (3) Cash flow from financing activities for 2013.
d. What is the amount of interest expense on this loan for 2015?

LO 2

Exercise 10-5A   *Journal entries for a line of credit*

Martin Company has a line of credit with Federal Bank. Martin can borrow up to $600,000 at any time over the course of the 2013 calendar year. The following table shows the prime rate expressed as an annual percentage along with the amounts borrowed and repaid during the first four months of 2013. Martin agreed to pay interest at an annual rate equal to 2 percent above the bank's prime rate. Funds are borrowed or repaid on the first day of each month. Interest is payable in cash on the last day of the month. The interest rate is applied to the outstanding monthly balance. For example, Martin pays 5 percent (3 percent + 2 percent) annual interest on $90,000 for the month of January.

Month	Amount Borrowed or (Repaid)	Prime Rate for the Month
January	$90,000	3.0%
February	50,000	3.5
March	(30,000)	4.0
April	20,000	4.5

Required

Provide all journal entries pertaining to Martin's line of credit for the first four months of 2013.

LO 3

Exercise 10-6A   *Two accounting cycles for bonds issued at face value*

Chapman Company issued $400,000 of 20-year, 6 percent bonds on January 1, 2013. The bonds were issued at face value. Interest is payable in cash on December 31 of each year. Chapman immediately invested the proceeds from the bond issue in land. The land was leased for an annual $60,000 of cash revenue, which was collected on December 31 of each year, beginning December 31, 2013.

Required

a. Prepare the journal entries for these events, and post them to T-accounts for 2013 and 2014.
b. Prepare the income statement, balance sheet, and statement of cash flows for 2013 and 2014.

LO 3

Exercise 10-7A   *Two accounting cycles for bonds issued at face value*

On January 1, 2013, Chavez Corp. issued $200,000 of 10-year, 6 percent bonds at their face value. Interest is payable on December 31 of each year with the first payment due December 31, 2013.

Required

Prepare all the general journal entries related to these bonds for 2013 and 2014.

LO 3

Exercise 10-8A   *Journal entries for callable bonds*

Truax Co. issued $250,000 of 6 percent, 10-year, callable bonds on January 1, 2013, at their face value. The call premium was 2 percent (bonds are callable at 102). Interest was payable annually on December 31. The bonds were called on December 31, 2016.

Required

Prepare the journal entries to record the bond issue on January 1, 2013, and the bond redemption on December 31, 2016. Assume that all entries to accrue and pay interest were recorded correctly.

LO 3

Exercise 10-9A   *Annual versus semiannual interest for bonds issued at face value*

Ellis Co. issued bonds with a face value of $150,000 on January 1, 2013. The bonds had a 6 percent stated rate of interest and a five-year term. The bonds were issued at face value.

Required

a. What total amount of interest will Ellis pay in 2013 if bond interest is paid annually each December 31?

b. What total amount of interest will Ellis pay in 2013 if bond interest is paid semiannually each June 30 and December 31?

c. Write a memo explaining which option Ellis would prefer.

Exercise 10-10A *Determining cash receipts from bond issues*   LO 3, 4

Required

Compute the cash proceeds from bond issues under the following terms. For each case, indicate whether the bonds sold at a premium or discount:

a. Few, Inc., issued $400,000 of 8-year, 8 percent bonds at 101.

b. Files Co. issued $250,000 of 4-year, 6 percent bonds at 98.

c. Fry Co. issued $300,000 of 10-year, 7 percent bonds at 102 ¼.

d. Ford, Inc., issued $200,000 of 5-year, 6 percent bonds at 97 ½.

Exercise 10-11A *Stated rate of interest versus the market rate of interest*   LO 4

Required

Indicate whether a bond will sell at a premium (P), discount (D), or face value (F) for each of the following conditions:

a. _____ The market rate of interest is higher than the stated rate.

b. _____ The stated rate of interest is higher than the market rate.

c. _____ The stated rate of interest is less than the market rate.

d. _____ The market rate of interest is equal to the stated rate.

e. _____ The market rate of interest is less than the stated rate.

Exercise 10-12A *Identifying bond premiums and discounts*   LO 4

Required

In each of the following situations, state whether the bonds will sell at a premium or discount:

a. Addy issued $400,000 of bonds with a stated interest rate of 7 percent. At the time of issue, the market rate of interest for similar investments was 6 percent.

b. Rigsby issued $200,000 of bonds with a stated interest rate of 6 percent. At the time of issue, the market rate of interest for similar investments was 8 percent.

c. Sanders Inc., issued callable bonds with a stated interest rate of 6 percent. The bonds were callable at 102. At the date of issue, the market rate of interest was 7 percent for similar investments.

Exercise 10-13A *Determining the amount of bond premiums and discounts*   LO 4

Required

For each of the following situations, calculate the amount of bond discount or premium, if any:

a. Wolfe Co. issued $120,000 of 6 percent bonds at 101.

b. Riley, Inc., issued $80,000 of 10-year, 8 percent bonds at 98.

c. Rais, Inc., issued $200,000 of 15-year, 9 percent bonds at 102 ¼.

d. Beaux Co. issued $400,000 of 20-year, 8 percent bonds at 99 ¾.

Exercise 10-14A *Straight-line amortization of a bond discount*   LO 4

Brock Company issued $300,000 face value of bonds on January 1, 2013. The bonds had a 6 percent stated rate of interest and a 10-year term. Interest is paid in cash annually, beginning December 31, 2013. The bonds were issued at 98.

Required

a. Use a financial statements model like the one shown below to demonstrate how (1) the January 1, 2013, bond issue and (2) the December 31, 2013, recognition of interest expense, including the amortization of the discount and the cash payment, affects the company's financial statements. Use + for increase, − for decrease, and NA for not affected.

Event No.	Assets	=	Liab.	+	Equity	Rev.	−	Exp.	=	Net Inc.	Cash Flow
1											

b. Determine the amount of interest expense reported on the 2013 income statement.

c. Determine the carrying value (face value less discount or plus premium) of the bond liability as of December 31, 2013.

d. Determine the amount of interest expense reported on the 2014 income statement.

e. Determine the carrying value (face value less discount or plus premium) of the bond liability as of December 31, 2014.

LO 4

Exercise 10-15A   *Straight-line amortization of a bond discount*

Delta Construction, Inc., issued $300,000 of 10-year, 6 percent bonds on July 1, 2013, at 96. Interest is payable in cash semiannually on June 30 and December 31.

Required

a. Prepare the journal entries to record issuing the bonds and any necessary journal entries for 2013 and 2014. Post the journal entries to T-accounts.

b. Prepare the liabilities section of the balance sheet at the end of 2013 and 2014.

c. What amount of interest expense will Delta Construction report on the financial statements for 2013 and 2014?

d. What amount of cash will Delta Construction pay for interest in 2013 and 2014?

LO 4

Exercise 10-16A   *Straight-line amortization for bonds issued at a discount*

On January 1, 2013, French Co. issued $400,000 of five-year, 6 percent bonds at 97. Interest is payable annually on December 31. The discount is amortized using the straight-line method.

Required

Prepare the journal entries to record the bond transactions for 2013 and 2014.

LO 4

Exercise 10-17A   *Straight-line amortization of a bond premium*

Asmus Company issued $300,000 face value of bonds on January 1, 2013. The bonds had a 6 percent stated rate of interest and a 10-year term. Interest is paid in cash annually, beginning December 31, 2013. The bonds were issued at 101 ½.

Required

a. Use a financial statements model like the one shown below to demonstrate how (1) the January 1, 2013 bond issue and (2) the December 31, 2013 recognition of interest expense, including the amortization of the premium and the cash payment, affects the company's financial statements. Use + for increase, − for decrease, and NA for not affected.

Event No.	Assets	=	Liab.	+	Equity	Rev.	−	Exp.	=	Net Inc.	Cash Flow
1											

b. Determine the carrying value (face value plus premium) of the bond liability as of December 31, 2013.

c. Determine the amount of interest expense reported on the 2013 income statement.

d. Determine the carrying value of the bond liability as of December 31, 2014.

e. Determine the amount of interest expense reported on the 2014 income statement.

Exercise 10-18A *Straight-line amortization for bonds issued at a premium*

LO 4

On January 1, 2013, Chu Company issued $300,000 of five-year, 6 percent bonds at 101. Interest is payable annually on December 31. The premium is amortized using the straight-line method.

Required

Prepare the journal entries to record the bond transactions for 2013 and 2014.

Exercise 10-19A *Determining the after-tax cost of debt*

LO 6

The following 2013 information is available for three companies:

	Almond Co.	Walnut Co.	Filbert Co.
Face value of bonds payable	$500,000	$600,000	$700,000
Interest rate	7%	8%	9%
Income tax rate	35%	20%	25%

Required

a. Determine the annual before-tax interest cost for each company *in dollars.*

b. Determine the annual after-tax interest cost for each company *in dollars.*

c. Determine the annual after-tax interest cost for each company as *a percentage* of the face value of the bonds.

Exercise 10-20A *Effective interest amortization of a bond discount*

LO 5

On January 1, 2013, Carrolton Condo Association issued bonds with a face value of $250,000, a stated rate of interest of 8 percent, and a 10-year term to maturity. Interest is payable in cash on December 31 of each year. The effective rate of interest was 10 percent at the time the bonds were issued. The bonds sold for $219,277. Carrolton used the effective interest rate method to amortize bond discount.

Required

a. Determine the amount of the discount on the day of issue.

b. Determine the amount of interest expense recognized on December 31, 2013.

c. Determine the carrying value of the bond liability on December 31, 2013.

d. Provide the general journal entry necessary to record the December 31, 2013, interest expense.

Exercise 10-21A *Effective interest amortization of a bond discount*

LO 5

On January 1, 2013, Seaside Enterprises issued bonds with a face value of $60,000, a stated rate of interest of 8 percent, and a five-year term to maturity. Interest is payable in cash on December 31 of each year. The effective rate of interest was 9 percent at the time the bonds were issued. The bonds sold for $57,666. Seaside used the effective interest rate method to amortize bond discount.

Required

a. Prepare an amortization table as shown below:

	Cash Payment	Interest Expense	Discount Amortization	Carrying Value
January 1, 2013				57,666
December 31, 2013	4,800	5,190	390	58,056
December 31, 2014	?	?	?	?
December 31, 2015	?	?	?	?
December 31, 2016	?	?	?	?
December 31, 2017	?	?	?	?
Totals	24,000	26,334	2,334	

b. What item(s) in the table would appear on the 2014 balance sheet?
c. What item(s) in the table would appear on the 2014 income statement?
d. What item(s) in the table would appear on the 2014 statement of cash flows?

LO 6

Exercise 10-22A   *Determining the effects of financing alternatives on ratios*

Husky Industries has the following account balances:

Current assets	$ 20,000	Current liabilities	$10,000
Noncurrent assets	80,000	Noncurrent liabilities	50,000
		Stockholders' equity	40,000

The company wishes to raise $40,000 in cash, and is considering two financing options. Either it can sell $40,000 of bonds payable, or it can issue additional common stock for $40,000. To help in the decision process, Husky's management wants to determine the effects of each alternative on its current ratio and debt to assets ratio.

Required

a. Help Husky's management by completing the following chart:

Ratio	Currently	If Bonds Are Issued	If Stock Is Issued
Current ratio			
Debt to asset ratio			

b. Assume that after the funds are invested, EBIT amounts to $12,000. Also assume the company pays $4,000 in dividends or $4,000 in interest depending on which source of financing is used. Based on a 30 percent tax rate, determine the amount of the increase in retained earnings that would result under each financing option.

LO 5

Exercise 10-23A   *Effective interest amortization of a bond premium*

On January 1, 2013, Janus Company issued bonds with a face value of $200,000, a stated rate of interest of 6 percent, and a 10-year term to maturity. Interest is payable in cash on December 31 of each year. The effective rate of interest was 5 percent at the time the bonds were issued. The bonds sold for $215,443. White used the effective interest rate method to amortize bond discount.

Required

a. Determine the amount of the premium on the day of issue.
b. Determine the amount of interest expense recognized on December 31, 2013.
c. Determine the carrying value of the bond liability on December 31, 2013.
d. Provide the general journal entry necessary to record the December 31, 2013, interest expense.

LO 5

Exercise 10-24A   *Effective interest amortization for a bond premium*

On January 1, 2013, Pitre Incorporated issued bonds with a face value of $120,000, a stated rate of interest of 8 percent, and a five-year term to maturity. Interest is payable in cash on December 31 of each year. The effective rate of interest was 7 percent at the time the bonds were issued. The bonds sold for $124,920. Pitre used the effective interest rate method to amortize bond discount.

Required

a. Prepare an amortization table as shown below:

	Cash Payment	Interest Expense	Premium Amortization	Carrying Value
January 1, 2013				124,920
December 31, 2013	9,600	8,744	856	124,064
December 31, 2014	?	?	?	?
December 31, 2015	?	?	?	?
December 31, 2016	?	?	?	?
December 31, 2017	?	?	?	?
Totals	48,000	43,080	4,920	

b. What item(s) in the table would appear on the 2015 balance sheet?

c. What item(s) in the table would appear on the 2015 income statement?

d. What item(s) in the table would appear on the 2015 statement of cash flows?

Exercise 10-25A   *Effective interest versus straight-line amortization*

LO 4, 5

On January 1, 2013, Purvis and Associates issued bonds with a face value of $800,000, a stated rate of interest of 8 percent, and a 20-year term to maturity. Interest is payable in cash on December 31 of each year. The effective rate of interest was 9 percent at the time the bonds were issued.

Required

Write a brief memo explaining whether the effective interest rate method or the straight-line method will produce the highest amount of interest expense recognized on the 2013 income statement.

PROBLEMS—SERIES A

All applicable Problems in Series A are available with McGraw-Hill's *Connect®* **Accounting.**

Problem 10-26A   *Effect of an installment note on financial statements*

LO 1

On January 1, 2013, Mixon Co. borrowed cash from First City Bank by issuing a $90,000 face value, three-year term note that had a 7 percent annual interest rate. The note is to be repaid by making annual payments of $34,295 that include both interest and principal on December 31. Mixon invested the proceeds from the loan in land that generated lease revenues of $45,000 cash per year.

CHECK FIGURES
a. 2013 Ending Principal Balance: $62,005
b. 2013 Net Income: $38,700

Required

a. Prepare an amortization schedule for the three-year period.

b. Prepare an income statement, balance sheet, and statement of cash flows for each of the three years. (*Hint:* Record the transactions for each year in T-accounts before preparing the financial statements.)

c. Does cash outflow from operating activities remain constant or change each year? Explain.

Problem 10-27A   *Effect of a line of credit on financial statements*

LO 2

Sims Company has a line of credit with Bay Bank. Sims can borrow up to $400,000 at any time over the course of the 2013 calendar year. The following table shows the prime rate expressed as an annual percentage along with the amounts borrowed and repaid during 2013. Sims agreed to pay interest at an annual rate equal to 1 percent above the bank's prime rate. Funds are borrowed or repaid on the first day of each month. Interest is payable in cash on the last day of the month. The interest rate is applied to the outstanding monthly balance. For example, Sims pays 6 percent (5 percent + 1 percent) annual interest on $60,000 for the month of January.

CHECK FIGURES
a. Interest Expense: $4,556
Total Assets: $60,444

Month	Amount Borrowed or (Repaid)	Prime Rate for the Month
January	$60,000	5%
February	40,000	5
March	(30,000)	6
April through October	No change	No change
November	(20,000)	6
December	(10,000)	5

Sims earned $25,000 of cash revenue during 2013.

Required

a. Prepare an income statement, balance sheet, and statement of cash flows for 2013.

b. Write a memo discussing the advantages to a business of arranging a line of credit.

LO 3

CHECK FIGURE
b. Interest Expense: $15,000
   Loss on Bond
   Redemption: $3,750

Problem 10-28A *Recording transactions for callable bonds*

Lewis Co. issued $250,000 of 10-year, 6 percent, callable bonds on January 1, 2013, with interest payable annually on December 31. The bonds were issued at their face amount. The bonds are callable at 101 ½. The fiscal year of the corporation is the calendar year.

Required

a. Show the effect of the following events on the financial statements by recording the appropriate amounts in a horizontal statements model like the following one. In the Cash Flow column, indicate whether the item is an operating activity (OA), investing activity (IA), or financing activity (FA). Use NA if an element was not affected by the event.

   (1) Issued the bonds on January 1, 2013.

   (2) Paid interest due to bondholders on December 31, 2013.

   (3) On January 1, 2017, Lewis Co. called the bonds. Assume that all interim entries were correctly recorded.

Event No.	Assets	=	Liab.	+	Equity	Rev.	−	Exp.	=	Net Inc.	Cash Flow
1											

b. Prepare journal entries for the three events listed in Requirement *a*.

LO 4

Problem 10-29A *Straight-line amortization of a bond discount*

Brown Co. was formed when it acquired cash from the issue of common stock. The company then issued bonds at a discount on January 1, 2013. Interest is payable on December 31 with the first payment made December 31, 2013. On January 2, 2013, Brown Co. purchased a piece of land that produced rent revenue annually. The rent is collected on December 31 of each year, beginning December 31, 2013. At the end of the six-year period (January 1, 2019), the land was sold at a gain, and the bonds were paid off at face value. A summary of the transactions for each year follows:

2013

1. Acquired cash from the issue of common stock.

2. Issued six-year bonds.

3. Purchased land.

4. Received land rental income.

5. Recognized interest expense, including the amortization of the discount, and made the cash payment for interest on December 31.

6. Prepared December 31 entry to close Rent Revenue.

7. Prepared December 31 entry to close Interest Expense.

2014–2018

8. Received land rental income.
9. Recognized interest expense, including the amortization of the discount, and made the cash payment for interest December 31.
10. Prepared December 31 entry to close Rent Revenue.
11. Prepared December 31 entry to close Interest Expense.

2019

12. Sold the land at a gain.
13. Retired the bonds at face value.

Required

Identify each of these 13 events and transactions as asset source (AS), asset use (AU), asset exchange (AE), or claims exchange (CE). Explain how each event affects assets, liabilities, equity, net income, and cash flow by placing a + for increase, − for decrease, or NA for not affected under each of the categories. In the Cash Flow column, indicate whether the item is an operating activity (OA), investing activity (IA), or financing activity (FA). The first event is recorded as an example.

Event No.	Type of Event	Assets	=	Liabilities	+	Common Stock	+	Retained Earnings	Net Income	Cash Flow
1	AS	+		NA		+		NA	NA	+ FA

Problem 10-30A *Straight-line amortization of a bond discount*

LO 4

CHECK FIGURES
d. 2013 Interest Expense: $10,625
e. 2013 Interest Paid: $6,000

During 2013 and 2014, Cook Co. completed the following transactions relating to its bond issue. The company's fiscal year ends on December 31.

2013

Mar. 1   Issued $200,000 of eight-year, 6 percent bonds for $194,000. The semiannual cash payment for interest is due on March 1 and September 1, beginning September 2013.

Sept. 1   Recognized interest expense including the amortization of the discount and made the semiannual cash payment for interest.

Dec. 31   Recognized accrued interest expense including the amortization of the discount.

Dec. 31   Closed the interest expense account.

2014

Mar. 1   Recognized interest expense including the amortization of the discount and made the semiannual cash payment for interest.

Sept. 1   Recognized interest expense including the amortization of the discount and made the semiannual cash payment for interest.

Dec. 31   Recognized accrued interest expense including the amortization of the discount.

Dec. 31   Closed the interest expense account.

Required

a. When the bonds were issued, was the market rate of interest more or less than the stated rate of interest? If the bonds had sold at face value, what amount of cash would Cook Co. have received?

b. Prepare the general journal entries for these transactions.

c. Prepare the liabilities section of the balance sheet at December 31, 2013 and 2014.

d. Determine the amount of interest expense Cook would report on the income statements for 2013 and 2014.

e. Determine the amount of interest Cook would pay to the bondholders in 2013 and 2014.

Problem 10-31A   *Straight-line amortization of a bond premium*

Jayroe Company was started when it issued bonds with $300,000 face value on January 1, 2013. The bonds were issued for cash at 103. They had a 15-year term to maturity and an 6 percent annual interest rate. Interest was payable annually. Jayroe immediately purchased land with the proceeds (cash received) from the bond issue. Jayroe leased the land for $36,000 cash per year. On January 1, 2016, the company sold the land for $310,000 cash. Immediately after the sale, Jayroe repurchased its bonds (repaid the bond liability) at 104. Assume that no other accounting events occurred in 2016.

Required

Prepare an income statement, statement of changes in equity, balance sheet and statement of cash flows for each of the 2013, 2014, 2015, and 2016 accounting periods. Assume that the company closes its books on December 31 of each year. Prepare the statements using a vertical statements format. (*Hint:* Record each year's transactions in T-accounts prior to preparing the financial statements.)

Problem 10-32A   *Effect of financing transactions on financial statements*

Required

Show the effect of each of the following independent accounting events on the financial statements using a horizontal statements model like the following one. Use + for increase, − for decrease, and NA for not affected. The first event is recorded as an example.

Event No.	Assets	=	Liab.	+	Equity	Rev.	−	Exp.	=	Net Inc.	Cash Flow
1	+		+		NA	NA		NA		NA	FA +

a. Issued a bond at a premium.
b. Made an interest payment on a bond that had been issued at a premium and amortized the premium.
c. Borrowed funds using a line of credit.
d. Made an interest payment for funds that had been borrowed against a line of credit.
e. Made a cash payment on a note payable for both interest and principal.
f. Issued a bond at face value.
g. Made an interest payment on a bond that had been issued at face value.
h. Issued a bond at a discount.
i. Made an interest payment on a bond that had been issued at a discount and amortized the discount.

Problem 10-33A   *Effective interest versus straight-line amortization*

On January 1, 2013, Wells Corp. sold $100,000 of its own 6 percent, 10-year bonds. Interest is payable annually on December 31. The bonds were sold to yield an effective interest rate of 5 percent. Wells Corp. uses the effective interest rate method. The bonds sold for $104,330.

Required

a. Prepare the journal entry for the issuance of the bonds.
b. Prepare the journal entry for the amortization of the bond premium and the payment of the interest on December 31, 2015. (Assume effective interest amortization.)
c. Prepare the journal entry for the amortization of the bond premium and the payment of interest on December 31, 2015. (Assume straight-line amortization.)
d. Calculate the amount of interest expense for 2016. (Assume effective interest amortization.)
e. Calculate the amount of interest expense for 2016. (Assume straight-line amortization.)

Problem 10-34A *Using ratios to make comparisons*

LO 6

CHECK FIGURE
a. Times Interest
Earned—Bell: 4.2

The following information pertains to Bell and Tower companies at the end of 2013:

Account Title	Bell	Tower
Current assets	$ 30,000	$ 30,000
Total assets	200,000	200,000
Current liabilities	20,000	15,000
Total liabilities	150,000	110,000
Stockholders' equity	55,000	90,000
Interest expense	13,000	10,000
Income tax expense	12,500	12,000
Net income	28,500	29,100

Required

a. Compute each company's debt to assets ratio, current ratio, and times interest earned (EBIT must be computed). Identify the company with the greater financial risk.

b. Compute each company's return on equity ratio and return on assets ratio. Use EBIT instead of net income when computing the return on assets ratio. Identify the company that is managing its assets more effectively. Identify the company that is producing the higher return from the stockholders' perspective. Explain how one company was able to produce a higher return on equity than the other.

EXERCISES—SERIES B

Exercise 10-1B *Interest only versus an installment note*

LO 1

Mize Co. borrowed $80,000 from the National Bank by issuing a note with a five-year term. Mize has two options with respect to the payment of interest and principal. Option 1 requires the payment of interest only on an annual basis with the full amount of the principal due at maturity. Option 2 calls for an annual payment that includes interest due plus a partial repayment of the principal balance. The effective annual interest rate on both notes is identical.

Required

Write a memo explaining how the two alternatives will affect *(a)* the carrying value of liabilities, *(b)* the amount of annual interest expense, *(c)* the total amount of interest that will be paid over the life of the note, and *(d)* the cash flow consequences.

Exercise 10-2B *Amortization schedule for an installment note*

LO 1

On January 1, 2013, Flick Co. borrowed $180,000 cash from Central Bank by issuing a five-year, 6 percent note. The principal and interest are to be paid by making annual payments in the amount of $42,731. Payments are to be made December 31 of each year, beginning December 31, 2013.

Required

Prepare an amortization schedule for the interest and principal payments for the five-year period.

Exercise 10-3B *Financial statement effects of an installment note*

LO 1

John Young started a business by issuing a $90,000 face value note to First State Bank on January 1, 2013. The note had a 10 percent annual rate of interest and a five-year term. Payments of $23,742 are to be made each December 31 for five years.

Required

a. What portion of the December 31, 2013, payment is applied to
   (1) Interest expense?
   (2) Principal?
b. What is the principal balance on January 1, 2014?
c. What portion of the December 31, 2014, payment is applied to
   (1) Interest expense?
   (2) Principal?

LO 1

Exercise 10-4B *Financial statement effects of an installment note*

A partial amortization schedule for a 10-year note payable issued on January 1, 2013, is shown below:

Accounting Period	Principal Balance January 1	Cash Payment	Applied to Interest	Applied to Principal
2013	$100,000	$22,961	$6,000	$16,961
2014	83,039	22,961	4,982	17,979
2015	65,060	22,961	3,904	19,057

Required

a. Using a financial statements model like the one shown here, record the appropriate amounts for the following two events:
   (1) January 1, 2013, issue of the note payable.
   (2) December 31, 2013, payment on the note payable.

Event No.	Assets	=	Liab.	+	Equity	Rev.	−	Exp.	=	Net Inc.	Cash Flow
1											

b. If the company earned $60,000 cash revenue and paid $42,000 in cash expenses in addition to the interest in 2013, what is the amount of each of the following?
   (1) Net income for 2013.
   (2) Cash flow from operating activities for 2013.
   (3) Cash flow from financing activities for 2013.
c. What is the amount of interest expense on this loan for 2016?

LO 2

Exercise 10-5B *Journal entries for a line of credit*

Ebanks Company has a line of credit with United Bank. Ebanks can borrow up to $200,000 at any time over the course of the 2013 calendar year. The following table shows the prime rate expressed as an annual percentage along with the amounts borrowed and repaid during the first three months of 2013. Ebanks agreed to pay interest at an annual rate equal to 2 percent above the bank's prime rate. Funds are borrowed or repaid on the first day of each month. Interest is payable in cash on the last day of the month. The interest rate is applied to the outstanding monthly balance. For example, Ebanks pays 6.5 percent (4.5 percent + 2 percent) annual interest on $70,000 for the month of February.

Month	Amount Borrowed or (Repaid)	Prime Rate for the Month
January	$40,000	4.0%
February	30,000	4.5
March	(20,000)	4.0

Required

Provide all journal entries pertaining to Ebanks's line of credit for the first three months of 2013.

Exercise 10-6B   *Two accounting cycles for bonds issued at face value*   LO 3

Zhang Company issued $600,000 of 10-year, 7 percent bonds on January 1, 2013. The bonds were issued at face value. Interest is payable in cash on December 31 of each year. Zhang immediately invested the proceeds from the bond issue in land. The land was leased for an annual $110,000 of cash revenue, which was collected on December 31 of each year, beginning December 31, 2013.

Required

a. Prepare the journal entries for these events, and post them to T-accounts for 2013 and 2014.
b. Prepare the income statement, balance sheet, and statement of cash flows for 2013 and 2014.

Exercise 10-7B   *Two accounting cycles for bonds issued at face value*   LO 3

On January 1, 2013, Ward Corp. issued $160,000 of 10-year, 7 percent bonds at their face amount. Interest is payable on December 31 of each year with the first payment due December 31, 2013.

Required

Prepare all the general journal entries related to these bonds for 2013 and 2014.

Exercise 10-8B   *Journal entries for callable bonds*   LO 3

Tsai Co. issued $600,000 of 6 percent, 10-year, callable bonds on January 1, 2013, at their face value. The call premium was 3 percent (bonds are callable at 103). Interest was payable annually on December 31. The bonds were called on December 31, 2017.

Required

Prepare the journal entries to record the bond issue on January 1, 2013, and the bond redemption on December 31, 2017. Assume that all entries for accrual and payment of interest were recorded correctly.

Exercise 10-9B   *Annual versus semiannual interest for bonds issued at face value*   LO 3

Osby Company issued bonds with a face value of $100,000 on January 1, 2013. The bonds had a 7 percent stated rate of interest and a six-year term. The bonds were issued at face value. Interest is payable on an annual basis.

Required

Write a memo explaining whether the total cash outflow for interest would be more, less, or the same, if the bonds pay semiannual versus annual interest.

Exercise 10-10B   *Determining cash receipts from bond issues*   LO 3, 4

Required

Compute the cash proceeds from bond issues under the following terms. For each case, indicate whether the bonds sold at a premium or discount:

a. Spring, Inc., issued $300,000 of 10-year, 8 percent bonds at 103.
b. Valley, Inc., issued $100,000 of five-year, 12 percent bonds at 97 ½.
c. River Co. issued $200,000 of five-year, 6 percent bonds at 102 ¼.
d. Snow, Inc., issued $80,000 of four-year, 8 percent bonds at 96.

Exercise 10-11B   *Stated rate of interest versus the market rate of interest*   LO 4

Required

Indicate whether a bond will sell at a premium (P), discount (D), or face value (F) for each of the following conditions:

a. _____ The stated rate of interest is less than the market rate.
b. _____ The market rate of interest is higher than the stated rate.

c. ____ The stated rate of interest is higher than the market rate.

d. ____ The market rate of interest is equal to the stated rate.

e. ____ The market rate of interest is less than the stated rate.

LO 4

Exercise 10-12B   *Identifying bond premiums and discounts*

Required

In each of the following situations, state whether the bonds will sell at a premium or discount:

a. Diaz issued $280,000 of bonds with a stated interest rate of 7 percent. At the time of issue, the market rate of interest for similar investments was 6 percent.

b. Baca issued $250,000 of bonds with a stated interest rate of 5 percent. At the time of issue, the market rate of interest for similar investments was 6 percent.

c. Ivy Inc. issued callable bonds with a stated interest rate of 5 percent. The bonds were callable at 102. At the date of issue, the market rate of interest was 6 percent for similar investments.

LO 4

Exercise 10-13B   *Determining the amount of bond premiums and discounts*

Required

For each of the following situations, calculate the amount of bond discount or premium, if any.

a. Holt Co. issued $70,000 of 6 percent bonds at 101 ¼.

b. Janus, Inc., issued $100,000 of 10-year, 6 percent bonds at 97 ½.

c. Mao, Inc., issued $200,000 of 20-year, 6 percent bonds at 103.

d. Hammi Co. issued $150,000 of 15-year, 7 percent bonds at 99.

LO 4

Exercise 10-14B   *Straight-line amortization of a bond discount*

Patal Company issued $150,000 face value of bonds on January 1, 2013. The bonds had a 7 percent stated rate of interest and a five-year term. Interest is paid in cash annually, beginning December 31, 2013. The bonds were issued at 98.

Required

a. Use a financial statements model like the one shown below to demonstrate how (1) the January 1, 2013, bond issue and (2) the December 31, 2013, recognition of interest expense, including the amortization of the discount and the cash payment, affects the company's financial statements. Use + for increase, − for decrease, and NA for not affected.

Event No.	Assets	=	Liab.	+	Equity	Rev.	−	Exp.	=	Net Inc.	Cash Flow
1											

b. Determine the carrying value (face value less discount or plus premium) of the bond liability as of December 31, 2013.

c. Determine the amount of interest expense reported on the 2013 income statement.

d. Determine the carrying value (face value less discount or plus premium) of the bond liability as of December 31, 2014.

e. Determine the amount of interest expense reported on the 2014 income statement.

LO 4

Exercise 10-15B   *Straight-line amortization of a bond discount*

The Grill, Inc., issued $300,000 of 10-year, 6 percent bonds on July 1, 2013, at 102. Interest is payable in cash semiannually on June 30 and December 31.

Required

a. Prepare the journal entries to record issuing the bonds and any necessary journal entries for 2013 and 2014. Post the journal entries to T-accounts.

b. Prepare the liabilities section of the balance sheet at the end of 2013 and 2014.

c. What amount of interest expense will Pet report on the financial statements for 2013 and 2014?

d. What amount of cash will Pet pay for interest in 2013 and 2014?

Exercise 10-16B *Straight-line amortization for bonds issued at a discount*   **LO 4**

On January 1, 2013, Berry Co. issued $180,000 of five-year, 6 percent bonds at 96 ½. Interest is payable annually on December 31. The discount is amortized using the straight-line method.

Required

Prepare the journal entries to record the bond transactions for 2013 and 2014.

Exercise 10-17B *Straight-line amortization of a bond premium*   **LO 4**

Forde Company issued $120,000 face value of bonds on January 1, 2013. The bonds had a 6 percent stated rate of interest and a five-year term. Interest is paid in cash annually, beginning December 31, 2013. The bonds were issued at 103.

Required

a. Use a financial statements model like the one shown below to demonstrate how (1) the January 1, 2013, bond issue and (2) the December 31, 2013, recognition of interest expense, including the amortization of the premium and the cash payment, affects the company's financial statements. Use + for increase, − for decrease, and NA for not affected.

Event No.	Assets	=	Liab.	+	Equity	Rev.	−	Exp.	=	Net Inc.	Cash Flow
1											

b. Determine the carrying value (face value less discount or plus premium) of the bond liability as of December 31, 2013.

c. Determine the amount of interest expense reported on the 2013 income statement.

d. Determine the carrying value of the bond liability as of December 31, 2014.

e. Determine the amount of interest expense reported on the 2014 income statement.

Exercise 10-18B *Straight-line amortization for bonds issued at a premium*   **LO 4**

On January 1, 2013, Waverly Company issued $250,000 of five-year, 6 percent bonds at 102. Interest is payable semiannually on June 30 and December 31. The premium is amortized using the straight-line method.

Required

Prepare the journal entries to record the bond transactions for 2013 and 2014.

Exercise 10-19B *Determining the after-tax cost of debt*   **LO 6**

The following 2013 information is available for three companies:

	Blue Co.	Yellow Co.	Green Co.
Face value of bonds payable	$500,000	$700,000	$900,000
Interest rate	8%	9%	10%
Income tax rate	30%	40%	35%

Required

a. Determine the annual before-tax interest cost for each company *in dollars.*

b. Determine the annual after-tax interest cost for each company *in dollars.*

c. Determine the annual after-tax interest cost for each company as *a percentage* of the face value of the bonds.

LO 5

Exercise 10-20B   *Effective interest amortization of a bond discount*

On January 1, 2013, the Magnolia Association issued bonds with a face value of $200,000, a stated rate of interest of 8 percent, and a 10-year term to maturity. Interest is payable in cash on December 31 of each year. The effective rate of interest was 9 percent at the time the bonds were issued. The bonds sold for $187,165. Magnolia used the effective interest rate method to amortize bond discount.

Required

a. Determine the amount of the discount on the day of issue.
b. Determine the amount of interest expense recognized on December 31, 2013.
c. Determine the carrying value of the bond liability on December 31, 2013.
d. Provide the general journal entry necessary to record the December 31, 2013, interest expense.

LO 5

Exercise 10-21B   *Effective interest amortization of a bond discount*

On January 1, 2013, Lesley Company issued bonds with a face value of $250,000, a stated rate of interest of 10 percent, and a five-year term to maturity. Interest is payable in cash on December 31 of each year. The effective rate of interest was 12 percent at the time the bonds were issued. The bonds sold for $231,976. Lesley used the effective interest rate method to amortize bond discount.

Required

a. Prepare an amortization table as shown below:

	Cash Payment	Interest Expense	Discount Amortization	Carrying Value
January 1, 2013				231,976
December 31, 2013	25,000	27,837	2,837	234,813
December 31, 2014	?	?	?	?
December 31, 2015	?	?	?	?
December 31, 2016	?	?	?	?
December 31, 2017	?	?	?	?
Totals	125,000	143,024	18,024	

b. What item(s) in the table would appear on the 2016 balance sheet?
c. What item(s) in the table would appear on the 2016 income statement?
d. What item(s) in the table would appear on the 2016 statement of cash flows?

LO 6

Exercise 10-22B   *Determining the effects of financing alternatives on ratios*

Parker Company has the following account balances:

Current assets	$ 80,000	Current liabilities	$ 50,000
Noncurrent assets	170,000	Noncurrent liabilities	120,000
		Stockholders' equity	80,000

The company wishes to raise $50,000 in cash, and is considering two financing options. Either it can sell $50,000 of bonds payable, or it can issue additional common stock for $50,000. To help in the decision process, Parker's management wants to determine the effects of each alternative on its current ratio and debt to assets ratio.

Required

a. Help Parker's management by completing the following chart:

Ratio	Currently	If Bonds Are Issued	If Stock Is Issued
Current ratio			
Debt to asset ratio			

b. Assume that after the funds are invested, EBIT amounts to $60,000. Also assume the company pays $10,000 in dividends or $10,000 in interest depending on which source of financing is used. Based on a 30 percent tax rate, determine the amount of the increase in retained earnings that would result under each financing option.

Exercise 10-23B *Effective interest amortization of a bond premium*

LO 5

On January 1, 2013, Stone Company issued bonds with a face value of $400,000, a stated rate of interest of 7 percent, and a 10-year term to maturity. Interest is payable in cash on December 31 of each year. The effective rate of interest was 6 percent at the time the bonds were issued. The bonds sold for $429,440. Stone used the effective interest rate method to amortize bond premium.

Required

a. Determine the amount of the premium on the day of issue.

b. Determine the amount of interest expense recognized on December 31, 2013.

c. Determine the carrying value of the bond liability on December 31, 2013.

d. Provide the general journal entry necessary to record the December 31, 2013, interest expense.

Exercise 10-24B *Effective interest amortization for a bond premium*

LO 5

On January 1, 2013, Mead Company issued bonds with a face value of $100,000, a stated rate of interest of 9 percent, and a five-year term to maturity. Interest is payable in cash on December 31 of each year. The effective rate of interest was 8 percent at the time the bonds were issued. The bonds sold for $103,993. Mead used the effective interest rate method to amortize bond premium.

Required

a. Prepare an amortization table as shown below:

	Cash Payment	Interest Expense	Premium Amortization	Carrying Value
January 1, 2013				103,993
December 31, 2013	9,000	8,319	681	103,312
December 31, 2014	?	?	?	?
December 31, 2015	?	?	?	?
December 31, 2016	?	?	?	?
December 31, 2017	?	?	?	?
Totals	45,000	41,007	3,993	

b. What item(s) in the table would appear on the 2016 balance sheet?

c. What item(s) in the table would appear on the 2016 income statement?

d. What item(s) in the table would appear on the 2016 statement of cash flows?

Exercise 10-25B *Effective interest versus straight-line amortization*

LO 4, 5

On January 1, 2013, the Simmons Companies issued bonds with a face value of $1,000,000, a stated rate of interest of 10 percent, and a 20-year term to maturity. Interest is payable in cash on December 31 of each year. The effective rate of interest was 8 percent at the time the bonds were issued.

Required

Write a brief memo explaining whether the effective interest rate method or the straight-line method will produce the highest amount of interest expense recognized on the 2013 income statement.

LO 1

Problem 10-26B   *Effect of an installment note on financial statements*

On January 1, 2013, Spain Co. borrowed cash from First Bank by issuing a $250,000 face value, four-year term note that had an 8 percent annual interest rate. The note is to be repaid by making annual cash payments of $75,480 that include both interest and principal on December 31 of each year. Spain used the proceeds from the loan to purchase land that generated rental revenues of $90,000 cash per year.

Required

a. Prepare an amortization schedule for the four-year period.

b. Prepare an income statement, balance sheet, and statement of cash flows for each of the four years. (*Hint:* Record the transactions for each year in T-accounts before preparing the financial statements.)

c. Given that revenue is the same for each period, explain why net income increases each year.

LO 2

Problem 10-27B   *Effect of a line of credit on financial statements*

Kemp Company has a line of credit with State Bank. Kemp can borrow up to $300,000 at any time over the course of the 2013 calendar year. The following table shows the prime rate expressed as an annual percentage along with the amounts borrowed and repaid during 2013. Kemp agreed to pay interest at an annual rate equal to 2 percent above the bank's prime rate. Funds are borrowed or repaid on the first day of each month. Interest is payable in cash on the last day of the month. The interest rate is applied to the outstanding monthly balance. For example, Kemp pays 7 percent (5 percent + 2 percent) annual interest on $120,000 for the month of January.

Month	Amount Borrowed or (Repaid)	Prime Rate for the Month
January	$120,000	5%
February	50,000	6
March	(40,000)	7
April through October	No change	No change
November	(80,000)	6
December	(20,000)	5

Kemp earned $40,000 of cash revenue during 2013.

Required

a. Prepare an income statement, balance sheet, and statement of cash flows for 2013. (*Note:* Round computations to the nearest dollar.)

b. Write a memo to explain how the business was able to generate retained earnings when the owner contributed no assets to the business.

LO 3

Problem 10-28B   *Recording transactions for callable bonds*

Laird Corp. issued $500,000 of 20-year, 8 percent, callable bonds on January 1, 2013, with interest payable annually on December 31. The bonds were issued at their face amount. The bonds are callable at 104. The fiscal year of the corporation ends December 31.

Required

a. Show the effect of the following events on the financial statements by recording the appropriate amounts in a horizontal statements model like the following one. In the Cash Flow column, indicate whether the item is an operating activity (OA), investing activity (IA), or financing activity (FA). Use NA if an element was not affected by the event.

(1) Issued the bonds on January 1, 2013.

(2) Paid interest due to bondholders on December 31, 2013.

(3) On January 1, 2018, Laird Corp. called the bonds. Assume that all interim entries were correctly recorded.

Event No.	Assets	=	Liab.	+	Equity	Rev.	−	Exp.	=	Net Inc.	Cash Flow
1											

b. Prepare journal entries for the three events listed in Requirement *a*.

Problem 10-29B   *Straight-line amortization of a bond premium*   LO 4

Delta Land Co. was formed when it acquired cash from the issue of common stock. The company then issued bonds at a premium on January 1, 2013. Interest is payable annually on December 31 of each year, beginning December 31, 2013. On January 2, 2013, Delta Land Co. purchased a piece of land and leased it for an annual rental fee. The rent is received annually on December 31, beginning December 31, 2013. At the end of the eight-year period (December 31, 2020), the land was sold at a gain, and the bonds were paid off. A summary of the transactions for each year follows:

2013

1. Acquired cash from the issue of common stock.
2. Issued eight-year bonds.
3. Purchased land.
4. Received land rental income.
5. Recognized interest expense including the amortization of the premium and made the cash payment for interest on December 31.
6. Prepared the December 31 entry to close Rent Revenue.
7. Prepared the December 31 entry to close Interest Expense.

2014–2019

8. Received land rental income.
9. Recognized interest expense including the amortization of the premium and made the cash payment for interest on December 31.
10. Prepared the December 31 entry to close Rent Revenue.
11. Prepared the December 31 entry to close Interest Expense.

2020

12. Sold land at a gain.
13. Retired bonds at face value.

Required

Identify each of these 13 events and transactions as asset source (AS), asset use (AU), asset exchange (AE), or claims exchange (CE). Explain how each event affects assets, liabilities, equity, net income, and cash flow by placing a + for increase, − for decrease, or NA for not affected under each category. In the Cash Flow column, indicate whether the item is an operating activity (OA), investing activity (IA), or financing activity (FA). The first event is recorded as an example.

Event No.	Type of Event	Assets	=	Liabilities	+	Common Stock	+	Retained Earnings	Net Income	Cash Flow
1	AS	+		NA		+		NA	NA	+ FA

Problem 10-30B   *Straight-line amortization of a bond discount*   LO 4

During 2013 and 2014, Davis Corp. completed the following transactions relating to its bond issue. The corporation's fiscal year is the calendar year.

2013

Jan. 1   Issued $200,000 of ten-year, 6 percent bonds for $197,000. The annual cash payment for interest is due on December 31.

Dec. 31   Recognized interest expense, including the amortization of the discount, and made the cash payment for interest.

Dec. 31   Closed the interest expense account.

2014

Dec. 31   Recognized interest expense, including the amortization of the discount, and made the cash payment for interest.

Dec. 31   Closed the interest expense account.

Required

a. When the bonds were issued, was the market rate of interest more or less than the stated rate of interest? If Davis had sold the bonds at their face amount, what amount of cash would Davis have received?

b. Prepare the general journal entries for these transactions.

c. Prepare the liabilities section of the balance sheet at December 31, 2013 and 2014.

d. Determine the amount of interest expense that will be reported on the income statements for 2013 and 2014.

e. Determine the amount of interest that will be paid in cash to the bondholders in 2013 and 2014.

LO 4

Problem 10-31B   *Straight-line amortization of a bond discount*

Pate Company was started when it issued bonds with a $400,000 face value on January 1, 2013. The bonds were issued for cash at 96. They had a 20-year term to maturity and an 8 percent annual interest rate. Interest was payable on December 31 of each year. Pate Company immediately purchased land with the proceeds (cash received) from the bond issue. Pate leased the land for $50,000 cash per year. On January 1, 2016, the company sold the land for $400,000 cash. Immediately after the sale of the land, Pate redeemed the bonds at 98. Assume that no other accounting events occurred during 2016.

Required

Prepare an income statement, statement of changes in equity, balance sheet, and statement of cash flows for the 2013, 2014, 2015, and 2016 accounting periods. Assume that the company closes its books on December 31 of each year. Prepare the statements using a vertical statements format. (*Hint:* Record each year's transactions in T-accounts prior to preparing the financial statements.)

LO 3, 4

Problem 10-32B   *Effect of bond transactions on financial statements*

The three typical accounting events associated with borrowing money through a bond issue are

1. Exchanging the bonds for cash on the day of issue.
2. Making cash payments for interest expense and recording amortization when applicable.
3. Repaying the principal at maturity.

Required

a. Assuming the bonds are issued at face value, show the effect of each of the three events on the financial statements, using a horizontal statements model like the following one. Use + for increase, − for decrease, and NA for not affected.

Event No.	Assets	=	Liab.	+	Equity	Rev.	−	Exp.	=	Net Inc.	Cash Flow
1											

b. Repeat the requirements in Requirement *a*, but assume instead that the bonds are issued at a discount.

c. Repeat the requirements in Requirement *a*, but assume instead that the bonds are issued at a premium.

Problem 10-33B *Effective interest versus straight-line amortization*   LO 4, 5

On January 1, 2013, Gandy Corp. sold $600,000 of its own 8 percent, 10-year bonds. Interest is payable annually on December 31. The bonds were sold to yield an effective interest rate of 9 percent. Gandy uses the effective interest rate method. The bonds sold for $561,495.

Required

a. Prepare the journal entry for the issuance of the bonds.

b. Prepare the journal entry for the amortization of the bond discount and the payment of the interest at December 31, 2013. (Assume effective interest amortization.)

c. Prepare the journal entry for the amortization of the bond discount and the payment of interest on December 31, 2013. (Assume straight-line amortization.)

d. Calculate the amount of interest expense for 2014. (Assume effective interest amortization.)

e. Calculate the amount of interest expense for 2014. (Assume straight-line amortization.)

Problem 10-34B *Using ratios to make comparisons*   LO 6

The following information pertains to Bierce Company and Crane, Inc. at the end of 2013:

Account Title	Bierce	Crane
Current assets	$ 35,000	$ 30,000
Total assets	350,000	350,000
Current liabilities	20,000	20,000
Total liabilities	280,000	200,000
Stockholders' equity	70,000	150,000
Interest expense	25,000	18,000
Income tax expense	17,000	16,000
Net income	31,500	36,000

Required

a. Compute each company's debt to assets ratio, current ratio, and times interest earned (EBIT must be computed). Identify the company with the greater financial risk.

b. Compute each company's return on equity ratio and return on assets ratio. Use EBIT instead of net income when computing the return on assets ratio. Identify the company that is managing its assets more effectively. Identify the company that is producing the higher return from the stockholders' perspective. Explain how one company was able to produce a higher return on equity than the other.

ANALYZE, THINK, COMMUNICATE

ATC 10-1 Business Application Case *Understanding real-world annual reports*

Use the Target Corporation's annual report in Appendix B to answer the following questions:

Required

a. What was the average interest rate on Target's long-term debt in the fiscal-year ended January 29, 2011 (2010)?

b. Target has a "unsecured revolving credit facility," (i.e., a line of credit). What is the total amount of credit available under this facility? How much of this total amount available had Target used as of January 29, 2011?

c. Target's balance sheet shows a line titled "Other noncurrent liabilities." What are the types of debt included in this category?

ATC 10-2 Group Assignment *Missing information*

The following three companies issued the following bonds:

1. Carr, Inc., issued $100,000 of 8 percent, five-year bonds at 102 ¼ on January 1, 2013. Interest is payable annually on December 31.
2. Kim, Inc., issued $100,000 of 8 percent, five-year bonds at 98 on January 1, 2013. Interest is payable annually on December 31.
3. Jay, Inc., issued $100,000 of 8 percent, five-year bonds at 104 on January 1, 2013. Interest is payable annually on December 31.

Required

a. Organize the class into three sections and divide each section into groups of three to five students. Assign each of the sections one of the companies.

Group Tasks

(1) Compute the following amounts for your company (use straight-line amortization):
    (a) Cash proceeds from the bond issue.
    (b) Interest paid in 2013.
    (c) Interest expense for 2013.
(2) Prepare the liabilities section of the balance sheet as of December 31, 2013.

Class Discussion

b. Have a representative of each section put the liabilities section for its company on the board.
c. Is the amount of interest expense different for the three companies? Why or why not?
d. Is the amount of interest paid different for each of the companies? Why or why not?
e. Is the amount of total liabilities different for each of the companies? Why or why not?

ATC 10-3 Real-World Case *Using accounting numbers to assess creditworthiness*

Costco Wholesale is the national membership-warehouse retailer. It has 58 million members and 147,000 employees.

Foot Locker sells athletic footwear and clothes in its 3,500 stores in the United States, Canada, Europe, Australia, and New Zealand.

Keystone Automotive Operations ". . . is a wholesale distributor and retailer of automotive after-market accessories and equipment, operating throughout the United States and in parts of Canada. The Company sells and distributes specialty automotive products, such as light truck/SUV accessories, car accessories and trim items, specialty wheels, tires, and suspension parts and high performance products."

Johnson & Johnson is a holding company, which, through its 250 subsidiary companies, develops, manufactures, and sells a broad range of prescription and nonprescription health care products. It has approximately 115,500 employees.

	Net Income	Cash Flow from Operations	Current Ratio	Debt to Assets Ratio	Times Interest Earned	Return on Assets Ratio
Costco Wholesale						
2010	$ 1,323,000	$ 2,780,000	1.16	0.54	19.5	0.06
2009	1,086,000	2,092,000	1.11	0.54	16.9	0.05
Foot Locker						
2010	48,000	346,000	4.09	0.31	8.4	0.02
2009	(80,000)	383,000	4.22	0.33	−19.2	−0.03
Keystone Automotive Operations						
2010	(26,617)	21,331	3.99	1.10	0.1	−0.06
2009	(206,613)	3,375	4.21	1.16	−6.2	−0.55
Johnson & Johnson						
2010	12,266,000	16,571,000	1.82	0.47	35.9	0.13
2009	12,949,000	14,972,000	1.65	0.50	39.9	0.15

Each company received a different rating from the S&P. In descending order, the ratings for these companies were AAA, A+, B+, and CC. These rating are as of February 7, 2011.

Required

Determine which credit rating was assigned to which company. Write a memorandum explaining the rationale for your decisions.

ATC 10-4   Business Applications Case   *Performing ratio analysis using real-world data*

Sonic Corporation began business in 1953. In 2010 it was operating 3,572 drive-in hamburger restaurants throughout the United States and Mexico. The following data were taken from the company's 2010 annual report. All dollar amounts are in thousands.

	Fiscal Years Ending	
Account Title	August 31, 2010	August 31, 2009
Current assets	$133,928	$ 202,132
Total assets	737,320	849,041
Current liabilities	118,608	117,319
Total liabilities	714,976	853,309
Stockholders' equity	22,344	(4,268)
Interest expense	36,073	35,657
Income tax expense	8,969	30,878
Net income	25,839	49,442

Required

a. Calculate the EBIT for each year.

b. Calculate the times interest earned ratio for each year.

c. Calculate the current ratio and debt to assets ratio for each year.

d. Did the company's level of financial risk increase or decrease from 2009 to 2010? Explain.

ATC 10-5   Business Applications Case   *Performing ratio analysis using real-world data*

Jos. A. Bank Clothiers, Inc., operated 506 retail clothing stores in 42 states and the District of Columbia as of January 31, 2011. The Men's Wearhouse, Inc., operated 1,075 men's clothing stores in the United States, and 117 in Canada, as of January 31, 2011. These stores do business under the names Men's Wearhouse, K&G Fashion Superstores, and Moores Clothing for Men. The following information was taken from these companies' January 31, 2011 annual reports. All dollar amounts are in thousands.

Account Title	Jos. A. Banks	Men's Wearhouse
Current assets	$533,097	$ 764,008
Total assets	662,037	1,320,318
Current liabilities	124,946	266,656
Total liabilities	179,361	336,465
Stockholders' equity	482,676	983,853
Interest expense	136	1,141
Income tax expense	56,261	32,852
Net income	85,799	67,678

Required

a. Calculate the EBIT for each company.

b. Calculate each company's debt to assets ratio, current ratio, and the times interest earned ratio.

c. Calculate each company's return on assets ratio using EBIT instead of net earnings. Calculate each company's return on equity ratio using net earnings.

d. Men's Wearhouse reported interest expense of $1,141, before taxes. What was its after-tax interest expense in dollars? (*Hint:* You will need to compute its tax rate by dividing income tax expense by *earnings before taxes,* which must be computed.)

ATC 10-6 Writing Assignment *Debt versus equity financing*

Mack Company plans to invest $50,000 in land that will produce annual rent revenue equal to 15 percent of the investment starting on January 1, 2013. The revenue will be collected in cash at the end of each year, starting December 31, 2013. Mack can obtain the cash necessary to purchase the land from two sources. Funds can be obtained by issuing $50,000 of 10 percent, five-year bonds at their face amount. Interest due on the bonds is payable on December 31 of each year with the first payment due on December 31, 2013. Alternatively, the $50,000 needed to invest in land can be obtained from equity financing. In this case, the stockholders (holders of the equity) will be paid a $5,000 annual cash dividend. Mack Company is in a 30 percent income tax bracket.

Required

a. Prepare an income statement and statement of cash flows for 2013 under the two alternative financing proposals.

b. Write a short memorandum explaining why one financing alternative provides more net income but less cash flow than the other.

ATC 10-7 Ethical Dilemma *I don't want to pay taxes*

Dana Harbert recently started a very successful small business. Indeed, the business had grown so rapidly that she was no longer able to finance its operations by investing her own resources in the business. She needed additional capital but had no more of her own money to put into the business. A friend, Gene Watson, was willing to invest $100,000 in the business. Harbert estimated that with Watson's investment, the company would be able to increase revenue by $40,000. Furthermore, she believed that operating expenses would increase by only 10 percent. Harbert and Watson agree that Watson's investment should entitle him to receive a cash dividend equal to 20 percent of net income. A set of forecasted statements with and without Watson's investment is presented here. (Assume that all transactions involving revenue, expense, and dividends are cash transactions.)

Financial Statements		
	Forecast 1 **Without Watson's** **Investment**	**Forecast 2** **With Watson's** **Investment**
Income Statements		
Revenue	$120,000	$160,000
Operating expenses	(70,000)	(77,000)
Income before interest and taxes	50,000	83,000
Income tax expense (effective tax rate is 30%)	(15,000)	(24,900)
Net income	$ 35,000	$ 58,100
Statements of Changes in Stockholders' Equity		
Beginning retained earnings	$ 15,000	$ 15,000
Plus: Net income	35,000	58,100
Less: Dividend to Watson (20% of $58,100)	0	(11,620)
Ending retained earnings	$ 50,000	$ 61,480
Balance Sheets		
Assets (computations explained in following paragraph)	$400,000	$511,480
Liabilities	$ 0	$ 0
Equity		
Common stock	350,000	450,000
Retained earnings	50,000	61,480
Total liabilities and equity	$400,000	$511,480

The balance for assets in Forecast 1 is computed as the beginning balance of $365,000 plus net income of $35,000. The balance for assets in Forecast 2 is computed as the beginning balance of $365,000, plus the $100,000 cash investment, plus net income of $58,100, less the $11,620 dividend. Alternatively, total assets can be computed by determining the amount of total claims (total assets = total claims).

Harbert tells Watson that there would be a $3,486 tax advantage associated with debt financing. She says that if Watson is willing to become a creditor instead of an owner, she could pay him an additional $697.20 (that is, 20 percent of the tax advantage). Watson tells Harbert that he has no interest in participating in the management of the business, but Watson wants an ownership interest to guarantee that he will always receive 20 percent of the profits of the business. Harbert suggests that they execute a formal agreement in which Watson is paid 11.62 percent interest on his $100,000 loan to the business. This agreement will be used for income tax reporting. In addition, Harbert says that she is willing to establish a private agreement to write Watson a personal check for any additional amount necessary to make Watson's total return equal to 20 percent of all profits plus a $697.20 bonus for his part of the tax advantage. She tells Watson, "It's just like ownership. The only difference is that we call it debt for the Internal Revenue Service. If they want to have some silly rule that says if you call it debt, you get a tax break, then we are foolish if we don't call it debt. I will call it anything they want, just as long as I don't have to pay taxes on it."

Required

a. Construct a third set of forecasted financial statements (Forecast 3) at 11.62 percent annual interest, assuming that Watson is treated as creditor (he loans the business $100,000).

b. Verify the tax advantage of debt financing by comparing the balances of the Retained Earnings account in Forecast 2 and Forecast 3.

c. If you were Watson, would you permit Harbert to classify the equity transaction as debt to provide a higher return to the business and to you?

d. Comment on the ethical implications of misnaming a financing activity for the sole purpose of reducing income taxes.

ATC 10-8   Research Assignment   *Analyzing long-term debt at Union Pacific Railroad*

Many companies have a form of debt called *capital leases*. A capital lease is created when a company agrees to rent an asset, such as equipment or a building, for such a long time that GAAP treats this lease as if the asset was purchased using borrowed funds. A capital lease creates a liability for the company that acquired the leased asset because it has promised to make payments to another company for several years in the future. If a company has any capital leases, it must disclose them in the notes to the financial statements, and will sometimes disclose them in a separate account in the liabilities section of the balance sheet.

Using the most current (Forms 10-K) for Union Pacific Corporation, complete the requirements below. To obtain the 10-Ks you can either use the EDGAR system following the instructions in Appendix A, or they can be found on the company's website.

Required

a. What was Union Pacific's debt to asset ratio?

b. How much interest expense did Union Pacific's incur?

c. What amount of liabilities did Union Pacific's have as a result of capital leases? Footnotes 14 and 16 present information about Union Pacific's leases.

d. What percentage of Union Pacific's long-term liabilities was the result of capital leases?

e. Many companies try to structure (design) leasing agreements so that their leases will *not* be classified as capital leases. Explain why a company such as Union Pacific might want to avoid having capital leases.

ATC 10-9   Spreadsheet Assignment   *Using Excel*

On January 1, 2013, Bainbridge Company borrowed $100,000 cash from a bank by issuing a 10-year, 9 percent note. The principal and interest are to be paid by making annual payments in the amount of $15,582. Payments are to be made December 31 of each year beginning December 31, 2013.

Required

a. Set up the spreadsheet as shown below. Notice that Excel can be set up to calculate the loan payment. If you're unfamiliar with this, see the following Spreadsheet Tips section. The Beginning Principal Balance (B12) and Cash Payment (C12) can be referenced from the Loan Information section. The interest rate used to calculate Interest Expense (D12) can also be referenced from the Loan Information section.

b. Complete the spreadsheet for the 10 periods.

c. In Row 23, calculate totals for cash payments, interest expense, and applied to principal.

d. Consider how the amounts would differ if Bainbridge were to borrow the $100,000 at different interest rates and time periods. The results of the original data (option 1) have been entered in the following schedule. In the spreadsheet, delete 9 percent and 10 from cells B4 and B5, respectively. Enter the data for the second option (8 percent and 10 years) in cells B4 and B5. Enter the recomputed payment and total interest in the schedule for the second option. Continue the same process for options 3 through 9 by deleting the prior rate and number of periods in the spreadsheet and entering in the next option's data. The number of years scheduled (rows 12 through 21) will have to be shortened for the 7-year options and lengthened for the 13-year options.

	Option								
	1	2	3	4	5	6	7	8	9
Rate	9%	8%	10%	9%	8%	10%	9%	8%	10%
Years	10	10%	10	7	7	7	13	13	13
Payment	15,582								
Total interest	55,820								

Spreadsheet Tips

1. Excel will calculate an installment loan payment. The interest rate (%), number of periods (nper), and amount borrowed or otherwise known as present value (PV) must be entered in the payment formula. The formula for the payment is =PMT(rate,nper,pv). The rate, number of periods, and amount borrowed (present value) may be entered as actual amounts or referenced to other cells. In the preceding spreadsheet, the payment formula can be either =PMT(9%,10,100000) or =PMT(B4,B5,B3). In our case, the latter is preferred so that variables can be altered in the spreadsheet without also having to rewrite the payment formula. Notice that the payment is a negative number.

2. Using positive numbers is preferred in the amortization schedule. The loan payment (cell B6) in the loan information section shows up as a negative number. Any reference to it in the amortization schedule should be preceded by a minus sign to convert it to a positive number. For example, the formula in cell C12 for the cash payment is =−B6.

3. Recall that to copy a fixed number, a $ sign must be positioned before the column letter and row number. The complete formula then for cell C12 is =−B6.

ATC 10-10   Spreadsheet Analysis   *Mastering Excel*

Wise Company was started on January 1, 2013, when it issued 20-year, 10 percent, $200,000 face value bonds at a price of 90. Interest is payable annually at December 31 of each year. Wise immediately purchased land with the proceeds (cash received) from the bond issue. Wise leased the land for $27,000 cash per year. The lease revenue payments are due every December 31.

Required

Set up the following horizontal statements model on a blank spreadsheet. The SCF Activity column is for the classifications operating, financing, or investing.

a. Enter the effects of the 2013 transactions. Assume that both the interest and lease payments occurred on December 31. Notice that the entry for the lease has already been entered as an example. Calculate the ending balances.

b. Enter the effects of the 2014 transactions. Assume that both the interest and lease payments occurred on December 31. Calculate the ending balances.

c. Enter the effects of the 2015 transactions. Assume that both the interest and lease payments occurred on December 31. Calculate the ending balances.

d. On January 1, 2016, Wise Company sold the land for $190,000 cash. Immediately after the sale of the land, Wise repurchased its bond at a price of 93. Assume that no other accounting events occurred during 2016. Enter the effects of the 2016 transactions. Calculate the ending balances.

COMPREHENSIVE PROBLEM

The trial balance of Pacilio Security Services Inc. as of January 1, 2020, had the following normal balances:

Cash	$122,475
Petty cash	100
Accounts receivable	27,400
Allowance for doubtful accounts	4,390
Supplies	165
Prepaid rent	3,000
Merchandise inventory (38 @ $290)	11,020
Equipment	9,000
Van	27,000
Accumulated depreciation	23,050
Sales tax payable	290
Employee income tax payable	500
FICA—Social Security tax payable	600
FICA—Medicare tax payable	150
Warranty payable	312
Unemployment tax payable	630
Interest payable	320
Notes payable	12,000
Common stock	50,000
Retained earnings	107,918

During 2020 Pacilio Security Services experienced the following transactions:

1. Paid the sales tax payable from 2019.
2. Paid the balance of the payroll liabilities due for 2019 (federal income tax, FICA taxes, and unemployment taxes).
3. On January 1, 2020, purchased land and a building for $150,000. The building was appraised at $125,000 and the land at $25,000. Pacilio paid $50,000 cash and financed the balance. The balance was financed with a 10-year installment note. The note had an interest rate of 7 percent and annual payments of $14,238 due on the last day of the year.
4. On January 1, 2020, issued $50,000 of 6 percent, five year bonds. The bonds were issued at 98.
5. Purchase $660 of supplies on account.
6. Purchased 170 alarm systems at a cost of $300. Cash was paid for the purchase.
7. After numerous attempts to collect from customers, wrote off $2,450 of uncollectible accounts receivable.
8. Sold 160 alarm systems for $580 each plus sales tax of 5 percent. All sales were on account. (Be sure to compute cost of goods sold using the FIFO cost flow method.)
9. Billed $120,000 of monitoring services for the year. Credit card sales amounted to $36,000, and the credit card company charged a 4 percent fee. The remaining $84,000 were sales on account. Sales tax is not charged on this service.
10. Replenished the petty cash fund on June 30. The fund had $11 cash and receipts of $65 for yard mowing and $24 for office supplies expense.
11. Collected the amount due from the credit card company.
12. Paid the sales tax collected on $85,000 of the alarm sales.
13. Collected $167,000 of accounts receivable during the year.
14. Paid installers and other employees a total of $82,000 for salaries for the year. Assume the Social Security tax rate is 6 percent and the Medicare tax rate is 1.5 percent. Federal income taxes withheld amounted to $9,600. The net amount of salaries was paid in cash.
15. Paid $1,250 in warranty repairs during the year.
16. On September 1, paid the note and interest owed to State Bank.

17. Paid $18,000 of advertising expense during the year.

18. Paid $5,600 of utilities expense for the year.

19. Paid the payroll liabilities, both the amounts withheld from the salaries plus the employer share of Social Security tax and Medicare tax, on $75,000 of the salaries plus $8,600 of the federal income tax that was withheld. (Disregard unemployment taxes in this entry.)

20. Paid the accounts payable.

21. Paid bond interest and amortized the discount.

22. Paid the annual installment on the amortized note.

23. Paid a dividend of $10,000 to the shareholders.

Adjustments

24. There was $210 of supplies on hand at the end of the year.

25. Recognized the expired rent for the office building for the year.

26. Recognized the uncollectible accounts expense for the year using the allowance method. Pacilio now estimates that 1.5 percent of sales on account will not be collected.

27. Recognized depreciation expense on the equipment, van, and building. The equipment has a five-year life and a $2,000 salvage value. The van has a four-year life and a $6,000 salvage value. The building has a 40-year life and a $10,000 salvage value. The company uses double-declining-balance for the van and straight-line for the equipment and the building. The equipment and van were purchased in 2018 and a full year of depreciation was taken for both in 2018.

28. The alarms systems sold in transaction 8 were covered with a one-year warranty. Pacilio estimated that the warranty cost would be 2 percent of alarm sales.

29. The unemployment tax on the three employees has not been paid. Record the accrued unemployment tax on the salaries for the year. The unemployment tax rate is 4.5 percent and gross wages for all employees exceeded $7,000.

30. Recognized the employer Social Security and Medicare payroll tax that has not been paid on $7,000 of salaries expense.

Required

a. Record the above transactions in general journal form. Round all amounts to nearest whole dollar.

b. Post the transactions to the T-accounts.

c. Prepare a trial balance.

d. Prepare an income statement, statement of changes in stockholders' equity, a classified balance sheet, and statement of cash flows.

e. Close the temporary accounts to retained earnings.

f. Post the closing entries to the T-accounts and prepare an after-closing trial balance.

CHAPTER 11

Proprietorships, Partnerships, and Corporations

LEARNING OBJECTIVES

After you have mastered the material in this chapter, you will be able to:

LO1   Identify the primary characteristics of sole proprietorships, partnerships, and corporations.

LO2   Explain how different types of capital stock affect financial statements.

LO3   Show how treasury stock transactions affect financial statements.

LO4   Explain how dividends, stock splits, and appropriations affect financial statements.

LO5   Explain some uses of accounting information in making stock investment decisions.

CHAPTER OPENING

You want to start a business. How should you structure it? Should it be a sole proprietorship, partnership, or corporation? Each form of business structure presents advantages and disadvantages. For example, a sole proprietorship allows maximum independence and control while partnerships and corporations allow individuals to pool resources and talents with other people. This chapter discusses these and other features of the three primary forms of business structure.

The Curious Accountant

Imagine your rich uncle rewarded you for doing well in your first accounting course by giving you $10,000 to invest in the stock of one company. After reviewing many recent annual reports, you narrowed your choice to two companies with the following characteristics:

Mystery Company A: This company began operations in 2003, but did not begin selling its stock to the public until June 28, 2010. It has lost money every year it has been in existence, and by December 31, 2010, it had total lifetime losses of approximately $415 million. Even so, its products have received lots of attention from the media and celebrities. At its current price of $25 you could buy 400 shares. A friend told you that a status-conscious person like you should at least buy this company's stock, since you cannot afford its products.

Mystery Company B: This company has been in existence since 1883 and has made a profit most years. In its 2010 fiscal year alone its net earnings were $1.2 billion, and it paid dividends of $238 million. Unlike Company A, Company B sells items that everyone needs and can afford. Its stock is selling for about $23 per share, so you can buy around 435 shares. Your friend said that buying this company's stock would be the most boring investment you would ever make.

The names of the real-world companies described above are disclosed later. Based on the information provided, which company's stock would you buy? (Answer on page 595.)

FORMS OF BUSINESS ORGANIZATIONS

LO 1

Identify the primary characteristics of sole proprietorships, partnerships, and corporations.

Sole proprietorships are owned by a single individual who is responsible for making business and profit distribution decisions. If you want to be the absolute master of your destiny, you should organize your business as a proprietorship. Establishing a sole proprietorship is usually as simple as obtaining a business license from local government authorities. Usually no legal ownership agreement is required.

Partnerships allow persons to share their talents, capital, and the risks and rewards of business ownership. Since two or more individuals share ownership, partnerships require clear agreements about how authority, risks, and profits will be shared. Prudent partners minimize misunderstandings by hiring attorneys to prepare a **partnership agreement** which defines the responsibilities of each partner and describes how income or losses will be divided. Since the measurement of income affects the distribution of profits, partnerships frequently hire accountants to ensure that records are maintained in accordance with generally accepted accounting principles (GAAP). Partnerships (and sole proprietorships) also may need professional advice to deal with tax issues.

A **corporation** is a separate legal entity created by the authority of a state government. The paperwork to start a corporation is complex. For most laypersons, engaging professional attorneys and accountants to assist with the paperwork is well worth the fees charged.

Each state has separate laws governing establishing corporations. Many states follow the standard provisions of the Model Business Corporation Act. All states require the initial application to provide **articles of incorporation** which normally include the following information: (1) the corporation's name and proposed date of incorporation; (2) the purpose of the corporation; (3) the location of the business and its expected life (which can be *perpetuity,* meaning *endless*); (4) provisions for capital stock; and (5) the names and addresses of the members of the first board of directors, the individuals with the ultimate authority for operating the business. If the articles are in order, the state establishes the legal existence of the corporation by issuing a charter of incorporation. The charter and the articles are public documents.

Each form of business organization presents a different combination of advantages and disadvantages. Persons wanting to start a business or invest in one should consider the characteristics of each type of business structure.

Regulation

Few laws specifically affect the operations of proprietorships and partnerships. Corporations, however, are usually heavily regulated. The extent of government regulation depends on the size and distribution of a company's ownership interests. Ownership interests in corporations are normally evidenced by **stock certificates.**

Ownership of corporations can be transferred from one individual to another through exchanging stock certificates. As long as the exchanges (buying and selling of shares of stock, often called *trading*) are limited to transactions between individuals, a company is defined as a **closely held corporation.** However, once a corporation reaches a certain size, it may list its stock on a stock exchange such as the New York Stock Exchange. Trading on a stock exchange is limited to the stockbrokers who are members of the exchange. These brokers represent buyers and sellers who are willing to pay the brokers commissions for exchanging stock certificates on their behalf. Although closely held corporations are relatively free from government regulation, companies whose stock is publicly traded on the exchanges by brokers are subject to extensive regulation.

The extensive regulation of trading on stock exchanges began in the 1930s. The stock market crash of 1929 and the subsequent Great Depression led Congress to pass the **Securities Act of 1933** and the **Securities Exchange Act of 1934** to regulate issuing stock and to govern the exchanges. The 1934 act also created the Securities and Exchange Commission (SEC) to enforce the securities laws. Congress gave the SEC legal authority to establish accounting principles for corporations that are registered on the exchanges. However, the SEC has generally deferred its rule-making authority to

Answers to The Curious Accountant

Mystery Company A is Tesla Motors, Inc., as of February 16, 2011. The company makes the Tesla Roadster. The Roadster is an electric-only sports car that can go from 0 to 60 miles per hour in under 4 seconds, reach a top speed of 125 MPH, and go up to 245 miles before having to recharge its batteries. It costs over $100,000. The company sold it first roadster in 2008 and had sold around 1,500 cars by the end of 2010. It plans to begin selling a second car-model in 2012, and it supplies electric car components to Daimler and Toyota.

Mystery Company B is Kroger Company, as of February 16, 2011. Of course, only the future will tell which company will be the better investment.

private sector accounting bodies such as the Financial Accounting Standards Board (FASB), effectively allowing the accounting profession to regulate itself.

A number of high-profile business failures around the turn of this century raised questions about the effectiveness of self-regulation and the usefulness of audits to protect the public. The **Sarbanes-Oxley Act of 2002** was adopted to address these concerns. The act creates a five-member Public Company Accounting Oversight Board (PCAOB) with the authority to set and enforce auditing, attestation, quality control, and ethics standards for auditors of public companies. The PCAOB is empowered to impose disciplinary and remedial sanctions for violations of its rules, securities laws, and professional auditing and accounting standards. Public corporations operate in a complex regulatory environment that requires the services of attorneys and professional accountants.

Double Taxation

Corporations pay income taxes on their earnings and then owners pay income taxes on distributions (dividends) received from corporations. As a result, distributed corporate profits are taxed twice—first when income is reported on the corporation's income tax return and a second time when distributions are reported on individual owners' tax returns. This phenomenon is commonly called **double taxation** and is a significant disadvantage of the corporate form of business organization.

To illustrate, assume Glide Corporation earns pretax income of $100,000. Glide is in a 30 percent tax bracket. The corporation itself will pay income tax of $30,000 ($100,000 × 0.30). If the corporation distributes the after-tax income of $70,000 ($100,000 − $30,000) to individual stockholders in 15 percent tax brackets,[1] the $70,000 dividend will be reported on the individual tax returns, requiring tax payments of $10,500 ($70,000 × .15). Total income tax of $40,500 ($30,000 + $10,500) is due on $100,000 of earned income. In contrast, consider a proprietorship that is owned by an individual in a 30 percent tax bracket. If the proprietorship earns and distributes $100,000 profit, the total tax would be only $30,000 ($100,000 × .30).

Double taxation can be a burden for small companies. To reduce that burden, tax laws permit small closely held corporations to elect "S Corporation" status. S Corporations

[1]As a result of the Jobs and Growth Tax Relief Reconciliation Act (JGTRRA) of 2003, dividends received in tax years after 2002 are taxed at a maximum rate of 15 percent for most taxpayers. Lower income individuals pay a 5 percent tax on dividends received on December 31, 2007, or earlier. This rate fell to zero in 2008. The provisions of JGTRRA were originally set to expire on December 31, 2008; however, they were extended by the Tax Increase Prevention and Reconciliation Act of 2005 through December 31, 2010. As this text goes to press, Congress has extended the tax rates for dividends through 2012.

are taxed as proprietorships or partnerships. Also, many states have enacted laws permitting the formation of **limited liability companies (LLCs)** which offer many of the benefits of corporate ownership yet are in general taxed as partnerships. Since proprietorships and partnerships are not separate taxable entities, company earnings are taxable to the owners rather than the company itself.

Limited Liability

Given the disadvantages of increased regulation and double taxation, why would anyone choose the corporate form of business structure over a partnership or proprietorship? A major reason is that the corporate form limits an investor's potential liability as an owner of a business venture. Because a corporation is legally separate from its owners, creditors cannot claim owners' personal assets as payment for the company's debts. Also, plaintiffs must sue the corporation, not its owners. The most that owners of a corporation can lose is the amount they have invested in the company (the value of the company's stock).

Unlike corporate stockholders, the owners of proprietorships and partnerships are *personally liable* for actions they take in the name of their companies. In fact, partners are responsible not only for their own actions but also for those taken by any other partner on behalf of the partnership. The benefit of **limited liability** is one of the most significant reasons the corporate form of business organization is so popular.

Continuity

Unlike partnerships or proprietorships, which terminate with the departure of their owners, a corporation's life continues when a shareholder dies or sells his or her stock. Because of **continuity** of existence, many corporations formed in the 1800s still thrive today.

Transferability of Ownership

The **transferability** of corporate ownership is easy. An investor simply buys or sells stock to acquire or give up an ownership interest in a corporation. Hundreds of millions of shares of stock are bought and sold on the major stock exchanges each day.

Transferring the ownership of proprietorships is much more difficult. To sell an ownership interest in a proprietorship, the proprietor must find someone willing to purchase the entire business. Since most proprietors also run their businesses, transferring ownership also requires transferring management responsibilities. Consider the difference in selling $1 million of Exxon stock versus selling a locally owned gas station. The stock could be sold on the New York Stock Exchange within minutes. In contrast, it could take years to find a buyer who is financially capable of and interested in owning and operating a gas station.

Transferring ownership in partnerships can also be difficult. As with proprietorships, ownership transfers may require a new partner to make a significant investment and accept management responsibilities in the business. Further, a new partner must accept and be accepted by the other partners. Personality conflicts and differences in management style can cause problems in transferring ownership interests in partnerships.

Management Structure

Partnerships and proprietorships are usually managed by their owners. Corporations, in contrast, have three tiers of management authority. The *owners* (**stockholders**) represent the highest level of organizational authority. The stockholders *elect* a **board of directors** to oversee company operations. The directors then *hire* professional executives to manage the company on a daily basis. Since large corporations can offer high salaries and challenging career opportunities, they can often attract superior managerial talent.

Ability to Raise Capital

Because corporations can have millions of owners (share-holders), they have the opportunity to raise huge amounts of capital. Few individuals have the financial means to build and operate a telecommunications network such as AT&T or a marketing distribution system such as Walmart. However, by pooling the resources of millions of owners through public stock and bond offerings, corporations generate the billions of dollars of capital needed for such massive investments. In contrast, the capital resources of proprietorships and part-nerships are limited to a relatively small number of private

owners. Although proprietorships and partnerships can also obtain resources by borrowing, the amount creditors are willing to lend them is usually limited by the size of the owners' net worth.

Appearance of Capital Structure in Financial Statements

The ownership interest (equity) in a business is composed of two elements: (1) owner/investor contributions and (2) retained earnings. The way these two elements are re-ported in the financial statements differs for each type of business structure (proprietor-ship, partnership, or corporation).

Presentation of Equity in Proprietorships

Owner contributions and retained earnings are combined in a single Capital account on the balance sheets of proprietorships. To illustrate, assume that Worthington Sole Proprietorship was started on January 1, 2013, when it acquired a $5,000 capital con-tribution from its owner, Phil Worthington. During the first year of operation, the company generated $4,000 of cash revenues, incurred $2,500 of cash expenses, and distributed $1,000 cash to the owner. Exhibit 11.1 displays 2013 financial statements for Worthington's company. Note on the *capital statement* that distributions are called **withdrawals.** Verify that the $5,500 balance in the Capital account on the balance sheet includes the $5,000 owner contribution and the retained earnings of $500 ($1,500 net income − $1,000 withdrawal).

EXHIBIT 11.1

WORTHINGTON SOLE PROPRIETORSHIP
Financial Statements
As of December 31, 2013

Income Statement		Capital Statement		Balance Sheet	
Revenue	$4,000	Beginning capital balance	$ 0	Assets	
Expenses	2,500	Plus: Investment by owner	5,000	Cash	$5,500
Net income	$1,500	Plus: Net income	1,500	Equity	
		Less: Withdrawal by owner	(1,000)	Worthington, capital	$5,500
		Ending capital balance	$5,500		

✓ CHECK YOURSELF 11.1

Weiss Company was started on January 1, 2013, when it acquired $50,000 cash from its owner(s). During 2013 the company earned $72,000 of net income. Explain how the equity section of Weiss's December 31, 2013, balance sheet would differ if the company were a proprietorship versus a corporation.

Answer   *Proprietorship* records combine capital acquisitions from the owner and earnings from operating the business in a single capital account. In contrast, *corporation* records separate capital acquisitions from the owners and earnings from operating the business. If Weiss were a proprietorship, the equity section of the year-end balance sheet would report a single capital component of $122,000. If Weiss were a corporation, the equity section would report two separate equity components, most likely common stock of $50,000 and retained earnings of $72,000.

Presentation of Equity in Partnerships

The financial statement format for reporting partnership equity is similar to that used for proprietorships. Contributed capital and retained earnings are combined. However, a separate capital account is maintained for each partner in the business to reflect each partner's ownership interest.

To illustrate, assume that Sara Slater and Jill Johnson formed a partnership on January 1, 2014. The partnership acquired $2,000 of capital from Slater and $4,000 from Johnson. The partnership agreement called for each partner to receive an annual distribution equal to 10 percent of her capital contribution. Any further earnings were to be retained in the business and divided equally between the partners. During 2014, the company earned $5,000 of cash revenue and incurred $3,000 of cash expenses, for net income of $2,000 ($5,000 − $3,000). As specified by the partnership agreement, Slater received a $200 ($2,000 × 0.10) cash withdrawal and Johnson received $400 ($4,000 × 0.10). The remaining $1,400 ($2,000 − $200 − $400) of income was retained in the business and divided equally, adding $700 to each partner's capital account.

Exhibit 11.2 displays financial statements for the Slater and Johnson partnership. Again, note that distributions are called *withdrawals.* Also find on the balance sheet a *separate capital account* for each partner. Each capital account includes the amount of the partner's contributed capital plus her proportionate share of the earnings.

Presentation of Equity in Corporations

Corporations have more complex capital structures than proprietorships and partnerships. Explanations of some of the more common features of corporate capital structures and transactions follow.

EXHIBIT 11.2

SLATER AND JOHNSON PARTNERSHIP
Financial Statements
As of December 31, 2014

Income Statement		Capital Statement		Balance Sheet	
Revenue	$5,000	Beginning capital balance	$ 0	Assets	
Expenses	3,000	Plus: Investment by owner	6,000	Cash	$7,400
Net income	$2,000	Plus: Net income	2,000	Equity	
		Less: Withdrawal by owner	(600)	Slater, capital	$2,700
		Ending capital balance	$7,400	Johnson, capital	4,700
				Total capital	$7,400

ACCOUNTING FOR CAPITAL STOCK

Stock issued by corporations may have a variety of different characteristics. For example, a company may issue different classes of stock that grant owners different rights and privileges. Also, the number of shares a corporation can legally issue may differ from the number it actually has issued. Further, a corporation can even buy back its own stock. Finally, a corporation may assign different values to the stock it issues. Accounting for corporate equity transactions is discussed in the next section of the text.

Explain how different types of capital stock affect financial statements.

Par Value

Many states require assigning a **par value** to stock. Historically, par value represented the maximum liability of the investors. Par value multiplied by the number of shares of stock issued represents the minimum amount of assets that must be retained in the company as protection for creditors. This amount is known as **legal capital.** To ensure that the amount of legal capital is maintained in a corporation, many states require that purchasers pay at least the par value for a share of stock initially purchased from a corporation. To minimize the amount of assets that owners must maintain in the business, many corporations issue stock with very low par values, often $1 or less. Therefore, *legal capital* as defined by par value has come to have very little relevance to investors or creditors. As a result, many states allow corporations to issue no-par stock.

Stated Value

No-par stock may have a stated value. Like par value, **stated value** is an arbitrary amount assigned by the board of directors to the stock. It also has little relevance to investors and creditors. Stock with a par value and stock with a stated value are accounted for exactly the same way. When stock has no par or stated value, accounting for it is slightly different. These accounting differences are illustrated later in this chapter.

Other Valuation Terminology

The price an investor must pay to purchase a share of stock is the **market value.** The sales price of a share of stock may be more or less than the par value. Another term analysts frequently associate with stock is *book value.* **Book value per share** is calculated by dividing total stockholders' equity (assets − liabilities) by the number of shares of stock owned by investors. Book value per share differs from market value per share because equity is measured in historical dollars and market value reflects investors' estimates of a company's current value.

Stock: Authorized, Issued, and Outstanding

As part of the regulatory function, states approve the maximum number of shares of stock corporations are legally permitted to issue. This maximum number is called **authorized stock.** Authorized stock that has been sold to the public is called **issued stock.** When a corporation buys back some of its issued stock from the public, the repurchased stock is called **treasury stock.** Treasury stock is still considered to be issued stock, but it is no longer outstanding. **Outstanding stock** (total issued stock minus treasury stock) is stock owned by investors outside the corporation. For example, assume a company that is authorized to issue 150 shares of stock issues 100 shares to investors, and then buys back 20 shares of treasury stock. There are 150 shares authorized, 100 shares issued, and 80 shares outstanding.

Classes of Stock

The corporate charter defines the number of shares of stock authorized, the par value or stated value (if any), and the classes of stock that a corporation can issue. Most stock issued is classified as either *common* or *preferred.*

Common Stock

All corporations issue **common stock.** Common stockholders bear the highest risk of losing their investment if a company is forced to liquidate. On the other hand, they reap the greatest rewards when a corporation prospers. Common stockholders generally enjoy several rights, including: (1) the right to buy and sell stock, (2) the right to share in the distribution of profits, (3) the right to share in the distribution of corporate assets in the case of liquidation, (4) the right to vote on significant matters that affect the corporate charter, and (5) the right to participate in the election of directors.

Preferred Stock

Many corporations issue **preferred stock** in addition to common stock. Holders of preferred stock receive certain privileges relative to holders of common stock. In exchange for special privileges in some areas, preferred stockholders give up rights in other areas. Preferred stockholders usually have no voting rights and the amount of their dividends is usually limited. Preferences granted to preferred stockholders include the following:

1. *Preference as to assets.* Preferred stock often has a liquidation value. In case of bankruptcy, preferred stockholders must be paid the liquidation value before any assets are distributed to common stockholders. However, preferred stockholder claims still fall behind creditor claims.

2. *Preference as to dividends.* Preferred shareholders are frequently guaranteed the right to receive dividends before common stockholders. The amount of the preferred dividend is normally stated on the stock certificate. It may be stated as a dollar value (say, $5) per share or as a percentage of the par value. Most preferred stock has **cumulative dividends,** meaning that if a corporation is unable to pay the preferred dividend in any year, the dividend is not lost but begins to accumulate. Cumulative dividends that have not been paid are called **dividends in arrears.** When a company pays dividends, any preferred stock arrearages must be paid before any other dividends are paid. Noncumulative preferred stock is not often issued because preferred stock is much less attractive if missed dividends do not accumulate.

To illustrate the effects of preferred dividends, consider Dillion, Incorporated, which has the following shares of stock outstanding:

> Preferred stock, 4%, $10 par, 10,000 shares
> Common stock, $10 par, 20,000 shares

Assume the preferred stock dividend has not been paid for two years. If Dillion pays $22,000 in dividends, how much will each class of stock receive? It depends on whether the preferred stock is cumulative.

Allocation of Distribution for Cumulative Preferred Stock		
	To Preferred	**To Common**
Dividends in arrears	$ 8,000	$ 0
Current year's dividends	4,000	10,000
Total distribution	$12,000	$10,000
Allocation of Distribution for Noncumulative Preferred Stock		
	To Preferred	**To Common**
Dividends in arrears	$ 0	$ 0
Current year's dividends	4,000	18,000
Total distribution	$ 4,000	$18,000

The total annual dividend on the preferred stock is $4,000 (0.04 × $10 par × 10,000 shares). If the preferred stock is cumulative, the $8,000 in arrears must be paid first. Then $4,000 for the current year's dividend is paid next. The remaining $10,000 goes to common stockholders. If the preferred stock is noncumulative, the $8,000 of dividends from past periods is ignored. This year's $4,000 preferred dividend is paid first, with the remaining $18,000 going to common.

Other features of preferred stock may include the right to participate in distributions beyond the established amount of the preferred dividend, the right to convert preferred stock to common stock or to bonds, and the potential for having the preferred stock called (repurchased) by the corporation. Detailed discussion of these topics is left to more advanced courses. Exhibit 11.3 indicates that roughly 25 percent of U.S. companies have preferred shares outstanding.

Accounting for Stock Transactions

Issuing stock with a par or stated value is accounted for differently from issuing no-par stock. For stock with either a par or stated value, the total amount acquired from the owners is divided between two separate equity accounts. The amount of the par or stated value is recorded in the stock account. Any amount received above the par or stated value is recorded in an account called **Paid-in Capital in Excess of Par** (or **Stated**) **Value.**

Issuing Par Value Stock

To illustrate the issue of common stock with a par value, assume that Nelson Incorporated is authorized to issue 250 shares of common stock. During 2013, Nelson issued 100 shares of $10 par common stock for $22 per share. The event increases assets and stockholders' equity by $2,200 ($22 × 100 shares). The increase in stockholders' equity is divided into two parts, $1,000 of par value ($10 per share × 100 shares) and $1,200 ($2,200 − $1,000) received in excess of par value. The income statement is not affected. The $2,200 cash inflow is reported in the financing activities section of the statement of cash flows. The journal entry and its effects on the financial statements are shown here.

Account Title	Debit	Credit
Cash	2,200	
Common Stock, $10 Par Value		1,000
Paid-in Capital in Excess of Par Value—Common		1,200

Assets	=	Liab.	+	Equity			Rev.	−	Exp.	=	Net Inc.	Cash Flow
Cash	=			Com. Stk.	+	PIC in Excess						
2,200	=	NA	+	1,000	+	1,200	NA	−	NA	=	NA	2,200 FA

The *legal capital* of the corporation is $1,000, the total par value of the issued common stock. The number of shares issued can be easily verified by dividing the total amount in the common stock account by the par value ($1,000 ÷ $10 = 100 shares).

Stock Classification

Assume Nelson Incorporated obtains authorization to issue 400 shares of Class B, $20 par value common stock. The company issues 150 shares of this stock at $25 per share. The event increases assets and stockholders' equity by $3,750 ($25 × 150 shares). The increase in stockholders' equity is divided into two parts, $3,000 of par value ($20 per share × 150 shares) and $750 ($3,750 − $3,000) received in excess of par value. The income statement is not affected. The $3,750 cash inflow is reported in the financing

EXHIBIT 11.3

Presence of Preferred Stock in the Capital Structure of U.S. Companies

With preferred stock 25%

Without preferred stock 75%

Data Source: AICPA, *Accounting Trends and Techniques.*

activities section of the statement of cash flows. The journal entry and its effects on the financial statements are shown here:

Account Title	Debit	Credit
Cash	3,750	
Common Stock, Class B, $20 Par Value		3,000
Paid-in Capital in Excess of Par Value—Class B Common		750

Assets	=	Liab.	+	Equity			Rev.	−	Exp.	=	Net Inc.	Cash Flow
Cash	=			Com. Stk.	+	PIC in Excess						
3,750	=	NA	+	3,000	+	750	NA	−	NA	=	NA	3,750 FA

As the preceding event suggests, companies can issue numerous classes of common stock. The specific rights and privileges for each class are described in the individual stock certificates.

Stock Issued at Stated Value

Assume Nelson is authorized to issue 300 shares of a third class of stock, 7 percent cumulative preferred stock with a stated value of $10 per share. Nelson issued 100 shares of the preferred stock at a price of $22 per share. The effect on the financial statements is identical to that described for the issue of the $10 par value common stock. The journal entry differs only to reflect the name of the different class of stock.

Account Title	Debit	Credit
Cash	2,200	
Preferred Stock, $10 Stated Value, 7% cumulative		1,000
Paid-in Capital in Excess of Stated Value—Preferred		1,200

Assets	=	Liab.	+	Equity			Rev.	−	Exp.	=	Net Inc.	Cash Flow
Cash	=			Pfd. Stk.	+	PIC in Excess						
2,200	=	NA	+	1,000	+	1,200	NA	−	NA	=	NA	2,200 FA

Stock Issued with No Par Value

Assume that Nelson Incorporated is authorized to issue 150 shares of a fourth class of stock. This stock is no-par common stock. Nelson issues 100 shares of this no-par stock at $22 per share. The entire amount received ($22 × 100 = $2,200) is recorded in the stock account. The journal entry and its effects on the financial statements are shown here:

Account Title	Debit	Credit
Cash	2,200	
Common Stock, No Par		2,200

Assets	=	Liab.	+	Equity			Rev.	−	Exp.	=	Net Inc.	Cash Flow
Cash	=			Com. Stk.	+	PIC in Excess						
2,200	=	NA	+	2,200	+	NA	NA	−	NA	=	NA	2,200 FA

Financial Statement Presentation

Exhibit 11.4 displays Nelson Incorporated's balance sheet after the four stock issuances described above. The exhibit assumes that Nelson earned and retained $5,000 of income during 2013. The stock accounts are presented first, followed by the paid-in capital in excess of par (or stated) value accounts. A wide variety of reporting formats is used in practice. For example, another popular format is to group accounts by stock class, with the paid-in capital in excess accounts listed with their associated stock accounts. Alternatively, many companies combine the different classes of stock into a single amount and provide the detailed information in notes to the financial statements.

EXHIBIT 11.4

NELSON, INCORPORATED
Balance Sheet
As of December 31, 2013

Assets	
Cash	$15,350
Stockholders' equity	
Preferred stock, $10 stated value, 7% cumulative,	
300 shares authorized, 100 issued and outstanding	$ 1,000
Common stock, $10 par value, 250 shares authorized,	
100 issued and outstanding	1,000
Common stock, class B, $20 par value, 400 shares	
authorized, 150 issued and outstanding	3,000
Common stock, no par, 150 shares authorized,	
100 issued and outstanding	2,200
Paid-in capital in excess of stated value—Preferred	1,200
Paid-in capital in excess of par value—Common	1,200
Paid-in capital in excess of par value—Class B common	750
Total paid-in capital	10,350
Retained earnings	5,000
Total stockholders' equity	$15,350

TREASURY STOCK

When a company buys its own stock, the stock purchased is called *treasury stock*. Why would a company buy its own stock? Common reasons include (1) to have stock available to give employees pursuant to stock option plans, (2) to accumulate stock in preparation for a merger or business combination, (3) to reduce the number of shares outstanding in order to increase earnings per share, (4) to keep the price of the stock high when it appears to be falling, and (5) to avoid a hostile takeover (removing shares from the open market reduces the opportunity for outsiders to obtain enough voting shares to gain control of the company).

    Conceptually, purchasing treasury stock is the reverse of issuing stock. When a business issues stock, the assets and equity of the business increase. When a business buys treasury stock, the assets and equity of the business decrease. To illustrate, return to the Nelson Incorporated example. Assume that in 2014 Nelson paid $20 per share to buy back 50 shares of the $10 par value common stock that it originally issued at $22 per share. The purchase of treasury stock is an asset use transaction. Assets and stockholders' equity decrease by the cost of the purchase ($20 × 50 shares = $1,000). The income statement is not affected. The cash outflow is reported in the financing activities section

LO 3

Show how treasury stock transactions affect financial statements.

of the statement of cash flows. The journal entry and its effects on the financial statements are shown here:

Account Title	Debit	Credit
Treasury Stock	1,000	
Cash		1,000

Assets	=	Liab.	+	Equity			Rev.	−	Exp.	=	Net Inc.	Cash Flow
Cash	=			Other Equity Accts.	−	Treasury Stk.						
(1,000)	=	NA	+	NA	−	1,000	NA	−	NA	=	NA	(1,000) FA

The Treasury Stock account is a contra equity account. It is deducted from the other equity accounts in determining total stockholders' equity. In this example, the Treasury Stock account is debited for the full amount paid ($1,000). The original issue price and the par value of the stock have no effect on the entry. Recording the full amount paid in the treasury stock account is called the **cost method of accounting for treasury stock** transactions. Although other methods could be used, the cost method is the most common.

Assume Nelson reissues 30 shares of treasury stock at a price of $25 per share. As with any other stock issue, the sale of treasury stock is an asset source transaction. In this case, assets and stockholders' equity increase by $750 ($25 × 30 shares). The income statement is not affected. The cash inflow is reported in the financing activities section of the statement of cash flows. The journal entry and its effects on the financial statements are shown here:

Account Title	Debit	Credit
Cash	750	
Treasury Stock		600
Paid-in Capital in Excess of Cost of Treasury Stock		150

Assets	=	Liab.	+	Equity					Rev.	−	Exp.	=	Net Inc.	Cash Flow
Cash	=			Other Equity Accounts	−	Treasury Stock	+	PIC from Treasury Stk.						
750	=	NA	+	NA	−	(600)	+	150	NA	−	NA	=	NA	750 FA

The decrease in the Treasury Stock account increases stockholders' equity. The $150 difference between the cost of the treasury stock ($20 per share × 30 shares = $600) and the sales price ($750) is *not* reported as a gain. The sale of treasury stock is a capital acquisition, not a revenue transaction. The $150 is additional paid-in capital. *Corporations do not recognize gains or losses on the sale of treasury stock.*

After selling 30 shares of treasury stock, 20 shares remain in Nelson's possession. These shares cost $20 each, so the balance in the Treasury Stock account is now $400 ($20 × 20 shares). Treasury stock is reported on the balance sheet directly below retained earnings. Although this placement suggests that treasury stock reduces retained earnings, the reduction actually applies to the entire stockholders' equity section. Exhibit 11.5 (page 609) shows the presentation of treasury stock in the balance sheet.

✓ CHECK YOURSELF 11.2

On January 1, 2013, Janell Company's Common Stock account balance was $20,000. On April 1, 2013, Janell paid $12,000 cash to purchase some of its own stock. Janell resold this stock on October 1, 2013, for $14,500. What is the effect on the company's cash and stockholders' equity from both the April 1 purchase and the October 1 resale of the stock?

Answer   The April 1 purchase would reduce both cash and stockholders' equity by $12,000. The treasury stock transaction represents a return of invested capital to those owners who sold stock back to the company.

The sale of the treasury stock on October 1 would increase both cash and stockholders' equity by $14,500. The difference between the sales price of the treasury stock and its cost ($14,500 − $12,000) represents additional paid-in capital from treasury stock transactions. The stockholders' equity section of the balance sheet would include Common Stock, $20,000, and Additional Paid-in Capital from Treasury Stock Transactions, $2,500.

DIVIDENDS, STOCK SPLITS, AND APPROPRIATIONS OF RETAINED EARNINGS

Cash Dividend

Cash dividends are affected by three significant dates: *the declaration date, the date of record,* and *the payment date.* Assume that on October 15, 2014, the board of Nelson Incorporated declared the cash dividend on the 100 outstanding shares of its $10 stated value preferred stock. The dividend will be paid to stockholders of record as of November 15, 2014. The cash payment will be made on December 15, 2014.

LO 4

Explain how dividends, stock splits, and appropriations affect financial statements.

Declaration Date

Although corporations are not required to declare dividends, they are legally obligated to pay dividends once they have been declared. They must recognize a liability on the **declaration date** (in this case, October 15, 2014). The increase in liabilities is accompanied by a decrease in retained earnings. The income statement and statement of cash flows are not affected. The journal entry and the effects on the financial statements of *declaring* the $70 (0.07 × $10 × 100 shares) dividend are shown here:

Account Title	Debit	Credit
Dividends	70	
Dividends Payable		70

Assets	=	Liab.	+		Equity		Rev.	−	Exp.	=	Net Inc.	Cash Flow
Cash	=	Div. Pay.	+	Com. Stk.	+	Ret. Earn.						
NA	=	70	+	NA	+	(70)	NA	−	NA	=	NA	NA

Date of Record

Cash dividends are paid to investors who owned the preferred stock on the **date of record** (in this case November 15, 2014). Any stock sold after the date of record but before the payment date (in this case December 15, 2014) is traded **ex-dividend,** meaning the buyer will not receive the upcoming dividend. The date of record is merely a cutoff date. It does not affect the financial statements.

REALITY BYTES

As you have learned, dividends, unlike interest on bonds, do not have to be paid. In fact, a company's board of directors must vote to pay dividends before they can be paid. Even so, once a company establishes a practice of paying a dividend of a given amount each period, usually quarterly, the company is reluctant to not pay the dividend. Furthermore, it is usually a significant news event when a company decides to increase the amount of its regular dividend.

When times are bad, however, dividends are often reduced, or eliminated entirely, as a quick way to conserve the company's cash. This occurred often as a result of the economic downturn of 2008. An article in the February 28, 2009, edition of *The Wall Street Journal* listed 10 large companies that had recently reduced or eliminated their common stock dividend. The companies named were: Blackstone Group, CBS, Citigroup, Dow Chemical, General Electric, JP Morgan Chase, Motorola, New York Times, Pfizer, and Textron. The article also noted that for the month of January 2009, dividends paid by companies in the S&P 500 Index were 24 percent lower than they had been in January 2008. A review of these companies showed that only two, GE and Pfizer, had raised their dividends as of the end of 2010, and neither of these had restored dividends to their previous levels.

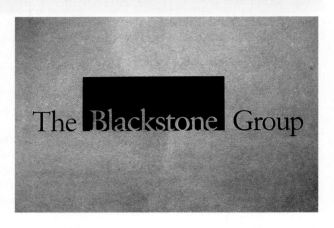

Payment Date

Nelson actually paid the cash dividend on the **payment date.** This event has the same effect as paying any other liability. Assets (cash) and liabilities (dividends payable) both decrease. The income statement is not affected. The cash outflow is reported in the financing activities section of the statement of cash flows. The journal entry and its effects on the financial statements are shown here:

Account Title	Debit	Credit
Dividends Payable	70	
Cash		70

Assets	=	Liab.	+		Equity			Rev.	−	Exp.	=	Net Inc.	Cash Flow	
Cash	=	Div. Pay.	+	Com. Stk.	+	Ret. Earn.								
(70)	=	(70)	+	NA	+	NA		NA	−	NA	=	NA	(70)	FA

Stock Dividend

Dividends are not always paid in cash. Companies sometimes choose to issue **stock dividends,** wherein they distribute additional shares of stock to the stockholders. To illustrate, assume that Nelson Incorporated decided to issue a 10 percent stock dividend on its class B, $20 par value common stock. Since dividends apply to outstanding shares only, Nelson will issue 15 (150 outstanding shares × 0.10) additional shares of class B stock.

Assume the new shares are distributed when the market value of the stock is $30 per share. As a result of the stock dividend, Nelson will transfer $450 ($30 × 15 new shares) from retained earnings to paid-in capital.[2] The stock dividend is an equity exchange transaction. The income statement and statement of cash flows are not affected. The journal entry and its effects on the financial statements are shown on the next page.

---

[2]The accounting here applies to small stock dividends. Accounting for large stock dividends is explained in a more advanced course.

Account Title	Debit	Credit
Retained Earnings	450	
Common Stock, Class B, $20 Par Value		300
Paid-in Capital in Excess of Par Value—Class B Common		150

Assets	=	Liab.	+	Equity						Rev.	−	Exp.	=	Net Inc.	Cash Flow
				Com. Stk.	+	PIC in Excess	+	Ret. Earn.							
NA	=	NA	+	300	+	150	+	(450)		NA	−	NA	=	NA	NA

Stock dividends have no effect on assets. They merely increase the number of shares of stock outstanding. Since a greater number of shares represents the same ownership interest in the same amount of assets, the market value per share of a company's stock normally declines when a stock dividend is distributed. A lower market price makes the stock more affordable and may increase demand for the stock, which benefits both the company and its stockholders.

Stock Split

A corporation may also reduce the market price of its stock through a **stock split.** A stock split replaces existing shares with a greater number of new shares. Any par or stated value of the stock is proportionately reduced to reflect the new number of shares outstanding. For example, assume Nelson Incorporated declared a 2-for-1 stock split

REALITY BYTES

WHAT IS A COMPANY WORTH?

Early in 2011 several news outlets reported that Facebook, a privately-held company, was worth $50 billion. How did they come to this conclusion? Goldman Sachs had recently agreed to purchase a 1 percent ownership in Facebook for $500 million. So, the argument went, if 1 percent of the company was worth half-a-billion dollars, then the whole company must be worth one-hundred times as much, or $50 billion.

This approach to assigning a value to a company is called *market capitalization.* In its simplest, and most common form, one multiplies the most recent price for which a single share of stock is traded, by the number of shares a company has outstanding; this amount is said to be its market capitalization. This approach, though simple, has limitations.

In early April 2011, Microsoft's stock was selling for around $26 per share. The company had 8.7 billion shares outstanding, of which Bill Gates owned approximately 621 million. This indicates that Microsoft's market capitalization was around $226 billion, and Mr. Gates's shares were worth $16.1 billion. Suppose Mr. Gates suddenly announced he was planning to immediately sell all 621 million of his shares; how would this affect the stock price? It might drop drastically if other investors thought Mr. Gates knew something they did not. Thus, the apparent market value of the company would decrease drastically even though the company itself had not changed at all.

Conversely, just because a person can buy one share of Microsoft for $26 does not mean one could buy *all* of the outstanding shares for that price. In March 2011, Warren Buffet, Bill Gates's good friend, announced that his company had agreed to purchase Lubrizol, a chemical company, for $9 billion. This price was *28 percent higher* than the company's market capitalization would have indicated. In fact, the price Mr. Buffett paid was 18 percent higher than the company's stock had ever traded. Usually, when one company wants to buy all of the stock of another company, it must pay a significantly higher price than its market capitalization would indicate.

Determining the market value of a company can be difficult. There are other ways to try to determine value besides market capitalization, but all of them provide only estimates. So, was Facebook really worth $50 billion in early 2011? Only future events will tell.

FOCUS ON INTERNATIONAL ISSUES

PICKY, PICKY, PICKY . . .

Considering the almost countless number of differences that could exist between U.S. GAAP and IFRS, it is not surprising that some of those that do exist relate to very specific issues. Consider the case of the timing of stock splits.

Assume a company that ends its fiscal year on December 31, 2013, declares a 2-for-1 stock split on January 15, 2014, before it has issued its 2013 annual report. Should the company apply the effects of the stock split retroactively to its 2013 financial statements, or begin showing the effects of the split on its 2014 statements? Under U.S. GAAP the split must be applied retroactively to the 2013 statements since they had not been issued at the time of the split. Under IFRS the 2013 statements would not show the effects of the split, but the 2014 statements would. By the way, an event that occurs between a company's fiscal year-end and the date its annual report is released is called a *subsequent event* by accountants.

Obviously no one can know every rule under GAAP, much less all of the differences between GAAP and IFRS. This is why it is important to learn how to find answers to specific accounting questions as well as to develop an understanding of the basic accounting rules. Most important, if you are not sure you know the answer, do not assume you do.

---

on the 165 outstanding shares (150 originally issued + 15 shares distributed in a stock dividend) of its $20 par value, class B common stock. Nelson notes in the accounting records that the 165 old $20 par shares are replaced with 330 new $10 par shares. Investors who owned the 165 shares of old common stock would now own 330 shares of the new common stock.

Stock splits have no effect on the dollar amounts of assets, liabilities, and stockholders' equity. They only affect the number of shares of stock outstanding and the par value per share. In Nelson's case, the ownership interest that was previously represented by 165 shares of stock is now represented by 330 shares. Since twice as many shares now represent the same ownership interest, the market value per share should be one-half as much as it was prior to the split. However, as with a stock dividend, the lower market price will probably stimulate demand for the stock. As a result, doubling the number of shares will likely reduce the market price to slightly more than one-half of the pre-split value. For example, if the stock were selling for $30 per share before the 2-for-1 split, it might sell for $15.50 after the split.

Appropriation of Retained Earnings

The board of directors may restrict the amount of retained earnings available to distribute as dividends. The restriction may be required by credit agreements, or it may be discretionary. A retained earnings restriction, often called an *appropriation,* is an equity exchange event. It transfers a portion of existing retained earnings to **Appropriated Retained Earnings.** Total retained earnings remains unchanged. To illustrate, assume that Nelson appropriates $1,000 of retained earnings for future expansion. The income statement and the statement of cash flows are not affected. The journal entry and its effects on the financial statements are shown here:

Account Title	Debit	Credit
Retained Earnings	1,000	
Appropriated Retained Earnings		1,000

Assets	=	Liab.	+	Equity					Rev.	−	Exp.	=	Net Inc.	Cash Flow
				Com. Stk.	+	Ret. Earn.	+	App. Ret. Earn.						
NA	=	NA	+	NA	+	(1,000)	+	1,000	NA	−	NA	=	NA	NA

Financial Statement Presentation

The 2013 and 2014 events for Nelson Incorporated are summarized below. Events 1 through 8 are cash transactions. The results of the 2013 transactions (nos. 1–5) are reflected in Exhibit 11.4. The results of the 2014 transactions (nos. 6–11) are shown in Exhibit 11.5.

1. Issued 100 shares of $10 par value common stock at a market price of $22 per share.
2. Issued 150 shares of class B, $20 par value common stock at a market price of $25 per share.
3. Issued 100 shares of $10 stated value, 7 percent cumulative preferred stock at a market price of $22 per share.
4. Issued 100 shares of no-par common stock at a market price of $22 per share.
5. Earned and retained $5,000 cash from operations.
6. Purchased 50 shares of $10 par value common stock as treasury stock at a market price of $20 per share.
7. Sold 30 shares of treasury stock at a market price of $25 per share.
8. Declared and paid a $70 cash dividend on the preferred stock.
9. Issued a 10 percent stock dividend on the 150 shares of outstanding class B, $20 par value common stock (15 additional shares). The additional shares were issued when the market price of the stock was $30 per share. There are 165 (150 + 15) class B common shares outstanding after the stock dividend.
10. Issued a 2-for-1 stock split on the 165 shares of class B, $20 par value common stock. After this transaction, there are 330 shares outstanding of the class B common stock with a $10 par value.
11. Appropriated $1,000 of retained earnings.

EXHIBIT 11.5

NELSON INCORPORATED
Balance Sheet
As of December 31, 2014

Assets		
Cash		**$21,030**
Stockholders' equity		
Preferred stock, $10 stated value, 7% cumulative,		
300 shares authorized, 100 issued and outstanding	$1,000	
Common stock, $10 par value, 250 shares authorized,		
100 issued, and 80 outstanding	1,000	
Common stock, class B, $10 par, 800 shares authorized,		
330 issued and outstanding	3,300	
Common stock, no par, 150 shares authorized,		
100 issued and outstanding	2,200	
Paid-in capital in excess of stated value—Preferred	1,200	
Paid-in capital in excess of par value—Common	1,200	
Paid-in capital in excess of par value—Class B common	900	
Paid-in capital in excess of cost of treasury stock	150	
Total paid-in capital		$10,950
Retained Earnings		
Appropriated	1,000	
Unappropriated	9,480	
Total retained earnings		10,480
Less: Treasury stock, 20 shares @ $20 per share		(400)
Total stockholders' equity		$21,030

The illustration assumes that Nelson earned net income of $6,000 in 2014. The ending retained earnings balance is determined as follows: Beginning balance $5,000 − $70 Cash dividend − $450 Stock dividend + $6,000 Net income = $10,480.

- -

THE FINANCIAL ANALYST

Stockholders may benefit in two ways when a company generates earnings. The company may distribute the earnings directly to the stockholders in the form of dividends. Alternatively, the company may retain some or all of the earnings to finance growth and increase its potential for future earnings. If the company retains earnings, the market value of its stock should increase to reflect its greater earnings prospects. How can analysts use financial reporting to help assess the potential for dividend payments or growth in market value?

- -

Receiving Dividends

Is a company likely to pay dividends in the future? The financial statements can help answer this question. They show if dividends were paid in the past. Companies with a history of paying dividends usually continue to pay dividends. Also, to pay dividends in the future, a company must have sufficient cash and retained earnings. These amounts are reported on the balance sheet and the statement of cash flows.

Increasing the Price of Stock

Is the market value (price) of a company's stock likely to increase? Increases in a company's stock price occur when investors believe the company's earnings will grow. Financial statements provide information that is useful in predicting the prospects for earnings growth. Here also, a company's earnings history is an indicator of its growth potential. However, because published financial statements report historical information, investors must recognize their limitations. Investors want to know about the future. Stock prices are therefore influenced more by forecasts than by history.

For example:

- On February 22, 2011, **Wal-Mart Stores, Inc.**, announced that revenues for its fiscal year ended January 31, 2011 were 3.4 percent higher than for 2010, and its earnings were up 14.2 percent from 2010. In reaction to this news, the price of stock *fell* by almost 4 percent. Why did the stock market respond in this way? Because the company's revenues for the quarter were less than had been expected by analysts who follow the company, and because the growth in revenues and profits were due to international operations. Revenues at stores in the United States that had been open for at least a year (same-store sales) were down 1.1 percent, and this was the seventh quarter in a row that same-store sales of U.S. stores were down.

- On February 8, 2011, **Avon Products, Inc.**, announced that earnings for 2010 were about 3 percent lower than they were for 2009, and the earnings for the fourth quarter of the year were over 14 percent lower than for the same quarter of 2009. The stock market's reaction to the news was to *increase* the price of Avon's stock by a little over 3 percent. The market reacted this way because even though earnings were down, revenues were up, and analysts seemed to think that as the economy continued to recover from its recent slump, Avon was positioned for improved growth in revenues and earnings.

In each case, investors reacted to the potential for earnings growth rather than the historical earnings reports. Because investors find forecasted statements more relevant to decision making than historical financial statements, most companies provide forecasts in addition to historical financial statements.

The value of a company's stock is also influenced by nonfinancial information that financial statements cannot provide. For example, suppose ExxonMobil announced in the middle of its fiscal year that it had just discovered substantial oil reserves on property to which it held drilling rights. Consider the following questions:

- What would happen to the price of ExxonMobil's stock on the day of the announcement?
- What would happen to ExxonMobil's financial statements on that day?

The price of ExxonMobil's stock would almost certainly increase as soon as the discovery was made public. However, nothing would happen to its financial statements on that day. There would probably be very little effect on its financial statements for that year. Only after the company began to develop the oil field and sell the oil would its financial statements reflect the discovery. Changes in financial statements tend to lag behind the announcements companies make regarding their earnings potential.

Stock prices are also affected by general economic conditions and consumer confidence as well as the performance measures reported in financial statements. For example, the stock prices of virtually all companies declined sharply immediately after the September 11, 2001, terrorist attacks on the World Trade Center and the Pentagon. Historically-based financial statements are of little benefit in predicting general economic conditions or changes in consumer confidence.

Price-Earnings Ratio

The **price-earnings ratio,** frequently called the *P/E ratio,* is the most commonly reported measure of a company's value. The P/E ratio is a company's market price per share of stock divided by the company's annual earnings per share (EPS).[3]

Assume Western Company recently reported annual earnings per share of $3. Western's stock is currently selling for $54 per share. Western's stock is therefore selling at a P/E ratio of 18 ($54 market price / $3 EPS). What does a P/E ratio of 18 mean? If Western continued earning $3 per share of stock each year and paid all its earnings out to stockholders in the form of cash dividends, it would take 18 years for an investor to recover the price paid for the stock.

In contrast, assume the stock of Eastern Company, which reported EPS of $4, is currently selling for $48 per share. Eastern's P/E ratio is 12 ($48 market price / $4 EPS). Investors who buy Eastern Company stock would get their money back six years faster (18 − 12) than investors who buy Western Company stock.

Why would investors buy a stock with a P/E ratio of 18 when they could buy one with a P/E ratio of 12? If investors expect Western Company's earnings to grow faster than Eastern Company's earnings, the higher P/E ratio makes sense. For example, suppose Western Company's earnings were to double to $6 per share while Eastern's remained at $4 per share. Western's P/E ratio would drop to 9 ($54 market price / $6 EPS) while Eastern's remains at 12. This explains why high-growth companies sell for higher P/E multiples than do low-growth companies.

Caution must be used when interpreting P/E ratios. A company can have a high P/E ratio due to very low earnings, rather than high optimism by investors. For example, if a company's EPS is $.02, and its stock is selling for $0.50, it will have a P/E ratio of 25, which is high. In this case the high P/E ratio is the result of very low earnings, not optimism. If a company has a net loss, the P/E ratio is not computed.

Also, be aware that P/E ratios reported in the financial press are often based on *projected* EPS, rather than its historical earnings. Sometimes P/E ratios based on historical earnings are referred to as being based on trailing earnings. In this course, compute the P/E ratio using the company's most recent, actual earnings amount rather than it forecasted earnings.

[3]The amount of earnings per share is provided on the face of the income statement. In its simplest form, it is computed by dividing the company's net income (net earnings) by the number of shares of common stock outstanding.

Exercising Control through Stock Ownership

The more influence an investor has over the operations of a company, the more the investor can benefit from owning stock in the company. For example, consider a power company that needs coal to produce electricity. The power company may purchase some common stock in a coal mining company to ensure a stable supply of coal. What percentage of the mining company's stock must the power company acquire to exercise significant influence over the mining company? The answer depends on how many investors own stock in the mining company and how the number of shares is distributed among the stockholders.

The greater its number of stockholders, the more *widely held* a company is. If stock ownership is concentrated in the hands of a few persons, a company is *closely held.* Widely held companies can generally be controlled with smaller percentages of ownership than closely held companies. Consider a company in which no existing investor owns more than 1 percent of the voting stock. A new investor who acquires a 5 percent interest would immediately become, by far, the largest shareholder and would likely be able to significantly influence board decisions. In contrast, consider a closely held company in which one current shareholder owns 51 percent of the company's stock. Even if another investor acquired the remaining 49 percent of the company, that investor could not control the company.

Financial statements contain some, but not all, of the information needed to help an investor determine ownership levels necessary to permit control. For example, the financial statements disclose the total number of shares of stock outstanding, but they normally contain little information about the number of shareholders and even less information about any relationships between shareholders. Relationships between shareholders are critically important because related shareholders, whether bound by family or business interests, might exercise control by voting as a block. For publicly traded companies, information about the number of shareholders and the identity of some large shareholders is disclosed in reports filed with the Securities and Exchange Commission.

 # A Look Back

Starting a business requires obtaining financing; it takes money to make money. Although some money may be borrowed, lenders are unlikely to make loans to businesses that lack some degree of owner financing. Equity financing is therefore critical to virtually all profit-oriented businesses. This chapter has examined some of the issues related to accounting for equity transactions.

The idea that a business must obtain financing from its owners was one of the first events presented in this textbook. This chapter discussed the advantages and disadvantages of organizing a business as a sole proprietorship versus a partnership versus a corporation. These advantages and disadvantages include the following:

1. *Double taxation*—Income of corporations is subject to double taxation, but that of proprietorships and partnerships is not.

2. *Regulation*—Corporations are subject to more regulation than are proprietorships and partnerships.

3. *Limited liability*—An investor's personal assets are not at risk as a result of owning corporate securities. The investor's liability is limited to the amount of the investment. In general proprietorships and partnerships do not offer limited liability. However, laws in some states permit the formation of limited liability companies which operate like proprietorships and partnerships yet place some limits on the personal liability of their owners.

4. *Continuity*—Proprietorships and partnerships dissolve when one of the owners leaves the business. Corporations are separate legal entities that continue to exist regardless of changes in ownership.

5. *Transferability*—Ownership interests in corporations are easier to transfer than those of proprietorships or partnerships.

6. *Management structure*—Corporations are more likely to have independent professional managers than are proprietorships or partnerships.

7. *Ability to raise capital*—Because they can be owned by millions of investors, corporations have the opportunity to raise more capital than proprietorships or partnerships.

Corporations issue different classes of common stock and preferred stock as evidence of ownership interests. In general, *common stock* provides the widest range of privileges including the right to vote and participate in earnings. *Preferred stockholders* usually give up the right to vote in exchange for preferences such as the right to receive dividends or assets upon liquidation before common stockholders. Stock may have a *par value* or *stated value,* which relates to legal requirements governing the amount of capital that must be maintained in the corporation. Corporations may also issue *no-par stock,* avoiding some of the legal requirements that pertain to par or stated value stock.

Stock that a company issues and then repurchases is called *treasury stock.* Purchasing treasury stock reduces total assets and stockholders' equity. Reselling treasury stock represents a capital acquisition. The difference between the reissue price and the cost of the treasury stock is recorded directly in the equity accounts. Treasury stock transactions do not result in gains or losses on the income statement.

Companies may issue *stock splits* or *stock dividends.* These transactions increase the number of shares of stock without changing the net assets of a company. The per share market value usually drops when a company issues stock splits or dividends.

A Look Forward

Chapter 12 examines the statement of cash flows in more detail than past chapters have. It introduces a more practical way to prepare the statement than analyzing every single entry in the cash account, and presents the more formal format for the statement of cash flows used by most real-world companies.

 SELF-STUDY REVIEW PROBLEM

A step-by-step audio-narrated series of slides is provided on the text website at www.mhhe.com/edmonds8e.

Edwards Inc. experienced the following events:

1. Issued common stock for cash.
2. Declared a cash dividend.
3. Issued noncumulative preferred stock for cash.
4. Appropriated retained earnings.
5. Distributed a stock dividend.
6. Paid cash to purchase treasury stock.
7. Distributed a 2-for-1 stock split.
8. Issued cumulative preferred stock for cash.
9. Paid a cash dividend that had previously been declared.
10. Sold treasury stock for cash at a higher amount than the cost of the treasury stock.

Required

Show the effect of each event on the elements of the financial statements using a horizontal statements model like the one shown here. Use + for increase, − for decrease, and NA for not affected. In the Cash Flow column, indicate whether the item is an operating activity (OA), investing activity (IA), or a financing activity (FA). The first transaction is entered as an example.

Event	Assets	=	Liab.	+	Equity	Rev.	−	Exp.	=	Net Inc.	Cash Flow
1	+		NA		+	NA		NA		NA	+ FA

Solution to Self-Study Review Problem

Event	Assets	=	Liab.	+	Equity	Rev.	−	Exp.	=	Net Inc.	Cash Flow
1	+		NA		+	NA		NA		NA	+ FA
2	NA		+		−	NA		NA		NA	NA
3	+		NA		+	NA		NA		NA	+ FA
4	NA		NA		− +	NA		NA		NA	NA
5	NA		NA		− +	NA		NA		NA	NA
6	−		NA		−	NA		NA		NA	− FA
7	NA		NA		NA	NA		NA		NA	NA
8	+		NA		+	NA		NA		NA	+ FA
9	−		−		NA	NA		NA		NA	− FA
10	+		NA		+	NA		NA		NA	+ FA

KEY TERMS

Appropriated Retained
   Earnings 608
articles of incorporation 594
authorized stock 599
board of directors 596
book value per share 599
closely held corporation 594
common stock 600
continuity 596
corporation 594
cost method of accounting
   for treasury stock 604

cumulative dividends 600
date of record 605
declaration date 605
dividends in arrears 600
double taxation 595
ex-dividend 605
issued stock 599
legal capital 599
limited liability 596
limited liability
   companies (LLCs) 596
market value 599

outstanding stock 599
Paid-in Capital in Excess of
   Par Value 601
par value 599
partnership
   agreement 594
partnerships 594
payment date 606
preferred stock 600
price-earnings ratio 611
Sarbanes-Oxley
   Act of 2002 595

Securities Act of 1933 and
   Securities Exchange
   Act of 1934 594
sole proprietorships 594
stated value 599
stock certificates 594
stock dividends 606
stockholders 596
stock split 607
transferability 596
treasury stock 599
withdrawals 597

QUESTIONS

1. What are the three major forms of business organizations? Describe each.

2. How are sole proprietorships formed?

3. Discuss the purpose of a partnership agreement. Is such an agreement

necessary for partnership formation?

4. What is meant by the phrase *separate legal entity?* To which type of business organization does it apply?

5. What is the purpose of the articles of incorporation? What information do they provide?

6. What is the function of the stock certificate?

7. What prompted Congress to pass the Securities Act

of 1933 and the Securities Exchange Act of 1934? What is the purpose of these laws?

8. What are the advantages and disadvantages of the corporate form of business organization?

9. What is a limited liability company? Discuss its advantages and disadvantages.

10. How does the term *double taxation* apply to corporations? Give an example of double taxation.

11. What is the difference between contributed capital and retained earnings for a corporation?

12. What are the similarities and differences in the equity structure of a sole proprietorship, a partnership, and a corporation?

13. Why is it easier for a corporation to raise large amounts of capital than it is for a partnership?

14. What is the meaning of each of the following terms with respect to the corporate form of organization?
   (a) Legal capital
   (b) Par value of stock
   (c) Stated value of stock
   (d) Market value of stock
   (e) Book value of stock
   (f) Authorized shares of stock

(g) Issued stock
(h) Outstanding stock
(i) Treasury stock
(j) Common stock
(k) Preferred stock
(l) Dividends

15. What is the difference between cumulative preferred stock and noncumulative preferred stock?

16. What is no-par stock? How is it recorded in the accounting records?

17. Assume that Best Co. has issued and outstanding 1,000 shares of $100 par value, 10 percent, cumulative preferred stock. What is the dividend per share? If the preferred dividend is two years in arrears, what total amount of dividends must be paid before the common shareholders can receive any dividends?

18. If Best Co. issued 10,000 shares of $20 par value common stock for $30 per share, what amount is credited to the Common Stock account? What amount of cash is received?

19. What is the difference between par value stock and stated value stock?

20. Why might a company repurchase its own stock?

21. What effect does the purchase of treasury stock have on the equity of a company?

22. Assume that Day Company repurchased 1,000 of its own shares for $30 per share and sold the shares two weeks later for $35 per share. What is the amount of gain on the sale? How is it reported on the balance sheet? What type of account is treasury stock?

23. What is the importance of the declaration date, record date, and payment date in conjunction with corporate dividends?

24. What is the difference between a stock dividend and a stock split?

25. Why would a company choose to distribute a stock dividend instead of a cash dividend?

26. What is the primary reason that a company would declare a stock split?

27. If Best Co. had 10,000 shares of $20 par value common stock outstanding and declared a 5-for-1 stock split, how many shares would then be outstanding and what would be their par value after the split?

28. When a company appropriates retained earnings, does the company set aside cash for a specific use? Explain.

29. What is the largest source of financing for most U.S. businesses?

30. What is meant by *equity financing*? What is meant by *debt financing*?

31. What is a widely held corporation? What is a closely held corporation?

32. What are some reasons that a corporation might not pay dividends?

MULTIPLE-CHOICE QUESTIONS

Multiple-choice questions are provided on the text website at www.mhhe.com/edmonds8e.

EXERCISES—SERIES A

All applicable Exercises in Series A are available with McGraw-Hill's *Connect® Accounting.*

Exercise 11-1A   *Effect of accounting events on the financial statements of a sole proprietorship*

LO 1

A sole proprietorship was started on January 1, 2013, when it received $30,000 cash from Alex Ard, the owner. During 2013, the company earned $50,000 in cash revenues and paid $22,300 in cash expenses. Ard withdrew $10,000 cash from the business during 2013.

Required

Prepare an income statement, capital statement (statement of changes in equity), balance sheet, and statement of cash flows for Ard's 2013 fiscal year.

LO 1

Exercise 11-2A *Effect of accounting events on the financial statements of a partnership*

Drake Cushing and Shawn Tadlock started the CT partnership on January 1, 2013. The business acquired $70,000 cash from Cushing and $140,000 from Tadlock. During 2013, the partnership earned $75,000 in cash revenues and paid $39,000 for cash expenses. Cushing withdrew $2,000 cash from the business, and Tadlock withdrew $4,000 cash. The net income was allocated to the capital accounts of the two partners in proportion to the amounts of their original investments in the business.

Required

Prepare an income statement, capital statement, balance sheet, and statement of cash flows for the CT partnership for the 2013 fiscal year.

LO 2

Exercise 11-3A *Effect of accounting events on the financial statements of a corporation*

Bozeman Corporation was started with the issue of 10,000 shares of $10 par common stock for cash on January 1, 2013. The stock was issued at a market price of $16 per share. During 2013, the company earned $71,000 in cash revenues and paid $46,500 for cash expenses. Also a $5,000 cash dividend was paid to the stockholders.

Required

Prepare an income statement, statement of changes in stockholders' equity, balance sheet, and statement of cash flows for Bozeman Corporation's 2013 fiscal year.

LO 2

Exercise 11-4A *Effect of issuing common stock on the balance sheet*

Newly formed Electronics Services Corporation has 100,000 shares of $10 par common stock authorized. On March 1, 2013, Electronics Services issued 20,000 shares of the stock for $12 per share. On May 2 the company issued an additional 30,000 shares for $15 per share. Electronics Services was not affected by other events during 2013.

Required

a. Record the transactions in a horizontal statements model like the following one. In the Cash Flow column, indicate whether the item is an operating activity (OA), investing activity (IA), or financing activity (FA). Use NA to indicate that an element was not affected by the event.

Assets	=	Liab.	+	Equity			Rev.	−	Exp.	=	Net Inc.	Cash Flow
Cash	=			Com. Stk.	+	PIC in Excess						

b. Determine the amount Electronic Services would report for common stock on the December 31, 2013, balance sheet.

c. Determine the amount Electronic Services would report for paid-in capital in excess of par.

d. What is the total amount of capital contributed by the owners?

e. What amount of total assets would Electronic Services report on the December 31, 2013, balance sheet?

f. Prepare journal entries to record the March 1 and May 2 transactions.

LO 2

Exercise 11-5A *Recording and reporting common and preferred stock transactions*

Goldman Inc. was organized on June 1, 2013. It was authorized to issue 500,000 shares of $10 par common stock and 100,000 shares of 4 percent cumulative class A preferred stock. The class A stock had a stated value of $50 per share. The following stock transactions pertain to Goldman Inc.:

1. Issued 40,000 shares of common stock for $16 per share.
2. Issued 20,000 shares of the class A preferred stock for $52 per share.
3. Issued 60,000 shares of common stock for $20 per share.

Required

a. Prepare general journal entries for these transactions.

b. Prepare the stockholders' equity section of the balance sheet immediately after these transactions.

Exercise 11-6A   *Effect of no-par common and par preferred stock on the horizontal statements model*

Bailey Corporation issued 10,000 shares of no-par common stock for $25 per share. Bailey also issued 3,000 shares of $40 par, 6 percent noncumulative preferred stock at $42 per share.

Required

a. Record these events in a horizontal statements model like the following one. In the cash flow column, indicate whether the item is an operating activity (OA), investing activity (IA), or financing activity (FA). Use NA to indicate that an element was not affected by the event.

Assets =	Equity			Rev. − Exp. = Net Inc.	Cash Flow
Cash =	Pfd. Stk. +	Com. Stk. +	PIC in Excess		

b. Prepare journal entries to record these transactions.

Exercise 11-7A   *Issuing stock for assets other than cash*

Hammond Corporation was formed when it issued shares of common stock to two of its shareholders. Hammond issued 10,000 shares of $5 par common stock to P. Coldwell in exchange for $80,000 cash (the issue price was $8 per share). Hammond also issued 3,500 shares of stock to M. Roberts in exchange for a one-year-old delivery van on the same day. Roberts had originally paid $39,000 for the van.

Required

a. What was the market value of the delivery van on the date of the stock issue?

b. Show the effect of the two stock issues on Hammond's books in a horizontal statements model like the following one. In the Cash Flow column, indicate whether the item is an operating activity (OA), investing activity (IA), or financing activity (FA). Use NA to indicate that an element was not affected by the event.

Assets	=	Equity		Rev. − Exp. = Net Inc.	Cash Flow
Cash + Van =		Com. Stk. +	PIC in Excess		

c. Prepare the journal entries to record these transactions.

Exercise 11-8A   *Treasury stock transactions*

Moore Corporation repurchased 4,000 shares of its own stock for $30 per share. The stock has a par of $10 per share. A month later Moore resold 2,500 shares of the treasury stock for $35 per share.

Required

a. Record the two events in general journal format.

b. What is the balance of the treasury stock account after these transactions?

LO 3

Exercise 11-9A   *Recording and reporting treasury stock transactions*

The following information pertains to Wise Corp. at January 1, 2013:

Common stock, $10 par, 50,000 shares authorized,	
3,000 shares issued and outstanding	$30,000
Paid-in capital in excess of par, common stock	12,000
Retained earnings	46,000

Wise Corp. completed the following transactions during 2013:

1. Issued 2,000 shares of $10 par common stock for $16 per share.
2. Repurchased 500 shares of its own common stock for $18 per share.
3. Resold 120 shares of treasury stock for $20 per share.

Required

a. How many shares of common stock were outstanding at the end of the period?
b. How many shares of common stock had been issued at the end of the period?
c. Prepare journal entries for these transactions and post them to T-accounts.
d. Prepare the stockholders' equity section of the balance sheet reflecting these transactions. Include the number of shares authorized, issued, and outstanding in the description of the common stock.

LO 4

Exercise 11-10A   *Effect of cash dividends on financial statements*

On October 1, 2013, Daster Corporation declared a $50,000 cash dividend to be paid on December 15 to shareholders of record on November 1.

Required

a. Record the events occurring on October 1, November 1, and December 15 in a horizontal statements model like the following one. In the Cash Flow column, indicate whether the item is an operating activity (OA), investing activity (IA), or financing activity (FA).

Date	Assets	=	Liab.	+	Com. Stock	+	Ret. Earn.		Rev.	−	Exp.	=	Net Inc.		Cash Flow

b. Prepare journal entries for all events associated with the dividend.

LO 4

Exercise 11-11A   *Accounting for cumulative preferred dividends*

When Higdon Corporation was organized in January 2013, it immediately issued 10,000 shares of $50 par, 5 percent, cumulative preferred stock and 15,000 shares of $10 par common stock. The company's earnings history is as follows: 2013, net loss of $18,000; 2014, net income of $50,000; 2015, net income of $90,000. The corporation did not pay a dividend in 2013.

Required

a. How much is the dividend arrearage as of January 1, 2014?
b. Assume that the board of directors declares a $65,000 cash dividend at the end of 2014 (remember that the 2013 and 2014 preferred dividends are due). How will the dividend be divided between the preferred and common stockholders?

LO 4

Exercise 11-12A   *Cash dividends for preferred and common shareholders*

J&J Corporation had the following stock issued and outstanding at January 1, 2013:

1. 200,000 shares of $10 par common stock.
2. 8,000 shares of $100 par, 4 percent, noncumulative preferred stock.

On May 10, J&J Corporation declared the annual cash dividend on its 8,000 shares of preferred stock and a $.50 per share dividend for the common shareholders. The dividends will be paid on June 15 to the shareholders of record on May 30.

Required

a. Determine the total amount of dividends to be paid to the preferred shareholders and common shareholders.

b. Prepare general journal entries to record the declaration and payment of the cash dividends (be sure to date your entries).

Exercise 11-13A   *Cash dividends: common and preferred stock*   LO 4

Yan Corp. had the following stock issued and outstanding at January 1, 2013:

1. 60,000 shares of no-par common stock.
2. 15,000 shares of $100 par, 4 percent, cumulative preferred stock. (Dividends are in arrears for one year, 2012.)

On February 1, 2013, Yan declared a $150,000 cash dividend to be paid March 31 to shareholders of record on March 10.

Required

a. What amount of dividends will be paid to the preferred shareholders versus the common shareholders?

b. Prepare the journal entries required for these transactions. (Be sure to include the dates of the entries.)

Exercise 11-14A   *Accounting for stock dividends*   LO 4

Tidwell Corporation issued a 4 percent stock dividend on 20,000 shares of its $10 par common stock. At the time of the dividend, the market value of the stock was $30 per share.

Required

a. Compute the amount of the stock dividend.

b. Show the effects of the stock dividend on the financial statements using a horizontal statements model like the following one.

Assets	=	Liab.	+	Com. Stock	+	PIC in Excess	+	Ret. Earn.	Rev.	−	Exp.	=	Net Inc.	Cash Flow

c. Prepare the journal entry to record the stock dividend.

Exercise 11-15A   *Determining the effects of stock splits on the accounting records*   LO 4

The market value of Dylan Corporation's common stock had become excessively high. The stock was currently selling for $240 per share. To reduce the market price of the common stock, Dylan declared a 3-for-1 stock split for the 200,000 outstanding shares of its $10 par common stock.

Required

a. How will Dylan Corporation's books be affected by the stock split?

b. Determine the number of common shares outstanding and the par value after the split.

c. Explain how the market value of the stock will be affected by the stock split.

Exercise 11-16A   *Accounting information*   LO 5

The Cutting Edge (TCE) is one of the world's largest lawn mower distributors. TCE is concerned about maintaining an adequate supply of the economy-line mowers that it sells in its stores. TCE currently obtains its economy-line mowers from two suppliers. To ensure a steady supply of mowers, the management of TCE is considering the purchase of an ownership interest in one of the companies that supply its mowers. More specifically, TCE wants to own enough stock of one of the suppliers to enable it to exercise significant influence over the management of the company. The following is a description of the two suppliers.

The first supplier, Dobbs Incorporated, is a closely held company. Large blocks of the Dobbs stock are held by individual members of the Dobbs family. TCE's investment advisor has discovered that one of the members of the Dobbs family is interested in selling her 5 percent share of the company's stock.

The second supplier, National Mowers Inc., has widely disbursed ownership with no one single stockholder owning more than 1 percent of the stock. TCE's investment advisor believes that 5 percent of this company's stock could be acquired gradually over an extended period of time without having a significant effect on the company's stock price.

Required

Provide a recommendation to TCE's management as to whether it should pursue the purchase of 5 percent of Dobbs Incorporated, or 5 percent of National Mowers Inc. Your answer should be supported by an explanation of your recommendation.

LO 5

Exercise 11-17A   *Using the P/E ratio*

During 2013 Catour, Inc., and Pavie, Inc., reported net incomes of $220,000 and $190,000, respectively. Both companies had 50,000 shares of common stock issued and outstanding. The market price per share of Catour's stock was $50, while Pavie's sold for $54 per share.

Required

a. Determine the P/E ratio for each company. (Round to the nearest whole number.)

b. Based on the P/E ratios computed in Requirement *a*, which company do investors believe has the greater potential for growth in income?

LO 5

Exercise 11-18A   *The P/E ratio*

Mace Company's earnings were approximately the same in 2013 and 2014. Even so, the company's P/E ratio dropped significantly.

Required

Speculate about why Mace's P/E ratio dropped significantly while its earnings remained constant.

PROBLEMS—SERIES A

All applicable Problems in Series A are available with McGraw-Hill's Connect® Accounting.

LO 1, 2

CHECK FIGURES
a. Net Income: $24,000
b. Moore Capital: $78,100

Problem 11-19A   *Effect of business structure on financial statements*

Auto Spa Company was started on January 1, 2013, when the owners invested $120,000 cash in the business. During 2013, the company earned cash revenues of $80,000 and incurred cash expenses of $56,000. The company also paid cash distributions of $5,000.

Required

Prepare a 2013 income statement, capital statement (statement of changes in equity), balance sheet, and statement of cash flows using each of the following assumptions. (Consider each assumption separately.)

a. Auto Spa is a sole proprietorship owned by B. Burns.

b. Auto Spa is a partnership with two partners, Sue Moore and Jim Pounds. Moore invested $72,000 and Pounds invested $48,000 of the $120,000 cash that was used to start the business. Pounds was expected to assume the vast majority of the responsibility for operating the business. The partnership agreement called for Pounds to receive 60 percent of the profits and Moore the remaining 40 percent. With regard to the $5,000 distribution, Pounds withdrew $1,500 from the business and Moore withdrew $3,500.

c. Auto Spa is a corporation. The owners were issued 10,000 shares of $10 par common stock when they invested the $120,000 cash in the business.

Problem 11-20A *Different forms of business organization*

Paul Salvy established a partnership with Lisa Witlow. The new company, S&W Fuels, purchased coal directly from mining companies and contracted to ship the coal via waterways to a seaport where it was delivered to ships that were owned and operated by international utilities companies. Salvy was primarily responsible for running the day-to-day operations of the business. Witlow negotiated the buy-and-sell agreements. She recently signed a deal to purchase and deliver $2,000,000 of coal to Solar Utilities. S&W Fuels purchased the coal on account from Miller Mining Company. After accepting title to the coal, S&W Fuels agreed to deliver the coal under terms FOB destination, Port of Long Beach. Unfortunately, Witlow failed to inform Salvy of the deal in time for Salvy to insure the shipment. While in transit, the vessel carrying the coal suffered storm damage that rendered the coal virtually worthless by the time it reached its destination. S&W Fuels immediately declared bankruptcy. The company not only was responsible for the $2,000,000 due to Miller Mining Company but also was sued by Solar for breach of contract. Witlow had a personal net worth of virtually zero, but Salvy was a wealthy individual with a net worth approaching $2,500,000. Accordingly, Miller Mining and Solar filed suit against Salvy's personal assets. Salvy claimed that he was not responsible for the problem because Witlow had failed to inform him of the contracts in time to obtain insurance coverage. Witlow admitted that she was personally responsible for the disaster.

Required

Write a memo describing Salvy's risk associated with his participation in the partnership. Comment on how other forms of ownership would have affected his level of risk.

Problem 11-21A *Recording and reporting treasury stock transactions*

Quality Corporation reports the following information in its January 1, 2013, balance sheet:

Stockholders' equity	
Common stock, $10 par value, 100,000 shares authorized, 50,000 shares issued and outstanding	$500,000
Paid-in capital in excess of par value	150,000
Retained earnings	120,000
Total stockholders' equity	$770,000

During 2013, Quality was affected by the following accounting events:

1. Purchased 2,000 shares of treasury stock at $15 per share.
2. Reissued 1,200 shares of treasury stock at $18 per share.
3. Earned $72,000 of cash revenues.
4. Paid $41,000 of cash operating expenses.

Required

a. Provide journal entries to record these transactions.
b. Prepare the stockholders' equity section of the year-end balance sheet.

Problem 11-22A *Recording and reporting stock dividends*

Concord Corp. completed the following transactions in 2013, the first year of operation:

1. Issued 30,000 shares of $10 par common stock for $15 per share.
2. Issued 6,000 shares of $100 par, 5 percent, preferred stock at $101 per share.
3. Paid the annual cash dividend to preferred shareholders.
4. Issued a 5 percent stock dividend on the common stock. The market value at the dividend declaration date was $19 per share.
5. Later that year, issued a 2-for-1 split on the 31,500 shares of outstanding common stock.
6. Earned $165,000 of cash revenues and paid $98,000 of cash operating expenses.
7. Closed the revenue, expense, and dividend accounts to retained earnings.

Required

a. Record each of these events in a horizontal statements model like the following one. In the Cash Flow column, indicate whether the item is an operating activity (OA), investing activity (IA), or financing activity (FA). Use NA to indicate that an element is not affected by the event.

Assets	=	Liab.	+	Equity					Rev.	−	Exp.	=	Net Inc.	Cash Flow
				Pfd. Stk. + Com. Stk. + PIC in Excess PS + PIC in Excess CS + Ret. Earn.										

b. Record the 2013 transactions in general journal form and post them to T-accounts.

c. Prepare the stockholders' equity section of the balance sheet at the end of 2013.

LO 2, 3, 4

eXcel

CHECK FIGURES
b. Preferred Stock, 2013: $160,000
c. Common Shares Outstanding, 2014: 44,000

Problem 11-23A *Recording and reporting stock transactions and cash dividends across two accounting cycles*

Malard Corporation was authorized to issue 100,000 shares of $8 par common stock and 50,000 shares of $80 par, 4 percent, cumulative preferred stock. Malard Corporation completed the following transactions during its first two years of operation:

2013

Jan.   2   Issued 25,000 shares of $8 par common stock for $10 per share.
       15   Issued 2,000 shares of $80 par preferred stock for $90 per share.
Feb. 14   Issued 20,000 shares of $8 par common stock for $12 per share.
Dec. 31   During the year, earned $280,000 of cash revenues and paid $165,000 of cash operating expenses.
       31   Declared the cash dividend on outstanding shares of preferred stock for 2013. The dividend will be paid on January 31 to stockholders of record on January 15, 2014.
       31   Closed revenue, expense, and dividend accounts to the retained earnings account.

2014

Jan. 31   Paid the cash dividend declared on December 31, 2013.
Mar.   1   Issued 4,000 shares of $80 par preferred stock for $92 per share.
June   1   Purchased 1,000 shares of common stock as treasury stock at $14 per share.
Dec. 31   During the year, earned $185,000 of cash revenues and paid $110,000 of cash operating expenses.
       31   Declared the dividend on the preferred stock and a $1.00 per share dividend on the common stock.
       31   Closed revenue, expense, and dividend accounts to the retained earnings account.

Required

a. Prepare journal entries for these transactions for 2013 and 2014 and post them to T-accounts.

b. Prepare the stockholders' equity section of the balance sheet at December 31, 2013.

c. Prepare the balance sheet at December 31, 2014.

LO 2, 3, 4

eXcel

CHECK FIGURE
b. Total Paid-In Capital: $411,200

Problem 11-24A *Recording and reporting treasury stock transactions*

Prairie Corp. completed the following transactions in 2013, the first year of operation:

1. Issued 15,000 shares of $10 par common stock at par.
2. Issued 5,000 shares of $50 stated value preferred stock at $52 per share.
3. Purchased 800 shares of common stock as treasury stock for $12 per share.
4. Declared a 5 percent cash dividend on preferred stock.
5. Sold 300 shares of treasury stock for $16 per share.
6. Paid the cash dividend on preferred stock that was declared in Event 4.
7. Earned revenue of $80,000 and incurred operating expenses of $48,000.
8. Closed revenue, expense, and dividend accounts to the retained earnings account.
9. Appropriated $6,000 of retained earnings.

Required

a. Prepare journal entries to record these transactions and post them to T-accounts.
b. Prepare the stockholders' equity section of the balance sheet as of December 31, 2013.

Problem 11-25A *Analyzing the stockholders' equity section of the balance sheet*

LO 2, 3, 4

The stockholders' equity section of the balance sheet for Gator Company at December 31, 2013, is as follows:

Stockholders' Equity		
Paid-in capital		
Preferred stock, ? par value, 5% cumulative, 100,000 shares authorized, 40,000 shares issued and outstanding	$400,000	
Common stock, $20 stated value, 150,000 shares authorized, 40,000 shares issued and ? outstanding	800,000	
Paid-in capital in excess of par—Preferred	30,000	
Paid-in capital in excess of stated value—Common	100,000	
Total paid-in capital		$1,330,000
Retained earnings		250,000
Treasury stock, 2,000 shares		(25,000)
Total stockholders' equity		$1,555,000

Note: The market value per share of the common stock is $40, and the market value per share of the preferred stock is $12.

Required

a. What is the par value per share of the preferred stock?
b. What is the dividend per share on the preferred stock?
c. What is the number of common stock shares outstanding?
d. What was the average issue price per share (price for which the stock was issued) of the common stock?
e. Explain the difference between the average issue price and the market price of the common stock.
f. If Gator declared a 2-for-1 stock split on the common stock, how many shares would be outstanding after the split? What amount would be transferred from the retained earnings account because of the stock split? Theoretically, what would be the market price of the common stock immediately after the stock split?

Problem 11-26A *Effects of equity transactions on financial statements*

LO 2, 3, 4

The following events were experienced by Carver Inc.:

1. Issued common stock for cash.
2. Distributed a 2-for-1 stock split on the common stock.
3. Appropriated retained earnings.
4. Issued cumulative preferred stock for cash.
5. Sold treasury stock for an amount of cash that was more than the cost of the treasury stock.
6. Issued noncumulative preferred stock for cash.
7. Paid cash to purchase treasury stock.
8. Declared a cash dividend.
9. Distributed a stock dividend.
10. Paid the cash dividend declared in Event 8.

Required

Show the effect of each event on the elements of the financial statements using a horizontal statements model like the following one. Use + for increase, − for decrease, and NA for not affected. In the Cash Flow column, indicate whether the item is an operating activity (OA), investing activity (IA), or financing activity (FA). The first transaction is entered as an example.

Event No.	Assets	=	Liab.	+	Equity	Rev.	−	Exp.	=	Net Inc.	Cash Flow
1	+		NA		+	NA		NA		NA	+ FA

EXERCISES—SERIES B

LO 1

Exercise 11-1B *Effect of accounting events on the financial statements of a sole proprietorship*

A sole proprietorship was started on January 1, 2013, when it received $40,000 cash from Jimmy Ross, the owner. During 2013, the company earned $28,300 in cash revenues and paid $14,100 in cash expenses. Ross withdrew $1,000 cash from the business during 2013.

Required

Prepare an income statement, capital statement (statement of changes in equity), balance sheet, and statement of cash flows for Ross 2013 fiscal year.

LO 1

Exercise 11-2B *Effect of accounting events on the financial statements of a partnership*

Katy Sneed and Rane Ellis started the S&E partnership on January 1, 2013. The business acquired $27,000 cash from Sneed and $63,000 from Ellis. During 2013, the partnership earned $36,000 in cash revenues and paid $17,500 for cash expenses. Sneed withdrew $1,000 cash from the business, and Ellis withdrew $2,000 cash. The net income was allocated to the capital accounts of the two partners in proportion to the amounts of their original investments in the business.

Required

Prepare an income statement, capital statement, balance sheet, and statement of cash flows for S&E's 2013 fiscal year.

LO 2

Exercise 11-3B *Effect of accounting events on the financial statements of a corporation*

Tronix Corporation was started with the issue of 2,000 shares of $5 par stock for cash on January 1, 2013. The stock was issued at a market price of $13 per share. During 2013, the company earned $29,000 in cash revenues and paid $19,000 for cash expenses. Also a $1,500 cash dividend was paid to the stockholders.

Required

Prepare an income statement, statement of changes in stockholders' equity, balance sheet, and statement of cash flows for Tronix Corporation's 2013 fiscal year.

LO 2

Exercise 11-4B *Effect of issuing common stock on the balance sheet*

Newly formed T&M Steel Corporation has 50,000 shares of $10 par common stock authorized. On March 1, 2013, T&M Steel issued 5,000 shares of the stock for $15 per share. On May 2 the company issued an additional 8,000 shares for $18 per share. T&M Steel was not affected by other events during 2013.

Required

a. Record the transactions in a horizontal statements model like the following one. In the Cash Flow column, indicate whether the item is an operating activity (OA), investing activity (IA), or financing activity (FA). Use NA to indicate that an element was not affected by the event.

Assets	=	Liab.	+	Equity			Rev.	−	Exp.	=	Net Inc.	Cash Flow
Cash	=			Com. Stk.	+	PIC in Excess						

b. Determine the amount T&M Steel would report for common stock on the December 31, 2013, balance sheet.

c. Determine the amount T&M Steel would report for paid-in capital in excess of par.

d. What is the total amount of capital contributed by the owners?

e. What amount of total assets would T&M Steel report on the December 31, 2013, balance sheet?

f. Prepare journal entries to record the March 1 and May 2 transactions.

Exercise 11-5B *Recording and reporting common and preferred stock transactions* LO 2

Clearpoint Inc. was organized on June 5, 2013. It was authorized to issue 300,000 shares of $10 par common stock and 50,000 shares of 5 percent cumulative class A preferred stock. The class A stock had a stated value of $40 per share. The following stock transactions pertain to Clearpoint Inc.:

1. Issued 10,000 shares of common stock for $12 per share.
2. Issued 3,000 shares of the class A preferred stock for $42 per share.
3. Issued 80,000 shares of common stock for $15 per share.

Required

a. Prepare general journal entries for these transactions.

b. Prepare the stockholders' equity section of the balance sheet immediately after these transactions.

Exercise 11-6B *Effect of no-par common and par preferred stock on the horizontal statements model* LO 2

A Plus Corporation issued 5,000 shares of no-par common stock for $40 per share. A Plus also issued 2,000 shares of $50 par, 5 percent noncumulative preferred stock at $55 per share.

Required

a. Record these events in a horizontal statements model like the following one. In the Cash Flow column, indicate whether the item is an operating activity (OA), investing activity (IA), or financing activity (FA). Use NA to indicate that an element was not affected by the event.

Assets	=	Equity				Rev.	−	Exp.	=	Net Inc.	Cash Flow
Cash	=	Pfd. Stk.	+	Com. Stk.	+ PIC in Excess						

b. Prepare journal entries to record these transactions.

Exercise 11-7B *Issuing stock for assets other than cash* LO 2

Bruce Brown, a wealthy investor, exchanged a plot of land that originally cost him $20,000 for 1,000 shares of $10 par common stock issued to him by Dunn Corp. On the same date, Dunn Corp. issued an additional 1,500 shares of stock to Brown for $35 per share.

Required

a. What was the value of the land at the date of the stock issue?

b. Show the effect of the two stock issues on Dunn's books in a horizontal statements model like the following one. In the Cash Flow column, indicate whether the item is an operating activity (OA), investing activity (IA), or financing activity (FA). Use NA to indicate that an element was not affected by the event.

Assets		=	Equity		Rev.	−	Exp.	=	Net Inc.	Cash Flow
Cash	+ Land	=	Com. Stk.	+ PIC in Excess						

c. Prepare the journal entries to record these transactions.

LO 3

Exercise 11-8B *Treasury stock transactions*

Schwartz Corporation repurchased 2,000 shares of its own stock for $35 per share. The stock has a par of $10 per share. A month later Schwartz resold 800 shares of the treasury stock for $40 per share.

Required

a. Record the two events in general journal format.

b. What is the balance of the treasury stock account after these transactions?

LO 3

Exercise 11-9B *Recording and reporting treasury stock transactions*

The following information pertains to MGM Corp. at January 1, 2013:

Common stock, $10 par, 20,000 shares authorized, 1,000 shares issued and outstanding	$10,000
Paid-in capital in excess of par, common stock	15,000
Retained earnings	82,000

MGM Corp. completed the following transactions during 2013:

1. Issued 3,000 shares of $10 par common stock for $35 per share.
2. Repurchased 500 shares of its own common stock for $38 per share.
3. Resold 200 shares of treasury stock for $40 per share.

Required

a. How many shares of common stock were outstanding at the end of the period?

b. How many shares of common stock had been issued at the end of the period?

c. Prepare journal entries for these transactions and post them to T-accounts.

d. Prepare the stockholders' equity section of the balance sheet reflecting these transactions. Include the number of shares authorized, issued, and outstanding in the description of the common stock.

LO 4

Exercise 11-10B *Effect of cash dividends on financial statements*

On May 1, 2013, Sturgis Corporation declared a $100,000 cash dividend to be paid on May 31 to shareholders of record on May 15.

Required

a. Record the events occurring on May 1, May 15, and May 31 in a horizontal statements model like the following one. In the Cash Flow column, indicate whether the item is an operating activity (OA), investing activity (IA), or financing activity (FA).

Date	Assets	=	Liab.	+	Com. Stock	+	Ret. Earn.	Rev.	−	Exp.	=	Net Inc.	Cash Flow

b. Prepare journal entries for all events associated with the dividend.

Exercise 11-11B *Accounting for cumulative preferred dividends*

When Dixie Corporation was organized in January 2013, it immediately issued 3,000 shares of $50 par, 6 percent, cumulative preferred stock and 40,000 shares of $20 par common stock. Its earnings history is as follows: 2013, net loss of $35,000; 2014, net income of $110,000; 2015, net income of $215,000. The corporation did not pay a dividend in 2013.

Required

a. How much is the dividend arrearage as of January 1, 2014?

b. Assume that the board of directors declares a $35,000 cash dividend at the end of 2014 (remember that the 2013 and 2014 preferred dividends are due). How will the dividend be divided between the preferred and common stockholders?

Exercise 11-12B *Cash dividends for preferred and common shareholders*

Molton Corporation had the following stock issued and outstanding at January 1, 2013:

1. 120,000 shares of $1 par common stock.
2. 10,000 shares of $100 par, 6 percent, noncumulative preferred stock.

On June 10, Molton Corporation declared the annual cash dividend on its 10,000 shares of preferred stock and a $1 per share dividend for the common shareholders. The dividends will be paid on July 1 to the shareholders of record on June 20.

Required

a. Determine the total amount of dividends to be paid to the preferred shareholders and common shareholders.

b. Prepare general journal entries to record the declaration and payment of the cash dividends (be sure to date your entries).

Exercise 11-13B *Cash dividends: common and preferred stock*

Sibley Inc. had the following stock issued and outstanding at January 1, 2013:

1. 100,000 shares of no-par common stock.
2. 20,000 shares of $50 par, 7 percent, cumulative preferred stock. (Dividends are in arrears for one year, 2012.)

On March 8, 2013, Sibley declared a $225,000 cash dividend to be paid March 31 to shareholders of record on March 20.

Required

a. What amount of dividends will be paid to the preferred shareholders versus the common shareholders?

b. Prepare the journal entries required for these transactions. (Be sure to include the dates of the entries.)

Exercise 11-14B *Accounting for stock dividends*

Hogan Corporation issued a 5 percent stock dividend on 20,000 shares of its $10 par common stock. At the time of the dividend, the market value of the stock was $15 per share.

Required

a. Compute the amount of the stock dividend.

b. Show the effects of the stock dividend on the financial statements using a horizontal statements model like the following one:

Assets	=	Liab.	+	Com. Stock	+	PIC in Excess	+	Ret. Earn.	Rev.	−	Exp.	=	Net Inc.	Cash Flow

c. Prepare the journal entry to record the stock dividend.

LO 4

Exercise 11-15B   *Determining the effects of stock splits on the accounting records*

The market value of Mason Corporation's common stock had become excessively high. The stock was currently selling for $180 per share. To reduce the market price of the common stock, Mason declared a 3-for-1 stock split for the 100,000 outstanding shares of its $10 par value common stock.

Required

a. What entry will be made on the books of Mason Corporation for the stock split?
b. Determine the number of common shares outstanding and the par value after the split.
c. Explain how the market value of the stock will be affected by the stock split.

LO 5

Exercise 11-16B   *Corporate announcements*

Super Drugs (one of the three largest drug makers) just reported that its 2013 third quarter profits are essentially the same as the 2012 third quarter profits. In addition to this announcement, the same day, Super Drugs also announced that the Food and Drug Administration has just approved a new drug used to treat high blood pressure that Super Drugs developed. This new drug has been shown to be extremely effective and has few or no side effects. It will also be less expensive than the other drugs currently on the market.

Required

Using the above information, answer the following questions:

a. What do you think will happen to the stock price of Super Drugs on the day these two announcements are made? Explain your answer.
b. How will the balance sheet be affected on that day by the above announcements?
c. How will the income statement be affected on that day by the above announcements?
d. How will the statement of cash flows be affected on that day by the above announcements?

LO 5

Exercise 11-17B   *Using the P/E ratio*

During 2014 the Channel Corporation and the Dock Corporation reported net incomes of $90,000 and $130,000, respectively. Both companies had 25,000 shares of common stock issued and outstanding. The market price per share of Channel's stock was $47, while Dock's sold for $52 per share.

Required

a. Determine the P/E ratio for each company.
b. Based on the P/E ratios computed in Requirement *a*, which company do investors believe has the greater potential for growth in income?

LO 5

Exercise 11-18B   *The P/E ratio*

Required

Write a memo explaining why one company's P/E ratio may be higher than another company's P/E ratio.

PROBLEMS—SERIES B

LO 1

Problem 11-19B   *Effect of business structure on financial statements*

Montana Company was started on January 1, 2013, when it acquired $50,000 cash from the owners. During 2013, the company earned cash revenues of $25,000 and incurred cash expenses of $16,200. The company also paid cash distributions of $5,000.

Required

Prepare a 2013 income statement, capital statement (statement of changes in equity), balance sheet, and statement of cash flows under each of the following assumptions. (Consider each assumption separately.)

a. Montana is a sole proprietorship owned by Steve Montana.

b. Montana is a partnership with two partners, Steve Montana and Jane Montana. Steve Montana invested $30,000 and Jane Montana invested $20,000 of the $50,000 cash that was used to start the business. Jane was expected to assume the vast majority of the responsibility for operating the business. The partnership agreement called for Jane to receive 60 percent of the profits and Steve to get the remaining 40 percent. With regard to the $5,000 distribution, Jane withdrew $3,000 from the business and Steve $2,000.

c. Montana is a corporation. It issued 5,000 shares of $5 par common stock for $50,000 cash to start the business.

Problem 11-20B   *Different forms of business organization*

LO 1

Shawn Bates was working to establish a business enterprise with four of his wealthy friends. Each of the five individuals would receive a 20 percent ownership interest in the company. A primary goal of establishing the enterprise was to minimize the amount of income taxes paid. Assume that the five investors are in a 35 percent personal tax bracket and that the corporate tax rate is 25 percent. Also assume that the new company is expected to earn $200,000 of cash income before taxes during its first year of operation. All earnings are expected to be immediately distributed to the owners.

Required

Calculate the amount of after-tax cash flow available to each investor if the business is established as a partnership versus a corporation. Write a memo explaining the advantages and disadvantages of these two forms of business organization. Explain why a limited liability company may be a better choice than either a partnership or a corporation.

Problem 11-21B   *Analyzing journal entries for treasury stock transactions*

LO 2, 3

The following correctly prepared entries without explanations pertain to Corners Corporation:

	Account Title	Debit	Credit
1.	Cash	1,000,000	
	Common Stock		600,000
	Paid-in Capital in Excess of Par Value		400,000
2.	Treasury Stock	24,000	
	Cash		24,000
3.	Cash	21,000	
	Treasury Stock		18,000
	Paid-in Capital in Excess of Cost of Treasury Stock		3,000

The original sale (Entry 1) was for 200,000 shares, and the treasury stock was acquired for $6 per share (Entry 2).

Required

a. What was the sales price per share of the original stock issue?

b. How many shares of stock did the corporation acquire in Entry 2?

c. How many shares were reissued in Entry 3?

d. How many shares are outstanding immediately following Entries 2 and 3, respectively?

LO 2, 4

Problem 11-22B *Recording and reporting stock dividends*

Inman Co. completed the following transactions in 2013, the first year of operation:

1. Issued 30,000 shares of no-par common stock for $10 per share.
2. Issued 6,000 shares of $20 par, 6 percent, preferred stock for $20 per share.
3. Paid a cash dividend of $7,200 to preferred shareholders.
4. Issued a 10 percent stock dividend on no-par common stock. The market value at the dividend declaration date was $12 per share.
5. Later that year, issued a 2-for-1 split on the shares of outstanding common stock. The market price of the stock at that time was $40 per share.
6. Produced $130,000 of cash revenues and incurred $68,000 of cash operating expenses.
7. Closed the revenue, expense, and dividend accounts to retained earnings.

Required

a. Record each of these events in a horizontal statements model like the following one. In the Cash Flow column, indicate whether the item is an operating activity (OA), investing activity (IA), or financing activity (FA). Use NA to indicate that an element is not affected by the event.

Assets	=	Equity			Rev.	−	Exp.	=	Net Inc.	Cash Flow
		P. Stk.	+ C. Stk.	+ Ret. Earn.						

b. Record the 2013 transactions in general journal form and post them to T-accounts.

c. Prepare the stockholders' equity section of the balance sheet at the end of 2013. (Include all necessary information.)

d. Theoretically, what is the market value of the common stock after the stock split?

LO 2, 3, 4

Problem 11-23B *Recording and reporting stock transactions and cash dividends across two accounting cycles*

Western Corporation received a charter that authorized the issuance of 100,000 shares of $10 par common stock and 50,000 shares of $50 par, 5 percent cumulative preferred stock. Western Corporation completed the following transactions during its first two years of operation:

2013

Jan.	5	Sold 5,000 shares of the $10 par common stock for $15 per share.
	12	Sold 1,000 shares of the 5 percent preferred stock for $55 per share.
Apr.	5	Sold 30,000 shares of the $10 par common stock for $20 per share.
Dec.	31	During the year, earned $140,000 in cash revenue and paid $85,000 for cash operating expenses.
	31	Declared the cash dividend on the outstanding shares of preferred stock for 2013. The dividend will be paid on February 15 to stockholders of record on January 10, 2014.
	31	Closed the revenue, expense, and dividend accounts to the retained earnings account.

2014

Feb.	15	Paid the cash dividend declared on December 31, 2013.
Mar.	3	Sold 20,000 shares of the $50 par preferred stock for $56 per share.
May	5	Purchased 900 shares of the common stock as treasury stock at $21 per share.

Dec. 31 During the year, earned $190,000 in cash revenues and paid $75,000 for cash operating expenses.
  31 Declared the annual dividend on the preferred stock and a $0.60 per share dividend on the common stock.
  31 Closed revenue, expense, and dividend accounts to the retained earnings account.

Required

a. Prepare journal entries for these transactions for 2013 and 2014 and post them to T-accounts.

b. Prepare the balance sheets at December 31, 2013 and 2014.

c. What is the number of common shares *outstanding* at the end of 2013? At the end of 2014? How many common shares had been *issued* at the end of 2013? At the end of 2014? Explain any differences between issued and outstanding common shares for 2013 and for 2014.

Problem 11-24B *Recording and reporting treasury stock transactions*   LO 2, 3, 4

Atalla Co. completed the following transactions in 2013, the first year of operation:

1. Issued 15,000 shares of $10 par common stock for $10 per share.
2. Issued 2,000 shares of $20 stated value preferred stock for $20 per share.
3. Purchased 1,000 shares of common stock as treasury stock for $11 per share.
4. Declared a $2,000 cash dividend on preferred stock.
5. Sold 500 shares of treasury stock for $12 per share.
6. Paid $2,000 cash for the preferred dividend declared in Event 4.
7. Earned cash revenues of $62,000 and incurred cash expenses of $34,000.
8. Closed revenue, expense, and dividend accounts to the retained earnings account.
9. Appropriated $6,000 of retained earnings.

Required

a. Prepare journal entries to record these transactions and post them to T-accounts.

b. Prepare a balance sheet as of December 31, 2013.

Problem 11-25B *Analyzing the stockholders' equity section of the balance sheet*   LO 2, 3, 4

The stockholders' equity section of the balance sheet for Quinn Equipment Co. at December 31, 2013, is as follows:

Stockholders' Equity		
Paid-in capital		
Preferred stock, ? par value, 6% cumulative, 100,000 shares authorized, 5,000 shares issued and outstanding	$ 125,000	
Common stock, $20 stated value, 200,000 shares authorized, 50,000 shares issued and outstanding	1,000,000	
Paid-in capital in excess of par—Preferred	25,000	
Paid-in capital in excess of stated value—Common	500,000	
Total paid-in capital		$1,650,000
Retained earnings		420,000
Total stockholders' equity		$2,070,000

Note: The market value per share of the common stock is $40, and the market value per share of the preferred stock is $28.

Required

a. What is the par value per share of the preferred stock?

b. What is the dividend per share on the preferred stock?

c. What was the average issue price per share (price for which the stock was issued) of the common stock?

d. Explain the difference between the par value and the market price of the preferred stock.

e. If Cross declares a 2-for-1 stock split on the common stock, how many shares will be outstanding after the split? What amount will be transferred from the retained earnings account because of the stock split? Theoretically, what will be the market price of the common stock immediately after the stock split?

LO 2, 3, 4

Problem 11-26B *Effects of equity transactions on financial statements*

The following events were experienced by Baskin, Inc.:

1. Issued cumulative preferred stock.
2. Issued common stock for cash.
3. Issued noncumulative preferred stock.
4. Paid cash to purchase treasury stock.
5. Sold treasury stock for an amount of cash that was more than the cost of the treasury stock.
6. Declared a cash dividend.
7. Declared a 2-for-1 stock split on the common stock.
8. Distributed a stock dividend.
9. Appropriated retained earnings.
10. Paid a cash dividend that was previously declared.

Required

Show the effect of each event on the elements of the financial statements using a horizontal statements model like the following one. Use + for increase, − for decrease, and NA for not affected. In the Cash Flow column indicate whether the item is an operating activity (OA), investing activity (IA), or financing activity (FA). The first transaction is entered as an example.

Event No.	Assets	=	Liab.	+	Equity	Rev.	−	Exp.	=	Net Inc.	Cash Flow
1	+		NA		+	NA		NA		NA	+ FA

ANALYZE, THINK, COMMUNICATE

ATC 11-1   Business Applications Case   *Understanding real-world annual reports*

Use the Target Corporation's annual report in Appendix B to answer the following questions:

Required

a. What is the par value per share of Target's stock? How was the par value established?

b. How many shares of Target's common stock were *outstanding* as of January 29, 2011?

c. Target's annual report provides some details about the company's executive officers. How many are identified? What is their minimum, maximum, and average age? How many are females?

d. Target's balance sheet does not show a balance for treasury stock. Does this mean the company has not repurchased any of its own stock? Explain.

ATC 11-2 Group Assignment *Missing information*

Listed here are the stockholders' equity sections of three public companies for years ending in 2010 and 2009:

	2010	2009
Wendy's/Arby's Group (in thousands)		
Stockholders' equity		
Common stock, ?? stated value per share, authorized:		
1,500,000; 470,424 shares issued	$ 47,042	$ 47,042
Capital in excess of stated value	2,771,126	2,761,433
Retained earnings	(412,464)	(380,480)
Acc. other comp. income (loss)	7,017	(5,685)
Treasury stock, at cost: 52,050 in 2010 and 17,492 in 2009	(249,547)	(85,971)
Coca-Cola (in millions)		
Stockholders' equity		
Common stock, ?? par value per share, authorized:		
5,600; issued: 3,520 shares in 2010 and 2009	880	880
Capital surplus	10,057	8,537
Reinvested earnings	49,278	41,537
Acc. other comp. inc. (loss)	(1,450)	(757)
Treasury stock, at cost: (1,228 shares in 2010;		
1,217 shares in 2009)	(27,762)	(25,398)
Harley-Davidson (in thousands)		
Stockholders' equity		
Common stock, ?? par value per share, authorized:		
800,000, issued: 338,260 in 2010 and		
336,801 shares in 2009	3,382	3,368
Additional paid-in capital	908,055	871,100
Retained earnings	6,336,077	6,324,268
Acc. other comp. inc. (loss)	(366,222)	(417,898)
Treasury stock, at cost: 102,740 for 2010 and		
102,487 for 2009	4,674,426	4,672,720

Required

a. Divide the class in three sections and divide each section into groups of three to five students. Assign each section one of the companies.

Group Tasks

Based on the company assigned to your group, answer the following questions:

b. What is the per share par or stated value of the common stock in 2010?

c. What was the average issue price of the common stock for each year?

d. How many shares of stock are outstanding at the end of each year?

e. What is the average cost per share of the treasury stock for 2010?

f. Do the data suggest that your company was profitable in 2010?

g. Can you determine the amount of net income from the information given? What is missing?

h. What is the total stockholders' equity of your company for each year?

Class Discussion

i. Have each group select a representative to present the information about its company. Compare the share issue price and the par or stated value of the companies.

j. Compare the average issue price to the current market price for each of the companies. Speculate about what might cause the difference.

ATC 11-3   Real-World Case   *Which stock is most valuable?*

Listed here are data for five companies. These data are from companies' annual reports for the fiscal year indicated. The market price per share is the closing price of the companies' stock as of April 20, 2011. Except for market price per share, all amounts are in thousands. The shares outstanding number is the number of shares reported on the companies' balance sheets.

Company	Fiscal Year	Net Earnings	Shares Outstanding	Stockholders' Equity	Market Price per Share
Brinks	12/31/2010	$ 57,100	48,200	$ 583,100	$33.01
Bristol-Myers Squibb	12/31/2010	4,513,000	1,713,000	15,638,000	27.88
eBay	12/31/2010	1,800,961	1,305,593	15,302,179	31.61
Ford	12/31/2010	6,561,000	3,449,000	(642,000)	14.71
Garmin	12/25/2010	584,603	196,979	3,049,562	33.90
Starbucks	10/03/2010	945,600	744,400	3,682,300	36.38

Required

a. Compute the earnings per share (EPS) for each company.

b. Compute the P/E ratio for each company.

c. Using the P/E ratios, rank the companies' stock in the order that the stock market appears to value the companies, from most valuable to least valuable. Identify reasons the ranking based on P/E ratios may not represent the market's optimism about one or two companies.

d. Compute the book value per share for each company.

e. Compare each company's book value per share to its market price per share. Based on the data, rank the companies from most valuable to least valuable. (The higher the ratio of market value to book value, the greater the value the stock market appears to be assigning to a company's stock.)

ATC 11-4   Business Applications Case   *Performing ratio analysis using real-world data*

Chevron Corporation is one of the world's largest oil and natural gas companies. The following data were taken from the company's 2010 annual report:

	Fiscal Years Ending	
	December 31, 2010	December 31, 2009
Net earnings (in millions)	$19,186	$10,483
Earnings per share	$9.53	$5.26
The following data were taken from public stock-price quotes:		
Stock price per share on February 28, 2011 (Two months after the end of Chevron's 2010 fiscal year.)		$103.75
Stock price per share on March 1, 2010 (Two months after the end of Chevron's 2009 fiscal year.)		$72.81

Required

a. Compute Chevron's price-earnings ratio for February 28, 2011, and March 1, 2010.

b. Did the financial markets appear to be more optimistic about Chevron's future performance on February 28, 2011, or March 1, 2010?

c. Based on the information provided, estimate approximately how many shares of stock Chevron had outstanding as of December 31, 2010.

ATC 11-5 Business Applications Case *Performing ratio analysis using real-world data*

Google, Inc., operates the world's largest Internet search engine. International Business Machines Corporation (IBM) is one of the world's largest computer hardware and software companies. The following data were taken from the companies' December 31, 2010, annual reports:

	Google, Inc.	IBM
Net earnings (in millions)	$8,505	$14,833
Earnings per share	$26.69	$11.69
The following data were taken from public stock-price quotes:		
Stock price per share on February 28, 2011 (Two months after the end of their 2010 fiscal years.)	$613.40	$161.88

Required

a. Compute the price-earnings ratios for each company as of February 28, 2011.

b. Which company's future performance did the financial markets appear to be more optimistic about as of February 28, 2011?

c. Provide some reasons why the market may view one company's future more optimistically than the other.

ATC 11-6 Writing Assignment *Comparison of organizational forms*

Jim Baku and Scott Hanson are thinking about opening a new restaurant. Baku has extensive marketing experience but does not know that much about food preparation. However, Hanson is an excellent chef. Both will work in the business, but Baku will provide most of the funds necessary to start the business. At this time, they cannot decide whether to operate the business as a partnership or a corporation.

Required

Prepare a written memo to Baku and Hanson describing the advantages and disadvantages of each organizational form. Also, from the limited information provided, recommend the organizational form you think they should use.

ATC 11-7 Ethical Dilemma *Bad news versus very bad news*

Louise Stinson, the chief financial officer of Bostonian Corporation, was on her way to the president's office. She was carrying the latest round of bad news. There would be no executive bonuses this year. Corporate profits were down. Indeed, if the latest projections held true, the company would report a small loss on the year-end income statement. Executive bonuses were tied to corporate profits. The executive compensation plan provided for 10 percent of net earnings to be set aside for bonuses. No profits meant no bonuses. While things looked bleak, Stinson had a plan that might help soften the blow.

After informing the company president of the earnings forecast, Stinson made the following suggestion: Since the company was going to report a loss anyway, why not report a big loss? She reasoned that the directors and stockholders would not be much more angry if the company reported a large loss than if it reported a small one. There were several questionable assets that could be written down in the current year. This would increase the current year's loss but would reduce expenses in subsequent accounting periods. For example, the company was carrying damaged inventory that was estimated to have a value of $2,500,000. If this estimate were revised to $500,000, the company would have to recognize a $2,000,000 loss in the current year. However, next year when the goods were sold, the expense for cost of goods sold would be $2,000,000 less and profits would be higher by that amount. Although the directors would be angry this year, they would certainly be happy next year. The strategy would also have the benefit of adding $200,000 to next year's executive bonus pool ($2,000,000 × 0.10). Furthermore, it could not hurt this year's bonus pool because there would be no pool this year since the company is going to report a loss.

Some of the other items that Stinson is considering include (1) converting from straight-line to accelerated depreciation, (2) increasing the percentage of receivables estimated to be uncollectible in the current year and lowering the percentage in the following year, and (3) raising the percentage of estimated warranty claims in the current period and lowering it in the following period. Finally, Stinson notes that two of the company's department stores have been experiencing losses. The company could sell these stores this year and thereby improve earnings next year. Stinson admits that the sale would result in significant losses this year, but she smiles as she thinks of next year's bonus check.

Required

a. Explain how each of the three numbered strategies for increasing the amount of the current year's loss would affect the stockholders' equity section of the balance sheet in the current year. How would the other elements of the balance sheet be affected?

b. If Stinson's strategy were effectively implemented, how would it affect the stockholders' equity in subsequent accounting periods?

c. Comment on the ethical implications of running the company for the sake of management (maximization of bonuses) versus the maximization of return to stockholders.

d. Formulate a bonus plan that will motivate managers to maximize the value of the firm instead of motivating them to manipulate the reporting process.

e. How would Stinson's strategy of overstating the amount of the reported loss in the current year affect the company's current P/E ratio?

ATC 11-8 Research Assignment *Analyzing Big Lots' equity structure*

Using either Big Lots, Inc.'s most current Form 10-K or the company's annual report, answer the questions below. To obtain the Form 10-K use either the EDGAR system following the instructions in Appendix A or the company's website. The company's annual report is available on its website.

Required

a. What is the *book value* of Big Lots' stockholders' equity that is shown on the company's balance sheet? What is its book value per share?

b. What is the par value of Big Lots' common stock?

c. Does Big Lots have any treasury stock? If so, how many shares of treasury stock does the company hold?

d. Why does the stock of a company such as a Big Lots have a market value that is higher than its book value?

ATC 11-9 Spreadsheet Analysis *Using Excel*

Annette's Accessories had the following stock issued and outstanding at January 1, 2013:

150,000 shares of $1 par common stock
10,000 shares of $50 par, 8%, cumulative preferred stock

On March 5, 2013, Annette's declared a $100,000 cash dividend to be paid March 31 to shareholders of record on March 21.

Required

Set up a spreadsheet to calculate the total amount of dividends to be paid to preferred and common shareholders under the following alternative situations:

a. No dividends are in arrears for preferred shareholders.

b. One year's worth of dividends is in arrears for preferred shareholders.

c. Two years' worth of dividends is in arrears for preferred shareholders.

d. Instead of a $100,000 dividend, Annette's paid a $70,000 dividend and one year of dividends was in arrears.

Spreadsheet Tips

The following spreadsheet provides one method of setting up formulas for all possible alternatives. The spreadsheet also reflects the results of Requirement *a*.

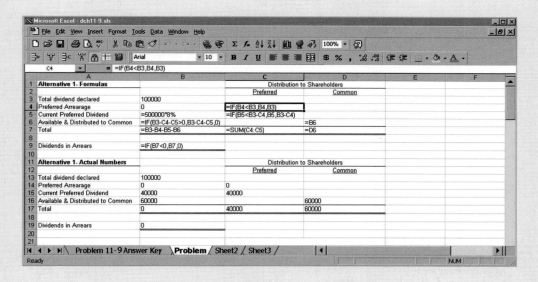

Notice the use of the IF function. The IF function looks like =IF(condition, true, false). To use the IF function, first describe a certain condition to Excel. Next indicate the desired result if that condition is found to be true. Finally, indicate the desired result if that condition is found to be false. Notice in cell C4 of the spreadsheet (dividends in arrears distributed to preferred shareholders) that the condition provided is B4<B3, which is asking whether the dividends in arrears are less than the total dividend. If this condition is true, the formula indicates to display B4, which is the amount of the dividends in arrears. If the condition is false, the formula indicates that B3 should be displayed, which is the total amount of the dividend.

The IF function can also be used to determine the amount of the current dividend distributed to preferred shareholders, the amount available for common shareholders, and the dividends in arrears after the dividend.

ATC 11-10   Spreadsheet Assignment   *Mastering Excel*

Required

Complete Requirement *a* of Problem 11-22B using an Excel spreadsheet.

COMPREHENSIVE PROBLEM

The trial balance of Pacilio Security Services Inc. as of January 1, 2021, had the following normal balances:

Cash	$113,718
Petty cash	100
Accounts receivable	39,390
Allowance for doubtful accounts	4,662
Supplies	210
Merchandise inventory (48 @ $300)	14,400
Equipment	9,000
Van	27,000
Building	125,000
Accumulated depreciation	28,075
Land	25,000
Sales tax payable	390
Employee income tax payable	1,000
FICA—Social Security tax payable	840
FICA—Medicare tax payable	210
Warranty payable	918
Unemployment tax payable	945
Notes payable—Building	92,762
Bonds payable	50,000
Discount on bonds payable	800
Common stock	50,000
Retained earnings	124,816

During 2021, Pacilio Security Services experienced the following transactions:

1. Paid the sales tax payable from 2020.
2. Paid the balance of the payroll liabilities due for 2020 (federal income tax, FICA taxes, and unemployment taxes).
3. Issued 5,000 additional shares of the $5 par value common stock for $8 per share and 1,000 shares of $50 stated value, 5 percent cumulative preferred stock for $52 per share.
4. Purchased $500 of supplies on account.
5. Purchased 190 alarm systems at a cost of $310. Cash was paid for the purchase.
6. After numerous attempts to collect from customers, wrote off $3,670 of uncollectible accounts receivable.
7. Sold 210 alarm systems for $600 each plus sales tax of 5 percent. All sales were on account. (Be sure to compute cost of goods sold using the FIFO cost flow method.)
8. Billed $125,000 of monitoring services for the year. Credit card sales amounted to $58,000, and the credit card company charged a 4 percent fee. The remaining $67,000 were sales on account. Sales tax is not charged on this service.
9. Replenished the petty cash fund on June 30. The fund had $10 cash and receipts of $75 for yard mowing and $15 for office supplies expense.
10. Collected the amount due from the credit card company.
11. Paid the sales tax collected on $105,000 of the alarm sales.
12. Collected $198,000 of accounts receivable during the year.
13. Paid installers and other employees a total of $96,000 for salaries for the year. Assume the Social Security tax rate is 6 percent and the Medicare tax rate is 1.5 percent. Federal income taxes withheld amounted to $10,600. No employee exceeded $110,000 in total wages. The net salaries were paid in cash.
14. On October 1, declared a dividend on the preferred stock and a $1 per share dividend on the common stock to be paid to shareholders of record on October 15, payable on November 1, 2021.

15. Paid $1,625 in warranty repairs during the year.
16. On November 1, 2021, paid the dividends that had been previously declared.
17. Paid $18,500 of advertising expense during the year.
18. Paid $6,100 of utilities expense for the year.
19. Paid the payroll liabilities, both the amounts withheld from the salaries plus the employer share of Social Security tax and Medicare tax, on $88,000 of the salaries plus $9,200 of the federal income tax that was withheld.
20. Paid the accounts payable.
21. Paid bond interest and amortized the discount. The bond was issued in 2020 and pays interest at 6%.
22. Paid the annual installment of $14,238 on the amortized note. The interest rate for the note is 7%.

Adjustments

23. There was $190 of supplies on hand at the end of the year.
24. Recognized the uncollectible accounts expense for the year using the allowance method. Pacilio now estimates that 1 percent of sales on account will not be collected.
25. Recognized depreciation expense on the equipment, van, and building. The equipment, purchased in 2018, has a five-year life and a $2,000 salvage value. The van has a four-year life and a $6,000 salvage value. The building has a 40-year life and a $10,000 salvage value. The company uses straight-line for the equipment and the building. The van is fully depreciated.
26. The alarms systems sold in transaction 7 were covered with a one-year warranty. Pacilio estimated that the warranty cost would be 2 percent of alarm sales.
27. The unemployment tax on the three employees has not been paid. Record the accrued unemployment tax on the salaries for the year. The unemployment tax rate is 4.5 percent and gross wages for all three employees exceeded $7,000.
28. Recognized the employer Social Security and Medicard payroll tax that has not been paid on $8,000 of salaries expense.

Required

a. Record the above transactions in general journal form. Round all amounts to the nearest whole dollar.
b. Post the transactions to the T-accounts.
c. Prepare a trial balance.
d. Prepare an income statement, a balance sheet, and a statement of cash flows.
e. Close the temporary accounts to retained earnings.
f. Post the closing entries to the T-accounts and prepare a post-closing trial balance.

Statement of Cash Flows

LEARNING OBJECTIVES

After you have mastered the material in this chapter, you will be able to:

LO1 Prepare the operating activities section of a statement of cash flows using the indirect method.

LO2 Prepare the operating activities section of a statement of cash flows using the direct method.

LO3 Prepare the investing activities section of a statement of cash flows.

LO4 Prepare the financing activities section of a statement of cash flows.

CHAPTER OPENING

To make informed investment and credit decisions, financial statement users need information to help them assess the amounts, timing, and uncertainty of a company's prospective cash flows. This chapter explains more about the items reported on the statement of cash flows and describes a more practical way to prepare the statement than analyzing every entry in the cash account. As previously shown, the statement of cash flows reports how a company obtained and spent cash during an accounting period. Sources of cash are **cash inflows,** and uses are **cash outflows.** Cash receipts (inflows) and payments (outflows) are reported as either operating activities, investing activities, or financing activities.

The Curious Accountant

As described in *The Curious Accountant* for Chapter 11, Tesla Motors, Inc., began operations in 2003. It did not sell its first car until 2008, and did not begin selling its stock to the public until June 2010. It has lost money every year it has been in existence, and by December 31, 2010, it had total lifetime losses of approximately $415 million. Its losses for 2010 alone were $154 million.

How could Tesla lose so much money and still be able to pay its bills? (Answer on page 647.)

AN OVERVIEW OF THE STATEMENT OF CASH FLOWS

The statement of cash flows provides information about cash coming into and going out of a business during an accounting period. Cash flows are classified into one of three categories: operating activities, investing activities, or financing activities. A separate section also displays any significant noncash investing and financing activities. Descriptions of these categories and how they are presented in the statement of cash flows follow.

Operating Activities

Routine cash inflows and outflows resulting from running (operating) a business are reported in the **operating activities** section of the statement of cash flows. Cash flows reported as operating activities include:

1. Cash receipts from revenues including interest and dividend revenue.
2. Cash payments for expenses including interest expense. Recall that dividend payments are not expenses. Dividend payments are reported in the financing activities section.

EXHIBIT 12.1

Operating Activities—Direct Method

Cash Flows from Operating Activities	
Cash receipts from customers	$400
Cash payments for expenses	(350)
Net cash flow from operating activities	$ 50

Under generally accepted accounting principles, the operating activities section of the statement of cash flows can be presented using either the *direct* or the *indirect* method. The **direct method** explicitly (*directly*) identifies the major *sources* and *uses* of cash. To illustrate, assume that during 2013 New South Company earns revenue on account of $500 and collects $400 cash from customers. Further assume the company incurs $390 of expenses on account and pays $350 cash to settle accounts payable. Exhibit 12.1 shows the operating activities section of the statement of cash flows using the *direct method.*

In contrast, the **indirect method** starts with net income as reported on the income statement followed by the adjustments necessary to convert the accrual-based net income figure to a cash-basis equivalent. To illustrate, begin with New South Company's income statement based on the above assumptions:

Revenues	$500
Expenses	(390)
Net income	$110

Converting the net income of $110 to the net cash flow from operating activities of $50 requires the following adjustments.

1. New South earned $500 of revenue but collected only $400 in cash. The remaining $100 will be collected in the next accounting period. This $100 *increase in accounts receivable* must be *subtracted* from net income to determine cash flow because it increased net income but did not increase cash.
2. New South incurred $390 of expense but paid only $350 in cash. The remaining $40 will be paid in the next accounting period. This $40 *increase in accounts payable* must be *added* back to net income to determine cash flow because it decreased net income but did not use cash.

EXHIBIT 12.2

Operating Activities—Indirect Method

Cash Flows from Operating Activities	
Net income	$110
Subtract: Increase in accounts receivable	(100)
Add: Increase in accounts payable	40
Net cash flow from operating activities	$ 50

Exhibit 12.2 shows the operating activities section of the statement of cash flows using the indirect method.

Compare the direct method presented in Exhibit 12.1 with the indirect method presented in Exhibit 12.2. Both methods report $50 of net cash flow from operating activities. They represent two different approaches to computing the same amount.

Because people typically find the direct method easier to understand, the Financial Accounting Standards Board (FASB) recommends it. Most companies, however, use the indirect method. Why? Back when the FASB adopted a requirement for companies to include a statement of cash flows in their published financial statements, most companies used accounting systems that were compatible with the indirect method. It was therefore easier to prepare the new statement under the indirect method using existing systems than to create new record-keeping systems compatible with the direct method.

The FASB continues to advocate the direct method and a growing number of companies use it. Since the majority of companies continue to use the indirect method, however, financial statement users should understand both methods.

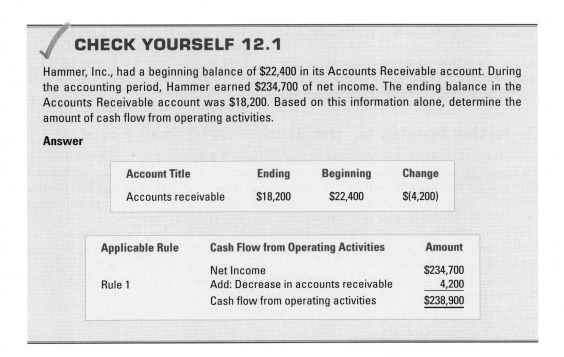

✓ CHECK YOURSELF 12.1

Hammer, Inc., had a beginning balance of $22,400 in its Accounts Receivable account. During the accounting period, Hammer earned $234,700 of net income. The ending balance in the Accounts Receivable account was $18,200. Based on this information alone, determine the amount of cash flow from operating activities.

Answer

Account Title	Ending	Beginning	Change
Accounts receivable	$18,200	$22,400	$(4,200)

Applicable Rule	Cash Flow from Operating Activities	Amount
	Net Income	$234,700
Rule 1	Add: Decrease in accounts receivable	4,200
	Cash flow from operating activities	$238,900

Investing Activities

For a business, long-term assets are investments. Cash flows related to acquiring or disposing of long-term assets are therefore reported in the **investing activities** section of the statement of cash flows. Cash flows reported as investing activities include:

1. Cash receipts (inflows) from selling property, plant, equipment, or marketable securities as well as collections from credit instruments such as notes or mortgages receivable.

2. Cash payments (outflows) for purchasing property, plant, equipment, or marketable securities as well as for making loans to borrowers.

Financing Activities

Cash flows related to borrowing (short- or long-term) and stockholders' equity are reported in the **financing activities** section of the statement of cash flows. Cash flows reported as financing activities include:

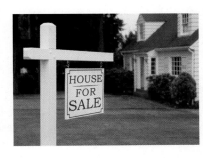

1. Cash receipts (inflows) from borrowing money and issuing stock.

2. Cash payments (outflows) to repay debt, purchase treasury stock, and pay dividends.

The classification of cash flows is based on the type of activity, not the type of account. For example, buying another company's common stock is an investing activity, but issuing a company's own common stock is a financing activity. Receiving dividends from a common stock investment is an operating activity, and paying dividends to a company's own stockholders is a financing activity. Similarly, loaning money is an investing activity, although borrowing it is a financing activity. Focus on the type of activity rather than the type of account when classifying cash flows as operating, investing, or financing activities.

Noncash Investing and Financing Activities

Companies sometimes undertake significant **noncash investing and financing activities** such as acquiring a long-term asset in exchange for common stock. Since these types of transactions do not involve exchanging cash they are not reported in the main body of the statement of cash flows. However, because the FASB requires that all material investing and financing activities be disclosed, whether or not they involve exchanging cash, companies must include with the statement of cash flows a separate schedule of any noncash investing and financing activities.

Reporting Format for the Statement of Cash Flows

Cash flow categories are reported in the following order: (1) operating activities; (2) investing activities; and (3) financing activities. In each category, the difference between the inflows and outflows is presented as a net cash inflow or outflow for the category. These net amounts are combined to determine the net change (increase or decrease) in the company's cash for the period. The net change in cash is combined with the beginning cash balance to determine the ending cash balance. The ending cash balance on the statement of cash flows is the same as the cash balance reported on the balance sheet. The schedule of noncash investing and financing activities is typically presented at the bottom of the statement of cash flows. Exhibit 12.3 outlines this format.

EXHIBIT 12.3	Format for Statement of Cash Flows

WESTERN COMPANY
Statement of Cash Flows
For the Year Ended December 31, 2013

Cash flows from operating activities	
Net increase (decrease) from operating activities	XXX
Cash flows from investing activities	
Net increase (decrease) from investing activities	XXX
Cash flows from financing activities	
Net increase (decrease) from financing activities	XXX
Net increase (decrease) in cash	XXX
Plus: Beginning cash balance	XXX
Ending cash balance	XXX
Schedule of Noncash Investing and Financing Activities	
List of significant noncash transactions	XXX

As indicated in Exhibit 12.4, most companies present the statement of cash flows as the last of the four primary financial statements. However, a sizable number of companies present it after the income statement and balance sheet but before the statement of changes in stockholders' equity. Some companies place the statement of cash flows first, before the other three statements.

EXHIBIT 12.4

Placement of Statement of Cash Flows Relative to Other Financial Statements

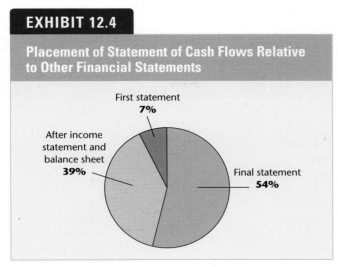

First statement 7%

After income statement and balance sheet 39%

Final statement 54%

Data Source: AICPA, *Accounting Trends and Techniques.*

PREPARING A STATEMENT OF CASH FLOWS

Most of the data needed to construct a statement of cash flows can be obtained from two successive balance sheets and the intervening income statement. Certain information from the long-term asset records is also usually required. To illustrate, refer to the financial statements for New South Company presented in Exhibit 12.5. Notice that cash decreased from $400 at the end of 2013 to $300 at the end of 2014. The statement of cash flows explains what caused this $100 decrease.

EXHIBIT 12.5   Financial Statements for New South Company

NEW SOUTH COMPANY
Balance Sheets
As of December 31

	2014	2013
Current assets:		
Cash	$ 300	$ 400
Accounts receivable	1,000	1,200
Interest receivable	400	300
Inventory	8,900	8,200
Prepaid insurance	1,100	1,400
Total current assets	11,700	$11,500
Long-term assets		
Investment securities	5,100	3,500
Store fixtures	5,400	4,800
Accumulated depreciation	(900)	(1,200)
Land	8,200	6,000
Total long-term assets	17,800	13,100
Total assets	$29,500	$24,600
Current liabilities:		
Accounts payable—inventory purchases	$ 800	$ 1,100
Salaries payable	1,000	900
Other operating expenses payable	1,500	1,300
Interest payable	300	500
Unearned rent revenue	600	1,600
Total current liabilities	4,200	5,400

continued

EXHIBIT 12.5   *concluded*

NEW SOUTH COMPANY
Balance Sheets
As of December 31

	2014	2013
Long-term liabilities		
Mortgage payable	2,200	0
Bonds payable	1,000	4,000
Total long-term liabilities	3,200	4,000
Stockholders' equity		
Common stock	10,000	8,000
Retained earnings	12,700	7,200
Treasury stock	(600)	0
Total stockholders' equity	22,100	15,200
Total liabilities and stockholders' equity	$29,500	$24,600

NEW SOUTH COMPANY
Income Statement
For the Year Ended December 31, 2014

Sales revenue		$20,600
Cost of goods sold		(10,500)
Gross margin		10,100
Operating expenses		
Depreciation expense	$(1,000)	
Salaries expense	(2,700)	
Insurance expense	(1,300)	
Other operating expenses	(1,400)	
Total operating expenses		(6,400)
Income from sales business		3,700
Other income—rent revenue		2,400
Operating income		6,100
Nonoperating revenue and expense		
Interest revenue	700	
Interest expense	(400)	
Gain on sale of store fixtures	600	
Total nonoperating items		900
Net income		$ 7,000

Note 1: No investment securities were sold during 2014.
Note 2: During 2014, New South sold store fixtures that had originally cost $1,700. At the time of sale, accumulated depreciation on the fixtures was $1,300.
Note 3: Land was acquired during 2014 by issuing a mortgage note payable. No land sales occurred during 2014.

PREPARING THE OPERATING ACTIVITIES SECTION OF A STATEMENT OF CASH FLOWS USING THE INDIRECT METHOD

LO 1

Prepare the operating activities section of a statement of cash flows using the indirect method.

Recall that the indirect approach begins with the amount of net income. Many aspects of accrual accounting, such as recognizing revenues and expenses on account, can cause differences between the amount of net income reported on a company's income statement and the amount of net cash flow it reports from operating activities.

Answers to The Curious Accountant

First, it should be remembered that GAAP requires earnings and losses be computed on an accrual basis. A company can have negative earnings and still have positive cash flows from operating activities. This was not the case at Tesla Motors. From 2008 through 2010 the company's cash flows from operating activities totaled a negative $261 million. Although this is less than the $293 million of cumulative net losses the company incurred during the same period, negative cash flows do not pay the bills.

In its early years of operations, Tesla, like many new companies, was able to stay in business because of the cash it raised through financing activities. Obviously, a company cannot operate indefinitely without generating cash from operating activities. Individuals and institutions who are willing to buy a company's stock or loan it cash in its early years will disappear if they do not believe the company will eventually begin earning profits, and positive cash flows from operations. Exhibit 12.6 presents Tesla's statements of cash flows from 2008 through 2010.

EXHIBIT 12.6

TESLA MOTORS, INC.
Consolidated Statements of Cash Flows
(in thousands)

	Year Ended December 31		
	2010	2009	2008
Cash flows from operating activities			
Net loss	$(154,328)	$(55,740)	$(82,782)
Adjustments to reconcile net loss to net cash used in operating activities:			
Depreciation and amortization	10,623	6,940	4,157
Change in fair value of warrant liabilities	5,022	1,128	2,800
Gain on extinguishment of convertible notes and warrants	—	(1,468)	(1,245)
Stock-based compensation	21,156	1,434	437
Excess tax benefits from stock-based compensation	(74)	—	—
Loss on abandonment of fixed assets	8	385	—
Inventory write-downs	951	1,353	4,297
Interest on convertible notes	—	2,686	3,692
Changes in operating assets and liabilities			
Accounts receivable	(3,222)	(168)	(3,261)
Inventory	(20,115)	(7,925)	(18,839)
Prepaid expenses and other current assets	(4,977)	(2,042)	750
Operating lease assets	(8,398)	—	—
Other assets	(463)	(445)	12
Accounts payable	(212)	902	8,815
Accrued liabilities	13,345	3,387	2,633
Deferred development compensation	(156)	(10,017)	10,173
Deferred revenue	4,801	(1,456)	4,073
Reservation payments	4,707	$(21,971)	10,684
Other long-term liabilities	3,515	2,192	1,192
Net cash used in operating activities	(127,817)	(80,825)	(52,412)

continued

EXHIBIT 12.6   *concluded*

TESLA MOTORS, INC.
Consolidated Statements of Cash Flows
(in thousands)

	Year Ended December 31		
	2010	**2009**	**2008**
Cash flows from investing activities			
Payments related to acquisition of Fremont manufacturing facility and related assets	(65,210)	—	—
Purchases of property and equipment excluding capital leases	(40,203)	(11,884)	(10,630)
Transfer of restricted cash into our dedicated Department of Energy account	(100,000)	—	—
Withdrawals out of our dedicated Department of Energy account	26,403	—	—
Increase in other restricted cash	(1,287)	(2,360)	(960)
Net cash used in investing activities	(180,297)	(14,244)	(11,590)
Cash flows from financing activities			
Proceeds from issuance of common stock in initial public offering	188,842	—	—
Proceeds from issuance of common stock in Toyota private placement	50,000	—	—
Proceeds from issuance of common stock in Panasonic private placement	30,000	—	—
Proceeds from issuance of Series F convertible preferred stock, net of issuance costs of $122	—	82,378	—
Proceeds from issuance of Series E convertible preferred stock, net of issuance costs of $556	—	49,444	—
Principal payments on capital leases and other debt	(315)	(322)	(191)
Proceeds from long-term debt and other long-term liabilities	71,828	—	1,000
Proceeds from issuance of convertible notes and warrants	—	25,468	54,782
Proceeds from exercise of stock options	1,350	497	477
Excess tax benefits from stock-based compensation	74	—	—
Common stock and loan facility issuance costs	(3,734)	(2,046)	—
Net cash provided by financing activities	338,045	$155,419	56,068
Net increase (decrease) in cash and cash equivalents	29,931	60,350	(7,934)
Cash and cash equivalents at beginning of period	69,627	9,277	17,211
Cash and cash equivalents at end of period	$ 99,558	$ 69,627	$ 9,277

Most of the differences between revenue and expense recognition and cash flows are related to changes in the balances of the noncash current assets and current liabilities.

Indirect Method—Reconciliation Approach

The following section of this chapter examines the relationships between items reported on the income statement and the related assets and liabilities. Begin by reconciling the *noncash* current asset and current liability amounts shown on the balance sheets in Exhibit 12.5. *Do not include Cash in this analysis.* The amount of the change in the cash balance is the result of not only operating activities but also investing and financing activities.

Reconciliation of Accounts Receivable

Use the information in Exhibit 12.5 to prepare the following reconciliation of Accounts Receivable. The beginning and ending balances appear on the balance sheets. The *increase due to revenue recognized on account* is the sales revenue reported on the income statement.

Table 1 Reconciliation of Accounts Receivable	
Beginning balance	$ 1,200
Increase due to revenue recognized on account	20,600
Decrease due to cash collections from customers	? = (20,800)
Ending balance	$ 1,000

To balance Accounts Receivable, the *decrease due to cash collections from customers* must be $20,800.[1]

The reconciliation shows that the $200 decrease in the accounts receivable balance occurred because *cash collections from customers* were $200 more than the amount of *revenue recognized on account* ($20,800 versus $20,600). Since the amount of cash collected is more than the amount of revenue recognized, we add $200 to the amount of net income to determine net cash flow from operating activities (Reference No. 1 in Exhibit 12.7, p. 653).

Reconciliation of Interest Receivable

The beginning and ending balances appear on the balance sheets in Exhibit 12.5. The *increase due to interest revenue recognized on account* is the interest revenue reported on the income statement.

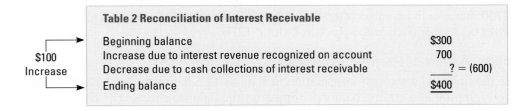

Table 2 Reconciliation of Interest Receivable	
Beginning balance	$300
Increase due to interest revenue recognized on account	700
Decrease due to cash collections of interest receivable	? = (600)
Ending balance	$400

To balance Interest Receivable, the *decrease due to cash collections of interest receivable* must be $600.

The reconciliation shows that the $100 increase in the interest receivable balance occurred because *cash collections of interest* were $100 less than the *interest revenue recognized on account* ($600 versus $700). Since the amount of cash collected is less than the amount of revenue recognized, we subtract the $100 from the amount of net income to determine net cash flow from operating activities (Reference No. 2 in Exhibit 12.7).

Reconciliation of Inventory and Accounts Payable

To simplify computing the amount of cash paid for inventory purchases, assume that all inventory purchases are made on account. The computation requires two steps. First, Inventory must be analyzed to determine the amount of inventory purchased. Second, Accounts Payable must be analyzed to determine the amount of cash paid to purchase inventory.

Use the financial statement information in Exhibit 12.5 to prepare the following Inventory reconciliation. The beginning and ending balances appear on the balance sheets. The *decrease due to recognizing cost of goods sold* is the cost of goods sold reported on the income statement.

[1]This text uses the simplifying assumption that all sales occur on account.

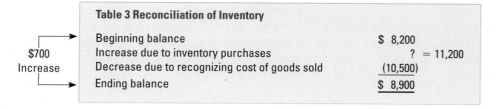

Table 3 Reconciliation of Inventory

Beginning balance	$ 8,200
Increase due to inventory purchases	? = 11,200
Decrease due to recognizing cost of goods sold	(10,500)
Ending balance	$ 8,900

$700 Increase

To balance Inventory, the *increase due to inventory purchases* must be $11,200.

Assuming the inventory was purchased on account, the $11,200 of inventory purchases determined above equals the *increase due to inventory purchases* used in the reconciliation of Accounts Payable below. The beginning and ending balances appear on the balance sheets in Exhibit 12.5.

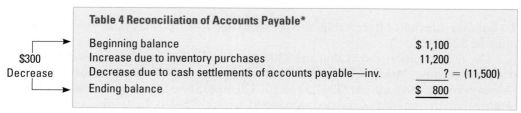

Table 4 Reconciliation of Accounts Payable*

Beginning balance	$ 1,100
Increase due to inventory purchases	11,200
Decrease due to cash settlements of accounts payable—inv.	? = (11,500)
Ending balance	$ 800

$300 Decrease

*Assume that Accounts Payable is used for purchases of inventory only.

To balance Accounts Payable, the *decrease due to cash settlements of accounts payable—inventory* (cash paid to purchase inventory) must be $11,500.

Since the amount of *cash paid to purchase inventory* is $1,000 more than the amount of *cost of goods sold* recognized on the income statement ($11,500 versus $10,500), we subtract the $1,000 difference from the amount of net income to determine net cash flow from operating activities. In Exhibit 12.7 the $1,000 subtraction is divided between a $700 increase in inventory (Reference No. 3 in Exhibit 12.7) and a $300 decrease in accounts payable (Reference No. 4 in Exhibit 12.7).

Reconciliation of Prepaid Insurance

Use the financial statement information in Exhibit 12.5 to reconcile Prepaid Insurance. The beginning and ending balances appear on the balance sheets. The *decrease due to recognizing insurance expense* is the insurance expense reported on the income statement.

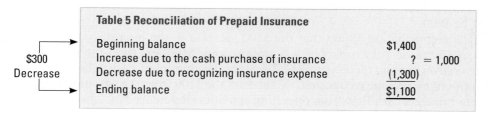

Table 5 Reconciliation of Prepaid Insurance

Beginning balance	$1,400
Increase due to the cash purchase of insurance	? = 1,000
Decrease due to recognizing insurance expense	(1,300)
Ending balance	$1,100

$300 Decrease

To balance Prepaid Insurance, the amount of the *increase due to the cash purchase of insurance* must be $1,000.

The reconciliation shows that the $300 decrease in the prepaid insurance balance occurred because *cash paid to purchase insurance* was $300 less than the amount of *insurance expense recognized* ($1,000 versus $1,300). Since the amount of cash paid is less than the amount of expense recognized, we add $300 to the amount of net income to determine the net cash flow from operating activities (Reference No. 5 in Exhibit 12.7).

Reconciliation of Salaries Payable

Use the financial statement information in Exhibit 12.5 to reconcile Salaries Payable. The beginning and ending balance appear on the balance sheets. The *increase due to recognizing salary expense on account* is the salaries expense reported on the income statement.

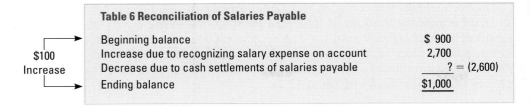

Table 6 Reconciliation of Salaries Payable

$100
Increase

Beginning balance	$ 900
Increase due to recognizing salary expense on account	2,700
Decrease due to cash settlements of salaries payable	? = (2,600)
Ending balance	$1,000

To balance Salaries Payable, the amount of the *decrease due to cash settlements of salaries payable* (cash paid for salaries expense) must be $2,600. The reconciliation shows that the $100 increase in the salaries payable balance occurred because the *cash paid for salary expense* is $100 less than the amount of *salary expense recognized on account* ($2,600 versus $2,700). Since the amount of cash paid is less than the amount of expense recognized, we add $100 to the amount of net income to determine the cash flow from operating activities (Reference No. 6 in Exhibit 12.7).

Reconciliation of Other Operating Expenses Payable

Use the financial statement information in Exhibit 12.5 to reconcile Other Operating Expenses Payable. The beginning and ending balances appear on the balance sheets. The *increase due to recognizing other operating expenses on account* is the other operating expenses amount reported on the income statement.

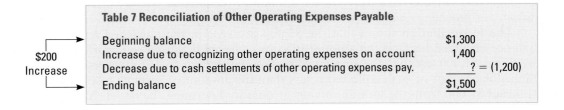

Table 7 Reconciliation of Other Operating Expenses Payable

$200
Increase

Beginning balance	$1,300
Increase due to recognizing other operating expenses on account	1,400
Decrease due to cash settlements of other operating expenses pay.	? = (1,200)
Ending balance	$1,500

To balance Other Operating Expenses Payable, the amount of the *decrease due to cash settlements of other operating expenses payable* must be $1,200.

The reconciliation shows that the $200 increase in the other operating expenses payable balance occurred because the *cash paid for other operating expenses* was $200 less than the amount of *other operating expenses recognized on account* ($1,200 versus $1,400). Since the amount of cash paid is less than the amount of expense recognized, we add $200 to the amount of net income to determine the net cash flow from operating activities (Reference No. 7 in Exhibit 12.7).

Reconciliation of Interest Payable

Use the financial statement information in Exhibit 12.5 to reconcile Interest Payable. The beginning and ending balances appear on the balance sheets. The *increase due to recognizing interest expense on account* is the interest expense reported on the income statement.

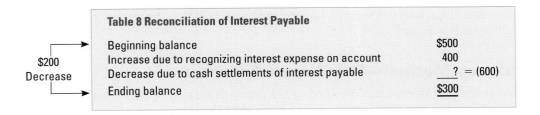

Table 8 Reconciliation of Interest Payable

$200
Decrease

Beginning balance	$500
Increase due to recognizing interest expense on account	400
Decrease due to cash settlements of interest payable	? = (600)
Ending balance	$300

To balance Interest Payable, the amount of the *decrease due to cash settlements of interest payable* (cash paid for interest expense) must be $600.

The reconciliation shows that the $200 decrease in the interest payable balance occurred because the amount of *cash paid for interest expense* is $200 more than the amount of *interest expense recognized on account* ($600 versus $400). Since the amount of cash paid is more than the amount of interest expense recognized, we subtract $200 from the amount of net income to determine the net cash flow from operating activities (Reference No. 8 in Exhibit 12.7).

Reconciliation of Unearned Rent Revenue

Use the financial statement information in Exhibit 12.5 to reconcile Unearned Rent Revenue. The beginning and ending balances appear on the balance sheets. The *decrease due to recognizing other income—rent revenue* is the other income—rent revenue reported on the income statement.

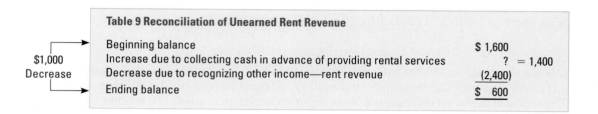

Table 9 Reconciliation of Unearned Rent Revenue	
Beginning balance	$ 1,600
Increase due to collecting cash in advance of providing rental services	? = 1,400
Decrease due to recognizing other income—rent revenue	(2,400)
Ending balance	$ 600

$1,000 Decrease

To balance Unearned Rent Revenue, the amount of the *increase due to collecting cash in advance of providing rental services* must be $1,400.

The reconciliation shows that the $1,000 decrease in the unearned rent revenue balance occurred because the amount of *cash collected in advance of providing rental services* is $1,000 less than the amount of *rent revenue recognized* ($1,400 versus $2,400). Since the amount of cash collected is less than the amount of revenue recognized, we subtract $1,000 from the amount of net income to determine the net cash flow from operating activities (Reference No. 9 in Exhibit 12.7).

Noncash Expenses

The calculation of accrual-based net income frequently includes noncash expenses such as depreciation expense. Since noncash expenses are deducted in determining net income, they must be added back to the amount of net income when computing net cash flow from operating activities (Reference No. 10 in Exhibit 12.7).

Gains and Losses

When a company retires a long-term asset, the company may receive cash from the sale of the asset being retired. If the asset is sold for more than book value (cost − accumulated depreciation), the gain increases net income; if the asset is sold for less than book value, the loss decreases net income. In either case, the cash inflow is the total amount of cash collected from selling the asset, not the amount of the gain or loss, and this cash inflow is reported in the investing activities section of the statement of cash flows. Since gains increase net income and losses decrease net income, but neither represents the amount of cash received from an asset sale, gains must be subtracted from and losses added back to net income to determine net cash flow from operating activities (Reference No. 11 in Exhibit 12.7).

Indirect Method—Rule-Based Approach

The reconciliation process described in the previous section of this chapter leads to a set of rules that can be used to convert accrual-based revenues and expenses to their cash flow equivalents. These rules are summarized in Exhibit 12.8.

Although the rule-based approach offers less insight, it is easy to apply. To illustrate, return to the financial statement data in Exhibit 12.5. The *noncash* current assets

EXHIBIT 12.7

Cash Flows from Operating Activities—Indirect Method

Reference No.	Cash Flows from Operating Activities	
	Net income	$7,000
	Adjustments to reconcile net income to net cash flow from operating activities:	
1	Decrease in accounts receivable	200
2	Increase in interest receivable	(100)
3	Increase in inventory	(700)
4	Decrease in accounts payable for inventory purchases	(300)
5	Decrease in prepaid insurance	300
6	Increase in salaries payable	100
7	Increase in other operating expenses payable	200
8	Decrease in interest payable	(200)
9	Decrease in unearned rent revenue	(1,000)
10	Depreciation expense	1,000
11	Gain on sale of store fixtures	(600)
	Net cash flow from operating activities	$5,900

EXHIBIT 12.8

Cash Flows from Operating Activities—Indirect Method

	Net income	XXX
Rule 1	Add decreases and subtract increases in noncash current assets.	XXX
Rule 2	Add increases and subtract decreases in noncash current liabilities.	XXX
Rule 3	Add noncash expenses (e.g., depreciation).	XXX
Rule 4	Add losses and subtract gains.	XXX
	Net cash flow from operating activities	XXX

and current liabilities reported on the balance sheets are summarized in Exhibit 12.9 for your convenience. The amount of the change in each balance is shown in the *Change* column.

Refer to the income statement to identify the amounts of net income, noncash expenses, gains, and losses. The income statement for New South Company in Exhibit 12.5 includes three relevant figures: net income of $7,000; depreciation expense of $1,000;

EXHIBIT 12.9

Noncash Current Assets and Current Liabilities

Account Title	2014	2013	Change
Accounts receivable	$1,000	$1,200	$ (200)
Interest receivable	400	300	100
Inventory	8,900	8,200	700
Prepaid insurance	1,100	1,400	(300)
Accounts payable—inventory purchases	800	1,100	(300)
Salaries payable	1,000	900	100
Other operating expenses payable	1,500	1,300	200
Interest payable	300	500	(200)
Unearned rent revenue	600	1,600	(1,000)

EXHIBIT 12.10	Cash Flows from Operating Activities—Indirect Method, Operating Activities

NEW SOUTH COMPANY
Statement of Cash Flows
For the Year Ended December 31, 2014

Applicable Rule	Cash Flows from Operating Activities	
	Net income	$7,000
	Adjustments to reconcile net income to net cash flow from operating activities:	
Rule 1	Decrease in accounts receivable	200
Rule 1	Increase in interest receivable	(100)
Rule 1	Increase in inventory	(700)
Rule 2	Decrease in accounts payable for inventory purchases	(300)
Rule 1	Decrease in prepaid insurance	300
Rule 2	Increase in salaries payable	100
Rule 2	Increase in other operating expenses payable	200
Rule 2	Decrease in interest payable	(200)
Rule 2	Decrease in unearned rent revenue	(1,000)
Rule 3	Depreciation expense	1,000
Rule 4	Gain on sale of store fixtures	(600)
	Net cash flow from operating activities	$5,900

and a $600 gain on sale of store fixtures. Applying the rules in Exhibit 12.8 produces the operating activities section of the statement of cash flows shown in Exhibit 12.10. The applicable rule for each item is referenced in the first column of the exhibit.

The operating activities section of the statements of cash flows shown in Exhibits 12.10 and 12.7 are identical. The rule-based approach is an alternative way to prepare this section when using the indirect method.

✓ CHECK YOURSELF 12.2

Q Magazine, Inc., reported $369,000 of net income for the month. At the beginning of the month, its Unearned Revenue account had a balance of $78,000. At the end of the month, the account had a balance of $67,000. Based on this information alone, determine the amount of net cash flow from operating activities.

Answer

Account Title	Ending	Beginning	Change
Unearned revenue	$67,000	$78,000	$(11,000)

Applicable Rule	Cash Flows from Operating Activities	Amount
	Net income	$369,000
Rule 2	Deduct: Decrease in unearned revenue	(11,000)
	Net cash flow from operating activities	$358,000

CHECK YOURSELF 12.3

The following account balances were drawn from the accounting records of Loeb, Inc.

Account Title	Ending Balance	Beginning Balance
Prepaid rent	$3,000	$4,200
Interest payable	2,650	2,900

Loeb reported $7,400 of net income during the accounting period. Based on this information alone, determine the amount of net cash flow from operating activities.

Answer   Based on Rule 1, the $1,200 decrease ($3,000 − $4,200) in Prepaid Rent (current asset) must be added to net income to determine the amount of net cash flow from operating activities. Rule 2 requires that the $250 decrease ($2,650 − $2,900) in interest Payable (current liability) must be deducted from net income. Accordingly, the cash flow from operating activities is $8,350 ($7,400 + $1,200 − $250). Note that paying interest is defined as an operating activity and should not be confused with dividend payments, which are classified as financing activities.

CHECK YOURSELF 12.4

Arley Company's income statement reported net income (all amounts are in millions) of $326 for the year. The income statement included depreciation expense of $45 and a net loss on the sale of long-term assets of $22. Based on this information alone, determine the net cash flow from operating activities.

Answer   Based on Rule 3 and Rule 4, both the depreciation expense and the loss would have to be added to net income to determine net cash flow from operating activities. Net cash flow from operating activities would be $393 million ($326 + $45 + $22).

PREPARING THE OPERATING ACTIVITIES SECTION OF A STATEMENT OF CASH FLOWS USING THE DIRECT METHOD

The reconciliation tables developed earlier to determine net cash flow from operating activities under the *indirect method* also disclose the information needed to present the amount of net cash flow from operating activities under the *direct method*. Remember that the amount of net cash flow from operating activities is the same whether it is presented using the indirect or the direct method.

The direct method shows the specific sources and uses of cash that are associated with operating activities. It does not show adjustments to net income. To illustrate, examine Exhibit 12.11. The information in the reference column identifies the reconciliation table from which the cash flow amounts were drawn. The page number indicates where the reconciliation table is located in this chapter.

Table 3 is not included above because it does not directly involve a cash flow. Also, noncash expenses, gains, and losses are not used in the determination of net cash flow from operating activities when using the direct method.

LO 2

Prepare the operating activities section of a statement of cash flows using the direct method.

EXHIBIT 12.11

Cash Flows from Operating Activities—Direct Method

Reference	Cash Flows from Operating Activities	
Table 1, page 649	Inflow from customers	$ 20,800
Table 2, page 649	Inflow from interest revenue	600
Table 4, page 650	Outflow for inventory purchases	(11,500)
Table 5, page 650	Outflow to purchase insurance	(1,000)
Table 6, page 651	Outflow to pay salary expense	(2,600)
Table 7, page 651	Outflow for other operating expenses	(1,200)
Table 8, page 651	Outflow to pay interest expense	(600)
Table 9, page 652	Inflow from rent revenue	1,400
	Net cash flow from operating activities	$ 5,900

PREPARING THE INVESTING ACTIVITIES SECTION OF A STATEMENT OF CASH FLOWS

LO 3

Prepare the investing activities section of a statement of cash flows.

The direct and indirect methods discussed above pertain only to the presentation of operating activities. The *investing activities* section of the statement of cash flows is the same regardless of whether the direct or indirect method is used for operating activities. The information necessary to identify cash inflows and outflows from investing activities is obtained by reconciling changes in a company's long-term assets. In general:

■ Increases in long-term asset balances suggest cash outflows to purchase assets.

■ Decreases in long-term asset balances suggest cash inflows from selling assets.

It is usually necessary to analyze data from the long-term asset records to determine details about long-term asset purchases and sales. In the New South Company example, these details are presented as notes at the bottom of the balance sheets.

To illustrate, return to the financial statements in Exhibit 12.5. New South Company reports the following three long-term assets on its balance sheets. *It is not necessary to reconcile accumulated depreciation since it does not affect cash flow.*

Long-Term Asset	2014	2013
Investment securities	$5,100	$3,500
Store fixtures	5,400	4,800
Land	8,200	6,000

For each long-term asset, reconcile the beginning and ending balances by identifying purchases and sales affecting it. Review the notes for additional relevant information. Begin with investment securities.

Reconciliation of Investment Securities

Reconciliation of Investment Securities	
Beginning balance in investment securities	$3,500
Increase due to purchase of investment securities	? = 1,600
Decrease due to sale of investment securities	0
Ending balance in investment securities	$5,100

Because Note 1 below the balance sheets indicates no investment securities were sold during 2014, the *decrease due to sale of investment securities* is zero. To balance Investment Securities, the *increase due to purchase of investment securities* must be $1,600. In the absence of contrary information, assume New South used cash to purchase the investment securities. This cash outflow is reported in the investing activities section of the statement of cash flows in Exhibit 12.12.

Reconciliation of Store Fixtures

Reconciliation of Store Fixtures		
Beginning balance in store fixtures	$4,800	
Increase due to purchase of store fixtures	?	= 2,300
Decrease due to sale of store fixtures	(1,700)	
Ending balance in store fixtures	$5,400	

Note 2 below the balance sheets indicates that the *decrease due to sale of store fixtures* is $1,700. What is the cash flow from this sale? The book value of these fixtures was $400 ($1,700 cost − $1,300 accumulated depreciation). Since the income statement reports a $600 gain on the sale of store fixtures, the cash collected from the sale was more than the book value of the store fixtures. Compute the amount of cash collected from the sale of store fixtures as follows:

$$\text{Cash inflow} = \text{book value} + \text{gain} = \$400 + \$600 = \$1,000$$

The $1,000 cash inflow from the sale of store fixtures is reported in the investing activities section of the statement of cash flows in Exhibit 12.12.

To balance Store Fixtures, the *increase due to purchase of store fixtures* must be $2,300. In the absence of contrary information, assume New South used cash to purchase store fixtures. The cash outflow is reported in the investing activities section of the statement of cash flows in Exhibit 12.12.

Reconciliation of Land

Reconciliation of Land		
Beginning balance in land	$6,000	
Increase due to purchase of land	?	= 2,200
Decrease due to sale of land	0	
Ending balance in land	$8,200	

Because Note 3 below the balance sheets indicates no land was sold during 2014, the *decrease due to sale of land* is zero. To balance Land, the *increase due to purchase of land* must be $2,200. Since the land was acquired by issuing a mortgage note payable, New South did not use cash for the purchase. This type of transaction is reported in the *noncash investing and financing activities* section of the statement of cash flows, discussed in more detail later in the chapter. The cash inflows and outflows from investing activities are summarized in Exhibit 12.12.

EXHIBIT 12.12

Cash Flows from Investing Activities

Cash Flows from Investing Activities

Cash outflow to purchase investment securities	$(1,600)
Cash inflow from the sale of store fixtures	1,000
Cash outflow to purchase store fixtures	(2,300)
Net cash outflow from investing activities	$(2,900)

CHECK YOURSELF 12.5

On January 1, 2013, Wyatt Company had an Equipment balance of $124,000. During 2013, Wyatt purchased equipment that cost $50,000. The balance in Equipment on December 31, 2013, was $90,000. The 2013 income statement included a $7,000 loss from the sale of equipment. On the date of sale, accumulated depreciation on the equipment sold was $49,000.

Required

a. Determine the cost of the equipment sold during 2013.

b. Determine the amount of cash flow from the sale of equipment that should be reported in the investing activities section of the 2013 statement of cash flows.

Solution

a.

Reconciliation of Equipment	
Beginning balance	$124,000
Increase due to the purchase of equipment	50,000
Decrease due to sale of equipment	? = (84,000)
Ending balance	$ 90,000

To balance Equipment, *decrease due to sale of equipment* must be $84,000.

b. The book value of the equipment sold was $35,000 ($84,000 − $49,000 accumulated depreciation). Since Wyatt recognized a loss on the equipment sale, the amount of cash collected from the sale was less than the book value of the equipment. The cash collected from the sale of the equipment was $28,000 ($35,000 book value − $7,000 loss on sale).

PREPARING THE FINANCING ACTIVITIES SECTION OF A STATEMENT OF CASH FLOWS

LO 4

Prepare the financing activities section of a statement of cash flows.

Because the differences between the direct and the indirect methods of presenting the statement of cash flows pertain only to operating activities, the *financing activities* section is the same under either approach. The information necessary to identify cash inflows and outflows from financing activities is obtained by reconciling changes in short-term notes payable, long-term liabilities, and stockholders' equity. In general

- Increases in short-term notes payable or long-term debt balances suggest cash inflows occurred from issuing debt instruments (notes or bonds).

- Decreases in short-term notes payable or long-term debt balances suggest cash outflows occurred for payment of debt (notes or bonds).

- Increases in contributed capital (common stock, preferred stock, or paid-in capital) suggest cash inflows occurred from issuing equity instruments.
- Increases or decreases in treasury stock suggest cash outflows or inflows occurred to purchase or sell a company's own stock.
- Decreases in retained earnings from cash dividends suggest cash outflows occurred to pay dividends.

To illustrate, return to the financial statements of the New South Company in Exhibit 12.5. The following long-term liability and stockholders' equity balances are reported on the New South balance sheets:

Account Title	2014	2013
Mortgage payable	$ 2,200	$ 0
Bonds payable	1,000	4,000
Common stock	10,000	8,000
Retained earnings	12,700	7,200
Treasury stock	600	0

For each account, reconcile the beginning and ending balances by identifying the increases and decreases affecting it. Review the notes for additional relevant information. Begin with the mortgage payable liability.

Reconciliation of Mortgage Payable

Reconciliation of Mortgage Payable

Beginning balance in mortgage payable	$ 0
Increase due to issuing mortgage payable	? = 2,200
Decrease due to payment of mortgage payable	0
Ending balance in mortgage payable	$2,200

As previously discussed, Note 3 indicates a mortgage payable was issued to acquire land. The *increase due to issuing mortgage payable* is $2,200. Since New South received land, not cash, by issuing the mortgage, the transaction is reported in the noncash investing and financing activities section of the statement of cash flows.

Reconciliation of Bonds Payable

Bonds Payable

Beginning balance in bonds payable	$4,000
Increase due to issuing bonds payable	0
Decrease due to payment of bonds payable	? = (3,000)
Ending balance in bonds payable	$1,000

Since there is no indication that New South issued bonds during 2014, assume the *increase due to issuing bonds payable* is zero. To balance Bonds Payable, the *decrease due to payment of bonds payable* must be $3,000. The cash outflow is reported in the financing activities section in Exhibit 12.13.

Reconciliation of Common Stock

Reconciliation of Common Stock	
Beginning balance in common stock	$ 8,000
Increase due to issuing common stock	? = 2,000
Ending balance in common stock	$10,000

To balance Common Stock, the *increase due to issuing common stock* has to be $2,000. The cash inflow is reported in the financing activities section in Exhibit 12.13.

Reconciliation of Retained Earnings

Reconciliation of Retained Earnings	
Beginning balance in retained earnings	$ 7,200
Increase due to net income	7,000
Decrease due to payment of dividends	? = (1,500)
Ending balance in retained earnings	$12,700

The *increase due to net income* comes from the income statement. To balance Retained Earnings, the decrease due to payment of dividends must be $1,500. In the absence of information to the contrary, assume the decrease is due to the cash payment of dividends. The cash outflow for payment of dividends is reported in the financing activities section of the statement of cash flows in Exhibit 12.13.

Reconciliation of Treasury Stock

Reconciliation of Treasury Stock	
Beginning balance in treasury stock	$ 0
Increase due to purchasing treasury stock	? = 600
Decrease due to reissuing treasury stock	0
Ending balance in treasury stock	$600

Since there is no indication that New South reissued treasury stock during 2014, the *decrease due to reissuing treasury stock* is zero. To balance Treasury Stock, the increase due to purchasing treasury stock must be $600. The cash outflow is reported in the financing activities section in Exhibit 12.13.

EXHIBIT 12.13

Cash Flows from Financing Activities

Cash Flows from Financing Activities	
Cash outflow to reduce bonds payable	$(3,000)
Cash inflow from issuing common stock	2,000
Cash outflow to pay dividends	(1,500)
Cash outflow to purchase treasury stock	(600)
Net cash outflow from financing activities	$(3,100)

Exhibits 12.14 and 12.15 illustrate the complete statement of cash flows for New South Company under the two alternative methods. Exhibit 12.14 presents operating activities using the indirect method. Exhibit 12.15 presents operating activities using the direct method. The investing and financing activities do not differ between methods. Under either method the combined effects of operating, investing, and financing activities result in a net decrease in cash of $100 for 2014. This $100 decrease is necessarily consistent with the difference between the December 31, 2014, and the December 31, 2013, cash balances shown in the balance sheets in Exhibit 12.5.

EXHIBIT 12.14   Statement of Cash Flows—Indirect Method

NEW SOUTH COMPANY
Statement of Cash Flows
For the Year Ended December 31, 2014

Cash Flows from Operating Activities

Net income	$ 7,000	
Adjustments to reconcile net income to net cash flow from operating activities:		
Decrease in accounts receivable	200	
Increase in interest receivable	(100)	
Increase in inventory	(700)	
Decrease in accounts payable for inventory purchases	(300)	
Decrease in prepaid insurance	300	
Increase in salaries payable	100	
Increase in other operating expenses payable	200	
Decrease in interest payable	(200)	
Decrease in unearned rent revenue	(1,000)	
Depreciation expense	1,000	
Gain on sale of store fixtures	(600)	
Net cash flow from operating activities		$5,900
Cash Flows from Investing Activities		
Cash outflow to purchase investment securities	(1,600)	
Cash inflow from the sale of store fixtures	1,000	
Cash outflow to purchase store fixtures	(2,300)	
Net cash outflow from investing activities		(2,900)
Cash Flows from Financing Activities		
Cash outflow to reduce bonds payable	(3,000)	
Cash inflow from issuing common stock	2,000	
Cash outflow to pay dividends	(1,500)	
Cash outflow to purchase treasury stock	(600)	
Net cash outflow from financing activities		(3,100)
Net decrease in cash		(100)
Plus: Beginning cash balance		400
Ending cash balance		$ 300
Schedule of Noncash Investing and Financing Activities		
Issue mortgage for land		$2,200

EXHIBIT 12.15   Statement of Cash Flows—Direct Method

NEW SOUTH COMPANY
Statement of Cash Flows
For the Year Ended December 31, 2014

Cash Flows from Operating Activities

Inflow from customers	$ 20,800	
Inflow from interest revenue	600	
Outflow for inventory purchases	(11,500)	
Outflow to purchase insurance	(1,000)	
Outflow to pay salary expense	(2,600)	
Outflow for other operating expenses	(1,200)	
Outflow to pay interest expense	(600)	
Inflow from rent revenue	1,400	
Net cash flow from operating activities		$5,900

continued

EXHIBIT 12.15 *concluded*

NEW SOUTH COMPANY
Statement of Cash Flows
For the Year Ended December 31, 2014

Cash Flows from Investing Activities

Cash outflow to purchase investment securities	(1,600)	
Cash inflow from the sale of store fixtures	1,000	
Cash outflow to purchase store fixtures	(2,300)	
Net cash outflow from investing activities		(2,900)

Cash Flows from Financing Activities

Cash outflow to reduce bonds payable	(3,000)	
Cash inflow from issuing common stock	2,000	
Cash outflow to pay dividends	(1,500)	
Cash outflow to purchase treasury stock	(600)	
Net cash outflow from financing activities		(3,100)
Net decrease in cash		(100)
Plus: Beginning cash balance		400
Ending cash balance		$ 300

Schedule of Noncash Investing and Financing Activities

Issue mortgage for land	$2,200

✓ CHECK YOURSELF 12.6

On January 1, 2013, Sterling Company had a balance of $250,000 in Bonds Payable. During 2013, Sterling issued bonds with a $75,000 face value. The bonds were issued at face value. The balance in Bonds Payable on December 31, 2013, was $150,000.

Required

a. Determine the cash outflow for repayment of bond liabilities assuming the bonds were retired at face value.

b. Prepare the financing activities section of the 2013 statement of cash flows.

Solution

a.

Reconciliation of Bonds Payable

Beginning balance	$250,000
Increase due to issuing bonds payable	75,000
Decrease due to payment of bonds payable	? = (175,000)
Ending balance	$150,000

In order to balance Bonds Payable, the decrease due to payment of bonds payable must be $175,000. In the absence of information to the contrary, assume cash was used to pay the bond liabilities.

b.

Cash Flows from Financing Activities

Inflow from issuing bond liabilities	$ 75,000
Outflow for reduction of bond liabilities	(175,000)
Net cash outflow from financing activities	$(100,000)

PREPARING THE SCHEDULE OF NONCASH INVESTING AND FINANCING ACTIVITIES

As mentioned earlier, companies may engage in significant noncash investing and financing activities. For example, New South Company acquired land by issuing a $2,200 mortgage note. Since these types of transactions do not involve exchanging cash, they are not reported in the main body of the statement of cash flows. However, the Financial Accounting Standards Board (FASB) requires disclosure of all material investing and financing activities whether or not they involve exchanging cash. Companies must therefore include with the statement of cash flows a separate schedule that reports noncash investing and financing activities. See the *Schedule of Noncash Investing and Financing Activities* at the bottom of Exhibits 12.14 and 12.15 for an example.

REALITY BYTES

How did Dillard's, Inc., the department store chain, acquire $25 million of property, plant, and equipment in its 2010 fiscal year *without* spending any cash? Oddly enough, the answer can be found on its statement of cash flows.

The supplemental "noncash transactions" information included at the bottom of Dillard's statement of cash flows revealed that it acquired the assets by exchanging debt directly for assets. A direct exchange of notes payable for assets was responsible for $23.6 million of these purchases. The remaining $1.7 million was purchased through "accrued capital transactions."

Had Dillard's borrowed $25 million from a bank and then used this cash to purchase $25 million of assets, it would have reported two separate cash events in the body of its statement of cash flows. A cash inflow would have been reported in the financing activities for the borrowing transaction, and a cash outflow would have been reported in the investing activities section for the purchase transaction. Acquiring large amounts of assets is considered important, even if there is no immediate exchange of cash, so generally accepted accounting principles require such events to be reported as a part of the statement of cash flows.

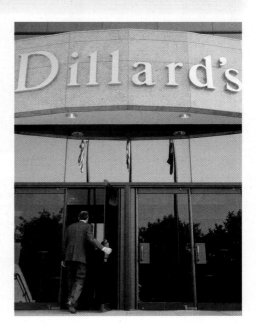

THE FINANCIAL ANALYST

Why are financial analysts interested in the statement of cash flows? Understanding the cash flows of a business is essential because cash is used to pay the bills. A company, especially one experiencing rapid growth, can be short of cash in spite of earning substantial net income. To illustrate, assume you start a computer sales business. You borrow $2,000 and spend the money to purchase two computers for $1,000 each. You sell one of the computers on account for $1,500. If your loan required a payment at this time, you could not make it. Even though you have net income of $500 ($1,500 sales − $1,000 cost of goods sold), you have no cash until you collect the $1,500 account receivable. A business cannot survive without managing cash flow carefully. It is little wonder that financial analysts are keenly interested in cash flow.

Real-World Data

The statement of cash flows frequently provides a picture of business activity that would otherwise be lost in the complexities of accrual accounting. For example, as *The Curious Accountant* in Chapter 10 explained, BP p.l.c. reported a net loss of $3.7 billion in 2010, but this was due to a $40.9 billion expense related to the oil spill in the Gulf of Mexico. Only $17.7 billion of this $40.9 billion had actually been paid in cash by the end of the year. In 2010, BP had positive cash flow from operating activities of $13.6 despite reporting its $3.7 billion net loss.

Investors consider cash flow information so important that they are willing to pay for it. Even though the FASB *prohibits* companies from disclosing *cash flow per share* in audited financial statements, one prominent stock analysis service, *Value Line Investment Survey,* sells this information to a significant customer base. Clearly, Value Line's customers value information about cash flows.

Exhibit 12.16 compares income from operations to cash flows from operating activities for six real-world companies for 2007 through 2010. Several things are apparent from this exhibit. The cash flow from operating activities exceeds income from operations for all but six of the 28 comparisons, and three of these are for one company, Green Mountain Coffee Roasters, and two are for Boeing. Cash flows often exceed income because depreciation, a noncash expense, is usually significant. The most dramatic example of the differences between cash flow and income is AOL. For the four years shown in Exhibit 12.16, AOL had a cumulative net loss of $665.2 million, but its cash flows from operations were a positive $3.5 *billion.* The difference between cash flow from operating activities and operating income helps explain how some companies can have significant losses over a few years and continue to stay in business and pay their bills.

The exhibit also shows that cash flow from operating activities can be more stable than operating income. Results for AOL and Alaska Air Group demonstrate this clearly.

EXHIBIT 12.16

Net Income versus Cash Flow from Operations (Amounts in $000)

	2010	2009	2008	2007
Alaska Air Group				
Net income	$ 251,100	$ 121,600	$ (135,900)	$ 125,000
Cash flow—operations	553,700	305,300	164,300	482,000
AOL				
Net income	(782,500)	248,500	(1,526,600)	1,395,400
Cash flow—operations	592,400	908,200	933,600	1,016,600
Boeing				
Operating income	3,307,000	1,312,000	2,672,000	4,074,000
Cash flow—operations	2,952,000	5,603,000	(401,000)	9,584,000
Green Mountain Coffee				
Net income	79,506	55,882	22,299	12,843
Cash flow—operations	(10,535)	38,498	1,946	29,834
Johnson & Johnson				
Net income	13,334,000	12,266,000	12,949,000	10,576,000
Cash flow—operations	16,385,000	16,571,000	14,972,000	15,249,000
McAfee				
Net income	184,112	173,420	172,209	166,980
Cash flow—operations	594,640	496,384	308,322	393,415

For the four years presented, Alaska Air reported a loss in one of the years and AOL had a loss in two of the years. However, operating cash flows were not only positive for both companies in every year, but they were never lower than $164.3 million.

What could explain why Green Mountain had *less* cash flow from operating activities than operating income in 2008, 2009, and 2010? Green Mountain was experiencing the kind of growth described earlier for your computer business. Its cash outflows were supporting growth in inventory and accounts receivable. Green Mountain Coffee Roasters is not a name familiar to many readers, but you have probably seen one of their main products. Green Mountain owns the Keurig coffee business, which make single serving "K-Cup" coffee machines and products. The other segment of its business is specialty coffees. Both segments have been experiencing rapid growth. Its growth rates based on sales were 52 percent, 46 percent, 61 percent, and 69 percent for 2007, 2008, 2009, and 2010. To keep up with these growth rates, Green Mountain has needed to increase its inventory, and as a result of increased sales, it has to carry larger balances of accounts receivable. From 2007 to 2010 when Green Mountain's earnings grew a total of 588 percent, its inventory level grew 675 percent and it accounts receivable grew 438 percent.

Finally, why did Boeing have negative cash flow from operations in 2008 even though its revenue and operating income were also declining? It was because of a growth in inventory, but not due to revenue growth. This situation was significant enough that Boeing explained it in the footnotes of its 2008 annual report, as follows:

> In 2008 inventory grew at a faster rate than customer advances. The 2008 increase in inventories was driven by continued spending on production materials, airplane engines, and supplier advances during the IAM strike, lower commercial airplane deliveries and the continued ramp-up of the 787 program. We expect to generate positive operating cash flows in 2009.

The Green Mountain Coffee Roasters situation highlights a potential weakness in the format of the statement of cash flows. Some accountants consider it misleading to classify all increases in long-term assets as *investing activities* and all changes in inventory as affecting cash flow from operating activities. They argue that the increase in inventory at Green Mountain that relates to expanding its business should be classified as an investing activity, just as the cost of a new warehouse is. Although inventory is classified as a current asset and buildings are classified as long-term assets, in reality there is a certain level of inventory a company must permanently maintain to stay in business. The GAAP format of the statement of cash flows penalizes cash flow from operating activities for increases in inventory that are really a permanent investment in assets.

Conversely, the same critics might argue that some purchases of long-term assets are not actually *investments* but merely replacements of old, existing property, plant, and equipment. In other words, the *investing activities* section of the statement of cash flows makes no distinction between expenditures that expand the business and those that simply replace old equipment (sometimes called *capital maintenance* expenditures).

Users of the statement of cash flows must exercise the same care interpreting it as when they use the balance sheet or the income statement. Numbers alone are insufficient. Users must evaluate numbers based on knowledge of the particular business and industry they are analyzing.

Accounting information alone cannot guide a businessperson to a sound decision. Making good business decisions requires an understanding of the business in question, the environmental and economic factors affecting the operation of that business, and the accounting concepts on which the financial statements of that business are based.

A Look Back

This chapter examined in detail only one financial statement, the statement of cash flows. The chapter provided a more comprehensive discussion of how accrual accounting relates to cash-based accounting. Effective use of financial statements requires understanding not only accrual and cash-based accounting systems but also how they relate to each other. That relationship is why a statement of cash flows can begin with a reconciliation of net income, an accrual measurement, to net cash flow from operating activities, a cash measurement. Finally, this chapter explained how the conventions for classifying cash flows as operating, investing, or financing activities require analysis and understanding to make informed decisions with the financial information.

>> A Look Forward

Chapter 13, which is available only online, provides expanded coverage of financial statement analysis. Your instructor will provide guidance as to how to access this chapter if he or she decides to cover it. If your journey ends here, we sincerely hope this text provided a meaningful learning experience that will serve you well as you progress through your academic training and, ultimately, your career. Good luck and best wishes.

SELF-STUDY REVIEW PROBLEM

A step-by-step audio-narrated series of slides is provided on the text website at www.mhhe.com/edmonds8e.

The following financial statements pertain to Schlemmer Company.

Balance Sheets As of December 31		
	2014	2013
Cash	$48,400	$ 2,800
Accounts receivable	2,200	1,200
Inventory	5,600	6,000
Equipment	18,000	22,000
Accumulated depreciation—equip.	(13,650)	(17,400)
Land	17,200	10,400
Total assets	$77,750	$25,000
Accounts payable (inventory)	$ 5,200	$ 4,200
Long-term debt	5,600	6,400
Common stock	19,400	10,000
Retained earnings	47,550	4,400
Total liabilities and equity	$77,750	$25,000

Income Statement For the Year Ended December 31, 2014	
Sales revenue	$67,300
Cost of goods sold	(24,100)
Gross margin	43,200
Depreciation expense	(1,250)
Operating income	41,950
Gain on sale of equipment	2,900
Loss on disposal of land	(100)
Net income	$44,750

Additional Data

1. During 2014 equipment that had originally cost $11,000 was sold. Accumulated depreciation on this equipment was $5,000 at the time of the sale.

2. Common stock was issued in exchange for land valued at $9,400 at the time of the exchange.

Required

Using the indirect method, prepare in good form a statement of cash flows for the year ended December 31, 2014.

Solution

SCHLEMMER COMPANY Statement of Cash Flows For the Year Ended December 31, 2014		
Cash Flows from Operating Activities		
Net income	$44,750	
Add:		
Decrease in inventory (1)	400	
Increase in accounts payable (2)	1,000	
Depreciation expense (3)	1,250	
Loss on disposal of land (4)	100	
Subtract:		
Increase in accounts receivable (1)	(1,000)	
Gain on sale of equipment (4)	(2,900)	
Net cash inflow from operating activities		$43,600
Cash Flows from Investing Activities		
Cash inflow from the sale of equipment (5)	8,900	
Cash outflow for the purchase of equipment (5)	(7,000)	
Cash inflow from sale of land (6)	2,500	
Net cash outflow from investing activities		4,400
Cash Flows from Financing Activities		
Cash outflow to repay long-term debt (7)	(800)	
Cash outflow to pay dividends (8)	(1,600)	
Net cash outflow from financing activities		(2,400)
Net Increase in Cash		45,600
Plus: Beginning cash balance		2,800
Ending cash balance		$48,400
Schedule of Noncash Investing and Financing Activities		
Issue of common stock for land (9)		$ 9,400

(1) Add decreases and subtract increases in current asset account balances to net income.

(2) Add increases and subtract decreases in current liability account balances to net income.

(3) Add noncash expenses (depreciation) to net income.

(4) Add losses on the sale of noncurrent assets to net income and subtract gains on the sale of long-term assets from net income.

(5) Information regarding the Equipment account is summarized in the following table.

Equipment Account Information	
Beginning balance in equipment	$22,000
Purchases of equipment (cash outflows)	?
Sales of equipment (cash inflows)	(11,000)
Ending balance in equipment	$18,000

To balance the account, equipments costing $7,000 must have been purchased. In the absence of information to the contrary, we assume cash was used to make the purchase.

Note 1 to the financial statement shows that equipment sold had a book value of $6,000 ($11,000 cost − $5,000 accumulated depreciation). The amount of the cash inflow from this sale is computed as follows:

$$\text{Cash inflow} = \text{book value} + \text{gain} = \$6,000 + \$2,900 = \$8,900$$

(6) The information regarding the Land account is as follows:

Land Account Information

Beginning balance in land	$10,400
Purchases of land (issue of common stock)	9,400
Sales of land (cash inflows)	?
Ending balance in land	$17,200

Note 2 indicates that land valued at $9,400 was acquired by issuing common stock. Since there was no cash flow associated with this purchase, the event is shown in the *noncash investing and financing activities* section of the statement of cash flows.

To balance the account, the cost (book value) of land sold had to be $2,600. Since the income statement shows a $100 loss on the sale of land, the cash collected from the sale is computed as follows:

$$\text{Cash inflow} = \text{book value} − \text{less} = \$2,600 − \$100 = \$2,500$$

(7) The information regarding the Long-Term Debt account is as follows:

Long-Term Debt Information

Beginning balance in long-term debt	$6,400
Issue of long-term debt instruments (cash inflow)	0
Payment of long-term debt (cash outflow)	?
Ending balance in long-term debt	$5,600

There is no information in the financial statements that suggest that long-term debt was issued. Therefore, to balance the account, $800 of long-term debt had to be paid off, thereby resulting in a cash outflow.

(8) The information regarding the Retained Earnings account is as follows:

Retained Earnings Information

Beginning balance in retained earnings	$ 4,400
Net income	44,750
Dividends (cash outflow)	?
Ending balance in retained earnings	$47,550

To balance the account, $1,600 of dividends had to be paid, thereby resulting in a cash outflow.

(9) Note 2 states that common stock was issue to acquire land valued at $9,400. This is a noncash investing and financing activity.

KEY TERMS

Cash inflows 640	Financing	Investing activities 643	Operating activities 642
Cash outflows 640	activities 643	Noncash investing and	
Direct method 642	Indirect method 642	financing activities 644	

QUESTIONS

1. What is the purpose of the statement of cash flows?

2. What are the three categories of cash flows reported on the cash flow statement? Discuss each and give an example of an inflow and an outflow for each category.

3. What are noncash investing and financing activities? Provide an example. How are such transactions shown on the statement of cash flows?

4. Albring Company had a beginning balance in accounts receivable of $12,000 and an ending balance of $14,000. Net income amounted to $110,000. Based on this information alone, determine the amount of net cash flow from operating activities.

5. Forsyth Company had a beginning balance in utilities payable of $3,300 and an ending balance of $5,200. Net income amounted to $87,000. Based on this information alone, determine the amount of net cash flow from operating activities.

6. Clover Company had a beginning balance in unearned revenue of $4,300 and an ending balance of $3,200. Net income amounted to $54,000. Based on this information alone, determine the amount of net cash flow from operating activities.

7. Which of the following activities are financing activities?
   (a) Payment of accounts payable.
   (b) Payment of interest on bonds payable.
   (c) Sale of common stock.
   (d) Sale of preferred stock at a premium.
   (e) Payment of a cash dividend.

8. Does depreciation expense affect net cash flow? Explain.

9. If Best Company sold land that cost $4,200 at a $500 gain, how much cash did it collect from the sale of land?

10. If Best Company sold office equipment that originally cost $7,500 and had $7,200 of accumulated depreciation at a $100 loss, what was the selling price for the office equipment?

11. In which section of the statement of cash flows would the following transactions be reported?
   (a) The amount of the change in the balance of accounts receivable.
   (b) Cash purchase of investment securities.
   (c) Cash purchase of equipment.
   (d) Cash sale of merchandise.
   (e) Cash sale of common stock.
   (f) The amount of net income.
   (g) Cash proceeds from loan.
   (h) Cash payment on bonds payable.
   (i) Cash receipt from sale of old equipment.
   (j) The amount of the change in the balance of accounts payable.

12. What is the difference between preparing the statement of cash flows using the direct method and using the indirect method?

13. Which method (direct or indirect) of presenting the statement of cash flows is more intuitively logical? Why?

14. What is the major advantage of using the indirect method to present the statement of cash flows?

15. What is the advantage of using the direct method to present the statement of cash flows?

16. How would Best Company report the following transactions on the statement of cash flows?
   (a) Purchased new equipment for $46,000 cash.
   (b) Sold old equipment for $8,700 cash. The equipment had a book value of $4,900.

17. Can a company report negative net cash flows from operating activities for the year on the statement of cash flows but still have positive net income on the income statement? Explain.

MULTIPLE-CHOICE QUESTIONS

Multiple-choice questions are provided on the text website at www.mhhe.com/edmonds8e.

EXERCISES—SERIES A

All applicable Exercises in Series A are available with McGraw-Hill's *Connect® Accounting.*

Exercise 12-1A   *Use the indirect method to determine cash flows from operating activities*

LO 1

An accountant for Southern Manufacturing Companies (SMC) computed the following information by making comparisons between SMC's 2013 and 2014 balance sheets. Further information was determined by examining the company's 2014 income statement.

1. The amount of cash dividends paid to the stockholders.
2. The amount of a decrease in the balance of an Unearned Revenue account.

3. The amount of an increase in the balance of an Inventory account.

4. The amount of an increase in the balance of a Land account.

5. The amount of a decrease in the balance of a Prepaid Rent account.

6. The amount of an increase in the balance of a Treasury Stock account.

7. The amount of an increase in the balance of the Accounts Receivable account.

8. The amount of a loss arising from the sale of land.

9. The amount of an increase in the balance of the other Operating Expenses Payable account.

10. The amount of a decrease in the balance of the Bonds Payable account.

11. The amount of depreciation expense shown on the income statement.

Required

For each item described above indicate whether the amount should be added to or subtracted from the amount of net income when determining the amount of net cash flow from operating activities. If an item does not affect net cash flow from operating activities, identify it as being not affected.

LO 1

Exercise 12-2A   Use the indirect method to determine cash flows from operating activities

Alfonza Incorporated presents its statement of cash flows using the indirect method. The following accounts and corresponding balances were drawn from the company's 2014 and 2013 year-end balance sheets:

Account Title	2014	2013
Accounts receivable	$16,200	$17,800
Accounts payable	$7,600	$9,100

The 2014 income statement showed net income of $31,600.

Required

a. Prepare the operating activities section of the statement of cash flows.

b. Explain why the change in the balance in accounts receivable was added to or subtracted from the amount of net income when you completed Requirement *a*.

c. Explain why the change in the balance in accounts payable was added to or subtracted from the amount of net income when you completed Requirement *a*.

LO 1

Exercise 12-3A   Use the indirect method to determine cash flows from operating activities

Shim Company presents its statement of cash flows using the indirect method. The following accounts and corresponding balances were drawn from Shim's 2014 and 2013 year-end balance sheets:

Account Title	2014	2013
Accounts receivable	$36,000	$37,200
Prepaid rent	2,400	1,800
Interest receivable	600	400
Accounts payable	9,300	10,400
Salaries payable	4,500	5,200
Unearned revenue	3,600	5,400

The income statement contained a $1,500 gain on the sale of equipment, an $800 loss on the sale of land, and $3,600 of depreciation expense. Net income for the period was $47,300.

Required

Prepare the operating activities section of the statement of cash flows.

Exercise 12-4A *Use the direct method to determine cash flows from operating activities*

The following accounts and corresponding balances were drawn from Avia Company's 2014 and 2013 year-end balance sheets:

Account Title	2014	2013
Unearned revenue	$7,600	$6,200
Prepaid rent	2,400	3,600

During the year, $46,000 of unearned revenue was recognized as having been earned. Rent expense for 2014 was $18,000.

Required

Based on this information alone, prepare the operating activities section of the statement of cash flows assuming the direct approach is used.

Exercise 12-5A *Use the direct method to determine cash flows from operating activities*

The following accounts and corresponding balances were drawn from Marinelli Company's 2014 and 2013 year-end balance sheets:

Account Title	2014	2013
Accounts receivable	$35,200	$31,600
Interest receivable	4,200	4,800
Other operating expenses payable	21,000	18,500
Salaries payable	6,500	7,200

The 2014 income statement is shown below:

Income Statement	
Sales	$530,000
Salary expense	(214,000)
Other operating expenses	(175,000)
Operating income	141,000
Nonoperating items: Interest revenue	16,500
Net income	$157,500

Required

a. Use the direct method to compute the amount of cash inflows from operating activities.
b. Use the direct method to compute the amount of cash outflows from operating activities.

Exercise 12-6A *Direct versus indirect method of determining cash flows from operating activities*

Expert Electronics, Inc. (EEI), recognized $3,800 of sales revenue on account and collected $2,100 of cash from accounts receivable. Further, EEI recognized $900 of operating expenses on account and paid $700 cash as partial settlement of accounts payable.

Required

Based on this information alone:

a. Prepare the operating activities section of the statement of cash flows under the direct method.
b. Prepare the operating activities section of the statement of cash flows under the indirect method.

LO 1, 2

Exercise 12-7A *The direct versus the indirect method of determining cash flows from operating activities*

The following accounts and corresponding balances were drawn from Jogger Company's 2014 and 2013 year-end balance sheets:

Account Title	2014	2013
Accounts receivable	$57,000	$62,000
Prepaid rent	1,100	1,300
Utilities payable	900	750
Other operating expenses payable	21,300	22,400

The 2014 income statement is shown below:

Income Statement	
Sales	$268,000
Rent expense	(36,000)
Utilities expense	(18,300)
Other operating expenses	(79,100)
Net Income	$134,600

Required

a. Prepare the operating activities section of the statement of cash flows using the direct method.

b. Prepare the operating activities section of the statement of cash flows using the indirect method.

LO 3

Exercise 12-8A *Determining cash flow from investing activities*

On January 1, 2013, Shelton Company had a balance of $325,000 in its Land account. During 2013, Shelton sold land that had cost $106,500 for $132,000 cash. The balance in the Land account on December 31, 2013, was $285,000.

Required

a. Determine the cash outflow for the purchase of land during 2013.

b. Prepare the investing activities section of the 2013 statement of cash flows.

LO 3

Exercise 12-9A *Determining cash flows from investing activities*

On January 1, 2013, Bacco Company had a balance of $72,350 in its Delivery Equipment account. During 2013, Bacco purchased delivery equipment that cost $22,100. The balance in the Delivery Equipment account on December 31, 2013, was $69,400. The 2013 income statement reported a gain from the sale of equipment for $5,000. On the date of sale, accumulated depreciation on the equipment sold amounted to $22,000.

Required

a. Determine the original cost of the equipment that was sold during 2013.

b. Determine the amount of cash flow from the sale of delivery equipment that should be shown in the investing activities section of the 2013 statement of cash flows.

LO 3

Exercise 12-10A *Determining cash flows from investing activities*

The following accounts and corresponding balances were drawn from Delsey Company's 2014 and 2013 year-end balance sheets:

Account Title	2014	2013
Investment securities	$110,000	$116,500
Machinery	486,000	437,000
Land	160,000	100,000

Other information drawn from the accounting records:

1. Delsey incurred a $6,000 loss on the sale of investment securities during 2014.
2. Old machinery with a book value of $8,000 (cost of $36,000 minus accumulated depreciation of $28,000) was sold. The income statement showed a gain on the sale of machinery of $4,500.
3. Delsey did not sell land during the year.

Required

a. Compute the amount of cash flow associated with the sale of investment securities.
b. Compute the amount of cash flow associated with the purchase of machinery.
c. Compute the amount of cash flow associated with the sale of machinery.
d. Compute the amount of cash flow associated with the purchase of land.
e. Prepare the investing activities section of the statement of cash flows.

Exercise 12-11A   *Determining cash flows from financing activities*   LO 4

On January 1, 2013, DIBA Company had a balance of $450,000 in its Bonds Payable account. During 2013, DIBA issued bonds with a $200,000 face value. There was no premium or discount associated with the bond issue. The balance in the Bonds Payable account on December 31, 2013, was $400,000.

Required

a. Determine the cash outflow for the repayment of bond liabilities assuming that the bonds were retired at face value.
b. Prepare the financing activities section of the 2013 statement of cash flows.

Exercise 12-12A   *Determining cash flows from financing activities*   ·   LO 4

On January 1, 2013, Hardy Company had a balance of $150,000 in its Common Stock account. During 2013, Hardy paid $20,000 to purchase treasury stock. Treasury stock is accounted for using the cost method. The balance in the Common Stock account on December 31, 2013, was $175,000. Assume that the common stock is no par stock.

Required

a. Determine the cash inflow from the issue of common stock.
b. Prepare the financing activities section of the 2013 statement of cash flows.

Exercise 12-13A   *Determining cash flows from financing activities*   LO 4

The following accounts and corresponding balances were drawn from Dexter Company's 2014 and 2013 year-end balance sheets:

Account Title	2014	2013
Bonds payable	$350,000	$400,000
Common stock	450,000	420,000

Other information drawn from the accounting records:

1. Dividends paid during the period amounted to $50,000.
2. There were no bond liabilities issued during the period.

Required

a. Compute the amount of cash flow associated with the repayment of bond liabilities.
b. Compute the amount of cash flow associated with the issue of common stock.
c. Prepare the financing activities section of the statement of cash flows.

PROBLEMS—SERIES A

All applicable Problems in Series A are available with McGraw-Hill's _Connect® Accounting._

LO 1, 2

CHECK FIGURE
Net cash flow from operating
activities: $105,200

Problem 12-14A   *The direct versus the indirect method to determine cash flow from operating activities*

Green Brands, Inc. (GBI), presents its statement of cash flows using the indirect method. The following accounts and corresponding balances were drawn from GBI's 2014 and 2013 year-end balance sheets:

Account Title	2014	2013
Accounts receivable	$48,000	$52,000
Merchandise inventory	78,000	72,000
Prepaid insurance	24,000	32,000
Accounts payable	31,000	28,000
Salaries payable	8,200	7,800
Unearned service revenue	2,400	3,600

The 2014 income statement is shown below:

Income Statement	
Sales	$ 720,000
Cost of goods sold	(398,000)
Gross margin	322,000
Service revenue	6,000
Insurance expense	(36,000)
Salaries expense	(195,000)
Depreciation expense	(12,000)
Operating income	85,000
Gain on sale of equipment	4,500
Net income	$ 89,500

Required

a. Prepare the operating activities section of the statement of cash flows using the direct method.

b. Prepare the operating activities section of the statement of cash flows using the indirect method.

LO 3

CHECK FIGURES
b. $4,700
c. $10,000

Problem 12-15A   *Determining cash flows from investing activities*

The following information was drawn from the year-end balance sheets of Mass Trading Company:

Account Title	2014	2013
Investment securities	$ 47,200	$ 42,400
Equipment	246,000	218,000
Buildings	646,000	720,000
Land	95,000	72,000

Additional information regarding transactions occurring during 2014:

1. Investment securities that had cost $6,100 were sold. The 2014 income statement contained a loss on the sale of investment securities of $1,400.

2. Equipment with a cost of $38,000 was purchased.

3. The income statement showed a gain on the sale of equipment of $8,000. On the date of sale, accumulated depreciation on the equipment sold amounted to $8,000.

4. A building that had originally cost $210,000 was demolished.

5. Land that had cost $30,000 was sold for $27,000.

Required

a. Determine the amount of cash flow for the purchase of investment securities during 2014.

b. Determine the amount of cash flow from the sale of investment securities during 2014.

c. Determine the cost of the equipment that was sold during 2014.

d. Determine the amount of cash flow from the sale of equipment during 2014.

e. Determine the amount of cash flow for the purchase of buildings during 2014.

f. Determine the amount of cash flow for the purchase of land during 2014.

g. Prepare the investing activities section of the 2014 statement of cash flows.

Problem 12-16A   *Determining cash flows from financing activities*

LO 4

The following information was drawn from the year-end balance sheets of Fox River, Inc.:

Account Title	2014	2013
Bonds payable	$600,000	$800,000
Common stock	210,000	180,000
Treasury stock	20,000	5,000
Retained earnings	86,000	75,000

Additional information regarding transactions occurring during 2014:

1. Fox River, Inc., issued $100,000 of bonds during 2014. The bonds were issued at face value. All bonds retired were retired at face value.

2. Common stock did not have a par value.

3. Fox River, Inc., uses the cost method to account for treasury stock.

4. The amount of net income shown on the 2014 income statement was $32,000.

Required

a. Determine the amount of cash flow for the retirement of bonds that should appear on the 2014 statement of cash flows.

b. Determine the amount of cash flow from the issue of common stock that should appear on the 2014 statement of cash flows.

c. Determine the amount of cash flow for the purchase of treasury stock that should appear on the 2014 statement of cash flows.

d. Determine the amount of cash flow for the payment of dividends that should appear on the 2014 statement of cash flows.

e. Prepare the financing activities section of the 2014 statement of cash flows.

Problem 12-17A   *Preparing a statement of cash flows*

LO 1, 3, 4

The following information can be obtained by examining a company's balance sheet and income statement information:

a. Increases in noncash current asset account balances.

b. Decreases in noncash current asset account balances.

c. Cash outflows made to purchase long-term assets.

d. Decreases in current liability account balances.

e. Cash outflows to repay long-term debt.

f. Gains recognized on the sale of long-term assets.

g. Noncash expenses (depreciation).

h. Cash outflows to purchase treasury stock.

i. Increases in current liability account balances.

j. Cash inflows from the sale of long-term assets.

k. Cash inflows from the issue of common stock.

l. Cash outflows to pay dividends.

m. Losses incurred from the sale of long-term assets.

n. Cash inflows from the issue of long-term debt.

Required

Construct a table like the one shown below. For each item, indicate whether it would be used in the computation of net cash flows from operating, investing, or financing activities. Also, indicate whether the item would be added or subtracted when determining the net cash flow from operating, investing, or financing activities. Assume the indirect method is used to prepare the operating activities section of the statement of cash flows. The first item has been completed as an example.

Item	Type of Activity	Add or Subtract
a.	Operating	Subtract
b.		
c.		
d.		
e.		
f.		
g.		
h.		
i.		
j.		
k.		
l.		
m.		
n.		

LO 1, 3, 4

Problem 12-18A *Using financial statements to prepare a statements of cash flows—Indirect method*

CHECK FIGURES
Net Cash Flow from Operating
Activities: $32,050
Net Increase in Cash: $16,050

The comparative balance sheets and income statements for Gypsy Company follow:

Balance Sheets As of December 31		
	2014	**2013**
Assets		
Cash	$ 32,500	$16,300
Accounts receivable	4,750	2,800
Inventory	11,200	9,800
Equipment	45,000	52,000
Accumulated depreciation—equipment	(17,800)	(21,800)
Land	28,000	12,000
Total assets	$103,650	$71,100
Liabilities and equity		
Accounts payable (inventory)	$ 3,750	$ 4,900
Long-term debt	5,800	7,800
Common stock	47,000	25,000
Retained earnings	47,100	33,400
Total liabilities and equity	$103,650	$71,100

Income Statement For the Year Ended December 31, 2014	
Sales revenue	$61,200
Cost of goods sold	(24,500)
Gross margin	36,700
Depreciation expense	(12,000)
Operating income	24,700
Gain on sale of equipment	1,500
Loss on disposal of land	(100)
Net income	$26,100

Additional Data

1. During 2014, the company sold equipment for $21,500; it had originally cost $36,000. Accumulated depreciation on this equipment was $16,000 at the time of the sale. Also, the company purchased equipment for $29,000 cash.

2. The company sold land that had cost $6,000. This land was sold for $5,900, resulting in the recognition of a $100 loss. Also, common stock was issued in exchange for title to land that was valued at $22,000 at the time of exchange.

3. Paid dividends of $12,400.

Required

Prepare a statement of cash flows using the indirect method.

Problem 12-19A *Using financial statements to prepare a statement of cash flows— Indirect method*

LO 1, 3, 4

The comparative balance sheets and an income statement for Raceway Corporation follow:

Balance Sheets As of December 31		
	2014	2013
Assets		
Cash	$ 6,300	$ 48,400
Accounts receivable	10,200	7,260
Merchandise inventory	45,200	56,000
Prepaid rent	700	2,140
Equipment	140,000	144,000
Accumulated depreciation	(73,400)	(118,000)
Land	116,000	50,000
Total assets	$245,000	$189,800
Liabilities		
Accounts payable (inventory)	$ 37,200	$ 40,000
Salaries payable	12,200	10,600
Stockholders' equity		
Common stock, $50 par value	150,000	120,000
Retained earnings	45,600	19,200
Total liabilities and equity	$245,000	$189,800

Income Statement	
For the Year Ended December 31, 2014	
Sales	$480,000
Cost of goods sold	(264,000)
Gross profit	216,000
Operating expenses	
Depreciation expense	(11,400)
Rent expense	(7,000)
Salaries expense	(95,200)
Other operating expenses	(76,000)
Net income	$ 26,400

Other Information

1. Purchased land for $66,000.
2. Purchased new equipment for $62,000.
3. Sold old equipment that cost $66,000 with accumulated depreciation of $56,000 for $10,000 cash.
4. Issued common stock for $30,000.

Required

Prepare the statement of cash flows for 2014 using the indirect method.

LO 2, 3, 4

CHECK FIGURE
Net Cash Flow from Operating
Activities: $(900)

Problem 12-20A *Using transaction data to prepare a statement of cash flows—Direct method*

York Company engaged in the following transactions for the year 2013. The beginning cash balance was $86,000 and ending cash balance was $59,100.

1. Sales on account were $548,000. The beginning receivables balance was $128,000 and the ending balance was $90,000.
2. Salaries expense for the period was $232,000. The beginning salaries payable balance was $16,000 and the ending balance was $8,000.
3. Other operating expenses for the period were $236,000. The beginning other operating expenses payable balance was $16,000 and the ending balance was $10,000.
4. Recorded $30,000 of depreciation expense. The beginning and ending balances in the Accumulated Depreciation account were $42,000 and $12,000, respectively.
5. The Equipment account had beginning and ending balances of $44,000 and $56,000 respectively. There were no sales of equipment during the period.
6. The beginning and ending balances in the Notes Payable account were $36,000 and $44,000, respectively. There were no payoffs of notes during the period.
7. There was $4,600 of interest expense reported on the income statement. The beginning and ending balances in the Interest Payable account were $8,400 and $7,500, respectively.
8. The beginning and ending Merchandise Inventory account balances were $22,000 and $29,400, respectively. The company sold merchandise with a cost of $83,600 (cost of goods sold for the period was $83,600). The beginning and ending balances of Accounts Payable were $8,000 and $6,400, respectively.
9. The beginning and ending balances of Notes Receivable were $60,000 and $100,000, respectively. Notes receivable result from long-term loans made to employees. There were no collections from employees during the period.
10. The beginning and ending balances of the Common Stock account were $120,000 and $160,000, respectively. The increase was caused by the issue of common stock for cash.
11. Land had beginning and ending balances of $24,000 and $14,000, respectively. Land that cost $10,000 was sold for $6,000, resulting in a loss of $4,000.

12. The tax expense for the period was $6,600. The Taxes Payable account had a $2,400 beginning balance and an $2,200 ending balance.

13. The Investments account had beginning and ending balances of $20,000 and $60,000, respectively. The company purchased investments for $50,000 cash during the period, and investments that cost $10,000 were sold for $22,000, resulting in a $12,000 gain.

Required

a. Determine the amount of cash flow for each item and indicate whether the item should appear in the operating, investing, or financing activities section of a statement of cash flows. If an item does not affect the cash flow statement, make a statement indicating that the cash flow statement will not be affected. Assume York Company uses the direct method for showing net cash flow from operating activities.

b. Prepare a statement of cash flows based on the information you developed in Requirement a.

Problem 12-21A *Using financial statements to prepare a statement of cash flows—*
Direct method

LO 2, 3, 4

The following financial statements were drawn from the records of Matrix Shoes:

Balance Sheets As of December 31		
	2014	**2013**
Assets		
Cash	$ 94,300	$ 14,100
Accounts receivable	36,000	40,000
Merchandise inventory	72,000	64,000
Notes receivable	0	16,000
Equipment	98,000	170,000
Accumulated depreciation—equipment	(47,800)	(94,000)
Land	46,000	30,000
Total assets	$298,500	$240,100
Liabilities		
Accounts payable	$ 24,000	$ 26,400
Salaries payable	15,000	10,000
Utilities payable	800	1,400
Interest payable	0	1,000
Notes payable (long-term)	0	24,000
Common stock	150,000	110,000
Retained earnings	108,700	67,300
Total liabilities and equity	$298,500	$240,100

Income Statement For the Year Ended December 31, 2014	
Sales revenue	$300,000
Cost of goods sold	(144,000)
Gross margin	156,000
Operating expenses	
Salary expense	(88,000)
Depreciation expense	(9,800)
Utilities expense	(6,400)
Operating income	51,800
Nonoperating items	
Interest expense	(2,400)
Loss on the sale of equipment	(800)
Net income	$ 48,600

Additional Information

1. Sold equipment costing $72,000 with accumulated depreciation of $56,000 for $15,200 cash.
2. Paid a $7,200 cash dividend to owners.

Required

Analyze the data and prepare a statement of cash flows using the direct method.

EXERCISES—SERIES B

LO 1

Exercise 12-1B *Use the indirect method to determine cash flows from operating activities*

An accountant for Farve Enterprise Companies (FEC) computed the following information by making comparisons between FEC's 2014 and 2013 balance sheets. Further information was determined by examining the company's 2014 income statement.

1. The amount of an increase in the balance of a Prepaid Rent account.
2. The amount of an increase in the balance of a Treasury Stock account.
3. The amount of a decrease in the balance of the Accounts Receivable account.
4. The amount of a gain arising from the sale of land.
5. The amount of an increase in the balance of the Salaries Payable account.
6. The amount of an increase in the balance of the Bonds Payable account.
7. The amount of depreciation expense shown on the income statement.
8. The amount of cash dividends paid to the stockholders.
9. The amount of an increase in the balance of an Unearned Revenue account.
10. The amount of a decrease in the balance of an Inventory account.
11. The amount of a decrease in the balance of a Land account.

Required

For each item described above, indicate whether the amount should be added to or subtracted from the amount of net income when determining the amount of net cash flow from operating activities using the indirect method. If an item does not affect net cash flow from operating activities, identify it as being not affected.

LO 1

Exercise 12-2B *Use the indirect method to determine cash flows from operating activities*

Napoleon Incorporated presents its statement of cash flows using the indirect method. The following accounts and corresponding balances were drawn from the company's 2014 and 2013 year-end balance sheets:

Account Title	2014	2013
Accounts receivable	$31,400	$28,600
Accounts payable	10,300	9,800

The 2014 income statement showed net income of $41,500.

Required

a. Prepare the operating activities section of the statement of cash flows.
b. Explain why the change in the balance in accounts receivable was added to or subtracted from the amount of net income when you completed Requirement *a*.
c. Explain why the change in the balance in accounts payable was added to or subtracted from the amount of net income when you completed Requirement *a*.

Exercise 12-3B *Use the indirect method to determine cash flows from operating activities*   **LO 1**

Pella Company presents its statement of cash flows using the indirect method. The following accounts and corresponding balances were drawn from Pella's 2014 and 2013 year-end balance sheets:

Account Title	2014	2013
Accounts receivable	$24,000	$21,000
Prepaid rent	1,650	1,900
Interest receivable	900	1,200
Accounts payable	10,200	8,500
Salaries payable	2,700	2,900
Unearned revenue	2,000	1,800

The income statement contained a $700 loss on the sale of equipment, a $900 gain on the sale of land, and $2,500 of depreciation expense. Net income for the period was $36,500.

Required

Prepare the operating activities section of the statement of cash flows.

Exercise 12-4B *Use the direct method to determine cash flows from operating activities*   **LO 2**

The following accounts and corresponding balances were drawn from Osprey Company's 2014 and 2013 year-end balance sheets:

Account Title	2014	2013
Unearned revenue	$4,500	$6,000
Prepaid rent	5,200	3,600

During the year, $84,000 of unearned revenue was recognized as having been earned. Rent expense for 2014 was $24,000.

Required

Based on this information alone, prepare the operating activities section of the statement of cash flows assuming the direct approach is used.

Exercise 12-5B *Use the direct method to determine cash flows from operating activities*   **LO 2**

The following accounts and corresponding balances were drawn from Pixi Company's 2014 and 2013 year-end balance sheets:

Account Title	2014	2013
Accounts receivable	$62,000	$56,000
Interest receivable	8,000	6,000
Other operating expenses payable	26,000	29,000
Salaries payable	12,000	9,000

The 2014 income statement is shown below:

Income Statement	
Sales	$650,000
Salary expense	(420,000)
Other operating expenses	(110,000)
Operating income	120,000
Nonoperating items: Interest revenue	15,000
Net income	$135,000

Required

a. Use the direct method to compute the amount of cash inflows from operating activities.

b. Use the direct method to compute the amount of cash outflows from operating activities.

LO 1, 2

Exercise 12-6B   *Direct versus indirect method of determining cash flows from operating activities*

Ragg Shop, Inc. (RSI), recognized $3,800 of sales revenue on account and collected $2,950 of cash from accounts receivable. Further, RSI recognized $1,200 of operating expenses on account and paid $900 cash as partial settlement of accounts payable.

Required

Based on this information alone:

a. Prepare the operating activities section of the statement of cash flows under the direct method.

b. Prepare the operating activities section of the statement of cash flows under the indirect method.

LO 1, 2

Exercise 12-7B   *The direct versus the indirect method of determining cash flows from operating activities*

The following accounts and corresponding balances were drawn from Geneses Company's 2014 and 2013 year-end balance sheets:

Account Title	2014	2013
Accounts receivable	$65,000	$72,000
Prepaid rent	1,400	1,950
Utilities payable	3,200	3,800
Other operating expenses payable	27,000	31,500

The 2014 income statement is shown below:

Income Statement	
Sales	$420,000
Rent expense	(52,000)
Utilities expense	(45,300)
Other operating expenses	(195,000)
Net income	$127,700

Required

a. Prepare the operating activities section of the statement of cash flows using the direct method.

b. Prepare the operating activities section of the statement of cash flows using the indirect method.

LO 3

Exercise 12-8B   *Determining cash flow from investing activities*

On January 1, 2013, Poole Company had a balance of $178,000 in its Land account. During 2013, Poole sold land that had cost $71,000 for $95,000 cash. The balance in the Land account on December 31, 2013, was $210,000.

Required

a. Determine the cash outflow for the purchase of land during 2013.

b. Prepare the investing activities section of the 2013 statement of cash flows.

Exercise 12-9B   *Determining cash flow from investing activities* LO 3

On January 1, 2013, Sanita Company had a balance of $76,300 in its Office Equipment account. During 2013, Sanita purchased office equipment that cost $30,300. The balance in the Office Equipment account on December 31, 2013, was $75,400. The 2013 income statement contained a gain from the sale of equipment for $6,000. On the date of sale, accumulated depreciation on the equipment sold amounted to $14,400.

Required

a. Determine the cost of the equipment that was sold during 2013.

b. Determine the amount of cash flow from the sale of office equipment that should be shown in the investing activities section of the 2013 statement of cash flows.

Exercise 12-10B   *Determining cash flows from investing activities* LO 3

The following accounts and corresponding balances were drawn from Teva Company's 2014 and 2013 year-end balance sheets:

Account Title	2014	2013
Investment securities	$102,000	$110,000
Machinery	480,000	465,000
Land	75,000	95,000

Other information drawn from the accounting records:

1. Teva incurred a $3,000 loss on the sale of investment securities during 2014.
2. Old machinery with a book value of $8,000 (cost of $34,000 minus accumulated depreciation of $26,000) was sold. The income statement showed a gain on the sale of machinery of $7,500.
3. Teva incurred a loss of $4,000 on the sale of land in 2014.

Required

a. Compute the amount of cash flow associated with the sale of investment securities.

b. Compute the amount of cash flow associated with the purchase of machinery.

c. Compute the amount of cash flow associated with the sale of machinery.

d. Compute the amount of cash flow associated with the sale of land.

e. Prepare the investing activities section of the statement of cash flows.

Exercise 12-11B   *Determining cash flows from financing activities* LO 4

On January 1, 2013, Van Company had a balance of $800,000 in its Bonds Payable account. During 2013, Van issued bonds with a $300,000 face value. There was no premium or discount associated with the bond issue. The balance in the Bonds Payable account on December 31, 2013, was $600,000.

Required

a. Determine the cash outflow for the repayment of bond liabilities assuming that the bonds were retired at face value.

b. Prepare the financing activities section of the 2013 statement of cash flows.

Exercise 12-12B   *Determining cash flows from financing activities* LO 4

On January 1, 2013, Milam Company had a balance of $300,000 in its Common Stock account. During 2013, Milam paid $18,000 to purchase treasury stock. Treasury stock is accounted for using the cost method. The balance in the Common Stock account on December 31, 2013, was $350,000. Assume that the common stock is no par stock.

Required

a. Determine the cash inflow from the issue of common stock.

b. Prepare the financing activities section of the 2013 statement of cash flows.

LO 4

Exercise 12-13B *Determining cash flows from financing activities*

The following accounts and corresponding balances were drawn from Cushing Company's 2014 and 2013 year-end balance sheets:

Account Title	2014	2013
Bonds payable	$200,000	$150,000
Common stock	650,000	400,000

Other information drawn from the accounting records:

1. Dividends paid during the period amounted to $50,000.
2. There were no bond liabilities repaid during the period.

Required

a. Compute the amount of cash flow associated with the issue of bond liabilities.
b. Compute the amount of cash flow associated with the issue of common stock.
c. Prepare the financing activities section of the statement of cash flows.

PROBLEMS—SERIES B

LO 1, 2

Problem 12-14B *The direct versus the indirect method to determine cash flows from operating activities*

The following accounts and corresponding balances were drawn from Crimson Sports, Inc.'s 2014 and 2013 year-end balance sheets:

Account Title	2014	2013
Accounts receivable	$31,000	$36,000
Merchandise inventory	70,000	65,000
Prepaid insurance	25,000	24,000
Accounts payable	18,000	20,000
Salaries payable	5,100	4,500
Unearned service revenue	10,200	9,500

The 2014 income statement is shown below:

Income Statement	
Sales	$495,000
Cost of goods sold	(215,000)
Gross margin	280,000
Service revenue	20,000
Insurance expense	(42,000)
Salaries expense	(122,000)
Depreciation expense	(12,000)
Operating income	124,000
Gain on sale of equipment	1,500
Net income	$125,500

Required

a. Prepare the operating activities section of the statement of cash flows using the direct method.
b. Prepare the operating activities section of the statement of cash flows using the indirect method.

Problem 12-15B   *Determining cash flows from investing activities*   **LO 3**

The following information was drawn from the year-end balance sheets of Vigotti Company:

Account Title	2014	2013
Investment securities	$ 51,000	$ 60,000
Equipment	310,000	275,000
Buildings	980,000	950,000
Land	135,000	110,000

Additional information regarding transactions occurring during 2014:

1. Investment securities that had cost $11,300 were sold. The 2014 income statement contained a loss on the sale of investment securities of $800.
2. Equipment with a cost of $80,000 was purchased.
3. The income statement showed a gain on the sale of equipment of $9,500. On the date of sale, accumulated depreciation on the equipment sold amounted to $38,000.
4. A building that had originally cost $90,000 was demolished.
5. Land that had cost $20,000 was sold for $15,000.

Required

a. Determine the amount of cash flow for the purchase of investment securities during 2014.
b. Determine the amount of cash flow from the sale of investment securities during 2014.
c. Determine the cost of the equipment that was sold during 2014.
d. Determine the amount of cash flow from the sale of equipment during 2014.
e. Determine the amount of cash flow for the purchase of buildings during 2014.
f. Determine the amount of cash flow for the purchase of land during 2014.
g. Prepare the investing activities section of the 2014 statement of cash flows.

Problem 12-16B   *Determining cash flows from financing activities*   **LO 4**

The following information was drawn from the year-end balance sheets of Long's Wholesale, Inc.:

Account Title	2014	2013
Bonds payable	$400,000	$600,000
Common stock	190,000	150,000
Treasury stock	20,000	15,000
Retained earnings	96,000	80,000

Additional information regarding transactions occurring during 2014:

1. Long's Wholesale, Inc., issued $90,000 of bonds during 2014. The bonds were issued at face value. All bonds retired were retired at face value.
2. Common stock did not have a par value.
3. Long's Wholesale, Inc., uses the cost method to account for treasury stock. Long's Wholesale, Inc., did not resell any treasury stock in 2014.
4. The amount of net income shown on the 2014 income statement was $49,000.

Required

a. Determine the amount of cash flow for the retirement of bonds that should appear on the 2014 statement of cash flows.
b. Determine the amount of cash flow from the issue of common stock that should appear on the 2014 statement of cash flows.

c. Determine the amount of cash flow for the purchase of treasury stock that should appear on the 2014 statement of cash flows.

d. Determine the amount of cash flow for the payment of dividends that should appear on the 2014 statement of cash flows.

e. Prepare the financing activities section of the 2014 statement of cash flows.

LO 1, 3, 4

Problem 12-17B *Preparing a statement of cash flows*

The following information can be obtained by examining a company's balance sheet and income statement information:

a. Increases in noncash current asset account balances.
b. Cash outflows made to purchase noncurrent assets.
c. Decreases in current liability account balances.
d. Noncash expenses (e.g., depreciation).
e. Cash outflows to purchase treasury stock.
f. Gains recognized on the sale of noncurrent assets.
g. Cash outflows to pay dividends.
h. Cash inflows from the issue of common stock.
i. Cash inflows from the sale of noncurrent assets.
j. Increases in current liability account balances.
k. Cash inflows from the issue of noncurrent debt.
l. Losses incurred from the sale of noncurrent assets.
m. Decreases in noncash current asset account balances.
n. Cash outflows to repay noncurrent debt.

Required

Construct a table like the one shown below. For each item, indicate whether it would be used in the computation of net cash flows from operating, investing, or financing activities. Also, indicate whether the item would be added or subtracted when determining the net cash flow from operating, investing, or financing activities. Assume the indirect method is used to prepare the operating activities section of the statement of cash flows. The first item has been completed as an example.

Item	Type of Activity	Add or Subtract
a.	Operating	Subtract
b.		
c.		
d.		
e.		
f.		
g.		
h.		
i.		
j.		
k.		
l.		
m.		
n.		

Problem 12-18B   *Using financial statements to prepare a statement of cash flows—*   **LO 1, 3, 4**
                     Indirect method

The following financial statements were drawn from the records of Culinary Products Co.:

Balance Sheets As of December 31		
	2014	**2013**
Assets		
Cash	$24,200	$ 2,800
Accounts receivable	2,000	1,200
Inventory	6,400	6,000
Equipment	19,000	42,000
Accumulated depreciation—equipment	(9,000)	(17,400)
Land	18,400	10,400
Total assets	$61,000	$45,000
Liabilities and stockholders' equity		
Accounts payable (inventory)	$ 2,600	$ 4,200
Long-term debt	2,800	6,400
Common stock	22,000	10,000
Retained earnings	33,600	24,400
Total liabilities and stockholders' equity	$61,000	$45,000

Income Statement For the Year Ended December 31, 2014	
Sales revenue	$35,700
Cost of goods sold	(14,150)
Gross margin	21,550
Depreciation expense	(3,600)
Operating income	17,950
Gain on sale of equipment	500
Loss on disposal of land	(50)
Net income	$18,400

Additional Data

1. During 2014, the company sold equipment for $18,500; it had originally cost $30,000. Accumulated depreciation on this equipment was $12,000 at the time of the sale. Also, the company purchased equipment for $7,000 cash.

2. The company sold land that had cost $4,000. This land was sold for $3,950, resulting in the recognition of a $50 loss. Also, common stock was issued in exchange for title to land that was valued at $12,000 at the time of exchange.

3. Paid dividends of $9,200.

Required

Prepare a statement of cash flows using the indirect method.

Problem 12-19B   *Using financial statements to prepare a statement of cash flows—*   **LO 1, 3, 4**
                     Indirect method

The comparative balance sheets and an income statement for Wang Beauty Products, Inc., shown on the next page.

Balance Sheets As of December 31		
	2014	**2013**
Assets		
Cash	$ 68,800	$ 40,600
Accounts receivable	30,000	22,000
Merchandise inventory	160,000	176,000
Prepaid rent	2,400	4,800
Equipment	256,000	288,000
Accumulated depreciation	(146,800)	(236,000)
Land	192,000	80,000
Total assets	$562,400	$375,400
Liabilities and equity		
Accounts payable (inventory)	$ 67,000	$ 76,000
Salaries payable	28,000	24,000
Stockholders' equity		
Common stock, $50 par value	250,000	200,000
Retained earnings	217,400	75,400
Total liabilities and equity	$562,400	$375,400

Income Statement For the Year Ended December 31, 2014	
Sales	$1,500,000
Cost of goods sold	(797,200)
Gross profit	702,800
Operating expenses	
Depreciation expense	(22,800)
Rent expense	(24,000)
Salaries expense	(256,000)
Other operating expenses	(258,000)
Net income	$ 142,000

Other Information

1. Purchased land for $112,000.
2. Purchased new equipment for $100,000.
3. Sold old equipment that cost $132,000 with accumulated depreciation of $112,000 for $20,000 cash.
4. Issued common stock for $50,000.

Required

Prepare the statement of cash flows for 2014 using the indirect method.

LO 2, 3, 4

Problem 12-20B *Using transaction data to prepare a statement of cash flows—Direct method*

The Electric Company engaged in the following transactions during 2014. The beginning cash balance was $43,000 and ending cash balance was $48,600.

1. Sales on account were $274,000. The beginning receivables balance was $86,000 and the ending balance was $74,000.
2. Salaries expense was $115,000. The beginning salaries payable balance was $9,600 and the ending balance was $7,500.
3. Other operating expenses were $118,000. The beginning other Operating Expenses Payable balance was $8,500 and the ending balance was $6,000.
4. Recorded $25,000 of depreciation expense. The beginning and ending balances in the Accumulated Depreciation account were $18,000 and $43,000, respectively.

5. The Equipment account had beginning and ending balances of $28,000 and $42,000, respectively. There were no sales of equipment during the period.

6. The beginning and ending balances in the Notes Payable account were $38,000 and $32,000, respectively. There were no notes payable issued during the period.

7. There was $4,600 of interest expense reported on the income statement. The beginning and ending balances in the Interest Payable account were $6,400 and $6,200, respectively.

8. The beginning and ending Merchandise Inventory account balances were $26,000 and $32,500, respectively. The company sold merchandise with a cost of $119,000. The beginning and ending balances of Accounts Payable were $10,000 and $12,500, respectively.

9. The beginning and ending balances of Notes Receivable were $80,000 and $20,000, respectively. Notes receivable result from long-term loans made to creditors. There were no loans made to creditors during the period.

10. The beginning and ending balances of the Common Stock account were $140,000 and $190,000, respectively. The increase was caused by the issue of common stock for cash.

11. Land had beginning and ending balances of $48,000 and $28,000, respectively. Land that cost $20,000 was sold for $16,000, resulting in a loss of $4,000.

12. The tax expense for the period was $6,600. The Tax Payable account had a $3,200 beginning balance and a $2,800 ending balance.

13. The Investments account had beginning and ending balances of $10,000 and $30,000, respectively. The company purchased investments for $40,000 cash during the period, and investments that cost $20,000 were sold for $26,000, resulting in a $6,000 gain.

Required

a. Determine the amount of cash flow for each item and indicate whether the item should appear in the operating, investing, or financing activities section of a statement of cash flows. If an item does not affect the cash flow statement, make a statement indicating that the cash flow statement will not be affected. Assume The Electric Company uses the direct method for showing net cash flow from operating activities.

b. Prepare a statement of cash flows based on the information you developed in Requirement a.

Problem 12-21B *Using financial statements to prepare a statement of cash flows—Direct method*   **LO 2, 3, 4**

The following financial statements were drawn from the records of Boston Materials, Inc.:

Balance Sheets As of December 31		
	2014	**2013**
Assets		
Cash	$ 99,700	$ 25,400
Accounts receivable	72,000	60,000
Inventory	86,000	75,000
Notes receivable (long-term)	0	24,000
Equipment	104,000	152,000
Accumulated depreciation—equipment	(67,500)	(75,000)
Land	60,000	45,000
Total assets	$354,200	$306,400
Liabilities and equity		
Accounts payable	$ 35,300	$ 36,200
Salaries payable	18,200	15,500
Utilities payable	1,400	2,800
Interest payable	600	1,200
Notes payable (long-term)	0	36,000
Common stock	120,000	100,000
Retained earnings	178,700	114,700
Total liabilities and equity	$354,200	$306,400

Income Statement For the Year Ended December 31, 2014	
Sales revenue	$450,000
Cost of goods sold	(212,000)
Gross margin	238,000
Operating expenses	
Salary expense	(96,000)
Depreciation expense	(18,500)
Utilities expense	(7,500)
Operating income	116,000
Nonoperating items	
Interest expense	(3,500)
Gain on sale of equipment	1,500
Net income	$114,000

Additional Information

1. Sold equipment costing $48,000 with accumulated depreciation of $26,000 for $23,500 cash.
2. Paid a $50,000 cash dividend to owners.

Required

Analyze the data and prepare a statement of cash flows using the direct method.

ANALYZE, THINK, COMMUNICATE

ATC 12-1   Business Applications Case   *Understanding real-world annual reports*

Required

Use the Target Corporation's annual report in Appendix B to answer the following questions.

a. For the year ended January 29, 2011 (2010), which was larger, Target's *net income* or its *cash flow from operating activities*? By what amount did they differ?

b. What two items are most responsible for the difference between Target's *net income* and its *cash flow from operating activities* in 2010?

c. In 2010 Target generated approximately $5.3 billion of cash from operating activities, and its cash balance decreased by about $0.5 billion. How did the company use this $5.8 billion of cash?

ATC 12-2   Real-World Case   *Following the cash*

Sirius XM Radio Inc. was created by a merger between Sirius Radio and XM Radio, in July 2008. Sirius Radio was formed in 1990, and XM Radio began in 1992, although these companies did not generate any significant amounts of revenue in the early years of their existence. Neither XM, Sirius, nor the combined company, Sirius XM Radio, earned a profit until 2010. Its cumulative net losses totaled $10 billion by the end of 2010. Sirius XM's statements of cash flows for 2008, 2009, and 2010 follow.

SIRIUS XM RADIO INC. AND SUBSIDIARIES
Consolidated Statements of Cash Flows
(dollar amounts in thousands)

	For the Years Ended December 31,		
	2010	2009	2008
Cash flows from operating activities:			
Net income (loss)	$ 43,055	$(352,038)	$(5,316,910)
Adjustments to reconcile net income (loss) to net cash provided by (used in) operating activities:			
Depreciation and amortization	273,691	309,450	203,752
Impairment of goodwill	—	—	4,766,190
			continued

continued

	For the Years Ended December 31,		
	2010	2009	2008
Non-cash interest expense, net of amortization of premium	$ 42,841	$ 43,066	$ (2,689)
Provision for doubtful accounts	32,379	30,602	21,589
Restructuring, impairments and related costs	66,731	26,964	—
Amortization of deferred income related to equity method investment	(2,776)	(2,776)	(1,156)
Loss on extinguishment of debt and credit facilities, net	120,120	267,646	98,203
Loss on investments, net	11,722	13,664	28,999
Loss on disposal of assets	1,017	—	4,879
Share-based payment expense	60,437	73,981	87,405
Deferred income taxes	2,308	5,981	2,476
Other non-cash purchase price adjustments	(250,727)	(202,054)	(68,330)
Other	—	—	1,643
Changes in operating assets and liabilities:			
Accounts receivable	(39,236)	(42,158)	(32,121)
Receivables from distributors	(11,023)	(2,788)	14,401
Inventory	(5,725)	8,269	8,291
Related party assets	(9,803)	15,305	(22,249)
Prepaid expenses and other current assets	75,374	10,027	(19,953)
Other long-term assets	17,671	86,674	(5,490)
Accounts payable and accrued expenses	5,420	(46,645)	(83,037)
Accrued interest	(884)	2,429	23,081
Deferred revenue	133,444	93,578	79,090
Related party liabilities	(53,413)	50,172	28,890
Other long-term liabilities	272	44,481	30,249
Net cash provided by (used in) operating activities	512,895	433,830	(152,797)
Cash flows from investing activities:			
Additions to property and equipment	(311,868)	(248,511)	(130,551)
Sales of property and equipment	—	—	105
Purchases of restricted and other investments	—	—	(3,000)
Acquisition of acquired entity cash	—	—	819,521
Merger related costs	—	—	(23,519)
Sale of restricted and other investments	9,454	—	65,869
Net cash provided by (used in) investing activities	(302,414)	(248,511)	728,425
Cash flows from financing activities:			
Proceeds from exercise of warrants and stock options	10,839	—	471
Preferred stock issuance, net of costs	—	(3,712)	—
Long-term borrowings, net of costs	1,274,707	582,612	531,743
Related party long-term borrowings, net of costs	196,118	362,593	—
Payment of premiums on redemption of debt	(84,326)	(17,075)	(18,693)
Payments to noncontrolling interest	—	—	(61,880)
Repayment of long term borrowings	(1,262,396)	(755,447)	(1,085,643)
Repayments of related party long-term borrowings	(142,221)	(351,247)	—
Net cash (used in) provided by financing activities	(7,279)	(182,276)	(634,002)
Net (decrease) increase in cash and cash equivalents	203,202	3,043	(58,374)
Cash and cash equivalents at beginning of period	383,489	380,446	438,820
Cash and cash equivalents at end of period	$ 586,691	$383,489	$ 380,446

Required

a. This chapter explained that many companies that report net losses on their earnings statements report positive cash flows from operating activities. How do Sirius XM's net incomes compare to its cash flows from operating activities?

b. Based only on the information in the statements of cash flows, does Sirius XM appear to be growing the capacity of its business? Explain.

c. In 2010 Sirius XM paid off over $1.262 billion of long-term borrowings and $142 million of related-party long-term borrowings. Where did it get the funds to repay this debt?

d. All things considered, based on the information in its statements of cash flows, did Sirius XM's cash position appear to be improving or deteriorating?

ATC 12-3 **Group Assignment** *Preparing a statement of cash flows*

The following financial statements and information are available for Blythe Industries Inc.

Balance Sheets As of December 31		
	2014	**2013**
Assets		
Cash	$ 160,200	$120,600
Accounts receivable	103,200	85,000
Inventory	186,400	171,800
Marketable securities (available for sale)	284,000	220,000
Equipment	650,000	490,000
Accumulated depreciation	(310,000)	(240,000)
Land	80,000	120,000
Total assets	$1,153,800	$967,400
Liabilities and equity		
Liabilities		
Accounts payable (inventory)	$ 36,400	$ 66,200
Notes payable—Long-term	230,000	250,000
Bonds payable	200,000	100,000
Total liabilities	466,400	416,200
Stockholders' equity		
Common stock, no par	240,000	200,000
Preferred stock, $50 par	110,000	100,000
Paid-in capital in excess of par—Preferred stock	34,400	26,800
Total paid-In capital	384,400	326,800
Retained earnings	333,000	264,400
Less: Treasury stock	(30,000)	(40,000)
Total stockholders' equity	687,400	551,200
Total liabilities and stockholders' equity	$1,153,800	$967,400

Income Statement For the Year Ended December 31, 2014		
Sales revenue		$1,050,000
Cost of goods sold		(766,500)
Gross profit		283,500
Operating expenses		
Supplies expense	$20,400	
Salaries expense	92,000	
Depreciation expense	90,000	
Total operating expenses		(202,400)
Operating income		81,100
Nonoperating items		
Interest expense		(16,000)
Gain from the sale of marketable securities		30,000
Gain from the sale of land and equipment		12,000
Net income		$ 107,100

Additional Information

1. Sold land that cost $40,000 for $44,000.
2. Sold equipment that cost $30,000 and had accumulated depreciation of $20,000 for $18,000.
3. Purchased new equipment for $190,000.

4. Sold marketable securities, classified as available-for-sale, that cost $40,000 for $70,000.

5. Purchased new marketable securities, classified as available-for-sale, for $104,000.

6. Paid $20,000 on the principal of the long-term note.

7. Paid off a $100,000 bond issue and issued new bonds for $200,000.

8. Sold 100 shares of treasury stock at its cost.

9. Issued some new common stock.

10. Issued some new $50 par preferred stock.

11. Paid dividends. (*Note:* The only transactions to affect retained earnings were net income and dividends.)

Required

Organize the class into three sections, and divide each section into groups of three to five students. Assign each section of groups an activity section of the statement of cash flows (operating activities, investing activities, or financing activities).

Group Task

Prepare your assigned portion of the statement of cash flows. Have a representative of your section put your activity section of the statement of cash flows on the board. As each section adds its information on the board, the full statement of cash flows will be presented.

Class Discussion

Have the class finish the statement of cash flows by computing the net change in cash. Also have the class answer the following questions:

a. What is the cost per share of the treasury stock?

b. What was the issue price per share of the preferred stock?

c. What was the book value of the equipment sold?

ATC 12-4   Business Applications Case   *Identifying different presentation formats*

In *Statement of Financial Accounting Standards No. 95,* the Financial Accounting Standards Board (FASB) recommended but did not require that companies use the direct method. In Appendix B, Paragraphs 106–121, of the standard, the FASB discussed its reasons for this recommendation.

Required

Obtain a copy of *Standard No. 95* and read Appendix B Paragraphs 106–121. Write a brief response summarizing the issues that the FASB considered and its specific reaction to those issues. Your response should draw heavily on paragraphs 119–121.

ATC 12-5   Writing Assignment   *Explaining discrepancies between cash flow and operating income*

The following selected information was drawn from the records of Fleming Company:

Assets	2013	2014
Accounts receivable	$ 400,000	$ 840,200
Merchandise inventory	720,000	1,480,000
Equipment	1,484,000	1,861,200
Accumulated depreciation	(312,000)	(402,400)

Fleming is experiencing cash flow problems. Despite the fact that it reported significant increases in operating income, operating activities produced a net cash outflow. Recent financial forecasts predict that Fleming will have insufficient cash to pay its current liabilities within three months.

Required

Write an explanation of Fleming's cash shortage. Include a recommendation to remedy the problem.

ATC 12-6   Ethical Dilemma   *Would I lie to you, baby?*

Andy and Jean Crocket are involved in divorce proceedings. When discussing a property settlement, Andy told Jean that he should take over their investment in an apartment complex because she would be unable to absorb the loss that the apartments are generating. Jean was somewhat distrustful and asked Andy to support his contention. He produced the following income statement, which was supported by a CPA's unqualified opinion that the statement was prepared in accordance with generally accepted accounting principles.

CROCKET APARTMENTS
Income Statement
For the Year Ended December 31, 2013

Rent revenue		$580,000
Less: Expenses		
Depreciation expense	$280,000	
Interest expense	184,000	
Operating expense	88,000	
Management fees	56,000	
Total expenses		(608,000)
Net loss		$ (28,000)

All revenue is earned on account. Interest and operating expenses are incurred on account. Management fees are paid in cash. The following accounts and balances were drawn from the 2012 and 2013 year-end balance sheets.

Account Title	2012	2013
Rent receivable	$40,000	$44,000
Interest payable	12,000	18,000
Accounts payable (oper. exp.)	6,000	4,000

Jean is reluctant to give up the apartments but feels that she must do so because her present salary is only $40,000 per year. She says that if she takes the apartments, the $28,000 loss would absorb a significant portion of her salary, leaving her only $12,000 with which to support herself. She tells you that while the figures seem to support her husband's arguments, she believes that she is failing to see something. She knows that she and her husband collected a $20,000 distribution from the business on December 1, 2013. Also, $150,000 cash was paid in 2013 to reduce the principal balance on a mortgage that was taken out to finance the purchase of the apartments two years ago. Finally, $24,000 cash was paid during 2013 to purchase a computer system used in the business. She wonders, "If the apartments are losing money, where is my husband getting all the cash to make these payments?"

Required

a. Prepare a statement of cash flows for the 2013 accounting period.

b. Compare the cash flow statement prepared in Requirement *a* with the income statement and provide Jean Crocket with recommendations.

c. Comment on the value of an unqualified audit opinion when using financial statements for decision-making purposes.

ATC 12-7   Research Assignment   *Analyzing cash flow information*

In 2008 Time Warner, Inc., reported a net loss of $13.4 billion. This loss occurred predominantly because Time Warner took a charge for "asset impairments" of $24,309 million, ($24.3 billion). (These amounts do not include tax benefits.) Without these special charges, Time Warner's net income would have been a positive $10.9 billion. Using the company's 2008 Form 10-K, complete the requirements below. Be sure to use the Form 10-K for *Time Warner, Inc.,* not *Time Warner Cable, Inc.* The Form 10-K can be found on the company's website. It can also be obtained using the EDGAR system following the instructions in Appendix A.

Required

a. How much cash flow from operating activities did Time Warner generate?

b. Based on the statement of cash flows, how much cash did the company pay out as a result of the asset impairments?

c. How much cash did Time Warner spend on investing activities (net)?

d. How much cash did the company use the repay debt? Where did it get the cash to make these payments?

Appendix A

Accessing the EDGAR Database through the Internet

Successful business managers need many different skills, including communication, interpersonal, computer, and analytical. Most business students become very aware of the data analysis skills used in accounting, but they may not be as aware of the importance of "data-finding" skills. There are many sources of accounting and financial data. The more sources you are able to use, the better.

One very important source of accounting information is the EDGAR database. Others are probably available at your school through the library or business school network. Your accounting instructor will be able to identify these for you and make suggestions regarding their use. By making the effort to learn to use electronic databases, you will enhance your abilities as a future manager and your marketability as a business graduate.

These instructions assume that you know how to access and use an Internet browser. Follow the instructions to retrieve data from the Securities and Exchange Commission's EDGAR database. Be aware that the SEC may have changed its interface since this appendix was written. Accordingly, be prepared for slight differences between the following instructions and what appears on your computer screen. Take comfort in the fact that changes are normally designed to simplify user access. If you encounter a conflict between the following instructions and the instructions provided in the SEC interface, remember that the SEC interface is more current and should take precedence over the following instructions.

Most companies provide links to their SEC filings from their corporate website. These links are often simpler to use and provide more choices regarding file formats than SEC's EDGAR site. On company websites, links to their SEC filings are usually found under one of the following links: "Investor Relations," "Company Info," or "About Us."

1. Connect to the EDGAR database through the following address: **http://www.sec.gov/.**

2. After the SEC homepage appears, under the heading **Filings and Forms,** click on **Search for Company Filings.**

3. On the screen that appears, click on **Company or Fund Name. . . .**

4. On the screen that appears, enter the name of the company whose file you wish to retrieve and click on the **Find Companies** button.

5. The following screen will present a list of companies that have the same, or similar, names to the one you entered. Identify the company you want and click on the CIK number beside it.

6. Enter the SEC form number that you want to retrieve in the window titled **Filing Type** that appears in the upper left portion of the screen. For example, if you want Form 10-K, which will usually be the case, enter **10-K** and click on the **Search** button.

7. A list of the forms you requested will be presented, along with the date they were filed. Click on the **Document** button next to the file you wish to retrieve.

8. You will be presented with a list of documents from which to select; usually you will want to choose the file **form10k.htm.**

9. Once the 10-K has been retrieved, you can search it online or save it on your computer.

10. Often the 10-K will have a table of contents that can help locate the part of the report you need. The financial statements are seldom located at the beginning of the Form 10-K. They are usually in either Section 8 or Section 15.

Appendix B

Portion of the Form 10-K for Target Corporation

This appendix contains a portion of the Form 10-K for the Target Corporation that was filed with the Securities and Exchange Commission on March 11, 2011. The document included in this appendix is Target's annual report, which was included *as a part* of its complete Form 10-K for the company's fiscal year ended January 29, 2011. Throughout this text this is referred to as the company's 2010 fiscal year.

This document is included for illustrative purposes, and it is intended to be used for educational purposes only. It should not be used for making investment decisions. Target Corporation's complete Form 10-K may be obtained from the SEC's EDGAR website, using the procedures explained in Appendix A. The Form 10-K may also be found at http://investors.target.com/phoenix.zhtml?c=65828&p=irol-IRHome. From this page, click on the "SEC Filings" tab and scroll to locate the appropriate 10-K report.

UNITED STATES
SECURITIES AND EXCHANGE COMMISSION
Washington, D.C. 20549

FORM 10-K

(Mark One)

☒   **ANNUAL REPORT PURSUANT TO SECTION 13 OR 15(d) OF THE SECURITIES EXCHANGE ACT OF 1934**
For the fiscal year ended January 29, 2011
OR

☐   **TRANSITION REPORT PURSUANT TO SECTION 13 OR 15(d) OF THE SECURITIES EXCHANGE ACT OF 1934**
For the transition period from   to
Commission file number **1-6049**

TARGET CORPORATION
(Exact name of registrant as specified in its charter)

Minnesota (State or other jurisdiction of   incorporation or organization)   **41-0215170**   (I.R.S. Employer   Identification No.)

1000 Nicollet Mall, Minneapolis, Minnesota   (Address   **55403**   (Zip Code)
of principal executive offices)
Registrant's telephone number, including area code: 612/304-6073

Securities Registered Pursuant To Section 12(B) Of The Act:

Title of Each Class	Name of Each Exchange on Which Registered
Common Stock, par value $0.0833 per share	New York Stock Exchange

Securities registered pursuant to Section 12(g) of the Act: **None**

Indicate by check mark if the registrant is a well-known seasoned issuer, as defined in Rule 405 of the Securities Act. Yes ☒ No ☐

Indicate by check mark if the registrant is not required to file reports pursuant to Section 13 or Section 15(d) of the Act. Yes ☐ No ☒

Note – Checking the box above will not relieve any registrant required to file reports pursuant to Section 13 or 15(d) of the Exchange Act from their obligations under those Sections.

Indicate by check mark whether the registrant (1) has filed all reports required to be filed by Section 13 or 15(d) of the Securities Exchange Act of 1934 during the preceding 12 months (or for such shorter period that the registrant was required to file such reports), and (2) has been subject to such filing requirements for the past 90 days. Yes ☒ No ☐

Indicate by checkmark whether the registrant has submitted electronically and posted on its corporate website, if any, every Interactive Data File required to be submitted and posted pursuant to Rule 405 of Regulation S-T (§232.405 of this chapter) during the preceding 12 months (or for such shorter period that the registrant was required to submit and post such files. Yes ☒ No ☐

Indicate by check mark if disclosure of delinquent filers pursuant to Item 405 of Regulation S-K (§229.405 of this chapter) is not contained herein, and will not be contained, to the best of registrant's knowledge, in definitive proxy or information statements incorporated by reference in Part III of this Form 10-K or any amendment to this Form 10-K. ☒

Indicate by check mark whether the registrant is a large accelerated filer, an accelerated filer, a non-accelerated filer or a smaller reporting company (as defined in Rule 12b-2 of the Act).

Large accelerated filer ☒   Accelerated filer ☐   Non-accelerated filer ☐   (Do not check if a smaller reporting company)   Smaller reporting company ☐

Indicate by check mark whether the registrant is a shell company (as defined in Rule 12b-2 of the Act). Yes ☐ No ☒

Aggregate market value of the voting stock held by non-affiliates of the registrant on July 31, 2010 was $37,014,234,947, based on the closing price of $51.32 per share of Common Stock as reported on the New York Stock Exchange Composite Index.

Indicate the number of shares outstanding of each of registrant's classes of Common Stock, as of the latest practicable date. Total shares of Common Stock, par value $0.0833, outstanding at March 7, 2011 were 693,063,352.

DOCUMENTS INCORPORATED BY REFERENCE

1.   Portions of Target's Proxy Statement to be filed on or about April 28, 2011 are incorporated into Part III.

TABLE OF CONTENTS

PART I
Item 1   Business   2
Item 1A Risk Factors   4
Item 1B Unresolved Staff Comments   8
Item 2   Properties   9
Item 3   Legal Proceedings   10
Item 4   Reserved   10
Item 4A Executive Officers   10
   PART II

Item 5   Market for Registrant's Common Equity, Related Stockholder Matters and Issuer Purchases of Equity
          Securities   12
Item 6   Selected Financial Data   14
Item 7   Management's Discussion and Analysis of Financial Condition and Results of Operations   14
Item 7A Quantitative and Qualitative Disclosures About Market Risk   29
Item 8   Financial Statements and Supplementary Data   31
Item 9   Changes in and Disagreements with Accountants on Accounting and Financial Disclosure   66
Item 9A Controls and Procedures   66
Item 9B Other Information   66
   PART III

Item 10 Directors, Executive Officers and Corporate Governance   67
Item 11 Executive Compensation   67
Item 12 Security Ownership of Certain Beneficial Owners and Management and Related Stockholder Matters   67
Item 13 Certain Relationships and Related Transactions, and Director Independence   67
Item 14 Principal Accountant Fees and Services   67
   PART IV

Item 15 Exhibits and Financial Statement Schedules   68
   Signatures   71
Schedule II – Valuation and Qualifying Accounts   72
Exhibit Index   73
Exhibit 12 – Computations of Ratios of Earnings to Fixed Charges for each of the Five Years in the Period Ended January 29,
2011   75

PART I

Item 1. Business

General

Target Corporation (the Corporation or Target) was incorporated in Minnesota in 1902. We operate as two reportable segments: Retail and Credit Card.

Our Retail Segment includes all of our merchandising operations, including our fully integrated online business. We offer both everyday essentials and fashionable, differentiated merchandise at discounted prices. Our ability to deliver a shopping experience that is preferred by our customers, referred to as "guests," is supported by our strong supply chain and technology infrastructure, a devotion to innovation that is ingrained in our organization and culture, and our disciplined approach to managing our current business and investing in future growth. As a component of the Retail Segment, our online presence is designed to enable guests to purchase products seamlessly either online or by locating them in one of our stores with the aid of online research and location tools. Our online shopping site offers similar merchandise categories to those found in our stores, excluding food items and household essentials.

Our Credit Card Segment offers credit to qualified guests through our branded proprietary credit cards, the Target Visa and the Target Card. Additionally, we offer a branded proprietary Target Debit Card. Collectively, these REDcards® help strengthen the bond with our guests, drive incremental sales and contribute to our results of operations.

Financial Highlights

Our fiscal year ends on the Saturday nearest January 31. Unless otherwise stated, references to years in this report relate to fiscal years, rather than to calendar years. Fiscal year 2010 ended January 29, 2011, and consisted of 52 weeks. Fiscal year 2009 ended January 30, 2010, and consisted of 52 weeks. Fiscal year 2008 ended January 31, 2009, and consisted of 52 weeks.

For information on key financial highlights, see the items referenced in Item 6, Selected Financial Data, and Item 7, Management's Discussion and Analysis of Financial Condition and Results of Operations, of this Annual Report on Form 10-K.

Seasonality

Due to the seasonal nature of our business, a larger share of annual revenues and earnings traditionally occurs in the fourth quarter because it includes the peak sales period from Thanksgiving to the end of December.

Merchandise

We operate Target general merchandise stores, the majority of which offer a wide assortment of general merchandise and a more limited food assortment than traditional supermarkets. During 2009 and 2010 we completed store remodels that enabled us to offer an expanded food assortment in many of our general merchandise stores. The expanded food assortment includes some perishables and some additional dry, dairy and frozen items. In addition, we operate SuperTarget® stores with general merchandise items and a full line of food items comparable to that of traditional supermarkets. Target.com offers a wide assortment of general merchandise including many items found in our stores and a complementary assortment, such as extended sizes and colors, sold only online. A significant portion of our sales is from national brand merchandise. We also sell many products under our owned and exclusive brands. Owned brands include merchandise sold under private-label brands including, but not limited to, Archer Farms®, Archer Farms® Simply Balanced, Boots & Barkley®, choxie®, Circo®, Durabuilt®, Embark®, Gilligan & O'Malley®, itso™, Market Pantry®, Merona®, Play Wonder®, Room Essentials®,

Smith & Hawken®, Sutton & Dodge®, Target Home, Vroom®, up & up, Wine Cube® and Xhilaration®. In addition, we sell merchandise under exclusive licensed and designer brands including, but not limited to, C9 by Champion®, Chefmate®, Cherokee®, Converse® One Star®, Eddie Bauer®, Fieldcrest®, Genuine Kids by OshKosh®, Kitchen Essentials® from Calphalon®, Liz Lange® for Target®, Michael Graves Design, Mossimo®, Nick & Nora®, Simply Shabby Chic®, Sonia Kashuk® and Thomas O'Brien® Vintage Modern. We also sell merchandise through unique programs such as ClearRx^{SM}, GO International® and The Great Save^{SM}. Additionally, we generate revenue from in-store amenities such as Target Café^{SM}, Target Clinic®, Target Pharmacy® and Target Photo®, and from leased or licensed departments such as Target Optical®, Pizza Hut, Portrait Studio and Starbucks.

Effective inventory management is key to our ongoing success. We utilize various techniques including demand forecasting and planning and various forms of replenishment management. We achieve effective inventory management by being in-stock in core product offerings, maintaining positive vendor relationships, and carefully planning inventory levels for seasonal and apparel items to minimize markdowns.

Sales by Product Category	Percentage of Sales		
	2010	2009	2008
Household essentials	24%	23%	22%
Hardlines	20	22	22
Apparel and accessories	20	20	20
Home furnishings and décor	19	19	21
Food and pet supplies	17	16	15
Total	100%	100%	100%

Household essentials includes pharmacy, beauty, personal care, baby care, cleaning and paper products.

Hardlines includes electronics (including video game hardware and software), music, movies, books, computer software, sporting goods and toys.

Apparel and accessories includes apparel for women, men, boys, girls, toddlers, infants and newborns. It also includes intimate apparel, jewelry, accessories and shoes.

Home furnishings and décor includes furniture, lighting, kitchenware, small appliances, home décor, bed and bath, home improvement, automotive and seasonal merchandise such as patio furniture and holiday décor.

Food and pet supplies includes dry grocery, dairy, frozen food, beverages, candy, snacks, deli, bakery, meat, produce and pet supplies.

Distribution

The vast majority of our merchandise is distributed through our network of distribution centers. We operated 37 distribution centers, including 4 food distribution centers, at January 29, 2011. General merchandise is shipped to and from our distribution centers by common carriers. In addition, third parties distribute certain food items. Merchandise sold through Target.com is distributed through our own distribution network, through third parties, or shipped directly from vendors.

Employees

At January 29, 2011, we employed approximately 355,000 full-time, part-time and seasonal employees, referred to as "team members." During our peak sales period from Thanksgiving to the end of December, our employment levels peaked at approximately 400,000 team members. We consider our team member relations to be good. We offer a broad range of company-paid benefits to our team members. Eligibility for, and the level of, these benefits varies, depending on team members' full-time or part-time status, compensation level, date of hire and/or length of service. These company-paid benefits include a pension plan, 401(k) plan, medical and dental plans, a retiree medical plan, disability insurance, paid vacation, tuition reimbursement, various team member assistance programs, life insurance and merchandise discounts.

Working Capital

Because of the seasonal nature of our business, our working capital needs are greater in the months leading up to our peak sales period from Thanksgiving to the end of December. The increase in working capital during this time is typically financed with cash flow provided by operations and short-term borrowings.

Additional details are provided in the Liquidity and Capital Resources section in Item 7, Management's Discussion and Analysis of Financial Condition and Results of Operations.

Competition

In our Retail Segment, we compete with traditional and off-price general merchandise retailers, apparel retailers, Internet retailers, wholesale clubs, category specific retailers, drug stores, supermarkets and other forms of retail commerce. Our ability to positively differentiate ourselves from other retailers largely determines our competitive position within the retail industry.

In our Credit Card Segment, our primary mission is to deliver financial products and services that drive sales and deepen guest relationships at Target. Our financial products compete with those of other issuers for market share of sales volume. Our ability to positively differentiate the value of our financial products primarily through our rewards programs, terms, credit line management, and guest service determines our competitive position among credit card issuers.

Intellectual Property

Our brand image is a critical element of our business strategy. Our principal trademarks, including Target, SuperTarget and our "Bullseye Design," have been registered with the U.S. Patent and Trademark Office. We also seek to obtain and preserve intellectual property protection for our private-label brands.

Geographic Information

Substantially, all of our revenues are generated and long-lived assets are located within the United States.

Available Information

Our Annual Report on Form 10-K, quarterly reports on Form 10-Q, current reports on Form 8-K and amendments to those reports filed or furnished pursuant to Section 13(a) or 15(d) of the Exchange Act are available free of charge at www.Target.com (click on "Investors" and "SEC Filings") as soon as reasonably practicable after we file such material with, or furnish it to, the Securities and Exchange Commission (SEC). Our Corporate Governance Guidelines, Business Conduct Guide, Corporate Responsibility Report and the position descriptions for our Board of Directors and Board committees are also available free of charge in print upon request or at www.Target.com (click on "Investors" and "Corporate Governance").

Item 1A. Risk Factors

Our business is subject to a variety of risks. The most important of these is our ability to remain relevant to our guests with a brand they trust. Meeting our guests' expectations requires us to manage various strategic, operational, compliance, and financial risks. Set forth below are the most significant risks that we face.

If we are unable to positively differentiate ourselves from other retailers, our results of operations could be adversely affected.

The retail business is highly competitive. In the past we have been able to compete successfully by differentiating our shopping experience by creating an attractive value proposition through a careful combination of price, merchandise assortment, convenience, guest service and marketing efforts. Guest perceptions regarding the cleanliness and safety of our stores, our in-stock levels and other factors also affect our ability to compete. No single competitive factor is dominant, and actions by our competitors on any of these factors could have an adverse effect on our sales, gross margin and expenses.

If we fail to anticipate and respond quickly to changing consumer preferences, our sales, gross margin and profitability could suffer.

A substantial part of our business is dependent on our ability to make trend-right decisions in apparel, home décor, seasonal offerings, food and other merchandise. Failure to accurately predict constantly changing consumer tastes, preferences, spending patterns and other lifestyle decisions may result in lost sales, spoilage and increased inventory markdowns, which would lead to a deterioration in our results of operations.

Our continued success is substantially dependent on positive perceptions of Target, including our owned and exclusive brands.

We believe that one of the reasons our guests prefer to shop at Target and our team members choose Target as a place of employment is the reputation we have built over many years of serving our four primary constituencies: guests, team members, the communities in which we operate and shareholders. To be successful in the future, we must continue to preserve, grow and leverage the value of Target's reputation. Reputational value is based in large part on perceptions of subjective qualities, and even isolated incidents that erode trust and confidence, particularly if they result in adverse publicity, governmental investigations or litigation, can have an adverse impact on these perceptions and lead to tangible adverse affects on our business, including consumer boycotts, loss of new store development opportunities, or team member recruiting difficulties.

In addition, we sell many products under our owned and exclusive brands, such as Market Pantry, up & up, Target Home, Merona and Mossimo. These brands generally carry higher margins than national brand products, and represent a growing portion of our overall sales, totaling approximately one-third of sales in 2010. If one or more of these brands experiences a loss of consumer acceptance or confidence, our sales and gross margin rate could be adversely affected.

We are highly susceptible to the state of macroeconomic conditions and consumer confidence in the United States.

All of our stores are located within the United States, making our results highly dependent on U.S. consumer confidence and the health of the U.S. economy. In addition, a significant portion of our total sales is derived from stores located in five states: California, Texas, Florida, Minnesota and Illinois, resulting in further dependence on local economic conditions in these states. Deterioration in macroeconomic conditions and consumer confidence could negatively affect our business in many ways, including slowing sales growth or reduction in overall sales, and reducing gross margins.

In addition to the impact of macroeconomic conditions on our retail sales, these same considerations impact the success of our Credit Card Segment. Deterioration in macroeconomic conditions can adversely affect cardholders' ability to pay their balances, and we may not be able to fully anticipate and respond to changes in the risk profile of our cardholders when extending credit, resulting in higher bad debt expense. Demand for consumer credit is also impacted by consumer choices regarding payment methods, and our performance could be adversely affected by consumer decisions to use debit cards or other forms of payment.

If we do not effectively manage our large and growing workforce, our results of operations could be adversely affected.

With approximately 355,000 team members, our workforce costs represent our largest operating expense, and our business is dependent on our ability to attract, train and retain a growing number of qualified team members. Many of those team members are in entry-level or part-time positions with historically high turnover rates. Our ability to meet our labor needs while controlling our costs is subject to external factors such as unemployment levels, prevailing wage rates, health care and other benefit costs and changing demographics. If we are unable to attract and retain adequate numbers of qualified team members, our operations, guest service levels and support functions could suffer. Those factors, together with increasing wage and benefit costs, could adversely affect our results of operations.

Lack of availability of suitable locations in which to build new stores could slow our growth, and difficulty in executing plans for new stores, expansions and remodels could increase our costs and capital requirements.

Our future growth is dependent, in part, on our ability to build new stores and expand and remodel existing stores in a manner that achieves appropriate returns on our capital investment. We compete with other retailers and businesses for suitable locations for our stores. In addition, for many sites we are dependent on a third party developer's ability to acquire land, obtain financing and secure the necessary zoning changes and permits for a larger project, of which our store may be one component. Turmoil in the financial markets may make it difficult for third party developers to obtain financing for new projects. Local land use and other regulations applicable to the types of stores we desire to construct may affect our ability to find suitable locations and also influence the cost of constructing, expanding and remodeling our stores. A significant portion of our expected new store sites are located in fully developed markets, which is generally a more time-consuming and expensive undertaking than expansion into undeveloped suburban and ex-urban markets.

Interruptions with our vendors and within our supply chain could adversely affect our results.

We are dependent on our vendors to supply merchandise in a timely and efficient manner. If a vendor fails to deliver on its commitments, whether due to financial difficulties or other reasons, we could experience merchandise out-of-stocks that could lead to lost sales. In addition, a large portion of our merchandise is sourced, directly or indirectly, from outside the United States, with China as our single largest source. Political or financial instability, trade restrictions, increased tariffs, currency exchange rates, the outbreak of pandemics, labor unrest, transport capacity and costs, port security or other events that could slow port activities and affect foreign trade are beyond our control and could disrupt our supply of merchandise and/or adversely affect our results of operations.

Failure to address product safety concerns could adversely affect our sales and results of operations.

If our merchandise offerings, including food, drug and children's products, do not meet applicable safety standards or our guests' expectations regarding safety, we could experience lost sales, experience increased costs and be exposed to legal and reputational risk. All of our vendors must comply with applicable product safety laws, and we are dependent on them to ensure that the products we buy comply with all safety standards. Events that give rise to actual, potential or perceived product safety concerns, including food or drug contamination, could expose us to government enforcement action or private litigation and result in costly product recalls and other liabilities. In addition, negative guest perceptions regarding the safety of the products we sell could cause our guests to seek alternative sources for their needs, resulting in lost sales. In those circumstances, it may be difficult and costly for us to regain the confidence of our guests.

If we fail to protect the security of personal information about our guests, we could be subject to costly government enforcement actions or private litigation and our reputation could suffer.

The nature of our business involves the receipt and storage of personal information about our guests. If we experience a data security breach, we could be exposed to government enforcement actions and private litigation. In addition, our guests could lose confidence in our ability to protect their personal information, which could cause them to discontinue usage of our credit card products, decline to use our pharmacy services, or stop shopping at our stores altogether. Such events could lead to lost future sales and adversely affect our results of operations.

Our failure to comply with federal, state or local laws, or changes in these laws could increase our expenses.

Our business is subject to a wide array of laws and regulations. Significant legislative changes that affect our relationship with our workforce could increase our expenses and adversely affect our operations. Examples of possible legislative changes affecting our relationship with our workforce include changes to an employer's obligation to recognize collective bargaining units, the process by which collective bargaining agreements are negotiated or imposed, minimum wage requirements, and health care mandates. In addition, changes in the regulatory environment regarding topics such as banking and consumer credit, Medicare reimbursements, privacy and information security, product safety or environmental protection, among others, could cause our expenses to increase without an ability to pass through any increased expenses through higher prices. In addition, if we fail to comply with applicable laws and regulations, particularly wage and hour laws, we could be subject to legal risk, including government enforcement action and class action civil litigation, which could adversely affect our results of operations.

Given the geographic concentration of our stores, natural disasters could adversely affect our results of operations.

Our three largest states, by total sales, are California, Texas and Florida, areas where hurricanes and earthquakes are prevalent. Such events could result in significant physical damage to or closure of one or more of our stores or distribution centers, and cause delays in the distribution of merchandise from our vendors to our distribution centers and stores, which could adversely affect our results of operations.

Changes in our effective income tax rate could affect our results of operations.

Our effective income tax rate is influenced by a number of factors. Changes in the tax laws, the interpretation of existing laws, or our failure to sustain our reporting positions on examination could adversely affect our effective tax rate. In addition, our effective income tax rate generally bears an inverse relationship to capital market returns due to the tax-free nature of investment vehicles used to economically hedge our deferred compensation liabilities.

If we are unable to access the capital markets or obtain bank credit, our growth plans, liquidity and results of operations could suffer.

We are dependent on a stable, liquid and well-functioning financial system to fund our operations and growth plans. In particular, we have historically relied on the public debt markets to raise capital for new store development and other capital expenditures, the commercial paper market and bank credit facilities to fund seasonal needs for working capital, and the asset-backed securities markets to partially fund our accounts receivable portfolio. In addition, we use a variety of derivative products to manage our exposure to market risk, principally interest rate and equity price fluctuations. Disruptions or turmoil in the financial markets could adversely affect our ability to meet our capital requirements, fund our working capital needs or lead to losses on derivative positions resulting from counterparty failures.

A significant disruption in our computer systems could adversely affect our operations.

We rely extensively on our computer systems to manage inventory, process guest transactions and summarize results. Our systems are subject to damage or interruption from power outages, telecommunications failures, computer viruses, security breaches and catastrophic events. If our systems are damaged or fail to function properly, we may incur substantial costs to repair or replace them, and may experience loss of critical data and interruptions or delays in our ability to manage inventories or process guest transactions, which could adversely affect our results of operations.

In 2011 we expect to migrate our online presence (Target.com) from a platform currently operated by Amazon, Inc. to our own proprietary platform. If this new platform does not function as designed, we may experience a loss of guest confidence, data security breaches, lost sales or be exposed to fraudulent purchases.

Our announced plan to expand retail operations into Canada could adversely affect our financial results.

Our plan to enter the Canadian retail market is our first expansion of retail operations outside of the United States. Our ability to convert the leased locations that we acquire from Zellers Inc. to Target stores depends in large measure upon our ability to negotiate acceptable modifications to existing lease terms, remodel existing assets and recruit, hire and retain qualified team members. In addition, access to local suppliers of certain types of goods may limit our ability to offer a full assortment of merchandise in certain markets. The effective execution of our strategy is also contingent on our ability to design new marketing and promotional programs that positively differentiate us from other retailers in Canada. If we do not effectively execute our expansion plans for Canada, our financial performance could be adversely affected.

Item 1B.   Unresolved Staff Comments

Not applicable.

Item 2. Properties

At January 29, 2011, we had 1,750 stores in 49 states and the District of Columbia:

	Number of Stores	Retail Sq. Ft. (in thousands)		Number of Stores	Retail Sq. Ft. (in thousands)
Alabama	20	2,867	Montana	7	780
Alaska	3	504	Nebraska	14	2,006
Arizona	48	6,363	Nevada	19	2,461
Arkansas	9	1,165	New Hampshire	9	1,148
California	248	32,818	New Jersey	43	5,671
Colorado	42	6,275	New Mexico	9	1,024
Connecticut	20	2,672	New York	66	9,000
Delaware	3	413	North Carolina	47	6,168
District of Columbia	1	179	North Dakota	4	554
Florida	125	17,552	Ohio	63	7,868
Georgia	55	7,517	Oklahoma	14	2,022
Hawaii	3	541	Oregon	19	2,318
Idaho	6	664	Pennsylvania	60	7,822
Illinois	87	11,895	Rhode Island	4	517
Indiana	33	4,377	South Carolina	18	2,224
Iowa	22	3,015	South Dakota	5	580
Kansas	19	2,577	Tennessee	32	4,096
Kentucky	13	1,525	Texas	148	20,838
Louisiana	15	2,108	Utah	12	1,818
Maine	5	630	Vermont	—	—
Maryland	36	4,663	Virginia	56	7,454
Massachusetts	34	4,437	Washington	35	4,098
Michigan	59	7,036	West Virginia	6	755
Minnesota	73	10,456	Wisconsin	37	4,482
Mississippi	6	743	Wyoming	2	187
Missouri	36	4,735			
			Total	**1,750**	**233,618**

The following table summarizes the number of owned or leased stores and distribution centers at January 29, 2011:

	Stores	Distribution Centers (b)
Owned	1,500	29
Leased	84	8
Combined (a)	166	—
Total	**1,750**	**37**

(a)   Properties within the "combined" category are primarily owned buildings on leased land.

(b)   The 37 distribution centers have a total of 48,022 thousand square feet.

We own our corporate headquarters buildings located in Minneapolis, Minnesota, and we lease and own additional office space in the United States. Our international sourcing operations have 27 office locations in 18 countries, all of which are leased. We also lease office space in Bangalore, India, where we operate various support functions. Our properties are in good condition, well maintained and suitable to carry on our business.

For additional information on our properties, see also the Capital Expenditures section in Item 7, Management's Discussion and Analysis of Financial Condition and Results of Operations and Notes 13 and 21 of the Notes to Consolidated Financial Statements included in Item 8, Financial Statements and Supplementary Data.

Item 3.   Legal Proceedings

The following governmental enforcement proceedings relating to environmental matters are reported pursuant to instruction 5(C) of Item 103 of Regulation S-K because they involve potential monetary sanctions in excess of $100,000:

We were a defendant in a civil lawsuit filed by the California Attorney General and a number of California District Attorneys in June 2009 alleging that we did not handle and dispose of certain unsold products as hazardous waste and that we violated California's hazardous waste laws. A settlement was reached in this case on January 27, 2011, which obligates Target to pay $22.5 million and consent to an injunction regarding future compliance with all California hazardous waste laws. The settlement was approved by the Alameda County Superior Court and judgment was entered on March 2, 2011.

We are the subject of an ongoing Environmental Protection Agency (EPA) investigation for alleged violations of the Clean Air Act (CAA). In March 2009, the EPA issued a Finding of Violation (FOV) related to alleged violations of the CAA, specifically the National Emission Standards for Hazardous Air Pollutants (NESHAP) promulgated by the EPA for asbestos. The FOV pertains to the remodeling of 36 Target stores that occurred between January 1, 2003 and October 28, 2007. The EPA FOV process is ongoing and no specific relief has been sought to date by the EPA.

The American Jobs Creation Act of 2004 requires SEC registrants to disclose if they have been required to pay certain penalties for failing to disclose to the Internal Revenue Service their participation in listed transactions. We have not been required to pay any of the penalties set forth in Section 6707A(e)(2) of the Internal Revenue Code.

Item 4.   Reserved

Item 4A.   Executive Officers

The executive officers of Target as of March 7, 2011 and their positions and ages are as follows:

Name	Title	Age
Timothy R. Baer	Executive Vice President, General Counsel and Corporate Secretary	50
Michael R. Francis	Executive Vice President and Chief Marketing Officer	48
John D. Griffith	Executive Vice President, Property Development	49
Beth M. Jacob	Executive Vice President, Technology Services and Chief Information Officer	49
Jodeen A. Kozlak	Executive Vice President, Human Resources	47
Tina M. Schiel	Executive Vice President, Stores	45
Douglas A. Scovanner	Executive Vice President and Chief Financial Officer	55
Terrence J. Scully	President, Financial and Retail Services	58
Gregg W. Steinhafel	Chairman of the Board, President and Chief Executive Officer	56
Kathryn A. Tesija	Executive Vice President, Merchandising	48
Laysha L. Ward	President, Community Relations and Target Foundation	43

Each officer is elected by and serves at the pleasure of the Board of Directors. There is neither a family relationship between any of the officers named and any other executive officer or member of the Board of Directors nor any arrangement or understanding pursuant to which any person was selected as an officer. The service period of each officer in the positions listed and other business experience for the past five years is listed below.

Timothy R. Baer	Executive Vice President, General Counsel and Corporate Secretary since March 2007. Senior Vice President, General Counsel and Corporate Secretary from June 2004 to March 2007.
Michael R. Francis	Executive Vice President and Chief Marketing Officer since August 2008. Executive Vice President, Marketing from January 2003 to August 2008.
John D. Griffith	Executive Vice President, Property Development since February 2005.
Beth M. Jacob	Executive Vice President and Chief Information Officer since January 2010. Senior Vice President and Chief Information Officer from July 2008 to January 2010. Vice President, Guest Operations, Target Financial Services from August 2006 to July 2008. Vice President, Guest Contact Centers, Target Financial Services from September 2003 to August 2006.
Jodeen A. Kozlak	Executive Vice President, Human Resources since March 2007. Senior Vice President, Human Resources from February 2006 to March 2007. Vice President, Human Resources and Employee Relations General Counsel from November 2005 to February 2006.
Tina M. Schiel	Executive Vice President, Stores since January 2011. Senior Vice President, New Business Development from February 2010 to January 2011. Senior Vice President, Stores from February 2001 to February 2010.
Douglas A. Scovanner	Executive Vice President and Chief Financial Officer since February 2000.
Terrence J. Scully	President, Financial and Retail Services since March 2003.
Gregg W. Steinhafel	Chief Executive Officer since May 2008. President since August 1999. Director since January 2007. Chairman of the Board since February 2009.
Kathryn A. Tesija	Executive Vice President, Merchandising since May 2008. Senior Vice President, Merchandising from July 2001 to May 2008.
Laysha L. Ward	President, Community Relations and Target Foundation since July 2008. Vice President, Community Relations from February 2003 to July 2008.

PART II

Item 5. Market for the
Registrant's Common Equity, Related Stockholder Matters and Issuer
Purchases of Equity Securities

Our common stock is listed on the New York Stock Exchange under the symbol "TGT." We are authorized to issue up to 6,000,000,000 shares of common stock, par value $0.0833, and up to 5,000,000 shares of preferred stock, par value $0.01. At March 7, 2011, there were 17,247 shareholders of record. Dividends declared per share and the high and low closing common stock price for each fiscal quarter during 2010 and 2009 are disclosed in Note 29 of the Notes to Consolidated Financial Statements, included in Item 8, Financial Statements and Supplementary Data.

In November 2007, our Board of Directors authorized the repurchase of $10 billion of our common stock. Since the inception of this share repurchase program, we have repurchased 151.4 million common shares for a total cash investment of $7,827 million ($51.70 per share).

The table below presents information with respect to Target common stock purchases made during the three months ended January 29, 2011, by Target or any "affiliated purchaser" of Target, as defined in Rule 10b-18(a)(3) under the Exchange Act.

Period	Total Number of Shares Purchased (a)	Average Price Paid per Share (a)	Total Number of Shares Purchased as Part of Publicly Announced Program (a)	Approximate Dollar Value of Shares that May Yet Be Purchased Under the Program
October 31, 2010 through November 27, 2010	1,632,664	$ 52.05	145,434,588	$ 2,501,898,442
November 28, 2010 through January 1, 2011	97,151 (b)	54.12	145,518,341	2,497,365,556
January 2, 2011 through January 29, 2011	5,872,428	55.31	151,390,769	2,172,553,879
	7,602,243	**54.60**	**151,390,769**	**2,172,553,879**

(a)   The table above includes shares reacquired upon settlement of prepaid forward contracts. For the three months ended January 29, 2011, 0.3 million shares were reacquired through these contracts. At January 29, 2011, we held asset positions in prepaid forward contracts for 1.2 million shares of our common stock, for a total cash investment of $51 million, or an average per share price of $44.09. Refer to Notes 24 and 26 of the Notes to Consolidated Financial Statements for further details of these contracts.

(b)   The number of shares above includes shares of common stock reacquired from team members who wish to tender owned shares to satisfy the tax withholding on equity awards as part of our long-term incentive plans or to satisfy the exercise price on stock option exercises. For the three months ended January 29, 2011, 13,398 shares were reacquired at an average per share price of $59.72 pursuant to our long-term incentive plan.

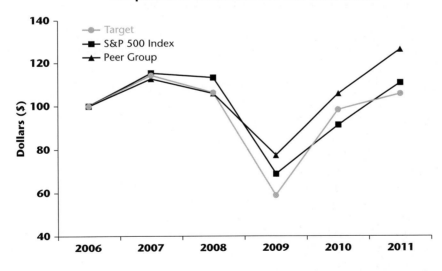

Comparison of Cumulative Five Year Total Return

	Fiscal Years Ended					
	January 28, 2006	February 3, 2007	February 2, 2008	January 31, 2009	January 30, 2010	January 29, 2011
Target	$ 100.00	$ 114.24	$ 106.01	$ 58.78	$ 98.20	$ 105.76
S&P 500 Index	100.00	115.32	113.24	68.66	91.41	110.85
Peer Group	100.00	112.67	105.89	77.34	105.84	126.16

The graph above compares the cumulative total shareholder return on our common stock for the last five fiscal years with the cumulative total return on the S&P 500 Index and a peer group consisting of the companies comprising the S&P 500 Retailing Index and the S&P 500 Food and Staples Retailing Index (Peer Group) over the same period. The Peer Group index consists of 40 general merchandise, food and drug retailers and is weighted by the market capitalization of each component company. The graph assumes the investment of $100 in Target common stock, the S&P 500 Index and the Peer Group on January 28, 2006, and reinvestment of all dividends.

Item 6. Selected Financial Data

(millions, except per share data)	2010	2009	2008	2007	2006(a)	2005
Financial Results:						
Total revenues	$ 67,390 $	65,357 $	64,948 $	63,367 $	59,490 $	52,620
Net earnings	2,920	2,488	2,214	2,849	2,787	2,408
Per Share:						
Basic earnings per share	4.03	3.31	2.87	3.37	3.23	2.73
Diluted earnings per share	4.00	3.30	2.86	3.33	3.21	2.71
Cash dividends declared per share	0.92	0.67	0.62	0.54	0.46	0.38
Financial Position:						
Total assets	43,705	44,533	44,106	44,560	37,349	34,995
Long-term debt, including current portion	15,726	16,814	18,752	16,590	10,037	9,872

(a)   Consisted of 53 weeks.

Item 7. Management's Discussion and Analysis of Financial Condition and Results of Operations

Executive Summary

Our 2010 Retail Segment sales increased 3.7 percent over last year due to a 2.1 percent comparable-store increase combined with the contribution from new stores. Our Retail Segment EBITDA and EBIT increased 4.9 percent and 5.8 percent, respectively, compared with the prior year. In the Credit Card Segment, we achieved a significant increase in segment profit primarily due to declining bad debt expense driven by improved trends in key measures of risk.

Cash flow provided by operations was $5,271 million, $5,881 million and $4,430 million for 2010, 2009 and 2008, respectively. We opened 13 new stores and 76 new stores in 2010 and 2009, respectively. In 2010 we remodeled 341 stores, significantly more than the 67 stores we remodeled in 2009. Additionally, during 2010 and 2009 we repurchased 47.8 million and 9.9 million shares of our common stock for a total cash investment of $2,508 million ($52.44 per share) and $479 million ($48.54 per share), respectively.

In January 2011, we entered into an agreement to purchase the leasehold interests in up to 220 sites in Canada currently operated by Zellers Inc., in exchange for C$1,825 million (Canadian dollars), due in two payments, one in May 2011 and one in September 2011. We believe this transaction will allow us to open 100 to 150 Target stores in Canada, primarily during 2013. We expect that renovation of these stores will require an investment of over C $1 billion, a portion of which may be funded by landlords. At January 29, 2011 the value of C$1.00 approximated the value of $1.00.

Additionally, in January 2011, we announced our plan to actively pursue the sale of our credit card receivables portfolio. As of January 29, 2011 the gross balance of our credit card receivables portfolio was $6,843 million, of which $3,954 million was funded by third parties and $2,889 million was funded by Target. Refer to Note 10 of the Notes to Consolidated Financial Statements for further description of historical financing transactions related to our credit card receivables.

Management's Discussion and Analysis is based on our Consolidated Financial Statements in Item 8, Financial Statements and Supplementary Data.

Analysis of Results of Operations

Retail Segment

Retail Segment Results (millions)		2010	2009	2008	Percent Change	
					2010/2009	2009/2008
Sales	$	**65,786** $	63,435 $	62,884	**3.7%**	0.9%
Cost of sales		**45,725**	44,062	44,157	**3.8**	(0.2)
Gross margin		**20,061**	19,373	18,727	**3.5**	3.5
SG&A expenses *(a)*		**13,367**	12,989	12,838	**2.9**	1.2
EBITDA		**6,694**	6,384	5,889	**4.9**	8.4
Depreciation and amortization		**2,065**	2,008	1,808	**2.8**	11.0
EBIT	$	**4,629** $	4,376 $	4,081	**5.8%**	7.3%

EBITDA is earnings before interest expense, income taxes, depreciation and amortization.

EBIT is earnings before interest expense and income taxes.

(a)   Loyalty Program discounts are recorded as reductions to sales in our Retail Segment. Effective with the October 2010 nationwide launch of our new 5% REDcard Rewards loyalty program, we changed the formula under which our Credit Card segment reimburses our Retail Segment to better align with the attributes of the new program. These reimbursed amounts were $102 million in 2010, $89 million in 2009 and $117 million in 2008. In all periods these amounts were recorded as reductions to SG&A expenses within the Retail Segment and increases to operations and marketing expenses within the Credit Card Segment.

Retail Segment Rate Analysis	2010	2009	2008
Gross margin rate	**30.5%**	30.5%	29.8%
SG&A expense rate	**20.3**	20.5	20.4
EBITDA margin rate	**10.2**	10.1	9.4
Depreciation and amortization expense rate	**3.1**	3.2	2.9
EBIT margin rate	**7.0**	6.9	6.5

Retail Segment rate analysis metrics are computed by dividing the applicable amount by sales.

Sales

Sales include merchandise sales, net of expected returns, from our stores and our online business, as well as gift card breakage. Refer to Note 2 of the Notes to Consolidated Financial Statements for a definition of gift card breakage. Total sales for the Retail Segment for 2010 were $65,786 million, compared with $63,435 million in 2009 and $62,884 million in 2008. All periods were 52-week years. Growth in total sales between 2010 and 2009 resulted from higher comparable-store sales and additional stores opened, whereas between 2009 and 2008, growth in total sales resulted from sales from additional stores opened, partially offset by lower comparable-store sales. In 2010, deflation affected sales growth by approximately 0.2 percentage points, compared with a deflationary impact of approximately 3.6 percentage points in 2009 and an inflationary impact of 2.2 percentage points in 2008.

Sales by Product Category	Percentage of Sales		
	2010	2009	2008
Household essentials	**24%**	23%	22%
Hardlines	**20**	22	22
Apparel and accessories	**20**	20	20
Home furnishings and décor	**19**	19	21
Food and pet supplies	**17**	16	15
Total	**100%**	100%	100%

Refer to the Merchandise section in Item 1, Business, for a description of our product categories.

Comparable-store sales is a measure that indicates the performance of our existing stores by measuring the growth in sales for such stores for a period over the comparable, prior-year period of equivalent length. The method of calculating comparable-store sales varies across the retail industry. As a result, our comparable-store sales calculation is not necessarily comparable to similarly titled measures reported by other companies.

Comparable-store sales are sales from our online business and stores open longer than one year, including:

- sales from stores that have been remodeled or expanded while remaining open

- sales from stores that have been relocated to new buildings of the same format within the same trade area, in which the new store opens at about the same time as the old store closes

Comparable-store sales do not include:

- sales from general merchandise stores that have been converted, or relocated within the same trade area, to a SuperTarget store format

- sales from stores that were intentionally closed to be remodeled, expanded or reconstructed

Comparable-Store Sales	2010	2009	2008
Comparable-store sales change	**2.1**%	(2.5)%	(2.9)%
Drivers of changes in comparable-store sales:			
Number of transactions	**2.0**%	(0.2)%	(3.1)%
Average transaction amount	**0.1**%	(2.3)%	0.2%
Units per transaction	**2.5**%	(1.5)%	(2.1)%
Selling price per unit	**(2.3)**%	(0.8)%	2.3%

The comparable-store sales increases or decreases above are calculated by comparing sales in fiscal year periods with comparable prior fiscal year periods of equivalent length.

In 2010, the change in comparable-store sales was driven by an increase in the number of transactions and a slight increase in the average transaction amount, reflecting an increase in units per transaction largely offset by a decrease in selling price per unit. In 2009, the change in comparable-store sales was driven by a decline in the average transaction amount, primarily due to a decrease in the number of units per transaction, as well as a slight decrease in the number of transactions. The collective interaction of a broad array of macroeconomic, competitive and consumer behavioral factors, as well as sales mix, and transfer of sales to new stores makes further analysis of sales metrics infeasible.

Beginning April 2010, all new qualified credit card applicants receive the Target Card, and we no longer issue the Target Visa to credit card applicants. Existing Target Visa cardholders are not affected. Beginning October 2010, guests receive a 5 percent discount on virtually all purchases at checkout every day when they use a REDcard at any Target store or on Target.com.

We monitor the percentage of store sales that are paid for using REDcards (REDcard Penetration), because our internal analysis has indicated that a meaningful portion of the incremental purchases on our REDcards are also incremental sales for Target, with the remainder of the incremental purchases on the REDcards representing a shift in tender type.

REDcard Penetration	2010	2009	2008
Target credit penetration	**5.2%**	5.2%	6.2%
Target debit penetration	**0.7%**	0.4%	0.3%
Total store REDcard penetration	**5.9%**	5.6%	6.5%

Since launching our new 5% REDcard Rewards program in October 2010, we have experienced an increase in REDcard penetration. REDcard penetration for the fourth quarter of 2010 was 7.4 percent compared to 5.6 percent in the fourth quarter of 2009.

Gross Margin Rate

Gross margin rate represents gross margin (sales less cost of sales) as a percentage of sales. See Note 3 of the Notes to Consolidated Financial Statements for a description of costs included in cost of sales. Markup is the difference between an item's cost and its retail price (expressed as a percentage of its retail price). Factors that affect markup include vendor offerings and negotiations, vendor income, sourcing strategies, market forces like raw material and freight costs, and competitive influences. Markdowns are the reduction in the original or previous price of retail merchandise. Factors that affect markdowns include inventory management, competitive influences and economic conditions.

Our gross margin rate was 30.5 percent in 2010, unchanged from prior year, as margin rates within categories were generally stable and the impact of sales mix was essentially neutral. There were no other significant variances in the drivers of gross margin rate.

Our gross margin rate was 30.5 percent in 2009, compared with 29.8 percent in 2008. Our 2009 gross margin rate benefitted from rate improvements within categories, partially offset by the mix impact of faster sales growth in lower margin rate categories (generally product categories of household essentials and food). The impact of rate performance within merchandise categories on gross margin rate was an approximate 1.1 percentage point increase for 2009. This increase is the result of improved markups and reduced markdowns. The impact of sales mix on gross margin rate was an approximate 0.4 percentage point reduction.

Selling, General and Administrative Expense Rate

Our selling, general and administrative (SG&A) expense rate represents SG&A expenses as a percentage of sales. See Note 3 of the Notes to Consolidated Financial Statements for a description of costs included in SG&A expenses. SG&A expenses exclude depreciation and amortization, as well as expenses associated with our credit card operations, which are reflected separately in our Consolidated Statements of Operations.

SG&A expense rate was 20.3 percent in 2010 compared with 20.5 percent in 2009 and 20.4 percent in 2008. The change in the rate in 2010 was primarily due to favorable leverage of overall compensation expenses. The change in the SG&A expense rate in 2009 was primarily driven by an approximate 0.4 percentage point impact from an increase in incentive compensation due to better than expected 2009 performance compared with 2008 results, which was partially offset by an approximate 0.2 percentage point impact from sustained productivity gains in our stores.

Depreciation and Amortization Expense Rate

Our depreciation and amortization expense rate represents depreciation and amortization expense as a percentage of sales. In 2010, our depreciation and amortization expense rate was 3.1 percent compared with 3.2 percent in 2009 and 2.9 percent in 2008. The rate was essentially unchanged from the same period last year. In 2009 the increase in the rate was primarily due to accelerated depreciation on assets that were replaced as part of our remodel program.

Store Data

Number of Stores	General merchandise	Expanded food assortment	SuperTarget	Total
January 30, 2010	1,381	108	251	1,740
Opened	—	13	—	13
Format conversion	(341)	341	—	—
Closed (a)	(3)	—	—	(3)
January 29, 2011	**1,037**	**462**	**251**	**1,750**

Retail Square Feet (b) (thousands)	General merchandise	Expanded food assortment	SuperTarget	Total
January 30, 2010	172,735	14,714	44,503	231,952
Opened	—	1,958	—	1,958
Format conversion	(45,138)	45,151	—	13
Closed (a)	(305)	—	—	(305)
January 29, 2011	**127,292**	**61,823**	**44,503**	**233,618**

(a)   Includes 1 store relocation in the same trade area and 2 stores closed without replacement.

(b)   Reflects total square feet less office, distribution center and vacant space.

Credit Card Segment

We offer credit to qualified guests through the Target Visa and the Target Card. Our credit card program supports our core retail operations and remains an important contributor to our overall profitability and engagement with our guests. Beginning April 2010, all new qualified credit card applicants receive the Target Card, and we no longer issue the Target Visa to credit card applicants. Existing Target Visa cardholders are not affected. Beginning October 2010, guests receive a 5 percent discount on virtually all purchases at checkout every day when they use a REDcard at any Target store or on Target.com. This new REDcard Rewards program replaced the existing rewards program in which account holders received an initial 10 percent-off coupon for opening the account and earned points toward a 10 percent-off coupon on subsequent purchases. These changes are intended to simplify the program and to generate profitable incremental retail sales.

Credit card revenues are comprised of finance charges, late fees and other revenue, and third party merchant fees, or the amounts received from merchants who accept the Target Visa credit card.

Credit Card Segment Results	2010		2009		2008	
(dollars in millions)	Amount	Rate (d)	Amount	Rate (d)	Amount	Rate (d)
Finance charge revenue	$ 1,302	18.3%	$ 1,450	17.4%	$ 1,451	16.7%
Late fees and other revenue	197	2.8	349	4.2	461	5.3
Third party merchant fees	105	1.5	123	1.5	152	1.7
Total revenues	1,604	22.6	1,922	23.0	2,064	23.7
Bad debt expense	528	7.4	1,185	14.2	1,251	14.4
Operations and marketing expenses (a)	433	6.1	425	5.1	474	5.4
Depreciation and amortization	19	0.3	14	0.2	17	0.2
Total expenses	980	13.8	1,624	19.4	1,742	20.0
EBIT	624	8.8	298	3.5	322	3.7
Interest expense on nonrecourse debt collateralized by credit card receivables	83		97		167	
Segment profit	$ 541		$ 201		$ 155	
Average receivables funded by Target (b)	$ 2,771		$ 2,866		$ 4,192	
Segment pretax ROIC (c)	19.5%		7.0%		3.7%	

(a) Loyalty Program discounts are recorded as reductions to sales in our Retail Segment. Effective with the October 2010 nationwide launch of our new 5% REDcard Rewards loyalty program, we changed the formula under which our Credit Card segment reimburses our Retail Segment to better align with the attributes of the new program. These reimbursed amounts were $102 million in 2010, $89 million in 2009 and $117 million in 2008. In all periods these amounts were recorded as reductions to SG&A expenses within the Retail Segment and increases to operations and marketing expenses within the Credit Card Segment.

(b) Amounts represent the portion of average gross credit card receivables funded by Target. For 2010, 2009 and 2008, these amounts exclude $4,335 million, $5,484 million and $4,503 million, respectively, of receivables funded by nonrecourse debt collateralized by credit card receivables.

(c) ROIC is return on invested capital, and this rate equals our segment profit divided by average gross credit card receivables funded by Target, expressed as an annualized rate.

(d) As an annualized percentage of average gross credit card receivables.

Spread Analysis – Total Portfolio	2010		2009		2008	
(dollars in millions)	Amount	Rate	Amount	Rate	Amount	Rate
EBIT	$ 624	8.8% (c)	$ 298	3.5% (c)	$ 322	3.7% (c)
LIBOR (a)		0.3%		0.3%		2.3%
Spread to LIBOR (b)	$ 604	8.5% (c)	$ 270	3.2% (c)	$ 118	1.4% (c)

(a) Balance-weighted one-month LIBOR.

(b) Spread to LIBOR is a metric used to analyze the performance of our total credit card portfolio because the majority of our portfolio earned finance charge revenue at rates tied to the Prime Rate, and the interest rate on all nonrecourse debt securitized by credit card receivables is tied to LIBOR.

(c) As a percentage of average gross credit card receivables.

Our primary measure of segment profit in our Credit Card Segment is the EBIT generated by our total credit card receivables portfolio less the interest expense on nonrecourse debt collateralized by credit card receivables. We analyze this measure of profit in light of the amount of capital we have invested in our credit card receivables. In addition, we measure the performance of our overall credit card receivables portfolio by calculating the dollar Spread to LIBOR at the portfolio level. This metric approximates overall financial performance of the entire credit card portfolio we manage by measuring the difference between EBIT earned on the portfolio and a hypothetical benchmark rate financing cost applied to the entire portfolio. The interest rate on all nonrecourse debt securitized by credit card receivables is tied to LIBOR.

Effective April 2009, we implemented a terms change to our portfolio that established a minimum annual percentage rate (APR) applied to cardholder account balances. Under these terms, finance charges accrue at a fixed APR if the benchmark Prime Rate is less than 6%; if the Prime Rate is greater than 6%, finance charges accrue at the benchmark Prime Rate, plus a spread. Because the Prime Rate was less than 6% during 2009, the majority of our portfolio accrued finance charges at a fixed APR subsequent to this terms change. As a result of regulatory actions that impact our portfolio, effective January 2010, we implemented a second terms change that converted the minimum APR for the majority of our accounts to a variable rate, and we eliminated penalty pricing for all current, or nondelinquent accounts. Penalty pricing is the charging of a higher interest rate for a period of time, generally 12 months, and is triggered when a cardholder repeatedly fails to make timely payments. Additionally, beginning in August 2010 late fee limitations went into effect that resulted in reduced late fee revenue.

In 2010, Credit Card Segment profit increased to $541 million from $201 million, driven mostly by favorability in bad debt expense. The reduction in our investment in the portfolio combined with these results produced a strong improvement in segment ROIC. Segment revenues were $1,604 million, a decrease of $318 million, or 16.5 percent, from the prior year, which was primarily driven by lower average receivables as well as reduced late fees. Segment expenses were $980 million, a decrease of $644 million, or 39.7 percent, from prior year driven primarily by lower bad debt expense due to lower actual and expected write-offs. Segment interest expense on nonrecourse debt declined due to a decrease in nonrecourse debt securitized by credit card receivables.

In 2009, Credit Card Segment profit increased to $201 million from $155 million as a result of improved portfolio performance (Spread to LIBOR) and significantly lower funding costs. The reduction in our investment in the portfolio combined with these results produced a strong improvement in segment ROIC. Segment revenues were $1,922 million, a decrease of $143 million, or 6.9 percent, from the prior year. The decrease in revenue was driven by a lower Prime Rate, lower average receivables, higher finance charge and late-fee write-offs, and lower late fees due to fewer delinquent accounts offset by the positive impacts of the terms changes implemented in late 2008 and April 2009. Segment expenses were $1,624 million, a decrease of $118 million, or 6.8 percent, from prior year driven by lower bad debt and operations and marketing expenses, on both a dollar and rate basis. Segment interest expense benefited from a significantly lower LIBOR rate compared to the prior year.

Receivables Rollforward Analysis (millions)	2010	2009	2008	Percent Change 2010/2009	2009/2008
Beginning gross credit card receivables	$ 7,982	$ 9,094	$ 8,624	(12.2)%	5.4%
Charges at Target	3,699	3,553	4,207	4.1	(15.5)
Charges at third parties	5,815	6,763	8,542	(14.0)	(20.8)
Payments	(11,283)	(12,065)	(13,482)	(6.5)	(10.5)
Other	630	637	1,203	(1.1)	(47.1)
Period-end gross credit card receivables	$ 6,843	$ 7,982	$ 9,094	(14.3)%	(12.2)%
Average gross credit card receivables	$ 7,106	$ 8,351	$ 8,695	(14.9)%	(4.0)%
Accounts with three or more payments (60+ days) past due as a percentage of period-end credit card receivables	4.2%	6.3%	6.1%		
Accounts with four or more payments (90+ days) past due as a percentage of period-end gross credit card receivables	3.1%	4.7%	4.3%		

Allowance for Doubtful Accounts (millions)	2010	2009	2008	Percent Change 2010/2009	2009/2008
Allowance at beginning of period	$ 1,016	$ 1,010	$ 570	0.6%	77.1%
Bad debt expense	528	1,185	1,251	(55.4)	(5.3)
Write-offs (a)	(1,007)	(1,287)	(912)	(21.8)	41.1
Recoveries (a)	153	108	101	40.2	8.3
Allowance at end of period	$ 690	$ 1,016	$1,010	(32.1)%	0.6%
As a percentage of period-end gross credit card receivables	10.1%	12.7%	11.1%		
Net write-offs as a percentage of average gross credit card receivables (annualized)	12.0%	14.1%	9.3%		

(a)   Write-offs include the principal amount of losses (excluding accrued and unpaid finance charges), and recoveries include current period principal collections on previously written-off balances. These amounts combined represent net write-offs.

Our 2010 period-end gross credit card receivables were $6,843 million compared to $7,982 million in 2009, a decrease of 14.3 percent. Average gross credit card receivables in 2010 decreased 14.9 percent compared with 2009 levels. In response to regulatory changes and credit card industry trends, we have undertaken risk management and underwriting initiatives that have reduced available credit lines for higher-risk cardholders. Additionally, we have experienced an increase in payment rates and a decrease in charges at third-parties.

Our 2009 period-end gross credit card receivables were $7,982 million compared with $9,094 million in 2008, a decrease of 12.2 percent. Average gross credit card receivables in 2009 decreased 4.0 percent compared with 2008 levels. This change was driven by the tighter risk management and underwriting initiatives described above, fewer new accounts being opened, and a decrease in charge activity resulting from reductions in card usage by our guests, partially offset by the impact of lower payment rates.

Other Performance Factors

Net Interest Expense

Net interest expense, which includes the interest expense on nonrecourse debt collateralized by credit card receivables detailed in the Credit Card Segment Results above, was $757 million for 2010, decreasing 5.5 percent, or $44 million from 2009 due to lower average debt balances and a $16 million charge related to the early retirement of long-term debt in 2009, partially offset by a higher average portfolio interest rate of 5.3 percent in 2010, compared with 4.8 percent in 2009. In 2009, net interest expense was $801 million, decreasing 7.5 percent, or $65 million from 2008. This decline was due to a lower average portfolio interest rate of 4.8 percent in 2009, compared with 5.3 percent in 2008, partially offset by a $16 million charge related to the early retirement of long-term debt.

Provision for Income Taxes

Our effective income tax rate was 35.1 percent in 2010 and 35.7 percent in 2009. The decrease in the effective rate between periods is primarily due to the favorable resolution of various income tax matters, which reduced income tax expense by approximately $100 million.

Our effective income tax rate was 35.7 percent in 2009 and 37.4 percent in 2008. The decrease in the effective rate between periods is primarily due to nontaxable capital market returns on investments used to economically hedge the market risk in deferred compensation plans in 2009, compared with nondeductible losses in 2008. The 2009 effective income tax rate is also lower due to federal and state discrete items.

Analysis of Financial Condition

Liquidity and Capital Resources

Our period end cash and cash equivalents balance was $1,712 million compared with $2,200 million in 2009. Marketable securities of $1,129 million and $1,617 million were included in cash and cash equivalents at the end of 2010 and 2009, respectively. Our investment policy is designed to preserve principal and liquidity of our marketable securities. This policy allows investments in large money market funds or in highly rated direct short-term instruments that mature in 60 days or less. We also place certain limitations on the aggregate dollars invested and percentage of total fund value held when making short-term investment decisions.

Our 2010 operations were funded by both internally and externally generated funds. Cash flow provided by operations was $5,271 million in 2010 compared with $5,881 million in 2009. This cash flow, combined with our prior year-end cash position and the debt issuance described below, allowed us to fund capital expenditures of $2,129 million and pay off $2,259 million of debt. In addition, in 2010 we increased our share repurchases and raised dividends paid to our shareholders.

Our 2010 period-end gross credit card receivables were $6,843 million compared with $7,982 million in 2009, a decrease of 14.3 percent. Average gross credit card receivables in 2010 decreased 14.9 percent compared with 2009 levels. This change was driven by the factors indicated in the Credit Card Segment above. This trend and the factors influencing it are likely to continue into 2011. Due to the decrease in gross credit card receivables, Target Receivables LLC (TR LLC), formerly known as Target Receivables Corporation (TRC), using cash flows from the receivables, repaid an affiliate of JPMorgan Chase (JPMC) $566 million and $163 million during 2010 and 2009, respectively, under the terms of our agreement with them as described in Note 10 of the Notes to Consolidated Financial Statements. To the extent the receivables balance continues to decline, TR LLC expects to continue to pay JPMC a prorata portion of principal collections such that the portion owned by JPMC would not exceed 47 percent.

Year-end inventory levels increased $417 million, or 5.8 percent from 2009. Inventory levels were higher to support traffic-driving strategic initiatives, such as our expanded food assortment in general merchandise stores and pharmacy, in addition to comparatively higher retail square footage. Accounts payable increased by $115 million, or 1.8 percent over the same period.

During 2010, we repurchased 47.8 million shares of our common stock for a total cash investment of $2,508 million ($52.44 per share) under a $10 billion share repurchase plan authorized by our Board of Directors in November 2007. In 2009, we repurchased 9.9 million shares of our common stock for a total cash investment of $479 million ($48.54 per share).

We paid dividends totaling $609 million in 2010 and $496 million in 2009, an increase of 22.7 percent. We declared dividends totaling $659 million ($0.92 per share) in 2010, an increase of 31.1 percent over 2009. In 2009, we declared dividends totaling $503 million ($0.67 per share), an increase of 6.8 percent over 2008. We have paid dividends every quarter since our first dividend was declared following our 1967 initial public offering, and it is our intent to continue to do so in the future.

Our financing strategy is to ensure liquidity and access to capital markets, to manage our net exposure to floating interest rate volatility, and to maintain a balanced spectrum of debt maturities. Within these parameters, we seek to minimize our borrowing costs. As described in Note 19, in July 2010, we issued $1 billion of long-term debt at 3.875% that matures in July 2020. There were no amounts issued in 2009.

Our ability to access the long-term debt, commercial paper and securitized debt markets has provided ample sources of liquidity to Target in the past. Our continued access to these markets depends on multiple factors including the economic environment, our operating performance and maintaining strong debt ratings. The ratings assigned to our debt by the credit rating agencies affect both the pricing and terms of any new financing. As of January 29, 2011 our credit ratings were as follows:

Credit Ratings	Moody's	Standard and	Poor's	Fitch
Long-term debt	A2		A+	A
Commercial paper	P-1		A-1	F1
Securitized receivables *(a)*	Aa2		n/a	n/a

(a)   These rated securitized receivables exclude the interest in our credit card receivables sold to JPMC.

If our credit ratings were lowered, our ability to access the debt markets and our cost of funds for new debt issuances could be adversely impacted. Each of the credit rating agencies reviews its rating periodically and there is no guarantee our current credit rating will remain the same as described above.

As a measure of our financial condition we monitor our interest coverage ratio, representing the ratio of pretax earnings before fixed charges to fixed charges. Fixed charges include interest expense and the interest portion of rent expense. Our interest coverage ratio as calculated by the SEC's applicable rules was 6.1x in 2010, 5.1x in 2009 and 4.3x in 2008.

At January 29, 2011 and January 30, 2010, there were no amounts outstanding under our commercial paper program. In past years, we funded our peak sales season working capital needs through our commercial paper program and then used the cash generated from that sales season to repay the commercial paper issued. In 2010 and 2009 we funded our working capital needs through internally generated funds and the long-term debt issuance indicated above.

Commercial Paper (millions)	2010	2009
Maximum daily amount outstanding during the year	$ —	$ 112
Average amount outstanding during the year	—	1
Amount outstanding at year-end	—	—
Weighted average interest rate	—	0.2%

An additional source of liquidity is available to us through a committed $2 billion unsecured revolving credit facility obtained through a group of banks in April 2007, which will expire in April 2012. No balances were outstanding at any time during 2010 or 2009 under this facility.

Most of our long-term debt obligations contain covenants related to secured debt levels. In addition to a secured debt level covenant, our credit facility also contains a debt leverage covenant. We are, and expect to remain, in compliance with these covenants. Additionally, at January 29, 2011, no notes or debentures contained provisions requiring acceleration of payment upon a debt rating downgrade, except that certain outstanding notes allow the note holders to put the notes to us if within a matter of months of each other we experience both (i) a change in control; and (ii) our long-term debt ratings are either reduced and the resulting rating is non-investment grade, or our long-term debt ratings are placed on watch for possible reduction and those ratings are subsequently reduced and the resulting rating is non-investment grade.

We believe our sources of liquidity will be adequate to maintain operations and to finance anticipated expansion and strategic initiatives during 2011, including our plan to enter the Canadian retail market by paying C$1,825 million to purchase the leasehold interests in up to 220 sites currently operated by Zellers Inc. We may issue new long-term debt for these and other initiatives, and we anticipate ample access to long-term financing. Further, in January 2011, we announced our plan to actively pursue the sale of our credit card receivables portfolio, which may provide additional funding. As of January 29, 2011 the gross balance of our credit card receivables portfolio was $6,843 million, of which $3,954 million was funded by third parties and $2,889 million was funded by Target.

Capital Expenditures

Capital expenditures were $2,129 million in 2010 compared with $1,729 million in 2009 and $3,547 million in 2008. This increase was driven by higher capital expenditures for remodels partially offset by reduced expenditures for new stores. Our 2010 capital expenditures include $482 million related to stores that will open in 2011 and later years. Net property and equipment increased $213 million in 2010 following a decrease of $475 million in 2009.

Capital Expenditures (millions)	2010	2009	2008
New stores	$ 574	$ 899	$ 2,341
Remodels and expansions	966	294	284
Information technology, distribution and other	589	536	922
Total	$ 2,129	$ 1,729	$ 3,547

In connection with the previously described agreement to purchase leasehold interests in Canada, we expect that renovation of these stores will require an investment of over C$1 billion, primarily during 2012 and 2013, a portion of which may be funded by landlords.

Commitments and Contingencies

At January 29, 2011, our contractual obligations were as follows:

Contractual Obligations (millions)	Total	Payments Due by Period			
		Less than 1 Year	1-3 Years	3-5 Years	After 5 Years
Recorded Contractual Obligations:					
Long-term debt (a)					
Unsecured	$11,287	$ 106	$ 2,002	$ 28	$ 9,151
Nonrecourse	4,061	—	4,061	—	—
Capital lease obligations (b)	617	32	66	62	457
Real estate liabilities (c)	65	65	—	—	—
Deferred compensation (d)	440	44	96	106	194
Tax contingencies (e)	—	—	—	—	—
Unrecorded Contractual Obligations:					
Interest payments – long-term debt					
Unsecured	10,080	678	1,214	1,127	7,061
Nonrecourse (f)	101	32	69	—	—
Operating leases (b)	3,954	190	376	288	3,100
Real estate obligations (g)	243	209	34	—	—
Purchase obligations (h)	1,907	713	747	348	99
Payment for Canadian leasehold interests (i)	1,825	1,825	—	—	—
Future contributions to retirement plans (j)	—	—	—	—	—
Contractual obligations	$34,580	$ 3,894	$ 8,665	$ 1,959	$ 20,062

(a)   Required principal payments only. Excludes fair market value adjustments recorded in long-term debt, as required by derivative and hedging accounting rules. Principal includes the 47 percent interest in credit card receivables sold to JPMC at the principal amount. In the event of a decrease in the receivables principal balance, accelerated repayment of this obligation may occur.

(b)   Total contractual lease payments include $1,949 million of operating lease payments related to options to extend the lease term that are reasonably assured of being exercised. These payments also include $28 million and $241 million of legally binding minimum lease payments for stores opening in 2011 or later for capital and operating leases, respectively. Capital lease obligations include interest.

(c)   Real estate liabilities include costs incurred but not paid related to the construction or remodeling of real estate and facilities.

(d)   Deferred compensation obligations include commitments related to our nonqualified deferred compensation plans. The timing of deferred compensation payouts is estimated based on payments currently made to former employees and retirees, forecasted investment returns, and the projected timing of future retirements.

(e)   Estimated tax contingencies of $397 million, including interest and penalties, are not included in the table above because we are not able to make reasonably reliable estimates of the period of cash settlement.

(f)   These payments vary with LIBOR and are calculated assuming LIBOR of 0.25 percent plus a spread, for each year outstanding.

(g)   Real estate obligations include commitments for the purchase, construction or remodeling of real estate and facilities.

(h)   Purchase obligations include all legally binding contracts such as firm minimum commitments for inventory purchases, merchandise royalties, equipment purchases, marketing related contracts, software acquisition/license commitments and service contracts. We issue inventory purchase orders in the normal course of business, which represent authorizations to purchase that are cancelable by their terms. We do not consider purchase orders to be firm inventory commitments; therefore, they are excluded from the table above. If we choose to cancel a purchase order, we may be obligated to reimburse the vendor for unrecoverable outlays incurred prior to cancellation. We also issue trade letters of credit in the ordinary course of business, which are excluded from this table as these obligations are conditioned on terms of the letter of credit being met.

(i)   *In January 2011, we entered into an agreement to purchase the leasehold interests in up to 220 sites in Canada currently operated by Zellers Inc., in exchange for C$1,825 million. At January 29, 2011 the value of C$1.00 approximated the value of $1.00. This commitment does not include future minimum lease payments on sites that may be selected in 2011.*

(j)   *We have not included obligations under our pension and postretirement health care benefit plans in the contractual obligations table above because no additional amounts are required to be funded as of January 29, 2011. Our historical practice regarding these plans has been to contribute amounts necessary to satisfy minimum pension funding requirements, plus periodic discretionary amounts determined to be appropriate.*

Off Balance Sheet Arrangements   We do not have any arrangements or relationships with entities that are not consolidated into the financial statements or financial guarantees that are reasonably likely to materially affect our liquidity or the availability of capital resources.

Critical Accounting Estimates

Our analysis of operations and financial condition is based on our consolidated financial statements, prepared in accordance with U.S. generally accepted accounting principles (GAAP). Preparation of these consolidated financial statements requires us to make estimates and assumptions affecting the reported amounts of assets and liabilities at the date of the consolidated financial statements, reported amounts of revenues and expenses during the reporting period and related disclosures of contingent assets and liabilities. In the Notes to Consolidated Financial Statements, we describe the significant accounting policies used in preparing the consolidated financial statements. Our estimates are evaluated on an ongoing basis and are drawn from historical experience and other assumptions that we believe to be reasonable under the circumstances. Actual results could differ under other assumptions or conditions. However, we do not believe there is a reasonable likelihood that there will be a material change in future estimates or assumptions. Our senior management has discussed the development and selection of our critical accounting estimates with the Audit Committee of our Board of Directors. The following items in our consolidated financial statements require significant estimation or judgment:

Inventory and cost of sales   We use the retail inventory method to account for substantially our entire inventory and the related cost of sales. Under this method, inventory is stated at cost using the last-in, first-out (LIFO) method as determined by applying a cost-to-retail ratio to each merchandise grouping's ending retail value. Cost includes the purchase price as adjusted for vendor income. Since inventory value is adjusted regularly to reflect market conditions, our inventory methodology reflects the lower of cost or market. We reduce inventory for estimated losses related to shrink and markdowns. Our shrink estimate is based on historical losses verified by ongoing physical inventory counts. Historically, our actual physical inventory count results have shown our estimates to be reliable. Markdowns designated for clearance activity are recorded when the salability of the merchandise has diminished. Inventory is at risk of obsolescence if economic conditions change. Relevant economic conditions include changing consumer demand, customer preferences, changing consumer credit markets or increasing competition. We believe these risks are largely mitigated because our inventory typically turns in less than three months. Inventory was $7,596 million and $7,179 million at January 29, 2011 and January 30, 2010, respectively, and is further described in Note 11 of the Notes to Consolidated Financial Statements.

Vendor income receivable   Cost of sales and SG&A expenses are partially offset by various forms of consideration received from our vendors. This "vendor income" is earned for a variety of vendor-sponsored programs, such as volume rebates, markdown allowances, promotions and advertising allowances, as well as for our compliance programs. We establish a receivable for the vendor income that is earned but not yet received. Based on the agreements in place, this receivable is computed by estimating when we have completed our performance and when the amount is earned. The majority of all year-end vendor income receivables are collected within the following fiscal quarter, and we do not believe there is a reasonable likelihood that the assumptions used in our estimate will change significantly. Historically, adjustments to our vendor income receivable have not been material. Vendor income receivable was $517 million and $390 million at January 29, 2011 and January 30, 2010, respectively, and is described further in Note 4 of the Notes to Consolidated Financial Statements.

Allowance for doubtful accounts   When receivables are recorded, we recognize an allowance for doubtful accounts in an amount equal to anticipated future write-offs. This allowance includes provisions for uncollectible finance charges and other credit-related fees. We estimate future write-offs based on historical experience of delinquencies, risk scores, aging trends and industry risk trends. Substantially all accounts continue to accrue finance charges until they are written off. Accounts are automatically written off when they become 180 days past due. Management believes the allowance for doubtful accounts is adequate to cover anticipated losses in our credit card accounts receivable under current conditions; however, unexpected, significant deterioration in any of the factors mentioned above or in general economic conditions could materially change these expectations. During 2010, we continued risk management and underwriting initiatives that reduced available credit lines for higher-risk cardholders. In addition, we experienced an increase in payment rates and a decrease in charge activity from reductions in card usage by our guests. As a result of these trends, our allowance for doubtful accounts related to our credit card receivables decreased $326 million, from $1,016 million, or 12.7 percent of gross credit card receivables, at January 30, 2010 to $690 million, or 10.1 percent of gross credit card receivables, at January 29, 2011. Credit card receivables and our allowance for doubtful accounts are described in Note 10 of the Notes to Consolidated Financial Statements.

Long-lived assets   Long-lived assets are reviewed for impairment whenever events or changes in circumstances indicate that the carrying amount of an asset (or asset group) may not be recoverable. An impairment loss would be recognized when estimated undiscounted future cash flows from the operation and disposition of the asset group are less than the carrying amount of the asset group. Asset groups have identifiable cash flows independent of other asset groups. Measurement of an impairment loss would be based on the excess of the carrying amount of the asset group over its fair value. Fair value is measured using discounted cash flows or independent opinions of value, as appropriate. A 10 percent decrease in the fair value of assets we intend to sell as of January 29, 2011 would result in additional impairment of approximately $12 million in 2010. Historically, we have not realized material losses upon sale of long-lived assets.

Goodwill and intangible assets   We evaluate goodwill and intangible assets for impairment annually, or whenever events or changes in circumstances indicate the carrying value of the asset may not be recoverable. Discounted cash flow models are used in determining fair value of goodwill and intangible assets. Growth rates for sales and profits are determined using inputs from our long-range planning process. We also make estimates of discount rates, perpetuity growth rates, and other factors. As of January 29, 2011 and January 30, 2010, we had $223 million and $239 million of goodwill and intangible assets, respectively. While we currently believe that the fair value of our goodwill and intangible assets exceeds its carrying value, materially different assumptions regarding future performance of our businesses or other factors could result in impairment losses.

Insurance/self-insurance   We retain a substantial portion of the risk related to certain general liability, workers' compensation, property loss and team member medical and dental claims. However, we maintain stop-loss coverage to limit the exposure related to certain risks. Liabilities associated with these losses include estimates of both claims filed and losses incurred but not yet reported. We use actuarial methods which consider a number of factors to estimate our ultimate cost of losses. General liability and workers' compensation liabilities are recorded at our estimate of their net present value; other liabilities referred to above are not discounted. Our workers' compensation and general liability accrual was $628 million and $653 million at January 29, 2011 and January 30, 2010, respectively. We believe that the amounts accrued are adequate; however, our liabilities could be significantly affected if future occurrences or loss developments differ from our assumptions. For example, a 5 percent increase or decrease in average claim costs would impact our self-insurance expense by approximately $30 million in 2010. Historically, adjustments to our estimates have not been material. Refer to Item 7A for further disclosure of the market risks associated with these exposures.

Income taxes   We pay income taxes based on the tax statutes, regulations and case law of the various jurisdictions in which we operate. Significant judgment is required in determining the timing and amounts of deductible and taxable items and in evaluating the ultimate resolution of tax matters in dispute with tax authorities. The benefits of uncertain tax positions are recorded in our financial statements only after determining whether it is likely the uncertain tax positions would withstand challenge by taxing authorities. We periodically reassess these probabilities, and record any changes in the financial statements as deemed appropriate. Liabilities for tax positions considered uncertain, including interest and penalties, were $397 million and $579 million at January 29, 2011 and January 30, 2010, respectively. We believe the resolution of these matters will not have a material adverse impact on our consolidated financial statements. Income taxes are described further in Note 22 of the Notes to Consolidated Financial Statements.

Pension and postretirement health care accounting   We fund and maintain a qualified defined benefit pension plan. We also maintain several smaller nonqualified plans and a postretirement health care plan for certain current and retired team members. The costs for these plans are determined based on actuarial calculations using the assumptions described in the following paragraphs. Eligibility for, and the level of, these benefits varies depending on team members' full-time or part-time status, date of hire and/or length of service.

Our expected long-term rate of return on plan assets is determined by the portfolio composition, historical long-term investment performance and current market conditions. Benefits expense recorded during the year is partially dependent upon the long-term rate of return used. A one percentage point decrease in the expected long-term rate of return used to determine net pension and postretirement health care benefits expense would increase annual expense by approximately $24 million.

The discount rate used to determine benefit obligations is adjusted annually based on the interest rate for long-term high-quality corporate bonds as of the measurement date, using yields for maturities that are in line with the duration of our pension liabilities. Therefore, these liabilities fluctuate with changes in interest rates. Historically, this same discount rate has also been used to determine net pension and postretirement health care benefits expense for the following plan year. Benefits expense recorded during the year is partially dependent upon the discount rates used, and a 0.5 percentage point decrease to the weighted average discount rate used to determine net pension and postretirement health care benefits expense would increase annual expense by approximately $23 million.

Based on our experience, we use a graduated compensation growth schedule that assumes higher compensation growth for younger, shorter-service pension-eligible team members than it does for older, longer-service pension-eligible team members.

Pension and postretirement health care benefits are further described in Note 27 of the Notes to Consolidated Financial Statements.

Legal contingencies   We are exposed to claims and litigation arising in the ordinary course of business and use various methods to resolve these matters in a manner that we believe serves the best interest of our shareholders and other constituents. Historically, adjustments to our estimates have not been material. We believe the recorded reserves in our consolidated financial statements are adequate in light of the probable and estimable liabilities. We do not believe that any of the currently identified claims or litigation matters will have a material adverse impact on our results of operations, cash flows or financial condition. However, litigation is subject to inherent uncertainties, and unfavorable rulings could occur. If an unfavorable ruling were to occur, there may be a material adverse impact on the results of operations, cash flows or financial condition for the period in which the ruling occurs, or future periods.

New Accounting Pronouncements

Recent Adoptions

In June 2009, the FASB issued SFAS No. 166, "Accounting for Transfers of Financial Assets an amendment of FASB Statement No. 140" (SFAS 166), codified in the Transfers and Servicing accounting principles, which amends the derecognition guidance in former FASB Statement No. 140 and eliminates the exemption from consolidation for qualifying special-purpose entities. We adopted this guidance at the beginning of 2010 and adoption had no impact on our consolidated net earnings, cash flows or financial position.

In June 2009, the FASB issued SFAS No. 167, "Amendments to FASB Interpretation No. 46(R)" (SFAS 167), codified in the Consolidation accounting principles, which amends the consolidation guidance applicable to variable interest entities. The amendments significantly affected the overall consolidation analysis under former FASB Interpretation No. 46(R). We adopted this guidance at the beginning of 2010 and the adoption had no impact on our consolidated net earnings, cash flows or financial position.

Outlook

Our outlook is based on the application of business judgment in light of current business trends, our assumptions regarding the macroeconomic environment, and estimates of the impact of current initiatives, the most significant of which are our store remodel program, the new 5 percent REDcard Rewards program, and our planned Canadian expansion.

In the Retail Segment, we expect that comparable-store sales will increase in the 4 to 5 percent range in 2011. We expect that our store remodel program will contribute incremental comparable-store sales, and net of the adverse impact of remodel disruption, this impact will grow to a run rate of about 1.5 percentage points as we progress through the year. Separately we expect that the sales contribution of our 5% REDcard Rewards program will grow more rapidly in its importance, adding up to 2 percentage points to our same store sales growth later in 2011. These estimates are based on extrapolations of the current performance of these programs.

In 2011 we expect to produce a full-year EBIT margin rate consistent with 2010, due to favorable leverage of SG&A and depreciation and amortization expenses offsetting the gross margin rate declines associated with our store remodel and new rewards strategies. This offsetting impact is unlikely to occur in the spring, particularly in the first quarter, resulting in modest pressure on EBIT margin rate in the spring, and modest favorability on this measure in the fall.

In our Credit Card Segment, we expect receivables will continue to decline in 2011, with the pace of the decline moderating as the year progresses. We expect that the allowance for doubtful accounts will continue to decline in 2011 as well, due to this decline in receivables and expected continued improvement in portfolio risks. We also expect measures of our rate of portfolio profitability to remain strong in 2011. Additionally, in January 2011 we announced our plan to actively pursue the sale of our credit card receivables portfolio. As of January 29, 2011 the gross balance of our credit card receivables portfolio was $6,843 million, of which $3,954 million was funded by third parties and $2,889 million was funded by Target.

In January 2011, we entered into an agreement to purchase the leasehold interests in up to 220 sites in Canada currently operated by Zellers Inc., in exchange for C$1,825 million, due in two payments, one in May 2011 and one in September 2011. We believe this transaction will allow us to open 100 to 150 Target stores in Canada, primarily during 2013. We expect that renovation of these stores will require an investment of over C$1 billion, a portion of which may be funded by landlords. Our direct costs associated with entry into Canada may add expenses equating to an earnings per share (EPS) equivalent in the range of $0.10 for 2011, an estimate that will continue to evolve over time. We currently believe the aggregate effect of our Canadian expansion could result in a $0.15 to $0.20 unfavorable impact on 2011 EPS, reflecting direct incremental expenses and the indirect impact of the Canadian investment on the pace of share repurchase. We expect that the 2012 dilutive EPS impact of the Canadian expansion will exceed the 2011 dilutive EPS impact, due primarily to a full year of lease-related expenses.

We expect 2011 capital expenditures related to our U.S. retail operations to be approximately $2.5 billion, driven primarily by a larger remodel program. We expect to open 21 new stores in the U.S. in 2011, adding approximately 15 new locations net of closings and relocations.

We also expect to continue to execute against our share repurchase plan, although at a slower pace due to our Canadian expansion, investing in the range of $1.5 billion to $2.0 billion during 2011. The timing and amount of share repurchase activity will be dependent on market conditions and the amount of future net earnings and cash flows.

We expect our 2011 effective tax rate to be in the range of 36 to 37 percent.

Forward-Looking Statements

This report contains forward-looking statements, which are based on our current assumptions and expectations. These statements are typically accompanied by the words "expect," "may," "could," "believe," "would," "might," "anticipates," or words of similar import. The principal forward-looking statements in this report include: For our Retail Segment, our outlook for sales, comparable-store sales trends, including the impact of our store remodel and 5% REDcard Rewards programs, and EBIT margin rates; for our Credit Card Segment, our outlook for year-end gross credit card receivables, future write-offs of current receivables, rate of portfolio profitability, the allowance for doubtful accounts, improvement in portfolio risks, and the pursuit of a portfolio sale; on a consolidated basis, details on the expected investment in Canada and its impact on our results, statements regarding the adequacy of our sources of liquidity, the continued execution of our share repurchase program, our expected capital expenditures and the number of stores to be opened in 2011, the expected effective income tax rate, the expected compliance with debt covenants, our intentions regarding future dividends, our expected future share-based compensation expense, our expected return on plan assets, our expected expense, contributions and benefit payments related to our pension and postretirement health care plans, the adequacy of our reserves for general liability, workers' compensation, property loss, and team member medical and dental, the potential impact of changes in our critical accounting estimates, the expected outcome of claims and litigation, and the resolution of tax uncertainties.

All such forward-looking statements are intended to enjoy the protection of the safe harbor for forward-looking statements contained in the Private Securities Litigation Reform Act of 1995, as amended. Although we believe there is a reasonable basis for the forward-looking statements, our actual results could be materially different. The most important factors which could cause our actual results to differ from our forward-looking statements are set forth on our description of risk factors in Item 1A to this Form 10-K, which should be read in conjunction with the forward-looking statements in this report. Forward-looking statements speak only as of the date they are made, and we do not undertake any obligation to update any forward-looking statement.

Item 7A.   Quantitative and Qualitative Disclosures About Market Risk

Our exposure to market risk results primarily from interest rate changes on our debt obligations, some of which are at a LIBOR-plus floating rate, and on our credit card receivables, the majority of which are assessed finance charges at a Prime based floating rate. To manage our net interest margin, we generally maintain levels of floating-rate debt to generate similar changes in net interest expense as finance charge revenues fluctuate. The degree of floating asset and liability matching may vary over time and in different interest rate environments. At January 29, 2011, the amount of floating-rate credit card assets exceeded the amount of net floating-rate debt obligations by approximately $2 billion. As a result, based on our balance sheet position at January 29, 2011, the annualized effect of a 0.1 percentage point decrease in floating interest rates on our floating rate debt obligations, net of our floating rate credit card assets and marketable securities, would be to decrease earnings before income taxes by approximately $2 million. See further description in Note 20 of the Notes to Consolidated Financial Statements.

We record our general liability and workers' compensation liabilities at net present value; therefore, these liabilities fluctuate with changes in interest rates. Periodically, in certain interest rate environments, we economically hedge a portion of our exposure to these interest rate changes by entering into interest rate forward contracts that partially mitigate the effects of interest rate changes. Based on our balance sheet position at January 29, 2011, the annualized effect of a 0.5 percentage point decrease in interest rates would be to decrease earnings before income taxes by approximately $10 million.

In addition, we are exposed to market return fluctuations on our qualified defined benefit pension plans. The annualized effect of a one percentage point decrease in the return on pension plan assets would decrease plan assets by $25 million at January 29, 2011. The value of our pension liabilities is inversely related to changes in interest rates. To protect against declines in interest rates we hold high-quality, long-duration bonds and interest rate swaps in our pension plan trust. At year-end, we had hedged approximately 55 percent of the interest rate exposure of our funded status.

As more fully described in Note 14 and Note 26 of the Notes to Consolidated Financial Statements, we are exposed to market returns on accumulated team member balances in our nonqualified, unfunded deferred compensation plans. We control the risk of offering the nonqualified plans by making investments in life insurance contracts and prepaid forward contracts on our own common stock that offset a substantial portion of our economic exposure to the returns on these plans. The annualized effect of a one percentage point change in market returns on our nonqualified defined contribution plans (inclusive of the effect of the investment vehicles used to manage our economic exposure) would not be significant.

We do not currently have significant direct exposure to foreign currency rates as all of our stores are located in the United States, and the vast majority of imported merchandise is purchased in U.S. dollars. Our previously described agreement to purchase leasehold interests in Canada will expose us to market risk associated with foreign currency exchange rate fluctuations between the Canadian dollar and the U.S. dollar beginning in 2011.

Overall, there have been no material changes in our primary risk exposures or management of market risks since the prior year.

Item 8. Financial Statements and Supplementary Data

Report of Management on the Consolidated Financial Statements

Management is responsible for the consistency, integrity and presentation of the information in the Annual Report. The consolidated financial statements and other information presented in this Annual Report have been prepared in accordance with accounting principles generally accepted in the United States and include necessary judgments and estimates by management.

To fulfill our responsibility, we maintain comprehensive systems of internal control designed to provide reasonable assurance that assets are safeguarded and transactions are executed in accordance with established procedures. The concept of reasonable assurance is based upon recognition that the cost of the controls should not exceed the benefit derived. We believe our systems of internal control provide this reasonable assurance.

The Board of Directors exercised its oversight role with respect to the Corporation's systems of internal control primarily through its Audit Committee, which is comprised of independent directors. The Committee oversees the Corporation's systems of internal control, accounting practices, financial reporting and audits to assess whether their quality, integrity and objectivity are sufficient to protect shareholders' investments.

In addition, our consolidated financial statements have been audited by Ernst & Young LLP, independent registered public accounting firm, whose report also appears on this page.

Gregg W. Steinhafel   Chief Executive Officer and President
March 11, 2011

Douglas A. Scovanner   Executive Vice President and   Chief Financial Officer

Report of Independent Registered Public Accounting Firm on Consolidated Financial Statements

The Board of Directors and Shareholders
Target Corporation

We have audited the accompanying consolidated statements of financial position of Target Corporation and subsidiaries (the Corporation) as of January 29, 2011 and January 30, 2010, and the related consolidated statements of operations, cash flows, and shareholders' investment for each of the three years in the period ended January 29, 2011. Our audits also included the financial statement schedule listed in Item 15(a). These financial statements and schedule are the responsibility of the Corporation's management. Our responsibility is to express an opinion on these financial statements and schedule based on our audits.

We conducted our audits in accordance with the standards of the Public Company Accounting Oversight Board (United States). Those standards require that we plan and perform the audit to obtain reasonable assurance about whether the financial statements are free of material misstatement. An audit includes examining, on a test basis, evidence supporting the amounts and disclosures in the financial statements. An audit also includes assessing the accounting principles used and significant estimates made by management, as well as evaluating the overall financial statement presentation. We believe that our audits provide a reasonable basis for our opinion.

In our opinion, the financial statements referred to above present fairly, in all material respects, the consolidated financial position of Target Corporation and subsidiaries at January 29, 2011 and January 30, 2010, and the consolidated results of their operations and their cash flows for each of the three years in the period ended January 29, 2011, in conformity with U.S. generally accepted accounting principles. Also, in our opinion, the related financial statement schedule, when considered in relation to the basic financial statements taken as a whole, presents fairly in all material respects the information set forth therein.

We also have audited, in accordance with the standards of the Public Company Accounting Oversight Board (United States), the Corporation's internal control over financial reporting as of January 29, 2011, based on criteria established in *Internal Control—Integrated Framework*, issued by the Committee of Sponsoring Organizations of the Treadway Commission and our report dated March 11, 2011, expressed an unqualified opinion thereon.

Ernst & Young LLP

Minneapolis, Minnesota   March 11, 2011

Report of Management on Internal Control

Our management is responsible for establishing and maintaining adequate internal control over financial reporting, as such term is defined in Exchange Act Rules 13a-15(f). Under the supervision and with the participation of our management, including our chief executive officer and chief financial officer, we assessed the effectiveness of our internal control over financial reporting as of January 29, 2011, based on the framework in *Internal Control—Integrated Framework*, issued by the Committee of Sponsoring Organizations of the Treadway Commission. Based on our assessment, we conclude that the Corporation's internal control over financial reporting is effective based on those criteria.

Our internal control over financial reporting as of January 29, 2011, has been audited by Ernst & Young LLP, the independent registered accounting firm who has also audited our consolidated financial statements, as stated in their report which appears on this page.

Gregg W. Steinhafel   Chief Executive Officer and President
March 11, 2011

Douglas A. Scovanner   Executive Vice President and   Chief
Financial Officer

Report of Independent Registered Public Accounting Firm on Internal Control over Financial Reporting

The Board of Directors and Shareholders
Target Corporation

We have audited Target Corporation and subsidiaries' (the Corporation) internal control over financial reporting as of January 29, 2011, based on criteria established in *Internal Control—Integrated Framework*, issued by the Committee of Sponsoring Organizations of the Treadway Commission (the COSO criteria). The Corporation's management is responsible for maintaining effective internal control over financial reporting, and for its assessment of the effectiveness of internal control over financial reporting included in the accompanying Report of Management on Internal Control over Financial Reporting. Our responsibility is to express an opinion on the Corporation's internal control over financial reporting based on our audit.

We conducted our audit in accordance with the standards of the Public Company Accounting Oversight Board (United States). Those standards require that we plan and perform the audit to obtain reasonable assurance about whether effective internal control over financial reporting was maintained in all material respects. Our audit included obtaining an understanding of internal control over financial reporting, assessing the risk that a material weakness exists, testing and evaluating the design and operating effectiveness of internal control based on the assessed risk, and performing such other procedures as we considered necessary in the circumstances. We believe that our audit provides a reasonable basis for our opinion.

A company's internal control over financial reporting is a process designed to provide reasonable assurance regarding the reliability of financial reporting and the preparation of financial statements for external purposes in accordance with generally accepted accounting principles. A company's internal control over financial reporting includes those policies and procedures that (1) pertain to the maintenance of records that, in reasonable detail, accurately and fairly reflect the transactions and dispositions of the assets of the company, (2) provide reasonable assurance that transactions are recorded as necessary to permit preparation of financial statements in accordance with generally accepted accounting principles and that receipts and expenditures of the company are being made only in accordance with authorizations of management and directors of the company, and (3) provide reasonable assurance regarding prevention or timely detection of unauthorized acquisition, use or disposition of the company's assets that could have a material effect on the financial statements.

Because of its inherent limitations, internal control over financial reporting may not prevent or detect misstatements. Also, projections of any evaluation of effectiveness to future periods are subject to the risk that controls may become inadequate because of changes in conditions or that the degree of compliance with the policies or procedures may deteriorate.

In our opinion, the Corporation maintained, in all material respects, effective internal control over financial reporting as of January 29, 2011, based on the COSO criteria.

We also have audited, in accordance with the standards of the Public Company Accounting Oversight Board (United States), the consolidated statements of financial position of Target Corporation and subsidiaries as of January 29, 2011 and January 30, 2010, and the related consolidated statements of operations, cash flows and shareholders' investment for each of the three years in the period ended January 29, 2011, and our report dated March 11, 2011, expressed an unqualified opinion thereon.

Ernst & Young LLP

Minneapolis, Minnesota   March 11, 2011

Consolidated Statements of Operations

(millions, except per share data)		2010	2009	2008
Sales	$	65,786 $	63,435 $	62,884
Credit card revenues		1,604	1,922	2,064
Total revenues		67,390	65,357	64,948
Cost of sales		45,725	44,062	44,157
Selling, general and administrative expenses		13,469	13,078	12,954
Credit card expenses		860	1,521	1,609
Depreciation and amortization		2,084	2,023	1,826
Earnings before interest expense and income taxes		5,252	4,673	4,402
Net interest expense				
Nonrecourse debt collateralized by credit card receivables		83	97	167
Other interest expense		677	707	727
Interest income		(3)	(3)	(28)
Net interest expense		757	801	866
Earnings before income taxes		4,495	3,872	3,536
Provision for income taxes		1,575	1,384	1,322
Net earnings	$	2,920 $	2,488 $	2,214
Basic earnings per share	$	4.03 $	3.31 $	2.87
Diluted earnings per share	$	4.00 $	3.30 $	2.86
Weighted average common shares outstanding				
Basic		723.6	752.0	770.4
Diluted		729.4	754.8	773.6

See accompanying Notes to Consolidated Financial Statements.

Consolidated Statements of Financial Position

(millions, except footnotes)		January 29, 2011	January 30, 2010
Assets			
Cash and cash equivalents, including marketable securities of **$1,129** and $1,617	$	1,712 $	2,200
Credit card receivables, net of allowance of **$690** and $1,016		6,153	6,966
Inventory		7,596	7,179
Other current assets		1,752	2,079
Total current assets		17,213	18,424
Property and equipment			
Land		5,928	5,793
Buildings and improvements		23,081	22,152
Fixtures and equipment		4,939	4,743
Computer hardware and software		2,533	2,575
Construction-in-progress		567	502
Accumulated depreciation		(11,555)	(10,485)
Property and equipment, net		25,493	25,280
Other noncurrent assets		999	829
Total assets	$	43,705 $	44,533
Liabilities and shareholders' investment			
Accounts payable	$	6,625 $	6,511
Accrued and other current liabilities		3,326	3,120
Unsecured debt and other borrowings		119	796
Nonrecourse debt collateralized by credit card receivables		—	900
Total current liabilities		10,070	11,327
Unsecured debt and other borrowings		11,653	10,643
Nonrecourse debt collateralized by credit card receivables		3,954	4,475
Deferred income taxes		934	835
Other noncurrent liabilities		1,607	1,906
Total noncurrent liabilities		18,148	17,859
Shareholders' investment			
Common stock		59	62
Additional paid-in-capital		3,311	2,919
Retained earnings		12,698	12,947
Accumulated other comprehensive loss		(581)	(581)
Total shareholders' investment		15,487	15,347
Total liabilities and shareholders' investment	$	43,705 $	44,533

Common Stock Authorized 6,000,000,000 shares, $0.0833 par value; **704,038,218** shares issued and outstanding at January 29, 2011; 744,644,454 shares issued and outstanding at January 30, 2010.

Preferred Stock Authorized 5,000,000 shares, $0.01 par value; no shares were issued or outstanding at January 29, 2011 or January 30, 2010.

See accompanying Notes to Consolidated Financial Statements.

Consolidated Statements of Cash Flows

(millions)	2010	2009	2008
Operating activities			
Net earnings	$ 2,920	$ 2,488	$ 2,214
Reconciliation to cash flow			
Depreciation and amortization	2,084	2,023	1,826
Share-based compensation expense	109	103	72
Deferred income taxes	445	364	91
Bad debt expense	528	1,185	1,251
Non-cash (gains)/losses and other, net	(145)	143	316
Changes in operating accounts:			
Accounts receivable originated at Target	(78)	(57)	(458)
Inventory	(417)	(474)	77
Other current assets	(124)	(129)	(99)
Other noncurrent assets	(212)	(114)	(55)
Accounts payable	115	174	(389)
Accrued and other current liabilities	149	257	(230)
Other noncurrent liabilities	(103)	(82)	(186)
Cash flow provided by operations	5,271	5,881	4,430
Investing activities			
Expenditures for property and equipment	(2,129)	(1,729)	(3,547)
Proceeds from disposal of property and equipment	69	33	39
Change in accounts receivable originated at third parties	363	(10)	(823)
Other investments	(47)	3	(42)
Cash flow required for investing activities	(1,744)	(1,703)	(4,373)
Financing activities			
Reductions of short-term notes payable	—	—	(500)
Additions to long-term debt	1,011	—	3,557
Reductions of long-term debt	(2,259)	(1,970)	(1,455)
Dividends paid	(609)	(496)	(465)
Repurchase of stock	(2,452)	(423)	(2,815)
Stock option exercises and related tax benefit	294	47	43
Other	—	—	(8)
Cash flow required for financing activities	(4,015)	(2,842)	(1,643)
Net increase/(decrease) in cash and cash equivalents	(488)	1,336	(1,586)
Cash and cash equivalents at beginning of year	2,200	864	2,450
Cash and cash equivalents at end of year	$ 1,712	$ 2,200	$ 864

Cash paid for income taxes was **$1,259,** $1,040 and $1,399 during 2010, 2009 and 2008, respectively. Cash paid for interest (net of interest capitalized) was **$752,** $805 and $873 during 2010, 2009 and 2008, respectively.

See accompanying Notes to Consolidated Financial Statements.

Consolidated Statements of Shareholders' Investment

(millions, except footnotes)	Common Stock Shares	Stock Par Value	Additional Paid-in Capital	Retained Earnings	Accumulated Other Comprehensive Income/(Loss)		Total
					Pension and Other Benefit Liability Adjustments	Derivative Instruments, Foreign Currency and Other	
February 2, 2008	818.7	$68	$2,656	$12,761	$(134)	$(44)	$15,307
Net earnings	—	—	—	2,214	—	—	2,214
Other comprehensive income/(loss)							
Pension and other benefit liability adjustments, net of taxes of $242	—	—	—	—	(376)	—	(376)
Net change on cash flow hedges, net of taxes of $2	—	—	—	—	—	(2)	(2)
Total comprehensive income							1,836
Dividends declared	—	—	—	(471)	—	—	(471)
Repurchase of stock	(67.2)	(5)	—	(3,061)	—	—	(3,066)
Stock options and awards	1.2	—	106	—	—	—	106
January 31, 2009	752.7	$ 63	$ 2,762	$ 11,443	$ (510)	$ (46)	$13,712
Net earnings	—	—	—	2,488	—	—	2,488
Other comprehensive income/(loss)							
Pension and other benefit liability adjustments, net of taxes of $17	—	—	—	—	(27)	—	(27)
Net change on cash flow hedges, net of taxes of $2	—	—	—	—	—	4	4
Currency translation adjustment, net of taxes of $0	—	—	—	—	—	(2)	(2)
Total comprehensive income							2,463
Dividends declared	—	—	—	(503)	—	—	(503)
Repurchase of stock	(9.9)	(1)	—	(481)	—	—	(482)
Stock options and awards	1.8	—	157	—	—	—	157
January 30, 2010	744.6	$ 62	$ 2,919	$ 12,947	$ (537)	$ (44)	$15,347
Net earnings	—	—	—	2,920	—	—	2,920
Other comprehensive income/(loss)							
Pension and other benefit liability adjustments, net of taxes of $4	—	—	—	—	(4)	—	(4)
Net change on cash flow hedges, net of taxes of $2	—	—	—	—	—	3	3
Currency translation adjustment, net of taxes of $1	—	—	—	—	—	1	1
Total comprehensive income							2,920
Dividends declared	—	—	—	(659)	—	—	(659)
Repurchase of stock	(47.8)	(4)	—	(2,510)	—	—	(2,514)
Stock options and awards	7.2	1	392	—	—	—	393
January 29, 2011	704.0	$59	$3,311	$12,698	$(541)	$(40)	$15,487

Dividends declared per share were $0.92, $0.67 and $0.62 in 2010, 2009 and 2008, respectively.

See accompanying Notes to Consolidated Financial Statements.

Notes to Consolidated Financial Statements

1. Summary of Accounting Policies

Organization   Target Corporation (Target or the Corporation) operates two reportable segments: Retail and Credit Card. Our Retail Segment includes all of our merchandising operations, including our fully integrated online business. Our Credit Card Segment offers credit to qualified guests through our branded proprietary credit cards, the Target Visa and the Target Card. Additionally, we offer a branded proprietary Target Debit Card. Collectively, these REDcards strengthen the bond with our guests, drive incremental sales and contribute to our results of operations.

Consolidation   The consolidated financial statements include the balances of the Corporation and its subsidiaries after elimination of intercompany balances and transactions. All material subsidiaries are wholly owned. We consolidate variable interest entities where it has been determined that the Corporation is the primary beneficiary of those entities' operations. The variable interest entity consolidated is a bankruptcy-remote subsidiary through which we sell certain accounts receivable as a method of providing funding for our accounts receivable.

Use of estimates   The preparation of our consolidated financial statements in conformity with U.S. generally accepted accounting principles (GAAP) requires management to make estimates and assumptions affecting reported amounts in the consolidated financial statements and accompanying notes. Actual results may differ significantly from those estimates.

Fiscal year   Our fiscal year ends on the Saturday nearest January 31. Unless otherwise stated, references to years in this report relate to fiscal years, rather than to calendar years. Fiscal year 2010 ended January 29, 2011, and consisted of 52 weeks. Fiscal year 2009 ended January 30, 2010, and consisted of 52 weeks. Fiscal year 2008 ended January 31, 2009, and consisted of 52 weeks.

Reclassifications   Certain prior year amounts have been reclassified to conform to the current year presentation. Accounting policies applicable to the items discussed in the Notes to the Consolidated Financial Statement are described in the respective notes.

2. Revenues

Our retail stores generally record revenue at the point of sale. Sales from our online business include shipping revenue and are recorded upon delivery to the guest. Total revenues do not include sales tax as we consider ourselves a pass-through conduit for collecting and remitting sales taxes. Generally, guests may return merchandise within 90 days of purchase. Revenues are recognized net of expected returns, which we estimate using historical return patterns as a percentage of sales. Commissions earned on sales generated by leased departments are included within sales and were $20 million in 2010, $18 million in 2009 and $19 million in 2008.

Revenue from gift card sales is recognized upon gift card redemption. Our gift cards do not have expiration dates. Based on historical redemption rates, a small and relatively stable percentage of gift cards will never be redeemed, referred to as "breakage." Estimated breakage revenue is recognized over time in proportion to actual gift card redemptions and was not material in 2010, 2009 and 2008.

Credit card revenues are recognized according to the contractual provisions of each credit card agreement. When accounts are written off, uncollected finance charges and late fees are recorded as a reduction of credit card revenues. Target retail sales charged on our credit cards totaled $3,455 million, $3,328 million and $3,948 million in 2010, 2009 and 2008, respectively.

Beginning April 2010, all new qualified credit card applicants receive the Target Card, and we no longer issue the Target Visa to credit card applicants. Existing Target Visa cardholders are not affected. Beginning October 2010, guests receive a 5 percent discount on virtually all purchases at checkout every day when they use a REDcard at any Target store or on Target.com. Target's REDcards include the Target Credit Card, Target Visa Credit Card and

Target Debit Card. This new REDcard Rewards program replaced the existing rewards program in which account holders received an initial 10 percent-off coupon for opening the account and earned points toward a 10 percent-off coupon on subsequent purchases. These changes are intended to simplify the program and to generate profitable incremental retail sales. The discounts associated with our REDcard Rewards program are included as reductions in sales in our Consolidated Statements of Operations and were $162 million in 2010, $94 million in 2009 and $114 million in 2008.

3. Cost of Sales and Selling, General and Administrative Expenses

The following table illustrates the primary costs classified in each major expense category:

Cost of Sales	Selling, General and Administrative Expenses
Total cost of products sold including • Freight expenses associated with moving merchandise from our vendors to our distribution centers and our retail stores, and among our distribution and retail facilities • Vendor income that is not reimbursement of specific, incremental and identifiable costs Inventory shrink Markdowns Outbound shipping and handling expenses associated with sales to our guests Payment term cash discounts Distribution center costs, including compensation and benefits costs	Compensation and benefit costs including • Stores • Headquarters Occupancy and operating costs of retail and headquarters facilities Advertising, offset by vendor income that is a reimbursement of specific, incremental and identifiable costs Pre-opening costs of stores and other facilities Other administrative costs

The classification of these expenses varies across the retail industry.

4. Consideration Received from Vendors

We receive consideration for a variety of vendor-sponsored programs, such as volume rebates, markdown allowances, promotions and advertising allowances and for our compliance programs, referred to as "vendor income." Vendor income reduces either our inventory costs or SG&A expenses based on the provisions of the arrangement. Promotional and advertising allowances are intended to offset our costs of promoting and selling merchandise in our stores. Under our compliance programs, vendors are charged for merchandise shipments that do not meet our requirements (violations), such as late or incomplete shipments. These allowances are recorded when violations occur. Substantially all consideration received is recorded as a reduction of cost of sales.

We establish a receivable for vendor income that is earned but not yet received. Based on provisions of the agreements in place, this receivable is computed by estimating the amount earned when we have completed our performance. We perform detailed analyses to determine the appropriate level of the receivable in the aggregate. The majority of year-end receivables associated with these activities are collected within the following fiscal quarter.

5. Advertising Costs

Advertising costs are expensed at first showing or distribution of the advertisement and were $1,292 million in 2010, $1,167 million in 2009 and $1,233 million in 2008. Advertising vendor income that offset advertising expenses was approximately $216 million, $179 million and $188 million in 2010, 2009 and 2008, respectively. Newspaper circulars and media broadcast made up the majority of our advertising costs in all three years.

6. Earnings per Share

Basic earnings per share (EPS) is calculated as net earnings divided by the weighted average number of common shares outstanding during the period. Diluted EPS includes the potentially dilutive impact of stock-based awards outstanding at period end, consisting of the incremental shares assumed to be issued upon the exercise of stock options and the incremental shares assumed to be issued under performance share and restricted stock unit arrangements.

Earnings Per Share (millions, except per share data)		2010	2009	2008
Net earnings	$	**2,920** $	2,488 $	2,214
Basic weighted average common shares outstanding		**723.6**	752.0	770.4
Dilutive impact of stock-based awards		**5.8**	2.8	3.2
Diluted weighted average common shares outstanding		**729.4**	754.8	773.6
Basic earnings per share	$	**4.03** $	3.31 $	2.87
Diluted earnings per share	$	**4.00** $	3.30 $	2.86

For the 2010, 2009 and 2008 EPS computations, 10.9 million, 22.9 million and 17.4 million stock options, respectively, were excluded from the calculation of weighted average shares for diluted EPS because their effects were antidilutive.

7. Other Comprehensive Income/(Loss)

Other comprehensive income/(loss) includes revenues, expenses, gains and losses that are excluded from net earnings under GAAP and are recorded directly to shareholders' investment. In 2010, 2009 and 2008, other comprehensive income/(loss) included gains and losses on certain hedge transactions, foreign currency translation adjustments and amortization of pension and postretirement plan amounts, net of related taxes. Significant items affecting other comprehensive income/(loss) are shown in the Consolidated Statements of Shareholders' Investment.

8. Fair Value Measurements

Fair value is the price at which an asset could be exchanged in a current transaction between knowledgeable, willing parties. A liability's fair value is defined as the amount that would be paid to transfer the liability to a new obligor, not the amount that would be paid to settle the liability with the creditor. Fair value measurements are categorized into one of three levels based on the lowest level of significant input used: Level 1 (unadjusted quoted prices in active markets); Level 2 (observable market inputs available at the measurement date, other than quoted prices included in Level 1); and Level 3 (unobservable inputs that cannot be corroborated by observable market data).

The following table presents financial assets and liabilities measured at fair value on a recurring basis:

Fair Value Measurements – Recurring Basis (millions)	Fair Value at January 29, 2011			Fair Value at January 30, 2010		
	Level 1	Level 2	Level 3	Level 1	Level 2	Level 3
Assets						
Cash and cash equivalents						
Marketable securities	$ 1,129	$ —	$ — $	1,617 $	— $	—
Other current assets						
Prepaid forward contracts	63	—	—	79	—	—
Other noncurrent assets						
Interest rate swaps *(a)*	—	139	—	—	131	—
Company-owned life insurance investments *(b)*	—	358	—	—	319	—
Total	$ 1,192	$ 497 $	— $	1,696 $	450 $	—
Liabilities						
Other noncurrent liabilities						
Interest rate swaps	$ —	$ 54 $	— $	— $	23 $	—
Total	$ —	$ 54 $	— $	— $	23 $	—

(a)   There were no interest rate swaps designated as accounting hedges at January 29, 2011 or January 30, 2010.

(b)   Company-owned life insurance investments consist of equity index funds and fixed income assets. Amounts are presented net of loans that are secured by some of these policies of $645 million at January 29, 2011 and $620 million at January 30, 2010.

Position	Valuation Technique
Marketable securities	Initially valued at transaction price. Carrying value of cash equivalents (including money market funds) approximates fair value because maturities are less than three months.
Prepaid forward contracts	Initially valued at transaction price. Subsequently valued by reference to the market price of Target common stock.
Interest rate swaps	Valuation models are calibrated to initial trade price. Subsequent valuations are based on observable inputs to the valuation model (*e.g.*, interest rates and credit spreads). Model inputs are changed only when corroborated by market data. A credit risk adjustment is made on each swap using observable market credit spreads.
Company-owned life insurance investments	Includes investments in separate accounts that are valued based on market rates credited by the insurer.

Certain assets are measured at fair value on a nonrecurring basis; that is, the assets are not measured at fair value on an ongoing basis but are subject to fair value adjustments only in certain circumstances (for example, when there is evidence of impairment). The fair value measurements related to long-lived assets held for sale and held and used in the following table were determined using available market prices at the measurement date based on recent investments or pending transactions of similar assets, third-party independent appraisals, valuation multiples or public comparables, less cost to sell where appropriate. We classify these measurements as Level 2. The fair value measurement of an intangible asset was determined using unobservable inputs that reflect our own assumptions regarding how market participants price the intangible assets at the measurement date. We classify these measurements as Level 3.

Fair Value Measurements – Nonrecurring Basis

(millions)	Other current assets Long-lived assets held for sale		Property and equipment Long-lived assets held and used (a)		Other noncurrent assets Intangible asset	
Measured during the year ended January 29, 2011:						
Carrying amount	$	9	$	127	$	—
Fair value measurement		7		101		—
Gain/(loss)	$	(2)	$	(26)	$	—
Measured during the year ended January 30, 2010:						
Carrying amount	$	74	$	98	$	6
Fair value measurement		57		66		—
Gain/(loss)	$	(17)	$	(32)	$	(6)

(a)   Primarily relates to real estate and buildings intended for sale in the future but not currently meeting the held for sale criteria.

The following table presents the carrying amounts and estimated fair values of financial instruments not measured at fair value in the Consolidated Statements of Financial Position. The fair value of marketable securities is determined using available market prices at the reporting date. The fair value of debt is generally measured using a discounted cash flow analysis based on our current market interest rates for similar types of financial instruments.

Financial Instruments Not Measured at Fair Value (millions)	January 29, 2011 Carrying Amount	Fair Value	January 30, 2010 Carrying Amount	Fair Value
Financial assets				
Other current assets				
Marketable securities (a)	$ 32	$ 32	27	$ 27
Other noncurrent assets				
Marketable securities (a)	4	4	5	5
Total	$ 36	$ 36	32	$ 32
Financial liabilities				
Total debt (b)	$ 15,241	$ 16,661	16,447	$ 17,487
Total	$ 15,241	$ 16,661	16,447	$ 17,487

(a)   Amounts include held-to-maturity government and money market investments that are held to satisfy the regulatory requirements of Target Bank and Target National Bank.

(b)   Represents the sum of nonrecourse debt collateralized by credit card receivables, unsecured debt and other borrowings, excluding unamortized swap valuation adjustments and capital lease obligations.

The carrying amounts of credit card receivables, net of allowance, accounts payable, and certain accrued and other current liabilities approximate fair value at January 29, 2011.

9. Cash Equivalents

Cash equivalents include highly liquid investments with an original maturity of three months or less from the time of purchase. Cash equivalents also include amounts due from third-party financial institutions for credit and debit card transactions. These receivables typically settle in less than five days and were $313 million at January 29, 2011 and January 30, 2010. Payables due to Visa resulting from the use of Target Visa Cards are included within cash equivalents and were $36 million and $40 million at January 29, 2011 and January 30, 2010, respectively.

10. Credit Card Receivables

Credit card receivables are recorded net of an allowance for doubtful accounts and are our only significant class of receivables. Substantially all accounts continue to accrue finance charges until they are written off. All past due accounts were incurring finance charges at January 29, 2011 and January 30, 2010. Accounts are written off when they become 180 days past due.

Age of Credit Card Receivables

(dollars in millions)	2010 Amount	Percent of Receivables	2009 Amount	Percent of Receivables
Current	$ 6,132	89.6%	$ 6,935	86.9%
1-29 days past due	292	4.3%	337	4.2%
30-59 days past due	131	1.9%	206	2.6%
60-89 days past due	79	1.1%	133	1.6%
90+ days past due	209	3.1%	371	4.7%
Period-end gross credit card receivables	$ 6,843	100%	$ 7,982	100%

Allowance for Doubtful Accounts

The allowance for doubtful accounts is recognized in an amount equal to the anticipated future write-offs of existing receivables and includes provisions for uncollectible finance charges and other credit-related fees. We estimate future write-offs on the entire credit card portfolio collectively based on historical experience of delinquencies, risk scores, aging trends and industry risk trends.

Allowance for Doubtful Accounts (millions)	2010	2009
Allowance at beginning of period	$ 1,016	$ 1,010
Bad debt expense	528	1,185
Write-offs (a)	(1,007)	(1,287)
Recoveries (a)	153	108
Allowance at end of period	$ 690	$ 1,016

(a) Write-offs include the principal amount of losses (excluding accrued and unpaid finance charges), and recoveries include current period principal collections on previously written-off balances. These amounts combined represent net write-offs.

Deterioration of the macroeconomic conditions in the United States would adversely affect the risk profile of our credit card receivables portfolio based on credit card holders' ability to pay their balances. If such deterioration were to occur, it would lead to an increase in bad debt expense. The Corporation monitors both the credit quality and the delinquency status of the credit card receivables portfolio. We consider accounts 30 or more days past due as delinquent, and we update delinquency status daily. We also monitor risk in the portfolio by assigning internally generated scores to each account and by periodically obtaining a statistically representative sample of current FICO scores, a nationally recognized credit scoring model. We update these FICO scores monthly, most recently in January 2011. The credit quality segmentation presented below is consistent with the approach used in determining our allowance for doubtful accounts.

Receivables Credit Quality (millions)		2010	2009
Nondelinquent accounts (Current and 1 - 29 days past due)			
FICO score of 700 or above	$	**2,819** $	2,886
FICO score of 600 to 699		**2,737**	3,114
FICO score below 600		**868**	1,272
Total nondelinquent accounts		**6,424**	7,272
Delinquent accounts (30+ days past due)		**419**	710
Period-end gross credit card receivables	$	**6,843** $	7,982

Under certain circumstances, we offer cardholder payment plans that modify finance charges and minimum payments, which meet the accounting definition of a troubled debt restructuring (TDR). These concessions are made on an individual cardholder basis for economic or legal reasons specific to each individual cardholder's circumstances. As a percentage of period-end gross receivables, receivables classified as TDRs were 5.9 percent at January 29, 2011 and 6.7 percent at January 30, 2010. Receivables classified as TDRs are treated consistently with other aged receivables in determining our allowance for doubtful accounts.

Funding for Credit Card Receivables

As a method of providing funding for our credit card receivables, we sell, on an ongoing basis, all of our consumer credit card receivables to Target Receivables LLC (TR LLC), formerly known as Target Receivables Corporation (TRC), a wholly owned, bankruptcy remote subsidiary. TR LLC then transfers the receivables to the Target Credit Card Master Trust (the Trust), which from time to time will sell debt securities to third parties, either directly or through a related trust. These debt securities represent undivided interests in the Trust assets. TR LLC uses the proceeds from the sale of debt securities and its share of collections on the receivables to pay the purchase price of the receivables to the Corporation.

We consolidate the receivables within the Trust and any debt securities issued by the Trust, or a related trust, in our Consolidated Statements of Financial Position based upon the applicable accounting guidance. The receivables transferred to the Trust are not available to general creditors of the Corporation.

In 2005, we entered into a public securitization of our credit card receivables. Note holders participating in this securitization were entitled to receive annual interest payments based on LIBOR plus a spread. The final payment on this securitization was made in April of 2010 as discussed in Note 19.

During 2006 and 2007, we sold an interest in our credit card receivables by issuing a Variable Funding Certificate. Parties who hold the Variable Funding Certificate receive interest at a variable short-term market rate. The Variable Funding Certificate matures in 2012 and 2013.

In the second quarter of 2008, we sold an interest in our credit card receivables to JPMorgan Chase (JPMC). The interest sold represented 47 percent of the receivables portfolio at the time of the transaction. In the event of a decrease in the receivables principal amount such that JPMC's interest in the entire portfolio would exceed 47 percent for three consecutive months, TR LLC (using the cash flows from the assets in the Trust) would be required to pay JPMC a pro rata amount of principal collections such that the portion owned by JPMC would not exceed 47 percent, unless JPMC provides a waiver. Conversely, at the option of the Corporation, JPMC may be required to fund an increase in the portfolio to maintain their 47 percent interest up to a maximum principal balance of $4.2 billion. Due to declines in gross credit card receivables, TR LLC repaid JPMC $566 million during 2010 and $163 million during 2009 under the terms of this agreement. No payments were made during 2008.

If a three-month average of monthly finance charge excess (JPMC's prorata share of finance charge collections less write-offs and specified expenses) is less than 2 percent of the outstanding principal balance of JPMC's interest, the Corporation must implement mutually agreed-upon underwriting strategies. If the three-month average finance charge excess falls below 1 percent of the outstanding principal balance of JPMC's interest, JPMC may compel the Corporation to implement underwriting and collections activities, provided those activities are compatible with the Corporation's systems, as well as consistent with similar credit card receivable portfolios managed by JPMC. If the Corporation fails to implement the activities, JPMC has the right to cause the accelerated repayment of the note payable issued in the transaction. As noted in the preceding paragraph, payments would be made solely from the Trust assets.

All interests in our Credit Card Receivables issued by the Trust are accounted for as secured borrowings. Interest and principal payments are satisfied provided the cash flows from the Trust assets are sufficient and are nonrecourse to the general assets of the Corporation. If the cash flows are less than the periodic interest, the available amount, if any, is paid with respect to interest. Interest shortfalls will be paid to the extent subsequent cash flows from the assets in the Trust are sufficient. Future principal payments will be made from the third party's prorata share of cash flows from the Trust assets.

Securitized Borrowings (millions)	2010		2009	
	Debt Balance	Collateral	Debt Balance	Collateral
2008 Series *(a)*	$ 2,954	$ 3,061	$ 3,475	$ 3,652
2006/2007 Series	1,000	1,266	1,000	1,266
2005 Series	—	—	900	1,154
Total	$ 3,954	$ 4,327	$ 5,375	$ 6,072

(a)   The debt balance for the 2008 Series is net of a 7% discount from JPMC. The unamortized portion of this discount was $107 million and $177 million as of January 29, 2011, and January 30, 2010, respectively.

11. Inventory

Substantially our entire inventory and the related cost of sales are accounted for under the retail inventory accounting method (RIM) using the last-in, first-out (LIFO) method. Inventory is stated at the lower of LIFO cost or market. Cost includes purchase price as reduced by vendor income. Inventory is also reduced for estimated losses related to shrink and markdowns. The LIFO provision is calculated based on inventory levels, markup rates and internally measured retail price indices.

Under RIM, inventory cost and the resulting gross margins are calculated by applying a cost-to-retail ratio to the retail value inventory. RIM is an averaging method that has been widely used in the retail industry due to its practicality. The use of RIM will result in inventory being valued at the lower of cost or market because permanent markdowns are currently taken as a reduction of the retail value of inventory.

We routinely enter into arrangements with vendors whereby we do not purchase or pay for merchandise until the merchandise is ultimately sold to a guest. Revenues under this program are included in sales in the Consolidated Statements of Operations, but the merchandise received under the program is not included in inventory in our Consolidated Statements of Financial Position because of the virtually simultaneous purchase and sale of this inventory. Sales made under these arrangements totaled $1,581 million in 2010, $1,470 million in 2009 and $1,538 million in 2008.

12. Other Current Assets

Other Current Assets (millions)	January 29, 2011	January 30, 2010
Vendor income receivable	$ 517	$ 390
Other receivables *(a)*	405	526
Deferred taxes	379	724
Other	451	439
Total	$ 1,752	$ 2,079

(a)   Includes pharmacy receivables and income taxes receivable.

13. Property and Equipment

Property and equipment are recorded at cost, less accumulated depreciation. Depreciation is computed using the straight-line method over estimated useful lives or lease terms if shorter. We amortize leasehold improvements purchased after the beginning of the initial lease term over the shorter of the assets' useful lives or a term that includes the original lease term, plus any renewals that are reasonably assured at the date the leasehold improvements are acquired. Depreciation expense for 2010, 2009 and 2008 was $2,060 million, $1,999 million and $1,804 million, respectively. For income tax purposes, accelerated depreciation methods are generally used. Repair and maintenance costs are expensed as incurred and were $726 million in 2010, $632 million in 2009 and $609 million in 2008. Facility pre-opening costs, including supplies and payroll, are expensed as incurred.

Estimated Useful Lives	Life (in years)
Buildings and improvements	8-39
Fixtures and equipment	3-15
Computer hardware and software	4-7

Long-lived assets are reviewed for impairment when events or changes in circumstances indicate that the asset's carrying value may not be recoverable. Impairments of $28 million in 2010, $49 million in 2009 and $2 million in 2008 were recorded as a result of the reviews performed. Additionally, due to project scope changes, we wrote off capitalized construction in progress costs of $6 million in 2010, $37 million in 2009 and $26 million in 2008.

14. Other Noncurrent Assets

Other Noncurrent Assets (millions)	January 29, 2011	January 30, 2010
Company-owned life insurance investments *(a)*	$ 358	$ 319
Goodwill and intangible assets	223	239
Interest rate swaps *(b)*	139	131
Other	279	140
Total	$ 999	$ 829

(a)   Company-owned life insurance policies on approximately 4,000 team members who are designated highly compensated under the Internal Revenue Code and have given their consent to be insured. Amounts are presented net of loans that are secured by some of these policies.

(b)   See Notes 8 and 20 for additional information relating to our interest rate swaps.

15. Goodwill and Intangible Assets

Goodwill and intangible assets are recorded within other noncurrent assets. Goodwill totaled $59 million at January 29, 2011 and January 30, 2010. Goodwill and indefinite-lived intangible assets are not amortized; instead, they are tested for impairment annually and whenever events or changes in circumstances indicate the carrying value of the asset may not be recoverable. Definite-lived intangible assets are amortized over their expected economic useful life and are tested for impairment whenever events or changes in circumstances indicate the carrying value of the asset may not be recoverable. Discounted cash flow models are used in determining fair value for the purposes of the required goodwill and intangible assets impairment tests. No material impairments were recorded in 2010, 2009 or 2008 as a result of the tests performed.

Intangible Assets	Leasehold Acquisition Costs		Other (a)		Total	
(millions)	Jan. 29, 2011	Jan. 30, 2010	Jan. 29, 2011	Jan. 30, 2010	Jan. 29, 2011	Jan. 30, 2010
Gross asset	$ 227	$ 246	$ 121	$ 101	$ 348	$ 347
Accumulated amortization	(111)	(110)	(73)	(57)	(184)	(167)
Net intangible assets	$ 116	$ 136	$ 48	$ 44	$ 164	$ 180

(a)   Other intangible assets relate primarily to acquired customer lists and trademarks.

Amortization is computed on definite-lived intangible assets using the straight-line method over estimated useful lives that typically range from 9 to 39 years for leasehold acquisition costs and from 3 to 15 years for other intangible assets. The weighted average life of leasehold acquisition costs and other intangible assets was 29 years and 4 years, respectively, at January 29, 2011. Amortization expense for 2010, 2009 and 2008 was $24 million, $24 million and $21 million, respectively.

Estimated Amortization Expense (millions)	2011	2012	2013	2014	2015
Amortization expense	$ 22	$ 16	$ 13	$ 11	$ 11

16. Accounts Payable

We reclassify book overdrafts to accounts payable at period end. Overdrafts reclassified to accounts payable were $558 million at January 29, 2011 and $518 million at January 30, 2010.

17. Accrued and Other Current Liabilities

Accrued and Other Current Liabilities (millions)	January 29, 2011	January 30, 2010
Wages and benefits	$ 921	$ 959
Taxes payable (a)	497	490
Gift card liability (b)	422	387
Straight-line rent accrual (c)	200	185
Dividends payable	176	127
Workers' compensation and general liability	158	163
Income tax payable	144	24
Interest payable	103	105
Other	705	680
Total	$ 3,326	$ 3,120

(a)   Taxes payable consist of real estate, team member withholdings and sales tax liabilities.

(b)   Gift card liability represents the amount of gift cards that have been issued but have not been redeemed, net of estimated breakage.

(c)   Straight-line rent accrual represents the amount of rent expense recorded that exceeds cash payments remitted in connection with operating leases.

18. Commitments and Contingencies

In January 2011, we entered into an agreement to purchase the leasehold interests in up to 220 sites in Canada currently operated by Zellers Inc., in exchange for C$1,825 million (Canadian dollars), due in two payments, one in May 2011 and one in September 2011. We believe this transaction will allow us to open 100 to 150 Target stores in

Canada, primarily during 2013. We expect that renovation of these stores will require an investment of over C$1 billion, a portion of which may be funded by landlords. At January 29, 2011 the value of C$1.00 approximated the value of $1.00.

Purchase obligations, which include all legally binding contracts, such as firm commitments for inventory purchases, merchandise royalties, equipment purchases, marketing-related contracts, software acquisition/license commitments and service contracts, were approximately $1,907 million and $2,016 million at January 29, 2011 and January 30, 2010, respectively. We issue inventory purchase orders, which represent authorizations to purchase that are cancelable by their terms. We do not consider purchase orders to be firm inventory commitments. If we choose to cancel a purchase order, we may be obligated to reimburse the vendor for unrecoverable outlays incurred prior to cancellation. We also issue trade letters of credit in the ordinary course of business, which are not obligations given they are conditioned on terms of the letter of credit being met.

Trade letters of credit totaled $1,522 million and $1,484 million at January 29, 2011 and January 30, 2010, respectively, a portion of which are reflected in accounts payable. Standby letters of credit, relating primarily to retained risk on our insurance claims, totaled $71 million and $72 million at January 29, 2011 and January 30, 2010, respectively.

We are exposed to claims and litigation arising in the ordinary course of business and use various methods to resolve these matters in a manner that we believe serves the best interest of our shareholders and other constituents. We believe the recorded reserves in our consolidated financial statements are adequate in light of the probable and estimable liabilities. We do not believe that any of the currently identified claims or litigation matters will have a material adverse impact on our results of operations, cash flows or financial condition.

19. Notes Payable and Long-Term Debt

We obtain short-term financing throughout the year under our commercial paper program, a form of notes payable.

Commercial Paper (millions)	2010	2009
Maximum daily amount outstanding during the year	$ —	$ 112
Average amount outstanding during the year	—	1
Amount outstanding at year-end	—	—
Weighted average interest rate	—	0.2%

An additional source of liquidity is available to us through a committed $2 billion unsecured revolving credit facility obtained through a group of banks in April 2007, which will expire in April 2012. No balances were outstanding at any time during 2010 or 2009 under this credit facility.

In July 2010, we issued $1 billion of long-term debt at 3.875% that matures in July 2020. There were no amounts issued in 2009.

As further explained in Note 10, we maintain an accounts receivable financing program through which we sell credit card receivables to a bankruptcy remote, wholly owned subsidiary, which in turn transfers the receivables to a Trust. The Trust, either directly or through related trusts, sells debt securities to third parties. The following summarizes this activity for 2009 and 2010.

Nonrecourse Debt Collateralized by Credit Card Receivables (millions)	2010	2009
Balance at beginning of period	$ 5,375	$ 5,490
Issued	—	—
Accretion (a)	45	48
Repaid (b)	(1,466)	(163)
Balance at end of period	$ 3,954	$ 5,375

(a)   Represents the accretion of the 7 percent discount on the 47 percent interest in credit card receivables sold to JPMC.

(b)   Includes repayments of $566 million and $163 million for the 2008 series of secured borrowings during 2010 and 2009 due to declines in gross credit card receivables and payment of $900 million to repurchase and retire in full the 2005 series of secured borrowings at par in April 2010, that otherwise would have matured in October 2010.

Other than debt backed by our credit card receivables and other immaterial borrowings, all of our outstanding borrowings are senior, unsecured obligations.

At January 29, 2011, the carrying value and maturities of our debt portfolio, including unamortized hedged debt valuation gains from terminated or de-designated interest rate swaps, were as follows:

Debt Maturities (millions)	January 29, 2011 Rate (a)	Balance
Due fiscal 2011-2015	3.2%	$ 6,090
Due fiscal 2016-2020	5.4	4,299
Due fiscal 2021-2025	8.9	120
Due fiscal 2026-2030	6.7	326
Due fiscal 2031-2035	6.6	906
Due fiscal 2036-2037	6.8	3,500
Total notes and debentures	5.0	15,241
Unamortized swap valuation adjustments		152
Capital lease obligations		333
Less:		
Amounts due within one year		(119)
Long-term debt		$ 15,607

(a)   Reflects the weighted average stated interest rate as of year-end.

Required principal payments on notes and debentures over the next five years, excluding capital lease obligations, are as follows:

Required Principal Payments (a) (millions)	2011	2012	2013	2014	2015
Unsecured	$ 106	$ 1,501	$ 501	$ 1	$ 27
Nonrecourse	—	750	3,311	—	—
Total required principal payments	$ 106	$ 2,251	$ 3,812	$ 1	$ 27

(a)   The required principal payments presented in this table do not consider the potential accelerated repayment requirements under our agreement with JPMC in the event of a decrease in credit card receivables.

Most of our long-term debt obligations contain covenants related to secured debt levels. In addition to a secured debt level covenant, our credit facility also contains a debt leverage covenant. We are, and expect to remain, in compliance with these covenants.

20. Derivative Financial Instruments

Derivative financial instruments are reported at fair value on the Consolidated Statements of Financial Position. Historically our derivative instruments have primarily consisted of interest rate swaps. We use these derivatives to mitigate our interest rate risk. We have counterparty credit risk resulting from our derivative instruments. This risk lies primarily with two global financial institutions. We monitor this concentration of counterparty credit risk on an ongoing basis.

Prior to 2009, the majority of our derivative instruments qualified for fair value hedge accounting treatment. The changes in market value of an interest rate swap, as well as the offsetting change in market value of the hedged debt, were recognized within earnings in the current period. We assessed at the inception of the hedge whether the hedging derivatives were highly effective in offsetting changes in fair value or cash flows of hedged items. Ineffectiveness resulted when changes in the market value of the hedged debt were not completely offset by changes in the market value of the interest rate swap. For those derivatives whose terms met the conditions of the "short-cut method," 100 percent hedge effectiveness was assumed. There was no ineffectiveness recognized in 2010, 2009 or 2008 related to our derivative instruments. As detailed below, at January 29, 2011, there were no derivative instruments designated as accounting hedges.

During the first quarter of 2008, we terminated certain "pay floating" interest rate swaps with a combined notional amount of $3,125 million for cash proceeds of $160 million, which are classified within other operating cash flows in the Consolidated Statements of Cash Flows. These swaps were designated as hedges; therefore, concurrent with their terminations, we were required to stop making market value adjustments to the associated hedged debt. Gains realized upon termination will be amortized into earnings over the remaining life of the associated hedged debt.

Additionally, during 2008, we de-designated certain "pay floating" interest rate swaps, and upon de-designation, these swaps no longer qualified for hedge accounting treatment. As a result of the de-designation, the unrealized gains on these swaps determined at the date of de-designation will be amortized into earnings over the remaining lives of the previously hedged items.

In 2010, 2009 and 2008, total net gains amortized into net interest expense for terminated and de-designated swaps were $45 million, $60 million and $55 million, respectively. The amount remaining on unamortized hedged debt valuation gains from terminated and de-designated interest rate swaps that will be amortized into earnings over the remaining lives of the previously hedged debt totaled $152 million, $197 million and $263 million, at the end of 2010, 2009 and 2008, respectively.

Simultaneous to the de-designations during 2008, we entered into "pay fixed" swaps to economically hedge the risks associated with the de-designated "pay floating" swaps. These swaps are not designated as hedging instruments and along with the de-designated "pay floating" swaps are measured at fair value on a quarterly basis.

Changes in fair value measurements are a component of net interest expense on the Consolidated Statements of Operations.

Outstanding Interest Rate Swap Summary   (dollars in millions)

	January 29, 2011	
	Pay Floating	**Pay Fixed**
Weighted average rate:		
Pay	one-month LIBOR	2.6% fixed
Receive	5.0% fixed	one-month LIBOR
Weighted average maturity	3.4 years	3.4 years
Notional	$1,250	$1,250

Derivative Contracts – Types, Balance Sheet Classifications and Fair Values
(millions)

		Asset			Liability		
			Fair Value At				Fair Value At	
Type	Classification	Jan. 29, 2011	Jan. 30, 2010	Classification	Jan. 29, 2011	Jan. 30, 2010
Not designated as hedging instruments:						
Interest rate swaps	Other noncurrent assets $	139	$ 131	Other noncurrent liabilities $	54	$ 23
Total		$ 139	$ 131		$ 54	$ 23

Periodic payments, valuation adjustments and amortization of gains or losses from the termination or de-designation of derivative contracts are summarized below:

Derivative Contracts – Effect on Results of Operations
(millions)

		Income/(Expense)		
Type	Classification	2010	2009	2008
Interest rate swaps	Other interest expense $	51	$ 65	$ 71
Total		$ 51	$ 65	$ 71

21. Leases

We lease certain retail locations, warehouses, distribution centers, office space, land, equipment and software. Assets held under capital leases are included in property and equipment. Operating lease rentals are expensed on a straight-line basis over the life of the lease beginning on the date we take possession of the property. At lease inception, we determine the lease term by assuming the exercise of those renewal options that are reasonably assured. The exercise of lease renewal options is at our sole discretion. The expected lease term is used to determine whether a lease is capital or operating and is used to calculate straight-line rent expense. Additionally, the depreciable life of leased buildings and leasehold improvements is limited by the expected lease term.

Rent expense is included in SG&A expenses. Some of our lease agreements include rental payments based on a percentage of retail sales over contractual levels. Certain leases require us to pay real estate taxes, insurance, maintenance and other operating expenses associated with the leased premises. These expenses are classified in

SG&A, consistent with similar costs for owned locations. Sublease income received from tenants who rent properties is recorded as a reduction to SG&A expense.

Rent Expense (millions)	2010	2009	2008
Property and equipment	$ 188	$ 187	$ 184
Software	25	27	24
Sublease income	(13)	(13)	(15)
Total rent expense	$ 200	$ 201	$ 193

Most long-term leases include one or more options to renew, with renewal terms that can extend the lease term from one to more than 50 years. Certain leases also include options to purchase the leased property.

Future Minimum Lease Payments (millions)	Operating Leases (a)	Capital Leases	Sublease Income	Total
2011	$ 190	$ 31	$ (11)	$ 210
2012	189	32	(8)	213
2013	187	32	(7)	212
2014	147	32	(6)	173
2015	141	30	(6)	165
After 2015	3,100	432	(35)	3,497
Total future minimum lease payments	$ 3,954	$ 589	$ (73)	$ 4,470
Less: Interest (b)		(256)		
Present value of future minimum capital lease payments (c)		$ 333		

(a)   Total contractual lease payments include $1,949 million related to options to extend lease terms that are reasonably assured of being exercised and also includes $241 million of legally binding minimum lease payments for stores that will open in 2011 or later.

(b)   Calculated using the interest rate at inception for each lease.

(c)   Includes the current portion of $12 million.

The future minimum lease payments above do not include any payments associated with the leases that may be acquired under our agreement with Zellers Inc., described in Note 18.

22. Income Taxes

Deferred tax assets and liabilities are recognized for the future tax consequences attributable to temporary differences between financial statement carrying amounts of existing assets and liabilities and their respective tax bases. Deferred tax assets and liabilities are measured using enacted income tax rates in effect for the year the temporary differences are expected to be recovered or settled. Tax rate changes affecting deferred tax assets and liabilities are recognized in income at the enactment date. We have not recorded deferred taxes when earnings from foreign operations are considered to be indefinitely invested outside the U.S. Such amounts are not significant.

Tax Rate Reconciliation	2010	2009	2008
Federal statutory rate	35.0%	35.0%	35.0%
State income taxes, net of federal tax benefit	1.4	2.8	3.8
Other	(1.3)	(2.1)	(1.4)
Effective tax rate	35.1%	35.7%	37.4%

Certain discrete state tax items reduced the impact of the state income tax rate, net of federal benefit, by 2.4 percentage points, 0.7 percentage points, and 0.6 percentage points in 2010, 2009, and 2008, respectively.

Provision for Income Taxes (millions)		2010	2009	2008
Current:				
Federal	$	1,086 $	877 $	1,034
State/other		44	143	197
Total current		1,130	1,020	1,231
Deferred:				
Federal		388	339	88
State/other		57	25	3
Total deferred		445	364	91
Total provision	$	1,575 $	1,384 $	1,322

Net Deferred Tax Asset/(Liability) (millions)		January 29, 2011	January 30, 2010
Gross deferred tax assets:			
Accrued and deferred compensation	$	451 $	538
Allowance for doubtful accounts		229	393
Accruals and reserves not currently deductible		373	380
Self-insured benefits		251	260
Other		67	92
Total gross deferred tax assets		1,371	1,663
Gross deferred tax liabilities:			
Property and equipment		(1,607)	(1,543)
Deferred credit card income		(145)	(166)
Other		(174)	(64)
Total gross deferred tax liabilities		(1,926)	(1,773)
Total net deferred tax asset/(liability)	$	(555) $	(110)

We file a U.S. federal income tax return and income tax returns in various states and foreign jurisdictions. We are no longer subject to U.S. federal income tax examinations for years before 2009 and, with few exceptions, are no longer subject to state and local or non-U.S. income tax examinations by tax authorities for years before 2003.

Reconciliation of Unrecognized Tax Benefit Liabilities (millions)		2010	2009
Balance at beginning of period	$	452 $	434
Additions based on tax positions related to the current year		16	119
Additions for tax positions of prior years		68	47
Reductions for tax positions of prior years		(222)	(61)
Settlements		(12)	(87)
Balance at end of period	$	302 $	452

If the Corporation were to prevail on all unrecognized tax benefit liabilities recorded, approximately $198 million of the $302 million reserve would benefit the effective tax rate. In addition, the reversal of accrued penalties and interest would also benefit the effective tax rate. Interest and penalties associated with unrecognized tax benefit liabilities are recorded within income tax expense. During the years ended January 29, 2011 and January 30, 2010, we recorded a net benefit from the reversal of accrued penalties and interest of approximately $28 million and $10 million, respectively. During the year ended January 31, 2009, we recorded a net expense for accrued penalties and interest of approximately $33 million. We had accrued for the payment of interest and penalties of approximately $95 million at January 29, 2011 and $127 million at January 30, 2010.

The January 30, 2010 liability for uncertain tax positions included $133 million for tax positions for which the ultimate deductibility was highly certain, but for which there was uncertainty about the timing of such deductibility. During 2010, we filed a tax accounting method change that resolved the uncertainty surrounding the timing of deductions for these tax positions, resulting in a $133 million decrease to our unrecognized tax benefit liability and no impact on income tax expense in 2010.

In addition, we resolved various state income tax matters in 2010, resulting in a reduction of approximately $80 million to our unrecognized tax benefit liability, which also reduced tax expense in 2010. It is reasonably possible that the amount of the unrecognized tax benefit liabilities with respect to our other unrecognized tax positions will increase or decrease during the next twelve months; however an estimate of the amount or range of the change cannot be made at this time.

During 2009, we filed income tax returns that included tax accounting method changes allowed under applicable tax regulations. These changes resulted in a substantial increase in tax deductions related to property and equipment, resulting in an increase in noncurrent deferred income tax liabilities of approximately $300 million and a corresponding increase in current income taxes receivable, which is classified as other current assets in the Consolidated Statements of Financial Position. These changes did not affect income tax expense for 2009.

23. Other Noncurrent Liabilities

Other Noncurrent Liabilities (millions)	January 29, 2011		January 30,	2010
General liability and workers' compensation *(a)*	$	470	$	490
Deferred compensation		396		353
Income tax		313		579
Pension and postretirement health care benefits		128		178
Other		300		306
Total	$	1,607	$	1,906

(a)   We retain a substantial portion of the risk related to certain general liability and workers' compensation claims. Liabilities associated with these losses include estimates of both claims filed and losses incurred but not yet reported. We estimate our ultimate cost based on analysis of historical data and actuarial estimates. General liability and workers' compensation liabilities are recorded at our estimate of their net present value.

24. Share Repurchase

In November 2007, our Board of Directors approved a share repurchase program totaling $10 billion that replaced a prior program. In November 2008, we announced that, in light of our business outlook, we were temporarily suspending our open-market share repurchase program. In January 2010, we resumed open-market purchases of shares under this program.

Share repurchases for the last three years, repurchased primarily through open market transactions, were as follows:

Share Repurchases (millions, except per share data)	Total Number of Shares Purchased	Average Price Paid per Share		Total Investment
2008	67.2	$	50.49	$ 3,395
2009	9.9		48.54	479
2010	47.8		52.44	2,508
Total	124.9	$	51.08	$ 6,382

Of the shares reacquired, a portion was delivered upon settlement of prepaid forward contracts as follows:

Settlement of Prepaid Forward Contracts (a)

(millions)	Total Cash	Investment	Aggregate	Market Value (b)
2008	$	249	$	251
2009		56		60
2010		56		61
Total	$	**361**	$	**372**

(a)   These contracts are among the investment vehicles used to reduce our economic exposure related to our nonqualified deferred compensation plans. The details of our positions in prepaid forward contracts have been provided in Note 26.

(b)   At their respective settlement dates.

Our share repurchases during 2008 included 30 million shares that were acquired through the exercise of call options.

Call Option Repurchase Details

Series	Number of Options	Exercised	Exercise Date	(amounts per share) Premium (a)	Strike Price	Total	Total Cost (millions)
Series I		10,000,000	April 2008	$ 11.04	$ 40.32	$51.36	$ 514
Series II		10,000,000	May 2008	10.87	39.31	50.18	502
Series III		10,000,000	June 2008	11.20	39.40	50.60	506
Total		**30,000,000**		$ **11.04**	$ **39.68**	**$50.71**	$ **1,522**

(a)   Paid in January 2008.

25. Share-Based Compensation

We maintain a long-term incentive plan (the Plan) for key team members and non-employee members of our Board of Directors. Our long-term incentive plan allows us to grant equity-based compensation awards, including stock options, stock appreciation rights, performance share units, restricted stock units, restricted stock awards or a combination of awards (collectively, share-based awards). The number of unissued common shares reserved for future grants under the Plan was 17,552,454 at January 29, 2011 and 21,450,009 at January 30, 2010.

Total share-based compensation expense recognized in the Consolidated Statements of Operations was $109 million, $103 million and $72 million in 2010, 2009 and 2008, respectively. The related income tax benefit was $43 million, $40 million and $28 million in 2010, 2009 and 2008, respectively.

Stock Options

We grant nonqualified stock options to certain team members under the Plan that generally vest and become exercisable annually in equal amounts over a four-year period and expire 10 years after the grant date. We also grant options to the non-employee members of our Board of Directors which vest immediately and become exercisable after one year with a term equal to the lesser of 10 years from date of grant or 5 years following departure from the Board. Starting in 2010, the options granted to our Board of Directors vest quarterly over a one-year period.

| Stock Option Activity | Stock Options *(a)* | | | | | | |
| | Total Outstanding | | | | Exercisable | | |
	No. of Options *(b)*	Exercise Price *(c)*	Intrinsic Value *(d)*	No. of Options *(b)*	Exercise Price *(c)*	Intrinsic Value *(d)*
January 30, 2010	38,242	$ 44.05	$ 331	22,453	$ 44.59	$ 189
Granted	4,584	55.33				
Expired/forfeited	(956)	44.87				
Exercised/issued	(7,220)	37.57				
January 29, 2011	**34,650**	**$ 46.87**	**$ 288**	**20,813**	**$ 47.06**	**$ 172**

(a)   Includes stock appreciation rights granted to certain non-U.S. team members.

(b)   In thousands.

(c)   Weighted average per share.

(d)   Represents stock price appreciation subsequent to the grant date, in millions.

We use a Black-Scholes valuation model to estimate the fair value of the options at grant date based on the assumptions noted in the following table. Volatility represents an average of market estimates for implied volatility of Target common stock. The expected life is estimated based on an analysis of options already exercised and any foreseeable trends or changes in recipients' behavior. The risk-free interest rate is an interpolation of the relevant U.S. Treasury security maturities as of each applicable grant date.

Valuation Assumptions	2010	2009	2008
Dividend yield	**1.8%**	1.4%	1.9%
Volatility	**26%**	31%	47%
Risk-free interest rate	**2.1%**	2.7%	1.5%
Expected life in years	**5.5**	5.5	5.5
Stock options grant date fair value	$ **12.51**	$ 14.18	$ 12.87

Stock Option Exercises (in millions)	2010	2009	2008
Cash received for exercise price	$ **271**	$ 62	$ 31
Intrinsic value	**132**	21	14
Income tax benefit	**52**	8	5

Compensation expense associated with stock options is recognized on a straight-line basis over the shorter of the vesting period or the minimum required service period. At January 29, 2011, there was $120 million of total unrecognized compensation expense related to nonvested stock options, which is expected to be recognized over a weighted average period of 1.3 years. The weighted average remaining life of currently exercisable options is 5.4 years, and the weighted average remaining life of all outstanding options is 6.7 years. The total fair value of options vested was $87 million, $85 million and $69 million, in 2010, 2009 and 2008, respectively.

Performance Share Units

We have issued performance share units to certain team members annually since January 2003. These units represent shares potentially issuable in the future; historically, the units have been issued based upon the attainment of certain compound annual growth rates in revenue and EPS over a three-year performance period. Beginning with the March 2009 grant, issuance is based upon our performance relative to a retail peer group over a three-year performance period on two measures: domestic market share change and EPS growth. The fair value of performance share units is calculated based on the stock price at the time of grant. The weighted average grant date fair value for performance share units was $52.62 in 2010, $27.18 in 2009 and $51.68 in 2008.

Performance Share Unit Activity	Total Nonvested Units			
	Performance	Share Units *(a)*	Grant Date	Price *(b)*
January 30, 2010		2,199	$	44.96
Granted		442		52.62
Forfeited		(657)		58.80
Vested		—		—
January 29, 2011		**1,984** *(c)* $		**42.10**

(a)   Assumes attainment of maximum payout rates as set forth in the performance criteria based in thousands of share units. Applying actual or expected payout rates, the number of outstanding units at January 29, 2011 was 1,046.

(b)   Weighted average per unit.

(c)   Because the performance criteria were not met, approximately 728 thousand of these performance share units outstanding at January 29, 2011 were not earned and will be forfeited in the first quarter of 2011.

Compensation expense associated with unvested performance share units is recognized on a straight-line basis over the shorter of the vesting period or the minimum required service period. The expense recognized each period is dependent upon our estimate of the number of shares that will ultimately be issued. Future compensation expense for currently unvested awards could reach a maximum of $16 million assuming payout of all unvested awards. The unrecognized expense is expected to be recognized over a weighted average period of 0.8 years. The fair value of performance share units vested and converted was $0 in 2010, $1 million in 2009, and $36 million in 2008.

Restricted Stock

We issue restricted stock units and restricted stock awards (collectively restricted stock) to certain team members with three-year cliff vesting from the date of grant. We also regularly issue restricted stock units to our Board of Directors, which vest quarterly over a one-year period and are settled in shares of Target common stock upon departure from the Board. Restricted stock units represent shares potentially issuable in the future whereas restricted stock awards represent shares issued upon grant that are restricted. The fair value for restricted stock units and restricted stock awards is calculated based on the stock price at the time of grant. The weighted average grant date fair value for restricted stock was $55.17 in 2010, $49.41 in 2009 and $34.64 in 2008.

Restricted Stock Activity	Total Nonvested Units			
	Restricted	Stock *(a)*	Grant Date	Price *(b)*
January 30, 2010		767	$	33.47
Granted		578		55.17
Forfeited		—		—
Vested		(207)		11.91
January 29, 2011		**1,138**	$	**48.29**

(a)   Represents the number of restricted stock units and restricted stock awards, in thousands.

(b)   Weighted average per unit.

Compensation expense associated with unvested restricted stock is recognized on a straight-line basis over the shorter of the vesting period or the minimum required service period. The expense recognized each period is dependent upon our estimate of the number of shares that will ultimately be issued. At January 29, 2011, there was $33 million of total unrecognized compensation expense related to restricted stock, which is expected to be recognized over a weighted average period of 1.2 years. The fair value of restricted stock vested and converted was $3 million in 2010, $12 million in 2009, and $3 million in 2008.

26. Defined Contribution Plans

Team members who meet certain eligibility requirements can participate in a defined contribution 401(k) plan by investing up to 80 percent of their compensation, as limited by statute or regulation. Generally, we match 100 percent of each team member's contribution up to 5 percent of total compensation. Company match contributions are made to the fund designated by the participant.

In addition, we maintain a nonqualified, unfunded deferred compensation plan for approximately 3,500 current and retired team members whose participation in our 401(k) plan is limited by statute or regulation. These team members choose from a menu of crediting rate alternatives that are the same as the investment choices in our 401(k) plan, including Target common stock. We credit an additional 2 percent per year to the accounts of all active participants in this plan, excluding executive officer participants, in part to recognize the risks inherent to their participation in a plan of this nature. We also maintain a nonqualified, unfunded deferred compensation plan that was frozen during 1996, covering substantially fewer than 100 participants, most of whom are retired. In this plan, deferred compensation earns returns tied to market levels of interest rates plus an additional 6 percent return, with a minimum of 12 percent and a maximum of 20 percent, as determined by the plan's terms. In response to changing requirements regarding the federal income tax treatment of nonqualified deferred compensation arrangements resulting from Section 409A to the Internal Revenue Code, we allowed participants to elect to accelerate the distribution dates for their account balances during 2009 and 2008. This election was not available in 2010. Participant elections resulted in payments of $29 million in 2009 and $86 million in 2008.

We mitigate some of our risk of offering the nonqualified plans through investing in vehicles, including company-owned life insurance and prepaid forward contracts in our own common stock, that offset a substantial portion of our economic exposure to the returns of these plans. These investment vehicles are general corporate assets and are marked to market with the related gains and losses recognized in the Consolidated Statements of Operations in the period they occur. The total change in fair value for contracts indexed to our own common stock recognized in earnings was pretax income/(loss) of $4 million in 2010, $36 million in 2009 and $(19) million in 2008. During 2010 and 2009, we invested approximately $41 million and $34 million, respectively, in such investment instruments, and this activity is included in the Consolidated Statements of Cash Flows within other investing activities. Adjusting our position in these investment vehicles may involve repurchasing shares of Target common stock when settling the forward contracts. In 2010, 2009 and 2008, these repurchases totaled 1.1 million, 1.5 million and 4.7 million shares, respectively, and are included in the total share repurchases described in Note 24.

Prepaid Forward Contracts on Target Common Stock (millions, except per share data)	Number of Shares	Contractual Price Paid per Share	Contractual Fair Value	Total Cash Investment
January 30, 2010	1.5	$ 42.77	$ 79	$ 66
January 29, 2011	**1.2**	**$ 44.09**	**$ 63**	**$ 51**

The settlement dates of these instruments are regularly renegotiated with the counterparty.

Plan Expenses (millions)	2010	2009	2008
401(k) Plan			
Matching contributions expense	$ 190	$ 178	$ 178
Nonqualified Deferred Compensation Plans			
Benefits expense/(income) *(a)*	$ 63	$ 83	$ (80)
Related investment loss/(income) *(b)*	(31)	(77)	83
Nonqualified plan net expense	$ 32	$ 6	$ 3

(a)   *Includes market-performance credits on accumulated participant account balances and annual crediting for additional benefits earned during the year.*

(b)   *Includes investment returns and life-insurance proceeds received from company-owned life insurance policies and other investments used to economically hedge the cost of these plans.*

27. Pension and Postretirement Health Care Plans

We have qualified defined benefit pension plans covering all U.S. team members who meet age and service requirements, including in certain circumstances, date of hire. We also have unfunded nonqualified pension plans for team members with qualified plan compensation restrictions. Eligibility for, and the level of, these benefits varies depending on team members' date of hire, length of service and/or team member compensation. Upon early retirement and prior to Medicare eligibility, team members also become eligible for certain health care benefits if they meet minimum age and service requirements and agree to contribute a portion of the cost. Effective January 1, 2009, our qualified defined benefit pension plan was closed to new participants, with limited exceptions.

We recognize that our obligations to plan participants can only be met over time through a combination of company contributions to these plans and earnings on plan assets. In light of this concept, we elected to contribute $153 million and $252 million to our qualified plans during 2010 and 2009, respectively. This restored the qualified plans to a fully-funded status at year-end on an ABO (Accumulated Benefit Obligation) basis.

During 2009, we amended our postretirement health care plan, resulting in a $46 million reduction to our recorded liability, with a corresponding increase to shareholders' equity of $28 million, net of taxes of $18 million. The financial benefits of this amendment will be recognized through a reduction of benefit plan expense over the six years subsequent to the amendment.

The following tables provide a summary of the changes in the benefit obligations, fair value of plan assets, and funded status and amounts recognized in our Consolidated Statement of Financial Position for our postretirement benefit plans:

| Change in Projected Benefit Obligation | Pension Benefits | | | | Postretirement Health Care Benefits | |
| | Qualified Plans | | Nonqualified Plans | | | |
(millions)	2010	2009	2010	2009	2010	2009
Benefit obligation at beginning of year	$ 2,227	$ 1,948	$ 33	$ 36	$ 87	$ 117
Service cost	114	99	1	1	9	7
Interest cost	127	123	2	2	4	6
Actuarial (gain)/loss	160	155	(2)	(3)	3	33
Participant contributions	2	1	—	—	6	6
Benefits paid	(105)	(99)	(3)	(3)	(15)	(18)
Plan amendments	—	—	—	—	—	(64)
Benefit obligation at end of year	$ 2,525	$ 2,227	$ 31	$ 33	$ 94	$ 87

| Change in Plan Assets | Pension Benefits | | | | Postretirement Health Care Benefits | |
| | Qualified Plans | | Nonqualified Plans | | | |
(millions)	2010	2009	2010	2009	2010	2009
Fair value of plan assets at beginning of year	$ 2,157	$ 1,771	$ —	$ —	$ —	$ —
Actual return on plan assets	308	232	—	—	—	—
Employer contributions	153	252	3	3	9	12
Participant contributions	2	1	—	—	6	6
Benefits paid	(105)	(99)	(3)	(3)	(15)	(18)
Fair value of plan assets at end of year	2,515	2,157	—	—	—	—
Benefit obligation at end of year	2,525	2,227	31	33	94	87
Funded status	$ (10)	$ (70)	$ (31)	$ (33)	$ (94)	$ (87)

Amounts recognized in the Consolidated Statements of Financial Position consist of the following:

Recognition of Funded/(Underfunded) Status (millions)	Qualified Plans		Nonqualified Plans (a)	
	2010	2009	2010	2009
Other noncurrent assets	$ 5	$ 2	$ —	$ —
Accrued and other current liabilities	(1)	(1)	(11)	(13)
Other noncurrent liabilities	(14)	(71)	(114)	(107)
Net amounts recognized	$ (10)	$ (70)	$ (125)	$ (120)

(a)   *Includes postretirement health care benefits.*

The following table summarizes the amounts recorded in accumulated other comprehensive income, which have not yet been recognized as a component of net periodic benefit expense:

Amounts in Accumulated Other Comprehensive Income	Pension Plans		Postretirement Health Care Plans	
(millions)	2010	2009	2010	2009
Net actuarial loss	$ 895	$ 900	$ 48	$ 50
Prior service credits	(1)	(5)	(51)	(62)
Amounts in accumulated other comprehensive income	$ 894	$ 895	$ (3)	$ (12)

The following table summarizes the changes in accumulated other comprehensive income for the years ended January 29, 2011 and January 30, 2010, related to our pension and postretirement health care plans:

Change in Accumulated Other Comprehensive Income	Pension Benefits		Postretirement Health Care Benefits	
(millions)	Pretax	Net of tax	Pretax	Net of tax
January 31, 2009	$ 821	$ 499	$ 19	$ 11
Net actuarial loss	96	58	33	20
Amortization of net actuarial losses	(24)	(14)	(2)	(1)
Amortization of prior service costs and transition	2	1	2	1
Plan amendments	—	—	(64)	(38)
January 30, 2010	$ 895	$ 544	$ (12)	$ (7)
Net actuarial loss	40	25	3	2
Amortization of net actuarial losses	(44)	(27)	(4)	(3)
Amortization of prior service costs and transition	3	1	10	6
January 29, 2011	$ 894	$ 543	$ (3)	$ (2)

The following table summarizes the amounts in accumulated other comprehensive income expected to be amortized and recognized as a component of net periodic benefit expense in 2011:

Expected Amortization of Amounts in Accumulated Other Comprehensive Income (millions)	Pretax	Net of tax
Net actuarial loss	$ 70	$ 42
Prior service credits	(12)	(7)
Total amortization expense	$ 58	$ 35

The following table summarizes our net pension and postretirement health care benefits expense for the years 2010, 2009 and 2008:

Net Pension and Postretirement Health Care Benefits Expense	Pension Benefits			Postretirement Health Care Benefits		
(millions)	2010	2009	2008	2010	2009	2008
Service cost benefits earned during the period	$ 115	$ 100	$ 94	$ 9	$ 7	$ 5
Interest cost on projected benefit obligation	129	125	116	4	6	7
Expected return on assets	(191)	(177)	(162)	—	—	—
Amortization of losses	44	24	16	4	2	—
Amortization of prior service cost	(3)	(2)	(4)	(10)	(2)	—
Total	$ 94	$ 70	$ 60	$ 7	$ 13	$ 12

Prior service cost amortization is determined using the straight-line method over the average remaining service period of team members expected to receive benefits under the plan.

Defined Benefit Pension Plan Information (millions)	2010	2009
Accumulated benefit obligation (ABO) for all plans (a)	$ 2,395	$ 2,118
Projected benefit obligation for pension plans with an ABO in excess of plan assets (b)	47	48
Total ABO for pension plans with an ABO in excess of plan assets	42	42
Fair value of plan assets for pension plans with an ABO in excess of plan assets	—	—

(a) The present value of benefits earned to date assuming no future salary growth.

(b) The present value of benefits earned to date by plan participants, including the effect of assumed future salary increases.

Assumptions

Weighted average assumptions used to determine benefit obligations as of the measurement date were as follows:

Weighted Average Assumptions	Pension Benefits		Postretirement Health Care Benefits	
	2010	2009	2010	2009
Discount rate	5.50%	5.85%	4.35%	4.85%
Average assumed rate of compensation increase	4.00%	4.00%	n/a	n/a

Weighted average assumptions used to determine net periodic benefit expense for each fiscal year were as follows:

Weighted Average Assumptions	Pension Benefits			Postretirement Health Care Benefits		
	2010	2009	2008	2010	2009	2008
Discount rate	5.85%	6.50%	6.45%	4.85%(a)	6.50%(a)	6.45%
Expected long-term rate of return on plan assets	8.00%	8.00%	8.00%	n/a	n/a	n/a
Average assumed rate of compensation increase	4.00%	4.25%	4.25%	n/a	n/a	n/a

(a) Due to the remeasurement from the plan amendment in the third quarter of 2009, the discount rate was decreased from 6.50 percent to 4.85 percent.

The discount rate used to measure net periodic benefit expense each year is the rate as of the beginning of the year (e.g., the prior measurement date). With an essentially stable asset allocation over the following time periods, our most recent annualized rate of return on qualified plans' assets has averaged 5.9 percent, 6.1 percent and 8.6 percent for the 5-year, 10-year and 15-year periods, respectively.

The expected Market-Related Value of Assets (MRV) is determined each year by adjusting the previous year's value by expected return, benefit payments and cash contributions. The expected MRV is adjusted for asset gains and losses in equal 20 percent adjustments over a five-year period.

Our expected annualized long-term rate of return assumptions as of January 29, 2011 were 8.5 percent for domestic and international equity securities, 5.5 percent for long-duration debt securities, 8.5 percent for balanced funds and 10.0 percent for other investments. Balanced funds primarily invest in equities, nominal and inflation-linked fixed income securities, commodities and public real estate. They seek to generate capital market returns while reducing market risk by investing globally in highly diversified portfolios of public securities. These estimates are a judgmental matter in which we consider the composition of our asset portfolio, our historical long-term investment performance and current market conditions. We review the expected long-term rate of return on an annual basis, and revise it accordingly. Additionally, we monitor the mix of investments in our portfolio to ensure alignment with our long-term strategy to manage pension cost and reduce volatility in our assets.

An increase in the cost of covered health care benefits of 7.5 percent was assumed for 2010 and is assumed for 2011. The rate will be reduced to 5.0 percent in 2019 and thereafter.

Health Care Cost Trend Rates—1% Change (millions)	1% Increase	1% Decrease
Effect on total of service and interest cost components of net periodic postretirement health care benefit expense	$ 1	$ (1)
Effect on the health care component of the accumulated postretirement benefit obligation	6	(5)

Plan Assets

Our asset allocation policy is designed to reduce the long-term cost of funding our pension obligations. The plan invests with both passive and active investment managers depending on the investment's asset class. The plan also seeks to reduce the risk associated with adverse movements in interest rates by employing an interest rate hedging program, which may include the use of interest rate swaps, total return swaps and other instruments.

Asset Category	Current targeted allocation	Actual allocation	
		2010	2009
Domestic equity securities (a)	19%	18%	19%
International equity securities	12	10	10
Debt securities	25	25	28
Balanced funds	30	26	19
Other (b)	14	21	24
Total	100%	100%	100%

(a)   Equity securities include our common stock in amounts substantially less than 1 percent of total plan assets as of January 29, 2011 and January 30, 2010.

(b)   Other assets include private equity, mezzanine and high-yield debt, natural resources and timberland funds, multi-strategy hedge funds, derivative instruments, and a 3 percent allocation to real estate.

Fair Value Measurements

(millions)		Total	Level 1		Level 2		Level 3	Total	Level 1		Level 2		Level 3
		Fair Value at January 29, 2011						**Fair Value at January 30, 2010**					
Cash and cash equivalents	$	195	$ —	$	195	$	—	$ 206	$ —	$	206	$	—
Common collective trusts (a)		490	—		490		—	464	—		464		—
Equity securities (b)		36	36		—		—	26	26		—		—
Government securities (c)		259	—		259		—	223	—		223		—
Fixed income (d)		397	—		397		—	365	—		365		—
Balanced funds (e)		596	—		596		—	404	—		404		—
Private equity funds (f)		327	—		—		327	336	—		—		336
Other (g)		130	—		3		127	133	—		14		119
Total		**$ 2,430**	**$ 36**	**$**	**1,940**	**$**	**454**	**$ 2,157**	**$ 26**	**$**	**1,676**	**$**	**455**
Contributions in transit (h)		85											
Total plan assets		**$ 2,515**											

(a)   Passively managed index funds with holdings in domestic and international equities.

(b)   Investments in U.S. small-, mid- and large-cap companies.

(c)   Investments in government securities and passively managed index funds with holdings in long-term government bonds.

(d)   Investments in corporate bonds, mortgage-backed securities and passively managed index funds with holdings in long-term corporate bonds.

(e)   Investments in equities, nominal and inflation-linked fixed income securities, commodities and public real estate.

(f)   Includes venture capital, mezzanine and high-yield debt, natural resources and timberland funds.

(g)   Investments in multi-strategy hedge funds (including domestic and international equity securities, convertible bonds and other alternative investments), real estate and derivative investments.

(h)   Represents $20 million in contributions to equity securities and $65 million in contributions to balanced funds held by investment managers, but not yet invested in the respective funds as of January 29, 2011.

Level 3 Reconciliation

(millions)	Balance at beginning of period	Actual return on plan assets (a)		Purchases, sales and settlements	Transfers in and/or out of Level 3	Balance at end of period
		Relating to still held reporting	assets at the date	Relating to assets sold during the period		
2009						
Private equity funds	$ 317	$ 19	$ 1	$ (1)	$ —	$ 336
Other	131	(20)	—	8	—	119
2010						
Private equity funds	$ 336	$ 28	$ 12	$ (49)	$ —	$ 327
Other	119	7	2	(1)	—	127

(a)   Represents realized and unrealized gains (losses) from changes in values of those financial instruments only for the period in which the instruments were classified as Level 3.

Position	Valuation Technique
Cash and cash equivalents	These investments are cash holdings and investment vehicles valued using the Net Asset Value (NAV) provided by the administrator of the fund. The NAV for the investment vehicles is based on the value of the underlying assets owned by the fund minus applicable costs and liabilities, and then divided by the number of shares outstanding.
Equity securities	Valued at the closing price reported on the major market on which the individual securities are traded.
Common collective trusts/ balanced funds/certain multi-strategy hedge funds	Valued using the NAV provided by the administrator of the fund. The NAV is a quoted transactional price for participants in the fund, which do not represent an active market.
Fixed income and government securities	Valued using matrix pricing models and quoted prices of securities with similar characteristics.
Private equity/real estate/ certain multi-strategy hedge funds/other	Valued by deriving Target's proportionate share of equity investment from audited financial statements. Private equity and real estate investments require significant judgment on the part of the fund manager due to the absence of quoted market prices, inherent lack of liquidity, and the long-term nature of such investments. Certain multi-strategy hedge funds represent funds of funds that include liquidity restrictions and for which timely valuation information is not available.

Contributions

In 2010 and 2009, we made discretionary contributions of $153 million and $252 million, respectively, to our qualified defined benefit pension plans. Even though we are not required to make any contributions, we may elect to make contributions depending on investment performance and the pension plan funded status in 2011. We expect to make contributions in the range of $10 million to $15 million to our postretirement health care benefit plan in 2011.

Estimated Future Benefit Payments

Benefit payments by the plans, which reflect expected future service as appropriate, are expected to be paid as follows:

Estimated Future Benefit Payments

(millions)	Pension	Benefits	Postretirement	Health Care	Benefits
2011	$	129	$		8
2012		138			7
2013		145			7
2014		154			8
2015		161			9
2016-2020		935			67

28. Segment Reporting

Our measure of profit for each segment is a measure that management considers analytically useful in measuring the return we are achieving on our investment.

Business Segment Results	2010			2009			2008		
(millions)	Retail	Credit Card	Total	Retail	Credit Card	Total	Retail	Credit Card	Total
Sales/Credit card revenues	$65,786 $	1,604	$67,390	$63,435 $	1,922	$65,357	$62,884 $	2,064	$64,948
Cost of sales	45,725	—	45,725	44,062	—	44,062	44,157	—	44,157
Bad debt expense *(a)*	—	528	528	—	1,185	1,185	—	1,251	1,251
Selling, general and administrative/ Operations and marketing expenses *(a)*, *(b)*	13,367	433	13,801	12,989	425	13,414	12,838	474	13,312
Depreciation and amortization	2,065	19	2,084	2,008	14	2,023	1,808	17	1,826
Earnings before interest expense and income taxes	4,629	624	5,252	4,376	298	4,673	4,081	322	4,402
Interest expense on nonrecourse debt collateralized by credit card receivables	—	83	83	—	97	97	—	167	167
Segment profit	$ 4,629 $	541	$ 5,169	$ 4,376 $	201	$ 4,576	$ 4,081 $	155	$ 4,236
Unallocated (income)/expense:									
Other interest expense			677			707			727
Interest income			(3)			(3)			(28)
Earnings before income taxes			$ 4,495			$ 3,872			$ 3,536

(a)   *The combination of bad debt expense and operations and marketing expenses within the Credit Card Segment represent credit card expenses on the Consolidated Statements of Operations.*

(b)   *Loyalty Program discounts are recorded as reductions to sales in our Retail Segment. Effective with the October 2010 nationwide launch of our new 5% REDcard Rewards loyalty program, we changed the formula under which our Credit Card segment reimburses our Retail Segment to better align with the attributes of the new program. These reimbursed amounts were $102 million in 2010, $89 million in 2009 and $117 million in 2008. In all periods these amounts were recorded as reductions to SG&A expenses within the Retail Segment and increases to operations and marketing expenses within the Credit Card Segment.*

Note: The sum of the segment amounts may not equal the total amounts due to rounding.

Total Assets by Business Segment	2010			2009			
(millions)	Retail	Credit Card	Total	Retail	Credit	Card	Total
Total assets	$ 37,324 $	6,381 $	43,705 $	37,200	$	7,333 $	44,533

Substantially all of our revenues are generated and long-lived assets are located within the United States.

29. Quarterly Results (Unaudited)

Due to the seasonal nature of our business, fourth quarter operating results typically represent a substantially larger share of total year revenues and earnings because they include our peak sales period from Thanksgiving through the end of December. We follow the same accounting policies for preparing quarterly and annual financial data. The table below summarizes quarterly results for 2010 and 2009:

Quarterly Results (millions, except per share data)	First Quarter		Second Quarter		Third Quarter		Fourth Quarter		Total Year	
	2010	2009	2010	2009	2010	2009	2010	2009	2010	2009
Total revenues	$ 15,593	$ 14,833	$ 15,532	$ 15,067	$ 15,605	$ 15,276	$ 20,661	$ 20,181	$ 67,390	$ 65,357
Earnings before income taxes	1,055	824	1,081	957	773	683	1,588	1,409	4,495	3,872
Net earnings	671	522	679	594	535	436	1,035	936	2,920	2,488
Basic earnings per share	0.91	0.69	0.93	0.79	0.75	0.58	1.46	1.25	4.03	3.31
Diluted earnings per share	0.90	0.69	0.92	0.79	0.74	0.58	1.45	1.24	4.00	3.30
Dividends declared per share	0.17	0.16	0.25	0.17	0.25	0.17	0.25	0.17	0.92	0.67
Closing common stock price										
High	58.05	41.26	57.13	43.79	55.05	51.35	60.77	52.02	60.77	52.02
Low	48.64	25.37	49.00	36.75	50.72	41.38	53.48	45.30	48.64	25.37

Note: Per share amounts are computed independently for each of the quarters presented. The sum of the quarters may not equal the total year amount due to the impact of changes in average quarterly shares outstanding and all other quarterly amounts may not equal the total year due to rounding.

Appendix C

Summary of Financial Ratios

CHAPTER 3

Debt to Assets Ratio

The debt to assets ratio reveals the percentage of a company's assets that is financed with borrowed money. The higher the debt to assets ratio is, the greater its financial risk, other things being equal. The debt to assets ratio is defined as

$$\frac{\text{Total debt}}{\text{Total assets}}$$

Return on Assets Ratio

The return on assets ratio (ROA) helps measure how well a company is using the assets available to it. The greater the amount of earnings that can be obtained for a given amount of assets, the better a company is doing at utilizing its assets. So, in general, the higher a company's ROA, the better. The ROA ratio is defined as

$$\frac{\text{Net income}}{\text{Total assets}}$$

Return on Equity Ratio

The return on equity ratio (ROE) helps to measure how much the owners of a company are earning on the money they have invested in the business. The higher a company's ROE, the better. The ROE is defined as

$$\frac{\text{Net income}}{\text{Stockholders' equity}}$$

CHAPTER 4

Gross Margin Percentage

The gross margin percentage helps explain a company's pricing strategy. It compares the amount a company pays for the goods it sells to the price the company is able to charge for those goods. The more a company marks up its goods, the higher the gross margin percentage will be. Specialty shops tend to have higher gross margin percentages while discount stores tend to have lower percentages. This ratio is sometimes called the gross profit percentage. The gross margin percentage is defined as

$$\frac{\text{Gross margin}}{\text{Net sales}}$$

Return on Sales Ratio

The return on sales ratio, expressed as a percentage, indicates how much of each dollar of sales remains as profit after all expenses have been deducted. Discount stores do not necessarily have lower return on sales percentages than specialty shops. The higher the return on sales ratio percentage, the better. The return on sales ratio is defined as

$$\frac{\text{Net income}}{\text{Net sales}}$$

CHAPTER 5

Inventory Turnover Ratio and Average Days to Sell Inventory

The inventory turnover ratio and the average days to sell inventory ratio indicate how long a company takes to sell the goods it has in merchandise inventory. The first ratio, inventory turnover, explains how many times per year a company's inventory is sold, or "turned over"; generally, the *higher* this ratio is the better. Because the inventory turnover ratio is not easily understood by everyone, the second ratio, average days to sell inventory, is often used. However, the average days to sell inventory ratio cannot be computed without first computing the inventory turnover ratio. Generally, the *lower* the average days to sell inventory ratio is, the better. The inventory turnover ratio is defined as

$$\frac{\text{Cost of goods sold}}{\text{Inventory}}$$

The average days to sell inventory ratio is defined as

$$\frac{\text{365 days}}{\text{Inventory turnover}}$$

A company's operating cycle is the time it takes it to convert cash into inventory, sell the inventory, and collect the cash from accounts receivable that resulted from the sale of the inventory. The time it takes a business to do this can be computed by adding the *average days to sell inventory* and the *average days to collect accounts receivable.*

CHAPTER 7

Accounts Receivable Turnover Ratio and Average Days to Collect Receivables

The accounts receivable turnover ratio and the average days to collect receivables ratio indicate how long a company takes to collect its accounts receivable. The first ratio, accounts receivable turnover, explains how many times per year a company's receivables are collected, or "turned over"; generally, the *higher* this ratio is, the better. Because the accounts receivable turnover ratios are not easily understood by everyone, the second ratio, average days to collect receivables, is often used. However, the average days to collect receivables ratio cannot be computed without first computing the accounts receivable turnover ratio. Generally, the *lower* the average days to collect receivables ratio is, the better. The accounts receivable turnover ratio is defined as

$$\frac{\text{Sales}}{\text{Accounts receivable}}$$

The average days to collect receivables ratio is defined as

$$\frac{\text{365 days}}{\text{Accounts receivable turnover ratio}}$$

CHAPTER 9

Current Ratio

Liquidity refers to how quickly noncash assets can be converted into cash. The more quickly assets can be converted into cash, the more liquid they are, and the more useful they are for paying liabilities that must be paid in the near future. The current ratio provides a measure of how much liquidity a company has. Specifically, it compares a company's more liquid assets (current assets) to its current liabilities. Other things being equal, the higher a company's current ratio, the easier it can pay its currently maturing debts. The current ratio is defined as

$$\frac{\text{Current assets}}{\text{Current liabilities}}$$

CHAPTER 10

Times Interest Earned Ratio

The times interest earned ratio helps assess a company's ability to make interest payments on its debt. Failure to make interest (or principal) payments can cause a company to be forced into bankruptcy. Other things being equal, a company with a higher times interest earned ratio is considered to have lower financial risk than a company with a lower ratio.

EBIT is an acronym for "earnings before interest and taxes." In other words, it is what net earnings would have been if the company had had no interest expense or income tax expense. Because net earnings are calculated after interest has been subtracted, a company might have $0 of earnings and still have been able to make its interest payments. Thus, the times interest earned ratio is based on EBIT and is defined as

$$\frac{\text{EBIT}}{\text{Interest expense}}$$

Return on Assets Ratio (refined)

As discussed in detail in Chapter 3, the return on assets ratio (ROA) helps measure how well a company is using the assets available to it. The greater the amount of earnings that can be obtained for a given amount of assets, the better a company is doing at utilizing its assets, so the higher this ratio is, the better. Throughout most of this textbook, ROA has been based on net earnings. However, the use of net earnings creates an ROA that is biased against companies with relatively more debt versus equity financing. Since the ROA ratio is intended to help assess how efficiently a company is using its assets, not how it is financed, the ROA that is used in the business world is often defined as

$$\frac{\text{EBIT}}{\text{Total assets}}$$

CHAPTER 11

Price-Earnings Ratio

The price-earnings ratio (P/E ratio) gives an indication of how optimistic the financial markets are about a company's future earnings. The higher a company's P/E ratio is, the more investors are willing to pay for each dollar of earnings that the company generates. Typically investors are willing to pay this higher price because they think the company will grow in the future. Lower P/E ratios indicate investors are less optimistic about the company's future growth. The price-earnings ratio is defined as

$$\frac{\text{Market price of one share of stock}}{\text{Earnings per share}}$$

Earnings per Share Ratio

The earnings per share ratio (EPS) provides an indication of the amount of a company's earnings that are attributable to each share of common stock outstanding. Obviously, the higher this ratio is the better. In companies that have complex equity structures, such as convertible preferred stock and stock option plans, the computation of EPS can be very complex, but in its simplest form, EPS is defined as

$$\frac{\text{Net earnings}}{\text{Outstanding shares of common stock}}$$

Appendix D

Annual Report and Financial Statement Analysis Projects

Authored By: Professor Linda Bell, William Jewell College

ANNUAL REPORT PROJECT FOR THE TARGET CORPORATION (SEE APPENDIX B FOR THE TARGET ANNUAL REPORT)

Target's 2008, 2009, and 2010 financial statements have been loaded in an Excel spreadsheet, which is available on the textbook's website. The income statement shown in the spreadsheet has been revised to better reflect the income statement format and wording used in the textbook. The revision moves credit card revenues (interest income) to the nonoperating section and enables the project solution for gross margin percentages to agree to those identified in the Management Discussion and Analysis section of the annual report. This Excel spreadsheet provides an excellent starting point for the vertical and horizontal analysis required in the project.

All references to the company's year-end data pertain to the fiscal year-end. For example, the company's 2010 year-end financial statements are dated January 29, 2011, which is the company's fiscal closing date.

Part 1: Items 1–4 and Part II: Items 5–7 (Management's Discussion and Analysis)

The annual report for Target Corporation opens with a general description of business operations, segments, financial highlights, and risk factors. This is followed by Management's Discussion and Analysis of Financial Condition, in which management talks about financial results and trends, liquidity, and other matters deemed necessary to provide adequate disclosure to users of the report. Refer to these items to answer questions 1–6.

1. What are the company's two reportable business segments?
2. Describe Target's competition for its retail segment.
3. Identify at least five risk factors for Target.
4. On what stock market exchange is the company's stock traded? What is Target's symbol?
5. What caused sales to increase 3.7 percent in 2010? Explain why the gross margin rate remained at 30.5 percent throughout 2009 and 2010.
6. When discussing its liquidity, management indicated that cash provided by operations in 2010 was $5,271 million. How did the company utilize these funds?

Report of Independent Registered Public Accounting Firm on Consolidated Financial Statements (Auditors)

7. What is the name of the company's independent auditors?
8. Who is responsible for the financial statements?
9. What is the outside auditors' responsibility?

10. What type of opinion did the independent auditors issue on the financial statements (unqualified, qualified, adverse, or disclaimer)? What does this opinion mean?

11. The auditors' report indicates the audit was concerned with material misstatements rather than absolute accuracy in the financial statements. What does "material" mean?

Income Statement—Vertical Analysis

12. Using Excel, compute common-size income statements for all three fiscal years. In common-size income statements, net sales is 100 percent and every other number is a percentage of sales. Attach the spreadsheet to the end of this project. (To help you get started, you can access Target's financial statements in Excel format on the student textbook website. The financial statements have been slightly reformatted to conform to the multistep income statement format utilized throughout the textbook.)

13. Using the common-size income statements, identify the significant trends.

14. What were the gross margin (gross profit) and the gross margin percentage for fiscal year-end 2010, 2009, and 2008?

15. If the gross margin changed over the three-year period, what caused the change? (The change in the two components of gross margin will reveal what caused any change in the gross margin.)

16. What was the percentage return on sales for fiscal year-end 2010, 2009, and 2008? What do these ratios indicate about Target?

Income Statement—Horizontal Analysis

17. Using Excel, compute annual changes for each line item on the income statement. For each of the two most recent years, insert a column for changes in absolute dollars and insert another column for the percentage changes. Attach the spreadsheet to the end of this project. (You can find Target's financial statements in Excel format on the student textbook website.)

18. What were the absolute dollar and the percentage changes in revenues between fiscal 2010 and 2009 and between 2009 and 2008?

19. Describe the trend in revenues. Be specific (e.g., slight/steady/drastic increase or decrease each year, or fluctuating with an initial modest/significant increase or decrease followed by a modest/significant increase or decrease, etc.) to precisely describe the company's situation.

20. What were the absolute dollar and the percentage changes in cost of sales (cost of goods sold) between fiscal 2010 and 2009 and between 2009 and 2008?

21. Describe the trend in cost of sales (cost of goods sold). Be specific (e.g., slight/steady/drastic increase or decrease each year, or fluctuating with an initial modest/significant increase or decrease followed by a modest/significant increase or decrease, etc.) to precisely describe the company's situation.

22. What were the absolute dollar and the percentage changes in selling, general, and administrative expenses (operating expenses) between fiscal 2010 and 2009 and between 2009 and 2008?

23. Describe the trend in selling, general, and administrative expenses. Be specific (e.g., slight/steady/drastic increase or decrease each year, or fluctuating with an initial modest/significant increase or decrease followed by a modest/significant increase or decrease, etc.) to precisely describe the company's situation.

24. What were the absolute dollar and the percentage changes in net income between fiscal 2010 to 2009 and between 2009 to 2008?

25. How would you describe the trend for net income? Be specific (e.g., slight/steady/drastic increase or decrease each year, or fluctuating with an initial modest/significant increase or decrease followed by a modest/significant increase or decrease, etc.) to precisely describe the company's situation. Do you expect the trend to continue?

26. Which items had the largest percentage change between fiscal 2010 to 2009 and between 2009 to 2008, revenues or expenses (selling, general, and administrative expenses and cost of sales)?

27. Summarize what is causing the changes in net income from fiscal 2008 to 2009 and 2009 to 2010 based on the percentages computed in questions 18 through 26. Do you expect the trend to continue?

Balance Sheet—Vertical Analysis

28. Using Excel, compute common-size balance sheets at the end of fiscal 2010 and 2009. In common-size balance sheets, total assets is 100 percent and every other number is a percentage of total assets. Attach the spreadsheet to the end of this project. (You can find Target's financial statements in Excel format on the student textbook website.)

29. What percentage were current assets of total assets at the end of fiscal 2010 and 2009? Which current asset had the largest balance at the end of fiscal 2010 and 2009?

30. Long-term assets constituted what percentage of total assets at the end of fiscal 2010 and 2009? (Note: solutions for percentages calculated for items 29 and 30 should total 100 percent.) Which long-term asset had the largest balance at the end of fiscal 2010 and 2009?

31. Current liabilities constituted what percentage of total assets at the end of fiscal 2010 and 2009? Which current liability had the largest balance at the end of fiscal 2010 and 2009?

32. Long-term liabilities constituted what percentage of total assets at the end of fiscal 2010 and 2009? Which long-term liability had the largest balance at the end of fiscal 2010 and 2009?

33. Calculate the ratio of total liabilities to total assets for fiscal year-end 2010 and 2009.

34. Calculate the ratio of stockholders' equity to total assets for fiscal year-end 2010 and 2009. (Recall percentages for items 33 and 34 should total 100 percent.) Identify whether Target finances its assets mostly with debt or equity.

Balance Sheet—Horizontal Analysis

35. Using Excel, compute annual changes for each line item on the balance sheet. Insert a column for changes in absolute dollars and insert another column for the percentage changes. Attach the spreadsheet to the end of this project. (You can find Target's financial statements in Excel format on the student textbook website.)

36. What were the absolute dollar change and the percentage change between the year-end 2010 and year-end 2009 net accounts receivable balance? Was the change an increase or decrease? What line item (account) on the income statement is directly related to accounts receivable? Did this account change in the similar direction as accounts receivable?

37. What were the absolute dollar change and the percentage change between year-end 2010 and year-end 2009 inventory? Was the change an increase or decrease? What line item (account) on the income statement is directly related to inventory? Did this account change in a similar direction as inventory?

38. Compared to year-end 2009, did the amounts reported for the following long-term assets increase or decrease? By how much? Include dollar amounts for each item.

	Fiscal Year-End 2010	
	Dollar Amount	Increase or Decrease
Property, plant, and equipment, net		
Other noncurrent assets		
Total long-term assets		

What line item on the income statement is directly related to long-term assets? Did this account change in a similar direction as long-term assets?

39. What were the absolute dollar change and the percentage change between fiscal year-end 2010 and fiscal year-end 2009 total liabilities? Was the change an increase or decrease? What line item (account) on the income statement is directly related to liabilities? Did this account change in a similar direction as total liabilities?

40. What was the amount of the change in the balance in retained earnings between fiscal year-end 2010 and 2009? What caused this change?

Balance Sheet—Ratio Analysis

41. Compute the current ratio at the end of fiscal 2010 and 2009. What does this ratio indicate about Target?

42. Calculate the accounts receivable turnover and the average number of days to collect accounts receivable for fiscal 2010 and 2009. In which year was the turnover and days to collect more favorable?

43. Calculate the inventory turnover ratios and the average number of days to sell inventory for fiscal 2010 and 2009. In which year was the turnover and days to sell inventory more favorable?

Balance Sheet—Stockholders' Equity Section

44. Does the company's common stock have a par value? If so, how much was the par value per share?

45. How many shares of common stock were issued at the end of fiscal 2010 and 2009?

46. How many shares of treasury stock did the company have at the end of fiscal 2010 and 2009? How were the treasury stock purchases reflected on the statement of cash flows? Include the type of cash flow activity.

47. What percentage of stockholders' equity do the following items represent at year-end?

	2010	2009
Total paid-in capital		
Retained earnings		
Other items		
	100%	100%

Statement of Cash Flows

48. Does Target report cash flows from operating activities using the direct or the indirect method? Describe how you can tell.

49. What was the dollar amount of the increase or decrease in cash and cash equivalents for the fiscal years ended 2010, 2009, and 2008?

50. Does the ending balance of cash and cash equivalents agree with the amount reported on the balance sheet?

	2010	2009
Balance sheet	$	$
Statement of cash flows	$	$

51. Target reported a $5,271 million cash flow provided by operations in 2010. Identify the four largest cash outflows for that year. Does this agree with management's comments identified in question 6?

52. On what statement(s) would you expect to find information regarding the declaration and payment of dividends? Did the company declare or pay dividends in 2010?

Notes to the Financial Statements

53. In your own words, briefly summarize two significant accounting policies.

54. How much is the estimated allowance for discounts and doubtful accounts for fiscal 2010?

55. What is the net realizable value of receivables at the end of fiscal 2010?

56. Complete the following schedule contrasting the effect the three inventory cost flow assumptions have on the balance sheet and income statement dollar amounts. Specify for each financial statement the account that is affected by the sale of inventory. Insert the most appropriate term (High, Middle, or Low) to indicate how the specified account would be affected by each of the given cost flow assumptions. Assume an inflationary environment.

Account Affected	Cost Flow Assumptions		
	FIFO	AVG	LIFO
1. Balance Sheet:			
2. Income Statement:			

57. What inventory cost flow method does Target use?

58. What are the estimated useful lives of the company's depreciable assets?

59. Complete the following schedule contrasting the effect the two types of depreciation methods have on the balance sheet and income statement dollar amounts. Specify for each financial statement the account affected by recording depreciation expense. Designate with an X the method (accelerated or straight-line) that would result in the higher balance in the specified account in the early years of the asset's life.

Account Affected	Depreciation Methods	
	Accelerated	Straight-Line
1. Balance Sheet:		
2. Income Statement:		
	(Higher balance early in asset's life)	

60. What method of depreciation does Target use?

61. Did the balance in the goodwill account increase or decrease? Speculate as to what caused this change.

62. In addition to goodwill, what kinds of intangible assets does the company have? What are their estimated lives?

63. Identify three different accrued expenses.

64. Identify two kinds of commitments and contingencies.

65. What is the amount of available unsecured revolving credit as of January 29, 2011? What was the balance outstanding at the end of each fiscal year?

66. What is the amount of total long-term borrowings at January 29, 2011? Are these obligations secured or unsecured? The amount reported in the notes does not agree with total long-term debt reported on the balance sheet. What are the two additional long-term items reported on the balance sheet?

Performance Measures

67. Compute the return on assets ratio (use net income rather than EBIT in the numerator) for fiscal years 2010 and 2009.

68. Compute the return on equity ratio for fiscal years 2010 and 2009.

69. For fiscal 2010, was the return on equity ratio greater than the return on assets ratio? Explain why.

70. What were Target's basic earnings per share (EPS) for fiscal 2010 and 2009? Identify what caused the ratio to change.

FINANCIAL STATEMENTS PROJECT (SELECTION OF COMPANY TO BE DECIDED BY INSTRUCTOR)

Date Due: _____

Required

Based on the annual report of the company you are reviewing, answer the following questions. If you cannot answer a particular question, briefly explain why. If the question is not applicable to your company's financial statements answer "N/A."

Show all necessary computations in good form. Label all numbers in your computations. If relevant, reference your answers to page(s) in the annual report.

"Current year" means the most recent fiscal year in the company's annual report. "Prior year" means the fiscal year immediately preceding the current year.

1. What products or services does the company sell? Be specific.

2. What do you think the outlook is for these products or services? Why do you think so?

3. By what percentage have sales increased or decreased in each of the last two fiscal years?

4. If the company reported sales by segments, which segment had the largest percentage of total sales? Which segment had the smallest percentage of total sales? **Show computations of the relevant percentages.**

Largest segment _____   Percentage of total sales _____
Smallest segment _____   Percentage of total sales _____

5. What is net income for the current year? _____

6. Did the current year's net income increase or decrease since the prior year? By how much? What caused the change?

7. If the company reported earnings by segments, which segment had the largest percentage of total earnings? Which segment had the smallest percentage of total earnings? **Show computations of the relevant percentages.**

Largest segment _____   Percentage of total earnings _____
Smallest segment _____   Percentage of total earnings _____

8. Did the company report any special, unusual, or otherwise nonroutine items in either current or prior year net income? If so, explain the item(s).

9. For the current year, how does net income compare to net cash provided (used) by operating activities?

10. For the current year, what one or two items were most responsible for the difference between net income and net cash provided (used) by operating activities?

11. Did the company pay cash dividends during the current year? If so, how much were they?

12. If the company paid cash dividends, what percentage of net income were the cash dividends? If the company did not pay cash dividends, why do you think it did not?

13. Which of the following is the company's largest asset category: accounts receivable, inventory, or land? What is the amount of that asset category?

14. If the company reported assets by segments, which segment had the largest percentage of total assets? Which segment had the smallest percentage of total assets? **Show computations of the relevant percentages.**

    Largest segment _____   Percentage of total assets _____

    Smallest segment _____   Percentage of total assets _____

15. How much **cash** did the company invest in property, plant, and equipment during the current year?

16. Which inventory method(s) did the company use?

17. Which depreciation method(s) did the company use?

18. If the company has any intangible assets, what kind are they?

19. Did the company report any contingent liabilities ("contingencies")? If so, briefly explain.

20. Does the company have any preferred stock authorized? If so, how many shares were authorized?

21. Does the company's common stock have a par value? If so, what was it?

22. In what price range was the company's common stock trading during the last quarter of the current year?

23. What was the market price of the company's common stock on DD/MM/Year?

24. Where (on what stock exchange) is the company's stock traded?

25. Who was the company's independent auditor?

26. Develop one question about the company's financial report that you do not know how to answer.

27. Compute the following ratios for the current year and the prior year. Show the appropriate formulas in the first column. Show all supporting computations in the second and third columns.

Ratio	Current Year	Prior Year
Gross Profit Formula:		
Inventory Turnover Formula:		
Current Ratio Formula:		
Debt to Equity Formula:		
Return on Assets Formula:		
Return on Equity Formula:		

Appendix E

Accounting for Investment Securities

TYPES OF INVESTMENT SECURITIES

A financial investment occurs when one entity provides assets or services to another entity in exchange for a certificate known as a *security*. The entity that provides the assets and receives the security certificate is called the **investor.** The entity that receives the assets or services and gives the security certificate is called the **investee.** This appendix discusses accounting practices that apply to securities held by investors.

There are two primary types of investment securities: debt securities and equity securities. An investor receives a **debt security** when assets *are loaned* to the investee. In general, a debt security describes the investee's obligation to return the assets and to pay interest for the use of the assets. Common types of debt securities include bonds, notes, certificates of deposit, and commercial paper.

An **equity security** is obtained when an investor acquires an *ownership interest* in the investee. An equity security usually describes the rights of ownership, including the right to influence the operations of the investee and to share in profits or losses that accrue from those operations. The most common types of equity securities are common stock and preferred stock. In summary, **investment securities** are certificates that describe the rights and privileges that investors receive when they loan or give assets or services to investees.

Transactions between the investor and the investee constitute the **primary securities market.** There is a **secondary securities market** in which investors exchange (buy and sell) investment securities with other investors. Securities that regularly trade in established secondary markets are called **marketable securities.** Investee companies are affected by secondary-market transactions only to the extent that their obligations are transferred to a different party. For example, assume that Tom Williams (investor) loans assets to American Can Company (investee). Williams receives a bond (investment security) from American Can that describes American Can's obligation to return assets and pay interest to Williams. This exchange represents a primary securities market transaction. Now assume that in a secondary-market transaction Williams sells his investment security (bond) to Tina Tucker. American Can Company is affected by this transaction only to the extent that the company's obligation transfers from Williams to Tucker. In other words, American Can's obligation to repay principal and interest does not change. The only thing that changes is the party to whom American Can makes payments. *An investee's financial statements are not affected when the securities it has issued to an investor are traded in the secondary market.*

The **fair value,** also called **market value,** is the amount that the investor would receive if the securities are sold in an orderly transaction. More specifically, the fair value is based on the amount that would be collected (an exit value) from the sale of an asset as opposed to the cost necessary to acquire a comparable asset. For a more detailed definition of fair value see *FASB Accounting Standards Codification Topic 820,* "Fair Value Measurements and Disclosures." Whether securities are reported at fair value or historical cost depends on whether the investor intends to sell or hold the securities. Generally accepted accounting principles require companies to classify their investment securities into one of three categories: (1) held-to-maturity securities, (2) trading securities, and (3) available-for-sale securities.

Held-to-Maturity Securities

Since equity securities representing ownership interests have no maturity date, the held-to-maturity classification applies only to debt securities. Debt securities should be classified as held-to-maturity securities if the investor has a *positive intent* and the *ability* to hold the securities until the maturity date. **Held-to-maturity securities** are reported on the balance sheet at *amortized historical cost.*[1]

Trading Securities

Both debt and equity securities can be classified as *trading securities.* **Trading securities** are bought and sold for the purpose of generating profits on the short-term appreciation of stock or bond prices. They are usually traded frequently and within short time spans from the time when they are acquired. Trading securities are reported on the investor's balance sheet at their fair value on the investor's fiscal closing date.

Available-for-Sale Securities

All marketable securities that are not classified as held-to-maturity or trading securities must be classified as **available-for-sale securities.** These securities are also reported on the investor's balance sheet at fair value as of the investor's fiscal closing date.

Two of the three classifications, therefore, must be reported at fair value, which is a clear exception to the historical cost concept. Other exceptions to the use of historical cost measures for asset valuation are discussed in later sections of this appendix.

REPORTING EVENTS THAT AFFECT INVESTMENT SECURITIES

The effects on the investor's financial statements of four distinct accounting events involving marketable investment securities are illustrated in the following section. The illustration assumes that the investor, Arapaho Company, started the accounting period with cash of $10,000 and common stock of $10,000.

EVENT 1   Investment Purchase
Arapaho paid $9,000 cash to purchase marketable investment securities.

This event is an asset exchange. One asset (cash) decreases, and another asset (investment securities) increases. The income statement is not affected. The $9,000 cash outflow is reported as either an operating activity or an investing activity, depending on how the securities are classified. Since *trading securities* are short-term assets that are regularly traded for the purpose of producing income, cash flows from the purchase or sale of trading securities are reported in the operating activities section of the statement of cash flows. In contrast, cash flows involving the purchase or sale of securities classified as *held to maturity* or *available for sale* are reported in the investing activities section of the statement of cash flows. The only difference among the three alternatives lies in the classification of the cash

[1]Debt securities are frequently purchased for amounts that are more or less than their face value (the amount of principal due at the maturity date). If the purchase price is above the face value, the difference between the face value and the purchase price is called a *premium.* If the purchase price is below the face value, the difference is called a *discount.* Premiums and discounts increase or decrease the amount of interest revenue earned and affect the carrying value of the bond investment reported on the balance sheet. The presentation in this section of the text makes the simplifying assumption that the bonds are purchased at a price equal to their face value. Accounting for discounts and premiums is discussed in Chapter 10.

outflow reported on the statement of cash flows, as shown in the following statements model:

Event No.	Type	Assets			=	Liab.	+	Equity	Rev.	−	Exp.	=	Net Inc.	Cash Flow	
		Cash	+	Inv. Sec.											
1	Held	(9,000)	+	9,000	=	NA	+	NA	NA	−	NA	=	NA	(9,000)	IA
1	Trading	(9,000)	+	9,000	=	NA	+	NA	NA	−	NA	=	NA	(9,000)	OA
1	Available	(9,000)	+	9,000	=	NA	+	NA	NA	−	NA	=	NA	(9,000)	IA

EVENT 2   Recognition of Investment Revenue
Arapaho earned $1,600 of cash investment revenue.

Investment revenue is reported the same way regardless of whether the investment securities are classified as held to maturity, trading, or available for sale. Investment revenue comes in two forms. Earnings from equity investments are called **dividends.** Revenue from debt securities is called **interest.** Both forms have the same impact on the financial statements. Recognizing the investment revenue increases both assets and stockholders' equity. Revenue and net income increase. The cash inflow from investment revenue is reported in the operating activities section of the statement of cash flows regardless of how the investment securities are classified.

Event No.	Assets	=	Liab.	+	Equity	Rev.	−	Exp.	=	Net Inc.	Cash Flow	
	Cash	=			Ret. Earn.							
2	1,600	=	NA	+	1,600	1,600	−	NA	=	1,600	1,600	OA

EVENT 3   Sale of Investment Securities
Arapaho sold securities that cost $2,000 for $2,600 cash.

This event results in recognizing a $600 realized (actual) gain that increases both total assets and stockholders' equity. The asset cash increases by $2,600 and the asset investment securities decreases by $2,000, resulting in a $600 increase in total assets. The $600 realized gain is reported on the income statement, increasing net income and retained earnings. The $600 gain does not appear on the statement of cash flows. Instead, the entire $2,600 cash inflow is reported in one section of the statement of cash flows. Cash inflows from the sale of held-to-maturity and available-for-sale securities are reported as investing activities. Cash flows involving trading securities are reported as operating activities. These effects are shown below:

Event No.	Type	Assets			=	Liab.	+	Equity	Rev. or Gain	−	Exp. or Loss	=	Net Inc.	Cash Flow	
		Cash	+	Inv. Sec.											
3	Held	2,600	+	(2,000)	=	NA	+	600	600	−	NA	=	600	2,600	IA
3	Trading	2,600	+	(2,000)	=	NA	+	600	600	−	NA	=	600	2,600	OA
3	Available	2,600	+	(2,000)	=	NA	+	600	600	−	NA	=	600	2,600	IA

EVENT 4   Market Value Adjustment
Arapaho recognized a $700 unrealized gain.

After Event 3, the historical cost of Arapaho's portfolio of remaining investment securities is $7,000 ($9,000 purchased less $2,000 sold). Assume that at Arapaho's fiscal closing date, these securities have a fair value of $7,700, giving Arapaho a $700 unrealized gain on its investment. This type of gain (sometimes called a *paper profit*) is classified as *unrealized* because the securities have not been sold. The treatment of **unrealized gains or losses** in the financial statements depends on whether the securities are classified as held to maturity, trading, or available for sale. Unrealized gains or losses on securities classified as *held to maturity* are not recognized in the financial statements; they have no effect on the balance sheet, income statement, and statement of cash flows. Even so, many companies choose to disclose the market value of the securities as part of the narrative description or in the notes that accompany the financial statements. Whether or not the market value is disclosed, held-to-maturity securities are reported on the balance sheet at amortized cost.

Investments classified as trading securities are reported in the financial statements at fair value. Unrealized gains or losses on *trading securities* are recognized in net income even though the securities have not been sold. In Arapaho's case, the $700 gain increases the carrying value of the investment securities. The gain increases net income, which in turn increases retained earnings. Unrealized gains and losses have no effect on cash flows.

Investments classified as available-for-sale securities are also reported in the financial statements at fair value. However, an important distinction exists with respect to how the unrealized gains and losses affect the financial statements. Even though unrealized gains or losses on available-for-sale securities are included in the assets on the balance sheet, they *are not* recognized in determining net income.[2] On Arapaho's balance sheet, the $700 gain increases the carrying value of the investment securities. A corresponding increase is reported in a separate equity account called Unrealized Gain or Loss on Available-for-Sale Securities. The statement of cash flows is not affected by recognizing unrealized gains and losses on available-for-sale securities.

The effects of these alternative treatments of unrealized gains and losses on Arapaho's financial statements are shown here:

Event No.	Type	Assets	=	Liab.	+	Equity			Rev. or Gain	−	Exp. or Loss	=	Net Inc.	Cash Flow
		Inv. Sec.	=			Ret. Earn.	+	Unreal. Gain						
4	Held	NA	=	NA	+	NA	+	NA	NA	−	NA	=	NA	NA
4	Trading	700	=	NA	+	700	+	NA	700	−	NA	=	700	NA
4	Available	700	=	NA	+	NA	+	700	NA	−	NA	=	NA	NA

FINANCIAL STATEMENTS

As the preceding discussion implies, the financial statements of Arapaho Company are affected by not only the business events relating to its security transactions but also the accounting treatment used to report those events. In other words, the same economic events are reflected differently in the financial statements depending on whether the

---

[2]GAAP permits companies to report unrealized gains and losses on available-for-sale securities as additions to or subtractions after net income with the result being titled *comprehensive income*. Alternatively, the unrealized gains and losses can be reported on a separate statement of net income and other comprehensive income.

EXHIBIT E.1

ARAPAHO COMPANY
Comparative Financial Statements
Income Statements

Investment Securities Classified as	Held	Trading	Available
Investment revenue	$ 1,600	$ 1,600	$ 1,600
Realized gain	600	600	600
Unrealized gain		700	
Net income	$ 2,200	$ 2,900	$ 2,200

Balance Sheets

	Held	Trading	Available
Assets			
Cash	$ 5,200	$ 5,200	$ 5,200
Investment securities, at cost (market value $7,700)	7,000		
Investment securities, at market (cost $7,000)		7,700	7,700
Total assets	$12,200	$12,900	$12,900
Stockholders' equity			
Common stock	$10,000	$10,000	$10,000
Retained earnings	2,200	2,900	2,200
Unrealized gain on investment securities			700
Total stockholders' equity	$12,200	$12,900	$12,900

Statements of Cash Flows

	Held	Trading	Available
Operating Activities			
Cash inflow from investment revenue	$ 1,600	$ 1,600	$ 1,600
Outflow to purchase securities		(9,000)	
Inflow from sale of securities		2,600	
Investing Activities			
Outflow to purchase securities	(9,000)		(9,000)
Inflow from sale of securities	2,600		2,600
Financing Activities*	0	0	0
Net decrease in cash	(4,800)	(4,800)	(4,800)
Beginning cash balance	10,000	10,000	10,000
Ending cash balance	$ 5,200	$ 5,200	$ 5,200

*The $10,000 of common stock is assumed to have been issued prior to the start of the accounting period.

securities are classified as held to maturity, trading, or available for sale. Exhibit E.1 displays the financial statements for Arapaho under each investment classification alternative.

The net income reported under the trading securities alternative is $700 higher than that reported under the held-to-maturity and available-for-sale alternatives because unrealized gains and losses on trading securities are recognized on the income statement. Similarly, total assets and total stockholders' equity are $700 higher under the trading and available-for-sale alternatives than they are under the held-to-maturity category because the $700 unrealized gain is recognized on the balance sheet for those two classifications. The gain is not reported on the income statement for available-for-sale securities; it is reported on the balance sheet in a special equity account called Unrealized

EXHIBIT E.2

Investment Category	Types of Securities	Types of Revenue Recognized	Reported on Balance Sheet at	Recognition of Unrealized Gains and Losses on the Income Statement	Cash Flow from Purchase or Sale of Securities Classified as
Held to maturity	Debt	Interest	Amortized cost	No	Investing activity
Trading	Debt and equity	Interest and dividends	Market value	Yes	Operating activity
Available for sale	Debt and equity	Interest and dividends	Market value	No	Investing activity

Gain on Investment Securities. The statements of cash flows report purchases and sales of trading securities as operating activities while purchases and sales of available-for-sale and held-to-maturity securities are investing activities. Exhibit E.2 summarizes the reporting differences among the three classifications of investment securities.

Alternative Reporting Practices for Equity Securities

If an investor owns 20 percent or more of an investee's equity securities, the investor is presumed able, unless there is evidence to the contrary, to exercise *significant influence* over the investee company. Investors owning more than 50 percent of the stock of an investee company are assumed to have control over the investee. The previous discussion of accounting rules for equity securities assumed the investor did not significantly influence or control the investee. Alternative accounting rules apply to securities owned by investors who exercise significant influence or control over an investee company. Accounting for equity investment securities differs depending on the level of the investor's ability to influence or control the operating, investing, and financing activities of the investee.

As previously demonstrated, investors who do not have significant influence (they own less than 20 percent of the stock of the investee) account for their investments in equity securities at fair value. Investors exercising significant influence (they own 20 to 50 percent of the investee's stock) must account for their investments using the **equity method.** A detailed discussion of the equity method is beyond the scope of this text. However, *be aware that investments reported using the equity method represent a measure of the book value of the investee rather than the cost or fair value of the equity securities owned.*

Investors that have a controlling interest (they own more than 50 percent of the investee's stock) in an investee company are required to issue **consolidated financial statements.** The company that holds the controlling interest is referred to as the **parent company,** and the company that is controlled is called the **subsidiary company.** Usually, the parent and subsidiary companies maintain separate accounting records. However, a parent company is also required to report to the public its accounting data along with that of its subsidiaries in a single set of combined financial statements. These consolidated statements represent a separate accounting entity consisting of the parent and its subsidiaries. A parent company that owns one subsidiary will produce three sets of financial statements: statements for the parent company, statements for the subsidiary company, and statements for the consolidated entity.

EXERCISES

Exercise E1 *Identifying asset values for financial statements*

Required

Indicate whether each of the following assets should be valued at fair market value (FMV), lower of cost or market (LCM), or historical cost (HC) on the balance sheet. For certain assets, historical cost may be called amortized cost (AC.)

Asset	FMV	LCM	HC/AC
Supplies			
Land			
Trading securities			
Cash			
Held-to-maturity securities			
Buildings			
Available-for-sale securities			
Office equipment			
Inventory			

Exercise E2   *Accounting for investment securities*

Winters Co. purchased $48,000 of marketable securities on March 1, 2013. On the company's fiscal year closing date, December 31, 2013, the securities had a market value of $27,000. During 2013, Winters Co. recognized $12,000 of revenue and $5,000 of expenses.

Required

a. Record a +, −, or NA in a horizontal statements model to show how the purchase of the securities affects the financial statements, assuming that the securities are classified as (1) held to maturity, (2) trading, or (3) available for sale. In the Cash Flow column, indicate whether the event is an operating activity (OA), investing activity (IA), or financing activity (FA). Record only the effects of the purchase event.

Event No.	Type	Cash	+	Inv. Sec.	=	Liab.	+	Equity	Rev.	−	Exp.	=	Net Inc.	Cash Flow
1	Held													
2	Trading													
3	Available													

b. Determine the amount of net income that would be reported on the 2013 income statement, assuming that the marketable securities are classified as (1) held to maturity, (2) trading, or (3) available for sale.

Exercise E3   *Effect of investment securities transactions on financial statements*

The following information pertains to Arnold Supply Co. for 2013:

1. Purchased $200,000 of marketable investment securities.
2. Earned $20,000 of cash investment revenue.
3. Sold for $60,000 securities that cost $50,000.
4. The fair value of the remaining securities at December 31, 2013, was $180,000.

Required

a. Record the four events in a statements model like the following one. Use a separate model for each classification: (1) held to maturity, (2) trading, and (3) available for sale. The first event for the first classification is shown as an example.

Held to Maturity

Event No.	Cash	+	Inv. Sec.	=	Liab.	+	Ret. Earn.	+	Unreal. Gain.	Rev. or Gains	−	Exp. or Loss	=	Net Inc.	Cash Flow
1	(200,000)	+	200,000	=	NA	+	NA	+	NA	NA	−	NA	=	NA	(200,000) IA

b. What is the amount of net income under each of the three classifications?

c. What is the change in cash from operating activities under each of the three classifications?

d. Are the answers to Requirements *b* and *c* different for each of the classifications? Why or why not?

Exercise E4   *Preparing financial statements for investment securities*

Media, Inc., began 2013 with $100,000 in both cash and common stock. The company engaged in the following investment transactions during 2013:

1. Purchased $40,000 of marketable investment securities.
2. Earned $1,200 cash from investment revenue.
3. Sold investment securities for $28,000 that cost $20,000.
4. Purchased $15,000 of additional marketable investment securities.
5. Determined that the investment securities had a fair value of $41,000 at the end of 2013.

Required

Use a vertical statements model to prepare income statements, balance sheets, and statements of cash flow for Media, Inc., assuming the securities were (*a*) held to maturity, (*b*) trading, and (*c*) available for sale.

Exercise E5   *Differences among marketable investment securities classifications*

Complete the following table for the three categories of marketable investment securities:

Investment Category	Types of Securities	Types of Revenue Recognized	Value Reported on Balance Sheet	Recognition of Unrealized Gains and Losses on the Income Statement	Cash Flow from Purchase or Sale of Securities Is Classified as
Held to maturity	Debt	Interest	Amortized cost	No	Investing activity
Trading					
Available for sale					

Exercise E6   *Effect of marketable investment securities transactions on financial statements*

The following transactions pertain to Glass Imports for 2013:

1. Started business by acquiring $50,000 cash from the issue of common stock.
2. Provided $180,000 of services for cash.
3. Invested $70,000 in marketable investment securities.
4. Paid $36,000 of operating expense.
5. Received $1,000 of investment income from the securities.
6. Invested an additional $30,000 in marketable investment securities.
7. Paid a $3,000 cash dividend to the stockholders.
8. Sold investment securities that cost $16,000 for $25,000.
9. Received another $2,000 in investment income.
10. Determined the market value of the investment securities at the end of the year was $81,000.

Required

Use a vertical model to prepare a 2013 income statement, balance sheet, and statement of cash flows, assuming that the marketable investment securities were classified as (a) held to maturity, (b) trading, and (c) available for sale. (*Hint:* Record the events in T-accounts prior to preparing the financial statements.)

Exercise E7   *Comprehensive horizontal statements model*

Cathy's Catering experienced the following independent events:

1. Acquired cash from issuing common stock.
2. Purchased inventory on account.
3. Paid cash to purchase marketable securities classified as trading securities.
4. Recorded unrealized loss on marketable securities that were classified as trading securities.
5. Recorded unrealized loss on marketable securities that were classified as available-for-sale securities.
6. Recorded unrealized loss on marketable securities that were classified as held-to-maturity securities.
7. Wrote down inventory to comply with lower-of-cost-or-market rule. (Assume that the company uses the perpetual inventory system.)
8. Recognized cost of goods sold under FIFO.
9. Recognized cost of goods sold under the weighted-average method.

Required

a. Show the effect of each event on the elements of the financial statements using a horizontal statements model like the following one. Use + for increase, − for decrease, and NA for not affected. In the Cash Flow column, indicate whether the item is an operating activity (OA), investing activity (IA), or financing activity (FA). The first transaction is entered as an example.

Event No.	Assets	=	Liab.	+	Equity	Rev. or Gain	−	Exp. or Loss	=	Net Inc.	Cash Flow
1	+		NA		+	NA		NA		NA	+ FA

b. Explain why there is or is not a difference in the way Events 8 and 9 affect the financial statements model.

Time Value of Money

Future Value

Suppose you recently won $10,000 cash in a local lottery. You save the money to have funds available to obtain a masters of business administration (MBA) degree. You plan to enter the program three years from today. Assuming you invest the money in an account that earns 8 percent annual interest, how much money will you have available in three years? The answer depends on whether your investment will earn *simple* or *compound* interest.

To determine the amount of funds available assuming you earn 8 percent **simple interest,** multiply the principal balance by the interest rate to determine the amount of interest earned per year ($10,000 × 0.08 = $800). Next, multiply the amount of annual interest by the number of years the funds will be invested ($800 × 3 = $2,400). Finally, add the interest earned to the principal balance to determine the total amount of funds available at the end of the three-year term ($10,000 principal + $2,400 interest = $12,400 cash available at the end of three years).

Investors can increase their returns by reinvesting the income earned from their investments. For example, at the beginning of the second year, you will have available for investment not only the original $10,000 principal balance but also $800 of interest earned during the first year. In other words, you will be able to earn interest on the interest that you previously earned. Earning interest on interest is called **compounding.** Assuming you earn 8 percent compound interest, the amount of funds available to you at the end of three years can be computed as shown in Exhibit F.1.

EXHIBIT F.1

Year	Amount Invested	×	Interest Rate	=	Interest Earned	+	Amount Invested	=	New Balance
1	$10,000.00	×	0.08	=	$ 800.00	+	$10,000.00	=	$10,800.00
2	10,800.00	×	0.08	=	864.00	+	10,800.00	=	11,664.00
3	11,664.00	×	0.08	=	933.12	+	11,664.00	=	12,597.12
Total interest earned				=	$2,597.12				

Obviously, you earn more with compound interest ($2,597.12 compound versus $2,400 simple). The computations required for **compound interest** can become cumbersome when the investment term is long. Fortunately, there are mathematical formulas, interest tables, and computer programs that reduce the computational burden. For example, a compound interest factor can be developed from the formula

$$(1 + i)^n$$

where i = interest

        n = number of periods

The value of the investment is determined by multiplying the compound interest factor by the principal balance. The compound interest factor for a three-year term and an 8 percent interest rate is 1.259712 ($1.08 × 1.08 × 1.08 = 1.259712$). Assuming a $10,000 original investment, the value of the investment at the end of three years is

$12,597.12 ($10,000 × 1.259712). This is, of course, the same amount that was computed in the previous illustration (see final figure in the New Balance column of Exhibit F.1).

The mathematical formulas have been used to develop tables of interest factors that can be used to determine the **future value** of an investment for a variety of interest rates and time periods. For example, Table I on page 778 contains the interest factor for an investment with a three-year term earning 8 percent compound interest. To confirm this point, move down the column marked n to the third period. Next move across to the column marked 8 percent, where you will find the value 1.259712. This is identical to the amount computed using the mathematical formula in the preceding paragraph. Here also, the value of the investment at the end of three years can be determined by multiplying the principal balance by the compound interest factor ($10,000 × 1.259712 = $12,597.12). These same factors and amounts can be determined using computer programs in calculators and spreadsheet software.

Clearly, a variety of ways can be used to determine the future value of an investment, given a principal balance, interest rate, and term to maturity. In our case, we showed that your original investment of $10,000 would be worth $12,597 in three years, assuming an 8 percent compound interest rate. Suppose you determine this amount is insufficient to get you through the MBA program you want to complete. Assume you believe you will need $18,000 three years from today to sustain yourself while you finish the degree. Suppose your parents agree to cover the shortfall. They ask how much money you need today in order to have $18,000 three years from now.

Present Value

The mathematical formula required to convert the future value of a dollar to its **present value** equivalent is

$$\frac{1}{(1 + i)^n}$$

where i = interest

n = number of periods

For easy conversion, the formula has been used to develop Table II, Present Value of $1 on page 778. At an 8 percent annual compound interest rate, the present value equivalent of $18,000 to be received three years from today is computed as follows: Move down the far left column to where n = 3. Next, move right to the column marked 8%. At this point, you should see the interest factor 0.793832. Multiplying this factor by the desired future value of $18,000 yields the present value of $14,288.98 ($18,000 × 0.793832). This means if you invest $14,288.98 (present value) today at an annual compound interest rate of 8 percent, you will have the $18,000 (future value) you need to enter the MBA program three years from now.

If you currently have $10,000, you will need an additional $4,288.98 from your parents to make the required $14,288.98 investment that will yield the future value of $18,000 you need. Having $14,288.98 today is the same as having $18,000 three years from today, assuming you can earn 8 percent compound interest. To validate this conclusion, use Table I to determine the future value of $14,288.98, given a three-year term and 8 percent annual compound interest. As previously indicated, the future-value conversion factor under these conditions is 1.259712. Multiplying this factor by the $14,288.98 present value produces the expected future value of $18,000 ($14,288.98 × 1.259712 = $18,000). The factors in Table I can be used to convert present values to future values, and the corresponding factors in Table II are used to convert future values to present values.

Future Value Annuities

The previous examples described present and future values of a single lump-sum payment. Many financial transactions involve a series of payments. To illustrate, we return to the example in which you want to have $18,000 available three years from today. We continue the assumption that you can earn 8 percent compound interest. However, now we assume that you do not have $14,288.98 to invest today. Instead, you decide to save part of the money during each of the next three years. How much money must you save each year to have $18,000 at the end of three years? *The series of equal payments made over a number of periods in order to acquire a future value is called an* **annuity.** The factors in Table III, Future Value of an Annuity of $1, on page 779 can be used to determine the amount of the annuity needed to produce the desired $18,000 future value. The table is constructed so that future values can be determined by multiplying the conversion factor by the amount of the annuity. These relationships can be expressed algebraically as follows:

Amount of annuity payment × Table conversion factor = Future value

To determine the amount of the required annuity payment in our example, first locate the future value conversion factor. In Table III, move down the first column on the left-hand side until you locate period 3. Next move to the right until you locate the 8 percent column. At this location you will see a conversion factor of 3.2464. This factor can be used to determine the amount of the annuity payment as indicated here:

Amount of annuity payment × Table conversion factor = Future value

Amount of annuity payment = Future value ÷ Table conversion factor

Amount of annuity payment = $18,000.00 ÷ 3.2464

Amount of annuity payment = $5,544.60

If you deposit $5,544.60 in an investment account at the end of each of the next three years,[1] the investment account balance will be $18,000, assuming your investment earns 8 percent interest compounded annually. This conclusion is confirmed by the following schedule:

End of Year	Beg. Acct. Bal.	+	Interest Computation	+	Payment	=	End. Acct. Bal.
1	NA	+	NA	+	$5,544.60	=	$ 5,544.60
2	$ 5,544.60	+	$ 5,544.60 × 0.08 = $443.57	+	5,544.60	=	11,532.77
3	11,532.77	+	11,532.77 × 0.08 = 922.62	+	5,544.60	=	18,000.00*

*Total does not add exactly due to rounding.

PRESENT VALUE ANNUITIES

We previously demonstrated that a future value of $18,000 is equivalent to a present value of $14,288.98, given annual compound interest of 8 percent for a three-year period. If the future value of a $5,544.60 annuity for three years is equivalent to $18,000, that same annuity should have a present value of $14,288.98. We can test this conclusion by using the conversion factors in Table IV, Present Value of an Annuity of $1 on page 779. The present value annuity table is constructed so that present values can be determined by multiplying the conversion factor by the amount of the annuity. These relationships can be expressed algebraically as follows:

Amount of annuity payment × Table conversion factor = Present value

To determine the present value of the annuity payment in our example, first locate the present value conversion factor. In Table IV, move down the first column on the left-hand side until you locate period 3. Next move to the right until you locate

[1]A payment made at the end of a period is known as an *ordinary annuity.* A payment made at the beginning of a period is called an *annuity due.* Tables are generally set up to assume ordinary annuities. Minor adjustments must be made when dealing with an annuity due. For the purposes of this text, we consider all annuities to be ordinary.

the column for the 8 percent interest rate. At this location you will see a conversion factor of 2.577097. This factor can be used to determine the amount of the present value of the annuity payment, as indicated:

Amount of annuity payment × Table conversion factor = Present value

$5,544.60   ×   2.577097   = $14,288.97*

*The 1 cent difference between this value and the expected value of $14,288.98 is due to rounding.

In summary, Tables III and IV can be used to convert annuities to future or present values for a variety of different assumptions regarding interest rates and time periods.

BUSINESS APPLICATIONS

Long-Term Notes Payable

In Chapter 10, we considered a case in which Blair Company borrowed $100,000 from National Bank. We indicated that Blair agreed to repay the bank through a series of annual payments (an *annuity*) of $25,709 each. How was this amount determined? Recall that Blair agreed to pay the bank 9 percent interest over a five-year term. Under these circumstances, we are trying to find the annuity equivalent to the $100,000 present value that the bank is loaning Blair. The first step in determining the annuity (annual payment) is to locate the appropriate present value conversion factor from Table IV. At the fifth row under the 9% column, you will find the value 3.889651. This factor can be used to determine the amount of the annuity payment as indicated here:

Amount of annuity payment × Table conversion factor = Present value

Amount of annuity payment = Present value ÷ Table conversion factor

Amount of annuity payment = $100,000 ÷ 3.889651

Amount of annuity payment = $25,709

There are many applications in which debt repayment occurs through annuities. Common examples with which you are probably familiar include auto loans and home mortgages. Payment schedules for such loans may be determined from the interest tables, as demonstrated here. However, most real-world businesses have further refined the computational process through the use of sophisticated computer programs. The software program prompts the user to provide the relevant information regarding the present value of the amount borrowed, number of payments, and interest rate. Given this information and a few keystrokes, the computer program produces the amount of the amortization payment along with an amortization schedule showing the amounts of principal and interest payments over the life of the loan. Similar results can be obtained with a spreadsheet software application such as Excel. Even many handheld calculators have present and future value functions that enable users to quickly compute annuity payments for an infinite number of interest rate and time period assumptions.

Bond Liabilities: Determine Price

We discussed the use of discounts and premiums as means of producing an effective rate of interest that is higher or lower than the stated rate of interest (see Chapter 10). For example, if the stated rate of interest is lower than the market rate of interest at the time the bonds are issued, the issuer can increase the effective interest rate by selling the bonds for a price lower than their face value. At maturity, the issuer will settle the obligation by paying the face value of the bond. The difference between the discounted bond price and the face value of the bond is additional interest. To illustrate, assume that Tower Company issues $100,000 face value bonds with a 20-year term and a 9 percent stated rate of annual interest. At the time the bonds are issued, the market rate of interest for bonds of comparable risk is 10 percent annual interest. For what amount would Tower Company be required to sell the bonds in order to move its 9 percent stated rate of interest to an effective rate of 10 percent?

Information from present value Tables II and IV is required to determine the amount of the discount required to produce a 10 percent effective rate of interest. First, we identify the future cash flows that will be generated by the bonds. Based on the stated interest rate, the bonds will pay $9,000 ($100,000 face value × 0.09 interest) interest per year. This constitutes a 20-year annuity that should be discounted back to its present value equivalent. Also, at the end of 20 years, the bonds will require a single $100,000 lump-sum payment to settle the principal obligation. This amount must also be discounted back to its present value in order to determine the bond price. The computations required to determine the discounted bond price are shown here:

Present value of principal	$100,000 × 0.148644	=	$14,864.40
	(Table II, $n = 20$, $i = 10\%$)		
Present value of interest	$9,000 × 8.513564	=	76,622.08
	(Table IV, $n = 20$, $i = 10\%$)		
Bond price (proceeds received)			$91,486.48

Tower Company bonds sell at an $8,513.52 discount ($100,000 − $91,486.48) to produce a 10 percent effective interest rate. Note that in these computations, the stated rate of interest was used to determine the amount of cash flow, and the effective rate of interest was used to determine the table conversion factors.

TABLE I — Future Value of $1

n	4%	5%	6%	7%	8%	9%	10%	12%	14%	16%	20%
1	1.040000	1.050000	1.060000	1.070000	1.080000	1.090000	1.100000	1.120000	1.140000	1.160000	1.200000
2	1.081600	1.102500	1.123600	1.144900	1.166400	1.188100	1.210000	1.254400	1.299600	1.345600	1.440000
3	1.124864	1.157625	1.191016	1.225043	1.259712	1.295029	1.331000	1.404928	1.481544	1.560896	1.728000
4	1.169859	1.215506	1.262477	1.310796	1.360489	1.411582	1.464100	1.573519	1.688960	1.810639	2.073600
5	1.216653	1.276282	1.338226	1.402552	1.469328	1.538624	1.610510	1.762342	1.925415	2.100342	2.488320
6	1.265319	1.340096	1.418519	1.500730	1.586874	1.677100	1.771561	1.973823	2.194973	2.436396	2.985984
7	1.315932	1.407100	1.503630	1.605781	1.713824	1.828039	1.948717	2.210681	2.502269	2.826220	3.583181
8	1.368569	1.477455	1.593848	1.718186	1.850930	1.992563	2.143589	2.475963	2.852586	3.278415	4.299817
9	1.423312	1.551328	1.689479	1.838459	1.999005	2.171893	2.357948	2.773079	3.251949	3.802961	5.159780
10	1.480244	1.628895	1.790848	1.967151	2.158925	2.367364	2.593742	3.105848	3.707221	4.411435	6.191736
11	1.539454	1.710339	1.898299	2.104852	2.331639	2.580426	2.853117	3.478550	4.226232	5.117265	7.430084
12	1.601032	1.795856	2.012196	2.252192	2.518170	2.812665	3.138428	3.895976	4.817905	5.936027	8.916100
13	1.665074	1.885649	2.132928	2.409845	2.719624	3.065805	3.452271	4.363493	5.492411	6.885791	10.699321
14	1.731676	1.979932	2.260904	2.578534	2.937194	3.341727	3.797498	4.887112	6.261349	7.987518	12.839185
15	1.800944	2.078928	2.396558	2.759032	3.172169	3.642482	4.177248	5.473566	7.137938	9.265521	15.407022
16	1.872981	2.182875	2.540352	2.952164	3.425943	3.970306	4.594973	6.130394	8.137249	10.748004	18.488426
17	1.947900	2.292018	2.692773	3.158815	3.700018	4.327633	5.054470	6.866041	9.276464	12.467685	22.186111
18	2.025817	2.406619	2.854339	3.379932	3.996019	4.717120	5.559917	7.689966	10.575169	14.462514	26.623333
19	2.106849	2.526950	3.025600	3.616528	4.315701	5.141661	6.115909	8.612762	12.055693	16.776517	31.948000
20	2.191123	2.653298	3.207135	3.869684	4.660957	5.604411	6.727500	9.646293	13.743490	19.460759	38.337600

TABLE II — Present Value of $1

n	4%	5%	6%	7%	8%	9%	10%	12%	14%	16%	20%
1	0.961538	0.952381	0.943396	0.934579	0.925926	0.917431	0.909091	0.892857	0.877193	0.862069	0.833333
2	0.924556	0.907029	0.889996	0.873439	0.857339	0.841680	0.826446	0.797194	0.769468	0.743163	0.694444
3	0.888996	0.863838	0.839619	0.816298	0.793832	0.772183	0.751315	0.711780	0.674972	0.640658	0.578704
4	0.854804	0.822702	0.792094	0.762895	0.735030	0.708425	0.683013	0.635518	0.592080	0.552291	0.482253
5	0.821927	0.783526	0.747258	0.712986	0.680583	0.649931	0.620921	0.567427	0.519369	0.476113	0.401878
6	0.790315	0.746215	0.704961	0.666342	0.630170	0.596267	0.564474	0.506631	0.455587	0.410442	0.334898
7	0.759918	0.710681	0.665057	0.622750	0.583490	0.547034	0.513158	0.452349	0.399637	0.353830	0.279082
8	0.730690	0.676839	0.627412	0.582009	0.540269	0.501866	0.466507	0.403883	0.350559	0.305025	0.232568
9	0.702587	0.644609	0.591898	0.543934	0.500249	0.460428	0.424098	0.360610	0.307508	0.262953	0.193807
10	0.675564	0.613913	0.558395	0.508349	0.463193	0.422411	0.385543	0.321973	0.269744	0.226684	0.161506
11	0.649581	0.584679	0.526788	0.475093	0.428883	0.387533	0.350494	0.287476	0.236617	0.195417	0.134588
12	0.624597	0.556837	0.496969	0.444012	0.397114	0.355535	0.318631	0.256675	0.207559	0.168463	0.112157
13	0.600574	0.530321	0.468839	0.414964	0.367698	0.326179	0.289664	0.229174	0.182069	0.145227	0.093464
14	0.577475	0.505068	0.442301	0.387817	0.340461	0.299246	0.263331	0.204620	0.159710	0.125195	0.077887
15	0.555265	0.481017	0.417265	0.362446	0.315242	0.274538	0.239392	0.182696	0.140096	0.107927	0.064905
16	0.533908	0.458112	0.393646	0.338735	0.291890	0.251870	0.217629	0.163122	0.122892	0.093041	0.054088
17	0.513373	0.436297	0.371364	0.316574	0.270269	0.231073	0.197845	0.145644	0.107800	0.080207	0.045073
18	0.493628	0.415521	0.350344	0.295864	0.250249	0.211994	0.179859	0.130040	0.094561	0.069144	0.037561
19	0.474642	0.395734	0.330513	0.276508	0.231712	0.194490	0.163508	0.116107	0.082948	0.059607	0.031301
20	0.456387	0.376889	0.311805	0.258419	0.214548	0.178431	0.148644	0.103667	0.072762	0.051385	0.026084

TABLE III   Future Value of an Annuity of $1

n	4%	5%	6%	7%	8%	9%	10%	12%	14%	16%	20%
1	1.000000	1.000000	1.000000	1.000000	1.000000	1.000000	1.000000	1.000000	1.000000	1.000000	1.000000
2	2.040000	2.050000	2.060000	2.070000	2.080000	2.090000	2.100000	2.120000	2.140000	2.160000	2.200000
3	3.121600	3.152500	3.183600	3.214900	3.246400	3.278100	3.310000	3.374400	3.439600	3.505600	3.640000
4	4.246464	4.310125	4.374616	4.439943	4.506112	4.573129	4.641000	4.779328	4.921144	5.066496	5.368000
5	5.416323	5.525631	5.637093	5.750739	5.866601	5.984711	6.105100	6.352847	6.610104	6.877135	7.441600
6	6.632975	6.801913	6.975319	7.153291	7.335929	7.523335	7.715610	8.115189	8.535519	8.977477	9.929920
7	7.898294	8.142008	8.393838	8.654021	8.922803	9.200435	9.487171	10.089012	10.730491	11.413873	12.915904
8	9.214226	9.549109	9.897468	10.259803	10.636628	11.028474	11.435888	12.299693	13.232760	14.240093	16.499085
9	10.582795	11.026564	11.491316	11.977989	12.487558	13.021036	13.579477	14.775656	16.085347	17.518508	20.798902
10	12.006107	12.577893	13.180795	13.816448	14.486562	15.192930	15.937425	17.548735	19.337295	21.321469	25.958682
11	13.486351	14.206787	14.971643	15.783599	16.645487	17.560293	18.531167	20.654583	23.044516	25.732904	32.150419
12	15.025805	15.917127	16.869941	17.888451	18.977126	20.140720	21.384284	24.133133	27.270749	30.850169	39.580502
13	16.626838	17.712983	18.882138	20.140643	21.495297	22.953385	24.522712	28.029109	32.088654	36.786196	48.496603
14	18.291911	19.598632	21.015066	22.550488	24.214920	26.019189	27.974983	32.392602	37.581065	43.671987	59.195923
15	20.023588	21.578564	23.275970	25.129022	27.152114	29.360916	31.772482	37.279715	43.842414	51.659505	72.035108
16	21.824531	23.657492	25.672528	27.888054	30.324283	33.003399	35.949730	42.753280	50.980352	60.925026	87.442129
17	23.697512	25.840366	28.212880	30.840217	33.750226	36.973705	40.544703	48.883674	59.117601	71.673030	105.930555
18	25.645413	28.132385	30.905653	33.999033	37.450244	41.301338	45.599173	55.749715	68.394066	84.140715	128.116666
19	27.671229	30.539004	33.759992	37.378965	41.446263	46.018458	51.159090	63.439681	78.969235	98.603230	154.740000
20	29.778079	33.065954	36.785591	40.995492	45.761964	51.160120	57.274999	72.052442	91.024928	115.379747	186.688000

TABLE IV   Present Value of an Annuity of $1

n	4%	5%	6%	7%	8%	9%	10%	12%	14%	16%	20%
1	0.961538	0.952381	0.943396	0.934579	0.925926	0.917431	0.909091	0.892857	0.877193	0.862069	0.833333
2	1.886095	1.859410	1.833393	1.808018	1.783265	1.759111	1.735537	1.690051	1.646661	1.605232	1.527778
3	2.775091	2.723248	2.673012	2.624316	2.577097	2.531295	2.486852	2.401831	2.321632	2.245890	2.106481
4	3.629895	3.545951	3.465106	3.387211	3.312127	3.239720	3.169865	3.037349	2.913712	2.798181	2.588735
5	4.451822	4.329477	4.212364	4.100197	3.992710	3.889651	3.790787	3.604776	3.433081	3.274294	2.990612
6	5.242137	5.075692	4.917324	4.766540	4.622880	4.485919	4.355261	4.111407	3.888668	3.684736	3.325510
7	6.002055	5.786373	5.582381	5.389289	5.206370	5.032953	4.868419	4.563757	4.288305	4.038565	3.604592
8	6.732745	6.463213	6.209794	5.971299	5.746639	5.534819	5.334926	4.967640	4.638864	4.343591	3.837160
9	7.435332	7.107822	6.801692	6.515232	6.246888	5.995247	5.759024	5.328250	4.946372	4.606544	4.030967
10	8.110896	7.721735	7.360087	7.023582	6.710081	6.417658	6.144567	5.650223	5.216116	4.833227	4.192472
11	8.760477	8.306414	7.886875	7.498674	7.138964	6.805191	6.495061	5.937699	5.452733	5.028644	4.327060
12	9.385074	8.863252	8.383844	7.942686	7.536078	7.160725	6.813692	6.194374	5.660292	5.197107	4.439217
13	9.985648	9.393573	8.852683	8.357651	7.903776	7.486904	7.103356	6.423548	5.842362	5.342334	4.532681
14	10.563123	9.898641	9.294984	8.745468	8.244237	7.786150	7.366687	6.628168	6.002072	5.467529	4.610567
15	11.118387	10.379658	9.712249	9.107914	8.559479	8.060688	7.606080	6.810864	6.142168	5.575456	4.675473
16	11.652296	10.837770	10.105895	9.446649	8.851369	8.312558	7.823709	6.973986	6.265060	5.668497	4.729561
17	12.165669	11.274066	10.477260	9.763223	9.121638	8.543631	8.021553	7.119630	6.372859	5.748704	4.774634
18	12.659297	11.689587	10.827603	10.059087	9.371887	8.755625	8.201412	7.249670	6.467420	5.817848	4.812195
19	13.133939	12.085321	11.158116	10.335595	9.603599	8.905115	8.364920	7.365777	6.550369	5.877455	4.843496
20	13.590326	12.462210	11.469921	10.594014	9.818147	9.128546	8.513564	7.469444	6.623131	5.928841	4.869580

EXERCISES

Exercise F1   *Future value and present value*

Required

Using Tables I, II, III, or IV in this appendix, calculate the following:

a. The future value of $60,000 invested at 8 percent for 10 years.

b. The future value of eight annual payments of $4,000 at 9 percent interest.

c. The amount that must be deposited today (present value) at 8 percent to accumulate $100,000 in five years.

d. The annual payment on a 10-year, 6 percent, $60,000 note payable.

Exercise F2   *Computing the payment amount*

June Money is a business major at State U. She will be graduating this year and is planning to start a consulting business. She will need to purchase computer equipment that costs $35,000. She can borrow the money from the local bank but will have to make annual payments of principal and interest.

Required

a. Compute the annual payment June will be required to make on a $35,000, four-year, 8 percent loan.

b. If June can afford to make annual payments of $9,000, how much can she borrow?

Exercise F3   *Saving for a future value*

John and Jane were recently married and want to start saving for their dream home. They expect the house they want will cost approximately $275,000. They hope to be able to purchase the house for cash in 10 years.

Required

a. How much will John and Jane have to invest each year to purchase their dream home at the end of 10 years? Assume an interest rate of 9 percent.

b. John's parents want to give the couple a substantial wedding gift for the purchase of their future home. How much must John's parents give them now if they are to have desired amount of $275,000 in 12 years? Assume an interest rate of 9 percent.

Exercise F4   *Sale of bonds at a discount using present value*

Zolf Corporation issued $60,000 of 6 percent, 10-year bonds on January 1, 2013, for a price that reflected a 7 percent market rate of interest. Interest is payable annually on December 31.

Required

a. What was the selling price of the bonds?

b. Prepare the journal entry to record issuing the bonds.

c. Prepare the journal entry for the first interest payment on December 31, 2013, using the effective interest rate method.

absolute amounts Dollar totals reported in accounts on financial reports that can be misleading because they make no reference to the relative size of the company being analyzed. *p. 13-3*

accelerated depreciation method Depreciation method that recognizes more depreciation expense in the early stages of an asset's life than the straight-line method and less later in the asset's life. *p. 425*

account Record of classified and summarized transaction data; component of financial statement elements. *p. 11*

account balance Difference between total debit and total credit amounts in an account. *p. 140*

accounting Service-based profession developed to provide reliable and relevant financial information useful in making decisions. *p. 3*

accounting controls Procedures companies implement to safeguard assets and to ensure accurate and reliable accounting records and reports. *p. 313*

accounting cycle For a given time period, the cycle of recording accounting data, adjusting the accounts, preparing the financial statements, and closing the temporary accounts; when one accounting cycle ends, a new one begins.

accounting equation Algebraic relationship between a company's assets and the claims on those assets, represented as Assets = Liabilities + Equity. *p. 13*

accounting event Economic occurrence that changes a company's assets, liabilities, or equity. *p. 14*

accounting period Time span covered by the financial statements; normally one year, but may be a quarter, a month or some other time interval. *p. 20*

accounts payable A liability account that represents the business's obligation to pay cash for operating expenses sometime in the future.

accounts receivable Expected future cash receipts arising from permitting customers to *buy now and pay later;* typically relatively small balances due within a short time period. *pp. 65, 360*

accounts receivable turnover Financial ratio that measures how fast accounts receivable are collected in cash; computed by dividing sales by accounts receivable. *pp. 360, 13-9*

accrual Accounting recognition of revenue or expense in a period before cash is exchanged. *p. 64*

accrual accounting Accounting system which recognizes revenues when earned and expenses when incurred regardless of when the related cash is exchanged. *p. 63*

Accumulated Depreciation Contra asset account that shows the sum of all depreciation expense recognized for an asset since the date of acquisition. *p. 422*

accrued expenses Expenses that are recognized before cash is paid. An example is accrued salaries expense. *p. 66*

accrued interest Interest revenue or expense that is recognized before cash has been exchanged. *p. 375*

acid-test ratio Measure of immediate debt-paying ability; calculated by dividing very liquid assets (cash, receivables, and marketable securities) by current liabilities. *p. 13-9*

adjusting entry Entry that updates account balances prior to preparing financial statements; a bookkeeping tool. Adjusting entries never affect the Cash account. *pp. 66, 375*

administrative controls Procedures companies implement to evaluate performance and monitor compliance with company policies and public laws. *p. 313*

adverse opinion Opinion issued by a certified public accountant that means one or more departures from GAAP in a company's financial statements are so very material the auditors believe the financial statements do not fairly represent the company's status; contrast with *unqualified opinion. p. 331*

aging of accounts receivable Classifying each account receivable by the number of days it has been outstanding. The purpose of the aging schedule is to develop a more accurate estimate of the amount of uncollectible accounts. *p. 370*

allocation Recognizing expense by systematically assigning the cost of an asset to periods of use.

Allowance for Doubtful Accounts Contra asset account used to record the amount of accounts receivable estimated to be uncollectible. *p. 362*

allowance method of accounting for uncollectible accounts An accounting practice that recognizes an estimated rather than the actual amount of uncollectible accounts expense. Estimated expenses are used to improve matching of revenues and expenses and/or to more accurately reflect the net realizable value of accounts receivable. *p. 362*

allowances Reductions in the selling price of goods extended to buyers because the goods are defective or of lower quality than the buyer ordered to encourage a buyer to keep merchandise that would otherwise be returned.

American Institute of Certified Public Accountants (AICPA) National association that serves the educational and professional interests of members of the public accounting profession; membership is voluntary. See also *Code of Professional Conduct. p. 85*

amortization (1) Systematic and periodic allocation of the costs of intangible assets to expense over their useful lives; (2) periodically transferring the discount on a note or a bond to interest expense. *pp. 418, 535*

amortization (of loan) Systematic repayment of principal and interest over the life of a loan. *p. 535*

amortizing Systematically allocating the cost of intangible assets to expense over their useful lives; also a term for converting the discount on a note or a bond to interest expense over a designated period. *p. 499*

annual report Document companies publish to provide information, including financial statements, to stockholders. *p. 26*

annuity Series of equal cash flows received or paid over equal time intervals at a constant rate of return. *p. 775*

appropriated retained earnings Retained earnings restricted by the board of directors for a specific purpose (e.g., to repay debt or for future expansion); part of total retained earnings, but not available for distribution as dividends. *p. 608*

articles of incorporation Information about a proposed corporation, such as its name, purpose, location, expected life, proposed capital stock, and a list of the members of its board of directors, filed with a state agency when applying for the legal formation of the corporation. *p. 594*

articulation   Characteristic of financial statements that means they are interrelated. For example, the amount of net income reported on the income statement is added to beginning retained earnings as a component in calculating the ending retained earnings balance reported on the statement of changes in stockholders' equity. *p. 20*

asset   Economic resource used to produce revenue which is expected to provide future benefit to the business. *p. 4*

asset exchange transaction   A transaction, such as the purchase of land with cash, that decreases one asset and increases another asset; total assets remain unchanged. *pp. 16, 65*

asset source transaction   A transaction that increases both an asset and a claim on assets; the three types of asset source transactions are acquisitions from owners (equity), borrowings from creditors (liabilities), or earnings from operations (revenues). *pp. 15, 64*

asset turnover ratio   The amount of net sales divided by average total assets. *pp. 13-14*

asset use transaction   A transaction that decreases both an asset and a claim on assets; the three types of asset use transactions are distributions (transfers to owners), liability payments (to creditors), or expenses (costs incurred to operate the business). *pp. 16, 65*

audit   Detailed examination of some aspect of a company's accounting records or operating procedures in order to report the results to interested parties. See *financial audit. p. 330*

authority manual   Written documentation outlining levels of authority and responsibility. The authority manual provides specific guidelines such as those for a personnel officer as well as general guidelines such as giving all vice presidents authorization to approve up to a designated spending limit. *p. 316*

authorized stock   Number of shares of stock a corporation has state approval to issue. *p. 599*

available-for-sale securities   Classification for marketable securities that are not considered held-to-maturity or trading securities. *p. 765*

average days to collect accounts receivable (average collection period)   Measure of how quickly, on average, a business collects its accounts receivable; calculated as 365 divided by the accounts receivable turnover. *pp. 380, 13-10*

average days to sell inventory (average days in inventory)   Financial ratio that measures the average number of days that inventory stays in stock before it is sold. *pp. 284, 13-10*

balance sheet   Financial statement that reports a company's assets and the corresponding claims (liabilities and equity) on those assets as of a specific date (usually as of the end of the accounting period). *p. 22*

bank reconciliation   Schedule that identifies and explains differences between the cash balance reported by the bank and the cash balance in the company's accounting records. *p. 321*

bank statement   Record issued by a bank (usually monthly) of all activity in the bank account for that period. *p. 320*

bank statement credit memo   Bank statement enclosure that describes an increase in the account balance. *p. 320*

bank statement debit memo   Bank statement enclosure that describes a decrease in the account balance. *p. 317*

basket purchase   Acquiring several assets at once for a single purchase price; no specific cost is attributed to the individual assets. *p. 419*

board of directors   Group of individuals elected by the stockholders of a corporation to oversee its operations. *p. 596*

bond certificate   Debt security used to obtain long-term financing in which a company borrows funds from a number of lenders, called *bondholders;* usually issued in denominations of $1,000. *p. 539*

bond discount   Difference between the selling price and the face amount of a bond sold for less than the face amount. *p. 547*

bondholder   The party buying a bond (the lender or creditor). *p. 539*

bond premium   Difference between the selling price and the face amount of a bond that is sold for more than the face amount. *p. 551*

book of original entry   A journal in which a transaction is first recorded. *p. 150*

book value   Historical (original) cost of an asset minus accumulated depreciation to date. *p. 422*

book value per share   An accounting measure of a share of common stock, computed by dividing total stockholders' equity less preferred rights by the number of common shares outstanding. *pp. 599, 13-16*

call premium   Difference between the call price (the price that must be paid for a called bond) and the face amount of the bond. *p. 542*

call price   Specified price an issuer must pay to call bonds; usually higher than the face amount of the bonds. *p. 542*

callable bonds   Bonds which the issuer, at its option, may pay off prior to maturity. *p. 542*

capital expenditures (for an existing asset)   Substantial amounts spent to improve an asset's quality or to extend its life. *p. 432*

capitalized   Initially recorded an expenditure in an asset account for subsequent transfer to expense as the asset is used to produce revenue.

carrying value   Face amount of a bond liability less any unamortized bond discount or plus any unamortized bond premium. *pp. 422, 547*

cash   Coins, currency, checks, balances in checking and certain savings accounts, money orders, bank drafts, certificates of deposit, and other items that are payable on demand. *p. 317*

cash discount   Price reduction on merchandise sold offered by sellers to encourage prompt payment; when taken, represents a sales discount to the seller and a purchase discount to the buyer of the merchandise. *p. 216*

cash inflows   Sources of cash. *p. 640*

cash outflows   Uses of cash. *p. 640*

Cash Short and Over   Account used to record the amount of cash shortages or overages; shortages represent expenses and overages represent revenues. *p. 326*

certified check   Check guaranteed by a bank to be drawn on an account with sufficient funds to pay the check. *p. 323*

certified public accountant (CPA)   Accountant who, by meeting certain educational and experiential requirements, is licensed by the state government to provide audit services to the public. *p. 330*

chart of accounts   List of all ledger accounts and their corresponding account numbers. *p. 151*

checks   Prenumbered forms, sometimes multicopy, preprinted on the face with the name of the business issuing them, authorizing the bank to disburse funds from the issuer's account. The issuer enters the transaction date, the desired payee, and the amount in the appropriate places on the check form. *p. 320*

claims   Owners' and creditors' interests in a business's assets. *p. 12*

claims exchange transaction   A transaction that decreases one claim and increases another claim; total claims remain unchanged. For example, accruing interest expense is a claims exchange transaction; liabilities increase, and the expense recognition decreases retained earnings. *p. 67*

classified balance sheet Balance sheet that distinguishes between current and noncurrent items. *p. 494*

closely held corporation Corporation whose stock is exchanged among a limited number of individuals. *p. 594*

closing the books or **closing** Bookkeeping technique of transferring balances from the temporary accounts (Revenue, Expense, and Dividends) to the permanent account (Retained Earnings). *p. 24*

closing entries Entries that transfer the balances in the temporary accounts (Revenue, Expense, and Dividends accounts) to the Retained Earnings account at the end of the accounting period. *p. 155*

Code of Professional Conduct Guidelines established by the American Institute of Certified Public Accountants (AICPA) to promote ethical conduct among certified public accountants; AICPA members agree to adhere to this code, which goes beyond legal requirements. *p. 85*

collateral Assets pledged as security for a loan. *pp. 374, 543*

common size financial statements Financial statements in which dollar amounts are converted to percentages to aid in comparing financial data among periods and among companies. *p. 228*

common stock Basic class of corporate stock that has no preferential claim on assets or dividends; certificates that evidence ownership in a company. *pp. 12, 600*

compound interest Interest earned on interest by reinvesting interest so that it is added to the initial principal. Contrast with *simple interest*. *p. 747*

compounding Earning interest on interest. *p. 747*

confidentiality Code of ethics requirement that prohibits CPAs from voluntarily disclosing information they acquire as a result of accountant-client relationships. *p. 332*

conservatism A principle that guides accountants in uncertain circumstances to select the alternative that produces the lowest amount of net income. *p. 72*

consistency The generally accepted accounting principle that a company should, in most circumstances, continually use the same accounting method(s) so that its financial statements are comparable across time. *p. 275*

consolidated financial statements Financial statements that represent the combined operations of a parent company and its subsidiaries. *p. 769*

contingent liability Obligations with amounts due that depend on events that will be resolved in the future. *p. 481*

continuity Presumption that a corporation's existence may extend well beyond the time at which any particular shareholder retires or sells his or her stock. *p. 596*

contra account Account with a normal balance opposite that of other accounts in the same category (e.g., Accumulated Depreciation is classified as an asset, but it normally has a credit balance).

contra asset account Account used to reduce the reported value of the asset to which it relates; e.g., subtracting the contra asset Allowance for Bad Debts from Accounts Receivable reduces receivables to their net realizable value. *pp. 364, 422*

contra liability account Account used to reduce the reported value of the liability to which it relates; e.g., subtracting the contra liability Discount on Note Payable from Notes Payable reduces the amount of liabilities on the balance sheet. *p. 498*

contributed capital The claim on assets resulting from asset contributions to a business by its owners.

convertible bonds Bonds which bondholders can convert (exchange) to ownership interests (stock) in the corporation. *p. 542*

copyright Legal protection of writings, musical compositions, and other intellectual property for the exclusive use of the creator or persons assigned the right by the creator. *p. 436*

corporation Legal entity separate from its owners, created by the state pursuant to an application submitted according to state laws by a group of individuals with a common purpose. *p. 594*

cost An amount paid to acquire a resource (asset) or to pay for a resource that has been consumed. Incurring a cost results in an asset exchange or expense recognition. *p. 73*

cost method of accounting for treasury stock Method of accounting for treasury stock in which treasury stock purchases are recorded in the Treasury Stock account at their cost to the company without regard to the original issue price or par value. *p. 604*

cost of goods available for sale Total costs paid to obtain goods and ready them for sale, including the cost of beginning inventory plus purchases and transportation-in costs, less purchase returns and allowances and purchase discounts. *p. 210*

cost of goods sold Total cost incurred for the goods sold during a specific accounting period. *p. 210*

credit Entry on the right side of an account; increases liability and equity accounts or decreases asset accounts. *p. 140*

creditor Individual or organization that has loaned goods or services to a business. *p. 4*

cumulative dividends Preferred dividends that accumulate from year to year until paid. *p. 600*

current (short-term) asset Asset that will be converted to cash or consumed within one year or an operating cycle, whichever is longer. *pp. 416, 493*

current (short-term) liability Obligation due within one year or an operating cycle, whichever is longer. *p. 493*

current ratio (working capital ratio) Measure of liquidity; calculated by dividing current assets by current liabilities. *pp. 495, 13-8*

date of record Date that establishes who will receive the dividend payment: shareholders who actually own the stock on the record date will receive the dividend even if they sell the stock before the dividend is paid. *p. 605*

debenture Unsecured bond backed by the general credit of the issuing company. *p. 541*

debit Entry on the left side of an account; increases asset accounts or decreases liability and equity accounts. *p. 140*

debt security Type of financial instrument that represents a liability to the investee company. *p. 764*

debt to assets ratio Financial measure of a company's level of risk, calculated as total debt divided by total assets. *pp. 158, 13-11*

debt to equity ratio Financial ratio that compares creditor financing to owner financing, expressed as the dollar amount of liabilities for each dollar of stockholder's equity. *p. 13-11*

declaration date Date on which the board of directors declares a dividend. *p. 605*

deferral Accounting recognition of revenue or expense in a period after cash is exchanged. *p. 64*

deferred tax liability Income tax payment postponed until future years because of the difference in accounting methods selected for financial reporting and methods required for tax purposes (e.g., a company may use straight-line depreciation in financial statements but use MACRS for tax reporting). *p. 431*

depletion The removal of natural resources from the land; the depletion costs of the natural resources are systematically transferred to expense as the resources are removed. *p. 418*

deposit ticket   Bank form submitted along with funds that identifies the account number, account name, and a record of the checks and cash being put in the account. *p. 320*

deposits in transit   Deposits added to a depositor's books but not received and recorded by the bank prior to the date of the bank statement. *p. 322*

depreciable cost   Original cost minus salvage value (of a long-term depreciable asset). *p. 420*

depreciation   Decline in value of long-term tangible assets such as buildings, furniture, or equipment. It is systematically recognized by accountants as depreciation expense over the useful lives of the affected assets. *p. 418*

depreciation expense   Portion of the original cost of a long-term tangible asset allocated to an expense account in a given period. *pp. 69, 420*

direct method   Method of reporting cash flows from operating activities on the statement of cash flows that shows individual categories of cash receipts from and cash payments for major activities (collections from customers, payments to suppliers, etc.). *p. 420*

direct write-off method   Accounting practice of recognizing uncollectible accounts expense when accounts are determined to be uncollectible, regardless of the period in which the related sale occurred. *p. 372*

disclaimer of opinion   Report on financial statements issued when the auditor is unable to obtain enough information to determine if the statements conform to GAAP; is neither positive nor negative. *p. 331*

discount   Amount of interest included in the face of a discount note; the discount (interest) is subtracted from the face amount of the note to determine the amount of cash borrowed (principal). *p. 497*

discount note   Note with interest included in its face value, which is also the maturity value. *p. 497*

Discount on Bonds Payable   Contra liability account used to record the amount of discount on a bond issue. *p. 547*

Discount on Notes Payable   Contra liability account subtracted from the Notes Payable account to determine the carrying value of the liability. *p. 498*

dividend   Transfer of wealth from a business to its owners. *pp. 17, 766*

dividend yield   Ratio for comparing stock dividends paid in relation to the market price; calculated as dividends per share divided by market price per share. *p. 13-17*

dividends in arrears   Cumulative dividends on preferred stock that were not paid in prior periods; must be paid before paying any dividends to holders of common stock. *p. 600*

double taxation   Recognition that corporate profits distributed to owners are taxed twice, once when the income is reported on the corporation's income tax return and again when the dividends are reported on the individual's return. *p. 573*

double-declining-balance depreciation   Depreciation computations that produce larger amounts of depreciation in the early years of an asset's life and progressively smaller amounts as the asset ages. *p. 425*

double-entry accounting (double-entry bookkeeping)   Recordkeeping system that provides checks and balances by recording two sides for every transaction. *p. 15*

earnings (net income)   The difference between revenues and expenses. Sometimes called *profit*. *p. 4*

earnings per share   Measure of the value of a share of common stock in terms of company earnings; calculated as net income available to common stockholders divided by the average number of outstanding common shares. *p. 13-17*

effective interest rate   Yield rate of bonds, equal to the market rate of interest on the day the bonds are sold. *p. 547*

effective interest rate method   Method of amortizing bond discounts and premiums that bases interest computations on the carrying value of liability. As the liability increases or decreases, the amount of interest expense also increases or decreases. *p. 54*

elements   The primary financial statement categories: assets, liabilities, equity, contributed capital, revenue, expenses, gains, losses, distributions, and net income. *p. 11*

employee   An individual whose labor is supervised, directed, and controlled by a business. *p. 485*

Employee's Withholding Allowance Certificate, Form W-4   A form used by an employee to report the number of withholding allowances claimed by the employee. Each withholding allowance reduces the amount of income tax withheld from the employee's pay. *p. 487*

Employer's Quarterly Federal Tax Return, Form 941   The form used to show the amounts due and paid to the government for federal tax withholdings. *p. 488*

entity   Economic unit (individual, business, or other organization) for which accounting records are separately maintained; it is distinct from its owners, creditors, managers, and employees.

equity method   Method of accounting for investments in marketable equity securities required when the investor company owns 20 percent or more of the investee company. Under the equity method, the amount of the investment asset represents a measure of the book value of the investee rather than the cost or market value of the investment security. *p. 769*

equity security   Type of financial instrument that evidences an ownership interest in a company, such as a common stock certificate. *p. 764*

estimated useful life   Time period for which a business expects to use an asset. *p. 420*

ex-dividend   Stock traded after the date of record but before the payment date; does not receive the benefit of the upcoming dividend. *p. 605*

expense   An economic sacrifice (decrease in assets or increase in liabilities) that is incurred in the process of generating revenue. *pp. 16, 84*

expense transactions   Business events that decrease assets or increase liabilities in order to produce revenue in the course of operating a business.

face value (of bond)   Amount to be paid to the bondholder at bond maturity; base for computing periodic cash interest payments. *p. 539*

fair value   The price at which securities or other assets sell in free markets. Also called market value. *p. 764*

Federal Unemployment Tax Act (FUTA)   The act that requires employers to pay unemployment tax for the establishment of a fund that is used to provide temporary relief to qualified unemployed persons. *p. 491*

fidelity bond   Insurance policy that a company buys to insure itself against loss due to employee dishonesty. *p. 315*

financial accounting   Branch of accounting focused on the business information needs of external users (creditors, investors, governmental agencies, financial analysts, etc.); its objective is to classify and record business events and transactions to produce external financial reports (income statement, balance sheet, statement of cash flows, and statement of changes in equity). *p. 6*

Financial Accounting Standards Board (FASB)   Private, independent standard-setting body established by the accounting profession that has been delegated the authority by the SEC to establish most of the accounting rules and regulations for public financial reporting. *p. 8*

financial statements audit   Detailed examination of a company's accounting records and the documents that support the information reported in the financial statements; includes testing the reliability of the underlying accounting system used to produce the financial reports. *p. 330*

financial leverage   Principle of increasing earnings through debt financing by investing money at a higher rate than the rate paid on the borrowed money. *pp. 158, 557*

financial resources   Money or credit supplied to a business by investors (owners) and creditors. *p. 4*

financial statements   Reports used to communicate a company's financial information to interested external parties. The four general-purpose financial statements are the income statement, statement of changes in equity, balance sheet, and statement of cash flows. *p. 11*

financing activities   Cash inflows and outflows from transactions with investors and creditors (except interest), including cash receipts from issuing stock, borrowing activities, and cash disbursements to pay dividends; one of the three categories of cash inflows and outflows reported on the statement of cash flows. This category shows the amount of cash supplied by these resource providers and the amount of cash that is returned to them. *pp. 23, 643*

first-in, first-out (FIFO) cost flow method   Inventory cost flow method in which cost of goods sold is computed as if the earliest items purchased are the first items sold. *p. 270*

fiscal year   The annual time period for which a company provides financial statements. *p. 139*

fixed interest rate   Interest rate (charge for borrowing money) that remains constant over the life of the loan. *p. 534*

FOB (free on board) destination   Shipping term that means the seller bears the freight (transportation-in) costs. *p. 210*

FOB (free on board) shipping point   Shipping term that means the buyer bears the freight (transportation-in) costs. *p. 217*

franchise   Exclusive right to sell products or perform services in certain geographic areas. *p. 437*

fraud triangle   A graphic that shows the common features of criminal and ethical misconduct with *opportunity* shown at the head of a triangle and *pressure* and *rationalization* shown at the base.

full disclosure   The accounting principle that financial statements should include all information relevant to an entity's operations and financial condition. Full disclosure frequently requires adding footnotes to the financial statements. *p. 275*

future value   Amount an investment will be worth at some point in the future, assuming a specified interest rate and the reinvestment of interest each period that it is earned. *p. 774*

gains   Increases in assets or decreases in liabilities that result from peripheral or incidental transactions. *pp. 220, 423*

general authority   Company guidelines that apply to various levels of a company's management, such as requiring everyone at that level to fly coach class. *p. 316*

general journal   Book of original entry in which any accounting transaction could be recorded, though commonly limited to adjusting and closing entries and unusual transactions. *p. 150*

general ledger   The set of all accounts used in given accounting system, typically organized in financial statement order. *pp. 18, 151*

general uncertainties   Uncertainties such as competition and damage from storms. These uncertainties are distinguished from contingent liabilities because they arise from future rather than past events. *p. 481*

generally accepted accounting principles (GAAP)   Rules and practices that accountants agree to follow in financial reports prepared for public distribution. *p. 8*

going concern assumption   Accounting presumption that a company will continue to operate indefinitely, benefiting from its assets and paying its obligations in full; justifies reporting assets and liabilities in the financial statements. *pp. 14, 476*

goodwill   Intangible added value of a successful business attributable to such factors as reputation, location, and superior products that enables the business to earn above-average profits; measured by an entity acquiring the business as the excess paid over the appraised value of the net assets. *p. 437*

gross earnings   The total amount of employee wages or salaries before any deductions or withholdings. Gross earnings include the total of regular pay plus any bonuses, overtime, or other additions. *p. 486*

gross margin (gross profit)   Difference between sales revenue and cost of goods sold; the amount a company makes from selling goods before subtracting operating expenses. *p. 210*

gross margin method   Technique for estimating the ending inventory amount without a physical count; useful when the percentage of gross margin to sales remains relatively stable from one accounting period to the next. *p. 210*

gross margin percentage   Expressing gross margin as a percentage of sales by dividing gross margin by net sales; the amount of each dollar of sales that is profit before deducting any operating expenses. *p. 229*

half-year convention   Tax rule that requires recognizing six months of depreciation expense on an asset both in the year of purchase and in the year of disposal regardless of the actual purchase date. *p. 430*

held-to-maturity securities   Classification for marketable debt securities the purchasing company intends to hold (rather than sell) until the securities mature. *p. 765*

historical cost concept   Accounting practice of reporting assets at the actual price paid for them when purchased regardless of estimated changes in market value. *pp. 17, 419*

horizontal analysis   Analysis technique that compares amounts of the same item over several time periods. *p. 13-3*

horizontal statements model   Concurrent representation of several financial statements horizontally across a page. *p. 25*

imprest basis   Maintaining an account at a specified fixed amount, such as periodically replenishing a petty cash fund to its imprest amount. *p. 327*

income   Increase in value created by providing goods and services through resource transformation. *p. 4*

income statement   Financial report of profitability; measures the difference between revenues and expenses for the accounting period (whether or not cash has been exchanged). *p. 20*

independent auditor   Licensed certified public accountant engaged to audit a company's financial statements; not an employee of the audited company. *p. 336*

independent contractor   An individual who is paid by a business but retains individual control and supervisory authority over the work performed. *p. 485*

indirect method   Method of reporting cash flows from operating activities on the statement of cash flows that starts with the net income from the income statement, followed by adjustments necessary to convert accrual-based net income to a cash-basis equivalent. *p. 642*

information overload   Situation in which presentation of too much information confuses the user of the information. *p. 13-2*

installment notes   Obligations that require regular payments of principal and interest over the life of the loan. *p. 536*

intangible assets   Long-term assets having no physical substance that benefit their owners through providing rights and privileges, such as a trademark. *p. 418*

interest   Fee paid for the use of funds; represents expense to the borrower and revenue to the lender. *pp. 4, 374, 766*

interest-bearing notes   Notes that require face value plus accrued interest be paid at maturity. *p. 497*

internal controls   Policies and procedures companies establish to provide reasonable assurance of reducing fraud, providing reliable accounting records, and accomplishing organization objectives. *pp. 86, 312*

International Accounting Standards Board (IASB)   Private, independent body that establishes International Financial Reporting Standards (IFRS). The IASB's authority is established by various governmental institutions that require or permit companies in their jurisdiction to use IFRS. To date, over 100 countries require or permit companies to prepare their financial statements using IFRS. One notable exception is the United States of America. *p. 9*

International Financial Reporting Standards (IFRS)   Pronouncement established by the International Accounting Standards Board that provide guidance for the preparation of financial statements. *p. 9*

inventory   Goods under production or finished and ready for sale; also stockpiles of supplies used in the business (office supplies, cleaning supplies).

inventory cost flow methods   Alternative ways to allocate the cost of goods available for sale between cost of goods sold and ending inventory. *p. 272*

inventory turnover   A measure of sales volume relative to inventory levels; calculated as the cost of goods sold divided by average inventory; indicates how many times a year, on average, the inventory is sold (turned over). *pp. 10, 284*

investee   Company that receives assets or services in exchange for a debt or equity security. *p. 764*

investing activities   Cash inflows and outflows associated with buying or selling long-term assets and cash inflows and outflows associated with lending activities and investments in the debt and equity of other companies; one of the three categories of cash inflows and outflows reported on the statement of cash flows. *pp. 23, 643*

investment   Commitment of assets (usually cash) by a business to acquire other assets that will be used to produce revenue.

investment securities   Certificates that describe the rights and privileges that investors receive when they loan or give assets or services to investees. *p. 764*

investor   Company or individual who gives assets or services in exchange for security certificates representing ownership interests. *pp. 4, 764*

issued stock   Stock a company has sold to the public. *p. 599*

issuer (of a bond)   Party that issues the bond (the borrower). *p. 539*

issuer of the note   Individual or business borrowing funds (the party receiving the cash when a note is issued). *p. 478*

journal   Book (or electronic record) of original entry in which accounting data are entered chronologically before posting to the ledger accounts. *p. 150*

labor resources   Both intellectual and physical efforts of individuals used in the process of providing goods and services to customers. *p. 5*

last-in, first-out (LIFO) cost flow method   Inventory cost flow method in which cost of goods sold is computed as if the most recently purchased items are the first items sold. *p. 270*

legal capital   Amount of assets that should be maintained as protection for creditors; the number of shares multiplied by the par value. *p. 599*

liabilities   Obligations of a business to relinquish assets, provide services, or accept other obligations. *p. 12*

limited liability   Concept that investors in a corporation may not be held personally liable for the actions or debts of the corporation; stockholders' liability is limited to the amount they paid for their stock. *p. 596*

limited liability company (LLC)   Organizational form that offers many of the favorable characteristics and legal benefits of a corporation (e.g., limited liability and centralized management) but is permitted by federal law to be taxed as a partnership, thereby avoiding double taxation of profits. *p. 596*

line of credit   Preapproved financing arrangement with a lending institution in which a business can borrow money up to the approved limit by simply writing a check. *p. 539*

liquidation   Process of dividing up an organization's assets and returning them to the resource providers. In business liquidations, creditors normally have first priority; after creditor claims have been satisfied, any remaining assets are distributed to the company's owners (investors). *p. 5*

liquidity   Ability to convert assets to cash quickly and meet short-term obligations. *pp. 22, 377, 495*

liquidity ratios   Measures of short-term debt-paying ability. *p. 13-7*

long-term liabilities   Liabilities with maturity dates beyond one year or the company's operating cycle, whichever is longer; noncurrent liabilities. *p. 534*

long-term operational assets   Assets used by a business, normally over multiple accounting periods, to generate revenue; contrast with assets that are sold (inventory) or held (investments) to generate revenue; also called *productive assets*. *p. 416*

losses   Decreases in assets or increases in liabilities that result from peripheral or incidental transactions. *pp. 220, 423*

lower-of-cost-or-market rule   Accounting principle of reporting inventory at its replacement cost (market) if replacement cost has declined below the inventory's original cost, regardless of the cause. *p. 278*

maker   The party issuing a note (the borrower). *p. 374*

management's discussion and analysis (MD&A)   Section of a company's annual report in which management explains many different aspects of the company's past performance and future plans. *p. 330*

managerial accounting   Branch of accounting focused on the information needs of managers and others working within the business; its objective is to gather and report information that adds value to the business. Managerial accounting information is not regulated or reported to the public. *p. 6*

manufacturing businesses   Companies that make the goods they sell customers. *p. 26*

market   Group of people or entities organized to buy and sell resources. *p. 4*

market interest rate   Interest rate currently available on a wide range of alternative investments with similar levels of risk. *p. 552*

market value   The price at which securities sell in the secondary market; also called *fair value*. *pp. 599, 764*

marketable securities   Securities that are readily traded in the secondary securities market. *p. 764*

matching concept   Accounting principle of recognizing expenses in the same accounting period as the revenues they produce, using one of three methods: match expenses directly with revenues (e.g. cost of goods sold); match expenses to the period in which they are incurred (e.g. rent expense), and match expenses systematically with revenues (e.g. depreciation expense). *pp. 20, 71, 375*

material error Error or other reporting problem that, if known, would influence the decision of an average prudent investor. *p. 331*

materiality The point at which knowledge of information would influence a user's decision; can be measured in absolute, percentage, quantitative, or qualitative terms. The concept allows nonmaterial matters to be handled in any convenient way, such as charging a pencil sharpener to expense rather than recording periodic depreciation over its useful life. *p. 13-3*

maturity date The date that a liability is due to be settled (the date the borrower is expected to repay a debt). *p. 374*

Medicare Health insurance provided by the government primarily for retired workers. *p. 488*

merchandise inventory Finished goods held for resale to customers. *p. 207*

merchandising businesses Companies that buy and resell merchandise inventory. *pp. 26, 206*

modified accelerated cost recovery system (MACRS) Prescribed method of depreciation for tax purposes that provides the maximum depreciation expense deduction permitted under tax law. *p. 429*

mortgage bond Type of secured debt that conditionally transfers title of designated property to the bondholder until the bond is paid. *p. 541*

multistep income statement Income statement format that matches various revenues with related expenses in order to present subtotals (steps) such as gross margin and operating income; distinguishes between routine operating items and nonoperating items such as gains, losses, and interest. Contrast with *single-step income statement. p. 222*

natural resources Wasting assets originally attached to land such as mineral deposits, oil and gas reserves, and reserves of timber, mines, and quarries; the land value declines as the resources are removed. *p. 418*

net assets See *equity.*

net income Increase in equity resulting from operating the business. *p. 20*

net income percentage See *return on sales. p. 229*

net loss Decrease in equity resulting from operating the business. *p. 20*

net margin Profitability measurement that indicates the percentage of each sales dollar resulting in profit; calculated as net income divided by net sales. *p. 13-13*

net pay Employee's gross pay less all deductions (withholdings). *p. 490*

net realizable value The amount of accounts receivable a company expects to actually collect in cash; the face amount of receivables less an allowance for estimated uncollectible accounts. *p. 362*

net sales Sales less returns from customers and allowances or cash discounts granted to customers. *p. 227*

noncash investing and financing activities Certain business transactions, usually long-term, that do not involve cash, such as exchanging stock for land or purchasing property by using debt; reported separately on the statement of cash flows. *p. 644*

non-sufficient-funds (NSF) check Customer's check deposited but returned by the bank on which it was drawn because the customer did not have enough money in its account to pay the check. *p. 323*

note payable Liability represented by a legal document called a *note* that describes pertinent details such as principal amount, interest charges, maturity date, and collateral. *p. 478*

notes to financial statements Written explanations accompanying the financial statements that provide information about such items as estimates used and accounting methods chosen when GAAP permits alternatives. *p. 329*

notes receivable Notes that evidence rights to receive cash in the future; usually specify the maturity date, rate of interest, and other credit terms. *p. 361*

not-for-profit entities Organizations (also called *nonprofit* or *nonbusiness entities*) established primarily for motives other than making a profit, such as providing goods and services for the social good. Examples include state-supported universities and colleges, hospitals, public libraries, and public charities. *p. 6*

operating activities Cash inflows from and outflows for routine, everyday business operations, normally resulting from revenue and expense transactions including interest; one of the three categories of cash inflows and outflows reported on the statement of cash flows. *pp. 23, 642*

operating cycle Process of converting cash into inventory, inventory into receivables, and receivables back to cash; its length can be measured in days using financial statement data. *pp. 381, 493*

operating income Income after subtracting operating expenses from operating revenues. Gains and losses and other peripheral activities are added to or subtracted from operating income to determine net income or loss. *p. 222*

opportunity An element of the fraud triangle that recognizes weaknesses in internal controls that enable the occurrence of fraudulent or unethical behavior. *p. 86*

outstanding checks Checks the depositor company has written and deducted from its cash account balance that have not yet been presented to its bank for payment. *p. 322*

outstanding stock Shares of stock a corporation has issued that are still owned by outside parties, i.e. all stock that has been issued less any treasury stock the corporation has repurchased. *p. 599*

Paid-In Capital in Excess of Par (or Stated) Value The account in which a company records any amount received above the par or stated value of stock when stock is issued. *p. 601*

par value Arbitrary value assigned to stock by the board of directors; like *stated value*, designates *legal capital. p. 599*

parent company Company that holds a controlling interest (more than 50 percent ownership) in another company. *p. 769*

partnership Business entity owned by at least two people who share talents, capital, and the risks of the business. *p. 594*

partnership agreement Legal document that defines the rights and responsibilities of each partner and describes how income and losses are to be divided. *p. 594*

patent Legal right granted by the U.S. Patent Office ensuring a company or an individual the exclusive right to a product or process. *p. 436*

payables Obligations to make future economic sacrifices, usually cash payments.

payee The party collecting cash. *p. 374*

payment date Date on which a dividend is actually paid. *p. 606*

percentage analysis Analysis of relationships between two different items to draw conclusions or make decisions. *p. 13-4*

percent of receivables method A method of estimating the amount of uncollectible accounts by taking a percent of the outstanding receivables balance. The percentage is frequently based on a combination of factors such as historical experience, conditions of the economy, and the company's credit policies. *p. 370*

percent of revenue method A method of estimating the amount of uncollectible account by taking a percent of revenue that was earned on account during the accounting period. The percentage is frequently based on a combination of factors such as historical experience, condition of the economy, and the company's credit policies. *p. 368*

period costs Expenses recognized in the period in which they are incurred regardless of when cash payments for them are made; costs that cannot be directly traced to products. *pp. 71, 209*

periodic inventory system   Method of accounting for inventory that requires a physical count of goods on hand at the end of the accounting period in order to determine the amount of cost of goods sold and to update the Inventory account. p. 233

permanent accounts   Balance sheet accounts; contain information carried forward from one accounting period to the next (ending account balance one period becomes beginning account balance next period). pp. 24, 76

perpetual inventory system   Method of accounting for inventory in which the amount of cost of goods sold is recorded for each sale of inventory; the Inventory account is increased and decreased with each purchase and sale of merchandise. p. 210

petty cash fund   Small amount of currency kept on company premises to pay for minor items when writing checks is not practical. p. 327

petty cash voucher   Document that verifies a petty cash disbursement, signed by the person who received the money. Supporting documents, such as an invoice, restaurant bill, or parking fee receipt, should be attached to the petty cash voucher. p. 327

physical flow of goods   Physical movement of goods through a business, normally on a FIFO basis so that the first goods purchased are the first goods delivered to customers, reducing the likelihood of inventory obsolescence. p. 270

physical resources   Natural resources businesses transform create more valuable resources. p. 5

posting   Copying transaction data from journals to ledger accounts. p. 151

preferred stock   Class of stock, usually nonvoting, that has preferential claims (usually to dividends) over common stock. p. 600

Premium on Bonds Payable   A liability account that represents reductions in the stated rate of interest. p. 552

prepaid items   Deferred expenses. An example is prepaid insurance. p. 73

present value   A measure of the value today of an amount of money expected to be exchanged on a specified future date. p. 774

pressure   An element of the fraud triangle that recognizes conditions that motivate fraudulent or unethical behavior. p. 87

price-earnings (P/E) ratio   Measure that reflects the values of different stocks in terms of earnings; calculated as market price per share divided by earnings (net income) per share; a higher P/E ratio generally indicates that investors are optimistic about a company's future. pp. 611, 13-16

primary securities market   Market in which investee companies issue debt and equity securities to investors in exchange for assets; contrast with *secondary securities market*. p. 764

principal   Amount of cash actually borrowed, to be repaid in the future with interest. pp. 374, 497

procedures manual   Written documentation of a company's accounting policies and procedures. p. 315

proceeds   The amount of cash received. An example is the principal amount borrowed on a discount note payable. p. 497

product costs   All costs directly traceable to acquiring inventory and getting it ready for sale, including transportation-in. Contrast with *selling and administrative costs*. p. 209

productive assets   See *long-term operational assets*.

profit   Value added by transforming resources into products or services desired by customers. p. 4

profitability ratios   Measurements of a firm's ability to generate earnings. p. 13-13

promissory note   A legal document representing a credit agreement between a lender and a borrower. The note specifies technical details such as the maker, payee, interest rate, maturity date, payment terms, and any collateral. p. 374

property, plant, and equipment   Assets such as machinery and equipment, buildings, and land, used to produce products or to carry on the administrative and selling functions of a business; sometimes called *plant assets*. p. 418

purchase discount   Reduction in the gross price of merchandise offered to a buyer if the buyer pays cash for the merchandise within a stated time (usually within 10 days of the date of the sale). p. 216

purchase returns and allowances   A reduction in the cost of purchases resulting from dissatisfaction with merchandise purchased. p. 215

qualified opinion   Opinion issued by a certified public accountant that means the company's financial statements are, for the most part, in compliance with GAAP, but there is some circumstance (explained in the auditor's report) about which the auditor has reservations; contrast with *unqualified opinion*. p. 331

quick ratio   Measure of immediate debt-paying ability; calculated by dividing very liquid assets (cash, receivables, and marketable securities) by current liabilities. p. 13-9

ratio analysis   Analysis of relationships between two different items to draw conclusions or make decisions. p. 13-6

rationalization   An element of the fraud triangle that recognizes a human tendency to justify fraudulent or unethical behavior. p. 87

realization   Accounting term that usually refers to actual cash collection (e.g., collecting accounts receivable). p. 63

recognition   Reporting an accounting event in the financial statements. p. 63

reinstate   Recording an account receivable previously written off back into the accounting records, generally when cash is collected long after the original due date. p. 365

relative fair market value method   Method of allocating the purchase price among individual assets acquired in a basket purchase; each asset is assigned a percentage of the total price paid for all assets. The percentage assigned equals the market value of a particular asset divided by the total of the market values of all assets acquired in the basket purchase. p. 419

reliability concept   The accounting principle that supports reporting most assets at historical cost, because historical cost, unlike the market value of many assets, can be independently verified. Reliable information is not subjective. p. 16

reporting entities   Businesses or other organizations for which financial statements are prepared. p. 10

residual interest   See *equity*.

restrictive covenants   Provisions specified in a loan agreement that are designed to reduce creditor risk, such as limiting additional borrowing or dividend payments. p. 543

retail companies   Businesses that sell merchandise directly to consumers. p. 207

retained earnings   Portion of stockholders' equity that includes all earnings retained in the business since inception (revenues minus expenses and distributions for all accounting periods). p. 12

return on assets   Profitability measure based on earnings a company generates relative to its asset base; calculated as net income divided by average total assets. pp. 157, 13-14

return on equity   Profitability measure based on earnings a company generates relative to its stockholders' equity; calculated as net income divided by average stockholders' equity. *pp. 158, 13-15*

return on investment   Measure of profitability based on the asset base of the firm; calculated as net income divided by average total assets. ROI is a product of net margin and asset turnover. *p. 13-14*

return on sales   Profitability measure that reflects the percent of net income each sales dollar generates; computed by dividing net income by net sales. Also called *net income percentage. p. 229*

revenue   The economic benefit (increase in assets or decrease in liabilities) gained by providing goods or services to customers. *pp. 16, 78*

revenue expenditures   Costs incurred for repair or maintenance of long-term assets: recorded as expense and subtracted from revenue in the accounting period in which incurred. *p. 432*

salaries   A term used to describe the amount due employees who are paid a set amount per week, month, or other earnings period regardless of how many hours they work during the period. *p. 486*

salaries payable   Amounts owed but not yet paid to employees for services they have already performed. *p. 66*

sales discount   Cash discount offered by the seller of merchandise to encourage a customer to pay promptly. When the customer takes the discount and pays less than the original selling price, the difference between the selling price and the cash collected is the sales discount. *p. 225*

sales returns and allowances   A reduction in sales revenue resulting from dissatisfaction with merchandise sold. *p. 227*

salvage value   Expected selling price of an asset at the end of its useful life. *pp. 89, 420*

Sarbanes-Oxley Act of 2002   Federal legislation enacted to promote ethical corporate governance and fair financial reporting. The act requires a company's chief executive officer (CEO) and chief financial officer (CFO) to certify in writing that the financial reports being issued present fairly the company's financial status. An executive who falsely certifies the company's financial reports is subject to significant fines and imprisonment. The act also establishes the Public Company Accounting Oversight Board (PCAOB) which has the primary responsibility for developing and enforcing auditing standards for CPAs who audit SEC companies. The Sarbanes-Oxley Act also prohibits auditors from providing most types of nonaudit services to companies they audit. *p. 595*

schedule of cost of goods sold   Internal report used with the periodic inventory system that reflects the computation of cost of goods sold. *p. 234*

secondary securities market   Market in which investors exchange securities with each other; contrast with *primary securities market. p. 764*

secured bonds   Bonds secured by specific identifiable assets. *p. 541*

Securities Act of 1933 and **Securities Exchange Act of 1934**   Federal legislation passed after the stock market crash of 1929 to regulate the issuance and subsequent trading of public company stocks and bonds; created the Securities and Exchange Commission (SEC). *p. 594*

Securities and Exchange Commission (SEC)   Federal agency authorized by Congress to establish financial reporting practices of public companies; requires companies that issue securities to the public to file audited financial statements with the government annually. *p. 332*

selling and administrative costs   Costs such as advertising expense and rent expense that cannot be directly traced to inventory; recognized as expenses in the period in which they are incurred. Contrast with *product costs. p. 209*

separation of duties   Internal control feature of assigning the functions of authorization, recording, and custody to different individuals. *p. 315*

serial bonds   Bonds that mature at specified intervals throughout the life of the total issue. *p. 541*

service businesses   Organizations such as accounting and legal firms, dry cleaners, and insurance companies that provide services to consumers. *p. 26*

service charges   Fees charged by a bank for such things as services performed or penalties for overdrawn accounts or failure to maintain a specified minimum cash balance. *p. 322*

shrinkage   Decreases in inventory for reasons other than sales to customers. *p. 224*

signature card   Bank form that documents the bank account number and signatures of persons authorized to write checks on an account. *p. 320*

simple interest   Interest computed by multiplying the principal by the interest rate by the number of periods. Previously earned interest is not added to the principal, so no interest is earned on the interest of past periods. Contrast with *compound interest. p. 747*

single-step income statement   Income statement format which presents net income in one step, the difference between total revenues and total expenses. Contrast with *multistep income statement. p. 223*

sinking fund   Fund to which the bond issuer contributes cash annually to ensure sufficient funds will be available to pay the face amount on the maturity date. *p. 542*

Social Security   Insurance provided by the federal government to qualified individuals. Also called old age, survivors, and disability insurance (OASDI). *p. 488*

sole proprietorship   Business (usually small) owned by one person. *p. 594*

solvency   Ability of a business to pay liabilities in the long run. *p. 495*

solvency ratios   Measures of a firm's long-term debt-paying ability. *p. 13-11*

source document   Record such as a cash register tape, invoice, time card, or check stub that provides accounting information to be recorded in the accounting journals and ledgers. *p. 149*

special journals   Journals designed to improve recording efficiency for specific routine, high-volume transactions such as credit sales. *p. 150*

specific authorizations   Policies and procedures that apply to designated levels of management, such as the policy that only the plant manager can authorize overtime pay. *p. 316*

specific identification   Inventory costing method in which cost of goods sold and ending inventory are computed using the actual costs of the specific goods sold or those on hand at the end of the period. *p. 270*

spread   Difference between the rate a bank pays to obtain money (e.g., interest paid on savings accounts) and the rate the bank earns on money it lends to borrowers. *p. 557*

stakeholders   Parties interested in the operations of a business, including owners, lenders, employees, suppliers, customers, and government agencies. *p. 6*

stated interest rate   Rate of interest specified in the bond contract that is the percentage of face value used to calculate the amount of interest paid in cash at specified intervals over the life of the bond. *p. 540*

stated value   Arbitrary value assigned to stock by the board of directors; like *par value*, designates *legal capital. p. 599*

statement of cash flows   The financial statement that reports a company's cash inflows and outflows for an accounting period, classifying them as operating, investing, or financing activities. *p. 23*

statement of changes in stockholders' equity   Statement that summarizes the transactions that affected the owners' equity during the accounting period. *p. 22*

stock certificate   Document showing ownership interest issued to an investor in exchange for contributing assets to a corporation; describes ownership rights and privileges. *p. 594*

stock dividend   Proportionate distribution of additional shares of the declaring corporation's stock. *p. 606*

stockholders   Owners of a corporation. *pp. 12, 596*

stockholders' equity   The interest in a corporation's assets that is owned by the stockholders. *p. 12*

stock split   Corporate action that proportionately reduces the par value and increases the number of outstanding shares; designed to reduce the market value of the split stock. *p. 607*

straight-line amortization   Method of amortization in which equal amounts of the account being reduced (e.g., Bond Discount, Bond Premium, Patent) are transferred to the appropriate expense account over the relevant time period. *p. 548*

straight-line depreciation   Depreciation computations that produce equal amounts of depreciation to allocate to expense each period over an asset's life; computed by subtracting the salvage value from the asset's cost and then dividing by the number of years of useful life. *pp. 90, 421*

subordinated debentures   Unsecured bonds with a lower claim on assets than general creditors; in the case of liquidation, holders are paid off after the general creditors are paid. *p. 541*

subsidiary company   Company controlled (more than 50 percent owned) by another company. *p. 769*

systematic allocation of cost   Process of allocating the cost of an asset to expense over several accounting periods in an orderly manner.

T-account   Simple account representation, using two bars arranged in the form of the letter "T"; the account title is written across the top on the horizontal bar, debit entries are recorded on the left side of the vertical bar, and credit entries on the right side. *p. 140*

tangible assets   Assets that have physical form, such as equipment, machinery, natural resources, and land. *p. 418*

temporary accounts   Accounts used to collect retained earnings data applicable to only the current accounting period (revenues, expenses and distributions); sometimes called *nominal accounts. p. 24*

term bonds   Bonds in an issue that mature on a specified date in the future. *p. 541*

time value of money   The concept that the present value of one dollar to be exchanged in the future is less than one dollar because of interest, risk, and inflation factors. For example, a person may be willing to pay $0.90 today for the right to receive $1.00 one year from today.

times interest earned   Ratio that measures a company's ability to make its interest payments; calculated by dividing the amount of earnings available for interest payments (net income before interest and income taxes) by the amount of the interest payments. *p. 559*

trademark   Name or symbol that identifies a company or an individual product. *p. 436*

trading securities   Classification for marketable securities companies plan to buy and sell quickly to generate profits from short-term appreciation in stock and bond prices. *p. 765*

transaction   Business event that involves transferring something of value between two entities. *p. 14*

transferability   Characteristic of corporations referring to the ease of exchanging ownership interests since ownership is divided into small, readily traded ownership units (shares of stock). *p. 596*

transportation-in (freight-in)   Cost of freight on goods purchased under FOB shipping point terms; a product cost usually added to the cost of inventory. *p. 217*

transportation-out (freight-out)   Freight cost for goods delivered to customers under FOB destination terms; a period cost expensed when incurred. *p. 218*

treasury stock   Stock previously issued to the public that the issuing corporation has bought back. Contrast with *outstanding stock. p. 599*

trend analysis   Study of the performance of a business over a period of time. *p. 13-3*

trial balance   Schedule listing the balances of all ledger accounts; verifies mathematical accuracy of the accounting records and provides a convenient reference of current account balances. *p. 153*

true cash balance   Actual amount of cash owned by a company at the close of business on the date of the bank statement. *p. 321*

2/10, n/30   Common payment terms indicating the seller is offering the purchaser a 2 percent discount off the gross invoice price if the purchaser pays the reduced amount in cash within 10 days from the merchandise purchase date. *p. 216*

unadjusted bank balance   Depositor's cash balance reported by the bank as of the date of the bank statement. *p. 321*

unadjusted book balance   Cash account balance in the depositor's accounting records as of the date of the bank reconciliation before making any adjustments. *p. 321*

uncollectible accounts expense   Expense associated with uncollectible accounts receivable; amount recognized may be estimated using the allowance method, or actual losses may be recorded using the direct write-off method. *p. 364*

unearned revenue   Liability arising when customers pay cash in advance for services a business will perform in the future. *p. 74*

units-of-production depreciation   Depreciation computations that produce varying amounts of depreciation based on the level of an asset's usage each period rather than a measure of time; for example, automobile depreciation may be based on total estimated miles to be driven rather than total estimated years to be used. *p. 427*

unqualified opinion   Opinion issued by a certified public accountant that means the company's financial statements are, in all material respects, in compliance with GAAP; the auditor has no reservations. Contrast with *qualified opinion. p. 331*

unrealized gains or losses   Paper gains or losses on investment securities the company still owns; not realized until the securities are sold or otherwise disposed of. *p. 767*

unsecured bonds (debentures)   Bonds backed by the general credit of the organization. *p. 541*

unsubordinated debentures   Unsecured bonds with claims on assets equal to those of general creditors. *p. 541*

users   Individuals or organizations that use financial information for decision making. *p. 6*

useful life   The period of time over which an asset is expected to be used in the normal operation of a business. *p. 89*

variable interest rate   Interest rate that fluctuates (changes) from period to period over the life of the loan. *p. 534*

vertical analysis   Analysis technique that compares items on financial statements to significant totals. *p. 13-6*

vertical statements model   Concurrent representation of several financial statements shown vertically on a page. *p. 80*

voluntarily disclosing   Professional responsibility to clients that prohibits CPAs, in most circumstances, from revealing information obtained as a result of their client–accountant relationships.

Wage and Tax Statement, Form W-2   Form used by employers to notify each employee of the amount of his or her gross earnings for the year and the amounts withheld by the employer. *p. 487*

wages   A term used to describe amounts due employees who are paid according to the number of hours they actually work. *p. 486*

warranties   Promises to correct deficiencies or dissatisfactions in quality, quantity, or performance of products or services sold. *p. 482*

weighted-average cost flow method   Inventory cost flow method in which the cost allocated between inventory and cost of goods sold is based on the weighted average cost per unit, which is determined by dividing total costs of goods available for sale during the accounting period by total units available for sale during the period. If the weighted average is recomputed with each successive purchase, the result is moving average. *p. 270*

wholesale companies   Companies that sell goods to other businesses. *p. 207*

withdrawals   Distributions of assets to the owners of proprietorships and partnerships. *p. 597*

working capital   Current assets minus current liabilities. *p. 13-8*

working capital ratio   Another term for the current ratio: calculated by dividing current assets by current liabilities. *p. 13-8*

Photo Credits

Index

Page numbers followed by n refer to notes.

A

Abercrombie & Fitch Co., 56, 139, 155, 156
Absences, required, for internal control, 315
Accelerated depreciation methods, 425
Account(s), 11–12
    chart of, 151
    ledger, financial statements and, 212–214
    permanent, 24
    temporary, 24
Account balance, 140
Accounting
    careers in, 7–8
    defined, 3
    information provided by, 6
    role in society, 4–10
Accounting cycle, 70, 71
    second, 72–84
    steps in, 70, 71
Accounting equation, 12–18
    asset exchange transactions and, 15–16
    asset source transactions and, 14–15, 16
    asset use transactions and, 16–18
Accounting events, 14
Accounting for deferrals, 72–84
Accounting information. See also Financial statements
    accounts to gather, 11–12
    types of, 6
    users of, 6
Accounting period, 20
Accounts Payable account, 72–73
Accounts receivable, 360
    uncollectible. See Uncollectible accounts
Accounts Receivable account, 65
Accounts receivable ratios, 380–381
Accounts receivable turnover ratio, 380, 755
Accrual, 63–64
Accrual accounting, 63–83
    accounting for deferrals and, 72–84
    accounts receivable and, 65
    accrued expenses and, 66–67
    interest expense and, 89–93
    long-term assets and, 89–93
    recognition under, 63–64
    salaries payable and, 66–67
    transaction classification and, 84
Accrued expenses, 66–67
Accumulated Depreciation account, 422
Active Wilderness Adventures, 57
Adjusted trial balance, 156–157
Adjusting entries, 66–67, 76–78, 80, 375
    prepaid items and, 76–77
Adjustments, double-entry accounting and, 147–149
Advanced Micro Devices, 262
Adverse opinions, 331
Aéropostale, Inc., 132
Aetna, 159–160
Aflac, 159–160
Aging of accounts receivable, 370–372
Alaska Air Group, 441, 664–665
Allowance for doubtful accounts, 362
Allowance method of accounting for uncollectible accounts, 362
American Eagle Outfitters, Inc., 132, 496
American Electric Power, 496

American Greetings Corporation, 470
American Heart Association (AHA), 2, 11
American Institute of Certified Public Accountants (AICPA)
    Code of Professional Conduct, 85
Amgen, Inc., 200
Amortization, 418, 438, 499, 535
Annual reports, 26–27, 329, 757–763
Annuities
    annuities due and, 775n
    future value, 774–775
    ordinary, 775n
    present value, 775–776
    table of future value, 779
    table of present value, 779
AOL, 664–665
Appropriated Retained Earnings account, 608
Appropriation of retained earnings, 608
Articles of incorporation, 594
Articulation, 20
Asset(s), 4, 5
    current (short-term), 416, 493
    intangible, 418–419, 435–439
    operational, long-term. See Depreciation;
        Long-term operational assets
    return on, 157, 159–160, 754, 755
    tangible, 418
Asset entries, double-entry accounting and, 161–162
Asset exchange transactions, 15–16, 84
    accounting for deferrals and, 73, 74, 75
    accrual accounting and, 65
    double-entry accounting and, 143–144
Asset source transactions, 14–15, 16, 84
    accounting for deferrals and, 72–73, 74, 76
    accrual accounting and, 64
    double-entry accounting and, 140–143
Asset use transactions, 16–18, 84
    accounting for deferrals and, 72, 74–75
    accrual accounting and, 65–66
    adjusting entries and, 76
    double-entry accounting and, 144–146
Atheros Communications, Inc., 56
AT&T, Inc., 262, 597
Audit(s), 330–332
Auditors' report, 27
Audit services, 7
Authority manuals, 316
Authorized stock, 599
AutoNation, Inc., 207, 208, 210, 230
AutoZone, Inc., 412
Available-for-sale securities, 765
Average number of days to collect accounts receivable, 380–381, 755
Average number of days to sell inventory (average days in inventory), 284, 755
Avon Products, Inc., 559, 610

B

Bain Capital Partners, 56
Balance sheet, 21, 22
    classified, 494
    inventory cost flow methods and, 271
    long-term operational assets and, 439
    preparation of, 68–70
    revenue recognition and, 377
Ball Co., 237

Bank balance
    adjustments to, 322
    unadjusted, 321
Bank of America, 529–530
Bank reconciliations, 321–326
    adjustments to bank balance and, 322
    adjustments to book balance and, 322–323
    certified checks and, 323
    correcting errors, 323
    determining true cash balance, 321
    illustration of, 323–324
Bank statement(s), 320–321
Bank statement credit memos, 320
Bank statement debit memos, 320
Basket purchases, 419–420
Bernard L. Madoff Investments (BMI), 313, 318, 333
Best Buy Company, 12, 161, 486
Big Lots, Inc., 636
Biogen Idec, Inc., 200
Blackstone Group, 606
Bloomberg BusinessWeek, 7
Boards of directors, 596
Boeing, 411, 664–665
Bond(s), 539–559
    advantages of issuing, 540–541
    amortization of. See Bond amortization
    callable, 542
    convertible, 542
    financial leverage and, 557–558
    financial statements and, 543–546
    issued at discount. See Bond discounts
    issued at face value, 542
    issued at premium. See Bond premiums
    maturity dates of, 541–542
    mortgage, 541
    price determination for, 776–777
    ratings of, 543
    ratio analysis and, 558–559
    redemption of, 552–553
    restrictive covenants and, 543
    secured, 541
    security of, 541
    serial, 541
    term, 541
    unsecured, 541
Bond amortization
    effective interest rate method for, 553–557
    straight-line method for, 548–549
Bond certificates, 539
Bond discounts, 546–551
    bond prices and, 547
    effective interest rate and, 547
    effective interest rate method and, 554–555
    financial statements and, 550–551
Bondholders, 539
Bond premiums, 551–552
    effective interest rate method and, 555–557
Book balance, adjustments to, 322–323
Books of original entry, 150
Book value, 90, 422
    of bonds, 547
    per share, 599
BorgWarner, Inc., 412
BP p.l.c., 28, 535, 537, 663–664
Brinks, 634
Bristol-Myers Squibb, 634

British Petroleum, 28, 535, 537, 663–664
Buffalo Wild Wings, Inc., 132–133
Buffet, Warren, 607
Burger King, 6
Business entities, 26
    forms of, 594–598. *See also specific forms*

C

California Pizza Kitchen (CPK), 262
Callable bonds, 542
Call premium, 542
Capital expenditures, for property, plant, and equipment, 432–433
Capital maintenance expenditures, 665
Capital stock. *See* Dividends; Stock *entries*
Careers in accounting, 7–8
Carmike Cinemas, Inc., 12
Carrying value. *See* Book value
Cash, 317–321
    checking account documents and, 320–321
    controlling, 318–320
    cost of protecting, 319
Cash balance, true, 321
Cash basis accounting, recognition under, 63
Cash discounts, 216
Cash dividends, 605–606
Cash flows. *See also* Statement of cash flows; Statement of cash flows preparation
    from operating activities, net income compared with, 70
Cash inflows, 23, 640
Cash outflows, 23, 640
Cash Short and Over account, 326
Caterpillar, Inc., 469
CBS, 606
Certified checks, 323
Certified Internal Auditor (CIA) designation, 8
Certified Management Accounting (CMA) designation, 8
Certified public accountants (CPAs), 7–8, 330
    confidentiality and, 332
    materiality and, 331
    types of audit opinions and, 331
Chart of accounts, 151
Check(s), 320
    certified, 323
    outstanding, 322
Checking accounts, documents associated with, 320–321
Chevron Corporation, 28, 160, 634–635
Citigroup, 606
Claims, 12–13
Claims exchange transactions, 84
    accrual accounting and, 66–67
    adjusting entries and, 77–78
    double-entry accounting and, 146–147
Classification of transactions, 84
Classified balance sheets, 494
Closely held corporations, 594
Closing, 24, 70, 71
Closing entries, double-entry accounting and, 155–156
Cloud Peak Energy, Inc., 470–471
Coca-Cola, 418, 436, 633
Code of Professional Conduct of AICPA, 85
Coke, 436
Collateral, 374, 543
Comcast Corp., 157, 441
Committee of Sponsoring Organizations of the Treadway Commission (COSO), 314
Common size financial statements, 228–229
Common stock, 12, 600
Communication, Information and, 314
Compounding, 773
Compound interest, 773
Concha y Toro, 284, 381

Confidentiality, 332
Conservatism, 72
Consistency, inventory cost flow methods and, 275–276
Consolidated Edison, Inc., 56
Consolidated financial statements, 769
Consulting services, 8
Consumers, 4
Contingent liabilities, 481–482
Continuity of corporations, 596
Contra asset accounts, 364, 422
Contra liability accounts, 498
Control. *See also* Internal controls
    through stock ownership, 612
Control activities, 314
Control environment, 314
Conversion agents, 4
Convertible bonds, 542
Copyrights, 436–437
Corporate governance, 85–88
    criminal and ethical misconduct and, 86–87
    ethics and, 85–88
    Sarbanes-Oxley Act and, 85–86
Corporations, 594
    capital raising by, 597
    closely held, 594
    continuity of, 596
    double taxation of, 595–596
    governance of. *See* Corporate governance
    limited liability of, 596
    management structure of, 596–597
    ownership of, transferability of, 596
    regulation of, 594–595
    reporting of capital structure in financial statements of, 598
    stock of. *See* Dividends; Stock *entries*
Cost(s), 73
    allocating between asset and expense accounts, 210
    depreciable, 420
    of financing inventory, 217
    inventory, flow of. *See* Inventory cost flow methods
    of long-term assets, determining, 419–420
    period, 71
    of protecting cash, 319
    transportation, 217–220
Costco Wholesale, 228, 284, 584–585
Cost method of accounting for treasury stock, 604
Cost of goods available for sale, allocating, 272–274
Cost of goods sold, 26
    schedule of, 234
Cost of Goods Sold account, 210
Cracker Barrel Old Country Store, 132
Credit, defined, 140
Credit card sales, 378–379
Credit lines, 539, 540
Creditors, 4, 5
Credit sales, cost of, 379–382
Criminal misconduct, 86–88
Cumulative dividends, 600
Current assets, 416, 493
Current liabilities, 493–494
Current ratio, 495–496, 755
CVS Caremark, 231

D

Daily trial balance, 157
Date of record, for dividends, 605
Debentures, 541
Debit, defined, 140
Debt, long-term. *See* Bond(s); Long-term debt
Debt securities, 764
Debt to assets ratio, 158–159, 754
Declaration date, for dividends, 605
Deere & Company, 262
Deferral, 63

Deferrals, accounting for, 72–84
    matching concept and, 72–73
    payables and, 72–73
    prepaid items and, 72–73
    purchase of supplies and, 72–73
    unearned revenue and, 74
Deferred tax liability, 431
Deflation, inventory cost flow methods and, 275
Delta Air Lines, 529–530
Denny's Corporation, 469
Depletion, 418, 434–435
Deposits in transit, 322
Deposit tickets, 320
Depreciable cost, 420
Depreciation, 418
Depreciation expense, 90, 420–429
    accelerated depreciation methods and, 425
    comparison of methods for computing, 429
    double-declining-balance, 420, 425–426
    entries for, double-entry accounting and, 161–162
    income taxes and, 429–431
    judgment and estimation and, 440–442
    revision of estimates of, 431–432
    straight-line, 90, 420, 421–423
    units-of-production, 420, 427–429
Dillard's, Inc., 663
Direct method for preparing operating activities section of statement of cash flows, 642, 655–656
Direct write-off method, 372–373
Disclaimers of opinion, 331
Discount(s), 497
    bond. *See* Bond discounts
Discount notes, 497–503
    financial statements and, 499–500, 502–503
    general ledger and, 499–500
Discount on Bonds Payable account, 547
Discount on Notes Payable account, 498
Dividends, 17
    appropriation of retained earnings for, 608
    in arrears, 600
    cash, 605–606
    cumulative, 600
    date of record for, 605
    declaration date for, 605
    financial statement presentation of, 609–610
    payment date for, 606
    receiving, 610
    stock, 606–607
    stock splits and, 607–608
Dominion Resources, 496
Double-declining-balance depreciation, 420, 425–426
Double-entry accounting, 138–162
    adjusting accounts and, 147–149
    asset exchange transactions and, 143–144
    asset source transactions and, 140–143
    asset use transactions and, 144–146
    claims exchange transactions and, 146–147
    closing entries and, 155–156
    debit/credit terminology and, 140
    debt to assets ratio and, 158–159, 754
    depreciation entries and, 161–162
    entries for long term assets and, 161–162
    financial leverage and, 158–159
    financial statements and, 153–160
    general journal and, 149–153
    interest expense and, 162
    notes payable and, 162
    post-closing trial balance and, 156–157
    return on assets ratio and, 157, 159–160
    return on equity ratio and, 158, 159–160
    T-accounts and, 140
    trial balance and, 153
    uncollectible accounts in, 369
Double-entry bookkeeping, 15
Double taxation, 595–596

Doubtful accounts. *See* Uncollectible accounts
Dow Chemical Company, 56, 606

E

Earnings, 4
gross, 486
retained, 12, 608
per share, 756
Earnings before interest and taxes (EBIT),
debt financing and, 558
eBay, 634
EDGAR database, 332
accessing, 696
Effective interest rate, 547
Effective interest rate method, 553–557
bond discounts and, 554–555
bond premiums and, 555–557
Elements of financial statements, 10–14
Employees. *See also* Payroll accounting
bonded, internal controls and, 315
defined, 485
independent contractors versus, 485–486
quality of, internal controls and, 315
Employee's Withholding Allowance Certificate (Form W-4),
487, 488
Employer payroll taxes, 491
Employer's Quarterly Federal Tax Return (Form 941), 488
Ending inventory balance, estimating, 282–285
Enron, 85–86, 314
Enterprise Risk Management (ERM)—An Integrated Framework
(COSO), 314
Equity, 12
return on, 158, 159–160, 754
stockholders.' *See* Stockholders' equity
Equity method for equity securities, 769
Equity securities, 764, 769
Estée Lauder, 559
Estimated useful life, 420
Ethical misconduct, 86–88
Ethics, 85–88
criminal and ethical misconduct and, 86–88
Sarbanes-Oxley Act and, 85–86
Ex-dividend stock, 605
Expenses, 16, 73
accrued, accrual accounting and, 66–67
depreciation. *See* Depreciation expense
for intangible assets, recognition of, 438–439
uncollectible accounts. *See* Uncollectible accounts
ExxonMobil, 28, 159–160, 596, 611

F

Facebook, 607
Face value, bonds issued at, 539, 543
Fair value, 764
Federal Deposit Insurance Corporation, 84
Federal Unemployment Tax Act (FUTA), 491
FICA taxes, 488–489
Fidelity bonds, 315
Financial accounting, 6
Financial Accounting Standards Board (FASB),
8, 595
on direct method for statement of cash flows, 643
Statement of Financial Accounting Standards (SFAS)
No. 95 issued by, 223–224
Financial audits, 330–332
Financial leverage, 158–159, 557
Financial resources, 4–5
Financial statements. *See also specific statements*
analysis of. *See* Ratio analysis
in annual report, 26–27
bonds and, 543–546
capital structure reporting in, 597–598

common size, 228–229
consolidated, 769
discount notes and, 499–500, 502–503
dividends and, 609–610
double-declining-balance depreciation and, 425–426
double-entry accounting and, 153–160
elements of, 10–14
footnotes to, 329
horizontal statements model and, 25–28
inventory cost flow methods and, 271, 274–276
investment securities and, 767–769
ledger accounts and, 212–214
of merchandising businesses, 210–214, 213
preparation of, 67–70
preparing, 20–25
ratio analysis and. *See* Ratio analysis
real-world, 26, 27–28
revenue recognition and, 377
straight-line depreciation and, 423–425
transactions involving stock and, 603, 609–610
uncollectible accounts and, 364–365, 370
vertical statements model for, 80, 82–83
Financing activities, statement of cash flows and,
23, 643–644
noncash financing activities, 644
preparation of financing activities section of statement of
cash flows and, 658–662
preparation of schedule of noncash investing and financing
activities and, 663–665
First-in, first-out (FIFO) cost flow method, 270, 272–273,
276–277
Fiscal year, 139
Fitch, 543
Fixed interest rate, 534
FOB destination, 217
FOB shipping point, 217
Foot Locker, 584–585
Ford Motor Company, 207, 209, 210, 230, 411, 634
Form 941 (Employer's Quarterly Federal Tax Return), 488
Form 10-K, 27, 332, 697–753
Form 10-Q, 332
Form W-2 (Wage and Tax Statement), 487–488, 489
Form W-4 (Employee's Withholding Allowance Certificate),
487, 488
Franchises, 437
Fraud, avoiding in merchandising businesses, 280–281
Freds, 445
Freeport-McMoRan Copper & Gold, Inc. (FCX),
417, 435
Friehling, David, 318, 333
Fringe benefits, 492
Full disclosure, inventory cost flow methods and, 275
Future value, 773–774
tables of, 778, 779
Future value annuities, 774–775

G

Gains, 423
recognition of, 220–222
unrealized, 767
Gap, Inc., 308, 496
Garmin, 634
Gates, Bill, 607
GEICO Insurance, 15
General authority, 316
General Electric, 278, 606
General journal, double-entry accounting and, 149–153
General ledger, 18, 67, 68, 151
discount notes and, 499–500
Generally accepted accounting principles (GAAP), 8–9
global, 9
IFRS compared with, 159, 608
General Mills, 559
General Motors Company, 56, 312

General uncertainties, 481
GlaxoSmithKline, 231
Going concern, 14
Going concern assumption, 476
Goldman Sachs, 607
Goods available for sale, 210
Goodwill, 437–438
Google, 2, 11, 456, 635
Green Mountain Coffee Roasters, 664–665
Greyhound, 456
Gross earnings, 486
Gross margin, 210
Gross margin method, 282
Gross margin percentage, 229, 230, 754
Gross profit, 210

H

Half-year convention, 430
Harley-Davidson Co., 382, 445, 633
Healthy Choice, 437
Held-to-maturity securities, 765
Hershey Foods Corporation, 411–412
Historical cost concept, 9, 17–18, 419
Home Depot, 496
Horizontal statements model, 25–28
H&R Block, Inc., 133–134

I

IBM (International Business Machines Corporation), 635
Imprest basis, 327
Income, 4
net, 20, 70, 222
operating, 222
Income statement, 20, 21
inventory cost flow methods and, 271, 275
matching concept and, 20
multistep, 222–224
preparation of, 68, 69
revenue recognition and, 377
single-step, 223
Income taxes
corporate, 595–596
debt financing and, 557–558
depreciation and, 429–431
inventory cost flow methods and, 274–275
payroll accounting and, 486–488, 489
Independent auditors, 330–332
Independent contractors, 485–486
Indirect method for preparing operating activities section of
statement of cash flows, 642, 646, 648–654
reconciliation approach for, 648–652
rule-based approach for, 652–654
Industries, characteristics of, financial performance measures
and, 441
Inflation, inventory cost flow methods and, 275
Information and Communication, 314
Intangible assets, 418–419, 435–439
expense recognition for, 438–439
Intel Corporation, 472
Interest, 4. *See also* Time value of money
compound, 773
on promissory note, 374
simple, 773
Interest-bearing notes, 497
Interest expense
accrual accounting and, 89–93
double-entry accounting and, 162
Interest rates
effective, 547
market, 552
stated, 540
Internal Control—An Integrated Framework (COSO), 314

Index

̣rnal controls, 86–87, 312–317
  accounting, 313
  administrative, 313
  key features of, 314–317
  limitations of, 317
Internal Revenue Service, 2
International Accounting Standards Board (IASB), 9
International Business Machines Corporation (IBM), 635
International Financial Reporting Standards (IFRS), 9, 159, 278, 280
  GAAP compared with, 159, 608
International issues
  balance sheets, 495
  GAAP, 9, 159
  IFRS, 159, 278, 280, 383, 495
  last-in, first-out, 278
  lower-of-cost-or-market rule, 280
  property, plant, and equipment, 430
  research and development, 436
Intuit, 151
Inventory, 209–214, 268–286, 306–311
  allocating cost between asset and expense accounts, 210
  avoiding fraud and, 280–281
  cost of financing, 217
  estimating ending balance of, 282–285
  financial statements and, 210–214
  lower-of-cost-or-market rule and, 278–280
  periodic inventory system and, 232–234
  perpetual inventory system and, 210
  purchase discounts and, 216
  purchase returns and allowances and, 215
  shrinkage of, 224–225
  transportation costs and, 217–220
Inventory cost flow methods, 270–278
  allocating cost of goods available for sale and, 272–274
  financial statements and, 271, 274–276
  first-in, first-out, 270, 272–273, 276–277
  last-in, first-out, 270, 273, 277–278
  multiple layers with multiple quantities and, 272
  physical flow, 270–271
  ratio analysis and, 285
  specific identification, 270
  weighted-average, 270, 274, 277–278
  when sales and purchases occur intermittently, 276–278
Inventory turnover ratio, 284, 755
Investees, 764
Investing activities, statement of cash flows and, 23, 643
  noncash infesting activities and, 644
  preparation of investing activities section of statement of cash flows and, 656–658
  preparation of schedule of noncash investing and financing activities and, 663–665
Investment securities, 764–772
  available-for-sale, 765
  events affecting, 765–767
  financial statements and, 767–769
  held-to-maturity, 765
  marketable, 764
  trading, 765, 767
  types of, 764–765
Investors, 4, 5, 764
Issued stock, 599
Issuers
  of bonds, 539
  of promissory notes, 478
ITV plc., 495

J

J. M. Smucker Company, 356–357
Jackson Hewitt Tax Services, Inc., 133–134
JCPenney, 207, 355
Jobs and Growth Tax Relief Reconciliation Act (JGTRRA) of 2003, 595n
Johnson & Johnson, 231, 584–585, 664–665

Jos. A. Bank Clothiers, Inc., 585
Journal(s), 150
  general, 149–153
  special, 150
Journal entries
  adjusting, 374
  closing, 155–156
JP Morgan Chase, 606

K

Kellogg's, 559
Kelly Services, 441
Keurig, 665
Keystone Automotive Operations, 584–585
K & G Fashion Superstore, 585
Kleenex, 436
Kmart, 228
The Kroger Co., 279
Kroger Company, 595

L

Labor resources, 5
Last-in, first-out (LIFO) cost flow method, 270, 273, 277–278
Las Vegas Sands Corporation, 542
Ledger accounts, financial statements and, 212–214
Legal capital, 599
Liabilities, 12
  contingent, 481–482
  current (short-term), 493–494
Life
  revision of, 431
  useful, estimated, 420
Limited liability, of corporations, 596
Limited liability companies (LLCs), 596
Lines of credit, 539, 540
Liquidation, 5
Liquidity, 22, 377
  solvency versus, 495–496
Lockheed Martin Corporation, 361, 363
Long-term assets, accrual accounting and, 89–93
Long-term debt, 534–560
  bonds. See Bond(s)
  installment notes payable, 536–538
  lines of credit, 539, 540
  time value of money and, 776
Long-term liabilities, 534
Long-term operational assets, 416–442
  continuing expenditures for plant assets and, 432–433
  cost of, 419–420
  depreciation expense and. See Depreciation expense
  intangible, 418–419, 435–439
  judgment and estimation and, 440–442
  natural resources, 418, 434–435
  tangible, 418
Losses, 423
  recognition of, 220–222
  unrealized, 767
Lower-of-cost-or-market rule, 278–280
Lowe's Companies, Inc., 161, 496
Lubrizol, 607

M

Macy's, 231
Madoff, Bernard, 313, 318, 333
Maker of promissory note, 374
Management, structure of, 596–597
Management's discussion and analysis (MD&A), 27, 330
Managerial accounting, 6
Manpower, Inc., 441
Manufacturing businesses, 26
Marathon Oil, 160

Market(s), 4
  resource priorities set by, 4–5
Marketable securities, 764
Market capitalization, 607
Market interest rate, 552
Market value, 764
  adjustment for, 767
  of stock, 599
Marriott, 559
Matching concept, 20, 70–72, 73, 374
Materiality, financial audits and, 331
Maturity dates
  of bonds, 541–542
  of promissory notes, 374
McAfee, 664–665
McDonald's Corporation, 284–285, 381, 418
Measurement rules, 8–9
Medicare tax, 488–489
The Men's Wearhouse, Inc., 585
Merchandise inventory, 207
Merchandising businesses, 26, 206–234
  avoiding fraud in, 280–281
  cost of financing inventory and, 217
  financial statements of, 210–214, 213, 222–224
  inventory and. See Inventory; Merchandise inventory
  lost, damaged, or stolen inventory and, 224–225
  purchase discounts and, 216
  purchase returns and allowances and, 215
  recognition of gains and losses and, 220–222
  sales and, 225–230
  transportation costs and, 217–220
Merck & Company, 26, 27, 231
Meredith Corporation, 64, 78–79
Michaels Stores, 199
Microsoft, 472, 607
Modified accelerated cost recovery system (MACRS), 429–431
Molson Coors Brewing, Inc., 469
Money, time value of. See Time value of money
Monitoring, 314
Moody's, 543
Moores Clothing for Men, 585
Mortgage bonds, 541
Motorola, 606
Multistep income statement, 222–224

N

NASDAQ, 318
National Semiconductor Corp., 530
Natural resources, 418, 434–435
Neiman Marcus, 228, 232, 284
Netflix, Inc., 135, 199–200
Net income, 20, 222
  cash flow from operating activities compared with, 70
Net income percentage, 229
Net losses, 20
Net pay, 490
Net realizable value, 362
Net sales, 227–228
Newell Rubbermaid, Inc., 530
Newmont Mining Corporation, 529–530
New York Stock Exchange, 594
New York Times, 606
Nike Company, 202, 436
Nonbusiness organizations, 6
Noncash investing and financing activities, statement of cash flows and, 644
  preparation of schedule of noncash investing and financing activities and, 663–665
Nonprofit organizations, 6
Nordstrom, 316
Notes payable, 478–479
  double-entry accounting and, 162
  installment, 536–538

Notes receivable, 361, 373-378
Notes to the financial statements, 329
Not-for-profit entities, 6
NSF checks, 323

O

Office Depot, 161, 231
Office Max, 351
Operating activities, 23
    cash flow from, net income compared with, 70
    statement of cash flows and, 642-643
Operating cycle, 381-382, 493
Operating income, 222
Opportunity, 86
Ordinary annuities, 775n
Outstanding checks, 322
Outstanding stock, 599

P

Paid-in Capital in Excess of Par (or Stated) Value account, 601
Papa John's International, Inc., 413
Paper profit, 767
Parent company, 769
Partnership(s), 594
    reporting of capital structure in financial statements of, 598
    transferring ownership of, 596
Partnership agreements, 594
Par value, 599
    stock issuance and, 601
Patents, 436
Payee of promissory note, 374
Payment date for dividends, 606
Payroll accounting, 485-492
    computing net pay and, 490
    deductions from gross earnings and, 486
    employer payroll taxes and, 491
    federal income taxes and, 486-488, 489
    fringe benefits and, 492
    gross earnings and, 486
    identifying employees and, 485-486
    Social Security and Medicare taxes and, 488-489
    voluntary withholdings and, 489-490
Peabody Energy Corporation, 470-471
Peace Corps, 6
Penske Automotive Group, Inc., 306-307
The Pep Boys—Manny, Moe & Jack, 531
Percent of receivables method, 370-372
Percent of revenue method for estimating uncollectible accounts expense, 368-370, 372
Performance evaluations, internal control and, 317
Period costs, 71, 209
Periodic inventory system, 232-234
    perpetual system versus, 234
Permanent accounts, 24
Perpetual inventory system, 210
    periodic system versus, 234
Petty cash funds, 327-329
Petty cash vouchers, 327
Pfizer, Inc., 262, 606
Physical control, internal control and, 316-317
Physical flow of goods, 270-271
Physical resources, 5
Polo, 436
Polo Ralph Lauren, 139, 155, 156
Post-closing trial balance, double-entry accounting and, 156-157
Posting, 151
Preferred stock, 600-601
Premium, bond. See Bond premiums
Premium on Bonds Payable account, 552
Prenumbered documents, internal control and, 316
Prepaid items
    accounting for deferrals and, 73
    adjusting entries and, 76-77

Present value, 774
    tables of, 778, 779
Present value annuities, 775-776
Pressure, 87
Price-earnings (P/E) ratio, 611, 755
Price of stock, increasing, 610-611
Primary securities market, 764
Princess Cruise Lines, 445
Principal, 374, 497
Private accounting, 8
Procedures manuals, internal control and, 315
Proceeds, 497
Procter & Gamble, 411
Product costs, 209
Profit, 4
    paper, 767
Progressive, 160
Promissory notes, 374, 478-479
Property, plant, and equipment, 418
    continuing expenditures for, 432-434
Prudential Insurance Co., 456
Public accounting, 7-8
Public Company Accounting Oversight Board (PCAOB), 333, 595
Publix, 280
Purchase(s), of investment security, 765-766
Purchase allowances, 216
Purchase returns, 215
Purchases discounts, 216

Q

Qualcomm, Inc., 56
Qualified opinions, 331
QuickBooks, 151

R

Ratio analysis
    accounts receivable turnover ratio and, 380-381, 755
    average number of days to collect accounts receivable and, 380-381, 755
    average number of days to sell inventory (average days in inventory) and, 284, 755
    current ratio and, 495-496, 755
    debt financing and, 559
    debt to assets ratio and, 158-159, 754
    earnings per share and, 756
    gross margin percentage and, 229, 230, 754
    inventory cost flow methods and, 285
    inventory turnover ratio and, 284, 755
    net income percentage and, 229
    price/earnings ratio and, 611, 756
    return on assets ratio and, 157, 159-160, 754, 756
    return on equity and, 159-160, 754
    return on sales ratio and, 229, 754
    times interest earned ratio and, 559, 756
Rationalization, 87
Realization, 63
Receivables, 360-384. See also Uncollectible accounts
Recognition, 63
    of investment revenue, 766
Reconciliation approach to indirect method for preparing operating activities section of statement of cash flows, 648-652
Reinstatement, 367
Relative fair market value method, 419-420
Reliability concept, 18
Rent-A-Center, 379-380
Reporting entities, 9-10
Resource(s)
    financial, 4-5
    labor, 5
    nonbusiness usage of, 6-7
    physical, 5
Resource allocation, market-based, 4-5

Resource owners, 4
Restrictive covenants, 543
Retail companies, 26, 207. See also Merchandising businesses
Retained earnings, 12
    appropriation of, 608
Return on assets, 157, 159-160, 754, 756
Return on equity, 159-160, 754
Return on sales ratio, 229, 754
Revenue(s), 16
    definition of, 78
    expenditures for property, plant, and equipment, 432-434
    investment, recognition of, 766
    unearned. See Unearned revenue
Risk assessment, 314
Rite Aid, 231
Ruby Tuesday's, Inc., 307
Rule-based approach, to indirect method for preparing operating activities section of statement of cash flows, 652-654

S

Safeway, Inc., 269, 283, 307
Saks Fifth Avenue, 228
Salaries, 486
Salaries payable account, 66-67
Sales, 225-230
    of investment securities, 766
    return on, 229
Sales discounts, 225, 227-228
Sales returns and allowances, 225, 226
Sales tax, 480-481
Salvage value, 89, 420
    revision of, 432
Sam's Club, 207
Sarbanes-Oxley Act of 2002 (SOX), 85-86, 314, 333, 595
Save-A-Lot, 262-263
Schedule of cost of goods sold, 234
Schedule of noncash investing and financing activities, preparation of, 663-665
Sears, Roebuck and Company, 15, 207
Second accounting cycle, 72-84
Secondary securities market, 764
Secured bonds, 541
Securities
    debt, 764
    equity, 764
    investment. See Investment securities
Securities Act of 1933, 594
Securities and Exchange Commission (SEC), 2, 332-333
    corporate regulation by, 594-595
    Form 10-K and, 27, 332, 697-753
    Form 10-Q and, 332
Securities Exchange Act of 1934, 594
Selling and administrative costs, 209
Separation of duties, 315
Serial bonds, 541
Service businesses, 26
Service charges, 322
Short-term assets, 416, 493
Short-term liabilities, 493-494
Shrinkage of inventory, 224-225
Signature cards, 320
Simple interest, 773
Single-step income statements, 223
Sinking funds, 542
Sirius XM Radio Inc., 690-691
Six Flags, Inc., 199
Social Security taxes, 488-489
Sole proprietorships, 594
    reporting of capital structure in financial statements of, 597
    transferring ownership of, 596
Solvency, liquidity versus, 495-496
Sonic, 59

Index

...ce documents, 149–150
Southwest Airlines, 441, 445
Special journals, 150
Specific authorizations, 316
Specific identification, 270
Spread, 557
Stakeholders, 2, 6, 10
Standard & Poor's, 543
Staples, 231
Starbucks, 284–285, 381, 634
Starwood Hotels, 559
Stated interest rate, 540
Stated value, 599
    stock issuance and, 602
Statement of cash flows, 21, 23, 640–666
    financing activities and, 643–644
    investing activities and, 643
    noncash investing and financing activities and, 644
    operating activities and, 642–643
    preparation of. See Statement of cash flows preparation
    reporting format for, 644–645
Statement of cash flows preparation, 68, 70, 645–646
    of financing activities section, 658–662
    of investing activities section, 656–658
    of operating activities section, 646, 648–656
    schedule of noncash investing and financing activities and, 663–665
Statement of changes in stockholders' equity, 21, 22
    preparation of, 68, 69
Statements of Financial Accounting Standards (SFAS)
    No. 95, 223–224
Stock, 599–612
    authorized, 599
    book value per share of, 599
    classes of, 599–601
    common, 600
    control through ownership of, 612
    dividends on. See Dividends
    earnings per share of, 756
    ex-dividend, 605
    financial statement presentation of transactions involving, 603, 609–610
    increasing price of, 610–611
    issuance of. See Stock issuance
    issued, 599
    market value of, 599
    outstanding, 599
    par value, 599, 601
    preferred, 600–601
    price/earnings ratio of, 611, 756
    splits and, 607–608
    stated value of, 599
    treasury, 599, 603–604
Stock certificates, 594
Stock dividends, 606–607
Stockholders, 12, 596
Stockholders' equity, 12
    statement of changes in, 21, 22, 68
Stock issuance
    with no par value, 602
    of par value stock, 601
    at stated value, 602
Stock splits, 607–608
Straight-line amortization of bonds, 548–549

Straight-line depreciation, 90, 420, 421–423
Subordinated debentures, 541
Subsidiary company, 769
Supervalu, Inc., 262–263
Supplies
    accounting for, 76
    purchase of, 72–73

T

T-accounts, 140. See also Double-entry accounting
Tangible assets, 418
Target Corporation, 26, 55–56, 131, 159, 198, 207, 229, 261, 285, 306, 354, 382, 410, 468, 528, 583, 632, 690, 697–753, 757–762
Tata Motors, 495
Taxes. See Income taxes; Payroll accounting; Sales tax
Tax Increase Prevention and Reconciliation Act of 2005, 595n
Tax liability, deferred, 431
Tax services, 8
Temporary accounts, 24
10-K report, 27, 332
10-Q report, 332
Term bonds, 541
Tesla Motors, Inc., 595, 641, 647–648
Texas Instruments, Inc., 530
Textron, 606
Times interest earned ratio, 559, 756
Time value of money, 773–779
    business applications of, 776–777
    future value and, 773–774
    future value annuities and, 774–775
    present value and, 774
    present value annuities and, 775–776
Time Warner, Inc., 695
Toll Brothers, Inc., 199
Toys R Us, Inc., 199
Trademarks, 436
Trading securities, 765
    unrealized gains or losses on, 767
Transaction classifications, 84
Transactions, 14
    asset exchange, 15–16, 65, 73, 74, 75, 84, 143–144
    asset source, 14–15, 16, 64, 72–73, 74, 76, 84, 140–143
    asset use, 16–18, 65–66, 72, 74–75, 76, 84, 144–146
    claims exchange, 77–78, 84, 146–147
Transferability of corporate ownership, 596
Transportation costs, 217–220
Transportation-in, 217
Transportation-out, 218
Treasury stock, 599, 603–604
Trial balance, double-entry accounting and, 153
True cash balance, 321
2/10, n/30, 216

U

Unadjusted bank balance, 321
Uncollectible accounts
    allowance method for, 362–367
    collection of, 366–367
    direct write-off method for, 372–373
    financial statements and, 364–365

    percent of receivables method for estimating, 370–372
    percent of revenue (sales) method for estimating, 368–370, 372
    reinstatement of, 367
    writing off, 366
Uncollectible accounts expense, 364
Unearned revenue
    adjusting entries and, 77–78
    deferral accounting and, 74
Union Pacific Corporation, 587
Units-of-production depreciation, 420, 427–429
Unqualified opinions, 331
Unsecured bonds, 541
Unsubordinated debentures, 541
UPS, 456
Useful life, 89
    estimated, 420
Users of accounting information, 6

V

Vail Resorts, Inc., 199
Value Line Investment Survey, 664
Variable interest rate, 534
Vaseline, 436
Verizon Communications, Inc., 131–132, 441
Vertical statements model, 67–70, 80, 82–83
Vulcan Materials Co., 279

W

Wage(s), 486
Wage and Tax Statement (Form W-2), 487–488, 489
Walgreens, 231
Walmart, 19, 161, 228, 229, 231, 232, 285, 312, 331, 382, 597, 610
The Walt Disney Company, 57–58
Warranties, 482–485
Washington Mutual Bank, 84
Weighted-average cost flow method, 270, 274, 277–278
Weight Watchers International, Inc., 469
Wendy's/Arby's Group, 6, 633
Whirlpool Corporation, 413
Whole Food Markets, 262–263
Wholesale companies, 26, 207. See also Merchandising businesses
Willamette Valley Vineyards, 284
Withdrawals, 597, 598
WorldCom, 85–86, 314

X

Xerox, 436

Y

Yum! Brands, 284–285, 381

Z

Zales, 307, 411